The Oxford Handbook of
Face Perception

The Oxford Handbook of Face Perception

Edited by

Andrew J. Calder

Gillian Rhodes

Mark H. Johnson

and

James V. Haxby

OXFORD
UNIVERSITY PRESS

OXFORD
UNIVERSITY PRESS

Great Clarendon Street, Oxford OX2 6DP

Oxford University Press is a department of the University of Oxford.
It furthers the University's objective of excellence in research, scholarship,
and education by publishing worldwide in

Oxford New York

Auckland Cape Town Dar es Salaam Hong Kong Karachi
Kuala Lumpur Madrid Melbourne Mexico City Nairobi
New Delhi Shanghai Taipei Toronto

With offices in

Argentina Austria Brazil Chile Czech Republic France Greece
Guatemala Hungary Italy Japan Poland Portugal Singapore
South Korea Switzerland Thailand Turkey Ukraine Vietnam

Oxford is a registered trade mark of Oxford University Press
in the UK and in certain other countries

Published in the United States
by Oxford University Press Inc., New York

British Library Cataloging in Publication Data
Data available

Library of Congress Cataloging in Publication Data

Library of Congress Control Number: 2011920651

Typeset by Glyph International, Bangalore, India
Printed in China
on acid-free paper by
Asia Pacific Offset

ISBN 978–0–19–955905–3

10 9 8 7 6 5 4 3 2 1

Whilst every effort has been made to ensure that the contents of this book are as complete, accurate and up-to-date as
possible at the date of writing, Oxford University Press is not able to give any guarantee or assurance that such is the case.
Readers are urged to take appropriately qualified medical advice in all cases. The information in this book is intended to
be useful to the general reader, but should not be used as a means of self-diagnosis or for the prescription of medication.

Preface

The human face is unique among social stimuli in conveying such a variety of different characteristics. A person's identity, sex, race, age, emotional state, focus of attention, facial speech patterns, and attractiveness are all detected and interpreted with relative ease from the face. Humans also display a surprising degree of consistency in the extent to which personality traits, such as trustworthiness and likeability, are attributed to faces. The chapters that follow are concerned with the scientific study of these different aspects of face perception. The idea for the book was conceived by two of the editors (Andy Calder and Gill Rhodes) during Calder's visit to the University of Western Australia. An edited book on face perception was on the cards, but both agreed that the area was unlikely to benefit a great deal from yet another edited volume focusing on one aspect of face research. In light of the increasing volume of studies addressing multiple aspects of face perception a handbook format was a surprising omission from the literature. This required a greater range of editorial expertise, and Mark Johnson and Jim Haxby were recruited to the team. Three years later, we are delighted to present *The Oxford Handbook of Face Perception.*

In contrast to other areas of psychological study, such as memory, language, and attention, the study of face perception was a minority interest during the early years of cognitive psychology, and the topic received little or no attention in early cognitive psychology textbooks. One potential reason why is illustrated by an anecdote from one of contributors, Vicki Bruce. Shortly after embarking on her PhD addressing face recognition, most likely one of the first, a highly respected vision scientist at the University of Cambridge advised her that the topic was unsuitable, since it provided insufficient material for a PhD and used stimuli that were too difficult to control. Thankfully, Vicki didn't heed his advice and over 30 years later the number of published studies in face perception has increased exponentially, with little evidence that the field is running out of ideas. However, the scientist's guarded attitude towards face perception has persisted in vision science until comparatively recently and goes some way to explaining the relatively late arrival of face perception in the history of cognitive research.

This increased interest in recent years has brought substantial advances in our understanding of the psychological and neurophysiological mechanisms underlying the various aspects of face perception, arising from cognitive studies of healthy participants, developmental studies of neonates to adolescents, impairments in neuropsychological, psychiatric, and developmental conditions, brain imaging techniques, computer simulations, and comparative research identifying homologues in non-human species. Although each has made a significant contribution, neuroimaging techniques, particularly magnetic resonance imaging, have probably attracted the greatest attention, providing a remarkable non-invasive window into the structure and function of the human brain. We are now seeing an impact of these techniques on theoretical frameworks of face perception. The box and arrow models of earlier years have been modified and given a neurological dimension; the issue of whether face perception has a special or "modular" status has been revisited; and developmental neuropsychological frameworks of face perception have been revised or proposed.

In the current volume, we have attempted to cover all of the above areas. Inevitably, there are others that we have been unable to include, or have only touched upon. For example, automated recognition of faces is a burgeoning area of current enquiry with numerous practical applications whose full consideration could easily justify a handbook of its own. Since the primary aim of the vast majority of this research is to achieve optimal machine performance rather than psychological validity, we have included only a limited discussion of work in this area with a clear psychological aim or application. Even within the narrower constraints of psychological studies of face perception, readers will no doubt identify other topics that they feel have been omitted, or researchers whose work has not been included. For practical reasons, primarily space, we were unable to cover all possible angles, and apologize for any omissions.

Despite the extensive interest in face research it is remarkable that this is the first edited book addressing multiple aspects of face perception for over 18 years. One potential reason is that it is only in more recent years that the various research topics included in the current edition have been considered a collective area of study. Prior to this, what we might refer to as the more "cognitive" aspects of face perception—face recognition, configural and part-based processing of faces, and their breakdown in various disorders—fell within the wider areas of *cognitive psychology* and *cognitive neuropsychology;* whereas more social facial properties—such as facial expression, eye gaze, attractiveness, and personality dimensions—tended to be studied within the separate discipline of *social psychology*. More recently, this division has become blurred, and frequently the same researchers are interested in both sets of characteristics. Interest in the perceptual and neurophysiological bases of the social facial properties has also contributed to the merging of these areas. Since these multiple facial characteristics emanate from the same source, this can only be a good thing when it comes to developing full theoretical accounts of how we extract and interpret the various facial properties from a single visual image.

The book's structure

The handbook is organized into five sections. *Part I* deals with central themes and methodological approaches in face perception and contains contributions from researchers who have played pivotal roles in the development of their fields. Where appropriate, contributors in this first section were asked to take a more "personal" approach, discussing how they became interested in the their respective areas of study, the route by which they arrived at a particular result or viewpoint, or problems they encountered when presenting new research or theoretical accounts. As with other sections of the book, we will not provide a synopsis of each chapter in this preface, since in many cases the titles speak for themselves and each chapter ends with a *Summary and conclusions* section that provides a brief overview of its content and main take home messages.

Part II is concerned with Perceiving and Remembering Faces. It explores the fundamental question of how we are able to discriminate and recognize many thousands of faces, despite their similarity as visual patterns and despite variability in the appearance of the same face due to facial movements and changing viewing conditions. Much has been learned about the nature of the mental representations and neural mechanisms that make this possible, how these develop, and whether they are specialized for faces. It is also clear that there are limits to our face expertise, as illustrated by difficulties with unfamiliar faces as well as other-race faces. These limitations, which can reveal a lot about the mechanisms underlying face expertise, are also considered in this section. Finally, we highlight the central role that sophisticated methods of manipulating, controlling and generating digitized facial images has played in increasing our understanding of face perception.

Part III explores the rapidly expanding literature addressing how social information is read from faces. In addition to conveying a person's identity, the face constitutes the principal source of a constantly varying array of verbal and non-verbal social signals, and the predominant medium by which we derive first impressions of others' attractiveness, trustworthiness or other personality traits. Although initially studied almost exclusively by social psychologists, the last 15 years has seen a vast expansion in research addressing perception of these various facial characteristics. This direction has been fuelled by new interest in the visuoperceptual and neurophysiological mechanisms underlying the perception of facial expression, eye gaze, facial speech, and personality traits, and their simulation and automated recognition by computer models. It is increasingly clear that these social facial properties are not processed in isolation, and research is beginning to uncover the manner in which they interact with one another, and with facial identity, wider cognitive systems, and other environmental cues, such as vocal expressions, body posture, and surrounding context.

Part IV addresses Comparative and Developmental Perspectives. The question of how things came to be the way they are in adult face processing is clearly a fundamental one, and has been addressed through work on both phylogeny (comparative) and ontogeny (development). Indeed, since Darwin, face perception has been used as an example domain or case study to address some of the most fundamental issues about the evolution and development of human brain functions. Sometimes this has involved claims about the extent to which either phylogeny or ontogeny contributes to emergence of the sophisticated and specialized mechanisms of face perception observed in human adults. Striking similarities in the neural and cognitive basis of face perception between different primate species have now been extended to other mammals, indicating that basic mechanisms of face processing have an extended evolutionary history in the mammalian line. Developmental and comparative studies provide evidence that this phylogenetic continuity is maintained by a combination of newborn biases, early experience, and common mechanisms of learning and skill acquisition.

Part V considers disorders of face perception. Observations of disordered face recognition following brain injury have been a major inspiration for proposals about neural mechanisms. The first detailed report of selective impairment of face recognition following brain injury, prosopagnosia, was published by Bodamer over 50 years ago and led to the hypothesis that face perception is mediated by neural mechanisms that are distinct from those for the perception of other objects. A further dissociation between two pathways for face recognition—one cognitive and the other emotional—has been proposed based on further observations of patients with prosopagnosia and another disorder of face recognition, Capgras syndrome. A congenital form of prosopagnosia has been described recently, but the relationship between the acquired and congenital variants is yet to be established. The extent to which the acquired and congenital forms affect other facial cues (e.g., expression, eye gaze, and facial speech) or object recognition varies considerably among the different reports. Disorders of face perception also provide an opportunity to apply models of face perception to help understand the symptoms and pathophysiology of conditions that affect social cognition, such as autism, schizophrenia, and depression. Additional discussion of neurological impairments affecting facial expressions, eye gaze and other social characteristics can also be found in *Part III*.

Our sincere thanks go to our friends and colleagues that agreed to contribute to this volume. We were delighted that with very few exceptions, all of those we approached agreed to take part. Consequently, the book contains perspectives from leading experts in the field. Special thanks go to a number of people for their continued support from the volume's initial conception to publication. To Martin Baum, Senior Commissioning Editor of Psychology and Psychiatry at the Oxford University Press (OUP), and Charlotte Green, Assistant Commissioning Editor, Brain Sciences, for their continued help and enthusiasm. To the editorial team at OUP, particularly Abigail Stanley, for the preparation of the complete published text. AC and MJ acknowledge long-term financial support from the UK Medical Research Council, GR acknowledges support from the Australian Research Council, and JH acknowledges support from the National Science Foundation and the National Institute of Mental Health. Finally, we are extremely grateful to Jill Keane at the MRC Cognition and Brain Sciences Unit, Cambridge, who coordinated all correspondence with contributors and played a central role in the preparation of the final manuscript. Her invaluable assistance was essential to preparing what we hope will be a key reference to the scientific study of face perception past and present, *The Oxford Handbook of Face Perception.*

Andy Calder
Gillian Rhodes
Mark Johnson
Jim Haxby

Contents

need

List of Contributors

Ralph Adolphs
Caltech
Pasadena, CA, USA

Nalini Ambady
Tufts University
Psychology Department
Medford, MA, USA

Gizelle Anzures
Institute of Child Study
University of Toronto
Toronto, ON, Canada

Galia Avidan
Department of Psychology
Ben-Gurion University of
the Negev
Beer Sheva, Israel

Marian Stewart Bartlett
Institute for Neural Computation
University of California San Diego
La Jolla, CA, USA

Jason J.S. Barton
Departments of Medicine (Neurology),
Opthalmology, and Visual Sciences
University of British Columbia
Vancouver, BC, Canada

Andrew P. Bayliss
School of Psychology
The University of Queensland
St Lucia, QLD, Australia

Marlene Behrmann
Department of Psychology
Carnegie Mellon University
Pittsburgh, PA, USA

Michael J. Bernstein
Psychological and Social Sciences
Penn State University-Abington
Abington, PA, USA

Michelle I. Bertrand
Department of Psychology
Queen's University at Kingston
Kingston, ON, Canada

Elina Birmingham
Simon Fraser University
Burnaby, BC, Canada

Vicki Bruce
School of Psychology
Newcastle University
Newcastle upon Tyne, UK

A. Mike Burton
Department of Psychology
University of Aberdeen
Aberdeen, UK

Andrew J. Calder
MRC Cognition and Brain Sciences Unit
Cambridge, UK

Ruth Campbell
Division of Psychology and Language Sciences
University College London
London, UK

Garrison W. Cottrell
Department of Computer Science and
Engineering
University of California San Diego
La Jolla, CA, USA

Gergely Csibra
Centre for Brain and Cognitive Development
School of Psychology
Birkbeck College
University of London
London, UK

Geraldine Dawson
Department of Psychiatry
University of North Carolina
Chapel Hill, NC, USA

Bradley Duchaine
Department of Psychological and Brain Sciences
Dartmouth College
Hanover, NH, USA

Martin Eimer
School of Psychology
Birkbeck College
London, UK

Susan Faja
Center on Human Development
and Disability
University of Washington
Seattle, WA, USA;
Center for Autism Research
Philadelphia, PA, USA

Jianfeng Feng
Department of Computer Science
Warwick University
Coventry, UK

Elaine Fox
Department of Psychology
University of Essex
Colchester, UK

Winrich Freiwald
Brain Research Institute
Department of Theoretical Neurobiology
Bremen, Germany;
The Rockefeller University
New York, NY, USA;
Division of Biology
Caltech, Pasadena, CA, USA

Beatrice de Gelder
Laboratory of Cognitive and Affective
Neuroscience
Tilburg University
Tilburg, The Netherlands

M. Ida Gobbini
Dipartimento di Psicologia
Facoltà di Medicina e Chirurgia
University of Bologna
Bologna, Italy

Iris Gordon
Department of Psychology
University of Victoria
Victoria, BC, Canada

Michelle de Haan
UCL Institute of Child Health
London, UK

James V. Haxby
Center for Cognitive Neuroscience
Department of Psychological &
Brain Sciences
Dartmouth College
Hanover, NH, USA

Erin E. Hecht
Division of Psychiatry and Behavioral
Sciences
Yerkes National Primate Research Center
Emory University
Atlanta, GA, USA

Janet H. Hsiao
Department of Psychology
University of Hong Kong
Hong Kong

Kurt Hugenberg
Department of Psychology
Miami University
Oxford, OH, USA

Rob Jenkins
Department of Psychology
University of Glasgow
Glasgow, UK

Mark H. Johnson
Department of Psychological Science
Birkbeck, University of London
London, UK

Natalie Kalmet
Department of Psychology
Queen's University at Kingston
Kingston, ON, Canada

Nancy Kanwisher
Brain and Cognitive Sciences
Massachusetts Institute
of Technology
Cambridge, MA, USA

Keith M. Kendrick
The Babraham Institute
Babraham Research Campus
Cambridge, UK

Robyn Langdon
Macquarie Centre for Cognitive Science
Macquarie University,
NSW, Australia

Kang Lee
Institute of Child Study
University of Toronto
Toronto, ON, Canada

David A. Leopold
National Institute of Mental Health
Bethesda, MD, USA

R.C.L. Lindsay
Department of Psychology
Queen's University at Kingston
Kingston, ON, Canada

Jamal K. Mansour
Department of Psychology
Queen's University at Kingston
Kingston, ON, Canada

Daphne Maurer
Department of Psychology, Neuroscience,
and Behaviour
McMaster University
Hamilton, ON, Canada

Gregory McCarthy
Department of Psychology
Yale University
New Haven, CT, USA

Elinor McKone
School of Psychology
The Australian National University
Canberra, ACT, Australia

Elisabeth I. Melsom
Department of Psychology
Queen's University at Kingston
Kingston, ON, Canada

Caroline Michel
Université catholique de Louvain (UCL);
Unité Cognition & Development (CODE);
Faculté de Psychologie
Louvain-La-Neuve, Belgium

Catherine J. Mondloch
Department of Psychology
Brock University
St. Catharines, ON, Canada

Edward R. Morrison
University of Portsmouth
Department of Psychology
Portsmouth, UK

Mayu Nishimura
Department of Psychology
Carnegie Mellon University
Pittsburgh, PA, USA

Alice J. O'Toole
School of Behavioral and Brain Sciences
The University of Texas at Dallas
Richardson, TX, USA

Lisa A. Parr
Yerkes National Primate Research Center
Center for Translational
Social Neuroscience
Emory University
Atlanta, GA, USA

Olivier Pascalis
Laboratoire de Psychologie et
NeuroCognition
Université Pierre Mendes France
Grenoble, France

Kevin A. Pelphrey
Yale Child Study Center and
Department of Psychology
Yale University
New Haven, CT, USA

Ian S. Penton-Voak
Department of Experimental Psychology
Bristol, UK

Mary L. Phillips
Department of Psychiatry
Western Psychiatric Institute and Clinic
University of Pittsburgh School
of Medicine
Pittsburgh, PA, USA

David Pitcher
McGovern Institute for Brain Research
Massachusetts Institute of
Technology
Cambridge, MA, USA

Paul C. Quinn
Department of Psychology
University of Delaware
Newark, DE, USA

Gillian Rhodes
ARC Centre of Excellence in Cognition and
its Disorders
School of Psychology
University of Western Australia
Perth, WA, Australia

Ruthger Righart
Laboratory for Social and Neural
Systems Research
University of Zürich
Zürich, Switzerland

Rachel Robbins
Macquarie Centre for Cognitive Sciences
Macquarie University
Macquarie, NSW, Australia

Edmund T. Rolls
Oxford Centre for Computational
Neuroscience
Oxford, UK

Bruno Rossion
Unité Cognition & Dévelopment
Université catholique de Louvain
Louvain-la-Neuve, Belgium

Donald F. Sacco
Department of Psychology
Miami University
Oxford, OH, USA

Christopher C. Said
Department of Psychology
New York University
New York, NY, USA

Stefan R. Schweinberger
Department of General Psychology
DFG Research Unit Person Perception
University of Jena
Jena, Germany

Lisa S. Scott
Department of Psychology
Neuroscience and Behavior Program
University of Massachusetts
Amherst, MA, USA

Alan M. Slater
University of Exeter
School of Psychology
Washington Singer Laboratories
Exeter, UK

James W. Tanaka
Department of Psychology
University of Victoria
Victoria, BC, Canada

Cibu Thomas
National Institute of Health
Bethesda, MD, USA

Steven P. Tipper
School of Psychology
Bangor University
Bangor, UK

Alexander Todorov
Psychology Department
Princeton University
Princeton, NJ, USA

Doris Tsao
Division of Biology
Caltech
Pasadena, CA, USA

Jan Van den Stock
Laboratory of Cognitive and Affective
Neuroscience
Tilburg University, Tilburg, the Netherlands;
Department of Neuroscience
KU Leuven, Leuven, Belgium

Brent C. Vander Wyk
Yale Child Study Center
Yale University
New Haven, CT, USA

Sara C. Verosky
Department of Psychology
Princeton University
Princeton, NJ, USA

Thomas Vetter
Computer Science Department
University of Basel
Basel, Switzerland

Patrik Vuilleumier
Laboratory for Behavioral Neurology and
Imaging of Cognition
Department of Neuroscience,
University Medical Center;
Department of Neurology
University Hospital
Geneva, Switzerland

Mirella Walker
Department of Psychology
University of Basel
Basel, Switzerland

Vincent Walsh
Institute of Cognitive Neuroscience and
Department of Psychology
University College London
London, UK

Sara Jane Webb
Center on Human Development and Disability
University of Washington
Seattle, WA, USA

Max Weisbuch
Department of Psychology
University of Denver
Denver, CO, USA

Jacob Whitehill
Department of Computer Science
and Engineering
University of California San Diego
La Jolla, CA, USA

Sylvia Wirth
Centre de Neuroscience Cognitive
Bron, France

Andrew W. Young
Department of Psychology
University of York
York, UK

Steven G. Young
Department of Psychology
Tufts University
Medford, MA, USA

Leslie A. Zebrowitz
Brandeis University
Department of Psychology
Waltham, MA, USA

Konstantina Zougkou
Department of Psychology
University of Essex,
Colchester, UK

Part I

Approaches to Studying Face Processing

Chapter 1

Face Perception: a Developmental Perspective

Mark H. Johnson

I have little interest in face perception for its own sake. This may seem like a shocking statement coming from someone who has devoted much of his career to the topic, but it reflects the fact that I have always viewed face perception as the ideal case study example for understanding the deeper principles underlying human neurodevelopment. In this chapter I will illustrate how face perception has been one of oldest battlegrounds for resolving key issues in human development. Conversely, I will argue that taking a developmental approach to face perception can resolve some of the major current debates in the adult face perception and cognitive neuroscience literature. Thus, face perception and development have been, and continue to be, mutually informative domains of study.

Ever since Darwin's (1872) book *The Expression of the Emotions in Man and Animals* the issue of whether the exquisite face perception skills we have as adults is due primarily to phylogeny (species adaptations) or ontogeny (individual development fuelled by experience) has motivated much research. Indeed, evidence from studies of face perception abilities at different ages has provided pillars to support domain-general nature or nurture arguments in human development. For example, in one of the very first scientific studies of human infants, Fantz (1963) showed that when given a choice of looking at a schematic face or a bull's-eye pattern, newborn babies generally preferred to look at the face. A decade or so later, Goren, Sarty, and Wu (1975) systematically tested human newborns—often within the first 10 minutes after birth—on their tendency to track slowly moving patterns. They observed that human newborns would turn their head and eyes further in order to keep a simple schematic face in view, than they would for equally complex "scrambled face" patterns. Viewed from the perspective of today's scientific standards, this study raised more questions than it answered, but at the very least it has generated a whole mini-field of scientific research (some of which will be discussed later).

In addition to the work on newborns designed to test what, if any, "innate knowledge" of faces we have, studying the development of face perception skills during infancy and childhood has proved to be fertile ground for domain-general theories of perceptual and cognitive development. Basic theories about mechanisms of learning (Nelson, 2003), pubertal dips in performance (Carey et al., 1980), the longitudinal stability of childhood performance, and the functional specialization of cortical regions (Johnson, 2001; Cohen-Kadosh and Johnson, 2007), have all been at least partly based on evidence from face perception studies.

Over the past decade an increasing number of cognitive neuroscientists who study aspects of face perception in adults have realized the importance of developmental data for addressing their key issues. In a later section I will review recent literature on the factors that contribute to the specialization of certain cortical areas for face processing. For example, the debate of whether the fusiform face area is specialized for face processing due to experience and training, or due to some kind of innate specification, remains unresolved and controversial based on the sometimes con-flicting data from adults. Data from infants and children not only allows this question to be addressed more directly, but also suggests an intriguing alternative middle-ground view in this polarized debate.

The two-process theory

Up until the late 1980s, the development of face perception was an actively researched field, but it was mainly dominated by issues in the nature versus nurture debate and related questions about the ages at which different face perception abilities might appear. After replicating the results with newborns of Goren et al. (1975), Johnson et al. (1991), and several of the key results supporting more gradual development of face processing abilities, John Morton and I proposed the "two-process" model of the development of face perception in 1991 (Johnson and Morton, 1991; Morton and Johnson, 1991; see also de Schonen and Mathivet, 1990 for a related view). The original two-process theory sought to reconcile the apparently conflicting lines of evidence about the development of face processing by postulating the existence of two systems: a tendency for newborns to orient to faces (CONSPEC), and an acquired specialization of cortical circuits for other aspects of face processing (CONLERN). This two-systems theory was partly based on my earlier animal work (e.g. Johnson et al., 1985). We hypothesized that CONSPEC serves to bias the input to developing cortical circuitry over the first weeks and months of life, thus ensuring that appropriate cortical specialization occurred in response to the social and survival-relevant stimulus of faces.

To this day the putative CONSPEC mechanism occupies the middle ground between those who argue that face preferences in newborns are due to low-level psychophysical biases, and others who propose that infants' representations of faces are richer and more complex. From birth, human infants preferentially attend to some face-like patterns suggesting a powerful mechanism to bias the input that is processed by the newborn's brain. Perhaps the most contro-versial aspect of the two-process theory was the proposal that "infants possess some information about the structural characteristics of faces from birth" (Morton and Johnson, 1991, p. 164). Although this committed us to the view that the general configuration that composes a face was important, we did not commit to a specific representation. Nevertheless, our empirical observation from the early experiments with newborns, and evidence from other species, indi-cated that a stimulus with three high-contrast blobs corresponding to the approximate location of the eyes and mouth might be sufficient (Figure 1.1). In 1991 the idea that infants were born with face-sensitive information had been rejected by most in the field, largely on the basis of experiments with 1- and 2-month-old infants that failed to show any preference for static face images (see Johnson and Morton, 1991 for review). Because infants shortly beyond the newborn stage did not prefer schematic face patterns over scrambled faces, it was generally assumed that newborns could not discriminate faces from other stimuli.

Over the ensuing years, more than 20 papers on newborns responses to faces and face-like patterns have been published (see Johnson, 2005 for review). All of these studies bar one found some evidence of discrimination of face-like patterns. Several types of explanation have now been advanced for newborn face preferences that have been observed in at least five different laborato-ries and in the vast majority of studies conducted.

1 *The sensory hypothesis* A number of authors have advanced the view that newborn visual pref-erences, including those for face-related stimuli, can be accounted for simply in terms of the relative visibility of the stimuli. Different versions of this account and a detailed discussion of their merits are reviewed in an article by Johnson et al. (2008). After more than a decade of

Fig. 1.1 Schematic illustration of the stimuli that might be optimal for eliciting a face-related preference in newborns. These hypothetical representations were created by putting together the results of several experiments on newborns' face-related preferences. Conclusions were combined from experiments showing the importance of the number of elements in the upper half of a bounded area or surface, the importance of a face-relevant pattern of phase contrast, and the importance of the basic face configuration as viewed at low spatial frequencies. Reprinted by permission from Macmillan Publishers Ltd: *Nature Reviews Neuroscience*, Subcortical face processing, Mark H. Johnson, **6**, 766–774, copyright 2005.

debate and empirical investigation about psychophysics, the upshot is that while some infant preferences for visual patterns can be predicted by the visibility of a stimulus as filtered through the limited visual system of infants, face patterns are nearly always more preferred over other psychophysically matched stimuli. That is, while the psychophysical properties of a stimulus do influence infants' looking preferences, when stimuli are carefully matched face patterns determine preference.

2 *Non-face structural preferences* This view is that newborn preference for faces can be explained by domain-general perceptual biases, such as those based on known adult Gestalt principles (see Simion et al., 2003). Simion and colleagues argue that "newborns' preference for faces may simply result from a number of non-specific attentional biases that cause the human face to be a frequent focus of newborns' visual attention" (Simion et al., 2003, p. 15). These authors still believe that the purpose of these biases is to direct attention to faces in the natural environment of the newborn, so that they are debating the nature of the representation(s) that underlie this bias, not the existence of the mechanism itself. At this point it is useful to differentiate between face-*specific* and face-*sensitive* mechanisms. The notion of CONSPEC was never claimed to be face-specific (tuned only and exclusively to faces), but merely sufficient in the natural environment of the newborn to pick out faces from other objects and stimuli (face-sensitive). Indeed, we (Johnson and Morton, 1991) speculated that it may be possible to create "super-normal" stimuli (such as high-contrast face patterns) that would actually be preferred over a realistic human face. While the arguments advanced about non-face structural preferences accept that newborns have face-sensitive mechanisms, they argue that these biases are not adapted for that purpose, but are general biases in visual processing that, in combination, just happen to pick out faces in most natural environments. In contrast, CONSPEC is assumed to be specifically adapted for detecting conspecifics in the environment.

Therefore, CONSPEC would be more consistent with evidence that the biases are related (act in concert) and respond to the natural conditions in which faces are typically observed (such as the contrast patterns caused by being illuminated from above). The non-face structural preferences view has spawned much empirical research. The upshot of some of this research is that only a complex combination of different biases can explain the results (see Johnson et al., 2008). For example, a most preferred stimulus for a newborn would involve an up–down asymmetrical pattern with more elements or features in the upper half, but only when it is within a congruently shaped bounded object or area such as an oval. Related recent research indicates that this near optimal stimulus is improved further with the addition of the appropriate phase-contrast relations for a top-lit face (see Farroni et al., 2005, figure 1). Further, these supposed different biases interact together in ways likely to be the product of one system or representation rather than being independent "non-specific" biases. Another line of research that casts doubt on non-specific structural preferences hypotheses is evidence supporting the existence of complex face processing abilities in newborns, discussed next.

3 *Newborns have complex face representations* Some empirical results have led to the hypothesis that newborns already have complex processing of faces (for review see Quinn and Slater, 2003). These findings, usually obtained with naturalistic face images, include a preference for attractive faces (Slater et al., 1998, 2000), a preference for face patterns with the appropriate phase-contrast relations (Farroni et al., 2005), a sensitivity to the presence of eyes in a face (Batki et al., 2000), and a preference to look at faces with direct gaze that engage them in eye contact (Farroni et al., 2002). Such findings have led some authors to conclude that ". . . face recognition abilities are well developed at birth" (Quinn and Slater, 2003, p. 4). A fuller consideration of the details of these effects reveal that while some of them can be accounted for by the original CONSPEC notion, other experiments force the conclusion that the bias is more specific than originally hypothesized. In Figure 1.2 you will see realistic face images filtered through the appropriate spatial frequency filters to simulate newborn vision. From these images it is evident that a mechanism sensitive to the arrangement of high-contrast, low-spatial frequency components of a face would be preferentially activated by (i) the typical configural arrangement of eye and mouth regions, (ii) the presence (or absence) of open eyes, and (iii) direct versus averted gaze (see Farroni et al., 2002).

Thus, the notion of CONSPEC as a mechanism that biases newborns to attend to faces has, in my view, stood the test of time fairly well. More recent conceptions, however, suggest the mechanism is further tuned to detect potential communicative partners, such as faces that engage them with direct gaze (Farroni et al., 2002) accompanied by a smile (Farroni et al., 2007). Thus, the function originally attributed to CONSPEC now needs to be expanded: it is not just for detecting and orienting to any faces, but also prioritizes faces likely to seek social interaction with the infant. In this way, it may provide a developmental basis, not just for face perception, but also for social cognition in the brain in general.

I should note that an important caveat to many, but not all, of the above studies is that they are conducted with newborns more than 1 day old. While age (in days) is commonly reported not to have an effect on the results obtained, studies of very early learning over the first few hours of face-to-face contact need to be a priority for the future.

While evidence for CONSPEC continues to strengthen and expand, there is no doubt that the notion of CONLERN was underspecified when we first proposed it in 1991. At that time CONLERN was described as "a device that acquires and retains specific information about the visual characteristics of individual conspecifics" (Johnson and Morton, 1991, p. 90). A large part

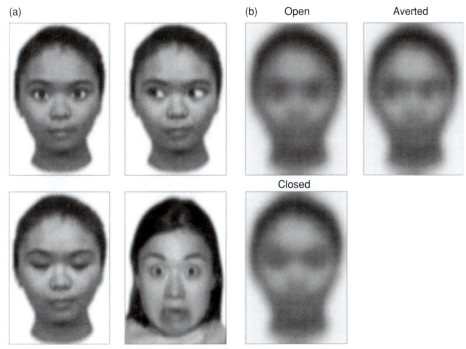

Fig. 1.2 How newborns see faces. (a) Realistic images of faces as viewed through the visual system of newborns at a typical distance for face-to-face interaction (~50 cm). A neutral face with direct gaze, averted gaze, and eyes closed, as well as a fearful face, are shown. These images support the view that, at close viewing distances, information around the eyes could activate the subcortical route. (b) The same realistic images of faces as viewed through the visual system of newborns, but from ~2 m. When viewed from a greater distance than in (a), or in the periphery, the configuration of shadowed areas that is characteristic of a naturally (top-) lit face could also activate the subcortical route. Reprinted by permission from Macmillan Publishers Ltd: *Nature Reviews Neuroscience*, Subcortical face processing, Mark H. Johnson, **6**, 766–774, copyright 2005.

of the reason for the lack of specificity in our original proposal, and why I did not go on to do much further research on the topic for another 4 or 5 years, was the lack of methods then available for child-friendly imaging of brain functions. My view was that without these methods we could never fully explore the mechanism(s) that underlie CONLERN. In the mid 1990s it became feasible to record high-density event-related potentials (ERPs), and, principally with Michelle de Haan, we began to exploit this method to provide evidence for the specialization of cortical processing of faces (see de Haan, Chapter 38, this volume). Some of the principles we discovered have now proved useful for functional magnetic resonance imaging (fMRI) studies of the neurodevelopment of face processing in children (see later section). Most recently, we have helped to pioneer near infrared spectroscopy (NIRS) as a method for studying cortical activation to faces and other social stimuli in infants and young children (Blasi et al., 2007; Grossman et al., 2008). Thus, the investigation of CONLERN illustrates the importance of available methods in the advancement of an area of scientific inquiry. Sometimes it is better to leave a burning question until the right methods become available for addressing it. Having said this, other researchers have made significant advances in understanding the development of the cognitive and perceptual aspects of face processing with behavioral studies alone (see Lee et al., Chapter 39, this volume).

A subcortical route?

In Johnson and Morton's original (1991) proposals we argued that subcortical processing was responsible for guiding the behavior of newborns toward face-like patterns. Although it was very controversial at the time, we made this proposal for a couple of reasons. First, evidence from other species indicated that inborn preferences for conspecifics are mediated by more primitive subcortical neural routes. This stands in contrast to early visual learning that is mediated by forebrain or cortical systems. Second, evidence on the maturation of the human visual system suggests that there is slower development of the cortical visual routes than the subcortical during postnatal development (e.g. Johnson, 1990). Subsequently to this and related proposals (e.g. Le Doux, 1996), neuroimaging, electrophysiological, and neuropsychological studies with adults have provided evidence for a rapid, low spatial frequency, subcortical face detection system in adults that involves the superior colliculus, pulvinar, and amygdala (see Johnson, 2005 for review). This route is hypothesized to be fast, operates on low spatial frequency visual information, and modulates cortical face processing, which led Le Doux (1996) to describe it as the "quick & dirty" pathway.

Evidence that the route is fast comes from ERP and magnetoencephalographic (MEG) studies showing that components associated with a "fast pathway" for face processing can occur at much shorter latencies than those generally associated with the "structural encoding" stage of cortical face processing (such as the N170 and M170) (Bailey et al., 2005).

Evidence that the route processes low spatial frequencies comes from fMRI studies in which the pulvinar, amygdala, and superior colliculus respond to low spatial frequency information about faces, and particularly fearful faces (Winston et al., 2003). This subcortical route was insensitive to the high spatial frequency information about faces that can activate the fusiform cortex. Finally, evidence consistent with the idea that the subcortical route modulates cortical processing comes from several functional imaging studies indicating that the degree of activation of structures in the subcortical route (amygdala, superior colliculus, and pulvinar) predicts or correlates with the activation of cortical face processing areas (George et al., 2001; Kleinhans et al., 2008). However, the causal direction of this correlation remains unknown.

What is the purpose of this putative subcortical route? The proposal that follows on from the two-process model is that it serves as a developmental basis for the emerging social brain network (see Johnson, 2005). This view assumes that newborns have widespread projections from the subcortical route to cortical structures, and as a consequence face detection initially activates widespread cortical activation of regions that will become incorporated into the adult social brain. Through the constraints imposed by architectural biases within different cortical regions, and through the process of interactive specialization discussed later, particular cortical regions become increasingly tuned for social stimulus processing. Thus, CONSPEC and the subcortical route is a critical foundation stone for each individual child to construct their cortical social brain network (Johnson, 2005).

Even if you grant that CONSPEC and the subcortical route are important for the ontogeny of face perception and the social brain, does this route have any relevance or importance for those who study face processing in adults? We have investigated this question recently (Tomalski et al., 2009a). Contrary to most cognitive and functional imaging paradigms in adults that involve foveal presentation of faces, we presented schematic face patterns similar to those used with newborns, but as briefly flashed peripheral stimuli. We observed more rapid saccadic orienting to flashed face-like configurations than similar patterns. Further, consistent with a subcortical basis, this effect is only evident with temporal (the visual hemifields away from the nose) rather than nasal (the visual hemifields next to the nose) visual field input (Tomalski et al., 2009b). The effect also seems be a product of fast oculomotor routes since it is not observed with manual key press responses.

While we may be able to detect subtle hallmarks of the subcortical route in laboratory experimental contexts in adults, is there any substantive consequence of this processing in the real world? Senju and Johnson (2009) marshal evidence that this route is engaged by eye contact in adults (as well as infants), and have proposed that it is one source of selective activation of cortical structures that contribute to the "eye contact effect." The eye contact effect is defined by these authors as the phenomenon that perceived eye contact modulates the concurrent and/or immediately following cognitive processing and/or behavioral response. If this hypothesis is correct, it means that the subcortical route continues to have a vital role in social perception and cognition in adults.

How do cortical regions come to be involved in face perception?

As discussed earlier, research on the mechanisms underlying CONLERN was delayed for several years due to a lack of necessary methods for progressing empirical research. While the use of ERPs has informed the neurodevelopment of face processing for some time now (see De Haan, Chapter 38, this volume), only in the past 5 years has fMRI been used with children on a regular basis.

Some of the hottest debates in adult cognitive neuroscience in recent years have focused on the degree to which face-sensitive markers of cortical function, such as the N170 ERP component, and activation of the fusiform face area (FFA) are selective for face processing, and how this degree of functional specificity arises in the first place (see Eimer, Chapter 17, this volume). In particular, for the FFA two opposing positions have emerged in accounting for the multitude of functional imaging data from adults. First, the "domain-specificity hypothesis" (Kanwisher et al., 1997) assumes that faces are processed in a modular and category specific fashion in the FFA. In opposition to this view is the "expertise hypothesis" that suggests that rather than being a dedicated face module, the FFA is a neural area involved in processing objects of expertise (Gauthier and Nelson, 2001). By the latter view, faces are the objects with which most adults have considerable expertise. While this debate has generated much further research with adults (see Kanwisher and Barton, Chapter 7; McKone and Robbins, Chapter 9; Scott, Chapter 11, this volume), the general question of the origin of functional specialization in human cortex is primarily a developmental issue. Specifically, the developmental question is what are the factors both intrinsic and extrinsic to the cortex that ensure that (1) we develop particular types of specialized cognitive functions relevant for our survival, such as face and language processing, and (2) these specialized functions usually end up located in approximately the same parts of cortex? The most obvious answer to these questions is that specific genes are expressed in particular parts of cortex and then "code for" patterns of wiring particular to certain computational functions. While this type of explanation appears to be valid for specialized computations within subcortical structures, a variety of genetic, neurobiological, and cognitive neuroscience evidence indicates that it is, at best, only part of the story for many human cognitive functions dependent on cerebral cortex.

I have previously outlined three viewpoints on human functional brain development (e.g. Johnson, 2001). According to a "maturational" perspective, functional brain development involves the sequential coming "on line" of a number of modular cortical regions. The maturation of a given region is thought to allow or enable advances in the perceptual, cognitive, or motor abilities of the child. As applied to the neurodevelopment of face perception, this implies that more complex aspects (such as "theory of mind" computations) will depend on the sequential maturation of associated cortical regions (possibly within the prefrontal cortex). This view fits best with the domain specificity hypothesis in the adult literature.

The second perspective on human functional brain development, "skill learning," argues for parallels between the dynamic brain events associated with the acquisition of complex perceptual and motor skills in adults, and the changes in brain function seen as infants and children come to successfully perform simpler tasks. From this perspective, it has been argued that some cortical regions become recruited for processing face stimulus information because typical humans become perceptual experts in this domain (Gauthier and Nelson, 2001). This view, then, clearly fits with the expertise hypothesis in the adult literature.

A third perspective, "interactive specialization," posits that functional brain development, at least in cerebral cortex, involves a process of specialization in which regions go from initially having very broadly-tuned functions, to having increasingly finely-tuned (more specialized) functions (Johnson 2001, 2002). A consequence of increased specialization of cortical regions is the increasingly focal patterns of cortical activation resulting from a given task demand or stimulus. By this view, some regions of cortex gradually become increasingly specialized for processing social stimuli and thus become recruited to face perception computations.

How does the empirical evidence from the neurodevelopment of face perception fit these views? The evidence available from positron emission tomography and electroencephalography/ERP studies suggests that most of the brain areas and mechanisms implicated in adult face processing can be activated relatively early in postnatal life. However, there are some additional effects, such as the activation of the inferior frontal and superior temporal gyrus in response to faces in 2-month-olds (Tzourio-Mazoyer et al., 2002), and the superior temporal sulcus generator of the face inversion effect found in 3- and 12-month-olds (Johnson et al., 2005), that do not directly map onto the mature face processing system. In addition to the extra regions involved while infants perceive faces, another important observation in the infant ERP work is that the infant face processing system possesses much broader response properties which are not yet as finely tuned to upright human faces (see de Haan, Chapter 38, this volume). This suggests that despite the gradual cortical specialization seen throughout the first year of life, the system continues to specialize well beyond infancy and into childhood.

More direct evidence for or against these models can be gained from fMRI developmental neuroimaging studies with children while they are engaged in face processing. The interactive specialization view predicts that with development there will be increased selectivity (fine tuning) in the activation of cortical areas for specific functions such as face processing. A consequence of this more selective activation of cortical areas is that the extent of cortical tissue activated in a given task context, or in response to a particular stimulus, will decrease and become more focal as the child gets older. This contrasts with the view that such cortical functional specializations are present from birth, or that they mature in a way relatively uninfluenced by experience.

We (Cohen-Kadosh and Johnson, 2007; Johnson et al., 2009) examined the currently available developmental fMRI literature on faces with regard to two hypotheses generated by the interactive specialization approach: 1) Does cortical activation in response to viewing faces become more focal and localized during development? 2) Does the degree of functional specialization (as measured by the degree of tuning to faces) increase in specificity during development? Encouragingly, we found some consistency across the seven developmental fMRI studies conducted to date. Collectively, these studies show that while faces activate specific areas of cortex in children, these areas may occupy more extensive or slightly different regions from those seen in adults. Further, the three most recent studies show evidence of increasing tuning of face-sensitive areas of cortex (Golarai et al., 2007; Passarotti et al., 2003; Scherf et al., 2007) accompanied in some cases by more focal patterns of activation in older children. In general, these dynamic developmental changes in cortical activation were consistent with the predictions of the interactive specialization view. Future studies will no doubt focus more on the emergence of specialized face processing networks during development using functional and structural connectivity measures. To date, the study of face perception during childhood provides perhaps the richest data source for comparing theories of functional specialization in human cortex, illustrating once again the two-way interaction between face perception studies and developmental science.

Summary and conclusions

In this chapter, I have illustrated that face perception has been one of the most important domains of study for our understanding of perceptual, cognitive, and neurocognitive aspects of human development. Additionally, the domain of face perception is one of the oldest battlegrounds for resolving key issues in the nature–nurture debate going back to Darwin and then to the origins of empirical work on human infants in the 1960s. This viewpoint on the history of the field has, of course, reflected my personal perspective and biases. Specifically, I highlighted Johnson and Morton's (1991) two-process theory of the development of face perception, and reviewed aspects of the theory that have stood the test of time, as well as other parts that have required modification in the light of additional empirical data.

In the next two sections of the chapter I examined how developmental thinking has influenced current research and issues on adult face perception. First, evidence for a putative subcortical route for face processing in adults has been bolstered by data from newborns where evidence suggests that cortical functioning is poor. Second, I suggested that debates about the role of expertise/experience in the activation of the "fusiform face area" could be resolved by theory and recent data from developmental fMRI studies supporting a gradual increase in functional specialization of the region.

Returning to the issue raised at the beginning of this chapter, we can now reconsider the factors, both intrinsic and extrinsic to the human cortex, that ensure that we both develop specialized processing of faces, and that this specialized function usually becomes located in the same parts of cortex in adults. With regard to developing a cortex specialized for face processing, I briefly reviewed evidence that newborns preferentially look toward faces. A number of lines of evidence suggested that this newborn preference is not mediated by the same cortical structures involved in face processing in adults, and may be due to a subcortical route for face detection. One purpose of this early tendency to fixate on faces may be to elicit bonding from adult caregivers. However, I suggest that an equally important purpose is to bias the visual input to plastic cortical circuits. This biased sampling of the visual environment over the first days and weeks of life may ensure the appropriate specialization of later developing cortical circuitry (Morton and Johnson, 1991). In addition to these findings, recent work has shown that newborns prefer to look at faces that engage them in direct (mutual) eye gaze (Farroni et al., 2002). Maintaining mutual gaze with another's face ensures foveation of that stimulus, a fact that may be relevant to the eventual location of "face areas" within the cortex (see Malach et al., 2004). Thus, I suggest, this newborn bias effectively "tutors" the developing cortex and early foveation of faces may, in part, determine the location of face-sensitive areas within cortex. In terms of the nature versus nurture issue, the research on faces has helped us understand the complex interplay between intrinsic and extrinsic factors in which each individual child's brain constructs its own specialized face-processing network. In my view headline claims about "innate face processing" (Sugita, 2009) or perceptual expertise (Gauthier and Nelson, 2001) do the field no justice in that they harp back to polarized debates from over 20 years ago. Usually, when we look more closely at the empirical details the subtle interweaving of nature and nurture is evident (see Maurer and Mondloch, Chapter 40, this volume). For example, the recent work of Sugita (2008, 2009) on monkeys reared without exposure to faces shows that they have abilities similar to those that have already been reported for human newborns, and that they subsequently show a process of perceptual tuning or specialization that is also very reminiscent of reports from human development (see Lee et al., Chapter 39, this volume). Sugita (2009) also speculates that the infant's proprioception or tactile contact with its own face may be important for establishing visual face perception skills, a suggestion that merits investigation with humans also.

What of the future? I believe that face perception will continue to be an important domain for our understanding of general issues in developmental science and vice versa. The application of theories based on typical development to developmental disorders with known atypicality in face processing such as autism, Williams syndrome, and developmental prosopagnosia (Webb et al., Chapter 43; Behrmann et al., Chapter 41; Duchaine, Chapter 42, respectively, this volume), will be a critical application of our basic research. Multimodal imaging offering good temporal and spatial resolution will be critical for discriminating between different theories of the emergence of cortical specialization for face perception (Grossman et al., 2008). Computational and neural network modeling of the emergence of specialization for face perception will be an essential bridge between brain and cognition (see Cottrell and Hsiao, Chapter 21, this volume). Moving from static and schematic to realistic and dynamic face images, presented in both foveal and peripheral visual fields, will be important to ensure that we are not just studying the brain responses to pictures of faces, rather than the real thing. Finally, studying how specific neural circuitry becomes tuned to face perception within the richer context of social cognition and interaction will help us unravel the complex dynamics between babies' experience of interaction with others, and their abilities to detect and analyze the signals from their faces.

References

Bailey, A.J., Braeutigam, S., Jousmaki, V., and Swithenby S.J. (2005). Abnormal activation of face processing systems at early and intermediate latency in individuals with autism spectrum disorder: a magnetoencephalographic study. *European Journal of Neuroscience*, **21**, 2575–2585.

Batki, A., Baron-Cohen, S., Wheelwright, S., Connellan, J., and Ahluwalia, J. (2000). Is there an innate gaze module? Evidence from human neonates. *Infant Behavior & Development*, **23**, 223–229.

Blasi, A., Lloyd-Fox, S., Everdell, N., *et al.* (2007). Investigation of depth dependent changes in cerebral haemodynamics during face perception in infants. *Physics in Medicine and Biology*, **52**, 6849–6864.

Carey, S., Diamond, R., and Woods, B. (1980). The development of face recognition: a maturational component? *Developmental Psychology*, **16**, 257–269.

Cohen-Kadosh, K. and Johnson, M.H. (2007). Developing a cortex specialized for face perception. *Trends in Cognitive Science*, **11**, 367–369.

Darwin, C. (1872). *The expression of emotion in man and animals*. London: John Murray.

de Schonen, S. and Mathivet, E. (1990). Hemispheric asymmetry in a face discrimination task in infants. *Child Development*, **61**, 1192–1205.

Fantz, R. (1963). Pattern vision in newborn infants. *Science*, **140**, 296–297.

Farroni, T., Csibra, G., Simion, F. and Johnson, M.H. (2002). Eye contact detection in humans from birth. *Proceedings of the National Academy of Sciences* (USA), **99**, 9602–9605.

Farroni, T., Johnson, M.H., Menon, E., Zulian, L., Faraguna, D., and Csibra G. (2005). Newborns' preference for face-relevant stimuli: Effects of contrast polarity. *Proceedings of National Academy of Sciences*, **102**, 17245–17250.

Farroni, T., Menon, E., Rigato, S., and Johnson, M.H. (2007). The perception of facial expressions in newborns. *European Journal of Developmental Psychology*, **4**, 2–13.

Gauthier, I. and Nelson, C. (2001). The development of face expertise. *Current Opinion in Neurobiology*, **11**, 219–224.

George, N., Driver, J., and Dolan, R. (2001). Seeing gaze-direction modulates fusiform activity and its coupling with other brain areas during face processing. *NeuroImage*, **13**, 1102–1112.

Golarai, G., Ghahremani, D.G., Whitfield-Gabrieli, S., *et al.* (2007). Differential development of high-level visual cortex correlates with category-specific recognition memory. *Nature Neuroscience*, **10**, 512–522.

Goren, C.C., Sarty, M., and Wu, P.Y.K. (1975). Visual following and pattern discrimination of face-like stimuli by newborn infants. *Pediatrics*, **56**, 544–549.

Grossman, T., Johnson, M.H., Lloyd-Fox, S., *et al.* (2008). Early cortical specialization for face-to-face communication in human infants. *Proceedings of the Royal Society B*, **275**, 2803–2811.

Johnson, M.H. (1990). Cortical maturation and the development of visual attention in early infancy. *Journal of Cognitive Neuroscience*, **2**, 81–95.

Johnson, M.H. (2001). Functional brain development in humans. *Nature Reviews Neuroscience*, **2**, 475–483.

Johnson, M.H. (2005). Sub-cortical face processing. *Nature Reviews Neuroscience*, **6**, 766–774.

Johnson, M. and Morton, J. (1991). *Biology and cognitive development. The case of face recognition.* Oxford: Blackwell.

Johnson, M.H., Bolhuis, J.J., and Horn, G. (1985). Interaction between acquired preferences and developing predispositions during imprinting. *Animal Behaviour*, **33**, 1000–1006.

Johnson, M.H., Dziurawiec, S., Ellis, H., and Morton, J. (1991). Newborns' preferential tracking of face-like stimuli and its subsequent decline. *Cognition*, **40**, 1–19.

Johnson, M.H., Griffin, R., Csibra, G., *et al.* (2005). The emergence of the social brain network: Evidence from typical and atypical development. *Development and Psychopathology*, **17**, 599–619.

Johnson, M.H., Grossman, T., and Farroni, T. (2008). The social cognitive neuroscience of infancy: illuminating the early development of the social brain functions. *Advances in Child Development and Behavior*, **36**, 331–372.

Johnson, M.H., Grossmann, T., and Cohen-Kadosh, K. (2009). Mapping functional brain development: Building a social brain through Interactive Specialization. *Developmental Psychology*, **45**, 151–159.

Kanwisher, N., McDermott, J., and Chun, M.M. (1997). The fusiform face area: A module in human extrastriate cortex specialized for face perception. *Journal of Neuroscience*, **17**, 4302–4311.

Kleinhans, N.M., Richards, T., Sterling, L., *et al.* (2008). Abnormal functional connectivity in autism spectrum disorders during face processing, *Brain*, **131**, 1000–1012.

Le Doux, J. (1996). *The Emotional Brain: The Mysterious Underpinnings of Emotional Life.* New York: Simon & Schuster.

Malach, R., Avidan, G., Lerner, V., Hasson, U. and Levy, I. (2004). The cartography of human visual object areas. In N. Kanwisher and J. Duncan (eds.), *Attention and Performance XX: Functional Neuroimaging of Visual Cognition*, pp. 195–204. Oxford: Oxford University Press.

Morton, J. and Johnson, M.H. (1991). CONSPEC and CONLERN: A two-process theory of infant face recognition. *Psychological Review*, **98**, 164–181.

Nelson, C.A. (2003). The development of face recognition reflects an experience-expectant and activity-dependent process. In O. Pascalis and A. Slater (eds.), *The development of face processing in infancy and early childhood: Current perspectives.* pp. 79–98. New York: Nova Science Publisher.

Passarotti, A.M., Smith, J., DeLano, M. and Huang, J. (2007). Developmental differences in the neural bases of the face inversion effect show progressive tuning of face-selective regions in the upright orientation. *Neuroimage*, **15**, 1708–1722

Quinn, P.C. and Slater, A. (2003). Face perception at birth and beyond. In O. Pascalis and A. Slater (eds.), *The development of face processing in infancy and early childhood: Current perspectives.* pp. 3–12. New York: Nova Science Publisher.

Scherf, K.S., Behrmann, M., Humphreys, K., and Luna, B. (2007). Visual category-selectivity for faces, places and objects emerges along different developmental trajectories. *Developmental Science*, **10**, F15–F31.

Senju, A. and Johnson, M.H. (2009). The eye contact effect: mechanisms and development. *Trends in Cognitive Science.* **13**, 127–134.

Simion, F., Macchi Cassia, V., Turati, C., and Valenza, E. (2003). Non-specific perceptual biases at the origins of face processing. In O. Pascalis and A. Slater (eds.), *The development of face processing in infancy and early childhood: Current perspectives.* pp. 13–26. New York: Nova Science Publisher.

Slater, A., Von der Schulenburg, C., Brown, E., and Badenoch, M. (1998). Newborn infants prefer attractive faces. *Infant Behavior and Development,* **21**, 345–354.

Slater, A., Quinn, P.C., Hayes, R., and Brown, E. (2000). The role of facial orientation in newborn infants' preference for attractive faces. *Developmental Science,* **3**, 181–185.

Sugita, Y. (2008). Face perception in monkeys reared with no experience to faces. *Proceedings of the National Academy of Sciences* (USA), **105**, 394–398.

Sugita, Y. (2009). Innate face processing. *Current Opinion in Neurobiology,* **19**, 39–44.

Tomalski, P., Csibra, G., and Johnson, M.H. (2009a). Rapid orienting toward face-like stimuli with gaze-relevant contrast information. *Perception,* **38**, 569–578

Tomalski, P., Johnson, M.H., and Csibra, G. (2009b). Temporal-nasal asymmetry of rapid orienting to face-like stimuli. *Neuroreport,* **20**, 1309–1312.

Tzourio-Mazoyer, N., de Schonen, S., Crivello, F., Reutter, B., Aujard, Y., and Mazoyer, B. (2002). Neural correlates of woman face processing by 2-month-old infants. *Neuroimage,* **15**, 454–461.

Winston, J.S., Vuilleumier, P. and Dolan, R.J. (2003). Effects of low-spatial frequency components of fearful faces on fusiform cortex activity. *Current Biology,* **13**, 1824–1829.

Chapter 2

Cognitive and Computational Approaches to Face Recognition

Alice J. O'Toole

The use of computational models for understanding human face perception and recognition has a long and intriguing history that runs parallel to efforts in the engineering literature to develop algorithms for computer-based face recognition systems. Over the years, intermittent collaborative interactions between computational and psychological approaches have offered numerous insights into the kinds of face representations capable of supporting the many tasks humans accomplish with faces. At the core of the intersection between cognitive and computational approaches is the physical reality of the human face itself, which is a complex three-dimensional object with overlapping pigmentation. Most of the time, we experience human faces in action, moving and deforming in complex and meaningful ways. The face is a primary source of the information we use for recognizing people and for classifying them into visually derived semantic classes (e.g. sex, race, age) (Bruce and Young, 1986). It also provides information useful for assessing a person's momentary emotional state (e.g. from smiles, frowns, etc.) and for determining their focus of attention (i.e. through gaze direction and head orientation).

Human expertise with faces is defined generally by the fact that we can remember hundreds, if not thousands, of faces as "individuals." This suggests an ability to extract and encode the information that makes a face unique. The computational challenges involved in this problem are of three sorts. The first is the general inverse optics problem of vision (henceforth, *Computational Challenge 1*), which is the fact that the visual system has, as input for the task of face recognition, two two-dimensional projections of the three-dimensional world—one image on each retina. The neural code for faces, and indeed, the rest of the visual world, must either recreate the lost third dimension (Marr, 1982) or must do without it (Gibson, 1966). Both strategies, by definition, force the visual system to rely on an error prone, or at least limited, estimate of the real visual world. The dissociable information at the core of this problem can be illustrated using data from a laser scan of a face (Figure 2.1), which separates the three-dimensional shape and reflectance/pigmentation in the face. Any unique combination of shape and reflectance information, (e.g. from an individual face) can produce a nearly limitless variety of two-dimensional retinal images, depending on the illumination conditions and the relative position of the viewer with respect to the head. This myriad of images must somehow be mapped to a single set of physical realities about the structure and reflectance properties of a face.

The second computational challenge is that, regardless of which strategy the neural system has evolved to deal with its limited quality sample of the world, it must ultimately encode and quantify the complex information in faces that we need to survive—the uniqueness of individual faces, the properties that specify age, sex, and race, and the social and emotional communication information faces convey (*Computational Challenge 2*). Thus, the single set of physical realities about the structure and reflectance properties of a face must be sufficient for the face processing tasks we do. Assuming that the visual system is capable of computing a reasonably veridical set of

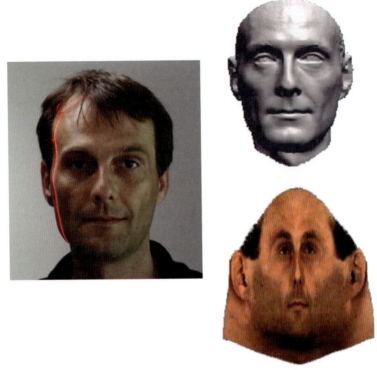

Fig. 2.1 A laser scan graphic that shows the sampling of the head (left), the three-dimensional shape information (right, top), and the reflectance information. The reflectance profile maps point for point onto the head surface and is a measure of how efficiently the pigmented surface reflects light across the spectrum.

measurements of faces, there is still the problem of finding the task-relevant information. Quantifying the complex variations in the three-dimensional shape and reflectance of a human face is by no means trivial. Again let's look at Figure 2.1. On the left, we see a laser scanner sampling the surface of a face. The output of the scan produces 512×512 (262,144) shape measurements expressible in x, y, z coordinates (Figure 2.1, upper right). The reflectance information is equally voluminous with the same number of samples expressed in r, g, b coordinates (somewhat analogous to the visual systems' filtering through the three cone channels) (Figure 2.1, lower right). From this complex input, which the human visual system likely processes in a highly different form, we are able identify to a "hooked nose," wide-set eyes, and a "perky" face.

The third computational challenge is that the "unique" information that specifies face identity does not exist in absolute terms, but rather is dependent on a reference population of relevant faces (*Computational Challenge 3*). A nose of a certain type has diagnostic value for identifying a person, only to the extent that is "unusual" within the context of a population of faces. A neural code for faces will be most efficient if it references the amount and type of variability in a relevant population of human faces. Some element of this population referencing is needed to account for several phenomena in human face recognition, including the recognition of other-race faces. In the case of other-race face recognition, the appropriate prototype or reference face is different and our limited experience with other-race face populations may constrain the quality of the representation we can create.

These three computational challenges apply to understanding human face representations from a neural and psychological point of view and are at the core of the productive dialog that has taken place between psychologists and computer vision researchers over the past two decades. Neuroscientists have come into this dialog more recently as functional neuroimaging studies have uncovered some of the basic structure of the neural organization of face processing. A further opportunity for dialog between neuroscientists and psychologists has arisen with findings of high-level visual after-effects for faces elicited with perceptual adaptation methods (Leopold et al., 2001; Webster and MacLin, 1999). We will return to this approach at the end of the chapter.

In this chapter, we will consider the insights gained from combining computational and cognitive approaches to the study of human face recognition. We will discuss the ways in which computational models have informed studies of human face processing and vice versa and how these interactions may be directed in the future to push progress in both fields forward. The chapter is organized as follows. We begin with the concept of a face space, in its abstract, psychological, and physical/computational forms. Next, we consider how physical face spaces have evolved via increasingly sophisticated kinds of inputs that alter the predictions we make about face processing as a function of the topography of these spaces. Different inputs change the nature of the space and its suitability as a model of human face representations. We will then look briefly at how adaptation as a method is beginning to reveal properties of neural representations in a way that connects with the cognitive/perceptual approach. Finally, we will discuss recent progress in state-of-the-art computational models of face recognition, which offer us a new perspective on the cognitive-computational dialog.

I will concentrate primarily on computer models of facial identity recognition, but readers can find information on computer recognition of other facial cues (e.g. facial expressions) in chapters by Cottrell and Hsiao (Chapter 21); Stewart-Bartlett and Whitehill (Chapter 25); and Calder (Chapter 22) elsewhere in this volume. Additional related studies of computational models of face processing for identification can be found in Chapter 20 by Vetter and Walker.

Representing faces

Measuring the information in a face and representing it in a face space

The *face space* model, introduced by Valentine (1991), serves as a metaphor for understanding human face representations. It is virtually impossible to explain the interaction between the computational and cognitive approaches to understanding face recognition without reference to this model. It serves as the glue that binds the theoretical and computational aspects of the problem together. The framework can be described simply with a few basic premises. First, faces are defined metaphorically as points in a multidimensional space. Second, the axes of the multidimensional face space define a "feature" set with which individual faces can be encoded. As such, each face has a value on each feature axis, and the combination of these feature values specifies its place in the space. Third, the similarity of two faces in the space can be measured as the Euclidean distance between them.

Abstract face space

As introduced by Valentine (1991), the face space was an *abstract* or theoretical construct for understanding some intrinsic factors underlying human face perception. In particular, the effect of face typicality on recognition (Light et al., 1979) and classification (Valentine and Bruce, 1986) are conceptually easy to assimilate in this framework. Typical faces are in the center of a crowded face space, and thus are recognized less accurately than unusual faces, because they are more easily confused with other faces. Typical faces are also classified as faces faster than unusual faces (Valentine and Bruce, 1986), presumably, because this classification involves a comparison between the object and the face prototype (though see Burton and Vokey, 1998, for a more technical account of a face space with higher dimensionality).

The concept of an abstract face space offers a framework for understanding the importance of *Computational Challenge 3*—that human face processing skills must be understood in the context of a relevant population of faces. The face space even in this simple abstract form forced psychologists to consider the statistical structure of populations of faces and its implications for human performance. I will argue later in this chapter that this is a challenge that the developers of computer-based face recognition algorithms have yet to appreciate fully.

Psychological face space

A psychological face space represents human judgments of face similarity in a direct, map-like way and can be helpful for understanding the "feature" space that underlies these judgments. To create a psychological face space, a similarity or distance matrix is created from similarity judgments made to pairs of faces. These judgments are averaged over a large number of subjects and are submitted to a multidimensional scaling analysis, often implemented as a simple linear principal components analysis (PCA). The analysis produces a face space, of n dimensions, with the dimensions ordered according to the proportion of variance explained in the human similarity judgments. A researcher decides the number of dimensions needed to provide a good account of the human similarity data—often as few as three or four. These dimensions can sometimes be interpreted visually, by simply placing individual face images on the graph at their derived locations and observing the differences between the faces that land at opposite ends of individual dimensions. Often these "features" include face shape (round faces at one end, thin faces at the other end), facial complexion (dark versus light complexions) and other generally Gestalt-like variations in facial appearance.

This psychological similarity map can be useful in sifting through the inferred feature dimensions that make faces more or less perceptually similar. It can be used also to test the validity of various types of physical face spaces. There are several problems with this approach, however, that have limited its broader use by researchers. First, the axes must be interpreted in an ad hoc way. Second, different subjects vary in the similarity criteria they use for generating these measures, making the technique susceptible to overt strategies applied by subjects ("I will look at the eyes"). Third, and perhaps the most limiting, is that the technique does not provide enough dimensions to capture all or even most of the information we represent from faces. At its best, a psychological face space highlights the role of the statistical structure of the face population (*Computational Challenge 3*) and offers a technique for inferring the saliency of some of the information we encode about faces (*Computational Challenge 2*).

Physical face space

A physical face space provides a method for quantifying the information in a set of faces and produces a statistically derived feature set for representing faces. This opens the door for asking whether a particular derived physical face space can account for various aspects of human face processing. A physical face space is created as follows. A set of physical measures is taken on a large set of faces, and encoded in individual vectors (one per face). The measures can include anything quantifiable about a face (e.g. nose length, pixel value, etc.). As with human similarity judgments, a covariance matrix of these physical measurements can be submitted to a PCA to produce a face space, of n dimensions, with the dimensions ordered according to the proportion of variance explained in the similarity matrix. These axes are now tangible, physical measures of the information in the set of faces from which they are derived.

This physical space represents the statistical structure of the similarity among faces in the set that depends directly on the types of measures made at the outset and on the variability of the population of faces analyzed. Although the interpretation of individual axes in the space must be made visually, a researcher has one additional interpretation tool for a physical face space that is not available with a psychological face space. Because the space is linear, and because the information is directly quantifiable from the face, it is usually possible to alter individual faces by tweaking the feature values within a face and re-synthesizing the face. By looking at how these manipulations change the face, often a guess about the nature of the information represented by the feature axes is possible.

The use of physical face space models to understand human face recognition has progressed over time with the creation of increasingly sophisticated spaces via the analysis of increasingly sophisticated face quantification schemes. In this way, computational face modeling progress has been front-loaded. By this, I mean that most of the insights we have gained have come from changes in what goes into the space rather than from more sophisticated ways of deriving the space. In fact, most researchers in both psychology and in some aspects of computer vision still use the simplest and least assumption-laden method available, PCA. In what follows, for simplicity, I will use PCA as a place-holder for any multidimensional space-creating analysis. Bear in mind that anything that works to create a graphic multidimensional space from the stimuli is an option.

Before proceeding, it is perhaps worth noting that the construct of the physical face space offers a basic framework for approaching *Computational Challenges 2* and *3*, but not *Computational Challenge 1*—the inverse optics problem. For the former two challenges, the face space lays theoretical groundwork for understanding the nature of the information in faces and how it relates to face populations as a whole. It does not directly address questions of how to overcome the inverse optics challenge to face recognition, which is tied to the specifics of the representation. In the next section, we consider the importance of *what goes into the space*, how it has changed over time, and the insights these changes have offered into understanding human face processing.

Feature quantification systems: input to the physical face space models

To make a long story short, in the era after Marr's (1982) classic book *Vision*, computer vision researchers were intent on extracting (or computing) representations of the three-dimensional structure of objects. This goal filtered into the first attempts to formalize computational approaches to face recognition. At a minimum, this required measuring the information in faces in a way that stayed true to the veridical three-dimensional, object-centered, invariant, attributes of the face—a goal that turned out to be unrealistic for both objects and faces given the technology and algorithms of the time. The post-Marr era began roughly with Poggio and Edelman's (1990) argument that extracting three-dimensional object-centered representations might not be necessary for object recognition. This approach was bolstered by psychological findings that indicated some degree of view-dependence in human performance for recognizing objects and faces (Bülthoff and Edelman, 1992; O'Toole et al., 1998a; Troje and Bülthoff, 1996; though see Biederman, 1987). The underlying assumption was that view-dependent object representations should yield view-dependent human performance. In hindsight, it is clear this assumption was overly simplistic. In particular, the assumption does not consider what happens to a face representation as a face becomes familiar (Jiang et al., 2009; Wallis and Bülthoff, 1999). Notwithstanding, computational trends and human object and face recognition data spurred the use of simpler image-based inputs, although at the beginning the use of these codes for psychological models was controversial.

In perspective, it is worth remembering that there are important differences between object and face recognition. Poggio and Edelman (1990), for example, explored computationally how much object recognition ("That is a chair") could be done using viewer-centered, image-based measurements. Object recognition researchers were mostly concerned with solving the problem of recognizing objects (classifying exemplars into object categories) over changes in viewpoint. Face recognition researchers, on the other hand, were more concerned with finding a recognition code that would capture enough of the subtle information in faces to quantify the uniqueness of individual faces ("That is Shimon"). Given that all faces have the same set of features, arranged in roughly the same configuration, it seemed evident that face codes would have to capture (implicitly or explicitly) more than a few simple discrete features. This provided an even stronger push in face recognition for assuming that an analysis of facial images might provide a good starting point for input to a face space.

Image-based representations

The first psychologically-motivated image-based face recognition model appeared under the name of auto-associative networks (O'Toole et al., 1988). Storing face images in an auto-associative memory allowed for content addressable retrieval of faces and used distributed storage mechanisms (i.e. individual face memories shared the same coding space rather than being assigned to different memory locations). In particular, this face code allowed generalization of recognition between images that varied in spatial frequency content (O'Toole et al., 1988). The paper was published in one of the first issues of the journal *Neural Networks* and was of interest to neural network researchers because it made use of Kohonen's (1984) auto-associative memory model. It further drew on Kohonen's use of face images to demonstrate that associative memory models could fill in missing information from occluded, blurred, or partial images previously stored in the memory. Of note, Kohonen (1984) made clear the link between auto-associative memory models and PCA (eigenvector analysis), which had not been explored in any detail within the context of an image memory application.

The second reason our paper ended up in *Neural Networks* was because it kept getting rejected from psychology journals, with reviewers expressing serious reservations about the use of image-based codes in a model of human face processing. I was sympathetic to these reviews, but I still thought that the model had some intriguing psychological properties that were worth exploring. First of all, it worked really well as a content addressable memory, having lossless encoding and relatively high-capacity storage. In other words, you could store many faces in the memory with no quality loss, using a single area of memory that shared resources. Thus, it did not force localized or separate storage of each face in a different place. Second, you could retrieve the stored images from "cue images" that were occluded, blurred, or otherwise frequency-filtered. Third, you did not have to do feature selection—a psychological perk that seemed to resonate with configural face codes. Fourth, retrieval of a face image did not require a serial search through a database of stored face images and the time required did not vary as a function of the number of images in the memory.

Although psychologists had reservations, computer vision researchers embraced the practical advantages of a simple, image-based PCA for face recognition applications. In a highly influential paper, Turk and Pentland (1991) proposed an image-based eigenanalysis (PCA) model for face recognition. Zhao et al. (2003), in their review of computational face recognition algorithms, describe Turk and Pentland's (1991) work as "the first really successful demonstration of machine recognition of faces" (p. 412). In addition to the fact that the image-based PCA could do face recognition better than it had been done before, other work suggested that the representation it used was amenable to being dissected and analyzed in interesting ways. Sirovich and Kirby (1987) had explored low-dimensional representations of faces in PCA, using only PCs/eigenvectors that explained large proportions of variance in the image set. O'Toole et al. (1993) found that PCs explaining large amounts of variance were better for face categorization tasks (e.g. by sex), whereas PCs explaining smaller amounts of variance were better for recognizing faces. This made intuitive sense, because the information that makes a face male or female is relevant for all faces in a population, whereas the information that makes individual faces unique is likely to explain little variance in a population of faces. It also gave us insight into understanding how the complex information in faces that could be used for different tasks (e.g. recognition, classification) could be dissociated.

In short, it was possible with this model to examine in some detail, the importance of computationally extracted features for different face processing tasks. With relatively little effort, this image-based version of a physical face space could be linked to some basic phenomena in the psychology of face perception, including the perception of face gender (Abdi et al., 1995; O'Toole et al., 1998b), and recognition of own- versus other-race faces (O'Toole et al., 1994).

The most critical problem with the pure image-based eigenface analysis was the fact that it required averaging face images without regard to the correspondence of feature locations. The correspondence problem for faces involves finding the locations of landmark features (e.g. tip of the nose, etc.) in all face images and coding these locations explicitly. This is easy to do by eye but challenging to do automatically. The problem with image-based eigenanalysis was quickly apparent to both psychologists and computer vision researchers. Because of its practical value, however, and the ease of roughly aligning and scaling face images (i.e. relative to difficulty of solving the correspondence problem), pure image-based models have persisted longer in machine-based face recognition algorithms (Zhao et al., 2003) than in psychological models of face recognition.

Two-dimensional morphable models

Researchers from both psychology and computer vision worked on going to the next step. From a computational perspective, Craw and Cameron (1991) were able to eliminate deviations from the average face shape from individual faces before submitting the faces to PCA. These "shape-free" faces were made by: (1) locating (by hand) a set of landmark feature points on each of a set of face; (2) averaging the locations of these points over a set of faces; and (3) morphing individual face images into the average shape. A PCA of these shape-free faces captures the image-based information in faces, free of the artifacts inherent in combining misaligned images. Unfortunately, a PCA on shape-free faces is also free of information about face configuration. More precisely, each face is morphed into the configuration of the average face, so that the features (nose, mouth, etc.) align with the features of the average face. Because facial configuration in this model does not vary across the set of faces, it loses its diagnostic value for identification. This is surely overkill for a psychological model of face perception. Hancock and colleagues (1996) added back the configural information, but in a form that allowed for separate shape and shape-free face image codes. The shape representation came from information about the two-dimensional deformation of individual faces (i.e. their landmark point locations) from the average face. The shape-free "texture" information came from the corresponded shape-free face. Next, they analyzed the shape and shape-free information in separate PCAs. The PCA predictions based on shape and shape-free face analyses dissociated hits and false positives in a face recognition task performed by humans. Hancock et al. (1996) found that the shape-free information predicted false positives and the shape information predicted hits. There was also evidence indicating that PCs explaining larger amounts of variance were generally more predictive of false positives. This physical framework made strong progress in modeling the effects of typicality on face recognition and in isolating the kinds of information in faces that contribute to different errors.

It is worth noting that two-dimensional morphable representations are also at the core of facial caricaturing. Caricaturing had long been possible using two-dimensional shape spaces that dragged the image points (pixel values) along with the shape deformation (cf. Rhodes, 1996 for a complete review), but did not alter pixel values. Benson and Perrett (1991), for example, were able to make precise photorealistic caricatures by two-dimensional shape deformations applied to photographs. They found that magnitude of the caricature advantage for human subjects recognizing faces correlated with the familiarity of the faces and with the quality of the caricaturing process as judged by caricature experts. They also showed an advantage for the speed of naming faces that were caricatured. Lee et al. (2000) found that this type of multidimensional face model accounted well for identification accuracy and distinctiveness ratings of veridical, caricatured, and anti-caricatured faces. The work of Lee and Perrett (1997) took this caricaturing process one step further to include caricaturing the color values in face images—a method that bridges to a more complete face representation.

It is worth pausing to consider the differences between the two-dimensional "semi-corre-sponded" face-space model and the pure image analysis. Semi-corresponded models code the shape, but not reflectance, in terms that relate individual faces to the average face. One difference is that it is possible to morph selectively through the part of the space that encodes the two-dimensional configural shape (i.e. via the facial landmark position codes). In the pure image-based face space, morphing can produce images that "leave the face space." This means that when there are correspondence artifacts or errors, a face with "two noses" or "two chins" can be synthesized in the morphing process. In the pure shape space, only valid faces lie on the trajectories between any two faces. A second difference is that the average of the shape space is necessarily a meaningful reference for all other faces, because the faces defined as deformations from the average. The representation of a face's shape in this space is a "point in the multidimensional space" (as in the image space), but one that is directly connected to the average face in the space. Concomitantly, the inclusion of the shape-free space also retains a measure of the image-based reflectance (although one that is not inherently dissociable from viewing parameters, e.g. illumination). The representation of a face's reflectance in this space is a point, similar to the point representation used in the image space (i.e. corresponded, but not linked formally to the average). Although it may look like a subtle difference, the Lee and Perrett (1997) model adds a "connected-to-the-average morphability" feature for color information. This is an important, but under-utilized, method in two-dimensional morphable spaces.

The idea of a dual shape- and shape-free space was an enormous improvement over a pure image-based space. One drawback in its use for computational modeling, however, was the work-intense pre-requisite involved in hand-locating enough landmark points (more than 30) in enough faces (over 100) to make a meaningful and clean morph in a face space that represented a sufficiently diverse, "psychologically interesting," population of faces. Although computer graphics researchers were making progress on the problem of automating the correspondence problem for faces (cf. Beymer et al., 1993; Lanitis et al., 1995; Vetter and Poggio, 1997), these techniques were sufficiently complex and technically demanding that they did not filter easily into psychology labs.

Three-dimensional morphable models

A completely automated solution to the correspondence problem for laser scan data on a large number of faces was put forth in 1999 by Blanz and Vetter (cf. Chapter 20, this volume, by Vetter and Walker). The laser scans they analyzed contained a direct and dense measure of the three-dimensional surface and a similarly dense measure of the point-for-point overlay of reflectance information. This latter measure did not confound viewing parameters, because of the use of an ambient light source by the scanner. Blanz and Vetter (1999) took several impressive steps forward from what had been accomplished previously. First, correspondence was established on all of the roughly quarter of a million head sample points, rather than on a subset of facial landmark points. Second, this corresponded representation was the first truly object-centered representation of faces analyzed in a face space (no light required). Third, the space was completely morphable, either in a way that cohesively combined the three-dimensional shape and reflectance information, or in a way that separated the space and reflectance subspaces. Fourth, because the face is represented in object-centered coordinates, face variations produced by morphing between faces, or by morphing in arbitrary directions in the space, can be viewed (with computer graphics) from any viewpoint and under any illumination condition (by putting back the light).

This space offered psychologists a myriad of options for manipulating the information in faces in precise and interesting ways. The representation of a face's shape and reflectance in this space is linked directly to the average face (with shape and reflectance included). An individual face's location in the space, therefore, is not just a point, but rather a trajectory that is defined by the line originating at the average face and continuing to the location of the individual face in the space. It is, therefore, the direction of this vector in the space that defines a face's *identity trajectory*.

In principle, any morphable space is useful for graphically altering human faces. The Blanz and Vetter (1999) space is an *object-centered* version of the more common *viewer-centered* two-dimensional morph spaces (Benson and Perrett, 1991; Hancock et al., 1996). In what follows, I will focus primarily on psychological findings that have emerged from work using the three-dimensional morphable model, incorporating data from two-dimensional morphable manipulations where relevant. Bear in mind, however, that the two-dimensional morphable model operates in an analogous viewer-centered way for shape.[1]

In the three-dimensional morphable space, the distinctiveness of faces can be manipulated easily by creating caricatures and anti-caricatures that incorporate both shape and reflectance information simultaneously. The caricature is made by stretching a face vector away from the average, while retaining the direction of its identity trajectory. Notably, caricatures can be made either with respect to the three-dimensional shape and/or reflectance. Caricaturing only the three-dimensional information in a face can age it decades, by enhancing slight creases in young faces into deep wrinkles (O'Toole et al., 1997; see Figure 2.2). This finding suggests that a part of information for face age is person-specific, rather than based on a general aging routine. Further, the finding complements Burt and Perrett's (1995) demonstration of aging a face in a two-dimensional morph space. They morphed younger faces in the direction of the average of the older faces and found a role for an aging algorithm that generalizes across individuals.

The importance of shape versus reflectance information has been tested also for face recognition using manipulations of faces in the three-dimensional morphing space. O'Toole et al. (1999) measured human recognition performance for a set of faces that varied only in shape and a set of faces that varied only in reflectance. These stimuli were created by morphing individual reflectance maps onto the shape average (shape-normalized faces) and by morphing the average reflectance map onto the shape of the individual faces (reflectance-normalized faces). Human recognition performance benefited from both shape and reflectance information. Recognition performance for the original faces, which varied both in shape and reflectance, was approximately equal to the sum of performance for the faces that varied only in shape and the faces that varied only in reflectance.

---

[1] One exception is Lee and Perrett's (1997) model, which implements reflectance codes also in terms of the face average.

Fig. 2.2 Caricaturing only the three-dimensional shape information in a face ages the face. The original scan is of a man in his early thirties (second from the left). An anti-caricature appears to the left of the original and three increasingly exaggerated caricatures appear to the right.

By far the weirdest invention of the Blanz and Vetter (1999) space has been the "anti-face" or face opposite (Figure 2.3; see also Rhodes and Leopold, Chapter 14, this volume, for a face space illustration). A face's anti-face is made in this space by reversing the direction of its identity trajectory, to pass back through the average face and continue along the line, roughly an equal distance in the opposite direction. This arrives at a point in space where the face's values on each of the many multidimensional axes in the space are inverted (opposite) to their original values (Blanz et al., 2000). I half-remember the first time Volker Blanz showed me an anti-face, almost incidentally. He said something like "Just set the caricature value on the morpher model to –1." What could be simpler? The anti-face was not designed into the morpher, it was just numerically there—on the other side of the mean. It can exist meaningfully only in a space where faces are in correspondence with the average. Although cognitively we understand that the face-anti-face pairs are a kind of opposite (round faces become elongated, dark complexions become light), there is a perceptual disconnect when the face crosses the mean and goes over to the other side. Faces retain their identity all along the identity trajectory from the average to the original face, but encounter a strong perceptual break with the original identity on the other side of the mean (Blanz et al., 2000). We found out soon after, however, that this perceptual break did not mean that these faces are disconnected from each other in the representational space. This connection became apparent in the form of high-level visual adaptation for faces.

Adaptation and the organization of the face space around the prototype

In recent years, one of the most fruitful methods for studying human face representation has been based on findings that face perception is susceptible to aftereffects elicited by adaptation.

Fig. 2.3 A face (left) and its anti-face opposite appear strongly dissimilar. The original face is thin and elongated with a dark complexion. The anti-face has a round shape with a light complexion.

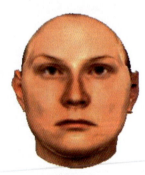

The effects are much the same as other lower-order visual aftereffects (e.g. color; Hering, 1878). Because the face adaptation literature is covered in detail elsewhere in this book (Rhodes and Leopold, Chapter 14), I will mention just a few effects and will focus on how these effects relate to the computational constructs presented in this chapter. The classic finding of Webster and MacLin (1999) demonstrated that adaptation to a grotesquely expanded or contracted face biases the perception of a subsequently presented normal face to appear distorted in the opposite direction. In other work, Leopold et al. (2001) found that adaptation to an anti-face biases the perception of an identity-neutral "average" face to appear as the original face. Further findings by Webster et al. (2004) showed face aftereffects for gender, race, and expression. All of these results suggest that the representations of faces that are quite distant in the perceptual and neural face space are strongly interconnected.

The opponent direction of the perceptual bias suggests the importance of a prototype or average face in the representation of individual faces. Thus, it seems that the feature values of an individual face in the space are defined with respect to average values across a relevant population. These findings fit comfortably into the framework of a morphable space, where "deformation from the average" is the basic unit of analysis, and where it is possible to reset or move the average in the short term, based on experience or exposure to a particular type of face. Again, the connectedness of faces in the space, and their codependence in coding is revealed in a compelling way by the fact that perceiving a particular face can influence one's subsequent perception of a highly dissimilar face, far away in the space.

Adaptation, and the psychological questions that have been addressed with this technique, rest heavily on predictions formulated in the computational construct of a face space. These findings have opened the door to addressing questions about the way faces are coded neurally. Numerous studies have demonstrated that face adaptation shows tolerance to two-dimensional affine transformations in the size, orientation, and retinal position of a face (Anderson and Wilson, 2005; Jeffrey et al., 2006; Leopold et al., 2001; Rhodes et al., 2003; Watson and Clifford, 2003; Zhao and Chubb, 2001). This eliminates low-level retinotopic visual processing areas as the neural locus of the effects. Moreover, recent studies using functional neuroimaging (Loffler et al., 2005) and neurophysiological methods (Leopold et al., 2006) support a prototype-centered organization of face representations. Both studies show a stronger neural response for faces distant from the average face.

Returning to questions about the nature of the information captured by the human face representations, using stimuli created with the three-dimensional morpher, Jiang et al. (2006) showed that identity adaptation effects can be elicited by faces that are opposites either in shape only or in reflectance only. This suggests that both shape and reflectance are encoded in this prototype-centered space. Further, Jiang et al. (2006) and Jeffrey et al. (2006) found partial transfer of face aftereffects across three-dimensional viewpoint change. Incorporating in the question of how face representations change with familiarity, Jiang et al. (2007) showed that the magnitude and viewpoint transferability of identity adaptation increases with the familiarity of a face. This suggests the exciting possibility that adaptation can track the development of individual face representations as they evolve with experience.

On the question of *Computational Challenge 1*, one can ask "To what extent do humans build a representation that includes inherently three-dimensional information about faces?" This stands as an alternative or complement to building a representation that incorporates multiple viewer-centered templates. Jiang et al. (2009) showed evidence for the inclusion of some *inherently* three-dimensional information in face representations when the faces were learned from multiple viewpoints. The strategy Jiang et al. applied for getting at inherently three-dimensional information involved testing the generality of information learned from one three-dimensional-refencing transformation (viewpoint change) for facilitating recognition across another three-dimensional-refencing transformation (illumination change). Identity adaptation over illumination change was facilitated for faces learned from multiple views, suggesting that learning a face from one type of three-dimensional transformation (e.g. viewpoint change) can benefit perceptual robustness to a different type of three-dimensional representation (e.g. illumination change). This provides a complementary role for three-dimensional codes to the well-established viewer-centered codes.

Although these results have been informative about the face representations that govern perception, more work needs to be done on the computational philosophy that connects adaptation findings to neural processing mechanisms. Non-opponent based explanations have been offered for other adaptation effects involving social attention cues, such as eye gaze (Calder et al., 2008) and body orientation (Lawson et al., 2009). This approach should be explored for other kinds of adaptation effects as well.

Humans versus machines

In the final part of this chapter, we will run a quick "reality check" on the progress of computational face recognition models and offer some observations about the future of the dialog between psychology and computer vision on face processing. It used to be possible for a psychologist (like me) to sit down and implement a simple version of a computational face recognition model and then run off and test some of the predictions the model made about human face processing. I could look at the nature of the representations used in a computational formulation of the problem and make some predictions about performance pitfalls or advantages that might go along with these representations. If human and machine performance were similar, I could infer that some properties of the computational model apply also to human representations, (and so on). Those days are gone. State-of-the-art computational models have come into their own as commercial products. They are now built from complex plug-in components, and solve a sequence of problems that span from getting a face out of the image, to running the information through pre-processing routines, to delivering a final response. They are also quite a bit more accurate than many of us would have predicted, even a few years ago.

United States government-sponsored evaluations, spanning more than a decade, have gauged the progress of these algorithms. In recent tests (the Face Recognition Grand Challenge, FRGC, and Face Recognition Vendor Test-2006, FRVT-06; Phillips et al., 2010), algorithms in one part of the competition were required to match face identity in over 128 million pairs of face images. The images comprising each pair varied substantially in illumination and the problem was quite challenging for algorithms, relative to tests where the illumination was controlled and matched.

We compared humans to algorithms on this FRGC test using a subset of computationally-defined "easy" and "difficult" face pairs (O'Toole et al., 2007a). In a head-to-head comparison on identical image pairs, three of the seven algorithms were more accurate than humans matching identity on the difficult face pairs. For the easy face pairs, six of seven algorithms were more accurate than humans. We replicated this result on two additional datasets used in the FRVT-06 tests. On the problem of matching identity in pairs of frontal face images, the best algorithms are now in range of human performance—though I will add some caveats to the generality of this claim shortly.

The next question we asked was whether the algorithms and humans were performing the task in qualitatively similar ways (i.e. were they making the same errors). In days gone by, we could have looked at the algorithm strategy to see what predictions it made for human accuracy. Now, however, the proprietary nature of many of the algorithms made this impossible. So, we decided to computationally fuse the algorithm and human identity match responses together to see if the combination would improve performance relative to the humans or algorithms operating alone (O'Toole et al., 2007b). Our rationale was that fusing together similar strategies results in only minimal performance improvements, whereas the fusion of highly different strategies will improve performance substantially. In fact, fusing the seven algorithms cut the error rate to about half of the error rate for best-performing algorithm alone—this suggested that the algorithms were not all qualitatively similar. Fusing humans with the seven algorithms pushed performance to nearly perfect, indicating that human strategies are at least partially different from the algorithms' strategies.

Finally, we looked to see if state-of-the-art algorithms from the FRVT-06 showed an "other-race effect" (O'Toole et al., 2008). First, we divided the algorithms into East Asian Algorithms ($n = 5$, originating in China, Korea, and Japan) and those originating in Western countries ($n = 8$, France, Germany, and the United States). Next, we created an East Asian and Western fusion algorithm by fusing together the identity match estimates from the five Western algorithms and the eight East Asian algorithms, separately. In two separate tests, we found evidence for an other-race effect in the performance of the East Asian and Western fusion algorithms matching identity in the Caucasian and East Asian face pairs. We surmise (but, cannot know for sure) that this other-race effect is due to differences in the "experience" of the algorithms. Experience in this context refers to the ethnic composition of the set of training faces used by the algorithms to extract a feature set for encoding the faces. This would make the root cause of the problem for algorithms similar to that of the human other-race effect. So, things now seem to come full circle, as we find ourselves looking to human performance to understand what the algorithms are doing. Maybe that's progress.

Before closing this section, I offer some caveats on the reality test. First, in these human–machine comparison tests, humans matched identity in pairs of unfamiliar faces. This is fair as a test of what security guards do, but does not represent human performance at its best. Humans are at their best with familiar faces (see Burton and Jenkins, Chapter 15, this volume). Indeed, we would expect human performance to exceed algorithm performance if the faces were familiar. Second, although there are stark changes in illumination between the images in the face pairs, the conditions under which algorithm performance surpassed human performance involved identity comparisons between images that did not vary in viewpoint, (specifically, frontal images). In fact, for algorithms, the inverse optics problem is still far from solved (*Computational Challenge 1*). Further, although it is clear that the algorithm developers have spent a great deal of effort working on Challenge 1, the other-race effect findings suggest that they have under-appreciated the complexities added when the task must be carried out in the context of a relevant face population, which may vary across locations (airports) and even by time of day (the Frankfurt and Tokyo flights arrive at 8am, the New York and Mumbai flights at 9 am, and so on).

Summary and conclusions

In summary, the use of computational models for understanding human face perception and recognition runs parallel to efforts in the engineering literature to develop algorithms for computer-based face recognition systems. Collaborative interactions between computational and psychological approaches to face recognition have offered numerous insights into the kinds of face representations capable of supporting the many tasks humans accomplish with faces. Combined with findings in functional neuroimaging and high-level face adaptation studies, computational formulations have increased our understanding of the complex tasks humans solve when they recognize faces. Beyond the expectations of many psychologists, state-of-the-art face recognition algorithms are now more accurate than humans on some challenging face recognition tasks. Moreover, recent studies show that optimal combinations of human and machine recognition judgments can improve recognition performance over that possible by either machines or humans alone. As machine recognition improves, however, there is clear evidence that they begin to show some of the weak points of human perception—such as the "other-race effect."

The computational challenges in face recognition have focused researchers in psychology and neuroscience on the problem of formulating theories of representation that meet these computational challenges. The face space framework, in all of its implementations, has productively bootstrapped this research. Although the dialog between cognitive and computational approaches has been active now for nearly two decades, important challenges remain. One part of face space framework that remains under-formulated is the gap between viewer- and object-centered representations. Even if human representations are primarily viewer-centered, there is still a need to link representations in ways that make them robust to changes in the viewing conditions. This leads to the second open issue—that of how representations change as faces become familiar. The face space formulation, as it stands, does not support representations that are more or less enriched by experience. These questions may begin to play a prominent role in the computational-cognitive dialog of the next decade of research.

Acknowledgments

Thanks are due to Andy Calder, Vicki Bruce, Vaidehi Natu, David Raboy, and Dana Roark for helpful comments on a previous version of the chapter. Thanks are also due to the Technical Support Working Group, U.S. DOD, for funding the human-machine comparisons.

References

Abdi, H., Valentin, D., Edelman, B., and O'Toole, A.J. (1996). A Widrow-Hoff learning rule for a generalization of the linear auto-associator. *Journal of Mathematical Psychology*, **40**, 175–182.

Anderson, N.D. and Wilson, H.R. (2005). The nature of synthetic face adaptation. *Vision Research*, **45**, 1815–1828.

Benson, P.J. and Perrett, D.I. (1991). Perception and recognition of photographic quality facial caricatures: implications for the recognition of natural images. *European Journal of Cognitive Psychology*, **3**, 105–135.

Beymer, D., Shashua, A., and Poggio T. (1993). *Example based image analysis and synthesis*. Cambridge, MA: Massachusetts Institute of Technology Artificial Intelligence Laboratory A I Memo 1431 CBCL Paper No. 80.

Biederman, I. (1987) Recognition-by-component: A theory of human image understanding. *Psychological Review*, **94**, 115–147.

Blanz, V. and Vetter, T. (1999). A morphable model for the synthesis of three-dimensional faces. *Computer Graphics Proceedings SIGGRAPH' 99*, 187–194.

Blanz, V., O'Toole, A.J., Vetter, T., and Wild, H.A. (2000). On the other side of the mean: The perception of dissimilarity in human faces. *Perception*, **29**, 885–891.

Bruce, V. and Young, A. (1986). Understanding face recognition. *British Journal of Psychology*, **77**, 305–327.

Bülthoff, H.H. and Edelman, S. (1992). Psychophysical support for a two-dimensional view interpolation theory of object recognition. *Proceedings of the National Academy of Sciences, USA*, **89**, 60–64.

Burt, D.M. and Perrett, D.I. (1995). Perception of age in adult Caucasian male faces: computer graphic manipulation of shape and colour information. *Proceedings of the Royal Society of London B*, **259**, 137–143.

Burton, A.M. and Vokey, J.R. (1998). The face-space typicality paradox: Understanding the face-space metaphor. *Quarterly Journal of Experimental Psychology A, Human Experimental Psychology* **51A**, 475–483.

Calder, A.J., Jenkins, R., Cassel, A., and Clifford, C.W.G. (2008). Visual representation of eye gaze is coded by a non-opponent multichannel system. *Journal of Experimental Psychology: General,* **137**, 244–261.

Craw, I. and Cameron, P. (1991). Parameterizing images for recognition and reconstruction. In P. Mowforth (ed.) Proceedings of the British Machine Vision Conference, pp. 367–370. London: Springer Verlag.

Gibson, J.J. (1966). *The Senses Considered as Perceptual Systems.* Boston, MA: Houghton Mifflin.

Hancock, P.J.B., Burton, A.M., and Bruce, V. (1996). Face processing: Human perception and principal components analysis. *Memory and Cognition,* **24**, 26–40.

Hering, E. (1878). *Zur Lehre vom Lichtsinn.* Vienna: Gerold.

Jeffery, L., Rhodes, G., and Busey, T. (2006). View-specific coding of face shape. *Psychological Science,* **17**, 501–505.

Jiang, F., Blanz, V., and O'Toole, A.J. (2006). Probing the visual representation of faces with adaptation: A view from the other side of the mean. *Psychological Science,* **17**, 493–500.

Jiang F., Blanz V., and O'Toole A.J. (2007). The role of familiarity in three-dimensional view transferability of face identity adaptation. *Vision Research,* **47**, 525–531.

Jiang, F., Blanz, V., and O'Toole, A.J. (2009). Three-dimensional information in face representation revealed by identity aftereffects. *Psychological Science,* **20**, 318–325.

Kohonen, T. (1984). *Self-organization and associative memory.* Berlin: Springer-Verlag.

Lanitis, A., Taylor, C.J., Cootes, T.F., and Ahmad, T. (1995). Automatic interpretation of human faces and hand gestures using flexible models. In M. Bichsel (ed.) *Proceedings of the International Workshop on Face and Gesture Recognition,* pp. 98–103. Zurich: University of Zurich Press.

Lawson, R.P., Clifford, C.W.G., and Calder, A.J. (2009). About turn: the visual representation of human body orientation revealed by adaptation. *Psychological Science,* **20**, 363–371.

Lee, K.J. and Perrett, D. (1997). Presentation-time measures of the effects of manipulations in colour space on discrimination of famous faces. *Perception,* **26**, 733–752.

Lee, K.J. and Perrett, D.I. (2000). Manipulation of colour and shape information and its consequence upon recognition and best-likeness judgments *Perception,* **29**, 1291–1312.

Leopold, D.A., O'Toole, A.J., Vetter, T., and Blanz, V. (2001). Prototype-referenced shape encoding revealed by high-level aftereffects. *Nature Neuroscience,* **4**, 89–94.

Leopold, D.A., Bondar, I.V., and Giese, M.A. (2006). Norm-based face encoding by single neurons in the monkey inferotemporal cortex. *Nature,* **442**, 572–575.

Light, L.L., Kayra-Stuart, F., and Hollander, S. (1979). Recognition memory for typical and unusual faces. *Journal of Experimental: Human Perception and Performance,* **5**, 212–228.

Loffler, G., Yourganov, G., Wilkinson, F., and Wilson, H.R. (2005). FMRI evidence for the neural representation of faces. *Nature Neuroscience,* **8**, 1386–1390.

Marr, D. (1982). *Vision.* San Francisco, CA: W.H. Freeman.

O'Toole, A.J., Millward, R.B., and Anderson, J.A. (1988). A physical system approach to recognition memory for spatially transformed faces. *Neural Networks,* **1**, 179–199.

O'Toole, A.J., Abdi H, Deffenbacher, K.A., and Valentin, D. (1993). Low dimensional representation of faces in higher dimensions of the face space. *Journal of the Optical Society of America A,* **10**, 405–410.

O'Toole, A.J., Deffenbacher, K.A., Valentin, D., and Abdi, H. (1994). Structural aspects of face recognition and the other-race effect. *Memory and Cognition,* **22**, 208–224.

O'Toole, A.J., Vetter, T., Volz, H. and Salter, E.M. (1997). Three-dimensional caricatures of human heads: Distinctiveness and the perception of facial age. *Perception,* **26**, 719–732.

O'Toole, A.J., Edelman, S., and Bülthoff, H.H. (1998a). Stimulus-specific effects in face recognition over changes in viewpoint. *Vision Research,* **38**, 2351–2363.

O'Toole, A.J., Deffenbacher, K.A., Valentin, D., McKee, K., Huff, D., and Abdi, H. (1998b). The perception of face gender: The role of stimulus structure in recognition and classification. *Memory and Cognition*, **26**, 146–160.

O'Toole, A.J., Vetter, T., and Blanz, V. (1999). Two-dimensional reflectance and three-dimensional shape contributions to recognition of faces across viewpoint. *Vision Research*, **39**, 3145–3155.

O'Toole, A.J., Phillips, P.J., Jiang, F., Ayyad, J., Pénard, N., and Abdi, H. (2007a). Face recognition algorithms surpass humans matching faces across changes in illumination. *IEEE: Transactions on Pattern Analysis and Machine Intelligence,* **29**, 1642–1646.

O'Toole, A.J., Abdi, H., Jiang, F., and Phillips, P.J. (2007b). Fusing face recognition algorithms and humans. *IEEE: Transactions on Systems, Man and Cybernetics*, **37**, 1149–1155.

O'Toole, A.J., Phillips, P. J., Narvekar, A., Jiang, F., and Ayyad, J. (2008). Face recognition algorithms and the other-race effect. 8th Annual Meeting of the Vision Science Society, Naples, FL, May, 2008.

Phillips, P.J., Scruggs, W.T., O'Toole, A.J., *et al.* (2010). FRVT 2006 and ICE 2006 large-scale experimental results. *IEEE: Transactions on Pattern Analysis and Machine Intelligence*, **32**, 831–846.

Poggio, T. and Edelman, S. (1990). A network that learns to recognize three-dimensional objects. *Nature*, **343**, 263–266.

Rhodes, G. (1996). *Superportraits: Caricatures and recognition.* Hove: The Psychology Press.

Rhodes, G., Jeffery, L., Watson, T., Clifford, C.W.G., and Nakayama, K. (2003). Fitting the mind to the world: face adaptation and attractiveness aftereffects. *Psychological Science* **14**, 558–566.

Sirovich, L. and Kirby, M. (1987). Low-dimensional procedure for the characterization of human. *Journal of the Optical Society of America A*, **4**, 519–524.

Troje, N. and Bülthoff, H.H. (1996). Face recognition under varying poses: The role of texture and shape. *Vision Research*, **36**, 1761–1771.

Turk, M. and Pentland, A. (1991). Eigenfaces for Recognition. *Journal of Cognitive Neurosicence*, **3**, 71–86.

Valentine, T. (1991). A unified account of the effects of distinctiveness, inversion, and race in face recognition. *Quarterly Journal of Experimental Psychology*, **43A**, 161–204.

Vetter, T. and Poggio, T. (1997). Linear object classes and image synthesis from a single example image. *IEEE Transactions on Pattern Analysis and Machine Intelligence*, **19**, 733–742

Valentine, T. and Bruce, V. (1986). The effects of distinctiveness in recognizing and classifying faces. *Perception*, **15**, 525–535.

Wallis, G. and Bülthoff, H.H. (1999). Learning to recognize objects. *Trends in Cognitive Sciences,* **3**, 22–31.

Watson, T.L. and Clifford, C.W.G. (2003). Pulling faces: an investigation of face-distortion aftereffect. *Perception*, **32**, 1109–1116.

Webster, M.A. and MacLin, O.H. (1999). Figural after-effects in the perception of faces. *Psychonomic Bulletin Review*, **6**, 647–653.

Webster, M.A., Kaping, D., Mizokami, Y., and Duhamel, P. (2004). Adaptation to natural facial categories. *Nature*, **428**, 557–561.

Zhao, L. and Chubb, C.F. (2001). The size-tuning of the face-distortion aftereffect. *Vision Research*, **41**, 2979–2994.

Zhao, W., Chellappa, R., Phillips, P. J., and Rosenfeld, A. (2003). Face recognition: A literature survey. *ACM Computing Surveys*, **35**, 399–459.

Chapter 3

Ecological and Social Approaches to Face Perception

Leslie A. Zebrowitz

The belief that faces provide cues to character spans the centuries, from Aristotle, who specified precise associations like "prominent ears and chattering," to 18th-century physiognomists, whose writings on the topic were assiduously followed by matchmakers and almost cost Darwin his passage on HMS Beagle,[1] to modern-day face readers, whom I encountered on the streets of Hong Kong. Faces also captured the attention of early psychologists, who conducted scientific investigations to determine whether there are facial markers of aptitude (Hull, 1928), personality (Brandenburg, 1926; Cleeton and Knight, 1924), and emotions (Dusenbury and Knower, 1938). Although contemporary research continues to examine the accurate emotion communication by facial expressions (Elfenbein and Ambady, 2003; Rosenberg and Ekman, 1994), the notion that faces accurately convey ability and personality traits was largely supplanted by research investigating perceptions of face-trait associations (Secord, 1958). In this chapter, I discuss an ecological theory of face perception that elucidates the basis of these perceptions. I then review research on first impressions elicited by facial qualities that are associated with fitness, emotion, race, age, and sex, in each case making links to ecological theory.

Origins of the ecological approach to face perception

The ecological approach to face perception is grounded in J.J. Gibson's writings, including *The Senses Considered as Perceptual Systems* (Gibson, 1966), which I initially read with great interest as a graduate student in a course taught by Wendell Garner. Hearing Gibson and Garner engage in a heated (but friendly) argument about perceptual processes at a department colloquium further sparked my interest in Gibson's theoretical viewpoint, and in 1979, I read his book, *The ecological approach to visual perception* (Gibson, 1979) together with writings of "neo-Gibsonians" Michael Turvey, Bob Shaw, and others at the University of Connecticut, including *Perceiving, Acting, and Knowing* (Shaw and Bransford, 1977). Although many themes in this monograph influenced my thinking, one chapter with a profound effect reported the results of research demonstrating that age perceptions of human profiles are tightly coupled to a growth-simulating mathematical transformation called cardioidal strain. I thought that if this transformation influences age perceptions, it must also influence other perceptions of interest to social psychologists, and that was the genesis of my research on the "babyface overgeneralization effect," which is discussed later in this chapter.

---

[1] Darwin reports in his autobiography that "I heard that I had run a very narrow risk of being rejected on account of the shape of my nose! He (the Captain) was an ardent disciple of Lavater, and was convinced that he could judge of a man's character by the outline of his features, and he doubted whether anyone with my nose could possess sufficient energy and determination for the voyage" (Darwin, 1887).

Having taken to heart Gibson's emphasis on understanding the stimulus information that guides perception even before reading his 1979 book, I had conducted some research in which I investigated the effects on social perceptions of variations in people's appearance (McArthur and Post, 1977). When my co-author was presenting our results at a professional conference, a psychologist sitting in front of me challenged him with questions about "top down" versus "bottom up" stimulus-linked determinants of our effects. I introduced myself, and told him that I totally agreed with what he had said. That was the beginning of many fruitful discussions with Reuben Baron, a social psychologist at the University of Connecticut, who had been greatly influenced by his neo-Gibsonian colleagues, and our mutual interests ultimately produced a paper in *Psychological Review* "Toward an ecological theory of social perception" (McArthur and Baron, 1983).

Although the value of applying Gibsonian ideas to social perception received a much welcomed stamp of approval from *Psychological Review*, all was not smooth sailing then or now. I still remember the first scathing review of my research examining impressions of babyfaced adults (McArthur and Apatow, 1983). It boiled down to "who cares" with the added barb "And probably people with pig-like faces are perceived to have pig-like qualities." Although I am not usually one to make lemonade out of lemons, I actually thought that this pig analogy was an interesting idea, and many years later I proposed an "animal analogies" principle, whereby people are judged to have the traits of the animals they resemble (Zebrowitz, 1996, 1997). Such a perceptual bias would mirror beliefs endorsed by Aristotle and "modern" humans are not immune to it (Zebrowitz et al., in press).

The reviewer's disdain for research that aimed to identify facial qualities that inform social perceptions reflected the zeitgeist at the time in social psychology. The emphasis was on understanding the cognitive mechanisms engaged in social perception, and this was typically accomplished by providing information about social qualities in lists of trait words. To understand the perception of social qualities in faces was not a valued pursuit, and it is only recently gaining favor among those interested in social perception (Zebrowitz, 2006). For example, there has never been a chapter on face perception in the *Handbook of Social Psychology,* the standard reference work in social psychology. So, I am particularly pleased to see due recognition accorded to the pivotal role of face perception in human psychology by this inaugural handbook of face perception.

Basic tenets of the ecological approach to face perception

The ecological approach to face perception has four significant principles: the assumption that perceiving is for doing, which emphasizes the functional nature of face perception; the related insight that perceivers detect behavioral affordances in their social environment; a stress on identifying the stimulus information to which perceivers respond; and the articulation of factors that influence perceivers' attunements to the affordances communicated in this stimulus information. Each tenet is described below.

Perceiving is for doing

The first tenet is Gibson's (1979) dictum that "perceiving is for doing." It has two significant components. One is that a full understanding of face perception requires theory and research that incorporates a "doing"—i.e. behaving—perceiver. The second is that face perception is not simply about recognizing a particular quality from facial cues. Rather, it is about the function of the perceptual system to guide actions that serve to solve specific adaptive problems or to facilitate other goal attainments of individuals. The focus on behavioral responses to faces is linked to the principle that faces communicate behavioral affordances.

Affordances are the objective

The emphasis on the adaptive function of face perception carries with it a second distinguishing feature of the ecological approach, namely an emphasis on the perception of social affordances. Affordances are defined by Gibson (1979, p. 127) as what the environment "offers the animal, what it provides or furnishes, either for good or ill." A more vivid explication of the concept is provided by the quotation from Koffka: "Each thing says what it is…a fruit says 'eat me'; water says 'drink me'; thunder says 'fear me'; and woman says 'love me'" (Gibson, 1979, p. 138). Although Gibson emphasizes the objective reality of affordances, he also emphasizes their emergence from the interaction of the environment and the perceiver. A woman may afford (erotic) loving by an adult but not a child; a heterosexual man, but not a homosexual one; a secular man, but not a priest; her spouse, but not a stranger.

Understanding the stimulus is central

A central feature of ecological theory is an emphasis on identifying the external stimulus environment that informs perception. Gibson (1966, 1979) argued that multimodal, dynamic changes over space and time are features that provide the most useful information to perceivers in non-social perception, and McArthur and Baron (1983) suggested that the same is true for social perception.[2] Thus, the dynamic and multifaceted facial information provided by facial structure, pigmentation, texture, and movement should provide the most accurate information about peoples' relatively invariant attributes (e.g. age, sex, ethnicity) and their more variable behavioral affordances. Information from other modalities, such as voice, may also contribute (see De Gelder and Van den Stock, Chapter 27, this volume). Moreover, impoverished stimulus information and a preparedness to respond to adaptively significant configurations of information are hypothesized to make predictable contributions to face perception, as discussed later in the section on overgeneralization hypotheses.

Attunements guide perceptions

The emergence of affordances from the interplay of perceiver and stimulus attributes is related to the fourth distinguishing tenet of the ecological approach. The detection of social affordances depends on the perceivers' attunements—their sensitivity to particular stimulus information. Attunements may be innate (e.g. men but not monkeys may be attuned to facial cues to a woman's sexual availability). Attunements also may be educated in a process of perceptual development that varies with perceivers' behavioral capabilities (men but not boys may be attuned to facial cues to a woman's sexual availability), social goals (secular men but not priests may be attuned to facial cues to a woman's sexual availability), or perceptual experiences (a lover but not a stranger may be attuned to facial cues to a woman's sexual availability).

Strong attunements are overgeneralized

A derivation from ecological theory that has been the focus of most of my own research on face perception is the hypothesis that innate or well-developed attunements to the affordances specified by facial cues can yield overgeneralized and erroneous perceptions, particularly when stimulus information is impoverished, as is typical in most research examining responses to static facial

---

2 Actually, Gibson himself argued that his theory should apply to social perception: "…it is no great step to admit that he can also learn to respond to the invariants of the social and the symbolic environments" (Gibson, 1963).

images. More specifically, a set of overgeneralization hypotheses holds that the psychological qualities that are accurately revealed by the facial qualities that characterize babies, emotion, identity, low fitness, or a particular animal are erroneously perceived in people whose facial appearance resembles one of those categories (Zebrowitz, 1996, 1997). Although sex overgeneralization has not been previously proposed, such an effect accommodates research on reactions to faces varying in masculinity/femininity, which will be discussed. Animal overgeneralization will not be discussed, as there is scant empirical research (see Zebrowitz et al., in press). According to ecological theory, the errors yielded by such overgeneralizations occur because they are less maladaptive than those that might result from failing to respond appropriately to persons of a particular age, emotional state, identity, health status, sex, or species. This postulate is consistent with error management theory posited by evolutionary psychologists (Haselton and Buss, 2000).[3]

Although overgeneralization effects will often yield erroneous perceptions, it is important to note that overgeneralization and accuracy are not mutually exclusive. Overgeneralization may sometimes produce accurate perceptions via self-fulfilling prophecy effects, whereby appearance elicits social interactions that contribute to the development or expression of the expected behaviors (Snyder et al., 1977). Overgeneralization can also produce significantly inaccurate perceptions via self-defeating prophecy effects, whereby the social interactions elicited by appearance may contribute to behaviors that defy expectations (Zebrowitz et al., 1998a). Other mechanisms that could yield actual relationships between appearance and behavior include biological links between facial appearance and traits, environmental factors that influence both, and an influence of traits on appearance (for a fuller discussion, see Zebrowitz and Collins, 1997).

Research bearing on the perception of socially relevant qualities in faces

In the following sections, I review face perception research pertinent to the detection of socially relevant qualities in faces—attractiveness, emotions, race, age, sex—as well as associated behavioral affordances, which have typically been assessed by trait ratings (see Todorov et al., Chapter 32, this volume). Due to space limitations, the burgeoning research on the neural bases of social face perception will not be discussed (for reviews, see Adolphs and Birmingham, Chapter 29, this volume; Zebrowitz and Zhang, in press). In addition, the review of behavioral research will be illustrative, not exhaustive. Within each section, I consider not only social perceptions but also evidence pertinent to ecological theory tenets—overgeneralization effects, behavioral reactions, stimulus information, and perceiver attunements—although the research evidence often fails to adequately incorporate these tenets.

Attractiveness

Social perceptions and behavioral responses

Social psychologists have focused much attention on the "attractiveness halo effect." Contrary to the adage "beauty is in the eye of the beholder," there is consensus in judgments of facial attractiveness. Furthermore, people with more attractive faces are perceived more positively on many trait dimensions (Eagly et al., 1991; Feingold, 1992; Langlois et al., 2000; Zebrowitz et al., 2002; Zebrowitz and Rhodes, 2004). Consistent with the ecological emphasis on links between perception and behavior, these trait impressions are accompanied by preferential treatment in a variety

---

[3] The overgeneralization hypotheses pertain to physical qualities besides facial appearance, including vocal, body, and gait characteristics.

of domains, including interpersonal relations, occupational settings, and the judicial system (Langlois et al., 2000; Zebrowitz, 1997). Attractive faces also facilitate approach responses whereas unattractive faces facilitate avoidance, even in infants (Langlois et al., 1990; Marsh et al., 2005b), and perceivers exert more effort to see attractive faces (Aharon et al., 2001).

For many years there was no conceptual framework to explain the positive effects of attractiveness other than the assumption that they reflected cultural teachings. Although that may be true, it begs the question of where those teachings originate. The fact that people from diverse cultures as well as infants and young children all show similar reactions to variations in attractiveness suggests that these impressions reflect some universal mechanism rather than arbitrary cultural influences (Cunningham et al., 1995; Dion, 2002; Kramer et al.,1995; Ramsey et al., 2004). One might suggest that universally positive responses to attractive faces reflects the spreading of positive affect from the face to other attributes. However, this fails to explain the origin of that positive affect. Anomalous face overgeneralization (AFO) holds that the adaptive value of recognizing individuals with disease or bad genes has produced a strong preparedness to respond to facial qualities that can mark low fitness (Zebrowitz, 1996, 1997). The accurately perceived affordances of unfit individuals, such as poor health and low intellectual and social skills, are then overgeneralized to normal, but unattractive, individuals whose faces resemble anomalous ones.

Stimulus information

AFO is a variant of the "good genes" hypothesis proposed by evolutionary psychologists to explain preferences for more attractive mates, with an emphasis on the greater fitness of highly attractive individuals (Buss, 1989). In contrast, AFO holds that appearance provides an accurate index only of low genetic fitness rather than a continuous index of genetic quality, and that the attractiveness halo effect is a perceptual by-product of reactions to low fitness. In support of AFO, a review of the literature on the halo effect concludes that it reflects the perception that "ugly is bad" more than the perception that "beautiful is good" (Griffin and Langlois, 2006). In addition, the facial qualities that differentiate faces of individuals with low fitness from normal faces include low averageness (i.e. typicality) and low symmetry (Krouse and Kauffman, 1982; Thornhill and Møller, 1997), which also mark the faces of normal individuals who are perceived as "unattractive" (see Penton-Voak and Morrison, Chapter 33, this volume). Further evidence that perceptions of normal unattractive faces can be accounted for by resemblance to anomalous ones is provided by research demonstrating that impressions of the attractiveness, health, intelligence, and sociability of normal faces were predicted by the extent to which their facial metrics resembled those of anomalous faces, as determined by connectionist modeling. Moreover, these effects could not be explained by corresponding variations in the actual health and intelligence of the people with normal faces (Zebrowitz et al., 2003).

Consistent with ecological theory, facial attractiveness is also influenced by dynamic and multimodal cues, with lower expressiveness associated with lower attractiveness (DePaulo et al., 1992; Riggio and Friedman, 1986). Although differences in the perceived affordances signaled by high versus low expressiveness provide a proximal explanation for this effect, it may also be influenced by anomalous face overgeneralization, since low facial expressiveness is a marker of physical and psychological disorders, such as Parkinson's disease (Pentland et al., 1987), depression, and schizophrenia (Schneider et al., 1990). The fact that vocal cues vary in attractiveness (Miyake and Zuckerman, 1993), as do body cues (Peters et al., 2007) suggests that multimodal, dynamic stimulus information may have a more profound influence on judged facial attractiveness and associated behavioral affordances than the standard two-dimensional faces. For example, judgments of speakers' facial attractiveness are influenced by their vocal attractiveness even when perceivers are instructed to ignore the voice (Zuckerman et al., 1991).

Perceiver attunements

Although there is a strong consensus in judgments of facial attractiveness, there are also variations across perceivers (cf. Little and Perrett, 2002). People from culturally isolated tribes in the Amazon rainforest show less agreement with Westerners than people from various Western cultures show with each other (Jones and Hill, 1993). Americans who share common perceptual experiences by virtue of being friends or relatives also show stronger consensus than do strangers (Bronstad and Russell, 2007). Even short-term perceptual experiences can influence judgments of attractiveness. Brief exposure to consistent distortions of normal faces yields a perceptual aftereffect marked by a shift in attractiveness judgments toward the distorted faces (Rhodes et al., 2003b).

In addition to the evidence for effects of perceptual experience, other findings suggest effects of social goals. Men with a more unrestricted approach to mating paid relatively more attention to attractive female faces (Duncan et al., 2007), and women showed a greater preference for facial symmetry in short term mates at the time of peak fertility, which has been interpreted as reflecting the greater adaptive value of responding to markers of good genes in this context (Little et al., 2007b). People also prefer faces that suggest the personality traits that they value (Little et al., 2006). Cultural variations in the halo effect provide further support for an effect of social goals. Social dominance is a stronger component of the halo effect in Western than East Asian cultures, where attractiveness is associated more with integrity and concern for others, consistent with the higher value placed on social harmony than individual agency (Wheeler and Kim, 1997). Research investigating the accuracy of impressions of individuals who vary in attractiveness is mixed, and none has examined an influence of perceiver attunements (Feingold, 1992; Langlois et al., 2000; Weeden and Sabini, 2005; Zebrowitz et al., 2002; Zebrowitz and Rhodes, 2004).

Emotions

Social perceptions and behavioral responses

At least six basic emotions can be communicated by facial expressions: happiness, fear, surprise, anger, disgust, and sadness. Whether posed in still photographs or in films or expressed spontaneously, these emotions are identified at better than chance levels, although surprise and fear are often confused (Buck et al., 1972; Ekman et al., 1987; Howell and Jorgensen, 1970; Wagner et al., 1986). Even people from a culturally isolated group in New Guinea are able to recognize posed expressions by Westerners (Ekman and Friesen, 1971).

From an ecological theory perspective, an important question is what behavioral affordances are perceived in facial expressions. Research indicates that expressions reveal not only affective states but also more stable behavioral intentions, an effect that Secord (1958) dubbed "temporal extension." People displaying transient happy expressions are perceived to have more stable traits associated with high affiliation and high dominance, although the latter effect is less reliable. Those with angry expressions are perceived as low in affiliation and high in dominance, and those with sad or fearful expressions are perceived as moderate in affiliation and low in dominance (Hess et al., 2000; Knutson, 1996; Montepare and Dobish, 2003; Zebrowitz et al., 2007b).

Consistent with the ecological dictum that perceiving is for doing, perceiving emotion expressions influences behavioral responses. For example, using anger expressions as a conditioned stimuli as compared with happy expressions facilitates aversive classical conditioning and increases resistance to extinction (Dimberg, 1986; Ohman and Dimberg, 1978). In addition, fear expressions potentiate startle responses to loud noises in infants (Balaban, 1995), and intensify adults' emotional reaction to a previously conditioned aversive stimulus as well as disrupting extinction (Lanzetta and Orr, 1981; Orr and Lanzetta, 1984). Interestingly, although fear expressions are unpleasant, they facilitate approach behaviors in perceivers in contrast to anger expressions that facilitate avoidance (Marsh et al., 2005b). One interpretation is that although fear expressions look unsociable, they invite help and assistance.

Not only do people perceive behavioral affordances in emotion expressions, but also they show emotion face overgeneralization (EFO), responding similarly to those whose neutral expression resembles an emotion. Neutral faces that show more resemblance to an angry expression, either as assessed by human raters (Montepare and Dobish, 2003) or by objective methods (Said et al., 2009; Zebrowitz et al., 2010), are perceived as less likeable and trustworthy and more powerful, hostile, and threatening, with opposite impressions of neutral faces showing greater resemblance to a happy expression. Moreover, these effects hold true with attractiveness, babyfaceness, and face sex controlled, demonstrating an independent effect of emotion overgeneralization (Montepare and Dobish, 2003; Zebrowitz et al., 2010). The converse is also true. Computer-generated neutral expression faces morphed to exaggerate features positively associated with trustworthiness look happy; those morphed to exaggerate features associated with low trustworthiness look angry; and those morphed to exaggerate features associated with submissiveness look fearful (Oosterhof and Todorov, 2008).

Stimulus information

The facial qualities that objectively differentiate emotion expressions have been extensively investigated, including specific two-dimensional static facial components (Ekman, 1971; Izard, 1977), specific facial muscle movements (Cohn et al., 2006), and trajectories of facial movements shown in point-light displays (Bassili, 1978; Bassili, 1979). Research examining what two-dimensional static facial components effectively communicate an emotion reveals that perceivers use information in different regions to recognize different emotions (Smith et al., 2005), and that emotion recognition is holistic (Calder et al., 2000). For example, abstract primitive masks from diverse cultures that communicated anger and threat were characterized by the configural qualities of diagonality and angularity in many regions (Aronoff et al., 1992). Facial orientation as well as structure may contribute to emotion perception. Adults with heads tilted backward are perceived as more likely to be proud than those with heads tilted forward, who are perceived as more likely to be ashamed (Mignault and Chaudhuri, 2003).

Investigations of specific emotion-related facial qualities that influence trait impressions demonstrate that lower eyebrows, a hallmark of an anger expression, create impressions of higher dominance, at least in Western cultures (Keating et al., 1981) as well as lower trustworthiness (Todorov et al., 2008). However, smiles, the primary component of a happy expression, sometimes elicit impressions of lower rather than the higher dominance that has been associated with happy expressions (Keating et al., 1981; Reis et al., 1990). These divergent results may reflect differences in definitions of dominance and/or subtle differences in types of smiles which can convey diverse social messages (LaFrance and Hecht, 1995).

The importance of dynamic cues is underscored by evidence that recognition of subtle emotion expressions is better from moving than static faces (Ambadar et al., 2005), and that dynamic facial expressions of emotion elicit stronger arousal in perceivers (Sato and Yoshikawa, 2007). Consistent with the ecological emphasis on multimodal stimulus information, not only are there vocal and bodily cues to emotion (de Gelder and Hadjikhani, 2006; Juslin and Scherer, 2005; Montepare et al., 1987), but also consistent multimodal information can yield more effective communication of emotion than the face alone (Hietanen et al., 2004; Van den Stock et al., 2007).

Most research investigating the specific facial qualities influencing emotion perception has been empirically rather than theoretically driven. A notable exception is provided by research that raised the question of why particular emotion expressions look the way they do (Marsh et al., 2005a). These authors argued that fear and anger expressions evolved to mimic baby faces and mature faces, respectively, because it is adaptive for those experiencing fear to elicit reactions paralleling those elicited by helpless babies and for those experiencing anger to elicit reactions paralleling those elicited by powerful adults. Consistent with this hypothesis, both subjective ratings of resemblance of emotions to babies as well as objective indices from connectionist models, showed that fear expressions or closely related surprise expressions resemble babies more than do neutral expressions, while anger expressions resemble babies less (Marsh et al., 2005a; Zebrowitz et al., 2007b). Anger expressions also resemble women less than they resemble men, whereas surprise resemble women more than men (Becker et al., 2007; Hess et al., 2004; Zebrowitz et al., 2010), which is consistent with the fact that faces of adult women retain more neotenous qualities than those of men (Enlow, 1990).

Perceiver attunements

In addition to effects of the perceiver's personality on emotion perception (see Fox and Zougkou, Chapter 26, this volume), there are hormonal influences on fear recognition, which may reflect some adaptive advantage to sensitivity to fear when conception is likely (Pearson and Lewis, 2005). Emotion recognition also is more accurate when judging expressions in faces from one's own culture, suggesting that perceptual experience attunes people to a particular non-verbal "dialect" (see Ambady and Weisbuch, Chapter 24, this volume). Similarly, there is some evidence for greater accuracy when judging emotion expressions in faces from one's own age group (Malatesta et al., 1987b). The accuracy of trait impressions from emotion expressions and emotion overgeneralizations has received little attention. However, one study suggests that neutral faces whose structural properties resemble an emotion expression may provide accurate trait information, at least in older adults (Malatesta et al., 1987a). Variations in attunements to the traits revealed through emotion-resemblance have not been investigated.

Race

Social perceptions and behavioral responses

Social psychologists have long been interested in understanding racial prejudice and stereotypes, and there is considerable evidence for ingroup favoritism, specific race stereotypes, and prejudicial behaviors (Jones, 1997; Schneider, 2004). However, until recently, attention to facial appearance was confined to its likely role in the categorization of people into one or another racial group. The scant attention to appearance is surprising, since many ethnic and racial groups look different from one another, something that is certainly not lost on perceivers. According to the familiar face overgeneralization hypothesis (FFO), the utility of differentiating known individuals from strangers has produced a tendency for strangers to elicit more negative responses when they show less resemblance to known individuals (Zebrowitz, 1996, 1997). This hypothesis suggests that own-race favoritism is, in part, a perceptual by-product of reactions to familiar people versus unfamiliar-looking strangers.

Because prototypical facial structure varies across racial groups and communities are often racially segregated, strangers from one's own racial group do indeed appear more familiar than strangers from a different racial group (Zebrowitz et al., 2007a). (For a related discussion, see Rossion and Michel, Chapter 12, this volume). Consistent with other evidence that unfamiliar stimuli are generally less liked (Bornstein, 1989; Hamm et al., 1975; Rhodes et al., 2001; Zajonc, 1968), faces of other-race strangers also are perceived as less likeable than those of own-race strangers (Zebrowitz et al., 2007a). More significant for FFO, this effect is partially mediated by the lower familiarity of other race faces, quite apart from other contributing social factors. Negative responses to the lesser familiarity of other-race faces also contributes to the strength of culturally-based race stereotypes, enhancing negative stereotypes of other-race faces and diminishing positive ones. For example, the tendency for white judges to perceive black faces as less competent than white ones was reduced when face familiarity was controlled, and the tendency for white judges to perceive Asian faces as more competent than white ones was increased when face familiarity was controlled (Zebrowitz, et al., 2007a).

Race-related facial qualities not only contribute to differential responses to own- versus other-race faces, but also to variations in reactions to faces that are all the same race, effects that may derive from FFO and/or learned associations between certain physical features and specific traits (Blair et al. 2002). More prototypically black faces prime negative concepts in white judges more than do less prototypical black faces or white faces (Livingston and Brewer, 2002), and black or ehite faces with more prototypically black features elicit trait impressions more consistent with African American stereotypes (Blair et al., 2002). Moreover, regardless of race, convicted criminals with a more prototypical black appearance received longer prison terms (Blair et al., 2004) and more frequent death sentences from judges who were predominantly white (Eberhardt et al., 2006). On the other hand, black raters formed more positive impressions of white faces with a more African appearance, with other facial qualities controlled, and they also found them more familiar-looking, while Korean raters formed more positive impressions of white faces with a more Asian appearance and found them more familiar-looking (Strom et al., 2008).

Stimulus information

Little research has directly investigated what facial qualities influence perceived racial prototypicality, which has been assessed by subjective ratings. In a recent study, discriminant function analysis of the facial metrics of black, white, and Korean faces revealed several metrics that objectively differentiated black, white, and Korean faces (Strom, 2008). Although some of the discriminating metrics seem unlikely to be explicitly recognized by perceivers, they nevertheless predicted how racially prototypical a face was judged to be. For example, black faces had narrower jaws than did white or Korean faces, and variations in this metric predicted how African-looking black, white, or Korean faces were judged to be by black American, white American, and Asian American raters. In addition to race-related variations in facial metrics, skin color is another salient difference. Interestingly, however, three-dimensional shape was as important as surface color when participants were asked to categorize faces as European or Japanese on the basis of one cue or the other, and shape influenced racial categorization even in the context of contradictory color cues (Hill et al., 1995). Dynamic facial movements and textural cues besides skin color, such as eyebrows and facial and scalp hair may also contribute to judgments of racial prototypicality, as may multimodal cues, such as vocal qualities (Walton and Orlikoff, 1994) and gesture (Johnson, 2006).

Attunements

As predicted by FFO, mere exposure to other race faces increases the subjective familiarity of new faces of that race as well as their likeability (Zebrowitz et al., 2008), which is consistent with the ameliorative effects on prejudice of interracial contact (Pettigrew and Tropp, 2006). Longer-term perceptual experiences and/or social goals also may yield different responses to race-related facial qualities, as suggested by perceiver variations in the relative influence of skin tone and facial metrics on racial prototypicality judgments (Strom et al., 2010).

Age

Social perceptions and behavioral responses

Like race stereotypes, age stereotypes have been of great interest to social psychologists. There is considerable evidence for negative impressions of older adults (Nelson, 2002), and it has been well-established that they are the targets of discriminatory and sometimes patronizing behaviors (for a review, see Zebrowitz and Montepare, 2000). Positive impressions of babies are also well-documented (Zebrowitz, 1997). Although that end of the age spectrum has received less attention, there is a well-documented babyface overgeneralization effect (BFO). Specifically, the accurately perceived affordances of babies are mirrored in reactions to babyfaced individuals at all ages, who are perceived by judges from diverse cultures to afford greater submissiveness, naïveté, warmth, honesty, and physical weakness than their peers. In addition to eliciting stereotyped impressions, babyfaced individuals also elicit different behavioral responses across the lifespan in a variety of domains. For example, consistent with the stereotyped trait impressions, they are passed over for mentally challenging tasks and leadership positions, albeit favored when a non-threatening appearance is advantageous (Livingston and Pearce, 2009). They also are more likely than their maturefaced peers to be exonerated when accused of intentional misdeeds, but more likely to be found at fault when accused of negligence (for reviews, see Montepare and Zebrowitz, 1998; Zebrowitz, 1997).

Whereas attention to facial appearance has been prominent in BFO research, it has been largely neglected in research on elder stereotypes. Indeed, although facial cues provide consensual and accurate judgments of an adult's chronological age (Henss, 1991), investigators have rarely used facial images to study elder stereotypes, relying instead on age labels. However, stereotypes of older adults are linked not simply to knowledge of their chronological age, but also to their physical appearance. For instance, some photographs of older adults yield positive stereotypes—"Grandmother types", who are accepting, helpful, and cheerful, and "Elder Statesmen types", who are aggressive, intelligent, and dignified, whereas other photographs yield negative stereotypes—"Senior citizen types", who are lonely, weak, and worried (Brewer et al., 1981)

Stimulus information

Connectionist modeling research suggests a role for AFO in social perceptions of older adults. A computer network trained to respond to the facial metrics of anomalous young adult faces was subsequently activated more by facial metrics from elderly than normal young adult faces, which may reflect an age-related increase in vulnerability to developmental instabilities that can yield facial asymmetries. In addition, greater confusion of elderly faces with anomalous ones mediated the stereotyped impressions of older adults as less attractive, less warm and sociable, and less strong and healthy than younger adults (Zebrowitz et al., 2003). Research investigating specific physical qualities has found that more positive impressions of elderly adults are associated with less wrinkling and gray hair (Hummert, 1994; Hummert et al., 1997), and perceptions of lower power in older men are associated with baldness (Muscarella and Cunningham, 1996). Some indirect evidence also suggests that babyfaceness may offset some negative impressions of older adults, since more babyfaced elderly adults report feeling fewer constraints in their lives than do their more maturefaced peers, an effect opposite to that shown for younger adults (Andreoletti et al., 2001).

The facial qualities that differentiate real babies from adults, including relatively larger eyes, a rounder face, and a larger ratio of cranium to chin (Enlow, 1990; Mark et al., 1981) also mark individuals from infancy to older adulthood who are perceived as more "babyfaced" than their peers (Zebrowitz and Montepare, 1992). Evidence that perceptions of babyfaced adults can be accounted for by facial resemblance to babies is provided not only by subjective ratings, but also by connectionist modeling, which demonstrated that impressions of adult faces' babyfaceness, as well as warmth, physical weakness, naïveté, and submissiveness were predicted by the extent to which their facial metrics resembled those of babies (Zebrowitz et al., 2003). The converse is also true. Computer-generated neutral expression faces that were morphed to exaggerate features associated with submissiveness looked more babyfaced and those morphed to exaggerate features associated with dominance looked more maturefaced (Oosterhof and Todorov, 2008).

Research has not investigated the influence of age-related dynamic facial cues on social perceptions. However, the fact that facial movement changes in systematic and noticeable ways from childhood to old age, allowing perceivers to extract age information from facial movement independent of its structure (Berry, 1990c), suggests that some facial movement cues may contribute to both elder and babyface stereotypes. Multimodal cues may strengthen effects of age-related facial cues on social perceptions. For example, vocal cues change with age (Helfrich, 1979), as do gait cues (Montepare and Zebrowitz-McArthur, 1988), and these variations are associated with different trait impressions (Berry, 1990b; Berry et al., 1994; Montepare and Zebrowitz-McArthur, 1987; Montepare and Zebrowitz-McArthur, 1988).

Attunements

The tendency for trait impressions of older adults to vary with their appearance qualities was more differentiated for older than younger perceivers (Brewer and Lui, 1984), which may reflect older adults' greater perceptual experience with their age peers. Social goals also can shape perceptual attunements: the preference for babyfaced people decreases when perceivers are experiencing threat, either in an experimental setting or during historic periods of social and economic hard times (Pettijohn and Jungeberg, 2004; Pettijohn and Tesser, 2005). Perceiver attunements may bear on the accuracy of impressions of people who vary in age-related facial qualities. Among the scant research on this topic is evidence that highly experienced health-care practitioners form more accurate impressions of the personality traits of older adults with Parkinson's disease than do novices, who are more mislead by the facial masking symptom (Tickle-Degnen and Lyons, 2004). Research investigating the general accuracy of impressions of babyfaced individuals is mixed, and none has examined effects of perceiver attunements (Berry, 1990a, 1991a; Berry and Brownlow, 1989; Darwin, 1887; Zebrowitz et al., 1998a,b; Zebrowitz and Collins, 1997).

Sex

Social perceptions and behavioral responses

Sex stereotypes also have been of great interest to social psychologists, with considerable evidence that men are generally perceived as more "agentic" or dominant than women, who in turn are perceived as more "communal" or warm than men (Kite et al., 2008). Corresponding differences in behavioral responses to men and women are legion. As in the case of race and age stereotypes, the contribution of facial appearance to sex stereotypes has received little attention. Yet, research providing descriptions of general appearance qualities as well as other cues demonstrated the central role of appearance, which predicted sex-stereotyped impressions of psychological traits and social roles more than the latter predicted each other (Deaux and Lewis, 1984).

Just as race- and age-related facial qualities contribute to variations in reactions to faces that are all the same race or age, so do sexually dimorphic facial qualities influence reactions to faces that are the same sex, a sex of face overgeneralization effect (SFO). For example, people attribute higher dominance and leadership ability to persons with a typically masculine appearance than to persons with a typically feminine appearance, regardless of the person's sex (Sczesny et al., 2006). More masculine-looking men and more feminine-looking women are also perceived as healthier (Luevano and Zebrowitz, 2007; Rhodes et al., 2007).

Stimulus information

Among the sexually dimorphic facial qualities that can contribute to masculinity/femininity of appearance (Russell, 2003; Samal et al., 2007), many overlap with facial qualities related to age and emotion. A more feminine appearance retains more neotenous qualities (Enlow, 1990), which is demonstrated by a positive relationship between facial masculinity and perceived age (Boothroyd et al., 2005), and by the finding that a computer network trained to respond to the facial metrics of babies was subsequently activated more by the facial metrics of adult female than male faces (Zebrowitz et al., 2003). A BFO contribution to sex stereotypes is supported by research manipulating the typical difference in babyfaceness between the sexes (Friedman and Zebrowitz, 1992). Typical male faces are perceived as less warm and more powerful than typical female faces. However, when male faces were made more babyfaced, by enlarging their eyes and forehead to chin ratio, and female faces were made more maturefaced by the reverse manipulations, then the men were perceived as less powerful than the women and equally warm, effects that were independent of attractiveness. Further evidence for interconnections among facial femininity, baby-faceness, and trait impressions is provided by the finding that computer-generated neutral expression faces that were morphed to exaggerate features associated with submissiveness not only looked more babyfaced, as noted above, but also more feminine. On the other hand, those morphed to exaggerate features associated with dominance looked more masculine as well as more maturefaced (Oosterhof and Todorov, 2008).

As noted above, a more masculine appearance looks more angry, while a more feminine appearance looks more surprised and happy, although the happy effect may reflect cultural stereotypes rather than facial structure (Becker et al., 2007; Hess et al., 2004; Zebrowitz et al., 2010). Thus, emotion overgeneralization, like babyface overgeneralization, may contribute to divergent impressions of the warmth and dominance of male versus female faces as well as faces of a single sex that vary in sexually dimorphic qualities. It is also possible that anomalous face overgenerali-zation contributes to the more positive overall impressions of females (Eagly and Mladinic, 1989), since vulnerability to developmental instabilities that can yield asymmetrical facial morphology is greater for males (Akabaliev and Sivkov, 2003; Riese, 1984). One implication of the commonali-ties in appearance across different face categories is that AFO, EFO, BFO, and SFO may all be partly driven by differential responses to facial qualities that are shared by people who tend to invite approach behaviors (babies, women, healthy people, afraid, surprised, or happy people) versus those that are shared by people who tend to invite avoidance (elderly adults, men, unhealthy people, angry people).

Although the contribution to sex stereotypes of sex differences in dynamic facial cues has not been assessed, the fact that people can accurately identify face sex from facial movement inde-pendent of its structure is consistent with this possibility (Berry, 1990c, 1991b; Morrison et al., 2007). Multimodal cues may strengthen effects of facial sexual dimorphism on sex stereotypes. For example, men and women have recognizably different gaits (Pollick et al., 2005) as well as vocal pitch, and more feminine, higher pitched, voices are perceived as less dominant (Apple et al., 1979; Robinson and McArthur, 1982).

Attunements

Evolutionary psychologists have devoted considerable attention to the question of perceiver sen-sitivity to variations in facial masculinity/femininity. Not only may there be a kernel of truth to the perception that more masculine-looking men are more healthy (Rhodes et al., 2003a; Thornhill and Gangestad, 2006) and more dominant and aggressive (Carré and McCormick, 2008), but also there are variations in perceiver attunement to these qualities. For example, the attractiveness of sexually dimorphic traits in male faces is more pronounced for women when conception is likely (Johnston et al., 2001) or when judging men as short-term, rather than long-term, mates (Little et al., 2007a), which has been interpreted as reflecting the greater adaptive value of responding to markers of good genes in these contexts (but see Koehler et al., 2006). The same explanation has been offered for the finding that women who live in a harsher environment show a stronger pref-erence for facial masculinity (Penton-Voak et al., 2004). It would be interesting to determine whether trait impressions also vary across the menstrual cycle, with different impressions of more masculine-looking men when conception is likely. Perceiver attunements to gender cues have also been investigated in studies of "gaydar." Not only can people of all sexual orientations identify gay men with better than chance accuracy from facial photos, but also homosexual men are more accurate than heterosexual men or women of any sexual orientation (Rule and Ambady, 2008; Rule et al., 2007). The stimulus information that supports these accurate perceptions has not yet been identified, although it has been shown that it is not simply hairstyles, and that sufficient cues are provided in many regions of the face (Rule et al., 2008).

Summary and conclusions

The ecological approach emphasizes the function of face perception to guide behavior through the detection of social affordances, with perceivers' attunement to this information influenced by perceptual experiences, behavioral capabilities, and social goals. It also postulates that strong attunements to the affordances specified by facial cues may be overgeneralized, a hypothesis that receives strong support in the research reviewed in this chapter. Like the early physiognomists, modern-day perceivers associate facial appearance with behavior, attributing different psychological attributes to people whose neutral expression faces vary in attractiveness, emotion resemblance, babyfaceness, racial prototypicality, or sex prototypicality. These effects can be explained by the overgeneralization of adaptive responses to people who differ in actual health status, emotional state, age, group identity, or sex to other individuals whose faces merely resemble people from one of those social categories. An even fuller understanding of social face perception awaits additional research that better incorporates ecological theory tenets emphasizing the function of perception to detect social affordances that guide behavior, the dynamic, multimodal stimulus information that reveals those affordances, and the experiential and motivational factors that differentially attune perceivers to them.

References

Aharon, I., Etcoff, N., Ariely, D., Chabris, C.F., O'Connor, E., and Breiter, H.C. (2001). Beautiful faces have variable reward value: fMRI and behavioral evidence. *Neuron*, 32, 537–551.

Akabaliev, V.H. and Sivkov, S.T. (2003). Sexual dimorphism in minor physical anomalies in schizophrenic and normal controls. *Comprehensive Psychiatry*, 44, 341–348.

Ambadar, Z., Schooler, J.W., and Cohen, J.F. (2005). Deciphering the enigmatic face: The importance of facial dynamics in interpreting subtle facial expressions. *Psychological Science*, 16, 403–410.

Andreoletti, C., Zebrowitz, L.A., and Lachman, M.E. (2001). Physical appearance and control beliefs in young, middle-aged, and older adults. *Personality & Social Psychology Bulletin*, 27, 969–981.

Apple, W., Streeter, L.A., and Krauss, R.M. (1979). Effects of pitch and speech rate on personal attributions. *Journal of Personality and Social Psychology*, 37, 715–727.

Aronoff, J., Woike, B.A., and Hyman, L.M. (1992). Which are the stimuli in facial displays of anger and happiness? Configurational bases of emotion recognition. *Journal of Personality and Social Psychology*, 62, 1050–1066.

Balaban, M.T. (1995). Affective influences on startle in five-month-old infants Reactions to facial expressions of emotion. *Child Development*, 58, 28–36.

Bassili, J.N. (1978). Facial motion in the perception of faces and of emotional expression. *Journal of Experimental Psychology: Human Perception and Performance*, 4, 373–379.

Bassili, J.N. (1979). Emotion recognition: The role of facial movement and the relative importance of upper and lower areas of the face. *Journal of Personality and Social Psychology*, 37, 2049–2058.

Becker, D.V., Kenrick, D.T., Neuberg, S.L., Blackwell, K.C., and Smith, D.M. (2007). The confounded nature of angry men and happy women. *Journal of Personality and Social Psychology*, 92, 179–190.

Berry, D.S. (1990a). Taking people at face value: Evidence for the kernel of truth hypothesis. *Social Cognition*, **8**, 343–361.

Berry, D.S. (1990b). Vocal attractiveness and vocal babyishness: Effects on stranger, self, and friend impressions. *Journal of Nonverbal Behavior*, **14**, 141–153.

Berry, D.S. (1990c). What can a moving face tell us? *Journal of Personality and Social Psychology*, **58**, 1004–1014.

Berry, D.S. (1991a). Accuracy in social perception: Contribution of facial and vocal information. *Journal of Personality and Social Psychology*, **61**, 298–307.

Berry, D.S. (1991b). Child and adult sensitivity to gender information in patterns of facial motion. *Ecological Psychology*, **3**, 349–366.

Berry, D.S. and Brownlow, S. (1989). Were the physiognomists right? Personality correlates of facial babyishness. *Personality and Social Psychology Bulletin*, **15**, 266–279.

Berry, D.S., Hansen, J.S., Landry-Pester, J.C., and Meier, J.A. (1994). Vocal determinants of first impressions of young children. *Journal of Nonverbal Behavior*, **18**, 187–197.

Blair, I.V., Judd, C.M., Sadler, M.S., and Jenkins, C. (2002). The role of Afrocentric features in person perception: Judging by features and categories. *Journal of Personality and Social Psychology*, **83**, 5–25.

Blair, I.V., Judd, C.M., and Chapleau, K.M. (2004). The influence of Afrocentric facial features in criminal sentencing. *Psychological Science*, **15**, 674–679.

Boothroyd, L.G., Jones, B.C., Burt, D.M., *et al.* (2005). Facial masculinity is related to perceived age but not perceived health. *Evolution and Human Behavior*, **26**, 417–431.

Bornstein, R.F. (1989). Exposure and affect: Overview and meta-analysis of research 1968–1987. *Psychological Bulletin*, **106**, 265–289.

Brandenburg, G.C. (1926). Do physical traits portray character? *Industrial Psychology*, **1**, 580–588.

Brewer, M.B. and Lui, L. (1984). Categorization of the elderly by the elderly: Effects of perceiver's category membership. *Personality and Social Psychology Bulletin*, **10**, 585–595.

Brewer, M.B., Dull, V., and Lui, L. (1981). Perceptions of the elderly: Stereotypes as prototypes. *Journal of Personality and Social Psychology*, **41**, 656–670.

Bronstad, P.M. and Russell, R. (2007). Beauty is in the 'we' of the beholder: Greater agreement on facial attractiveness among close relations. *Perception*, **36**, 1674–1681.

Buck, R.W., Savin, V.J., Miller, R.E., and Caul, W.F. (1972). Communication of affect through facial expressions in humans. *Journal of Personality and Social Psychology*, **23**, 362–371.

Buss, D.M. (1989). Sex differences in human mate preferences: evolutionary hypotheses tested in 37 cultures. *Behavioral and Brain Sciences*, **12**, 1–49.

Calder, A.J., Young, A.W., Keane, J., and Dean, M. (2000). Configural information in facial perception. *Journal of Experimental Psychology: Human Perception and Performance*, **26**, 527–551.

Carré, J.M. and McCormick, C.M. (2008). In your face: facial metrics predict aggressive behaviour in the laboratory and in varsity and professional hockey players. *Proceedings of the Royal Society*, **275**, 2651–2656.

Cleeton, G.C. and Knight, F.B. (1924). Validity of character judgments based on external criteria. *Journal of Applied Psychology*, **8**, 215–231.

Cohn, J.F., Ekman, P., Harrigan, J.A., Rosenthal, R., and Scherer, K.R. (2006). Measuring facial action. In J.A. Harrigan, R. Rosenthal, and K.R. Scherer (eds.) *The New Handbook of Methods in Nonverbal Behavior Research*, pp. 9–64. New York: Oxford University Press.

Cunningham, M.R., Roberts, A.R., Barbee, A.P., and Druen, P.B. (1995). 'Their ideas of beauty are, on the whole, the same as ours': Consistency and variability in the cross-cultural perception of female physical attractiveness. *Journal of Personality and Social Psychology*, **68**, 261–279.

Darwin, C. (1887). The Autobiography of Charles Darwin: 1809–1882 Project Gutenberg. EBook #2010. http://www.gutenberg.org.

de Gelder, B. and Hadjikhani, N. (2006). Non-conscious recognition of emotional body language. *Neuroreport: For Rapid Communication of Neuroscience Research*, **17**, 583–586.

Deaux, K. and Lewis, L.L. (1984). Structure of gender stereotypes: Interrelationships among components and gender label. *Journal of Personality and Social Psychology*, **46**, 991–1004.

DePaulo, B.M., Blank, A.L., and Swaim, G.W. (1992). Expressiveness and expressive control. *Personality and Social Psychology Bulletin*, **18**, 276–285.

Dimberg, U. (1986). Facial expressions as excitatory and inhibitory stimuli for conditioned autonomic responses. *Biological Psychology*, **22**, 37–57.

Dion, K.K. (2002). Cultural perspectives on facial attractiveness. In G. Rhodes and L.A. Zebrowitz (eds.) *Facial attractiveness: Evolutionary, cognitive, and social perspectives*, pp. 239–259. Westport, CT: Ablex Publishing.

Duncan, L.A., Park, J.H., Faulkner, J., Schaller, M., Neuberg, S.L., and Kenrick, D.T. (2007). Adaptive allocation of attention: Effects of sex and sociosexuality on visual attention to attractive opposite-sex faces. *Evolution and Human Behavior*, **28**, 359–364.

Dusenbury, D. and Knower, F.H. (1938). Experimental studies of the symbolism of action and voice. I. A study of the specificity of meaning in facial expression. *Quarterly Journal of Speech*, **24**, 424–435.

Eagly, A.H. and Mladinic, A. (1989). Gender stereotypes and attitudes toward women and men. *Personality and Social Psychology Bulletin*, **15**, 543–558.

Eagly, A.H., Ashmore, R.D., Makhijani, M.G., and Longo, L.C. (1991). What is beautiful is gooD, but: A meta-analytic review of research on the physical attractiveness stereotype. *Psychological Bulletin*, **110**, 109–128.

Eberhardt, J.L., Davies, P.G., Purdie-Vaughns, V.J., and Johnson, S.L. (2006). Looking deathworthy: perceived stereotypicality of black defendants predicts capital-sentencing outcomes. *Psychological Science*, **17**, 383–386.

Ekman, P. (1971). Universals and cultural differences in facial expressions of emotion. *Nebraska Symposium on Motivation*, **19**, 207–283.

Ekman, P. and Friesen, W.V. (1971). Constants across cultures in the face and emotion. *Journal of Personality and Social Psychology*, **17**, 124–129.

Ekman, P., Friesen, W.V., O'Sullivan, M., *et al.* (1987). Universals and cultural differences in the judgments of facial expressions of emotion. *Journal of Personality and Social Psychology*, **53**, 712–717.

Elfenbein, H.A. and Ambady, N. (2003). When familiarity breeds accuracy: Cultural exposure and facial emotion recognition. *Journal of Personality and Social Psychology*, **85**, 276–290.

Enlow, D.H. (1990). *Facial growth*. Philadelphia, PA: Harcourt Brace.

Feingold, A. (1992). Good-looking people are not what we think. *Psychological Bulletin*, **111**, 304–341.

Friedman, H. and Zebrowitz, L.A. (1992). The contribution of typical sex differences in facial maturity to sex role stereotypes. *Personality & Social Psychology Bulletin*, **18**, 430–438.

Gibson, J.J. (1963). The useful dimensions of sensitivity. *American Psychologist*, **18**, 1–15.

Gibson, J.J. (1966). *The senses considered as perceptual systems*. Oxford: Houghton Mifflin.

Gibson, J.J. (1979). *The ecological approach to visual perception*. Boston, MA: Houghton Mifflin.

Griffin, A.M. and Langlois, J.H. (2006). Stereotype directionality and attractiveness stereotyping: Is beauty good or is ugly bad? *Social Cognition*, **24**, 187–206.

Hamm, N.H., Baum, M.R., and Nikels, K.W. (1975). Effects of race and exposure on judgments of interpersonal favorability. *Journal of Experimental Social Psychology*, **11**, 14–24.

Haselton, M.G. and Buss, D.M. (2000). Error management theory: A new perspective on biases in cross-sex mind reading. *Journal of Personality and Social Psychology*, **78**, 81–91.

Helfrich, H. (1979). Age markers in speech. In K.R. Scherer, and H. Giles (eds.) *Social markers in speech*, pp. 63–107. New York: Cambridge University Press.

Henss, R. (1991). Perceiving age and attractiveness in facial photographs. *Journal of Applied Social Psychology*, **21**, 933–946.

Hess, U., Blairy, S., and Kleck, R.E. (2000). The influence of facial emotion displays, gender, and ethnicity on judgments of dominance and affiliation. *Journal of Nonverbal Behavior*, **24**, 265–283.

Hess, U., Adams, R.B., Jr., and Kleck, R.E. (2004). Facial appearance, gender, and emotion expression. *Emotion*, **4**, 378–388.

Hietanen, J.K., Leppänen, J.M., Illi, M., and Surakka, V. (2004). Evidence for the integration of audiovisual emotional information at the perceptual level of processing. *European Journal of Cognitive Psychology*, **16**, 769–790.

Hill, H., Bruce, V., and Akamatsu, S. (1995). Perceiving the sex and race of faces: The role of shape and colour. *Proceedings of the Royal Society of London, Series B: Biological Sciences*, **261**, 367–373.

Howell, R.J. and Jorgensen, E.C. (1970). Accuracy of judging unposed emotional behavior in a natural setting: A replication study. *Journal of Social Psychology*, **81**, 269–270.

Hull, C.L. (1928). *Aptitude testing*. Oxford: World Book.

Hummert, M. (1994). Physiogonomic cues and the activation of stereotypes of the elderly in interaction. *International Journal of Aging and Human Development*, **39**, 5–19.

Hummert, M.L., Garstka, T.A., and Shaner, J.L. (1997). Stereotyping of older adults: The role of target facial cues and perceiver characteristics. *Psychology and Aging*, **12**, 107–114.

Izard, C.E. (1977). *Human emotions*. New York: Plenum Press.

Johnson, R.R. (2006). Confounding influences on police detection of suspiciousness. *Journal of Criminal Justice*, **34**, 435–442.

Johnston, V.S., Hagel, R., Franklin, M., Fink, B., and Grammer, K. (2001). Male facial attractiveness: Evidence for hormone-mediated adaptive design. *Evolution and Human Behavior*, **22**, 251–267.

Jones, D. and Hill, K. (1993). Criteria of facial attractiveness in five populations. *Human Nature*, **4**, 271–296.

Jones, J.M. (1997). *Prejudice and Racism*. New York: McGraw-Hill.

Juslin, P.N. and Scherer, K.R. (2005). Vocal expression of affect. In J.A. Harrigan, R. Rosenthal, and K.R. Scherer (eds.) *The New Handbook of Methods in Nonverbal Behavior Research*, pp. 65–135. New York: Oxford University Press.

Keating, C.F., Mazur, A., and Segall, M.H. (1981). A cross-cultural exploration of physiognomic traits of dominance and happiness. *Ethology and Sociobiology*, **2**, 41–48.

Kite, M.E., Deaux, K., Haines, E.L., Denmark, F.L., and Paludi, M.A. (2008). Gender stereotypes. *Psychology of women: A handbook of issues and theories* (2nd edn.). Westport, CT: Praeger Publishers/Greenwood Publishing Group.

Knutson, B. (1996). Facial expressions of emotion influence interpersonal trait inferences. *Journal of Nonverbal Behavior*, **20**, 165–182.

Koehler, N., Rhodes, G., Simmons, L.W., and Zebrowitz, L.A. (2006). Do cyclic changes in women's face preferences target cues to long-term health? *Social Cognition*, **24**, 641–656.

Kramer, S., Zebrowitz, L.A., San Giovanni, J.P, and Sherak, B. (1995). Infants' preferences for attractiveness and babyfaceness. In B.G. Bardy, R.J. Bootsma, and Y. Guiard (eds.) *Studies in perception and action III*, pp. 389–392. Mahwah, NJ: Lawrence Erlbaum Associates, Inc.

Krouse, J.P. and Kauffman, J.M. (1982). Minor physical anomalies in exceptional children: A review and critique of research. *Journal of Abnormal Child Psychology*, **10**, 247–264.

LaFrance, M. and Hecht, M.A. (1995). Why smiles generate leniency. *Personality and Social Psychology Bulletin*, **21**, 207–214.

Langlois, J.H., Roggman, L.A., and Rieser-Danner, L.A. (1990). Infants' differential social responses to attractive and unattractive faces. *Developmental Psychology*, **26**, 153–159.

Langlois, J.H., Kalakanis, L., Rubenstein, A.J., Larson, A., Hallam, M., and Smoot, M. (2000). Maxims or myths of beauty? A meta-analytic and theoretical review. *Psychological Bulletin*, **126**, 390–423.

Lanzetta, J.T. and Orr, S.P. (1981). Stimulus properties of facial expressions and their influence on the classical conditioning of fear. *Motivation and Emotion*, **5**, 225–234.

Little, A.C. and Perrett, D.I. (2002). Putting beauty back into the eye of the beholder: evolution and individual differences in face preference. *The Psychologist*, **15**, 28–32.

Little, A.C., Burt, D.M., and D.I., P. (2006). What is good is beautiful: Face preference reflects desired personality. *Personality and Individual Differences*, **41**, 1107–1118.

Little, A.C., Cohen, D.L., Jones, B.C., and Belsky, J. (2007a). Human preferences for facial masculinity change with relationship type and environmental harshness. *Behavioral Ecology and Sociobiology*, **61**, 967–973.

Little, A.C., Jones, B.C., Burt, D.M., and Perrett, D.I. (2007b). Preferences for symmetry in faces change across the menstrual cycle. *Biological Psychology*, **76**, 209–216.

Livingston, R.W. and Brewer, M.B. (2002). What are we really priming? Cue-based versus category-based processing of facial stimuli. *Journal of Personality and Social Psychology*, **82**, 5–18.

Livingston, R.W. and Pearce, N.A. (2009). The teddy-bear effect: Does having a baby face benefit black chief executive officers? *Psychological Science*, **20**, 1229–1236.

Luevano, V.X. and Zebrowitz, L.A. (2007). Do impressions of health, dominance, and warmth explain why masculine faces are preferred more in a short-term mate? *Evolutionary Psychology*, **5**, 15–27.

Malatesta, C.Z., Fiore, M.J., and Messina, J.J. (1987a). Affect, personality, and facial expressive characteristics of older people. *Psychology and Aging*, **2**, 64–69.

Malatesta, C.Z., Izard, C.E., Culver, C., and Nicolich, M. (1987b). Emotion communication skills in young, middle-aged, and older women. *Psychology and Aging*, **2**, 193–203.

Mark, L.S., Todd, J.T., and Shaw, R.E. (1981). Perception of growth: A geometric analysis of how different styles of change are distinguished. *Journal of Experimental Psychology: Human Perception and Performance*, **7**, 855–868.

Marsh, A.A., Adams, R.B., Jr., and Kleck, R.E. (2005a). Why do fear and anger look the way they do? Form and social function in facial expressions. *Personality and Social Psychology Bulletin*, **31**, 73–86.

Marsh, A.A., Ambady, N., and Kleck, R.E. (2005b). The effects of fear and anger facial expressions on approach and avoidance related behaviors. *Emotion*, **5**, 119–124.

McArthur, L. and Apatow, K. (1983). Impressions of baby-faced adults. *Social Cognition*, **2**, 315–342.

McArthur, L.Z. and Baron, R.M. (1983). Toward an ecological theory of social perception. *Psychological Review*, **90**, 215–238.

McArthur, L.Z. and Post, D.L. (1977). Figural emphasis and person perception. *Journal of Experimental Social Psychology*, **13**, 520–535.

Mignault, A. and Chaudhuri, A. (2003). The many faces of a neutral face: Head tilt and perception of dominance and emotion. *Journal of Nonverbal Behavior*, **27**, 111–132.

Miyake, K. and Zuckerman, M. (1993). Beyond personality impressions: Effects of physical and vocal attractiveness on false consensus, social comparison, affiliation, and assumed and perceived similarity. *Journal of Personality*, **61**, 411–437.

Montepare, J.M. and Dobish, H. (2003). The contribution of emotion perceptions and their overgeneralizations to trait impressions. *Journal of Nonverbal Behavior*, **27**, 237–254.

Montepare, J.M. and Zebrowitz-McArthur, L. (1987). Perceptions of adults with childlike voices in two cultures. *Journal of Experimental Social Psychology*, **23**, 331–349.

Montepare, J.M. and Zebrowitz-McArthur, L. (1988). Impressions of people created by age-related qualities of their gaits. *Journal of Personality and Social Psychology*, **55**, 547–556.

Montepare, J.M. and Zebrowitz, L.A. (1998). 'Person perception comes of age': The salience and significance of age in social judgments. In M. Zanna (ed.) *Advances in Experimental Social Psychology*, pp. 203–222. San Diego, CA: Academic Press.

Montepare, J.M., Goldstein, S.B., and Clausen, A. (1987). The identification of emotions from gait information. *Journal of Nonverbal Behavior*, **11**, 33–42.

Morrison, E.R., Gralewski, L., Campbell, N., and Penton-Voak, I.S. (2007). Facial movement varies by sex and is related to attractiveness. *Evolution and Human Behavior*, **28**, 186–192.

Muscarella, F. and Cunningham, M.R. (1996). The evolutionary significance and social perception of male pattern baldness and facial hair. *Ethology & Sociobiology*, **17**, 99–117.

Nelson, T.D. (ed.) (2002). *Ageism: Stereotyping and prejudice against older persons.* Cambridge, MA: The MIT Press.

Ohman, A. and Dimberg, U. (1978). Facial expressions as conditioned stimuli for electrodermal responses: A case of 'preparedness'? *Journal of Personality and Social Psychology,* **36**, 1251–1258.

Oosterhof, N.N. and Todorov, A. (2008). The functional basis of face evaluation. *Proceedings of the National Academy of Sciences of the U S A,* **105**, 11087–11092.

Orr, S.P. and Lanzetta, J.T. (1984). Extinction of an emotional response in the presence of facial expressions of emotion. *Motivation and Emotion,* **8**, 55–66.

Pearson, R. and Lewis, M. B. (2005). Fear recognition across the menstrual cycle. *Hormones and Behavior,* **47**, 267–271.

Pentland, B., Pitcairn, T.K., Gray, J.M., and Riddle, W.J.R. (1987). The effects of reduced expression in Parkinson's disease on impression formation by health professionals. *Clinical Rehabilitation,* **1**, 307–313.

Penton-Voak, I.S., Jacobson, A., and Trivers, R. (2004). Populational differences in attractiveness judgments of male and female faces: Comparing British and Jamaican samples. *Evolution and Human Behavior,* **25**, 355–370.

Peters, M., Rhodes, G., and Simmons, L.W. (2007). Contributions of the face and body to overall attractiveness. *Animal Behaviour,* **73**, 937–942.

Pettijohn, T.F., II and Jungeberg, B.J. (2004). Playboy playmate curves: changes in facial and body feature preferences across social and economic conditions. *Personality and Social Psychology Bulletin,* **30**, 1186–1197.

Pettijohn, T.F., II and Tesser, A. (2005). Threat and social choice: When eye size matters. *Journal of Social Psychology,* **145**, 547–570.

Pettigrew, T.F. and Tropp, L.R. (2006). A meta-analytic test of intergroup contact theory. *Journal of Personality and Social Psychology,* **90**, 751–783.

Pollick, F.E., Kay, J.W., Heim, K., and Stringer, R. (2005). Gender recognition from point-light walkers. *Journal of Experimental Psychology: Human Perception and Performance,* **31**, 1247–1265.

Ramsey, J.L., Langlois, J.H., Hoss, R.A., Rubenstein, A.J., and Griffin, A.M. (2004). Origins of a stereotype: Categorization of facial attractiveness by 6-month-old infants. *Developmental Science,* **7**, 201–211.

Reis, H.T., Wilson, I.M., Monestere, C., *et al.* (1990). What is smiling is beautiful and good. *European Journal of Social Psychology,* **20**, 259–267.

Rhodes, G., Halberstadt, J., and Brajkovich, G. (2001). Generalization of mere exposure effects to averaged composite faces. *Social Cognition,* **19**, 57–70.

Rhodes, G., Chan, J., Zebrowitz, L.A., and Simmons, L.W. (2003a). Does sexual dimorphism in human faces signal health? *Proceedings of the Royal Society of London B Biological Sciences,* **270**(Suppl 1), S93–5.

Rhodes, G., Jeffery, L., Watson, T.L., Clifford, C.W.G., and Nakayama, K. (2003b). Fitting the mind to the world: Face adaptation and attractiveness aftereffects. *Psychological Science,* **14**, 558–566.

Rhodes, G., Yoshikawa, S., Palermo, R., *et al.* (2007). Perceived health contributes to the attractiveness of facial symmetry, averageness, and sexual dimorphism. *Perception,* **36**, 1244–1252.

Riese, M.L. (1984). Minor physical anomalies and behavior in neonates: Sex and gestational age differences. *Journal of Pediatric Psychology,* **9**, 257–266.

Riggio, R.E. and Friedman, H. (1986). Impression formation: The role of expressive behavior. *Journal of Personality and Social Psychology,* **50**, 421–427.

Robinson, J. and McArthur, L.Z. (1982). Impact of salient vocal qualities on causal attribution for a speaker's behavior. *Journal of Personality and Social Psychology,* **43**, 236–247.

Rosenberg, E.L. and Ekman, P. (1994). Coherence between expressive and experiential systems in emotion. *Cognition & Emotion,* **8**, 201–229.

Rule, N.O. and Ambady, N. (2008). Brief exposures: Male sexual orientation is accurately perceived at 50ms. *Journal of Experimental Social Psychology,* **44**, 1100–1105.

Rule, N.O., Ambady, N., Adams, R.B., and Macrae, C.N. (2007). Us and them: Memory advantages in perceptually ambiguous groups. *Psychonomic Bulletin & Review,* **14**, 687–692.

Rule, N.O., Ambady, N., Adams, R.B., Jr., and Macrae, C.N. (2008). Accuracy and awareness in the perception and categorization of male sexual orientation. *Journal of Personality and Social Psychology*, **95**, 1019–1028.

Russell, R. (2003). Sex, beauty, and the relative luminance of facial features. *Perception*, **32**, 1093–1107.

Said, C.P., Sebe, N., and Todorov, A. (2009). Structural resemblance to emotional expressions predicts evaluation of emotionally neutral faces. *Emotion*, **9**, 260–264.

Samal, A., Subramani, V., and Marx, D. (2007). Analysis of sexual dimorphism in human face. *Journal of Visual Communication and Image Representation*, **18**, 453–463.

Sato, W. and Yoshikawa, S. (2007). Enhanced experience of emotional arousal in response to dynamic facial expressions. *Journal of Nonverbal Behavior*, **31**, 119–135.

Schneider, D.J. (2004). *The psychology of stereotyping*. New York: Guilford Press.

Schneider, F., Heimann, H., Himer, W., and Huss, D. (1990). Computer-based analysis of facial action in schizophrenic and depressed patients. *European Archives of Psychiatry and Clinical Neuroscience*, **240**, 67–76.

Sczesny, S., Spreemann, S., and Stahlberg, D. (2006). Masculine = competent? Physical appearance and sex as sources of gender-stereotypic attributions. *Swiss Journal of Psychology*, **65**, 15–23.

Secord, P. (1958). *Facial features and inference processes in interpersonal perception*. In R. Tagiuri and L. Petrullo (eds.) *Person Perception and Interpersonal Behavior*. Stanford, CA: Stanford University Press.

Shaw, R. and Bransford, J. (1977). *Perceiving, acting, and knowing: Toward an ecological psychology*. Oxford: Lawrence Erlbaum.

Smith, M.L., Cottrell, G.W., Gosselin, F., and Schyns, P.G. (2005). Transmitting and Decoding Facial Expressions. *Psychological Science*, **16**, 184–189.

Snyder, M., Tanke, E.D., and Berscheid, E. (1977). Social perception and interpersonal behavior: On the self-fulfilling nature of social stereotypes. *Journal of Personality and Social Psychology*, **35**, 656–666.

Strom, M., Zebrowitz, L.A., Zhang, S., Bronstad, P.M., and Lee, H.K. (2010). *Skin and Bones: The contribution of skin tone and facial structure to racial prototypicality ratings*. Waltham, MA: Brandeis University.

Strom, M., Zhang, S., Zebrowitz, L.A., Bronstad, P.M., and Lee, H.K. (2008). *Black Americans and Koreans Favor Whites Who Look Like Them?* Waltham, MA: Brandeis University.

Thornhill, R. and Gangestad, S.W. (2006). Facial sexual dimorphism, developmental stability, and susceptibility to disease in men and women. *Evolution and Human Behavior*, **27**, 131–144.

Thornhill, T. and Møller, A.P. (1997). Developmental stability, disease and medicine. *Biological Reviews*, **72**, 497–548.

Tickle-Degnen, L. and Lyons, K.D. (2004). Practitioner's impressions of patients with Parkinson's disease: The social ecology of the expressive mask *Social Science & Medicine*, **58**, 603–614.

Todorov, A., Baron, S.G., and Oosterhof, N.N. (2008). Evaluating face trustworthiness: A model based approach. *Social Cognitive and Affective Neuroscience*, **3**, 119–127.

Van den Stock, J., Righart, R., and de Gelder, B. (2007). Body expressions influence recognition of emotions in the face and voice. *Emotion*, **7**, 487–494.

Wagner, H.L., MacDonald, C.J., and Manstead, A.S. (1986). Communication of individual emotions by spontaneous facial expressions. *Journal of Personality and Social Psychology*, **50**, 737–743.

Walton, J.H. and Orlikoff, R.F. (1994). Speaker race identification from acoustic cues in the vocal signal. *Journal of Speech & Hearing Research*, **37**, 738–745.

Weeden, J. and Sabini, J. (2005). Physical attractiveness and health in Western Societies: A review. *Psychological Bulletin*, **131**, 635–653.

Wheeler, L. and Kim, Y. (1997). What is beautiful is culturally good: The physical attractiveness stereotype has different content in collectivistic cultures. *Personality and Social Psychology Bulletin*, **23**, 795–800.

Zajonc, R.B. (1968). Attitudinal effects of mere exposure. *Journal of Personality and Social Psychology*, **9**, 1–27.

Zebrowitz, L.A. (1996). Physical appearance as a basis for stereotyping. In N. McRae, M. Hewstone and C. Stangor (eds.) *Foundation of stereotypes and stereotyping*. New York: Guilford Press.

Zebrowitz, L.A. (1997). *Reading faces: Window to the soul?* Boulder, CO: Westview Press.

Zebrowitz, L.A. (2006). Finally, faces find favor. *Social Cognition, 24*, 657–701.

Zebrowitz, L.A. and Collins, M.A. (1997). Accurate social perception at zero acquaintance: The affordances of a Gibsonian approach. *Personality and Social Psychology Review, 1*, 204–223.

Zebrowitz, L.A. and Montepare, J.M. (1992). Impressions of babyfaced individuals across the life span. *Developmental Psychology, 28*, 1143–1152.

Zebrowitz, L.A. and Montepare, J.M. (2000). 'Too young, too old': Stigmatizing adolescents and elders. In T.F. Heatherton, R.E. Kleck, M.R. Hebl, and J.G. Hull (eds.) *Social psychology of stigma*, pp. 334–373. New York: Guilford Press.

Zebrowitz, L.A. and Rhodes, G. (2004). Sensitivity to 'bad genes' and the anomalous face overgeneralization effect: Cue validity, cue utilization, and accuracy in judging intelligence and health. *Journal of Nonverbal Behavior, 28*, 167–185.

Zebrowitz, L.A. and Zhang, Y. (in press). Origins of impression formation in animal and infant face perception. In J. Decety and J. Cacioppo (eds.) *The Handbook of Social Neuroscience*. New York: Oxford University Press.

Zebrowitz, L.A., Andreoletti, C., Collins, M.A., Lee, S.Y., and Blumenthal, J. (1998a). Bright, bad, babyfaced boys: appearance stereotypes do not always yield self-fulfilling prophecy effects. *Journal of Personality And Social Psychology, 75*, 1300–1320.

Zebrowitz, L.A., Collins, M.A., and Dutta, R. (1998b). The relationship between appearance and personality across the life span. *Personality & Social Psychology Bulletin, 24*, 736–749.

Zebrowitz, L.A., Hall, J.A., Murphy, N.A., and Rhodes, G. (2002). Looking smart and looking good: Facial cues to intelligence and their origins. *Personality and Social Psychology Bulletin, 28*, 238–249.

Zebrowitz, L.A., Fellous, J.M., Mignault, A., and Andreoletti, C. (2003). Trait impressions as overgeneralized responses to adaptively significant facial qualities: evidence from connectionist modeling. *Personality and Social Psychology Review, 7*, 194–215.

Zebrowitz, L.A., Bronstad, P.M., and Lee, H.K. (2007a). The contribution of face familiarity to ingroup favoritism and stereotyping. *Social Cognition, 25*, 306–338.

Zebrowitz, L.A., Kikuchi, M., and Fellous, J.-M. (2007b). Are effects of emotion expression on trait impressions mediated by babyfaceness? Evidence from connectionist modeling. *Personality and Social Psychology Bulletin, 33*, 648–662.

Zebrowitz, L.A., White, B., and Weineke, K. (2008). Mere exposure and racial prejudice: Exposure to other-race faces increases liking for strangers of that race. *Social Cognition, 26*, 259–275.

Zebrowitz, L.A., Kikuchi, M., and Fellous, J.M. (2010). Facial Resemblance to Emotions: Group Differences, Impression Effects, and Race Stereotypes. *Journal of Personality and Social Psychology, 98*, 175–189.

Zebrowitz, L.A., Wadlinger, H.A., Luevano, V.X., White, B.M., Xing, C. and Zhang, Y. (in press). Animal analogies in first impressions of faces. *Social Cognition*.

Zuckerman, M., Miyake, K., and Hodgins, H.S. (1991). Cross-channel effects of vocal and physical attractiveness and their implications for interpersonal perception. *Journal of Personality & Social Psychology, 60*, 545–554.

Chapter 4

Face Neurons

Edmund T. Rolls

The discovery of face neurons

In 1976 we recorded from single neurons in the awake behaving non-human primate to investigate reward systems in the brain. We had shown that neurons in the hypothalamus and orbitofrontal cortex were activated from brain sites where electrical stimulation produced reward, and wished to know whether neurons in these areas were activated by natural rewards (Rolls, 1976; Rolls et al., 1980). We discovered that single neurons in the lateral hypothalamus responded not only to the taste of food, but enormously interestingly, to the sight of food (Rolls et al., 1976). We showed that the neurons were involved in food reward, for they only responded to the sight and taste of food when hunger was present (Burton et al., 1976). Indeed, it was uncanny at the time that we could predict the behavior of the monkey on a single trial, whether he would eat the food, by the responses of these neurons that responded to the sight of food, a topic quantified later with information theoretic approaches (Rolls, 2008b; Rolls et al., 2009). These investigations triggered a whole area of research which showed how taste, olfactory, visual, and somatosensory reward was decoded and represented in the orbitofrontal cortex (which connects to the hypothalamus), and led to a theory of emotion, of how and why the brain implements emotion, of some emotional disorders produced by brain damage, of the reward systems involved in appetite control, and of the brain mechanisms of decision-making (Rolls, 2005; Rolls and Deco, 2010; Rolls and Grabenhorst, 2008).

   We wished to test where the reward value of visual stimuli discovered in these hypothalamic recordings was decoded and represented. We wanted to test whether reward was represented in the highest visual cortical processing area, the inferior temporal visual cortex, or whether this was added in a later structure such as the orbitofrontal cortex that connects the inferior temporal visual cortex to the hypothalamus. We discovered that the reward value of visual stimuli is not represented in the inferior temporal visual cortex, as shown by the facts that the neurons did not reverse their responses when the reward association of the stimuli was reversed, and that the neurons' responses to a visual stimulus, even the sight of food, did not decrease after feeding to satiety (Rolls et al., 1977). The same rule that cortical object representations are computed before reward value then becomes a property of the representations at a later cortical stage has now been shown to apply in the taste and olfactory systems (Rolls, 2005; Rolls and Grabenhorst, 2008). During these recordings, we found neurons that responded to complex stimuli such as faces, and reported in the paper that "neurons were found which could apparently only be excited by more complicated stimuli" (than simple geometrical stimuli) (Rolls et al., 1977), and cited earlier observations of Charles Gross and colleagues (Gross et al., 1972) on the effectiveness of complex stimuli for some of these neurons in anesthetized macaques. (They reported that "For at least three TE units, complex colored patterns (e.g. photographs of faces, trees) were more effective than the standard stimuli, but the crucial features of these stimuli were never determined" (Gross et al., 1972).) In 1977, we (Rolls et al., 1977) needed more evidence before we were ready to describe face-selective neurons, with visual neurophysiology so dominated by the inspiring discoveries of Hubel and Wiesel on neurons responding to bars and edges in the primary visual cortex (Hubel and Wiesel, 1968).

By 1979 we (Sanghera et al. (1979), with an abstract in 1977 (Sanghera et al. (1977)) were sufficiently convinced to report in the journal *Experimental Neurology* the presence of face-selective neurons in the amygdala and inferior temporal visual cortex, as follows:

> It should also perhaps be noted that nine of the amygdaloid neurons with visual responses were found to respond primarily to faces or photographs of faces, and two more to respond to all stimuli except these. It is possible that innate or learned factors contributed to the responses of these neurons, as well as to the responses of a comparable group of neurons from which we have recorded in the anterior inferotemporal cortex.

A neuron with good responses to faces is illustrated in figure 1 of that paper (Sanghera et al., 1979), even if that neuron was chosen to illustrate different tuning than that of a face-selective neuron. Further reports on these amygdala face-selective neurons, and on comparable face-selective neurons in the temporal lobe cortex within the superior temporal sulcus, soon appeared (Rolls, 1981a,b, 1984). For example, Rolls (1981a,b) reported that in the cortex in the superior temporal sulcus eighteen neurons

> responded selectively to faces . . . Masking out, or presenting isolated, parts of faces showed that some cells responded on the basis of different features. Some required eyes, some hair, some the mouth, and others showed parallel responses to each of a number of features. Some cells responded more strongly when such component features of faces were combined. Presenting a face in profile failed to elicit a response from some cells. Transformations of the face such as isomorphic rotation or alterations of color, size, or distance did not greatly affect the magnitude of the neuronal responses.

At about the time that we were making these recordings in the amygdala and inferior temporal visual cortex, David Perrett and Simon Thorpe joined the lab, and both were very interested in the face-selective neurons in the inferior temporal visual cortex (and also reported as present in the orbitofrontal cortex; Thorpe et al., 1983). By 1979 we (Perrett et al. (1979), with a fuller report in 1982 (Perret et al., 1982)) had published a report describing some of the properties of these neurons, including their face selectivity, their invariance (for size, color, distance, and isomorphic rotation), their frequent tuning to a particular view of a face such as profile or front view, the responsiveness of some neurons to face parts such as eyes, mouth, or hair and of other neurons only to combinations of all these features in the correct relative spatial positions, and the fact that they do not respond on the basis of arousal.

Our 1979 report was as follows:

> While recording from visual cells in the temporal lobe, we have observed a small number of cells which responded strongly to faces. Analysis of the responses of 50 such neurons in the vicinity of the fundus of the superior temporal sulcus in three hemispheres of two alert rhesus monkeys showed the following. (1) All 50 neurons responded to faces (which were human or rhesus monkey, 3-D or projected, and shown to the monkey through a large-aperture shutter with visual fixation monitored), and were almost unresponsive to gratings, simple geometrical, and other complex 3-D stimuli. (2) The neuronal responses to the sight of a face were sustained and had latencies of 110±20 ms. (3) 32 neurons responded also to some arousing or aversive visual stimuli. (4) 18 neurons responded selectively to faces, and had the following properties. (5) These neurons were in general unresponsive to auditory or tactile stimulation which was aversive, or arousing as shown by the GSR, or to stimuli such as a hand which signified a human or monkey. (6) Masking out, or presenting isolated parts of faces showed that some cells responded on the basis of different features. Some required eyes, some hair, some the mouth, and others showed parallel responses to each of a number of features. (7) Some cells responded more when such component features were combined. (8) Presenting the face in profile failed to elicit a response

for some cells. (9) Transformations of the face such as isomorphic rotation, or alterations of color, size or distance, did not greatly affect the magnitude of the neuronal responses. This evidence suggests that in the temporal lobe of the primate there are neurons specialized to respond to the component visual features present in faces. (Perrett et al., 1979.)

In 1981, Bruce and colleagues, citing our 1979 report of face-selective neurons in the cortex in the superior temporal sulcus (Perrett et al., 1979), described seven neurons in the same region that confirmed our findings in that their 7 neurons "appeared to be selective for faces"; "responded to a variety of human and monkey faces (real faces, slides, and photographs) differing in size, color, and movement"; "covering the eyes on the photograph reduced but did not eliminate the response"; and "scrambling the photographs eliminated the response" (Bruce et al., 1981).

Soon after our initial reports of face-selective neurons in the amygdala, inferior temporal visual cortex (Perrett et al., 1979, 1982; Rolls, 1984; Sanghera et al., 1977, 1979) and orbitofrontal cortex (Thorpe et al., 1983), others (Desimone, 1991; Desimone et al., 1984; Gross et al., 1985; Perrett et al., 1985a) as well as ourselves (Baylis et al., 1985; Leonard et al., 1985; Perrett and Rolls, 1983; Rolls, 1981b, 1984, 1991, 1992, 2000a, 2007b, 2008a,b) provided further descriptions and analyses of face-selective neurons, and these and many more recent discoveries are described in the remainder of this chapter.

These face-selective neurons have been helpful in many of the discoveries about the cortical mechanisms that implement face and object recognition at the neuronal and computational levels (Rolls, 2007a, 2008b, 2009; Rolls and Stringer, 2006b), and the further processing of faces beyond the visual cortical areas. Some of these discoveries are described in the following sections.

The specialization of neuronal responses found in different temporal lobe cortex visual areas

Considerable specialization of function is found in the architectonically defined areas of temporal visual cortex (Baylis et al., 1987; Rolls, 2008a) (Figure 4.1). Areas TPO, PGa and IPa are multimodal, with neurons that respond to visual, auditory and/or somatosensory inputs; the inferior temporal gyrus and adjacent areas (TE3, TE2, TE1, Tea, and TEm) are primarily unimodal visual areas; areas in the cortex in the anterior and dorsal part of the superior temporal sulcus (e.g. TPO, IPa, and IPg) have neurons specialized for the analysis of moving visual stimuli; and neurons responsive primarily to faces are found more frequently in areas TPO, Tea, and TEm, where they comprise approximately 20% of the visual neurons responsive to stationary stimuli, in contrast to the other temporal cortical areas in which they comprise 4% to 10%. The stimuli which activate other cells in these TE regions include simple visual patterns such as gratings, and combinations of simple stimulus features (Gross et al., 1985; Tanaka et al., 1990). Due to the fact that face-selective neurons, though found in high proportion in some subregions (Tsao et al., 2006), nevertheless are found in lower proportions in many temporal lobe architectonic regions (Baylis et al., 1987), it might be expected that only large lesions, or lesions that interrupt outputs of these visual areas, would produce readily apparent face-processing deficits.

Neurons with responses related to facial expression, head and face movement, and gesture are more likely to be found in the cortex in the superior temporal sulcus, whereas neurons with activity related to facial identity are more likely to be found in the TE areas (Hasselmo et al., 1989a).

The face-selective temporal cortex neurons we have studied are found mainly between 7 mm and 3 mm posterior to the sphenoid reference, which in a 3 to 4 kg macaque corresponds to approximately 11 to 15 mm anterior to the interaural plane (Baylis et al., 1987). The "middle face patch" of Tsao et al. (2006) identified with functional magnetic resonance imaging (fMRI) in the

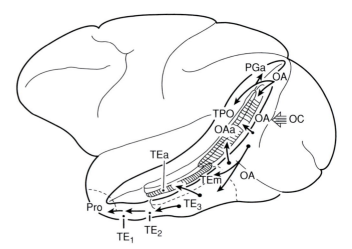

Fig. 4.1 Lateral view of the macaque brain showing the different architectonic areas (e.g. TEm, TPO) in and bordering the anterior part of the superior temporal sulcus (STS) of the macaque (see text). After Seltzer and Pandya (1978), with permission.

macaque was at A6, which is probably part of the posterior inferior temporal cortex; see Freiwald and Tsao (Chapter 36, this volume). Tsao et al. (2006) also described "anterior face patches" at A15 to A22 (see also Rajimehr et al., 2009). A15 might correspond to where we have analyzed face-selective neurons (it might translate to 3 mm posterior to our sphenoid reference).

Correspondingly, in human fMRI studies, evidence for specialization of function is described (Grill-Spector and Malach, 2004; Haxby et al., 2002; O'Toole et al., 2005; Spiridon et al., 2006; Spiridon and Kanwisher, 2002) related to face processing (in the fusiform face area, which may correspond to parts of the macaque inferior temporal visual cortex in which face neurons are common); to face expression and gesture (i.e. moving faces) (in the cortex in the superior temporal sulcus, which corresponds to the macaque cortex in the superior temporal sulcus); to objects (in an area that may correspond to the macaque inferior temporal cortex in which object but not face representations are common, as described above); and to spatial scenes (in a parahippocampal area which probably corresponds to the macaque parahippocampal gyrus areas in which neurons are tuned to spatial view and to combinations of objects and the places in which they are located) (Georges-François et al., 1999; Robertson et al., 1998; Rolls, 1999c; Rolls and Kesner, 2006; Rolls et al., 1997a, 1998, 2005; Rolls and Xiang, 2006). See chapters by Kanwisher and Barton (Chapter 7) and Haxby and Gobbini (Chapter 6) in this volume for further discussion of human neuroimaging research.

The single neuron studies in macaques described in this chapter provide evidence on a number of questions difficult to resolve with fMRI. The neuronal recording studies show that individual neurons can be highly tuned in that they convey information about face identity, *or* about face expression, *or* about head movement, *or* about objects, *or* about spatial view. The recording studies show that within these different classes, individual neurons by responding differently to different members of the class convey information about whose face it is, what the face expression is, etc., using a sparse distributed code with an approximately exponential firing rate probability distribution. The neuronal recording studies also show that each cytoarchitectonically defined area contains different proportions of face identity versus object neurons, but that the proportion of face-selective neurons in any one area is not higher than 20% of the visually responsive neurons in a cytoarchitectonically defined area, so that considerable intermixing of specifically tuned neurons is the rule (Baylis et al., 1987), although there are subregions with high proportions of face-selective neurons (Tsao et al., 2006). The neuronal recording studies also show that at the fine spatial scale, clusters of neurons extending for approximately 1 to several mm with tuning to one aspect of stimuli are common (e.g. face identity, or the visual texture of stimuli, or a particular class of head motion), and this can be understood as resulting from self-organizing mapping based on local cortical connectivity when a high dimensional space of objects, faces, etc. must be represented on a two-dimensional cortical sheet (Rolls, 2008b; Rolls and Deco, 2002). Indeed, consistent with self-organizing map principles (Rolls, 2008b), there is a high concentration of face-selective neurons within a patch identified by fMRI (Tsao et al., 2006). Consistent with our neuronal recording studies, mapping with activity-dependent cellular markers shows that there is a patchy distribution of areas with predominantly face-selective neurons, placed between areas with object-selective neurons, throughout the monkey inferior temporal visual cortical area, with the face-selective patches having estimated widths of several mm (Zangenehpour and Chaudhuri, 2005). Thus overall the evidence is consistent with a patchy distribution of face-selective neurons in the inferior temporal cortical areas, consistent with self-organizing map principles that arise because of the predominance of short-range excitatory (1–several mm) connections in the neocortex, and the resulting minimization of wiring length between neurons that are interconnected for computational reasons (Rolls, 2008). There are likely to be differences in neuronal activity between the different patches, at least in the sense that in more posterior areas it is often difficult to obtain clear responses without careful control of visual fixation (consistent with smaller receptive fields), whereas it is a computationally useful property of the neurons we have investigated, which are in the more anterior parts of the temporal cortical visual areas, that they respond under natural conditions during normal visual viewing of an object without precise control of eye position, consistent with larger receptive fields of the more anterior neurons (Aggelopoulos and Rolls, 2005; Rolls et al., 2003a).

The selectivity of one population of neurons for faces

The inferior temporal cortex neurons described in our studies as having responses selective for faces are selective in that they respond two to 20 times more (and statistically significantly more) to faces than to a wide range of gratings, simple geometrical stimuli, or complex three-dimensional objects (Baylis et al., 1985, 1987; Rolls, 1984, 1992, 1997, 2000a; Rolls and Deco, 2002). The recordings are made while the monkeys perform a visual fixation task in which after the fixation spot has disappeared, a stimulus subtending typically 8 degrees is presented on a video monitor (or, in some earlier studies, while monkeys perform a visual discrimination task). The responses to faces are excitatory with firing rates often reaching 100 spikes/s, sustained, and have typical latencies of 80 to 100 ms.

These neurons are specialized to provide information about faces in that they provide much more information (on average 0.4 bits) about which (of 20) face stimuli is being seen than about which (of 20) non-face stimuli is being seen (on average 0.07 bits) (Rolls and Tovee, 1995b; Rolls et al., 1997b). These information theoretic procedures provide an objective and quantitative way to show what is "represented" by a particular neuron and by a particular population of neurons (Rolls, 2008b).

The selectivity of these neurons for individual face features or for combinations of face features

The fact that many face-selective neurons respond only to a combination of face features in the correct spatial configuration (Perrett et al., 1982; Rolls, 1981a, 2008b; Rolls et al., 1994; Tanaka et al., 1990) (with one example also provided by Bruce et al., 1981) are consistent with the hypotheses that they are formed by competitive self-organization which provides a computational mechanism for the spatial binding of features in neural networks (Elliffe et al., 2002; Rolls, 2008b; Rolls and Deco, 2002).

Distributed encoding of face and object identity

Barlow (1972) speculated that a particular object (or face) is represented in the brain by the firing of one or a few gnostic (or "grandmother") cells. We showed that this is not the case, and that although a face-selective cell may respond only to faces, its firing rate is graded to a set of faces with some faces producing large responses, and more and more producing lower and lower responses, with each neuron having a different profile of responses to each face with an approximately exponential firing rate probability distribution (Baylis et al., 1985; Rolls and Tovee, 1995b), with the average sparseness being 0.65 (Baddeley et al., 1997; Baylis et al., 1985; Franco et al., 2007; Rolls and Tovee, 1995b; Treves et al., 1999) (see Figure 4.2). The sparseness of the representation provided by a neuron can be defined as:

$$a = (\Sigma_{s=1,S} \, r_s/S)^2 / \Sigma_{s=1,S}(r_s^2/S)$$

where r_s is the mean firing rate of the neuron to stimulus s in the set of S stimuli.

Complementary evidence comes from applying information theory to analyze how information is represented by a population of these neurons. The information required to identify which of S equiprobable events occurred (or stimuli were shown) is $\log_2 S$ bits. (Thus 1 bit is required to specify which of two stimuli was shown, 2 bits to specify which of 4 stimuli was shown, 3 bits to specify which of 8 stimuli was shown, etc.) The important point for the present purposes is that if the encoding was local (or grandmother cell-like), the number of stimuli encoded by a population of neurons would be expected to rise approximately linearly with the number of neurons in the population. In contrast, with distributed encoding, provided that the neuronal responses are sufficiently independent, the number of stimuli encodable by the population of neurons might be expected to rise exponentially as the number of neurons in the sample of the population was increased. The information available about which of 20 equiprobable faces had been shown that was available from the responses of different numbers of these neurons is shown in Figure 4.3. First, it is clear that some information is available from the responses of just one neuron—on average approximately 0.34 bits. Thus knowing the activity of just one neuron in the population does provide some evidence about which stimulus was present. This evidence that information is available in the responses of individual neurons in this way, without having to know the state of all the other neurons in the population, indicates that information is made explicit in the firing of individual neurons in a way that will allow neurally plausible decoding, involving computing a sum of input activities each weighted by synaptic strength, a dot product, to work (see below). Second, it is clear (Figure 4.3) that the information rises approximately linearly, and the number of stimuli encoded thus rises approximately exponentially, as the number of cells in the sample increases (Abbott et al., 1996; Rolls and Treves, 1998; Rolls et al., 1997b), confirmed with simultaneous recordings from different neurons (Panzeri et al., 1999a; Rolls et al., 2004, 2006b). Consistently, Gawne and Richmond (1993) showed that even adjacent pairs of neurons recorded simultaneously from the same electrode carried information that was approximately 80% independent.

Some have postulated that there might be information available if neurons became temporally synchronized to some but not other stimuli in a set (Engel et al., 1992; Singer, 1999). With rigorous information theoretic techniques (Rolls, 2008b), we showed that for static faces and objects most of the information is available in the firing rates of the neurons (the number of spikes in a

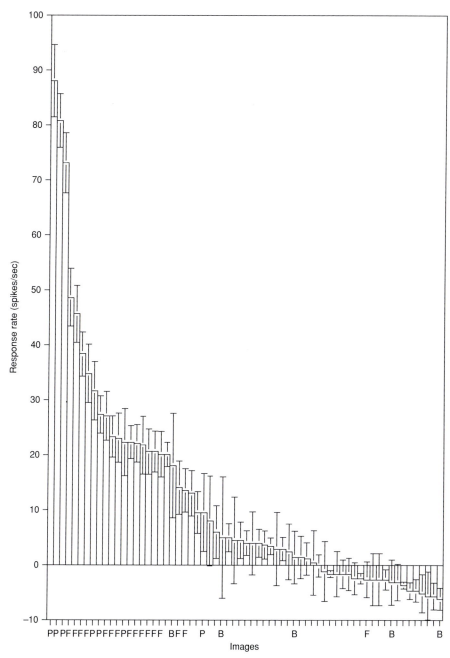

Fig. 4.2 Firing rate distribution of a single neuron in the temporal visual cortex to a set of 23 face (F) and 45 non-face images of natural scenes. The firing rate response (± the standard error) to each of the 68 stimuli is shown, i.e. the spontaneous firing rate has been subtracted so that the 0 baseline is the spontaneous firing rate. P indicates a face profile stimulus, a B a body part stimulus such as a hand. With kind permission from Springer Science+Business Media: *Experimental Brain Research*, The responses of single neurons in the temporal visual cortical areas of the macaque when more than one stimulus is present in the receptive field, **103**(3), 1995, Edmund T. Rolls and Martin J. Tovee.

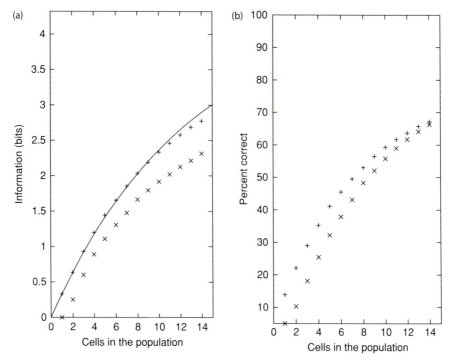

Fig. 4.3 (a) The values for the average information available in the responses of different numbers of inferior temporal cortex neurons on each trial, about which of a set of 20 face stimuli has been shown. The decoding method was Dot Product (DP, x) or Bayesian Probability Estimation (PE, +), and the effects obtained with cross validation procedures utilizing 50% of the trials as test trials are shown. The remainder of the trials in the cross-validation procedure were used as training trials. Probability estimation refers to estimating the probability from the neuronal responses for a single trial that each of the 20 faces was shown, thus utilizing the neuronal evidence available about how likely it was that each stimulus was shown (see Rolls et al., 1997). The full line indicates the amount of information expected from populations of increasing size, when assuming random correlations within the constraint given by the ceiling (the information in the stimulus set, I = 4.32 bits). (b) The per cent correct for the corresponding data to those shown in Figure 4.3a. After Rolls et al. (1997), with permission.

short time period), and that there is little additional information (less than 5% of the total) in the relative time of firing of simultaneously recorded neurons (Franco et al., 2004; Panzeri et al., 1999a; Rolls et al., 2003b, 2004). This has been shown to apply to natural vision in natural scenes in which two test images had to be segmented from a complex background, the features of each object had to be bound together, and the monkey had to use top-down attention to search for one of two images in a complex scene (Aggelopoulos et al., 2005).

Advantages of the sparse distributed representation of faces and objects for brain processing

The advantages of the distributed encoding found include the following explained in more detail elsewhere (Rolls, 2005, 2007b, 2008b; Rolls and Deco, 2002; Rolls and Treves, 1998), with a full analysis of how information theory has helped in the understanding of neural representations in the brain provided by Rolls (2008b).

Exponentially high coding capacity

This property arises from a combination of the encoding being sufficiently close to independent by the different neurons (i.e., factorial), and sufficiently distributed, and is illustrated by the evidence shown in Figure 4.3.

Ease with which the code can be read by receiving neurons

For brain plausibility, it is also a requirement that neurons should be able to read the code. This is why when we have estimated the information from populations of neurons, we have used in addition to a probability estimating measure (optimal, in the Bayesian sense), also a dot product measure, which is a way of specifying that all that is required of decoding neurons would be the property of adding up postsynaptic potentials produced through each synapse as a result of the activity of each incoming axon (Abbott et al., 1996; Rolls et al., 1997b). It was found that with such a neurally plausible algorithm (the Dot Product, DP, algorithm), which calculates which average response vector the neuronal response vector on a single test trial was closest to by performing a normalized dot product (equivalent to measuring the angle between the test and the average vector), the same generic results were obtained, with only a 40% reduction of information compared to the more efficient (Bayesian) algorithm. This is an indication that the brain could utilize the exponentially increasing capacity for encoding stimuli as the number of neurons in the population increases.

Higher resistance to noise

Because the information is decoded from a large population of neurons by inner product multiplication with the synaptic weight vector, there is less dependence on the random (almost Poisson) firing times for a given mean rate of single neurons, and thus there is resistance to noise inherent in the activity of single neurons (Rolls and Deco, 2010).

Generalization

Generalization to similar stimuli is again a property that arises in neuronal networks if distributed but not if local encoding is used. The generalization arises as a result of the fact that a neuron can be thought of as computing the inner or dot product of the stimulus representation expressed as the firing rate on the set of input neurons with its synaptic weight vector (see further Rolls, 2008b; Rolls and Deco, 2002; Rolls and Treves, 1998).

Completion

Completion occurs in associative memory networks by a similar process. Completion is the property of recall of the whole of a pattern in response to any part of the pattern.

Graceful degradation or fault tolerance

Again, because the information is decoded from a large population of neurons by inner product multiplication with the synaptic weight vector, there is less dependence on the firing of any one neuron or on any particular subset of neurons, so that if some neurons are damaged, the performance of the system only gradually degrades, and is in this sense fault tolerant.

Speed of readout of the information

The information available in a distributed representation can be decoded by an analyzer more quickly than can the information from a local representation, given comparable firing rates. Within a fraction of an interspike interval, with a distributed representation, much information can be extracted (Panzeri et al., 1999b; Rolls et al., 1997b, 2006b; Treves, 1993; Treves et al., 1996, 1997). In effect, spikes from many different neurons can contribute to calculating the angle between a neuronal population and a synaptic weight vector within an interspike interval (Franco et al., 2004; Rolls, 2008b; Rolls and Deco, 2002). With local encoding, the speed of information readout depends on the exact model considered, but if the rate of firing needs to be taken into account, this will necessarily take time, because of the time needed for several spikes to accumulate in order to estimate the firing rate.

Invariance in the neuronal representation of stimuli

One of the major problems that must be solved by a visual system is the building of a representation of visual information which allows recognition to occur relatively independently of size, contrast, spatial frequency, position on the retina, angle of view, etc. This is required so that if the receiving associative networks (in, e.g. the amygdala, orbitofrontal cortex, and hippocampus) learn about one view, position, etc., of the object, generalization occurs correctly to other positions, views, etc. of the object. It has been shown that the majority of face-selective inferior temporal cortex neurons have responses that are relatively invariant with respect to the size of the stimulus (Rolls and Baylis, 1986). The median size change tolerated with a response of greater than half the maximal response was 12 times. Also, the neurons typically responded to a face when the information in it had been reduced from three-dimensional to a two-dimensional representation in gray on a monitor, with a response which was on average 0.5 of that to a real face. Another transform over which recognition is relatively invariant is spatial frequency. For example, a face can be identified when it is blurred (when it contains only low spatial frequencies), and when it is high-pass spatial frequency filtered (when it looks like a line drawing). It has been shown that if the face images to which these neurons respond are low-pass filtered in the spatial frequency domain (so that they are blurred), then many of the neurons still respond when the images contain frequencies only up to eight cycles per face (cpf). Similarly, the neurons still respond to high-pass filtered images (with only high spatial frequency edge information) when frequencies down to only eight cycles per face are included (Rolls et al., 1985). Face recognition shows similar invariance with respect to spatial frequency (Rolls et al., 1985). Further analysis of these neurons with narrow (octave) bandpass spatial frequency filtered face stimuli shows that the responses of these neurons to an unfiltered face can not be predicted from a linear combination of their responses to the narrow band stimuli (Rolls et al., 1987). This lack of linearity of these neurons, and their responsiveness to a wide range of spatial frequencies, indicate that in at least this part of the primate visual system recognition does not occur using Fourier analysis of the spatial frequency components of images.

Inferior temporal visual cortex neurons also often show considerable translation (shift) invariance, not only under anesthesia (see Gross et al., 1985), but also in the awake behaving primate (Tovee et al., 1994), and selectivity between faces is maintained.

Until recently, research on translation invariance (and much visual neurophysiology) considered the case in which there is only one object or stimulus in the visual field. What happens in a cluttered, natural environment? Do all objects that can activate an inferior temporal neuron do so whenever they are anywhere within the large receptive fields of inferior temporal cortex neurons

(Rolls and Tovee, 1995a)? If so, the output of the visual system might be confusing for structures that receive inputs from the temporal cortical visual areas. It has now been shown that the receptive fields of inferior temporal cortex neurons while large (typically 70 degrees in diameter) when a test stimulus is presented against a blank background, become much smaller, as little as several degrees in diameter, when objects are seen against a complex natural background (Rolls et al., 2003a) (cf. DiCarlo and Maunsell, 2003; Op De Beeck and Vogels, 2000). Thus the neurons provide information biased towards what is present at the fovea, and not equally about what is present anywhere in the visual field. This makes the interface to action simpler, in that what is at the fovea can be interpreted (e.g. by an associative memory in the orbitofrontal cortex or amygdala) partly independently of the surroundings, and choices and actions can be directed if appropriate to what is at the fovea (Ballard, 1993; Rolls and Deco, 2002). These findings are an important step towards understanding how the visual system functions in a natural environment (Aggelopoulos and Rolls, 2005; Gallant et al., 1998; Rolls, 2008b; Rolls and Deco, 2002; Stringer and Rolls, 2008; Stringer et al., 2007).

A view-invariant representation of faces and objects

It has also been shown that some temporal cortical neurons reliably responded differently to the faces of two different individuals independently of viewing angle (Hasselmo et al., 1989b), although in most cases (16/18 neurons) the response was not perfectly view-independent. Mixed together in the same cortical regions there are neurons with view-dependent responses (Hasselmo et al., 1989b). Such neurons might respond for example to a view of a profile of a monkey but not to a full-face view of the same monkey (Perrett et al., 1985a). These findings, of view-dependent, partially view independent, and view independent representations in the same cortical regions are consistent with the hypothesis discussed below that view-independent representations are being built in these regions by associating together neurons that respond to different views of the same individual. View-independent representations are important for face and object recognition. View-independent object neurons are also found in the inferior temporal cortex (Booth and Rolls, 1998), as well as view-dependent neurons (Logothetis and Pauls, 1995).

Further evidence that some neurons in the temporal cortical visual areas have object-based rather than view-based responses comes from a study of a population of neurons that responds to moving faces (Hasselmo et al., 1989b). For example, neurons responded to ventral flexion of the head irrespective of whether the head was upright or inverted. In this procedure, retinally encoded or viewer-centered movement vectors are reversed, but the object-based description remains the same. It is an important property of these neurons that they can encode a description of an object that is based on relative motions of different parts of the object, and that is not based on flow relative to the observer. The implication of this type of encoding is that the upper eyelids closing could be encoded as the same social signal that eye contact is being broken independently of the particular in-plane rotation (tilt, as far as being fully inverted) of the face being observed (or of the observer's head).

Also consistent with object-based encoding is the discovery of a small number of neurons that respond to images of faces of a given *absolute* size, irrespective of the retinal image size or distance (Rolls and Baylis, 1986).

Learning of new representations in the temporal cortical visual areas

To investigate the hypothesis that visual experience might guide the formation of the responsiveness of neurons so that they provide an economical and ensemble-encoded representation of items actually present in the environment, the responses of inferior temporal cortex face-selective neurons have been analyzed while a set of new faces were shown. It was found that some of the neurons studied in this way altered the relative degree to which they responded to the different members of the set of novel faces over the first few (one to two) presentations of the set (Rolls, 1995; Rolls et al., 1989b). This evidence is consistent with the categorization being performed by self-organizing competitive neuronal networks, as described elsewhere (Rolls, 1989, 2008b; Rolls and Deco, 2002; Rolls and Treves, 1998; Rolls et al., 1989a).

Further evidence that these neurons can learn new representations very rapidly comes from an experiment in which binarized black and white images of faces which blended with the background were used. These did not activate face-selective neurons. Full gray-scale images of the same photographs were then shown for ten 0.5-s presentations. It was found that in a number of cases, if the neuron happened to be responsive to that face, when the binarized version of the same face was shown next, the neurons responded to it (Tovee et al., 1996). This is a direct parallel to the same phenomenon that is observed psychophysically, and provides dramatic evidence that these neurons are influenced by only a very few seconds (in this case 5 s) of experience with a visual stimulus. We have shown a neural correlate of this effect using similar stimuli and a similar paradigm in a PET (positron emission tomography) neuroimaging study in humans, with a region showing an effect of the learning found for faces in the right temporal lobe, and for objects in the left temporal lobe (Dolan et al., 1997).

Such rapid learning of representations of new faces and objects appears to be a major type of learning in which the temporal cortical areas are involved. Ways in which this learning could occur are considered briefly below, and in detail elsewhere (Rolls, 2008b, 2009; Rolls and Deco, 2002; Rolls and Stringer, 2006b).

The speed of processing in the temporal cortical visual areas

Given that there is a whole sequence of visual cortical processing stages including V1, V2, V4, and the posterior inferior temporal cortex to reach the anterior temporal cortical areas, and that the response latencies of neurons in V1 are about 40 to 50 ms, and in the anterior inferior temporal cortical areas approximately 80 to 100 ms, each stage may need to perform processing for only 15 to 30 ms before it has performed sufficient processing to start influencing the next stage. Consistent with this, response latencies between V1 and the inferior temporal cortex increase from stage to stage (Thorpe and Imbert, 1989).

In a first approach to this issue, we measured the information available in short temporal epochs of the responses of temporal cortical face-selective neurons about which face of a set of faces had been seen. We found that if a period of the firing rate of 50 ms was taken, then this contained 84.4% of the information available in a much longer period of 400 ms about which of four faces had been seen. If the epoch was as little as 20 ms, the information was 65% of that available from the firing rate in the 400 ms period (Tovee et al., 1993). We were able to extend this finding to the case when a much larger stimulus set, of 20 faces, was used. Again, we found that the information available in short (e.g. 50-ms) epochs was a considerable proportion (e.g. 65%) of that available in a 400-ms long firing-rate analysis period (Tovee and Rolls, 1995). We extended these results by showing that although there is considerable information in the first spike of each neuron that arrives after a stimulus has been shown, there is more information if the number of spikes in a short window of, for example, 20 ms is used, and that the order of arrival of the spikes from different neurons is not an important factor, whereas the number of spikes in a short window is an important factor (Rolls et al., 2006b).

The next approach has been to use a visual backward masking paradigm. In this paradigm there is a brief presentation of a test stimulus which is rapidly followed (within 1 to 100 ms) by the presentation of a second stimulus (the mask), which impairs or masks the perception of the test stimulus. It has been shown (Rolls and Tovee, 1994) that when there is no mask, inferior temporal cortex neurons respond to a 16-ms presentation of the test stimulus for 200 to 300 ms, far longer than the presentation time. It is suggested that this reflects the operation of a short-term memory system implemented in cortical circuitry, which we propose is important in learning invariant representations (Rolls, 2008b). If the pattern mask followed the onset of the test face stimulus by 20 ms (a stimulus onset asynchrony of 20 ms), face-selective neurons in the inferior temporal cortex of macaques responded for a period of 20 to 30 ms before their firing was interrupted by the mask (Rolls and Tovee, 1994; Rolls et al., 1999). We went on to show that under these conditions (a test-mask stimulus onset asynchrony of 20 ms), human observers looking at the same displays could just identify which of six faces was shown (Rolls et al., 1994).

These results provide evidence that a cortical area can perform the computation necessary for the recognition of a visual stimulus in 20 to 30 ms (although it is true that for conscious perception, the firing needs to occur for 40 to 50 ms; see Rolls, 2003). This provides a fundamental constraint which must be accounted for in any theory of cortical computation. The results emphasize just how rapidly cortical circuitry can operate, a topic that is treated elsewhere (Panzeri et al., 2001; Rolls, 2008b; Rolls and Treves, 1998; Treves, 1993; Treves et al., 1996).

Computational mechanisms in the visual cortex for face and object recognition

One of the enormous computational problems solved by the brain is forming a representation of a face or object that is selective, and invariant with respect to position, view, scale, and even partly rotation, and that can be read by neurons performing dot-product decoding using multiple neurons for recognition, association, and action. The neurophysiological findings described above, and wider considerations on the possible computational properties of the cerebral cortex, have led to a theory of how invariant representations of objects are formed using hierarchical self-organizing competitive networks with the temporal and spatial continuity as an object transforms providing the basis for neurons learning to respond to the different transforms of objects (Figure 4.4). Due to space limitations, the theory is described elsewhere (Elliffe et al., 2002; Perry et al., 2006, 2010; Rolls, 1992, 2007a, 2008b, 2009; Rolls and Deco, 2002; Rolls and Milward, 2000; Rolls and Stringer, 2001, 2006b; Stringer et al., 2006; Stringer and Rolls, 2000, 2002; Wallis and Rolls, 1997). The theory proposes that neurons in these visual areas use a modified Hebb synaptic modification rule with a short-term memory trace to capture whatever can be captured at each stage that is invariant about faces or objects as they change in retinal view, position, size, and rotation. The statistics of the visual input are used to help build invariant representations. The model can use temporal continuity in an associative synaptic learning rule with a short-term memory trace, and/or it can use spatial continuity in spatial continuous transformation learning. The model of visual processing in the ventral cortical stream can build representations of objects that are invariant with respect to translation, view, size, and lighting. The model has been extended to incorporate top-down feedback connections to model the control of attention by biased competition in, for example, spatial and object search tasks (Deco and Rolls, 2004). Recent developments include a theory of how several faces or objects and their spatial positions can be represented simultaneously in a scene using asymmetries in the receptive fields revealed in crowded scenes

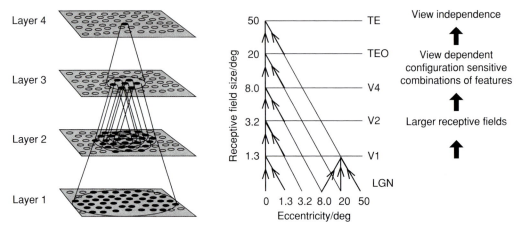

Fig. 4.4 Right. Schematic diagram showing convergence achieved by the forward projections in the visual system, and the types of representation that may be built by competitive networks operating at each stage of the system from the primary visual cortex (V1) to the inferior temporal visual cortex (area TE) (see text). LGN, lateral geniculate nucleus. Area TEO forms the posterior inferior temporal cortex. The receptive fields in the inferior temporal visual cortex (e.g. in the TE areas) cross the vertical midline (not shown). Left. Hierarchical network structure of VisNet. A description of the operation of this model of cortical invariant face and object recognition is provided in chapter 4 of *Memory, Attention, and Decision-Making* (Rolls, 2008b), available online at http://www.oxcns.org/papers/MemoryAttentionAndDecisionMakingContentsAndSampleChapter4.pdf.

(Aggelopoulos and Rolls, 2005; Rolls et al., 2008b), how spatial information about the position of objects in the inferior temporal cortex can be used to build spatial scene representations in the hippocampal system (Rolls et al., 2008b), how invariant representations of individual faces or objects can be learned even when multiple faces or objects are present during learning (Stringer and Rolls, 2008; Stringer et al., 2007), and how a similar computational mechanism could lead to object global motion encoding in the dorsal visual system (e.g. looming, rotation, and object-based movement) (Rolls and Stringer, 2006a). This approach is more biologically plausible than some complementary approaches that assume a MAX function to help compute invariant representations (Riesenhuber and Poggio, 1999; Serre et al., 2007) or which implement slow learning (captured by our synaptic trace learning rule) using non-local backpropagation algorithms (Wiskott and Sejnowski, 2002), but which nevertheless in terms of the concepts support the computational hypotheses incorporated in the biologically plausible approach we have developed, and modeled with VisNet.

Attentional effects, models of attention, and their implications for neuropsychology

In complex natural scenes, the receptive fields of inferior temporal cortex neurons shrink to a few degrees in diameter close to the fovea, and this helps to solve the binding problem in visual perception, for then IT neurons encode the object that is close to the fovea, and which is being fixated, providing the coordinates for actions directed to the object or face (Rolls et al., 2003a). Under these conditions, attention to a particular face or object increases the receptive field size for that face or object (Rolls et al., 2003a) by a top-down biased competition process analyzed in an extended model of VisNet in which there are top-down effects implemented by cortico-cortical backprojections (Deco and Rolls, 2004).

Top-down biased competition models of attention (Desimone and Duncan, 1995) are now becoming sufficiently developed that they can provide an account of interactions between the dorsal and ventral visual systems (Deco and Rolls, 2004, 2005a; Rolls and Deco, 2002), of how non-linearities important in attention are implemented at the neuronal and biophysical level (Deco and Rolls, 2005b), of how fMRI signals may reflect the synaptic and neuronal mechanisms involved in attention (Deco et al., 2004), and of the psychophysics (Rolls and Deco, 2002) and neuropsychiatry (Loh et al., 2007; Rolls and Deco, 2010; Rolls et al., 2008a) of attention. These concepts are also being applied to the neuropsychology of attention, including object-based visual neglect understood in terms of a gradient of damage increasing to the right of the parietal cortex; the difficulty of disengaging attention; extinction and visual search; the effect on neglect of top-down knowledge; alterations in the search of hierarchical patterns after brain damage; and alterations in conjunction search after brain damage (Deco et al., 2002; Deco and Zihl, 2001; Rolls, 2008b; Rolls and Deco, 2002). It was possible to account for example for the neglect of the left half of each object (or face) arranged in a row of objects by local lateral inhibition interacting with damage increasing in a graded way to the right of the parietal cortex (Deco and Rolls, 2002).

Different neural systems are specialized for face expression decoding and for face recognition

It has been shown that some neurons respond to face identity, and others to face expression (Hasselmo et al., 1989a). The neurons responsive to expression were found primarily in the cortex in the superior temporal sulcus, while the neurons responsive to identity (described in the preceding sections) were found in the inferior temporal gyrus including areas TEa and TEm. Information about facial expression is of potential use in social interactions (Rolls, 1984, 1986a,b, 1990, 1999a, 2005). Damage to this population may contribute to the deficits in social and emotional behavior which are part of the Kluver–Bucy syndrome produced by temporal lobe damage in monkeys (see Leonard et al., 1985; Rolls, 1981b, 1984, 1986a,b, 1990, 1999a, 2005).

A further way in which some of these neurons in the cortex in the superior temporal sulcus may be involved in social interactions is that some of them respond to gestures, e.g. to a face undergoing ventral flexion, as described above (Hasselmo et al., 1989a) and by Perrett et al. (1985b). Moreover, the neuronal responses to head motion are in head-based coordinates, that is they show invariance (Hasselmo et al., 1989a), and this has been modeled in a version of VisNet that includes visual motion flow inputs and computes invariant representations of global flow (Rolls and Stringer, 2006a). The interpretation of these neurons as being useful for social interactions is that in some cases these neurons respond not only to ventral head flexion, but also to the eyes lowering and the eyelids closing (Hasselmo et al., 1989a). These two movements (head lowering and eyelid lowering) often occur together when a monkey is breaking social contact with another. It is also important when decoding facial expression to retain some information about the head direction of the face stimulus being seen relative to the observer, for this is very important in determining whether a threat is being made in your direction. The presence of view-dependent, head and body gesture (Hasselmo et al., 1989b), and eye gaze (Perrett et al., 1985b), representations in some of these cortical regions where face expression is represented is consistent with this requirement. In contrast, the TE areas (more ventral, mainly in the macaque inferior temporal gyrus), in which neurons tuned to face identity (Hasselmo et al., 1989a) and with view-independent responses (Hasselmo et al., 1989b) are more likely to be found, may be more related to a view invariant representation of identity. Of course, for appropriate social and emotional responses, both types of subsystem would be important, for it is necessary to know both the direction of a social gesture, and the identity of the individual, in order to make the correct social or emotional response.

A representation of faces in the amygdala

Outputs from the temporal cortical visual areas reach the amygdala and the orbitofrontal cortex, and evidence is accumulating that these brain areas are involved in social and emotional responses to faces (Rolls, 1990, 1999a, 2000b, 2005; Rolls and Deco, 2002). For example, lesions of the amygdala in monkeys disrupt social and emotional responses to faces, and we have identified a population of neurons with face-selective responses in the primate amygdala (Leonard et al., 1985), some of which may respond to facial and body gesture (Brothers et al., 1990).

A representation of faces in the orbitofrontal cortex

Rolls et al. (2006a) have found a number of face-responsive neurons in the orbitofrontal cortex, and they are also present in adjacent prefrontal cortical areas (Wilson et al., 1993). The orbitofrontal cortex face-responsive neurons, first observed by Thorpe and colleagues (1983), then by Rolls et al. (2006a), tend to respond with longer latencies than temporal lobe neurons (140–200 ms typically, compared with 80–100 ms); they also convey information about which face is being seen, by having different responses to different faces (see Figure 4.5); and are typically rather harder to activate strongly than temporal cortical face-selective neurons, in that many of them respond much better to real faces than to two-dimensional images of faces on a video monitor (Rolls and Baylis, 1986). Some of the orbitofrontal cortex face-selective neurons are responsive to face gesture or movement, and others to face expression (Rolls et al., 2006a). The findings are consistent with the likelihood that these neurons are activated via the inputs from the temporal cortical visual areas in which face-selective neurons are found. The significance of the neurons is likely to be related to the fact that faces convey information that is important in social reinforcement, both by conveying face expression (cf. Hasselmo et al., 1989a), which can indicate reinforcement, and by encoding information about which individual is present, also important in evaluating and utilizing reinforcing inputs in social situations. Consistent with a role in reinforcement for face-selective neurons in the orbitofrontal cortex, activations in the orbitofrontal cortex are related to the attractiveness of a face (O'Doherty et al., 2003).

We have also been able to obtain evidence that non-reward used as a signal to reverse behavioral choice is represented in the human orbitofrontal cortex (for background, see Rolls, 2005). Kringelbach and Rolls (2003) used the faces of two different people, and if one face was selected then that face smiled, and if the other was selected, the face showed an angry expression. After good performance was acquired, there were repeated reversals of the visual discrimination task. Kringelbach and Rolls (2003) found that activation of a lateral part of the orbitofrontal cortex in the fMRI study was produced on the error trials, that is when the human chose a face, and did not obtain the expected reward. The study reveals that the human orbitofrontal cortex is very sensitive to social feedback from face expression when it must be used to change behavior (Kringelbach and Rolls, 2003, 2004; Rolls, 2005).

To investigate the possible significance of face-related inputs to the orbitofrontal cortex visual neurons described above, we also tested the responses to faces of patients with orbitofrontal cortex damage. Impairments in the identification of facial and vocal emotional expression were demonstrated in a group of patients with ventral frontal lobe damage who had socially

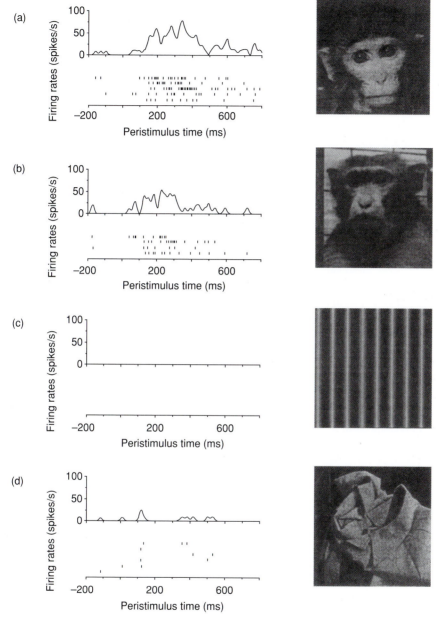

Fig. 4.5 Orbitofrontal cortex face-selective neuron as found in macaques. Peristimulus rastergrams and time histograms are shown. Each trial is a row in the rastergram. Several trials for each stimulus are shown. The ordinate is in spikes/s. The neuron responded best to face (a), also responded, though less to face (b), had different responses to other faces (not shown), and did not respond to non-face stimuli (e.g. (c) and (d)). The stimulus appeared at time 0 on a video monitor. After Rolls et al. (2006a), with permission.

inappropriate behavior (Hornak et al., 1996, 2003; Rolls, 1999b). The results (Hornak et al., 2003) also extend these investigations to the anterior cingulate cortex (including some of medial prefrontal cortex area BA9) by showing that lesions in these regions can produce voice and/or face expression identification deficits, and marked changes in subjective emotional state (see further Rolls, 2008a).

Summary and conclusions

Neurophysiological evidence is described showing that some neurons in the macaque inferior temporal visual cortex and cortex in the superior temporal sulcus have responses that are invariant with respect to the position, size, and in some cases view of faces, and that these neurons show rapid processing and rapid learning. Which face (or object) is present is encoded using a distributed representation in which each neuron conveys independent information in its firing rate, with little information evident in the relative time of firing of different neurons. This ensemble encoding has the advantages of maximizing the information in the representation useful for discrimination between stimuli using a simple synaptically weighted sum of the neuronal firing by the receiving neurons, and with the properties of generalization and graceful degradation. These invariant representations are ideally suited to provide the inputs to brain regions such as the orbitofrontal cortex and amygdala, where face-selective neurons are also found, that learn the reinforcement associations of an individual's face. This enables the learning in the orbitofrontal cortex and amygdala, and the appropriate social and emotional responses, to generalize to other views of the same face (Rolls, 2005, 2008b). These representations are also ideally suited for face recognition, and as an input to systems that implement episodic memory (Rolls, 2008b, 2010; Rolls and Kesner, 2006). In complex natural scenes the neuronal responses remain face-selective, but the receptive fields become reduced in size and asymmetric around the fovea, enabling several objects and their relative spatial positions to be simultaneously represented close to the fovea. Multiple instances of the same face or object can be represented simultaneously in this way. A different population of neurons in the cortex in the superior temporal sulcus responses encodes face gesture (movement) and face expression, and many of these neurons have view-dependent responses.

The responses of these neurons thus reflect solution of some of the major problems of visual perception. Analysis of their responses has helped in the development of a computational theory and model of how invariant representations of faces and objects may be produced in a hierarchically organized set of visual cortical areas with convergent connectivity and synaptic plasticity that reflects the statistics of the temporal and spatial continuity of objects in natural scenes (Rolls, 2008b, 2009).

Acknowledgments

The author has worked on some of the investigations described here with L. Abbott, N. Aggelopoulos, P. Azzopardi, R. Baddeley, G.C. Baylis, F. Battaglia, M. Booth, A.S. Browning, H. Critchley, G. Deco, R.J. Dolan, M.C.M. Elliffe, G.R. Fink, P. Földiák, L. Franco, K. Friston, F. Grabenhorst, M.E. Hasselmo, J. Hornak, B. Horwitz, K. Inoue, S.J. Judge, M. Kadohisa, M. Kringelbach, C.M. Leonard, T.J. Milward, R. Morris, J. O'Doherty, S. Panzeri, D.I. Perrett, G. Perry, D.G. Purcell, V.S. Ramachandran, S. Reece, M.K. Sanghera, M. Simmen, S.M. Stringer, M.J. Tovee, A. Treves, S.J. Thorpe, J. Tromans, T.W. Vidyasagar, D. Wade, E.A. Wakeman, G. Wallis, and F.A.W. Wilson, and their collaboration is sincerely acknowledged. Different parts of the research described were supported by the Medical Research Council, PG8513790; by The Wellcome Trust; by a Human Frontier Science Program grant; by an EC Human Capital and Mobility grant; by the MRC Oxford Interdisciplinary Research Centre in Cognitive

Neuroscience; and by the Oxford McDonnell Centre in Cognitive Neuroscience. A description of the computational implications of some of the findings described here is provided in chapter 4 of *Memory, Attention, and Decision-Making* (Rolls, 2008b), available online at http://www. oxcns.org/papers/MemoryAttentionAndDecisionMakingContentsAndSampleChapter4.pdf.
   Some of the publications referred to here are available at http://www.oxcns.org.

References

Abbott, L.F., Rolls, E.T., and Tovee, M.J. (1996). Representational capacity of face coding in monkeys. *Cerebral Cortex*, **6**, 498–505.

Aggelopoulos, N.C. and Rolls, E.T. (2005). Natural scene perception: inferior temporal cortex neurons encode the positions of different objects in the scene. *European Journal of Neuroscience*, **22**, 2903–2916.

Aggelopoulos, N.C., Franco, L., and Rolls, E.T. (2005). Object perception in natural scenes: encoding by inferior temporal cortex simultaneously recorded neurons. *Journal of Neurophysiology*, **93**, 1342–1357.

Baddeley, R.J., Abbott, L.F., Booth, M.J.A., *et al.* (1997). Responses of neurons in primary and inferior temporal visual cortices to natural scenes. *Proceedings of the Royal Society of London B*, **264**, 1775–1783.

Ballard, D.H. (1993). Subsymbolic modelling of hand-eye coordination. In D.E. Broadbent (ed.) *The Simulation of Human Intelligence*, pp. 71–102. Oxford: Blackwell.

Barlow, H.B. (1972). Single units and sensation: A neuron doctrine for perceptual psychology? *Perception*, **1**, 371–394.

Baylis, G.C., Rolls, E.T., and Leonard, C.M. (1985). Selectivity between faces in the responses of a population of neurons in the cortex in the superior temporal sulcus of the monkey. *Brain Research*, **342**, 91–102.

Baylis, G.C., Rolls, E.T., and Leonard, C.M. (1987). Functional subdivisions of the temporal lobe neocortex. *Journal of Neuroscience*, **7**, 330–342.

Booth, M.C.A. and Rolls, E.T. (1998). View-invariant representations of familiar objects by neurons in the inferior temporal visual cortex. *Cerebral Cortex*, **8**, 510–523.

Brothers, L., Ring, B., and Kling, A. (1990). Response of neurons in the macaque amygdala to complex social stimuli. *Behavioral Brain Research*, **41**, 199–213.

Bruce, C., Desimone, R., and Gross, C.G. (1981). Visual properties of neurons in a polysensory area in superior temporal sulcus of the macaque. *Journal of Neurophysiology*, **46**, 369–384.

Burton, M.J., Rolls, E.T., and Mora, F. (1976). Effects of hunger on the responses of neurones in the lateral hypothalamus to the sight and taste of food. *Experimental Neurology*, **51**, 668–677.

Deco, G. and Rolls, E.T. (2002). Object-based visual neglect: a computational hypothesis. *European Journal of Neuroscience*, **16**, 1994–2000.

Deco, G. and Rolls, E.T. (2004). A neurodynamical cortical model of visual attention and invariant object recognition. *Vision Research*, **44**, 621–644.

Deco, G. and Rolls, E.T. (2005a). Attention, short-term memory, and action selection: a unifying theory. *Progress in Neurobiology*, **76**, 236–256.

Deco, G. and Rolls, E.T. (2005b). Neurodynamics of biased competition and co-operation for attention: a model with spiking neurons. *Journal of Neurophysiology*, **94**, 295–313.

Deco, G. and Zihl, J. (2001). Top-down selective visual attention: a neurodynamical approach. *Visual Cognition*, **8**, 119–140.

Deco, G., Heinke, D., Zihl, J., and Humphreys, G. (2002). A computational neuroscience account of visual neglect. *Neurocomputing*, **44–46**, 811–816.

Deco, G., Rolls, E.T., and Horwitz, B. (2004). "What" and "where" in visual working memory: a computational neurodynamical perspective for integrating fMRI and single-neuron data. *Journal of Cognitive Neuroscience*, **16**, 683–701.

Desimone, R. (1991). Face-selective cells in the temporal cortex of monkeys. *Journal of Cognitive Neuroscience*, **3**, 1–8.

Desimone, R. and Duncan, J. (1995). Neural mechanisms of selective visual attention. *Annual Review of Neuroscience*, **18**, 193–222.

Desimone, R., Albright, T.D., Gross, C.G., and Bruce, C. (1984). Stimulus-selective properties of inferior temporal neurons in the macaque. *Journal of Neuroscience*, **4**, 2051–2062.

DiCarlo, J.J. and Maunsell, J.H. (2003). Anterior inferotemporal neurons of monkeys engaged in object recognition can be highly sensitive to object retinal position. *Journal of Neurophysiology*, **89**, 3264–3278.

Dolan, R.J., Fink, G.R., Rolls, E.T., *et al.* (1997). How the brain learns to see objects and faces in an impoverished context. *Nature*, **389**, 596–599.

Elliffe, M.C.M., Rolls, E.T., and Stringer, S.M. (2002). Invariant recognition of feature combinations in the visual system. *Biological Cybernetics*, **86**, 59–71.

Engel, A.K., Konig, P., Kreiter, A.K., Schillen, T.B., and Singer, W. (1992). Temporal coding in the visual system: new vistas on integration in the nervous system. *Trends in Neurosciences*, **15**, 218–226.

Franco, L., Rolls, E.T., Aggelopoulos, N.C., and Treves, A. (2004). The use of decoding to analyze the contribution to the information of the correlations between the firing of simultaneously recorded neurons. *Experimental Brain Research*, **155**, 370–384.

Franco, L., Rolls, E.T., Aggelopoulos, N.C., and Jerez, J.M. (2007). Neuronal selectivity, population sparseness, and ergodicity in the inferior temporal visual cortex. *Biological Cybernetics*, **96**, 547–560.

Gallant, J.L., Connor, C.E., and Van Essen, D.C. (1998). Neural activity in areas V1, V2 and V4 during free viewing of natural scenes compared to controlled viewing. *Neuroreport*, **9**, 85–89.

Gawne, T.J. and Richmond, B.J. (1993). How independent are the messages carried by adjacent inferior temporal cortical neurons? *Journal of Neuroscience*, **13**, 2758–2771 .

Georges-François, P., Rolls, E.T., and Robertson, R.G. (1999). Spatial view cells in the primate hippocampus: allocentric view not head direction or eye position or place. *Cerebral Cortex*, **9**, 197–212.

Grill-Spector, K. and Malach, R. (2004). The human visual cortex. *Annual Review of Neuroscience*, **27**, 649–677.

Gross, C.G., Rocha Miranda, C.E., and Bender, D.B. (1972). Visual properties of neurons in inferotemporal cortex of the macaque. *Journal of Neurophysiology*, **35**, 96–111.

Gross, C.G., Desimone, R., Albright, T.D., and Schwartz, E.L. (1985). Inferior temporal cortex and pattern recognition. *Experimental Brain Research*, **11**, 179–201.

Hasselmo, M.E., Rolls, E.T., and Baylis, G.C. (1989a). The role of expression and identity in the face-selective responses of neurons in the temporal visual cortex of the monkey. *Behavioral Brain Research*, **32**, 203–218.

Hasselmo, M.E., Rolls, E.T., Baylis, G.C., and Nalwa, V. (1989b). Object-centred encoding by face-selective neurons in the cortex in the superior temporal sulcus of the the the monkey. *Experimental Brain Research*, **75**, 417–429.

Haxby, J.V., Hoffman, E.A., and Gobbini, M.I. (2002). Human neural systems for face recognition and social communication. *Biological Psychiatry*, **51**, 59–67.

Hornak, J., Rolls, E.T., and Wade, D. (1996). Face and voice expression identification in patients with emotional and behavioural changes following ventral frontal lobe damage. *Neuropsychologia*, **34**, 247–261.

Hornak, J., Bramham, J., Rolls, E.T., *et al.* (2003). Changes in emotion after circumscribed surgical lesions of the orbitofrontal and cingulate cortices. *Brain*, **126**, 1691–1712.

Hubel, D.H. and Wiesel, T.N. (1968). Receptive fields and functional architecture of macaque monkey striate cortex. *Journal of Physiology*, **195**, 215–243.

Kringelbach, M.L. and Rolls, E.T. (2003). Neural correlates of rapid reversal learning in a simple model of human social interaction. *Neuroimage*, **20**, 1371–1383.

Kringelbach, M.L. and Rolls, E.T. (2004). The functional neuroanatomy of the human orbitofrontal cortex: evidence from neuroimaging and neuropsychology. *Progress in Neurobiology*, **72**, 341–372.

Leonard, C.M., Rolls, E.T., Wilson, F.A.W., and Baylis, G.C. (1985). Neurons in the amygdala of the monkey with responses selective for faces. *Behavioral Brain Research*, **15**, 159–176.

Logothetis, N.K. and Pauls, J. (1995). Psychophysical and physiological evidence for viewer-centered object representations in the primate. *Cerebral Cortex*, **5**, 270–288.

Loh, M., Rolls, E.T., and Deco, G. (2007). A dynamical systems hypothesis of schizophrenia. *PLoS Computational Biology*, 3, e228. doi:10.1371/journal.pcbi.0030228.

O'Doherty, J., Winston, J., Critchley, H., Perrett, D., Burt, D.M., and Dolan, R.J. (2003). Beauty in a smile: the role of medial orbitofrontal cortex in facial attractiveness. *Neuropsychologia*, **41**, 147–155.

O'Toole, A.J., Jiang, F., Abdi, H., and Haxby, J.V. (2005). Partially distributed representations of objects and faces in ventral temporal cortex. *Journal of Cognitive Neuroscience*, **17**, 580–590.

Op De Beeck, H. and Vogels, R. (2000). Spatial sensitivity of macaque inferior temporal neurons. *Journal of Comparative Neurology*, **426**, 505–518.

Panzeri, S., Schultz, S.R., Treves, A., and Rolls, E.T. (1999a). Correlations and the encoding of information in the nervous system. *Proceedings of the Royal Society of London B*, **266**, 1001–1012.

Panzeri, S., Treves, A., Schultz, S., and Rolls, E.T. (1999b). On decoding the responses of a population of neurons from short time epochs. *Neural Computation*, **11**, 1553–1577.

Panzeri, S., Rolls, E.T., Battaglia, F., and Lavis, R. (2001). Speed of feedforward and recurrent processing in multilayer networks of integrate-and-fire neurons. *Network: Computation in Neural Systems*, **12**, 423–440.

Perrett, D.I. and Rolls, E.T. (1983). Neural mechanisms underlying the visual analysis of faces. In J.-P. Ewert, R.R. Capranica & D.J. Ingle (eds.) *Advances in Vertebrate Neuroethology*, pp. 543–566. New York, Plenum Press.

Perrett, D.I., Rolls, E.T., and Caan, W. (1979). Temporal lobe cells of the monkey with visual responses selective for faces. *Neuroscience Letters*, **S3**, S358.

Perrett, D.I., Rolls, E.T., and Caan, W. (1982). Visual neurons responsive to faces in the monkey temporal cortex. *Experimental Brain Research*, **47**, 329–342.

Perrett, D.I., Smith, P.A., Potter, D.D., *et al.* (1985a). Visual cells in the temporal cortex sensitive to face view and gaze direction. *Proceedings of the Royal Society of London B*, **223**, 293–317.

Perrett, D.I., Smith, P.A.J., Mistlin, A.J., *et al.* (1985b). Visual analysis of body movements by neurons in the temporal cortex of the macaque monkey: a preliminary report. *Behavioural Brain Research*, **16**, 153–170.

Perry, G., Rolls, E.T., and Stringer, S.M. (2006). Spatial vs temporal continuity in view invariant visual object recognition learning. *Vision Research*, **46**, 3994–4006.

Perry, G., Rolls, E.T., and Stringer, S.M. (2010). Continuous transformation learning of translation invariant representations. *Experimental Brain Research*, **204**, 255–270 .

Rajimehr, R., Young, J.C., and Tootell, R.B. (2009). An anterior temporal face patch in human cortex, predicted by macaque maps. *Proceedings of the National Academy of Sciences U S A*, **106**, 1995–2000.

Riesenhuber, M. and Poggio, T. (1999). Hierarchical models of object recognition in cortex. *Nature Neuroscience*, **2**, 1019–1025.

Robertson, R.G., Rolls, E.T., and Georges-François, P. (1998). Spatial view cells in the primate hippocampus: Effects of removal of view details. *Journal of Neurophysiology*, **79**, 1145–1156.

Rolls, E.T. (1976). The neurophysiological basis of brain-stimulation reward. In A. Wauquier and E.T. Rolls (eds.) *Brain-stimulation Reward*, pp. 65–87. Amsterdam: North-Holland.

Rolls, E.T. (1981a). Processing beyond the inferior temporal visual cortex related to feeding, learning, and striatal function. In Y. Katsuki, R. Norgren & M. Sato (eds.) *Brain Mechanisms of Sensation*, pp. 241–269. New York, Wiley.

Rolls, E.T. (1981b). Responses of amygdaloid neurons in the primate. In Y. Ben-Ari (ed.) *The Amygdaloid Complex*, pp. 283–393. Amsterdam, Elsevier.

Rolls, E.T. (1984). Neurons in the cortex of the temporal lobe and in the amygdala of the monkey with responses selective for faces. *Human Neurobiology*, **3**, 209–222.

Rolls, E.T. (1986a). Neural systems involved in emotion in primates. In R. Plutchik & H. Kellerman (eds.) *Emotion: Theory, Research, and Experience. Vol. 3. Biological Foundations of Emotion*, pp. 125–143. New York, Academic Press.

Rolls, E.T. (1986b). A theory of emotion, and its application to understanding the neural basis of emotion. In Y. Oomura (ed.) *Emotions. Neural and Chemical Control*, pp. 325–344. Basel: Karger.

Rolls, E.T. (1989). Functions of neuronal networks in the hippocampus and neocortex in memory. In J.H. Byrne & W.O. Berry (eds.) *Neural Models of Plasticity: Experimental and Theoretical Approaches*, pp. 240–265. San Diego, CA: Academic Press.

Rolls, E.T. (1990). A theory of emotion, and its application to understanding the neural basis of emotion. *Cognition and Emotion*, **4**, 161–190.

Rolls, E.T. (1991). Neural organisation of higher visual functions. *Current Opinion in Neurobiology*, **1**, 274–278.

Rolls, E.T. (1992). Neurophysiological mechanisms underlying face processing within and beyond the temporal cortical visual areas. *Philosophical Transactions of the Royal Society of London B*, **335**, 11–21.

Rolls, E.T. (1995). Learning mechanisms in the temporal lobe visual cortex. *Behavioural Brain Research*, **66**, 177–185.

Rolls, E.T. (1997). A neurophysiological and computational approach to the functions of the temporal lobe cortical visual areas in invariant object recognition. In M. Jenkin and L. Harris (eds.) *Computational and Psychophysical Mechanisms of Visual Coding*, pp. 184–220. Cambridge: Cambridge University Press.

Rolls, E.T. (1999a). *The Brain and Emotion*. Oxford: Oxford University Press.

Rolls, E.T. (1999b). The functions of the orbitofrontal cortex. *Neurocase*, **5**, 301–312.

Rolls, E.T. (1999c). Spatial view cells and the representation of place in the primate hippocampus. *Hippocampus*, **9**, 467–480.

Rolls, E.T. (2000a). Functions of the primate temporal lobe cortical visual areas in invariant visual object and face recognition. *Neuron*, **27**, 205–218.

Rolls, E.T. (2000b). Neurophysiology and functions of the primate amygdala, and the neural basis of emotion. In J.P. Aggleton (ed.) *The Amygdala: A Functional Analysis*, Second edn., pp. 447–478. Oxford: Oxford University Press.

Rolls, E.T. (2003). Consciousness absent and present: a neurophysiological exploration. *Progress in Brain Research*, **144**, 95–106.

Rolls, E.T. (2005). *Emotion Explained*. Oxford: Oxford University Press.

Rolls, E.T. (2007a). Invariant representations of objects in natural scenes in the temporal cortex visual areas. In S. Funahashi (ed.) *Representation and Brain*, pp. 47–102. Tokyo: Springer.

Rolls, E.T. (2007b). The representation of information about faces in the temporal and frontal lobes. *Neuropsychologia*, **45**, 125–143.

Rolls, E.T. (2008a). Face processing in different brain areas, and critical band masking. *Journal of Neuropsychology*, **2**, 325–360.

Rolls, E.T. (2008b). *Memory, Attention, and Decision-Making: A Unifying Computational Neuroscience Approach*. Oxford: Oxford University Press.

Rolls, E.T. (2009). The neurophysiology and computational mechanisms of object representation. In S. Dickinson, M. Tarr, A. Leonardis, and B. Schiele. (eds.) *Object Categorization: Computer and Human Vision Perspectives*, pp. 257–287. Cambridge: Cambridge University Press.

Rolls, E.T. (2010). A computational theory of episodic memory formation in the hippocampus. *Behavioural Brain Research*, 215, 180–196.

Rolls, E.T. and Baylis, G.C. (1986). Size and contrast have only small effects on the responses to faces of neurons in the cortex of the superior temporal sulcus of the monkey. *Experimental Brain Research*, **65**, 38–48.

Rolls, E.T. and Deco, G. (2002). *Computational Neuroscience of Vision*. Oxford: Oxford University Press.

Rolls, E.T. and Deco, G. (2010). *The Noisy Brain: Stochastic Dynamics as a Principle of Brain Function.* Oxford: Oxford University Press.

Rolls, E.T. and Grabenhorst, F. (2008). The orbitofrontal cortex and beyond: from affect to decision-making. *Progress in Neurobiology*, **86**, 216–244.

Rolls, E.T. and Kesner, R.P. (2006). A computational theory of hippocampal function, and empirical tests of the theory. *Progress in Neurobiology*, **79**, 1–48.

Rolls, E.T. and Milward, T. (2000). A model of invariant object recognition in the visual system: learning rules, activation functions, lateral inhibition, and information-based performance measures. *Neural Computation*, **12**, 2547–2572.

Rolls, E.T. and Stringer, S.M. (2001). Invariant object recognition in the visual system with error correction and temporal difference learning. *Network: Computation in Neural Systems*, **12**, 111–129.

Rolls, E.T. and Stringer, S.M. (2006a). Invariant global motion recognition in the dorsal visual system: a unifying theory. *Neural Computation*, **19**, 139–169.

Rolls, E.T. and Stringer, S.M. (2006b). Invariant visual object recognition: a model, with lighting invariance. *Journal of Physiology - Paris*, **100**, 43–62.

Rolls, E.T. and Tovee, M.J. (1994). Processing speed in the cerebral cortex and the neurophysiology of visual masking. *Proceedings of the Royal Society of London B*, **257**, 9–15.

Rolls, E.T. and Tovee, M.J. (1995a). The responses of single neurons in the temporal visual cortical areas of the macaque when more than one stimulus is present in the visual field. *Experimental Brain Research*, **103**, 409–420.

Rolls, E.T. and Tovee, M.J. (1995b). Sparseness of the neuronal representation of stimuli in the primate temporal visual cortex. *Journal of Neurophysiology*, **73**, 713–726.

Rolls, E.T. and Treves, A. (1998). *Neural Networks and Brain Function*, Oxford: Oxford University Press.

Rolls, E.T. and Xiang, J.-Z. (2006). Spatial view cells in the primate hippocampus, and memory recall. *Reviews in the Neurosciences*, **17**, 175–200.

Rolls, E.T., Burton, M.J., and Mora, F. (1976). Hypothalamic neuronal responses associated with the sight of food. *Brain Research*, **111**, 53–66.

Rolls, E.T., Judge, S.J., and Sanghera, M. (1977). Activity of neurones in the inferotemporal cortex of the alert monkey. *Brain Research*, **130**, 229–238.

Rolls, E.T., Burton, M.J., and Mora, F. (1980). Neurophysiological analysis of brain-stimulation reward in the monkey. *Brain Research*, **194**, 339–357.

Rolls, E.T., Baylis, G.C., and Leonard, C.M. (1985). Role of low and high spatial frequencies in the face-selective responses of neurons in the cortex in the superior temporal sulcus in the monkey. *Vision Research*, **25**, 1021–1035.

Rolls, E.T., Baylis, G.C., and Hasselmo, M.E. (1987). The responses of neurons in the cortex in the superior temporal sulcus of the monkey to band-pass spatial frequency filtered faces. *Vision Research*, **27**, 311–326.

Rolls, E.T., Baylis, G.C., Hasselmo, M., and Nalwa, V. (1989a). The representation of information in the temporal lobe visual cortical areas of macaque monkeys. In J.J. Kulikowski, C.M. Dickinson and I.J. Murray (eds.) *Seeing Contour and Colour*. Oxford: Pergamon.

Rolls, E.T., Baylis, G.C., Hasselmo, M.E., and Nalwa, V. (1989b). The effect of learning on the face-selective responses of neurons in the cortex in the superior temporal sulcus of the monkey. *Experimental Brain Research*, **76**, 153–164.

Rolls, E.T., Tovee, M.J., Purcell, D.G., Stewart, A.L., and Azzopardi, P. (1994). The responses of neurons in the temporal cortex of primates, and face identification and detection. *Experimental Brain Research*, **101**, 473–484.

Rolls, E.T., Robertson, R.G., and Georges-François, P. (1997a). Spatial view cells in the primate hippocampus. *European Journal of Neuroscience*, **9**, 1789–1794.

Rolls, E.T., Treves, A., and Tovee, M.J. (1997b). The representational capacity of the distributed encoding of information provided by populations of neurons in the primate temporal visual cortex. *Experimental Brain Research*, **114**, 177–185.

Rolls, E.T., Treves, A., Robertson, R.G., Georges-François, P., and Panzeri, S. (1998). Information about spatial view in an ensemble of primate hippocampal cells. *Journal of Neurophysiology*, **79**, 1797–1813.

Rolls, E.T., Tovee, M.J., and Panzeri, S. (1999). The neurophysiology of backward visual masking: information analysis. *Journal of Cognitive Neuroscience*, **11**, 335–346.

Rolls, E.T., Aggelopoulos, N.C., and Zheng, F. (2003a). The receptive fields of inferior temporal cortex neurons in natural scenes. *Journal of Neuroscience*, **23**, 339–348.

Rolls, E.T., Franco, L., Aggelopoulos, N.C., and Reece, S. (2003b). An information theoretic approach to the contributions of the firing rates and correlations between the firing of neurons. *Journal of Neurophysiology*, **89**, 2810–2822.

Rolls, E.T., Aggelopoulos, N.C., Franco, L., and Treves, A. (2004). Information encoding in the inferior temporal cortex: contributions of the firing rates and correlations between the firing of neurons. *Biological Cybernetics*, **90**, 19–32.

Rolls, E.T., Xiang, J.-Z., and Franco, L. (2005). Object, space and object-space representations in the primate hippocampus. *Journal of Neurophysiology*, **94**, 833–844.

Rolls, E.T., Critchley, H.D., Browning, A.S., and Inoue, K. (2006a). Face-selective and auditory neurons in the primate orbitofrontal cortex. *Experimental Brain Research*, **170**, 74–87.

Rolls, E.T., Franco, L., Aggelopoulos, N.C., and Perez, J.M. (2006b). Information in the first spike, the order of spikes, and the number of spikes provided by neurons in the inferior temporal visual cortex. *Vision Research*, **46**, 4193–4205.

Rolls, E.T., Loh, M., Deco, G., and Winterer, G. (2008a). Computational models of schizophrenia and dopamine modulation in the prefrontal cortex. *Nature Reviews Neuroscience*, **9**, 696–709.

Rolls, E.T., Tromans, J., and Stringer, S.M. (2008b). Spatial scene representations formed by self-organizing learning in a hippocampal extension of the ventral visual system. *European Journal of Neuroscience*, **28**, 2116–2127.

Rolls, E.T., Grabenhorst, F., and Franco, L. (2009). Prediction of subjective affective state from brain activations. *Journal of Neurophysiology*, **101**, 1294–1308.

Sanghera, M.K., Rolls, E.T., and Roper-Hall, A. (1977). Visual responses of neurones in the lateral amygdala of the rhesus monkey. *Proceedings of the International Union of Physiological Sciences*, III, 1950.

Sanghera, M.K., Rolls, E.T., and Roper-Hall, A. (1979). Visual responses of neurons in the dorsolateral amygdala of the alert monkey. *Experimental Neurology*, **63**, 610–626.

Seltzer, B. and Pandya, D.N. (1978). Afferent cortical connections and architectonics of the superior temporal sulcus and surrounding cortex in the rhesus monkey. *Brain Research*, **149**, 1–24.

Serre, T., Oliva, A., and Poggio, T. (2007). A feedforward architecture accounts for rapid categorization. *Proceedings of the National Academy of Sciences U S A*, **104**, 6424–6449.

Singer, W. (1999). Neuronal synchrony: A versatile code for the definition of relations? *Neuron*, **24**, 49–65.

Spiridon, M. and Kanwisher, N. (2002). How distributed is visual category information in human occipito-temporal cortex? An fMRI study. *Neuron*, **35**, 1157–1165.

Spiridon, M., Fischl, B., and Kanwisher, N. (2006). Location and spatial profile of category-specific regions in human extrastriate cortex. *Human Brain Mapping*, **27**, 77–89.

Stringer, S.M. and Rolls, E.T. (2000). Position invariant recognition in the visual system with cluttered environments. *Neural Networks*, **13**, 305–315.

Stringer, S.M. and Rolls, E.T. (2002). Invariant object recognition in the visual system with novel views of 3D objects. *Neural Computation*, **14**, 2585–2596.

Stringer, S.M. and Rolls, E.T. (2008). Learning transform invariant object recognition in the visual system with multiple stimuli present during training. *Neural Networks*, **21**, 888–903.

Stringer, S.M., Perry, G., Rolls, E.T., and Proske, J.H. (2006). Learning invariant object recognition in the visual system with continuous transformations. *Biological Cybernetics*, **94**, 128–142.

Stringer, S.M., Rolls, E.T., and Tromans, J. (2007). Invariant object recognition with trace learning and multiple stimuli present during training. *Network: Computation in Neural Systems*, **18**, 161–187.

Tanaka, K., Saito, C., Fukada, Y., and Moriya, M. (1990). Integration of form, texture, and color information in the inferotemporal cortex of the macaque. In E. Iwai and M. Mishkin (eds.) *Vision, Memory and the Temporal Lobe*, pp. 101–109. New York: Elsevier.

Thorpe, S.J. and Imbert, M. (1989). Biological constraints on connectionist models. In R. Pfeifer, Z. Schreter, and F. Fogelman-Soulie (eds.) *Connectionism in Perspective*, pp. 63–92. Amsterdam, Elsevier.

Thorpe, S.J., Rolls, E.T., and Maddison, S. (1983). Neuronal activity in the orbitofrontal cortex of the behaving monkey. *Experimental Brain Research*, **49**, 93–115.

Tovee, M.J. and Rolls, E.T. (1995). Information encoding in short firing rate epochs by single neurons in the primate temporal visual cortex. *Visual Cognition*, **2**, 35–58.

Tovee, M.J., Rolls, E.T., Treves, A., and Bellis, R.P. (1993). Information encoding and the responses of single neurons in the primate temporal visual cortex. *Journal of Neurophysiology*, **70**, 640–654.

Tovee, M.J., Rolls, E.T., and Azzopardi, P. (1994). Translation invariance in the responses to faces of single neurons in the temporal visual cortical areas of the alert macaque. *Journal of Neurophysiology*, **72**, 1049–1060.

Tovee, M.J., Rolls, E.T., and Ramachandran, V.S. (1996). Rapid visual learning in neurones of the primate temporal visual cortex. *Neuroreport*, **7**, 2757–2760.

Treves, A. (1993). Mean-field analysis of neuronal spike dynamics. *Network*, **4**, 259–284.

Treves, A., Rolls, E.T., and Tovee, M.J. (1996). On the time required for recurrent processing in the brain. In V. Torre and F. Conti (eds.) *Neurobiology: Ionic Channels, Neurons, and the Brain*, pp. 325–353. New York: Plenum.

Treves, A., Rolls, E.T., and Simmen, M. (1997). Time for retrieval in recurrent associative memories. *Physica D*, **107**, 392–400.

Treves, A., Panzeri, S., Rolls, E.T., Booth, M., and Wakeman, E.A. (1999). Firing rate distributions and efficiency of information transmission of inferior temporal cortex neurons to natural visual stimuli. *Neural Computation*, **11**, 611–641.

Tsao, D.Y., Freiwald, W.A., Tootell, R.B., and Livingstone, M.S. (2006). A cortical region consisting entirely of face-selective cells. *Science*, **311**, 617–618.

Wallis, G. and Rolls, E.T. (1997). Invariant face and object recognition in the visual system. *Progress in Neurobiology*, **51**, 167–194.

Wilson, F.A.W., O'Scalaidhe, S.P.O., and Goldman-Rakic, P.S. (1993). Dissociation of object and spatial processing domains in primate prefrontal cortex. *Science*, **260**, 1955–1958.

Wiskott, L. and Sejnowski, T.J. (2002). Slow feature analysis: unsupervised learning of invariances. *Neural Computation*, **14**, 715–770.

Zangenehpour, S. and Chaudhuri, A. (2005). Patchy organization and asymmetric distribution of the neural correlates of face processing in monkey inferotemporal cortex. *Current Biology*, **15**, 993–1005.

Chapter 5

Disorders of Face Perception

Andrew W. Young

Hard times

Until the 1970s, neuropsychological studies of the effects of brain injury and brain disease were a highly specialist enterprise that often had little impact on the rest of psychology. In part, this lack of impact reflected the fact that most studies were addressed to correlations between observed functional deficits and disease locus. With only limited brain imaging methods available, the possibility of identifying the affected brain regions from a patient's symptoms was a major goal for many neuropsychological studies.

Unfortunately, it was easy to make mistakes. For example, symptoms in the early stages of brain damage might reflect "diaschisis" (disruption of function in distant but connected regions), whereas longstanding symptoms could be mild or even masked by compensatory strategies. In practice, avoiding such pitfalls required considerable skill, and substantial parts of the literature remained contradictory and confusing. In his seminal review of studies of face recognition, Hadyn Ellis (1975) noted case reports where inability to recognize familiar faces (prosopagnosia) had been thought to follow damage to bilateral occipital lobes, bilateral parieto-occipital regions, in the parietotemporo-occipital junction, and even the left frontal lobe. He commented that this diversity of putative lesion sites might suggest that face recognition involves "a number of scattered sub-processes any of which, if interfered with, can lead to a total inability to recognize faces" (Ellis, 1975, p. 421). The sceptic's alternative, though, was that much of the localization information was imprecise or simply incorrect. In fact, a remarkably astute contemporary review of the neuroanatomical basis of prosopagnosia by Meadows (1974) offered a quite different emphasis, identifying lesions in the right inferior occipitotemporal junction as critical, largely from a careful analysis of visual field defects in reported cases and the small number of postmortem reports.

Dramatic developments in brain imaging have, of course, borne out Meadows' (1974) neuroanatomical conclusions through structural imaging of the brains of people with prosopagnosia and through functional brain imaging of face perception by neurologically normal individuals (Kanwisher, 2000; Kanwisher and Barton, Chapter 7, this volume). High quality structural images have also largely replaced the craft of inferring lesion locations from patterns of symptoms, and ability to do this is no longer a recognized pillar of a skilled clinician's competence (Kapur, 2009). However, ground-breaking studies by Marshall and Newcombe (1966) and Warrington and Shallice (1969) pointed the way to a very different use of neuropsychological evidence; namely, to use the effects of brain injury as tests of psychological theories. From this perspective, the sites of the brain lesions are less informative than their behavioral consequences.

Cognitive neuropsychology

Let's take Warrington and Shallice's (1969) study as an example. They investigated case KF, a patient who was severely impaired at repeating auditory stimuli following a left hemisphere brain injury. KF had a verbal memory span of only one digit yet, despite this severely impaired verbal short-term memory, his verbal learning and verbal long-term memory were remarkably unaffected. This pattern of impaired short-term and preserved long-term memory was, in effect, the opposite of the pattern of preserved short-term and impaired long-term memory found in the more commonly reported "amnesic syndrome." This double dissociation of impairments of short- and long-term memory following different types of brain damage supported the idea of separate short- and long-term memory functions.

What was ground-breaking about Warrington and Shallice's approach was that it used the effects of brain injury to address an issue which was an important fundamental question in psychology ("are there separate short-term and long-term memory stores?"), and whose impact therefore extended well beyond the specific province of brain–behavior relationships. Importantly, the finding of preserved long-term with impaired short-term memory for KF rendered it highly unlikely that then standard accounts of material entering long-term memory by passing through short-term memory could be correct, because such accounts clearly predict that short-term memory problems will always have a consequential impact on long-term memory. From this then-standard perspective, KF's pattern of preserved long-term with severely impaired short-term memory was impossible, so its existence clearly falsified or brought into serious question the standard account.

This approach is now known as "cognitive neuropsychology." At its heart is the idea that an adequate model of normal performance of a particular mental ability should be able to account for the effects of brain injury, and that to the extent which such a model does not account for effects of brain injury, it should be revised or abandoned. The consequences of brain injury thus become another way to test accounts of normal cognition. As well as Warrington and Shallice's (1969) study of memory impairments, Marshall and Newcombe (1966) had used this general approach to account for a patient's errors in reading printed words (acquired dyslexia), and in a more wide-ranging theoretical paper (Marshall and Newcombe, 1973) they spelt out its key features:

> We wish to emphasize the essential "normality" of the errors characteristic of acquired dyslexia. That is, we shall interpret dyslexic mistakes in terms of a *functional analysis* of normal reading processes. Many of the error types observed as a consequence of brain injury may also be observed – in certain conditions – in normal subjects, both children and adults. (Marshall and Newcombe, 1973, p.188.)

Cognitive neuropsychology caught on quickly in the 1970s and early 80s—especially for studies of reading and language. The possibility of doing something similar with face recognition was one of the things that motivated Dennis Hay and myself to look at the neuropsychological literature and sketch out what it might be telling us (Hay and Young, 1982). We were particularly struck by two things. First, a lot of studies were focused almost exclusively on the question as to whether or not faces are special (see McKone and Robbins, Chapter 9; Scott, Chapter 11, this volume), but this debate was confusing because different people had different ideas of what being "special" might entail; they seldom defined what they meant by "special", and seemed often to be arguing at cross-purposes. Typically, the issue would be approached through investigating whether or not a particular case of prosopagnosia involved a face-specific deficit. The implicit assumption was that special status would be confirmed by face-specific deficits, but less thought was given to whether non-specific deficits might also be consistent with some of the meanings of "special."

A second, striking approach came from the work of Arthur Benton and Ennio De Renzi. Reasoning that prosopagnosia was too rare a deficit for a large-scale study, they had developed tests involving matching photographs of unfamiliar faces, to allow them to investigate milder forms of face recognition impairment. Instead, they found that their prosopagnosic patients were not as impaired as they expected on these unfamiliar face matching tests, and that people who were impaired (scoring less well than people with prosopagnosia) often did not experience any obvious problems with familiar face recognition (Benton, 1980). To our way of thinking, this double dissociation (reviewed by Benton, 1980) offered an interesting parallel with "dual-route" models then commonly used in cognitive neuropsychological studies of reading, in which familiar (words) and unfamiliar (non-words) collections of letters are read using different mechanisms.

There were also potential neuropsychological impairments that had not received much attention. The definition of prosopagnosia emphasized that recognition of people by other means than the face (for example, recognizing the person from his or her voice, or simply their name) could be relatively preserved—that is, people with prosopagnosia had not simply forgotten who familiar people are. Yet Warrington (1975) had described cases of loss of semantic memory for objects, involving a multimodal deficit of core knowledge in which objects could not be recognized from seeing them, hearing characteristic sounds, holding them, or from their names. It seemed likely that some form of comparable loss of memory for familiar people might exist, but it was a few years before cases were documented (Ellis et al., 1989; Hanley et al., 1989). Similarly, problems in name retrieval ("anomias") were a known consequence of brain injuries involving parts of the left hemisphere, but Flude et al. (1989) were the first to look in detail at how the naming of familiar people might be affected.

Vicki Bruce and I (Bruce and Young, 1986) developed Hay and Young's (1982) approach to face recognition into something more systematic that placed recognition in the context of other abilities involved in face perception. Faces carry a range of social meanings other than identity (age, sex, expression, and so on), yet most studies of prosopagnosia only reported anecdotally whether or not patients were also impaired at reading these social signals from the face and, conversely, the literature on patients with neuropsychological deficits of facial expression recognition seldom asked whether they also experienced difficulties in recognizing identity.

No royal road to understanding

Some of the early successes of cognitive neuropsychology were persuasive, exciting, and have stood the test of time (e.g. Warrington and Shallice, 1969). In the field of face perception differences between familiar and unfamiliar faces, between recognition of identity and expression, and between impairments that seem more perceptual or more mnestic in nature have been recurrent research motifs.

This is not to say, though, that we understand how correctly to interpret such studies (Calder and Young, 2005; Calder, Chapter 22, this volume). Inevitably, people got over-enthusiastic and began to fantasize that the brain would readily yield many of its secrets to this new approach. Instead, of course, it has turned out that progress is hard-won. To see why, it's worth looking briefly at some of the fundamentals.

The first thing to note is that it wasn't obvious at the time that the cognitive neuropsychological approach would work at all. Influential arguments put forward by Gregory (1961, 2005) and others noted that the effects of damaging a highly interactive system with complex operating characteristics could themselves be unpredictable:

> the removal of any of several widely spaced resistors may cause a radio set to emit howls, but it does not follow that howls are immediately associated with these resistors, or indeed that the causal relation is anything but the most indirect. In particular, we should not say that the function of the resistors in a normal circuit is to inhibit howling. (Gregory, 2005, p.123.)

A more formal way to put the point is to say that there are a priori grounds for doubting that the effects of brain injury will be transparent in revealing underlying functional organization.

Gregory agreed, of course, that someone with a circuit diagram and a good knowledge of electronics might well be able to correctly diagnose the fault; his argument was that looking at the faults themselves would not readily create this level of understanding.

Against this, the cognitive neuropsychological approach does often seem fruitful. Certainly, it works better than Gregory's analogy with electronics would lead one to expect. Why should this be?

In truth, we don't really know, which remains disconcerting. However, the standard answer usually involves some mixture of two ideas; levels of description, and modularity. Both of these can be seen with the counter-analogy of a domestic hi-fi. When this goes wrong, most of us are capable of deducing whether the fault is in the CD player, the radio tuner, the amplifier, or the left or right speaker. The components of the system are modular; each has a designated function, and this usually makes the logic of working out which function is missing fairly straightforward. Moreover, because we are usually interested in a fairly broad-brush characterization of the problem (is it a speaker or the amplifier?), we can sidestep some of the detailed issues (it doesn't matter so much to us what the exact nature of the problem is, as long as we replace the correct component).

Often, cognitive neuropsychological approaches seem to work for similar reasons. They help us to identify putative "functional components" of cognition. Initially, it was thought that this happens because modularity is a design principle used by the brain. Marr (1976, 1982), for example, pointed out that it is easier to modify a modular than a non-modular system, because a change in one component of a modular system need not impact on other components; this could be useful in organizing change both in ontogeny and phylogeny. Of course, Marr was not himself a neuropsychologist, but he used examples taken from Warrington's neuropsychological studies of object recognition (Warrington and Taylor, 1973). Fodor's (1983) more extended discussion of modularity and what it might entail remains very well known. However, the extent to which the brain has a genuinely modular organization remains contentious. All that can be said with certainty is that a number of neuropsychological deficits meet at least some of the appropriate criteria for modularity. It seems possible, though, that this could reflect a truly modular structure (as in a hi-fi) or more limited forms of modularity resulting from the nature of underlying neural representations (Haxby et al., 2001) or reliance on different neurological pathways (Milner and Goodale, 1995).

The hi-fi analogy also offers a useful way to think about a further complicating factor highlighted by Geschwind (1965a,b), namely that neuropsychological deficits may reflect damage to particular brain regions or disconnection of nerve fiber pathways linking one region to another. The distinction maps easily onto the difference between breaking a component of your hi-fi (e.g. kicking a speaker) or cutting a connecting cable.

Where the functional components approach seems to be less successful is in pointing towards details as to how these components actually do their respective jobs. For instance, the observation that some forms of brain injury can severely affect recognition of identity from the face whilst the recognition of emotional expression is relatively unaffected doesn't tell us whether this is because there is something fundamentally different between mechanisms needed for recognizing identity and expression, or whether they are simply kept separate to some degree because information about identity and expression is needed for different social purposes. There are plenty of pertinent potential factors one can think of—identity is relatively fixed, expressions change from moment to moment, and so on—but the existence of a neuropsychological dissociation does not in itself seem to favor any one explanation over another.

At worst, overinterpreting dissociations can be misleading. Calder and Young (2005) and Calder (Chapter 22, this volume) discuss a range of alternative ways of thinking about the identity versus expression dissociation, not all of which require different modules for identity and expression. A clear example of the dangers of overinterpretation comes from the phenomenon of covert recognition in prosopagnosia. In a seminal study, Bauer (1984) demonstrated that LF, a person who was prosopagnosic following a road accident, showed some form of preserved autonomic nervous system response to the match between a familiar person's face and name. He did this by reading out a list of five possible names for each face, and measuring LF's skin conductance response (SCR) when the correct or when an incorrect name was given. On around 60% of trials, LF's SCR change was greatest to the correct name, whereas chance responding would be at 20%. Yet when LF was asked explicitly to pick which name went with each face, he did perform at chance level.

Differences between severely impaired overt recognition and some form of "recognition without awareness" in prosopagnosia were noted in other studies using psychophysiological (Tranel and Damasio, 1985) and behavioral (Bruyer et al., 1983; de Haan et al., 1987) indices, though it was also clear that not all patients showed covert recognition (Newcombe et al., 1989). Taken at face value, the dissociation seemed to point to a separation between functional components involved in recognition and awareness of recognition, but this raised all kinds of conceptual and philosophical problems. Bauer's (1984) own explanation in terms of a difference between neurological pathways subserving overt recognition and emotional orienting responses to stimuli with personal significance was relatively neat, but didn't seem to sit well with the findings based on behavioral measures of priming, learning, and interference. Something was obviously amiss.

Help was not long in arriving. Mike Burton and his colleagues (Burton et al., 1990) had developed a computer simulation of the recognition route in Bruce and Young's (1986) box and arrow model. Their aim was to create a model that would generate unequivocal predictions and be testable against detailed patterns of experimental data. They noticed, however, that an unintended consequence of the way the model was implemented was that degrading the quality of its face input connections would lead to a pattern of performance comparable to that seen in behavioral studies of prosopagnosia, namely severely impaired recognition with relatively preserved priming and interference effects. This happened simply because a degraded input could propagate sufficient activation in the implemented model to create behavioral consequences for recognition of related stimuli (such as the person's name) without approaching the threshold at which successful classification of the input could be achieved (Burton et al., 1991). This offered a simple, mechanistic approach to modeling the behavioral observations that could be worked through in a fair degree of detail (Young and Burton, 1999). The moral, though, is that this neat solution came from outside neuropsychology—an important point whose implications we will return to later.

The nitty gritty

As well as the "big picture" points we have just discussed, there are a lot of details that need to be well managed for a neuropsychological study to make a genuine contribution.

Traditional studies often used a design where the performance of one or more groups of patients with brain injuries would be compared to that of a group of matched "controls." The brain-injured group was often defined by lesion location (e.g. left- vs. right-sided brain damage), or sometimes in terms of a particular form of symptom (such as inability to speak). This became a reasonably well-developed craft, in which a range of techniques were used in the best studies to avoid what turned out to be otherwise common pitfalls. For example, deficits affecting face perception seemed to be more severe following right than left hemisphere lesions, but in the absence of brain scanning techniques it was important to match patients on some independent index of lesion severity (such as visual field defects). Without such matching, there was a real risk that the left-hemisphere group would have smaller lesions, because the presence of language deficits created an immediately obvious symptom that could lead to their being differentially represented in clinical samples.

Cognitive neuropsychology typically operates in a very different way, in which the emphasis is on detailed analysis of individual patients with theoretically interesting impairments. In this context, interesting impairments are usually those that exemplify a striking dissociation, such as the relatively preserved ability to match unfamiliar faces found in some cases of prosopagnosia. The logic is that a dissociable deficit will often reflect damage to a distinct functional component, so that by studying dissociable deficits we can gain insight into what the functional components are that underpin human mental abilities. This logic works best if the pattern of a "double dissociation" can be demonstrated. Using our example of the dissociation between relatively preserved ability to match unfamiliar faces and severely impaired recognition of familiar faces in prosopagnosia, we can see that alternative interpretations of this single dissociation are possible. It might arise because different functional components are needed for matching unfamiliar faces and recognizing familiar faces, with the familiar face recognition component being primarily affected in prosopagnosia, or it might arise because matching pictures of unfamiliar faces is so easy that the tests simply don't pick up any deficit in cases of prosopagnosia. However, the existence of the opposite pattern of difficulty in other brain-injured patients—preserved recognition of familiar faces with impaired matching of unfamiliar faces—shows that the idea that unfamiliar face matching is inherently easy will not suffice as an explanation. Double dissociations, in which patient X is impaired at Task A but not Task B whilst patient Y is impaired at Task B but not Task A, thus have a privileged status in ruling out alternative explanations in terms of factors like task difficulty.

A clever variant of the dissociable deficits approach has been to focus on what is preserved, as well as the deficit itself. A path-breaking study by Moscovitch, Winocur, and Behrmann (1997) investigated CK, a person with impaired visual object and word recognition but normal face recognition following a closed head injury. Moscovitch et al. (1997) were able to show that CK performed as well as neurologically normal controls on face perception tasks as long as the face was upright and retained the correct pattern of spacing of internal features. They reasoned that CK has lost a part-based mechanism needed for the recognition of words and objects, but only required for face recognition if the face is presented in an unusual manner (such as being inverted or fragmented). In a particularly telling experiment, Moscovitch et al. (1997) showed that CK could outperform controls when searching for faces in a picture where they were hidden among overlapping rocks and trees. This happened, of course, because CK could not properly recognize the obscuring rocks and trees (due to impairment of the part-based recognition mechanism). The demonstration of a performance enhancement (however unlikely to be of real-life value) resulting from a brain injury gives a strong indication that the underlying theory is on the right lines (Kapur, 1996).

In general, then, cognitive neuropsychology has thrived on investigations of dissociable deficits. Taken to its logical limit, it has even been argued that dissociations are all that matters, because associated deficits are very difficult to interpret. If a person with a brain injury is impaired at both Task A and Task B, this may be because A and B both depend on some common process, or it may be because A and B depend on independent functional components that both happen to be compromised by this type of brain injury. This possibility is, of course, especially likely if the putative components are in anatomical proximity. A good example concerns the debate as to whether or not prosopagnosia is a face-specific deficit. Empirically, it is clear that most patients with prosopagnosia are poor at recognizing individual members of other visually homogeneous categories. However, Kanwisher and others have downgraded the potential significance of this observation, and argued instead that it is the comparatively rare instances of relatively face-specific deficits that are critical. To do this, Kanwisher (2000) used the analogy that the chance that a stroke or head trauma to visual cortex will obliterate all of the hypothesized face-processing region of cortex without affecting nearby cortical areas is similar to the chance that an asteroid hitting New England would obliterate all of the state of Rhode Island without affecting Massachusetts or Connecticut. (Kanwisher, 2000, p. 760.)

Paradoxically, the force of the argument that only dissociations really matter has been more readily acknowledged outside neuropsychology—e.g. by cognitive psychologists who adopted the cognitive neuropsychological agenda—than by neuropsychologists themselves. In many ways, it goes against the grain of traditional approaches that have often been based on identifying distinct neuropsychological syndromes to inform the diagnosis and management of underlying brain disease. Since a syndrome is itself simply a cluster of associated deficits, some or all of which may themselves dissociate across patients, the value of syndrome groupings in research studies can be questioned. For example, a series of patients categorized as "aphasics" may show deficits that do not greatly overlap with each other on a more fine-grained analysis, and for this reason the influential journal *Cognitive Neuropsychology* explicitly rejected syndrome-based group studies and favored single-case approaches (Coltheart, 1984).

Even so, interpreting dissociations is not always straightforward, and some of the main reasons for problems of interpretation were thoroughly discussed by Shallice (1988). In the first place, most dissociations are not of what Shallice called the "classical" type. In a classical dissociation, performance on Task A is perfectly preserved, whilst performance of Task B is severely impaired. Instead, it is more common to find a "trend" dissociation, in which performance of Task A is perhaps low normal or a bit impaired, whereas Task B seems worse. These trend dissociations can be susceptible to technical problems resulting from non-linearity of the measures used, and need to be treated with a degree of circumspection. Secondly, even classical dissociations are not problem-free. A tricky issue concerns what counts as perfectly preserved, normal performance. Often, accuracy scores that fall within the range of normal controls or that meet some statistical criterion (such as a z-score) are taken as evidence of normality, but these can themselves be influenced by technical properties of the measures (especially ceiling performance by normal controls, which can suggest the test is too easy to be able to discriminate at the higher-scoring end).

It is also sometimes necessary to question the assumption that a normal score reflects normal cognitive mechanisms. Newcombe (1979) noted that although her prosopagnosic patient RB could match pictures of unfamiliar faces, he took a long time to do this and seemed to rely on careful feature by feature comparison. This led Newcombe to suggest that RB's apparent dissociation between impaired familiar face recognition and preserved unfamiliar face matching might reflect the availability of alternative strategies in face matching paradigms. From this point of view, reaction time measures might form a useful additional source of information, since unusual strategies will often be time-consuming. The danger, of course, is that people with brain injuries may often be slow and careful for reasons other than that they are deploying unusual strategies. In fact, subsequent studies of neurologically normal people tend to show that matching photos of unfamiliar faces is sufficiently tricky that all of us try various techniques to see which will help solve what can be a surprisingly problematic perceptual puzzle (Hancock et al., 2001).

One of the thorniest questions of all concerns the implicit assumption that all neurologically normal adults share some form of common "functional architecture" of the mind. Why should we assume that the functional components person A uses to perceive faces will be the same as person B's? Without this assumption, the dissociation logic quickly runs into trouble—it would not be easy to draw conclusions about normal cognitive abilities from cases of cognitive impairment if there is more than one premorbid pattern of organization.

Again, the strongest defense seems to be simply that the approach works. If there are alternative variants of the "normal" functional architecture, we don't seem to get many pointers to their existence. Of course, this is not meant to deny the existence of striking differences in ability between different individuals, but what it does say is that such differences must be superimposed on a common underlying pattern. None the less, in some cases (e.g. in congenital prosopagnosia—see below) the differences are sufficiently marked that it does seem likely that the underlying brain organization may differ from normal in important ways, and this suspicion is reinforced by findings of a genetic link to face recognition ability (de Haan, 1999; Schmalzl et al., 2008). A potentially powerful approach is therefore to document abilities across a systematic set of tests applied to a series of cases. This can show what is typical and what is unusual, and from the perspective that atypical functional architectures might exist, it is the atypical cases that need to be treated most carefully. The approach has yielded important insights in other areas, notably studies of semantic dementia (Woollams et al., 2007). It has yet to be as extensively pursued with impairments of face perception, but there have been some studies using case series with unilateral focal lesions (Young et al., 1993a) or clinical prosopagnosia (Barton, 2008) and work on the development of appropriate test batteries (Herzmann et al., 2008; Young et al., 2002).

These complexities don't make cognitive neuropsychology impossible, but they do create pitfalls that need carefully to be avoided, and caveats that must often be set against possible interpretations. In addition, attention needs to be given to the background nature of the deficits investigated. Broadly, three main sources of evidence have been used:

- Acquired impairments due to brain injury or disease, such as strokes, head injuries, neurodegenerative diseases
- Congenital and neurodevelopmental differences, such as autism, Williams syndrome, congenital prosopagnosia
- Psychiatric and neuropsychiatric problems, now often called "cognitive neuropsychiatry."

In each case, the rules of the game can be different. What we have focused on so far is mainly acquired impairments due to adult brain injury, where the individual would be expected to have developed a "normal" premorbid cognitive system and the neurological effects of the brain injury are either relatively fixed (e.g. strokes, head injuries after the initial period of recovery) or progressively severe (neurodegenerative diseases). Either way, the observed effects can reasonably be interpreted in terms of damage to a normal functional architecture.

In congenital and neurodevelopmental cases (see Behrmann et al., Chapter 41; Duchaine, Chapter 42, this volume), the same logic need not hold. A person with a neurodevelopmental disorder may start life with some form of atypical brain organization, and then continue developing along a trajectory that leads to something that will be more or less atypical in terms of normal functional architecture. This makes the value of interpreting the final pattern of abilities in terms of a comparison to normal development potentially questionable and problematic (Bishop, 1997). It doesn't mean that observations of dissociations such as good ability to read facial expressions with impaired recognition of facial identities in some cases of congenital prosopagnosia (Duchaine et al., 2003) are uninteresting, but it does make it problematic to equate them with patterns found in adult acquired prosopagnosia. In our example of good ability to interpret facial expressions with impaired recognition of facial identities in congenital prosopagnosia, it is clear that this implies that it is not necessary to be able to recognize facial identities normally to recognize facial expressions, and that the brain is therefore capable of achieving a degree of separation between these abilities. However, what the observation does not address directly is the question of whether such separation exists in the normal brain? It is possible that the degree of separation seen in congenital prosopagnosia would not be found after normal development of face recognition ability.

The dissociation logic also works differently in cognitive neuropsychiatry. In cognitive neuropsychology, the primary aim is to create a symbiosis in which models of the normal performance of a cognitive ability are used to account for the effects of brain injury and the effects of brain injury are used to refine models of normal performance. Cognitive neuropsychiatry pushes this logic to the limit, trying to bring aberrant abilities that would often be considered "psychiatric" in nature into the same ambit as other neuropsychological phenomena. One of the starting points that has been tried involves delusional beliefs, where there was a prima facie case that a neuropsychological approach might be valuable because comparable delusions are sometimes observed in both neuropsychological (i.e. after brain injury) and psychiatric settings (i.e. with no obvious brain morbidity). For face perception, the most well-known example is Capgras delusion—the delusional belief that close relatives have been replaced by near-exact duplicates.

The claim that relatives are impostors is so bizarre that it has been very difficult to see what might lie behind it. Traditional accounts were mostly purely psychodynamic. For example, the idea that there will always be things we like and things we dislike about someone close to us, and that splitting the loved one into good ("real") or bad ("impostor") variants allows the dislikeable things to be hated without guilt. Such theories were intriguing, but entirely fanciful and unsupported by evidence. In fact they were contradicted by a number of basic observations, such as that Capgras delusion patients are not always hostile to the duplicates.

It was Hadyn Ellis who had the insight that we should try to account for Capgras and related misidentification delusions in terms of impairments of normal recognition (Ellis and Young, 1990). He also generated the clever suggestion that the Capgras delusion itself might reflect a loss of appropriate "emotional" responses to familiar faces. This had the virtue of both being testable (by measuring SCRs to faces as an index of autonomic nervous system activity) and of being predicted by no other theory. Findings or reduced SCRs to faces in patients with organic or psychiatric Capgras delusion (Ellis et al., 1997; Hirstein and Ramachandran, 1997) thus offer strong support to the theory. However, it is equally evident that many people who suffer brain injuries that compromise their emotional responses to familiar faces do not experience the Capgras delusion (Tranel et al., 1995), so the loss of emotional responsiveness can only be part of the explanation of the delusion.

One way to resolve the paradox that reduced autonomic responses seem to form a necessary but not sufficient condition for Capgras delusion is to suggest that the delusion reflects a misinterpretation of an anomalous perceptual experience in which things seem devoid of emotional significance (Young et al., 1993b). Such an anomalous experience can, of course, be interpreted in many different ways, ranging from the non-delusional ("I feel peculiar") to the bizarre ("my wife has been replaced by an impostor"). From this perspective, the Capgras delusion results from an interaction of different contributory factors which create the anomalous experience and lead to its misinterpretation.

This idea has been pushed further by Langdon and Coltheart (2000; Langdon, Chapter 45, this volume), who suggest that the origins of many delusional beliefs are of this (interacting contributory factors) form. The point is important not just as a neat piece of theory, but because if correct it implies that cognitive neuropsychiatry will need different methods from those typically used in cognitive neuropsychology (Young, 2000). The idea of interacting contributory factors underlying delusional beliefs suggests a critical status for what in cognitive neuropsychology would be regarded as relatively uninteresting "associated deficits." In cognitive neuropsychiatry, then, the logic of how associated and dissociable deficits are treated is having to be rethought.

Converging operations

By now, readers of nervous or impetuous dispositions are probably in despair. It seems that, if looked at skeptically and critically, almost any neuropsychological observation can be brought into question and reinterpreted. How then are we to make progress?

I believe the answer is both simple and encouraging. What is needed is to take into account as many sources of evidence and pertinent theory as possible, including approaches that are not themselves neuropsychological. For many of the questions we are interested in, a whole range of observations are relevant. For instance, the idea that names are stored separately from other semantic information was a feature of the Hay and Young (1982) and Bruce and Young (1986) functional models that is supported by neuropsychological evidence (Flude et al., 1989), but is also supported by non-neuropsychological studies:

♦ The "tip of the tongue" state—in which we seem to be able to bring to mind everything we know about an object except its name—is fairly common for people's names (Yarmey, 1973; Young et al., 1985)

♦ Naming a face generally takes longer than making judgments based on other types of semantic information, such as deciding whether it is an actor or a politician (Young et al., 1986)

♦ Learning to associate names with faces is harder than learning information such as the person's occupation (McWeeny et al., 1987).

In each case, we can try to pick holes in the line of reasoning, just as we saw for neuropsychological studies. But it is impressive that all of these different lines of evidence point to the same conclusion, that there is something problematic about putting names to faces. Moreover, the ways in which each line of evidence might be at fault are themselves quite different. Let's call the different possible conclusions from each line of evidence C1 (names are especially hard to retrieve), alternative A1, A2, etc. Put formally, we could say that line of evidence E1 points to one of the conclusions C1, A1, or A2 being the case, where A1 and A2 represent our alternative potential explanations of the data that might otherwise point to C1. Importantly, though, the alternatives for each line of evidence are usually different, so evidence E2 points to conclusions C1, A3, or A4 being the case, whilst E3 implicates C1, A5, or A6, E4 implicates C1, A7, or A8, and so on. It quickly becomes clear that as more lines of evidence are adduced, the possibility of C1s being true looks increasingly more likely than some arbitrary combination of the alternatives (A1, A2, A3, etc.).

This technique of putting the weight on what is consistently indicated across different techniques is often called "converging operations" in the literature on research methods. It doesn't give a privileged status to any one line of argument; instead it tries to weigh the evidence by how consistently it points in the same direction. Of course, this doesn't guarantee we will reach the right conclusion, but it does enhance confidence that a phenomenon is interesting and important.

As well as bringing together converging lines of evidence, it is useful to systematize what is known. The simplest technique is the "box and arrow" functional modeler's diagram. Though often looked down upon, these diagrams are useful in succinctly representing what is being claimed, and highlighting what needs further work. They can also have some predictive value. For instance, a clear prediction of the sequential recognition model proposed by Hay and Young (1982) and Bruce and Young (1986) is that, whilst we will often find ourselves recognizing a face but being unable to recall the person's name, we should never find ourselves able to put a name to a familiar face without being able to produce other identity-specific semantic information. This prediction follows naturally from the proposed order of sequential access of different types of information (familiarity, then semantic information, then name retrieval), and several experimental and neuropsychological studies show that the overwhelming majority of errors fit the predicted type. The most notable exceptions are errors made by children (Scanlan and Johnston, 1997)—possibly a special case—and Brennen et al.'s (1996) isolated report of sporadic errors in a patient with dementia.

The limitation of box and arrow models is that because they don't make explicit what happens at each stage, they offer only a partial account and they are limited to relatively coarse predictions.

To model phenomena that have been studied in detail, it is preferable to create an implemented computer simulation. Implemented models have the advantages both of greater precision and of suggesting new ways to interpret complex phenomena. We have already seen how Burton et al.'s (1990) simulation of Bruce and Young's (1986) account of face recognition offered a new approach to the previously baffling phenomenon of covert recognition of familiar faces in prosopagnosia (Burton et al., 1991). At the same time, it was able to offer an alternative account of the particular difficulty of name retrieval that did not simply involve assigning names to a separate store (Burton and Bruce, 1992).

The value of bringing together data and theories from neuropsychology and experimental psychology is therefore clear. But the examples we've looked at are very much of a type where the issue investigated is fairly "psychological" in nature, so they might be thought to stack the odds in favor of the advocated approach. I don't think, though, that this is correct. Certainly, there are different types of question we can ask. Wanting to know how we recognize familiar faces is not the same as wanting to know whether there are differences between the cerebral hemispheres in face recognition ability. The former concern ("How do we recognize faces?") is clearly psychological, the latter ("Are there hemisphere differences?") more strictly neuropsychological or neurological.

This brings us back to where we came in. From the 1960s to the 1980s, there was an explosion of interest in cerebral hemisphere differences. This was in large part stimulated by split-brain studies, but commissurotomy operations were rare and it was recognized that patients needing this operation might have atypically organized brains, so there was a lot of interest in the possibility of studying cerebral asymmetry in the intact brain. Without brain imaging, the most popular way to do this was to make use of the existence of contralateral projections in the nervous system. In the case of face recognition, we could present pictures of faces to the left visual field so that they were initially projected to the primary visual cortex of the right hemisphere, or in the right visual field to the left hemisphere (Rizzolatti et al., 1971).

The resulting performance differences between left and right visual field presentations were not large, but findings such as reduced asymmetry in left-handers suggested they were related to cerebral asymmetry. However, as the literature grew it became increasingly complex and often inconsistent. Something was amiss.

One of the most promising attempts to sort things out was by Moscovitch, Scullion, and Christie (1976). Their approach involved looking more carefully at the kinds of tasks used, and in particular the stages of perceptual analysis required successfully to perform different tasks. In general, it seemed to Moscovitch et al. (1976) that cerebral asymmetries in recognizing faces are not found for early stages of precategorical perceptual analysis, and that the right hemisphere superiority becomes more evident when higher-order processing is needed. The idea is an excellent example of how a more general theoretical background can help even in approaching a specifically neuropsychological question. At the time, Dennis Hay and I were both primarily interested in cerebral asymmetry for face recognition. We saw the value of Moscovitch et al.'s (1976) line of reasoning, but also thought that its ultimate success would depend on developing a more detailed underlying theoretical model of functional components involved in face perception. This was critical in inspiring us to give theorizing a try.

So there is a case for bringing together theories and data from different areas. In the modern era, the new kid on the block in this respect is functional brain imaging. It has had a rather mixed reception. Henson (2005) has led the welcoming committee, seeing neuroimaging as a useful adjunct to other ways of gaining evidence that can be used to test psychological theories. Henson's (2005) view is that, as long as there is some systematic mapping between psychological functions and underlying brain structure, functional neuroimaging findings can be used in the same way as other data to test psychological theories.

In contrast, Coltheart (2006) is more reserved. He draws a sharp distinction between testing theories expressed at the psychological level and localizing functions to specific brain regions. Coltheart (2006) recognizes that neuroimaging studies have provided plenty of data relevant to the localizationist enterprise but argues that, to date, they have not successfully been used to distinguish psychological theories.

To me, this is reminiscent of debates in the 1980s about whether information about lesion locations was needed in cognitive neuropsychological studies. Logically, there was a case that knowing the lesion location might not be seen as essential, but pragmatically it made sense to have this information available whenever possible; it could both highlight other deficits that might need to be evaluated and it could be a clear pointer to an unexpected or atypical pattern (e.g. if the lesion seemed to be in the "wrong" location for the observed behavioral deficit). More specifically, Coltheart's (2006) criterion that a line of evidence should be able decisively to arbitrate between competing psychological theories if it is to be taken on board seems very strict. We have seen here that neuropsychological evidence also often fails to live up to such high expectations, yet it remains very valuable.

The debate is important because a recent neurological model of face perception by Haxby, Hoffman and Gobbini (2000; Haxby and Gobbini, Chapter 6, this volume), which was created largely around data from brain imaging, actually relates well to explicitly "functional" models such as Bruce and Young (1986), as Calder and Young (2005) point out. Something that is particularly appealing about Haxby et al.'s (2000) position, though, is that it explains a potential organizing principle underlying part of the "division of labor" in face perception, by emphasizing the differences between those aspects of face perception that depend on the interpretation of cues that are changeable from moment to moment (e.g. emotional expression, gaze direction) or relatively invariant (age, sex, identity). Moreover, this can be linked to a more general system of visual pathways for perceiving motion and static form in the cerebral cortex, making the neuroanatomy and psychology fit neatly alongside each other.

As already discussed, one of the strongest features of Bruce and Young (1986) was that it sought to use ideas that were consistent across as wide a range of evidence as possible. The emerging convergence with neuroanatomy thus seems to me to give additional grounds for thinking the approach of bringing together different lines of evidence remains our best way forward.

Summary and conclusions

This chapter takes an overview of what we can learn about face perception from studying its disorders. The term "disorders" is broadly interpreted to include acquired brain injury and disease, neurodevelopmental differences, and neuropsychiatric problems. I show why opinions about what can be learnt from disorders have ranged the entire spectrum from "nothing that isn't misleading" to "everything worth knowing." I then highlight a number of the assumptions that get made, explain why things are often complicated, and emphasize the value of a pragmatic "converging operations" approach in which evidence from disorders of face perception is brought together with other sources of data and theory.

References

Barton, J.J.S. (2008). Structure and function in acquired prosopagnosia: lessons from a series of 10 patients with brain damage. *Journal of Neuropsychology*, **2**, 197–225.

Bauer, R.M. (1984). Autonomic recognition of names and faces in prosopagnosia: a neuropsychological application of the guilty knowledge test. *Neuropsychologia*, **22**, 457–469.

Benton, A.L. (1980). The neuropsychology of facial recognition. *American Psychologist*, **35**, 176–186.

Bishop, D.V.M. (1997). Cognitive neuropsychology and developmental disorders: uncomfortable bedfellows. *Quarterly Journal of Experimental Psychology*, **50A**, 899–923.

Brennen, T., David, D., Fluchaire, I., and Pellat, J. (1996). Naming faces and objects without comprehension - a case study. *Cognitive Neuropsychology*, **13**, 93–110.

Bruce, V. and Young, A. (1986). Understanding face recognition. *British Journal of Psychology*, **77**, 305–327.

Bruyer, R., Laterre, C., Seron, X., *et al.* (1983). A case of prosopagnosia with some preserved covert remembrance of familiar faces. *Brain and Cognition*, **2**, 257–284.

Burton, A.M. and Bruce, V. (1992). I recognise your face but I can't remember your name: a simple explanation? *British Journal of Psychology*, **83**, 45–60.

Burton, A.M., Bruce, V., and Johnston, R.A. (1990). Understanding face recognition with an interactive activation model. *British Journal of Psychology*, **81**, 361–380.

Burton, A.M., Young, A.W., Bruce, V., Johnston, R., and Ellis, A.W. (1991). Understanding covert recognition. *Cognition*, **39**, 129–166.

Calder, A.J. and Young, A.W. (2005). Understanding the recognition of facial identity and facial expression. *Nature Reviews Neuroscience*, **6**, 645–651.

Coltheart, M. (1984). Editorial. *Cognitive Neuropsychology*, **1**, 1–8.

Coltheart, M. (2006). What has functional neuroimaging told us about the mind (so far)? *Cortex*, **42**, 323–331.

de Haan, E.H.F. (1999). A familial factor in the development of face recognition deficits. *Journal of Clinical and Experimental Neuropsychology*, **21**, 312–315.

de Haan, E.H.F., Young, A., and Newcombe, F. (1987). Face recognition without awareness. *Cognitive Neuropsychology*, **4**, 385–415.

Duchaine, B.C., Parker, H., and Nakayama, K. (2003). Normal recognition of emotion in a prosopagnosic. *Perception*, **32**, 827–838.

Ellis, A.W., Young, A.W., and Critchley, E.M.R. (1989). Loss of memory for people following temporal lobe damage. *Brain*, **112**, 1469–1483.

Ellis, H.D. (1975). Recognizing faces. *British Journal of Psychology*, **66**, 409–426.

Ellis, H.D. and Young, A.W. (1990). Accounting for delusional misidentifications. *British Journal of Psychiatry*, **157**, 239–248.

Ellis, H.D., Young, A.W., Quayle, A.H., and de Pauw, K.W. (1997). Reduced autonomic responses to faces in Capgras delusion. *Proceedings of the Royal Society: Biological Sciences*, **B264**, 1085–1092.

Flude, B.M., Ellis, A.W., and Kay, J. (1989). Face processing and name retrieval in an anomic aphasic: names are stored separately from semantic information about familiar people. *Brain and Cognition*, **11**, 60–72.

Fodor, J. (1983). *The modularity of mind*. Cambridge, MA: MIT Press.

Geschwind, N. (1965a). Disconnexion syndromes in animals and man. *Part I. Brain*, **88**, 237–294.

Geschwind, N. (1965b). Disconnexion syndromes in animals and man. *Part II. Brain*, **88**, 585–644.

Gregory, R.L. (1961). The brain as an engineering problem. In W.H. Thorpe and O.L. Zangwill (eds.) *Current Problems in Animal Behaviour*, pp. 307–330. Cambridge: Cambridge University Press.

Gregory, R.L. (2005). Images of mind in brain. *Word and Image*, **21**, 120–123.

Hancock, P.J.B., Bruce, V., and Burton, A.M. (2001). Recognition of unfamiliar faces. *Trends in Cognitive Sciences*, **4**, 330–337.

Hanley, J.R., Young, A.W., and Pearson, N. (1989). Defective recognition of familiar people. *Cognitive Neuropsychology*, **6**, 179–210.

Haxby, J.M., Gobbini, M.I., Furey, M.L., Ishai, A., Schouten, J.L., and Pietrini, P. (2001). Distributed and overlapping representations of faces and objects in ventral temporal cortex. *Science*, **293**, 2425–2430.

Haxby, J.V., Hoffman, E.A., and Gobbini, M.I. (2000). The distributed human neural system for face perception. *Trends in Cognitive Sciences*, **4**, 223–233.

Hay, D.C. and Young, A.W. (1982). The human face. In A.W. Ellis (ed.) *Normality and pathology in cognitive functions*, pp. 173–202. London: Academic Press.

Henson, R.N.A. (2005). What can functional neuroimaging tell the experimental psychologist? *Quarterly Journal of Experimental Psychology*, **58A**, 193–233.

Herzmann, G., Danthiir, V., Schacht, A., Sommer, W., and Wilhelm, O. (2008). Toward a comprehensive test battery for face cognition: assessment of the tasks. *Behavior Research Methods*, **40**, 840–857.

Hirstein, W. and Ramachandran, V.S. (1997). Capgras syndrome: a novel probe for understanding the neural representation of the identity and familiarity of persons. *Proceedings of the Royal Society: Biological Sciences*, **B264**, 437–444.

Kanwisher, N. (2000). Domain specificity in face perception. *Nature Neuroscience*, **3**, 759–763.

Kapur, N. (1996). Paradoxical functional facilitation in brain-behaviour research: a critical review. *Brain*, **119**, 1775–1790.

Kapur, N. (2009). On the pursuit of clinical excellence. *Clinical Governance*, **14**, 24–37.

Langdon, R. and Coltheart, M. (2000). The cognitive neuropsychology of delusions. *Mind and Language*, **15**, 183–216.

Marr, D. (1976). Early processing of visual information. *Philosophical Transactions of the Royal Society of London*, **B, 275**, 483–519.

Marr, D. (1982). *Vision*. San Francisco, CA: Freeman.

Marshall, J.C. and Newcombe, F. (1966). Syntactic and semantic errors in paralexia. *Neuropsychologia*, **4**, 169–176.

Marshall, J.C. and Newcombe, F. (1973). Patterns of paralexia: a psycholinguistic approach. *Journal of Psycholinguistic Research*, **2**, 175–199.

McWeeny, K.H., Young, A.W., Hay, D.C., and Ellis, A.W. (1987). Putting names to faces. *British Journal of Psychology*, **78**, 143–149.

Meadows, J.C. (1974). The anatomical basis of prosopagnosia. *Journal of Neurology, Neurosurgery, and Psychiatry*, **37**, 489–501.

Milner, A.D. and Goodale, M.A. (1995). *The visual brain in action*, Oxford Psychology Series, 27. Oxford: Oxford University Press.

Moscovitch, M., Scullion, D., and Christie, D. (1976). Early versus late stages of processing and their relation to functional hemispheric asymmetries in face recognition. *Journal of Experimental Psychology: Human Perception and Performance*, **2**, 401–416.

Moscovitch, M., Winocur, G., and Behrmann, M. (1997). What is special about face recognition? Nineteen experiments on a person with visual object agnosia and dyslexia but normal face recognition. *Journal of Cognitive Neuroscience*, **9**, 555–604.

Newcombe, F. (1979). The processing of visual information in prosopagnosia and acquired dyslexia: functional versus physiological interpretation. In D.J. Oborne, M.M. Gruneberg, and J.R. Eiser (eds.) *Research in psychology and medicine*, Vol 1, pp. 315–322. London: Academic Press.

Newcombe, F., Young, A.W., and de Haan, E.H.F. (1989). Prosopagnosia and object agnosia without covert recognition. *Neuropsychologia*, **27**, 179–191.

Rizzolatti, G., Umiltà, C., and Berlucchi, G. (1971). Opposite superiorities of the right and left cerebral hemispheres in discriminative reaction time to physiognomical and alphabetical material. *Brain*, **94**, 431–442.

Scanlan, L.C. and Johnston, R.A. (1997). I recognize your face, but I can't remember your name: a grown-up explanation? *Quarterly Journal of Experimental Psychology*, **50A**, 183–198.

Schmalzl, L., Palermo, R., and Coltheart, M. (2008). Cognitive heterogeneity in genetically-based prosopagnosia: a family study. *Journal of Neuropsychology*, **2**, 99–117.

Shallice, T. (1988). *From neuropsychology to mental structure*. Cambridge: Cambridge University Press.

Tranel, D. and Damasio, A.R. (1985). Knowledge without awareness: an autonomic index of facial recognition by prosopagnosics. *Science*, **228**, 1453–1454.

Tranel, D., Damasio, H., and Damasio, A.R. (1995). Double dissociation between overt and covert recognition. *Journal of Cognitive Neuroscience*, **7**, 425–432.

Warrington, E.K. (1975). The selective impairment of semantic memory. *Quarterly Journal of Experimental Psychology*, **27**, 635–657.

Warrington, E.K. and Shallice, T. (1969). The selective impairment of auditory verbal short-term memory. *Brain*, **92**, 885–896.

Warrington, E.K. and Taylor, A.M. (1973). The contribution of the right parietal lobe to object recognition. *Cortex*, **9**, 152–164.

Woollams, A.M., Lambon Ralph, M.A., Plaut, D., and Patterson, K. (2007). SD-squared: on the association between semantic dementia and surface dyslexia. *Psychological Review*, **114**, 316–339.

Yarmey, A.D. (1973). I recognize your face but I can't remember your name: further evidence on the tip-of-the-tongue phenomenon. *Memory and Cognition*, **1**, 287–290.

Young, A.W. (2000). Wondrous strange: the neuropsychology of abnormal beliefs. *Mind and Language*, **15**, 47–73.

Young, A.W. and Burton, A.M. (1999). Simulating face recognition: implications for modelling cognition. *Cognitive Neuropsychology*, **16**, 1–48.

Young, A.W., Hay, D.C., and Ellis, A.W. (1985). The faces that launched a thousand slips: everyday difficulties and errors in recognizing people. *British Journal of Psychology*, **76**, 495–523.

Young, A.W., McWeeny, K.H., Ellis, A.W., and Hay, D.C. (1986). Naming and categorizing faces and written names. *Quarterly Journal of Experimental Psychology*, **38A**, 297–318.

Young, A.W., Newcombe, F., de Haan, E.H.F., Small, M., and Hay, D.C. (1993a). Face perception after brain injury: selective impairments affecting identity and expression. *Brain*, **116**, 941–959.

Young, A.W., Reid, I., Wright, S., and Hellawell, D.J. (1993b). Face-processing impairments and the Capgras delusion. *British Journal of Psychiatry*, **162**, 695–698.

Young, A.W., Perrett, D.I., Calder, A.J., Sprengelmeyer, R., and Ekman, P. (2002). *Facial expressions of emotion: stimuli and tests (FEEST)*. Bury St. Edmunds: Thames Valley Test Company.

Chapter 6

Distributed Neural Systems for Face Perception

James V. Haxby and M. Ida Gobbini

Introduction

Face perception plays a central role in social communication and is, arguably, one of the most sophisticated visual perceptual skills in humans. Consequently, face perception has been the subject of intensive investigation and theorizing in both visual and social neuroscience.

The organization of neural systems for face perception has stimulated intense debate. Much of this debate has focused on models that posit the existence of a module that is specialized for face perception (Kanwisher et al., 1997; Kanwisher and Yovel, 2006) versus models that propose that face perception is mediated by distributed processing (Haxby et al., 2000, 2001; Ishai et al., 2005; Ishai 2008). These two perspectives on the neural systems that underlie face perception are not necessarily incompatible (see Kanwisher and Barton, Chapter 7, this volume). In our work, we have proposed that face perception is mediated by distributed systems, both in terms of the involvement of multiple brain areas and in terms of locally distributed population codes within these areas (Haxby et al., 2000, 2001). Specifically, we proposed a model for the distributed neural system for face perception that has a Core System of visual extrastriate areas for visual analysis of faces and an Extended System that consists of additional neural systems that work in concert with the Core System to extract various types of information from faces (Haxby et al., 2000). We also have shown that in visual extrastriate cortices, information that distinguishes faces from other categories of animate and inanimate objects is not restricted to regions that respond maximally to faces, i.e. the fusiform and occipital face areas (Haxby et al., 2001; Hanson et al., 2004).

In this chapter we present an updated model of distributed human neural systems for face perception. We will begin with a discussion of the Core System for visual analysis of faces with an emphasis on the distinction between perception of invariant features for identity recognition and changeable features for recognition of facial gestures such as expression and eye gaze. The bulk of the chapter will be a selective discussion of neural systems in the Extended System for familiar face recognition and for extracting the meaning of facial gestures, in particular facial expression and eye gaze. We will discuss the roles of systems for the representation of emotion, for person knowledge, and for action understanding in face recognition and perception of expression and gaze. The neural systems that are recruited for extracting socially-relevant information from faces are an unbounded set whose membership accrues with further investigations of face perception. Rather than attempt an exhaustive review, our intention is to present systems that we believe are of particular relevance for social communication and that are illustrative of how distributed systems are engaged by face perception. Many of the chapters in this volume provide a more detailed account for areas that we touch on in this chapter. Our review also is biased towards work that we have been directly involved in, with selective references to closely related work by other investigators. We will finish with a discussion of modularity and distributed processing in neural representation.

The path that has led to our current model has been neither direct nor predictable. Our path was guided by empirical results that forced us repeatedly to question the ideas that motivated our experiments and to redirect our subsequent efforts. The work began in the late 1980s in the early days of imaging brain blood flow with positron emission tomography. One of us (JVH) was working at the National Institutes of Health with Cheryl Grady, Barry Horwitz, and Leslie Ungerleider, with critical support from Mortimer Mishkin and Stanley Rapoport. We set out to investigate whether the human visual system was organized into ventral object vision and dorsal spatial vision pathways. We used a face perception task to activate the ventral pathway (Haxby et al., 1991, 1994), reasoning that face processing, as compared to visual processing of other objects, is more restricted to the ventral pathway. It was soon obvious, however, that faces had a distinct representation within the ventral pathway and were, therefore, a poor choice for revealing the full functional architecture of the ventral visual pathway. We began to conduct our own studies of differential responses to faces and other objects in the ventral temporal cortex (Chao et al., 1999; Haxby et al., 1999; Ishai et al., 1999). When we examined the data from these experiments, it was apparent that the functional architecture of the ventral pathway was not a simple division into regions that responded preferentially to faces and regions that responded preferentially to other object categories. The two of us began working together at this point. We explored how the distinct responses to faces and other object categories were, in fact, organized, leading to the development of multivariate pattern (MVP) analysis and understanding the response to faces in ventral temporal cortex as a distributed population code (Haxby et al., 2001). At the same time, we became interested in the role of face perception in social communication, leading notably to studies of familiar face recognition (Gobbini et al., 2004, 2006; Leibenluft et al., 2004; Gobbini and Haxby, 2007) and the perception of gaze direction and facial expressions (Hoffman and Haxby, 2000; Engell and Haxby, 2007; Montgomery and Haxby, 2008; Montgomery et al., 2009; Said et al., 2010). It soon became apparent that the functional architecture for these face perception operations was not restricted to the ventral temporal cortex, and we were forced, again by the data, to look at the role played by other areas in visual extrastriate cortex and by areas in non-visual neural systems. The result of these repeated reformulations is the model that we present in this chapter. The broad outlines of our model have been relatively stable for the past 9 to 10 years, but we know from experience that future empirical research may well lead to further, possibly radical, revisions. We cannot predict what form the next revision may take.

The core system for visual analysis of faces

Three extrastriate visual regions that respond maximally to faces

Functional neuroimaging consistently has shown that three bilateral regions in occipital-temporal extrastriate visual cortex respond more strongly when viewing faces than when viewing other visual images. These areas are in the inferior occipital gyrus—the occipital face area (OFA), the lateral fusiform gyrus—the fusiform face area (FFA), and the posterior superior temporal sulcus (pSTS) (Figure 6.1). Although these regions can usually be identified in both the right and left hemispheres, they tend to be larger and more reliably found in the right hemisphere. In addition to these areas that respond maximally to faces, nearby cortices also respond significantly during face recognition, and these non-maximal responses carry information about the distinction between faces and other stimuli (Haxby et al., 2001; Hanson et al., 2004) and are related to successful face identification (Grill-Spector et al., 2004).

We proposed that these three areas—along with adjacent cortex that responds significantly, albeit not maximally, to faces—constitute a "Core System" for the visual analysis of face images

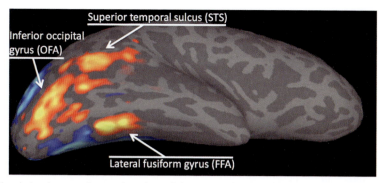

Fig. 6.1 Three visual extrastriate regions in occipitotemporal cortex that respond strongly to face stimuli. This figure shows the areas that responded more strongly to images of faces than to images of houses in a single subject. The activations are on a cortical surface that has been inflated to reveal sulcal cortex and tipped to show both lateral and ventral surfaces. Adapted from Haxby et al. (2000).

(Haxby et al., 2000). We proposed further that different regions within the Core System have representations that emphasize different types of visual information about faces.

Two classes of face perception operations

In their classic paper on cognitive systems for face perception, Bruce and Young (1986) distinguished between processes for recognizing facial identity and processes for analyzing facial expression and speech-related facial movements. Their model focused primarily on face identity recognition. We have emphasized how these complementary processes are dissociated in the Core System.

Identity recognition is dependent on perceiving facial features that are invariant across facial movements, such as facial expression and speech-related movements, and across variable viewing conditions, such as angle of profile and lighting. Face recognition has a virtually unlimited capacity for representing distinct identities. The representations of these identities must be generative and robust in that they allow recognition of a familiar face from a novel image—a particular image that one has never seen before—with a wide range of variations in expression, gaze, and mouth movements. Furthermore, the face recognition system is capable of perceiving that a previously unfamiliar face is unique and distinct from all faces that one has seen previously. By contrast, analysis of facial expression is targeted at nuanced perception of changes that are associated with facial movement. For facial expression perception, precisely the variations that are irrelevant for identity recognition are of paramount importance. Moreover, categories of facial expressions—such as smiling, scowling, disgust, disdain, boredom—are perceived as the same expression even though they are produced by different familiar or unfamiliar individuals. Thus, these two classes of face perception operations are distinct and have the potential to interfere with each other. A change in expression should not be perceived as a change in identity. A particular expression should be interpreted as carrying similar information if produced by different individuals.

We have proposed that these two classes of face perception operations are kept distinct within the Core System by anatomic segregation of representational spaces that emphasize invariant features for identification versus changeable features such as expression and eye gaze changes

(Haxby et al., 2000). We formulated this hypothesis based on findings from single-unit recordings in macaque cortex (Hasselmo et al., 1989) that showed that neurons that were tuned to variations in identity were located more ventrally in the convexity of inferior temporal (IT) cortex whereas neurons that were tuned to variations in expression were found in greater concentrations in the STS. We hypothesized that a similar dissociation exists between face-responsive regions in the human fusiform and STS cortices.

Perception of both eye and mouth movements selectively evoke responses in the pSTS but not the FFA (Puce et al., 1998). Subsequent work has supported our hypothesis that the pSTS is involved both in the perception of facial movements and in the perception of features, such as eye gaze and expression, that are changed by movements. We found that selective attention to identity increased the neural response in the FFA but not in pSTS, whereas selective attention to eye gaze direction increased the neural response in pSTS but not in the FFA (Hoffman and Haxby, 2000), supporting our hypothesis that the FFA is involved more in the representation of identity whereas the pSTS is involved more in eye gaze perception. In another study, we compared the FFA and pSTS responses to dynamic changes in the eye gaze direction and identity (Engell et al., 2006) and found that the FFA responded more strongly to identity than gaze changes, whereas the pSTS responded more to gaze than identity changes. The response to faces shows adaptation to repeated expression in the pSTS as well as in a more anterior STS region but not in the fusiform cortex (Winston et al., 2004). In addition the STS responses to faces are significantly stronger for dynamic facial expressions than for still images of expressions, but no such enhancement is seen in the FFA (Figure 6.2). A functional localizer that uses dynamic videos of faces reveals a much larger face responsive STS region than does a localizer that uses static images of faces, whereas the addition of facial motion had little effect on the size of the fusiform face-responsive area (Hasson et al., 2004).

Although there is abundant evidence that the representation of faces in the FFA plays a greater role in recognizing identity and the representation of faces in the pSTS plays a greater role in perception of changeable features, such as expression and gaze, the distinction is not black and white. Consequently, the dominant roles of the FFA in face identity perception and the pSTS in expression perception have been challenged (Calder and Young, 2005; see Calder, Chapter 22, this volume). Perception of gaze changes appears to be more restricted to the pSTS than is perception of expression, and within the STS expression perception appears to involve more rostral locations than does gaze perception (Winston et al., 2004; Engell and Haxby, 2007) (Figure 6.3).

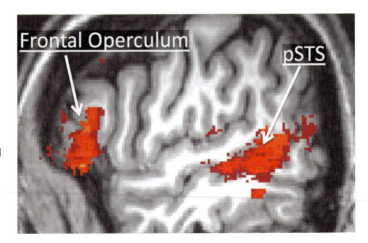

Fig. 6.2 Brain areas that showed a significantly stronger response while viewing dynamic videos of actors producing facial expressions than while viewing still images of the same expressions. (Kirkland and Haxby, previously unpublished.)

Emotional facial expressions, however, evoke stronger responses than do neutral expressions in both the pSTS and the FFA (Vuilleumier et al., 2001; Engell and Haxby, 2007), and the response to faces shows adaptation to repeated identity in both the FFA and pSTS (Winston et al., 2004).

Naïvely, one might expect that making trait inferences, such as trustworthiness or competence based on facial appearance would rely on the same class of invariant features that are involved in the recognition of identity. Todorov and colleagues, however, have shown that these inferences appear to be based on subtle variations that suggest facial expressions, such as anger and happiness (Todorov et al., 2008; see Todorov et al., Chapter 32, this volume). Consistent with Todorov et al.'s hypothesis, which was based on a model of face space and behavioral findings, a study by Winston et al. (2001) showed that explicit judgments of trustworthiness increased the response to faces in the pSTS but not in fusiform cortex.

The full extent of the Core System is not restricted to the OFA, FFA, and pSTS. Within ventral occipitotemporal and superior temporal sulcal cortices, the full extent of cortex that responds significantly to faces extends beyond cortex that responds maximally to faces (see next section) (Haxby et al., 1999, 2001; Ishai et al., 1999; Grill-Spector et al., 2004; Rajimehr et al., 2009). Moreover, face-selective regions—regions that respond more to faces than other stimuli—in ventral temporal and STS cortex do not appear to be restricted to the FFA and the pSTS. An anterior face-responsive ventral temporal region has been identified (Rajimehr et al., 2009) that appears to be involved in discrimination of identities (Kriegeskorte et al., 2007). More anterior regions in the STS appear to be involved in the representation of specific gaze directions (Calder et al., 2007) and expressions (Winston et al., 2004).

Distributed representation within extrastriate cortex

In our work on distributed representations of faces and objects, we have emphasized both distribution of complex or multifaceted processes across multiple brain areas (Haxby et al., 2000) and distribution of population codes within a cortical area (Haxby et al., 2001). In this chapter we are presenting a model for distribution of face perception across multiple brain regions. For clarity and simplicity, we have indicated the location of Core System areas in terms of regions that show greater responsiveness to faces than other stimuli. Consistent with our other work, however, we argue that face perception in the Core System is not limited to the regions that respond maximally to faces but rather extends beyond into neighboring cortical fields that respond significantly, but not maximally, to faces.

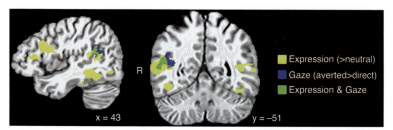

Fig. 6.3 Brain areas that show a stronger response to still images of facial expressions, as compared to a neutral expression, or to still images of faces with averted gaze, as compared to direct gaze. Reprinted from *Neuropsychologia*, **45**(14), Andrew D. Engell, James V. Haxby, Facial expression and gaze-direction in human superior temporal sulcus, Copyright (2007), with permission from Elsevier.

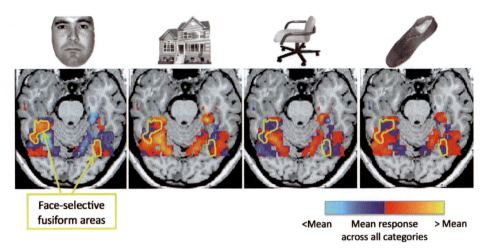

Fig. 6.4 Patterns of response in ventral temporal cortex to faces and three categories of objects—houses, chairs, and shoes. Data shown are in one axial section from one subject. The face-responsive fusiform areas are outlined in yellow. Note that the distinctive pattern of response to faces extends into areas outside of the face-selective areas. Data are from Haxby et al. (2001).

We have shown that the pattern of neural response to viewed faces in cortex that responds maximally to other visual stimuli distinguishes faces from other objects and different types of faces from each other (Figure 6.4) (Haxby et al., 2001; Connolly et al., in press). These distinctions were detected using multivariate pattern analysis (MVPA), which is more sensitive than conventional univariate analysis methods (Haynes and Rees, 2006; Norman et al., 2006; O'Toole et al., 2007). Whereas the mean response in the FFA does not distinguish between human faces and nonhuman mammalian faces (Tong et al., 1999), MVPA of responses, both within the FFA and in ventral temporal cortex that responds maximally to other visual stimuli, does detect such distinctions (Connolly et al., in press). Grill-Spector et al. (2004) showed that half of the ventral temporal cortex that correlated with successful face identification, relative to face detection, was outside of the FFA. In macaque IT cortex, high concentrations of face-selective neurons are found in face-selective patches (Tsao et al., 2006; see Freiwald and Tsao, Chapter 36, this volume), but face-selective cells also are found outside of these patches, albeit in lower concentrations. Moreover, many face-responsive IT cells show coarse tuning profiles, with significant responses to both faces and other stimuli (Kiani et al., 2007). Thus, the full extent of cortex that participate in face perception in extrastriate visual areas is not restricted to the face-selective OFA, FFA, and pSTS and includes neurons that respond significantly to both faces and other stimuli.

The extended system for extracting information from faces

Recognition of familiar faces

Although recognition of a familiar face is accompanied by modulation of activity in the Core System FFA, this modulation can be positive or negative (for a review, see Gobbini and Haxby, 2007). Consequently, the strength of the FFA response may be more a reflection of top-down modulation than a signal of familiarity. Although facial identity may be encoded in the population response in the FFA (Rolls, 2000; Tsao et al., 2006; Freiwald et al., 2009; see Rolls, Chapter 4, and Freiwald and Tsao, Chapter 36, this volume) and other ventral temporal areas (e.g. anterior temporal cortex, Kriegeskorte et al., 2007), the contribution of other systems may modulate the overall strength of Core System responses. We have proposed that these other systems, which are outside of visual extrastriate cortex, play a central role in familiar face recognition—specifically in the automatic retrieval of person knowledge and in the emotional response to familiar individuals. These systems are key parts of the Extended System for face perception.

Immediate retrieval of information about familiar individuals—such as their personality traits, their relationships with oneself and others, and their probable intentions—is a fundamental process that lays the foundation for appropriate social interactions. Therefore, recognition of the visual features of a familiar face is only the initial and relatively minor stage in the processes involved in familiar face recognition. A key component of the neural representation of familiar individuals is the retrieval of person knowledge. A second fundamental component of the neural representation of familiar individuals concerns one's emotional response to that individual. Person knowledge refers to a broad class of information that encompasses personal traits, intentions, attitudes, transient mental states, biographical information and episodic memories related to specific individuals.

Research in social psychology has shown evidence for the spontaneous activation of traits and attitudes associated with the perceived individuals (Greenwald and Banaji, 1995; Bargh et al., 1996; Todorov and Uleman, 2002; Todorov et al., 2007). Furthermore, there is evidence that the representation of significant others is richer in thoughts, feelings and emotions as compared to non-significant others (Andersen and Cole, 1990; Andersen et al., 1998). As someone becomes more familiar the type of inferences made about these personally familiar individuals relates more to "psychological mediating variables" (such as goals and beliefs) and less to broad uncontextualized traits (e.g. "aggressive" or "friendly") (Idson and Mischel, 2001).

The pattern of neural activity evoked by viewing a familiar face is modulated by the knowledge one has about that individual and by one's emotional response to that person. We found that comparing faces with different levels of familiarity modulated the neural response in a distributed set of areas (Figure 6.5). We recorded a stronger response in areas associated with mentalizing or

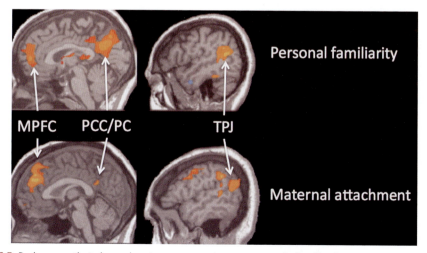

Fig. 6.5 Brain areas that showed a stronger response to personally familiar faces, as compared to famous faces (upper panel, Gobbini et al., 2004), and to pictures of one's own child, as compared to familiar, but unrelated, other children (lower panel, Leibenluft et al., 2004).

theory of mind (ToM), such as the medial prefrontal cortex (MPFC) and the temporoparietal junction (TPJ), for faces of relatives and friends as compared to faces of famous individuals (politicians, actors, singers, athletes) and as compared to faces of strangers (Gobbini et al., 2004). The TPJ region that is involved in familiar face recognition and mentalizing can be dissociated from the nearby face-responsive pSTS (Gobbini et al., 2007). In a study of mothers of young children, the face of one's own child as compared to faces of familiar but unrelated children (Leibenluft et al., 2004) also evoked stronger responses in these areas. Faces that are only visually familiar (through a behavioral training session in a laboratory prior to the functional magnetic resonance imaging (fMRI) experiment) but not associated with any semantic information, did not modulate the MPFC and TPJ (Gobbini and Haxby, 2006). We have hypothesized that the MPFC and the TPJ encode those aspects of person knowledge (Mitchell et al., 2002) that are related to the representation of personal traits and mental states characteristic of a familiar individual.

The more familiar faces also evoked a stronger response in the posterior cingulate cortex and precuneus (PCC/PC) (Gobbini et al., 2004; Leibenluft et al., 2004). Faces that are visually familiar but with no associated person knowledge also evoked an increased response in the PCC/PC, suggesting that this region plays a role in the acquisition of simple visual familiarity (Kosaka et al., 2003; Gobbini and Haxby, 2006). The stronger response for the more familiar faces recorded in PCC/PC found in our studies and the involvement of the anterior temporal regions reported by others (Gorno-Tempini et al., 1998; Leveroni et al., 2000; Nakamura et al., 2000; Douville et al., 2005; Rotshtein et al., 2005) might indicate the involvement of these areas in retrieval of episodic memories and biographical information associated with familiar individuals.

Viewing faces of familiar individuals also modulated neural activity in regions usually involved in emotional responses, such as the amygdala and the insula. Faces of strangers evoked a stronger response in the amygdala as compared to the faces of relatives and friends. The stronger response of the amygdala to faces of strangers could reflect the wary attitude we experience when seeing someone new. On the other hand, mothers viewing the face of their own child evoked a stronger response in the amygdala as compared to faces of familiar unrelated children. Seeing the face of one's own child also evoked a stronger response in the anterior insula. The insula responds to negatively valenced stimuli, such as expressions of disgust (Calder et al., 2001; Phillips et al., 2003), to being treated unfairly during negotiation games (Sanfey et al., 2003), but also might play a role also in mediating empathic reactions (Bartels and Zeki, 2000; Carr et al., 2003; Singer et al., 2004), and strong, positive emotions such as romantic love (Bartels and Zeki, 2000). The increased activity in the amygdala and in the insula elicited by viewing the face of one's child might reflect the intense attachment and vigilant protectiveness that characterize the maternal relationship.

Emotional response plays an essential role in familiar face recognition but is dissociable from conscious recognition. The dissociation of these complementary processes is demonstrated by physiological data from prosopagnosic patients and patients with Capgras syndrome (see Langdon, Chapter 45, this volume). Prosopagnosia is characterized by the inability to consciously recognize familiar faces, but when prosopagnosics see pictures of familiar faces, their skin conductance response differs significantly from their skin conductance response to strangers (Tranel et al., 1995; Ellis and Lewis, 2001). This response must be elicited by sufficient processing to identify the face for an emotional response but these processes are insufficient to evoke the conscious experience of recognition. By contrast, patients with Capgras syndrome can consciously recognize the visual features of a specific face as belonging to a familiar individual but believe that an impostor took the place of that familiar individual. Unlike prosopagnosics, patients with Capgras syndrome do not show a differential skin conductance response to familiar faces (Ellis and Lewis, 2001). These findings indicate that when the emotional response to a familiar face is altered or missing, as it is in Capgras syndrome, familiar face recognition can be disrupted. The absence of the emotional "glow" that accompanies familiar face recognition can lead to the failure of conscious recognition, which is complete only after one is certain of another's identity.

Extracting the meaning of facial expressions

The visual analysis of facial expression involves primarily extrastriate cortex in the pSTS, but extracting the significance of facial expression involves a distributed set of brain areas that are involved in action understanding and emotion. Perception of facial expression engages the putative human mirror neuron system (hMNS), in particular the frontal operculum, supposedly reflecting the role of engaging motor representations for producing facial expressions in understanding the meaning of facial expressions (Carr et al., 2004; Montgomery and Haxby, 2008; Montgomery et al., 2009). The similarity structure of patterns of response to particular facial expressions in the frontal operculum correlates highly with the similarity structure in the pSTS (Said et al., 2010), showing that the representational spaces for facial expressions in these two areas are closely related. Perception of facial expressions that convey particular emotions also engages areas that are associated with emotion processing (Breiter et al., 1996; Morris et al., 1996; Phillips et al., 1997; Whalen, 1998; Whalen et al., 1998, 2004; Wicker et al., 2003).

Mirror neurons were discovered in single-unit recording studies in monkeys and are characterized by their responses during both the execution of specific actions and the perception of others performing the same actions (Di Pellegrino et al., 1992; Gallese et al., 1996; Rizzolatti et al., 2001; Grafton, 2009). In humans the location of putative mirror neurons is established with fMRI by finding areas that respond both during the execution and perception of actions. FMRI adaptation and MVPA have provided ambiguous evidence for the specificity of these common responses to particular actions in humans (Lingnau et al., 2007; Dinstein et al., 2007, 2008; Kilner et al., 2009); nonetheless, the common responses to a range of actions are taken as a sufficient demonstration of mirror neuron properties. The areas that show these properties for the execution and perception of facial expressions are in the inferior parietal lobe, the frontal operculum, and premotor cortex (Figure 6.6).

The frontal opercular area that responds during the perception of facial expression has a more anterior and inferior location than a nearby area that responds during the perception of hand movements. This result shows that the representation of facial expression in the frontal hMNS can be distinguished from the representation of other types of actions (Montgomery and Haxby, 2008).

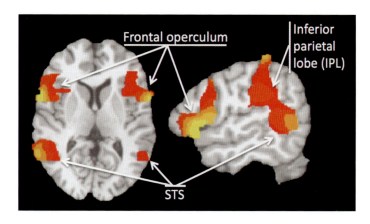

Fig. 6.6 Brain areas that responded during viewing, imitation, and production of facial expressions. From Montgomery et al., 2009, reprinted with permission from Sage Publications Ltd.

The response in the frontal opercular area is related to social cognition. We found that this response is enhanced for the perception of dynamic facial expressions, which have social meaning, as compared to the perception of non-social facial movements, but only in individuals who were rated as having average or high levels of empathy (Montgomery et al., 2009) (Figure 6.7). Individuals with low empathy ratings showed equivalent responses in this region to facial expressions and non-social facial movements. Thus, the response to facial expressions in the hMNS is better tuned to the social content of those expressions in more empathic individuals. No such differential response was seen in the pSTS. Previous behavioral work showed that individuals with higher empathy ratings are more likely to imitate others in social interactions (Chartrand and Bargh, 1999). The role of the frontal operculum in social cognition has also been implied from studies of action understanding in autism (Oberman et al., 2005; Dapretto et al., 2006; Oberman and Ramachandran, 2007).

Perception of expression also evokes activity in brain areas associated with emotion. The amygdala responds to many facial expressions but most strongly to fear (Breiter et al., 1996; Morris et al., 1996; Whalen, 1998; Whalen et al., 1998, 2004). The anterior insula responds to facial expressions of disgust (Phillips et al., 1997). The same insular region that responds when viewing an expression of disgust also responds when experiencing the emotion of disgust in response to an unpleasant odor (Wicker et al., 2003). The activity in these areas suggests that understanding the emotional meaning of expressions involves evoking the emotion itself—a simulation or mirroring of another's emotion that is analogous to the putative role of the hMNS in simulating or mirroring the motor actions of another. Perception of a facial expression, however, does not necessarily lead to a strong experience of the associated emotion. Similarly, viewing another's action need not elicit an automatic imitation of that action, although imitation of the actions and expressions of others is common and usually is not deliberate (Dimberg, 1982; Dimberg et al., 2000; Chartrand and Bargh, 1999). Subthreshold activation of muscles that would mimic a viewed expression can be detected with electromyography (Dimberg et al., 2000). Similarly, the activation of the insula and amygdala may reflect evocation of the representation of an emotion that plays a role in understanding others' emotions but does not lead to the explicit experience of that emotion, either because the conscious experience is actively suppressed or because the evoked representation is weak and below threshold.

Fig. 6.7 Stronger response to facial expressions than non-social facial movements in the frontal operculum in subjects with low, average, and high scores on a self-report measure of empathy (the Perspective Taking scale on the Interpersonal Reactivity Index). From Montgomery et al., 2009, reprinted with permission from Sage Publications Ltd.

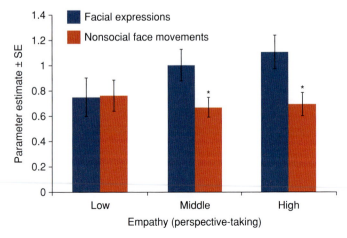

The role of the amygdala in facial expression perception appears multifaceted. The amygdala is critical for fear conditioning, but it appears to involve more than simply mirroring the emotion of fear. The amygdala can also be engaged by positive emotions and positive experiences. Whalen (1998) has proposed that the amygdala is part of a vigilance system that is activated in ambiguous situations with biological relevance. In this formulation, the ambiguity, not the emotion of fear, is the critical factor and can be either positive or negative.

Action understanding: eye gaze perception

Eye gaze is another changeable feature of faces that plays an important role in social communication. The pSTS plays a central role in the perception of others' eye gaze direction, but the modulation of pSTS activity by direct and averted eye gaze is variable (Nummenmaa and Calder, 2009). Analogous to the variable modulation of fusiform responses by familiarity, the variable response of the pSTS may be due to the ambiguous meaning of direct and averted eye gaze. Direct eye gaze—eye contact—can be a sign of interest, an attempt to catch one's attention, a sign of engagement in a social interaction, or a sign of threat. Averted gaze can signify lack of interest, lack of threat, or, conversely, can indicate another's attention to an event or presence elsewhere in the environment that one should also be aware of oneself. Consequently, small differences in psychological experiments can lend different meanings to direct and averted eye gaze and, thus, have variable effects on responses. The extraction of these different meanings is mediated by other neural systems that we include in the Extended System for face perception. Similar to the top-down effect of Extended System areas for person knowledge and emotion on fusiform responses to familiar faces, Extended System areas for spatial attention and mentalizing can exert a modulating influence on the pSTS response to eye gaze.

Perception of another's averted eye gaze evokes a spontaneous shift of one's own attention in the same direction (Friesen and Kingstone, 1998; Driver et al., 1999; Hietanen, 1999; Langton et al., 1999). We found that viewing faces with eye gaze averted unpredictably to the right and left evoked a stronger response in the intraparietal sulcus than did viewing faces with direct eye gaze (Hoffman and Haxby, 2000). The intraparietal sulcus plays a central role in shifting the direction of attention and in oculomotor control, along with the frontal eye fields (Beauchamp et al., 2001). The frontal eye fields were not included in the imaging volume in our study of gaze perception, which was restricted to coronal sections through posterior cortices (Figure 6.8a). Subsequent studies by others, however, have shown that the frontal eye fields also are engaged by eye gaze perception (Nummenmaa and Calder, 2009) (Figure 6.8b). The role of the neural system for shifting attention and eye movements in gaze perception is analogous to the role of the hMNS in the perception of facial expression.

Eye gaze perception additionally activates several other brain areas that play other roles in extracting information from the gaze of others. In a meta-analysis of imaging studies, Nummenmaa and Calder (2009) found consistent evidence for the engagement of the amygdala and MPFC, in addition to other areas. They proposed that the amygdala involvement reflects a role for this area in eye contact and the emotional response to being looked at. The role of the MPFC may relate to making inferences about the mental states that are implied by gaze, such as the focus of attention and intentions to act.

Modularity and distributed processing in neural representation

We present here a model of face perception that involves multiple brain regions that work in concert in various configurations to extract different types of information from faces. Our perspective contrasts with the emphasis others have placed on a dominant role for a single region

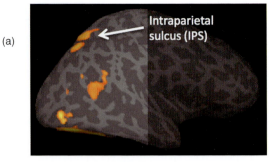

(a)

Intraparietal sulcus (IPS)

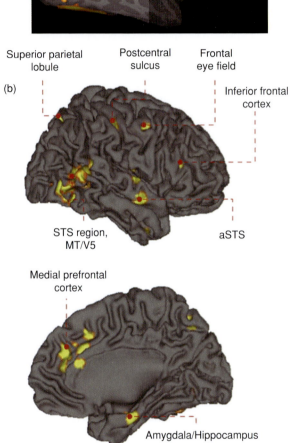

Superior parietal lobule

Postcentral sulcus

Frontal eye field

(b)

Inferior frontal cortex

STS region, MT/V5

aSTS

Medial prefrontal cortex

Amygdala/Hippocampus

Fig. 6.8 (a) A region in the intraparietal sulcus that responded during an eye gaze perception task. Frontal cortices are darkened to indicate that the imaging volume in this study (Hoffman and Haxby, 2000) did not include those areas. (b) Right hemisphere areas that showed involvement in gaze perception from a meta-analysis of PET and fMRI studies. Reprinted from *Trends in Cognitive Sciences*, **13**(3), Lauri Nummenmaa and Andrew J. Calder, Neural mechanisms of social attention, copyright (2009), with permission from Elsevier.

in fusiform cortex, the FFA (Kanwisher et al., 1997; Kanwisher and Yovel, 2006). The modular and distributed system perspectives on the neural architecture that underlies face perception, however, are not necessarily incompatible (see Kanwisher and Barton, Chapter 7, this volume). We are not casting doubt on the existence of the FFA as an area that responds more during perception of faces than during perception of other objects, or even denying that the FFA plays a major role in many face perception operations. Our position also is not that all parts of the distributed systems that we describe play an equipotential role in face perception. We propose, instead, that an adequate account of the neural architecture that underlies face perception, which accounts both for the data from neuroimaging experiments on face perception and for the full scope of cognitive operations that fall within the domain of face perception, cannot be achieved with an exclusive focus on a single area. Studies of face perception consistently find that the occipitotemporal extrastriate visual cortices that respond significantly to faces includes inferior occipital and STS cortices, in addition to fusiform cortex, and extends into regions that do not respond maximally to faces. Similarly, multiple face-selective regions have been found in monkey IT cortex (see Freiwald and Tsao, Chapter 36, this volume). Studies of familiar face recognition, facial expression perception, and gaze perception consistently find activations in numerous, widely-distributed brain areas, such as the MPFC, TPJ, frontal operculum, IPS, FEF, amygdala, and anterior insula. Cognitively, face perception involves more than passive viewing of still face images or matching face images. Face perception also includes recognition of familiar faces, interpretation of facial expressions, and processing eye gaze, among other functions. These face perception operations are dependent upon the activation of person knowledge, the activation of motor programs for producing facial expressions and for oculomotor control, and emotional responses. The contribution of a single region, such as the FFA, to face perception must take into account the context in which that region functions, both in terms of the distributed system of cortical areas and in terms of the full range of cognitive operations that fall within the domain of face perception.

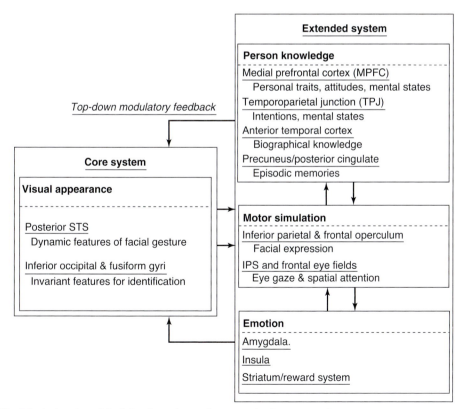

Fig. 6.9 Updated model of distributed neural systems for face perception.

Summary and conclusion

Face perception plays a multifaceted role in social communication, conveying many different types of information about the identity and mental states of others. Here we present an update of our model of the distributed system for face perception, which we first proposed in 2000 (Figure 6.9). This model divides brain areas that are involved in face perception into a Core System—occipitotemporal visual extrastriate areas that play a central role in the visual analysis of faces—and an Extended System—neural systems whose functions are not primarily visual but play critical roles in extracting information from faces. In the Core System, we emphasize a distinction between representation of invariant features that are critical for recognizing facial identity and representation of changeable features that are critical for facial gestures, such as expressions and eye gaze. We emphasize three sets of brain areas in the Extended System that are involved, respectively, in the representation of person knowledge, in action understanding (including gaze and attention), and in emotion. Familiar face recognition involves visual codes for familiar individuals in Core System areas in the fusiform, and possibly anterior temporal, cortex, along with the automatic activation of person knowledge and emotional responses. Facial expression involves visual codes in the STS, along with activation of representations of emotion and motor programs for producing expressions. Perception of eye gaze similarly involves visual codes in the STS, along with activation of brain areas for shifting attention and oculomotor control.

References

Bargh, J.A., Chen, M., and Burrows, L. (1996). Automaticity of social behavior: direct effects of trait construct and stereotype-activation on action. *Journal of Personality and Social Psychology*, **71**, 230–244.

Bartels, A. and Zeki, S. (2000). The neural basis of romantic love. *Neuroreport*, **11**, 3829–3834.

Beauchamp, M.S., Petit, L., Ellmore, T.M., Ingeholm, J., and Haxby J.V. (2001). A parametric fMRI study of overt and covert shifts of visuospatial attention. *Neuroimage*, **14**, 310–321.

Breiter, H.C., Etcoff, N.L., Whalen, P.J., *et al.* (1996). Response and habituation of the human amygdala during visual processing of facial expression. *Neuron*, **17**, 875–887.

Bruce, V. and Young, A. (1986). Understanding face recognition. *British Journal of Psychology*, **77**, 305–327.

Calder, A.J., Burton, A.M., Miller, P., Young, A.W., and Akamatsu, S. (2001). A principal component analysis of facial expressions. *Vision Research*, **41**, 1179–1208.

Calder, A.J. and Young, A.W. (2005). Understanding the recognition of facial identity and facial expression. *Nature Reviews Neuroscience*, **6**, 641–651.

Calder, A.J., Beaver, J.D., Davis, M.H., van Ditzhuijzen, J., Keane, J., and Lawrence, A.D. (2007). Disgust sensitivity predicts the insula and pallidal response to pictures of disgusting foods. *European Journal of Neuroscience*, **25**, 3422–3428.

Carr, L., Iacoboni, M., Dubeau, M.C., Mazziotta, J.C., and Lenzi GL. (2003). Neural mechanisms of empathy in humans: a relay from neural systems for imitation to limbic areas. *Proceedings of the National Academy of Science USA*, **100**, 5497–5502.

Chao, L.L., Martin, A., and Haxby, J.V. (1999). Are face-responsive regions selective only for faces? *Neuroreport*, **10**, 2945–2950.

Chartrand, T.L. and Bargh, J.A. (1999). The chameleon effect: the perception-behavior link and social interaction. *Journal of Personality and Social Psychology*, **76**, 893–910.

Connolly, A.C., Gobbini, M.I., and Haxby, J.V. (in press). Three virtues of similarity-based multi-voxel pattern analysis. In N. Kriegeskorte and G. Kreiman (eds.) *Understanding visual population codes (UVPC)–toward a common multivariate framework for cell recording and functional imaging*. Boston, MA: MIT Press.

Dapretto, M., Davies, M.S., Pfeifer, J.H., *et al.* (2006). Understanding emotions in others: mirror neuron dysfunction in children with autism spectrum disorders. *Nature Neuroscience*, **9**, 28–30.

Dimberg, U. (1982). Facial reactions to facial expressions. *Psychophysiology*, **19**, 643–647.

Dimberg, U., Thunberg, M., and Elmehed K. (2000). Unconscious facial reactions to emotional facial expressions. *Psychological Science*, **11**, 86–89.

Dinstein, I., Hasson, U., Rubin, N., and Heeger, D.J. (2007). Brain areas selective for both observed and executed movements. *Journal of Neurophysiology*, **98**, 1415–1427.

Dinstein, I., Gardner, J.L., Jazayeri, M., and Heeger, D.J. (2009). Executed and observed movements have different distributed representations in human aIPS. *Journal of Neuroscience*, **28**, 11231–11239.

di Pellegrino, G., Fadiga, L., Fogassi, L., Gallese, V., and Rizzolatti, G. (1992). Understanding motor events: a neuropsychological study. *Experimental Brain Research*, **91**, 176–180.

Douville, K., Woodard, J.L., Seidenberg, M., *et al.* (2005). Medial temporal lobe activity for recognition of recent and remote famous names: an event-related fMRI study. *Neuropsychologia*, **43**, 693–703.

Ellis, H.D. and Lewis, M.B. (2001). Capgras delusion: A window on face recognition. *Trends in Cognitive Sciences*, **5**, 149–156.

Engell, A.D., Gobbini, M.I., and Haxby, J.V. (2006). Gaze-change perception in the early visual cortex. *Society for Neuroscience Abstracts*, **438**.12.

Engell, A.D. and Haxby, J.V. (2007). Facial expression and gaze-direction in human superior temporal sulcus. *Neuropsychologia*, **45**, 3234–3241.

Freiwald, W.A., Tsao, D.Y., and Livingstone, M.S. (2009). A face feature space in the macaque temporal lobe. *Nature Neuroscience*, **12**, 1187–1196.

Gallese, V., Fadiga, L., Fogassi, L., and Rizzolatti, G. (1996). Action recognition in the premotor cortex. *Brain*, **119**, 593–609.

Greenwald, A.G. and Banaji, M.R. (1995). Implicit social cognition: attitudes, self-esteem, and stereotypes. *Psychological Review*, **102**, 4–27.

Gobbini, M. I., Leibenluft, E., Santiago, N., and Haxby, J. V. (2004). Social and emotional attachment in the neural representation of faces. *NeuroImage*, **22**, 1628–1635.

Gobbini, M.I. and Haxby, J.V. (2006). Neural response to the visual familiarity of faces. *Brain Research Bulletin*, **71**, 76–82.

Gobbini, M. I. and Haxby, J. V. (2007). Neural systems for recognition of familiar faces. *Neuropsychologia*, **45**, 32–41.

Gobbini, M.I., Koralek, A.C., Bryan, R.E., Montgomery, K.J., and Haxby, J.V. (2007). Two takes on the social brain: A comparison of theory of mind tasks. *Journal of Cognitive Neuroscience*, **19**, 1803–1814.

Gorno-Tempini, M.L., Price, C.J., Josephs, O., *et al.* (1998).The neural systems sustaining face and proper-name processing. *Brain*, **121**, 2103–2118.

Grafton, S.T. (2009). Embodied cognition and the simulation of action to understand others. *Annals of the New York Academy of Sciences*, **1156**, 97–117.

Grill-Spector, K., Knouf, N., and Kanwisher, N. (2004). The fusiform face area subserves face perception, not generic within-category identification. *Nature Neuroscience*, **7**, 555–562.

Hanson, S.J., Matsuka, T., and Haxby, J.V. (2004). Combinatorial codes in ventral temporal lobe for object recognition: Haxby (2001) revisited: is there a "face" area? *Neuroimage*, **23**, 156–166.

Hasselmo, M.E., Rolls, E.T., and Baylis, G.C. (1989). The role of expression and identity in the face-selective responses of neurons in the temporal visual cortex of the monkey. *Behavioral Brain Research*, **32**, 203–218.

Hasson, U., Nir, Y., Levy, I., Fuhrmann, G., and Malach, R. (2004). Intersubject synchronization of cortical activity during natural vision. *Science*, **303**, 1634–1640.

Haxby, J.V. Grady, C.L., Horwitz, B., *et al.* (1991). Dissociation of object and spatial visual processing pathways in human extrastriate cortex. *Proceedings of the National Academy of Science, U S A*, **88**, 1621–1625.

Haxby, J.V., Horwitz, B., Ungerleider, L.G., Maisog, J.M., Pietrini, P., and Grady, C.L. (1994) The functional organization of human extrastriate cortex: A PET-rCBF study of selective attention to faces and locations. *Journal of Neuroscience*, **14**, 6336–6353.

Haxby, J.V., Ungerleider, L.G., Clark, V.P., Schouten, J.L., Hoffman, E.A., and Martin, A. (1999). The effect of face inversion on activity in human neural systems for face and object perception. *Neuron*, **22**, 189–199.

Haxby, J.V., Hoffman, E.A., and Gobbini, M.I. (2000). The distributed human neural system for face perception. *Trends in Cognitive Sciences*, **4**, 223–233.

Haxby, J.V., Gobbini, M.I., Furey, M.L., Ishai, A., Schouten, J.L., and Pietrini, P. (2001). Distributed and overlapping representations of faces and objects in ventral temporal cortex. *Science*, **293**, 2425–2430.

Haynes, J.D. and Rees, G. (2006). Decoding mental states from brain activity in humans. *Nature Reviews Neuroscience*, **7**, 523–534.

Hoffman, E.A. and Haxby, J.V. (2000). Distinct representations of eye gaze and identity in the distributed human neural system for face perception. *Nature Neuroscience*, **3**, 80–84.

Idson, L.C. and Mischel, W. (2001). The personality of familiar and significant people: the lay perceiver as a social-cognitive theorist. *Journal of Personality and Social Psychology*, **80**, 585–96.

Ishai, A. (2008). Let's face it: It's a cortical network. *NeuroImage*, **40**, 415–419.

Ishai, A., Ungerleider, L.G., Martin, A., Schouten, J.L., and Haxby, J.V. (1999). Distributed representation of objects in the human ventral visual pathway. *Proceedings of the National Academy of Sciences, USA*, **96**, 9379–9384.

Ishai, A., Schmidt, C.F., and Boesiger, P. (2005). Face perception is mediated by a distributed cortical network. *Brain Research Bulletin*, **67**, 87–93.

Kanwisher, N. and Yovel, G. (2006). The fusiform face area: a cortical region specialized for the perception of faces. *Philosophical Transactions of the Royal Society B*, **361**, 2109–2128.

Kanwisher, N., McDermott, J., and Chun, M.M. (1997). The fusiform face area: a module in human extrastriate cortex specialized for face perception. *Journal of Neuroscience*, **17**, 4302–4311.

Kiani, R., Esteky, H., Mirpour, K., and Tanaka, K. (2007). Object category structure in response patterns of neuronal population in monkey inferior temporal cortex. *Journal of Neurophysiology*. **97**, 4296–4309.

Kilner, J.M., Neal, A., Weiskopf, N., Friston, K.J., and Frith C.D. (2009). Evidence of mirror neurons in human inferior frontal gyrus. *Journal of Neuroscience*, **29**, 10153–10159.

Kosaka, H. Omori, M., Iidaka, T. *et al.* (2003). Neural substrates participating in acquisition of facial familiarity: an fMRI study. *Neuroimage*, **20**, 1734–1742.

Kriegeskorte, N., Formisano, E., Sorger, B., and Goebel, R. (2007). Individual faces elicit distinct response patterns in human anterior temporal cortex. *Proceedings of the National Academy of Sciences, USA*, **104**, 20600–20605.

Leibenluft, E., Gobbini, M.I., Harrison, T., and Haxby J.V. (2004). Mothers' neural activation in response to pictures of their children and other children. *Biological Psychiatry*, **56**, 225–32.

Leveroni, C.L., Seidenberg, M., Mayer, A.R., Mead, L.A., Binder, J.R., and Rao SM. (2000). Neural systems underlying the recognition of familiar and newly learned faces. *Journal of Neuroscience*, **20**, 878–86.

Lingnau, A., Gesierich, B., and Caramazza, A. (2009). Asymmetric fMRI adaptation reveals no evidence for mirror neurons in humans. *Proceedings of the National Academy of Sciences, USA*, **106**, 9925–9930.

Mitchell, J.P., Heatherton, T.F., and Macrae, C.N. (2002). Distinct neural systems subserve person and object knowledge. *Proceedings of the National Academy of Sciences, USA*, **99**, 15238–15234.

Montgomery, K.J. and Haxby J.V. (2008). Mirror neuron system differentially activated by facial expressions and social hand gestures: a functional magnetic resonance imaging study. *Journal of Cognitive Neuroscience*, **20**, 1866–1877.

Montgomery, K.J., Seeherman, K.R., and Haxby, J.V. (2009). The well-tempered social brain. *Psychological Science*, **20**, 1211–1213.

Morris, J.S., Frith, CD., Perrett, D.I., *et al*. (1996). A differential neural response in the human amygdala to fearful and happy facial expressions. *Nature*, **383**, 812–815.

Nakamura, K., Kawashima, R., Sato, N., *et al*. (2000). Functional delineation of the human occipito-temporal areas related to face and scene processing. *A PET study. Brain*, **123**, 1903–1912.

Norman, K.A., Polyn, S.M., Detre, G.J., and Haxby, J.V. (2006). Beyond mind-reading: multi-voxel pattern analysis of fMRI data. *Trends in Cognitive Science*, **10**, 424–430.

Nummenmaa, L. and Calder, A.J. (2009). Neural mechanisms of social attention. *Trends in Cognitive Sciences*. **13**, 135–143.

Oberman, L.M., Hubbard, E.M., McCleery, J.P., Altschuler, E.L., Ramachandran, V.S., and Pineda, J.A. (2005). EEG evidence for mirror neuron dysfunction in autism spectrum disorders. *Brain Research, Cognitive Brain Research*, **24**, 190–198.

Oberman, L.M. and Ramachandran, V.S. (2007). The simulating social mind: the role of the mirror neurons system and simulation in the social and communicative deficits of autism spectrum disorders. *Psychological Bulletin*, **133**, 310–327.

O'Toole, A.J., Jiang, F., Abdi, H., Penard, N., Dunlop, J.P., and Parent, M.A. (2007) Theoretical, statistical, and practical perspectives on pattern-based classification approaches to the analysis of functional neuroimaging data. *Journal of Cognitive Neuroscience*, **18**, 1735–1752.

Phillips, M.L., Young, A.W., Senior, C., *et al*. (1996). A specific neural substrate for perceiving facial expressions of disgust. *Nature*, **389**, 495–498.

Phillips, M.L., Drevets, W.C., Rauch, S.L., and Lane, R. (2003). Neurobiology of emotion perception. I: the neural basis of normal emotion perception. *Biological Psychiatry*, **54**, 504–514.

Puce, A., Allison, R., Bentin, S., Gore, J.C., and McCarthy, G. (1998). Temporal cortex activation in humans viewing eye and mouth movements. *Journal of Neuroscience*, **18**, 2188–2199.

Rajimehr, R., Young, J.C., and Tootell, R.B.H. (2009). An anterior temporal face patch in human cortex, predicted by macaque maps. *Proceedings of the National Academy of Sciences, USA*, **106**, 1995–2000.

Rizzolatti, G., Fogassi, L., and Gallese, V. (2001). Neurophysiological mechanisms underlying the understanding and imitation of action. *Nature Reviews Neuroscience*, **2**, 661–670.

Rolls, E.T. (2000). Functions of the primate temporal lobe visual cortices in invariant visual object and face recognition. *Neuron*, **27**, 205–218.

Rotshtein, P., Henson, R. N., Treves, A., Driver, J., and Dolan, R. J. (2005). Morphing Marilyn into Maggie dissociates physical and identity face representations in the brain. *Nature Neuroscience*, **8**, 107–113.

Said, C.P., Moore, C.D., Engell, A.D., Todorov, A., and Haxby J.V. (2010). Distributed representations of dynamic facial expression in the superior temporal sulcus. *Journal of Vision*, **10**: 11, 1–12.

Sanfey, A.G., Rilling, J.K., Aronson, J.A., Nystrom, L.E., and Cohen, J.D. (2003). The neural basis of economic decision-making in the ultimatum game. *Science*, **300**, 1755–1758.

Singer, T., Seymou, B., O'Doherty, J., Kaube, H., Dolan, R.J., and Frith, C.D. (2004). Empathy for pain involves the affective but not sensory components of pain. *Science*, **303**, 1157–1162.

Todorov, A. and Uleman, J.S. (2002). Spontaneous trait inferences are bound to actors' faces: evidence from a false recognition paradigm. *Journal of Personality and Social Psychology*, **83**, 1051–1065.

Todorov, A., Gobbini, M.I., Evans, K.K., and Haxby, J.V. (2007). Spontaneous retrieval of affective person knowledge in face perception. *Neuropsychologia*, **45**, 163–173.

Todorov, A., Said, C.P., Engell, A.D., and Oosterhof, N.N. (2008). Understanding evaluation of faces on social dimensions. *Trends in Cognitive Sciences*, **12**, 455–460.

Tranel, D., Damasio, A.R., and Damasio, H. (1995). Double dissociation between overt and covert recognition. *Journal of Cognitive Neurosciences*, **7**, 425–432.

Vuilleumier, P., Armony, J.L., Driver, J., and Dolan, R.J. (2001). Effects of attention and emotion on face processing in the human brain: An event-related fMRI study. *Neuron*, **30**, 829–841.

Whalen, P.J. (1998). Fear, vigilance, and ambiguity: initial neuroimaging studies of the human amygdala. *Current Directions in Psychological Science*, 7, 177–188.

Whalen, P.J., Rauch, S.L., Etcoff, N.L., McInerney, S.C., Lee, M.B., and Jenike, M.A. (1998). Masked presentations of emotional face expressions modulate amygdala activity without explicit knowledge. *Journal of Neuroscience*, 18, 411–418.

Whalen, P.J., Kagan, J., Cook, R.G., *et al.* (2004). Human amygdala responsivity to masked fearful eye whites. *Science*, 306, 2061.

Wicker, B., Keysers, C., Plailly, J., Royet, J.-P., Gallese, V., and Rizzolatti, G. (2003). Both of us disgusted in *my* insula: The common neural basis of seeing and feeling disgust. *Neuron*, 40, 655–664.

Winston, J.S., Henson, R.N.A., Fine-Goulden, M.R., and Dolan, R.J. (2004). fMRI-adaptation reveals dissociable neural representations of identity and expression in face perception. *Journal of Neurophysiology*, 92, 1830–1839.

Chapter 7

The Functional Architecture of the Face System: Integrating Evidence from fMRI and Patient Studies

Nancy Kanwisher and Jason J.S. Barton

Introduction

Like all complex cognitive processes, face perception is neither a single function nor served by a single cortical region. Many different types of information can be extracted from faces. These can depend on very different properties of the face, and are used for very different cognitive purposes. Anatomically, functional neuroimaging has revealed a core set of areas that are selectively activated during face perception, including the fusiform face area or FFA (Kanwisher et al., 1997; McCarthy et al., 1997), the occipital face area or OFA (Gauthier et al., 2000b), and the face-selective region in the posterior superior temporal sulcus or fSTS (Puce et al., 1998). These regions show a right hemisphere dominance: while there are similar face-selective regions in the left hemisphere, these are less consistently detected, show statistically weaker patterns of activation by faces, and have fewer voxels than their right hemispheric counterparts.

Current neuroanatomic models link these core face-processing regions with a number of other regions comprising the "extended face-processing system" (Gobbini and Haxby 2007). This includes the anterior temporal lobe (Rajimehr et al., 2009; Tsao et al., 2008), the inferior frontal gyrus, precuneus, and amygdala. These additional regions likely participate by processing emotional and semantic information (e.g. biographical information, episodic experiences about the people identified), are probably not specific to either faces or even visual stimuli, and will not be the focus of this review.

Our goal in the present chapter is to ask what functions are performed by each of the "core" face processing regions: the FFA, OFA, and fSTS. We review the data from two complementary sources: functional imaging in healthy subjects and behavioral data from neurological subjects with damage to these regions. Data from functional neuroimaging (mainly functional magnetic resonance imaging; fMRI) enable us to determine which regions are specifically engaged by which stimuli and which tasks; fMRI adaptation and pattern classification methods even enable us to characterize the representations extracted in each. However, fMRI can only tell us that a given region is sensitive to a particular stimulus property, or (in some cases) that activity or patterns of responses in a given area are correlated with behavior. FMRI cannot tell us if the processing required to perceive that property occurs in that area, or if it occurs elsewhere and merely modulates the activity in the cortical region in question. In contrast, lesion data can answer the crucial question of whether a given brain region is necessary for a given computation. In the case of face processing in humans, such data comes mainly from subjects with acquired prosopagnosia, the loss of the ability to recognize faces (Barton et al., 2003).

Human lesion data regarding a process as complex as face perception have limitations, however. First, many lesions are large and affect more than one cortical area. Second, interpretation is complicated when critical regions exist in both right and left hemispheres. We do not know, for example, whether the left FFA performs a function complementary to that of the right FFA, or if the system has some redundancy. With redundancy, intact performance after a unilateral lesion cannot be taken to imply that the lesioned area is not involved in that task or process. Third, on a practical level, localizing small cortical lesions is not always easy, and the imaging in many older reports suffers from imprecision that renders it impossible to know which if any of the regions identified with fMRI are compromised. Fortunately, newer studies incorporating both high-resolution structural MRI and fMRI from neurological patients are starting to appear (Fox et al., 2009a; Marotta et al., 2001; Schiltz et al., 2006; Steeves et al., 2006). Despite these limitations of the standard methods, emerging data from both fMRI and lesion studies permit some tentative conclusions about the function of each of the "core" face processing regions. We begin with a discussion of the possible functional components of face perception. We then discuss each of the face processing regions in turn, first considering the evidence from fMRI concerning their possible functions, and then the evidence from human lesion studies.

Functional components of face perception

Face detection

Many computer-vision algorithms separate face detection from face identification (Tsao and Livingstone, 2008), and certainly it is possible to detect a face without processing the identity of the person. This is the classic situation of subjects with acquired prosopagnosia, who have lost the ability to recognize the identity of faces but can still recognize that a face is a face and not a car (Barton et al., 2003). This distinction between intact basic-level detection but impaired "within-category" identification for faces is an integral part of the definition of prosopagnosia, and distinguishes it from general visual agnosia, in which subjects lose the ability to discriminate between objects of different categories. These considerations support the possibility that face detection could be a distinct stage of face processing, perhaps even serving a "gating function" for activating the face perception system (Liu et al., 2002; Tsao and Livingstone, 2008,). However, there is no definitive evidence for separate functional modules or anatomic substrates for detection versus subsequent stages of face perception. Also, in some computational models, detection and discrimination are regarded merely as tasks that vary along a continuum of specificity in terms of the information demanded, but which both engage the same neural substrate (Riesenhuber et al., 2004). Indeed, some brain regions have been implicated in both face detection and the more fine-grained processing necessary for discriminating one face from another (Grill-Spector et al., 2004).

Structural encoding of faces

Once a face has been detected, its structural properties must be extracted and represented in sufficient detail to support the many types of information we routinely extract from faces, such as gender, age, ethnicity, attractiveness, mood, direction of attention, and personal identity. Although sometimes depicted as a single stage, there may be different levels and varieties of structural encoding (Bruce and Young, 1986). Thus some evidence suggests that the OFA is sensitive to any variation in the physical shape of the face, whereas the FFA is sensitive to changes that correlate with an alteration in the perceived identity (Rotshtein et al., 2005), both of which could be considered aspects of structural encoding. Neural network models often incorporate distinct levels of processing, with a layer of viewpoint-specific representations for the two-dimensional facial image converging upon a second layer of viewpoint-independent representations of three-dimensional facial structure (Rosen 2003).

There may also be variation in the type of structural facial properties encoded, for example between processing of the basic parts of the face (eyes, nose, mouth) versus the precise configuration or spacing of those parts (Maurer et al., 2002; Liu et al., 2010; McKone and Yovel, 2008; Pitcher et al., 2007). Another important distinction is a contrast between static and dynamic properties of faces (Gobbini and Haxby, 2007) discussed in more detail below. While classic cognitive models portray a common encoding stage that feeds into both identity and expression processing (Bruce and Young, 1986), different types of perceptual information may be important for these different kinds of information. For all these reasons, it may be incorrect to treat "perceptual encoding" as a single cognitive process or unitary stage. Whether these distinctions are also reflected in the anatomy of the face-processing network will be considered below.

Visual recognition of faces

The most obvious information we extract from a face is the identity of the person. Identity recognition requires a system for storing perceptual descriptions of the appearance of each person we know, plus the ability to compare incoming perceptual representations to these stored representations. Furthermore, recognizing that a face is familiar usually but not always triggers additional multimodal cognitive processes that are not face-specific in nature (Gobbini and Haxby, 2007). Thus face recognition may lead to retrieval of a name and a variety of semantic information about the person, such as their occupation and social relation to us, specific episodes we have experienced with them, and our emotional response to them. These data are multimodal because their retrieval can also be activated through other routes, such as hearing the person's voice or being given their name. By "visual recognition" we mean the process of matching the input to a stored visual description (or "face recognition unit" in the Bruce and Young 1986 model), not the subsequent and separate process of accessing a semantic representation of the person (or "person identity nodes" in the Bruce and Young 1986 model). The distinction between the two is apparent from the common occurrence of realizing you have seen someone before, yet not being able to say how you know them or who they are (Young et al., 1985).

Neuropsychological evidence also supports the dissociation between visual recognition of faces, and retrieval of semantic information or names from faces. While subjects with right anterior temporal lobectomies have difficulty recognizing faces as familiar, subjects with lobectomies on the left perform normally on familiarity decisions about faces but are impaired in retrieving the person's name (Glosser et al., 2003). Damage to the right temporal pole can lead to failure to access people-related semantic information without other semantic deficits (Ellis et al., 1989; Evans et al., 1995; Hanley et al., 1989; Thompson et al., 2004). Prosopagnosic subjects, on the other hand, usually have preserved semantic information about people, when tested through other modalities and stimuli than faces (Barton et al., 2001).

Extracting dynamic social information from faces

Much of the information we extract from a face is dynamic in nature. Facial movements help in speech interpretation, as in the McGurk effect (Campbell 2008, Chapter 31, this volume), and faces change over seconds and minutes as people show different emotional expressions. People shift their eyes repeatedly: gaze direction is an important cue to the focus of attention and social engagement of the individual before you. Although mannerisms can provide cues to identity also, dynamic information is probably more critical for the interpretation of social signals than for individual recognition.

Facial expressions are sometimes reduced to six basic types (happiness, sadness, anger, fear, disgust, and surprise). However, we are also capable of subtler expression judgments, as indicated in the wide range of answers for mental states in the "Reading the Mind in the Eyes test" (Baron-Cohen et al., 2001). Other complex social judgments such as likeability or trustworthiness are also possible from a face (Todorov et al, Chapter 32; Zebrowitz, Chapter 3, this volume). The "thin slice" paradigms show that, when asked to rate the effectiveness of a person as a teacher from a very brief and silent movie clip of the person, judges' ratings are highly correlated with the ratings of the filmed person by students at the end of the semester (Ambady and Rosenthal, 1993). The extent to which dynamic rather than static information is used in various social judgments is an important question for future investigation.

Extracting other information from faces

Besides identity and the social signals of expression, speech and gaze, other information can be gleaned from a face, such as gender, ethnicity, age, and attractiveness. The degree to which extraction of these attributes shares neural machinery with either identity or dynamic social processing is uncertain. In a functional sense, at least some of these would appear to be linked. Thus, gender and ethnicity can be considered broad categories within identity, in which a perceptual class is constructed from structural features common to members of that group. Also, while expression and identity are orthogonal properties (e.g. George can look sad or he can look happy, and this does not change the fact that he is George), gender and ethnicity are not orthogonal to identity. The identity of a face inevitably carries a specific ethnicity and gender as a part of its identity (e.g. George is always Chinese and always male), and to some degree this is also true of attractiveness. Age has a more ambiguous relationship to identity: while at any given moment a specific individual must be of a certain age range (e.g. George in 2009 is in his 30s, so I would not mistake a 60-year-old man for George), it is also possible to recognize the same person from images taken at different points in life (e.g. recognizing George in his Grade 7 yearbook). Also, age, gender, ethnicity, and possibly attractiveness, are stable across changes in mood, just as identity is. Hence it is reasonable to expect that these variables may be properties that emerge from the encoding in the identity stream. Consistent with this idea, prosopagnosic subjects are frequently impaired in attractiveness judgments, and an fMRI study suggests modulation of face responses in the FFA by attractiveness (Iaria et al., 2008).

Regarding other properties of faces, the lesion literature is highly variable: some prosopagnosics can make judgments about age, gender, expression, or direction of gaze from faces (Bruyer et al., 1983; Evans et al., 1995; Sergent and Poncet 1990; Sergent and Villemure, 1989; Mangini and Biederman, 2001; Tranel et al., 1988), but others have difficulty (Campbell et al., 1990; de Haan and Campbell, 1991; Kracke, 1994; Young and Ellis, 1989). The implications of a single dissociation between identity processing and that for age, gender or ethnicity must be treated cautiously, though. Given that the required specificity regarding facial structure is likely lower with a category judgment for age or gender than with identification of one unique individual, sparing of the former may merely indicate that such judgments can be supported by weak residual output from a partially damaged face network, while identification cannot. Furthermore, some of these broader categorical judgments may be supported by external or partial data that do not involve face mechanisms: for example, cues like wrinkling may support age judgments, without actually tapping into encoding of facial structure (Young and Ellis, 1989).

Division of labor among brain regions

Which brain regions are involved in each of these components of face processing? We now review the evidence from fMRI and patient studies on this question, addressing each core face-processing region in turn.

The fusiform face area

The best-studied cortical region engaged in face perception is the FFA, a small region on the lateral aspect of the fusiform gyrus, on the inferior surface of the right hemisphere of every normal subject (Kanwisher et al., 1997; McCarthy et al., 1997). This region can be identified in virtually all normal subjects by its higher response to faces than to objects in fMRI (see Figure 7.1, top row). Neuroimaging studies across many labs have replicated the existence of this region and investigated its properties. Furthermore, damage to the fusiform gyrus is frequent in subjects with some forms of prosopagnosia (Barton, 2008). Whether or not such damage specifically involves the FFA is a matter of current investigation. The specificity for faces is the key defining feature of both the FFA and the phenomenon of prosopagnosia; evidence on both is discussed next.

Face specificity in the FFA

The FFA responds at least twice as strongly when subjects view faces (even schematic faces or cat faces) as it does for other non-face stimuli. Three lines of evidence indicate that the FFA responds specifically to *faces*, and not simply to lower-level stimulus features usually present in faces (such as a pair of horizontally-arranged eye-like dark regions). First, the FFA responds vigorously and similarly to a variety of face stimuli that differ widely in their low-level features, including front and profile photographs of faces (Tong et al., 2000), line drawings of faces (Spiridon and Kanwisher, 2002), cat faces (Tong et al., 2000), and two-tone stylized "Mooney faces." Second, the FFA response to upright Mooney faces is much higher than to inverted Mooney stimuli, in which the face is difficult to detect (Kanwisher et al., 1998; Rhodes et al., 2004), even though most low-level features such as luminance and spatial frequency composition are identical in upright and inverted images. Finally, for bistable stimuli such as the Rubin face-vase illusion (Hasson et al., 2001), or for binocularly rivalrous stimuli in which a face is presented to one eye and a non-face object is presented to the other eye (Pasley et al., 2004; Tong et al., 1998; Williams et al., 2004), the FFA response is greater when subjects report perceiving a face than when they do not, even though the retinal image has not changed (Andrews et al., 2002). For all these reasons, it is difficult to account for the selectivity of the FFA in terms of lower-level features that co-vary with faces. Instead, these findings support the idea that the FFA is selectively engaged in the perception of faces.

It has been argued that the strong FFA response to faces is not necessarily a marker for face-specificity, but may reflect engagement of a mechanism required whenever subjects discriminate

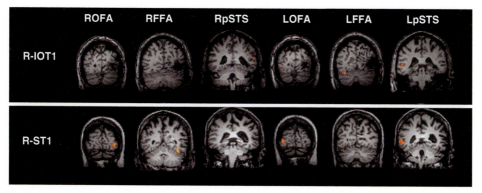

Fig. 7.1 Coronal structural MRI with functional MRI data contrasting face and object-viewing in two patients. Subject R-IOT1 has lost the right FFA and OFA, while subject R-STS1 has lost the right STS alone from the core face network. Orange marks regions with greater response to faces. (Right hemisphere is on the right of each brain image.) Courtesy of Chris Fox.

between highly similar exemplars within a category (Gauthier et al., 1999a). This idea was refuted in a number of studies, such as (Yovel and Kanwisher, 2004), who showed that when subjects perform within-category discrimination for faces and houses that have been matched for discriminability, the FFA still responds about three times as strongly during face discrimination as house discrimination. The "expertise" variant of this hypothesis states that the FFA responds more strongly not only to faces but also to objects for which the observer has a particular expertise. While some evidence for this hypothesis was presented early on (Gauthier et al., 1999b, 2000a; Xu, 2005), the fMRI evidence since then has consistently argued against the expertise hypothesis (for reviews see McKone et al., 2007; McKone and Robbins, Chapter 9, this volume).

Face specificity of prosopagnosia

Paralleling the debate on the specificity of the FFA for face processing is a more longstanding controversy about whether the prosopagnosic deficit is limited to faces. Integral to the definition of prosopagnosia is the idea that the recognition impairment is not part of a more general agnostic or amnestic disorder. That is, while impaired face recognition can be part of a broader range of impairments in disorders such as Alzheimer's disease and general visual agnosia, such subjects should not be considered prosopagnosic. Although many prosopagnosic subjects do have mild deficits in other object recognition or memory processes, this is not surprising given the usually large size of their lesions. Still, these additional deficits must not be severe enough to explain their prosopagnosia.

While prosopagnosic subjects can discriminate between broad visual object categories, a more relevant question is whether, as with faces, they have trouble distinguishing between objects of a similar type (e.g. different models of cars). If so, this would support suggestions that their problem with faces may merely be the most dramatic example of a more general difficulty in discriminating different versions of the same object type–so-called "within-category" judgments (Davidoff and Landis 1990; Gauthier et al., 1999a). If not, this would support the proposal that prosopagnosia arises from damage to a face-specific process.

Face selectivity has proved to be a logically slippery concept in prosopagnosia, however. First, what can be made of the demonstrations that prosopagnosic subjects are impaired in discriminations involving other object classes (Gauthier et al., 1999a)? As already stated, prosopagnosic lesions are often large and sometimes multiple. Additional difficulties recognizing non-face objects do not necessarily imply that both faces and non-face objects use the same processes and structures; rather, these problems may arise through damage to structures adjacent to face-processing modules. Second, what should we make of demonstrations that a prosopagnosic subject performs normally on some test of non-face object recognition? This is also problematic. For one, only a finite number of object classes can be tested, and the question is open as to how many classes need to be tested before concluding that no other object type is affected. For another, an important confound in testing non-face object recognition is determining and calibrating for premorbid expertise with other object classes (Diamond and Carey 1986, Gauthier et al., 2000b). Universal expertise can be assumed for very few other objects besides faces in human experience: thus, a test of bird recognition may be too hard for someone with no interest in birds but too easy for an enthusiast.

With these caveats in mind, we can examine the prosopagnosic data. The older literature contains many examples of subjects with trouble identifying subtypes ("subordinate categories") of items such as cars, food, or coins, or specific individuals ("exemplars") of items such as buildings, handwriting, or personal clothing (Damasio et al., 1982; de Haan and Campbell, 1991; Lhermitte et al., 1972; Whiteley and Warrington, 1977). There are also examples of prosopagnosic subjects who can identify personal belongings (De Renzi 1986), individual animals (Bruyer et al., 1983; McNeil and Warrington, 1993), specific places (Bruyer et al., 1983; Evans et al., 1995), cars (Bruyer et al., 1983; Henke et al., 1998), and different eyeglasses (Farah et al., 1995), though measures of reaction time and signal detection parameters may suggest subtle deficits in non-face processing even when accuracy rates are good (Gauthier et al., 1999a). The effect of premorbid expertise was seldom considered in any of these reports, however, and the limited neuroimaging data of these early reports makes it difficult to relate the findings to lesion anatomy.

Nevertheless, additional support for face-specificity of the processes affected in prosopagnosia comes from a study of a non-prosopagnosic subject, CK (Moscovitch et al., 1997). This subject was severely impaired at even very simple object discrimination tasks, yet normal on a range of face perception tasks. This type of double dissociation is useful for excluding the greater difficulty of face tasks as an account of prosopagnosia. Unfortunately, CK's neuroimaging did not reveal any clear lesion.

A more recent study of nine prosopagnosic subjects examined recognition of fruit and vegetables, arguing that, like faces, food is a reasonably universal human interest (Barton et al., 2004). This study found impairments in almost all subjects, despite the marked variability of their lesions, with the exception of a borderline normal result in one subject with a small right fusiform and occipital lesion that an fMRI study confirmed had eliminated the FFA (de Gelder et al., 2003). From this subject's data, one may tentatively suggest that relatively modest damage involving the FFA may result in face-specific impairments, though more data is required to establish this firmly. Though not studied with fMRI, another subject with a hematoma in the region of the FFA was said to have an isolated impairment in face recognition, but this was based solely on the fact that he recognized 6/6 animal faces and 6/6 famous places (Wada and Yamamoto 2001). Prosopagnosic subject FB, with structural MRI showing somewhat more extensive damage to the right fusiform gyrus, inferior temporal gyrus and inferior occipital gyrus, did as well as her husband and controls on tests of identifying fruits, vegetables, flowers, and birds (Riddoch et al., 2008).

In summary, many prosopagnosic subjects do not have deficits for faces only. Whether the deficits for non-face objects in these patients result from damage to the FFA or nearby regions remains unclear. Lack of face specificity is not in itself surprising given the large and multiple lesions present in many patients. In principle, a single subject with a small lesion whose deficit was face-specific would be sufficient to prove that the essential prosopagnosic deficit is limited to faces. At present, there are tantalizing data from a few subjects with lesions limited to the vicinity of the FFA, but more testing with more categories and better calibration for expertise are needed to establish this point.

What processes are conducted in the FFA?

If we accept that the FFA may make a special and specific contribution to face processing, the next question is: What function does it actually perform? That is, in which of the many aspects of face perception outlined in Part II of this book is the FFA engaged?

Face detection The greater response of the FFA to faces than other objects may suggest a role in face detection. However, the fact that prosopagnosic subjects are not impaired in discriminating basic categories of objects, and easily recognize that a face is a face and not a hat, would argue that face detection is preserved in this disorder. Given the evidence that damage to the vicinity of the right FFA is present in at least some cases of prosopagnosia (Barton 2008) and not necessarily in general visual agnosia (Steeves et al., 2006), this would argue against the hypothesis that the FFA is necessary for discriminating faces from other objects. However, more demanding tests of face detection, such as the perception of hidden faces in complex scenes, or Mooney faces in two-tone stimuli, suggest subtle face detection deficits in developmental prosopagnosia (Garrido et al., 2008). Unfortunately, these subjects do not have visible lesions on neuroimaging, and the current evidence indicates that the FFA is preserved in developmental prosopagnosia (Avidan et al.,

2005). Similar difficulties with face detection in Mooney faces and Arcimboldo paintings (by the 16th-century Italian painter, depicting bowls of fruit that could also be seen as faces) occur in patients with general visual agnosia, as in one patient with bilateral lesions of the lateral occipital complex and OFA (Steeves et al., 2006), but have seldom been studied in subjects with a more selective acquired prosopagnosia. Thus, more evidence is required regarding a possible role for the FFA in face detection.

Structural encoding Many lines of evidence implicate the FFA in the structural encoding of faces, consistent with the overall model of Haxby et al. (2000). First, the FFA is sensitive to the basic physical structure of a face, including both the presence of face features (eyes, nose, mouths), as well as the proper configuration of facial features (Liu et al., 2010). The FFA also shows greater adaptation for upright than inverted faces (Mazard et al., 2005; Yovel and Kanwisher, 2005): consistent with the behavioral face inversion effect, the FFA better discriminates faces when they are upright than inverted. Another behavioral effect cited as evidence of configural encoding is the composite face effect, in which recognition of one vertical half of a face is difficult when it is combined with the lower half from a different face (Young et al., 1987). A correlate of this composite effect has also been shown in the FFA (Mazard et al., 2005; Schiltz and Rossion, 2005, 2006).

Second, numerous studies using fMRI adaptation (Grill-Spector et al., 1999; Kourtzi and Kanwisher 2001) have demonstrated sensitivity of the FFA to differences in face identity (e.g. (Avidan et al., 2005; Eger et al., 2005; Gauthier and Nelson 2001; Pourtois et al., 2005; Rotshtein et al., 2005; Yovel and Kanwisher 2004). This adaptation across repeated images of the same face is found even when those images differ in position (Grill-Spector et al., 1999) image size (Andrews and Schluppeck, 2004; Grill-Spector et al., 1999) and spatial scale (Eger et al., 2004). These findings indicate that the FFA does not simply encode low-level properties of the image of the face, but the structure of the face, and furthermore that these are structural properties that are relevant to the processing of identity. Indeed, adaptation in the FFA was found not only for identical faces but also for faces that were perceived as from the same identity despite morph-induced changes in the image, whereas adaptation was not found across changes in perceived identity (Rotshtein et al., 2005). Similarly, Fox et al. (2009b) showed that release from adaptation occurred in the FFA only when subjects responded that they perceived a change in identity.

Data from individuals with prosopagnosia support a role for the FFA in structural encoding of faces. While not all prosopagnosic subjects have lesions that encompass the fusiform gyrus, many do, with either right or bilateral fusiform damage being the classic lesion (Barton, 2008). While prosopagnosic subjects are rare, a survey of the largest recent series suggested that damage to the fusiform gyrus was particularly associated with an apperceptive variant of prosopagnosia (Barton 2008), meaning that their deficit lies in the formation of an accurate percept of the face before them, rather than in matching what they are seeing with stored facial memories, the problem in the associative variant. These subjects were shown to have a severe perceptual deficit in the encoding of configural relationships of facial features, which was not present in a prosopagnosic subject with more anterior temporal damage (Barton et al., 2002). Of note, this configural deficit could also be demonstrated with non-face stimuli (Barton and Cherkasova, 2005; Barton, 2009; Barton et al., 2007). In at least one of these subjects with apperceptive prosopagnosia, fMRI showed loss of the FFA (de Gelder et al., 2003).

Individual identification Does the FFA discriminate between familiar and unfamiliar faces? If so, this might indicate a role beyond simply encoding the structural properties relevant to identity, to the matching of that information to previously stored facial memories.

Two studies that investigated faces learned in the laboratory found opposite results, one showing an increase in FFA response to familiar compared to unfamiliar faces (Lehmann et al., 2004) and the other (using positron emission tomography) finding a decrease (Rossion et al., 2003b). Although this discrepancy may be due to the use of different tasks in the two experiments (Henson et al., 2002; Rossion et al., 2003b), studies of responses to famous faces, which provide a stronger manipulation of familiarity, do not give a clearer picture. One study found a small but significantly greater response to famous compared to anonymous faces (Avidan et al., 2005) and another found a higher FFA response on trials in which subjects correctly identified a famous face than on trials in which they failed to recognize the same individual (Grill-Spector et al., 2004). However, two other studies found no difference in the response to famous versus anonymous faces in the FFA (Eger et al., 2005; Pourtois et al., 2005; see also Gorno-Tempini and Price, 2001; Gorno-Tempini et al., 1998). All told, these studies do not show a consistently different mean FFA response for familiar versus unfamiliar faces.

Lack of consistent familiarity effects in the FFA may indicate that the FFA is involved in generating a perceptual representation of faces, with actual recognition (i.e. matching to stored representations) occurring at a later stage. However, other evidence that the FFA is sensitive to stored representations comes from fMRI adaptation studies (Ewbank and Andrews, 2008) which found greater invariance to changes in the viewpoint of a face when that face was familiar than when it was unfamiliar (Eger et al., 2005). Another fMRI adaptation study found greater release from adaptation for changes in face stimuli that resulted in a change in identity, compared to changes of similar physical magnitude that did not produce a change in identity (Rotshtein et al., 2005). These results suggest some sensitivity to stored representations of individual faces in the FFA. It is also possible that information about face familiarity is represented not by an overall difference in the mean response, but by the pattern of response across voxels within the FFA (Haxby et al., 2001; but see Kriegeskorte et al., 2007). Nevertheless, the idea that recognition—that is, the matching of incoming perceptual information to stored visual representations in memory—is primarily performed by structures other than the FFA is supported by some data from the prosopagnosic literature. Using tests of imagery to probe the status of facial memories, it was shown that prosopagnosic subjects with right or bilateral lesions of the fusiform gyri had only mild deficits in facial imagery, whereas subjects with lesions of more anterior temporal cortex had severe deficits, suggesting that stored facial representations mainly involve structures anterior to the FFA (Barton, 2008; Barton and Cherkasova, 2003; Barton et al., 2003).

Social signals The neuroimaging data would suggest that the FFA is particularly sensitive to static aspects of facial structure relevant to identity processing. Whether it is involved in the processing of dynamic properties that may be more relevant to social signals is less clear. Some studies show higher responses to emotional than neutral faces in the fusiform gyrus (Breiter et al., 1996; Dolan et al., 2001; Vuilleumier et al., 2001, 2003; Williams et al., 2004)). However, this effect could reflect a general attentional enhancement for expressive faces (Wojciulik et al., 1998) perhaps via amygdala input (Dolan et al., 2001), particularly since this type of effect is not specific to the FFA. Better evidence may come from fMRI adaptation studies. One found that the FFA was sensitive to changes in identity but not changes in expression (Winston et al., 2004). However, two other adaptation studies found that the FFA was sensitive to changes in both identity and expression (Fox et al., 2009b; Ganel et al., 2005), casting some doubt on the idea that the FFA is involved in processing face identity only (Calder, Chapter 22, this volume). Consistent with these last two reports is a recent study in which neural responses were recorded directly from the cortex of nine human subjects undergoing epilepsy monitoring (Tsuchiya et al., 2008). This study applied decoding analyses and found better representation of both face identity and face expression (whether in static or dynamic stimuli) in ventral regions (i.e. in the vicinity of the FFA) than in lateral temporal cortex (i.e. in the vicinity of the fSTS).

While prosopagnosic observations support the fMRI data implicating the FFA in encoding facial structure, the lesion data is less clear on whether this encoding deficit is selective for stimulus properties relevant to identity, or if it also affects the encoding of expression and other social signals. It is clear from the older literature that the processing of facial expression can be affected in some prosopagnosic subjects (Campbell et al., 1990; de Haan and Campbell, 1991; Kracke, 1994; Young and Ellis, 1989,) but spared in others (Bruyer et al., 1983; Evans et al., 1995; Sergent and Poncet, 1990; Sergent and Villemure, 1989; Tranel et al., 1988). Given standard neuroanatomic models in which the FFA is involved in encoding structure relevant to identity but not expression, the assumption would be that expression processing would only be affected in prosopagnosic subjects when damage to the FFA is combined with damage to other structures, like the STS or OFA. Verifying this conjecture from the older literature is difficult if not impossible, given the lack of detailed neuroimaging in many.

More recently, though, the ability to reliably identify core regions of the face-processing network in single subjects (Fox et al., 2009a) has allowed us to correlate the pattern of damage across these regions with the pattern of behavioral deficits. Using morphed faces to probe sensitivity to changes in face structure induced by expression or identity separately, it was reported that one prosopagnosic subject whose lesion damaged the right FFA and OFA but spared the right STS had reduced sensitivity to changes in identity but not expression on an oddity paradigm that required participants to indicate which face had been altered on the probed dimension (Fox et al., 2008, 2009a) . Such data support the assertion that the FFA is dedicated specifically to the encoding of aspects of facial structure relevant to identity, and suggest that the expression signals detected in the FFA may reflect a modulatory role of social information rather than the extraction of these signals in the FFA.

Summary The results reviewed in this section provide the beginnings of a characterization of the computations and representations that occur in the FFA. The FFA has higher responses to faces than other objects, and this differential signal may contribute to face detection. More significantly, the FFA is likely involved in a structural encoding stage, particularly for information related to face identity, and therefore for static structural properties that are stable for the individual over time. The neuroimaging data are mixed on whether the FFA plays a role in encoding facial expressions, but some neuropsychological evidence indicates that unilateral loss of the right FFA does not impair discrimination of face expressions. Similarly, there is no consistent evidence that the FFA is the site where face identity is retrieved; rather, facial memories may be stored in more anterior temporal cortex.

The occipital face area

Based on its anatomic location (see Figure 7.1, bottom row), the OFA is often assumed to be an earlier stage of the face-processing network that sends its output to the FFA. Although the responses of the OFA are similar to those of the FFA, they do differ in some important respects that are consistent with this hypothesis.

First, the OFA is slightly less face-selective than the FFA (Schwarzlose et al., 2008), and pattern analyses show that this region contains more information about stimulus position than the FFA (Kovacs et al., 2008; Schwarzlose et al., 2008), including a stronger contralateral-field bias than the FFA (Hemond et al., 2007). Second, three different fMRI-adaptation studies have shown that the OFA is sensitive to changes in face stimuli whether or not these identity changes are perceived by the viewer, in contrast to the FFA, which is sensitive only to *perceived* changes in the face (Fox et al., 2009b; Large et al., 2008; Rotshtein et al., 2005). Third, one study (Yovel and Kanwisher,

2005) found that the magnitude of the OFA response was similar for upright and inverted faces, and there was with no correlation across subjects between the magnitude of the behavioral face inversion effect and the difference in the response of the OFA to upright and inverted faces (OFA-face inversion effect). In contrast, the FFA showed higher response to upright than inverted faces, and this difference was correlated across subjects with the behavioral face inversion effect. Finally, whereas the FFA responds to first-order stimulus information about both face parts and face configurations, the OFA is sensitive only to face parts (Liu et al., 2002). Consistent with these findings, a recent TMS study (Pitcher et al., 2007) showed that that OFA stimulation that takes place 60 to 100ms after stimulus onset disrupts discrimination of faces that differ in parts but not in spacing among them.

Taken together, these findings suggest that the OFA constitutes an earlier stage of face processing, which represents information that is more closely tied to the face stimulus, more local, and more tied to retinotopic position, whereas the FFA represents the perceived appearance of the face.

What do the lesion data tell us? At this time, there are only a few reports of patients with OFA damage confirmed by fMRI (Fox et al., 2009a; Rossion et al., 2003a; Steeves et al., 2006). The data from these patients are complicated by the fact that additional lesions were present. Thus, prosopagnosic subject PS has a lesion of the right OFA and the left FFA (Rossion et al., 2003a), and prosopagnosic subject R-IOT1 has a lesion of the right OFA and the right FFA (Fox et al., 2008). Subject DF has a lesion not only of right and left OFA, but also of the right and left lateral occipital complex, and given the etiology of carbon monoxide poisoning may have had more extensive damage than was visible on MRI (Steeves et al., 2006). Also, DF has general visual agnosia rather than prosopagnosia.

Current models that show the OFA as an early stage of face processing suggest that it may send information to both the FFA and STS, and therefore may contribute to a wide range of facial perceptions. Subject PS was most severely impaired in identity judgments and face-matching tasks, but also showed milder deficits in judgments of expression and gender, but not of age (Rossion et al., 2003a). Subject R-IOT1, on the other hand, did well on a variety of expression tests, and on a test of sensitivity to changes in expression or identity in morphed faces, showed a selective deficit for identity processing, with normal sensitivity to expression changes (Fox et al., 2009a). Subject DF could discriminate faces from non-faces in the natural context, but not in more demanding and complex stimuli, and was severely impaired in gender and expression judgments (Steeves et al., 2006). While not strictly speaking a lesion study, disruption of right OFA function by transcranial magnetic stimulation appears to impair expression judgments (Pitcher et al., 2007, 2008, Chapter 19, this volume).

The fact that fMRI found face-selective activation in the right FFA and fSTS in patient PS (Sorger et al., 2007) and both right and left FFA and right and left STS in patient DF also deserves comment. This implies that the right OFA is not the only source of face-selective signals that provides input to the FFA and fSTS. In PS, this additional input may come from the left OFA; however, in DF, this input must arise from other regions, since she lacks both OFAs. In both PS and healthy subjects, fMRI-adaptation experiments have shown sensitivity to facial identity in the ventral lateral occipital complex, an object-processing region that is not face-selective (Dricot et al., 2008). Nevertheless, despite this potential source of signals, PS is prosopagnosic and her right FFA does not show normal adaptation effects for facial identity (Dricot et al., 2008; Schiltz et al., 2006). Thus discrimination of facial identity at both a behavioral level and also a physiological level in the FFA may depend upon the integrity of the right OFA. Whether this is also true of discriminative signals in the fSTS is not yet known.

In summary, the OFA appears to constitute an early stage of face processing, with sensitivity to all aspects of facial structure, though its activity is not correlated with perception of identity or expression, as seen in the FFA and fSTS. The available lesion data are limited, complex, and confounded by loss of other object and face processing regions; nevertheless, they suggest a possible contribution of the OFA to a wide array of facial perception tasks.

The superior temporal sulcus

Although the FFA can be found in essentially all normal subjects, face-selective regions in the STS (fSTS) are less reliable, and are found in only half (Kanwisher et al., 1997) to three quarters (Fox et al., 2009a; Yovel and Kanwisher, 2005) of subjects scanned individually with standard static localizers. (Further studies will be enhanced by the ability of new localizers using dynamic images that identify the fSTS in almost all subjects (Fox et al., 2009a).) For this reason the fSTS has been studied less extensively than the FFA. Nonetheless, evidence to date suggests important functional distinctions between the fSTS and other face-selective regions of cortex, with the fSTS more involved in processing dynamic and social aspects of faces such as emotional expression and gaze (Haxby et al., 2000).

Several studies have provided compelling evidence that the fSTS is involved in the processing of eye gaze, emotional expression, and dynamic information about faces. First, Hoffman and Haxby showed that although the FFA responds more strongly when subjects performed a 1-back task on face identity than on gaze information, the fSTS showed a slightly higher response for the gaze task than the identity task (Hoffman and Haxby, 2000). Second, an fMR-adaptation study (Winston et al., 2004) in which expression and identity were manipulated in a factorial manner found significant sensitivity to information about emotional expression in faces in the fSTS but none in the fusiform gyrus (see also Andrews and Ewbank, 2004). Another adaptation study showed that the fSTS was sensitive to perceived changes in expression but only when subjects were explicitly attending to expression (Fox et al., 2009b). Numerous other studies have shown strong responses in fSTS to dynamic face stimuli in which expression or gaze changes (Calvert and Campbell, 2003; Thompson et al., 2007).

In contrast, the fSTS does not show the same involvement in face detection and identity processing that has been found in the FFA. Two studies have found that the FFA but not the fSTS is correlated with successful face detection (Andrews and Schluppeck 2004; Grill-Spector et al., 2004). Regarding facial identity, Grill-Spector et al. found no correlation of the fSTS response with successful identification of faces (Grill-Spector et al., 2004). Similarly, studies that used fMRl-adaptation found sensitivity to face identity in the FFA but not in the fSTS (Andrews and Schluppeck, 2004; Yovel and Kanwisher, 2005). Several studies have found a robust face inversion effect (higher response to upright than inverted faces) in the fSTS (Yovel and Kanwisher, 2005), but in contrast to the FFA, this difference between upright and inverted faces was not correlated with the behavioral face inversion effect measured in a face identity discrimination task (Yovel and Kanwisher, 2005).

On the other hand, there is evidence that identity signals may be present in some component of the fSTS. Two fMRl-adaptation studies have found sensitivity to identity in the posterior STS, with selectivity to expression alone emerging in the anterior or middle STS (Fox et al., 2009b; Winston et al., 2004). The role of these identity signals is uncertain. While they may contribute to identity judgments, it is also possible that identity signals may reflect a stage where expression representations retain some identity specificity, prior to the generation of an identity-independent representation of expression. The presence of identity-dependent and identity-independent layers in expression processing is also suggested by some behavioral adaptation studies (Fox and Barton, 2007).

Even less lesion data are available for the fSTS than for the OFA or FFA. In most prosopagnosic subjects, the region of the STS is likely spared. This was confirmed in R-IOT1, in whom the processing of facial expression was normal. This report also contains a single subject, R-ST1 (Figure 7.1), with damage to the STS but sparing the right FFA and right OFA (Fox et al., 2009a). This subject was impaired on expression judgments in a test of discrimination in morphed facial images. With identity judgments, he was normal except when the images also contained irrelevant changes in expression. These data suggest that the fSTS makes a specific contribution to expression processing and is also important in providing signals to identity processing that allow for changes in expression to be discounted, to allow for expression-invariant identity recognition.

Summary and conclusions

Cognitive models have long suggested that face perception is accomplished by a number of distinct processing components (Bruce and Young 1986; Damasio et al., 1990). Functional neuroimaging has revealed a set of cortical areas that respond selectively to faces (Haxby et al., 2000). Here we have reviewed the evidence from fMRI and patient studies in an attempt to link the two, by determining the function of each of the core face-processing regions (Gobbini and Haxby, 2007).

Current data support the hypothesis that the FFA is involved in the structural encoding of faces, particularly for static facial structure related to identity, including the configural relations between features. The OFA is sensitive to all aspects of physical structure, and likely does not differentiate between changes related to identity and those related to expression. Both neuroimaging and patient data implicate the STS in the processing of social signals such as expression and gaze direction.

The findings reviewed here have only scratched the surface in our quest to discover the function of each of the cortical regions that collectively make up the face-processing system. All of the conclusions reached here remain tentative and all require further testing. In addition, we know little about the functional division of labor among regions in the "extended face network" (Fox et al., 2009a). For example, anterior temporal lesions can cause prosopagnosia, without damage to the core network (Barton 2008; Barton et al., 2003; Fox et al., 2009a). This result is consistent with evidence for the existence of face-selective regions in anterior inferior temporal cortex in both humans and monkeys (Kriegeskorte et al., 2007; Rajimehr et al., 2009; Rossion et al., 2001). Are these anterior regions the site of the stored memories of known faces? Consistent with this hypothesis is the recent report that developmental prosopagnosics, most of whom show normal FFAs, have reduced connectivity to anterior temporal regions (Thomas et al., 2009), as predicted if access to stored face memories in anterior temporal regions are crucial in face recognition. Inconsistent with this hypothesis is the fact that these same individuals are often also impaired at perceptual discriminations on faces that do not require access to stored face memories. Discovering the contribution of anterior temporal and other regions of the extended face system will be a major task for future research.

Beyond the functional division labor among the components of the core and extended face system, numerous other fundamental questions remain unanswered. First, we know almost nothing about the actual circuits that produce the face selectivity evident in fMRI studies. Second, we know very little about the connections between the cortical regions discussed here, or about the interactions between these regions and the role those interactions may play in shaping the representations achieved in each region. Third, we do not know how these regions arise in typical and atypical development. The possibility of answering all three questions has received a major boost from the recent discovery of face-selective cortical regions in macaques. This work has opened up the possibility of using single-unit recording to characterize the neural representations extracted in those regions, and the use of novel methods for tracing the connections between these regions (Moeller et al., 2008). The applicability of the results from macaques to humans will however depend on further work establishing homologies between face-selective regions in macaques and face-selective regions in humans (Tsao et al., 2008). It will also be crucial to test whether face perception in macaques operates similarly to face perception in humans at a cognitive level, by testing whether the behavioral "signatures" of face perception in humans are also seen in macaques.

Finally, we have treated the adult face-processing network as a fixed system, with lesions to components of this system equivalent to permanent deletions of those components. However, might there be some ability of the face processing system to adapt to damage, such that functions can shift between components of the face processing system, or even move to new cortical regions not previously implicated in face perception? Answering this question will require not just the juxtaposition of data from fMRI and lesion studies, as we have done here, but the execution of functional imaging studies in individual patients over time, and possibly with rehabilitative efforts (Fox et al., 2009a; Marotta et al., 2001; Schiltz et al., 2006; Steeves et al., 2006).

References

Ambady, N. and Rosenthal, R. (1993). Half a minute: Predicting teacher evaluations from thin slices of nonverbal behavior and physical attractiveness. *Journal of Personality and Social Psychology*, **64**, 431–441.

Andrews, T., Schluppeck, D., Homfray, D., Matthews, P., and Blakemore, C. (2002). Activity in the fusiform gyrus predicts conscious perception of Rubin's vase-face illusion. *NeuroImage*, **17**, 890–901.

Andrews, T.J. and Ewbank, M.P. (2004). Distinct representations for facial identity and changeable aspects of faces in the human temporal lobe. *Neuroimage*, **23**, 905–913.

Andrews, T.J. and Schluppeck, D. (2004). Neural responses to Mooney images reveal a modular representation of faces in human visual cortex *Neuroimage*, **21**, 91–98.

Avidan, G., Hasson, U., Malach, R., and Behrmann, M. (2005). Detailed exploration of face-related processing in congenital prosopagnosia: 2. *Functional neuroimaging findings. Journal of Cognitive Neuroscience*, **17**, 1150–1167.

Baron-Cohen, S., Wheelwright, S., Hill, J., Raste, Y., and Plumb, I. (2001). The "Reading the Mind in the Eyes" Test revised version: a study with normal adults, and adults with Asperger syndrome or high-functioning autism. *Journal of Child Psychology and Psychiatry*, **42**, 241–251.

Barton, J.J.S. (2008). Structure and function in acquired prosopagnosia: lessons from a series of ten patients with brain damage. *Journal of Neuropsychology*, **2**, 197–225.

Barton, J.JS .(2009). What is meant by impaired configural processing in acquired prosopagnosia? *Perceptio*, **38**, 242–260.

Barton, J.J. and Cherkasova, M. (2003). Face imagery and its relation to perception and covert recognition in prosopagnosia. *Neurology*, **61**, 220–225.

Barton, J.J. and Cherkasova, M.V. (2005). Impaired spatial coding within objects but not between objects in prosopagnosia. *Neurology*, **65**, 270–274.

Barton JJ, Cherkasova M and O'Connor M (2001). Covert recognition in acquired and developmental prosopagnosia *Neurology*, **57**, 1161–1167.

Barton, J.J., Press, D.Z., Keenan, J.P., and O'Connor, M. (2002). Lesions of the fusiform face area impair perception of facial configuration in prosopagnosia. *Neurology*, **58**, 71–78.

Barton, J., Cherkasova, M., Press, D., Intriligator, J., and O'Connor, M. (2003). Developmental prosopagnosia: a study of three patients. *Brain and Cognition*, **51**, 12–30.

Barton, J.J., Cherkasova, M.V., Press, D.Z., Intriligator, J.M. and O'Connor, M. (2004). Perceptual functions in prosopagnosia *Perception*, **33**, 939–956.

Barton, J.J., Malcolm, G.L., and Hefter, R.L. (2007). Spatial processing in Balint syndrome and prosopagnosia: a study of three patients *Journal of Neuro-ophthalmology*, **27**, 268–274.

Breiter, H.C., Etcoff, N.L., Whalen, P.J., *et al.* (1996). Response and habituation of the human amygdala during visual processing of facial expression *Neuron,* **17,** 875–887.

Bruce, V. (1986). Influences of familiarity on the processing of faces. *Perception,* **15,** 387–397.

Bruce, V. and Young, A. (1986). Understanding face recognition. *British Journal of Psychology,* **77** 305–327.

Bruyer, R., Laterre, C., Seron, X., *et al.* (1983). A case of prosopagnosia with some preserved covert remembrance of familiar faces *Brain Cognition,* **2,** 257–284.

Calvert, G.A. and Campbell, R. (2003). Reading speech from still and moving faces: the neural substrates of visible speech. *Journal of Cognitive Neuroscience,* **15,** 57–70.

Campbell, R. (2008). The processing of audio-visual speech: empirical and neural bases. *Philosophical Transactions of the Royal Society of London - Series B: Biological Sciences,* **363,** 1001–1010.

Campbell, R., Heywood, C.A., Cowey, A., Regard, M., and Landis, T. (1990). Sensitivity to eye gaze in prosopagnosic patients and monkeys with superior temporal sulcus ablation *Neuropsychologia,* **28,** 1123–1142.

Damasio, A.R., Damasio, H., and Van Hoesen, G.W. (1982). Prosopagnosia: anatomic basis and behavioral mechanisms *Neurology,* **32,** 331–341.

Damasio, A.R., Tranel, D., and Damasio, H. (1990). Face agnosia and the neural substrates of memory. *Annual Review of Neuroscience,* **13,** 89–109.

Davidoff, J. and Landis, T. (1990). Recognition of unfamiliar faces in prosopagnosia. *Neuropsychologia,* **28,** 1143–1161.

de Gelder, B., Frissen, I., Barton, J., and Hadjikhani, N. (2003). A modulatory role for facial expressions in prosopagnosia. *Proceedings of the National Academy of Sciences USA,* **100,** 13105–13110.

de Haan, E. and Campbell, R. (1991). A fifteen year follow-up of a case of developmental prosopagnosia. *Cortex,* **27,** 489–509.

De Renzi, E. (1986). Current issues in prosopagnosia. In Ellis, H.D., Jeeves, M.A., Newcombe, F., and Young, A. (eds.) *Aspects of face processing.* Dordecht: Martinus-Nijhoff.

Diamond, R. and Carey, S. (1986). Why faces are and are not special: an effect of expertise *Journal of Experimental Psychology: General,* **115,** 107–117.

Dolan, R.J., Morris, J.S., and de Gelder, B. (2001). Crossmodal binding of fear in voice and face. *Proceedings of the National Academy of Sciences, USA,* 98, 10006–10010.

Dricot, L., Sorger, B., Schiltz, C., Goebel, R., and Rossion, B. (2008). The roles of "face" and "non-face" areas during individual face perception: evidence by fMRI adaptation in a brain-damaged prosopagnosic patient. *Neuroimage,* **40,** 318–332.

Eger, E., Schyns, P.G., and Kleinschmidt, A. (2004). Scale invariant adaptation in fusiform face-responsive regions. *Neuroimage,* **22,** 232–242.

Eger, E., Schweinberger, S.R., Dolan, R.J., and Henson, R.N. (2005). Familiarity enhances invariance of face representations in human ventral visual cortex: fMRI evidence. *Neuroimage,* **26,** 1128–1139.

Ellis, H.D., Young, A.W., and Critchley, E.M.R. (1989). Loss of memory for people following temporal lobe damage. *Brain,* **1989,** 1469–83.

Evans, J.J., Heggs, A.J., Antoun, N., and Hodges, J.R .(1995). Progressive prosopagnosia associated with selective right temporal lobe atrophy. *Brain,* **118,** 1–13.

Ewbank, M.P. and Andrews, T.J. (2008). Differential sensitivity for viewpoint between familiar and unfamiliar faces in human visual cortex. *Neuroimage,* **40,** 1857–1870.

Farah, M., Levinson, K.L., and Klein, K.L. (1995). Face perception and within-category discrimination in prosopagnosia *Neuropsychologia,* **33,** 661–674.

Fox, C.J. and Barton, J.J.S. (2007). What is adapted in face adaptation? The neural representations of expression in the human visual system *Brain Research,* **1127,** 80–89.

Fox, C.J., Iaria, G., Duchaine, B.C., and Barton, J.J. (2008). Behavioral and fMRI studies of identity and expression perception in acquired prosopagnosia *Journal of Vision,* **8,** 708.

Fox, C.J., Iaria, G., and Barton, J.J. (2009). Defining the face processing network: Optimization of the functional localizer in fMRI. *Human Brain Mapping,* **30,** 1637–1651.

Fox, C.J., Moon, S.-Y., Iaria, G., and Barton, J.J.S. (2009). The correlates of subjective perception of identity and expression in the face network: an fMRI adaptation study. *Neuroimage* **44**, 569–580.

Ganel, T., Valyear, K.F., Goshen-Gottstein, Y., and Goodale, M.A. (2005). The involvement of the "fusiform face area" in processing facial expression *Neuropsychologia*, **43**, 1645–1654.

Garrido, L., Duchaine, B., and Nakayama, K. (2008). Face detection in normal and prosopagnosic individuals. *Journal of Neuropsychology*, **2**, 119–140.

Gauthier, I. and Nelson, C.A. (2001). The development of face expertise *Current Opinion in Neurobiology*, **11**, 219–224.

Gauthier, I., Behrmann, M., and Tarr, M.J. (1999a). Can face recognition really be dissociated from object recognition? *Journal of Cognitive Neuroscience*, **11**, 349–370.

Gauthier, I., Tarr, M.J., Anderson, A.W., Skudlarski, P., and Gore, J.C. (1999b). Activation of the middle fusiform "face area" increases with expertise in recognizing novel objects. *Nature Neuroscience*, **2**, 568–573.

Gauthier I, Skudlarski P, Gore JC and Anderson AW (2000a). Expertise for cars and birds recruits brain areas involved in face recognition. *Nature Neuroscience*, **3**, 191–197.

Gauthier, I., Tarr, M.J., Moylan, J., *et al.* (2000b). The fusiform "face area" is part of a network that processes faces at the individual level *Journal of Cognitive Neuroscience*, **12**, 495–504.

Glosser, G., Salvucci, A.E., and Chiaravalloti, N.D. (2003). Naming and recognizing famous faces in temporal lobe epilepsy *Neurology*, **61**, 81–86.

Gobbini, M.I. and Haxby, J.V. (2007). Neural systems for recognition of familiar faces *Neuropsychologia*, **45**, 32–41.

Gorno-Tempini, M.L. and Price, C.J. (2001). Identification of famous faces and buildings: a functional neuroimaging study of semantically unique items. *Brain*, **124**, 2087–2097.

Gorno-Tempini, M.L., Price, C.J., Josephs, O., *et al.* (1998). The neural systems sustaining face and proper name processing. *Brain*, **121**, 2103–2118.

Grill-Spector, K., Kushnir, T., Edelman, S., *et al.* (1999). Differential processing of objects under various viewing conditions in the human lateral occipital complex *Neuron*, **24**, 187–203.

Grill-Spector, K., Knouf, N., and Kanwisher, N. (2004). The fusiform face area subserves face perception, not generic within-category identification. *Nature Neuroscience*, **7**, 555–562.

Hanley, J.R., Young, A.W., and Pearson, N.A. (1989). Defective recognition of familiar people. *Cognitive Neuropsychology*, **6**, 179–210.

Hasson, U., Hendler, T., Ben Bashat, D., and Malach, R. (2001). Vase or face? A neural correlate of shape-selective grouping processes in the human brain. *Journal of Cognitive Neuroscience*, **13**, 744–753.

Haxby, J.V., Gobbini, M.I., Furey, M.L., *et al.* (2001). Distributed and overlapping representations of faces and objects in ventral temporal cortex *Science*, **293**, 2425–2430.

Haxby, J.V., Hoffman, E.A., and Gobbini, M.I. (2000). The distributed human neural system for face perception. *Trends in Cognitive Science*, **4**, 223–233.

Hemond, C.C., Kanwisher, N., and Op de Beeck, H.P. (2007). A preference for contralateral stimuli in human object- and face-selective cortex. *PLoS ONE*, **2**, e574.

Henke, K., Schweinberger, S.R., Grigo, A., Klos, T., and Sommer, W. (1998). Specificity of face recognition: recognition of exemplars of non-face objects in prosopagnosia *Cortex*, **34**, 289–296.

Henson, R.N., Shallice, T., Gorno-Tempini, M.L., and Dolan, R.J. (2002). Face repetition effects in implicit and explicit memory tests as measured by fMRI. *Cerebral Cortex*, **12**, 178–186.

Hoffman, E.A. and Haxby, J.V. (2000). Distinct representations of eye gaze and identity in the distributed human neural system for face perception *Nature Neuroscience*, **3**, 80–84.

Iaria, G., Fox, C.J., Waite, C., Aharon, I., and Barton, J.J.S. (2008). The contribution of the fusiform gyrus and superior temporal sulcus in processing facial attractiveness: Neuropsychological and neuroimaging evidence. *Neuroscience*, **155**, 409–422.

Kanwisher, N.G., McDermott, J., and Chun, M.M. (1997). The fusiform face area: A module in human extrastriate cortex specialized for face perception *Journal of Neuroscience*, **17**, 4302–4311.

Kanwisher, N., Tong, F., and Nakayama, K. (1998). The effect of face inversion on the human fusiform face area *Cognition*, **68**, B1–B11.

Kourtzi, Z. and Kanwisher, N. (2001). Representation of perceived object shape by the human lateral occipital complex. *Science*, **293**, 1506–1509.

Kovacs, G., Cziraki, C., Vidnyanszyk, Z., Schweinberger, S.R., and Greenlee, M.W. (2008). Position-specific and position-invariant face aftereffects reflect the adaptation of different cortical areas. *Neuroimage*, **43**, 156–164.

Kracke, I. (1994). Developmental prosopagnosia in Asperger syndrome: presentation and discussion of an individual case. *Developmental Medicine and Child Neurology*, **36**, 873–886.

Kriegeskorte, N., Formisano, E., Sorger, B., and Goebel, R. (2007). Individual faces elicit distinct response patterns in human anterior temporal cortex. *Proceedings of the National Academy of Sciences, USA*, **104**, 20600–20605.

Large, M.E., Cavina-Pratesi, C., Villis, T., and Culham, J.C. (2008). The neural correlates of change detection in the face perception network. *Neuropsychologia*, **46**, 2169–2176.

Lehmann, C., Mueller, T., Federspiel, A., *et al.* (2004). Dissociation between overt and unconscious face processing in fusiform face area. *Neuroimage*, **21**, 75–83.

Lhermitte, F., Chain, F., Escourolle, R., Ducarne, B., and Pillon, B. (1972). Étude anatomo-clinique d'un cas de prosopagnosie. *Revue Neurologique*, **126**, 329–346.

Liu, J., Harris, A., and Kanwisher, N. (2002). Stages of processing in face perception: an MEG study. *Nature Neuroscience*, **5**, 910–916.

Liu, J., Harris, A., and Kanwisher, N. (2010). Perception of face parts and face configurations: An fMRI study. *Journal of Cognitive Neuroscience*, **22**, 203–211.

Marotta, J.J., Genovese, C.R., and Behrmann, M. (2001). A functional MRI study of face recognition in patients with prosopagnosia. *NeuroReport*, **12**, 1581–1587.

Maurer, D., LeGrand, R., and Mondloch, J. (2002). The many faces of configural processing. *Trends Cognitive Sciences*, **6**, 225–260.

Mazard, A., Laou, L., Joliot, M., and Mellet, E. (2005). Neural impact of the semantic content of visual mental images and visual percepts. *Brain Research. Cognitive Brain Research*, **24**, 423–435.

McCarthy, G., Puce, A., Gore, J.C., and Allison, T. (1997). Face-specific processing in the human fusiform gyrus *Journal of Cognitive Neuroscience*, **9**, 605–610.

McKone, E., Kanwisher, N., and Duchaine, B.C. (2007). Can generic expertise explain special processing for faces? *Trends in Cognitive Sciences*, **11**, 8–15.

McKone, E. and Yovel, G. (2008). A single holistic representation of spacing and feature shape in faces. *Journal of Vision*, **8**, 163a.

McNeil, J.E. and Warrington, E.K. (1993). Prosopagnosia: a face-specific disorder. *Quarterly Journal of Experimental Psychology. A, Human Experimental Psychology*, **46**, 1–10.

Moeller, S., Freiwald, W.A., and Tsao, D.Y. (2008). Patches with links: a unified system for processing faces in the macaque temporal lobe. *Science*, **320**, 1355–1359.

Moscovitch, M., Winocur, G., and Behrmann, M. (1997). What is special about face recognition? Nineteen experiments on a person with visual object agnosia and dyslexia but normal face recognition. *Journal of Cognitive Neuroscience*, **9**, 555–604.

Pasley, B.N., Mayes, L.C., and Schultz, R.T. (2004). Subcortical discrimination of unperceived objects during binocular rivalry. *Neuron*, **42**, 163–172.

Pitcher, D., Garrido, L., Walsh, V., and Duchaine, B. (2008). Transcranial Magnetic Stimulation Disrupts the Perception and Embodiment of Facial Expressions *Journal of Neuroscience*, **28**, 8929–8933.

Pitcher, D., Walsh, V., Yovel, G., and Duchaine, B. (2007). TMS evidence for the involvement of the right occipital face area in early face processing. *Current Biology*, **17**, 1568–1573.

Pourtois, G., Schwartz, S., Seghier, M.L., Lazeyras, F., and Vuilleumier, P. (2005). Portraits or people? Distinct representations of face identity in the human visual cortex. *Journal of Cognitive Neuroscience*, **17**, 1043–1057.

Puce, A., Allison, T., Bentin, S., Gore, J.C., and McCarthy, G. (1998). Temporal cortex activation in humans viewing eye and mouth movements *Journal of Neuroscience,* **18**, 2188–2199.

Rajimehr, R., Young, J.C., and Tootell, R.B. (2009). An anterior temporal face patch in human cortex, predicted by macaque maps. *Proceedings of National Academy of Sciences, USA,* **106**, 1995–2000.

Rhodes, G., Byatt, G., Michie, P.T., and Puce, A. (2004). Is the fusiform face area specialized for faces, individuation, or expert individuation? *Journal of Cognitive Neuroscience,* **16**, 189–203.

Riddoch, M.J., Johnson, R., Bracewell, M., Boutsen, L., and Humphreys, G.W. (2008). Are faces special: a case of pure prosopagnosia. *Cognitive Neuropsychology,* **25**, 3–26.

Riesenhuber, M., Jarudi, I., Gilad, S., and Sinha, P. (2004). Face processing in humans is compatible with a simple shape-based model of vision *Proceedings. Biological Sciences,* **271**, S448–450.

Rosen, E. (2003). Face representation in cortex: Studies using a simple and not so special model. *Electrical Engineering and Computer Science.* Cambridge, MA: Massachusetts Institute of Technology.

Rossion, B., Schiltz, C., Robaye, L., Pirenne, D., and Crommelinck, M. (2001). How does the brain discriminate familiar and unfamiliar faces?: a PET study of face categorical perception. *Journal of Cognitive Nueroscience,* **13**, 1019–1034.

Rossion, B., Caldara, R., Seghier, M., *et al.* (2003a). A network of occipito-temporal face-sensitive areas besides the right middle fusiform gyrus is necessary for normal face processing. *Brain,* **126**, 2381–2395.

Rossion, B., Schiltz, C., and Crommelinck, M. (2003b). The functionally defined right occipital and fusiform "face areas" discriminate novel from visually familiar faces *Neuroimage,* **19**, 877–883.

Rotshtein, P., Henson, R.N., Treves, A., Driver, J., and Dolan, R.J. (2005). Morphing Marilyn into Maggie dissociates physical and identity face representations in the brain. *Nature Neuroscience,* **8**, 107–113.

Schiltz, C. and Rossion, B. (2005). Faces are processed holistically in the right middle fusiform gyrus. *Vision Sciences Society.* Sarasota, Florida.

Schiltz, C. and Rossion, B. (2006). Faces are represented holistically in the human occipito-temporal cortex. *NeuroImage,* **32**, 1385–1394.

Schiltz, C., Sorger, B., Caldara, R., *et al.* (2006). Impaired face discrimination in acquired prosopagnosia is associated with abnormal response to individual faces in the right middle fusiform gyrus. *Cerebral Cortex,* **16**, 574–586.

Schwarzlose, R.F., Swisher, J.D., Dang, S., and Kanwisher, N. (2008). The distribution of category and location information across object-selective regions in human visual cortex. *Proceedings of National Academy of Sciences, USA,* **105**, 4447–4452.

Sergent, J. and Poncet, M. (1990). From covert to overt recognition of faces in a prosopagnosic patient. *Brain,* **113**, 989–1004.

Sergent, J. and Villemure, J.-G. (1989). Prosopagnosia in a right hemispherectomized patient. *Brain,* **112**, 975–995.

Sorger, B., Goebel, R., Schiltz, C., and Rossion, B. (2007). Understanding the functional neuroanatomy of acquired prosopagnosia. *Neuroimage,* **35**, 836–852.

Spiridon, M. and Kanwisher, N. (2002). How distributed is visual category information in human occipito-temporal cortex? An fMRI study *Neuron,* **35**, 1157–1165.

Steeves, J.K., Culham, J.C., Duchaine, B.C., *et al.* (2006). The fusiform face area is not sufficient for face recognition: evidence from a patient with dense prosopagnosia and no occipital face area. *Neuropsychologia,* **44**, 594–609.

Thomas, C., Avidan, G., Humphreys, K., *et al.* (2009). Reduced structural connectivity in ventral visual cortex in congenital prosopagnosia. *Nature Neuroscience,* **12**, 29–31.

Thompson, J.C., Hardee, J.E., Panayiotou, A., Crewther, D., and Puce, A. (2007). Common and distinct brain activation to viewing dynamic sequences of face and hand movements. *Neuroimage,* **37**, 966–973.

Thompson, S.A., Graham, K.S., Williams, G., *et al.* (2004). Dissociating person-specific from general semantic knowledge: roles of the left and right temporal lobes *Neuropsychologia,* **42**, 359–370.

Tong, F., Nakayama, K., Moscovitch, M., Weinrib, O., and Kanwisher, N. (2000). Response properties of the human fusiform face area *Cognitive Neuropsychology*, **17**, 257–279.

Tong, F., Nakayama, K., Vaughan, J.T., and Kanwisher, N. (1998). Binocular rivalry and visual awareness in human extrastriate cortex *Neuron*, **21**, 753–759.

Tranel, D., Damasio, A.R., and Damasio, H. (1988). Intact recognition of facial expression, gender, and age in patients with impaired recognition of face identity *Neurology*, **38**, 690–696.

Tsao, D.Y. and Livingstone, M.S. (2008). Mechanisms of face perception. *Annual Review of Neuroscience*, **31**, 411–437.

Tsao, D.Y., Moeller, S., and Freiwald, W.A. (2008). Comparing face patch systems in macaques and humans. *Proceedings of National Academy of Sciences, USA*, **105**, 19514–19519.

Tsuchiya, N., Kawasaki, H., Oya, H., Howard, M.Ar., and Adolphs, R. (2008). Decoding face information in time, frequency and space from direct intracranial recordings of the human brain. *PLoS ONE*, **3**, 3892.

Vuilleumier, P., Armony, J.L., Driver, J., and Dolan, R.J. (2001). Effects of attention and emotion on face processing in the human brain: an event-related fMRI study. *Neuron*, **30**, 829–841.

Vuilleumier, P., Armony, J.L., Driver, J., and Dolan, R.J. (2003). Distinct spatial frequency sensitivities for processing faces and emotional expressions *Nature Neuroscience*, **6**, 624–631.

Wada, Y. and Yamamoto, T. (2001). Selective impairment of facial recognition due to a haematoma restricted to the right fusiform and lateral occipital region. *Journal of Neurology, Neurosurgery & Psychiatry*, **71**, 254–257.

Whiteley, A.M. and Warrington, E.M. (1977). Prosopagnosia: a clinical, psychological, and anatomical study of three patients. *Journal of Neurology, Neurosurgery & Psychiatry*, **40**, 395–403.

Williams, M.A., Moss, S.A. and Bradshaw, J.L. (2004). A unique look at face processing: the impact of masked faces on the processing of facial features *Cognition*, **91**, 155–172.

Winston, J.S., Henson, R.N., Fine-Goulden, M.R., and Dolan, R.J. (2004). fMRI-adaptation reveals dissociable neural representations of identity and expression in face perception. *Journal of Neurophysiology*, **92**, 1830–1839.

Wojciulik, E., Kanwisher, N., and Driver, J. (1998). Covert visual attention modulates face-specific activity in the human fusiform gyrus: fMRI study. *Journal of Neurophysiology*, **79**, 1574–1578.

Xu, Y. (2005). Revisiting the role of the fusiform face area in visual expertise *Cerebral Cortex*, **15**, 1234–1242.

Young, A.W. and Ellis, H.D. (1989). Childhood prosopagnosia. *Brain and Cognition*, **9**, 16–47.

Young, A.W., Hay, D.C., and Ellis, A.W. (1985). The faces that launched a thousand slips: everyday difficulties and errors in recognizing people. *British Journal of Psychology*, **76**, 495–523.

Young, A.W., Hellawell, D., and Hay, D.C. (1987). Configurational information in face perception. *Perception*, **16**, 747–759.

Yovel, G. and Kanwisher, N. (2004). Face perception domain specific, not process specific. *Neuron*, **44**, 889–898.

Yovel, G. and Kanwisher, N. (2005). The neural basis of the behavioral face-inversion effect. *Current Biology*, **15**, 2256–2262.

Chapter 8

Applied Research in Face Processing

Vicki Bruce

As I write this chapter, government agencies funding research in the UK, and academics in receipt of funding, continue to debate the extent to which publicly funded research should be actually or potentially "useful." Research ratings for submitted project proposals or for the judged quality of research in the Research Assessment Exercises are increasingly influenced by perceived impact beyond the academic community and/or perspectives from non-academic "users" of research. Studying something just because it is intrinsically interesting appears mildly old-fashioned. But research into face perception and recognition has always been driven strongly by applied problems, and has the potential to make a difference to policy or practice in various areas, as I will illustrate here.

I myself became interested in face recognition because of a dilemma between observed high performance in face recognition observed in the laboratory and a real problem of eyewitness memory for faces seen in criminal incidents. In the early 1970s, when I was a student, cognitive psychologists interested in memory were becoming intrigued by memory for non-verbal materials. Roger Shepard, Lionel Standing, and others had demonstrated remarkable capacities for recognition memory for many hundreds of pictures. Faces were particularly accurately remembered compared with other kinds of picture (Shepard, 1967; Standing et al., 1970). And yet, in the same period, there was a public enquiry chaired by Lord Devlin (1976) into cases of mistaken identification made by eyewitnesses to a crime in England. It concluded that eyewitness memory for faces was so prone to error that a person should not normally be convicted on the basis of such evidence alone. Around that time too, Hadyn Ellis and his colleagues Graham Davies and John Shepherd at Aberdeen were evaluating some of the tools that police were using to help track down villains. I will elaborate on this research later in this chapter.

While I became intrigued by the contrast between laboratory and everyday memory for faces, there were a number of important "blue skies" discoveries at about that time indicating that faces were of special interest to brains. Charles Gross and colleagues first reported cells in macaque inferotemporal lobe that were particularly responsive to faces (Gross et al., 1972), while a group of pediatricians (Goren et al., 1975) demonstrated that newborn babies track face-like images more than other kinds of patterns.

I believe that the explosion of research interest in faces and face processing, and the engagement of a wide range of disciplines has been fueled by theoretical fascination combined with applied importance. Sparks were kindled in the 1970s and the fire really took hold in the 80s and 90s. In this chapter I will stress applications. Many other chapters in this book will elaborate the theory.

In selecting applications areas to discuss, I have chosen to emphasize those which have involved a wide range of psychological questions or where the contribution of psychology is particularly significant. There is a huge research industry looking at the automation of face recognition for security applications, and the animation of facial expressions for entertainment applications, as evidenced, for example, by the regular IEEE International Conference on Automatic Face and

Gesture Recognition, a series of meetings held biennially since the early 1990s. On the whole, however, this work is not well connected with matters psychological. Readers will find more about this topic in the chapters by O'Toole (Chapter 2), and by Stewart Bartlett and Whitehill (Chapter 25) in this volume.

Here I focus on the three areas of face-to-face communication; reconstruction and alteration of faces; and the use of facial images in crime investigations.

Face-to-face communication

With advances in *video-based communication (VMC) systems*, through which conversations between remote participants can be held with visual as well as audio channels, have come two kinds of applied research question.

The first is how the quality of images in VMC systems may affect whether they can usefully substitute for face-to-face communication. The second area explores similarities and differences between remote (VMC) and co-present face-to-face interaction. Images are electronically bulky items and their transmission generally requires compression in some way. Twenty years ago bandwidth limitations for most users were extremely severe. Early research by Don Pearson aimed at developing communication devices for deaf people (see Pearson, 1992) showed that reducing images to one bit per pixel (i.e. black and white, rather than grayscale) yielded well-recognizable images provided that the compression included a "thresholding" function which preserved information about shading and gross pigmentation and not just "edges." So, to be recognizable, a black and white picture of a face must preserve areas of relative light and dark from the original image and not just outline significant features as would happen if contrast edges alone were depicted (see Figure 8.1). This practical observation had interesting theoretical implications. It showed that however faces are represented for their different uses by the human brain, representations were unlikely to be based upon simple measurements made on face features, since these should be preserved in simple line drawings (see also Davies et al., 1978). Remarkably, though, compression preserving "mass" (shading and pigmentation) conveys extremely recognizable and usable images even when these only contain one bit per pixel.

Compression algorithms have moved on since this research, and this, plus improved bandwidth, means that we can view and download color movies on home computers.

Fig. 8.1 A photograph of Michael Caine's face shown thresholded (left), with edges alone (centre), or as "full cartoon" of edges plus thresholded regions (see Pearson, 1992). Figure reproduced from V. Bruce et al. (1992). The importance of "mass" in line drawings of faces. *Applied Cognitive Psychology*, **6**, 619–628. Reprinted here with permission from Wiley-Blackwell Publishing.

Even though the quality of transmitted images of faces can now be very high, there are still human factors issues surrounding the use of video-links rather than conducting conversations face to face. Real-time images via web-cam applications may still appear jerky, and it seems likely that it is these temporal factors rather than pictorial image quality per se that is likely to impact upon the quality of interaction. When people converse remotely there are other limitations that might influence their interaction too. Eye contact can only rarely be established, though it may be simulated, and the interlocutors do not share the same physical space and so the meaning of different eye gaze patterns cannot readily be established.

Boyle and colleagues (1994) investigated how visual signals complemented verbal interaction when two people worked together on a conversational task known as the "map task." In this, each person has a map that only they can see. One person has a map with a route drawn on it, and that person must describe this route so that their partner can reproduce the route on their own map. However, each member of the pair has a map with different landmarks shown and labeled and so the task requires clarification and negotiation on both sides. Both the conversation structure and its success (in terms of accuracy of the reproduced route and time taken to complete it) can be measured. Boyle et al. (1994) found that partners who could see as well as hear each other required shorter dialogues to achieve similar levels of success on the task than those who could only hear each other. Conversation analysis conducted by Doherty-Sneddon et al. (1997) showed that words such as "uh-huh; yes; ok" were used in the audio-only condition to signal that messages had been understood, and it was the reduction of this kind of "back-channel" or alignment response that yielded shorter dialogues when partners could see each other.

Doherty-Sneddon et al. (1997) then used the same task but with partners collaborating via high-quality video-links that either allowed or prevented eye contact between members of the pairs. They found that video-mediated communication was similar to face-to-face in the reduction of verbal alignments needed to complete the task. But video-mediated communication that involved eye contact provoked longer dialogues and was accompanied by more gazing between participants than was observed face to face. In the VMC conditions partners checked each other's understanding more often than when communicating with words alone. This may be because the novelty of a remote communication device that enabled eye contact was disruptive of regular interpersonal interaction in some way, or made participants less confident of their means of communication.

There are other demonstrations of differences between VMC and face-to-face interaction. It has been common practice in the past 20 years or so to allow child witnesses in cases involving physical or sexual abuse to be questioned via a live video-link, so that the child is not intimidated by the court room setting and/or the presence of their alleged abuser in the court room. Early evaluations of the use of live video-links in courtrooms in England (Davies and Noon, 1991) and Scotland (Flin et al., 1996) and in "mock" trials in the US (Goodman et al., 1998) revealed some differences in the evidence elicited in the two settings, but different studies found slightly different effects. However, an interesting effect in two of these three studies was that children interviewed via video were more resistant to misleading questions than were children interviewed live. This makes sense if the children feel more social presence from the authoritative adult in face-to-face settings, and thus under more pressure to comply.

This finding was replicated by Doherty-Sneddon et al. (2000) who compared live with video-based recall of information about a sequence of events that had taken place earlier the same day. The video condition used video tunnels, where an arrangement of mirrors combined with the cameras allowed eye contact to be established even in the video-based interview condition. Interspersed with a series of open-ended and closed questions about the child's journey to the laboratory and events on arrival at the university, there were three misleading questions, such as

"The cartoon you watched with Sandra was really funny wasn't it?" The correct response to this was to say they had not watched a cartoon.

The research revealed few significant differences between the two modes of communication, though in general 10-year-old children performed better than 6-year-olds, as one might expect. The older children also produced longer narratives when questioned face to face than on video. Importantly, though, in closed questions, the 6-year-olds were significantly more able to resist misleading questions when asked these via the video-link. Fewer incorrect responses were given in the video-mediated condition too, by both age groups.

If these "facilitative" effects of video-mediated communication arise because children are less intimidated by adults when these are not actually there, perhaps other situations may yield similar effects. Tachakra and Rajani (2002) compared interactions between a doctor, an emergency nurse practitioner, and a series of patients attending a minor accident and treatment service when all three were present together and when the doctor was available through a live video-link from a more distant location. There were no differences in interaction between the patients and the nurse across conditions (suggesting the patients in the two groups were probably comparable) but there were significant differences in the interactions with the doctor. For both the patients and the nurse, video-mediated communication with the doctor yielded longer and more interactive sessions, with patients more likely to interrupt and interrogate the doctor when he or she was located remotely. This suggests that the video-link made the patient feel more empowered—or less intimidated—than when the doctor was physically present. So, if the video-link removes some aspects of social pressure which is exerted more effectively when the person is physically present, this can have advantages.

Video-links may be constructed to allow participants to have eye contact, but some interesting work has examined the important role played by gaze *aversion* in managing cognitive load. Glenberg et al. (1998) noted that adults may avert their gaze when trying to answer difficult questions and suggested that this was a strategy to avoid cognitive overload by reducing the load of simultaneous non-verbal processing. Doherty-Sneddon and her colleagues (Doherty-Sneddon et al., 2001, 2002) extended Glenberg et al.'s findings to show that this gaze aversion strategy seems to be developed by the time children are 8 years old, but is not found in younger children.

Doherty-Sneddon and Phelps (2005) investigated whether gaze aversion was principally due to avoidance of cognitive overload, or whether it was driven in part as a way of avoiding embarrassment, e.g. when questions were difficult and attempts might be unsuccessful. Eight-year-olds were questioned live or via a video-link on questions varying in content and difficulty. Although children averted their gaze more in face-to-face than video interviews, in both conditions the amount of gaze aversion was related to question difficulty. Thus there may be a social factor that leads people to avert their gaze when they are thinking, and this is stronger in live conversation, but there appears also to be a cognitive driver too. As gaze aversion is often believed to be associated with people who are lying rather than telling the truth (Vrij et al., 2006) there are important implications of this research in understanding what behavior may lead someone to judge that a witness or defendant is being untruthful.

This section has demonstrated that face-to-face interaction is rather complex, and the rich variety of social cues can inhibit as well as help performance, depending on task and circumstances. Sometimes it is advantageous to reduce social distance while maintaining a rich variety of non-verbal signals—as when children are interviewed or patients interrogate their doctors. Sometimes, as in gaze aversion, interlocutors need to escape from the demands of face processing, even when social distance has already been reduced by video-links. Adding video to audio channels may not always be helpful, for example where two collaborators must do cognitively demanding work.

Such factors will need to be considered carefully when designing remote communication links for future applications.

Reconstruction of faces

The cosmetics industry is big business and as surgical procedures advance, and facial cosmetic surgery becomes more acceptable, there is potentially lots of interest in being able to simulate the effects of surgical interventions on the face to anticipate how these will impact upon appearance. At a superficial level, two-dimensional (2D) computer graphics allow people to explore the effects of simple changes in hairstyle, smoothing of wrinkles, or removal of blemishes. But facial surgery has developed to address much more significant and serious conditions than is implied by the term "cosmetic."

Harcourt and Rumsey (2008) suggest that almost one in 100 people in the UK have a significant facial disfigurement, with some 66,000 disfigurements arising from accidents (e.g. burns) and 40,000 with disfigurements arising from cancer or cancer treatments. Facial disfigurement can be extremely traumatic and threatening to the person's self-image and self-esteem. This itself raises interesting and important psychological questions, since there is no apparent relationship between the severity of the disfigurement in terms of the person's appearance, and their psychological adjustment to it. Rumsey et al. (2004) studied 458 adults with a range of conditions affecting their facial appearance and found that almost half of them had symptoms of anxiety, and over a quarter of depression, but this was not obviously linked to the actual extent of their disfigurement. This study confirms many others which suggest that some individuals are extraordinarily resilient to potentially distressing conditions, but for others the effects of disfigurement are extremely destructive.

Over the past 20 years or so the development of three-dimensional (3D) graphics and structural imaging tools has made it possible for surgeons to plan particular surgical operations and predict what appearance effects might result from different interventions. Such techniques usually rely on the imaging of bony structures using 3D computed tomography (CT) or other kinds of structural scans. The surface of the face may also be scanned using 3D laser or other techniques and the effects of changes to the underlying structures on the appearance of the surface modeled by fitting the old surface over the new underlying structures. This technique of mapping a surface onto an underlying skeletal structure also provides a way of trying to build a representation of the appearance of a person from a skull. This may be of interest in historical/archaeological contexts but also in certain criminal or accident investigations where the identity of a particular person's remains needs to be established.

It is in this context that an understanding of the psychology of identity of 3D structures becomes relevant. If 3D structure is accurate (and this depends on the reconstructed person having skin/soft tissue measurements that are average or near average) would the surface alone prove recognizable? Bruce et al. (1991) showed that accurate high-density 3D surface models created by laser scanning of familiar faces (who could be identified 99% accurately from regular photographs) were difficult to identify, particularly for female heads (72.5% accurate identification for males in three-quarter views; but just 25% for females) compared with fully textured photographs of the same people with eyes closed and wearing bathing caps (85% accurate for males; 87.5% accurate for females). What are the practical implications of this result? Without knowledge of the person's likely coloring, it may be difficult for superficial details of the resulting model to be anything other than a guess. This may be one of the reasons that the unidentified victim of the King's Cross underground fire in 1987 remained unknown for so long. Chambers (2007) describes the painstaking forensic investigation, including the reconstruction of a possible face for the unidentified person, who remained unknown for a full 16 years after the original accident that resulted in his death.

Such observations have theoretical importance too. During the 1980s many of us were influenced by an approach to understanding object recognition building on the insights of the late David Marr (1982) and developed by scientists such as Irv Biederman (1987). In this approach, 2D images of objects present features indicative of their 3D shape—and the recognition of an object from any viewpoint is held to be achieved via some stored representation of the 3D structure of the object. The observation that 3D shape alone leads to very poor recognition (something that was known by the artists of the classical world who painted features onto their sculptures) is suggestive of a rather different representational system for faces than for basic level object categories (see O'Toole, Chapter 2, this volume).

Face transplants

At the time of writing there have been three reported cases of face transplantation, where a person with a facial disfigurement has been given a significant amount of facial tissue from a "donor." All three reported cases have achieved a significant improvement in appearance and quality of life for the recipients. Nonetheless the procedure remains extremely controversial, for a number of reasons, many of them psychological.

Living with another person's face is the stuff of science fiction (e.g. see Hiroshi Teshigahara's 1966 film *The Face of Another* based on Kōbō Abe's 1959 novel). But the donor's identity and its possible impact on the recipient is probably not the main psychological issue that arises from face transplantation. Of the three reported cases, two had had a recent and traumatic change to their facial appearance as a result of attack by an animal (one dog; one bear) and so they were already having to cope with a transformation of their underlying self-image. Moreover, since a "face" transplant is really a process by which soft tissue from one face is pulled over the bones of another, the soft tissues will assume a good deal of underlying shape from the recipient. Moreover, the procedures to date have been partial transplants. Many of the recipients' original features remain intact. Pictures of the first reported case in France (see Dubernard et al., 2007) reveal a high degree of resemblance in the image of the person post-recovery and her original face before her injury, at least to someone unfamiliar with her.

The psychological issues arising from face transplantation are more subtle than those of wearing "another's" identity. First there is the issue of the loss of identity of the *donor* as a result of the transplant. The surgical teams involved make considerable effort to reconstruct the face of the donor with synthetic materials after the facial tissue is removed in order to minimize the impact of this disfigurement at death on the families and friends of the donor. Second, there is the prospective and very serious risk of rejection of the transplant by the recipient. In all three reported cases rejection problems have been reported postoperatively, and while these have been controlled with changed drug regimens there remains the real problem of long-term rejection (with the necessity of further surgery, and yet another new face) and significant health risks from the drugs themselves. Third there is the uncertain extent of the recovery of function as well as appearance of the face. A face must be able to move—to smile, speak, eat—it does much more than provide a bland identity, and the recovery of these functions is slow and uncertain. The French patient was able to drink without dribbling after 12 months and recovered sensitivity to heat and cold within the first few months. Recovery of motor function was slower but the patient was able to smile normally 18 months after the operation. The ability to express emotions facially may be of more than cosmetic importance. Recent research has shown that the administration of "Botox", which can be used to paralyze expressive muscles in the face such as those used to frown in anger, attenuates responses in the amygdala and other brain structures involved in the expression of such emotions (Hennenlotter et al., 2009).

The face transplant procedure remains experimental and as such is governed by ethical guidelines of the particular country. Morris et al. (2007) describe the results of the discussion about the ethical procedures needed to inform any request for such an intervention in the UK. Rapid progress in the surgical and immunosuppressive techniques will be needed for this to become anything other than a rare experimental treatment, but as these techniques develop so there will be need for further consideration of the wide range of psychological issues surrounding the donor, the recipient, and their families and friends.

Eyewitness research

I began this chapter as I began my own career, noting the public interest that was taken in cases of mistaken identity during the 1970s. Since that time there has been an enormous amount of research conducted on factors contributing to successful—or more often unsuccessful—recognition of faces by eyewitnesses. Eyewitnesses may be asked to try to identify the person seen committing a crime from live line-ups, photo-spreads and frequently these days, video parades. I will not review this work here because it forms the content of the chapter by Lindsay and colleagues later in this volume (see Chapter 16). However, there is an important conclusion from this work which resonates with that drawn from work on CCTV images and recall of composites that I review here. A witness who picks someone out from a parade or collection of photographs is making an important statement that is of relevance to the courts. The statement that they are making is that the person they pick _resembles_ their memory of the criminal more closely than any of the other available choices, and resembles their memory sufficiently strongly that they believe this was indeed the person that they saw. But resemblance and identity are not the same thing, and we must be cautious about inferring identity from a statement that can only be based on resemblance.

Composite images and their improvement

If a witness to a crime is able to describe the appearance of someone they saw then they may be asked to try to build an image of the criminal's face. Such images are now collectively called "composite" images because they usually involve the witness working with some kind of "kit" of face features or face variations to build an image. However, before the invention of any such composite kits, witnesses were interviewed by police artists who would work with the witness to draw an image, and police artists still do such work today.

Before computer-based composite systems were developed, two "manual" systems gained prominence—the Identikit system in the US and the Photo-fit system predominantly in Europe. Identikit was initially based on line-drawn face features, but evolved into a photo-based system, like Photo-fit. Photo-fit was developed by the French photographer Jacques Penry. It was built from photographs of faces from which local areas containing different features were cut and stored. The result was that both Identikit and Photo-fit systems required that the witness build a face by choosing from a variety of different face features (e.g. one nose from a set of noses; one mouth from a set of mouths) and assembling a whole face from these different local choices. The systems were developed pragmatically and/or intuitively rather than being based on any particular understanding of how witnesses perceive or recall faces. In the UK a group of psychologists at Aberdeen—Hadyn Ellis, Graham Davies, and John Shepherd—conducted some formal evaluations of the efficacy of these systems for helping witnesses to recall faces and came up with some rather damning findings.

For example, witnesses who were asked to make their own drawings of faces in front of them could produce images rated as better likenesses of the target faces than if they built a face from Photo-fit (Ellis et al., 1978a). Moreover, working from memory, the quality of likenesses produced by drawing dropped off dramatically—but that made with Photo-fit did not—but only because performance was effectively at floor (Ellis et al., 1978a). A US team led by Ken Laughery found similar problems with Identikit (e.g. Laughery and Fowler, 1980). Likenesses made by a police sketch artist showed sensitivity to delay while those built from Identikit did not.

The visible lines between the features selected to build up a Photo-fit also contributed to their poor likeness. Ellis et al. (1978b) showed that recognition of photographs of faces with lines drawn on them was poorer than the same faces without these lines. This particular problem should now have gone with the development of computerized systems such as "E-FIT." Computerized systems have several advantages. Features can be moved around allowing modification of the overall configuration of the face, which is so important for face recognition (see later; and Tanaka and Gordon, Chapter 10, this volume). There are no longer sharp boundaries between the features because of the image processing applied to the features. Various alterations can be made to the composites using additional paint functions. As a result a skilled operator can produce an extremely good likeness of a target face they try to copy (see Figure 8.2)—there are no longer limitations with the art work. Nonetheless, once mock witnesses attempt to build images of faces from memory, the rated likeness of such composites is poor, and the resulting composites are rarely recognized by people who should know them (see examples in Figure 8.3).

In Table 8.1, I reproduce data from Frowd et al. (2005) which compares performance of four contemporary composite systems with that from a human sketch artist. Composites were produced of a series of target faces, from memory, after each was studied in a single photograph by a participant unfamiliar with the individual shown. Other participants familiar with these targets then tried to identify them. All current systems gave extremely poor identification rates when the composites were built after a forensically realistic delay of two days from seeing the target face.

There seem to be several different problems of recall using composite systems.

Fig. 8.2 An experienced operator's E-FIT composite of a well-known face (former Prime Minister John Major, constructed by John Shepherd). Reproduced from Bruce and Young, *In the eye of the beholder: The science of face perception*, 1998, with permission from Oxford University Press.

Fig. 8.3 Four composite images produced using different systems by experienced operators working with mock witnesses who were not familiar with the target face. Top left: Brad Pitt by police sketch artist; Top right: Robbie Williams by EvoFIT; bottom left: Michael Owen by PRO-fit; bottom right Noel Gallagher by E-FIT. Images courtesy of Charlie Frowd, University of Central Lancashire.

One is the kind of information that can be remembered well with a composite technique. We have known since seminal work by Hadyn Ellis and colleagues (Ellis et al., 1979) that the external features of unfamiliar faces, which include the hair, are remembered better than their internal features, while the internal features—probably the eyes in particular (O'Donnell and Bruce, 2001)—are more strongly represented in familiar faces. This immediately raises a problem

Table 8.1 Percentage correct naming of composites of famous faces produced by a sketch artist and four different computer-based composite systems in Frowd et al. (2005).

Technique	Naming
Sketch	8.1
EvoFIT	3.6
FACES	3.2
PROfit	1.3
E-FIT	0.0
Mean	3.2

for the eyewitness working to build a face composite. By definition, someone building a composite is unfamiliar with the person they are trying to remember—and thus likely to be able to remember the external features of the face better than the internal features—confirmed in a study by Frowd et al. (2007a). But the composite, once created, is intended to provoke recognition by people familiar with the identity of the composite—for them, it is the internal features that matter more. This may be one of the reasons why overall rates of identification of composites remain very low.

A second and fundamental problem is that most composite systems require witnesses to try to *recall* individual face features. But faces appear to be represented in memory much more holistically—as evidenced by extensive work on the inversion effect (Yin, 1969; see Tanaka and Gordon, Chapter 10, this volume), and various effects of relative influences of the whole face on parts within it such as Tanaka and Farah (1993), Young et al. (1987), etc. (see Tanaka and Gordon, Chapter 10, this volume). In view of this, it might be better if witnesses were asked to build a composite by exploiting their capacities to recognize whole faces rather than recall individual features. Such reasoning has led to the development of new systems such as EvoFIT (http://www. uclan.ac.uk/scitech/psychology/research/evofit/research.php).

In this, witnesses inspect one or more whole faces generated from underlying holistic features (created through principal components analysis of a large data base of face images) and on the basis of choices a face is "evolved" to more closely match what the witness remembers of the person they saw.

Evaluation of EvoFIT alongside other more conventional composite systems in use has shown mixed results. It sometimes outperforms other systems, but not always, though there are some pleasing demonstrations of its efficacy in real policing. However, EvoFIT does have some further advantages over the E-FIT-like systems.

Alongside the problems of recalling individual features are the rather limited ways that witnesses can interact with the resulting composite as it develops. Making a face look "meaner" or "younger" or "prettier" is just not possible with the kit-based composite systems used today. But such global transformations are possible with a holistic recognition based system like EvoFIT. Frowd et al. (2006) describe the implementation of systems that allow an EvoFIT composite to be made "more threatening" or "more dishonest" or "older." Such manipulations enhanced the likenesses produced.

Nevertheless, perhaps it is too much to expect a single witness to produce a good likeness with any of the current systems. A person's memory for an event is likely to be imperfect however wonderful the system for eliciting it. Bruce et al. (2002) reasoned that where there was more than a single witness to a specific crime, we might be able to combine their different memories in a way which reinforced correct features and minimized the impact of errors. After all, if three independent witnesses to a crime stated that the getaway car was blue, this is likely to be seen as a stronger pointer to guide investigation than if each witness recollected a different color. Why not do the same with faces? By morphing different composite images together, similar features across the different individual composites will be emphasized and deviations minimized. Bruce et al. (2002) found, in two separate experiments, that the average of four individual composites was always at least as good—in terms of rated likeness or other measures of identifiability—as the best of the four individual composites (see Figure 8.4 for an illustration). This demonstration, often replicated since, has now been used to amend the guidance given to investigating officers so that individual composites may be used in combination in certain circumstances.

One consequence of morphing together the composite images created independently by different witnesses is that the resulting morph looks a little more "average" in appearance than any of the contributing composites. We reasoned that if the morphed composite reinforced correct memories and minimized incorrect ones, a compensatory caricature of the resulting morphed composite should enhance the likeness further. This was found in a recent study by Frowd et al. (2007b). Positive caricatures of morphed composites were rated as better likenesses and recognized at least as well as the non-caricatured morphs. Frowd et al. (2007b) also demonstrated that it was *anti-caricatures*—not caricatures—of individual composites that improved their likeness to the required identity. Arguably, anti-caricaturing a composite has an effect a little like morphing—by making the composite a bit more average it will reduce the impact of any errors of

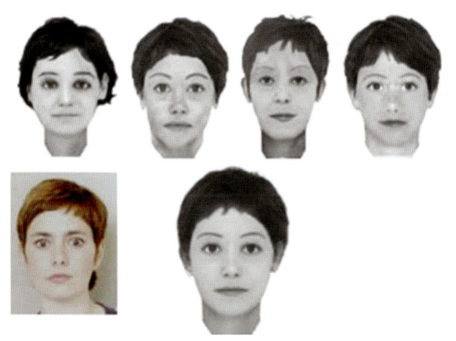

Fig. 8.4 Four individual witness attempts to produce composite images of a woman (shown in the photograph) following study of her on video. Below is shown the result of morphing all these four composites together. Reproduced from Bruce et al. (2002), courtesy of the American Psychological Association.

memory that result in extreme feature values. However, the greatest improvement of all was observed when a series of morphed images ranging from anti-caricatures to positive caricatures of the original composite were shown for identification. Showing a caricature series raised identification rates substantially, so that composites of famous faces were correctly named by the majority of participants.

Closed circuit television

The UK has more CCTV (closed circuit television) cameras in public places per head of the population than any other country. Most incidents that occur in public places such as car parks, shopping centers, or within individual shops or banks will be recorded by at least one and some-times several cameras. Given this, we should ask whether there remains any need to rely on evi-dence about appearance from eye-witnesses at all? Unfortunately, or fortunately, depending on your point of view, there remain many areas of life which are outside the reach of CCTV. Assaults may take place in the countryside, within our own homes, or down dark back alleys beyond the reach of cameras. Although the cameras on nearby streets might help point to suspects, only the person or people directly affected by these assaults can help pinpoint which of many passers-by were those involved.

Moreover, even where a camera has captured an image of a person committing a crime, we must be extremely careful how this image is used subsequently. On the positive side, broadcasting images from security cameras on programmes such as the BBC's *Crimewatch* is likely to prove extremely useful in any investigation. Burton et al. (1999) showed that participants who were familiar with people who were filmed on poor-quality CCTV images were extremely accurate at identifying them from short video-clips despite the poverty of these images, provided the face was shown in the image. On the negative side, however, Bruce et al. (1999) showed that even when video images were of high quality, participants unfamiliar with the faces were extremely poor at verifying whether or not the person shown in a particular image was present in an array of face images shown for comparison.

Zoe Henderson followed up this rather surprising finding using a more realistic scenario by making use of some simulated crime footage produced by a television company under extremely realistic conditions (Henderson et al., 2001; see Figure 8.5). Actors played the roles of robbers entering a bank and demanding money. Even the images taken by the broadcast quality cameras proved hard to verify for identity when the task was to decide whether each image shown matched a photograph of the target or a similar-looking foil. Davis and Valentine (2009) have demon-strated even more ecological validity by showing that confusions indeed extend to the matching of camera images against live targets as would be the case if a CCTV image was used for com-parison with a suspect in court.

To sum up, even poor quality images can be extremely useful in a criminal investigation, because people familiar with someone shown in such an image have a very good chance of recog-nizing them correctly. Leads such as this following the broadcast of such images can help reveal other evidence, and have proved extremely useful in the hunt for criminals. However, using an image to help narrow down the field of enquiry is quite different from using an image to prove identity in court. Our research on the confusions that can be made between different camera images points to the extreme caution that should be used over the presentation of CCTV images in court. Two different images of the same person can look very different, and two images of dif-ferent people can look highly similar. A CCTV image can, and should, be used to point to a resemblance, but not to prove identity, a recommendation that echoes that applying to witness identification of suspects from line-ups.

(a)

CCTV images of robber 21

(b)   Photo array for robber 1

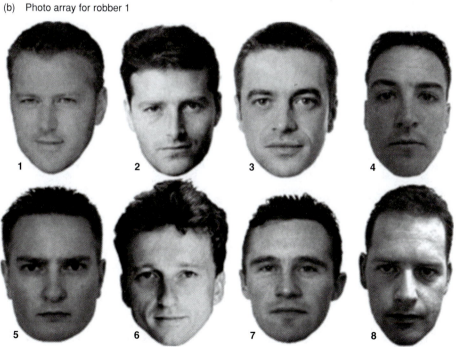

1   2   3   4

5   6   7   8

Fig. 8.5 (a) CCTV images of one of the robbers in Henderson et al. (2001) study. (b) the array within which the robber may or may not be seen. Reproduced from Henderson, Bruce, and Burton (2001). Matching the faces of robbers captured on video, *Applied Cognitive Psychology*, **15**, 445–464. Reprinted here with permission from Wiley-Blackwell Publishing.

Summary and conclusions

This chapter has described some of the psychological research that has accompanied the recent rapid development or deployment of systems for showing, building, or manipulating faces for a variety of purposes. I have had to be selective in my review, but I hope nonetheless to have succeeded in illustrating the psychological issues that arise in a range of engineering, medical, and legal contexts.

However, as the chapter has illustrated, technological development has not always been matched by an appreciation of the psychological issues that need to be overcome to take full advantage of new systems. In some areas the advances raise new psychological issues (e.g. facial transplants). In others, new technology has simply replicated old problems— e.g. that witnesses cannot recall individual face features; or that resemblance and identity are not the same thing. For the future it would be good to see more developments start with these psychological issues and build the technologies around them.

References

Biederman, I. (1987). Recognition-by-components. A theory of human image understanding. *Psychological Review*, **94**, 115–147.

Boyle, E.A., Anderson, A.H., and Newlands, A. (1994). The effects of visibility on dialogue and performance in a cooperative problem-solving task. *Language and Speech*, **37**, 1–20.

Bruce, V., Healey, P., Burton, M., Doyle, T., Coombes, A., and Linney, A. (1991). Recognising facial surfaces. *Perception*, **20**, 755–769.

Bruce, V., Henderson, Z., Greenwood, K., Hancock, P.J.B., Burton, A.M., and Miller, P. (1999). Verification of face identities from images captured on video. *Journal of Experimental Psychology: Applied*, **5**, 339–360.

Bruce, V., Ness, H., Hancock, P.J.B., Newman, C., and Rarity, J. (2002). Four heads are better than one: Combining face composites yields improvements in face likeness. *Journal of Applied Psychology*, **87**, 894–902.

Burton, A.M., Wilson, S., Cowan, M., and Bruce, V. (1999). Face recognition in poor-quality video: Evidence from security surveillance. *Psychological Science*, **10**, 243–248.

Chambers, P. (2007). *Body 115. The mystery of the last victim of the King's Cross Fire*. Chichester: Wiley.

Davies, G.M. and Noon, E. 1991. *An evaluation of the Live Link for child witnesses*. London: The Home Office.

Davis, J.P and Valentine, T. (2009). CCTV on trial: Matching video images with the defendant in the dock. *Applied Cognitive Psychology*, **23**, 482–505.

Davies, G., Ellis, H.D., and Shepherd, J. (1978). Face recognition accuracy as a function of mode of representation. *Journal of Applied Psychology*, **63**, 180–187.

Devlin, Lord (1976) *Report to the Secretary of State for the Home Department of the Departmental Committee on Evidence of Identification in Criminal Cases*. London: HMSO.

Doherty-Sneddon, G., Anderson, A., O'Malley, C., Langton, S., Garrod, S., and Bruce, V. (1997). Face-to-face and video-mediated communication: A comparison of dialogue structure and task performance. *Journal of Experimental Psychology: Applied*, **3**, 105–125.

Doherty-Sneddon, G., Bonner, L., and Bruce, V. (2001). Cognitive demands of face monitoring: Evidence for visuospatial overload. *Memory & Cognition*, **29**, 909–919.

Doherty-Sneddon, G., Bruce, V., Bonner, L., Longbotham, S., and Doyle, C. (2002). Development of gaze aversion as disengagement from visual information. *Developmental Psychology*, **38**, 438–445.

Doherty-Sneddon, G. and McAuley, S. (2000). Influence of video-mediation on adult-child interviews: Implications for the use of the live link with child witnesses. *Applied Cognitive Psychology*, **14**, 379–392.

Doherty-Sneddon, G. and Phelps, F.G. (2005). Gaze aversion: A response to cognitive or social difficulty? *Memory & Cognition*, **33**, 727–733.

Dubernard, J.-M., Lengele, B., Morelon, E., *et al.* (2007). Outcomes 18 months after the first human partial face transplantation. *New England Journal of Medicine*, **357**, 2451–2460.

Ellis, H.D., Davies, G.M., and Shepherd, J.W. (1978a). A critical examination of the Photofit system for recalling faces. *Ergonomics*, **21**, 297–307.

Ellis, H.D., Davies, G.M., and Shepherd, J.W. (1978b). Remembering pictures of real and unreal faces–some practical and theoretical considerations. *British Journal of Psychology*, **69**, 467–474.

Ellis, H.D., Shepherd, J.W., and Davies, G.M. (1979). Identification of familiar and unfamiliar faces from internal and external features–some implications for theories of face recognition. *Perception*, **8**, 431–439.

Flin R., Kearney, B., and Murray, K. (1996). Children's evidence: Scottish research and law. *Criminal Justice and Behaviour*, **23**, 358–376.

Frowd, C.D., Carson, D., Ness, H., *et al.* (2005). Contemporary Composite Techniques: the impact of a forensically-relevant target delay. *Legal & Criminological Psychology*, **10**, 63–81

Frowd, C.D., Bruce, V., McIntyre, A., and Hancock, P. (2006). Adding holistic dimensions to a facial composite system. *Proceedings of the Seventh International Conference on Automatic Face and Gesture Recognition*, 183–188.

Frowd, C., Bruce V., McIntyre A., and Hancock, P. (2007). The relative importance of external and internal features of facial composites. *British Journal of Psychology*, **98**, 61–77.

Frowd, C., Bruce, V., Ross, D., McIntyre, A., and Hancock, P.J.B. (2007). An application of caricature: How to improve the recognition of facial composites. *Visual Cognition*, **15**, 954–984.

Frowd, C.D., Bruce, V., Smith, A.J., and Hancock, P.J.B. (2008). Improving the quality of facial composites using a holistic cognitive interview. *Journal of Experimental Psychology—Applied*, **14**, 276–287.

Glenberg, A.M., Schroeder, J.L., and Robertson, D.A. (1998). Averting the gaze disengages the environment and facilitates remembering. *Memory & Cognition*, **26**, 651–658.

Goodman, G.S, Tobey, A.E., Batterman-Faunce, J.M., *et al.* (1998). Face-to-face confrontation: Effects of closed-circuit technology on children's eyewitness testimony and jurors' decisions. *Law & Human Behaviour*, **22**, 165–203.

Goren, C.C., Sarty, M., and Wu, P.H.K. (1975). Visual following and pattern discrimination of face-like stimuli by new-born infants. *Pediatrics*, **56**, 544–549.

Gross, C.G., Rocha-Miranda, C.E., and Bender, D.B. (1972) Visual properties of neurons in inferotemporal cortex of the macaque. *Journal of Neurophysiology*, **35**, 96–111.

Harcourt, D. and Rumsey, N. (2008). Psychology and visible difference. *The Psychologist*, **21**, 486–489.

Henderson, Z., Bruce, V., and Burton, A.M. (2001). Matching the faces of robbers captured on video. *Applied Cognitive Psychology*, **15**, 445–464.

Hennenlotter, A., Dresel, C., Castrop, F., Ceballos Baumann, A.O., Wohlschlager, A.M., and Haslinger, B. (2009). The link between facial feedback and neural activity within central circuitries of emotion–new insights from botulinum toxin-indiced denervation of frown muscles. *Cerebral Cortex*, **19**, 537–542.

Laughery, K. and Fowler, R. (1980). Sketch artist and identikit procedures for generating facial images, *Journal of Applied Psychology*, **65**, 307–316.

Marr, D. (1982). *Vision: A computational investigation into the human representation and processing of visual information.* San Francisco, CA: WH Freeman.

Morris, P., Bradley, A., Doyal, L., *et al.* (2007). Face transplantation: A review of the technical, immunological, psychological and clinical issues with recommendations for good practice. *Transplantation*, **83**, 109–128.

O'Donnell, C. and Bruce, V. (2001). Familiarisation with faces selectively enhances sensitivity to changes made to the eyes. *Perception*, **30**, 755–764.

Pearson, D. (1992). The extraction of use of facial features in low bit-rate visual communication. *Philosophical Transactions of the Royal Society of London, B*, **335**, 79–85.

Rumsey, N., Clarke, A., White, P., Wyn-Williams, M., and Garlick, W. (2004). Altered body image: appearance-related concerns of people with visible disfigurement. *Journal of Advanced Nursing*, **48**, 443–453.

Shepard, R.N. (1967). Recognition memory for words, sentences and pictures. *Journal of Verbal Learning and Verbal Memory*, **6**, 156–163.

Standing, L. (1970). Perception and memory for pictures–single trial learning of 2500 visual stimuli. *Psychonomic Science*, **19**, 73–74.

Tachakra, S., and Rajani R. (2002). Social presence in telemedicine. *Journal of Telemedicine and Telecare*, **8**, 226–230.

Tanaka, J. and Farah, M. (1993). Parts and wholes in face recognition. *Quarterly Journal of Experimental Psychology*, **46A**, 225–246.

Vrij, A., Akehurst, L., and Knight, S. (2006). Police officers', social workers' and the general public's beliefs about deception in children, adolescents and adults. *Legal and Criminological Psychology*, **11**, 297–312.

Yin, R.K. (1969). Looking at upside-down faces. *Journal of Experimental Psychology*, **81**, 141–145.

Young, A.W., Hellawell, D.J., and Hay, D.C. (1987). Configural information in face perception. *Perception*, **16**, 747–759.

Part II

Perceiving and Remembering Faces

Chapter 9

Are Faces Special?

Elinor McKone and Rachel Robbins

In many ways, of course, the answer to the question "Are faces special?" is obvious. There is no doubt that faces are special *functionally*—that is, faces provide unique information about expression, gaze direction, identity, and visual cues to speech. In the literature, however, the debate about whether "faces are special" has referred to the specific question of whether there are special *visual processing mechanisms* unique to faces, presumably deriving from the social importance of faces and developed either across the course of evolution or the course of childhood. Further, because it is obvious that mechanisms involved in recognizing facial expression, eye gaze direction, and speech cues must be special to faces—these types of information are available in no other objects—the question of "Are faces special?" has essentially referred to whether there are unique visual mechanisms for processing *identity*-related information in faces as compared to other objects.

It is this question we address here. We provide historical background to the question, and then an updated review of the empirical evidence.

The theoretical proposals: faces are special

Historically, several strands can be identified to the proposal that visual representations of faces are special. First, it has been suggested that infants might be born with an innate representation of the structural form of a face (Morton and Johnson, 1991). This would make faces special, because innateness is a property that clearly cannot hold for non-face objects in general: humans can learn totally new forms of objects even as adults (e.g. new inventions such as computers or mobile phones). Second, it has been proposed that a key processing style used for recognizing faces— variously referred to as holistic, configural, or second-order relational[1]—might be unique to faces and does not occur for other objects (Diamond and Carey, 1986; Yin, 1969). Third, it has been proposed that there might be face-specific neural representations (e.g. Kanwisher et al., 1997): common ideas are that: (1) face-selective neurons are clustered together such that they form face-selective regions visible in functional magnetic resonance imaging (fMRI) (the fusiform face area (FFA) and occipital face area (OFA) being the most relevant for present purposes), (2) face and object regions are capable of being selectively damaged, and (3) there are face-selective event-related potential (ERP) responses (the N170 being the most relevant here).

---

[1] Researchers differ as to whether holistic, configural, and second-order relational processing are independent aspects of the "special" processing style used for faces (D. Maurer et al., 2002), or not (McKone and Yovel, 2009; Tanaka and Sengco, 1997; Yovel and Duchaine, 2006). For present purposes, it is not necessary to distinguish between them, and we use the term "holistic" throughout.

The theoretical proposals: faces are not special

Two theoretical challenges have been proposed to the idea that faces are special. The first is that apparently face-specific mechanisms are in fact engaged by any within-class discrimination task (Damasio et al., 1982). The logic here is that, with faces, the task (actual or implied) is almost always to identify a face at the individual level of "Mary" or "Jane" rather than merely as "a face," while for objects the natural level of identification for most people is the general level such as "dog" rather than as individuals "Fido" or "Rex"; this could matter because within-class (subordinate level) judgments are perceptually more taxing than basic level categorization. The *within-class discrimination hypothesis* then proposes that apparently face-specific or face-selective mechanisms will be engaged by individual-level recognition of objects, just as they are by individual-level recognition of faces. In general, it seems well accepted that the within-class discrimination hypothesis has been disproved, and we collate the evidence against it here.

Second, there has been ongoing debate about the *expertise hypothesis* (Diamond and Carey, 1986). This is derived from the within-class discrimination hypothesis. However, rather than proposing that claimed face-specific or face-selective mechanisms are tapped by *all* within-class discrimination situations, it proposes that these mechanisms are tapped by individual-level recognition tasks only in the *special situation in which a person is an expert* at recognizing exemplars of a non-face object category (e.g. in gun dog judges for the stimulus class of Labrador dogs). The logic here is that because people typically are experts at individuating faces but not other objects, apparently face-specific visual mechanisms could in fact be expertise-specific mechanisms. People expert in within-class discrimination of objects are rare, but the case is still theoretically important: if such people show "face-specific" processing for their objects-of-expertise then this would demonstrate that this type of processing is not limited to the face structural form.

Empirical review

We now turn to evaluating the empirical evidence testing whether or not faces are special. This material overlaps with our earlier reviews and discussions (McKone, 2010; McKone, Crookes, and Kanwisher, 2009; McKone and Kanwisher, 2005; McKone, Kanwisher, and Duchaine, 2007; McKone and Robbins, 2007; Robbins and McKone, 2007), but is expanded to include a number of important new results. We will argue the latest evidence supports the view that faces are special in *all* the ways that have been proposed in the literature: that is, in terms of innate coding, holistic processing, and face-specific neural representation in adults.

An evolved face representation

Supporting the view that faces are special, recent studies have provided the first compelling evidence of an evolved and innate representation of face structure, which is involved in discriminating individual faces.

First, the ability to tell apart highly similar faces is found in newborn babies (even when the faces are novel, hair is removed, and there is a viewpoint change between habituation and test; Turati et al., 2006, 2008), and also in young monkeys raised without visual face exposure (Sugita, 2008). These results indicate individuation ability *in the absence or near absence of any prior experience* with faces. Second, *perceptual narrowing across the course of infancy* occurs for faces: experience with faces of one human race tunes out the initial ability to individuate faces of other races and other primate species (Kelly et al., 2007; Pascalis et al., 2002; Sugita, 2008). In other domains (notably language), perceptual narrowing has been taken as strong evidence of innate mechanisms that are experience-expectant. Finally, there is evidence of *heritability* of face recognition ability and neural mechanisms. The lifelong inability to recognize faces revealed in developmental prosopagnosia can affect multiple members of the same family (Duchaine et al., 2007; Grueter et al., 2007; Kennerknecht et al., 2008) including across three generations (Schmalzl et al., 2008). And, in the first twin study of face recognition, the pattern of fMRI activation across visual areas in the ventral stream was more similar for monozygotic than dizygotic twins, but only when the stimuli were faces and not when they were classes for which it is clear there could be no evolutionary basis for the observed selective cortical regions (i.e. written words, and chairs; Polk et al., 2007).

Other findings are also consistent with the idea of an evolutionarily old face representation. Monkeys, like humans, show face selective cells (e.g. Tsao et al., 2006). Also, chimpanzees, monkeys, and indeed even sheep, demonstrate some key behavioral properties of face recognition found in humans, such as inversion effects that are much larger for faces than objects (chimpanzees: Parr et al., 2009; sheep: Kendrick et al., 1996), and a Thatcher illusion (monkeys: Adachi et al., 2009). (For more detailed discussion of the animal literature, see Kendrick and Feng, Chapter 34; Parr and Hecht, Chapter 35, this volume.)

Finally, evidence suggests the innate representation of face structure is specifically of the *upright orientation*. In newborns, individual-level discrimination occurs only for upright faces, and not inverted faces (Turati et al., 2006), and newborn preference for attractive over unattractive faces is also found upright but not inverted (Slater et al., 2000).

Testing the within-class discrimination hypothesis

We now turn to behavioral and neural results relevant to testing the first alternative theory to the view that faces are special, namely the *within-class discrimination hypothesis*. Crucially, all results reviewed in this section come from studies in human adults contrasting face and object recognition in tasks in which the object condition has involved, like the face condition, *recognition of the objects at the individual level*. (For example, a behavioral experiment might require learning a set of 15 Labradors followed by a memory test presenting the 15 learned Labradors paired with 15 novel Labradors.) The present section deals only with the typical situation in which participants have no particular expertise at discriminating individual exemplars of the tested object class; such participants are referred to as "novices."

A review of the results show that requiring within-class discrimination of objects does not produce face-like processing. This conclusion is derived from multiple paradigms, clearly rejecting the within-class discrimination hypothesis.

Holistic/configural processing

Considering behavioral methods first, the procedures of classic paradigms associated with holistic/configural processing for faces are illustrated in Figures 9.1 and 9.2 (also see Tanaka and Gordon, Chapter 10, this volume). These paradigms produce a strong and replicable dissociation between faces and within-class discrimination of objects.

First, there is a *disproportionate inversion effect* on recognition memory and perceptual matching. Inversion effects on memory (measured as the absolute difference between per cent correct for upright and per cent correct for inverted) are typically 20 to 25 percentage points for faces, and 0 to 8 percentage points for within-class discrimination of objects. Sample findings are listed in the first two data columns of Table 9.1, and similar results exists for airplanes, costumes, and stick figures (Yin, 1969), landscapes (Diamond and Carey, 1986), shoes (de Gelder et al., 1998), buildings and dog faces (Scapinello and Yarmey, 1970), houses and chairs (Boutet and Faubert, 2006), houses (Leder and Carbon, 2006), cats, dogs, and birds (Minnebusch et al., 2009), and racehorses

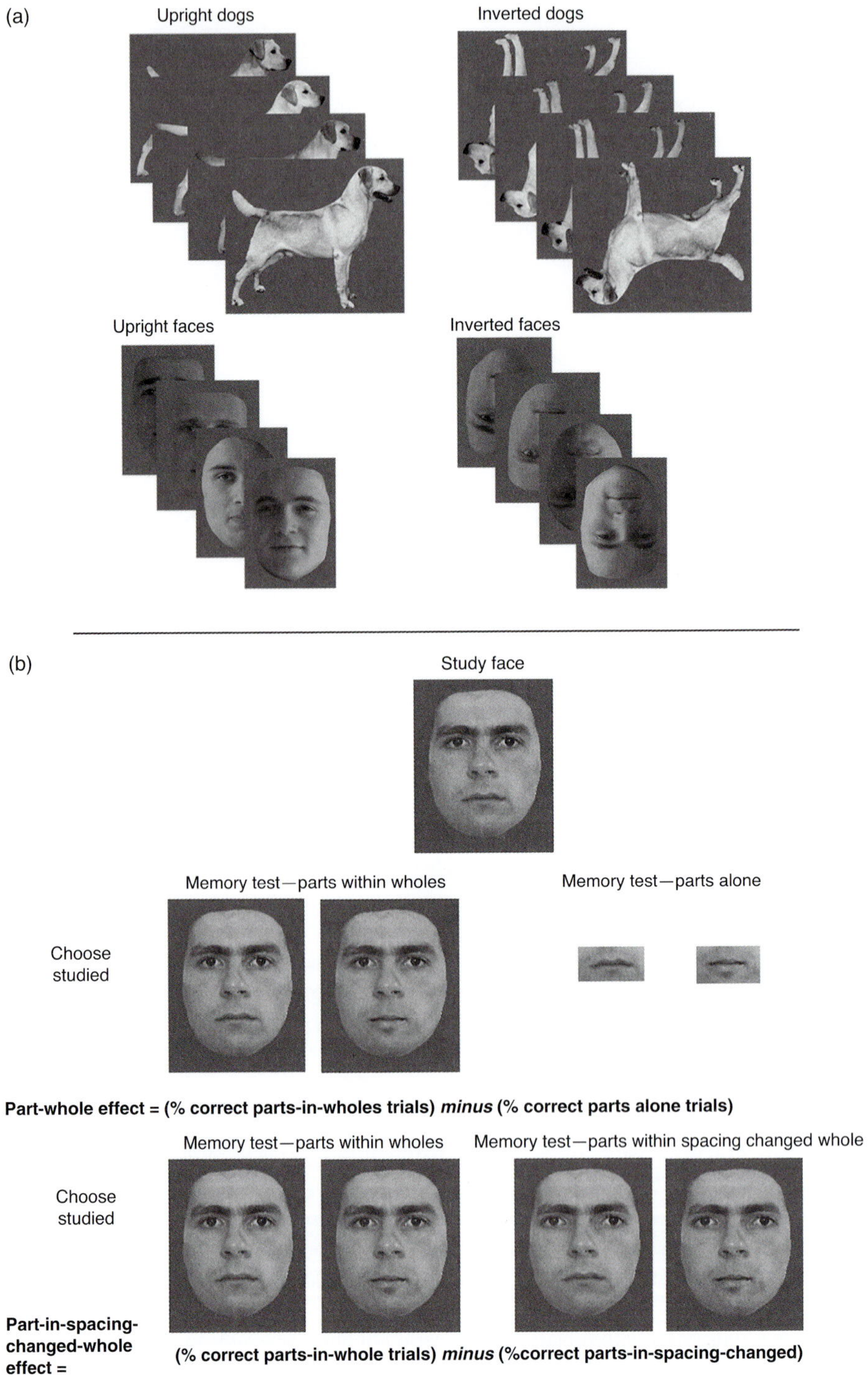

(a)

(b)

Fig. 9.1 Standards tasks: (a) inversion effect on memory or discrimination, (b) part-whole (Tanaka and Farah, 1993) and part-in-spacing-changed-whole (Tanaka and Sengco, 1997) tasks. Original faces are from the PICS (http://pics.psych.stir.ac.uk/) and CVL face databases (http://lrv.fri.uni-lj.si/facedb.html).

(a)

The "naming" version of the composite task

Name top half

Different identity
irrelevant half

Composite effect =   (RT for aligned trials) *minus* (RT for misaligned trials)

(b)

The "same-different" version of the composite task

"same" trial misaligned   "same" trial aligned

Match top halves

Irrelevant half
always different

Composite effect =   (% correct for same misaligned trials)   *Minus*   (% correct for same aligned trials)

"diifferent" trial misaligned   "diifferent" trial aligned

(diifferent trials not used in the calculation of the composite effect)

(c)

The "congruency effect" using composite stimuli

"congruent-same" trial   "incongruent-same" trial

Match top halves

Response suggested
by irrelevant half
agrees/disagress
with correct response
for target half

"congruent-different" trial   "incongruent-different" trial

Congruency effect =   (d' congruent trials)   *minus*   (d' incongruent trials)

Fig. 9.2 The composite illusion together with: (a) the standard naming version of the composite task, contrasting perception of the target half across aligned and misaligned conditions; (b) the standard same-different version of the composite task. (c) The Gauthier and Curby task that uses composite stimuli but measures a congruency effect rather than the composite effect. Unfamiliar faces are from the PICS (http://pics.psych.stir.ac.uk/) and CVL face databases (http://lrv.fri.uni-lj.si/facedb.html); famous faces are taken from the public domain.

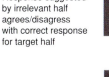
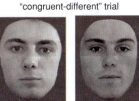

Table 9.1 Inversion decrement (upright-inverted) for faces and objects. Because there are too many studies testing faces vs objects in novices to list all of them, only studies that also tested experts on the objects are shown; all such studies are included. Studies reported various measures, including percent correct (%), d', reaction time (ms), and short-term memory capacity (K-max). For novices and experts, the significance or otherwise of each inversion effect is indicated; a separate column indicates whether the increase in the size of the inversion effect from novices to experts was significant. Studies are approximately ordered from smallest inversion effect in objects-of-expertise to largest. Reprinted from *Cognition*, **103**(1), Rachel Robbins and Elinor McKone, No face-like processing for objects-of-expertise in three behavioural tasks, Copyright 2007, with permission from Elsevier

	Expert type	Task	Faces	Objects novices	Objects experts	sig of expertise increase
Dogs (Robbins and McKone, 2007, Experiment 3)	Real world	Simultaneous matching	11%*	1%^{ns}	2%^{ns}	ns
Dogs (Robbins and McKone, 2007, Experiment 1)	Real world	Long-term memory	23%*	3%^{ns}	7%^{ns}	ns
Fingerprints (Busey and Vanderkolk 2005)	Real world	Face/print classification	16%*	6%^{ns}	8%^{ns}	ns
Birds (Gauthier et al., 2000)	Real world	Sequential matching	—	d'=0.05^{ns}	d'=.30^{ns}	—
Houses [a][b] (Husk et al., 2007)	Lab trained	Sequential matching	35%*	1%$^{-}$	4%*	—
Cars (Xu et al., 2005)	Real world	Sequential matching	—	8%$^{-}$	8%$^{-}$	ns
			—	d'=0.44^{-}	d'=0.87^{-}	*
Handwriting (Bruyer and Crispeels, 1992)	Real world	Long-term memory	20%*	5%^{ns}	9%*	ns
Cars (Gauthier et al., 2000)	Real world	Sequential matching	—	d'=.57*	d'=.84*	—
Greebles [a] (Rossion et al., 2002)	Lab trained	Sequential matching	75ms^{-}	25 ms^{-}	46 ms^{-}	*
Cars (Curby et al., 2009)	Real world	Short-term memory capacity (Cowan's K)	0.519*	0.053^{ns}	0.435*	*
Dogs (Diamond and Carey, 1986 - Experiment 3)	Real world	Long-term memory	20%*	5%^{ns}	22%*	*

Notes: * = $p<0.05$; ns = $p>0.05$; reverse = trend in opposite-to-predicted direction for expertise effect; — = not tested or not reported. Means for Busey and Vanderkolk (2005) provided by Thomas Busey (pers comm, 21.7.06).

[a] In all lab training studies, results are reported for discrimination of novel exemplars of the trained class, not the trained exemplars.

[b] Husk et al. (2007) created experts with a particular type of house, by training participants to discriminate very similar exemplars all sharing the same first order configuration.

(Crookes and McKone, 2008). Inversion effects on identification of overlearned stimuli in peripheral vision (*peripheral inversion effect*; McKone, 2004) also occur for faces but not objects (dachshund dogs; McKone, Brewer et al., 2007). Importantly, inversion effects for objects remain small or absent even for object classes in which, like faces, all exemplars share a basic "first order" configuration (i.e. cats, Labradors, dachshunds and racehorses; although see Ashworth et al., 2007, for a contradictory result using the artificial objects "greebles"). Also, the key to a large inversion effect is perception as a face: a large inversion effect occurs when an ambiguous stimulus is primed as face, but disappears when the same stimulus is primed as a Chinese character (Ge et al., 2006).

We turn next to tasks that more directly assess style of processing, in that they address, in a given orientation, whether perception involves a strong integration of information from across the face or object (i.e. holistic/configural processing) which includes access specifically to information about exact distances between parts (i.e. an aspect of "second-order relational" information). Figure 9.1b illustrates the *part-whole effect* (Tanaka and Farah, 1993), in which memory for a face part (e.g. Bill's nose) is much better in the context of the original whole face (e.g. Bill's nose vs. Jim's nose in Bill's face) than when presented alone (Bill's nose vs. Jim's nose); Figure 9.1b also illustrates the part-in-spacing-changed-whole variant, in which memory for the face part is better in the original face than when presented in a version of the original whole that includes a distance alteration in another region of the face (e.g. Bill's nose vs. Jim's nose in Bill's face with the eyes shifted slightly apart). Figures 9.2a and b illustrate the *composite effect* in which aligning the top half-face of one individual with the bottom half-face of a different individual makes it difficult to name the top half (famous face version, Figure 9.2a; Young et al., 1987) or produces an effect in which two physically same top halves appear different when aligned with two different bottom halves (novel face version, Figure 9.2b; Le Grand et al., 2004)—in both cases the control condition against which reaction time or accuracy is compared is a version of the same stimuli with the two halves misaligned.

Regarding tests of the within-class discrimination hypothesis, Table 9.2 shows that the part-whole effect for objects in novices is small, and far smaller than that for recognition of faces. Table 9.3 shows that the *part-in-spacing-changed-whole effect* for objects is absent in novices, as compared to a significant 7% effect for faces. Table 9.4 shows that the *composite effect* for objects is absent in novices, as compared to a strong effect in faces. Finally, sensitivity to the *exact spacing between internal elements* is usually much weaker in objects than in faces; for example, to match sensitivity to spacing changes in upright faces and upright houses requires much larger physical changes in the houses than in the faces (Yovel and Kanwisher, 2008).

A final observation is that inversion effects can be far more stable for faces than for other stimuli. Inversion effects for letter and object identification disappear rapidly with repeated trials (Corballis et al., 1978; McKone and Grenfell, 1999). In contrast, large inversion effects remain after practice for faces (but not objects) under difficult viewing conditions (e.g. peripheral presentation: McKone, 2004; noise: McKone et al., 2001), and holistic processing for faces remains impossible for inverted faces even with thousands or tens of thousands of learning trials (McKone et al, 2001; Robbins and McKone, 2003).

In summary, both indirect evidence (disproportionate inversion effect) and direct tests of processing style (part-whole, part-in-spacing-changed-whole, composite, spacing sensitivity) confirm a lack of holistic processing for individual-level recognition of objects. The only potential exception of which we are aware is human bodies, and even here the evidence is currently uncompelling. The most relevant situation is recognition of body *identity*: this does not show inversion effects when the head is removed (Minnebusch et al., 2009), although there is a strong part-whole effect for body identity with heads (Seitz, 2002). Also note that even inversion effects for body *pose* (Reed et al., 2003) have recently been shown to depend entirely on the presence of a head

Table 9.2 Results of previous studies using the Tanaka and Farah (1993) part-whole paradigm, showing size of the whole-part difference, averaged over all parts tested. All stimuli were upright unless otherwise stated. All studies including objects-of-expertise are included, as are sample extra studies that tested objects only in novices. Example results are also provided for faces. Scores are percent correct (%) or d-prime discriminability (d'). Greebles are an artificial object class. Reprinted from *Cognition*, **103**(1), Rachel Robbins and Elinor McKone, No face-like processing for objects-of-expertise in three behavioural tasks, Copyright 2007, with permission from Elsevier

	Faces	Inverted faces	Objects (novices)	Objects (experts)	sig of expertise increase
No objects (Pellicano et al., 2006)	13%*	$-2\%^{ns}$	—	—	—
Houses (Tanaka and Farah, 1993)	11%*	$-1\%^{ns}$	$-2\%^{ns}$	—	—
Houses (Tanaka and Sengco, 1997)	15%*	$0\%^{ns}$	$1\%^{ns}$	—	—
Chairs (Davidoff and Donnelly, 1990)	11%*	—	$4\%^{ns}$	—	—
Dog faces (Tanaka et al., 1996)	20%*	—	$2\%^{ns}$	$8\%^{ns}$	ns
Cars (Tanaka et al., 1996)	18%*	—	$8\%^{-}$	$6\%^{-}$	Reverse
Biological cells (Tanaka et al., 1996)	26%*	—	16%*	10%*	Reverse
Greebles (Gauthier and Tarr, 1997)	—	—	$5\%^{ns}$	11%*	ns
Greebles (Gauthier et al., 1998)	—	—	$7\%^{-}$	$0\%^{-}$	Reverse
Greebles (Gauthier and Tarr, 2002)	—	—	$d' = 0.75^{-}$	$d' = 0.68^{-}$	Reverse

Notes: * = p<.05; ns = p>.05; reverse = trend in opposite-to-predicted direction for expertise effect; — = not tested or not reported. Data from Tanaka et al. (1996) are as cited in Tanaka and Gauthier (1997).

(Yovel et al., 2010). Thus, although it is possible that holistic processing might extend to cover bodies as well as faces, a reasonable alternative hypothesis is that holistic processing for bodies occurs only when the body contains a face.

Overall, results reviewed in this section are consistent with the view that "faces are special" compared to a very wide range of objects (with the possible exception of human bodies). Results clearly reject the within-class discrimination hypothesis.

Face selective neurons and cortical regions.

Turning to neural findings, results show the existence of strongly face-selective cells that cluster together in regions large enough to be detectable with fMRI.

In humans, multiple fMRI studies reveal face selective areas which can respond two to three times more strongly to within-class discrimination of faces than to within-class discrimination of other objects, including houses, flowers, hands, birds, and cars (for review see Kanwisher and

Table 9.3 Results of previous studies using the Tanaka and Sengco's (1997) paradigm, showing part-in-whole minus part-in-spacing-altered-whole, averaged over all parts tested. All stimuli were upright unless otherwise stated. All studies that tested objects-of-expertise are included, as is the original study that tested objects only in novices. Reprinted from *Cognition*, **103**(1), Rachel Robbins and Elinor McKone, No face-like processing for objects-of-expertise in three behavioural tasks, Copyright 2007, with permission from Elsevier

	Faces	Objects (novices)	Objects (experts)	sig of expertise increase
Houses (Tanaka and Sengco, 1997)	7%*	0%ns	—	—
Greebles (Gauthier and Tarr, 1997)	—	−4%ns	0%ns	ns
Greebles (Gauthier et al., 1998)	—	1%ns	0%ns	Reverse
Greebles (Gauthier and Tarr, 2002)	—	$d' = 0.69^-$	$d' = 0.64^-$	Reverse

Notes: * = $p<0.05$; ns = $p>0.05$; reverse = trend in opposite-to-predicted direction for expertise effect; — = not tested or not reported.

Yovel, 2006). Regions identified include the FFA[2] and the OFA. In contrast, there are other areas of extrastriate cortex that are object-general; for example, lateral occipital complex (LOC, defined as a region responding more strongly to objects than scrambled objects) typically responds at close to equal levels for objects and faces (Op de Beeck et al., 2006). Importantly, face-selective regions are dissociated from other regions in fMRI even when, like faces, all exemplars of the object set share a basic "first-order" configuration (e.g. hands; also, houses all made from a common template, Husk et al., 2006). High-resolution fMRI also dissociates face-selective regions from regions selective for headless bodies (extrastriate body area: Downing et al., 2001; fusiform body area: Schwarzlose et al., 2005).

Monkey fMRI also reveals face-selective regions in temporal cortex (Tsao et al., 2006). Recording from one of these (the "middle face patch") revealed that, of more than 100 cells tested, 97% of visually-responsive neurons were strongly face-selective in comparison to a wide range of objects including clocks, bodies and hands (Tsao et al., 2006). Thus, when search for face-selective cells is guided by fMRI, dense clusters of colocated face cells can be identified (in contrast to early single unit studies, in which unguided electrode placement suggested face cells were more widely dispersed; e.g. Perrett et al., 1985).

Selective disruption of the network

The fact that face cells cluster into regions argues it should be possible to damage face recognition without object recognition, and vice versa. This double dissociation has indeed been demonstrated.

---

[2] Using higher-resolution fMRI, Grill-Spector et al. (2006) claimed the FFA was not uniformly face selective, reporting it contained many finer-scale voxels highly selective for non-face objects (e.g. sculptures). However, this claim relied on invalid data analysis (Baker et al., 2007; Simmons et al., 2007).

Using transmagnetic stimulation (TMS) to temporarily disrupt cortical regions in healthy adults, Pitcher et al. (2009) found a triple dissociation between within-class face, body, and object recognition in extrastriate cortex (note face and object areas located in inferotemporal cortex cannot be accessed with TMS). Participants performed discrimination tasks involving faces, bodies, and an artificial-object category while TMS was delivered over the right occipital face area (rOFA), the right extrastriate body area (rEBA), or the right lateral occipital area (rLO). Results argued category-selective areas contributed to behavioral performance solely within their preferred categories. TMS over rOFA impaired discrimination of faces but not objects or bodies. TMS over rEBA impaired discrimination of bodies but not faces or objects. Finally, TMS over rLO impaired discrimination of objects but not faces or bodies.

We now turn to evidence from neuropsychology; that is, to cases of acquired brain injury and of atypical development. Before evaluating the evidence in this field, an important theoretical point is that pure cases of face-object dissociations would be expected to be rare. Most injuries will damage broad swathes of cortex, covering both face and object areas (and/or also damage broad swathes of connecting white matter; see Thomas et al., 2008, for the importance of white matter in prosopagnosia). Similarly, many neural development problems (e.g. a neural migration problem during a particular week of fetal development) would also be expected to damage the development of both face and object perception mechanisms. Of strong theoretical importance, however, is that pure cases *can* be identified, and that these form a *double dissociation* between face and object recognition. There exist prosopagnosics who have extremely poor recognition of faces in combination with perfectly normal within-class discrimination of objects (e.g. Duchaine et al., 2006; McNeil and Warrington, 1993; Sergent and Signoret, 1992). A few cases have also been reported of the reverse pattern (e.g. Assal et al., 1984): best known is Mr CK who was severely object agnosic but could individuate faces at normal or above-normal levels, even in very difficult formats (e.g. overlaid cartoons of multiple individuals; Moscovitch et al., 1997).

Taken together, the results of fMRI, single-cell recording, TMS, and neuropsychology make a strong case that faces are "special" in terms of tight clusterings of colocated face-selective neurons. Moreover, the results indicate dissociations not only between faces and objects in general, but also specifically between faces and other parts of the body (headless bodies, hands).

Face selective ERP/MEG response: the N170/M170

The N170 is an ERP response peaking 170 ms after stimulus onset which is stronger to faces than objects at occipitotemporal electrode sites (Jeffreys, 1996; for review see Eimer, Chapter 17, this volume); there is an equivalent M170 measured with MEG (Halgren et al., 2000; Liu et al., 2000). For our purposes, the critical finding is that the N170/M170 face-selectivity occurs even when the object exemplars are all from the same category with highly similar structural forms (for references to 17 articles containing this result, see Rossion and Jacques, 2008, p. 1962), and cannot be attributed to image variability amongst the object pictures (Rossion and Jacques, 2008). For faces, inversion produces a delay and increases the amplitude of the N170, a pattern which does not occur, or is much smaller, for objects (e.g. Rossion et al., 2000). Also, for human bodies, inversion produces delay and increased amplitude for bodies with heads, but not bodies without heads (Minnebusch et al., 2009). Results again reject the within-class discrimination hypothesis.

Summary

The results reviewed in this section clearly reject the "within-class discrimination hypothesis." When within-class discrimination of faces is contrasted with within-class discrimination of objects, results show that: (1) holistic processing remains restricted to faces, (2) face-selective cortical regions and single neurons still occur (3) selective damage to face or object recognition is still possible, and (4) face-selective ERP responses still occur. Moreover, a number of studies have identified associations between face-selective neural phenomena and face-specific behavioral properties: in particular, the FFA demonstrates holistic processing (composite effect; Schiltz and Rossion, 2006), better identity discrimination for upright than inverted faces (Mazard et al., 2006; Yovel and Kanwisher, 2005), and identity discrimination for faces but not objects ("blobs," Yue et al., 2006). Overall, results make a compelling case that, in the typical situation in which people have no particular expertise with an object class, faces are "special."

Testing the expertise hypothesis

We next evaluate the *expertise hypothesis*. All results discussed in this section come from the situation in which faces are compared with an object class for which the participant has developed demonstrated expertise at within-class discrimination, either through many years of real world interest and experience (e.g. car, bird, or dog experts), or through several hours of laboratory training (e.g. "greeble" experts). Results refute the expertise hypothesis and again support the view that "faces are special."

Holistic/configural processing: "gold standard" tasks

Three tasks are available which can be considered "gold standards" for testing expertise hypothesis predictions about holistic processing: the part-whole task, the part-in-spacing-changed-whole task, and the composite task. We emphasize these tasks for three reasons: (1) well-established results show they produce face-specificity in object novices; (2) the tasks *directly* assess processing style (i.e. part-based versus holistic); and (3) logically, the tasks provide measures of "face-type" holistic processing (a point which will become clearer when we cover one much weaker use of the term "holistic" in a later section).

Results for all studies testing objects-of-expertise in these tasks are shown in Tables 9.2 to 9.4. Findings are straightforward, and clearly reject the expertise hypothesis.

If holistic processing emerged with expertise, then we would expect the part-whole, part-in-spacing-changed-whole and composite effects to be significant in object experts and significantly larger in object experts than in object novices. In contrast, Table 9.2 shows the part-whole effect is no larger in experts than in novices (in fact, 4/6 studies show trend in reverse-to-predicted direction); also, in a related method, detection of a small nodule in a cued region of a chest X-ray remains only slightly facilitated by a whole chest as opposed to a scrambled one in radiology experts (i.e. no more facilitated than in novices; Harley et al., 2009). Similarly, the part-in-spacing-changed effect (Table 9.3) is no larger in experts than in novices (2/3 showing trend in reverse-to-predicted direction). Regarding the composite effect (Table 9.4), a significant composite effect has never been obtained in object experts (in four published attempts plus two others mentioned in a footnote by Gauthier et al., 1998), and statistical tests comparing experts to novices have either not been conducted or show non-significant or reverse-to-predicted-direction differences in the size of the composite effect. Thus, results of the three "gold standard" tasks clearly argue that expertise with objects does not induce face-like holistic processing.

It is worth noting that, although the original results of these studies very clearly *reject* the expertise hypothesis, exactly the opposite conclusion could easily be reached by the casual reader of much of the face recognition literature. Several of the articles whose results are shown in Tables 9.2 to 9.4 have been regularly miscited as having shown evidence of holistic processing in object experts on these standard tasks when (as can be seen) they did not. Given this common miscitation, we note that we are confident we have correctly presented the original results.

Table 9.4 Results of the Young et al. (1987) composite paradigm, showing the aligned–unaligned difference for reaction times, or unaligned–aligned for accuracy; in both cases, a positive number corresponds to the direction for a positive composite effect, (i.e. aligned should be the more difficult condition). All stimuli were upright unless otherwise stated. All studies including objects-of-expertise are included, as are some sample studies that reported data for inverted faces. Reprinted from *Cognition*, **103**(1), Rachel Robbins and Elinor McKone, No face-like processing for objects-of-expertise in three behavioural tasks, Copyright 2007, with permission from Elsevier

	Task	Faces	Inverted faces	Objects (novices)	Objects (experts)	sig of expertise increase
No objects (Young et al., 1987)	Speeded naming	212 ms*	9 ms[ns]	—	—	—
No objects (McKone, 2008)	Speeded naming	74 ms*	14 ms[ns]	—	—	—
No objects (Robbins and McKone, 2003)	Naming twins	8.8%*	−1.2%[ns]	—	—	—
Cars (Macchi Cassia et al., 2009)	Sequential matching	58 ms	—	0 ms	—	—
Greebles, same-family halves (Gauthier et al., 1998)	Speeded naming	—	—	—	115 ms[ns] 0%	—
Greebles, different-family halves (Gauthier et al., 1998)	Speeded naming	—	—	—	−37 ms[reverse] −3%[reverse]	—
Greebles, same-family halves (Gauthier and Tarr, 2002)	Speeded naming	—	—	−42 ms[−]	12 ms[−]	—[a]
Dogs (Robbins and McKone, 2007)	Simultaneous matching	6.1% *	−3.5%[ns]	−0.8%[ns] 0.8%[ns b]	0.7%[ns]	ns Reverse

Notes: * = p<0.05; ns = p>0.05; reverse = trend in opposite-to-predicted direction for expertise effect; — = not tested or not reported.

[a] Across 5 sessions (we show only session 1 = novices, session 5 = experts), there was a close-to-significant interaction between session and aligned vs. unaligned. This did not reflect an increase with expertise: the composite effect started close to zero, strangely became more negative in sessions 2-4, then returned to close to zero. The 12 ms composite effect in experts was in the context of 35 ms SEMs for the aligned and unaligned conditions.

[b] Results for two independent groups of subjects.

We previously presented the expertise values in Tables 9.1 to 9.4 in Robbins and McKone (2007), on which Gauthier, as the major recent proponent of the expertise hypothesis, wrote a commentary (Gauthier and Bukach, 2007): no mistakes or omissions were indicated.

Holistic/configural processing: attempts to discredit the standard tasks

Several articles by Gauthier and colleagues have tried to discredit two of the "gold standard" tasks, suggesting that the part-whole and composite effects are not good measures of holistic perceptual integration (despite their wide acceptance as such in the face literature). Regarding the part-whole effect, Gauthier and Tarr (2002) argued that the effect may arise from the general memory advantage which arises from match as opposed to mismatch in stimulus format between study and test: study-test match is greater in the whole condition (whole at study, whole at test) than in the part condition (whole at study, part at test). In response, we have pointed out (Robbins and McKone, 2007) that, although there may indeed be some contribution of general memory-match effects on this task (see Leder and Carbon, 2005), Gauthier and Tarr's (2002) proposal fails to mention that inverted faces produce no whole-over-part advantage despite the degree of study-test match in the whole and part conditions being the same as for upright faces, and also provides no explanation of why the part-whole effect is consistently so much larger for faces than for objects. To our minds, these findings imply that the large part-whole effect for upright faces can only be attributed to holistic processing.

Regarding the composite effect, the argument (Gauthier and Bukach, 2007; Richler et al., 2008) is that the composite effect in the same-different version of the task arises at a decisional level rather than a perceptual level. Again, however, Gauthier and colleagues have failed to mention two key points: (1) making a decisional-perceptual distinction requires analyzing *different* trials in the composite procedure and this is invalid because, while there is a clear prediction that holistic processing will make aligned harder than unaligned for "same" trials, the predicted direction of any effect on "different" trials will vary depending on the similarity of the non-target halves (see Robbins and McKone, 2007, p. 54); and (2) on the *naming* version of the task, in which the issue of decisional bias does not arise, the composite effect is also present for faces (Young et al., 1987) and not for objects (greebles, Table 4).

Overall, we see no reason to discount the results of the "gold standard" holistic processing tasks, which clearly support the view that faces are special.

Holistic/configural processing: disproportionate inversion effect

We now turn to results for objects-of-expertise in other tasks which have been suggested to be measures of "holistic processing," but in which we believe the link between the task and holistic processing is either more tenuous or entirely absent.

We first consider the classic disproportionate inversion effect. Valentine (1988) pointed out many years ago that the fact that an inversion effect is larger in one condition (e.g. faces) than in another (e.g. objects) does not per se show that this arises from holistic processing: the task does not address processing style in either orientation (as do part-whole, part-in-spacing-changed-whole, and composite). For *faces*, research has subsequently made a very strong case that the large inversion effect on memory and discrimination *does* derive from holistic processing. However, this does not guarantee that the origin of any large inversion effects for *other objects* must derive from holistic processing. Many authors now explicitly state that the inversion effect is merely indirect evidence for holistic processing (e.g. Michel et al., 2006), and D. Maurer et al. (2002) explicitly noted that the mere presence of an inversion effect is not diagnostic of holistic/configural processing in the absence of more direct evidence.

Do results for objects-of-expertise show even indirect support for holistic processing, using the inversion effect? If inversion effects for objects-of-expertise reflect holistic processing, the expertise hypothesis predicts that studies should find an increase in the size of the inversion effect with expertise. Table 9.1 shows that this result is found only very occasionally. Instead, the findings are highly variable. Inversion effects for objects in experts range from nothing to an inversion effect as large as that for faces. Four tests have found only small and non-significant inversion effects in experts that are only very slightly and non-significantly larger in experts than in novices (dogs with both memory and sequential matching: Robbins and McKone, 2007; fingerprints: Busey and

Vanderkolk, 2005; birds: Gauthier et al., 2000); similarly, a fifth test found no change in inversion effect at all with expertise on a per cent-correct measure (cars: Xu et al., 2005). Next, three tests have found either significant inversion effects in experts, or a significant novice-expert difference, but with the inversion effects for objects-of-expertise remaining fairly small: the effect was either strikingly smaller than for faces (4% houses vs. 35% faces in Husk et al., 2007; 9% handwriting vs. 20% faces in Bruyer and Crispeels, 1992), and/or the difference from objects in novices was not great in numerical terms (cars in Gauthier et al., 2000; also the d' measure in Xu et al., 2005). Next, one study produced a quite large inversion effect in experts, with the effect for objects 85% larger in experts than in novices, and 60% the size of that for faces (greebles, Rossion et al., 2002). Finally, two studies have produced very large inversion effects for objects of expertise, equal in size to the inversion effects for faces (dogs, Diamond and Carey, 1986; cars, Curby et al., 2009). Taken together, these studies argue there is some effect of expertise on inversion effects for objects which is typically small, but can sometimes be very large.

What explains the variability across studies? The expertise hypothesis could account for it if the variable driving the size of the inversion effect was the experts' level of expertise. However, results in Table 9.1 contradict this interpretation: for example, the dog experts in Robbins and McKone (2007) had a mean of 23 years experience (and were as good at discriminating dogs as faces), yet showed no inversion effect; while, at the other extreme, the greeble experts in Rossion et al. (2002) had only a few hours of laboratory training, yet showed quite a sizeable expertise-related change in the inversion effect.

Alternatively, the expertise hypothesis could perhaps account for the variability if it were proposed that expertise effects on holistic processing emerge only with expertise specifically in *individual*-level discrimination (an idea proposed by Wong et al., 2009) noting that several studies with small inversion effects tested bird and car experts and these people typically have expertise at discriminating class exemplars at the "subordinate" rather than individual level (e.g. Mazda 626 vs. Mazda 323, not a particular Mazda 626). Again, however, Table 9.1 contradicts this hypothesis: small inversion effects have been found in people highly expert in individual-level discrimination of labradors (Robbins and McKone, 2007) and fingerprints (Busey and Vandervolk, 2005); and, one of the two findings of extremely large inversion effects was obtained with car experts (Curby et al., 2009).

We thus conclude that results of inversion effect studies do not provide even indirect support for the expertise hypothesis: level of expertise does not appear to correlate with the size of the inversion effect; and nor does expertise specifically in individual-level discrimination.

This does leave us with an interesting open question, however, which is what *does* explain the variability in inversion effects? Robbins and McKone (2007) suggested that the large inversion effect in Diamond and Carey (1986) could have been explained if the experts in that study had been pre-experimentally familiar with *the particular dog images* (but not the face images) used as stimuli (this was plausible given the source of the participants and stimulus images). However, this critique does not apply to Rossion et al. (2002), where the test stimuli were all novel greebles. Also, although in Curby et al. (2009) some of the particular car images could plausibly have been pre-experimentally familiar to participants, this is equally true of all the other car studies which produced only small inversion effects in experts. We therefore suggest it may be worthwhile exploring the effect of other variables in future studies. For example, for faces, the size of the inversion effect is affected by *distinctiveness* (Valentine, 1991). Perhaps, if object recognition inversion effects are also affected by distinctiveness, and we make the plausible assumption that experts are more sensitive to distinctiveness than novices, then we could potentially explain why inversion effects vary across studies in experts (but not novices) by hypothesizing that the particular stimulus sets used in particular studies happened to comprise items that were either more distinctive or more typical exemplars of their class. Importantly, this explanation requires no reference to the concept of holistic processing.

Holistic/configural processing: definition as merely a generic failure of selective attention

In claiming support for the expertise hypothesis, one approach by Gauthier and colleagues has been to weaken the definition of holistic processing from the traditional face-literature definition—that is, some form of very strong perceptual integration (Tanaka and Gordon, Chapter 10, this volume)—to merely any failure of selective attention (specifically, "obligatory processing of all features of an object, when subjects are instructed to attend selectively to one feature while ignoring others," Gauthier et al., 2003, p. 1). Corresponding tasks (e.g. Gauthier et al., 2003; Wong et al., 2009) have then relied on measuring a *congruency effect* (see Figure 9.2c). In a sequential same-different task, using some form of composite stimuli, two conditions are contrasted in which the response suggested by matching the to-be-ignored half is either consistent with the response suggested by the target half (e.g. the non-target bottom halves are the same when the target top halves are the same; congruent trials) or inconsistent with the response suggested by the target half (e.g. the non-target bottom halves are different when the target top halves are the same; incongruent trials). The difference between congruent and incongruent trials is then taken as the measure of "holistic processing."

This congruency measure can sometimes produce patterns in objects of expertise that are similar to patterns in faces: that is, patterns in which failures of selective attention to parts are strong for faces, weak or absent for objects in novices, and significantly stronger for objects in experts than in novices (cars: Gauthier et al., 2003; novel objects ziggerins: Wong et al., 2009). In other cases, however, the results do not show face-like patterns (e.g. a strong congruency effect in *novices* for misaligned greebles, Richler et al., 2009; or no expertise influence on the congruency effect, Hsiao and Cottrell, 2009).

Even where face-like patterns are obtained, however, the question is whether this should be taken as evidence of claimed "special" processing for objects of expertise. We argue not. The selective attention approach weakens the definition of holistic processing to such an extent as to make it of no theoretical value in the present context. Under the Gauthier definition, practically any two things one cared to test would be processed "holistically": for example, the Stroop effect would be interpreted as showing that ink color and word identity are processed together "holistically," despite the fact that color and word form/names are clearly *not* integrated at a perceptual level. Thus, the congruency effect revealed for car experts in Gauthier et al. (2003; or for ziggerins in Wong et al., 2009) is, to our minds, not an expertise effect on *face*-like holistic processing; instead, it merely shows that competition for attentional resources from the to-be-ignored half is stronger when subjects are experts with the object class. This seems unsurprising. (As an analogy, the Stroop effect would not occur for English readers if the written word was in Chinese.) Consistent with our explanation, the circumstances in which the congruency effect in experts weakens or disappears (when the non-target half is either flipped upside down or misaligned to one side; cars, Gauthier et al., 2003; ziggerins, Wong et al., 2009) correspond to a circumstance known from the spatial attention literature to disrupt global processing and facilitate attention to parts (i.e. sudden discontinuities in the outline suggest the presence of "two things" not "one thing").

We thus conclude that the results of the *congruency effect* tasks do not demonstrate *face*-like processing for objects of expertise, but instead reflect general Stroop-like attentional phenomena. The theory that "faces are special" remains intact.

Face selective neurons and cortical regions

No single-cell recording studies have addressed the question of whether face-selective cells respond strongly to objects-of-expertise. The available evidence regarding cortical location of face-selectivity and expertise comes from fMRI. These studies have focused on the FFA.

The expertise hypothesis predicts that the FFA should be more strongly engaged by objects of expertise than by objects for which the participant is a novice; also, where expertise levels are high, activation should approach face levels. Twelve studies have reported relevant data. One failed to properly localize the FFA, reporting a significant expertise effect in a larger region centered around the FFA that would be expected to include much object-general cortex (greebles: Gauthier et al., 1999). Of those that localized the FFA, only two found small but significant increases in responses to objects of expertise compared with control objects in the FFA (cars and birds: Gauthier et al, 2000; cars: Xu et al., 2005), and one a significant correlation between level of behavioral expertise and FFA activation (chest X-rays: Harley et al., 2009). Two report non-significant trends towards expertise effects in the FFA (Lepidoptera: Rhodes et al., 2004; novel polygon-based objects: Moore et al., 2006) and four report no change with expertise (cars: Grill-Spector et al., 2004; "blobs": Yue et al., 2006; novel objects: Op de Beeck et al., 2006; dance actions: Calvo-Merino et al., 2005). Another study failed to find a change in the degree of overlap between the FFA and a "greeble selective fusiform area" with expertise training (Kung et al., 2007). Finally, Liu et al. (2008) found activity in the right FFA was substantially greater for faces than for a non-face class for which their subjects were highly expert at individual-level discrimination (Chinese characters).

Thus, most studies find that the FFA is not strongly activated in response to objects-of-expertise. Even more compellingly, some studies have examined expertise effects in cortical regions *not* selective for faces. Of six relevant studies, all have found larger effects of expertise in these regions than in the FFA (Calvo-Merino et al., 2005; Gauthier et al., 2000; Moore et al., 2006; Op de Beeck et al., 2006; Rhodes et al., 2004; Yue et al., 2006). Overall, then, the results indicate a dissociation between the FFA and areas related to object expertise, rather than the strong association predicted by the expertise hypothesis.

Why does the FFA sometimes show greater activation in experts than novices? For many of the studies reviewed, a plausible idea (Xu et al., 2005) is that the effects do not reflect a special role for the FFA in processing objects of expertise but rather an overall increased attentional engagement for these stimuli: for example, bird experts will find birds more interesting than novices, and will thus pay more attention to bird stimuli than to other objects. This will elevate neural responses to objects of expertise, which produce a small response in the FFA even in non-experts (possibly because limits in the spatial resolution of fMRI can conflate adjacent functional regions). This idea is consistent with evidence that greater attention raises BOLD response and that hemodynamic signals in the FFA include late responses that can be modulated by feedback connections (Furey et al., 2006). It is also directly supported in cases where correlations between FFA response to objects of expertise and behaviorally measured expertise have been shown in *location*-discrimination tasks, where subjects are free to attend to item identity as they wish, but not in *identity*-discrimination tasks, where all subjects, regardless of intrinsic interest level, are forced to attend to item identity (Grill-Spector et al., 2004; Gauthier et al., 2000; also see Kung et al., 2007).

One study, however, provided good evidence against an attentional explanation, and so requires more detailed consideration. Using novice and expert radiologists, Harley et al. (2009) found that behavioral performance during scanning on a radiograph abnormality diagnosis task correlated positively with level of FFA activation, and negatively with activation of voxels (in LO) selective for radiographs. This could potentially indicate a role for the FFA in expert processing of radiographs. An alternative explanation, however, arises from the fact that the voxel resolution used in the study cannot discriminate between responses from the true FFA and the neighboring fusiform body area (higher resolution is required; see Schwarzlose, et al., 2005). Given that chest radiographs show body parts and not faces, and that radiologists are trained to associate radiographs to real bodies, it seems plausible that the expertise effects arose from body-selective neurons not from face-selective neurons. In support of this interpretation, the location of the strong LO activation apparent for the radiographs appears to correspond closely to the typical location of the extrastriate body area (e.g. see figure 6 in Arzy et al., 2006); thus, it is possible that the expertise effect in the Harley et al. study represents expert radiologists increasing their reliance on the FBA, and decreasing their reliance on the EBA, relative to first-year intern radiologists.

In summary, the data provide no compelling evidence for the special relationship between expertise and the FFA predicted by the expertise hypothesis (and in many cases no evidence at all). Instead, fMRI studies are more consistent with the view that "faces are special."

Selective disruption of the network: TMS and neuropsychology

There are no TMS studies of objects-of-expertise. Regarding neuropsychology, the expertise hypothesis states that the same "special" neural mechanisms used for recognizing faces are also used for recognizing objects-of-expertise. It thus predicts that damage to, or atypical development of, these mechanisms should *always* damage both face recognition *and* object-of-expertise recognition; in contrast, evidence that objects of expertise dissociate from faces would reject the expertise hypothesis and support the view that faces are special.

Few studies have tested this prediction (for the obvious reason that few individuals with acquired prosopagnosia happened to be experts in another object class prior to their brain injury), but results refute the expertise hypothesis. Some individuals show extremely poor face recognition but excellent recognition of objects of expertise: following brain injury, RM retained his expertise with cars (Sergent and Signoret, 1992); WJ lost face recognition but learned to individuate sheep (McNeil and Warrington, 1993); and developmental prosopagnosic Edward learned greeble expertise at completely normal levels (both accuracy and reaction time; Duchaine et al., 2006). In the other half of the double dissociation, individuals have lost recognition of former objects-of-expertise, but retained face recognition: cases include MX, a farmer who could recognize faces but no longer recognize his cows (Assal et al., 1984), and CK, who retained perfect face recognition but lost interest in his toy-soldier collection, which numbered in the thousands (Moscovitch et al., 1997). No cases have been reported in which recognition of faces and objects of expertise have both been impaired while recognition of non-expert objects is unimpaired, or vice versa.

Face selective ERP/MEG response: the N170/M170

Several studies have shown that an N170 response can be altered by expertise with non-face stimuli. This includes increased amplitude in experts compared to novices (birds and cars: Tanaka and Curran, 2001; greebles: Rossion et al., 2004; fingerprints: Busey and Vanderkolk, 2005; words in both alphabetic and character-based scripts: Wong et al., 2005), and the emergence of a time delay in peak amplitude for inverted relative to upright stimulus orientations (greebles: Rossion et al., 2002; fingerprints: Busey and Vanderkolk, 2005).

Perhaps the most relevant question here is whether or not these effects derive from the same neural generators as the N170 to faces. The N170 is a complex ERP response that provides far from a pure measure of face-selective cortical regions. A recent review of source localization studies (Rossion and Jacques, 2009) concludes the N170 over occipitotemporal sensors most likely derives from an equivalent dipole combining neural processes in and between multiple regions activated in interlocked time-courses, some of which are face-selective (including OFA and FFA) and some of which are object-general (e.g. the lateral occipital complex, LOC).

If objects-of-expertise activate "face" neural generators, a minimum prediction is that the spatial distribution on the scalp of the N170 to objects-of-expertise should shift towards that of faces and away from that of objects in novices. However, in general results favor the view that this does not occur, consistent with the idea that "faces are special." Xu et al. (2005), using MEG, found face selective sensors showed absolutely no magnitude increase in the car M170 response in experts compared to novices. Tanaka and Curran (2001) found significant expertise effects on car and bird N170 amplitudes but, crucially, the result was obtained from a selection of sensors that barely overlaps with the sensors usually used in face N170 studies (see Figure 9.3); moreover, scalp distribution data showed no suggestion of a shift towards a more face-like distribution of the peak sensors with expertise. Two other studies have measured at T5 and T6, sensors for which the N170 is highly face-selective. Rossion et al. (2002) found the development of an inversion delay with greeble expertise occurred in the *left* hemisphere (T5) but not the right hemisphere (T6), in contrast to the bilateral occurrence of this delay for faces (Rossion et al., 2000). Busey and Vanderkolk (2005) found the opposite pattern of an inversion delay in fingerprint experts in the right but not left hemisphere; but, the study also showed *no* amplitude increase in the *right* hemisphere (T6) with fingerprint expertise (i.e. not a face-like pattern). Further, neither of these studies reported the expertise effects on any other sensors, and so it cannot be determined whether

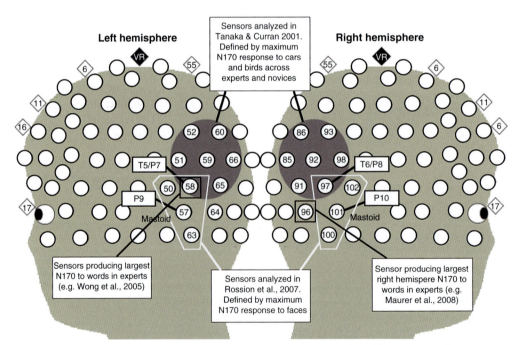

Fig. 9.3 Approximate scalp locations reported in N170 expertise studies of faces, objects (cars, birds) and words (both alphabetic and character-based languages). Numbers refer to sensor numbers in the 128-channel Geodesic Sensor Net™. Corresponding values in the 10-20 system are indicated for T5, T6, P9 and P10. James W. Tanaka and Tim Curran, *Psychological Science*, **12**(1), © 2001 by SAGE. Reprinted by permission of SAGE Publications.

the scalp distribution for objects-of-expertise matched that for faces (i.e. expertise effects on object processing may have been larger at other sensors). Turning to word studies, experts with a given word script show a strong *left* hemisphere bias in amplitude of the word N170 including for character-based scripts (U. Maurer et al., 2008a,b; Wong et al., 2005), in contrast to a more bilateral pattern in novices (U. Maurer et al., 2008b), and in contrast to the typical right hemisphere bias for the N170 to faces. Even within the right hemisphere the word N170 responses are strongest at a different sensor location from that which typically produces the largest face N170 (sensor 96, rather than 97/T5; U. Maurer et al., 2008a,b).

Overall, the pattern emerging across studies argues that expertise induces an N170 that has different properties of spatial localization from the N170 for faces. This suggests that the neural generators producing the N170 for objects of expertise are different from those producing the N170 for faces.

Interference between faces and objects-of-expertise on the N170

Another approach using the N170 has examined competition effects between faces and objects-of-expertise. Results show that, at traditional face-selective sensors, the amplitude of the N170 to faces is reduced more by simultaneous presentation of objects of expertise than by the same objects in novices (greebles: Rossion et al., 2004; cars: Rossion et al., 2007). Rossion et al. (2007) also found that the degree of reduction correlates with level of expertise, and showed the competition effects were unlikely to be attributable to attention differences between experts and novices (e.g. no group differences on P1 were observed).

How should these results be interpreted? It is possible that they could reflect the activation of "face-selective" neural generators by objects of expertise, and thus be consistent with the expertise hypothesis. However, there is an equally valid alternative explanation. The N170 to face stimuli almost certainly includes a component arising from non-face selective cortical regions—for example, faces activate the LOC (e.g. Yovel and Kanwisher, 2005), and this is an area very likely to contribute to the N170 (Rossion and Jacques, 2009). The interference effect could then arise from competition for resources between faces and objects-of-expertise *within these object-general regions* and, because expertise with objects has been shown to increase LOC activation (e.g. Op de Beeck et al., 2006), this competition between faces and objects will be larger in experts than in novices. Thus, these studies cannot answer the crucial question of whether claimed *face-specific* neural generators contributing to the face N170 are also used by objects-of-expertise.

Other arguments for the expertise hypothesis

We now describe, and discard, four other arguments sometimes made for the expertise hypothesis.

"Null effects don't count"

Gauthier and Bukach (2007) have argued that results failing to support the expertise hypothesis should be ignored because many of these rely on statistical null effects; that is, findings of no significant difference between objects in experts and novices.

This argument ignores the fact that many relevant studies find statistically significant effects in other parts of their design (e.g. significant effects for faces, or significant differences in the size of the effect for faces and objects-of-expertise; e.g. see Tables 9.2–9.4), arguing against poor experimental methods or a general lack of statistical power. It also ignores the fact that trends in the reverse-to-predicted direction are often obtained (e.g. see Tables 9.2–9.4), in contrast to the pattern that would be expected if statistical power was the problem. Finally, we believe it represents poor scientific practice—and a misunderstanding of the role of statistics—to ignore consistent evidence of null findings on a given task. This approach allows only for one theoretical outcome: "proof" of the hypothesis that happens to predict the "positive" statistical finding. For example, the logic of Gauthier and Bukach (2007) would never allow us conclude that women's height does *not* change between the ages of 20 and 30 years, regardless of how many studies showing null effects of age were conducted. Another useful example to consider is that of a pharmaceutical company that wishes to bring its new product to market: no scientist would consider it acceptable that this company could choose to count as valid only studies in which their product produced a significant improvement in health outcomes and ignore those in which it failed to produce any significant improvement or produced a significant worsening of health.

"Children show late emergence of holistic processing"

Early studies claimed that children needed 10 years of experience of faces to develop the hallmarks of adult holistic processing (Carey et al., 1980), which was taken as strong support for the expertise hypothesis (Diamond and Carey, 1986). However, this early evidence was rapidly refuted. All holistic effects for faces have been demonstrated in children as young as 4 years, and there are even good reasons to argue that holistic processing is at *full adult levels of strength* by 5 to 6 years (see Crookes and McKone, 2009). Thus, developmental results do not provide support for the expertise hypothesis.

The other-race effect

Some have argued in favor of the expertise hypothesis because face recognition is sensitive to experience. For example, holistic processing, and FFA activation can be affected by race of the face (Golby et al., 2001; Tanaka et al., 2004). However, such findings are not evidence that learning has taken place within a generic expertise system. The effects are equally consistent with experience-based tuning within face-specific mechanisms.

Downward shift in preferred categorization level

The fact that expertise with objects causes a downward shift in entry level of categorization (i.e. faster reaction times for judgments at individual or subordinate levels as compared to basic or superordinate levels, Tanaka and Taylor, 1991) has been taken by some as support for the expertise hypothesis. However, this is based on out-of-date evidence. It has recently been shown that: (1) for objects, preference for the individual level can be obtained without expertise (towers: Anaki and Bentin, 2009), and (2) for faces, preference for the individual level for faces occurs only under certain circumstances (D'Lauro et al., 2008).

Summary

Taken together, results reviewed in this section argue compellingly against the expertise hypothesis. The relevant findings are: (1) on the gold standard measures of face-type holistic processing, expertise does not induce holistic processing for other objects; (2) evidence of expertise effects on other behavioral tasks sometimes presented as measures of "holistic processing" can be explained on the basis of things other than face-type holistic processing; (3) in fMRI, expertise-related changes in BOLD are usually greater in object general areas than in the FFA; (4) where expertise effects are found in the FFA these are open to an attentional explanation or a confound of neighboring face and body areas; (5) neuropsychological cases show a double dissociation between faces and objects-of-expertise; (6) the expertise-related changes in the N170 for objects produce patterns that are typically not face-like in terms of spatial distribution; (7) interference from objects-of-expertise on the face N170 could potentially arise from competition within object-general areas; and (8) other arguments that have been made in favor of the expertise hypothesis are either based on out-of-date evidence (childhood development, downwards categorization shift) or are theoretically invalid (null effects, other-race effects). We also note that the expertise hypothesis provides no explanation of the evidence of an evolved and innate face representation: if processing mechanisms claimed to be special to faces were instead general to objects-of-expertise, then it is impossible to explain why infants are born with the ability to individuate faces but are not born experts with, say, cars.

Should faces and objects be different in all possible ways?

It is important to note that, theoretically, the idea that "faces are special" does not predict that faces should be different from objects in *all* possible ways. For one thing, many stages of the total processing stream will of course be shared by faces and objects: these stages include early visual processing (e.g. no-one would propose that area V1 processes only face stimuli and not object stimuli, or vice versa), and general cognitive processes such as working memory, control of spatial attention, and general decision-making strategies. It is also unsurprising that certain basic properties that improve perceptual efficiency will be shared by both face and object modules: for example, both faces and objects show the property that recently repeated stimuli are processed faster with fewer neural resources than previously unseen items. Our point here is that a finding that object processing is similar to face processing in some way is not evidence against the idea that "faces are special" unless the underlying process was originally a serious candidate for face-specificity.

Summary and conclusions

This chapter addressed whether there are unique visual mechanisms for processing identity-related information in faces compared to other objects. We reviewed literature on an evolved face representation, including studies of newborns, face-deprived monkeys and twins; on holistic/configural behavioral processing in object novices and object experts; and on neural processing in object novices and object experts including single-unit recording, fMRI, ERPs, TMS, and neuropsychological studies. Results clearly favored the view that faces are special. Evidence argued that neither individual-level categorization (within-class discrimination hypothesis) nor individual-level categorization with extensive expertise (expertise hypothesis) leads to face-like processing for objects. Instead, results showed that holistic/configural processing is limited to faces, argued that there are dissociable cortical regions dedicated to processing faces per se, and showed that there exists an evolved representation of the structure of an upright face that is able to support individual level discrimination of faces apparently from birth.

Very recent studies support our conclusions. Key theoretical findings are that (a) twin studies have demonstrated heritability of behavioural face recognition ability independent of object recognition and general cognitive abilities (e.g., IQ); results include heritability of holistic processing for upright faces (composite effect, face inversion) but no heritability of recognition of inverted or split faces (Wilmer et al., 2010; Zhu et al., 2010; for summary and discussion see McKone and Palermo, 2010); and (b) a whole-brain analysis showed object-expertise was associated with increased activation across extensive regions of visual cortex (even V1), that expertise effects were much stronger outside the FFA than inside it, and provided evidence that expertise effects reflect top-down attentional modulation (Harel et al., 2010). Key methodological findings supporting our views about appropriateness of tasks are: (a) the Gauthier 'congruency effect' is nearly as large for inverted faces as for upright faces at typical presentation times (Richler et al.,

2011), in contrast to the substantial inversion effects on the traditional tasks (e.g. composite illusion as assessed by naming or standard same-different version); and (b) ERPs have confirmed the standard same-different composite effect arises from perceptual integration, not later decisional processes (Kuefner, Jacques, Prieto, and Rossion, 2010).

References

Adachi, I., Chou, D.P., and Hampton, R.R. (2009). Thatcher effect in monkeys demonstrates conservation of face perception across primates. *Current Biology*, **19**, 1270–1273.

Anaki, D. and Bentin, S. (2009). Familiarity effects on categorization levels of faces and objects. *Cognition*, **111**, 144–149.

Arzy, S., Thut, G., Mohr, C., Michel, C.M., and Blanke, O. (2006). Neural basis of embodiment: distinct contributions of temporoparietal junction and extrastriate body area. *Journal of Neuroscience*, **26**, 8074–8081.

Ashworth, A.R.S., Vuong, Q.C., Rossion, B., and Tarr, M.J. (2007). Recognizing rotated faces and Greebles: What properties drive the face inversion effect? *Visual Cognition*, **16**, 754–784.

Assal, G., Favre, C., and Anderes, J.P. (1984). Nonrecognition of familiar animals by a farmer: Zooagnosia or prosopagnosia for animals. *Revue Neurologique (Paris)*, **140**, 580–584.

Baker, C.I., Hutchison, T.L., and Kanwisher, N. (2007). Does the fusiform face area contain subregions highly selective for nonfaces? *Nature Neuroscience*, **10(1)**, 3.

Boutet, I. and Faubert, J. (2006). Recognition of faces and complex objects in younger and older adults. *Memory and Cognition*, **34**, 854–864.

Bruyer, R. and Crispeels, G. (1992). Expertise in person recognition. *Bulletin of the Psychonomic Society*, **30**, 501–504.

Busey, T.A. and Vanderkolk, J.R. (2005). Behavioral and electrophysiological evidence for configural processing in fingerprint experts. *Vision Research*, **45**, 431–448.

Calvo-Merino, B., Glaser, D.E., Grèzes, J., Passingham, R.E., and Haggard, P. (2005). Action observation and acquired motor skills: An fMRI study with expert dancers. *Cerebral Cortex*, **15**, 1243–1249.

Carey, S., Diamond, R., and Woods, B. (1980). Development of face recognition - A maturational component? *Developmental Psychology*, **16**, 257–269.

Corballis, M.C., Zbrodoff, N.J., Shetzer, L.I. and Butler, P.B. (1978). Decisions about identity and orientation of rotated letters and digits. *Memory & Cognition*, **6**, 98–107.

Crookes, K. and Mckone, E. (2008). Perceptual narrowing during development: How broad is the innate representation driving adult face-specificity? [Conference abstract]. *Australian Journal of Psychology*, **60(Supp)**, 66.

Crookes, K. and Mckone, E. (2009). Early maturity of face recognition: No childhood development of holistic processing, novel face encoding, or face-space. *Cognition*, **111**, 219–247.

Curby, K.M., Glazek, K., and Gauthier, I. (2009). Perceptual expertise increases visual short-term memory. *Journal of Experimental Psychology: Human Perception and Performance*, **35**, 94–107.

D'lauro, C., Tanaka, J.W., and Curran, T. (2008). The preferred level of face categorization depends on discriminability. *Psychonomic Bulletin and Review*, **15**, 623–629.

Damasio, A.R., Damasio, H., and Van Hoesen, G.W. (1982). Prosopagnosia: Anatomic basis and behavioral mechanisms. *Neurology*, **32**, 331–341.

Davidoff, J. and Donnelly, N. (1990) Object superiority: A comparison of complete and part probes. *Acta Psychologica*, **73**, 225–243.

De Gelder, B., Bachoud-Levi, A.C., and Degos, J.D. (1998). Inversion superiority in visual agnosia may be common to a variety of orientation polarised objects besides faces. *Vision Research*, **38**, 2855–2861.

Diamond, R., and Carey, S. (1986). Why faces are and are not special: An effect of expertise. *Journal of Experimental Psychology: General*, **115**, 107–117.

Downing, P.E., Jiang, Y.H., Shuman, M., and Kanwisher, N. (2001). A cortical area selective for visual processing of the human body. *Science*, **293**, 2470–2473.

Duchaine, B.C., Yovel, G., Butterworth, E., and Nakayama, K. (2006). Prosopagnosia as an impairment to face-specific mechanisms: Elimination of the alternative hypotheses in a developmental case. *Cognitive Neuropsychology*, **23**, 714–747.

Duchaine, B.C., Germine, L., and Nakayama, K. (2007). Family resemblance: Ten family members with prosopagnosia and within-class object agnosia. *Cognitive Neuropsychology*, **24**, 419–430.

Furey, M.L., Tanskanen, T., Beauchamp, M.S., *et al.* (2006). Dissociation of face-selective cortical responses by attention. *Proceedings of the National Academy of Sciences of the United States of America*, **103**, 1065–1070.

Gauthier, I. and Bukach, C. (2007). Should we reject the expertise hypothesis? *Cognition*, **103**, 322–330.

Gauthier, I. and Tarr, M.J. (1997) Becoming a "Greeble" expert: exploring mechanisms for face recognition. *Vision Research*, **37(12)**, 1673–1682.

Gauthier, I. and Tarr, M.J. (2002). Unravelling mechanisms for expert object recognition: bridging brain activity and behavior. *Journal of Experimental Psychology: Human Perception and Performance*, **28**, 431–446.

Gauthier, I., Williams, P.C., Tarr, M.J., and Tanaka, J.W. (1998). Training "greeble" experts: a framework for studying expert object recognition processes. *Vision Research*, **38**, 2401–2428.

Gauthier, I., Tarr, M.J., Anderson, A.W., Skudlarski, P., and Gore, J.C. (1999). Activation of the middle fusiform "face area" increases with expertise in recognizing novel objects. *Nature Neuroscience*, **2**, 568–573.

Gauthier, I., Skudlarski, P., Gore, J.C., and Anderson, A.W. (2000). Expertise for cars and birds recruits brain areas involved in face recognition. *Nature Neuroscience*, **3**, 191–197.

Gauthier, I. and Tarr, M.J. (2002) Unravelling mechanisms for expert object recognition: bridging brain activity and behavior. *Journal of Experimental Psychology: Human Perception and Performance*, **28**, 431–446.

Gauthier, I., Curran, T., Curby, K.M., and Collins, D. (2003). Perceptual interference supports a non-modular account of face processing. *Nature Neuroscience*, **6**, 428–432.

Ge, L., Wang, Z., Mccleery, J.P., and Lee, K. (2006). Activation of face expertise and the inversion effect. *Psychological Science*, **17**, 12–16.

Golby, A.J., Gabrieli, J.D.E., Chiao, J.Y., and Eberhardt, J.L. (2001). Differential responses in the fusiform region to same-race and other-race faces. *Nature Neuroscience*, **4**, 845–850.

Grill-Spector, K., Knouf, N., and Kanwisher, N. (2004). The fusiform face area subserves face perception, not generic within-category identification. *Nature Neuroscience*, **7**, 555–562.

Grill-Spector, K., Sayres, R., and Ress, D. (2006). High-resolution imaging reveals highly selective nonface clusters in the fusiform face area. *Nature Neuroscience*, **9**, 1177–1185.

Grueter, M., Grueter, T., Bell, V., *et al.* (2007). Hereditary prosopagnosia: The first case series. *Cortex*, **43**, 734–749.

Halgren, E., Raij, T., Marinkovic, K., Jousmaki, V., and Hari, R. (2000). Cognitive response profile of the human fusiform face area as determined by MEG. *Cerebral Cortex*, **10**, 69–81.

Harel, A., Gilaie-Dotan, S., Malach, R., and Bentin, S. (2010). Top-down engagement modulates the neural expressions of visual expertise. *Cerebral Cortex*, **20**, 2304–2318.

Harley, E.M., Pope, W.B., Villablanca, J.P., *et al.* (2009). Engagement of fusiform cortex and disengagement of lateral occipital cortex in the acquisition of radiological expertise. *Cerebral Cortex*, **19**, 2746–2754.

Hsiao, J.H.-W. and Cottrell, G. (2009). Not all visual expertise is holistic, but it may be leftist: The case of Chinese character recognition. *Psychological Science*, **20(4)**, 455–463.

Husk, J.S., Bennett, P.J., and Sekuler, A.B. (2007). Inverting houses and textures: Investigating the characteristics of learned inversion effects. *Vision Research*, **47**, 3350–3359.

Husk, J.S., Betts, L.R., O'craven, K.M., Bennett, P.J., and Sekuler, A.B. (2006). House training: Neural correlates of object learning [Abstract]. *Journal of Vision*, **6**, 664a.

Jeffreys, D.A. (1996). Evoked potential studies of face and object processing. *Visual Cognition*, **3**, 1–38.

Kanwisher, N., Mcdermott, J., and Chun, M.M. (1997). The fusiform face area: A module in human extrastriate cortex specialized for face perception. *Journal of Neuroscience*, **17**, 4302–4311.

Kanwisher, N. and Yovel, G. (2006). The fusiform face area: a cortical region specialized for the perception of faces. *Proceedings of the Royal Society B: Biological Sciences*, **361**, 2109–2128.

Kelly, D.J., Quinn, P.C., Slater, A., Lee, K., Ge, L., and Pascalis, O. (2007). The other-race effect develops during infancy: Evidence of perceptual narrowing. *Psychological Science*, **18**, 1084–1089.

Kendrick, K.M., Atkins, K., Hinton, M.R., Heavens, P., and Kevern, B. (1996). Are faces special for sheep? Evidence from facial and object discrimination learning tests showing effects of inversion and social familiarity. *Behavioural processes*, **38**, 19–35

Kennerknecht, I., Pluempe, N., and Welling, B. (2008). Congenital prosopagnosia: A common hereditary cognitive dysfunction in humans. *Frontiers in Bioscience*, **1**, 3150–3158.

Kuefner, D., Jacques, C., Prieto, E.A., and Rossion, B. (2010). Electrophysiological correlates of the composite face illusion: disentangling perceptual and decisional components of holistic face processing in the human brain. *Brain and Cognition*, **74**, 225–238.

Kung, C.-C., Peissig, J.J., and Tarr, M.J. (2007). Is region-of-interest overlap comparison a reliable measure of category specificity? *Journal of Cognitive Neuroscience*, **19**, 2019–2034.

Le Grand, R., Mondloch, C.J., Maurer, D., and Brent, H.P. (2004). Impairment in holistic face processing following early visual deprivation. *Psychological Science*, **15**, 762–768.

Leder, H. and Carbon, C.-C. (2005). When context hinders! Lean-test compatibility in face recognition. *Quarterly Journal of Experimental Psychology*, **58**, 235–250.

Leder, H. and Carbon, C.-C. (2006). Face-specific configural processing of relational information. *British Journal of Psychology*, **97**, 19–29.

Liu, J., Tian, J., Lee, K., and Li, J. (2008). A study on neural mechanism of face processing based on fMRI. *Progress in Natural Science*, **18**, 201–207.

Liu, J., Higuchi, M., Marantz, A., and Kanwisher, N. (2000). The selectivity of the occipitotemporal M170 for faces. *Neuroreport*, **11**, 337–341.

Macchi Cassia, V., Picozzi, M., Kuefner, D., Bricolo, E., and Turati, C. (2009) Holistic processing for faces and cars in preschool-aged children and adults: Evidence from the composite effect. *Developmental Science*, **12**, 236–248.

Maurer, D., Le Grand, R., and Mondloch, C.J. (2002). The many faces of configural processing. *Trends in Cognitive Sciences*, **6**, 255–260.

Maurer, U., Rossion, B., and Mccandliss, B.D. (2008a). Category specificity in early perception: Face and word N170 responses differ in both lateralization and habituation properties. *Frontiers in Human Neuroscience*, **2**, 1–7.

Maurer, U., Zevin, J.D., and Mccandliss, B.D. (2008b). Left-lateralized N170 effects of visual expertise in reading: Evidence from Japanese syllabic and logographic scripts. *Journal of Cognitive Neuroscience*, **20**, 1878–1891.

Mazard, A., Schiltz, C., and Rossion, B. (2006). Recovery from adaptation to facial identity is larger for upright than inverted faces in the human occipito-temporal cortex. *Neuropsychologia*, **44**, 912–922.

McKone, E. (2004). Isolating the special component of face recognition: Peripheral identification and a Mooney face. *Journal of Experimental Psychology: Learning, Memory and Cognition*, **30**, 181–197.

McKone, E. (2008). Configural processing and face viewpoint. *Journal of Experimental Psychology: Human Perception and Performance*, **34**, 310–327.

McKone, E. (2010). Face and object recognition: How do they differ? In V. Coltheart (ed.), *Tutorials in Visual Cognition*, pp. 261–303. New York: Psychology Press.

McKone, E. and Grenfell, T. (1999). Orientation invariance in naming rotated objects: individual differences and repetition priming. *Perception and Psychophysics*, **61**, 1590–603.

McKone, E. and Kanwisher, N. (2005). Does the human brain process objects of expertise like faces? A review of the evidence. In S. Dehaene, J.-R. Duhamel, M. Hauser, and G. Rizzolatti (eds.), *From Monkey Brain to Human Brain*, pp. 339–356. Cambridge, MA: The MIT Press.

McKone, E. and Palermo, R. (2010). A strong role for nature in face recognition. *Proceedings of the National Academy of Sciences of the USA*, **107**(11), 4795–4796.

McKone, E. and Robbins, R. (2007). The evidence rejects the expertise hypothesis: Reply to Gauthier & Bukach. *Cognition*, **103**, 331–336.

McKone, E. and Yovel, G. (2009). Why does picture-plane inversion sometimes dissociate perception of features and spacing in faces, and sometimes not? Towards a new theory of holistic processing. *Psychonomic Bulletin & Review*, **16**, 778–797.

McKone, E., Kanwisher, N., and Duchaine, B.C. (2007). Can generic expertise explain special processing for faces? *Trends in Cognitive Sciences*, **11**, 8–15.

McKone, E., Martini, P. and Nakayama, K. (2001). Categorical perception of face identity in noise isolates configural processing. *Journal of Experimental Psychology: Human Perception and Performance*, **27**, 573–599

McKone, E., Brewer, J.L., Macpherson, S., Rhodes, G., and Hayward, W.G. (2007). Familiar other-race faces show normal holistic processing and are robust to perceptual stress. *Perception*, **36**, 224–248.

McKone, E., Crookes, K., and Kanwisher, N. (2009). The cognitive and neural development of face recognition in humans. In M. S. Gazzaniga (ed.), *The Cognitive Neurosciences* (IV edn.), pp. 467–482. Cambridge, MA: Bradford Books.

McNeil, J.E. and Warrington, E.K. (1993). Prosopagnosia: a face-specific disorder. *Quarterly Journal of Experimental Psychology: A*, **46**, 1–10.

Michel, C., Rossion, B., Han, J., Chung, C.-S., and Caldara, R. (2006). Holistic processing is finely tuned for face of one's own race. *Psychological Science*, **17**, 608–615.

Minnebusch, D.A., Suchan, B., and Daum, I. (2009). Losing your head: Behavioral and electrophysiological effects of body inversion. *Journal of Cognitive Neuroscience*, **21**, 865–874.

Moore, C.D., Cohen, M.X., and Ranganath, C. (2006). Neural mechanisms of expert skills in visual working memory. *Journal of Neuroscience*, **26**, 11187–11196.

Morton, J. and Johnson, M.H. (1991). CONSPEC and CONLERN: A two-process theory of infant face recognition. *Psychological Review*, **98**, 164–181.

Moscovitch, M., Winocur, G., and Behrmann, M. (1997). What is special about face recognition? Nineteen experiments on a person with visual object agnosia and dyslexia but normal face recognition. *Journal of Cognitive Neuroscience*, **9**, 555–604.

Op De Beeck, H., Baker, C., Dicarlo, J., and Kanwisher, N. (2006). Discrimination training alters object representations in human extrastriate cortex. *Journal of Neuroscience*, **26**, 13025–13036.

Parr, L.A., Hecht, E., Barks, S.K., Preuss, T.M., and Votaw, J.R. (2009). Face processing in the chimpanzee brain. *Current Biology*, **19**, 50–53.

Pascalis, O., De Haan, M., and Nelson, C.A. (2002). Is face processing species-specific during the first year of life? *Science*, **296**, 1321–1323.

Pellicano, E., Rhodes, G., and Peters, M. (2006). Are preschoolers sensitive to configural information in faces? *Developmental Science*, **9**, 270–277.

Perrett, D.I., Smith, P.A.J., Potter, D.D., *et al.* (1985). Visual cells in the temporal cortex sensitive to face view and gaze direction. *Proceedings of the Royal Society B: Biological Sciences*, **223**, 293–317.

Pitcher, D., Charles, L., Devlin, J.T., Walsh, V., and Duchaine, B.C. (2009). Triple dissociation of faces, bodies and objects in extrastriate cortex. *Current Biology*, **19**, 319–324.

Polk, T.A., Park, J., Smith, M.R., and Park, D. (2007). Nature versus nurture in ventral visual cortex: A functional magnetic resonance imaging study of twins. *The Journal of Neuroscience*, **27**, 13921–13925.

Reed, C.L., Stone, V.E., Bozova, S., and Tanaka, J. (2003). The body-inversion effect. *Psychological Science*, **14**, 302–308.

Rhodes, G., Byatt, G., Michie, P.T., and Puce, A. (2004). Is the fusiform face area specialized for faces, individuation, or expert identification? *Journal of Cognitive Neuroscience*, **16**, 189–203.

Richler, J.J., Gauthier, I., Wenger, M.J., and Palmeri, T.J. (2008). Holistic processing of faces: Perceptual and decisional components. *Journal of Experimental Psychology: Learning, Memory and Cognition*, **34**, 328–342.

Richler, J.J., Mack, M.L., Palmeri, T.J., and Gauthier, I. (2011). Inverted faces are (eventually) processed holistically. *Vision Research*, **51**, 333–342.

Richler, J.J., Bukach, C.M. and Gauthier, I. (2009). Context influences holistic processing of nonface objects in the composite task. *Attention Perception & Psychophysics*, **71**, 530–540.

Robbins, R. and McKone, E. (2003). Can holistic processing be learned for inverted faces? *Cognition*, **88**, 79–107.

Robbins, R. and McKone, E. (2007). No face-like processing for objects-of-expertise in three behavioural tasks. *Cognition*, **103**, 34–79.

Rossion, B., Collins, D., Goffaux, V., and Curran, T. (2007). Long-term expertise with artificial objects increases visual competition with early face categorization processes. *Journal of Cognitive Neuroscience*, **19**, 543–555.

Rossion, B., Gauthier, I., Goffaux, V., Tarr, M.J., and Crommelinck, M. (2002). Expertise training with novel objects leads to left-lateralized facelike electrophysiological responses. *Psychological Science*, **13**, 250–257.

Rossion, B., Gauthier, I., Tarr, M.J., *et al.* (2000). The N170 occipito-temporal component is delayed and enhanced to inverted faces but not to inverted objects: An electrophysiological account of face-specific processes in the human brain. *NeuroReport*, **11**, 69–72.

Rossion, B. and Jacques, C. (2008). Does physical interstimulus variance account for early electrophysiological face sensitive responses in the human brain? Ten lessons on the N170. *NeuroImage*, **39**, 1959–1979.

Rossion, B. and Jacques, C. (2009). The N170: Understanding the time-course of face perception in the human brain. In S. Luck and E. Kappenman (eds.) *The Oxford Handbook of ERP Components*. Oxford: Oxford University Press.

Rossion, B., Kung, C.-C., and Tarr, M.J. (2004). Visual expertise with nonface objects leads to competition with the early perceptual processing of faces in the human occipitotemporal cortex. *Proceedings of the National Academy of Sciences of the United States of America*, **101**, 14521–14526.

Scapinello, K.F. and Yarmey, A.D. (1970). The role of familiarity and orientation in immediate and delayed recognition of pictorial stimuli. *Psychonomic Science*, **21**, 329–331.

Schiltz, C. and Rossion, B. (2006). Faces are represented holistically in the human occipito-temporal cortex. *NeuroImage*, **32**, 1385–1394.

Schmalzl, L., Palermo, R., and Coltheart, M. (2008). Cognitive heterogeneity in genetically based prosopagnosia: A family study. *Journal of Neuropsychology*, **2**, 99–117.

Schwarzlose, R.F., Baker, C.I., and Kanwisher, N. (2005). Separate face and body selectivity on the fusiform gyrus. *The Journal of Neuroscience*, **25**, 11055–11059.

Seitz, K. (2002). Parts and wholes in person recognition: Developmental trends. *Journal of Experimental Child Psychology*, **82**, 367–381.

Sergent, J. and Signoret, J.-L. (1992). Varieties of functional deficits in prosopagnosia. *Cerebral Cortex*, **2**, 375–388.

Simmons, W.K., Bellgowan, P.S.F., and Martin, A. (2007). Measuring selectivity in fMRI data. *Nature Neuroscience*, **10**, 4–5.

Slater, A., Quinn, P.C., Hayes, R., and Brown, E. (2000). The role of facial orientation in newborn infants' preference for attractive faces. *Developmental Science*, 3, 181–185.

Sugita, Y. (2008). Face perception in monkeys reared with no exposure to faces. *Proceedings of the National Academy of Sciences of the United States of America*, 105, 394–398.

Tanaka, J.W. and Curran, T. (2001). A neural basis for expert object recognition. *Psychological Science*, 12, 43–47.

Tanaka, J.W. and Farah, M.J. (1993). Parts and wholes in face recognition. *The Quarterly Journal of Experimental Psychology*, 46A, 225–245.

Tanaka, J.W. and Gauthier, I. (1997). Expertise in object and face recognition. In R. L. Goldstone, D. L. Medin & P. G. Schyns (Eds.), *Mechanisms of perceptual learning*, Vol. 36, pp. 83–125. San Diego, CA: Academic Press.

Tanaka, J.W., Kiefer, M., and Bukach, C.M. (2004) A holistic account of the own-race effect in face recognition: evidence from a cross-cultural study. *Cognition*, 93, B1–B9.

Tanaka, J.W. and Sengco, J.A. (1997). Features and their configuration in face recognition. *Memory and Cognition*, 25, 583–592.

Tanaka, J.W. and Taylor, M. (1991). Object categories and expertise: Is the basic level in the eye of the beholder. *Cognitive Psychology*, 23, 457–482.

Tanaka, J.W., Kiefer, M., and Bukach, C.M. (2004). A holistic account of the own-race effect in face recognition: evidence from a cross-cultural study. *Cognition*, 93, B1–B9.

Thomas, C., Avidan, G., Humphreys, K., Jung, K.-J., Gao, F., and Behrmann, M. (2008). Reduced structural connectivity in ventral cortex in congenital prosopagnosia. *Nature Neuroscience*, 12, 29–31.

Tsao, D.Y., Freiwald, W.A., Tootell, R.B.H., and Livingstone, M.S. (2006). A cortical region consisting entirely of face-selective cells. *Science*, 311, 670–674.

Turati, C., Bulf, H., and Simion, F. (2008). Newborns' face recognition over changes in viewpoint. *Cognition*, 106, 1300–1321.

Turati, C., Macchi Cassia, V., Simion, F., and Leo, I. (2006). Newborns' face recognition: Role of inner and outer facial features. *Child Development*, 77, 297–311.

Valentine, T. (1988). Upside-down faces: A review of the effect of inversion upon face recognition. *British Journal of Psychology*, 79, 471–491.

Valentine, T. (1991). A unified account of the effects of distinctiveness, inversion, and race in face recognition. *The Quarterly Journal of Experimental Psychology*, 43A, 161–204.

Wilmer, J.B., Germine, L., Chabris, C.F., Chatterjee, G., Williams, M., Loken, E., *et al.* (2010). Human face recognition ability is highly heritable. *Proceedings of the National Academy of Sciences USA*, 107, 5238–5241.

Wong, A.C.N., Gauthier, I., Woroch, B., Debuse, C., and Curran, T. (2005). An early electrophysiological response associated with expertise in letter perception. *Cognitive, Affective, & Behavioral Neuroscience*, 5, 306–318.

Wong, A.C.N., Palmeri, T.J., and Gauthier, I. (2009). Conditions for face-like expertise with objects: Becoming a Ziggerin expert - but which type? *Psychological Science*, 20, 1108–1117.

Xu, Y., Liu, J., and Kanwisher, N. (2005). The M170 is selective for faces, not for expertise. *Neuropsychologia*, 43, 588–597.

Yin, R.K. (1969). Looking at upside-down faces. *Journal of Experimental Psychology*, 81, 141–145.

Young, A.W., Hellawell, D., and Hay, D.C. (1987). Configurational information in face perception. *Perception*, 16, 747–759.

Yovel, G. and Duchaine, B.C. (2006). Specialized face perception mechanisms extract both part and spacing information: Evidence from developmental prosopagnosia. *Journal of Cognitive Neuroscience*, 18, 580–593.

Yovel, G. and Kanwisher, N. (2005). The neural basis of behavioral face-inversion effect. *Current Biology*, 15, 2256–2262.

Yovel, G. and Kanwisher, N. (2008). The representations of spacing and part-based information are associated for upright faces but dissociated for objects: Evidence from individual differences. *Psychonomic Bulletin and Review*, **15**, 933–939.

Yovel, G., Pelc, T. and Lubetzky, I. (2010). It's all in your head: Why is the body inversion effect abolished for headless bodies? *Journal of Experimental Psychology: Human Perception and Performance*, **36**, 759–767.

Yue, X., Tjan, B.S., and Biederman, I. (2006). What makes faces special. *Vision Research*, **26**, 3802–3811.

Zhu, Q., Song, Y., Hu, S., Li, X., Tian, M., Zhen, Z., *et al.* (2010). Heritability of the specific cognitive ability of face perception. *Current Biology*, **20**, 137–142.

Chapter 10

Features, Configuration, and Holistic Face Processing

James W. Tanaka and Iris Gordon

Since the days of Galton (1879), psychologists have been aware that a face is not identified by the recognition of its isolated, individual features, but by the integration of these features into a perceived whole. For example, Brad Pitt is not readily recognized by the shape of his eyes, the slant of his nose, or the contour of his lips. Instead, it is the combination of these features that create the unique, immediate, and holistic impression of the famous actor. Of course, holistic face perception is not reserved for the recognition of well known celebrities, but a process that typifies the recognition of all faces.

In this chapter, we will explore what it means to recognize a face holistically and examine the experimental paradigms that serve as the "gold standards" for holistic perception. Next, we will discuss the contribution of featural and configural information to the holistic process and the controversy surrounding these often misunderstood concepts. This discussion will focus on the kind of featural and configural information that is impaired in an inverted face as well as the information that is spared. Finally, we will consider Rossion's (2008) concept of a "perceptual field" that allows for the preservation of both featural and configural information within a restricted spatial region of an inverted face.

Holistic representation and the demands of face recognition

The pragmatics of everyday face recognition require us to identify faces at the subordinate level of the individual (e.g. Mary, Bob) rather than the basic level of the "person" or "face." Despite the increased perceptual demands required for subordinate level judgments (Jolicoeur et al., 1984), humans are able to recognize familiar faces (e.g. Brad Pitt, Kate Winslet) as quickly and accurately as individuals as they are to recognize them at a basic level of human (D'Lauro et al., 2008; Tanaka, 2001). Recent behavioral (Grill-Spector and Kanwisher, 2005) and neurophysiological (Jacques and Rossion, 2006; Liu et al., 2002) evidence suggests that 250 ms is enough time to individuate a familiar face. The speed and accuracy with which people can identify a familiar face at the very specific level of the individual suggests that most of us qualify as bona fide "face experts" (Carey, 1992).

From a perceptual standpoint, the feat of everyday face recognition is remarkable given that faces share, an underlying structural geometry. That is, all faces have the same features of two eyes, a nose, and a mouth arranged in a similar spatial configuration with the eyes horizontally aligned above the midline nose which is above the mouth. Diamond and Carey (1986) have referred to this information as the first-order relational properties of a face. However, recognition of an individual person and therefore cannot be based on first-order information because of its similarity to other faces, and therefore must depend on recognition of the subtle differences in the features and their configuration that form the impression of unique face. This is the essence of Galton's claim: the face is perceived holistically as an integrated whole that is more than the combined sum of it individual parts.[1]

Three tests of holistic face perception

According to theories of holistic face perception, facial features are simultaneously encoded so that the individual components are integrated into a "global percept" (Sergent, 1984). The holistic view does not deny that the individual features of a face play a role in face perception, only that their contribution is secondary to the percept of the whole face. Although the notion of holistic perception is intuitively appealing, it is critical to ground this concept in experimental methods that operationally define holistic perception and pose tests of holistic perception based on these definitions. In this sub-section, we will discuss three empirical paradigms involving inversion, composite faces, and part-whole recognition that explicitly manipulate the factors that influence the holistic (and analytic) perception of faces.

The disproportional face inversion effect

While many objects are more difficult to identify upside down than right side up, faces seem to be *disproportionately* impaired by inversion relative to the recognition of most mono-oriented objects—this phenomenon is referred to as the so-called face inversion effect (Yin, 1969).[2] In the typical face inversion experiment, a series of faces and contrast objects (e.g. airplanes, building, costumes) are presented for study in their upright or inverted orientation and then tested for recognition when presented either in their upright or inverted orientation. The main finding is that faces are more difficult to recognize than other objects when either studied, tested or both studied and tested in their inverted orientations. For example, Brad Pitt (Figure 10.1a) is easily recognized compared to the foil face (e.g. Tom Cruise embedded in Brad Pitt's face) when the faces are presented in their upright orientations (Figure 10.1b). However, recognition is much more challenging when the faces are presented in their inverted orientations (Figure 10.1c).

The face inversion effect has been obtained with a variety of face stimuli including famous and novel faces (Scapinello and Yarmey, 1970; Yarmey, 1971), schematic faces (Yin, 1969) and photographs of faces (Carey and Diamond, 1977; Diamond and Carey, 1986). Furthermore, this effect has been tested under different paradigms employing immediate and delayed matching tasks (Freire et al., 2000), utilizing forced-choice (Yin, 1969), and "old/new" responses (Valentine and Bruce, 1986). Other work has shown that inversion disrupts the perception of the whole face more than perception of its parts presented in isolation (Rhodes et al., 1993). An important advantage of the inversion manipulation is that the low level properties of the face (e.g. luminance, contrast, spatial frequency) remain constant yet the recognition of the face is severely impaired. Thus, impaired performance of the inverted face cannot be attributed to changes in the low level properties of the face but to differences in the cognitive processes brought to bear in the recognition of upright versus inverted faces.

---

[1] The terms "configural" and "holistic" processing have sometimes been used interchangeably in the literature. In this chapter, we use the term "holistic" processing to refer to the process by which the featural and configural information are integrated into a face representation. We use the term "configural processing" in a more limited sense, to refer to encoding of metric distances between features (i.e. second-order relational properties).

[2] Since the Yin finding, inversion effects has been demonstrated for human bodies (Reed et al., 2003) and artificial "greeble" objects by laboratory trained greeble experts (Gauthier and Tarr, 1998; Gauthier et al., 2000). These findings suggest that inversion effects can be shown for objects with which people have extensive familiarity or expertise.

(a)

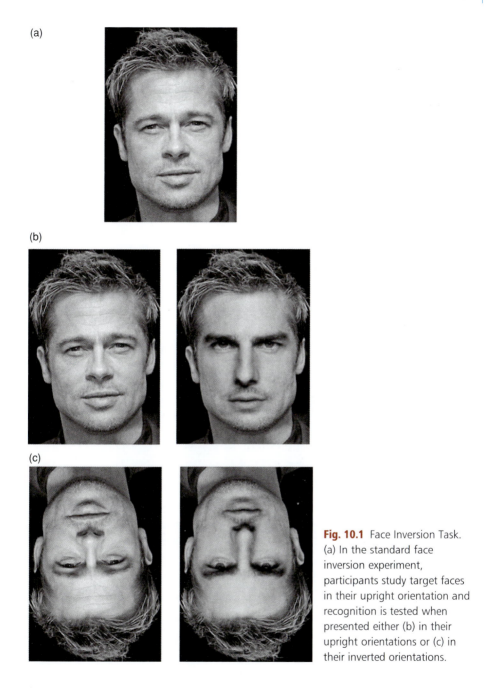

(b)

(c)

Fig. 10.1 Face Inversion Task. (a) In the standard face inversion experiment, participants study target faces in their upright orientation and recognition is tested when presented either (b) in their upright orientations or (c) in their inverted orientations.

A limitation of the inversion paradigm is that the source of the inversion effect is left unspecified. That is, the face inversion paradigm doesn't provide any direct clues about the nature of the cognitive mechanism that is impaired as a consequence of face inversion. Yin (1969) speculated that a "special factor" is suppressed or inhibited when a face is turned upside down. The precise nature of this "special factor" can be more directly manipulated in the face composite and parts-wholes tasks.

Face composite task

A compelling demonstration of whole face perception is the face composite task (Young et al., 1987). In this paradigm, a composite face stimulus is produced by merging the top half of a well-known person with the bottom half of another famous individual (as shown in Figure 10.2). The impression of the composite image is a novel face that resembles neither the original person depicted in the top nor the bottom portion, but a face with a new, emergent identity. In the face composite task, the participant reports the identity of the person in the cued half -face while ignoring information in the uncued portion. The main finding is that participants have difficulty in selectively attending to the cued portion of the face due to holistic interference caused by the to-be-ignored half. Critically, the interference effect is attenuated if the configural information in the face is disrupted by misaligning the top and bottom halves (Young et al., 1987). Interestingly, inverting the composite face also abolishes the interference effect, suggesting that inversion induces a piecemeal mode of perceptual analysis (Young et al., 1987). These results suggest that the features of a face are not perceived independently of one another, but are integrated into a complete face representation. However, interpretation of the composite results is not as straightforward as researchers initially thought. Recent work has shown that judgments about aligned

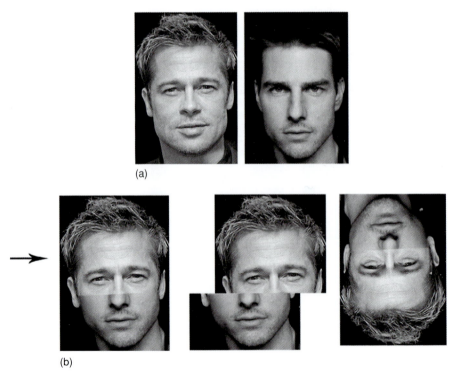

(a)

(b)

Fig. 10.2 Composite Face Task. (a) Original images of Brad Pitt and Tom Cruise. (b) A composite face is created by the joining the top half of one famous face (Brad Pitt) with the bottom half of another famous face (Tom Cruise). At test, participants are asked to identify the face shown in the cued half of the composite face while ignoring information in the uncued half. The test face is either an intact composite face (left), misaligned composite face (middle face) or inverted composite (right face).

and misaligned faces can also be influenced by decisional (Cheung et al., 2008) and attentional (Richler et al., 2008) factors.

The argument for a qualitative difference between the holistic processing of upright and the analytic processing of inverted faces is further supported by studies examining perception of faces presented at multiple degrees of rotation. As a measure of holistic perception, Murray et al. (2000) asked observers to make grotesqueness judgments to "Thatcher faces" (i.e. a face that is made to look bizarre by inverting the local orientations of the eye and mouth features) presented at multiple degrees of orientation. When an inverted Thatcher face was systematically rotated from 180 to 0 degrees, a discrete increase in grotesque judgments was reported at about 90 degrees orientation that was similar to judgments made to the upright face. This non-linearity was interpreted as a qualitative shift from an analytic to a holistic perception in which the individual elements were abruptly integrated into a unified percept of a grotesque face. Similar non-linear effects of orientation have been reported in a face composite task (Rossion and Boremanse, 2011) and categorical perception of faces presented in noise (McKone et al., 2001).

Parts-wholes task

Further evidence for holistic representation emerges from the parts-wholes task. In this paradigm, a series of study faces (e.g. Joe, Bob, Fred) are learned and memory for a face part from one of the study faces (Joe's eyes) is then tested either in isolation, or in the context of the whole face in a two-alternative force choice design. In the whole face test condition, the target and foil faces are identical with the exception of the critical part under examination. As shown in the Figure 10.3 example, recognition for Brad Pitt's nose is tested in a whole face in which the eyes and mouth are kept constant in the target and foil faces. The whole face hypothesis predicts that if memory for the individual features of a face is integrated into the whole face representation, recognition of the face part should be better when presented in the whole face context (Figure 10.3d) than when tested in isolation (Figure 10.3b). Consistent with this prediction, part recognition was superior when presented in the context of whole face (Tanaka and Farah, 1993). However, no evidence of holistic recognition was found when the studied and test stimuli were scrambled faces, non-face stimuli (houses) or inverted faces. In these cases, the recognition of the individual part did not benefit from the context of the whole stimulus forcing an analytic approach to encoding (Tanaka and Farah, 1993). Based on this evidence, it has been argued that faces are represented as unified, non-decomposable forms where part and configural information are integrated in a *holistic* face representation (see also Donnelly and Davidoff, 1999).

A prediction of the holistic hypothesis is that modifications to one source of information (e.g. changing the spatial distances between the eyes) should affect the perception of the other type of information (e.g. perception of individual eyes and mouth). To test this prediction, Tanaka and Sengco (1997) asked participants to learn faces in one configuration and then tested their recognition for a part when the part was presented in isolation, in a new configuration or in an old configuration. Participants studied a version of the face with its eyes spaced close together. They were then asked to recognize a part of the studied face, such as the mouth, when the target and foil mouth were presented in isolation, in the previously learned whole face with the eyes spaced close together and in a new configuration with eyes spaced far apart. The results showed that recognition of a part was best when tested in the old configuration, followed by performance in the new configuration, and was poorest when tested in isolation. Critically, altering the spatial distance between the eyes impaired recognition of the nose and mouth features—features whose spatial locations were not directly changed. This effect is illustrated in Figure 10.3, where memory for Brad Pitt's nose is best when tested in its original configuration (Figure 10.3c) as compared to

(a) Study face

(b) Isolated part test item

(c) New configuration test item

Fig. 10.3 Parts-wholes Faces Task. (a) In the "Parts-Wholes" task, participants are shown a target face (e.g., Brad Pitt). At test, participants are asked to identify a "part" of the target face (e.g., Brad Pitt's nose) presented either (b) in isolation, (c) in the whole face with an altered inter-ocular distance and (d) in the whole face with the same inter-ocular distance. In the isolated part and whole face test conditions, the target and foil items differ only with respect to part under test (e.g. Brad Pitt's nose).

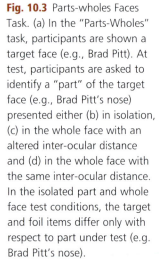 

(d) Old configuration test item

a new configuration where the space between the eye features is increased (Figure 10.3d). These findings provide a powerful demonstration of how the features of a face and their configuration are closely linked in a holistic representation in which a local change in spatial distance alters the global perception of all features in the face.

To sum up, evidence from the inversion, composite, and parts-wholes experiments demonstrate that faces are processed more holistically than the other types of non-face objects (e.g. airplanes, buildings, costumes) tested in these paradigms. Results from these studies have been informative for identifying the specific characteristics of holistic face processing. First, holistic processing can be disrupted by manipulations of spatial misalignment, feature scrambling and inversion. Second, holistic representations are resistant to the influences of selective attention, such that it is difficult to attend to one half of a holistic stimulus, while disregarding information in the to-be-ignored half. Third, changes in configural information influence the perception of featural information.

While the above experiments emphasize the holistic aspects of faces, this does not imply that face representations are devoid of any part structure. In the parts-wholes task, for example, the participants performed well above chance when identifying features presented in isolation, indicating that information about the individual parts of the face was encoded along with the whole face. Farah (1991, 1992) has proposed that visual patterns lay on a holistic-to-feature continuum depending on their proportion of whole and part-based representations (for similar models, see McKone, 2004; Moscovitch et al., 1997). On one end of the continuum are stimuli such as faces and bodies (Reed et al., 2003) whose recognition relies primarily on the whole stimulus and less on the part structure. On the other end of the continuum are visual patterns, such as words whose representations emphasize the decomposition of the word into its individual letter units (Johnston and McClelland, 1980). Human-made and natural objects (e.g. cars, chairs, birds) are somewhere in the middle of the two extremes containing a mixture of both whole- and part-based representations. According to this view, face recognition is not distinctive because it depends exclusively on holistic representations. It is only distinguished because its representation is disproportionately more holistic than the representation of most other types of objects.

The inversion debate: Is configuration special?

While there is little disagreement that face recognition requires information about the whole face, there is much debate regarding the kind of information that is lost when a face is turned upside down. Common to all theories of face perception is the assumption that the face-specific processes engaged by upright faces are disabled or suppressed when a face is turned upside down. Thus, knowing the type of information and processes that are compromised in an inverted face provides important clues for understanding what makes face perception distinct from other forms of object recognition (Valentine, 1988). The controversy revolves around the relative contribution of featural and configural information to the whole face representation. On one side of the issue, proponents of the configural view argue that sensitivity to the spatial relations between the features of a face is differentially disrupted through inversion (Freire et al., 2000; LeGrand et al., 2001; Maurer et al., 2002; Mondloch et al., 2002). On the other side of the issue, advocates of the featural+configural view have argued that there is nothing special about the effects of inversion on the configural properties of a face. According to this position, feature coding is equally vulnerable to the inversion as configural coding when the two types of information are equated for discrimination in their upright orientations (Riesenhuber et al., 2004; McKone and Yovel, 2009; Yovel and Kanwisher, 2004; see also McKone and Robbins, Chapter 9, this volume). In the following section, we will consider the evidence supporting the configural and featural+configural accounts of the face inversion effect and discuss recent studies that reconcile the two positions.

The configural view

Diamond and Carey (1986) hypothesized that the ability to discriminate the spatial relations between the face parts is what distinguishes face recognition from other types of object recognition. According to Diamond and Carey, it is our sensitivity to the *second-order relational properties* of a face that is selectively compromised when a face is inverted (see McKone and Yovel, 2009, for a detailed discussion of second-order relational properties). As a test of this claim, Friere et al. (2000) presented pairs of upright and inverted faces that differed either in their configuration (distances between the eyes and nose and mouth) or features (eyes and mouths). Consistent with the second-order relational view, the main finding was that a larger inversion effect was found for configural discriminations than featural discriminations. Other studies have also shown that identification involving the spatial distances between the eyes or distances between the nose and mouth is more susceptible to inversion than identification of the eyes, nose or mouth features (Leder and Bruce, 2000; Rhodes, 1993).

While these results demonstrate that the coding of spatial relations are impaired in an inverted face, an important question that arises is whether this impairment is specific to faces or characteristic of other non-face objects? To address this question, Leder and Carbon (2006) presented participants with house stimuli that varied in their window or door features or their spatial distances between the features. When recognition for the houses was tested in the upright and inverted orientations, inversion had little effect on judgments involving featural or configural changes. Based on these results, the authors argued that face-specific processes are recruited for differentiating spatial relations.

Over the past decade, the configural position has gained traction as a processing account of the face inversion effect. Using a standard set of stimuli (i.e. the Jane stimuli), studies have shown that configural discriminations are selectively compromised due to early visual deprivation (LeGrand et al., 2001) and are slower to develop in children (Mondloch et al., 2002). Thus, many behavioral studies suggest that configural information is selectively compromised in an inverted face. However, the configural view has not gone unchallenged.

The featural+configural view

Proponents of the featural+configural position have argued that both featural and configural information are equally disrupted in an inverted face. The featural+configural researchers have challenged the "configural only" evidence on several fronts. Methodologically, some studies testing featural and configural discrimination have employed a blocked design procedure in which the faces differed either in their configural properties or their featural properties. This method might promote strategies that are more optimum for featural or configural approaches (Freire et al., 2000; Mondloch et al., 2002). Participants in the featural block, for example, might adopt a localist strategy that focuses on changes in the either the isolated eye or mouth region thereby ignoring whole face information. The advantage of the local encoding strategy is that single parts are less susceptible to the effects of inversion than whole-face information. In the configural block, a localist strategy is not optimal because spacing changes occur over a broader spatial area of the facial image. In the configural block then, participants are less likely to use the local strategy and adopt a whole face approach that is typical to normal face processing and therefore prone to inversion effects. In support of the strategic account, Riesenhuber et al. (2004) showed that the featural-configural difference disappeared when face discrimination was tested in an unblocked design and reappeared when the same stimuli were tested using a blocked procedure. Recently, Rossion (2008) has taken issue with Riesenhuber et al.'s strategic account. Rossion cites numerous studies showing that when randomized (i.e. non-blocked) versions of the inversion paradigm are tested, a greater cost is found in spacing manipulations than featural manipulations (Freire et al., Experiment 3 and 4; Leder and Bruce, 2000; Rhodes et al., 2007) suggesting that the source of the configural impairment is not necessarily methodological.

The configural view has been criticized for other reasons. Yovel and Kanwisher (2004) observed that in many of the studies showing greater configural inversion effects, part judgments were easier than spacing judgments (Le Grand et al., 2001; Mondloch et al., 2002) which might explain the diminished inversion effect in the featural condition. To control for baseline differences, they argued that featural and configural discriminations should be equated for difficulty and properly calibrated to avoid ceiling and floor effects. When these considerations were taken in account, they found that featural part differences were as difficult to discriminate as configural differences (Yovel and Kanwisher, 2004).

Representation of featural and configural information in the brain

Are the features and the configurations of a face coded in different parts of the brain? Neuroimaging studies have focused on the BOLD response to faces in the fusiform face area (FFA)–an area of the brain that has been implicated in the perception of individual faces (Gauthier et al., 2000; Kanwisher and Yovel, 2006). In support of the configural view, some studies have shown that judgments involving feature spacing produce increased activity in or near the right fusiform face area (FFA) (Maurer et al., 2007; Rhodes et al., 2009), whereas judgments about features themselves more strongly activate areas in the left prefrontal cortex (Maurer et al., 2007). Consistent with the featural+configural view, other studies have shown that during a discrimination task, detection of featural and spacing changes produced equivalent levels of BOLD activation in the FFA (Yovel and Kanwisher, 2004; but see Rhodes et al., 2009).

Definitional problems: What is a feature? What is configuration?

Much of the controversy surrounding the configural versus featural+configural debate has to do with the varied and sometimes confusing array of terms that researchers have used to explain the phenomenon (McKone and Yovel, 2009). As shown in Table 10.1, on some occasions, the same terms have been used to mean different things and on others, different terms mean the same thing. For example, the term "feature" has been most commonly described as the internal parts of a face including the eyes and eyebrows, nose and mouth (Freire et al., 2000; Lee and Freire, 1999) corresponding to points of discontinuity in its surface geometry (Biederman, 1987; Hoffman and Richards, 1985). Typically, the pair of eyes is treated as a single feature, but there are also exceptions in which the left and right eyes are independently manipulated (Cooper and Wojan, 2000). In other studies, the inferior contour of the face (i.e. jaw-line) has been treated as a "feature" (Sergent, 1984). In other instances, surface properties such the color of the lips (Rhodes et al., 2006) and eyes (Barton et al., 2001) or brightness of the eyes (Leder and Bruce, 1998) were manipulated and treated as featural properties. Presumably, these types of "surface" features (e.g. color, brightness) are less vulnerable to manipulations of inversion than part features because they are orientation invariant (e.g. blue is still blue regardless of its orientation). As discussed in the next section, whether a "feature" is vulnerable to inversion depends on how it is defined.

The concept of configuration is equally difficult to define and empirically quantify. Configuration refers to the spatial distances or spacing between features. Whereas the categorical arrangement

Table 10.1 The different ways researchers have described facial features, configural processing, and holistic processing

Feature		Description
Part	Donnelly and Davidoff, 1999; Rhodes 1988; Tanaka and Farah, 1993	The individual parts of the face (eyes, nose and mouth)
External contour	Sergent, 1984	The external face outline including the chin and jaw contours
Color	Barton et al., 2001; Leder and Carbon, 2006; Leder and Bruce, 2000	Eye color, hair color, mouth color
Non-face	Carey and Diamond, 1977; Rhodes et al., 1985	Glasses, clothing
Configural processing		**Description**
First-order relational properties	Diamond and Carey, 1986	The categorical spatial relations between parts of a face (e.g. the eyes are above the nose)
Second-order relational properties	Diamond and Carey, 1986	The metric spacing between the parts of a face (e.g. inter-ocular distance is wide versus narrow)
Configural processing	Maurer et al., 2002	Three types: (1) first-order relational properties, (2) second-order relational properties, and (3) holistic processing
Holistic processing		**Description**
Holistic Processing	Donnelly and Davidoff, 1999; Tanaka and Farah, 1993; Tanaka and Sengco, 1997	The integration of part features and second-order relational properties into a whole face representation

of the eyes and mouth region above and below the nose respectively (the so-called first-order relational properties) is straightforward, the precise manipulation and measurement of the spatial distances between these features is problematic. It is not obvious, for example, whether configuration is best calculated as the distance between features using the external contours of the landmark features (i.e. edge-to-edge distances) or by utilizing the centroids of features (i.e. centroid-to-centroid) as the reference points. Furthermore, it is not possible to isolate the local spatial relations given that changes in one feature (e.g. interocular distance) affect its spatial relations to other features in the face (e.g. distance between eyes and nose). Attempts to isolate the configural properties of a face by low spatial frequency filtering are also problematic because this filtering smears the edge-to-edge spatial distances between features. In summary, without explicit rules for quantification, it is not obvious how the configural properties of a face can be measured and manipulated independently of its features.

A more insidious problem for studying the independent contributions of the featural and configural information in face perception is that the two dimensions are inherently confounded. As Sergent (1984) pointed out "changing a single feature in a face also modifies the interrelation between the components and, therefore, the configuration of the face." In other words, when a feature from one face (e.g. Brad Pitt's eyes) is swapped for a feature in another face (e.g. Tom Cruise's eyes), changes in both featural and configural information occur. Moreover, featural manipulations can affect the spatial distances between features based on either their centroids or their edges. For example, scaling the size of a feature does not change the location of its centroid, but will affect edge-to-edge relations. Conversely, changing the shape of an eye may affect its centroid, but not affect the distance of its edge to the edge of the nose. Changes in configuration can also affect the perception of facial features. For example, shifting the eyes and eyebrows upward on a face creates the unintended illusion of an elongated nose in a face stimulus.

In summary, investigating the effects of inversion on the perception of features and configuration in a face has proven challenging for several reasons. First, changes to the features of a face invariably affect the spatial relations between the part features and conversely, alterations in configuration can impact the perception of face features. Second, researchers have adopted different ways of operationalizing and testing the concept of a "feature" leading to conflicting claims about how inversion affects feature perception. In the next sub-section, we will discuss recent attempts to bring clarity to the field by carefully defining what is meant by the terms "features" and "configuration."

What's lost and what's preserved in the inverted face

Recently, McKone and Yovel (2009) reviewed 22 published papers in the literature examining the relative effects of inversion on the perception of featural and configural information. Their findings were revealing. If "feature" was defined as a surface property (e.g. color, brightness), inversion produced little impairment in recognition relative to its upright condition (Barton et al., 2001; Leder and Bruce, 2000; Leder and Carbon, 2006; Searcy and Bartlett, 1996; Murray et al., 2000). However, if feature was defined in terms of shape, the magnitude of the inversion effect for feature changes was at least as large as the effect for spacing changes (Rhodes et al., 1993, Riesenhuber et al., 2004; Yovel and Kanwisher, 2004; Yovel and Duchaine, 2006). Whereas surface changes are orientation invariant and resistant to the effects of inversion, the perception of face parts are vulnerable to the effects of misorientation.

Recent work suggests inversion does not disrupt all configural relations equally–some relations appear to be more susceptible to inversion than others. In their experiment, Goffaux and Rossion (2007) manipulated two kinds of spacing in the eye region: the vertical displacement of the eyes and eyebrows relative to the rest of the face and the horizontal distance between these features. They found that inversion drastically impaired the perception of vertical displacements, but had a weaker effect on the perception of horizontal changes. Sekunova and Barton (2008) also showed that if the eyes, but not the eyebrows, are vertically displaced, the magnitude of the inversion is greatly diminished. According to Skeunova and Barton, configural discriminations, such as the distance between the eyes or distance between the eye and eyebrows, can be computed on the basis of local information and are therefore less affected by the influences of inversion. In contrast, metric distances that are calculated over a large spatial extent (e.g. nose-mouth distances, vertical position of the eyes and eyebrows) are more vulnerable to the effects of inversion.

The eye region is not the only area of the face that is disrupted by inversion. Vertical displacements between the nose and mouth are similarly compromised when a face is turned upside to down (Barton et al., 2001, 2003). The neglect of the lower region of the face seems not to be restricted to spatial separation between the nose and mouth, but extends to the perception of the mouth feature. In a recent study, Tanaka et al. (2009) designed the Face Dimensions Task where participants were asked to detect changes in eye spacing (distance between the eyes), mouth spacing (distance between nose and mouth), eye features (size of the eyes) and mouth features (size of the mouth) for easy, moderate and difficult levels of discrimination (see Figure 10.4). Discrimination difficulty was equated across the four conditions for faces presented in the

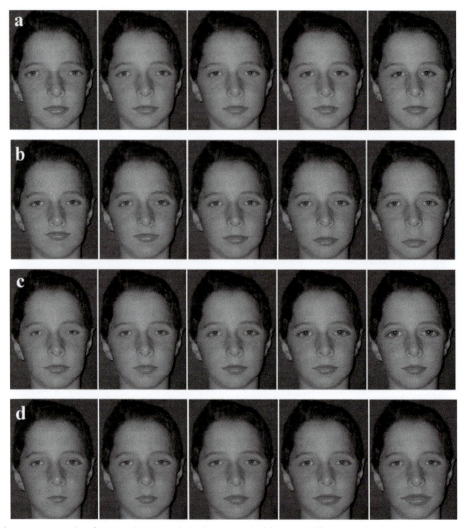

Fig. 10.4 Example of a complete set of the face stimuli. (a) Faces differing in the distances separating the eyes (configural/eyes manipulation). (b) Faces differing in the distance between the nose and mouth (configural/mouth manipulation). (c) Faces differing in the size of the eyes (featural/eyes manipulation). (d) Faces differing in size of the mouth (featural/mouth manipulation). The original upon which the manipulations were made is the middle face of each row. Reproduced with permission from the *Journal of Neurosychology* © The British Psychological Society.

upright orientations. The critical question was what would happen when the same faces are tested in their inverted orientation?

The main finding was that inversion disrupted the perception of featural (i.e. size of the mouth) and configural (i.e. distance between the nose and the mouth) changes in the lower region of the face. For inverted faces, the magnitude of impaired perception was stunning such that detection was only slightly above chance levels even in the easy discrimination condition. It is unlikely that the impaired mouth perception reflected a lower visual field deficit because in a control study with house stimuli, inversion had little effect on the discrimination of featural and configural information in the bottom half of the houses (Tanaka et al., 2009). In contrast to the impaired perception of the lower half of the face, inversion had relatively little impact on the perception in the upper region of the face. In the Face Dimensions task, discrimination of featural (i.e. size of the eyes) and configural (i.e. distance between the eyes) eye differences were only marginally affected by inversion.

Contrary to the configural view, the evidence indicates that inversion neither selectively disrupts configural information nor selectively spares featural information. Both types of information are simultaneously impaired and preserved during inversion. Inversion adversely affects configural coding of the vertical position of the eyes/eyebrows, vertical spacing between nose and mouth features (Goffaux and Rossion, 2007; Sekunova and Barton, 2008) and featural coding of the size and shape of the mouth feature (Tanaka et al., 2009). At the same time, inversion does little to perturb the featural perception of eye shape or eye size. Inversion also leaves intact configural perception involving the horizontal spacing between the eyes (Goffaux and Rossion, 2007; Tanaka et al., 2009). These results show that featural and configural information in the eye region of the face is selectively spared during inversion whereas information outside this area is severely impaired. Thus, the differential effects of inversion on face perception are determined by the location of featural and configural information in the face rather than by the nature of the information itself.

Inversion, fractured faces, and perceptual fields

The foregoing results produce an interesting puzzle: if critical eye information is essentially preserved in an inverted face, then why are upside down faces so difficult to recognize? Many face perception studies have shown that the eyes are critical for the perception of upright faces. The eyes are highly diagnostic for identity, expression and gender judgments (Vinette et al., 2004), are essential for monitoring ongoing social communication (Klin et al., 2002) and are sufficient to drive the so-called face N170 component in ERPs (Bentin et al., 2002). Failure to encode eye information can also lead to breakdowns in face recognition in individuals with autism (Wolf et al., 2008) and patients with prosopagnosia (Bukach et al., 2008; Caldara et al., 2005; Rossion et al., 2009). These experiments demonstrate the importance of eye information in face perception.

While the eyes may be crucial to face processing, the holistic account proposes that accurate coding of eye information by itself is not sufficient. In an upright face, facial features (eyes, nose, mouth) and their configural relationships are fused together into a single perceptual representation. If the stimulus is inverted, this interdependence is lost causing a disruption in holistic face perception. In an inverted face, the holistic representation is shattered; the eyes become disconnected from the external contours of the face (Goffaux and Rossion, 2007; Lee and Freire, 1999), the nose-to-mouth spacing is disrupted (Goffaux and Rossion, 2007; Sekunova and Barton, 2008) and coding of the mouth feature is lost (Tanaka et al., 2009). The inversion studies show that successful face recognition demands more than the coding of eyes, but requires the holistic integration of the eyes with the rest of the face (McKone and Yovel, 2009; Rossion, 2008).

Rossion (2008) speculates that inversion causes the observer's "perceptual field" of the face to decrease in size. As shown in Figure 10.5, the perceptual field for an upright face is expansive encompassing the facial features of the eyes, nose, mouth and their configural relations to each other and to the external face contour. Inversion causes the perceptual field to shrink in size, forcing the observer to process a face in a feature-by-feature manner (Rossion, 2008). Having to rely on this piecemeal approach, it follows that judgments requiring spatial judgments between *two* features will be more susceptible to inversion than judgments involving just one feature. According

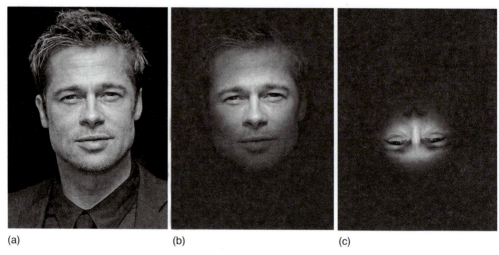

(a)   (b)   (c)

Fig. 10.5 Rossion's Perceptual Field. (a) Complete face image. (b) In an upright face, the perceptual field encompasses the entire face binding featural and configural information in a holistic representation. (c) Inversion reduces the perceptual field and shifts focus to the eye region.

to the perceptual field account, if the perceptual field is narrowly focused on the eye region in an inverted face, information within this field will be preserved (e.g. eye features and spacing) whereas information outside the perceptual field (e.g. nose-to-mouth spacing, mouth features) will be lost.

The perceptual field is not necessarily fixed on the eyes in the inverted face, but can be redirected to other face regions. Sekunova and Barton (2008) employed a spatial cuing paradigm in which participants were cued to the eye or the mouth region of upright and inverted faces. Faces varied either with respect to the vertical location of the eyes and eye brows or the vertical spacing between the nose and mouth. When cued to the mouth region, participants showed a reduced inversion effect relative to effects of cueing on the eye region. Thus, while attention is not spontaneously drawn to the mouth region in an inverted face, discrimination of spatial distances between the nose and mouth features can be enhanced if spatial attention is directed to this area.

During normal upright face perception, the perceptual field unifies the individual parts of a face and their relations in a holistic representation. However, holistic processing of upright faces can also be disrupted by either asking participants to encode multiple faces in a display (Palermo and Rhodes, 2002) or by introducing an attentionally demanding secondary task (Reinitz et al., 1994). In one study (Palermo and Rhodes, 2002), participants completed a parts-wholes task to a centrally presented face that was flanked by two peripheral faces. When told to ignore the flanking faces, participants showed normal holistic recognition of the central face. However, in a divided attention task, where participants were instructed to complete the parts-wholes task while matching the identities of the flanker faces, they showed no evidence of holistic encoding. These results suggest that face-specific holistic resources are limited, such that only one face can be holistically encoded at a time (see also Bindemann et al., 2005 and Boutet et al., 2002).

Summary and conclusions

In this chapter, we define holistic face processing as the recognition of the face stimulus as "all of one piece" in which the features of a face and their spatial relations are fused together in a unified representation. It has been claimed that the recruitment of holistic processes is what distinguishes faces from most types of object recognition. This claim is validated in holistic tests of inversion, misalignment and parts-whole recognition where these manipulations affect the recognition of faces more than the recognition of non-face objects. Some research has indicated that discrimination of the distances between the parts of a face (i.e. its configural information) is sometimes more vulnerable to inversion than discrimination of the parts themselves. By extension, it has been proposed that configural information is more essential to the distinctive properties of the holistic face representation than featural information. However, this claim has been challenged by researchers who attribute the configural deficit in these studies to experimental procedures that may have favored a featural strategy (Risienhuber et al., 2004), the relative ease of featural discriminations compared to configural discriminations (Yovel and Kanwwisher, 2004) or the definition of a feature in terms of surface rather than shape properties (McKone and Yovel, 2009). When these factors are taken into account, there is little evidence to suggest the configural information is selectively compromised in an inverted face compared to part features (McKone and Yovel, 2009).

While much of the research has focused on what is *lost* in an inverted face, it is equally important to know what information is *preserved*. As in upright faces, people are drawn to the eyes of inverted faces. To a remarkable degree, the ability to discriminate featural information about the size and shape of the eyes and configural information regarding their inter-ocular distance is retained. However, as a consequence of inversion, discrimination of featural (i.e. mouth) and configural (i.e. nose-to-mouth distances) information in the lower half of the face is compromised. In addition, the ability to localize the relative position of the eyes along the vertical axis is impaired. These results suggest that the face inversion effect cannot be explained simply by the loss of eye information or by the selective impairment or sparing of configural or featural information. Rather, inverting a face disrupts the holistic process that binds the eyes, nose and mouth features, and their configural relationships together in a unified representation of the whole face.

Acknowledgments

We would like to thank the National Sciences and Engineering Research Council of Canada, the James S. McDonnell Foundation, and the Temporal Dynamics of Learning Center (NSF Grant #SBE-0542013) for supporting this research. We are grateful to Elinor McKone and Gill Rhodes for their incisive comments and suggestions.

References

Barton, J.J.S., Keenan, J.P., and Bass, T. (2001) Discrimination of spatial relations and features in faces: Effects of inversion and viewing duration. *British Journal of Psychology*, **92**, 527–549.

Barton, J.J., Press, D.Z., Keenan, J.P., and O'Connor, M. (2002). Lesions of the fusiform face area impair perception of facial configuration in prosopagnosia. *Neurology*, **58**, 71–78.

Barton, J.J., Zhao, J., and Keenan, J.P. (2003). Perception of global facial geometry in the inversion effect and prosopagnosia. *Neuropsychologia*, **41**, 1703–1711.

Bentin, S., Sagiv, N., Mecklinger, A., Friederici, A., and von Cramon, Y.D. (2002). Priming visual face-processing mechanisms: electrophysiological evidence. *Psychological Science*, **13**, 190–193.

Biederman, I. (1987). Recognition-by-Components: A theory of human image understanding. *Psychological Review*, **94**, 115–145.

Bindemann, M., Burton, A.M., and Jenkins, R. (2005). Capacity limits for face processing. *Cognition*, **98**, 177–197.

Boutet, I., Gentes-Hawn, A., and Chaudhuri, A. (2002). The influence of attention on holistic face encoding. *Cognition, 84*, 321–341.

Bukach, C.M., LeGrand, R., Kaiser, M., Bub, D., and Tanaka, J.W. (2008). Preservation of featural and configural processing for the mouth region in a case of prosopagnosia. *Journal of Neuropsychology, 2*, 227–244.

Caldara, R., Schyns, P., Mayer, E., Smith, M.L., Gosselin, F., and Rossion, B. (2005). Does prosopagnosia take the eyes out of face representations? Evidence for a defect in representing diagnostic facial information following brain damage. *Journal of Cognitive Neuroscience, 17*, 1652–1666.

Carey, S. (1992). Becoming a face expert. *Philosophical Transactions Royal Society of London B, 335*, 95–103.

Carey, S. and Diamond, R. (1977). From piecemeal to configurational representation of faces. *Science, 195*, 312–314.

Cheung O.S., Richler J.J., Palmeri T.J., Gauthier I. (2008). Revisiting the role of spatial frequencies in the holistic processing of faces. *Journal of Experimental Psychology: Human Perception and Performance, 34*, 1327–1336

Cooper, E.E. and Wojan, T.J. (2000). Differences in the coding of spatial relations in face identification and basic-level object recognition. *Journal of Experimental Psychology: Learning, Memory and Cognition, 26*, 470–488.

Diamond, R. and Carey, S. (1986). Why faces are not special: An effect of expertise. *Journal of Experimental Psychology: General, 115*, 107–117.

D'Lauro, C., Tanaka, J.W., and Curran, T. (2008). The preferred level of face categorization depends on discriminability. *Psychonomic Bulletin and Review, 15*(3), 623–629.

Donnelly, D. and Davidoff, J. (1999). The mental representations of faces and houses: issues concerning parts and wholes. *Visual Cognition, 6*, 319–343.

Farah, M.J. (1991). Patterns of co-occurence among the associative agnosics: Implications for visual object representation. *Cognitive Neuropsychology, 8*, 1–19.

Farah, M.J. (1992). Is an object an object an object? Cognitive and neuropsychological investigations of domain-specificity in visual object recognition. *Current Directions in Psychological Science, 1*, 164–169.

Freire, A., Lee, K., and Symons, L.A. (2000). The face-inversion effect as a deficit in the encoding of configural information: Direct evidence. *Perception, 29*, 159–170.

Galton, F. (1879). Composite portraits, made by combining those of many different persons into a single, resultant figure. *Journal of the Anthropological Institute, 8*, 132–144.

Gauthier, I. and Tarr, M.J. (1997). Becoming a "Greeble" expert: exploring the face recognition mechanism. *Vision Research, 37*, 1673–1682.

Gauthier, I., Williams, P., Tarr, M.J., and Tanaka, J.W. (1998). Training "Greeble" experts: a framework for studying expert object recognition processes. *Vision Research, 38*, 2401–2428.

Gauthier, I., Tarr, M.J., Moylan, J., Skudlarski, P., Gore, J.C., and Anderson, A. W. (2000). The fusiform "face area" is part of a network that processes faces at the individual level. *Journal of Cognitive Neuroscience, 12*, 495–504.

Goffaux, V. and Rossion, B. (2007). Face inversion disproportionately impairs the perception of vertical but not horizontal relations between features. *Journal of Experimental Psychology: Human Perception and Performance, 33*, 995–1002.

Grill-Spector, K. and Kanwisher, N. (2005). Visual recognition: as soon as you know it is there, you know what it is. *Psychological Science, 16*, 152–160.

Hoffman, D. and Richards, D. (1985). Parts in recognition. *Cognition, 18*, 65–96.

Jacques, C. and Rossion, B. (2006). The speed of individual face categorization. *Psychological Science, 17*, 485–492.

Johnston, J.C. and McClelland, J.L. (1980). Experimental tests of a hierarchical model of word identification. *Journal of Verbal Learning and Verbal Behavior, 19*, 503–524.

Jolicoeur, P., Gluck, M.A., and Kosslyn, S.M. (1984). Pictures and names: Making the connection. *Cognitive Psychology, 16*, 243–275.

Kanwisher, N. and Yovel, G. (2006). The fusiform face area: a cortical region specialized for the perception of faces. *Philosophical Transactions of the Royal Society of London B*, **361**, 2109–2128.

Klin, A., Jones, W., Schultz, R., Volkmar, F., and Cohen, D. (2002). Visual fixation patterns during viewing of naturalistic social situations as predictors of social competence in individuals with autism. *Archives of General Psychiatry*, **59**, 809–816.

Leder, H. and Bruce, V. (1998). Local and relational aspects of face distinctiveness. *Quarterly Journal of Experimental Psychology A*, **51**, 449–473.

Leder, H. and Bruce, V. (2000). When inverted faces are recognized: the role of configural information in face recognition. *Quarterly Journal of Experimental Psychology A*, **53**, 513–536.

Leder, H. and Carbon, C. C. (2006). Face-specific configural processing of relational information. *British Journal of Psychology*, **97**, 19–29.

Lee, K. and Freire, A. (1999). Effects of face configuration change on shape perception: a new illusion. *Perception*, **28**, 1217–1226.

Le Grand, R., Mondloch, C.J., Maurer, D., and Brent, H.P. (2001). Early visual experience and face processing. *Nature*, **410**, 890.

Liu, J., Harris, A., and Kanwisher, N. (2002). Stages of processing in face perception: an MEG study. *Nature Neuroscience*, **5**, 910–916.

Malcolm, G.L., Leung, C., and Barton, J.J. (2004). Regional variation in the inversion effect for faces: differential effects for feature shape, feature configuration, and external contour. *Perception*, **33**, 1221–1231.

Maurer, D., Le Grand, R., and Mondloch, C.J. (2002). The many faces of configural processing. *Trends in Cognitive Sciences*, **6**, 255–260.

Maurer, D., O'Craven, K.M., Le Grand, R., *et al.* (2007). Neural correlates of processing facial identity based on features versus their spacing. *Neuropsychologia*, **45**, 1438–1451.

McKone, E. (2004). Isolating the special component of face recognition: peripheral identification and a Mooney face. *Journal of Experimental Psychology: Learning, Memory and Cognition*, **30**, 181–197.

McKone, E. and Yovel, G. (2009). Why does picture-plane inversion sometimes dissociate perception of features and spacing in faces, and sometimes not? Toward a new theory of holistic processing. *Psychonomic Bulletin and Review*, **16**, 778–797.

McKone, E., Martini, P., and Nakayama, K. (2001). Categorical perception of face identity in noise isolates configural processing. *Journal of Experimental Psychology: Human Perception and Performance*, **27**, 573–599.

Mondloch, C.J., Le Grand, R., and Maurer, D. (2002). Configural face processing develops more slowly than featural face processing. *Perception*, **31**, 553–566.

Moscovitch, M., Winocur, G., and Behrmann, M. (1997). What is special about face recognition? Nineteen experiments on a person with visual object agnosia and dyslexia but normal face recognition. *Journal of Cognitive Neuroscience*, **9**, 555–604.

Murray, J.E., Yong, E., and Rhodes, G. (2000). Revisiting the perception of upside-down faces. *Psychological Science*, **11**, 492–496.

Palermo, R. and Rhodes, G. (2002). The influence of divided attention on holistic face perception. *Cognition*, **82**, 225–257.

Reed, C.L., Stone, V.E., Bozova, S., and Tanaka, J. (2003). The body-inversion effect. *Psychological Science*, **14**, 302–308.

Reinitz, M., Morrissey, J., and Demb, J. (1994). Role of attention in face encoding. *Journal of Experimental Psychology: Learning, Memory and Cognition*, **20**, 161–168.

Rhodes, G. (1988). Looking at faces: first-order and second-order features as determinants of facial appearance. *Perception*, **17**, 43–63.

Rhodes, G., Brake, S., and Atkinson, A. (1993). What's lost in inverted faces? *Cognition*, **17**, 25–57.

Rhodes, G., Hayward, W.G., and Winkler, C. (2006) Exert face coding: configural and component coding of own-race and other-race faces. *Psychonomic Bulletin and Review* **13**, 499–505.

Rhodes, G., Michie, P.T., Hughes, M.E., and Byatt, G. (2009). The fusiform face area and occipital face area show sensitivity to spatial relations in faces. *European Journal of Neuroscience*, **30**, 721–733.

Richler. J.J, Tanaka, J.W., Brown, D.D., and Gauthier, I. (2008). Why does selective attention to parts fail in face processing? *Journal of Experimental Psychology: Learning, Memory and Cognition*, **34**, 1356–1368.

Riesenhuber, M., Jarudi, I., Gilad, S., and Sinha, P. (2004). Face processing in humans is compatible with a simple shape-based model of vision. *Proceedings of the Royal Society of London Series B-Biological Sciences*, **271**, S448–S450.

Rossion, B. (2008). Picture-plane inversion leads to qualitative changes of face perception. *Acta Psychol (Amst)*, **128**, 274–289.

Rossion, B. and Boremanse, A. (2011). Nonlinear relationship between holistic processing of individual faces and picture-plane rotation: Evidence from the face composite illusion. *Journal of Vision*, **11**(2):16, 1–21.

Rossion, B., Le Grand, R., Kaiser, M., Bub, D., and Tanaka, J.W. (2009). Preserved discrimination of mouth information in Patient PS. *Journal of Neuropsychology*, **3**, 69–78

Scapinello, K.F., and Yarmey, A.D. (1970). The role of familiarity and orientation in immediate and delayed recognition of pictorial stimuli. *Psychonomic Science*, **21**, 329–330.

Searcy, J.H. and Bartlett, J.C. (1996). Inversion and processing of component and spatial-relational information in faces. *Journal of Experimental Psychology: Human Perception and Performance*, **22**, 904–915.

Sekuler, A. B., Gaspar, C.M., Gold, J.M., and Bennett, P.J. (2004). Inversion leads to quantitative, not qualitative, changes in face processing. *Current Biology*, **14**, 391–396.

Sekunova, A. and Barton, J.J. (2008). The effects of face inversion on the perception of long-range and local spatial relations in eye and mouth configuration. *Journal of Experimental Psychology: Human Perception and Performance*, **34**, 1129–1135.

Sergent, J. (1984). An investigation into component and configural processes underlying face perception. *The British Journal of Psychology*, **75**, 221–242.

Tanaka, J.W. (2001). The entry point of face recognition: evidence for face expertise. *Journal of Experimental Psychology: General*, **130**, 534–543.

Tanaka, J.W. and Farah, M.J. (1993) Parts and wholes in face recognition, *The Quarterly Journal of Experimental Psychology Section A*, **46**, pp. 225–245

Tanaka, J.W., and Sengco, J. (1997). Features and their configuration in face recognition. *Memory and Cognition*, **25**, 583–592.

Tanaka, J.W., Kaiser, M.J., Bub, D.N. and Butler, S. (2009). *Generalized impairment of featural and configural information in the lower half of the face through inversion.* Poster presented at the Vision Science Society, Naples, Florida, May, 2008.

Valentine, T. (1988). Upside-down faces: A review of the effect of inversion upon face recognition. *British Journal of Psychology*, **79**, 471–491.

Valentine, T. and Bruce, V. (1986). The effect of race inversion and encoding activity upon face recognition. *Acta Psychologica*, **61**, 259–273.

Vinette, C., Gosselin, F., and Schyns, P.G. (2004). Spatio-temporal dynamics of face recognition in a flash: it's in the eyes. *Cognitive Science*, **28**, 289–301.

Wolf, J.M., Tanaka, J.W., Klaiman, C., *et al.* (2008). Specific impairment of face-processing abilities in children with autism spectrum disorder using the Let's Face It! skills battery. *Autism Research*, **1**, 329–340.

Yarmey, A. (1971). Recognition memory for familiar "public" faces: Effects of orientation and delay. *Psychonomic Science*, **24**, 286–288.

Yin, R. (1969). Looking at upside-down faces. *Journal of Experimental Psychology*, **81**, 141–145.

Young, A., Hellawell, D., and Hay, D.C. (1987). Configural information in face perception. *Perception*, **10**, 747–759.

Yovel, G. and Duchaine, B. (2006). Specialized face perception mechanisms extract both part and spacing information: evidence from developmental prosopagnosia. *Journal of Cognitive Neuroscience*, **18**, 580–593.

Yovel, G. and Kanwisher, N. (2004). Face perception: domain specific, not process specific. *Neuron*, **44**, 889–898.

Chapter 11

Face Perception and Perceptual Expertise in Adult and Developmental Populations

Lisa S. Scott

Introduction

Both developmental and adult investigations of perception unequivocally suggest that experience shapes perceptual abilities beginning early in development and throughout the lifespan
(e.g. Gauthier and Nelson, 2001; McKone et al., 2007; Bukach et al., 2006; Scott and Monesson,
2009; Scott et al., 2007). Investigators studying perceptual expertise typically consider how
domain-general cognitive and neural mechanisms are recruited when individuals learn about
and become experts at recognizing and distinguishing visual categories, including faces and
objects (Bukach et al., 2006). The term perceptual expertise has been used in various ways, but
generally refers to an increased ability to discriminate and recognize among exemplars within
some categories of visual stimuli relative to others. Investigations of perceptual expertise are usually designed to uncover the underlying representational and neural changes accompanying the
acquisition of expertise using a variety of methods (e.g. behavioral measures of accuracy and
reaction time, functional magnetic resonance imaging (fMRI), event-related potentials (ERPs),
magnetoencephalography (MEG), eye-tracking, and computational modeling) and with various
study designs and populations (e.g. real-world experts, training studies, clinical populations,
developmental populations, and non-human primates). This interdisciplinary and multimethod
approach has significantly contributed to understanding how humans, animals, and computers
solve complex visual problems. The present chapter will review how behavioral methods, ERPs,
and fMRI have been used to understand the acquisition of perceptual expertise in both adult and
developmental populations.

   As will be discussed further, in the context of specific studies reviewed below, behavioral tasks
designed to assess perceptual expertise in adults include: perceptual discrimination and matching
tasks and categorization and recognition memory tasks (e.g. Tanaka and Taylor, 1991; Gauthier
et al., 1998; Scott et al., 2006a). In infants, visual preference tasks are used to measure their ability
to discriminate stimuli (e.g. Pascalis et al., 2002, 2005; Kelly et al., 2007; Scott and Monesson,
2009). In both adults and infants, ERPs are used to assess neural responses before and after training or in experts. ERPs are recorded non-invasively from a net or cap of recording electrodes
placed on the head and have very high temporal resolution. ERP amplitude and latency responses
reflect the activity of simultaneously active populations of neurons in the cerebral cortex. This
activity results in electrical signals that propagate up to the scalp and can be recorded in response
to the presentation of images or sounds. Researchers typically examine two ERP components, the
N170 and the N250, when adults view faces, trained objects, or objects of expertise (e.g. Tanaka and
Curran 2001; Scott et al., 2006a, 2008; Tanaka and Pierce, 2009). Analogous infant components,

the N290 and P400, have also been identified in response to faces and objects. The advantage of using ERPs with developmental populations is that no verbal or motor response is required and, given the appropriate equipment, recording electrodes can be applied easily.

Unlike ERPs, which have excellent temporal resolution, fMRI has been used to examine the hemodynamic consequences of neural activity and allows for an examination of spatial resolution on the order of a few millimeters (Hu et al., 1997). Investigators using fMRI with adults have examined how regions of the occipital and temporal cortex respond to faces, trained objects, or objects of expertise (e.g. Gauthier et al., 1999; 2000a,b; Kanwisher et al., 1997, 2000).

Using these various methods and techniques, studies of perceptual expertise have proven useful to our understanding of specialization of perceptual skills and categorization abilities and have expanded our understanding of the function and plasticity of the visual system (Bukach et al., 2006). The purpose of the present review is to provide an overview of the research focused on understanding the role and nature of experience in both the acquisition of perceptual expertise and the development of expert face processing.

The acquisition of expertise in adults

Training studies have been used to mimic the natural acquisition of face and non-face percep-tual expertise. Although training in the laboratory cannot be equated to years of real-world expertise, training novices in the laboratory allows for careful control and manipulation of experience. The use of training designs to study perceptual expertise began with training par-ticipants with novel objects, called greebles (Gauthier and Tarr, 1997). Greebles are a class of non-face, novel, cartoon-like objects that can be classified at multiple levels (i.e. the individual level, the subordinate level, and the basic level). Greebles have four protruding parts originating from a central cylinder-like body. Based on the configuration and orientation of these parts each individual greeble belongs to one of two "genders" and one of five "families". In a now clas-sic investigation, Gauthier and Tarr (1997) trained adult participants to discriminate greebles and found that training led greebles to be treated similarly to faces. Relative to object process-ing, face processing requires attention to the relations between the parts within the face (i.e. configural relations; Diamond and Carey, 1986; Farah, 1990; Rhodes, 1988; Sergent, 1988). Gauthier and Tarr (1997) confirmed that laboratory-trained greeble experts, but not novices, were faster at identifying trained greeble configurations as compared to untrained greeble con-figurations suggesting that training increased configural processing of previously novel non-face objects. Subsequent greeble training studies also suggest that face-selective areas of the cortex are recruited after training (Gauthier and Tarr 2002; Gauthier et al., 1999) and that an electrophysiological index of face processing, the N170 ERP component, increases in response to greebles after training (Rossion et al., 2002).

Researchers use training designs to investigate the behavioral and neural correlates of the fac-tors influencing the acquisition of expertise in both adult and developmental populations. These studies will be summarized below and special attention will be paid to understanding: (1) how the level of category specificity is related to increased perceptual expertise (i.e. whether a stimulus is identified at the individual, subordinate, basic, or exposure levels), (2) how perceptual expertise leads to transfer and generalization within and across domains of expertise, (3) how stable exper-tise effects are over time, (4) how perceptual expertise in one domain interferes with learning or performance within another domain, and (5) how feedback during learning influences later per-ceptual expertise (Gillebert et al., 2009; Gauthier and Tarr 1997; Gauthier et al., 1998; Lebrecht et al., 2009; Rossion et al., 2002, 2004, 2007; Tanaka et al., 2005; Tanaka and Pierce 2009; Scott and Monesson 2009; Scott et al., 2006a, 2008).

Level of categorization and perceptual expertise

From the adult categorization literature we know that visual object and face categorization is unconstrained in the sense that a single object or face can be classified at multiple levels of abstraction. For example, Barack Obama can be categorized as a "human" at the superordinate level, a "man" at the basic level, an "African American man" at the general or subordinate level, and "Barack Obama" at the individual level. Consistent with this example, research has shown that when recognizing and discriminating familiar groups of faces, humans typically do so at the level of the individual (e.g. Johnny versus Billy; see Tanaka, 2001). In contrast, when recognizing and discriminating objects, such as the Eastern Screech Owl, people typically classify them at the basic level (i.e. bird or owl; Jolicoeur et al., 1984; Murphy and Smith, 1982; Rosch et al., 1976). However, as expertise is acquired for a certain object category (such as expert bird watchers or car enthusiasts) individuals identify objects within this category at more subordinate levels (e.g. Barred Owl, BMW Z4) compared to non-experts (Tanaka and Taylor, 1991). Moreover, people who learn objects at more specific ("This is Mary's mug") compared to more general ("This is a mug") levels extract different perceptual features during encoding, which subsequently improves performance on a change-detection task involving the trained objects (Archambault et al., 1999). Combined, these findings suggest that perceptual expertise can arise when discrimination and recognition demands require that exemplars within a category be differentiated from one another at more specific levels of abstraction (as is the case with faces).

Evidence for perceptual expertise arising when it becomes important to discriminate among category exemplars also comes from investigations which manipulated the level at which participants learn birds (Tanaka et al., 2005; Scott et al., 2006a), cars (Scott et al., 2008), other-race faces (Tanaka and Pierce 2009), four-circle blob stimuli (Nishimura and Maurer 2008), and artificial objects called "Ziggerins" (Wong et al., 2009). These investigations consistently find that subordinate- or individual-level learning leads to increased within-category discrimination abilities, greater configural processing, and more specialized neural responses. For example, in one study, adult participants were trained to categorize one family of birds (e.g. owls) at the subordinate level and another family of birds (e.g. wading birds) at the basic level across six training sessions over a two-week period (Scott et al., 2006a). Before and after training, participants completed a sequential species-level discrimination task while behavioral measures of accuracy and cortical ERPs were recorded. Results showed increased accuracy, as measured by d', after species-level training (the subordinate-level) but not after family-level training (the basic level). This improvement generalized to untrained exemplars within the trained species as well as untrained species within the same family. These behavioral differences were also mirrored in the electrophysiological response. The N170 is recorded over occipitotemporal brain regions and is thought to be an index of face processing and perceptual expertise as it is consistently larger in response to faces relative to objects (Carmel and Bentin 2002; Bentin et al., 1996; Botzel et al., 1995; Eimer 2000; Rossion et al., 2000; see Eimer, Chapter 17, this volume) and in response to objects of expertise relative to other objects (Tanaka and Curran, 2001). The N250 component is also related to face processing and is evoked in response to repeated and familiar faces compared to novel or unfamiliar faces (Schweinberger et al., 2002, 2004; Tanaka et al., 2006). Expertise training with birds increased the amplitude of both the N170 and N250 ERP components (Scott et al., 2006a). However, the N170 increased equally for both subordinate-level, and basic-level training whereas the N250 only increased in response to subordinate-level training. These results suggest that N170 amplitude is likely influenced by general effects of category experience resulting in expert categories, such as faces or objects of expertise, eliciting greater amplitude N170s.

Both the behavioral and ERP results reported by Scott and colleagues (2006a) were replicated in a subsequent investigation with car stimuli (Scott et al., 2008). In this study an additional exposure-only condition was added and participants returned for post-test assessments immediately after training and 1 week after training ended. Training included antique cars, modern SUVs, and modern sedans and each participant was trained with exemplars from each of these three categories at either the subordinate, basic, and exposure-only level. Results revealed increased behavioral performance after subordinate-, but not basic-level or exposure training and an increased N170 in response to all three types of training. Similar to the behavioral results, the N250 increased only in response to subordinate-level training. The results from both of these investigations suggest that subordinate-level training leads to an increased ability to discriminate exemplars within a category, which is indexed by the N250 ERP component. Figure 11.1 shows both the N170 and N250 results in response to basic- and subordinate-level training.

The increased accuracy and differential ERP responses after subordinate-level training were recently replicated using face stimuli (Tanaka and Pierce, 2009). In this study, Caucasian adults were trained with African or Hispanic faces at either the individual (each face was assigned a different label) or category (all faces were labeled the same) levels. Post-training recognition accuracy increased after subordinate-level but not category-level individuation training regardless of race. In addition, the N250 ERP response also increased after subordinate-level individuation

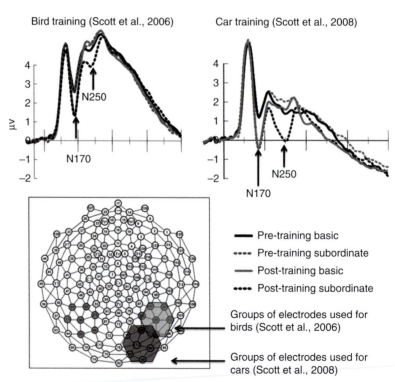

Fig. 11.1 Event-related potentials (ERPs) before and after basic-, and subordinate-level expertise training in two recent adult investigations (Scott et al., 2006a, 2008). Groups of electrodes (shaded regions), recorded over occipital and temporal brain regions, were averaged for both the N170 and N250 components.

training, further suggesting that the N250 is an index of increased subordinate-level discriminatory abilities for faces and objects. In another investigation, individual-level training with other-race faces also decreased implicit racial biases, suggesting a link between the perceptual and social face biases (Lebrecht et al., 2009).

Holistic and configural visual processing are hallmarks of both face processing and real-world perceptual expertise (see Tanaka and Gordon, Chapter 10, this volume; Busey and Vanderkolk, 2005; Diamond and Carey, 1986) and previous studies reported increases in holistic and configural processing after perceptual training (Gauthier and Tarr, 1997; Gauthier et al., 1998; Wong et al., 2009). Although definitions of holistic and configural processing vary, three types of configural processing have been examined in relation to face processing (for review see Maurer et al., 2002). First-order configural processing occurs during the general detection of a face (two eyes above a nose, above a mouth). Second-order configural processing involves detecting spatial relations among face features. Finally, holistic processing involves integrating information across the face.

To examine second-order configural processing of non-face objects, one investigation trained participants with stimuli comprised of four circular blobs (Nishimura and Maurer, 2008). Two groups of participants learned these stimuli at either the individual (Bobo 1, Bobo 2, Bobo 3) or the basic (all stimuli named Bobo) level and were tested before and after training using a same/different discrimination task. Results revealed increased sensitivity to second-order configural stimulus changes after adults were trained at the individual level relative to the basic level. Recently, two groups of adults were trained with artificial objects called "Ziggerins" (Wong et al., 2009). In this study individuation, but not categorization, training led to increased holistic processing as measured by a composite task in which the top and bottom halves of the stimuli were manipulated.

In sum, the results from studies using perceptual training suggest that subordinate- or individual-level learning leads to increased perceptual expertise as indexed by both behavioral and electrophysiological indices. Behaviorally, adults trained at more specific levels of abstraction show increased performance on a change-detection task with objects (Archambault et al., 1999), increased ability to discriminate exemplars within trained categories of faces and objects (Scott et al., 2006a, 2008; Tanaka et al., 2004; Tanaka and Pierce, 2009), decreased implicit racial biases (Lebrecht et al., 2009), and increased configural processing (Nishimura and Maurer, 2008; Wong et al., 2009). In addition, training at the subordinate level increased the amplitude of both the N170 and the N250 ERP components (Scott et al., 2006a; 2008; Tanaka and Pierce, 2009). However, the N170 also increased after basic-level category training as well as exposure training (Scott et al., 2008) suggesting that it may index increased exposure to object categories whereas the N250 is an index of subordinate or individual level learning.

Generalization of perceptual expertise

One question that permeates the study of perceptual learning as well as the study of perceptual expertise is whether or not training effects generalize to novel exemplars of trained categories. Investigations of low-level perceptual learning (e.g. Ahissar et al., 1998; Fiorentini and Berardi, 1980; Poggio et al., 1992) often find little if any generalization of learning after training. Failure to generalize learning has also been found in more complex forms of perceptual learning including domains of expertise. For example, although radiologists are experts at finding and detecting radiological anomalies they do not show a general advantage in visual search tasks such as "Where's Waldo" or the "NINA" drawings from The New York Times (Nodine and Krupinski, 1998). In another investigation, parents of monozygotic twins were faster at discriminating their own twins' faces, but this increased discrimination did not generalize to unfamiliar twin pairs (Saether and Laeng, 2008). However, other investigations have found at least partial generalization after expertise training. For example, after greeble training, learning generalizes to structurally similar, but not structurally dissimilar, exemplars of greebles (Gauthier et al., 1998).

Generalization of learning was also found after training with birds (Scott et al., 2006a) and cars (Scott et al., 2008). Training with birds led to an increased ability to discriminate untrained exemplars of trained species and untrained species of birds within the trained family (i.e. owls or wading birds; see Figure 11.2). Car training, on the other-hand, led to a small increase in ability to discriminate untrained exemplars of trained models but this increase did not generalize to untrained models within the trained car family (i.e. SUVs or Sedans). This generalization discrepancy after bird and car training suggests that stimulus features within the trained category may influence generalization. There are several differences between birds and cars that might lead to more or less generalization. For example, features like color, texture and contrast are helpful diagnostic cues for subordinate-level bird learning, but not subordinate-level car learning. In addition, participants in the car training study likely had more previous experience categorizing and labeling cars than those in the bird training study had with birds, which might interfere with their ability to learn new subordinate-level labels. Finally, the generalization differences may also reflect differences between natural kinds and artifacts (or living versus non-living things). These hypotheses can be tested using computer-generated categories of objects that are previously unfamiliar to participants and can be made to be more car- or bird-like.

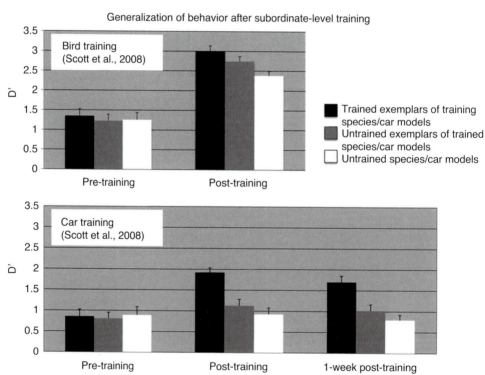

Fig. 11.2 D′ before and after and subordinate-level expertise training in two recent adult investigations (Scott et al., 2006a, 2008). Generalization of training was tested in two conditions (untrained exemplars of trained species/car models and untrained exemplars of untrained species/car models). The top panel pictures results after bird training and the bottom panel pictures results after car training.

Despite the less than perfect behavioral generalization for birds and cars after training, both the N170 and the N250 responses generalized perfectly for untrained exemplars of trained species/models of birds/cars and untrained species/models of birds/cars (see Figure 11.3 for an example from Scott et al., 2008). Thus, the electrophysiological increases are not limited to the specific episodic experiences because they generalize to untrained exemplars. It is currently unclear why this disconnect between behavioral and electrophysiological generalization exists. However, given that the electrophysiological responses reported by Scott and colleagues (2006, 2008) index early visual processing, it would not be surprising if additional later occurring perceptual and cognitive processes contributed to the observed behavioral responses resulting in this discrepancy.

Stability of perceptual expertise

Training studies are also useful for understanding how people maintain perceptual expertise over time. Scott and colleagues (2008) used a pre- and post-test design that included an immediate post-test and a 1-week post-test. After training at the subordinate, basic and exposure levels with three different classes of cars, ERPs and behavioral discriminability were measured at both post-tests. Neither basic-level nor exposure training led to increased discrimination after training. However, subordinate-level training led to increased discrimination immediately and one week after the end of training. An increased N170 response was found at the immediate post-test for all three types of training. However, this increase did not carry over to the 1-week post-test. This lack of stability suggests that continued category exposure over time is necessary to maintain amplitude increases seen for the N170. It is possible that previous reports of increased N170 amplitudes to faces are due to the consistent exposure humans have with faces. The N250 only increased in

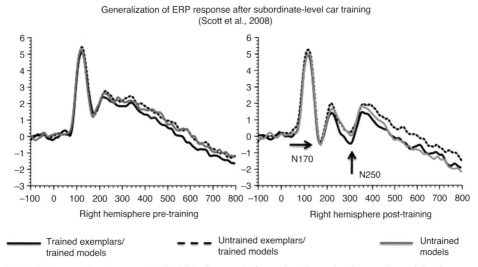

Fig. 11.3 Event-related potentials (ERPs) before and after subordinate-level expertise training in a recent adult investigation (Scott et al., 2008). Pictured are the N170 and N250 components, recorded from averaged electrodes over occipital and temporal brain regions. Generalization of training was tested in two conditions (untrained exemplars of trained species/car models and untrained exemplars of untrained species/car models). N170 and N250 ERP increases generalized across all conditions.

response to subordinate-level training and this increase remained stable at the immediate-and 1-week post-test. These results further support the notion that more specific levels of training lead to enhanced perceptual expertise, as indexed by increased discrimination, which is reflected in increases in the N250 ERP component.

Interference across domains of perceptual expertise

Evidence from real-world and from laboratory-trained experts suggests that perceptual expertise with non-face objects leads to neural competition with faces within occipitotemporal regions of the cortex (Gauthier et al., 2003; Jacques and Rossion 2004; Rossion et al., 2004). In one study, holistic processing of cars in car experts reduced holistic processing of faces and the N170 amplitude difference between cars and faces was reduced with increased car expertise (Gauthier et al., 2003). In addition, after greeble training, the amplitude of the N170 is significantly decreased in response to faces when they are viewed concurrently with greebles compared to other (non-expert) objects (Rossion et al., 2004). Interference across expertise domains suggests that non-face perceptual expertise and face processing may rely on shared neural resources (Gauthier and Curby 2005).

Feedback during the acquisition of perceptual expertise

Results reported by Scott et al. (2008) suggest that mere exposure is not sufficient for improved perceptual expertise, but that subordinate- or individual-level learning is required for the acquisition of perceptual expertise for categories of objects and faces. Thus, increases in perceptual expertise may require category exposure coupled with learning at more specific levels of abstraction. These results are consistent with a neurocomputational model of basic- and subordinate-level learning that relies on both unsupervised and supervised mechanisms to simulate expert perceptual discrimination (Nguyen and Cottrell, 2005). In this computational model and in human training studies, feedback during learning appears to plays a critical role. When learning to categorize or discriminate visual stimuli both explicit and implicit rules are formed via feedback-dependent mechanisms (Ashby and O'Brien, 2005; Ashby et al., 1998). Several brain regions, including the inferior temporal cortex, the basal ganglia, the anterior cingulate cortex, and the frontal cortex, mediate these feedback-dependent processes.

To understand the role of feedback in the acquisition of expertise Krigolson and colleagues (2009) trained adult participants with several exemplars of two different categories of computer generated blob stimuli, which were labeled "A" or "B" and then recorded ERPs while they completed a category-verification task and were given positive and negative feedback. The category verification task included exemplars from the A and the B category as well as a morphed category (50% A and 50% B). Participants were required to indicate whether or not images of blobs matched or did not match the provided label. Feedback for the morph category had a 50% probability of being positive or negative. Behaviorally, two groups emerged, including: (1) low learners and (2) high learners (greater than 70% performance). The high-learner, but not low-learner group, exhibited a greater amplitude N250 and ERN (error related negativity) response during the category verification task. The ERN is an ERP component that occurs in response to internal error detection (response ERN) or external error detection (feedback ERN) and is thought to be mediated by the anterior cingulate cortex (Holroyd et al., 2004). Krigolson and colleagues (2009) found increased amplitude for both types of ERNs in the high, but not low, learners. These findings support a link between the reinforcement learning system in medial-frontal regions of the brain (as indexed by the ERN) and the perceptual category learning systems in the occipital and temporal regions of the brain (as indexed by the N250) during the acquisition of perceptual expertise.

Summary of perceptual expertise in adults

Investigations using training designs with adults have provided us with invaluable information about the neural and behavioral mechanisms whereby people acquire perceptual expertise. From these studies it is clear that subordinate- and/or individual-level learning, mediated by feedback, is important for the acquisition of expertise. Moreover, increased perceptual expertise is associated with increased configural processing, increased neural competition when concurrently processing faces and objects of expertise, and increased generalization to similar non-expert domains for some stimuli. However, increased perceptual expertise with faces may also lead to perceptual biases such as the other-race effect, the other-age effect, and the other-species effect (see Pascalis and Wirth, Chapter 37; Lee et al., Chapter 39, this volume). These naturally occurring biases likely originate early in development and are a result of greater individual-level experience with familiar groups of faces (Scott and Monesson, 2009).

The acquisition of perceptual expertise during development

Recently, the acquisition of perceptual expertise in adulthood has been hypothesized as a model for understanding the development of face processing abilities in infancy and childhood (Scott and Monesson, 2009; Quinn, 2010). However, the study of development has also helped inform our understanding of adult perceptual expertise (Gauthier and Nelson 2001). Researchers studying perceptual expertise and face processing in development typically use both behavioral and ERP methods. Preferential looking paradigms, which measure infant looking duration and direction of visual fixations, have been used to examine infant preferences and discrimination. One such paradigm is the visual-paired comparison (VPC) method. This method capitalizes on infants' preference for novelty after either a familiarization or habituation period (for review see Synder et al., 2007). Studies using ERPs have helped elucidate the neural mechanisms involved in the development of face and object processing during the first year of life (e.g. de Haan and Nelson, 1999; de Haan et al., 2002; Halit et al., 2003; Scott and Nelson, 2006; Scott et al., 2006b).

The ontogeny of face processing abilities is still a matter of active debate. Some have argued that expertise with faces stems from an innate neural module (e.g. Farah et al., 2000; de Schonen and Mathivet, 1989; Morton and Johnson 1991) and others argue that face processing abilities and the underlying neural specialization are acquired through experience (e.g. Gauthier and Nelson 2001; Le Grand et al., 2001, 2003). A close examination of the literature related to this debate reveals several important theoretical subtleties. Early work suggests that newborns prefer to look at face-like stimuli relative to inverted and scrambled control stimuli (Goren et al., 1975; Johnson et al., 1991). Although this early preference for faces is not debated, the mechanisms responsible for this preference are debated. One view is that the newborn preference for faces stems from an innate subcortical mechanism (CONSPEC) (Morton and Johnson 1991). CONSPEC leads infants to prefer face-like stimuli (two blobs over another blob). After the second month of life, CONSPEC is replaced by CONLERN, an experientially based mechanism that involves a diffuse network of cortical areas and allows for continued cortical specialization and tuning (Johnson 2000; Morton and Johnson 1991). An alternate account of the newborn face preference suggests that general, as opposed to specific, biases within the visual system lead newborns to prefer face-like stimuli (Simion et al., 2001, 2002). For example, newborns prefer stimuli with more elements in the upper relative to the lower half of a stimulus (i.e. "T"-like stimuli) (Simion et al., 2001, 2002). These researchers posit that the newborn face preference is not face-specific, but can be found to any stimulus whose inner and outer parts are congruent and top-heavy. Although important for understanding the origins of face processing, it has proven very difficult for researchers to determine whether newborns prefer faces and stimuli with more elements in the upper half because they are face-like or because they have more elements in the upper half.

This debate notwithstanding, several studies have focused on understanding how early perceptual experience influences the behavioral and neural specificity of face processing during the first year of life. Research in this area has revealed several perceptual biases arising within the first year of life, including the other-race (Hayden et al., 2007; Kelly et al., 2005, 2007, 2009) and the other-species effects (Pascalis et al., 2002, 2005; Scott and Monesson, 2009), as well as a specific preference for female relative to male faces in infants whose primary caregiver is female (Quinn et al., 2002). The development of these perceptual biases is not surprising given a recent report suggesting that the majority of infants' time is spent interacting with same-race females (Rennels and Davis, 2008).

Perceptual narrowing

Nelson (2001) proposed a model of the development of face perception, which suggests that infants tune their face processing system to better recognize and differentiate commonly experienced face groups. Thus, during development, infants' perceptual abilities are tuned to the demands of their environment, a process Nelson called *perceptual narrowing*. Perceptual narrowing is a form of developmental tuning that is present across several domains of perceptual development (for review see Scott et al., 2007). Results from investigations with infants are consistent with this model in that there appears to be a decline, from 6 to 9 months of age, in the ability to differentiate between two faces within a rarely experienced face category (e.g. other-species faces: Pascalis et al., 2002, 2005; Scott and Monesson, 2009, or other-race faces: Kelly et al., 2007, 2009; for review see Pascalis and Wirth, Chapter 37, this volume). For example, after familiarization to a single monkey face 6-month-old infants look longer at a novel monkey face when paired with the recently familiarized face, indicating discrimination of these two faces (Pascalis et al., 2002, 2005; Scott and Monesson, 2009). However, neither 9-month-olds nor adults show discrimination of a recently familiarized monkey face from a novel monkey face, unless they have had prior experience with monkey faces (Pascalis et al., 2002; Scott and Monesson, 2009).

In a recent non-human primate training study, infant monkeys were reared without exposure to faces for a period of between 6 and 24 months (Sugita, 2008). After this deprivation period monkeys did not show a preference for human or monkey faces, whereas control, non-deprived, monkeys preferred to look at monkey faces. After deprivation, one group of monkeys was exposed to human faces and another group of monkeys was exposed to monkey faces for one month. Using the VPC task, control monkeys discriminated familiar and novel monkey, but not human, faces. Deprived monkeys exposed to human faces preferred to look at human faces, looked equally at monkey faces and non-face objects, and could discriminate human but not monkey faces. Deprived monkeys with monkey face experience preferred to look at monkey faces and exhibited discrimination for monkey, but not human, faces. Finally, monkeys deprived of monkey face experience continued to showed deficits discriminating monkey faces 1 year after being placed in a typical environment with other monkeys. These results are consistent with reports of perceptual narrowing in human infants and support the existence of a sensitive period for the development of face expertise. However, the timing of this sensitive period is not well understood and may not be limited to the first year of life.

Initially, our understanding of perceptual narrowing was limited in that several investigations (Kelly et al., 2007, 2009; Pascalis et al., 2002, 2005) found a decline from 6 to 9 months of age, but none examined the early experiences that contribute to this decline. Pascalis and colleagues (2005) designed an infant training study to determine whether three months of experience with monkey faces (six individually named monkey faces presented in a picture book) resulted in maintenance of the ability to distinguish these faces after training. Results revealed that 9-month-old infants with book training not only discriminated trained monkey from novel monkey faces, but also maintained the ability to discriminate a newly familiarized monkey face from a novel monkey face. This evidence of generalization is important for our understanding of category learning and the development of expertise with faces. However, following the pattern reported by Pascalis et al., (2002), 9-month-olds without training did not show evidence of discrimination. These results suggest that during the first 9 months of life, infants may be drawn to make perceptual distinctions among faces within commonly experienced, relative to uncommonly experienced, face groups. Furthermore, this increased sensitivity to familiar groups of faces may function to shape later perceptual abilities.

Level of categorization and perceptual expertise

Scott and Monesson (2009) hypothesized that the manner in which perceptual expertise is acquired in adults (e.g. Scott et al., 2006a, 2008; Tanaka and Pierce 2009) is similar to the manner in which face expertise is acquired through experience in the course of normal development. Six-month-old infants were trained to recognize six monkey faces at the individual level (i.e. each face is individually labeled during training) over a 3-month period and, similar to previous findings, they maintained the ability to discriminate monkey faces. However, infants trained with these same six faces categorically (i.e. all faces are labeled "monkey") or who were simply exposed (i.e. no label control group) to these faces, showed a decline in the ability to discriminate monkey faces (Scott and Monesson, 2009; see Figure 11.4). These results suggest that during the first year of life, the decline in infants' ability to distinguish between two faces within an unfamiliar category (i.e. two other-species faces) is critically dependent on the lack of experience individuating these unfamiliar types of faces. These results are noteworthy because they suggest that face biases originate in infancy and are dependent on the relative lack of experience individuating unfamiliar groups of faces. Moreover, it appears that learning multiple exemplars at more specific levels may lead to greater expertise for familiar face groups.

In adults, the N170 component differentiates faces and objects (e.g. Carmel and Bentin, 2002) and is delayed (e.g. Bentin et al., 1996) and enhanced (e.g. Rossion et al., 1999) to inverted relative to upright faces (but not inverted relative to upright objects). However, in adults, inverting monkey faces, similar to objects, has no effect on the N170 (deHaan et al., 2002) (see Eimer, Chapter 17, this volume for further discussion of the adult N170). In infants, the N170 response is distributed across two components, a negative N290 component and a positive P400 component (de Haan et al., 2002; Halit et al., 2003; Scott and Nelson, 2006; Scott et al., 2006b). In 6-month old infants, the P400 is greater for upright versus inverted faces (de Haan et al., 2002) and delayed for objects compared to faces (de Haan and Nelson, 1999). Future work is needed to more clearly determine the relation between the adult N170 and N250 components and the infant N290 and P400 components.

In contrast to previous behavioral findings (Pascalis et al, 2002), the 9-month-old ERP response discriminates pictures of newly familiarized and unfamiliar monkey and human faces, as evidenced by clear amplitude (N290 and P400) differences (Scott et al., 2006b). However, infants' amplitude response distinguished frontal and profile views of individual human faces better than frontal and profile views of individual monkey faces. These results support the hypothesis that by 9 months of age the face processing system is tuned to human faces. However, even in the absence of behavioral discrimination, the brain may continue to differentiate unfamiliar types of faces, albeit less efficiently. The results from Scott et al. (2006b) suggest that perceptual narrowing should be characterized as a decline and not a loss of ability.

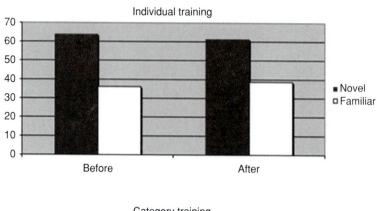

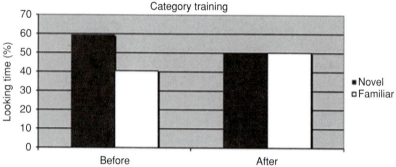

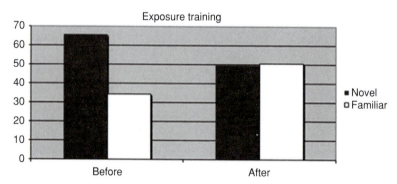

Fig. 11.4 Mean percent looking time toward the novel and familiar monkey faces before and after 3 months of training at the individual (top), category (middle), and exposure (bottom) levels. Whereas individual training led to maintenance in ability to discriminate monkey faces, category and exposure training led to a decline. Reprinted with permission (Psychological Science).

It is possible that neural discrimination may allow for later behavioral discrimination if the environment demands change. In another investigation, ERPs were recorded before and after 3 months of monkey-face book training in order to better understand the neural bases of perceptual narrowing over time (Scott and Monesson, 2010). Infants viewed trained (or to-be-trained) and untrained monkey faces presented in the upright and inverted orientation. It was hypothesized that if individual-level training led to more face-like neural responses then infants with individual-level, but not category-level or exposure training, should exhibit a differential ERP response to inverted monkey faces after training (similar to their response to human faces). Results confirmed that infants trained at the individual level exhibited a differential neural response to inverted monkey faces at post-training relative to the pre-training (see Figure 11.5). This differential response was recorded over occipital and temporal electrode locations and began at the N290 and continued to the P400 component. These results suggest that experience individuating faces during the first year of life leads to adult-like face inversion effects. Moreover, combined with behavioral results (Scott and Monesson, 2009) these data suggest that early labeling may be driving the development of perceptual representations for faces and objects. However, it is currently unclear whether verbal labels are necessary or simply sufficient for individuation learning to occur. It is possible that any correlated, individual-level cue, will lead to similar behavioral and neural specialization.

Face misperceptions and perceptual deficits are prevalent in a variety of developmental disorders, most notably in autism spectrum disorders (ASD) (for review see Webb et al., Chapter 43, this volume). For example, individuals with an ASD have difficulty remembering faces (Hauck et al., 1999) and have aberrant processing of emotional expressions (Ashwin et al., 2007). ASD individuals use feature-based, rather than holistic-based, face processing (Joseph and Tanaka, 2003; Senju et al., 2008) and spend less time directing their attention to the eye area of the face relative neurotypical children (Klin et al., 2002; Pelphrey et al., 2002). In addition, unlike typically developing individuals, individuals with an ASD do not show recognition deficits when faces are presented upside down (Hobson et al., 1998) and show aberrant electrophysiological responses to faces (Dawson et al., 2002). Recently, perceptual expertise training methods (Gauthier and Tarr, 1997) were adapted for autistic populations, to determine whether adolescents and young adults diagnosed with autism benefit from face training (Faja et al., 2008). Five individuals with autism were trained using explicit, rule-based instruction across several different training tasks. Training included learning to label faces at the individual level. Results revealed improvements in the

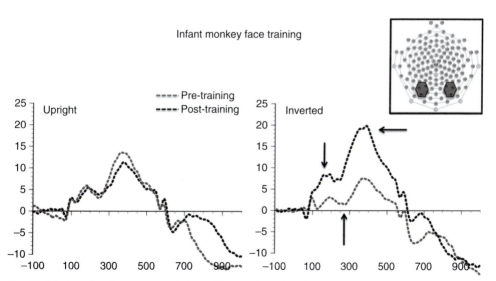

Fig. 11.5 Infant ERP changes to upright and inverted monkey faces before and after 3 months of individual-level training. After training, the amplitude response to inverted, but not upright, faces increased significantly.

ability to detect configuration changes and an increase in reaction time to inverted relative to upright faces (Faja et al., 2008). These inversion effects are consistent with previously reported adult (Tanaka and Pierce, 2009) and infant training studies (Scott and Monesson 2009, 2010) and further strengthen the argument that individual level learning plays an important role in the acquisition and development of perceptual expertise.

Summary and conclusions

The acquisition of perceptual expertise and the development of face and object categorization have recently become mutually informative. This chapter provided an overview of studies, in both adult and developmental populations, examining visual perceptual learning over time using both behavioral and cognitive neuroscience methods.

The study of the acquisition of perceptual expertise in adults and in developing populations suggests that neural systems responsible for face and object processing are especially sensitive to the level of abstraction at which these categories are learned (Scott and Monesson, 2010; Scott et al., 2006a, 2008). In adults, developing infants, and individuals with autism, learning to discriminate exemplars at more specific levels may lead to an increased emphasis on unique and individuating visual features whereas learning to categorize leads learners to focus on the visual features that stimuli within categories have in common. Labeling and feedback during perceptual learning with objects (in adults; Scott et al., 2006a, 2008) or with faces (in infants: Scott and Monesson, 2009; in adults: Tanaka and Pierce, 2009; in individuals with autism: Faja et al., 2008) enhances learning and leads to specialized behavioral and neural responses consistent with perceptual expertise. In adults, learning appears to generalize for some classes of stimuli (birds: Scott et al., 2006a) more than others (cars: Scott et al., 2008). In addition, learning in one domain may interfere with previously acquired perceptual expertise in another domain, leading to neural competition (Gauthier and Curby, 2005).

Here it is suggested that perceptual expertise arises similarly in adults and during development. Moreover, an effort to conduct experiments utilizing both adult and developmental populations may lead to a better understanding of how humans parse the world into categories of objects and people. In infants, we do not fully understand generalization and stability of learning, whether learning in one domain interferes with learning in another domain, or the role of labels and feedback during the acquisition perceptual expertise. Future work in the area of development is needed to determine whether: (1) cortical regions, responsible for face and object processing, compete during development, (2) labeling objects at the individual level will lead to similar behavioral and neural response as has been found with faces, and (3) perceptual narrowing in human infants represents a sensitive period during development or whether the development of specialized face representations can develop at any time.

References

Ahissar, M., Laiwand, R., Kozminsky, G., and Hochstein, S. (1998). Learning pop-out detection: Building representations for conflicting target-distracter relationships. *Vision Research*, **38**, 3095–3107.

Archambault, A., O'Donnell, C., and Schyns, P. (1999). Blind to object changes: when learning the same object at different levels of categorization modifies its perception. *Psychological Science*, **10**, 249–255.

Ashby, F.G., Alfonso-Reese, L.A., Turken, U., and Waldron, E.M. (1998). A neuropsychological theory of multiple systems in category learning. *Psychological Review*, **105**, 442–481.

Ashby, F.G. and O'Brien, J.B. (2005). Category learning and multiple memory systems. *Trends in Cognitive Science*, **9**, 83–89.

Ashwin, C., Baron-Cohen, S., Wheelwright, S., O'Riordan, M., and Bullmore, E.T. (2007). Differential activation of the amygdala and the "social brain" during fearful face-processing in Asperger Syndrome. *Neuropsychologia*, **45**, 2–14.

Carey, S. (1996). Perceptual classification and expertise. In R. Gelman and T. Au (eds.) *Handbook of Perception and Cognition: Perceptual and Cognitive Development*, pp. 49–69. New York: Academic Press.

Carmel, D. and Bentin, S. (2002). Domain specificity versus expertise: Factors influencing distinct processing of faces. *Cognition*, **83**, 1–29.

Bentin, S., Allison, T., Puce, A., Perez, E., and McCarthy G. (1996). Electrophysiological studies of face perception in humans. *Journal of Cognitive Neuroscience*, **8**, 551–565.

Bötzel, K., Schultze, S., and Stodieck, S.R. (1995). Scalp topography and analysis of intracranial sources of face-evoked potentials. *Experimental Brain Research*, **104**, 135–143.

Bukach, C.M., Gauthier, I., and Tarr, M.J. (2006). Beyond faces and modularity: the power of an expertise framework. *Trends in Cognitive Sciences*, **10**, 159–166.

Busey, T.A. and Vanderkolk, J.R. (2005). Behavioral and electrophysiological evidence for configural processing in fingerprint experts. *Vision Research*, **45**, 431–448.

Dawson, G., Carver, L., Meltzoff, A., *et al.* (2002). Neural correlates of face and object recognition in young children with autism spectrum disorder, developmental delay and typical development. *Child Development*, **73**, 700–717.

de Haan, M. and Nelson, C.A. (1999). Brain activity differentiates face and object processing in 6-month-old infants. *Developmental Psychology*, **35**, 1113–1121.

de Haan, M., Pascalis, O., and Johnson, M.H. (2002). Face-sensitive cortical processing in early infancy. *Journal of Child Psychology and Psychiatry*, **45**, 1228–1234.

de Schonen, S. and Mathivet, E. (1989). First come, first served: A scenario about the development of hemispheric specialization in face recognition during infancy. *European Bulletin of Cognitive Psychology*, **9**, 3–44.

Diamond, R. and Carey, S. (1986). Why faces are not special: an effect of expertise. *Journal of Experimental Psychology: General*, **115**, 107–117.

Eimer, M. (2000). Event-related brain potentials distinguish processing stages involved in face perception and recognition. *Clinical Neurophysiology*, **111**, 694–705.

Faja, S., Aylward, E., Bernier, R., and Dawson, G. (2008). Becoming a face expert: a computerized face-training program for high-functioning individuals with autism spectrum disorders. *Developmental Neuropsychology*, **33**, 1–24.

Farah, M.J. (1990). *Visual Agnosia*. Cambridge, MA: MIT Press.

Farah, M.J., Rabinowitz, C., Quinn, G.E., and Lie, G.T. (2000). Early commitment of neural substrates for face recognition. *Cognitive Neuropsychology*, **17**, 117–123.

Fiorentini, A. and Berardi, N. (1980). Perceptual learning is specific for orientation and spatial frequency. *Nature*, **287**, 43–44.

Gauthier, I. and Curby, K.M. (2005). A perceptual traffic jam on highway N170: Interference between face and car expertise. *Current Directions in Psychological Science*, **14**, 30–33.

Gauthier, I. and Nelson, C.A. (2001). The development of face expertise. *Current Opinion in Neurobiology*, **11**, 219–224.

Gauthier, I. and Tarr, M.J. (1997). Becoming a "greeble" expert: exploring mechanisms for face recognition. *Vision Research*, **37**, 1673–1682.

Gauthier, I. and Tarr, M.J. (2002). Unraveling mechanisms for expert object recognition: Bridging brain activity and behavior. *Journal of Experimental Psychology: Human Learning and Memory*, **28**, 431–446.

Gauthier, I., Williams, P., Tarr, M.J., and Tanaka, J. (1998). Training "greeble" experts: a framework for studying expert object recognition processes. *Vision Research*, **38**, 2401–2428.

Gauthier, I., Tarr, M.J., Anderson, A.W., Skudlarski, P., and Gore, J.C. (1999). Activation of the middle fusiform "face area" increases with expertise in recognizing novel objects. *Nature Neuroscience*, **2**, 568–573.

Gauthier, I., Tarr, M.J., Moylan, J., Skudlarski, P., Gore, J.C., and Anderson, A.W. (2000a). The fusiform "face area" is part of a network that processes faces at the individual level. *Journal of Cognitive Neuroscience.* **12**, 495–504.

Gauthier, I., Skudlarski, P., Gore, J.C., and Anderson, A.W. (2000b). Expertise for cars and birds recruits brain areas involved in face recognition. *Nature Neuroscience*, **3**, 191–197.

Gauthier, I., Curran, T., Curby, K.M., and Collins, D. (2003). Perceptual interference supports a non-modular account of face processing. *Nature Neuroscience*, **6**, 428–432.

Gillebert, C.R., Op de Beeck, H.P., Panis, S. and Wagemans, J. (2009). Subordinate categorization enhances the neural selectivity in human object-selective cortex for fine shape differences. *Journal of Cognitive Neuroscience*, **21**, 1054–1064.

Goren, C., Sarty, M., and Wu, P., (1975). Visual following and pattern discrimination of face-like stimuli by newborn infants. *Pediatrics*, **56**, 544–549.

Halit, H., de Haan, M., and Johnson, M.H. (2003). Cortical specialisation for face processing: Face-sensitive event-related potential components in 3- and 12-month-old infants. *Neuroimage*, **19**, 1180–1193.

Hauck, M., Fein, D., Maltby, N., *et al.* (1999). Memory for faces in children with autism. *Child Neuropsychology*, **4**, 187–198.

Hayden, A., Bhatt, RS., Joseph, J.E., and Tanaka, J.W. (2007). The other-race effect in infancy: Evidence using a morphing technique. *Infancy*, **12**, 95–104.

Hobson, R.P. and Lee, A. (1998). Hello and goodbye: A study of social engagement in autism. *Journal of Autism and Developmental Disorders*, **28**, 117–127.

Hobson, R.P., Ouston, J., and Lee, A. (1988). What's in a face? The case of autism. *British Journal of Psychology*, **79**, 441–453.

Holroyd, C.B., Nieuwenhuis, S., Yeung, N., *et al.* (2004). Dorsal anterior cingulate cortex shows fMRI response to internal and external error signals. *Nature Neuroscience*, **7**, 497–498.

Hu, X., Le, T.H., and Ugurbil, K. (1997). Evaluation of the early response in fMRI in individual subjects using short stimulus duration. *Magnetic Resonance in Medicine*, **37**, 855–864.

Jacques, C. and Rossion, B. (2004). Concurrent processing reveals competition between visual representations of faces. *Neuroreport*, **15**, 2417–2421.

Johnson, M.H. (2000). Functional brain development in infants: Elements of an interactive specialization framework. *Child Development*, **71**, 74–81.

Johnson, M.H., Dziurawiec, S., Ellis, H., and Morton, J. (1991). Newborns' preferential tracking of face-like stimuli and its subsequent decline. *Cognition*, **40**, 1–19.

Jolicoeur, P., Gluck, M.A., and Kosslyn, S.M. (1984). Pictures and names: making the connection. *Cognitive Psychology*, **16**, 243–275.

Joseph, R.M. and Tanaka, J. (2003). Holistic and part-based face recognition in children with autism. *Journal of Child Psychology and Psychiatry and Allied Disciplines*, **44**, 529–542.

Kanwisher, N. (2000). Domain specify in face perception. *Nature Neuroscience*, **3**, 759–763.

Kanwisher, N., McDermott, J., and Chun, M.M. (1997). The fusiform face area: A module in human extrastriate cortex specialized f or face perception. *Journal of Neuroscience*, **17**, 4302–4311.

Kelly, D.J., Quinn, P.C., Slater, A.M., *et al.* (2005). Three-month-olds, but not newborns, prefer own-race faces. *Developmental Science*, **8**, F31–F36.

Kelly, D., Quinn, P., Slater, A., Lee, K., Ge, L., and Pascalis, O. (2007). The other-race effect develops during infancy. *Psychological Science*, **18**, 1084–1089.

Kelly, D., Liu, S., Lee, K., *et al.* (2009). Development of the other-race effect during infancy: evidence towards universality? *Journal of Experimental Child Psychology*, **104**, 105–114.

Klin, A., Jones, W., Schultz, R., Volmar, F., and Cohen, D. (2002). Visual fixation patterns during viewing of naturalistic social situations as predictors of social competence in individuals with autism. *Archives of General Psychiatry*, **59**, 809–816.

Krigolson, O.E., Pierce, L.J., Holroyd, C.B., and Tanaka, J.W. (2009). Learning to become an expert: reinforcement learning and the acquisition of perceptual expertise. *Journal of Cognitive Neuroscience*, **21**, 1834–1841.

Le Grand, R., Mondloch, C.J., Maurer, D., and Brent, H.P. (2001). Early visual experience and face processing. *Nature*, **410**, 890.

Le Grand, R., Mondloch, C.J., Maurer, D., and Brent, H.P. (2003). Expert face processing requires visual input to the right hemisphere during development. *Nature Neuroscience*, **6**, 1108–1112.

Lebrecht, S., Pierce, L.J., Tarr, M.J., and Tanaka, J.W. (2009). Perceptual other-race training reduces implicit racial bias. *PLoS ONE*, **4**, e4215 1–6.

Maurer, D., Grand, R.L., and Mondloch, C.J. (2002). The many faces of configural processing. *Trends in Cognitive Sciences*, **6**, 255–260.

McKone, E., Kanwihser, N., and Duchaine, B. (2007) Can generic expertise explain special processing for faces? *Trends in Cognitive Science*, **11**, 8–15.

Meissner, C.A. and Brigham, J.C. (2001). Thirty years of investigating the own-race bias in memory for faces: A meta-analytic review. *Psychology, Public Policy, and Law*, 7, 3–35.

Morton, J. and Johnson, M.H. (1991). CONSPEC and CONLERN: A two-process theory of infant face recognition. *Psychological Press*, **98**, 164–181

Murphy, G.L. and Smith, E.E. (1982). Basic-level superiority in picture categorization. *Journal of Verbal Learning and Verbal Behavior*, **21**, 1–20.

Nelson, C.A. (2001). The development and neural bases of face recognition. *Infant and Child Development*, **10**, 3–18.

Nguyen, N. and Cottrell, G.W. (2005). Owls and wading birds: Generalization gradients in expertise. Paper presented at the 27th Annual Cognitive Science Society, July, Stresa, Italy.

Nishimura, M. and Maurer, D. (2008). The effect of categorization on sensitivity to second-order relations in novel objects. *Perception*, **37**, 584–601.

Nodine, C.F. and Krupinski, E.A. (1998). Perceptual skill, radiology expertise, and visual test performance with NINA and WALDO. *Academic Radiology*, **5**, 603–612.

Pascalis, O., de Haan, M., and Nelson, C.A. (2002). Is face processing species-specified during the first year of life? *Science*, **296**, 1321–1323.

Pascalis, O., Scott, L.S., Kelly, D.J., *et al.* (2005). Plasticity of face processing in infancy. *Proceedings of the National Academy of Sciences*, **102**, 5297–5300.

Pelphrey, K.A., Sasson, N.J., Reznich, J., Paul, G., Goldman, B.D., and Piven, J. (2002). Visual scanning of faces in autism. *Journal of Autism and Developmental Disorders*, **32**, 249–261.

Poggio, T., Fahle, M., and Edelman, S. (1992). Fast perceptual learning in visual hyperacuity. *Science*, **256**, 1018–21.

Quinn, P.C. (2010). The acquisition of expertise as a model for the growth of cognitive structure. In S.P. Johnson (ed.), *Neoconstructivism: The new science of cognitive development*, pp. 252–273. New York: Oxford University Press.

Quinn, P.C., Yahr, J., Kuhn, A., Slater, A.M., and Pascalis, O. (2002). Representations of the gender of human faces by infants: A preference for female. *Perception*, **31**, 1109–1121.

Rennels, J.L. and Davis, R.E. (2008). Facial experience during the first year of life. *Infant Behavior and Development*, **4**, 665–678.

Rhodes, G. (1988). Looking at faces: first-order and second-order features as determinants of facial appearance. *Perception*, **17**, 43–63.

Rosch, E., Mervis, C.B., Gray, W.D., Johnson, D.M., and Boyes-Braem, P. (1976). Basic objects in natural categories. *Cognitive Psychology*, **8**, 382–452.

Rossion, B. and Gauthier, I. (2002). How does the brain process upright and inverted faces? *Behavioral and Cognitive Neuroscience Review*, **1**, 63–75.

Rossion, B., Delvenne, J-F., Debatisse, D., *et al.* (1999). Spatio-temporal localization of the face inversion effect: an event-related potentials study. *Biological Psychology*, **50**, 173–189.

Rossion, B., Gauthier, I., Tarr, M.J., *et al.* (2000). The N170 occipito-temporal component is delayed and enhanced to inverted faces but not to inverted objects: an electrophysiological account of face-specific processes in the human brain. *Cognitive Neuroscience*, **11**, 69–72.

Rossion, B., Gauthier, I., Goffaux, V., Tarr, M.J., and Crommelinck, M. (2002). Expertise training with novel objects leads to left-lateralized facelike electrophysiological responses. *Psychological Science*, **13**, 250–257.

Rossion, B., Kung, C.C., and Tarr, M.J. (2004). Visual expertise with nonface objects leads to competition with the early perceptual processing of faces in the human occipitotemporal cortex. *Proceedings of the National Academy of Sciences*, **101**, 14521–14526.

Rossion, B., Collins, D., Goffaux, V., and Curran, T. (2007). Long-term expertise with artificial objects increases visual competition with early face categorization processes. *Journal of Cognitive Neuroscience*, **19**, 543–555.

Saether, L. and Laeng, B. (2008). On facial expertise: Processing strategies of twins' parents. *Perception*, **37**, 1227–1240.

Schweinberger, S.R., Pickering, E., Jentzsch, I., Burton, A.M., and Kaufmann, J.M. (2002). Event-related brain potential evidence for a response of inferior temporal cortex to familiar face repetitions. *Cognitive Brain Research*, **14**, 398–409.

Schweinberger, S.R., Huddy, V., and Burton, M. (2004). N250r: a face-selective brain response to stimulus repetitions. *Neuroreport*, **15**, 1501–1505.

Scott, L.S. and Monesson, A. (2009). The origin of biases in face perception. *Psychological Science*, **20**, 676–680.

Scott, L.S. and Monesson, A. (2010). Experience-dependent neural specialization during infancy. *Neuropsychologia*, **48**, 1857–1861.

Scott, L.S., Tanaka, J.W., Sheinberg, D.L., and Curran, T. (2006a). A reevaluation of the electrophysiological correlates of expert object processing. *Journal of Cognitive Neuroscience*, **18**, 1453–1465.

Scott, L.S., Shannon, R.W., and Nelson, C.A. (2006b). Neural correlates of human and monkey face processing by 9-month-old infants. *Infancy*, **10**, 171–186.

Scott, L.S., Pascalis, O., and Nelson, C.A. (2007) A domain general theory of perceptual development. *Current Directions in Psychological Science*, **16**, 197–201.

Scott, L.S., Tanaka, J.W., Sheinberg, D.L., and Curran, T. (2008). The role of category learning in the acquisition and retention of perceptual expertise: a behavioral and neurophysiological study. *Brain Research*, **1210**, 204–215.

Senju, A., Kikuchi, Y., Hasegawa, T., Tojo, Y., and Osanai, H. (2008). Is anyone looking at me? Direct gaze detection in children with and without Autism. *Brain and Cognition*, **67**, 127–139.

Sergent, J. (1988) Face perception and the right hemisphere. In L. Weiskrantz (ed.) *Thought without language*, pp. 108–131. Oxford: Oxford University Press.

Simion, F., Macchi Cassia, V., Turati, C., *et al.* (2001). The origins of face perception: Specific versus non-specific mechanisms. *Infant and Child Development*, **10**, 59–65.

Simion, F., Valenza, E., Macchi Cassia, V., Turati, C., and Umiltà, C. (2002). Newborns' reference for up-down asymmetrical configurations. *Developmental Science*, **4**, 427–434.

Suigita, Y. (2008). Face perception in monkeys reared with no exposure to faces. *Proceedings of the National Academy of Sciences*, **105**, 394–398.

Synder, K.A. (2007). Neural mechanisms underlying memory and attention in preferential-looking tasks. In LM Oakes and PJ Bauer (eds.) *Short- and Long-Term Memory in Infancy and Early Childhood*, pp. 179–208. New York: Oxford University Press.

Tanaka, J.W. and Curran, T. (2001). A neural basis for expert object recognition. *Psychological Science,* **12(1)**, 43–47.

Tanaka, J.W. and Pierce L.J. (2009). The neural plasticity of other-race face recognition. *Cognitive, Affective, and Behavioral Neuroscience,* 9, 122–131.

Tanaka, J. and Taylor, M. (1991). Object categories and expertise: is the basic level in the eye of the beholder? *Cognitive Psychology,* **23**, 457–482.

Tanaka, J.W., Kiefer, M., and Bukach, C.M. (2004). A holistic account of the own-race effect in face recognition: Evidence from a cross-cultural study. *Cognition,* **93**, B1–B9.

Tanaka, J.W., Curran, T., and Sheinberg, D.L. (2005). The training and transfer of real-world perceptual expertise. *Psychological Science,* **16**, 145–151.

Tanaka, J.W., Curran, T., Porterfield, A.L., and Collins, D. (2006). Activation of preexisting and acquired face representations: The n250 event-related potential as an index of face familiarity. *Journal of Cognitive Neuroscience,* **18**, 1488–1497.

Wong, AC-N., Palmeri, T.J., and Gauthier, I. (2009). Conditions for facelike expertise with objects. *Psychological Science,* **20**, 1108–1117.

Chapter 12

An Experience-Based Holistic Account of the Other-Race Face Effect

Bruno Rossion and Caroline Michel

Variations between human populations in face structure and the concept of "face race"

Since populations of the modern human race left Africa around 100,000 years ago and settled in different continents, their body morphology, including the face, has been transformed in response to different natural selection pressures[1] (i.e. different environments; e.g. Katzmarzyk and Leonard, 1998; Ruff, 1994, 2002). Consequently, despite the extremely high genetic similarity between different human populations (e.g. Altshuler et al., 2005; Cavalli-Sforza and Cavalli-Sforza, 1994), there are important and clearly visible differences between their faces, both in terms of the bone structure and the reflectance of light on the skin (surface reflectance, i.e. color and texture) (Bruce and Young, 1998; see Figure 12.1). For instance, sub-Saharan Africans have a darker skin and wider, more bulbous noses than Asians or Western Europeans, the latter being characterized by the thinnest pointy noses (see Choe et al., 2004; Farkas, 1994; Le et al., 2002; Porter, 2004; Porter and Olson, 2001).

The term of "race," and the concept it traditionally refers to, namely genetically different human populations in the world, is one of the most intellectually and emotionally charged in society, and in science as well. While some scientists claim that there is no biological reality to racial categories in the human population, others argue that different human groups can be distinguished based on genetic factors (see e.g. Edwards, 2003; Jorde and Wooding, 2004, Risch et al., 2002; and the whole special issue of *Nature Genetics*, volume 36, 2004). Even though one has to acknowledge that the genetic borders between human populations are fuzzy, that there is no point in trying to define a number of different human races on earth, and that the variance in genetic diversity can be much greater within a given population than between populations (Lewontin, 1972; Witherspoon et al., 2007) if the genes are considered in isolation (rather than collectively; see Edwards, 2003), a substantial part of the variance in the skin color and texture, as well as in the bone structure of the face (and the whole body) (e.g. Rosenberg et al., 2002), is at least accounted for by genetic differences between human populations. In short, biologically, race is real, though it involves superficial traits and fuzzy categories. In this chapter, we will focus on how human beings recognize individual faces of their own versus another "racial group," and we will use the term "face race" in the context of visual recognition, as traditionally done in this scientific literature.

---

[1] Some traits of the body and face may also have, as Darwin (1871) suggested, spread through sexual selection (e.g. an arbitrary preference for blue eyes).

Fig. 12.1 Illustration of the variations of the human face between a few populations. Top row, left to right: the (2009) leaders of Malawi, Bolivia, France, and Laos; second row: Slovenia, China, Nigeria, and Egypt; third row: Lebanon, Senegal, Sweden, and Japan; fourth row: North Korea, Germany, Israel, and Rwanda; fifth row: Cambodia, Mongolia, Ecuador, and US.

The "other-race" face effect

Race is in the face. We first notice it there. And we notice it particularly quickly when the person belongs to another racial group. By means of both shape and surface reflectance information (Hill et al., 1995), an observer is able to distinguish between two faces belonging to two different races (e.g. a Western European versus a sub-Saharian African) accurately and rapidly (e.g. Caldara et al., 2004; Levin, 1996, 2000; Valentine and Endo, 1992).

Within a given human race, identifying specific individuals from their face is more complex, since it requires us to perceive much subtler variations of shape and surface-based properties among faces (O'Toole et al., 1999), both at the level of local distinct facial features (e.g. eyes, eyebrows, nose, mouth, ears, etc.) and at the global level of the face (e.g. head shape, relative distances between features such as the eyes and the mouth; Rhodes, 1988). Despite this complexity of individual face recognition, normal adult human observers are quite accurate at making differences between distinct individual unfamiliar faces, and in particular at recognizing previously seen individuals from their face (e.g. Bahrick et al., 1975; Bruce and Young, 1998).

However, this expertise holds only if the individual faces are from the same racial group that the observer encounters regularly in his/her environment, i.e. generally his/her own racial group. In contrast, people are not that good at individualizing faces belonging to another racial group and may find that faces from other races "all look alike," whereas faces of one's own race appear easily distinguishable (Feingold, 1914).

Using a face recognition task, Malpass and Kravitz (1969) reported the first empirical demonstration that observers perform significantly better with their own-race as compared to other-race faces. Since this first demonstration, this "other-race effect" (ORE, also called "own-race bias," "cross-race effect," and "cross-racial facial identification effect" in the scientific literature) has been replicated in numerous studies, with different racial groups (see Meissner and Brigham, 2001).

In most empirical studies, the ORE is demonstrated through a standard recognition paradigm, in which participants have to discriminate between faces encoded during a (incidental or explicit) learning phase (targets) and novel faces (distractors). The ORE is classically reflected by a crossover interaction between the race of participants and the race of faces in discrimination accuracy (Figure 12.2). In some studies, a response time advantage for same-race (SR) relative to other-race (OR) faces has also been found (e.g. Chance and Goldstein, 1987; Michel et al., 2006b; Valentine, 1991).

In some studies guided by an applied research concern—i.e. the understanding of the psychological factors affecting eyewitness identifications, a context in which the phenomenon is currently largely acknowledged (e.g. Brigham and Wolfskeil, 1983; Brigham et al., 1999; Deffenbacher and Loftus, 1982; Kassin et al., 1989)—the ORE has also been demonstrated in more forensically relevant paradigms. These paradigms include lineup identification (e.g. Berger, 1969; Brigham et al., 1982; Doty, 1998; Fallshore and Schooler, 1995; Platz and Hosch, 1988), facial reconstruction tasks (Ellis et al., 1979), and photo lineup construction by law enforcement officers (Brigham and Ready, 1985). Finally, the ORE has also been observed in perceptual matching tasks with unfamiliar faces (e.g. Lindsay et al., 1991; Malpass et al., 1988; Sangrigoli and de Schonen, 2004; Walker and Hewstone, 2006; Walker and Tanaka, 2003), even though it is not always found, and never as large as in an old/new recognition paradigm (see Papesh and Goldinger, 2009).

The results of these numerous studies conducted in adult human observers have been reviewed in several meta-analyses (Anthony et al., 1992; Bothwell et al., 1989; Lindsay and Wells, 1983; Shapiro and Penrod, 1986), the most recent one (Meissner and Brigham, 2001) reviewing over 30 years of research on the ORE, with nearly 5000 participants involved.

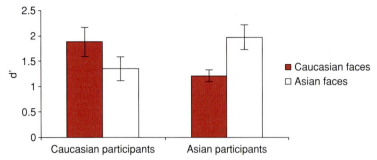

Fig. 12.2 A typical other-race effect as observed in an old/new face recognition task. In this study (Michel et al., 2006a), participants were first presented with 20 faces of each race one by one (3-s duration, ISI 1-s) to encode in memory. Then, they performed an old/new recognition task on 40 faces (20 learned, 20 new) presented individually, for same- and other-race faces separately. Each face was presented until the participant's response, or for a maximum of 2 s. Participants did not know the ratio of old and new faces, and did not receive any feedback for their responses. The order of presentation for the blocks of same- and other-race faces was counterbalanced across participants. The other-race effect is reflected by the cross-over interaction between the race of participants and the race of faces in discrimination accuracy (d'), participants of both groups performing better at recognizing their own-race than other-race faces. Errors bars represent standard errors of the mean.

Overall, these meta-analyses confirm the robust nature of the ORE. The advantage of recognizing SR faces is consistent across different experimental paradigms and racial groups, even though it is not always reflected by a perfect cross-over interaction (Anthony et al., 1992; Meissner and Brigham, 2001).

The size of the ORE varies across studies. While we have found quite large OREs in our own studies with an old/new recognition paradigm (Figure 12.2), other authors have referred to the ORE as a fairly weak effect (Meissner and Brigham, 2001). However, the ORE has been replicated numerous times and is one of the few reliable empirical phenomena in the face recognition literature. The small size of the effect—relative to interindividual variability in face recognition performance—in an experimental context may have more to do with the limitations of the paradigms to capture a phenomenon that can nevertheless be dramatic in one's real life experience (Feingold, 1914). Moreover, the large majority of researchers who study the ORE perform their experiments with participants raised in largely multiracial societies (e.g. North America, Australia) in which the ORE may be smaller than when it is assessed in populations living in fairly homogenous racial societies (e.g. Africa, Western Europe, or East Asia).

Proposed explanations of the ORE

Different explanations have been proposed to account for the ORE. They will simply be mentioned in this section without expanding (for details, see e.g. Meissner and Brigham, 2001).

1 A *difference of intrinsic discriminability* between different populations of faces (e.g. Malpass and Kravitz, 1969): there would be less physiognomic variability between individual faces within one race than within another race.

2 A *lack of contact or visual experience with OR faces*, as initially proposed by Feingold (1914, p.50): "it is well known that, other things being equal, individuals of a given race are distinguishable from each other in proportion to our familiarity, to our contact with the race as a whole".

3 A *difficulty in processing OR faces holistically or configurally* OR faces would be treated using a more piecemeal, and less efficient process (e.g. Rhodes et al., 1989).

4 A *differential depth of encoding* for SR versus OR faces: SR faces would be encoded deeply in memory while OR faces would be encoded in a shallow way (Chance and Goldstein, 1981).

5 *Prejudiced racial attitudes*: observers, particularly those with more prejudiced racial attitudes, would not be motivated to differentiate members of another race, which would result in a weaker memory for OR faces (e.g. Berger, 1969; Galper, 1973).

6 An *emphasis on visual information specifying race for OR faces*: observers would limit their encoding of OR faces at a superordinate level of categorization, focusing on race-specifying features ("It's a Chinese person") at the expense of individuating information (e.g. Anthony et al., 1992; Levin, 1996, 2000).

7 A *differential coding of OR and SR faces in a multidimensionally organized face-space* (Valentine, 1991): individual faces encountered would be organized in a multidimensional face-space in memory. The dimensions of the face-space would be the most diagnostic for discriminating own-race faces. Individual faces from another race would be densely clustered in the space, and thus easily confused.

8 An inherent difference in the most diagnostic cues for individualization of SR and OR faces which would lead to *a reduced sensitivity to diagnostic features for OR faces* (e.g. Furl et al., 2002): the utility of the facial dimensions for individualization, which would include both features and the relative distances between these features (Rhodes, 1988), would vary between races. For example, eye color could be less useful for discriminating Asian than Caucasian faces. The observer's sensitivity to these diagnostic dimensions would develop through visual experience (generally limited to SR faces). As a result, sensitivity to diagnostic features would be lower for OR than SR faces.

The only account that is usually rapidly dismissed in reviews of the ORE is the difference of intrinsic discriminability between different populations of faces, because the ORE can be observed in participants of many different races (e.g. Byatt and Rhodes, 2004; Chance et al., 1975; Luce, 1974; O'Toole et al., 1994; Valentine and Endo, 1992). However, one should remain aware that there *are* probably real intrinsic differences in the potential discriminability of individual faces from different populations of the world. For instance, Africans differ among each other genetically far more than other races do (Cavalli-Sforza and Cavalli-Sforza, 1994), since the African's DNA continued to diversify after the ancestors of Australian aboriginals, Europeans, and Asians left Africa. Hence, there is certainly much more variance in the face (and body) morphology within the African population than within the Caucasian or Aboriginal populations. In other words, for an "ideal observer," individual faces of a given population considered as a single race may in fact be more heterogeneous than individual faces of another race. Therefore, at least for that reason, one should not expect a perfect cross-over ORE in any given study, even if experience with OR faces and all other factors were perfectly controlled.

As for the other accounts of the ORE, they are not always situated at the same level of explanation, and are not all mutually exclusive. Here we will argue in favor of an experience-based holistic account of the ORE, as an integrated theoretical proposal.

An experience-based holistic account of the ORE

The necessity of experience

At the highest level of explanation, the ORE *has to* be due to the *differential visual experience* one has with a group of faces sharing a certain given morphology, generally one's own facial morphology, as compared to a group of faces sharing another kind of morphology, the other-race faces. The only alternative account would be that the human face processing system is genetically pre-specified to an extreme degree of precision such that one is only able to efficiently individualize faces of his/her own racial group. This latter account can be definitely dismissed by recent results observed in human adults who have been adopted at a young age (3–9 years old) into another racial group: they present an advantage at processing these other-race faces over their own-race faces (Sangrigoli et al., 2004), a finding that could not be explained by a genetic account. The role of visual experience in the ORE is further supported by developmental studies indicating that although 3-month-old Western European infants can discriminate faces within four different racial groups (faces of their own racial group, sub-Saharan Africans, Middle Eastern, and Chinese faces), 9-month-old infants can only discriminate own-race faces (Kelly et al., 2007). Together, these studies show that visual experience early in life with one racial group of faces tunes the face recognition system to the characteristics that allow individualizing faces of this group. However, the face recognition system remains flexible for years at least, since the ORE can be reversed in large part (de Heering et al., 2010), or even completely (Sangrigoli et al., 2004), if one is exposed to another racial group throughout development.

The experience-based account of the ORE, or "contact hypothesis," is sometimes questioned because the ORE does not always go away, or even get smaller with experience (e.g. Ng and Lindsay, 1994; Wright et al., 2003) or training (e.g. Malpass et al., 1973; Lavrakas et al., 1976). However, the claim that experience does not affect the ORE (e.g. Levin, 2000) is not always correct (e.g. Chiroro and Valentine, 1995; Cross et al., 1971; Dunning et al., 1998; Hancock and Rhodes, 2008; Rhodes et al., 2009; see also the training studies of Tanaka and Pierce, 2009; for a review, see McKone et al., 2007). Most importantly, this is an entirely different issue: whether, *in adulthood, after* one's face recognition system has been tuned to individualize SR faces efficiently during development, it is still possible to learn to individualize OR faces as efficiently as SR faces. Irrespective of the answer to this latter question, which is still unresolved, it remains clear that, at the highest level of explanation, the differential visual experience with SR versus OR faces *during development* of the face recognition system accounts for the ORE.

An experience-based holistic account

Face perception is a high-level visual process, i.e. it results from the interaction of the incoming information and internal representations (Cavanagh, 1991; Gregory, 1997). Therefore, it is necessary to understand the nature and characteristics of this interaction to explain it. With early and extensive exposure to a set of visual stimuli sharing a common structure, the face recognition system appears to build what Goldstein and Chance (1980) referred to as a "schema." The schema can be considered as a generic face representation derived from visual experience with a rapidly growing number of exemplars early in life. Importantly, this generic representation is a *global* face configuration, also called a *holistic* representation (Galton, 1883; Sergent, 1984, 1986; Tanaka and Farah, 1993).

In most societies, people's visual experience during development is limited to faces that share a certain morphology, i.e. faces of a certain racial group. Hence, with increasing experience, the holistic representation, originally *broadly tuned*, becomes more fine-grained, or *finely tuned* for a certain racial group of faces (Kelly et al., 2007). That is, it becomes centered around the physical characteristics of these SR faces (e.g. a relatively large eye-eyebrow distance as in Eastern Asian faces). The holistic representation is also optimally tuned to take into account the *variations* of these features in the population of faces encountered (e.g. how variable is the distance between the eye and eyebrow within the population). The representation of a given facial attribute (e.g. nose width, interocular distance) within this face schema is thus finely (small variance) or rather broadly (large variance) specified, around an average value.

In this context, let us consider the perception of a face belonging to another race. The OR face input differs substantially from the observer's experience-based holistic representation, on multiple morphological aspects. For instance, the interocular distance of the OR face may be very small, and so out of range of the variations encountered before. As a result, this OR face input does not fit well the experience-based holistic template of the observer. Consequently, the new OR face is not—or less well—encoded and represented holistically. Rather, the OR face has to be analyzed feature-by-feature, i.e. analytically. Fine-grained information can of course be extracted from the new morphological input (OR face), and the individual face can be encoded in the system, but it requires a greater amount of resources, at the expense of speed and accuracy.

Such a relatively simple proposal, inspired by Goldstein and Chance's (1980) early proposal and encompassing more recent data (see below) and concepts from the face recognition literature, can form the basic theoretical account of the ORE. This view is particularly interesting because, as we will explain below, it could account for the ORE even if the *variance* between facial features in two sets of faces—and thus their diagnosticity—from different races was strictly identical.

This experience-based holistic (EBH) account is based on the reduced holistic/configural processing mode observed for OR faces (Michel et al., 2006a,b; Tanaka et al., 2004) and can account for its consequences (the reduced sensitivity to feature-based properties and relative distances between features; Hayward et al., 2008; Rhodes et al., 2006). It can incorporate, as we will discuss below, the notion of face-space (Valentine, 1991), and is not incompatible with the idea of a differential depth of encoding (Chance and Goldstein, 1981), which is rather seen as a consequence of a lack of holistic processing. This account can also predict, to some extent, the inverse relationship between the ability to individualize OR faces and race-categorization judgments (Levin, 2000) without the need to call upon the social notions of stereotypes towards "outgroup" members as causes of the ORE (see section "The sociocognitive account of the ORE: a brief critical review").

This theoretical proposal is, however, fundamentally incompatible with the view that the ORE is caused exclusively, or even to a large extent, by motivational, attentional, or more generally by sociocognitive factors (e.g. Hugenberg et al., 2007; Levin, 1996, 2000; Sporer, 2001). It does not deny that sociocognitive factors can greatly influence face identification, and thus the ORE, in experimental or ecological contexts (see Hugenberg et al., Chapter 13, this volume), or that these studies are of great interest in order to understand social cognition. However, according to the EBH account, modulatory sociocognitive factors are not at the root of the ORE, which we propose primarily results from the way the human brain perceives and represents faces.

Some clarifications and evidence for the EBH account

Holistic processing of individual faces

There is considerable evidence that individual faces are represented holistically or configurally, even though there is much less agreement on what this exactly means (e.g. Farah et al., 1998; Galton, 1883; Goldstein and Chance, 1980; Peterson and Rhodes, 2003; Rossion, 2008, 2009; Tanaka and Gordon, Chapter 10, this volume). Here, as in early studies in this area (Sergent, 1984;

Tanaka and Farah, 1993; Young et al., 1987), the terms "holistic" and "configural" are used as synonyms. Importantly, "holistic/configural" refers to both a way of *representing* faces and a *perceptual process*: it is by matching the incoming visual face-stimulus to an internal holistic representation that this face can be *perceived* holistically (see Rossion, 2009; Rossion and Boremanse, 2008).

The empirical evidence in favor of the holistic view of face perception shows essentially that facial features are *interdependent* during face processing: the processing of a facial feature (e.g. eyes, nose, mouth, etc.) is affected by identity or position alterations of one or several other facial feature(s) (e.g. Farah et al., 1998; Homa et al., 1976; Mermelstein et al., 1979; Sergent, 1984; Suzuki and Cavanagh, 1995; Tanaka and Farah, 1993; Tanaka and Sengco, 1997; Young et al., 1987). This interdependency of facial features during face processing is nicely illustrated by the "composite-face illusion," adapted from the "composite-face effect" (Young et al., 1987): identical attended top halves of faces tend to be perceived as being different if they are aligned (but not if they are spatially misaligned) with distinct unattended bottom parts (Figure 12.3), illustrating that the parts of a face (here the two halves) cannot be perceived independently (for empirical demonstrations in face matching tasks, e.g. Goffaux and Rossion, 2006; Hole, 1994; Le Grand et al., 2004; Rossion and Boremanse, 2008).

What is "holistic" in this framework is the *perception* of the face, as indicated by the perceptual nature of the composite-face illusion (Figure 12.3), the fact that the locus of this illusion lies

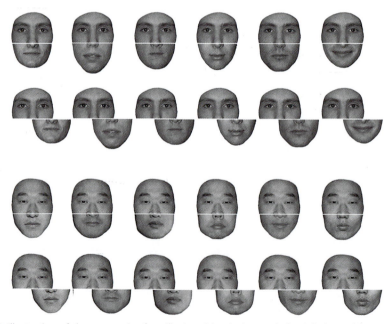

Fig. 12.3 Illustration of the composite-face illusion. Identical attended top halves of faces tend to be perceived as being different when they are aligned with distinct unattended bottom parts. Here, the top half of a face is aligned with six different bottom halves (first row: example for a Western European face; third row: example for an Eastern Asian face). The illusion disappears if the two halves of the face are spatially misaligned (second and fourth rows). It has been demonstrated that the composite-face illusion is stronger for same- than for other-race faces, leading to a larger face-composite effect for the former (Michel et al., 2006b, 2007, 2010).

primarily in high-level visual areas sensitive to faces, such as the right "fusiform face area" (Schiltz and Rossion, 2006), and that it occurs at about 160 ms over the visual occipitotemporal cortex (Jacques and Rossion, 2009) (for an alternative view, with a locus of holistic processing at a decisional level, see Richler et al., 2008; Wenger and Ingvalson, 2002). The perception is holistic because the incoming face-stimulus has to be matched to the holistic internal *representation* of the face (Tanaka and Farah, 1993), *derived from experience*, for the stimulus to by fully perceived. This view has been indirectly supported by showing, for instance, that if the exact same face input deviates from the usually seen upright orientation (i.e. an inverted face), holistic face perception breaks down (e.g. Tanaka and Farah, 1993; Young et al., 1987). This phenomenon is best illustrated by the fact that the composite-face illusion vanishes if faces are presented upside down. In addition, this loss of holistic face perception in the composite face effect is abrupt, taking place between 60 and 90 degrees of angle of face rotation, rather than being linearly related with the angle of rotation of the face (Rossion and Boremanse, 2008; see also McKone, 2004; Murray et al., 2000, 2003). This observation suggests that the face input is perceived by means of an experience-based internal face representation (i.e. we are used to seeing faces upright and tilted up to a certain angle, but almost never from 90 degrees to 180 degrees).

This holistic representation is applied to *all* information that is potentially diagnostic to individualize the face: both the local facial features *and* the relative distances between these features, without giving any special representational status to the latter (sometimes referred to as "configural," "configurational," or "second-order relational" cues in the literature, e.g. Carey, 1992; Maurer et al., 2002) (Rossion, 2008, 2009; Tanaka and Farah, 2003). Nevertheless, some kinds of facial information (i.e. diagnostic cues that are used to individualize the face) may be more dependent on holistic processing than other cues. For instance, large-scale information, conveyed by lower spatial frequency ranges, such as global head shape or relative distance between eyes and mouth, may be more dependent on holistic processing than local details or fine-grained variations of texture, contained in higher spatial frequency ranges (Goffaux and Rossion, 2006; Sergent, 1986).

Importantly, this holistic mode of processing faces, which is already present in 4 to 6-year-old children (Carey and Diamond, 1994; de Heering et al., 2007; Pellicano and Rhodes, 2003; Tanaka et al., 1998), and perhaps even in 7-month-old infants (e.g. Bhatt et al., 2005; Cohen and Cashon, 2001), is *functional*, in the sense that it allows efficient encoding of an individual face, i.e. as a single representation, with all its diagnostic cues being encoded at once. The importance of the holistic mode of face processing is supported by evidence that acquired prosopagnosia, the inability to recognize and discriminate individual faces following brain damage (Bodamer, 1947), is related to an inability to process faces holistically (e.g. Levine and Calvanio, 1989; Sergent and Villemure, 1989; see Ramon et al., 2010 for a review).

Other-race faces are processed less holistically/configurally than same-race faces

Four studies have shown directly that OR faces are processed less holistically than SR faces. Using the "whole-part advantage" effect (i.e. the fact that it is easier to recognize a facial feature when it is presented within the whole context of the face than when it is presented in isolation; Tanaka and Farah 1993; see Tanaka and Gordon, Chapter 10, this volume), Tanaka and colleagues (2004) showed that Western Europeans (Germany), who had been living in a largely unicultural society and had minimal experience with Asian faces, processed Caucasian (SR) faces, but not Asian (OR) faces, holistically. Michel and colleagues (2006a) replicated this finding in Belgian participants, who presented a strong ORE as measured in a preliminary face recognition task. Interestingly, in both studies, the Eastern Asian participants (Chinese), who had experience with

Caucasian faces (for their entire life in the study of Tanaka et al., 2004; for a year on average in the study of Michel et al., 2006a), showed holistic face processing for both races of faces (Caucasians and Asians), suggesting that visual experience may lead to, or increase, holistic processing for OR faces.

In a subsequent study (Michel et al., 2006b), Caucasian participants presented a composite-face effect (i.e. a difference in performance between misaligned and aligned face-stimuli in a composite-face matching task) in accuracy rates for Caucasian faces exclusively (Figure 12.4). These Caucasian participants presented a composite face effect for both race of faces in response times. Interestingly, in this study, Eastern Asian participants, who had no significant experience with Caucasian faces, showed a significant composite-face effect for Caucasian faces in accuracy rates, but marginally smaller than the composite-face effect exhibited for Asian faces (Figure 12.4). Moreover, their composite effect was also significantly smaller for Caucasian than for Asian faces in response times. These results showed that more holistic processing for SR than OR faces is found also for Asian observers. They also showed that holistic processing can be applied to OR faces (to a lesser extent than SR faces) even when observers do not have visual experience with these OR faces, an observation which is valid also for Caucasian observers presented with Asian faces (Michel et al., 2007).

In summary, there is direct evidence from two well-validated experimental paradigms measuring the interdependence between facial features, a marker of holistic face processing, that SR faces are processed, i.e. perceived, more holistically than OR faces. There is also indirect evidence in favor of this view: the decrease of performance for processing inverted faces (Farah et al., 1995; Rossion, 2008, 2009), an indirect marker of holistic processing, is larger for SR than OR faces (Hancock and Rhodes, 2008; Rhodes et al., 1989, 2006; Sangrigoli and de Schonen, 2004; see also Murray et al., 2003), at least when SR and OR faces are tested under the same conditions (unlike in Valentine and Bruce, 1986, where OR faces were given an advantage by being presented for a longer time). A lack of verbal overshadowing effect, the phenomenon that describing verbally a previously seen face impairs recognition of this face, for OR faces is also generally taken in support of the view that these faces are not or less processed holistically (Fallshore and Schooler, 1995).

A theoretical framework

The experience-based holistic account of the ORE outlined above is reasonably simple, and in agreement with many different proposals and observations about the ORE, as we will try to explain below.

PC analysis of SR and OR faces, and global components

Several studies have applied principal components analysis (PCA) to face images to extract the main dimensions that account for variance in a face set (e.g. Kirby and Sirovich, 1990; Turk and Pentland, 1991). PCA does a good job of accounting for some aspects of human memory performance with SR and OR face images (e.g. O'Toole et al., 1994; O'Toole, Chapter 2, this volume). Most interestingly, the PCs (or "eigenfaces") that account for most of the variations within races of faces are not only different for different races—indicating that there are distinct diagnostic features to individualize faces in different races—but they are global: they are identifiable at the level of the whole face and do not correspond to common sense local cues such as the size of the nose, or the thickness of the eyebrows for instance (O'Toole et al., 1994). This observation suggests that in order to accurately and rapidly identify an individual face within a given race, observers should consider many elements covarying together. Note that in a PC analysis of faces, the early components can carry information about subordinate-level categorization (sex,

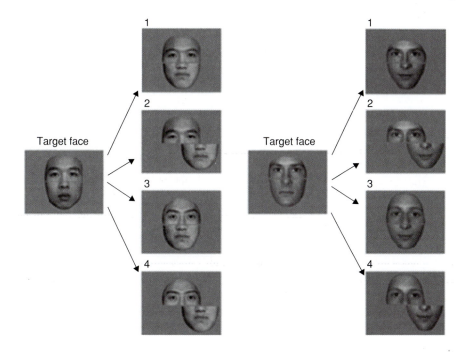

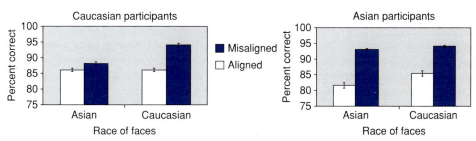

Fig. 12.4 Top: examples of Asian (on the left) and Caucasian (on the right) original (target) and composite faces used in the experiment of Michel et al. (2006b). The target face could be followed by a composite face with (1) the same top part aligned with a different bottom part, (2) the same top part misaligned with that different bottom part, (3) a different top part aligned with that different bottom part, or (4) a different top part misaligned with that different bottom part. For each pair of faces, participants were required to judge if the top parts were "same" or "different," ignoring the lower parts. Bottom: the composite-face effect in accuracy rates showed by Caucasian and Asian participants for Asian and Caucasian faces in the experiment of Michel et al. (2006b). The effect is reflected by the difference in performance for the trials requiring a "same" response (conditions 1 and 2) between "aligned" and "misaligned" conditions. Caucasian participants presented a composite-face effect for Caucasian faces but not for Asian faces. Asian participants showed a significant composite-face effect for Caucasian faces, but weaker than the composite-face effect exhibited for Asian faces. Errors bars represent standard errors of the mean. From Michel et al. (2006b), reprinted with permission from Wiley-Blackwell.

race, etc.; see Abdi et al., 1994; O'Toole et al., 1994) while the later PCs apparently carry finer details, being potentially important for coding identity (O'Toole et al., 1994). However, even these later components are essentially global. This observation is consistent with a coarse-to-fine mode of processing face identity in which an initial global coarse representation is progressively refined, yet remains holistic throughout the processing of the face (Sergent, 1986).

Distinct diagnostic features for SR and OR faces

As stated above, the PCs accounting for variations within races of faces appear to be different for different races, indicating that there are distinct diagnostic features to individualize faces in different races (O'Toole et al., 1991, 1994). There are other sources of evidence that the main sources of variability between features of faces (i.e. diagnostic information for individualization) are different between races. In an early behavioral study, Ellis and colleagues (1975) found that Africans did not use the same facial features as Caucasians in their verbal descriptions of own-race faces, suggesting that the diagnostic features differ in these two races (see also Shepherd and Deregowski, 1981). Anthropometric studies also report large variations between different human populations, not only in terms of the average size and shape of certain features (allowing race categorization of the faces), but also in terms of their degree of variance within a given population (see Farkas, 1994). Interestingly, members of different racial groups, who may not look at faces the same way during identification (see Blais et al., 2008), appear to rely on different features to discriminate individual faces, irrespective of the race of the face with which they are presented (Ellis et al., 1975; although see Shepherd and Deregowski, 1981).

In principle, if faces from different races differ from each other along different (diagnostic) dimensions, and people rely on information that is diagnostic in their own race when they have to individualize faces, it is not very surprising that our face recognition system has great difficulties in discriminating individual OR faces. Throughout development, people would become particularly sensitive to the facial information that is diagnostic to individualize SR faces (e.g. interocular distance if it varies a lot between individual SR faces). When faced with OR faces, they would tend to rely on the same facial information, without much success because the source of variance in individual OR faces would be different (e.g. interocular distance would not vary a lot between OR faces).

In itself, such an experience-based account would be sufficient to account for the ORE, without the need to call upon the notion of a holistic representation. However, we argue that this account is not fully satisfactory. First, under this account, it is difficult to explain the larger holistic processing effects found for SR than OR faces. Second, Rhodes and colleagues (2006) found a clear ORE for participants of two races tested with stimuli on which *strictly identical* variations of local features or relative distances between features were applied to SR and OR faces. If the ORE was entirely due to naturally differential diagnostic cues for different races, an experiment in which *the exact same variations* were created on a set of SR and OR stimuli should not have led to any ORE. This finding *cannot* be explained by an account of the ORE in terms of differentially diagnostic features across races. Indeed, why would one be more sensitive to featural/relational changes applied on SR than on OR faces if they are identical, and do not respect the normal variations of cues encountered in real life? In contrast, according to the EBH account, participants in that study did not perceive OR faces as holistically as SR faces because, irrespective of the fact that the exact same variations were diagnostic for SR and OR faces, OR faces did not fit well with the observer's holistic template, contrary to SR faces. Therefore, OR faces were not encoded and recognized well. Thus, while there are certainly different diagnostic cues for different races of faces, and this factor probably contributes to the ORE, it is not sufficient.

A more efficient processing of both local features and relative distances between them for SR faces

Since holistic/configural processing is applied to *all* kinds of information that is potentially diagnostic to individualize the face, the EBH account of the ORE is entirely compatible with the observation that one is less efficient at processing both the local features of OR faces *and* the relative distances between these features (see Hayward et al., 2008; Rhodes et al., 2006, 2009a). However, the EBH account makes an interesting prediction: since the perception of long-range relative distances between features may be the most vulnerable to a loss of holistic perception (Goffaux and Rossion, 2007; Rossion, 2008; 2009; Sekunova and Barton, 2008), if anything, the ORE could be larger when only long-range relative distances between features are manipulated (e.g. eyes-mouth distance) than when diagnostic cues which can be resolved locally (e.g. eyes color, eye-eyebrow distance) are modified. This would be particularly the case in conditions of uncertainty, i.e. when the observer is not told about the nature of the diagnostic cues in a given task (see Rossion, 2008, 2009).

OR faces more densely clustered than SR faces in face-space memory

Valentine (1991) provided an account of the ORE (among other effects) in terms of "face-space." A face would be uniquely represented as a point, or a vector, in a memory-space defined by a number of dimensions along which faces vary. Since the diagnostic facial dimensions would differ between different races, the dimensions of the face-space would be relevant mainly for SR faces. Therefore, OR faces would be more densely clustered in that space, and thus more confusable (Byatt and Rhodes, 2004; Valentine, 1991; Valentine and Endo, 1992). This account is clearly an experience-based account, in the sense that an observer would have developed sensitivity through experience to the different dimensions (i.e. interrelated group of features) characterizing SR faces.

The EBH account is largely compatible with this view, or at least the main aspects of it. The average (SR) face, or "norm," that is supposed to be the centre of the face-space (Valentine, 1991) would be used as a holistic template to perceive an individual face and encode it. The dense cluster of OR faces is merely a way of representing the fact that the aspects coded, i.e. the dimensions of the space (e.g. interocular distance, from small to large), or the range covered by these dimensions, may be inappropriate to encode an OR face (OR faces would thus be all out of range in the space). OR faces would be far from the average because they differ a lot from the template. However, there are a few aspects of Valentine (1991)'s proposal that would differ or need to be specified in an EBH account. First, according to Valentine (1991), the phenomenon essentially reflects a memory problem. However, according to the EBH account, perception and memory of individual faces cannot be disentangled: an internal representation is necessary to perceive the incoming face-stimulus in full: OR faces are *perceived and represented* less holistically than SR faces. Second, obviously, the dimensions that are used to encode a face must be interdependent in the EBH account. Third, the EBH account is more compatible with "norm-based" coding (Rhodes et al., 1987; Rhodes and Leopold, Chapter 14, this volume), i.e. a face being encoded as a vector in the face-space with reference to a central norm calculated as the "average" of the known population of faces, than with exemplar-based coding (Nosofsky, 1986).[2]

---

[2] With respect to this issue, recent studies have showed that opposite figural "adaptation aftereffects" (see Rhodes and Leopold, Chapter 14, this volume) can be induced simultaneously for faces of different races (Jaquet et al., 2007, 2008). These effects are often interpreted as evidence of different norms for faces of different races but we suspect that these experiments do not allow making such direct inferences about the

A perceptual phenomenon: neural measures

According to an EBH account, OR faces are *perceived* less holistically than SR faces. One should thus expect to observe a difference between SR and OR face coding at the level of visual areas of the human brain, in particular the areas of the cortical network that are sensitive to faces (see Haxby et al., 2000; Sergent et al., 1992). Consistent with this suggestion, it has been shown in functional magnetic resonance imaging (fMRI) studies that the "fusiform face area," an area which codes individual faces holistically (Schiltz and Rossion, 2006) responds less well to OR than SR faces (Golby et al., 2001). Note that rather than reflecting an intrinsically lower response to OR than SR faces in this area, these latter results most likely reflect a larger adaptation to facial identity for OR faces (since they all look more alike), which would lead to a decrease of fMRI signal due to adaptation (see Gauthier et al., 2000; Grill-Spector and Malach, 2001; see also the discussion of a related issue about face inversion in Mazard et al., 2006). According to the EBH account, OR faces, which are perceived less holistically, could however recruit part-based processes to a larger extent, perhaps recruiting more general object perception regions such as the lateral occipital cortex (LOC, Malach et al., 1995), as found for faces presented upside-down (e.g. Yovel and Kanwisher, 2005).

Event-related potential (ERP) recordings from the human scalp provide more direct evidence in favor of the perceptual basis of the ORE. The parameters (amplitude, latency, scalp topography) of the face-sensitive N170 component (Bentin et al., 1996; Eimer, Chapter 17, this volume), which is thought to reflect the earliest activation of face representations in the human brain (Rossion and Jacques, 2008), do not vary in a consistent way between OR and SR faces (e.g. Caldara et al., 2004; Ito and Urland, 2003; Stahl et al., 2008). However, most interestingly, there is recent evidence that the release from adaptation to face identity as observed on the N170 amplitude (Jacques et al., 2007) is larger for SR than OR faces (Vizioli et al., 2010). This latter finding supports the view that the ORE is based on a perceptual encoding of individual face representations. Interestingly, the same ERP adaptation paradigm applied with upright and inverted faces, as well as composite faces, indicates that the individual face is encoded holistically during the time range of the N170 (Jacques and Rossion, 2009; Jacques et al., 2007). Altogether, these observations support the EBH account of the ORE.

Summary and some implications

To summarize, we propose that the full percept of an individual SR face results from the matching between the face input and an internal generic holistic template, possibly an average face. This matching allows a simultaneous perception of the individual face's deviations from the template, which concern both local and global aspects of the face (e.g. bigger nose, thicker eyebrows, smaller interocular distance, smaller head shape than the template). Depending on its specific deviations, the face could be registered as a vector in a multidimensional space, defined by interdependent, relevant, dimensions. In contrast, an individual OR face cannot fit well with the holistic template because its morphology is beyond the range of morphologies generally encountered in the perceiver's environment. It could then be processed, at least relatively more, by means of analytic, general (i.e. non-face specific) visual recognition mechanisms.
Let us now briefly discuss a few implications of this proposal.

---

nature of face representation. Indeed, if different aftereffects for different races of faces imply different norms, then following this logic, one must also have different norms for upright and inverted faces (Rhodes et al., 2004), male and female faces (Little et al., 2005), or perhaps even different individual faces (Robbins and Heck, 2009).

First, this mode of coding could also account for related phenomena to the ORE, such as the "other-age effect," the reduced ability to recognize faces of another age group, differing substantially in morphology (the "all kids look alike effect"; e.g. Anastasi and Rhodes, 2005; Kuefner et al., 2008; Lamont et al., 2005). Interestingly, it has been recently shown that faces of another age-group are perceived less holistically than same-age faces, an effect which can be overturned only with extensive experience with another age group of faces (de Heering and Rossion, 2008; Kuefner et al., 2010).

Second, in this framework, there is only a *single* holistic template.[3] For a given observer, this template is relatively broadly or narrowly tuned to a specific morphology of faces, depending on his/her range of visual experience with faces. If it is finely tuned to SR faces only, OR faces will not be processed holistically. If it is broadly tuned, for instance for an observer who had visual experience with several races of faces, OR faces may also be processed holistically. Importantly, such a broad tuning would make the observer process SR faces *relatively* less holistically than another observer with a representation that is tuned to SR faces only. In other words, trade-offs of holistic effects between SR and OR faces should be observed. Interestingly, there is evidence for such trade-offs in the data of some recent studies that have investigated the other-age face effect. For instance, de Heering and Rossion (2008) found that adult preschool teachers (experts) processed children faces more holistically than adults without visual experience with child faces (novices). However, the data suggested a reverse effect for adult faces, with more holistic processing for child-face novices than experts (see also Kuefner et al., 2010). In the context of SR and OR faces, we predict a similar observation: observers who process OR faces more holistically following experience with OR faces, should process SR faces relatively less holistically than observers who have experience only with SR faces.

In the same vein, a third interesting prediction that can be made from the EBH account concerns observers who are exposed to multiple races of faces during development (e.g. Western European and sub-Saharan African faces). Because their holistic representation would be rather broadly tuned, they would handle more holistically faces of another race never encountered before (e.g. Eastern Asians) as compared to observers who have mainly been exposed to a single race of faces throughout their life.

Fourth, minimal experience may be sufficient to recalibrate the system temporarily (as shown by face adaptation studies; e.g. Webster and MacLin, 1999; Webster et al., 2004), and to be able to process a specific set of OR faces holistically (McKone et al., 2007). However extensive visual experience would be necessary to recalibrate the perceptual face system for the long term and for perceiving unfamiliar OR faces as holistically as SR faces (see de Heering and Rossion, 2008). What "extensive" exactly means cannot be assessed independently of the "quality" of experience, and of the age at which it is acquired. Another important factor to consider would be the degree of morphological difference between the visually experienced regime of faces and the new race of faces. If the latter differs substantially in morphology from the experienced race of faces, as would be the case for faces from another species, the system may take more time to recalibrate. Note also that, according to this view, the ORE would not only concern faces that present quite different morphologies, but should also be observed between different groups of a given human population, in relation to their morphological differences (e.g. Scandinavians and Mediterraneans within the Western European population; see Chiroro et al., 2008).

---

[3] At least for a given face view, without excluding the possibility of multiple viewpoint dependent representations in the system (Bruce and Young, 1986; Tarr, 1995).

Fifth, if the observer's holistic representation is broadly tuned, he/she may be able to distinguish an OR face from a SR face less efficiently and rapidly than an observer who has a holistic representation tuned only to SR faces. This is because, for the first observer, *both* SR and OR faces could be matched with the internal template and perceived holistically. In contrast, the second observer will categorize the OR face as belonging to another race more easily, since it will not even be encoded holistically. Thus, there may be an inverse relationship between the ability to individualize OR faces and to categorize these faces as OR faces. Interestingly, the "other-race advantage" observed in race-categorization tasks (i.e. the fact that people are generally faster at categorizing OR than SR faces along their race-dimension; e.g. Caldara et al., 2004; Levin, 1996, 2000; Valentine and Endo, 1992; Zhao and Bentin, 2008) might indeed be inversely related to the ORE in face identification tasks (Levin, 2000). Importantly, this observation can be accounted for by an experience-based holistic account of the ORE without the need to call upon an alternative sociocognitive explanation, to which we will turn in the next section.

Finally, according to this framework, the ability to perceive individual faces holistically is considered as *necessary* for efficient face recognition. Nevertheless, once the individual face has been encoded holistically, a wealth of detailed information, which can enrich its representation and consolidate it in memory, can be accumulated in the face recognition system. Hence, while being able to perceive faces holistically would be *necessary* for efficient face recognition (as shown indirectly by our inability to recognize inverted faces, or by the prosopagnosic patients' recognition difficulties), it is certainly not *sufficient*. It follows that the ability of the face processing system to perceive a face holistically may not be necessarily correlated with the accuracy of face memory in a population of normal individuals. For instance, even though their composite face effect was the largest for SR faces, Asian participants in the study of Michel et al. (2006a) showed holistic processing also for OR (Caucasian) faces. Nevertheless, these Asian participants still showed a substantial ORE as measured in an old/new face recognition task. Moreover, the differential composite effect for SR and OR faces in the study of Michel and colleagues (2006b) was not correlated with the amplitude of the ORE, neither for Asian nor Caucasian participants.

The sociocognitive account of the ORE: a brief critical review

According to the experience-based holistic account of the ORE, the nature of our face representation and processes would be *constrained* by our perceptual experience with different facial morphologies. That is, visual experience would fine-tune the system such that OR faces would be *perceived* less holistically. However, according to an alternative view, it is largely for social reasons that people are less accurate in recognizing OR faces. For instance, people would have prejudices towards members of another racial group, or would lack motivation/attention to encode OR faces, or would focus on the race of these faces at the expense of their individuality. This proposal is fairly old (see e.g. Berger, 1969; Galper, 1973) and has several variants, which have received much attention over the past few years (see e.g. Hugenberg et al., 2007; Levin, 2000; Sporer, 2001).

This sociocognitive account differs fundamentally from the EBH account because, according to the former, the face processing system would remain *broadly tuned*, and thus perfectly *able* in adulthood to deal with a wide variety of facial morphologies from different human populations (or even perhaps beyond human faces, see below). Thus, from a theoretical point of view, the fundamental difference between the sociocognitive and the EBH account is that the latter considers the ORE as a phenomenon occurring at the level of our internal face representation and processes, which are modified by experience and adaptive, whereas the former considers the ORE as a phenomenon that is largely independent from how we represent and process faces. Rather, the ORE would be due to the modulation of face recognition performance by social representations, motivation and/or attentional factors.

In terms of predictions, the difference between the sociocognitive and the EBH account of the ORE is that of a *capability*. According to the EBH account, a human adult observer with no visual experience with OR faces will have more difficulty individualizing these faces than SR faces, *all other factors* (motivation, attention, etc.) *being equal*. According to the sociocognitive account, i.e. if an observer is as motivated and attentive to OR as SR faces and has no prejudicial attitudes towards the OR faces, then he/she should be perfectly *able* to individualize these faces as efficiently as SR faces.

What about the evidence supporting the latter view? The sociocognitive view can in fact be divided into two variants that we will briefly review in turn.

Attention, motivation, and affective factors

The idea that people would not be *motivated* to encode the individualizing information on OR faces because of prejudiced racial attitudes (e.g. Berger, 1969; Galper, 1973) has not been supported (Brigham and Barkowitz, 1978; Ferguson et al., 2001; Lavrakas et al., 1976; Platz and Hosch, 1988; Slone et al., 2000). Chance and Goldstein (1981)'s proposal, according to which we would not be motivated to encode OR faces *deeply* (irrespective of our racial attitudes), or Malpass' (1990) view, according to which we would not *pay attention to* OR faces' particularities because we would not find it useful to do so, have been either dismissed (Burgess and Weaver, 2003; Devine and Malpass, 1985; see also Rhodes et al., 2009b) or not tested (e.g. Malpass' hypothesis).

However, several recent findings appear to support the sociocognitive account of the ORE. For instance, motivation to individualize OR faces induced by a verbal instruction, a positive emotional state, or a larger functional importance experimentally provided to SR and OR face-stimuli through an angry expression can reduce, or even eliminate, the ORE (Hugenberg et al., 2007; Johnson and Fredrickson, 2005; Ackerman et al., 2006, respectively). It has also been shown that a pattern of performance similar to the ORE (i.e. one group of faces being more accurately recognized than the other) can be reproduced if one arbitrary group of SR faces is considered as "in-group" and the other as "out-group" (Bernstein et al., 2007; MacLin and Malpass, 2001; Pauker et al., 2009; Shriver et al., 2008).

However, there are a number of issues with these studies and their interpretation. First, participants' differential visual experience with OR faces has not been controlled in any of the above-mentioned studies performed with SR and OR faces, except in that of Rhodes et al. (2009b) who did not observe a significant interaction between condition of encoding and face race.

Second, and more fundamentally, as mentioned above, according to the EBH account of the ORE, a human adult observer has more difficulty individualizing OR faces than SR faces, *all other factors* (motivation, attention, etc.) *being equal*. This account does not state that attentional, motivational, or more generally social factors do not play any role in face recognition memory. Obviously, they do (e.g. Hugenberg et al., Chapter 13, this volume). If, for reasons provided by the experimenter, an observer becomes *more* motivated to encode OR than SR faces, pays more attention to OR faces, associates these OR faces with particular emotional experiences, etc., he/she may indeed end up being able to recall OR faces equally well or even better than SR faces (see Hugenberg et al., 2007). However, this is an unfair comparison.

In the same vein, telling subjects of an experiment that some faces of a set belong to their own group is likely to increase the attention devoted to these particular faces. Hence, it is not surprising that subjects will recognize these "own group" faces better than the other faces of the set (see Shriver et al., 2008). It is unclear to us how this finding can be relevant for understanding the nature of the ORE.

To understand this issue better, let us make an analogy. It is well known that face recognition performance is massively affected by inversion of the stimulus (Yin, 1969). Even though the nature of the phenomenon is still debated, it is largely believed that upright and inverted faces are not encoded and perceived the same way. According to the most influential view of the face inversion effect, an inverted face cannot be encoded holistically (Farah et al., 1995; Galton, 1883; Rossion, 2008, 2009; Yin, 1969). Now, let us make the hypothesis that people are poor at recognizing inverted faces because of a lack of motivation and attention, or because they have stereotypes towards inverted faces. We design an experiment in which we ask people to encode upright and inverted faces, and ask them to pay particularly attention to the inverted faces "because it is well known that they are harder to recognize." It is likely that the inversion effect will be reduced in these conditions, just because people would pay much more attention to inverted than upright faces. Could we conclude that motivational and attentional factors explain why we perform poorly with inverted faces in general?

Focusing on race rather than individuality for OR faces

According to an old version of the sociocognitive account of the ORE (e.g. Sheperd, 1981), categorical race-specifying information would be more salient in OR than SR faces. Consequently, the observer would focus on this race-specifying information when processing OR faces ("It's a Chinese"), at the expense of individualizing information ("It's Fang"). Levin (1996, 2000; Levin and Angelone, 2001), provided the strongest evidence for this claim by adapting a visual search paradigm (Treisman and Souther, 1985), in which Caucasian observers detected an OR-target face (Sub-Saharan African) among SR distractor-faces more easily than the reverse (detecting a SR-target face among OR distractor faces). This finding is consistent with the "other-race advantage" observed in race-categorization tasks: observers categorize OR faces according to race faster than SR faces (Caldara et al., 2004; Levin, 1996, 2000; Valentine and Endo, 1992; Zhao and Bentin, 2008). Importantly, Levin (1996, 2000) showed that participants who do not present the ORE in an old/new face-recognition task do not show this OR advantage either in a visual search task, a race-categorization task, or both, suggesting that the two phenomena are linked.

However, Levin's (1996, 2000) observations have not always been replicated (see Chiao et al., 2006; Levin, 1996, sixth experiment), and the "OR advantage" observed in a discrimination task in his study conflicts with more recent results (Walker and Hewstone, 2006; Walker and Tanaka, 2003). Moreover, coding race-specifying information for both SR and OR faces does not reduce the ORE, contrary to Levin's hypothesis (Rhodes et al., 2009b). Finally, and most importantly, the OR advantage in a race-categorization task (Caldara et al., 2004; Levin, 1996, 2000; Valentine and Endo, 1992) and its inverted relationship to the ORE (SR advantage) in a face-recognition task (Levin, 1996, 2000) do not necessarily imply a sociocognitive explanation. In fact, as indicated at the end of the earlier section "Summary and some implications," this observation would be perfectly compatible with the EBH account outlined here: if the observer's holistic representation is broadly tuned, he/she may be able to distinguish an OR face from a SR face less efficiently and rapidly than an observer who has a holistic representation tuned only to SR faces. This is because, for the first observer, *both* SR and OR faces could be matched with the internal template and perceived holistically. In contrast, the second observer will categorize the OR face as belonging to another race more easily, since it will not even be encoded holistically.

In summary, it may well be that sociocognitive factors that are not concerned directly with the nature of our face representation, such as a reduced attention or motivation, or an overemphasis on race at the expense of individuality for OR faces, play a role in the poorer recognition performance for OR than SR faces observed in real life. However, the experimental evidence in favor of these factors is rather mixed and subject to caution. Moreover, we argue that these factors are certainly not at the heart of the ORE, which rather appears to concern the nature of our face perception mechanisms. We will try to illustrate this point by raising two final, and more general, issues regarding the sociocognitive as opposed to an experience-based holistic account of the ORE.

General issues

The assumption of a non-adaptive face recognition system, and the under-specification of the sociocognitive account

While the face of all modern humans (*Homo sapiens sapiens*) had the same (African) morphology before human populations came out of Africa and spread on the different continents, the human face and the body have, since then, truly evolved in sometimes dramatically different ways due to environmental pressures (heat, humidity, etc.; Ruff, 1994, 2002). According to the EBH account, the human face recognition system adapts to the regime of faces that one experiences, and becomes finely tuned to the characteristics of these particular faces. In contrast, the sociocognitive view of the ORE depicts a view of our face recognition system that would not have been very adaptive in human evolution: given that human populations have coevolved separately and that multiracial societies are recent, a face recognition system that would have maintained a broad tuning would have been less efficient. In fact, unless one considers that variations in morphology between different world populations are negligible, which is hardly the case (see earlier section "Variations between human populations in face structure and the concept of 'face race'"), there is no reason to expect that the face recognition system would have remained broadly tuned to accommodate all variations of human faces throughout human evolution over the past 100,000 to 200,000 years.

However, let us imagine for one second that the face recognition system remains, as hypothesized by the sociocognitive account of the ORE, broadly tuned. Where does this broad tuning stop? Why do we find it difficult to individualize faces of non-human primates for instance (e.g. Pascalis and Bachevalier, 1998)? Could it be because humans lack the necessary motivation, attention, or because they emphasize the species categorization at the expense of the individualization?

This point illustrates the underspecification of the sociocognitive account of the ORE. Many animal species have faces that resemble those of humans in their configuration (Bruce and Young, 1998). Yet, without extensive experience, humans find it difficult to individualize faces from another species, even of non-human primate faces (see figure 1 in Sergent, 1994; Pascalis and Bachevalier, 1998). It is difficult to believe that this difficulty would be due to social stereotypes or motivational factors, and that by increasing their motivation and positive feelings towards non-human primates or other animal species, humans would be able to discriminate these individuals from their face as well as human faces, without extensive experience training. Yet, this is exactly what would be predicted, in principle, by a sociocognitive account of such an "other-species face effect."

The relevance of studies testing the ORE in multiracial societies

Another important issue to consider is that many studies claiming to find effects supporting the sociocognitive account are performed in multiracial societies (e.g. North America, Australia). Even though this is understandable—researchers would like to clarify phenomena that are particularly relevant for the community they live in—the generalization of results from these studies to observers living in largely uniracial societies is debatable. Indeed, the tuning to faces with different morphologies is certainly broader in populations of multiracial societies in general than in populations who are exposed almost exclusively to one race of faces. Consequently, in multiracial societies, the ORE is likely to be relatively smaller, and may be eliminated more easily by training participants to individuate other-race faces (McKone et al., 2007; Tanaka and Pierce, 2009) or providing them with an extra-motivation to pay attention to other-race faces (Hugenberg et al., 2007) than in populations who are mainly exposed to a single race of faces. Hence, it may be relatively easy to get rid of the ORE in an experiment performed with participants coming from a multiracial society, and one should be careful in generalizing the outcome of such studies to populations who have never been exposed to OR faces.

Conclusion

In conclusion, given the arguments mentioned here, we very much doubt that sociocognitive factors are at the heart of the ORE phenomenon. To be clear, it is extremely important to acknowledge that motivational, attentional, and social factors in general may modulate face recognition performance, and thus may contribute to our difficulty in recognizing OR faces. However, we argue that what is truly at the heart of the phenomenon is the reduced ability to encode OR faces as holistically as SR faces, and that a full understanding of this robust and fascinating phenomenon will go a long way towards a clarification of the nature of our face representation and processes.

Summary and conclusions

There are important and clearly visible differences in terms of bone structure, defining shape, and skin reflectance (color and texture) between faces originating from different human populations of the world. In this chapter, we have reviewed the well-known phenomenon that people have greater difficulty distinguishing and recognizing individual faces from a different human population, or "race," than their own. We integrated a large corpus of data and previous proposals into an experience-based holistic (EBH) account of the ORE. According to this EBH account, an individual face is perceived in full when it matches a holistic representation, a template, derived from visual experience during development. This holistic representation, originally broadly tuned, is refined during development to become tuned to the morphological characteristics of the most common population of faces encountered. Consequently, in adulthood, the individual face belonging to another "racial" group cannot register well with the holistic template. The other-race (OR) face is thus not perceived as holistically as a same-race (SR) face, and is encoded in a more piecemeal, less efficient, fashion. The holistic template is plastic enough to become tuned to OR faces following a reversal of face race experience during childhood, and perhaps during adulthood following extensive experience. We suggest that the EBH account encompasses and extends most other proposals, such as a more densely clustered organization of OR faces in an internal face-space centered on a "norm," and it leads to a number of interesting predictions about the processing of SR and OR faces. In contrast, we argue that while motivational, attentional and sociocognitive factors in general may contribute to lower recognition performance for OR faces, they are not at the heart of the ORE, a phenomenon that is important for understanding the nature of face perception and representation.

Acknowledgements

We thank Gillian Rhodes for her careful reading of several previous versions of this chapter and her insightful comments. We also thank Kurt Hugenberg for his critical comments on a previous version of this chapter, which has been greatly improved thanks to these comments. The authors are supported by the Belgian National Fund for Scientific Research (FNRS).

References

Abdi, H., Valentin, D., Edelman, B., and O'Toole, A.J. (eds.) (1994). *Neural Networks and Biological Systems*. Special issue of *Journal of Biological Systems*, **2**(4).

Ackerman, J.M., Shapiro, J.R., Neuberg, S.L. *et al.* (2006). They all look the same to me (unless they're angry). *Psychological Science*, **17**, 836–840.

Altshuler, D., Brooks, L.D., Chakravarti, A., Collins, F.S., Daly, M.J., and Donnelly, P. (2005). A haplotype map of the human genome. *Nature*, **437**, 1299–1320.

Anastasi, J.S. and Rhodes, M.G. (2005) An own-age bias in face recognition for children and older adults. *Psychonomic Bulletin & Review*, **12**, 1043–1047.

Anthony, T., Copper, C., and Mullen, B. (1992). Cross-racial facial identification: A social cognitive integration. *Personality and Social Psychology Bulletin*, **18**, 296–301.

Bahrick, H.P., Bahrick, P.O., and Wittlinger, R. (1975). Fifty years on memory for names and faces: A cross-sectional approach. *Journal of Experimental Psychology: General*, **104**, 54–75.

Bentin, S., Allison, T., Puce, A., Perez, A., and McCarthy, G. (1996). Electrophysiological studies of face perception in humans. *Journal of Cognitive Neuroscience*, **8**, 551–565.

Berger, D.G. (1969). They all look alike. Unpublished doctoral dissertation, Vanderbilt University.

Bernstein, M.J., Young, S.G., and Hugenberg, K. (2007). The cross-category effect. Mere social categorization is sufficient to elicit an own-group bias in face recognition. *Psychological Science*, **18**, 706–712.

Bhatt, R.S., Bertin, E., Hayden, A., and Reed, A. (2005). Face processing in infancy: Developmental changes in the use of different kinds of relational information. *Child Development*, **76**, 169–181.

Blais, C., Jack, R.E., Scheepers, C., Fiset, D., and Caldara, R. (2008). Culture shapes how we look at faces. *PLoS ONE*, **3**(8): e3022.

Bodamer, J. (1947). Die-Prosop-agnosie. *Archive für Psychiatrie und Nervenkrankheiten*, **179**, 6–54. (English translation by Ellis, H.D. and Florence, M. (1990)). *Cognitive Neuropsychology*, **7**, 81–105.

Bothwell, R.K., Brigham, J.C., and Malpass, R.S. (1989). Cross-racial identification. *Personality and Social Psychology Bulletin*, **15**, 19–25.

Brigham, J.C. and Barkowitz, P. (1978). Do "They all look alike"? The effect of race, sex, experience, and attitudes on the ability to recognize faces. *Journal of Applied Psychology*, **8**, 306–318.

Brigham, J.C. and Ready, D.J. (1985). Own-race bias in lineup construction. *Law and Human Behavior*, **9**, 415–424.

Brigham, J.C. and Wolfskeil, M.P. (1983). Opinions of attorneys and law enforcement personnel on the accuracy of eyewitness identifications. *Law and Human Behavior*, **7**, 337–349.

Brigham, J.C., Maass, L.D., Snyder, L.D., and Spaulding, K. (1982). The accuracy of eyewitness in a field setting. *Journal of Personality and Social Psychology*, **442**, 673–678.

Brigham, J.C., Wasserman, A.W., and Meissner, C.A. (1999). Disrupted eyewitness identification evidence: Important legal and scientific issues. *Court Review, Summer* **99**, 12–25.

Bruce, V. and Young, A. (1986). Understanding face recognition. *British Journal of Psychology*, **77**, 305–327.

Bruce, V. and Young, A.W. (1998). *In the eye of the beholder: The science of face perception.* Oxford: Oxford University Press.

Burgess, M.C.R. and Weaver, G.E. (2003). Interest and attention in facial recognition. *Perceptual & Motor Skills,* **96**, 467–480.

Byatt, G. and Rhodes, G. (2004). Identification of own-race and other-race faces: Implications for the representation of race in face space. *Psychonomic Bulletin & Review,* **11**, 735–741.

Caldara, R., Rossion, B., Bovet, P., and Hauert, C.A. (2004). Event-related potentials and time course of the "other-race" face classification advantage. *NeuroReport,* **15**, 905–910.

Carey, S. (1992). Becoming a face expert. *Philosophical Transactions of the Royal Society of London: Series B. Biological Sciences,* **335**, 95–102.

Carey, S. and Diamond, R. (1994). Are faces perceived as configurations more by adults than by children? *Visual Cognition,* **1**, 253–274.

Cavalli-Sforza, L.L. and Cavalli-Sforza, F. (1994). *Qui sommes-nous? Une histoire de la diversité humaine.* Paris: Albin Michel.

Cavanagh, P. (1991). What's up in top-down processing? In A. Gorea (ed.) *Representations of Vision: Trends and Tacit Assumptions in Vision Research,* pp. 295–304. Cambridge: Cambridge University Press.

Chance, J. and Goldstein, A.G. (1981). Depth of processing in response to own- and other-race faces. *Personality and Social Psychology Bulletin,* **7**, 475–480.

Chance, J.E. and Goldstein, A.G. (1987). Retention interval and face recognition: Response latency measures. *Bulletin of the Psychonomic Society,* **25**, 415–418.

Chance, J., Goldstein, A.G., and McBride, L. (1975). Differential experience and recognition memory for faces. *Journal of Social Psychology,* **97**, 243–253.

Chiao, J.Y., Heck, H.E., Nakayama, K., and Ambady, N. (2006). Priming race in biracial observers affects visual search for black and white faces. *Psychological Science,* **17**, 387–392.

Chiroro, P. and Valentine, T. (1995). An investigation of the contact hypothesis of the ownrace bias in face recognition. *Quarterly Journal of Experimental Psychology: Human Experimental Psychology,* **48A**, 879–894.

Chiroro, P.M., Tredoux, C.G., Radaelli, S., and Meissner, C.A. (2008). Recognizing faces across continents: The effect of within-race variations on the own-race bias in face recognition. *Psychonomic Bulletin & Review,* **15**, 1089–1092.

Choe, K.S., Sclafani, A.P., Litner, J.A., Yu, G.P., and Romo, T. (2004). The Korean American woman's face. *Archives of Facial Plastic Surgery,* **6**, 244–252.

Cohen, L.B. and Cashon, C.H. (2001). Do 7-month-old infants process independent features or facial configurations? *Infant and Child Development,* **10**, 83–92.

Cross, J.F., Cross, J., and Daly, J. (1971). Sex, race, age, and beauty as factors in recognition of faces. *Perception & Psychophysics,* **10**, 393–396.

Darwin, C. (1871). *The Descent of Man and Selection in Relation to Sex.* London: John Murray.

Deffenbacher, K.A. and Loftus, E.F. (1982). Do jurors share a common understanding concerning eyewitness behavior? *Law and Human Behavior,* **6**, 15–30.

de Heering, A. and Rossion, B. (2008). Prolonged visual experience in adulthood modulates holistic face perception. *PLoS One,* **3(5)**: e2317.

de Heering, A., Houthuys, S., and Rossion, B. (2007). Holistic face processing is mature at 4 years of age: Evidence from the composite face effect. *Journal of Experimental Child Psychology,* **96**, 57–70.

de Heering, A., de Liederkerke, C., Deboni, M., and Rossion, B. (2010). The role of experience during childhood in shaping the other-race effect. *Developmental Science,* **13**, 181–187.

Devine, P.G. and Malpass, R.S. (1985). Orienting strategies in differential face recognition. *Personality and Social Psychology Bulletin,* **11**, 33–40.

Doty, N.D. (1998). The influence of nationality on the accuracy of face and voice recognition. *American Journal of Psychology,* **111**, 191–214.

Dunning, D., Li, J., and Malpass, R.S. (1998). Basketball fandom and cross-race identification among European-Americans: Another look at the contact hypothesis. Paper presented at the biennial conference of the American Psychology-Law Society, Redondo Beach, California.

Edwards, A.W.F. (2003). Human genetic diversity: Lewontin's fallacy. *BioEssays*, **25**, 798–801.

Ellis, H.D., Deregowski, J.B., and Sherperd, J.W. (1975). Description of white and black faces by white and black subjects. *American Journal of Psychology*, **10**, 119–123.

Ellis, H.D., Davies, G.M., and McMurran, M.M. (1979). Recall of white and black faces by white and black witnesses using the Photofit system. *Human Factors*, **21**, 55–59.

Fallshore, M. and Schooler, J.W. (1995). Verbal vulnerability of perceptual expertise. *Journal of Experimental Psychology: Learning, Memory, and Cognition*, **21**, 1608–1623.

Farah, M.J., Tanaka, J.W., and Drain, H.M. (1995). What causes the face inversion effect. *Journal of Experimental Psychology: Human Memory and Performance*, **21**, 628–634.

Farah, M.J., Wilson, K.D., Drain, M., and Tanaka, J. (1998). What is "special" about face perception? *Psychological Review*, **105**, 482–498.

Farkas, L.G. (1994). *Anthropometry of the Head and Face*. New York: Raven Press.

Feingold, C.A. (1914). The influence of the environment on identification of persons and things. *Journal of Criminal Law and Police Science*, **5**, 39–51.

Ferguson, D.P., Rhodes, G., Lee, K., and Sriram, N. (2001). "They all look alike to me." Prejudice and cross-race face recognition. *British Journal of Psychology*, **92**, 567–577.

Furl, N., Phillips, P.J., and O'Toole, A.J. (2002). Face recognition algorithms and the other-race effect: Computational mechanisms for a developmental contact hypothesis. *Cognitive Science*, **26**, 797–815.

Galper, R.E. (1973). "Functional race membership" and recognition of faces. *Perceptual & Motor Skills*, **37**, 455–462.

Galton, F. (1883). *Inquiries into human faculty and its development*. London: Macmillan.

Gauthier, I., Tarr, M.J., Moylan, J., Skudlarski, P., Gore, J.C., and Anderson, A.W. (2000). The fusiform face area is part of a network that processes faces at the individual level. *Journal of Cognitive Neuroscience*, **12**, 495–504.

Goffaux, V. and Rossion, B. (2006). Faces are "spatial"– Holistic face perception is supported by low spatial frequencies. *Journal of Experimental Psychology: Human Perception and Performance*, **32**, 1023–1039.

Goffaux, V. and Rossion, B. (2007). Face inversion disproportionately impairs the perception of vertical but not horizontal relations between features. *Journal of Experimental Psychology: Human Perception and Performance*, **33**, 995–1002.

Golby, A.J., Gabrieli, J.D., Chiao, J.Y., and Eberhardt, J.L. (2001). Differential responses in the fusiform region to same-race and other-race faces. *Nature Neuroscience*, **4**, 845–850.

Goldstein, A.G. and Chance, J.E. (1980). Memory for faces and schema theory. *Journal of Psychology*, **105**, 47–59.

Gregory, R.L. (1997). Knowledge in perception and illusion. *Philosophical Transactions of the Royal Society of London B*, **352**, 1121–1128.

Grill-Spector, K. and Malach, R. (2001). fMR-adaptation: A tool for studying the functional properties of human cortical neurons. *Acta Psychologica*, **107**, 293–321.

Hancock, K.J. and Rhodes, G. (2008). Contact, configural coding and the other-race effect in face recognition. *British Journal of Psychology*, **99**, 45–56.

Haxby, J.V., Hoffman, E.A., and Gobbini, M.I. (2000). The distributed human neural system for face perception. *Trends in Cognitive Sciences*, **4**, 223–233.

Hayward, W.G., Rhodes, G., and Schwaninger, A. (2008). An own-race advantage for components as well as configurations in face recognition. *Cognition*, **106**, 1017–1027.

Hill, H., Bruce, V., and Akamatsu, S. (1995). Perceiving the sex and race of faces: the role of shape and colour. *Proceedings. Biological sciences*, **261**, 367–373.

Hole, G.J. (1994). Configurational factors in the perception of unfamiliar faces. *Perception*, **23**, 65–74.

Homa, D., Haver, B., and Schwartz, T. (1976). Perceptibility of schematic face stimuli: Evidence for a perceptual Gestalt. *Memory & Cognition*, **4**, 176–185.

Hugenberg, K., Miller, J., and Claypool, H.M. (2007). Categorization and individuation in the cross-race recognition deficit: Toward a solution to an insidious problem. *Journal of Experimental Social Psychology*, **43**, 334–340.

Ito, T.A. and Urland, G.R. (2003). Race and gender on the brain: Electrocortical measures of attention to race and gender of multiply categorizable individuals. *Journal of Personality and Social Psychology*, **85**, 616–626.

Jacques, C. and Rossion, B. (2009). The initial representation of individual faces in the right occipito-temporal cortex is holistic: Electrophysiological evidence from the composite face illusion. *Journal of Vision*, **9**(6):8, 1–16.

Jacques, C., d'Arripe, O., and Rossion, B. (2007). The time course of the face inversion effect during individual face discrimination. *Journal of Vision*, **7**(8):3, 1–9.

Jaquet, E., Rhodes, G., and Hayward, W.G. (2007). Opposite aftereffects for Chinese and Caucasian faces are selective for social category information and not just physical face differences. *Quarterly Journal of Experimental Psychology*, **60**, 1457–1467.

Jaquet, E., Rhodes, G., and Hayward, W.G. (2008). Race-contingent aftereffects suggest distinct perceptual norms for different race faces. *Visual Cognition*, **16**, 734–753.

Johnson, K.J. and Fredrickson, B.L. (2005). "We all look the same to me." Positive emotions eliminate the own-race bias in face recognition. *Psychological Science*, **16**, 875–881.

Jorde, L.B. and Wooding, S.P. (2004). Genetic variation, classification and "race". *Nature Genetics*, **36**, S28–33.

Kassin, S.M., Ellsworth, P.C., and Smith, V.L. (1989). The general acceptance of psychological research on eyewitness testimony: A survey of the experts. *American Psychologist*, **46**, 1089–1098.

Katzmarzyk, P.T. and Leonard, W.R. (1998). Climatic influences on human body size and proportions: Ecological adaptations and secular trends. *American Journal of Physical Anthropology*, **106**, 483–503.

Kelly, D.J., Quinn, P.C., Slater, A.M., Lee, K., Ge, L., and Pascalis, O. (2007). The other-race effect develops during infancy. *Psychological Science*, **18**, 1084–1089.

Kirby, M. and Sirovich, L. (1990). Application of the Karhunen-Loeve procedure for the characterization of human faces. *IEEE Transactions of Pattern Analysis and Machine Intelligence*, **12**, 103–108.

Kuefner, D., Macchi Cassia, V., Picozzi, M., and Bricolo, E. (2008). Do all kids look alike? Evidence for an other-age effect in adults. *Journal of Experimental Psychology: Human Perception and Performance*, **34**, 811–817.

Kuefner, D., Macchi Cassia, V., Vescovo, E., and Picozzi, M. (2010). Natural experience acquired in adulthood enhances holistic processing of other-age faces. *Visual Cognition*, **18**, 11–25.

Lamont, A.C., Stewart-Williams, S., and Podd, J. (2005) Face recognition and aging: Effects of target age and memory load. *Memory & Cognition*, **33**, 1017–1024.

Lavrakas, P.J., Bun, J.R., and Mayzner, M.S. (1976). A perspective on the recognition of other race faces. *Perception & Psychophysics*, **20**, 475–481.

Le, T.T., Farkas, L.G., Ngim, R.C.K., Scott Levin, L., and Forrest, C.R. (2002). Proportionality in Asian and North American Caucasian faces using neoclassical facial canons as criteria. *Aesthetic Plastic Surgery*, **26**, 64–69.

Le Grand, R., Mondloch, C., Maurer, D., and Brent, H. (2004). Impairment in holistic face processing following early visual deprivation. *Psychological Science*, **15**, 762–768.

Levin, D.T. (1996). Classifying faces by race: The structure of face categories. *Journal of Experimental Psychology: Learning, Memory, and Cognition*, **22**, 1364–1382.

Levin, D.T. (2000). Race as a visual feature: Using visual search and perceptual discrimination tasks to understand face categories and the cross race recognition deficit. *Journal of Experimental Psychology: General*, **129**, 559–574.

Levin, D.T. and Angelone, B.L. (2001). Visual search for a socially defined feature: What causes the search asymmetry favoring cross-race faces? *Perception & Psychophysics*, **63**, 423–435.

Levine, D.N. and Calvanio, R. (1989). Prosopagnosia: A defect in visual configural processing. *Brain and Cognition*, **10**, 149–170

Lewontin, R.C. (1972) The apportionment of human diversity. In T. Dobzhansky, M.K. Hecht, and W.C. Steere (eds.) *Evolutionary Biology* 6, pp. 381–398. New York: Appleton-Century-Crofts.

Lindsay, D.S., Jack, P.C., and Christian, M.A. (1991). Other-race face perception. *Journal of Applied Psychology*, **76**, 587–589.

Lindsay, R.C.L. and Wells, G.L. (1983). What do we really know about cross-race eyewitness identification? In S. Lloyd-Bostock and B.R. Clifford (eds.) *Evaluating witness evidence: Recent psychological research and new perspectives*, pp. 219–233. Chichester: Wiley.

Little, T., DeBruine, L.M., and Jones, B.C. (2005). Sex-contingent face aftereffects suggest distinct neural populations code male and female faces. *Proceedings of the Royal Society of London B*, **272**, 2283–2287.

Luce, T.S. (1974). Blacks, whites and yellows: They all look alike to me. *Psychology Today*, **8**, 105–108.

MacLin, O.H. and Malpass, R.S. (2001). Racial categorization of faces. The ambiguous race face effect. *Psychology, Public Policy, and Law*, **7**, 98–118.

Malach, R., Reppas, J., Benson, R., *et al.* (1995). Object-related activity revealed by functional magnetic resonance imaging in the human occipital cortex. *Proceedings of the National Academy of Sciences USA*, **92**, 8135–8139.

Malpass, R.S. (1990). An excursion into utilitarian analysis, with side trips. *Behavior Science Research*, **24**, 1–5.

Malpass, R.S. and Kravitz, J. (1969). Recognition for faces of own and other race. *Journal of Personality and Social Psychology*, **13**, 330–334.

Malpass, R.S., Lavigueur, H., and Weldon, D.E. (1973). Verbal and visual training in face recognition. Perception and Psychophysics, **14**, 285–292.

Malpass, R.S., Erskine, D.M., and Vaughn, L.L. (1988). Matching own- and other- race faces. Paper presented at the annual meeting of the Eastern Psychological Association, Buffalo, New York.

Maurer, D., Le Grand, R., and Mondloch, C.J. (2002). The many faces of configural processing. *Trends in Cognitive Sciences*, **6**, 255–260.

Mazard, A., Schiltz, C., and Rossion, B. (2006). Recovery from adaptation to facial identity is larger for upright than inverted faces in the human occipito-temporal cortex. *Neuropsychologia*, **44**, 912–922.

McKone, E. (2004). Isolating the special component of face recognition: Peripheral identification and a Mooney face. *Journal of Experimental Psychology: Learning, Memory, and Cognition*, **30**, 181–197.

McKone, E., Brewer, J.L., MacPherson, S., Rhodes, G., and Hayward, W.G. (2007). Familiar other-race faces show normal holistic processing and are robust to perceptual stress. *Perception*, **36**, 224–248.

Meissner, C.A. and Brigham, J.C. (2001). Thirty years of investigating the own-race bias in memory for faces: A meta-analysis review. *Psychology, Public Policy, and Law*, **7**, 3–35.

Mermelstein, R., Banks, W., and Prinzmetal, W. (1979). Figural goodness effects in perceprtion and memory. *Perception & Psychophysics*, **26**, 472–480.

Michel, C., Caldara, R., and Rossion, B. (2006a). Same-race faces are perceived more holistically than other-race faces. *Visual Cognition*, **14**, 55–73.

Michel, C., Rossion, B., Han, J., Chung, C.H., and Caldara, R. (2006b). Holistic processing is finely tuned for faces of one's own race. *Psychological Science*, **17**, 608–615.

Michel, C., Corneille, O., and Rossion, B. (2007). Race-categorization modulates holistic face encoding. *Cognitive Science*, **31**, 911–924.

Michel, C., Corneille, O., and Rossion, B. (2010). Holistic face encoding is modulated by perceived face race: Evidence from perceptual adaptation. *Visual Cognition*, **18**, 434–455.

Nature Genetics (2004). *Genetics for the human race*, **36 (11s)**.

Murray, J.E., Yong, E., and Rhodes, G. (**2000**). Revisiting the perception of upside-down faces. *Psychological Science*, **11**, 498–502.

Murray, J.E., Rhodes, G., and Schuchinsky, M. (**2003**). When is a face not a face? The effects of Misorientation on Mechanisms of Face Perception. In M.A. Peterson and G. Rhodes (eds.) *Perception of Faces, Objects, and Scenes: Analytic and Holistic Processes*, pp. 75–91. Oxford: Oxford University Press.

Ng, W.J. and Lindsay, R.C.L. (1994). Cross-race facial recognition: Failure of the contact hypothesis. *Journal of Cross-Cultural Psychology*, **25**, 217–232.

Nosofsky, R.M. (1986). Attention, similarity, and the identification-categorization relationship. *Journal of Experimental Psychology: General*, **115**, 39–57.

O'Toole, A.J., Abdi, H., Deffenbacher, K.A., and Bartlett, J.C. (1991). Simulating the "other-race effect" as a problem in perceptual learning. *Connection Science*, **3**, 163–178.

O'Toole, A.J., Deffenbacher, K.A., Valentin, D., and Abdi, H. (1994). Structural aspects of face recognition and the other race effect. *Memory & Cognition*, **22**, 208–224.

O'Toole, A.J., Vetter, T., and Blanz, V. (1999). Two-dimensional reflectance and three-dimensional shape contributions to recognition of faces across viewpoint. *Vision Research*, **39**, 3145–3155.

Papesh, M.H. and Goldinger, S.D. (2009). Deficits in other-race face recognition: no evidence for encoding-based effects. *Canadian Journal of Experimental Psychology*, **63**, 253–262.

Pascalis, O. and Bachevalier, J. (1998). Face recognition in primates: a cross-species study. *Behavioural Processes*, **43**, 87–96.

Pauker, K., Weisbuch, M., Ambady, N., Sommers, S.R., Adams, R.B., and Ivcevic, Z. (2009). Not so black and white: Memory for ambiguous group members. *Journal of Personality and Social Psychology*, **96**, 795–810.

Pellicano, E. and Rhodes, G. (2003). Holistic processing of faces in preschool children and adults. *Psychological Science*, **14**, 618–622.

Peterson, M.A. and Rhodes, G. (eds.) (2003), *Perception of Faces, Objects, and Scenes: Analytic and Holistic Processes*. Oxford: Oxford University Press.

Platz, S.J. and Hosch, H.M. (1988). Cross-racial/ethnic eyewitness identification: A field study. *Journal of Applied Social Psychology*, **18**, 972–984.

Porter, J. (2004). The average African American male face. *Archives of Facial Plastic Surgery*, **6**, 78–81.

Porter, J. and Olson, K.L. (2001). Anthropometric facial analysis of the African American woman. *Archives of Facial Plastic Surgery*, **3**, 191–197.

Ramon, M., Busigny, T., and Rossion, B. (2010). Impaired holistic processing of unfamiliar individual faces in acquired prosopagnosia. *Neuropsychologia*, **48**, 933–944.

Richler, J.J., Gauthier, I., Wenger, M.J., and Palmeri, T.J. (2008). Holistic processing of faces: Perceptual and decisional components. *Journal of Experimental Psychology: Learning, Memory, and Cognition*, **34**, 328–342.

Rhodes, G. (1988). Looking at faces: First-order and second-order features as determinants of facial appearance. *Perception*, **17**, 43–63.

Rhodes, G., Brennan, S., and Carey, S. (1987). Identification and ratings of caricatures: Implications for mental representations of faces. *Cognitive Psychology*, **19**, 473–497.

Rhodes, G., Tan, S., Brake, S., and Taylor, K. (1989). Expertise and configural coding in face recognition. *British Journal of Psychology*, **80**, 313–331.

Rhodes, G., Jeffery, L., Watson, T.L., Jaquet, E., Winkler, C., and Clifford, C.W. (2004). Orientation-contingent face aftereffects and implications for face-coding mechanisms. *Current Biology*, **14**, 2119–223.

Rhodes, G., Hayward, W.G., and Winkler, C. (2006). Expert face coding: Configural and component coding of own-race and other-race faces. *Psychonomic Bulletin & Review*, **13**, 499–505.

Rhodes, G., Ewing, L., Hayward, W.G., Maurer, D., Mondloch, C.J., and Tanaka, J.W. (2009a). Contact and other-race effects in configural and component processing of faces. *British Journal of Psychology*, **100**, 717–723.

Rhodes, G., Locke, V., Ewing, L., and Evangelista, E. (2009b). Race coding and the other-race effect in face recognition. *Perception*, **38**, 232–241.

Risch, N., Burchard, E., Ziv, E., and Tang, H. (2002). Categorization of humans in biomedical research: Genes, race and disease. *Genome Biology*, **3**, comment2007.

Robbins, R. and Heck, P. (2009). Brad Pitt & Jude Law: Individual-contingent face aftereffects and norm-versus exemplar-based models of face-space. [Abstract]. *Journal of Vision*, **9**(8):516, 516a.

Rodin, M.J. (1987). Who is memorable to whom: A study of cognitive disregard. *Social Cognition*, **5**, 144–165.

Rosenberg, N.A., Pritchard, J.K., Weber, J.L., *et al.* (2002). Genetic structure of human populations. *Science*, **298**, 2381–2385.

Rossion, B. (2008). Picture-plane inversion leads to qualitative changes of face perception. *Acta Psychologica*, **128**, 274–289.

Rossion, B. (2009). Distinguishing the cause and consequence of face inversion: the perceptual field hypothesis. *Acta Psychologica*, **132**, 300–312.

Rossion, B. and Boremanse, A. (2008). Nonlinear relationship between holistic processing of individual faces and picture-plane rotation: Evidence from the face-composite illusion. *Journal of Vision*, **8**, 3.1–3.13.

Rossion, B. and Jacques, C. (2008). Does physical interstimulus variance account for early electrophysiological face sensitive responses in the human brain? Ten lessons on the N170. *NeuroImage*, **39**, 1959–1979.

Ruff, C.B. (1994). Morphological adaptation to climate in modern and fossil hominids. *Yearbook of Physical Anthropology*, **37**, 65–107.

Ruff, C. (2002). Variation in human body size and shape. *Annual Review of Anthropology*, **31**, 211–232.

Sangrigoli, S. and de Schonen, S. (2004). Effect of visual experience on face processing: A developmental study of inversion and non-native effects. *Developmental Science*, **7**, 74–87.

Sangrigoli, S., Pallier, C., Argenti, A.M., Venturevra, V.A.G., and de Schonen, S. (2004). Reversibility of the othe-race effect in face recognition during childhood. *Psychological Science*, **16**, 440–444.

Schiltz, C. and Rossion, B. (2006). Faces are represented holistically in the human occipito-temporal cortex. *NeuroImage*, **32**, 1385–1394.

Sekunova, A. and Barton, J.J. (2008). The effects of face inversion on the perception of long-range and local spatial relations in eye and mouth configuration. *Journal of experimental psychology: Human Perception and Performance*, **34**, 1129–135.

Sergent, J. (1984). An investigation into component and configural processes underlying face perception. *British Journal of Psychology*, **75**, 221–242.

Sergent, J. (1986). Microgenesis of face perception. In H.D. Ellis, M.A. Jeeves, F. Newcombe, and A.M. Young (eds.) *Aspects of face processing*, pp. 17–33. Dordrecht: Martinus Nijhoff.

Sergent, J. (1994). Cognitive and neural structures in face processing. In A. Kertesz, (ed.) *Localization and neuroimaging in neuropsychology*, pp. 473–494. San Diego, CA: Academic Press.

Sergent, J. and Villemure, J.G. (1989). Prosopagnosia in a right hemispherectomized patient. *Brain*, **112**, 975–995.

Sergent, J., Ohta, S., and MacDonald, B. (1992). Functional neuroanatomy of face and object processing. *A positron emission tomography study. Brain*, **115**, 15–36.

Shapiro, P.N. and Penrod, S. (1986). Meta-analysis of facial identification studies. *Psychological Bulletin*, **100**, 139–156.

Sheperd, J.W. (1981). Social factors in face recognition. In G. Davies, H. Ellis, and J.W. Sheperd (eds.) *Perceiving and Remembering Faces*, pp. 55–79. London: Academic Press.

Shepherd, J.W. and Deregowski, J.B. (1981). Races and faces–a comparison of the responses of Africans and Europeans to faces of the same and different races. *British Journal of Social Psychology*, **20**, 125–133.

Shriver, E., Young, S.G., Hugenberg, K., Bernstein, M.J., and Lanter, J. (2008). Outgroup contextual cues attenuate the own-race advantage in face recognition. *Personality and Social Psychology Bulletin*, **34**, 260–274.

Slone, A.E., Brigham, J.C., and Meissner, C.A. (2000). Social and cognitive factors affecting the own-race bias in Whites. *Basic and Applied Social Psychology*, **22**, 71–84.

Sporer, S.L. (2001). Recognizing faces of other ethnic groups - An integration of theories. *Psychology, Public Policy, and Law*, **7**, 36–97.

Stahl, J., Wiese, H., and Schweinberger, S.R. (2008). Expertise and own-race bias in face processing: An event-related potential study. *NeuroReport*, **19**, 583–587.

Suzuki, S. and Cavanagh, P. (1995). Facial organization blocks access to low-level features–an object inferiority effect. *Journal of Experimental Psychology: Human Perception and Performance*, **21**, 901–913.

Tanaka, J.W. and Farah, M. (1993). Parts and wholes in face recognition. *Quarterly Journal Of Experimental Psychology*, **46(A)**, 225–245.

Tanaka, J.W. and Farah, M. (2003). The holistic representation of faces. In Peterson, M.A. and Rhodes, G. (eds.) *Perception of Faces, Objects, and Scenes: Analytic and Holistic Processes*, pp.53–74. Oxford: Oxford University Press.

Tanaka, J.W. and Pierce, L.J. (2009). The neural plasticity of other-race face recognition. Journal of Cognitive and Behavioral Neuroscience, **9**, 122–131.

Tanaka, J.W. and Sengco, J.A. (1997). Features and their configuration in face recognition. *Memory & Cognition*, **25**, 583–592.

Tanaka, J.W., Kay, J.B., Grinell, E., Stansfield, B., and Szetchter, L. (1998). Face recognition in young children: When the whole is greater than the sum of its parts. *Visual Cognition*, **5**, 479–496.

Tanaka, J.W., Kiefer, M., and Bukach, C.M. (2004). A holistic account of the own-race effect in face recognition: Evidence from a cross-cultural study. *Cognition*, **93**, B1–B9.

Tarr, M.J. (1995). Rotating objects to recognize them: A case study of the role of viewpoint dependency in the recognition of three-dimensional objects. *Psychonomic Bulletin & Review*, **2**, 55–82.

Treisman, A. and Souther, J. (1985). Search asymmetry: A diagnostic for preattentive processing of separable features. *Journal of Experimental Psychology: General*, **114**, 285–310.

Turk, M. and Pentland, A. (1991). Eigenfaces for recognition. *Journal of Cognitive Neuroscience*, **3**, 71–86.

Valentine, T. (1991). A unified account of the effects of distinctiveness, inversion, and race in face recognition. *Quarterly Journal of Experimental Psychology*, **43A**, 161–204.

Valentine, T. and Bruce, V. (1986). The effect of race, inversion and encoding activity upon face recognition. *Acta Psychologica*, **61**, 259–273.

Valentine, T. and Endo, M. (1992). Towards an exemplar model of face processing: The effects of race and distinctiveness. *Quarterly Journal of Experimental Psychology*, **44A**, 671–703.

Vizioli, L., Rousselet, G., and Caldara, R. (2010). Neural repetition suppression to identity is abolished by other-race faces. *Proc Natl Acad Sci USA*, **107**(46), 20081–20086.

Walker, P.M. and Hewstone, M. (2006). A perceptual discrimination investigation of the own-race effect and intergroup experience. *Applied Cognitive Psychology*, **20**, 461–475.

Walker, P.M. and Tanaka, J.W. (2003). An encoding advantage for own-race versus other-race faces. *Perception*, **32**, 1117–1125.

Webster, M.A. and MacLin, O.H. (1999). Figural after-effects in the perception of faces. *Psychonomic Bulletin & Review*, **6**, 647–653.

Webster, M.A., Kaping, D., Mizokami, Y., and Duhamel, P. (2004). Adaptation to natural face categories, *Nature*, **428**, 557–56

Wenger, M.J. and Ingvalson, E.M. (2002). A decisional component of holistic encoding. *Journal of Experimental Psychology: Learning, Memory, and Cognition*, **28**, 872–892.

Witherspoon, D.J., Wooding, S., Rogers, A.R., *et al.* (2007). Genetic similarities within and between human populations. *Genetics.* **176**, 351–359.

Wright, D.B., Boyd, C.E., and Tredoux, C.G. (2003). Inter-racial contact and the own-race bias for face recognition in South Africa and England. *Applied Cognitive Psychology*, **17**, 365–373.

Yin, R.K. (1969). Looking at upside-down faces. *Journal of Experimental Psychology*, **81**, 141–145

Young, A.W., Hellawell, D., and Hay, D.C. (1987). Configurational information in face perception. *Perception*, **16**, 747–759.

Yovel, G. and Kanwisher, N. (2005). The neural basis of the behavioral face-inversion effect. *Current Biology*, **15**, 2256–2262.

Zhao, L. and Bentin, S. (2008). Own- and other-race categorization of faces by race, gender, and age. *Psychonomic Bulletin & Review*, **15**, 1093–1099.

Chapter 13

Social Categorization Influences Face Perception and Face Memory

Kurt Hugenberg, Steven G. Young, Donald F. Sacco, and Michael J. Bernstein

Introduction

Given the wealth of information communicated via the human face, it is perhaps no surprise that faces are central to our social cognition. Contained in the face is a vast body of social information, both fixed (e.g. race, sex, age, identity) and flexible (e.g. facial expressions; see Calder, Chapter 22, this volume; Haxby et al., 2000). For example, simply knowing an individual's category membership can yield powerful, if imperfect predictions as to their motives and future behaviors. Indeed, extensive research shows that such category-based predictions (i.e. stereotypes) can powerfully bias how we interpret our social world. For example, the race of a target can lead to the same behavior being interpreted differently. What appears to be a mere request among white children appears to be a dangerous threat when a black child is involved (e.g. Sagar and Schofield, 1980). What appears to be a harmless cell phone in the hand of a white person is commonly mistaken for a firearm when held by a black person (Correll et al., 2003; Payne, 2001).

Beyond such category-based biases in social judgment, recent evidence also suggests that social categorization affects face perception and face memory (Hugenberg and Sacco, 2008). In this chapter, we review this research at the juncture of social psychology and face perception showing the interplay between social categorization and face processing. We first lay out evidence indicating that social categories are extracted easily from faces, suggesting that the effects of social categories can occur quickly and unintentionally. Building on this, we next discuss recent evidence that social categories can affect perception of both invariant (e.g. facial structure) and variant (e.g. facial expression) facial characteristics. Finally, we summarize recent evidence indicating that the motivational consequences of social categories can affect which faces are remembered and how faces are processed.

Social categories are extracted quickly and easily from faces

The distinction between visually apparent social categories such as race, sex, and age can occur rapidly in the visual system (e.g. Ito and Urland, 2003; Mouchetant-Rostaing and Girard, 2003; Mouchetant-Rostaing et al., 2000). For example, Ito and Urland (2003) found that racial differences among target faces appear to elicit differential responses due to their low-level perceptual differences as early as 100ms after stimulus onset (N100), with sex-specifying distinctions eliciting differences as early as 200ms (P200). The race and sex of a stimulus face continued to have effects throughout the early cognitive stream (N200) and also on later event-related potentials (ERPs) associated with attention and working memory (P300), as well as on subsequent explicit evaluations of racial outgroups (Ito et al., 2004).

Importantly, behavioral research has also demonstrated the speed and ease with which categorical information can be extracted from faces. For example, social category information can be accurately processed even when face stimuli are presented under suboptimal viewing conditions such as visual noise or inversion. Extracting individual identity from these same stimuli under such difficult conditions, however, is often impaired and requires greater time and effort. To illustrate, Clouthier et al. (2005) found that when participants viewed inverted faces, reaction times to make target identity judgments were slowed to a greater degree than reaction times to make target sex category judgments. Clouthier et al. (2005) found similar results when faces were blurred or presented at very short exposure times. Additionally, this efficient extraction of category information has been shown to occur even when a face is not the focal stimulus, again highlighting how easily categorical information can be gathered from faces (Macrae et al., 2005).

Moreover, social categories can be activated even by subliminally presented faces. For example, Bargh et al. (1996, Exp. 3) had non-black American participants complete a visual task in which participants were unwittingly exposed to subliminal presentations of the faces of black or white males (13–26-ms presentation times). All participants were then exposed to a frustrating experience (a computer failure) and their average levels of hostility were surreptitiously observed. Simply observing subliminally-presented black faces during the visual task led participants to become more aggressive during the subsequent interaction with the experimenter. Bargh and colleagues argue that the mere presence of the black faces led to the activation of black-stereotypic concepts (such as hostility and aggression; see Devine, 1989), which then affected subsequent behavior. Although there are a handful of situations where the mere presence of a face will not activate a social category (see Macrae et al., 1997, 1999), social category activation is efficient and ubiquitous when attending to faces.

Social categories bias face perception

Across multiple lines of work, it seems clear that social categories are extracted quickly and easily from faces, apparently even more easily than facial identity (Clouthier et al., 2005). Moreover, the ease with which social categories can be extracted means that categorical effects on face processing can affect the perception of, interpretation of, and memory for faces (Hugenberg and Sacco, 2008). In short, social categories can elicit *assimilation*, pulling targets toward the category prototype (see Corneille et al., 2004). Below we discuss how both the perception of invariant features (e.g. facial structure, skin tone) and interpretations of malleable features (e.g. facial expressions) of faces can be biased by social categories.

Categories bias perception of facial characteristics

Recent studies provide provocative evidence suggesting that social categories, and in particular race categories, can influence the perception of facial characteristics. In an initial demonstration, MacLin and Malpass (2001, 2003) found evidence that social categories can influence the perception of a series of race-linked facial features. In what they dub the Ambiguous Race Illusion, MacLin and Malpass (2001) created a series of racially-ambiguous faces that were identical across facial features, but would be categorized as either black or Hispanic, depending on the target's hairstyle. Thus, the same target face appears black when drawn with a black-typical hairstyle, but appears Hispanic when drawn with a Hispanic-typical hairstyle. This minor manipulation of hairstyle affected participants' reports of the characteristics of the faces. Indeed, the same face drawn with a black-typical hairstyle was rated as more prototypical of black people (i.e. darker complexion, narrower face, deeper eyes, wider mouth) on Likert-type scales than the identical facial structure drawn with an Hispanic-typical hairstyle. MacLin and Malpass argue that merely changing a race-specifying cue external to facial features can change the perception of the facial features themselves.

Despite the strength of this initial demonstration, one possible alternate explanation for these effects is that they are judgmental rather than perceptual in nature. That is, perhaps participants reported that they saw darker skin tone on a target with black-typical hair due to a reporting bias. More recently, however, research from Levin and Banaji (2006) show a similar effect using perceptual judgments (rather than Likert-type scale ratings). In their experiments, they had participants adjust the lightness/darkness of a stimulus (a face or a patch of gray) to match the skin tone of a previously seen black or white target. For example, in their second experiment, participants were shown grayscale images of ambiguous-race black-white morphed targets on a computer, and were asked to adjust the lightness of a patch of gray pixels to match that of the target. Critically, Levin and Banaji manipulated the race of the ambiguous faces via labeling, with some participants believing the targets were black and others believing the same targets were white. On average, simply categorizing the same target as black led participants to choose a darker skin tone, as compared to when the target was categorized as white. Thus, by using a more perceptual measure, Levin and Banaji confirmed MacLin and Malpass' earlier conclusion that categories do appear to affect the perception of facial characteristics.

Categories bias perception of facial expressions (and vice versa)

Social categories can also affect how facial expressions are perceived and interpreted. First, social category membership can moderate the accuracy with which facial expressions are recognized. Although cross-cultural recognition of basic emotional expressions is universally above chance (Ekman and Friesen, 1971), recent evidence has revealed an ingroup emotion recognition advantage. For example, even among same-race faces, facial expressions displayed by members of one's own culture (e.g. white American) are more accurately decoded than are expressions displayed by members of another closely-related culture (e.g. white Australian; see Ambady and Weisbuch, Chapter 24, this volume, Elfenbein and Ambady, 2003). To explain these findings, Dialect Theory (Elfenbein and Ambady, 2002) posits that across cultures there are subtle, yet distinct differences in how discrete emotions are expressed, thereby adding local variations—analogous to dialects of a shared spoken language—to a universally shared non-verbal language. Thus, these local variations may cause relative difficulty recognizing cultural outgroup expressions of emotion.

More recently, however, Young and Hugenberg (2010) have found that even minimal ingroup/outgroup differences can elicit analogous results, even when holding the "dialect" of the emotion sender constant. Across four studies, white American participants were randomly assigned to an ingroup based on the results of a bogus personality inventory. For example, participants were assigned to "red" and "green" personality types, although were given no description of the personality type itself. Participants were then shown a series of faces displaying unambiguous facial expressions (e.g. anger, fear, happiness), displayed on red and green backgrounds. Critically, the colored background ostensibly indicated the personality type of the face displaying the expression. Results indicated that participants more accurately recognized the expressions on faces they believed were fellow ingroup members (i.e. shared "personality types"), as compared to outgroup members, even though all participants and all emotional face stimuli were from the same larger cultural ingroup (i.e. white Americans). Thus, how accurately expressions can be decoded appears to be subject to ingroup/outgroup social categorizations as well as dialect differences.

Social categories can also bias how ambiguous facial expressions are interpreted. For example, Hugenberg and Bodenhausen (2003) found that the race of a face (in concert with perceivers' prejudices) affected the perceived intensity of an expression. In one study, white Americans were shown movies of both black and white faces, matched for facial structure changing in facial expression from angry to happy. Participants responded when they observed the initial angry expression disappearing. Thus, participants responded to the offset of the angry expression. At each point in time in the angry-to-happy movies, the black and white targets were displaying identical expressions, the only difference being the skin tone and the hairstyle of the targets. Critically, anger was seen to linger for longer on the black as compared to the white faces, an effect that was strongest for perceivers high in implicit anti-black prejudice. Hostility is stereotypic of the social category "black" in the US (e.g. Devine, 1989). This stereotype appears to bias interpretations of the ambiguous facial expressions on black relative to white targets, and thus black targets were seen as threatening for longer than are identical white targets. Importantly, the category-expression relationship appears to be a bidirectional one. In other research (Hugenberg and Bodenhausen, 2004), white Americans saw a series of computer generated racially-ambiguous black/white faces, manipulated to display either anger or happiness. In this study, participants categorized these targets as either white or black. Replicating the anger–black link found in the previous research, the same ambiguous race face was categorized as black more frequently when it displayed an angry expression, relative to when it displayed a happy expression. As in the previous work, this effect was stronger for perceivers with stronger implicit anti-black prejudice. In this case, the expression on the face appears to have been used to disambiguate the race of otherwise ambiguous social targets.

These category-expression links are not unique to racial categories. Eagly and Mladinic (1989) have consistently found that although men and women are both judged favorably, women are reliably more positively evaluated than men overall, a phenomenon known as the "women are wonderful" effect. This female–positivity link reliably plays out in facial expression perception. For example, individuals interpret ambiguous facial expressions on men and women in manner consistent with social category membership. Hess and colleagues (1997) found that ambiguously happy faces are rated as happier when the faces are female as opposed to when they are male. Thus, the interpretation of the expression is assimilated to the evaluative associations typical of the sex category (see Plant et al., 2004 for a related finding). Moreover, happiness is recognized more quickly and more accurately on female as compared to male faces (Hugenberg and Sczesny, 2005), whereas anger is detected more quickly on male as compared to female faces (Becker et al., 2007).

Although part of these sex-expression effects may be due to top-down effects of the ubiquitous female–positivity stereotype (Eagly and Mladinic, 1989), the more specific female-happiness and male–anger links are due at least in part to bottom-up effects of the facial structural differences between female and male faces. On average, male and female faces differ on their babyfacedness; female faces, relative to male faces, have more babyfaced characteristics (e.g. small chin, large eyes). Importantly, babyfacedness affects both trait inferences and expression perception. Thus, individuals with more immature or "babyish" faces are not only believed to have more babyish personality traits (e.g. warm but incompetent; Berry and McArthur, 1985, 1986; Zebrowitz and Montepare, 1992), but are also judged to display more intense expressions that are typical of babies (e.g. supplication; see Sacco and Hugenberg, 2009) Because female faces have more baby-faced characteristics (e.g. large eyes) and male faces have more mature characteristics (e.g. small eyes), this facial structural difference facilitates the recognition of happy expressions on female and angry expressions on male faces, respectively (Becker et al., 2007; Marsh et al., 2005). Thus, the facial features that specify categories can act in a bottom-up manner, just as the categories themselves can act in a top-down manner (see Hugenberg and Bodenhausen, 2003 where structure was held constant), to influence the perception of facial expressions.

Finally, it appears that the category–expression relationship can also influence the perceptual discriminability of faces. In recent work, Corneille and colleagues (2007) created angry-to-happy morph continua separately for black faces and for white faces. Participants were then shown either identical pairs of faces from these continua or two subtly different faces from these continua, and were asked to determine if the faces were identical or slightly different. On trials where the facial expression matched the stereotype of the target social category, discrimination accuracy was greater than when the expression was counter-stereotypical of the target social group. That is, discrimination accuracy was maximized on trials where pairs of white targets were smiling (i.e. taken from the smiling end of the morph continuum), and when pairs of black targets were angry, as compared to when pairs of white targets were angry or black targets were smiling. Corneille and colleagues explain these effects using an attractor field model, arguing that the stereotypic expressions have smaller attractor basins in a multidimensional face space than do counterstereotypic expressions (i.e. the attractor basins cover less "space" in the multidimensional face space). These smaller attractor basins allow for more fine-grained perceptual distinctions among similar stimuli, but the weaker attractor basins lead to difficulty in subsequent memory. Thus, congruency or incongruency between expressions and the stereotypes of social categories can affect perceptual discriminability as well.

Taken together, this recent body of findings indicates that the perception and interpretation of both fixed (e.g. facial structure; skin tone) and flexible (e.g. facial expressions) facial characteristics is clearly influenced by social categorization. First, expectancies about categories bias the perception and interpretation of faces. For example, activating a social category leads both facial characteristics (skin tone; Levin and Banaji, 2006; MacLin and Malpass, 2003) and expressions (e.g. Hess et al., 1997; Hugenberg and Bodenhausen, 2003) to be interpreted as more typical of the category. Second, shared ingroup memberships also appear to improve the accuracy of expression recognition (see Ambady and Weisbuch, Chapter 24, this volume). Finally, categories and expressions can work together to affect perceptual discriminability (Corneille et al., 2007). Despite these recent advances, more evidence is needed to investigate the links between perceptual processes and the behavioral outcomes observed to understand where in the perception-to-response stream these phenomena occur. Nonetheless, the preliminary behavioral evidence seems clear; social categories bias the perception of both stable and flexible facial characteristics.

Social categories influence face memory

Not only do categories affect the perception of faces and facial expressions, but they also appear to play a potent role in face memory. One of the best known phenomena in this regard is the cross-race effect (CRE; known alternately as the own-race bias or other-race effect): recognition memory is reliably better for same-race (SR) compared to cross-race (CR) faces. This phenomenon has been reliably documented and shows a substantial effect size in both laboratory and applied settings (Meissner and Brigham, 2001). Perhaps more importantly the CRE also has substantial legal ramifications, with cross-race eyewitness misidentifications accounting for a troubling percentage of wrongful incarcerations (Schenk et al., 2003). Certainly, part of the culprit for the CRE is a lack of cross-race exposure (see Rossion and Michel, Chapter 12, this volume). De facto segregation in even ostensibly multicultural societies means that many perceivers may have weak expertise with CR faces, debilitating recognition (Rhodes et al., 1989). Beyond these deficits in perceptual expertise, however, it appears that the sequelae of social categorization also have a direct and sometimes debilitating effect on face recognition as well. Indeed, social categorization itself appears to affect face memory, with targets being assimilated to the category prototype, thereby reducing subsequent recognition (e.g. Corneille et al., 2004; Young et al., 2009). More than that, the motivational effects of social categorization can also be quite potent, with members of outgroups eliciting less attention and encoding (e.g. Rodin, 1987).

Thus, it appears that both weak expertise and social categorization conspire in many real-world instances to create the robust CRE in face memory (see Hugenberg et al., 2010). Next, we briefly describe how social categories can affect face memory, and finally discuss multiple mechanisms that have been proposed whereby social categories may affect face processing.

Categories can bias the memory of faces toward face prototypes

As discussed above, social categories can affect the perception of facial features; ambiguous race faces categorized as "Black" were seen as having darker skin tone than when categorized as "white" (Levin and Banaji, 2006) or "Hispanic" (MacLin and Malpass, 2001, 2003). Remarkably, this perceptual effect also appears to affect face memory as well. MacLin and Malpass (2001) found that manipulating the race of the face using non-facial characteristics (i.e. hairstyle) creates a CRE, even when holding the structure of the facial features constant. In their work, Hispanic participants recognized faces better when the same facial structure was drawn with a Hispanic-typical hairstyle than when drawn with a black-typical hairstyle. According to MacLin and Malpass (2001, 2003), categorizing a face as an ingroup member appeared to improve face memory. Thus, this study provided preliminary evidence consistent with the argument that the effects of social categorization may also play out in subsequent face memory. However, because this research manipulated the target stimuli to manipulate categorization, these effects are not definitively due to categorization.

More recently, Corneille et al. (2004) provided evidence that more directly addressed the relationship between social categories and perceptions of prototypicality. In this research, Corneille and colleagues (2004) found that memory for a face is biased in the direction of the racial category prototype. Specifically, they showed participants Asian–white morphed faces, with either a preponderance of white-prototypic (70% white/30% Asian) or a preponderance of Asian-prototypic (30% white/70% Asian) features. During a later recognition phase, participants were then shown a series of five faces from the same Asian–white morph continuum, and decide which of those five faces had been previously seen. Critically, the five faces participants selected from always included the target face (e.g. 70% Asian) and four distracters. Two of the distracters were always more prototypic of the target's category (e.g. an 80% and a 90% Asian morph) and the other two distracters were always less prototypic of the target's category (e.g. a 50% Asian and a 60% Asian morph). Corneille and colleagues found that face memory was distorted in the direction of the category prototype. Thus, when participants originally saw a 70% Asian face, perceivers most commonly selected faces that were more prototypically Asian (i.e. the 80% or 90% Asian version of the face). In short, participants remembered faces as being more racially prototypic than they actually were. More recently, Huart et al. (2005) showed that similar memory distortions were caused by sex categorization, as well. Taken together, these data indicate that simply categorizing a target (e.g. by race or sex) can lead it to be assimilated to the category, affecting memory.

Similarly, we have found that this categorical assimilation can affect face memory for even high-expertise SR faces: making the race category for SR faces salient reduces SR recognition (Young et al., 2009). The salience of a racial identity or category is situationally dependent (Tajfel and Turner, 1979). Thus, most white people in the US do not spontaneously think of themselves or other SR faces as white, unless the situation dictates otherwise (the "white male norm"; Stroessner, 1996). One common context that does elicit strong salience of the SR category is interracial contexts. Simply being in the context of people of other races can make one's own race salient. Therefore, we manipulated whether white participants saw SR faces in the context of CR faces (black targets) or not. Across two studies we found that the mere presence of CR targets significantly reduces SR recognition. Although not all means of manipulating category salience appear equally powerful in creating such memory reductions for SR faces (see Rhodes et al., 2009), it does appear that the mere presence of CR faces is sufficient to reduce SR recognition. In a conceptually analogous line of work, Wilson and Hugenberg (2010) manipulated the perceived inter-group context of SR and CR targets via a paragraph read in a task prior to face encoding. In this experiment, some white American participants read that Hispanic migration to the US was creating a multicultural context that would ostensibly become omnipresent in the US in the near future, whereas other participants read a control paragraph unrelated to race. Again, the belief that whites and Hispanics would be in close contact in the near future reduced SR recognition. Thus, even for high-expertise SR faces, it seems that categorizing the group by race reduces the accuracy of face recognition.

Categories can affect motivation for individuation

Beyond the potential assimilative effects of social categories (e.g. Corneille et al., 2004), social categories can have a potent influence on the motivation with which faces are processed. For example, social psychologists have long recognized that many of the effects of spontaneous categorization can be overcome with motivated individuation (Brewer, 1988; Fiske and Neuberg, 1990). Critically, stereotypes of social categories include beliefs about outcome dependency or personal utility (Malpass, 1990). That is, some people and some categories are simply believed to be of low personal relevance. Consequently, members of many outgroups (especially low-status outgroups) may elicit little if any processing resources (Rodin, 1987). Indeed, many individuals we encounter on a daily basis may only be encoded at the category level if deemed to be of low personal relevance, whereas faces believed to be of high relevance may be encoded quite well even after only a fleeting encounter. Therefore, the faces of the elderly cashier and the teenage bagger in the grocery store this morning may be difficult to remember, but the face of the new dean seen only once in the school newspaper may remain etched in one's mind. Some categories signify that a target's identity is important (e.g. ingroups, powerful figures), whereas others signify that the target's individual identity seems irrelevant. Thus, categories can differentially motivate individuation (i.e. encoding characteristics of faces that distinguish among category members). This differential individuation motivation plays out in face memory.

As one example of this, ingroup/outgroup differences in face memory occur for groups well beyond race. Although it has received less empirical investigation, a cross-sex effect in face memory has been observed, with superior face memory for own-sex relative to cross-sex targets (e.g. Cross et al., 1971; Wright and Sladden, 2003). Similarly, cross-age effects have also been observed (e.g. Rodin, 1987; Wright and Stroud, 2002). More recently, Rule et al. (2007) have even shown a cross-sexual orientation effects. In this study, Rule and colleagues presented homosexual and heterosexual participants with a series of (unlabeled) homosexual and heterosexual faces. Not only could participants accurately extract the sexual orientation of the faces at substantially above chance levels, but that ingroup/outgroup categorization affects face memory. Targets of one's own sexual orientation were better recognized than were targets in the outgroup (i.e. of the other orientation).

Importantly, even mere ingroup/outgroup distinctions, when holding constant the actual faces and a priori expertise with the categories, appears to generate identical effects. In one such demonstration, Bernstein et al. (2007) manipulated the apparent ingroup/outgroup status of faces. In the first study, white Miami University students engaged in a face memory task with only SR targets. Importantly, all SR faces appeared on either a red or green background, manipulated on a within-subjects basis. For half the participants, these background colors were given no explanation. The remaining participants were instructed that the colors were indicative of university affiliation (red for the ingroup university (Miami University), green for the outgroup university (Marshall University, Miami's perennial football rival)). Whereas control participants showed no effect of background color on face memory, participants who believed the background was indicative of an ingroup/outgroup distinction showed both a decrement in recognition for outgroup faces and an increase in ingroup face recognition. The mere presence of ingroup/out-group category labels elicited a CRE-like phenomenon, even though counterbalancing proce-dures held the a priori expertise with the faces constant. A follow-up study was conducted using a minimal-group style manipulation of personality types, identical to that described above (Young and Hugenberg, 2010) led to analogous effects; ingroup members were recognized better than outgroup members, even holding the faces themselves constant via counterbalancing.

More recently, Shriver and colleagues (2008) showed that the socioeconomic status of targets was also sufficient to elicit similar ingroup/outgroup effects for SR faces. In this work, upper-income white participants were shown both SR (white) and CR (black) targets on different back-grounds, some indicating wealth (e.g. a well-appointed boardroom) with others indicating poverty (e.g. dilapidated housing). Thus, some SR targets were believed to be relatively well-off, while oth-ers were presented as quite poor. Replicating Bernstein et al. (2007), these beliefs about the socio-economic status of the SR targets affected recognition. Recognition of impoverished SR faces (i.e. whites shown in impoverished contexts) was significantly weaker than "wealthy" SR targets. Further, this decrement in SR recognition was powerful, reducing recognition for impoverished SR faces to the level of CR recognition. Thus, even SR faces may be poorly recognized when the SR targets belong to subjectively "unimportant" categories (e.g. low socioeconomic status).

Recent work by Pauker and colleagues (2009) shows an analogous effect using racially ambigu-ous faces. In this work, white and black American participants were presented with white, black, and racially ambiguous faces in a face memory task. In the US, race is determined by a *hypodescent* (or "one drop" rule; see Peery and Bodenhausen, 2008). As such, racially ambiguous faces are commonly categorized as black rather than white. In line with this, not only did white and black participants show the common CRE for the unambiguous white and black faces, but black par-ticipants recognized the ambiguous faces as well as SR (black) faces, but white participants recog-nized them as poorly as CR (black) faces. In a follow-up study, Pauker and colleagues manipulated whether participants were motivated to include the ambiguous targets in the racial ingroup. This inclusion manipulation changed the categorization of the ambiguous faces, thus changing face memory. When the same ambiguous targets were categorized as ingroup members, face memory was as good as SR face memory. When those same ambiguous targets were categorized as out-group members, face memory dropped to CR levels. Similar to Bernstein and colleagues (2007), these data clearly indicate that merely including a target as an ingroup member is sufficient to powerfully modulate face memory.

Taken together, these results provide clear evidence that social categories can differentially motivate individuation; the members' identities of some categories (e.g. ingroups) simply seem more important to encode than members of other groups (e.g. outgroups, the poor). However, these motives to individuate can come from multiple sources. Although categories are one such source, the behaviors, the characteristics, or even the facial expressions of the targets can create the motive to individuate CR faces. Critically, regardless of the source, increasing motivation to individuate appears to improve face recognition, even for outgroup targets with which perceivers commonly lack expertise (e.g. CR faces).

For example, Hugenberg et al. (2007) have shown that motivating perceivers to attend to the individuating characteristics of CR faces can eliminate the CRE via an increase in CR recognition.

In this set of studies, white Americans engaged in face encoding and recognition tasks. However, some participants were informed, before encoding, about the CRE and given explicit instructions to "pay close attention to what differentiates one particular face from another face of the same race, especially when that face is not" an SR face. Across three studies, these instructions were sufficient to eliminate the CRE via an increase in CR recognition without affecting SR recognition. Thus, inducing perceivers to attend to individuating characteristics of CR faces appears to substantially improve CR recognition, in this case eliminating the CRE (see Rhodes et al., 2009 for a replication using a white Australian population).

Beyond heavy-handed instructions, simply making CR targets powerful also appears to have similar effects. For example, longstanding power differentials can motivate strong face encoding. Wright et al. (2003) found that black South Africans showed a reversed CRE, a *same-race recognition deficit*, such that CR white faces were better recognized than SR black faces. Wright and colleagues (2003) suggested that the historical distribution of power in South Africa may explain this unusual finding. Although black people constitute an overwhelming majority of South Africans, until recently South Africa was an apartheid state wherein the majority black population suffered from institutional discrimination perpetrated by the minority white population.

More recently, Ackerman and colleagues (2006) have shown that anger, another means of demonstrating power, is also sufficient to substantially improve face memory. In this research, white Americans were shown neutral and angry SR (white) and CR (black) faces. They reliably found that whereas neutral expression faces showed the typical CRE, the angry CR faces were as well recognized or even *better* recognized than were the SR faces. In our own lab, we have also found direct experimental evidence that powerful CR targets are very well recognized (Shriver and Hugenberg, 2010). In this work, participants encoded both SR and CR faces, which were paired with behaviors implying either physical power (e.g. violence), social power (e.g. wealth), or behaviors that did not imply power. Power is one of the most potent means of signaling importance, and powerful others are commonly processed in detail (Fiske, 1993). In line with the findings of Wright and colleagues and Ackerman and colleagues, both physically and socially powerful CR targets (i.e. violent or wealthy) were remembered just as well as SR targets, eliminating the CRE. Low power CR targets, however, were poorly recognized as usual. In short, whereas the CRE was observed for low power targets, it was eliminated via an increase in CR recognition among high power targets.

Taken together, this research shows that social categories can serve as signals to individuate faces. Members of certain social categories tend to elicit more individuation; both long-standing category differences, and mere minimal-group style ingroup/outgroup distinctions appear sufficient to elicit potent biases in face memory. Similarly, faces that are believed to be important, whether ingroup members or powerful outgroup members, are relatively well recognized compared with faces believed to be unimportant, such as members of outgroups, and the disenfranchised. Importantly, however, it seems clear that individuation motives resulting outside of social categories can influence face memory as well. Even simply being motivated to attend to the individuating characteristics of CR targets appears sufficient to improve CR recognition, eliminating the commonly-observed CRE.

Social categories influence face processing

Finally, research from multiple theoretical perspectives offers evidence that social categories can affect how faces are processed. Above, we have discussed one mechanism by which the CRE can be elicited: quantitatively more processing of SR and CR targets. Beyond this quantitative difference, there also appears to be good evidence that SR and CR targets are processed qualitatively differently. Indeed, it appears that the additional motivation elicited by ingroups or powerful targets may do more than simply elicit more processing. Rather, it may lead perceivers to process using qualitatively different mechanisms. We discuss two perspectives on this possibility: race-coding and holistic processing. Both propose differences in the processing of SR and CR targets, both have been proposed as mechanisms for the CRE, and both have been shown to be affected by social categorization.

First, Levin's (1996, 2000) race-coding model proposes that features within same-race and cross-race faces are attended to differently. From this perspective, people pay attention to the unique, identity-specifying characteristics in SR faces. Thus, perceivers attend to characteristics of SR faces that distinguish them from other faces (i.e. individuating characteristics), which facilitates subsequent recognition. However, in cross-race faces people instead attend to category-specifying characteristics. Thus, for CR faces, perceivers attend to characteristics that are shared by members of the category, rather than to characteristics that are unique to that individual, leading to difficulty in subsequent recognition. Levin provides some support for this model. First, CR targets are categorized by race more quickly, and found more easily in visual displays, than are SR targets, suggesting strong levels of category activation. Moreover, this categorization advantage for CR targets appears linked to the CRE, with those who show a CRE also showing the CR categorization advantage. Hugenberg and colleagues' (2007) demonstration that inducing perceivers to attend to the individuating characteristics of CR targets improves CR recognition could also be interpreted as support for this perspective. More recently, Ge and colleagues (2009) found that the speed advantage for cross-race categorization is correlated with the speed disadvantage for cross-race recognition, which is consistent with the hypothesis that categorical information competes with identifying information when processing faces. Relatedly, Quinn and colleagues have found that face individuation appears antagonistic to face categorization, with strongly individuated exemplars inhibiting category activation (Quinn et al., 2009, 2010). Thus, from this perspective, differential processing of SR and CR targets is about differentially attending to category or individuating characteristics during face encoding.

However, despite this supporting evidence, other research has failed to support this race-coding hypothesis. First, although some researchers have found evidence for a categorization (e.g. Caldara et al., 2004; Levin, 1996, 2000) and search advantage for CR faces (Levin, 1996, 2000), other research has failed to find such evidence for either the categorization (Lipp et al., 2009; Stroessner, 1996; Zarate and Smith, 1990) or the search advantage (Chaio et al., 2006), indicating that task or perceiver characteristics can modulate these effects. Second, whether there is a functional tradeoff between categorization and individuation is also a matter of some debate. On one hand, Ge and colleagues (2009) find a negative correlation between categorization speed and recognition speed, Quinn and colleagues (2009; 2010) find that individuation inhibits categorization, and Young and colleagues (2009) find that enhancing the salience of the SR category reduces SR recognition. On the other hand, Rhodes et al. (2009) recently reported evidence that attention to race specifying characteristics (i.e. categorization) was unrelated to face memory. Thus, the extent to which the strength of category activation affects processing from the perspective of the race-coding model is still a matter for some debate.

An alternative position is that SR and CR faces elicit differential *configural* processing, or the encoding of the relative positions of features across the face as a whole. Although a full review of the literature on configural processing is beyond the scope of this article (see McKone and Robbins, Chapter 9; Rossion and Michel, Chapter 12; Tanaka and Gordon, Chapter 10, this volume), it does appear that SR faces do typically elicit superior configural processing, relative to CR faces (but see Hayward et al., 2008 and Rhodes et al., 2006 for similar effects on feature processing). For example, inverting faces, a manipulation known to reduce configural processing, has stronger effects for SR than CR faces (Rhodes et al., 1989; see also Hancock and Rhodes, 2008). Similarly, Michel and colleagues (2006) used the face composite paradigm to show that SR faces are processed more holistically (i.e. perceptually integrated into a "gestalt") than are CR faces, another procedural hallmark of configural processing. In this paradigm, perceivers tend to perceive identical top halves of two face stimuli as being different when they are aligned with different bottom halves. Simply replacing the bottom half of one face with a different bottom half creates a different gestalt, making the top half appear different. However, the gestalt effect is disrupted when the top and bottom halves of the faces are misaligned (laterally offset). Using this paradigm, Michel and colleagues found that this composite-face effect was larger for SR than CR faces (see also Tanaka et al., 2004), indicating stronger holistic processing of SR than CR faces.

However, although holistic processing is commonly attributed to differential expertise with SR and CR faces, it appears that social categorization also affects the extent to which stimuli are processed holistically. For example, Michel et al. (2007) used the face composite paradigm to show that ambiguous race faces are more likely to be processed holistically when believed to be SR than CR. In this work, merely categorizing an ambiguous race face as SR increased holistic processing, relative to categorizing it as CR. Michel and colleagues (2010) have also replicated this finding using a face adaptation paradigm. Here, ambiguous race faces were processed more holistically when adapted with a cross-race face than when adapted with a same-race face, presumably because of their race categorization. Again using the face composite paradigm, research indicates that even the holistic processing of SR faces is subject to ingroup/outgroup social categorizations (Hugenberg and Corneille, 2009). In this case, SR faces believed to belong to an ingroup (i.e. fellow university students) were processed more holistically than were SR faces believed to belong to an outgroup (i.e. a competing university). Although face memory was not tested, these categorization findings suggest a process whereby mere social categorization may contribute to deficits in face memory, even holding perceptual expertise constant (see Bernstein et al., 2007; Shriver et al., 2008; Young et al., 2010). More research is certainly needed to clarify this plausible, but untested link. Importantly, these latter results may be important in that they indicate that the holistic processing commonly observed for SR faces may be surprisingly fragile. Insofar as holistic processing is resource dependent (Palermo and Rhodes, 2002; for an alternate view, see Boutet et al., 2002) it may be reserved only for situations in which there is sufficient motivation; such as motivation elicited by a shared ingroup membership.

Finally, it is also the case that there is some uncertainty in the literature as to whether configural (or holistic) encoding itself empirically predicts the CRE. In one recent study, Michel and colleagues (2006) found that SR faces were better recognized than CR faces (i.e. showed the CRE), and SR faces were processed more holistically than CR faces, but that these two phenomena were unrelated (i.e. holistic processing did not predict the CRE). However, other recent research has found that the greater configural processing of SR relative to CR faces does predict the CRE (see Hancock and Rhodes, 2008). Thus, although the extent to which configural (or holistic) encoding reliably predicts the CRE is a matter for additional research, there is clear evidence from multiple perspectives that social categorization can affect the mechanisms whereby faces are processed.

Future research and open questions

Although research from multiple laboratories has shown how social categorization affects face processing, this work is by no means complete. Indeed, a number of exciting research questions remain. One key question is the time course of categorical effects on face processing. That is, when do the effects of social categories emerge in the perception-through-memory stream? In our own lab, we have found that the effects of social categories on face memory act during the encoding rather than during the recognition stage (Young et al., 2010). However, this is still a very rough distinction, with face encoding involving a number of distinct processes.

A second issue that remains important to address is how the effects of categorization on face processing summarized herein would play out across different social category distinctions. Indeed, much of our own work has focused on the racial distinctions between blacks and whites using white American participants. Would similar phenomena occur across racial groups or across cultures? To a great extent this is still an open question, but we hypothesize that the basic phenomena would still occur, although they will likely take different forms in different situations. Take, for example, our findings for ingroup advantages in face processing and memory. In this research, we find that white American participants become better at SR face recognition (Bernstein et al., 2007; Shriver et al., 2008), better at SR expression recognition (Young and Hugenberg, 2010), and show enhanced holistic processing of SR faces (Hugenberg and Corneille, 2009) when they believe those SR faces belong to their own ingroup, relative to an outgroup. In this case, we have no reason to believe that this same phenomenon would not occur cross culturally. However, what ingroups and outgroups may induce these effects are certainly culturally defined. Whereas university affiliations and personality differences may seem important to our participant population, other populations may be more sensitive to other culturally specific ingroup/outgroup distinctions. Thus, although we predict ingroup/outgroup distinctions are likely to affect face processing, expression recognition, and face memory in many different contexts, which ingroup/outgroup distinctions are subjectively important enough to elicit these effects will likely differ for different populations of people.

In another case, consider our recent findings that target power influences CR face recognition (Shriver and Hugenberg, 2010), such that powerful CR targets are as well recognized as are SR targets. In the US, black persons are stereotypically low in status, whereas white persons are commonly seen as at the top of the power and status hierarchy (e.g. Thomas and Hughes 1986). Thus, for our white American participants, the increase in target power affects CR but not SR targets. Would increasing CR power necessarily increase CR recognition in all cultures and in all situations? We think not. For example, South African black people show a *cross-race* (white) recognition advantage (Wright et al., 2003), likely in part because black South Africans have until recently been subjected to the institutionalized low power situation of apartheid. Thus for black South African participants, increasing CR (white) power would likely have little effect on CR recognition, because white people are already chronically high in power. Instead, if increasing South African black people's perception of SR (black) power would likely increase SR recognition. Thus, the effects of target power on face memory are likely dependent on the local context, and who typically holds power.

Similarly, in other research we have found that warning participants about the CRE and instructing them to individuate CR faces improves CR recognition and eliminates the CRE (Hugenberg et al., 2007). Would this phenomenon occur in all cultures and across contexts? Perhaps not. Although this phenomenon has been conceptually replicated using a white Australian population (see Rhodes et al., 2009), both such populations are parts of multicultural societies in which they are exposed to many CR faces in popular media and in person. Perhaps this latent ability to successfully eliminate the CRE via individuation of CR faces is due to the *simultaneous* combination of sufficient prior experience with CR faces and sufficient motivation at the time of encoding. Alternately, it is plausible that individuation motivation alone, even without extensive prior expertise with CR faces may be sufficient. Thus, it is an open question as to whether motivation to individuate will have an effect (or as large of an effect) for target groups with which perceivers have little exposure (highly unfamiliar racial groups; greebles, see Gauthier and Tarr, 1997). Research in our own laboratory is currently investigating this exciting possibility of interactions between perceiver expertise and motivations on face memory.

That said, it seems clear that many participant populations in which the CRE is investigated involve multiethnic societies that involve everyday exposure to both SR and CR faces (e.g. black-white in the US, Turkish-white in Germany, white-Chinese in Hong Kong), yet this substantial exposure to CR faces alone appears insufficient to eliminate the CRE. Moreover, this fact is important to understand if one's interest in the CRE stems from difficulties in eyewitness misidentification (Sporer, 2001) or the potential for social harm stemming from CR confusions (Doyle, 2001). Fortunately, that individuation motives can improve CR recognition (e.g. Hugenberg et al., 2007; Rhodes et al., 2009) suggests that the multiethnic societies within which such misidentifications are most likely (because of high frequency inter-racial contact) are exactly the same societies whose citizens likely have sufficient experience with CR faces to eliminate the CRE when sufficiently motivated to do so.

From our perspective, the hypothesis that the same basic phenomena (ingroup/outgroup distinctions affecting face processing; social categories affecting facial expression perception; etc.) will play out differently in different cultural contexts is one of the exciting implications of this social cognitive perspective on face processing and face memory. However, just because the phenomena have different manifestations in different social contexts does not undermine the power of social categories to affect face processing.

Summary and conclusions

Across multiple lines of converging evidence it has become increasingly clear that face processing is subject to one of the most potent and best understood of social cognitive phenomena: social categorization. Social category information is extracted quickly and efficiently from faces, and social categories have potent effects on how people process and respond to faces. From stable facial characteristics to expressions, from encoding through memory, longstanding social categories, such as race, sex, age, and even mere ingroup/outgroup distinctions, can have potent effects on face perception and face memory. Although more research is certainly needed to clarify the nature and boundaries of these effects, we believe that this recent spate of evidence can both inform our theories of face processing and can also provide a fertile ground in which social cognition and cognitive science can work together to yield a complete perspective on that most social of stimuli: the human face.

Acknowledgments

Preparation of this manuscript was supported by National Science Foundation grants BCS-0642525 and BCS-0951463, awarded to KH.

References

Ackerman, J.M., Shapiro, J.R., Neuberg, S.L., *et al.* (2006). They all look the same to me (unless they're angry): From out-group homogeneity to out-group heterogeneity. *Psychological Science*, **17**, 836–840.

Becker, D.V., Kenrick, D.T., Neuberg, S.L., Blackwell, K.C., and Smith, D.M. (2007). The confounded nature of angry men and happy women. *Journal of Personality and Social Psychology*, **92**, 179–190.

Bernstein, M.J., Young, S.G., and Hugenberg, K. (2007). The cross-category effect: Mere social categorization is sufficient to elicit an own-group bias in face recognition. *Psychological Science*, **18**, 706–712.

Berry, D.S. and McArthur, L.Z. (1985). Some components and consequences of a babyish face. *Journal of Personality and Social Psychology*, **48**, 312–323.

Berry, D.S. and McArthur, L.Z. (1986). Perceiving character in faces: The impact of age-related craniofacial changes on social perception. *Psychological Bulletin*, **15**, 266–279.

Boutet, I., Gentes-Hawn, A., and Chaudhuri, A. (2002). The influence of attention on holistic face encoding. *Cognition*, **84**, 321–341.

Brewer, M.B. (1988). A dual process model of impression formation. In R.S. Wyer and T.K. Srull (eds.) *Advances in social cognition* (Vol. 1, pp. 1–36). Hillsdale, NJ: Erlbaum.

Caldara, R., Rossion, B., Bovet, P., and Hauert, C.A. (2004). Event-related potentials and time course of the "other-race" face classification advantage. *NeuroReport*, **15**, 905–910.

Clouthier, J., Mason, M.F., and Macrea, C.N. (2005). The perceptual determinants of person construal: Re-opening the social cognitive toolbox. *Journal of Personality and Social Psychology*, **88**, 885–894.

Corneille, O., Huart, J., Becquart, E., and Brédart, S. (2004). When memory shifts towards more typical category exemplars: Accentuation effects in the recollection of ethnically ambiguous faces. *Journal of Personality and Social Psychology*, **86**, 236–250.

Corneille, O., Hugenberg, K., and Potter, T. (2007) Applying the attractor field model to social cognition: perceptual discrimination is facilitated but memory is impaired for faces displaying evaluatively-congruent expressions. *Journal of Personality and Social Psychology*, **93**, 335–352.

Correll, J., Park, B., Judd, C.M., and Wittenbrink, B. (2003). The police officer's dilemma: Using ethnicity to disambiguate potentially threatening individuals. *Journal of Personality and Social Psychology*, **83**, 1314–*1329*.

Cross, J.F., Cross, J., and Daly, J. (1971). Sex, race, age, and beauty as factors in recognition of faces. *Perception and Psychophysics*, **10**, 393–396.

Devine, P.G. (1989). Stereotypes and prejudice: Their automatic and controlled components. *Journal of Personality and Social Psychology*, **56**, 5–18.

Doyle, J.M. (2001). Discounting the error costs: Cross-racial false alarms in the culture of contemporary criminal justice. *Psychology, Public Policy, and Law*, 7, 253–262.

Eagly, A.H. and Mladinic, A. (1989). Gender stereotypes and attitudes toward women and men. *Personality and Social Psychology Bulletin*, **15**, 543–558.

Elfenbein, H.A. and Ambady, N. (2002). On the universality and cultural specificity of emotion recognition: A meta-analysis. *Psychological Bulletin*, **128**, 203–235.

Elfenbein, H.A. and Ambady, N. (2003). When familiarity breeds accuracy: Cultural exposure and facial emotion recognition. *Journal of Personality and Social Psychology*, **85**, 276–290.

Ekman, P. and Friesen, V. (1971). Constants across cultures in the face and emotion. *Journal of Personality and Social Psychology*, **17**, 124–129.

Fiske, S.T. (1993). Controlling other people: The impact of power on stereotyping. *American Psychologist*, **48**, 621–628.

Fiske, S.T. and Neuberg, S.L. (1990). A continuum model of impression formation: From category-based to individuating processes as a function of information, motivation, and attention. In M. P. Zanna (Ed.), *Advances in experimental social psychology*, Vol. 23, pp. 1–74. New York, NY: Academic Press.

Gaulthier, I. and Tarr, M.J. (1997). Becoming a "Greeble" expert: Exploring mechanisms for face recognition. *Vision Research*, **37**, 1673–1682.

Ge, L, Zhang, H., Wang, Z., *et al.* (2009). Two faces of the other-race effect: Recognition and categorisation of Caucasian and Chinese faces. *Perception*, **38**, 1199–1210.

Hancock, K.J. and Rhodes, G. (2008). Contact, configural coding and the other-race effect in face recognition. *British Journal of Psychology*, **99**, 45–56.

Haxby J., Hoffman, E., and Gobbini, M. (2000). The distributed human neural system for face perception. *Trends in Cognitive Sciences*, **4**, 223–233.

Hayward, W.G., Rhodes, G., and Schwaninger, A. (2008). An own-race advanteage for components as well as configurations in face recognition. *Cognition*, **106**, 1017–1027.

Hess, U., Blairy, S., and Kleck, R.E. (1997). The intensity of emotional facial expressions and decoding accuracy. *Journal of Nonverbal Behavior*, **21**, 241–257.

Huart, J., Corneille, O., and Becquart, E. (2005). Face-based categorization, context-based categorization, and distortions in the recollection of gender ambiguous faces. *Journal of Experimental Social Psychology*, **41**, 598–608.

Hugenberg, K., Young, S.G., Bernstein, M.J., and Sacco, D.F. (2010). The Categorization-Individuation Model: An integrative account of the cross race recognition deficit. *Psychological Review*, **117**, 1168–1187.

Hugenberg, K. and Bodenhausen, G.V. (2003). Facing prejudice: Implicit prejudice and the perception of facial threat. *Psychological Science*, **14**, 640–643.

Hugenberg, K. and Bodenhausen, G.V. (2004). Ambiguity in social categorization: The role of prejudice and facial affect in face categorization. *Psychological Science*, **15**, 342–345.

Hugenberg, K. and Corneille, O. (2009). Holistic processing is tuned for in-group faces. *Cognitive Science*, **33**, 1173–1181.

Hugenberg, K., Miller, J., and Claypool, H. (2007). Categorization and individuation in the Cross-Race Recognition Deficit: Toward a solution to an insidious problem. *Journal of Experimental Social Psychology*, **43**, 334–340.

Hugenberg, K. and Sacco, D.F. (2008). Social categorization and stereotyping: How social categorization biases person perception and face memory. *Social and Personality Psychology Compass*, **2**, 1052–1072.

Hugenberg, K. and Sczesny, S. (2005). On wonderful women and seeing smiles: Social categorization moderates the happy face response latency advantage. *Social Cognition*, **24**, 516–539.

Ito, T.A. and Urland, G.R. (2003). Race and gender on the brain: electrocortical measures of attention to race and gender of multiply categorizable individuals. *Journal of Personality and Social Psychology*, **85**, 616–26.

Ito, T.A., Thompson, E., and Cacioppo, J.T. (2004). Tracking the timecourse of social perception: the effects of racial cues on event related brain potentials. *Personality and Social Psychology Bulletin*, **30**, 1267–80.

Levin, D.T. (1996). Classifying faces by race: The structure of face categories. *Journal of Experimental Psychology: Learning, Memory, and Cognition*, **22**, 1364–1382.

Levin, D.T. (2000). Race as a visual feature: Using visual search and perceptual discrimination tasks to understand face categories and the cross-race recognition deficit. *Journal of Experimental Psychology: General*, **129**, 559–574.

Levin, D.T. and Banaji, M.R. (2006). Distortions in the perceived lightness of faces: The role of race categories. *Journal of Experimental Psychology: General*, **135**, 501–512.

Lipp, O.V., Terry, D.J., Smith, J.R., Tellegen, C.L., Kuebbeler, J., and Newey, M. (2009). Searching for differences in race: Is there evidence for preferential detection of other-race faces? *Emotion*, **9**, 350–360.

MacLin, O.H. and Malpass, R.S. (2001). Racial categorization of faces: The ambiguous race face effect. *Psychology, Public Policy, and Law*, **7**, 98–118.

MacLin, O.H. and Malpass, R.S. (2003). The ambiguous-race face illusion. *Perception*, **32**, 249—252.

Macrae, C.N., Bodenhausen, G.V., Milne, A.B., and Calvini, G. (1999). Seeing more than we can know: Visual attention and category activation. *Journal of Experimental Social Psychology*, **35**, 590–602.

Macrae, C.N., Bodenhausen, G.V., Milne, A.B., Thorn, T.M.J., and Castelli, L. (1997). On the activation of social stereotypes: The moderating role of processing objectives. *Journal of Experimental Social Psychology*, **33**, 471–489.

Macrae, C.N., Quinn, K.A., Mason, M.F., and Quadflieg, S. (2005). Understanding others: The face and person construal. *Journal of Personality and Social Psychology*, **89**, 686–695.

Malpass, R.S. (1990). An excursion into utilitarian analysis. *Behavior Science Research*, **24**, 1–15.

Marsh, A.A., Adams, Jr. R.B., Kleck, R.E. (2005). Why do fear and anger look the way they do? Form and social function in facial expressions. *Personality and Social Psychology Bulletin*, **31**, 73–86.

Meissner, C.A. and Brigham, J.C. (2001). Thirty years of investigating the own-race bias in memory for faces: A meta-analytic review. *Psychology, Public Policy, and Law*, **7**, 3–35.

Michel, C., Corneille, O., and Rossion, B. (2007). Race categorization modulates holistic face encoding. *Cognitive Science*, **31**, 911–924.

Michel, C., Corneille, O., and Rossion, B. (2010). Holistic face encoding is modulated by perceived face race: Evidence from perceptual adaptation. *Visual Cognition*, **18**, 434–455.

Michel, C., Rossion, B., Han, J., Chung, C.H., and Caldara, R. (2006). Holistic processing is finely tuned for faces of one's own race. *Psychological Science*, **17**, 608–615.

Mouchetant-Rostaing, Y. and Girard, M.H. (2003). Electrophysiological correlates of age and gender perception on human faces. *Journal of Cognitive Neuroscience*, **15**, 900–910.

Mouchetant-Rostaing, Y., Girard, M.H., Bentin, S., Aguera, P.E., and Pernier, J. (2000). Neurophysiological correlates of face gender processing in humans. *European Journal of Neuroscience*, **12**, 303–310.

Palermo, R. and Rhodes, G. (2002). The influence of divided attention on holistic face perception. Cognition, **82**, 225–257.

Pauker, K., Weisbuch, M., Ambady, N., Sommers, S.R., Adams, R.B., and Ivcevic, Z. (2009). Not so black and white: Memory for ambiguous group members. *Journal of Personality and Social Psychology*, **96**, 795–810.

Payne, B.K. (2001). Prejudice and perception: The role of automatic and controlled processes in misperceiving a weapon. *Journal of Personality and Social Psychology*, **81**, 181–192.

Peery, D. and Bodenhausen, G.V. (2008). Black + white = black: Hypodescent in reflexive categorization of racially ambiguous faces. *Psychological Science*, **19**, 973–977.

Plant, E.A., Kling, K.C., and Smith, G.L. (2004). The influence of gender and social role on the interpretation of facial expressions. *Sex Roles*, **51**, 187–196.

Quinn, K.A., Mason, M.F., and Macrae, C.N. (2009). Familiarity and person construal: Individuating knowledge moderates the automaticity of category activation. *European Journal of Social Psychology*, **39**, 852–861.

Quinn, K.A., Mason, M.F., and Macrae, C.N. (2010). When Arnold is "The Terminator," we no longer see him as a man: The temporal determinants of person perception. *Experimental Psychology*, **57**, 27–35.

Rodin, M.J. (1987). Who is memorable to whom: A study of cognitive disregard. *Social Cognition*, **5**, 144–165.

Rhodes, G., Brake, S., Taylor, K., and Tan, S. (1989). Expertise and configural coding in face recognition. *British Journal of Psychology*, **80**, 313–331.

Rhodes, G., Hayward, W.G., and Winkler, C. (2006). Expert face coding: Configural and component coding of own-race and other-race faces. *Psychonomic Bulletin & Review*, **13**, 499–505.

Rhodes, G., Locke, V., Ewing, L., and Evangelista, E. (2009). Race coding and the other-race effect in face recognition. *Perception*, **38**, 232–241.

Sacco, D.F. and Hugenberg, K. (2009). The look of fear and anger: Facial maturity modulates recognition of fearful and angry expressions. *Emotion*, **9**, 39–49.

Sagar, H.A. and Schofield, J.W. (1980). Racial and behavioral cues in black and white children's perceptions of ambiguously aggressive acts. *Journal of Personality and Social Psychology*, **39**, 590–598.

Shriver, E.R. and Hugenberg, K. (2010). Power, individuation, and the cross-race recognition deficit. *Journal of Experimental Social Psychology*, **46**, 767–774.

Shriver, E.R., Young, S.G., Hugenberg, K., Bernstein, M.J., and Lanter, J.R. (2008). Class, race, and the face: Social context modulates the cross-race effect in face recognition. *Personality and Social Psychology Bulletin*, **34**, 260–274.

Sporer, S.L. (2001). The cross-race effect: Beyond recognition of faces in the laboratory. *Psychology, Public Policy, and Law*, **7**, 36–97.

Stroessner, S.J. (1996). Social categorization by race or by sex: Effects of perceived non-normalcy on response times. *Social Cognition*, **14**, 247–276.

Tanaka, J.W., Kiefer, M., and Bukach, C.M. (2004). A holistic account of the own-race effect in face recognition: Evidence from a cross-cultural study. *Cognition*, **93**, B1–B9.

Tajfel, H. and Turner, J.C. (1979). An integrative theory of intergroup conflict. In W.G. Austin and S. Worchel (eds.) *The social psychology of intergroup relations*, pp. 33–47. Monterey, CA: Brooks/cole.

Thomas, M.E. and Hughes, M. (1986). The continuing significance of race: A study of race, class, and quality of life in America, 1972–1985. *American Sociological Review*, **51**, 830–841.

Wilson, J.P. and Hugenberg, K. (2010). When under threat, we all look the same: Distinctiveness threat induces in group homogeneity in face memory. *Journal of Experimental Social Psychology*, **46**, 1004–1010.

Wright, D.B. and Sladden, B. (2003). An own gender bias and the importance of hair in face recognition. *Acta Psychologica*, **114**, 101–114.

Wright, D.B. and Stroud, J.N. (2002). Age differences in lineup identification accuracy: People are better with their own age. *Law and Human Behavior*, **26**, 641–654.

Wright, D.B., Boyd, C.E., and Tredoux, C.G. (2003). Inter-racial contact and the own-race bias for face recognition in South Africa and England. *Applied Cognitive Psychology*, **17**, 365–373.

Young, S.G. and Hugenberg, K. (2010). Mere social categorization modulates identification of facial expressions of emotion. *Journal of Personality and Social Psychology*, **99**, 964–977.

Young, S.G., Hugenberg, K., Bernstein, M.J., and Sacco, D.F. (2009). Inter-racial contexts debilitate same-race face recognition. *Journal of Experimental Social Psychology*, **45**, 1123–1126.

Young, S.G., Bernstein, M.J., and Hugenberg, K. (2010). When do own-group biases in face recognition occur? Encoding versus recognition. *Social Cognition*, **28**, 240–250.

Zarate, M.A. and Smith, E.R. (1990). Social categorization and stereotyping. *Social Cognition*, **8**, 161–185.

Zebrowitz, L.A. and Montepare, J.M. (1992). Impressions of babyish faced individuals across the life span. *Developmental Psychology*, **28**, 1143–1152.

Chapter 14

Adaptive Norm-Based Coding of Face Identity

Gillian Rhodes and David A. Leopold[1]

Introduction

Faces convey a wealth of information that guides our social interactions. At a glance we can assess a person's identity, gender, ethnicity, age, attractiveness, emotional state, and focus of attention. This fluency, however, belies the difficulty of the underlying perceptual discriminations. Consider the problem of determining someone's identity. The first-order configural properties of the internal facial features are the same in all people, a pair of eyes above a midline nose and mouth, and cannot serve as a basis for recognition. Moreover, changes in viewing perspective, illumination, and emotional expression mean that the brain must extract the identity of a particular face from very different retinal images. Facial appearance also changes with age, health, and cosmetic decisions affecting skin color as well as facial and head hair. Yet somehow the brain is able to see past shared structure, dynamic deformations, and irrelevant image variation, to focus on subtle details that distinguish one face from another. A central goal of face perception research is to understand how this is done.

In this chapter we will argue that the brain takes an efficient approach to this problem, using prior knowledge about the structure of faces in its analysis. Specifically, it employs intrinsic, learned reference points, called *norms*, to focus on subtle variations in the shared face configuration (sometimes called second-order, relational properties) that differentiate one face from another. We will review evidence that the brain uses multiple norms to extract face identity, that these norms are shaped by visual experience, and that norm-based coding is well-suited to meeting the challenges of image-based face perception mentioned above. By encoding faces with reference to stored perceptual norms the visual system can focus on what is unique to each individual, allowing us to discriminate and remember thousands of faces despite their similarity as visual patterns (Bahrick et al., 1975). We refer to this representational system as "adaptive" because it tailors itself to the diet of faces experienced in order to code the identity of a face.

Adaptation and aftereffects

Adaptation, defined broadly, refers to a change in the operating characteristics of a system in response to a change in its inputs. The term describes diverse phenomena found in a variety of biological and artificial systems, and occurring over multiple timescales, from milliseconds to millions of years. Adaptive processes are central to the functioning of the central nervous system,

[1] Author's or Editor's contribution to the Work was done as part of the Author's or Editor's official duties as a NIH employee and is a Work of the United States Government. Therefore, copyright may not be established in the United States.

and particularly perceptual coding systems, which routinely adjust their sensitivity based on the external world. Adaptation of perceptual systems can occur over periods of weeks, months, and years, as in the perceptual learning of a fine discrimination, but can also act rapidly, producing dramatic perceptual aftereffects following only a few seconds of stimulus exposure (Clifford and Rhodes, 2005; Favreau and Corballis, 1976; Frisby, 1980). The adaptive processes underlying such diverse phenomena may have little in common at the neurobiological level, but may share a common function of fitting the mind to the world (Clifford and Rhodes, 2005; Schwartz et al., 2007; Wark et al., 2007).

Perceptual aftereffects resulting from short-term adaptation (seconds to minutes) have been widely used to explore the computations or functional principles underlying perceptual coding, leading them to be dubbed the psychologist's microelectrode (Frisby, 1980). A classic example is the waterfall illusion, in which stationary objects appear to move upwards to an observer after viewing a downward-flowing waterfall (Mather et al., 1998). This motion aftereffect provides insight into motion perception, suggesting that it depends on a balance of activity from cell populations tuned to different directions of motion, and that when activity corresponding to one direction is selectively reduced, perceived movement shifts in the opposite direction (Sutherland, 1961, see Mather et al., 2008 for more complex, contemporary models derived from the study of motion aftereffects). Similar aftereffects have provided insight into coding properties of color, orientation, curvature, and a number of other basic visual stimulus attributes.

The discovery of face aftereffects in the last decade has sparked interest in using short-term adaptation to probe the brain's principles for encoding faces. Aftereffects have been reported for numerous facial attributes, including perceived identity, sex, race, expression, normality, attractiveness, and eye gaze direction (Hurlbert, 2001; Jenkins et al., 2006; Leopold et al., 2001; MacLin and Webster, 2001; O'Leary and McMahon, 1991; Rhodes and Jeffery, 2006; Rhodes et al., 2003; Rutherford et al., 2008; Watson and Clifford, 2003; Webster and MacLin, 1999; Webster et al., 2004). For example, just a few seconds of adaptation[2] to a face produces an *identity aftereffect*, in which the perception of a subsequently presented face is biased towards the "opposite" identity (Figure 14.1). In the related *figural face aftereffect*, several minutes of exposure to consistently distorted faces causes subsequently viewed faces to appear distorted in the opposite direction (Figure 14.2). In the next sections we see what these two kinds of face aftereffects have revealed about the way faces are mentally represented and recognized.

Norm-based coding of identity

Many theorists have suggested that an elegant and economical way to represent faces would be to code how each face deviates from a perceptual norm or prototype, which represents the central tendency (average value) of a distribution of faces (Diamond and Carey, 1986; Goldstein and Chance, 1980; Hebb, 1949; Hochberg, 1978; Leopold et al., 2001; Rhodes, 1996; Rhodes et al., 1987; Valentine 1991). In this framework, the norm occupies the center of a mental face-space (Figure 14.1), whose dimensions correspond to whatever information we use to discriminate faces (Valentine, 1991, 2001).

By making explicit what is distinctive about a face, norm-based coding may allow the visual system to see past the shared structure of faces and code those subtle variations that define individuals. Such a coding system may be more efficient than one that stores a complete structural description of each face, most elements of which are shared by all faces and therefore redundant.

---

[2] The term 'adaptation' is often used informally to refer to the prolonged viewing of visual stimuli, because this act is closely linked to adaptation of the underlying coding mechanisms.

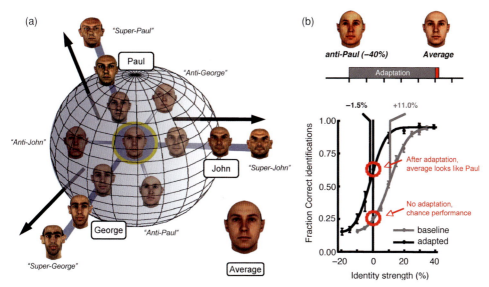

Fig. 14.1 (a) A simplified (three-dimensional) face-space with three identities. The statistical average of many such faces lies at the center (yellow circle—see also inset). The identity strength of a face can be varied along a trajectory from the average face (light blue lines). Caricatures (e.g. Super-John), which exaggerate how a face differs from the average, have increased identity strength. On the opposite side of the average lies a face's antiface (e.g. AntiJohn), which has opposite values on all the dimensions of face-space. These faces appear simply as different individuals, but based on their "opposite" structure, they hold a special relationship to the face on the other side of the mean, as revealed through adaptation. (b) Identity aftereffect. Adaptation to face biases participants to see the opposite identity. For example, after adapting to antiPaul for 5 seconds, the psychometric function shifts so that the identification threshold for Paul is reduced (from +11.0% to −1.5%) (Leopold et al., 2001).

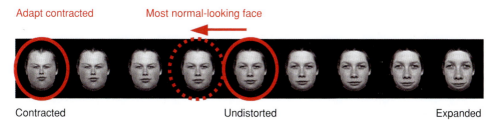

Fig. 14.2 A few minutes of adaptation to consistently distorted faces (e.g., contracted) produces a *figural aftereffect* in which the most normal looking face configuration shifts towards the adapting distortion and undistorted faces appear slightly distorted in the opposite direction (e.g. expanded) (e.g. Rhodes et al., 2003; Webster and MacLin, 1999). Adaptation therefore appears to shift the norm towards the adapting distortion.

Norm-based coding would also allow flexible updating in response to changes in the statistical distribution of dimension values in a population of faces encountered over time. These changes could occur abruptly, as when one is immersed in a population of faces with new features (e.g. a different ethnicity), or gradually, as in the aging of one's cohort.

In simpler domains, adaptive processes allow a system with a limited response range to calibrate itself to the external environment, thereby increasing coding efficiency (Barlow, 1990; Bartlett, 2007; Blakemore and Sutton, 1969; Dodwell and Humprey, 1990; Helson, 1948, 1964; Hosoya et al., 2005; Webster, 2003; Webster and Leonard, 2008; Werblin, 1973). This adaptation sometimes shifts an internal norm or reference point, such as what looks *stationary* in the perception of motion, or what looks *white* in the perception of color (Webster and Leonard, 2008). Here, we review evidence that a similar adaptive process underlies our perception of facial identity.

Norm-based coding of face identity receives support from several lines of experimental evidence. First, people appear to spontaneously abstract averages or prototypes from sets of seen faces, as indicated by the familiarity of unseen averages (Bruce et al., 1991; Cabeza and Kato, 2000; Cabeza et al., 1999; De Haan et al., 2001; Haberman and Whitney, 2007; Inn et al., 1993; MacLin and Webster, 2001; Reed, 1972; Rhodes et al., 2003, 2004; Solso and McCarthy 1981a,b; Strauss, 1979; Wallis et al., 2008; Walton and Bower, 1993; Webster and MacLin, 1999). In addition, the proximity of faces to the average face affects recognition, with more distinctive faces recognized better than less distinctive ones (Valentine, 1991, 2001). Furthermore, caricatures, which exaggerate how a face differs from the average, are sometimes recognized even better than the original faces (Benson and Perrett, 1994; Byatt and Rhodes, 1998; Calder et al., 1996; Lee et al., 2000; Rhodes, 1996; Rhodes et al., 1987) (Figure 14.3).

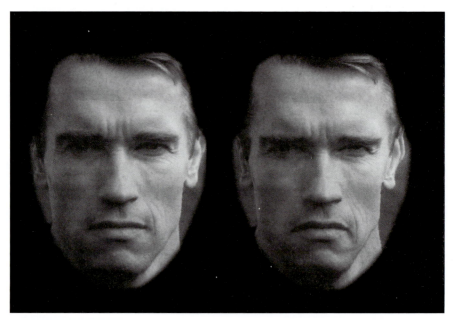

Fig.14.3 Which is the real Arnie? The image on the right is Super-Arnie, a caricature that exaggerates how Arnie differs from an average male by 50%. At brief exposures, caricatures can be identified more accurately than undistorted faces (Lee et al., 2000).

However, these results, while providing prima facie support for the model, are not conclusive. The familiarity of unseen averages or prototypes could result from their similarity to stored exemplars and better recognition of distinctive faces and caricatures could result from fewer neighboring distractors (e.g. Rhodes et al., 1998) (cf. the long-standing dispute over prototype vs. exemplar models of categorization, Nosofsky, 2000). Moreover, even if averages are abstracted, they might not function as perceptual norms.

We suggest that face aftereffects provide more compelling evidence for norm-based coding of identity (Anderson and Wilson, 2005; Leopold et al., 2001, 2005; Rhodes and Jeffery, 2006; Rhodes et al., 2007a; Tsao and Freiwald, 2006). Consider the example in Figure 14.1. A few seconds of viewing a face (e.g. antiPaul) biases perception of a subsequent face towards the identity that lies opposite, relative to the average, in face-space (i.e. Paul). The bias can be conceived of as a temporary shift in the average face towards the adapting face, so that low identity strength versions of Paul now lie further from the (new) average, making them more distinctive and more recognizable (Rhodes and Jeffery, 2006). The shift in the norm can even cause an "identity-neutral" average face to take on the identity opposite to the adapting face (Leopold et al., 2001, 2005; Rhodes et al., 2007a). These results strongly suggest that identity is coded relative to the average face—when the internal representation of the average temporarily shifts, the perceived identity of viewed faces shifts with it.

Crucially, this interpretation requires that the aftereffect is a selective bias towards the opposite identity and not a generalized contrast effect whereby perception is biased non-selectively away from an adapting identity, in all directions in face-space. Leopold et al., (2001) sought to rule out a generalized effect by comparing aftereffects for opposite and non-opposite adapting faces. However, the non-opposite adapting faces were more similar to the test faces than were the opposite adapting faces (Leopold et al., 2001, figure 1; see Anderson and Wilson, 2005). This difference is problematic because more similar adapt-test pairs can produce smaller aftereffects (Clifford, 2002). However, subsequent studies have shown that identity aftereffects are larger for opposite adapt-test pairs than for equally perceptual dissimilar, but non-opposite, pairs (Rhodes and Jeffery, 2006; see also Benton and Burgess, 2008) (Figure 14.4). This result rules out a simple contrast account.

Further evidence that the average face functions as a perceptual norm for coding identity comes from the finding that a blend of two faces shows less resemblance to its parent faces when they are opposite than non-opposite identities (Rhodes and Jeffery, 2006). Figure 14.4a shows two face test blends: a 50/50 blend of opposite faces (Dan and antiDan) and a blend of non-opposite, but equally perceptually dissimilar, faces. The "opposites" blend approximates the average face and should be identity-neutral with little resemblance to either parent. In contrast, the non-opposite blend will deviate from the average in some direction (Figure 14.4a, short gray arrow) and will resemble its parent faces to the extent that they also deviate from the average in this direction. As predicted, participants see much less resemblance to the parent faces in the opposite than non-opposite blends (Rhodes and Jeffery, 2006). Just as opponent colors cancel perceptually, making it difficult to see a reddish-green, so it appears do opposite identities. These results provide further evidence that opposites in face-space are perceptual opposites, and for the special status of the average face in coding identity.

Norms and experience

The identity aftereffect suggests that even a single brief exposure to a face can influence the norm, at least temporarily (Leopold et al., 2005; Rhodes et al., 2007a). More direct evidence that norms are updated by experience comes from figural face aftereffects in which a few minutes of exposure

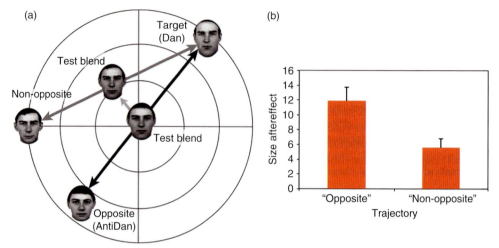

Fig. 14.4 (a) A simplified (two-dimensional) face-space showing a face (Target "Dan"), together with its opposite antiface (antiDan) and a non-opposite adapting face that is equally perceptually dissimilar to the target. Test blends are shown for both the target-opposite and target-non-opposite trajectories. The light gray arrow shows the deviation of the non-opposite blend from the center of face-space (norm). (b) Adaptation to both opposite and non-opposite adapting faces biases perception towards Dan, but the aftereffect is much bigger for opposite than non-opposite pairs, indicating selectivity for the opposite identity (Rhodes and Jeffery, 2006).

to consistently distorted faces changes subjects' perception of what looks normal (MacLin and Webster, 2001; Rhodes et al., 2003, 2004; Watson and Clifford, 2003; Webster and MacLin, 1999; Webster et al., 2005). For example, after viewing faces whose internal features have been "expanded," slightly expanded faces appear normal, and after viewing "contracted" faces, slightly contracted faces appear normal (e.g. Rhodes et al., 2003) (Figure 14.2). In each case, undistorted faces appear distorted in the opposite way to the adapting faces. These figural face aftereffects are not driven solely by low-level adaptation, because they survive changes in retinal position between adapt and test faces (Rhodes et al., 2003; Watson and Clifford, 2003, 2006; Zhao and Chubb, 2001). Importantly, these aftereffects influence the perception of new faces, suggesting that adaptation has altered the norm used to code faces.

In many domains the aftereffects produced by brief exposures have long-term, as well as short-term, components (Favreau and Corballis, 1976; Harris, 1980; Masland, 1969; Vul et al., 2008; Wolfe and O'Connell, 1986). It is interesting to speculate that the same may be true for face aftereffects. Time-course studies indicate that, like aftereffects in many domains, face aftereffects decay exponentially, with an initial rapid decay that flattens out (with above-zero asymptote), raising the possibility of a longer-term component (Leopold et al., 2005; Rhodes et al., 2007a). Interestingly, after a few seconds of exposure, a small aftereffect remained even at the longest duration tested (albeit only 16 seconds) in these studies. Furthermore, several minutes of exposure to consistently distorted faces can produce aftereffects 15 minutes later (McKone et al., 2005). Even longer-lasting effects (up to 24 hours) have also been reported, although it remains to be seen whether these effects reflect changes in the norm, because reliable generalization to new faces has not been established (Carbon and Leder, 2006; Carbon et al., 2007; Morikawa, 2005). Although more research is clearly needed, these initial findings suggest that face adaptation may have cumulative effects on the face norm, allowing it to represent the central tendency (average) of the diet of faces experienced.

Face aftereffects indicate that face-coding mechanisms retain considerable plasticity into adulthood, with a norm that is continuously updated by experience. But how does a norm arise in the first place? It is possible that a crude face norm or template is innate, allowing newborns to orient to, and learn about, face-like patterns in the environment (Johnson, Chapter 1, this volume). Although the relationship between an initial template and subsequent norms is unknown, it is clear that sensitivity to differences between faces develops rapidly with experience (de Haan et al., 2001; Kelly, et al., 2005; Walton and Bower, 1993). Adaptation studies suggest further that norm-based coding is in place by the age of four (Jeffery and Rhodes, 2008) with adult-like identity aftereffects by the age of 8 years (Jeffery et al., 2009; Nishimura et al., 2008; Pimperton et al., 2009).

One norm or many?

So far we have treated norm-based coding of identity as if a single, special face serves as the norm in all cases. However, the brain is opportunistic, and depending on the information needed, might exploit multiple internal reference points. In this section we see how aftereffects can reveal the nature of norms used.

Different norms for different social categories

In addition to individuating faces, we also categorize them, according to race, sex, and other important social categories. These categories are often visually distinct, raising the possibility that distinct visual norms are used to represent identities within the different categories. Might the identities of Caucasian and Asian faces, for example, or male and female faces, be coded using distinct norms?

Evidence for multiple norms comes from *category-contingent* aftereffects, whereby opposite aftereffects can be generated simultaneously for different kinds of faces (Figure 14.5). For example, viewing interleaved "contracted" Caucasian and "expanded" Asian faces for a few minutes produces opposite aftereffects for each race (Jaquet et al., 2007, 2008; Little et al., 2008). After this adaptation, undistorted Caucasian faces look slightly expanded, undistorted Asian faces look slightly contracted, and the most normal-looking configuration for each race shifts in opposite directions, towards the adapting distortion for that race (Figure 14.5). These category-contingent aftereffects suggest that different norms are used for each category. If they were not, then the adaptation to opposite distortions in Asian and Caucasian faces would have competing effects on the single, generic norm, pulling it in opposite directions, resulting in little net aftereffect (e.g. Jeffery et al., 2007). Aftereffects can also be contingent on sex (Beselmeyer et al., 2008; Jaquet and Rhodes, 2008; Little et al., 2005), species (Little et al., 2008), and even age of faces (Little et al., 2008). These results suggest that the brain has *multiple* face norms.

The flip-side of contingent adaptation is *transfer* of adaptation and aftereffects from one category to another (Figure 14.5b). This transfer results from adaptation of dimensions that are *common* to both categories of faces. In contrast, category-contingent aftereffects reflect adaptation of dimensions that are *selective* for a particular category of faces.[3] Not surprisingly, given the similarity of all faces as visual patterns, face aftereffects show considerable transfer between

---

[3] So long as the adapting distortions affect common dimensions, some transfer should occur—see Little et al. (2005) for a case where adaptation to male-specific dimensions may have prevented transfer to female faces.

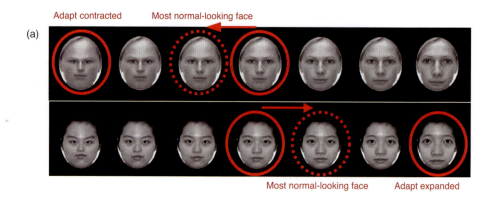

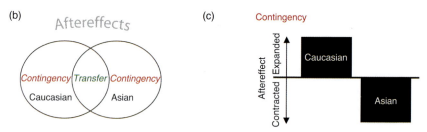

Fig. 14.5 (a) After viewing "contracted" Caucasian and "expanded" Asian faces for a few minutes, opposite aftereffects occur for each race, with undistorted Caucasian faces looking slightly expanded and undistorted Asian faces looking slightly contracted. The most normal-looking configuration shifts towards the adapting distortion, consistent with a shift in the norm. (b) Contingent aftereffects reflect adaptation of race-selective coding mechanisms, whereas transferred aftereffects (adapt to one category and test with the other) reflects adaptation of common coding mechanisms. (c) Typical race-contingent aftereffect results for the adaptation shown in (a). Undistorted Caucasian faces now look slightly expanded and Asian faces look slightly contracted.

categories, in addition to the category-contingent effects described above (Jaquet and Rhodes, 2008; Jaquet et al., 2008).

This pattern of results suggests that the visual system represents both generic and category-specific information about faces, analogous to the basic-level and subordinate-level representations in the conceptual system. In the face-space framework, some dimensions would be used for all faces, whereas others would be selective for a particular race or sex. A similar model has been proposed to handle the dissociable coding of facial identity and expression (Calder, Chapter 22, this volume; Calder and Young, 2005; Calder et al., 2001). In summary, we suggest that multiple category-specific face norms may be used to code identity.

Different norms for different viewpoints

Successful identification requires that we can recognize a face from different viewpoints. In principle, this could be done by having multiple view-specific norms tuned to distinct viewpoints, or a single view-invariant norm. Aftereffect studies suggest that multiple, view-specific norms are used to code identity. Both identity and figural aftereffects decrease as the difference in viewpoint between the adapt and test identities increases (Benton et al., 2006; Jeffery et al., 2006; Jiang et al., 2006, 2007). Moreover, figural aftereffects at one viewpoint are not completely canceled by concurrent adaptation to the opposite distortion at another view, with no cancellation between 30°- and 90°-views, and only partial cancellation between 30°- and 60°-views (Jeffery et al., 2007).

These results suggest that faces are coded using view-specific, albeit broadly tuned, norms. This conclusion appears consistent with the difficulty people have in generalizing face identity across viewpoints, at least for unfamiliar faces (for a review see Jeffery et al., 2006). Familiar faces, which are easier to match and recognize across changes in viewpoint, may have more broadly tuned representations (Ewbank and Andrews, 2008; Jiang et al., 2007, 2009). However, even in that case a change in viewpoint between adapt and test faces still reduces the identity aftereffect, suggesting view-specific norms (e.g. Benton et al., 2006; Jiang et al., 2007).

Norm-based versus exemplar-based coding

Norm-based coding can be contrasted with exemplar-based coding, in which individual faces are coded as absolute values on the dimensions of face-space, and the average face does not function as a perceptual norm (Valentine, 1991, 2001). In neural terms, norm-based coding has been linked with opponent coding models and exemplar-based coding has been linked with multichannel models (Calder et al., 2008; Robbins et al., 2007; Tsao and Freiwald, 2006) (Figures 14.6 and 14.7). In this section we describe a simple model of each type and argue that the evidences favors an opponent coding over a multichannel model of face coding.

A simple opponent coding model

A simple opponent coding model has been proposed for norm-based coding of faces (Rhodes and Jeffery, 2006; Rhodes et al., 2005; Robbins et al., 2007; Tsao and Freiwald, 2006), similar to those used for norm-based coding of simpler properties like direction of motion and aspect ratio

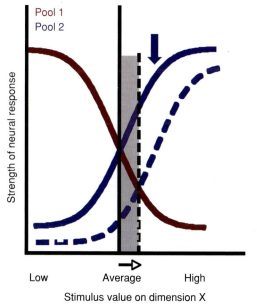

Fig. 14.6 A simple model in which each face dimension is coded by two opponent populations, one responding to below-average and the other to above-average values. Average values are coded implicitly, by equal (and low) activation of the two populations. Following adaptation to a face with a certain dimension value (large arrow), the relative contribution of the corresponding population is diminished, shifting the balance point (perceived average) towards the adapting value (small arrow, shaded area) and biasing subsequent perception away from the adapting value.

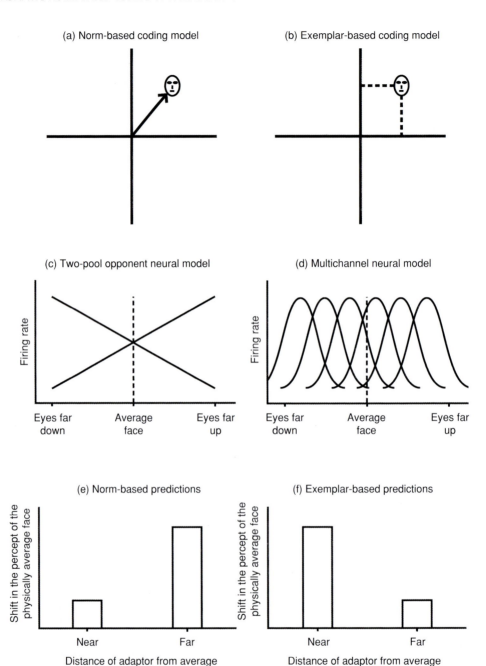

Fig. 14.7 Row 1. Simplifed face-space models, showing only two dimensions, illustrating (a) norm-based coding, in which a face is coded as a deviation from the average, and (b) exemplar-based coding, in which a face is represented by the absolute value on the dimensions. Row 2. Neural coding of a single dimension of face-space (eye height) using (c) norm-based coding, implemented as a two-pool opponent neural model, and (d) exemplar-based coding, implemented as a multichannel neural model, Row 3. The predicted effects of adaptation on the perception of a physically average face when the adaptors are near to, and far from, the average face for (e) a norm-based coding model and (f) an exemplar-based coding model. Figure kindly supplied by Linda Jeffery.

(Mather, 1980; Regan and Hamstra, 1982; Sutherland, 1961; Suzuki, 2005). In the model, each dimension of face-space is coded by a pair of neural populations, one tuned to above-average and the other to below-average values on that dimension (Figures 14.6 and 14.7). For example, for the dimension of eye size, one population would be tuned to above-average (large) and the other to below-average (small) eyes. The model does not contain neurons that are tuned to average values. Instead the average face is represented by equal activation in both members of the paired populations.

According to the opponent coding model, aftereffects occur because brief exposure to a face temporarily suppresses the responsivity of neurons that are activated by that face (Figure 14.6). For each dimension, one population will typically be suppressed more than the other (unless the face is average on that dimension), thus biasing the observer to see the opposite value. The model, therefore, offers a mechanism for the short-term adaptation seen in typical face aftereffect studies. We might speculate that longer-term adaptation reflects the accumulation of residual effects whereby responsivity does not return fully to the initial, pre-adaptation state.

Opponent coding versus multichannel coding

Figure 14.7 shows a simple multichannel model, in which each dimension is coded by activation in multiple populations of neurons (channels) that are tuned to different values along that dimension. Multichannel coding is used for some low-level properties like spatial frequency and orientation (for a review see Suzuki, 2005) and for some higher-level dimensions, such as body direction (Lawson et al., 2009), and eye-gaze direction (Calder et al., 2008; but see Kloth and Schweinberger, 2008). This last finding raises the question of whether a multichannel model could also be used for face dimensions used to code identity.

Robbins and colleagues sought to address this question using the dimension of eye height (Robbins et al., 2007). They adapted people to distortions in eye height (both eyes up or both eyes down) and examined the effects on perceptions of normality for learned identities shown with various eye heights. Robbins et al. (2007) derived different predictions from the two models about the relationship between adaptor distortion level and size of the aftereffect on perception of the physically average face. The multichannel model predicts that weakly distorted adaptors, which lie close to the average face, should produce a stronger aftereffect than strongly distorted adaptors, which lie further from the average (and thus do not activate channels that respond to the average) (Figure 14.7). The opponent coding model makes the opposite prediction because the neurons are tuned to extreme values (above or below the average) and so are more affected by extreme than typical adaptors. The results supported the opponent coding model, providing further evidence for norm-based coding of faces.

Robbins and colleagues also derived opposite predictions for test stimuli that are slightly more extreme (i.e. further from average) than the adapting stimuli. The opponent coding model predicts that these test stimuli should look less extreme after adapting, because adaptation shifts the neutral point (average) towards the adaptor, and therefore, towards those extreme faces. However, on a multichannel model these test stimuli may look *more* extreme than before, because adaptation suppresses activity in channels on the neutral side of those, resulting in asymmetric activation consistent with a more extreme value. Again, the results supported norm-based coding (Robbins et al., 2007).

Insights from neurophysiology and neuroimaging

Direct measurements of the brain's responses to faces provide additional support for norm-based coding, although they also highlight the difficulty of translating computational models of face encoding into predicted patterns of neural responses. Human neuroimaging results suggest that neural responses may increase with distance from the average face (Loffler et al., 2005). As synthetically generated faces were moved away from the average, increasing identity strength (distinctiveness), activation increased in face-selective cortex. Moreover, functional magnetic resonance (fMR)-adaptation (reduced responses to repeated stimuli) was stronger during blocks containing faces that all deviated in the same direction from the average than during blocks containing faces from multiple directions. This result suggests that neural populations are sensitive to direction from the norm, although the conclusion would be stronger if the physical variability of images in the same- and different-direction blocks had been equated. That said, lower-level visual areas (V1/V2) did not respond differently, as might be expected if the blocks had differed in physical variability. Clearly, further research is needed here. It would also be interesting to compare fMR-adaptation for pairs that lie opposite in face-space (face–antiface pairs), with equally perceptually dissimilar pairs that do not lie opposite in face-space. If mutually opponent neural populations code a face and its antiface, then we should see less fMR-adaptation for opposite than non-opposite pairs.

Single-cell recordings in macaque monkey inferotemporal cortex (area TEv) suggest that responses often increased with distance from the average (Leopold et al., 2006) (Figure 14.8). In another recent study, responses in face-selective cortex (lower bank of the superior temporal sulcus) showed broad, monotonic tuning across the full dimension range for many dimensions of cartoon faces (Freiwald et al., 2009). Such tuning is not consistent with multichannel coding, which predicts narrower tuning curves (Figure 14.7). In addition, across the population maximal responses were seen to both extremes on many dimensions, consistent with norm-based coding.

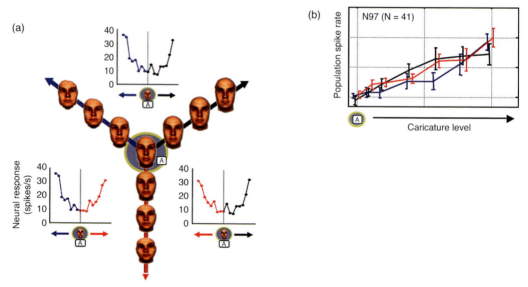

Fig. 14.8 (a) Example of a neuron in monkey anterior inferotemporal cortex showing increased firing rate in response to faces further from the average face (Leopold et al., 2006). Three trajectories are depicted (red, blue, black), with the corresponding tuning functions shown. Firing generally increased with distance from the average. (b) Mean normalized spiking trend as a function of caricature level (identity strength) across a population of 41 AIT neurons in one monkey (Leopold et al., 2006). This plot illustrates the monotonic, near-linear tuning of neurons to face identity for three directions in face-space.

Face selectivity and neural origins

Face perception depends on activity throughout the entire ventral visual system, not just activity in high-level, face-selective areas (Haxby and Gobbini, Chapter 6; Kanwisher and Barton, Chapter 7, this volume). Therefore, face aftereffects could potentially reflect adaptation at any point in this pathway, including adaptation of low-level, retinotopically organized mechanisms that code simple image features (e.g. brightness, contrast, orientation, spatial frequency). Here we consider whether figural and identity aftereffects reflect higher-level, and possibly face-selective, adaptation or whether they can be explained solely by low-level adaptation. Clearly, face aftereffects will provide a more useful tool for studying face perception if high-level mechanisms are adapted.

We know that face-selective cortex adapts (becomes less responsive) when a face is repeated, and that it recovers from this adaptation when the identity changes (Loffler et al., 2005; Mazard et al., 2006; Rotshtein et al., 2005; Winston et al., 2004). This neural adaptation was first seen in the general object-processing area LOC (lateral occipital cortex) and may not be confined to areas that respond more strongly to faces than other objects (Grill-Spector et al., 1999). However, identity-specific face adaptation seems confined to higher-level, face-selective cortex (Rotshtein et al., 2005). Adaptation in face-selective cortex is also sensitive to face-viewpoint, and is reduced by a change of viewpoint (e.g. Andrews and Ewbank, 2004; Ewbank and Andrews, 2008). It seems like that these adaptation effects would be linked to face identity aftereffects (cf. Calder et al., 2007), but this has yet to be demonstrated.

At the moment, the best evidence regarding the source of adaptation underlying face aftereffects comes from psychophysical experiments. These show that both identity and figural face aftereffects are larger when the adapt and test faces have the same retinal location than when they don't, indicating some contribution of low-level adaptation (Afraz and Cavanagh, 2007; Zhao and Chubb, 2001). Importantly, however, they are not eliminated by changes in retinal size and/ or position, ruling out a purely low-level account (Afraz and Cavanagh, 2007; Leopold et al., 2001; Rhodes et al., 2003, 2007a; Watson and Clifford, 2003, 2006; Zhao and Chubb, 2001).

Although we can rule out a low-level account, face aftereffects might still reflect adaptation of mid-level (non-retinotopic) mechanisms that code general shape properties, such as curvature, taper, convexity, skew, aspect ratio, and relative size, many of which use perceptual norms, just like face identity (Suzuki, 2005; Suzuki and Cavanagh, 1998). If such mechanisms are involved, as seems likely, then we should see substantial transfer of aftereffects between face- and non-face categories. Some transfer between simple shapes and faces has been reported for face expression aftereffects, but these aftereffects did not survive changes in retinal position, suggesting a low-level locus for the effects (Xu et al., 2008). Another study reported that a figural face aftereffect, produced by viewing horizontally-distorted faces, showed some transfer to ellipses (O'Leary and McMahon, 1991). Interestingly, however, transfer was only observed when participants had to estimate the height and width of the ellipses and not when they had to rate how *normal* the ellipses looked. These results suggest that there may be distinct perceptual norms for faces and shapes, and perhaps some face selectivity of face adaptation. Clearly more transfer studies are needed, although face and shape adaptation will likely be difficult to tease apart.

High-level face-coding mechanisms are strongly tuned to upright faces (McKone and Robbins, Chapter 9, this volume) and adaptation of such mechanisms should result in orientation-selective aftereffects. Several studies have found that aftereffects do not transfer fully between upright and inverted faces (Watson and Clifford, 2003; Webster and MacLin, 1999) and that opposite aftereffects can be induced simultaneously for upright and inverted faces (Rhodes et al., 2004; Watson and Clifford, 2006). These results are consistent with a contribution of higher-level, face-selective adaptation to aftereffects for upright faces. However, given that upright and inverted faces contain different shapes (e.g. the nose is a wedge shape with the widest part at the bottom in an upright face and at the top in an inverted face), it is difficult to completely rule out a mid-level shape account of these orientation effects. Recent evidence that identity aftereffects can be larger for upright than inverted faces, however, seems difficult to explain by mid-level shape adaptation (Rhodes et al., 2009a).

So too is evidence that face aftereffects are sensitive to higher-level semantic category membership (e.g. race, sex) and not just purely physical differences. As described above, opposite aftereffects can be generated for faces from different semantic categories, by adapting people to opposite distortions in the two kinds of faces (e.g. contracted Asian, expanded Caucasian). These aftereffects are reduced or eliminated for adapting sets of faces that are not perceived as different categories even though they may be just as physically distinct (Beselmeyer et al., 2008; Jaquet et al., 2007). These results implicate adaptation of high-level face-coding mechanisms that are sensitive to social category information (Golby et al., 2001; Kim et al., 2006; Rotshtein et al., 2005). Finally, face identity aftereffects are linked to conscious awareness of the adapting faces (Moradi et al., 2005), which also suggests high-level adaptation (e.g. George et al., 1999; Sheinberg and Logothetis, 1997).

We conclude that figural and identity aftereffects reflect adaptation of higher-level, face-coding mechanisms, and cannot be explained solely by adaptation of low-level (retinotopic) mechanisms that code simple visual attributes or mid-level (non-retinotopic) shape-coding mechanisms. This is good news for those who would use face aftereffects to probe the mechanisms of face perception. Ultimately, however, the challenge will be to understand how low-level and high-level stimulus features are integrated in face perception, rather than to isolate them completely.

Advantages of adaptive norm-based coding

In this final section we review the possible benefits of coding identity relative to norms and of using norms that are continuously updated by experience (see also Webster et al., 2005).

Coding economy

An important benefit of norm-based coding is surely that it highlights what is distinctive about a face, facilitating successful recognition. This approach is economical, as the processing and encoding of redundant facial structure is minimized. In our norm-based coding model, face dimensions are coded by pairs of neural populations, tuned to above-average and below-average values, respectively (Figures 14.6 and 14.7). Splitting the coding of inputs in this way reduces responses to common or average stimuli relative to more extreme stimuli, as observed in face-coding regions of the brain (e.g. Leopold et al., 2006; Loffler, et al., 2005), which seems useful given the metabolic cost of action potentials (Laughlin, 2001). It also doubles the precision of representation, and may provide an optimal code for representing sensory inputs (MacLeod and von der Twer, 2003).

Calibration and performance

The fact that face norms can be updated by experience may also be useful. In low-level vision, adaptation calibrates a limited neural response range to prevailing inputs (Barlow, 1990; Brenner et al., 2000; Clifford and Rhodes, 2005; Clifford et al., 2007; Kohn, 2007; Mather et al., 2008; Schwartz et al., 2007; Wark et al., 2007). A classic example is lightness adaptation in the retina, which enables exquisite sensitivity (although not at the same time) over an enormous range

(10 log units) (Werblin, 1973). Visual adaptation can also operate over much longer timescales, as with recalibration of color vision following cataract surgery over several weeks (for a review see Webster et al., 2005).

Most face adaptation studies have focused on short timescales, with brief adaptation and short delays between adaptation and test stimuli. Even under these conditions, however, it may be possible to discern beneficial effects. For example, 5 minutes of adaptation to an average Caucasian or Asian face can facilitate identification of faces from the adapted, relative to the unadapted, race (Rhodes et al., 2010). Enhanced discrimination around a population average has also been reported for synthetic faces (Wilson et al., 2002). This facilitation was observed in the absence of explicit adaptation and could reflect long-term (pre-experimental) adaptation to a population of faces. A similar study using more realistic faces, however, did not find enhanced discrimination around the average either with or without explicit adaptation (Rhodes et al., 2007b). This variability of results parallels that found in simpler domains (e.g. orientation and motion processing), where enhanced discrimination around the average stimulus is also found inconsistently (for reviews see Kohn, 2007; Rhodes et al., 2007b). Nevertheless, there are an increasing number of reports of enhanced discrimination of faces around the adapted state (Chen et al., 2010; Oruç and Barton, 2011; Yang et al., 2011). Little is known about face adaptation over longer timescales, but we can speculate that it might contribute to our face expertise, including better recognition of own-race than other-race faces (Rossion and Michel, Chapter 12, this volume).

As well as updating face norms, adaptation shifts perceptual category boundaries between different kinds of faces, moving them towards the adapting category (Webster et al., 2004). These shifts occur for faces of different races and sexes and for different emotional expressions (Rutherford et al., 2008; Webster et al., 2004). In principle, such shifts could reduce the range of stimuli that fall within a category, thereby spreading a fixed response range over a smaller stimulus range and increasing sensitivity to differences within that range. However, extensive investigations have found little evidence for such changes in sensitivity, so that it remains unclear whether these changes to face category boundaries have functional benefits (Ng et al., 2008).

Atypical adaptation in autism spectrum disorders

Another line of evidence for a functional role of face adaptation is that adaptation is reduced in a population with face processing difficulties (Pellicano et al., 2007). Individuals with autism spectrum disorders (ASD) can experience a variety of such problems, including difficulty discriminating and recognizing faces (Behrmann et al., 2006a,b; Blair et al., 2002; Boucher and Lewis, 1992; Dawson et al., 2005; Klin et al., 1999). Pellicano and colleagues (2007) found that children with autism had substantially smaller identity aftereffects than typically developing children. Moreover, in the autism group, the size of the aftereffects was strongly negatively correlated with current autistic symptomatology (Figure 14.9). These results suggest that children with autism may have difficulty abstracting and/or using norms to code faces. They also raise the possibility that reduced adaptation contributes to the face processing deficits in this group, and point, more generally, to a functional role for face adaptation.

Beyond identity: adaptation and the perception of beauty

Perceptual adaptation and norms play an important role in the perception of beauty, as well as in the coding of identity. Average faces are attractive (Langlois and Roggman, 1990; Rhodes, 2006) and when adaptation to consistently distorted faces shifts the most normal-looking distortion towards the adapting distortion, there is a parallel shift in what looks most attractive (Anzures

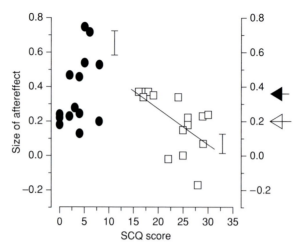

Fig. 14.9 Size of the identity aftereffect for typically developing children (filled circles) and children with an autism spectrum disorder (ASD) (open squares) as a function of Social Communication Questionnaire (SCQ) scores. The SCQ measures current autistic symptomatology (Rutter, 2003). The vertical bars near each cluster show the average standard error of measurement of individual participants in each group, and the filled and open arrows show the mean aftereffects for the typical and ASD groups respectively. A regression line is shown for the ASD group. These results show that face adaptation is reduced autism, a disorder associated with face processing difficulties. Adapted from Pellicano et al., 2007.

et al., 2009; Buckingham, et al., 2006; Little et al., 2005; Rhodes et al., 2003).[4] With extended exposure, this calibration of preferences by experience may contribute to the well-known appeal of average faces (Rhodes, 2006), as well as to individual variation in preferences (Honekopp, 2006) due to variation in experience (cf. Bronstad and Russell, 2007; Cooper et al., 2006; Perrett et al., 2002; but see Rhodes et al., 2005).

Perceptual adaptation may also play a role in our preference for symmetric faces (Rhodes, 2006). Fluctuating asymmetries (with a random distribution of directional bias across the population) have been linked to developmental stability and mate quality, making a preference for symmetric faces evolutionarily adaptive (Penton-Voak and Morrison, Chapter 33, this volume; Rhodes, 2006). Interestingly, perceptions of facial symmetry are driven by fluctuating asymmetries, with little impact of asymmetries that show a consistent direction of asymmetry across the population and are unrelated to mate quality (Simmons et al., 2004). This focus on fluctuating asymmetries seems to be mediated by perceptual adaptation to consistent directional asymmetries in faces—after viewing faces with a consistent asymmetry (e.g. left eye always larger than right eye), new faces with that asymmetry look more symmetric and more attractive (Rhodes et al., 2009b).

These effects of adaptation on perceptions of attractiveness suggest that another function of adaptation may be to calibrate preferences to the diet of faces experienced. This calibration may

---

[4] Note, however, that it may not be possible to adapt to attractiveness per se (De Bruine et al. 2007), perhaps because of its multidimensional nature (Rhodes, 2006).

even help us find high quality mates, because averageness and symmetry can signal mate quality (for a review, see Rhodes, 2006).

Summary and conclusions

We suggest that faces are coded relative to perceptual norms that are continuously updated by experience. This norm-based coding allows the visual system to ignore the shared structure of faces and code the subtle variations that define individuals. Support for norm-based coding of faces comes from identity aftereffects in which adaptation to a face selectively biases perception towards the opposite identity. These aftereffects suggest that faces are coded by pairs of neural populations, tuned to above-average and below-average values, respectively on face-coding dimensions, with the average face (norm) producing equal activity in these pairs. The norm is represented implicitly in these tuning functions, which can be modified (adapted) by experience. The short-term effects of such adaptation are seen in figural face aftereffects, where exposure to consistently distorted faces shifts perceptions of normality and attractiveness towards the adapting distortion. If such changes accumulate over time, as seems likely, then the norm can be calibrated to the diet of faces experienced, and contribute to our expertise with those faces.

Studies of face aftereffects also suggest that the brain adopts a flexible approach to norm-based coding, with different norms for faces of different races and sexes, and for faces seen in different viewpoints. For example, opposite aftereffects can be generated simultaneously for visually distinct sets of faces drawn from different social categories. Interestingly, these "category-contingent" aftereffects are larger than the "structure-contingent" aftereffects that can be obtained for equally visually distinct sets of faces that fall within the same social category. This result implicates high-level face adaptation in face aftereffects and confirms their usefulness as a tool for exploring face perception.

Norm-based coding can be contrasted with exemplar-based coding of faces, in which faces are coded as absolute values on face dimensions and the average face plays no special functional role. These forms of coding have been linked to opponent (two pool) and multichannel neural coding models, respectively. Both psychophysical and neuroimaging evidence supports opponent, norm-based coding rather than multichannel exemplar-based coding of face identity. Recent psychophysical evidence suggests that norm-based coding is also used to represent facial expressions of emotion (Skinner and Berton, 2010).

We also reviewed preliminary evidence for impaired face adaptation in children with autism spectrum disorders, a disorder characterized by face processing difficulties. This association points to a functional role for adaptive processes in face perception. Evidence that face adaptation can facilitate recognition of faces from a familiar (adapted) population also supports a functional role. We conclude that by allowing the visual system to focus on how each face differs from the average, norm-based coding provides an elegant and economical solution to the problem of face recognition.

However, many interesting questions remain and we hope that researchers will be inspired to address them. These include:

1 How are the short-term effects seen in face aftereffects related to longer-term changes in face norms?

2 How does face adaptation contribute to face expertise, and particularly the acquisition of expertise with new face populations?

3 Is the reduced face adaptation seen in children with autism spectrum disorders causally related to the face-processing difficulties often experienced by that group?

4 Are there stable individual differences in adaptability of face-coding mechanisms and are these related to differences in face expertise?

5 Do developmental changes in adaptability contribute to developmental improvements in face recognition?

6 Why is norm-based coding used for some dimensions (e.g. identity-related face dimensions, expression-related face dimensions, aspect ratio, color) and multichannel coding for others (e.g. gaze direction, body orientation, spatial frequency)?

Acknowledgments

This work was supported by the Australian Research Council. We thank Linda Jeffery, Emma Jaquet, Liz Pellicano, and Colin Clifford for their important contributions to ideas presented in this chapter. Thanks to Linda Jeffery and Louise Ewing for comments on the chapter. Correspondence should be addressed to Gillian Rhodes, School of Psychology, University of Western Australia, 35 Stirling Highway, Crawley, Perth, WA 6009, Australia, or emailed to gill@psy.uwa.edu.au. DAL was supported by the intramural research program of the National Institute of Mental Health

References

Afraz, S.R. and Cavanagh, P. (2007). Retinotopy of the face aftereffect. *Vision Research*, **48**, 42–54.

Anderson, N.D. and Wilson, H.R. (2005). The nature of synthetic face adaptation. *Vision Research*, **45**, 1815–1828.

Andrews, T.J. and Ewbank, M.P. (2004). Distinct representations for facial identity and changeable aspects of faces in the human temporal lobe. *Neuroimage*, **23**, 905–913.

Anzures, G., Mondloch, C.J., and Lackner, C. (2009). Face adaptation and attractiveness aftereffects in 8-year-olds and adults. *Child Development*, **80**, 178–191.

Bahrick, H.P., Bahrick, P.O., and Wittlinger, R.P. (1975). Fifty years of memory for names and faces: a cross-sectional approach. *Journal of Experimental Psychology: General*, **104**, 54–75.

Barlow, H.B. (1990). A theory about the functional role and synaptic mechanism of visual after-effects. In C. Blakemore (ed.) *Vision: Coding and Efficiency*, pp. 363–375. Cambridge: Cambridge University Press.

Bartlett, M.S. (2007). Information maximization in face processing. *Neurocomputing*, **70**, 2204–2217.

Behrmann, M., Avidan, G., Leonard, G.L., *et al.* (2006a). Configural processing in autism and its relationship to face processing. *Neuropsychologia*, **44**, 110–129.

Behrmann, M., Thomas, C., and Humphreys, K. (2006b). Seeing it differently: visual processing in autism. *Trends in Cognitive Sciences*, **10**, 258–264.

Benson, P.J. and Perrett, D.I. (1994). Visual processing of facial distinctiveness. *Perception*, **23**, 75–93.

Benton, C.P. and Burgess, E.C. (2008). The direction of measured face aftereffects. *Journal of Vision*, **8(15):1**, 1–6.

Benton, C.P., Jennings, S.J., and Chatting, D.J. (2006). Viewpoint dependence in adaptation to facial identity. *Vision Research*, **46**, 3313–3325.

Beselmeyer, P.E.G., Jones, B.C., DeBruine, L.M., *et al.* (2008). Sex-contingent face aftereffects depend on perceptual category rather than structural coding. *Cognition*, **107**, 353–365.

Blair, R.J.R., Frith, U., Smith, N., Abell, F., and Cipolotti, L. (2002). Fractionation of visual memory: Agency detection and its impairment in autism. *Neuropsychologia*, **40**, 108–118.

Blakemore, C. and Sutton, P. (1969). Size adaptation: a new aftereffect. *Science*, **166**, 245–247.

Boucher, J. and Lewis, V. (1992). Unfamiliar face recognition in relatively able autistic children. *Journal of Child Psychology & Psychiatry*, **33**, 843–859.

Brenner, N., Bialek, W., and de Ruyter van Steveninck, R. (2000). Adaptive rescaling maximizes information transmission. *Neuron*, **26**, 695–702.

Bronstad, P.M. and Russell, R. (2007). Beauty is in the "we" of the beholder: Greater agreement on facial attractiveness among close relatives. *Perception*, **36**, 1674–1681.

Bruce, V., Doyle, T., Dench, N., and Burton, M. (1991). Remembering facial configurations. *Cognition*, **38**, 109–144.

Buckingham, G., DeBruine, L.M., Little, A.C., *et al.* (2006). Visual adaptation to masculine and feminine faces influences generalized preferences and perceptions of trustworthiness. *Evolution & Human Behavior*, **27**, 381–389.

Byatt, G. and Rhodes, G. (1998). Recognition of own-race and other-race caricatures: Implications for models of face recognition. *Vision Research*, **38**, 2455–2468.

Cabeza, R. and Kato, T. (2000). Features are also important: Contribution of featural and configural processing to face recognition. *Psychological Science*, **11**, 429–433.

Cabeza, R., Bruce, V., Kato, T., and Oda, M. (1999). The prototype effect in face recognition: Extension and limits. *Memory & Cognition*, **27**, 139–151.

Calder, A.J., Beaver, J.D., Winston, J.S., *et al.* (2007). Separate coding of different gaze directions in the superior temporal sulcus and inferior parietal lobule. *Current Biology*, **17**, 20–25.

Calder, A.J., Burton, A.M., Miller, P., Young, A.W., and Akamatsu, S. (2001). A principal component analysis of facial expressions. *Vision Research*, **41**, 1179–1208.

Calder, A.J., Jenkins, R., Cassel, A., and Clifford, C.W.G. (2008). Visual representation of eye gaze is coded by nonopponent multichannel system. *Journal of Experimental Psychology: General*, **137**, 244–261.

Calder, A.J. and Young, A.W. (2005). Understanding the recognition of facial identity and facial expression. *Nature Reviews Neuroscience*, **6**, 641–651.

Calder, A.J., Young, A.W., Benson, P.J., and Perrett, D.I. (1996). Self priming from distinctive and caricatured faces. *British Journal of Psychology*, **87**, 141–62.

Carbon, C-C. and Leder, H. (2006). The Mona Lisa effect: is "our" Lisa fame or fake? *Perception*, **35**, 411–414.

Carbon, C-C., Strobach, T., Langton, S.R.H., Harsanyi, G., Leder, H., and Kovacs, G. (2007). Adaptation effects of highly familiar faces: Immediate and long lasting. *Memory & Cognition*, **35**, 1966–1976.

Chan, J., Yang, H., Wang, A., and Fang, F. (2010). Perceptual consequences of face viewpoint adaptation: face viewpoint aftereffect, changes of differential sensitivity to face view, and their relationship. *Journal of Vision*, **10**, 1–11.

Clifford, C.W.G. (2002). Adaptation-induced plasticity in perception: motion parallels orientation. *Trends in Cognitive Sciences*, **6**, 136–143.

Clifford, C.W.G. and Rhodes, G. (eds.) (2005). *Fitting the mind to the world: Adaptation and aftereffects in high-level vision*. Oxford: Oxford University Press.

Clifford, C.W.G., Webster, M.A., Stanley, G.B. *et al.* (2007). Visual adaptation: Neural, psychological and computational aspects. *Vision Research*, **47**, 3125–3131.

Cooper, P.A., Geldart, S.S., Mondloch, C.J., and Maurer, D. (2006). Developmental changes in perceptions of attractiveness: a role of experience. *Developmental Science*, **9**, 530–543.

Dawson, G., Webb, S.J., and McPartland, J. (2005). Understanding the nature of the face processing impairment in autism: Insights from behavioral and electrophysiological studies. *Developmental Neuropsychology*, **27**, 403–424.

DeBruine, L.M., Jones, B.C., Little, A.C., Unger, L., and Feinberg, D.R. (2007). Dissociating averageness and attractiveness: Attractive faces are not always average. *Journal of Experimental Psychology: Human Perception & Performance*, **33**, 1420–1430.

De Haan, M., Johnson, M.H., Maurer, D., and Perrett, D.I. (2001). Recognition of individual faces and average face prototypes by 1- and 3-month-old infants. *Cognitive Development*, **16**, 659–678.

Diamond, R. and Carey, S. (1986). Why faces are and are not special: An effect of expertise. *Journal of Experimental Psychology: General*, **115**, 107–117.

Dodwell, P.C. and Humphrey, G.K. (1990). A functional theory of the McCollough effect. *Psychological Review*, **97**, 78–89.

Ewbank, M.P. and Andrews, T.J. (2008). Differential sensitivity for viewpoint between familiar and unfamiliar faces in human visual cortex. *Neuroimage*, **40**, 1857–1870.

Favreau, O.E. and Corballis, M.C. (1976). Negative aftereffects in visual perception. *Scientific American*, **235**, 42–48.

Freiwald, W.A., Tsao, D.Y., and Livingstone, M. (2009). A face feature space in the macaque temporal lobe. *Nature Neuroscience*, **12(9)**, 1187–1196.

Frisby, J.P. (1980). *Seeing: Illusion, mind and brain.* Oxford: Oxford University Press.

George, N., Dolan, R. J., Fink, G.R., Baylis, G.C., Russell, C., and Driver, J. (1999). Contrast polarity and face recognition in the human fusiform gyrus. *Nature Neuroscience*, **2**, 574–580.

Golby, A.J., Gabrieli, J.D.E., Chiao, J.Y., and Eberhardt, J.L. (2001). Differential responses in the fusiform region to same-race and other-race faces. *Nature Neuroscience*, **4**, 845–850.

Goldstein, A.G. and Chance, J.E. (1980). Memory for faces and schema theory. *Journal of Psychology*, **105**, 47–59.

Grill-Spector, K., Kushnir, T., Edelman, S., Avidan, G., Itzchak, Y., and Malach, R. (1999). Differential processing of objects under various viewing conditions in the human lateral occipital cortex. *Neuron*, **24**, 187–203.

Haberman, J. and Whitney, D. (2007). Rapid extraction of mean emotion and gender from sets of faces. *Current Biology*, **17**, R751–753.

Harris, C.S. (1980). Insight or out of sight? Two examples of plasticity in the human adult. in C.S. Harris (ed.) *Visual coding and adaptability*, pp. 95–150. Hillsdale, NJ: L. Erlbaum Associates.

Haxby, J.V., Hoffman, E.A., and Gobbini, M.I. (2000). The distributed human neural system for face perception. *Trends in Cognitive Science*, **4**, 223–233.

Hebb, D.O. (1949). *The organisation of behaviour.* New York: Wiley.

Helson, H. (1948). Adaptation-level as a basis for a quantitative theory of frames of reference. *Psychological Review*, **55**, 297–313.

Helson, H. (1964). *Adaptation level theory.* New York: Harper & Row.

Hochberg, J.E. (1978). *Perception (2nd ed.).* Englewood Cliffs, New Jersy: Prentice-Hall.

Honekopp, J. (2006). Once more: Is beauty in the eye of the beholder? Relative contributions of private and shared taste to judgments of facial attractiveness. *Journal of Experimental Psychology: Human Perception & Performance*, **32**, 199–209.

Hosoya, T., Baccus, S.A. and Meister, M. (2005). Dynamic predictive coding by the retina. *Nature*, **436**, 71–77.

Hurlbert, A. (2001). Trading faces. *Nature Neuroscience*, **4**, 3–5.

Inn, D., Walden, K.J., and Solso, R.L. (1993). Facial prototype formation in children. *Bulletin of the Psychonomic Society*, **31**, 197–200.

Jaquet, E. and Rhodes, G. (2008). Face aftereffects indicate dissociable, but not distinct, coding of male and female faces. *Journal of Experimental Psychology: Human Perception & Performance*, **34**, 101–112.

Jaquet, E., Rhodes, G., and Hayward, W.G. (2007). Opposite aftereffects for Chinese and Caucasian faces are selective for social category information and not just physical face differences. *Quarterly Journal of Experimental Psychology*, **60**, 1457–1467.

Jaquet, E., Rhodes, G., and Hayward, W.G. (2008). Race-contingent aftereffects suggest distinct perceptual norms for different race faces. *Visual Cognition*, **16**, 734–753.

Jeffery, L. and Rhodes, G. (2008). Aftereffects reveal enhanced face-coding plasticity in young children. *Journal of Vision*, **8**, 187.

Jeffery, L., Rhodes, G., and Busey, T. (2006). View-specific norms code face shape. *Psychological Science*, **17**, 501–505.

Jeffery, L., Rhodes, G., and Busey, T. (2007). Broadly tuned, view-specific coding of face shape: Opposing figural aftereffects can be induced in different views. *Vision Research*, **47**, 3070–3077.

Jeffery, L., Rhodes, G., and Pellicano, E. (2009). Adaptive norm-based coding of facial identity in children: The face identity aftereffect is selective for opposite identities. Unpublished manuscript.

Jenkins, R., Beaver, J.D., and Calder, A.J. (2006). I thought you were looking at me: Direction specific aftereffects in gaze perception. *Psychological Science*, **17**, 506–513.

Jiang, F., Blanz, V., and O'Toole, A.J. (2006). Probing the visual representation of faces with adaptation: A view from the other side of the mean. *Psychological Science*, **17**, 493–500.

Jiang, F., Blanz, V., and O'Toole, A.J. (2007). The role of familiarity in three-dimensional view-transferability of face identity adaptation. *Vision Research*, **47**, 525–531.

Kelly, D.J., Quinn, P.C., Slater, A.M., *et al.* (2005). Three-month-olds but not newborns, prefer own-race faces. *Developmental Science*, **8**, F31–F36.

Kim, J.S., Yoon, H.W., Kim, B.S., Jeun, S.S., Jung, S.L., and Choe, B.Y. (2006). Racial distinction of the unknown facial identity recognition mechanism by event-related fMRI. *Neuroscience Letters*, **397**, 279–284.

Klin, A., Sparrow, S.S., de Bildt, A., Cicchetti, D.V., Cohen, D.J., and Volkmar, F.R. (1999). A normed study of face recognition in autism and related disorders. *Journal of Autism & Developmental Disorders*, **29**, 499–508.

Kloth, N. and Schweinberger, S.R. (2008). The temporal decay of eye gaze adaptation effects. *Journal of Vision*, **8**, 1–11.

Kohn, A. (2007). Visual adaptation: Physiology, mechanisms, and functional benefits. *Journal of Neurophysiology*, **97**, 3155–3164.

Langlois, J.H. and Roggman, L.A. (1990). Attractive faces are only average. *Psychological Science*, **1**, 115–121.

Laughlin, S.B. (2001). Energy as a constraint on the coding and processing of sensory information. *Current Opinion in Neurobiology*, **11**, 475–480.

Lawson, R.P., Clifford, C.W.G., and Calder, A.J. (2009). About turn: The visual representation of human body orientation revealed by adaptation. *Psychological Science*, **20**, 363–371.

Lee, K., Byatt, G., and Rhodes, G. (2000). Caricature effects, distinctiveness and identification: Testing the face-space framework. *Psychological Science*, **11**, 379–385.

Leopold, D.A. and Bondar, I. (2005). Adaptation to complex visual patterns in humans and monkeys. In C.W.G. Clifford and G. Rhodes (eds.) *Fitting the mind to the world: Adaptation and aftereffects in high-level vision*, pp. 189–211. Oxford: Oxford University Press.

Leopold, D.A., O'Toole, A.J., Vetter, T., and Blanz, V. (2001). Prototype-referenced shape encoding revealed by high-level aftereffects. *Nature Neuroscience*, **4**, 89–94.

Leopold, D.A., Rhodes, G., Müller, K-M., and Jeffery, L. (2005). The dynamics of visual adaptation to faces. *Proceedings of the Royal Society of London, Series B*, **272**, 897–904.

Leopold, D.A., Bondar, I. and Giese, M.A. (2006). Norm-based face encoding by single neurons in the monkey inferotemporal cortex. *Nature*, **442**, 572–575

Lie, H.C., Rhodes, G., and Simmons, L.W. (2008). Genetic diversity revealed in human faces. *Evolution*, **62**, 2473–2486.

Little, A.C., DeBruine, L.M., and Jones, B.C. (2005). Sex-contingent face aftereffects suggest distinct neural populations code male and female faces. *Proceedings of the Royal Society of London, Series B*, **272**, 2283–2287.

Little, A.C., DeBruine, L.M., Jones, B.C., and Watt, C. (2008). Category contingent aftereffects for faces of different races, ages and species. *Cognition*, **106**, 1537–1547.

Loffler, G., Yourganov, G., Wilkinson, F., and Wilson, H. (2005). fMRI evidence for the neural representation of faces. *Nature Neuroscience*, **8**, 1386–1391.

Lord, C., Rutter, M., and Le Couteur, A. (1994). Autism Diagnostic Interview–Revised. *Journal of Autism and Developmental Disorders*, **24**, 659–685.

MacLeod, D.I.A. and von der Twer, T. (2003). The pleistochrome: Optimal opponent codes for natural colours. In R. Mausfield, and D. Heyer (eds.) *Color perception: Mind and the physical world*, pp. 155–184. Oxford: Oxford University Press.

MacLin, O.H. and Webster, M.A. (2001). Influence of adaptation on the perception of distortions in natural images. *Journal of Electronic Imaging*, **10**, 100–109.

Masland, R.H. (1969). Visual motion perception: Experimental modification. *Science*, **165**, 819–821.

Mather, G. (1980). The movement aftereffect and a distribution-shift model for coding the direction of visual movement. *Perception*, **9**, 379–392.

Mather, G., Verstraten, F., and Anstis, S. (eds.) (1998). *The Motion Aftereffect: A Modern Perspective*. Cambridge, MA: MIT Press.

Mather, G., Pavan, A., Campana, G., and Casco, C. (2008). The motion aftereffect reloaded. *Trends in Cognitive Sciences*, **12**, 481–487.

Mazard, A., Schiltz, C., and Rossion, B. (2006). Recovery from adaptation to facial identity is larger for upright than inverted faces in the human occipito-temporal cortex. *Neuropsychologia*, **44**, 912–922.

McKone, E., Edwards, M., Robbins, R., and Anderson, R. (2005). The stickiness of face adaptation aftereffects. *Journal of Vision*, **5**, 822a.

Moradi, F., Koch, C., and Shimojo, S. (2005). Face adaptation depends on seeing the face. *Neuron*, **45**, 169–175.

Morikawa, K. (2005). Adaptation to asymmetrically distorted faces and its lack of effect on mirror images. *Vision Research*, **45**, 3180–3188.

Moscovitch, M. Moscovitch, M., Winocur, G., and Behrmann, M. (1997). What is special about face recognition: Nineteen experiments on a person with visual object agnosia and dyslexia but normal face recognition. *Journal of Cognitive Neuroscience*, **9**, 555–604.

Nishimura, M., Maurer, D., Jeffery, L., Pellicano, E., and Rhodes, G. (2008). Fitting the child's mind to the world: Adaptive norm-based coding of facial identity in 8-year-olds. *Developmental Science*, **11**, 620–627.

Ng, M., Boynton, G. M. and Fine, I. (2008). Face adaptation does not improve performance on search or discrimination tasks. *Journal of Vision*, **8**, 1–20.

Nosofsky, R.M. and Johansen, M.K. (2000). Exemplar-based accounts of "multiple-system" phenomena in perceptual categorization. *Psychonomic Bulletin & Review*, **7**, 375–402.

O'Leary, A. and McMahon, M. (1991). Adaptation to form distortion of a familiar shape. *Perception & Psychophysics*, **49**, 328–332.

Oruç, I. and Barton, J.J.S. (2011). Adaptation improves discrimination of face identity. *Proceedings of the Royal Society of London, Series B*. January 26. Epub ahead of print.

Pellicano, E., Jeffery, L., Burr, D., and Rhodes, G. (2007). Abnormal adaptive face-coding mechanisms in children with autism spectrum disorder. *Current Biology*, **17**, 1508–1512.

Perrett D.I, Penton-Voak I, Little A.C, *et al.* (2002). Facial attractiveness judgements reflect learning of parental age characteristics. *Proceedings of the Royal Society of London Series B*, **269**, 873–880.

Pimperton, H., Pellicano, E., Jeffery, L., and Rhodes, G. (2009). The role of higher-level adaptive coding mechanisms in the development of face recognition. *Journal of Experimental Child Psychology*, **104**, 229–238.

Reed, S.K. (1972). Pattern recognition and categorization. *Cognitive Psychology*, **3**, 382–407.

Regan, D. and Hamstra, S.J. (1992). Shape discrimination and the judgment of perfect symmetry: Dissociation of shape from size. *Vision Research*, **32**, 1845–1864.

Rhodes, G. (1988). Looking at faces: First-order and second-order features as determinants of facial appearance. *Perception*, **17**, 48–63.

Rhodes, G. (1996). *Superportraits: Caricatures and recognition*. Hove: The Psychology Press.

Rhodes, G. (2006). The evolution of facial attractiveness. *Annual Review of Psychology*, **57**, 199–226.

Rhodes, G. and Jaquet, E. (2010). Aftereffects reveal that adaptive face-coding mechanisms are selective for race and sex. In R.A. Adams Jr, N. Ambady, K. Nakayama, and S. Shimojo (eds.) *Social Vision*, pp. 347–362. New York: Oxford University Press.

Rhodes, G. and Jeffery, L. (2006). Adaptive norm-based coding of facial identity. *Vision Research*, **46**, 2977–2987.

Rhodes, G., Brennan, S., and Carey, S. (1987). Identification and ratings of caricatures: Implications for mental representations of faces. *Cognitive Psychology*, **19**, 473–497.

Rhodes, G., Carey, S., Byatt, G., and Proffitt, F. (1998). Coding spatial variations in faces and simple shapes: A test of two models. *Vision Research*, **38**, 2307–2321.

Rhodes, G., Jeffery, L., Watson, T.L., Clifford, C.W.G., and Nakayama, K. (2003). Fitting the mind to the world: Face adaptation and attractiveness aftereffects. *Psychological Science*, **14**, 558–566.

Rhodes, G., Jeffery, L., Watson, T., Jaquet, E., Winkler, C., and Clifford, C.W.G. (2004). Orientation-contingent face aftereffects and implications for face coding mechanisms. *Current Biology*, **14**, 2119–2123.

Rhodes, G., Robbins, R., Jaquet, E., McKone, E., Jeffery, L., and Clifford, C.W.G. (2005). Adaptation and face perception: How aftereffects implicate norm-based coding of faces. In C.W.G. Clifford and G. Rhodes (eds.) *Fitting the mind to the world: Adaptation and aftereffects in high-level vision*, pp. 213–240. Oxford: Oxford University Press.

Rhodes, G., Jeffery, L., Clifford, C.W.G., and Leopold, D.A. (2007a). The timecourse of higher-level face aftereffects. *Vision Research*, **47**, 2291–2296.

Rhodes, G., Maloney, L.T., Turner, J., and Ewing, L. (2007b). Adaptive face coding and discrimination around the average face. *Vision Research*, **47**, 974–989.

Rhodes, G., Evangelista, E., and Jeffery, L. (2009a). Orientation-sensitivity of face identity aftereffects. *Vision Research*, **49**, 2379–2385.

Rhodes, G., Louw, K., and Evangelista, E. (2009b). Perceptual adaptation to facial asymmetries. *Psychonomic Bulletin & Review*, **16**, 503–508.

Rhodes, G., Watson, T.L., Jeffery, L., and Clifford, C.W.G. (2010). Perceptual adaptation helps us identify faces from a familiar population. *Vision Research*, **50**, 963–968.

Robbins, R., McKone, E., and Edwards, M. (2007). Aftereffects for face attributes with different natural variability: Adaptor position effects and neural models. *Journal of Experimental Psychology: Human Perception and Performance*, **33**, 570–592.

Rotshtein, P., Henson, R.N.A., Treves, A., Driver, J., and Dolan, R.J. (2005). Morphing Marilyn into Maggie dissociates physical and identity representations in the brain. *Nature Neuroscience*, **8**, 107–113.

Rutherford, M.D., Chattha, H.M. and Krysko, K.M. (2008). The use of aftereffects in the study of the relationships among emotion categories. *Journal of Experimental Psychology: Human Perception & Performance*, **34**, 27–40.

Rutter, M., Bailey, A., and Lord, C. (2003). *SCQ: Social Communication Questionnaire*. Los Angeles, CA: Western Psychological Services.

Schwartz, O., Hsu, A., and Dayan, P. (2007). Space and time in visual context. *Nature Reviews: Neuroscience*, **8**, 522–535.

Sheinberg, D.L. and Logothetis, N.K. (1997). The role of temporal cortical areas in perceptual organization. *Proceedings of the National Academy of Sciences USA*, **94**, 3408–3413.

Simmons, L. W., Rhodes, G., Peters, M., and Koehler, N. (2004). Are human preferences for facial symmetry focused on signals of developmental instability? *Behavioral Ecology*, **15**, 864–871.

Skinner, A.L. and Berton, C.P. (2010). Anti-expression after effects reveal prototype-referenced coding of facial expressions. *Psychological Science*, **21**, 1248–1253.

Solso, R.L. and McCarthy, J.E. (1981a). Prototype formation of faces: A case of pseudomemory. *British Journal of Psychology*, **72**, 499–503.

Solso, R.L. and McCarthy, J.E. (1981b). Prototype formation: Central tendency models vs. attribute frequency model. *Bulletin of the Psychonomic Society*, **17**, 10–11.

Strauss, M.S. (1979). Abstraction of prototype information by adults and 10-month-old infants. *Journal of Experimental Psychology: Human Learning & Memory*, **5**, 618–632.

Sutherland, N.S. (1961). Figural aftereffects and apparent size. *Quarterly Journal of Experimental Psychology*, **13**, 222–228.

Suzuki, S. (2005). High-level pattern coding revealed by brief shape aftereffects. In C.W.G. Clifford and G. Rhodes (eds.) *Fitting the mind to the world: Adaptation and aftereffects in high-level vision*, pp. 135–172. Oxford: Oxford University Press.

Suzuki, S. and Cavanagh, P. (1998). A shape-contrast effect for briefly presented stimuli. *Journal of Experimental Psychology: Human Perception & Performance*, **24**, 1315–1341.

Tsao, D.Y. and Freiwald, W.A. (2006). What's so special about the average face? *Trends in Cognitive Sciences*, **10**, 391–393.

Valentine, T. (1991). A unified account of the effects of distinctiveness, inversion and race on face recognition. *Quarterly Journal of Experimental Psychology*, **43A**, 161–204.

Valentine, T. (2001). Face-space models of face recognition. In M.J. Wenger and J.T. Townsend (eds.) *Computational, geometric, and process perspectives on facial cognition: Contexts and challenges*, pp. 83–113. Hillsdale, NJ: Erlbaum.

Vul, E., Krizay, E., and MacLeod, D.I.A. (2008). The McCollough effect reflects permanent and transient adaptation in early visual cortex. *Journal of Vision*, **8(12):4**, 1–12.

Wallis, G., Siebeck, U.E., Swann, K., Blanz, V., and Bülthoff, H.H. (2008). The prototype effect revisited: Evidence for an abstract feature model of face recognition. *Journal of Vision*, **8**, 1–15.

Walton, G.E. and Bower, T.G.R. (1993). Newborns form "prototypes" in less than 1 minute. *Psychological Science*, **4**, 203–205.

Wark, B., Lundstrom, B.N., and Fairhall, A. (2007). Sensory adaptation. *Current Opinion in Neurobiology*, **17**, 423–429.

Watson, T.L. and Clifford, C.W.G. (2003). Pulling faces: An investigation of the face-distortion aftereffect. *Perception*, **32**, 1109–1116.

Watson, T.L. and Clifford, C.W.G. (2006). Orientation dependence of the orientation-contingent face aftereffect. *Vision Research*, **46**, 3422–3429.

Webster, M.A. (2003). Light adaptation, contrast adaptation, and human vision. In R. Mausfeld and D. Heyer (eds.) *Colour Perception: Mind and the Physical World*, pp. 67–110. Oxford: Oxford University Press.

Webster, M.A. and Leonard, D. (2008). Adaptation and perceptual norms in color vision. *Journal of the Optical Society of America, A*, **25**, 2817–2825.

Webster, M.A. and MacLin, O.H. (1999). Figural aftereffects in the perception of faces. *Psychonomic Bulletin & Review*, **6**, 647–653.

Webster, M.A., Kaping, D., Mizokami, Y., and Duhamel, P. (2004). Adaptation to natural face categories. *Nature*, **428**, 557–560.

Webster, M.A., Werner, J.S. and Field, D.J. (2005). Adaptation and the phenomenology of perception. In C.W.G. Clifford and G. Rhodes (eds.) *Fitting the Mind to the World: Adaptation and Aftereffects in High-Level Vision*, pp. 241–277. Oxford: Oxford University Press.

Werblin, F.S. (1973). The control of sensitivity in the retina. *Scientific American*, **228**, 70–79.

Wilson, H.R., Loffler, G., and Wilkinson, F. (2002). Synthetic faces, face cubes, and the geometry of face space. *Vision Research*, **42**, 2909–2923.

Winston, J.S., Henson, R.N.A., Fine-Goulden, M.R., and Dolan, R.J. (2004). fMRI-Adaptation reveals dissociable neural representations of identity and expression in face perception. *Journal of Neurophysiology*, **92**, 1830–1839.

Wolfe, J.M. and O'Connell, K.M. (1986). Fatigue and structural change: Two consequences of visual pattern adaptation. *Investigative Ophthalmology & Visual Science*, **27**, 538–543.

Xu, H., Dayan, P., Lipkin, R.M., and Qian, N. (2008). Adaptation across the cortical hierarchy: Low-level curve adaptation affects high-level facial-expression judgments. *Journal of Neuroscience*, **28**, 3374–3383.

Yamashita, J.A., Hardy, J.L., De Valois, K.K., and Webster, M.A. (2005). Stimulus selectivity of figural aftereffects for faces. *Journal of Experimental Psychology: Human Perception and Performance*, **31**, 420–437.

Yang, H., Shen, J., Chen, J., and Fang, F. (2011). Face adaptation improves gender discrimination. *Vision Research*, **51**, 105–110.

Yin, R.K. (1969). Looking at upside-down faces. *Journal of Experimental Psychology*, **81**, 141–145.

Zhao, L. and Chubb, C. (2001). The size-tuning of the face-distortion after-effect. *Vision Research*, **41**, 2979–2994.

Chapter 15

Unfamiliar Face Perception

A. Mike Burton and Rob Jenkins

Introduction

For purposes of identification, we are not face experts. It is certainly true to say that human observers show expertise in the perception of *some* faces: we can recognize our family and colleagues across large variations in lighting, pose, age, health, and expression. However, our abilities with unfamiliar faces are much less impressive. When asked to make judgments about the identity of strangers, either by remembering a face, or matching a person to their photograph, observers are very poor. Indeed, unfamiliar face recognition is not only bad, it is *surprisingly* bad.

In this chapter, we will describe some differences between familiar and unfamiliar face processing. We will start by presenting the evidence that unfamiliar face recognition is poor. Since this poor performance has implications both practically and theoretically, it is important to establish the facts first. We will then ask why it is that people appear to have little insight into their own poor performance with unfamiliar faces, and why it is that some sectors of society seem so keen to use faces as a means of proving identity. Following this, we will review some historical research comparing familiar and unfamiliar face processing. It will become clear that this distinction was important to early researchers, but that some early lessons have not been incorporated into modern theorizing. Finally, we will suggest that the modern tendency to conflate familiar and unfamiliar face processing, and to theorize about "face recognition" in general, lies at the heart of practical failures in this field. In a time of high security, we still do not have automated face recognition devices operating at anything near useful levels of accuracy. If psychological research is to benefit automatic systems, it is important to understand *both* expert performance and poor performance in humans.

Let us start by considering a situation in which unfamiliar face recognition is well-known to be poor: eyewitness testimony. There is a very large literature, some of it reviewed in this collection, demonstrating that eyewitnesses are fallible (Lindsay et al., Chapter 16, this volume). Indeed, understanding this fact may be regarded as an important success of psychological research; many national jurisdictions now incorporate measures to explain to jurors that eyewitnesses can be honestly mistaken, even when appearing confident in their identification of a suspect. The psychological study of this human fallibility has tended to emphasize the error-prone nature of memory. Since eyewitness testimony, by definition, requires recall of an event, or recognition of an individual, it is natural to explain errors in terms of fallible memory. So, for example, there is considerable research demonstrating that performance can be improved somewhat by trying to match the encoding and recall contexts, or by conducting psychologically-informed interview protocols (e.g. Malpas and Devine, 1981; Searcy et al., 1999; Meissner, 2002; Wells and Olson, 2003).

In recent years, the problem of unfamiliar face *matching* has come to be just as important practically as face *memory*. In daily life, we are increasingly asked to prove our identity by showing photo identification (ID), not only at airports and border crossings, but also in more mundane settings such as entry to the workplace. Furthermore, the rapid expansion of security surveillance means that many crimes are captured on film. The task of an observer is to verify matches in this setting, either person-to-photo, for example with passports, or photo-to-photo when comparing crime-scene footage to potential suspects. Despite eliminating the memory-load of normal eye-witness situations, it turns out that people are surprisingly bad at *matching* two images of the same unfamiliar person. In the next section we will review the evidence for this assertion.

Unfamiliar face matching

In a series of experiments, Bruce et al. (1999, 2001) showed participants 1-in-10 lineups of the type illustrated in Figure 15.1 (solutions given in endnote). Viewers were asked, for each array, whether the target person was present among the ten candidates, and if so to pick out the matching person. One way to think of these arrays is as a photographic version of police lineups, without the requirement to remember an incident. As with real lineups, all the faces fit the same general description (they were all clean-shaven young men with short hair). Participants performed surprisingly badly on this task, with 30% error rates on both target-present arrays and target-absent arrays.

This poor level of performance is particularly striking when one considers the nature of the photos. These images were all taken on the same day. The target photos (top of Figure 15.1) were taken with a different camera to the array photos, and this turns out to be a very important variable in unfamiliar face recognition. However, the individuals portrayed had no opportunity to change their hair, weight, health etc., and all were shown in near-identical pose, in excellent lighting. The people shown were not chosen to be particularly homogenous (they were a graduating class of police trainees), and while they all meet the same general description, this mirrors the real forensic situation well: typically, police line-ups are populated with foils who broadly resemble the suspect. Overall accuracy would doubtless be higher if foils were selected at random, as observers would seldom confuse faces of very different appearance. However, the problem of facial misidentification typically arises in situations of visual similarity. For this reason, foils in experimental settings should not be too dissimilar to targets, if the research is to capture the applied problem.

To examine viewers' poor matching performance further, we note that in target-present arrays, participants failed to pick anyone on roughly 20% of occasions, and on 10% of occasions they picked the wrong person (Bruce et al., 1999). So, in the presence of the correct person, with a photo taken on the same day, in the same pose, in good light, people choose the wrong person from a line-up 10% of the time. This is perhaps a surprising result. In the target-absent arrays, people are also willing to identify the target as the wrong man, doing so on 30% of occasions. These results have now been replicated many times, and with different stimulus sets and observers. For example, Figure 15.2 shows an example from Megreya and Burton (2008), in which arrays of Egyptian faces were shown to Egyptian subjects. Similar levels of performance were demonstrated to those in the original Bruce et al. studies.

Poor performance in the 1-in-10 simultaneous matching task suggests that part of the difficulty in eyewitness identification may be the encoding of unfamiliar faces in the first place. Even when memory load is practically eliminated, viewers are very severely impaired. However, this situation does add the extra difficulty of distractor processing. It may be that presenting participants with a choice of 10 possible matches makes this too difficult a task. The phenomenology of the task offers a clue to this. Participants often report that in attempting to solve the match, they find themselves resorting to a serial comparison of relatively isolated image features such as the angle of an eyebrow or a particular lock of hair. Reducing the number of possible matches should decrease the cognitive demands of this strategy.

(a)

(b)

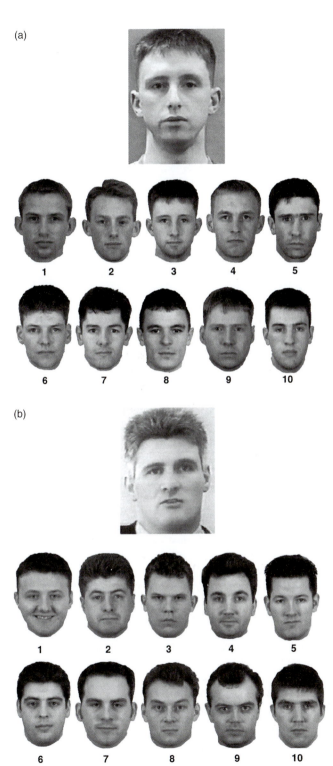

Fig. 15.1 (a) The person shown at the top may or may not be one of the 10 in the array. (b) The person shown at the top may or may not be one of the 10 in the array.

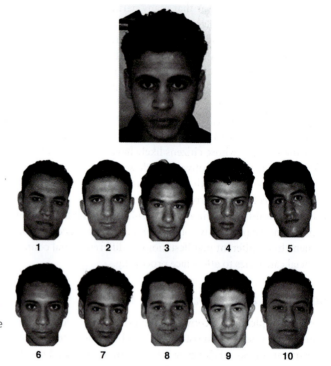

Fig. 15.2 The person shown at the top may or may not be one of the 10 in the array. A 1-in-10 line-up with Egyptian faces.

More recently, we have studied viewers' ability to make simple match/mismatch decisions to pairs of faces. We have conducted these tests with the same faces as used by Bruce et al. (Megreya and Burton 2006), with the Egyptian faces (Megreya and Burton, 2008), and with a new set of faces which vary in age, gender, and ethnicity. Using this latter set, we have developed the Glasgow Face Matching Test (GFMT; Burton et al., 2010), a psychometric instrument for measuring an individual's matching ability.

Figure 15.3 shows examples from the GFMT. Using all these different stimulus sets, we have found the same thing: viewers are very poor at matching pairs of unfamiliar faces, typically getting between 10% and 25% of pairs wrong, even when the photos are taken on the same day, in excellent lighting, and in the same pose. In all cases, different cameras have been used to capture the two photos, and the image-specific differences inherent in this camera-change appear to be enough to affect matching badly. Note that foils were always chosen to give rise to similar verbal descriptions (i.e. young men were never paired with old women), but the population of faces was not chosen to be particularly homogenous—in fact all these sources represented students with particular courses in common. Pairs of photos gathered from the real world present an even greater challenge than those taken in research settings, as real world photos encompass a natural range of variability. Figure 15.4 illustrates this problem. The top row shows photos of two *different* people, taken by the same photographer in the same town on the same day. The bottom row shows photos of the *same* person, taken by the same photographer in the same room, 18 years apart.

So, it appears that face matching is difficult. But is this a particular problem with matching photos? Perhaps if viewers were asked to match a live person to their photo, as with passport inspections, observers would perform better. In fact, the data show that a real-life setting does not improve performance. Kemp et al. (1997) were the first to demonstrate poor ability to match

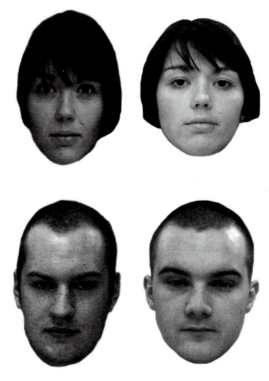

Fig. 15.3 Two items from the Glasgow Face Matching Test— a match (top row), and a mismatch (bottom row).

people to their photo IDs. In an experiment performed after-hours in a large supermarket, experienced cashiers were asked to verify shoppers' ID by means of a photo on their credit cards. Shoppers were a diverse group (men and women, with a range of age and ethnicity). Despite the fact that cashiers knew they were taking part in an experiment, and that accuracy was emphasized, a very large number of errors were made. For example, when a shopper presented a fraudulent card which matched the bearer for sex and ethnicity, cashiers made 34% errors, falsely accepting incorrect photo-ID. To follow up these results, Megreya and Burton (2008) compared photo–photo face matching to live–photo face matching for both 1-in-10 and pairwise matching. In this experimental setting, we were able to rotate stimuli around conditions, such that all actors were seen equally often live, and as photographs. The results showed no difference at all between matching a person to their photo, and matching two photos of that person. In both cases, observers were highly error-prone making roughly 17% errors in the pairwise case. Very recently, results from Davies and Valentine (2009) have demonstrated similar findings. These researchers asked participants to match a live person to moving CCTV footage. As with other research described here, they found that observers were highly error prone in this task, even when the CCTV footage showed very high quality close-up sequences.

Unfamiliar face recognition is very poor: Why do people not know this?

The results reviewed above show a level of face matching performance which could certainly not be regarded as demonstrating expertise. In this context, it is interesting to ask why our poor levels of performance seem to be so little understood. In practical settings, security experts and legislators

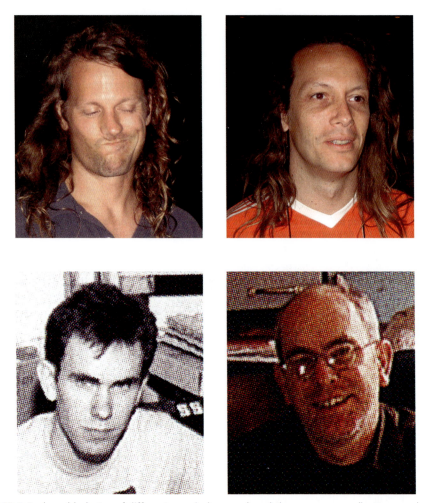

Fig. 15.4 Real world photos of different people (top row) and the same person (bottom row). Bottom row photos from 20 years of Dischord, 2002, Washington DC: Dischord Records. Copyright (2002) by Glen E. Friedman. Reprinted with permission.

continue to expand the use of photo ID, thus asking inspectors to perform a task which we know to be highly error-prone. In psychological theorizing, models continue to be produced which conflate familiar and unfamiliar face recognition, ignoring the very large differences between the two. In the following section we will consider the underlying reasons for differences between familiar and unfamiliar face processing, but first, it is worth asking how we came to the present state of affairs in which this distinction is often ignored.

Use of repeated images in tests of face recognition

In many tests of face recognition, for example in recognition memory, the same image is used at learning and test. In very early studies (e.g. Hochberg and Galper, 1967; Nickerson, 1965), high rates of recognition memory for faces were reported, but later studies demonstrated a severe drop

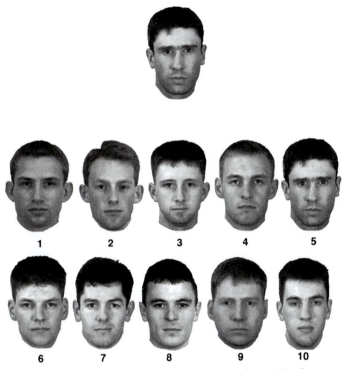

Fig. 15.5 The person shown at the top may or may not be one of the 10 in the array. An easy task with identical images.

in performance when the particular photo of an individual was changed between presentations (e.g. Bruce, 1982). In short, it is now clear that *image* recognition is very good, and when this is confounded with *face* recognition, misleading results can be obtained. For example, consider Figure 15.5. Although this presents a situation more starkly than in normal experiments, the ease with which the task can be solved contrasts well with the difficulty observers have with tasks such as those illustrated in Figures 15.1 and 15.2. In short, confounding image recognition with face recognition gives the wrong answer—because the former task is easy, and the latter is hard when the faces are unfamiliar.

Familiar face recognition is easy

Perhaps the most compelling reason why people tend to assume that we have general expertise in face recognition is because *familiar* face recognition is so good. Figure 15.6 shows a match which is very easy for viewers who are familiar with the person. In contrast to Figure 15.3, observers are not distracted by change in cameras, viewing angle, or change in the person's physical appearance. Viewers do not report trying to match physical aspects of the two photos, but instead simply recognize the same person separately in the two instances. In fact, familiar face recognition is robust over very severe degradation of images. Figure 15.7 shows a CCTV image taken from an operational security camera in our home university. Despite the very poor resolution, lighting, and viewing angle, students can recognize their (familiar) lecturers in these images almost perfectly (Burton et al., 1999).

Fig. 15.6 Two different photos of the same familiar person, taken on the same day. Photo taken from the public domain. Source: the United States Department of Defense. http://www.defense. gov/multimedia.

Fig. 15.7 An image from a working CCTV system. Viewers familiar with these people can identify them with very high accuracy.

We propose that non-psychologists addressing security issues are drawn to the use of face recognition because of our impressive ability to recognize familiar people. Unfortunately, we all tend intuitively to over-generalize this expertise to unfamiliar faces, even though the formal evidence does not support this. It is easy to see how this misplaced confidence can come about. A great deal of the time that we spend looking at faces is spent looking at familiar faces. After accounting for family and friends, colleagues, acquaintances, and media celebrities, rather little of our contact time with faces involves people who we have never seen before. However, virtually all of the applied interest in face recognition is in that atypical case; when an identity check is performed, it is generally to verify the identity of an unfamiliar person. To make matters worse, insight into our over-generalization of expertise is difficult to achieve, for at least two reasons. First, outside of psychology laboratories, we seldom receive feedback on our errors. If we encounter an unfamiliar person on one day, and then fail to recognize the same person the next day, this raises no dilemma. We can simply assume that the second encounter was with a different person. In the absence of any corrective feedback, this is an entirely plausible interpretation, but it adds to the mistaken impression that we never miss a face. The second reason is that familiarity is rapidly acquired, so that we leave behind our poor performance with new faces after rather modest exposure. We return to the issue of face learning in a later section.

Neuroscientific evidence does not highlight differences between familiar and unfamiliar faces

Although we hope to have demonstrated the clear behavioral differences between familiar and unfamiliar face recognition, there does not seem to be such clear evidence for a neurological distinction. A great many neuroimaging studies have presented faces as stimuli, and face perception researchers have increasingly turned to neuroimaging methods. As this trend gathered pace, the absence of a clear neuroscientific marker for face familiarity may have led to this issue being overlooked, in favor of other aspects of face perception that are more amenable to neuroimaging. For example, the extensive work on the electrophysiological component N170 shows clear sensitivity to faces (e.g. Bentin et al., 1996; see Eimer, Chapter 17, this volume). However, this early component is not readily modulated by familiarity (Bentin and Deouell, 2000; Eimer, 2000). Similarly, functional magnetic resonance imaging (fMRI) work on the fusiform face area (FFA) (Kanwisher et al., 1997; reviewed elsewhere in this volume) does not show a clear distinction between familiar and unfamiliar faces (e.g. Haxby et al., 2000; Leveroni et al., 2000), though there are some reports of marginal sensitivity (Dubois et al., 1999; Rossion et al., 2003). These major loci of neuroscientific face recognition research tend not to highlight effects of face familiarity, instead apparently reflecting more general face processing, or more general familiarity that extends to non-face stimuli (e.g. Haxby et al., 2000). Recently however, some specific markers have been proposed. The MEG component, M170, is sometimes taken as an analog of the event-related potential (ERP) N170 component. There is some evidence that M170 is modulated by familiarity (Kloth et al., 2006), although a familiarity distinction does not emerge in all M170 studies (Ewbank et al., 2007).

Within electrophysiological work there are some subtle effects which are more reliable markers of familiarity. For example, the ERP component N250r is sensitive to repetitions of familiar faces only (Engst et al., 2006; Schweinberger et al., 2002, 2004; Tanaka et al., 2006). This component is driven by visual recognition of a familiar person, and is sensitive to change in picture (i.e. it is reduced, though continues to exist, for repetitions in which the photograph of the person is changed). It has been argued (Bindemann et al., 2008; Kaufmann et al., 2009) that this component reflects a higher level of visual recognition, akin to the view-independent representations which are the core of many models of face recognition (Bruce and Young, 1986).

In fMRI research, evidence is beginning to accrue for an effect of familiarity in fMR-adapation. In a series of experiments Ewbank and Andrews (2008) found adaptation to repeated presentations of faces in FFA (though not in superior temporal sulcus). Furthermore, this adaptation was strongly modulated by familiarity. A change in viewing angle between repetitions of a face was enough to provide release from adaptation for unfamiliar faces. However, for familiar faces, adaptation was observed across changes in viewpoint. This generalization across viewing angles, for familiar faces only, leads the authors to suggest that this marker is a good index of familiarity in BOLD response.

The main message from the neuroscientific literature is that a reliable marker for face familiarity has been surprisingly difficult to find. This contrasts with the behavioral case, where the distinction between familiar and unfamiliar face processing is strong, clear, and reliable across a wide range of measures.

Theoretical distinctions between familiar and unfamiliar face processing

We have argued that, despite the applied importance of this distinction, contemporary research does not pay sufficient attention to the difference between familiar and unfamiliar face recognition. This has not always been the case. Early experiments using recognition memory tests consistently found that familiar faces were recognized faster and more accurately than unfamiliar faces (e.g. Bruce, 1986; Ellis, 1981; Ellis et al., 1979; Klatzky and Forest, 1984). In addition to overall differences in task performance, there is also evidence that changes in photo between first exposure and test lead to sharper reductions in performance for unfamiliar than for familiar faces. Changes in expression (Patterson and Baddeley, 1997), lighting (Hill and Bruce, 1996) and viewpoint (O'Toole et al., 1998; Roberts and Bruce, 1989) have all been shown to have a severe effect on recognition memory for unfamiliar faces, but not for familiar faces.

In the neuropsychological field, dissociations between familiar and unfamiliar face processing are also long-established. Skin conductance measures show a marked difference as a result of viewing familiar versus unfamiliar faces, and this is observed in some prosopagnosic patients (Bauer, 1984; Tranel and Damasio, 1985) as well as in typical viewers (Ellis et al., 1993, 1999).

All these demonstrations show responses modulated by familiarity, but none have the power to differentiate quantitative from qualitative effects. The evidence just reported could all be due to reduced response to unfamiliar items on the measure of interest. However a qualitative difference is suggested by some neuropsychological evidence, in the form of a double dissociation between familiar and unfamiliar face recognition. Several prosopagnosic patients have been reported who show preserved ability to match unfamiliar faces, despite having lost the ability to recognize familiars (e.g. Bauer, 1984; Benton et al., 1983; Young et al., 1993). On the other side of the dissociation, Malone et al., (1982) report a patient who had relatively preserved ability to recognize familiar faces, but was severely impaired in matching unfamiliars.

There are also some suggestions of a qualitative familiarity effect from behavioral studies. Many of these have focused on the apparent differences in those aspects of the face which are used by viewers. For example, there is an "internal feature advantage" for familiar faces. When asked to recognize parts of faces, viewers are reliably faster and more accurate with the internal features of a familiar face than the external features. However, this distinction is not present for unfamiliar faces (Ellis et al., 1979; Young et al., 1985). Recently, Osborne and Stevenage (2008) have demonstrated that this internal feature advantage increases with increasing familiarity, and is entirely eliminated by inverting the face.

Jackson and Raymond (2008) have examined the capacity of visual working memory (WM) for faces, using a change-detection procedure. They found that visual WM performance was significantly better, and that capacity was significantly higher, for familiar rather than unfamiliar faces. These results held even under high verbal-WM loads (so that viewers could not label familiar people). Once again, the familiar/unfamiliar distinction was eliminated by inversion. Upside-down familiar faces behave just like upright unfamiliar faces under these conditions—a pattern to which we will return. Finally, Jackson and Raymond (2006) demonstrated an interesting familiarity-based distinction in a low-level attentional task. Unfamiliar faces were prone to being missed in an "attentional blink" experiment, at ISIs which allowed detection of familiar faces. These relatively low-level effects provide further converging evidence for a distinction between familiar and unfamiliar face processing.

If there is a *qualitative* difference between familiar and unfamiliar faces, where might it lie? The argument is articulated directly by Hancock and colleagues (2000), who suggest that unfamiliar face processing is based on "relatively low-level image descriptions." That is to say, that while familiar faces appear to be processed in some abstractive way, allowing flexible perception (for example which will survive a change in camera), unfamiliar faces in contrast are coded as *pictures*. This is a very strong statement of the argument, probably too strong, but in the remainder of this section we will try to illustrate why such a suggestion might be warranted.

One way to investigate processes involved in familiar and unfamiliar face processing is to examine the individual variation among perceivers. To this end, Megreya and Burton (2006), investigated individual differences in unfamiliar face matching. Although not the topic of this chapter, it is important to point out that the poor average levels of performance described above mask very large individual differences which are stable–some viewers are simply better at face matching tasks than others (see Russell et al., 2009, for more recent evidence of this). These differences allow one to examine the relationship between viewers' performance on different face tasks. Using different types of face matching task (both 1-in-10 and pairwise matching), we discovered no correlation between subjects' ability to match familiar and unfamiliar faces. However, there was a very large correlation between their ability to match unfamiliar faces, and their ability to match these same unfamiliar faces upside-down. For familiar faces, this correlation did not exist—there was no association between the ability to match familiar faces upright and inverted. Finally, there was a strong correlation between subjects' ability to match *upright unfamiliar* and *inverted familiar* faces.

These results are quite striking. It is well known that inverting a face makes it harder to process for identity, and this is commonly held to be due to the fact that face-specific processing ("configural processing") is disengaged while viewing inverted faces (Tanaka and Gordon, Chapter 10, this volume). What we appear to be observing in the results above is that upright familiar faces behave in one way, while unfamiliar faces, inverted familiar faces, and inverted unfamiliar faces all behave in a different way. In short, whatever is lost in the comparison between familiar upright and inverted faces, is also lost in the comparison between familiar and unfamiliar faces. For this reason, we called our paper "Unfamiliar faces are not faces," a strong title, but a position we would like further to develop here. As with Hancock et al. (2000), we propose that unfamiliar faces are processed in mainly image-specific ways, and benefit less from abstracted processing. For this reason, poor performance in matching tasks, reviewed above, arises because viewers are forced into a strategy of image matching. This is a difficult task, and one which is not necessary for familiar face processing (compare Figures 15.3 and 15.6). Note that this hypothesis is consistent with the research of Jackson and Raymond (2008) and Osborne and Stevenage (2008), described above. In those (very different) tasks, perception of familiar faces also dissociated from inverted familiar faces, which in turn behaved like upright unfamiliar faces. The problem is that it is difficult to find a task that is suitable for both familiar and unfamiliar faces, so the definitive experiments have not been done.

In more recent work we have observed a further dissociation between familiar and unfamiliar faces. It has been known for some time that unfamiliar faces do not demonstrate a "mirror effect" in recognition memory, an interesting observation first reported by Vokey and Read (1992). The mirror effect refers to the fact that items which are easy to remember when they have been seen, are also easy to reject as unseen when they have not been shown previously. This phenomenon has been observed for many classes of stimulus (for a review see Glanzer et al., 1993). However, this effect does not hold for unfamiliar faces, and Vokey and Read's results have now been replicated using several different methods by several different groups (e.g. Hancock et al., 1996; Lewis and Johnston, 1997). The result is perhaps surprising—one might think that for an unusual-looking face it would be easy to know when one had seen it, and easy to know when one had not, but in fact these two tasks are unrelated (a result which holds across observers, as well across faces).

In Megreya and Burton (2007), we presented a set of matching studies which demonstrate the same dissociation for unfamiliar face *matching*. So, across an experiment in which pairs of faces are matched, it is possible to ask how many times a particular face is matched to its partner correctly, as well as how many times it is correctly rejected when presented in a mismatch. It turns out that these measures are uncorrelated—faces are neither easy nor hard to match overall, instead, some faces are easy to match correctly, and some easy to reject correctly, but these sets of faces are unrelated. Of most interest here, is that the standard mirror effect returns when the faces are familiar. Using a learning procedure in which some of the faces within an experiment have previously been learned, it was possible to demonstrate a clear mirror effect for familiar faces, in the absence of an equivalent effect for unfamiliar faces. In common with many of the effects reviewed in this section, it seems that we have evidence here for another index of face familiarity. This brings us to the topic of the next section, face learning.

Face learning

We have argued above that there are qualitative differences between face processing for familiar and unfamiliar faces. If this is true, then it poses a major challenge—how do faces become familiar in the first place? We have noted that there are large performance differences between identity-based tasks for familiar and unfamiliar faces—this much is indisputable, whether or not one accepts the argument that these reflect qualitative processing differences. It is also true to say that we are constantly learning faces, and that this process continues through life. It is therefore a great mystery how the system moves from "unintelligent" image-based processing typical of unfamiliar faces, to sophisticated and generalizable processing which characterizes familiar face processing.

Given the importance of the topic, it is perhaps surprising that relatively little research has been published on how faces are learned. One of the problems with conducting such research is measuring how well a face has been learned. In a typical experiment viewers are exposed to a set of faces, and subsequently asked whether or not they have seen particular faces before (e.g. Bonner et al., 2003; Kaufmann et al., 2009). The problem with this approach is that it tends to be blunt—faces are typically learned quite fast, and there is little room in the dependent variable to pick up the effects of within-experimental manipulations.

In a series of studies, Clutterbuck and Johnston (2002, 2004, 2005) have demonstrated that pairwise face matching is an excellent index of familiarity. The task has the advantage that no measure of explicit knowledge is required (neither "old/new," nor "familiar/unfamiliar" judgments). Instead, subjects are simply presented with pairs of faces and asked whether each pair match or not. Clutterbuck and Johnston demonstrate quite convincingly that this index is sensitive to levels of familiarity–and measures of response latency continue to show graded effects of familiarity, even when accuracy reaches ceiling levels.

In recent work we have begun to ask how faces might come to be familiar. In doing so, we have appealed to the notion of an "average" face, a concept introduced to modern face research by Benson and Perrett (1993), which we have extended for the purpose of theoretical and practical facial recognition (Burton et al., 2005, Jenkins and Burton, 2008; Jenkins et al., 2006). Figure 15.8 shows how individual images ("instances") of a particular person's face may be successively combined to form a running average of that person. Figure 15.9 shows four averages of famous people, each constructed from 16 original photographs. Our proposal is that face learning can be understood in these terms, and it relies on two hypotheses: (1) the long-run average of a person's face forms a good representation, capable of supporting the generalizable face recognition typical of familiar faces; (2) the successive refinement of the average, through exposure to different instances, works as a good model of face learning. We will examine these two hypotheses in turn.

Using computer-based face recognition algorithms, we have demonstrated that the average face works extremely well as a basis for recognition. The problem of automatic face recognition is typically to match an incoming image with all the images held in a database. In this way, systems compare two different images of an individual. If a sufficiently close match is found, then a hit is registered.

In the computer-based face recognition literature, the focus of attention is almost always on the nature of the matching algorithm. Faces have to be matched across a range of views, lighting conditions, and so forth, and so highly sophisticated matching algorithms are required. However, our approach has been very different. Instead of concentrating on the nature of the matching algorithm, we have considered the nature of the images to be matched. It is here that the advantage for averages has been apparent. It turns out, across different matching algorithms, that the match

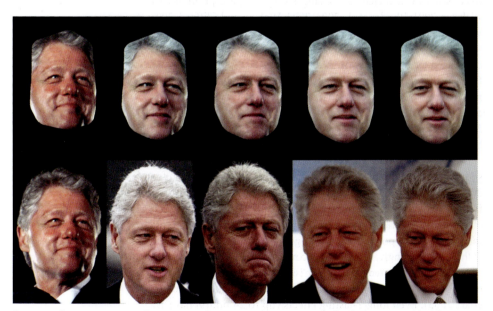

Fig. 15.8 The construction of an average face. As each new image of Bill Clinton is added (bottom row), the average is updated (top row). Photo taken from the public domain. Source: the United States Department of Defense. http://www.defense.gov/multimedia.

Fig. 15.9 Some average photos of celebrities. 16 images were used to construct each average.

between a photo of someone and an average of that person, is typically closer than the match between two individual images. Using this approach we have tested the two most prevalent classes of automatic face recognition device. One system, based on principal components analysis (PCA) of images, extracts matching dimensions based on the statistical variation in facial images. Using such a system, we demonstrated that storing a database of face averages, rather than a database of face images, significantly improved performance (Burton et al., 2005). Using a completely different system, based on wavelet decomposition (Wiskott et al., 1997), we also showed a very significant increase in performance when the system was required to match a photo to an average, as compared to matching two photos (Jenkins and Burton, 2008). In short, the pairwise difference between two individual photos can be very large, but the distance between a photo and that person's average is very frequently much smaller. This is illustrated in Figure 15.10.

This practical demonstration of the usefulness of facial averages leads one to ask how they confer a recognition advantage. Our proposal is that any particular image of a person has image-specific characteristics which will tend to dominate a match. Consider figure 15.10. One approach to computer-based matching using an example (the left in figure 15.10) would be to attempt to "partial out" those aspects of the image which are not specific to the person, prior to attempting a match. This is a very difficult problem. It requires an understanding of the light and lighting conditions, good estimates of the reflectance properties of skin and hair, the position and focal properties of the camera, and an assumption that the person has not changed very much himself between this photo and any to which it is to be matched. In contrast, the use of an average simply eliminates much of this variability. For example, over several images, the direction and strength of the lighting is likely to vary in ways that are uncorrelated to the person under view, and so simply averaging over these eliminates them without the need for any complex calculation to partial them away. We therefore propose that the advantage for averages relies as much on *eliminating* spurious (image-based) information, as it does on the formation of a prototype across instances of the same person.

In fact, this idea is a very old one. Frances Galton was the first to propose the use of facial averages, which he called *composite portraits*, though he is better known for producing averages across different people of a similar type (particularly criminals convicted of the same offense). In fact, he was also interested in the idea of producing averages within an identity, and wrote the following in 1878:

> Another use of this process [composite portraiture] is to obtain by photography a really good likeness of a living person. The inferiority of photographs to the best works of artists, so far as resemblance is concerned, lies in their catching no more than a single expression. If many photographs of a person

Fig. 15.10 A photograph (left) and average image (right) of the same famous face. Photo taken from the public domain. Source: the United States Department of Defense. http://www.defense.gov/multimedia.

were taken at different times, perhaps even years apart, their composite would possess that in which a single photograph is deficient. (Galton, 1878, p. 140.)

This quotation exactly captures the proposal being developed here: individual photographs are the product of the moment, capturing all kinds of information which is irrelevant to the *identity* of the individual, and it is this information which stands in the way of a "really good likeness."

This brings us to the proposal for how faces are learned. We suggest that unfamiliar face processing is predominantly image-based—simply because one has no information about how a person looks beyond the information shown in a particular photo. Since it is impossible from a single shot to know which aspects of the photo are due to the person depicted, and which are due to the image-characteristics, one is forced into a simple image-bound strategy to perform tasks such as matching. In contrast, familiar face matching need not rely on this unsophisticated process. Instead, one can use a stored representation of a person (an average built-up over many instances), and this will match a large variety of images. So, the case of a familiar face match, such as that in Figure 15.6, relies on comparison to a stable abstract representation. Under this scheme, learning corresponds to successive refinement of one's representation of a face. Early in the process, one has to use an unrefined representation: either a single image or an average of two or three. As learning takes place, this representation is successively refined, incorporating novel instances into the same average representation.

In domains other than face recognition, this type of distinction between familiar and unfamiliar elements is commonplace and uncontroversial. We offer the following analogy with language, which provides a useful point of reference for managing expectations about what should and should not be possible with faces. Consider the Dutch sentence "Een goede onderzoeker moet kunnen leiden." As non-Dutch speakers, we are able to make some progress with this—it is relatively clear how to read the words, and one can formulate some reasonable hypotheses about how the sentence is constructed. However, if we asked readers to compare this with the second sentence "Een goede onderzoeker moet kunnen lijden," one would be reduced to simple part-by-part matching. A Dutch speaker would have to make no such comparison: the sentences have completely different meanings, and may be rejected as dissimilar immediately. (The first means "A good researcher must be able to lead," whereas the second translates as "A good researcher must be able to suffer.")

The point of this illustration is that sentences with different meanings can look and sound more similar than sentences with the same meaning. Language users are, of course, aware of this possibility. As such, we are unlikely to take superficial similarity to imply semantic similarity in languages that we know. However, in unfamiliar languages we are much more vulnerable to this type of error: we have nothing else to go on but superficial appearances. The main interest from our point of view is that the analogous problem also applies to face recognition. Photos of different people can be more similar than photos of the same person. The language analogy is helpful because it provides an intuitive touchstone for guiding our expectations about face recognition performance. We properly understand that we cannot deal with unknown languages. If we are to improve our face recognition infrastructure, we need to understand that we cannot deal with unknown faces.

Summary and conclusions

The research reviewed in this chapter illustrates very large differences in viewers' ability to recognize familiar and unfamiliar faces. In brief, we are very good at recognizing the people we know (even in difficult conditions) whereas we are very poor at identifying people we do not know (even in near-perfect conditions). Perhaps surprisingly, this distinction is not well-known outside the scientific community, leading to unrealistic expectations of what can be achieved in unfamiliar face recognition. The distinction is also sometimes under-played in scientific theorizing about face perception. We believe that these results have potentially significant consequences both practically and theoretically, and so we conclude by highlighting the most important of these.

Police procedures should incorporate an understanding of the differences between familiar and unfamiliar face recognition

While there is a general understanding of the fallibility of face *memory* in legal settings, this does not currently extend to face *matching*. So, for example, officers are regularly required to testify that images from security surveillance match a person subsequently arrested. In the UK, jurors are sometimes shown security camera footage, and invited by counsel to identify a defendant in such footage (Davis and Valentine, 2009). There is now considerable evidence that this is a more difficult task than people commonly imagine.

In contrast, there is also little understanding of the *accuracy* of familiar face recognition. For example, the utility of surveillance footage is often discussed in court, where advocates are interested to establish whether the quality of particular images is sufficiently high to support recognition. In fact, this issue relies more on the familiarity of the viewer than on the quality of the image–observers can recognize people they know well in very severely degraded images. These and related issues should be disseminated widely among legal professionals.

Engineers need to build an understanding of familiarity into their automatic face recognition systems

Why have automated face recognition devices failed so far? Our proposal is that this is partly because automatic systems typically emulate a human task which psychologists know to be difficult—matching two photos of the same person with no other context. Given the evidence from human perception, it is not even clear whether this type of matching is possible—certainly there are no natural systems which can achieve it. Instead, high performance in human face recognition relies very greatly on familiarity. This suggests that a good way to make progress in automated systems would be somehow to emulate human familiarity within the system. We have suggested one way in which this might be achieved—by basing the match on an abstracted representation, the face average. Of course, there will be many other proposals for capturing familiarity—including some based on storage of multiple exemplars. We do not know which approach will eventually prove most fruitful. However, it does seem clear that some acknowledgment of familiarity effects in face recognition need to be built in to future systems. Forty years of attempting image-based matching has singularly failed to produce a working system.

Theoretical models of face recognition should incorporate face learning

We started this chapter with a provocative statement that people are not face experts. The reader will be aware that the issue of expertise is important to face researchers, and the "are faces special?" debate is discussed elsewhere (McKone and Robbins, Chapter 9, this volume). Our suggestion is that this debate does not address the most fundamental question in face recognition. Instead, the most important question is how we come to be expert in *some* faces. How is it that we are able to acquire information about particular people which allows us to recognize them subsequently over a huge range of conditions—including those which have not previously been encountered? This is an apparently easy process—we meet new people throughout life, and it seems that relatively little exposure can shift the viewer from unsophisticated image-bound strategies to expert performance. Considering the fluidity with which we can learn faces, it might be more appropriate to inquire whether faces are special in the sense that there are special mechanisms to support *learning* faces. In addition to research on the characteristics of face representations (for example in neuroscientific programs) it may be especially fruitful to focus on the processes involved as we learn to recognize particular faces so well.

Endnote: solutions to line-up displays

Figure 15.1a–3; Figure 15.1b–Target absent; Figure 15.2–Target absent; Figure 15.5–5.

References

Bauer, R.M. (1984). Autonomic recognition of names and faces in prosopagnosics: A neuropsychological application of the Guilty Knowledge Test. *Neuropsychologia*, **22**, 457–469.

Benson, P.J. and Perrett, D.I. (1993). Extracting prototypical facial images from exemplars. *Perception*, **22**, 257–262.

Bentin, S. and Deouell, L.Y. (2000). Structural encoding and identification in face processing: ERP evidence for separate mechanisms. *Cognitive Neuropsychology*, **17**, 35–54.

Bentin, S., Allison. T., Puce, A., Perez, E., and McCarthy, G. (1996). Electrophysiological studies of face perception in human. *Journal of Cognitive Neuroscience*, **8**, 551–565.

Benton, A.L., Hamsher K.S., Varney, N.R., and Spreen, O. (1983). *Contributions to neuropsychological assessment.* New York: Oxford University Press.

Bindemann, M., Burton, A.M., Leuthold, H., and Schweinberger, S.R. (2008). Event-related potentials of face recognition: Geometric distortions and the N250r brain response to stimulus repetitions. *Psychophysiology*, **45**, 535–544.

Bonner, L., Burton, A.M., and Bruce, V. (2003). Getting to know you: How we learn new faces. *Visual Cognition*, **10**, 527–536.

Bruce, V. (1982). Changing faces: Visual and non-visual coding processes in face recognition. *British Journal of Psychology*, **73**, 105–116.

Bruce, V. (1986). Influences of familiarity on the processing of faces. *Perception*, **15**, 387–97.

Bruce, V., and Young, A.W. (1986). Understanding face recognition. *British Journal of Psychology*, **77**, 305–327.

Bruce, V., Henderson, Z., Greenwood, K., Hancock, P., Burton, A.M., and Miller, P. (1999). Verification of face identities from images captured on video. *Journal of Experimental Psychology: Applied*, **5**, 339–360.

Bruce, V., Henderson, Z., Newman, C., and Burton, A.M. (2001). Matching identities of familiar and unfamiliar faces caught on CCTV images. *Journal of Experimental Psychology: Applied*, **7**, 207–218.

Burton, A.M, Wilson, S., Cowan, M., and Bruce, V. (1999). Face recognition in poor quality video: evidence from security surveillance. *Psychological Science*, **10**, 243–248.

Burton, A.M., Jenkins, R., Hancock, P.J.B., and White, D. (2005). Robust representations for face recognition: The power of averages. *Cognitive Psychology*, **51**, 256–284.

Burton, A.M., White, D., and McNeill, A. (2010). The Glasgow Face Matching Test. *Behavior Research Methods*, **42**, 286–291.

Clutterbuck, R. and Johnston, R.A. (2002). Exploring levels of face familiarity by using an indirect face-matching measure. *Perception*, **31**, 985–994.

Clutterbuck, R. and Johnston, R.A. (2004). Matching as an index of face familiarity. *Visual Cognition*, **11**, 857–869.

Clutterbuck, R. and Johnston, R.A. (2005). Demonstrating how unfamiliar faces become familiar using a face matching task. *European Journal of Cognitive Psychology*, **17**, 97–116.

Davis, J. and Valentine, T. (2009). CCTV on trial: Matching video images with the defendant in the dock. *Applied Cognitive Psychology*, **23**, 482–505.

Dubois, S., Rossion, B., Schiltz, C., Bodart, J.M., Michel, C., Bruyer, R., and Crommelinck, M. (1999). Effect of familiarity on the processing of human faces. *Neuroimage*, **9**, 278–289.

Eimer, M. (2000). Event-related brain potentials distinguish processing stages involved in face perception and recognition. *Clinical Neurophysiology*, **111**, 694–705.

Ellis, H.D., Shepherd, J.W., and Davies, G.M. (1979). Identification of familiar and unfamiliar faces from internal and external features: Some implications for theories of face recognition. *Perception*, **8**, 431–439.

Ellis H.D. (1981). Theoretical aspects of face recognition. In G.M. Davies, H.D. Ellis, and J.W. Shepherd (eds.) *Perceiving and Remembering Faces*, pp. 171–197. London: Academic Press.

Ellis, H.D., Young, A.W., and Koenken, G. (1993). Covert face recognition without prosopagnosia. *Behavioural Neurology*, **6**, 27–32.

Ellis, H.D., Quayle, A.H., and Young, A.W. (1999). The emotional impact of faces (but not names): Face specific changes in skin conductance responses to familiar and unfamiliar people. *Current Psychology*, **18**, 88–97.

Engst, F.M., Martin-Loeches, M., and Sommer, W. (2006). Memory systems for structural and semantic knowledge of faces and buildings. *Brain Research*, **1124**, 70–80.

Ewbank, M.P. and Andrews, T.J. (2008). Differential sensitivity for viewpoint between familiar and unfamiliar faces in human visual cortex. *NeuroImage*, **40**, 1857–1870.

Ewbank, M.P., Smith, W.A.P, Hancock, E.R. and Andrews, T.J. (1997). The M170 reflects a viewpoint-dependent representation for both familiar and unfamiliar faces. *Cerebral Cortex*, **18**, 364–370.

Galton F. (1878). Composite portraits. *Journal of the Anthropological Institute*, **8**, 132–144.

Glanzer, M., Adams, J.K., Iverson, G.J., and Kim, K. (1993). The regularities of recognition memory. *Psychological Review*, **100**, 546–567.

Hancock, P.J.B., Burton, A.M., and Bruce, V. (1996). Face processing: Human perception and principal components analysis. *Memory and Cognition*, **24**, 26–40.

Hancock, P.J.B., Bruce, V., and Burton, A.M. (2000). Recognition of unfamiliar faces. *Trends in Cognitive Science*, **4**, 330–337.

Haxby, J.V., Hoffman, E.A., and Gobbini, M.I. (2000). The distributed neural system for face perception. *Trends in Cognitive Sciences*, **4**, 223–233.

Hill, H. and Bruce, V. (1996). Effects of lighting on the perception of facial surfaces. *Journal of Experimental Psychology: Human Perception and Performance*. **22**, 986–1004.

Hochberg, J. and Galper, R.E. (1967). Recognition of faces: 1. An exploratory study. *Psychonomic Science*, **9**, 619–620.

Jackson, M.C. and Raymond, J.E. (2006). The role of attention and familiarity in face identification. *Perception and Psychophysics*, **68**, 543–557.

Jackson, M.C. and Raymond, J.E. (2008). Familiarity Enhances Visual Working Memory for Faces, *Journal of Experimental Psychology: Human Perception and Performance*. **34**, 556–568.

Jenkins, R. and Burton, A.M. (2008). 100% accuracy in automatic face recognition. *Science*, **319**, 435.

Jenkins, R., Burton, A.M., and White, D. (2006) Face recognition from unconstrained images: Progress with prototypes. *Proceedings of the Seventh IEEE International Conference on Automatic Face and Gesture Recognition*, pp. 25–30.

Kanwisher, N., McDermitt, J., and Chun, M.M. (1997). The fusiform face area: a module in human extrastriate cortex specialized for face perception. *Journal of Neuroscience*, **17**, 4302–4411.

Kaufmann, J.M., Schweinberger, S.R., and Burton, A.M. (2009). N250 ERP correlates of the acquisition of face representations across different images. *Journal of Cognitive Neuroscience*, **21**, 625–641.

Kemp, R., Towell, N., and Pike, G. (1997). When seeing should not be believing: Photographs, credit cards and fraud. *Applied Cognitive Psychology*, **11**, 211–222.

Klatzky, R.L. and Forrest, F.H. (1984). Recognizing familiar and unfamiliar faces. *Memory and Cognition*, **12**, 60–70.

Kloth, N., Dobel, C., Schweinberger, S.R., Zwitserlood, P., Bolte, J., and Junghofer, M. (2006). Effects of personal familiarity on early neuromagnetic correlates of face perception. *European Journal of Neuroscience*. **24**, 3317–3321.

Leveroni, C.L., Seidenberg, M., Mayer, A.R., Mead, L.A., Binder, J.R., and Rao, S.M. (2000). Neural systems underlying the recognition of familiar and newly learned faces. *Journal of Neuroscience*, **20**, 878–886.

Lewis, M.B. and Johnston, R.A. (1997). Familiarity, target set, and false positives in face recognition. *European Journal of Cognitive Psychology*, **9**, 437–459.

Malone, D.R., Morris, H.H., Kay, M.C., and Levin, H.S. (1982). Prosopagnosia: a double dissociation between the recognition of familiar and unfamiliar faces. *Journal of neurology, Neurosurgery and Psychiatry*, **45**, 820–822.

Malpass, R. S. and Devine, P.G. (1981). Eyewitness identification: Lineup instructions and the absence of the offender. *Journal of Applied Psychology*, **66**, 482–489.

Megreya, A.M. and Burton, A.M. (2006). Unfamiliar faces are not faces: Evidence from a matching task. *Memory and Cognition*, **34**, 865–876.

Megreya, A.M. and Burton, A.M. (2007). Hits and false positives in face matching: A familiarity-based dissociation. *Perception and Psychophysics*, **69**, 1175–1184.

Megreya, A.M. and Burton, A.M. (2008). Matching faces to photographs: Poor performance in eyewitness memory (without the memory). *Journal of Experimental Psychology: Applied*, **14**, 364–372.

Meissner, C.A. (2002). Applied aspects of the instructional bias effect in verbal overshadowing. *Applied Cognitive Psychology*, **16**, 911–928.

Nickerson, R.S. (1965). Short-term memory for complex meaningful visual configurations: A demonstration of capacity. *Canadian Journal of Psychology*, **19**, 155–160.

Osborne, C.D. and Stevenage, S.V. (2008). Internal feature saliency as a marker of familiarity and configural processing. *Visual Cognition*, **16**, 23–43.

O'Toole, A.J., Edelman, S., and Bülthoff, H.H. (1998). Stimulus-specific effects in face recognition over changes in viewpoint. *Vision Research*, **38**, 2351–263.

Patterson, K.E. and Baddeley, A.D. (1977). When face recognition fails. *Journal of Experimental Psychology: Human Learning and Memory*, **3**, 406–417.

Roberts T. and Bruce, V. (1989). Repetition priming of face recognition in a serial choice reaction-time task. *British Journal of Psychology*, **8**, 201–211.

Rossion, B., Schiltz, C. and Crommelinck, M. (2003). The functionally defined right occipital and fusiform "face areas" discriminate novel from visually familiar faces. *NeuroImage*, **19**, 877–883.

Russell, R., Duchaine, B. and Nakayama, K. (2009). Super-recognizers: People with extraordinary face recognition ability. *Psychonomic Bulletin and Review*, **16**, 252–257.

Schweinberger, S.R., Pickering, E.C., Jentzsch, I., Burton, A.M., and Kaufmann, J.M. (2002). Event-related brain potential evidence for a response of inferior temporal cortex to familiar face repetitions. *Cognitive Brain Research*, **14**, 398–409.

Schweinberger, S.R., Huddy, V., and Burton, A.M. (2004). N250r: a face-selective brain response to stimulus repetitions. *Neuroreport*, **15**, 1501–105.

Searcy, J.H., Bartlett, J. C., and Memon, A. (1999). Age differences in accuracy and choosing in eyewitness identification and face recognition. *Memory and Cognition*, **27**, 538–552.

Tanaka, J.W., Curran, T., Porterfield, A.L., and Collins, D. (2006). Activation of preexisting and acquired face representations: The N250 event-related potential as an index of face familiarity. *Journal of Cognitive Neuroscience*, **18**, 1488–1497.

Tranel, D. and Damasio, A.R. (1985). Knowledge without awareness: An autonomic index of facial recognition by prosopagnosics. *Science*, **228**, 1453–1454.

Vokey, J.R. and Read, J.D. (1992). Familiarity, memorability, and the effect of typicality on the recognition of faces. *Memory and Cognition*, **20**, 291–302.

Wells, G.L. and Olson, E. (2003). Eyewitness identification. *Annual Review of Psychology*, **54**, 277–295.

Wiskott, L., Fellous, J-M., Kruger, N., and von der Malsburg, C. (1997). Face recognition by elastic bunch graph matching. *IEEE Transactions on Pattern Analysis and Machine Intelligence*, **17**, 775–779.

Young, A.W., Hay, D.C., McWeeny, K.H., Flude, B.M., and Ellis, A.W. (1985). Matching familiar and unfamiliar faces on internal and external features. *Perception*, **14**, 737–746.

Young, A.W., Newcombe, F., de Haan, E.H.F., Small, M., and Hay, D.C. (1993). Face perception after brain injury: selective impairments affecting identity and expression. *Brain*, **116**, 941–959.

Chapter 16

Face Recognition in Eyewitness Memory

R.C.L. Lindsay, Jamal K. Mansour,
Michelle I. Bertrand, Natalie Kalmet,
and Elisabeth I. Melsom

Introduction

People's ability to remember faces is impressive. If someone showed you a set of six faces, could you pick your mother out of that set of faces? What about your favorite actor? We remember thousands of familiar faces seemingly without effort. However, would you be able to select the person who served you at the last restaurant you visited? What about someone you saw run in and out of your neighbor's house in the middle of the night? You would probably be much less accurate identifying these individuals. Examples such as these reflect the nature of eyewitness memory: under some conditions people are likely to accurately recognize faces, and under others they are less likely to do so. Worse still, people are prone to false positive choices (mistakenly selecting individuals they did not actually see). Such false positive choices are the single leading cause of wrongful conviction (Connors et al., 1996). In this chapter, we address some of the reasons that eyewitnesses are prone to making errors, particularly false identifications.

Commonly, witnesses to crimes are asked to perform tasks that involve memory for faces such as describing or creating a composite of the perpetrator and examining lineups or mug books to indicate whether the perpetrator is present. Face recognition is impacted by two types of variables: estimator variables that cannot be controlled and system variables that are under direct control by the criminal justice system (Wells 1978). Estimator variables include situational factors (e.g. viewing conditions), factors particular to the eyewitness (e.g. age, sex), and factors related to the perpetrator (e.g. distinctiveness). Estimator variables are explored both by eyewitness researchers and traditional facial memory researchers.

In this chapter we provide a cursory discussion of differences between typical facial memory and eyewitness studies and conclude that the two areas generally find similar results. We then provide a brief review of estimator variable effects. Finally, an important focus of the chapter is a discussion of system variables. System variables are rarely studied by traditional facial recognition researchers but reveal important factors that police and policy makers should consider with regard to eyewitness identification and the courts. We will conclude that there is still room for considerable improvement in identification procedures and encourage more system variable research as a means of reducing wrongful convictions.

Eyewitness memory paradigms versus facial recognition paradigms

Eyewitness researchers are generally interested in how well people remember a perpetrator they have seen commit a crime. People who witness a crime are commonly asked to describe the person they saw and/or to identify the individual. Studies of eyewitness memory commonly involve the viewing of some event (live, video, image), followed by a delay and subsequent identification (recognition) procedure (mugshots, showup, lineup). Eyewitness and face recognition researchers use different methods to learn about memory for faces in terms of the number of targets, type of exposure, and nature of the recognition task.

Facial recognition studies present participants with multiple target faces to be remembered, often dozens or even hundreds (Pozzulo 2007). Eyewitness memory studies most often present a single target (e.g. Lindsay and Wells, 1985). Facial recognition studies tend to present face images one at a time and on blank backgrounds with no competing information. As well, some facial recognition studies include faces that are devoid of information commonly used to determine identity, such as hair color or faces that are computer-generated images (e.g. Hill and Bruce, 1996). In contrast, eyewitness studies normally present to-be-remembered faces as part of a more complex scene that often includes other objects and possibly other faces. Eyewitness studies also involve a much greater range of exposure durations (e.g. Dysart and Lindsay, 2007b). In facial recognition paradigms, participants frequently do not attempt to remember the targets until after they have seen all of the target faces (e.g. Shepherd et al., 1991) and are normally aware of the upcoming memory test (e.g. Chance and Goldstein 1979; Troje and Kersten, 1999). In terms of the recognition task, facial recognition paradigms generally include both the target faces and additional, previously unseen faces in the set of photos shown, and sometimes use the same image or pose at study and test. In contrast, in eyewitness paradigms the recognition task normally follows exposure to the to-be-remembered individual without exposure to other faces and participants are often not told about the upcoming recognition task until after encoding (e.g. Lindsay and Wells, 1985). Eyewitness studies frequently present lineups that are either target-present (target is in the lineup) or target-absent (target is not in the lineup) and the targets almost never appear exactly as they appeared at encoding (Pozzulo 2007).

Methodological differences between facial recognition and eyewitness research are not absolute. Some eyewitness studies are specifically designed to test the impact of other faces as a source of interference (e.g. Dysart et al., 2001) or inform participants of the upcoming recognition task before the staged crime (e.g. Beaudry et al., 2006a). Both facial recognition and eyewitness studies manipulate the quality of exposure to faces (e.g. De Jong et al., 2005; Lindsay et al., 2008). Eyewitness research frequently utilizes theory and methodology arising from face recognition research (e.g. Loftus and Harley, 2005). In addition, eyewitness researchers are turning to face recognition paradigms to maximize the amount of data collected from participants. For example, Meissner et al. (2005) allowed participants to view lineups only after they had seen a series of target faces.

Beyond methodology, the two paradigms differ in how data are interpreted and how the results of the research are used. Facial recognition studies tend to focus on understanding the mechanisms of face recognition. Results of eyewitness memory research are discussed and evaluated primarily with regard to their usefulness for policy in police investigations and trials. Although researchers in the eyewitness field often believe mundane realism (e.g. presenting live or taped staged events rather than still photos as stimuli) is required in order to apply their results to policy, a meta-analysis by Shapiro and Penrod (1986), including both eyewitness and face recognition studies, found that type of study accounted for only 3% of the variance in hit rates and 2% of the variance in false alarm rates. Thus, the mundane realism often employed by eyewitness researchers may not be critical.

Influence of estimator variables on eyewitness facial recognition accuracy

Estimator variables are those that *cannot* be controlled by the justice system. The factors discussed below do not represent an exhaustive list but reflect the majority of research in the area to date. Certainly other estimator variables remain to be examined (e.g. sleep deprivation).

Intrinsic factors

Distinctiveness

The more distinctive a face is, the more likely it is to be remembered (Brigham, 1990; Courtois and Mueller, 1981; Light et al., 1979; Shapiro and Penrod, 1986; Shepherd et al., 1991), though not all studies have found significant effects (e.g. Brigham, 1990; Valentine, 1991). Distinctive faces produce both more hits and fewer false alarms[1] (Shapiro and Penrod, 1986). Distinctiveness may act at the retrieval stage by providing distinguishing cues matching the target to the photo. Or, distinctiveness could act at the encoding stage because distinctive faces, by definition, provide unusual cues that may be processed more deeply or extensively (Fleishman et al., 1976; Shapiro and Penrod, 1986). Facial distinctiveness has been shown to influence accuracy in both face recognition (Light et al., 1979) and eyewitness memory studies (Courtois and Mueller, 1981).

Ethnicity

An individual is more likely to correctly identify, and less likely to falsely identify, a person of their own ethnicity compared to people of other ethnicities. This phenomenon is known as the cross-race effect or the own-race bias and is commonly found in both eyewitness and facial recognition studies (Brigham et al., 2007; Meissner and Brigham, 2001a; Shapiro and Penrod, 1986; and Hugenberg et al., Chapter 13; Rossion and Michel, Chapter 12, this volume). For example, Hispanic participants were better at recognizing Hispanic as compared to black faces across variations in encoding duration, retention interval, arousal, and attentional demands (MacLin et al., 2001). The effect is consistent but not equally strong across ethnicities (Brigham, 2002; Chance et al., 1975; Geiselman et al., 1996). A meta-analysis found a larger cross-race effect for participants of European ancestry than other participants on false alarms (Meissner and Brigham, 2001a). The cross-race effect also exists for children, although it becomes more pronounced with age and may not exist for very young children (Chance et al., 1982; Goodman et al., 2007). However; research also exists demonstrating cross-race effects with infants (Kelly et al., 2007).

When Meissner and Brigham (2001a) compared studies using face recognition versus eyewitness methodologies, they found no difference in false alarms for the cross-race effect. However, they did find that eyewitness studies tended to obtain more hits for own-race faces than for other-race faces compared to face recognition studies. This finding is interesting, as more real-world suspect identifications are made when the suspect is of the same versus a different race than the criminal (Behrman and Davey, 2001; Valentine et al., 2003).

Age

For facial memory studies, age of participants influences the accuracy of facial recognition. For children, hits increase and false alarms decrease with age (Carey et al., 1980; Flin, 1980; Goldstein and Chance, 1964). Once adulthood is reached however, there is a monotonic decline in accuracy of facial memory with a substantial decline occurring after the age of 50 (O'Rourke et al., 1989). Children and the elderly are as accurate as young adults at correctly identifying a previously seen face from lineups, but they are much more inclined to make false positive recognition responses in eyewitness studies (Bartlett and Memon, 2007; Pozzulo, 2007).

---

[1] Hit refers to any correct decision about a stimulus that was previously presented (saying a face was seen before when it was seen before). False alarm refers to an incorrect decision about a stimulus not previously presented (saying a face was seen before when it was not seen before). Eyewitness researchers often use the terms correct and false identification instead of hit and false alarm respectively. Both sets of terms are used here interchangeably.

The age effects with children may be related to less developed language abilities, a lower memory load capacity, a poorer understanding of the task, or a sense of pressure to choose (Brigham, 2002; Pozzulo, 2007). Comparing the standard face recognition and eyewitness paradigms, face recognition studies show that the performance of children between the ages of 10 to 12 years is on par with adults for both hits and false alarms (e.g. Chance and Goldstein, 1979). Eyewitness studies show that by around age 5 years, children's performance is on par with adults for hits, but they do not perform like adults in terms of false alarms until the ages of 10 to 12 years, or possibly older (Cross et al., 1971; Flin, 1980; Parker and Ryan, 1993; Pozzulo and Lindsay, 1998).

The age effect with elderly adults shows a pattern similar to that of children (Bartlett and Fulton, 1991; Bartlett et al., 1989; Fulton and Bartlett, 1991; Mason, 1986). In this case, false alarms increase with age (Anastasi and Rhodes, 2006; Bartlett and Memon, 2007; Fulton and Bartlett, 1991; Wright and Stroud, 2002). However, this age effect is not always found—while it clearly holds for seniors over age 70, the effects are sometimes absent or reversed for those under 70 (Bartlett and Memon, 2007). Recently, Bartlett and Memon (2007) analyzed 17 data sets and found an age-related performance difference only when young adults do very well.

Large sets of homogeneous face images may be particularly difficult for seniors to process (Koutstaal and Schacter 1997; Koutstaal et al., 1999). Long delays may also cause seniors to experience a greater detriment to their identification accuracy, although this may only be the case for individuals over age 70 (Bartlett and Memon, 2007). Finally, the similarity of the age between the perpetrator and witness can also influence recognition. Younger adults tend to obtain more hits with young faces than old faces, and seniors are either better with old faces compared to young, or show no difference (Anastasi and Rhodes, 2006; Bartlett and Memon, 2007; Fulton and Bartlett, 1991; Wright and Stroud, 2002).

Stress

Deffenbacher (1983) reviewed 21 published studies of the effect of stress on identification accuracy. Ten studies showed an increase in performance with increasing stress and the remaining 11 showed a decrease in performance with increasing stress. Deffenbacher concluded that the results were consistent with the Yerkes–Dodson law—task performance improves as stress increases up to a critical point after which performance worsens. Christianson's (1992) meta-analysis suggested that negative emotional events increased memory for central information but decreased memory for peripheral information of the event, and thus the Yerkes–Dodson law did not properly characterize the relationship between stress and eyewitness memory. Consistent with Christianson's reasoning, Read et al. (1992) found that arousal produced no change in identification accuracy for individuals considered peripheral to an event but increased identification accuracy for individuals central to an event.

However, a problem with the work reviewed by Christianson (1992) is its focus on anxiety production that may involve orienting (i.e. information receptive) rather than defensive responses (e.g. avoidance, aggression) and thus may not be truly representative of stress responses for witnesses of crime. Recently, Deffenbacher et al. (2004) reviewed 27 studies that focused on the more defensive stress response. They found an overall negative effect of stress on identification accuracy from target-present, but not target-absent, lineups. Of interest, five of the 27 studies in this review were face recognition studies and for these, the effect of stress was non-significant and only about one-third the size of that seen in eyewitness studies. This suggests that there may be something fundamentally different about experiencing stress in an eyewitness context. Deffenbacher et al. also examined the effect of study paradigm and found that in high stress situations the proportion of correct responses was lower in eyewitness (0.39) than in face recognition studies (0.56). No significant difference was found in the low-stress situation. Deffenbacher et al. also reviewed studies with children and adults and found both age groups showed similar effects of stress. Stress is a complex mechanism that influences numerous physical and psychological systems. Systematic research differentiating types of stress and its impact on different human systems is needed (and ongoing) to resolve this issue.

Weapons and violence

The weapon focus effect (WFE) refers to inferior recall for aspects of an experienced event if a weapon (versus a neutral object) was present and visible during the event (Kramer et al., 1990; Loftus et al., 1987; Steblay, 1992; Tooley et al., 1987). For example, in Loftus et al. (1987) participants who viewed a slide sequence that included a weapon were less accurate on a lineup identification task than those who viewed a sequence without a weapon. The WFE on correct identifications has been demonstrated under many different circumstances and with a variety of weapons (e.g. guns, knives, syringes, bottles, meat cleaver; Cutler et al., 1987a,b; Kramer et al., 1990; Loftus et al., 1987; Maass and Köhnken, 1989; Pickel, 1998, 1999).

A meta-analysis conducted by Steblay (1992) confirmed that this effect exists for identifications in eyewitness studies. However, an archival analysis of actual crimes by Behrman and Davey (2001) did not find a relationship between suspect identification and the presence or absence of a weapon. Possible reasons for the difference in findings between experimental and actual cases may be related to crime seriousness (Cutler et al., 1987b; Leippe et al., 1978) and event duration (Mansour et al., 2008).

Threat and violence can occur in the absence or presence of weapons, and have been associated with improved recognition memory for adults, as well as children (e.g. Cutler et al., 1987b; Kinzler and Shutts, 2008), though not all studies find a significant effect (e.g. Clifford and Hollin, 1981). The literature on weapons, threat, and violence is necessarily related and it is not yet clear which component of an event or interaction of components is responsible for particular memorial results. Clearly the pattern of results is complex and somewhat contradictory. Only further research can clarify this situation.

Involvement

The degree of direct involvement in a criminal event, such as being the teller actually robbed versus a teller several wickets away during a bank robbery, has been associated with stronger memory for an event (e.g. Stanny and Johnson, 2000). However, only a few studies have examined the impact of involvement on recognition. Hosch and Cooper (1982) found that identification accuracy was no better when participants were victims of crime compared to bystanders. Behrman and Davey's (2001) archival analysis showed a small, non-significant effect whereby victims of crimes made slightly more suspect identifications than witnesses to the same crimes. There is insufficient data at this time to draw strong conclusions but the common sense notion that more involved witnesses must be more accurate is not supported by the data to date.

Drugs

In general, when a person's physical state at the time of recognition is the same as it was during encoding, they demonstrate greater accuracy in their memory for the event compared to when their physical states are incongruent (Morris et al., 1977). However, witnesses much more frequently observe crimes while under the influence of drugs than attempt identifications while under the influence. Overall, the influence of drugs on recognition—in laboratory-based eyewitness memory studies at least—seems to be non-existent or marginal (Yuille and Tollestrup, 1990; Yuille et al., 1998). For example, when participants were intoxicated at study (but not at test), Read et al. (1992) found a marginal effect of intoxication on recognition from lineups, and then only for participants in a low arousal condition. In contrast, Dysart et al. (2002) found that participants with low blood-alcohol levels at study and test were less likely than participants with higher blood alcohol levels to falsely identify innocent people from a single photo (a "showup").

Extrinsic factors

Distance

Face recognition studies on accuracy and distance have shown that the amount of information available to a witness decreases as the distance between him/her and the perpetrator increases (De Jong et al., 2005; Loftus and Harley, 2005). As such, there is an inverse relationship between identification accuracy and distance (Lindsay et al., 2008; Uelmen, 1980; Wagenaar and Van Der Schrier, 1996), though the detrimental effect of distance on accuracy is mitigated by familiarity with the target (Greene and Fraser, 2002). Wagenaar and Van Der Schrier (1996) showed that the effect of distance held for both target-present and target-absent lineups. Lindsay et al. (2008) had participants make lineup decisions after viewing a target individual from a variety of distances (5 to 50 m). Importantly, they found that while hits decreased as distance increased, the proportion of correct rejections did not vary with distance (cf. Valentine et al., 2003). Thus, as distance between a perpetrator and witness increases, the credibility of lineup identification decreases because witnesses are just as likely to choose but less likely to choose correctly.

Obstruction

The topic of obstruction has received little attention in the face recognition literature. Valentine et al. (2003) found no difference in suspect identifications for partial obstruction versus absence of obstruction. Some work has evaluated how shadows affect face recognition (Braje, 2003; Braje et al., 1998), as shadows may obscure or enhance three-dimensional information about the face. While Braje et al. (1998) found shadows impair recognition, Braje (2003) did not find an effect of shadows and suggested task differences may explain why shadows did not impair recognition in his study. Braje et al. (1998) presented faces in only one position, while Braje (2003) presented faces in two different positions for recognition. When to-be-compared faces are presented in different positions, shadow information may not be a useful cue and thus is not processed; as such, there would be no impact of shadows on recognition.

Disguise

Research confirms a significant detrimental effect of disguise on eyewitness identification accuracy which generalizes across age groups (Beaudry et al., 2007; Cutler et al., 1987a,b; Mansour et al., 2007). Face recognition and eyewitness research often considers the impact of disguising individual features (e.g. Sadr et al., 2003; Terry, 1993) for example by masking eye and hair information (Beaudry et al., 2007; Cutler and Penrod, 1988; Mansour et al., 2007; McKelvie, 1976; Terry, 1993). The eyes are the most looked at feature in a face so it is not surprising that masking them affects face recognition (Schyns et al., 2002). For example, McKelvie (1976) found that masking eyes led to poorer recognition than masking mouths, which in turn led to poorer recognition than no masking.

Hair information also may be particularly important to identification because hairstyles vary greatly from person to person. Wright and Sladden (2003) found a significant decrease in hits when hair information was absent versus present during encoding (and present at recognition in both cases). Yarmey (2004) presented targets in no disguise or with both a hat and sunglasses, but found no effect of disguise; interestingly, hair cues were still visible in the disguise condition. The bottom line is that disguise works, but generally because important cues to face recognition (hair, eyes) are disrupted or masked.

Encoding duration

Face recognition research demonstrates that more correct identifications are obtained when the exposure to the target is long and more false identifications are obtained when the exposure is short (Laughery et al., 1971; Light et al., 1979; Shepherd et al., 1991). For example, MacLin et al., (2001) looked at the effect of encoding duration on the cross-race effect and found a systematic decrease in accuracy with decreased exposure time, regardless of whether the targets were black or Hispanic. Ellis et al. (1977) systematically varied exposure duration (0.25, 0.5, 1, 2, or 4 seconds) for 30 faces and found a linear increase in sensitivity (d') in a later recognition task with increasing exposure times. Findings are similar using face recognition and eyewitness paradigms (Cutler et al., 1987a,b; Meissner and Brigham, 2001a). Longer exposures have been associated with greater accuracy for both real faces (e.g. Memon et al., 2003) and Identikit faces (Reynolds and Pezdek, 1992). On the other hand, some DNA exoneration cases involved very long exposures. For example, Jennifer Thompson saw the man who raped her over a period close to 30 minutes but still misidentified Ronald Cotton as the rapist a few days later and failed to correctly recognize Bobby Poole, the man who actually raped her, when she saw him in court later (Loeterman, 1997).

Pose

The pose of a face at the time of encoding and retrieval affects the accuracy of face recognition. Some have argued that the three-quarter pose (45-degree view) leads to the most accurate recognition of unfamiliar faces (Bruce et al., 1987; Krouse, 1981; Logie et al., 1987). Other research has shown that the three-quarter advantage only occurs when lighting is from the top (Hill and Bruce, 1996). Still other research fails to find a three-quarter advantage, particularly when pose at exposure and the recognition test are the same or taken into account (Hill et al., 1997; Laughery et al., 1971; Logie et al., 1987; Liu and Chaudhuri, 2002). In their meta-analysis of both eyewitness and face recognition studies, Shapiro and Penrod (1986) found pose to be a significant predictor of hits, but not false alarms, with the three-quarter pose at encoding eliciting the best recognition performance, followed by front and then profile. Pose accounted for 3% of variance in performance.

Unfortunately, no published research has specifically manipulated pose in an eyewitness study; all published research on the effects of pose have been face recognition research. Kalmet (2008) recently showed participants videos of a target turning 180 degrees and then showed them three different lineups: straight on, profile, and three-quarter pose. She found no difference in identification accuracy based on pose at retrieval when participants were unaware of a forthcoming identification. However, when participants were aware they would be doing an identification task they made more innocent suspect identifications when they were shown lineup members in a three-quarter pose (followed by straight on and then profile poses). Interestingly, in a second experiment where pose at encoding and retrieval were counterbalanced, Kalmet found that for target-present lineups, a three-quarter view of the target at exposure led to more correct identifications than any other exposure, regardless of the pose of lineup members (retrieval).

A match of poses between encoding and retrieval consistently leads to better recognition performance than a change of pose (Hill and Bruce, 1996; Krouse, 1981; O' Toole et al., 1998) though Stephan and Caine (2007) found this to be true only for a profile view. In contrast, Kalmet's (2008) second experiment found that match between exposure pose and retrieval pose was beneficial only for straight on views of the target. Troje and Bülthoff (1996) found that pose at encoding but not pose at retrieval affected accuracy and that the ideal pose depended on surface properties of the face. Logie et al. (1987) showed that presentation of three poses led to better recognition accuracy than presentation of only one pose. Similarly, Bertrand et al. (2006) reported superior hit rates from lineups using profile photos in addition to straight on rather than just straight on photos (false positive rates varied little). Overall, much more research on the impact of pose would be useful in both the facial recognition and eyewitness literatures.

Lighting

Intuitively, we expect that when a perpetrator was witnessed committing a crime in the dark, recognition will be poorer than when a perpetrator was witnessed committing a crime in day-light, although there is little research in this area using the eyewitness paradigm. What has been done shows a systematic increase in eyewitness identification accuracy as illumination increases, for both target-present and target-absent lineups (Wagenaar and Van Der Schrier, 1996) and these results are similar to those found in face recognition studies (De Jong et al., 2005). Yarmey (1986) manipulated illumination and found no significant differences in correct identifications but correct rejections were significantly higher with better illumination. In a field study, Valentine et al. (2003) examined lighting by coding daylight or good indoor lighting as "good" and twilight, night, or poor indoor lighting as "bad." Suspect identification rates did not differ as a function of lighting.

Face recognition studies have evaluated the role of lighting systematically: recognition is affected by changes in illumination direction (Braje, 2003; Hill and Bruce, 1996). When identical pictures of a face are illuminated from different directions, participants take longer to match these versions than when they are illuminated from the same direction (Braje et al., 1998; Hill and Bruce, 1996; Troje and Bülthoff, 1996). Hill and Bruce (1996) also found lighting from above facilitated face recognition relative to lighting from below.

Delay

Courts have recognized that delay, or the amount of time between an event and identification, influences the reliability of eyewitness identification (*Commonwealth v. Bumpus* 1968; *Neil v. Biggers* 1972; *Wright v. United States* 1969). Meta-analyses evaluating studies that included a delay between encoding and the recognition task, but did not manipulate delay, support a general delay effect such that identification accuracy is better with smaller delays (Shapiro and Penrod, 1986; Steblay et al., 2001, 2003). Yet Shapiro and Penrod (1986) found that retention interval did not account for any unique variance in the false alarm rate. However, the data are consistent with the existence of a delay effect and field studies support the data, even though it is not yet appropriate to rule out the effect of other variables (Shapiro and Penrod, 1986). For example, Ellis et al. (1977) suggest that the delay itself is likely not as important as what occurs during the delay, which is consistent with contemporary perspectives on memory—that memory does not decay, but can be interfered with to such an extent that retrieval becomes very improbable (Tulving and Pearlstone, 1966). In general, and consistent with either perspective, memory errors increase over time (Behrman and Davey, 2001; Valentine et al., 2003; Wright and McDaid, 1996).

Eyewitness studies where delay is specifically manipulated have not been systematic, making it difficult to form broad conclusions about its effects. Empirical studies manipulating delay sometimes find an impact of delay on correct rejections, sometimes find a small to moderate effect on false positive identifications, and very infrequently find an effect on correct identifications (Dysart and Lindsay, 2007b). However, Krouse (1981) employed a combination of eyewitness and face recognition paradigms (participants viewed 16 photos, then identified "old" photos from 16 arrays of four images), and found a significant main effect of delay (immediate versus 2–3 days) on hits. Similar results have been found by others using hybrid and face recognition paradigms (e.g. Courtois and Mueller, 1981; Shepherd et al., 1991).

Familiarity

Recognition of familiar people (e.g. a parent) is generally very easy and is accurate even under poor viewing conditions (Bruce et al., 2001; 2007; Bonner et al., 2003; Burton and Jenkins, Chapter 15, this volume; Hancock et al., 2000). Recognition of unfamiliar faces is much poorer and much more susceptible to errors when there are even small changes (e.g. perspective, lighting, pose, etc.; Hancock et al., 2000; Henderson et al., 2001; Liu and Chaudhuri, 2000). These effects have been shown for suspect identifications in field studies as well (Valentine et al., 2003; Wright and McDaid, 1996). Troje and Kersten (1999) found a viewpoint dependence effect for recognition (naming) of people's own faces, such that people were significantly faster recognizing their own frontal face view than their own profile face view. There was no viewpoint dependence for other familiar faces, and participants were generally slower naming faces other than their own. Troje and Kersten (1999) speculated that familiarity effects are a product of experience with different views of a face. Much has been done in this area using face recognition studies, but little has been done using the eyewitness paradigm (Burton et al., 1999) though the few existing results are consistent with the face-recognition literature.

Unconscious transference

Unconscious transference is the confusion of familiarity and source. For example, a person may witness a crime committed by one person immediately before, during, or after an interaction with another person (Loftus, 1976). If the person later identifies the other person as being the criminal, unconscious transference has occurred as the person has unconsciously confused a familiar, yet innocent, person with the actual criminal.

Unconscious transference has rarely been tested with a face recognition paradigm (but see Brown et al., 1977 for an example). The effect has been studied using two different eyewitness paradigms (Deffenbacher et al., 2006). In the first, participants view an event in which two individuals could be confused as the perpetrator of a crime (e.g. Read et al., 1990; Ross et al., 1994). In the second, participants view an event and then view a mug book (e.g. Brown et al., 1977; Dysart et al., 2001; Gorenstein and Ellsworth, 1980). In both types of studies, these tasks are followed by lineup identifications. Unconscious transference occurs in the first case when participants identify an innocent bystander as the perpetrator when viewing the lineup, and in the second case when participants erroneously identify a person seen only in the mug book as the perpetrator when viewing a lineup.

Researchers have sometimes found improved rather than deteriorated recognition of a perpetrator when a bystander was present at the time of the target event (Geiselman et al., 1996; Read et al., 1990). Read et al. (1990) concluded that unconscious transference occurs only under specific conditions of physical and situational similarity. Shallow processing has also been found to exacerbate the unconscious transference effect (Davis et al., 2008). Moreover, memory for the event must be both good enough that a recognition response is elicited and poor enough that the true identity or context of seeing the innocent bystander is not recalled, and the poorly recalled context must be accepted as the correct context for viewing the misidentified bystander (Ross et al., 1994; Philips et al., 1997). Ross et al. (1994) have called this process conscious inference.

Unconscious transference (Ross et al., 1994; Perfect and Harris, 2003; Phillips et al., 1997) is a form of source monitoring error (Lindsay, 1994). Indeed, Brown et al. (1977) showed that while participants could very accurately identify whether or not they previously had seen a face, they were much less accurate at identifying *where* the face had been seen. In line with these findings, Deffenbacher et al. (2006) conducted a meta-analysis examining the bystander paradigm (eight published studies) and the mug shot paradigm (11 published studies). A significant negative effect on identification accuracy was found for transference versus control groups in these studies, with the effect on accuracy in the mug shot paradigm being twice what was found in the bystander paradigm.

Misinformation

Misinformation has rarely been tested in a face recognition paradigm. However, much research on misinformation has been conducted using the eyewitness paradigm (e.g. Loftus, 1992, 2005; Loftus and Hoffman, 1989). Misinformation refers to incorrect information passed on to a witness from any source after an event is witnessed. The source can be other people, such as police officers, co-witnesses, or lawyers, or the witness themselves. The misinformation effect occurs when this incorrect information is incorporated into the witness' account of their experience, meaning a witness may come to believe the guilty person has some particular attribute when they do not have that attribute. The effect is more likely to occur when one's memory is less clear, for peripheral (versus central) details, and with the elderly and children (Bartlett and Memon, 2007; Bless and Strack, 1998; Hoffman et al., 2001; Pozzulo, 2007; Strack and Bless, 1998).

Verbal overshadowing

Verbal overshadowing (Schooler and Engstler-Schooler, 1990) is a decrease in identification accuracy when a witness gives a description of a perpetrator prior to attempting an identification (Dodson et al., 1997; Fallshore and Schooler, 1995; Meissner and Brigham, 2001b; Meissner et al., 2007; Ryan and Schooler, 1998). Some studies have not found an effect of verbal overshadowing under specific circumstances (e.g. Fallshore and Schooler, 1995 with other-race faces; Finger and Pezdek, 1999 with a 24-min delay) and a few others have shown that if you ask witnesses not to guess, the effect is eliminated and the description actually enhances recognition accuracy (MacLin et al., 2002; Meissner, 2002; Meissner and Brigham, 2001b). Meissner and Brigham's (2001b) meta-analysis concluded the effect was present, but small, and most likely to occur when identification occurred immediately after the description was given and when witnesses were given elaborative instructions for the description. The effect can occur when participants provide a description regardless of whether they describe the target or another face and also occurs even when participants review an already prepared description (Dodson et al., 1997).

The mechanisms of this self-generated effect are not clear, though some have suggested it may be due to recoding interference; i.e. because some aspects of events are difficult or impossible to verbalize, the process of verbalization causes a mismatch between one's visual memory of the event and one's verbal description of the event (Schooler et al., 1997). Others have suggested that it is due to a transfer inappropriate processing shift because witnesses become stuck in a verbal processing mode which is inappropriate for recognition tasks like lineups (Brown and Lloyd-Jones, 2002, 2003; Schooler, 2002). Still others have suggested it is due to a "processing shift" whereby witnesses raise their response criterion for making positive identifications, correct or incorrect (Finger, 2002; Hunt and Carrol, 2008). Unfortunately, none of these accounts adequately explains the research findings. There may be multiple mechanisms for the verbal overshadowing effect depending on the circumstances of witnessing or retrieval (Meissner et al., 2007), or the true mechanism may remain to be discovered.

System variables: the impact of the identification process on eyewitness accuracy

Composites

A composite is a picture of a criminal created with the assistance of a witness that is then used in police investigations to help identify and/or find the criminal. There have been four "generations" of methods used to produce composites (Davies and Valentine, 2007): artists' impressions, mechanical systems, software systems, and genetic algorithms.

When a composite is developed by an artist, a witness meets with an artist who interviews them and draws a representation of the target individual based on the interview. Almost no research has been conducted on the method itself, likely because of the wide range of procedures used by different artists and the rarity of such artists. However, when composites produced with this method are compared to the other methods, it is the most effective (Davies and Valentine, 2007).

Mechanical systems are more widely used and researched. In these systems, drawings (e.g. Identikit) or photos (e.g. Photokit) of individual features are presented on clear plastic. There may be, for example, 50 different types of noses from which witnesses select the best match to their memory of the perpetrator's nose. The process is repeated for all other features and then all the features are assembled (overlaid) to create a composite. These systems are limited by the limited availability of features, the inflexibility of using discrete feature images, the verbal ability of the witness, and the skill of the person who administers the task to the witness. Research suggests that the utility of these methods is low (Ellis et al., 1978; Frowd et al., 2005). Software systems, like Mac-a-Mug Pro and E-FIT, use a system similar to mechanical ones but offer more flexibility in adjustment of features because they use digital images. However, composites constructed via software systems still produce composites that are recognized with a lower level of accuracy than those produced by artists (Davies and Valentine, 2007; Davies et al., 2000). Consensus among researchers is that these systems fail because they are feature based while facial memory and recognition more likely relies on holistic processes (see McKone and Robbins, Chapter 9; Tanaka and Gordon, Chapter 10, this volume).

Finally, genetic algorithms use statistical methods (e.g. principal components analysis) to generate a multidimensional similarity space (face-space) from a set of faces from which the algorithm can construct a likeness. These systems utilize selection from randomly generated sets of faces and genetic algorithms to generate subsequent sets of faces to progress towards a better and better likeness of the target. The system takes advantage of the fact that people normally recognize faces as a whole rather than parts of faces (features). Accuracy in identifying faces constructed using this type of method has been shown to be poorer than when E-FIT or an artist's sketch was used (Frowd et al., 2005). Thus, this method likely requires further refinement before its potential can be realized.

Presentation of faces

Mug books

Mug books are collections of photos of people who have been arrested. They are used by the police to find suspects. Mug book images can be presented in different ways, such as sequentially (one after another), or grouped with each page having multiple images (McAllister, 2007). Mug books are presented on a computer or in printed photo format.

Mug book recognition performance has been shown to be unaffected by pose or whether photos are in color or not (Laughery et al., 1971). Increasing the number of mug book faces that are similar to the perpetrator decreases the likelihood the perpetrator will be identified (Lindsay et al., 1994b; McAllister et al., 2003), though innocent suspects are not at greater risk with larger mug books (McAllister et al., 2003). Because face recognition research supports the use of motion cues for recognition (e.g. Lander and Bruce, 2000), some researchers explored the use of dynamic information in mug books by permitting people to see video clips of selected individuals on request. Although there was no difference in the likelihood of selecting a guilty suspect (McAllister et al., 1997, 2000, 2003), McAllister et al. (1997, 2000) found fewer false positive selections from mug books when the viewer could access motion information. Moreover, McAllister et al. (2003) found participants became significantly less likely to view motion information the later the position of the target individual in the mug book. Given motion cues reduce the number of possible suspects without increasing the likelihood of selecting the guilty suspect and given the expense of instituting such a policy, providing motion cues with mug books is unlikely to be utilized by the police.

Generally, mug books are used to find rather than identify suspects. The same witness will on occasion be asked to identify a suspect from a lineup after having completed a search of a mug book. Research has shown that the mug book task does not interfere with lineup identification when the target is not present in the mug book (Cutler et al., 1987a; Dysart et al., 2001). However, when the target is present in the mug book, the likelihood of identifying that individual in the lineup is higher than if a mug book had not been reviewed, or if a non-target was viewed in the mug book and lineup (familiarity effect). A commitment effect has also been shown, whereby an incorrect person selected from the mug book is as likely to be selected from a subsequent lineup as the actual target (Brigham and Cairns, 1988; Dysart et al., 2001; Goodsell et al., 2009; Gorenstein and Ellsworth, 1980; Memon et al., 2002). This source of identification error is a serious concern for the criminal justice system. Weaker evidence supports a form of transference error whereby innocent people seen in, but not selected from, mug books are at increased risk of misidentification from subsequent lineups (Deffenbacher et al., 2006).

Showups

A showup is the presentation of a single person to a witness, either live or via photo, for the purpose of determining whether the individual is the person the witness saw commit the crime. Police often use showups for the purpose of quickly eliminating suspects (e.g. people fitting the description and found near the scene of a crime). Little research has been conducted on showups, despite their widespread use (Dysart and Lindsay, 2007a). Steblay et al. (2003) conducted a meta-analysis comparing lineup identification and showup identification accuracy. They note that showups lead to more correct decisions relative to lineups (0.69 vs. 0.51), with slightly more correct identifications (target-present conditions) but more incorrect selections (target-absent conditions) of innocent suspects. This apparent anomaly (more correct decisions overall but more false identifications with showups) occurs because many false selections from lineups are of fillers, or non-suspect individuals in the lineup (e.g. a false positive rate of 30% spread across six lineup members resulting in an average of 5% incorrect suspect choices), while all false selections from showups are suspects (so the 15% false positive rate is all selections of innocent suspects). This pattern provides a clear example of data that could be misleading if not interpreted within the applied context. The lower overall error rate seems desirable until the applied implications are considered.

Showups can be particularly susceptible to clothing bias. Dysart et al. (2006) manipulated the clothing worn by the person in the photo such that it was the same as that worn by the target when seen by the witness, similar to his clothing, or dissimilar. The person shown in the target-absent photo was either similar to the target or different (selected because he had never been selected from a lineup after seeing the same target). When seen in dissimilar clothing, the similar innocent suspect was selected much more often (25%) than the dissimilar suspect (0%). When wearing the same clothing as the criminal, selections of the similar innocent suspect doubled (50%). Choices of the dissimilar innocent suspect increased even more dramatically (37%). Clothing bias was shown to occur even when the clothing was dissimilar but matched the witness' memory of the clothing as indicated in a description of the target. This pattern is of considerable practical significance as witnesses (both in the laboratory and field) frequently provide vague descriptions and half or more of all information provided describes what the criminal was wearing (Lindsay et al., 1994a).

Lineups

Lineups involve the presentation of one or more suspects embedded in a set of fillers. The task for the witness is to indicate whether any of the lineup members are familiar and, in particular, if one of them is the perpetrator they witnessed committing the crime. Lineups are widely used by police. A selection from a lineup, usually referred to as an "identification," is powerful evidence in court and can lead to a conviction even in the absence of other evidence (Devlin, 1976). Lineup identification has been demonstrated to be a major source of wrongful conviction in cases where DNA evidence has exonerated innocent people (Connors et al., 1996).

Lineup procedures have been extensively researched. Overall, correct selection rates from line-ups are somewhat lower, and false positive selection rates higher, than hit and false alarm rates in facial recognition studies. The overall lower accuracy rate for lineups is further exacerbated by a variety of biases and procedural issues that can reduce accuracy further, mostly by inflating false positive selection rates.

Multiple suspect lineups

Perhaps the most dangerous lineup bias is the inclusion of multiple suspects in the same lineup which reaches the pinnacle of bias when all lineup members are suspects. To the extent that witnesses feel pressure to choose, an all suspect lineup functions like a multiple choice test with no wrong answer. Approximately 40% of witnesses will choose from a target-absent lineup (Steblay et al., 2001). Researchers strongly recommend the use of single suspect lineups (Wells and Turtle, 1986).

Lineup size

Assuming that a single-suspect model is employed, the larger a lineup is, the lower the probability that an innocent suspect will be selected by chance. Real-world lineup practice includes lineups as small as three and as large as 20. Relatively little research has been conducted on the impact of lineup size on identification accuracy, but the studies to date indicate that there is some loss of correct identification (e.g. Bertrand et al., 2006), as well as a reduction in false identifications as lineups become very large (e.g. Beaudry et al., 2006b).

Instruction bias

Instruction bias occurs when the person presenting a lineup to a witness indicates that the perpe-trator is in the lineup rather than cautioning the witness that the perpetrator may not be in the lineup. Instructions to the witness that suggest the guilty person is present in the lineup increase the likelihood that a witness will choose someone from a target-absent lineup (e.g. Malpass and Devine, 1981). Steblay's (1997) meta-analysis shows that instruction bias occurs from both lead-ing instructions implying that the criminal is in the lineup (Malpass and Devine, 1981) and high pressure instructions that do not give a "no choice" option. Biased lineup instructions decrease accuracy for elderly witnesses (Rose et al., 2005) and child witnesses (Beresford and Blades, 2006), as well as young adult witnesses (Steblay, 1997). From a face recognition perspective, biased lineup instructions serve to lower the witness' response criterion.

Filler bias

Filler bias exists when the suspect stands out in the lineup because he or she is a better match to the witness' description of the criminal than are the fillers. When an innocent suspect is the only lineup member who matches the description, false identification rates can be virtually equal to correct identification rates (Lindsay and Wells, 1980). Lineup size and filler bias can interact as a lineup can contain large numbers of fillers but of varying quality. Measures have been developed to reflect the degree of fairness of lineups independent of the nominal size of the lineup. Lineups are considered fair when the suspect does not stand out based on the description provided by the witness (Malpass and Lindsay, 1999).

Clothing bias

Clothing bias occurs when only the suspect in a lineup (or, simply "the suspect" in the case of a showup) is wearing clothing that is similar or identical to the clothing described by the witness as being worn by the criminal during the crime. Clothing bias does not influence correct identifications; however, there is a significant increase in false identifications. The clothing bias effect is reliable for lineups (Lindsay et al., 1987), mugshots (Lindsay et al., 1994b) and showups (Dysart et al., 2006). Clothing bias has been shown to occur with children, though children also produce more correct identifications in biased as compared to unbiased conditions (Friere et al., 2004; Seitz, 2003).

Investigator bias

Investigator bias potentially exists whenever the person conducting a lineup procedure is aware of which lineup member is the suspect. This bias is similar to an experimenter expectancy effect and has long led researchers to recommend double-blind testing (witness and the lineup administrator are unaware of who is the suspect; Lindsay and Wells, 1985; Wells et al., 1999). Phillips et al. (1999) demonstrated that when the lineup administrator was aware of the identity of the suspect in a lineup, participant witnesses were more likely to choose from the lineup, depending on the type of lineup used. This occurred despite instructions to the lineup administrator to present the lineup fairly. Moreover, the presence of an observer seemed to exacerbate the effect. Administrator awareness of which lineup member is the suspect also interacts with other biases such that double blind testing can reduce the impact of other biases (Greathouse and Kovera, 2009).

Summary and conclusions

People are good at recognizing faces, particularly of those they know. The eyewitness memory situation frequently is much more difficult than recognizing a familiar other. The eyewitness may not have devoted much attention to the criminal. Often, the criminal will have been viewed under imperfect viewing conditions. Some conditions are more harmful to recognition accuracy than others (e.g. delay has a small effect while disguise can have a dramatic effect on recognition accuracy). Of particular importance in the applied context, face identification accuracy is reasonably good if the target is present. Unfortunately, in situations where the face shown has not been seen before, or was seen but is not the criminal, (in)accuracy is a concern. Many factors can lead people to say they recognize a face that they did not actually see.

Moreover, the nature of the justice system can exacerbate biases that have already occurred. Identification procedures are under the control of the system but are far from ideal in many cases (biased lineups, for example). These conditions can and do lead innocent people to be wrongfully convicted. Identification procedures should be based on sound empirical evidence. Our review has noted that empirical evidence from the basic face recognition literature and the eyewitness memory literature are generally in agreement, though they offer different types of experimental controls. Research in both areas should be monitored for findings that can contribute to increasing the probability that the guilty, and not the innocent, are punished.

References

Anastasi, J.F., and Rhodes, M.G. (2006). Evidence for an own-race bias in face recognition. *North American Journal of Psychology*, **8**, 232–257.

Bartlett, J.C., and Fulton, A. (1991). Familiarity and recognition of faces: The factor of age. *Memory and Cognition*, **19**, 229–23.

Bartlett, J.C., and Memon, A. (2007). Eyewitness memory in young and old adults. In R. Lindsay, D. Ross, J. Read, and M. Toglia (eds.) *Handbook of Eyewitness Psychology: Memory for People*, pp. 309–338. Mahwah, NJ: Lawrence Erlbaum.

Bartlett, J.C., Leslie, J.E., Tubbs, A., and Fulton, A. (1989). Aging and memory for pictures of faces. *Psychology and Aging*, **4**, 276–283.

Beaudry, J.L., Leach, A.-M., Mansour, J.K., Bertrand, M., and Lindsay, R.C.L. (2006a). The element of surprise: The impact of participants' knowledge of a subsequent lineup task. Presentation to the American Psychology-Law Society, March, St. Petersburg, Florida.

Beaudry, J.L., Dupuis, P.R., Mansour, J. K., Bertrand, M.I., and Lindsay, R.C.L. (2006b). A cautionary tale? The impact of instructions on the Multiple-choice, Sequential, Large lineup. Presentation to the American Psychology-Law Society, March, St. Petersburg, Florida.

Beaudry, J.L., MacLennan, K., and Lindsay, R.C.L. (2007). Does disguise reduce correct identification more rapidly for sequential than simultaneous lineups? Paper presented to the Society for Applied Research in Memory and Cognition, July, Lewiston, Maine.

Behrman, B.W. and Davey, S.L. (2001). Eyewitness identification in actual criminal cases: An archival analysis. *Law and Human Behavior*, **25**, 475–491.

Beresford, J., and Blades, M. (2006). Children's identification of faces from lineups: The effects of lineup presentation and instructions on accuracy. *Journal of Applied Psychology*, **91**, 1102–1113.

Bertrand, M.I., Beaudry, J.L., Mansour, J.K., and Lindsay, R.C.L. (2006). *Is increasing lineup size an alternative to sequential presentation?* Poster presented at the American Psychology-Law Society, March, St. Petersburg, Florida.

Bless, H. and Strack, F. (1998). Social influence on memory. In V.Y. Yzerbyt, G. Lories, and B. Dardenne (eds.) *Metacognition: Cognitive and Social Dimensions*, pp. 90–106. Thousand Oaks, CA: Sage Publications, Inc.

Bonner, L., Burton, A.M., Jenkins, R., and McNeill, A. (2003). Meet the Simpsons: Top-down effects in face learning. *Perception*, **32**, 1159–1168.

Braje, W.L. (2003). Illumination encoding in face recognition: Effect of position shift. *Journal of Vision*, **3**, 161–170.

Braje, W.L., Kersten, D., Tarr, M.J., and Troje, N.F. (1998). Illumination effects in face recognition. *Psychobiology*, **26**, 371–380.

Brigham, J.C. (1990). Target person distinctiveness and attractiveness as moderator variables in the confidence-accuracy relationship in eyewitness identifications. *Basic and Applied Social Psychology*, **11**, 101–115.

Brigham, J.C. (2002). Face identification: Basic processes and developmental changes. In M.L. Eisen, J.A. Quas, and G.S. Goodman (eds.) *Memory and Suggestibility in the Forensic Interview*, pp. 115–140. Mahwah, NJ: Lawrence Erlbaum.

Brigham, J.C., and Cairns, D.L. (1988). The effect of mugshot inspections on identification accuracy. *Journal of Applied Social Psychology*, **18**, 1394–1420.

Brigham, J.C., Maass, A., Snyder, L.D., and Spaulding, K. (1982). Accuracy of eyewitness identifications in a field setting. *Journal of Personality and Social Psychology*, **42**, 673–681.

Brigham, J.C., Bennett, L.B., Meissner, C.A., and Mitchell, T. L. (2007). The influence of race on eyewitness memory. In R. Lindsay, D. Ross, J. Read, and M. Toglia (eds.) *Handbook of Eyewitness Psychology: Memory for People*, pp. 257–281. Mahwah, NJ: Lawrence Erlbaum.

Brown, C. and Lloyd-Jones, T.J. (2002). Verbal overshadowing in a multiple face presentation paradigm: Effects of description instruction. *Applied Cognitive Psychology: Special Issue: Investigations of the effects of verbalization on memory,* **16**, 873–885.

Brown, C. and Lloyd-Jones, T. J. (2003). Verbal overshadowing of multiple face and car recognition: Effects of within- versus across-category verbal descriptions. *Applied Cognitive Psychology,* **17**, 183–201.

Brown, E., Deffenbacher, K., and Sturgill, W. (1977). Memory for faces and the circumstances of the encounter. *Journal of Applied Psychology,* **62**, 311–318.

Bruce, V., Valentine, T., and Baddeley, A. (1987). The basis of the ¾ advantage in face recognition. *Applied Cognitive Psychology,* **1**, 109–120.

Bruce, V., Henderson, Z., Newman, C., and Burton, A.M. (2001). Matching identities of familiar and unfamiliar faces caught on CCTV images. *Journal of Experimental Psychology: Applied,* **7**, 207–218.

Bruce, V., Burton, M., and Hancock, P. (2007). Remembering faces. In R. Lindsay, D. Ross, J. Read, and M. Toglia (eds.) *Handbook of Eyewitness Psychology: Memory for People,* pp. 87–100. Mahwah, NJ: Lawrence Erlbaum.

Burton, A. M., Wilson, S., Cowan, M., and Bruce, V. (1999). Face recognition in poor quality video: Evidence from security surveillance. *Psychological Science,* **10**, 243–248.

Carey, S., Diamond, R., and Woods, B. (1980). Development of face recognition - a maturational component? *Developmental Psychology,* **16**, 257–269.

Chance, J.E., and Goldstein, A.G. (1979). Reliability of face recognition performance. *Bulletin of the Psychonomic Society,* **14**, 115–117.

Chance, J., Goldstein, A.G., and McBride, L. (1975). Differential experience and recognition memory for faces. *Journal of Social Psychology,* **97**, 243–253.

Chance, J.E., Turner, A.L., and Goldstein, A.G. (1982). Development of differential recognition for own- and other-race faces. *Journal of Psychology,* **112**, 29–37.

Christianson, S̊-A. (1992). Emotional stress and eyewitness memory: A critical review. *Psychological Bulletin,* **112**, 284–309.

Clifford, B.R., and Hollin, C.R. (1981). Effects of the type of incident and the number of perpetrators on eyewitness memory. *Journal of Applied Psychology,* **66**, 364–370.

Commonwealth v. Bumpus. (1968). Mass, *238 N.E.2d 343,* 347.

Connors, E., Miller, N., Lundregan, T., and McEwan, T. (1996). Convicted by Juries, Exonerated by Science: Case Studies in the Use of DNA Evidence to Establish Innocence After Trial. National Institute of Justice, NCJ 161258, Research Report.

Courtois, M.R., and Mueller, J.H. (1981). Target and distractor typicality in facial recognition. *Journal of Applied Psychology,* **66**, 639–645.

Cross, J.F., Cross, J., and Daly, J. (1971). Sex, age, and beauty as factors in recognition of faces. *Perception and Psychophysics,* **10**, 393–396.

Cutler, B.L., and Penrod, S.D. (1988). Improving the reliability of eyewitness identification: Lineup construction and presentation. *Journal of Applied Psychology,* **73**, 281–290.

Cutler, B.L., Penrod, S.D., and Martens, T.K. (1987a). Improving the reliability of eyewitness identification: Putting context into context. *Journal of Applied Psychology,* **72**, 629–637.

Cutler, B.L., Penrod, S.D., and Martens, T.K. (1987b). The reliability of eyewitness identification: The role of system and estimator variables. *Law and Human Behavior,* **11**, 233–258.

Davies, G.M., and Valentine, T. (2007). Facial composites: Their utility and psychological research. In R. Lindsay, D. Ross, J. Read, and M. Toglia (eds.) *Handbook of Eyewitness Psychology: Memory for People,* pp. 59–83. Mahwah, NJ: Lawrence Erlbaum.

Davies, G.M., van der Willik, P., and Morrison, L. (2000). Facial composite production: A comparison of mechanical and computer-driven systems. *Journal of Applied Psychology,* **85**, 119–124.

Davis, D., Loftus, E.F., Vanous, S., and Cucciare, M. (2008). 'Unconscious transference' can be an instance of 'change blindness.' *Applied Cognitive Psychology,* **22**, 605–623.

Deffenbacher, K.A. (1983). The influence of arousal on reliability of testimony. In S.M.A. Lloyd-Bostock and B.R. Clifford (eds.) *Evaluating witness evidence*, pp. 235–251. Chichester: Wiley.

Deffenbacher, K.A., Bornstein, B.A., Penrod, S.D., and McGorty, E.K. (2004). A meta-analytic review of the effects of high stress on eyewitness memory. *Law and Human Behavior*, **28**, 687–706.

Deffenbacher, K.A., Bornstein, B.A., and Penrod, S.D. (2006). Mugshot exposure effects: Retroactive interference, mugshot commitment, source confusion, and unconscious transference. *Law and Human Behavior*, **30**, 287–307.

De Jong, M., Wagenaar, W.A., Wolters, G., and Verstijnen, I. M. (2005). Familiar face recognition as a function of distance and illumination: A practical tool for use in the courtroom. *Psychology, Crime, and Law*, **11**, 87–97.

Devlin Report (1976). *Report to the Secretary of State for the Home Department of the departmental committee on evidence of identification in criminal cases.* London: Her Majesty's Stationery Office.

Dodson, C.S., Johnson, M.K., and Schooler, J.W. (1997). The verbal overshadowing effect: Why descriptions impair face recognition. *Memory and Cognition*, **25**, 129–139.

Dysart, J.E. and Lindsay, R.C.L. (2007a). Show-up identifications: Suggestive technique or reliable method? In R. Lindsay, D. Ross, J. Read, and M. Toglia (eds.) *Handbook of Eyewitness Psychology: Memory for People*, pp. 137–153. Mahwah, NJ: Lawrence Erlbaum.

Dysart, J.E. and Lindsay, R.C.L. (2007b). The effects of delay on eyewitness identification accuracy: Should we be concerned? In R. Lindsay, D. Ross, J. Read, and M. Toglia (eds.) *Handbook of Eyewitness Psychology: Memory for People*, pp. 361–375. Mahwah, NJ: Lawrence Erlbaum.

Dysart, J.E., Lindsay, R.C.L., Hammond, R., and Dupuis, P. (2001). Mug shot exposure prior to lineup identification: Interference, transference, and commitment effects. *Journal of Applied Psychology*, **86**, 1280–1284.

Dysart, J.E., Lindsay, R.C.L., MacDonald, T.K., and Wicke, C. (2002). The intoxicated witness: Effects of alcohol on identification accuracy from showups. *Journal of Applied Psychology*, **87**, 170–175.

Dysart, J.E., Lindsay, R.C.L., and Dupuis, P.R. (2006). Show-ups: The critical issue of clothing bias. *Applied Cognitive Psychology*, **20**, 1009–1023.

Ellis, H.D., Davies, G.M., and Shepherd, J.W. (1977). Experimental studies of face identification. *National Journal of Criminal Defense*, **3**, 219–234.

Ellis, H.D., Davies, G.M., and Shepherd, J.W. (1978). A critical examination of the Photofit system for recalling faces. *Ergonomics*, **21**, 297–307.

Fallshore, M., and Schooler, J.W. (1995). Verbal vulnerability of perceptual expertise. *Journal of Experimental Psychology: Learning, Memory, and Cognition*, **21**, 1608–1623.

Finger, K. (2002). Mazes and music: Using perceptual processing to release verbal overshadowing. *Applied Cognitive Psychology: Special Issue: Investigations of the effects of verbalization on memory*, **16**, 887–896.

Finger, K. and Pezdek, K. (1999). The effect of the cognitive interview on face identification accuracy: Release from verbal overshadowing. *Journal of Applied Psychology*, **84**, 340–348.

Fleishman, J.J., Buckley, M.L., Klosinsky, M.J., Smith, N., and Tuck, B. (1976). Judged attractiveness in recognition memory of women's faces. *Perceptual and Motor Skills*, **43**, 709–710.

Flin, R.H. (1980). Age effects in children's memory for unfamiliar faces. *Developmental Psychology*, **16**, 373–374.

Friere, A., Lee, K., Williamson, K.S., Stuart, S.J.E., and Lindsay, R.C.L. (2004). Lineup identification by children: Effects of clothing bias. *Law and Human Behavior*, **28**, 339–354.

Frowd, C.D., Carson, D., Ness, H., *et al.* (2005). A forensically valid comparison of facial composite systems. *Psychology, Crime, and Law*, **11**, 33–52.

Fulton, A. and Bartlett, J.C. (1991). Young and old faces in young and old heads: The factor of age in face recognition. *Psychology and Aging*, **6**, 623–630.

Geiselman, R.E., Haghighi, D., and Stown, R. (1996). Unconscious transference and characteristics of accurate and inaccurate eyewitnesses. *Psychology, Crime, and Law*, **2**, 197–209.

Goldstein, A.G. and Chance, J. (1964). Recognition of children's faces. *Child development*, **35**, 129–136.

Goodman, G.S., Sayfan, L., Lee, J.S., *et al.* (2007). The development of memory for own- and other-race faces. *Journal of Experimental Child Psychology*, **98**, 233–242.

Goodsell, C.A., Neuschatz, J.S., and Gronlund, S.D. (2009). Effects of *mugshot* commitment on *lineup* performance in young and older adults. *Applied Cognitive Psychology*, **23**, 788–803.

Gorenstein, G.W., and Ellsworth, P.C. (1980). Effect of choosing an incorrect photograph on later identification by an eyewitness. *Journal of Applied Psychology*, **65**, 616–622.

Greathouse, S.M. and Kovera, M.B. (2009). Instruction *bias* and *lineup* presentation moderate the effects of administrator knowledge on eyewitness identification. *Law and Human Behavior*, **33**, 70–82.

Greene, E. and Fraser, S.C. (2002). Observation distance and recognition of photographs of celebrities' faces. *Perceptual and Motor Skills*, **95**, 637–651.

Hancock, J.B., Bruce, V., and Burton, A.M. (2000). Recognition of unfamiliar faces. *Trends in Cognitive Science*, **4**, 330–336.

Henderson, Z., Bruce, V., and Burton, A.M. (2001). Matching the faces of robbers captured on video. *Applied Cognitive Psychology*, **15**, 445–464.

Hill, H. and Bruce, V. (1996). Effects of lighting on the perception of facial surfaces. *Journal of Experimental Psychology: Human Perception and Performance*, **22**, 986–1004.

Hill, H., Schyns, P.G., and Akamatsu, S. (1997). Information and viewpoint dependence in face recognition. *Cognition*, **62**, 201–222.

Hoffman, H.G., Granhag, P.A., Kwong See, S.T., and Loftus, E.F. (2001). Social influences on reality-monitoring decisions. *Memory and Cognition*, **29**, 394–404.

Hosch, H.M. and Cooper, D.S. (1982). Victimization as a determinant of eyewitness accuracy. *Journal of Applied Psychology*, **67**, 649–652

Hunt, C. and Carroll, M. (2008). Verbal overshadowing effect: How temporal perspective may exacerbate or alleviate the processing shift. *Applied Cognitive Psychology*, **22**, 85–93.

Kalmet, N. (unpublished). Multiple lineup identification procedure: Utility with face-only lineups. Unpublished Master's thesis.

Kelly, D.J., Quinn, P.C., Slater, A.M., Lee, K., Ge, L., and Pascalis, O. (2007). The other race effect develops during infancy: Evidence of perceptual narrowing. *Psychological Science*, **18**, 1084–1089.

Kinzler, K.D. and Shutts, K. (2008). Memory for 'mean' over 'nice': The influence of threat on children's face memory. *Cognition*, **107**, 775–783.

Koutstaal, W. and Schacter, D. (1997). Gist based false recognition of pictures in older and younger adults. *Journal of Memory and Language*, **37**, 555–583.

Koutstaal, W., Schacter, D.L., Galluccio, L., and Stofer, K.A. (1999). Reducing gist-based false recognition in older adults: Encoding and retrieval manipulations. *Psychology and Aging*, **14**, 220–237.

Kramer, T.H., Buckhout, R., and Eugenio P. (1990). Weapon focus, arousal, and eyewitness memory: Attention must be paid. *Law and Human Behavior*, **14**, 167–184.

Krouse, F.L. (1981). Effects of pose, pose change, and delay on face recognition performance. *Journal of Applied Psychology*, **66**, 651–654.

Lander, K. and Bruce, V. (2000). Recognizing famous faces: The benefits of facial motion. *Ecological Psychology*, **12**, 259–272.

Laughery, K.R., Alexander, J.F., and Lane, A.B. (1971). Recognition of human faces: Effects of target exposure time, target position, pose position, and type of photograph. *Journal of Applied Psychology*, **5**, 477–483.

Leippe, M.R., Wells, G.L., and Ostrom, T.M. (1978). Crime seriousness as a determinant of accuracy in eyewitness identification. *Journal of Applied Psychology*, **63**, 345–351.

Light, L.L., Kayra-Stuart, F., and Hollander, S. (1979). Recognition memory for typical and unusual faces. *Journal of Experimental Psychology: Human Learning and Memory*, **5**, 212–228.

Lindsay, D.S. (1994). Memory source monitoring and eyewitness testimony. In D.F. Ross, J.D. Read, and M.P. Toglia (eds.) *Adult eyewitness testimony: Current trends and developments*, pp. 27–55. New York: Cambridge University Press.

Lindsay, R.C.L., Martin, R., and Webber, L. (1994a). Default values in eyewitness descriptions: A problem for the match-to-description lineup foil selection strategy. *Law & Human Behavior*, **18**, 527–541.

Lindsay, R.C.L., Nosworthy, G.J., Martin, R., and Martynchuk, C. (1994b). Using mugshots to find suspects. *Journal of Applied Psychology*, **79**, 121–130.

Lindsay, R.C.L., Semmler, C., Weber, N., Brewer, N. and Lindsay, M.R. (2008). How variations in distance affect eyewitness reports and identification accuracy. *Law and Human Behavior*, **32**, 526–535.

Lindsay, R.C.L., Wallbridge, H., and Drennan, D. (1987). Do the clothes make the man? An exploration of the effect of lineup attire on eyewitness identification accuracy. *Canadian Journal of Behavioural Science*, **19**, 463–478.

Lindsay, R.C.L. and Wells, G.L. (1980). What price justice? Exploring the relationship of lineup fairness to identification accuracy. *Law and Human Behavior*, **4**, 303–313.

Lindsay, R.C.L. and Wells, G.L. (1985). Improving eyewitness identifications from lineups: Simultaneous versus sequential lineup presentation. *Journal of Applied Psychology*, **70**, 556–564.

Liu, C.H. and Chaudhuri, A. (2000). Recognition of unfamiliar faces: three kinds of effects. *Trends in Cognitive Science*, **4**, 445–446.

Liu, C.H. and Chaudhuri, A. (2002). Reassessing the ¾ view effect in face recognition. *Cognition*, **83**, 31–48.

Loftus, E.F. (1976). Unconscious transference in eyewitness identification. *Law and Psychology Review*, **2**, 93–98.

Loftus, E.F. (1992). When a lie becomes memory's truth: Memory distortion after exposure to misinformation. *Current Directions in Psychological Science*, **1**, 121–123.

Loftus, E.F. (2005). Planting misinformation in the human mind: A 30 year investigation of the malleability of memory. *Learning & Memory*, **12**, 361–366.

Loftus, E.F. and Hoffman, H.G. (1989). Misinformation and memory: The creation of new memories. *Journal of Experimental Psychology: General*, **118**, 100–104.

Loftus, E.F., Loftus, G.R., and Messo, J. (1987). Some facts about 'weapon focus.' *Law and Human Behavior*, **11**, 55–62.

Loftus, G.R., and Harley, E.M. (2005). Why is it easier to identify someone close than far away? *Psychonomic Bulletin and Review*, **12**, 43–65.

Logie, R.H., Baddeley, A.D., and Woodhead, M.M. (1987). Face recognition, pose, and ecological validity. *Applied Cognitive Psychology*, **1**, 53–69.

Loeterman, B. (Producer). (1997). *What Jennifer Saw*. [TV Program] PBS, February 25 1997.

Maass, A. and Köhnken, G. (1989). Eyewitness identification: Simulating the 'weapon effect.' *Law and Human Behavior*, **13**, 397–408.

MacLin, O.H., MacLin, M.K., and Malpass, R.S. (2001). Race, arousal, attention, exposure, and delay. An examination of factors moderating face recognition. *Psychology, Public Policy, and Law*, **7**, 134–152.

MacLin, O.H., Tapscott, R.L., and Malpass, R.S. (2002). The development of a computer system to obtain descriptions of culprits. *Applied Cognitive Psychology*, **16**, 937–945.

Malpass, R.S. and Devine, P.G. (1981). Eyewitness identification: Lineup instructions and the absence of the offender. *Journal of Applied Psychology*, **66**, 482–489.

Malpass, R.S. and Lindsay, R.C.L. (1999). Measuring lineup fairness. *Applied Cognitive Psychology*, **13(SI)**, S1-S7.

Mansour, J.K., Lindsay, R.C.L., and Munhall, K.M. (2008). *The Flamingo Focus Effect*. Paper presented at the American Psychology-Law Society, March, Jacksonville, Florida.

Mansour, J.K., Mateus, T., and Lindsay, R.C.L. (2007). *Disguise Effects on Identification Accuracy from Sequential and Simultaneous Lineups*. Paper presented at the Society of Applied Research in Memory and Cognition, July, Lewiston, Maine.

Mason, S.E. (1986). Age and gender as factors in facial recognition and identification. *Experimental Aging Research*, **12**, 151–154.

McAllister, H.A. (2007). Mug books: More than just large photospreads. In R. Lindsay, D. Ross, J. Read, and M. Toglia (eds.) *Handbook of Eyewitness Psychology: Memory for People*, pp. 35–58. Mahwah, NJ: Lawrence Erlbaum.

McAllister, H.A., Bearden, J.N., Kohlmaier, J.R., and Warner, M.D. (1997). Computerized mug books: Does adding multimedia Help? *Journal of Applied Psychology*, **82**, 688–698.

McAllister, H.A., Blair, M.J., Cerone, L.G., and Laurent, M.J. (2000). Multimedia mug books: How multi should the media be? *Applied Cognitive Psychology*, **14**, 277–291.

McAllister, H.A., Stewart, H.A., and Loveland, J. (2003). Effects of mug book size and computerized pruning on the usefulness of dynamic mug book procedures. *Psychology, Crime, and Law*, **9**, 265–278.

McKelvie, S.J. (1976). The roles of eyes and mouth in the memory of a face. *American Journal of Psychology*, **89**, 311–323.

Meissner, C. A. (2002). Applied aspects of the instructional bias effect in verbal overshadowing. *Applied Cognitive Psychology*, **16**, 911–928.

Meissner, C. A. and Brigham, J. C. (2001a). Thirty years of investigating the own-race bias in memory for faces. *Psychology, Public Policy, and Law*, **7**, 3–35.

Meissner, C.A. and Brigham, J. C. (2001b). A meta-analysis of the verbal overshadowing effect in face identification. *Applied Cognitive Psychology*, **15**, 603–616.

Meissner, C.A., Sporer, S.L., and Schooler, J.W. (2007). Person descriptions as eyewitness evidence. In R. Lindsay, D. Ross, J. Read, and M. Toglia (eds.) *Handbook of Eyewitness Psychology: Memory for People*, pp. 3–34. Mahwah, NJ: Lawrence Erlbaum.

Meissner, C.A., Tredoux, C.G., Parker, J.F., and MacLin, O.H. (2005). Eyewitness decisions in simultaneous and sequential lineups: A dual process signal detection theory analysis. *Memory and Cognition*, **33**, 783–792.

Memon, A., Hope, L., Bartlett, J., and Bull, R. (2002). Eyewitness recognition errors: The effect of mugshot viewing and choosing in young and old adults. *Memory and Cognition*, **30**, 1219–1227.

Memon, A., Hope, L., and Bull, R. (2003). Exposure duration: Effects on eyewitness accuracy and confidence. *British Journal of Psychology*, **94**, 339–354.

Morris, C.D., Bransford, J.D., and Franks, J.J. (1977). Levels of processing versus transfer appropriate processing. *Journal of Verbal Learning and Verbal Behavior*, **16**, 519–533.

Neil v. Biggers. (1972). 409 U.S. 188.

O'Rourke, T.E., Penrod, S.D., Cutler, B.L., and Stuve, T.E. (1989). The external validity of eyewitness identification research: Generalizing across subject populations. Law and Human Behavior, **13**, 385–395.

O'Toole, A.J., Edelman, S., and Bülthoff, H.H. (1998). Stimulus-specific effects in face recognition over changes in viewpoint. *Vision Research*, **38**, 2351–2363.

Parker, J.F., and Ryan, V. (1993). An attempt to reduce guessing behavior in children's and adults' eyewitness identifications. *Law and Human Behavior*, **17**, 11–26.

Perfect, T.J. and Harris, L.J. (2003). Adult age differences in unconscious transference: Source confusion or identity blending? *Memory and Cognition*, **31**, 570–580.

Phillips, M.R., Geiselman, R.E., Haghighi, D., and Lin, C. (1997). Some boundary conditions for bystander misidentification. *Criminal Justice and Behavior*, **24**, 370–390.

Phillips, M.R., McAuliff, B.D., Bull-Kovera, M., and Cutler, B.L. (1999). Double-blind photoarray administration as a safeguard against investigator bias. *Journal of Applied Psychology*, **84**, 940–951.

Pickel, K.L. (1998). Unusualness and threat as possible causes of 'weapon focus.' *Memory*, **6**, 277–295.

Pickel, K.L. (1999). The influence of context on the 'weapon focus' effect. *Law and Human Behavior*, **23**, 299–311.

Pozzulo, J.D. (2007). Person description and identification by child witnesses. In R. Lindsay, D. Ross, J. Read, and M. Toglia (eds.) *Handbook of Eyewitness Psychology: Memory for People*, pp. 283–307. Mahawah, NJ: Lawrence Erlbaum.

Pozzulo, J.D. and Lindsay, R.C.L. (1998). Identification accuracy of children versus adults: A meta-analysis. *Law and Human Behavior*, **22**, 549–570.

Read, J.D., Tollestrup, P., Hammersley, R., McFazden, E., and Christianson, A. (1990). The unconscious transference effect: Are innocent bystanders ever misidentified? *Applied Cognitive Psychology*, **4**, 3–31.

Read, J.D., Yuille, J.C., and Tollestrup, P. (1992). Recollections of a robbery: Effects of arousal and alcohol upon recall and person identification. *Law and Human Behavior*, **16**, 425–446.

Reynolds, J.K. and Pezdek, K. (1992). Face recognition memory: The effects of exposure duration and encoding instruction. *Applied Cognitive Psychology*, **6**, 279–292.

Rose, R.A., Bull, R., and Vrij, A. (2005). Non-biased lineup instructions do matter - a problem for older witnesses. *Psychology, Crime, and Law*, **11**, 147–159.

Ross, D.F., Ceci, S.J., Dunning, D., and Toglia, M.P. (1994). Unconscious transference and mistaken identity: When a witness misidentifies a familiar but innocent person. *Journal of Applied Psychology*, **79**, 918–930.

Ryan, R. A. and Schooler, J. W. (1998). Whom do words hurt? Individual differences in verbal overshadowing. *Applied Cognitive Psychology*, **12**, S105–S125.

Sadr, J., Jarudi, I., and Sinha, P. (2003). The role of eyebrows in face recognition. *Perception*, **32**, 285–293.

Schooler, J.W. (2002). Verbalization produces a transfer-inappropriate processing shift. *Applied Cognitive Psychology*, **16**, 989–997.

Schooler, J.W. and Engstler-Schooler, T.Y. (1990). Verbal overshadowing of visual memories: Some things are better left unsaid. *Cognitive Psychology*, **22**, 36–71.

Schooler, J.W., Fiore, S.M. and Brandimonte, M.A. (1997). At a loss from words: Verbal overshadowing of perceptual memories. In D.L. Medin (ed), *The psychology of learning and motivation: Advances in research and theory*, Vol. **37**. pp. 291–340. San Diego, CA: Academic Press.

Schyns, P. G., Bonnar, L. and Gosselin, F. (2002). Show me the features! Understanding recognition from the use of visual information. *Psychological Science*, **13**, 402–409.

Searcy, J.H., Bartlett, J.C., and Memon, A. (1999). Age differences in accuracy and choosing in eyewitness identification and face recognition. *Memory and Cognition*, **27**, 538–552.

Searcy, J.H., Bartlett, J.C., Memon, A., and Swanson, K. (2001). Aging and lineup performance at long retention intervals: Effects of meta-memory and context reinstatement. *Journal of Applied Psychology*, **86**, 207–214.

Seitz, K. (2003). The effect of changes in posture and clothing on the development of unfamiliar person recognition. *Applied Cognitive Psychology*, **17**, 819–832.

Shapiro, P.N., and Penrod, S. (1986). Meta-analysis of facial identification studies. *Psychological Bulletin*, **2**, 139–156.

Shepherd, J.W., Gibling, F., and Ellis, H.D. (1991). The effects of distinctiveness, presentation time and delay on face recognition. *European Journal of Cognitive Psychology*, **3**, 137–145.

Stanny, C.J. and Johnson, T.C. (2000). Effects of stress induced by a simulated shooting on recall by police and citizen witnesses. *American Journal of Psychology*, **113**, 359–386.

Steblay, N.M. (1992). A meta-analytic review of the weapon focus effect. *Law and Human Behavior*, **16**, 413–424.

Steblay, N.M. (1997). Social influence in eyewitness recall: A meta-analytic review of lineup instruction effects. *Law and Human Behavior*, **21**, 283–297.

Steblay, N., Dysart, J., Fulero, S., and Lindsay, R.C.L. (2001). Eyewitness accuracy rates in sequential and simultaneous lineup presentations: A meta-analytic comparison. *Law and Human Behavior*, **25**, 459–473.

Steblay, N., Dysart, J., Fulero, S., and Lindsay, R.C.L. (2003). Eyewitness accuracy rates in police showup and lineup presentations: A meta-analytic comparison. *Law and Human Behavior,* **27**, 523–540.

Stephan, B.C.M., and Caine, D. (2007). What is in a view? The role of featural information in the recognition of unfamiliar faces across viewpoint transformation. *Perception,* **36**, 189–198.

Strack, F. and Bless, H. (1998). Memory for nonoccurrences: Metacognitive and presuppositional strategies. *Journal of Memory and Language,* **33**, 203–217.

Terry, R.L. (1993). How wearing eyeglasses affects facial recognition. *Current Psychology,* **12**, 151–162.

Tooley, V., Brigham, J.C., Maass, A., and Bothwell, R.K. (1987). Facial recognition: Weapon effect and attentional focus. *Journal of Applied Social Psychology,* **17**, 845–859.

Troje, N.F. and Bülthoff, H.H. (1996). Face recognition under varying poses: The role of texture and shape. *Vision Research,* **36**, 1761–1771.

Troje, N.F. and Kersten, D. (1999). Viewpoint dependent recognition of familiar faces. *Perception,* **28**, 483–487.

Tulving, E. and Pearlstone, Z. (1966). Availability versus accessibility of information in memory for words. *Journal of Verbal Learning and Verbal Behavior,* **5**, 381–91.

Uelmen, G.F. (1980). Testing the assumptions of *Neil v. Biggers:* An experiment in eyewitness identification. *Criminal Law Bulletin,* **16**, 358–368.

Valentine, T. (1991). A unified account of the effects of distinctiveness, inversion, and race in face recognition. *Quarterly Journal of Experimental Psychology,* **43A**, 161–204.

Valentine, T., Pickering, A., and Darling, S. (2003). Characteristics eyewitness identifications that predict the outcome of real lineups. *Applied Cognitive Psychology,* **17**, 969–993.

Wagenaar, W.A. and Van Der Schrier, J.H. (1996). Face recognition as a function of distance and illumination: A practical tool for use in the courtroom. *Psychology, Crime, and Law,* **2**, 321–332.

Wells, G.L. (1978). Applied eyewitness-testimony research: System and estimator variables. *Journal of Personality and Social Psychology,* **36**, 1546–1557.

Wells, G.L., Small, M., Penrod, S., Malpass, R.S. Fulero, S.M., and Brimacombe, C.A.E. (1999). Eyewitness identification procedures: Recommendations for lineups and photospreads. *Law & Human Behavior,* **22**, 603–647.

Wells, G.L. and Turtle, J. (1986). Eyewitness identification: The importance of lineup models. *Psychological Bulletin,* **99**, 320–329.

Wright, D.B. and McDaid, A.T. (1996). Comparing system and estimator variables using data from real line-ups. *Applied Cognitive Psychology,* **10**, 75–84.

Wright, D.B. and Sladden, B. (2003). An own-gender bias and the importance of hair in face recognition. *Acta Psychologica,* **114**, 101–114.

Wright, D.B. and Stroud, J. (2002). Age differences in lineup identification accuracy: People are better with their own age. *Law and Human Behavior,* **26**, 641–654.

Wright v. United States (1969) 404 F.2d 1256 (D.C.Cir).

Yarmey, A.D. (1986). Verbal, visual, and voice identification of a rape suspect under different levels of illumination. *Journal of Applied Psychology,* **71**, 363–370.

Yarmey, A.D. (2004). Eyewitness recall and photo identification: A field experiment. *Psychology, Crime, and Law,* **10**, 53–68.

Yuille, J.C. and Tollestrup, P.A. (1990). Some effects of alcohol on eyewitness memory. *Journal of Applied Psychology,* **75**, 268–273.

Yuille, J.C., Tollestrup, P.A., Marxsen, D., Porter, S., and Herve, H.F.M. (1998). An exploration of the effects of marijuana on eyewitness memory. *International Journal of Law and Psychiatry,* **21**, 117–128.

Chapter 17

The Face-Sensitive N170 Component of the Event-Related Brain Potential

Martin Eimer

Faces are perhaps the most important object category in visual perception, as faces of conspecifics frequently convey behaviourally, socially, and emotionally relevant information that is critical for the adaptive control of action. Given this undisputed significance of faces, it is not surprising that the study of human face processing has long been one of the most active research areas in visual cognition. In recent years, numerous new insights into the mechanisms and neural processes that underlie our ability to perceive and recognize faces have come from studies that have investigated face processing with neuroscientific methods. Functional brain imaging studies have identified the fusiform face area (FFA; Kanwisher et al., 1997), the right lateral occipital face area (OFA; Gauthier et al., 2000b), and the superior temporal sulcus (Hoffman and Haxby, 2000) as regions that are specifically involved in the processing of faces (see Haxby et al., 2000, for a review of the neural network involved in human face perception; Haxby and Gobbini, Chapter 6, this volume). Electrophysiological evidence for face-specific brain processes has been obtained through intracranial recordings (Allison et al., 1999), as well as in many studies using event-related brain potentials (ERPs). These ERP studies have uncovered several components that are linked to different stages in face perception, face recognition, and the processing of emotional facial expression (e.g. Eimer, 2000c; Eimer and Holmes, 2007).

The earliest, most prominent, and by far the most widely studied face-sensitive ERP component is the N170. When compared to different categories of non-face objects, human faces consistently elicit a larger negative-going ERP component at occipitotemporal electrodes. The presence of an N170 component in response to faces has been demonstrated in two early ERP investigations of human face perception (Bentin et al., 1996; Bötzel et al., 1995), and the N170 has since featured prominently in face perception research. There are currently more than 200 published studies that have used this component to investigate different aspects of face processing in the human brain. More recently, an "M170" component with response properties that are very similar but perhaps not identical to the N170 has been identified in experiments that used magnetoencephalographic (MEG) measures to study face processing (e.g. Halgren et al., 2000; Harris and Nakayama, 2008).

The purpose of this chapter is to introduce the N170 component to readers who may not be intimately familiar with the details of ERP methodology and interpretation, and to provide a brief review of some important research questions that have been addressed by employing the N170 as an electrophysiological marker of face processing. The first section will discuss basic properties of the N170 component, its neural basis, as well as some methodological issues that need to be kept in mind when using this component to study face-specific processes, and when evaluating the results from previous N170 experiments. In the next section, a recent methodological challenge to the claim that the N170 reliably reflects face-specific brain processes (Thierry et al., 2007a) will be evaluated and rejected. The following two sections review research that has employed the N170 component to investigate two central and interrelated issues in face processing. First, the relative roles of configural versus feature-based processes in face perception will be addressed. The fourth section discusses the domain-specificity or generality of face processing, as well as the possible role of expertise. Finally, some avenues for future research will be outlined.

The N170 component—measurement, cortical generators, and relationship with the "vertex positive potential" (VPP)

Before reviewing recent research that has used the N170 component to study different aspects of face processing, it is essential to clarify what precisely is claimed when this component is described as face-selective. This claim does emphatically *not* imply that this component is triggered exclusively in response to faces. The N170 belongs to the family of visually evoked (or "exogenous") N1 components that are elicited over visual brain areas in response to most types of visual stimuli regardless of their category. The N170 has acquired its status as a face-sensitive component because ERP amplitudes elicited at occipitotemporal electrodes between 140 ms and 200 ms after stimulus onset are virtually always larger in response to faces than in response to non-face objects. It is this *amplitude difference* between faces and non-face stimuli with its characteristic scalp topography (see below) that is thought to reflect the activation of face-selective brain areas. Given that research on the N170 is essentially based on such amplitude differences, the common description of the N170 as a *face-specific* ERP component is potentially misleading, since it incorrectly implies that this component is triggered exclusively in response to faces. The N170 response should be more accurately characterized as *face-sensitive*, and this label will be used in this chapter.

The fact that the N170 is a visual evoked ERP component implies that, similar to earlier visual components such as the P1, it is strongly affected by variations in the low-level perceptual attributes of visual stimuli, such as their size, contrast, luminance, retinal eccentricity, or spatial frequency. Therefore, for any comparison of N170 amplitude differences between face and non-face objects to be meaningful, it is essential to ensure that such low-level visual features do not differ systematically across the visual object categories of interest. A careful control of physical stimulus properties is extremely important for any ERP experiment that employs naturalistic stimuli such as photographs of faces and other visual objects. Even though enhanced occipito-temporal negativities in the N170 time range to faces as compared to pictures of non-face objects such as houses, hands, cars, household objects or animals have been consistently observed in several hundred ERP studies, it has recently been argued that this apparent face-sensitivity of the N170 does in fact result from the uncontrolled variation of low-level visual stimulus attributes (Thierry et al., 2007a). This specific challenge will be discussed in detail in the next section.

Figure 17.1 (top panel) shows a typical pattern of ERP responses to face versus non-face objects that was obtained in the author's lab in response to centrally presented faces and houses. ERPs are shown separately for left and right occipitotemporal electrodes P7 and P8 and for the vertex electrode Cz. An enhanced negativity to faces is clearly visible at both lateral posterior electrodes in the N170 time range, and this differential effect is more pronounced over the right hemisphere. Figure 17.1 also makes clear that in addition to the N170, an enhanced positivity to faces as compared to houses was elicited at electrode Cz. This "vertex positive potential" (VPP) usually accompanies the N170 component, and is elicited in the same time range. In fact, early ERP studies of face processing (Bötzel and Grüsser, 1989; Jeffreys, 1989) identified the VPP as an electrophysiological correlate of face processing well before the N170 component became the major focus of ERP research.

ERPs to faces and houses

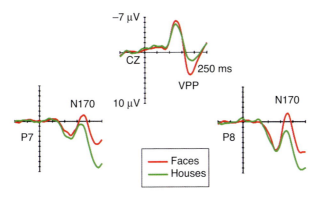

Face-house difference amplitudes
(160–200 ms post-stimulus)

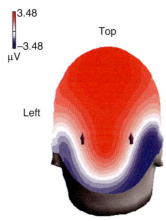

Fig. 17.1 Top panel: Grand-averaged ERP waveforms in response to faces and houses presented at fixation, shown for the first 250 ms after stimulus onset. Negative amplitudes are plotted upward. ERPs at midline electrode Cz are characterized by an enhanced positivity to faces relative to houses. This "vertex positive potential" (VPP) has its maximum at about 180 ms after stimulus onset. At lateral occipitotemporal electrodes (P7, P8), the VPP is accompanied by an enhanced negativity for faces relative to houses (N170), which here also peaks at about 180 ms post-stimulus. Bottom panel: Scalp topography of ERP differences between houses and faces, measured for the N170 time window (160–200 ms after stimulus onset). Enhanced negativity for faces versus houses is shown in blue, enhanced positivity for faces versus houses in red. The face-sensitive N170 (marked in blue) is maximal over lateral occipitotemporal areas, and disappears rapidly at more medial and dorsal posterior electrode sites. The face-sensitive VPP (marked in red) is maximal at the vertex, but extends into more posterior and inferior areas. N170 and VPP are likely to reflect the activity of the same underlying neural generator processes. A plausible location for bilateral symmetric dipoles in lateral temporal cortex is indicated here by the two forward-pointing arrows.

There has been considerable debate as to whether the N170 and the VPP reflect the same underlying neural processes, or whether they represent the activity of two functionally distinct electrical sources. Although some studies have reported small latency differences between N170 and VPP (e.g. Bentin et al., 1996) or a differential sensitivity of these components to peripherally presented face versus non-face objects (Eimer, 2000a), there is now substantial evidence that the response properties of the N170 and VPP are closely associated across a range of stimulus and task manipulations (Jemel et al., 2003; Itier and Taylor, 2002; Joyce and Rossion, 2005), which suggests that they represent the same underlying face-sensitive brain processes. This is also intuitively plausible when examining the topography of these two components: Figure 17.1 (bottom panel) shows an ERP scalp distribution map obtained by subtracting ERPs to houses from ERPs to faces in the N170 time range (160–200 ms poststimulus). The lateral posterior negativity (N170) and centrally distributed positivity (VPP) shown here can both be accounted for by a pair of symmetrical dipoles in lateral temporal cortex that point towards the vertex. Joyce and Rossion (2005) have recently demonstrated that relative amplitude differences observed between the N170 and the VPP in earlier studies are largely due to the choice of reference electrodes during EEG recording: with mastoid reference, N170 amplitudes were small and VPP amplitudes were maximal, while the reverse pattern of results was observed when a nose reference was used instead. Joyce and Rossion (2005) recommend a common average reference as the most suitable method for recording face-sensitive ERP components with minimal distortion.

Although the scalp topography of face-sensitive brain responses in the N170 time range, as shown in Figure 17.1 (bottom panel), strongly suggests bilateral posterior temporal cortical generator processes, source localization studies of the N170 and its magnetic counterpart (M170) have yielded somewhat inconclusive results. Some of these discrepancies between studies may be linked to the different methods used to estimate the cortical sources of these components. Studies that employed dipole fitting methods to explain the pattern of electrical activity observed on the scalp surface have suggested bilateral occipitotemporal cortex and the posterior fusiform gyrus as likely origins of the N170 (e.g. Bötzel et al., 1995; Rossion et al., 2003) and M170 (e.g. Halgren et al., 2000; Deffke et al., 2007). These posterior regions overlap more closely with the localization of the occipital face area (OFA; Gauthier et al., 2000b) than with the fusiform face area (FFA; Kanwisher et al., 1997), as described in functional imaging studies (but see Sams et al., 1997 for evidence that more anterior fusiform regions including the FFA might also contribute to the M170). Source localization studies that have estimated the cortical origins of scalp-recorded ERP topographies not by dipole fitting, but by computing distributed brain activation patterns have obtained different results, with sources for the N170/M170 localized in the posterior superior temporal sulcus (STS; Itier and Taylor, 2004; Watanabe et al., 2003), or right fusiform gyrus (e.g. Henson et al., 2007). Such discrepancies between source localization studies are partly due to the limited spatial resolution of EEG and MEG, and to the fact that different methods for estimating the locus of neural generator processes were used. However, they also suggest that N170 and M170 components are not linked to a single source, but are instead generated by multiple simultaneously active face-sensitive brain processes that are primarily located in lateral occipitotemporal areas. One important focus for future research on the N170 component will be the study of possible functional dissociations between these different cortical generator processes and their respective contributions to face processing.

Is the face-sensitivity of the N170 an artifact of uncontrolled interstimulus perceptual variance?

In the past 10 years, the face-sensitive N170 component has been employed in a large number of ERP studies to investigate the time course, neural basis, and functional organization of face perception.

This research has by no means resolved all questions about the interpretation of the N170 and its links to the specific mechanisms that are involved in face processing. Some of these issues will be discussed in the following two sections. However, the basic consensus is that the N170 component is a valid electrophysiological reflection of face-sensitive brain processes. A recent article (Thierry et al., 2007a) has challenged this assumption. According to Thierry and colleagues, the core finding of numerous studies that N170 amplitudes are larger in response to faces than for any other object category is based on a critical, and hitherto unrecognized methodological artifact: in all of these experiments, enhanced N170 components for faces relative to non-face objects were observed because the face images that were used in these studies were physically more similar to each other than were the images within non-face object categories.

Thierry et al. (2007a) introduced the concept of "interstimulus perceptual variance" (ISPV) to describe the physical similarity between tokens within a given object category. ISPV is low when all tokens share a basic structure (e.g. when images of individual faces all show the same frontal view, are all presented at fixation, and are identical in size). ISPV is high when individual tokens differ substantially in terms of their basic physical attributes (e.g. when images of non-face objects are presented from different viewpoints, or vary in their size or location). According to Thierry et al. (2007a), the apparent face-sensitivity of the N170 component is an artifact of inadequate stimulus control, and specifically of systematic ISPV differences between faces and other stimulus categories, because in typical N170 experiments, ISPV is generally low for faces, and higher for non-face objects. High ISPV increases the variability of ERP peak latencies across single trials, and this latency jitter results in a systematic reduction of ERP peaks in averaged waveforms. Reduced N170 amplitudes for non-face objects as compared to faces would thus be the consequence of systematic between-category differences in ISPV. Once ISPV is controlled, the face-sensitivity of the N170 would be abolished. Thierry et al. (2007a) support this provocative claim by presenting data from two experiments where they manipulated the ISPV of faces and non-face objects (cars or butterflies). Larger N170 components for faces were found only when the ISPV of faces was low and the ISPV of non-faces was high. In contrast, when the ISPV level was the same for faces and non-faces, no N170 amplitude differences were observed.

Not surprisingly, these results, and in particular the conclusions that were drawn by Thierry and colleagues, have elicited a hostile and extremely critical response from the N170 community (Bentin et al., 2007; Rossion and Jacques, 2008). Can it really be the case that all previous studies that have used the N170 component as a critical marker of face processing are now invalidated due to the presence of an unrecognized methodological confound? Fortunately for researchers that have used or intend to use the N170 to study face processing, any such reports on the demise of this face-sensitive component are definitely premature. In fact, the arguments put forward by Thierry and colleagues have already been conclusively refuted (see Rossion and Jacques, 2008, for detailed arguments). However, the fact that these arguments were originally published in a highly visible multidisciplinary journal may still lead researchers who are not familiar with the intricacies of ERP methodology to assume that the N170 component cannot provide any valid insights into the brain mechanisms that underlie face processing. It will therefore be useful to briefly summarize the case against Thierry et al. (2007a) in this chapter.

As described in the previous section, the N170 is a visual evoked ERP component, and is therefore not only sensitive to faces, but is also affected by variations of low-level visual features. Because of this fact, absolute N170 amplitudes can vary substantially as a result of differences in visual stimulus parameters such as luminance, spatial frequency, contrast, symmetry, and retinal eccentricity. It is therefore not very surprising that ISPV may be another low-level variable that has the potential to affect N170 amplitudes. However, Thierry et al. (2007a) do not just claim that ISVP can modulate the size of the N170, but instead, and much more controversially, that uncontrolled ISPV differences across object categories can account for all previously reported N170 amplitude differences between faces and non-face stimuli, and that the face-sensitivity of the N170 disappears when ISPV is held constant.

The case against Thierry and colleagues (2007a) includes two main lines of argument: on the one hand, there appear to be substantial methodological flaws in their own experiments, specifically with respect to the measurement of the N170, which may have obscured the real face-sensitivity of this component. On the other hand, and even more importantly, the claim by Thierry et al. (2007a) that previous N170 studies failed to control for ISPV is simply wrong, and their conclusion that the N170 is no longer face-sensitive when ISPV is held constant is therefore plainly inconsistent with existing data.

With respect to the internal methodological problems of the experiments reported by Thierry et al. (2007a), it is likely that they may have missed face-sensitive N170 modulations because their choice of electrodes used to measure N170 amplitudes was inappropriate. As can be seen in Figure 17.1, N170 amplitude enhancements to faces relative to non-face objects have a distinct lateral occipitotemporal distribution. This face-sensitive effect is usually maximal at lateral posterior electrodes such as P7 and P8, and its amplitude declines rapidly at more medial occipital electrodes. Likewise, face-specific N170 modulations are rarely observed at more dorsal occipitoparietal electrode sites. If anything, these electrodes are more likely to pick up the posterior part of the VPP component (the positive-going counterpart of the N170, see Figure 17.1). In spite of these well-known facts about N170 scalp distribution patterns, Thierry and colleagues chose to quantify N170 amplitudes by including medial occipital and parietal electrodes. It is therefore not very surprising that they observed generally very small N170 amplitudes, and no systematic differences between faces and non-faces. This diagnosis is further supported by inspecting the ERP waveforms from more appropriate occipitotemporal electrodes that were provided by Thierry and colleagues (2007b) in their response to a critique of their original paper by Bentin et al. (2007). Here, the N170 was indeed larger for faces than for cars, at least when ISPV was high for both categories, which appears to directly contradict their original claims.

Not only do the N170 data that Thierry and colleagues have put forward to support their controversial conclusions suffer from an inappropriate choice of electrode sites, but their claims also do not stand up in the light of existing studies of the N170 component. First of all, it is simply not correct that previous experiments on the N170 have not considered ISPV as a possible confounding factor. In fact, in the vast majority of these studies, including those conducted by the author of this review, great care has been taken to equate the size, location, and viewpoint for images of face and non-face objects, in order to minimize any differences between object categories in terms of the low-level physical attributes of individual stimuli (see Rousselet et al., 2008 for a recent example). There is therefore no reason to assume that ISPV was generally much higher for non-face images than for faces in all previous N170 experiments. Although ISPV has usually not been explicitly measured for different stimulus categories, closer scrutiny of existing studies reveals that ISVP is not a critical factor for N170 amplitudes in general, and for the face-sensitivity of this component in particular. Bentin et al. (2007) present a re-analysis of the N170 results obtained by Rossion et al. (2000) in response to faces, houses, cars, and novel visual objects ("greebles"). ISPV values for each of these categories were estimated by computing the pixel-by-pixel correlation between all images within the same category. N170 amplitudes were maximal in response to faces, and were basically unrelated to differences in ISPV between object categories. Perhaps most tellingly, N170 amplitudes were much larger for faces than for houses, in spite of the fact that ISPV was minimal for houses (i.e. individual houses were more similar to each other than were the items in the other three categories), and substantially larger for faces. In another study (Goffaux et al., 2003), substantially larger N170 amplitudes were observed to faces than to cars, in spite of the fact that ISVP was virtually identical across these two stimulus categories. In addition to these two examples, similar dissociations between ISPV and N170 amplitudes could be easily demonstrated on the basis of numerous other existing studies (see Bentin et al., 2007, and Rossion and Jacques, 2008, for more examples). Further strong evidence against the claim that the apparent face-sensitivity of the N170 is due to a confound with ISPV comes from numerous studies that have shown that the N170 is modulated by face inversion. These studies will be reviewed in the next section. Because stimulus inversion leaves ISPV unaffected, such N170 face inversion effects cannot be due to an uncontrolled variation of this factor.

To summarize, the strong claims put forward by Thierry et al. (2007a) can be safely refuted not only on the basis of internal problems related to the measurement of the N170, but most compellingly because of the conclusive evidence from many other studies which demonstrates that the face-sensitivity of the N170 component bears virtually no relationship to variations in ISVP across stimulus categories. The systematic methodological artifact that might threaten to invalidate all previous research on the N170 does simply not exist. Nevertheless, the contribution by Thierry and colleagues may still serve as an important reminder that careful control of low-level visual stimulus attributes remains an essential aspect of research in visual cognition, and in particular in experiments that measure brain responses to natural images, such as photographs of faces and non-face objects. If stimulus control is not sufficiently rigid, the unrecognized variance of elementary perceptual features between image categories could indeed lead to mistaken claims about category-specific processing.

The N170 as a marker for the structural encoding and configural processing of faces

The face-sensitivity of the N170 strongly suggests that this component is linked to cortical processes that are involved in the category-selective processing of faces. Several studies have demonstrated that the N170 is unaffected by the familiarity of faces (e.g. Bentin and Deouell, 2000; Eimer 2000c; but see Caharel et al., 2002 for diverging results), indicating that this component is associated with face processing stages that precede the identification of individual faces. It has therefore been suggested (e.g. Eimer, 2000d; Sagiv and Bentin, 2001) that the N170 is an electrophysiological marker for the perceptual structural encoding of faces that takes place prior to face recognition. The existence of face-specific structural encoding was originally postulated in the influential face processing model by Bruce and Young (1986) as the stage where visual representations of the features of individual faces are generated. Even though the N170 is typically unaffected by the long-term familiarity of faces, it does show systematic repetition effects for individual unfamiliar faces: N170 amplitudes are reduced when the same face is presented twice in rapid succession, relative to trials where the second face image shows a different individual (e.g. Jemel et al., 2005). Such identity-dependent N170 adaptation effect can even be observed when the two successively presented faces differ in their viewpoint (Caharel et al., 2009). These observations are fully in line with the hypothesis that the N170 is linked to the structural encoding of individual faces. In addition, the N170 typically shows little sensitivity to the emotional expression of a face (Eimer and Holmes, 2002; Eimer et al., 2003; but see Batty and Taylor, 2003 for different results). The observation that facial expression modulates ERPs at anterior electrodes in the 140–200 ms post-stimulus latency window, whereas the face-sensitive N170 that emerges in the same time window at lateral posterior electrodes is not affected by emotional expression (see Eimer and Holmes, 2002, 2007) is in line with the assumption of Bruce and Young (1986) that structural encoding and the detection of the emotional expression of faces represent two parallel and independent stages of face processing (see also Chapter 22 by Calder, this volume, for a more detailed and critical discussion of this assumption).

The question of how the structural encoding of faces, as reflected by the N170 component, differs from the perceptual processing of other types of objects is still a subject of considerable debate. One key difference between face and object processing is that that inversion has a much larger negative effect on the perception and recognition of faces than on the perception and recognition of non-face objects. This "face inversion effect" (e.g. Yin, 1969) is usually explained by assuming that inversion specifically disrupts the processing of configural information, and that this type of information is much more important for the perception and recognition of faces than for the processing of other types of visual objects (for more details, see McKone and Robbins, Chapter 9; Tanaka and Gordon, Chapter 10, this volume). While some authors (e.g. Tanaka and Farah, 1993) postulate that faces are analyzed in a holistic fashion, others (Leder and Bruce, 2000) assume that relational information (e.g. the spatial configuration of specific face parts) is the key aspect in the configural processing of faces (see Rossion, 2008; and Rossion and Gauthier, 2002 for more detailed discussions of the difference between the holistic and relational interpretation of face-specific configural processing). Still others (e.g. Valentine, 1988) have claimed that inversion does not primarily affect the perception of faces, but instead their post-perceptual encoding in memory, which is less efficient when faces are inverted.

The N170 has played an important part in this debate, as this component is highly sensitive to face inversion. One of the most reliable and replicable features of the N170 is that it is delayed by about 10 ms in response to inverted as compared to upright faces (Bentin et al., 1996; Eimer, 2000b; Itier et al., 2006, 2007; Rossion et al., 2000; Sagiv and Bentin, 2001). A similar effect of face inversion on the latency of the face-sensitive VPP (the positive counterpart of the N170 at midline electrodes, see the first section in this chapter) was already reported by Jeffreys (1989). Although some small inversion-induced N170 latency delays have recently also been observed for some non-face objects (Itier et al., 2006), this latency shift is generally much more pronounced and consistent for inverted faces. The delay of the N170 in response to inverted faces has been attributed to the disruption of configural face processing that is caused when prototypical spatial relationships between face parts are altered as a result of face inversion. The fact that face inversion systematically affects an early visually evoked component such as the N170 provides conclusive evidence for a perceptual locus of the face inversion effect, and against the view that this effect is primarily generated during the encoding of inverted faces in memory (Valentine, 1988).

However, face inversion does not just result in a delay of the N170 component, but is also typically reflected by an enhancement of N170 amplitudes (Bentin et al., 1996; Eimer, 2000b; Rossion et al., 2000; Sagiv and Bentin, 2001). The fact that the N170 is larger for inverted than for upright faces is often considered as puzzling: if face inversion disrupts configural processing, an ERP marker such as the N170 that is supposed to be sensitive to this type of processing should be attenuated rather than enhanced in response to inverted faces. Several explanations have been put forward to account for the paradoxical increase in N170 amplitude for inverted faces. According to one hypothesis (Itier et al., 2007), the inversion-induced enhancement of N170 amplitudes is linked to the additional recruitment of eye-sensitive cells by inverted faces. These authors assume that the N170 component is primarily generated in STS, which includes both face-selective and eye-selective neurons. Upright faces activate only face-selective, but not eye-selective cells, because the latter are assumed to be inhibited when presented in the context of an upright face (see also Perrett et al., 1988). The disruption of prototypical face configurations induced by face inversion releases eye-sensitive neurons from context-induced inhibition. In line with their account, Itier et al. (2007) demonstrated that face inversion effects on N170 amplitude disappeared for faces without eyes. One problem for this explanation of enhanced N170 amplitudes for inverted faces in terms of an additional recruitment of eye-selective cells in STS is that that most source localization studies have pointed to occipitotemporal cortex and the posterior fusiform gyrus, but not to STS, as the most likely primary origin of the N170 (see the first section in this chapter).

According to an alternative hypothesis (Rossion et al., 2000), both inverted and upright faces activate face-specific neurons, but only inverted faces will additionally recruit object-sensitive neurons. This additional neural input results in an enhancement of the N170 in response to inverted faces. In support of this hypothesis, an earlier fMRI study (Haxby et al., 1999) has shown that inverted faces produce an increased activation of a ventral extrastriate region that respond preferentially to non-face objects. Even though several studies measuring fMRI (e.g. Kanwisher et al., 1998) and intracranially recorded brain activity (McCarthy et al., 1999) have observed stronger activations of face-selective areas for upright relative to inverted faces, other studies (e.g. Yovel and Kanwisher 2005) did find an increased activation of the object-selective lateral occipital complex (LOC) to inverted faces. In line with this observation, Rosburg et al. (2010) recently reported an inversion-induced enhancement of a face-sensitive component that was intracranially recorded from lateral occipital cortex at around 180 ms after stimulus onset. This face inversion effect was observed over face-selective as well as over object-selective lateral occipital areas. Given that the N170 is assumed to originate at least partially from lateral occipital cortex (see the first section in this chapter), these findings are also in line with the hypothesis that inversion-induced N170 amplitude enhancements are associated with the additional recruitment of object-selective neurons (Rossion et al., 2000).

Even though a comprehensive and generally accepted explanation for the effects of face inversion on N170 latencies and amplitudes has not yet been developed, the presence of such effects does in itself indicate that this component is linked to stages of face processing that code the configuration of individual faces. Additional support for this conclusion comes from studies demonstrating that N170 amplitudes are modulated when facial features are scrambled (George et al., 1996) and when face halves are spatially misaligned (Letourneau and Mitchell, 2008), as well as from the observation that N170 components triggered by two-tone Mooney stimuli in an explicit face detection task were enhanced on trials where these stimuli were perceived as faces (George et al., 2005). However, the link between the N170 component and configural face processing is not universally accepted. For example, a recent MEG study (Harris and Nakayama, 2008) measured the reduced sensitivity of the M170 (the magnetic counterpart of the N170) to upright faces when these were immediately preceded by an adapting stimulus. While the M170 was strongly attenuated when a face was preceded by another face, and much less so when the adapting stimulus was a non-face, M170 adaptation effects were equal in size regardless of whether upright faces, inverted faces, or isolated face parts were shown as adapting stimuli. This observation was interpreted as evidence that the M170 is primarily sensitive to face components, and not to the overall configuration of a face. Unlike EEG, MEG is more sensitive to lateral than medial sources, which suggests that M170 and N170 components do not necessarily reflect exactly the same neural generators, and may therefore show different patterns of adaptation. For example, the fact that N170 adaptation effects have been observed when the face of the same individual is presented twice in rapid succession, even when the viewpoint is changed (Caharel et al., 2009), strongly suggests that the N170 is sensitive to facial configuration, and not just to the presence of face components. An important focus of future N170 research will be to further clarify which aspects of a face are coded at the level of the N170, and how exactly this component is linked to configural face processing.

The N170 component, domain specificity, and perceptual expertise

One fundamental question in research on face perception and recognition is whether face-selective brain processes should be understood as domain-specific mechanisms (or "modules").

On the one hand, it has been argued that face processing is based on dedicated, special-purpose, and possibly innate mechanisms that are selectively and exclusively involved in the processing of faces (Kanwisher, 2000). On the other hand, the subordinate level expertise model (Tarr and Gauthier, 2000) claims that specific brain areas are selectively and consistently activated by faces because the classification of faces is usually made at the subordinate (i.e. individual) level, and is based on a subtle analysis of configural information, whereas most other object categories are recognized at the basic level (e.g. as cars, houses, or birds). An important implication of this model is that once observers have acquired sufficient perceptual expertise with a non-face object category to use configural information in order to discriminate objects at a subordinate level, the processing of these objects will recruit the same brain areas that are activated during face percep-tion and recognition. In other words, these areas are not dedicated to a specific category of visual objects (faces), but instead to a specific type of visual processing (recognition of individual object tokens based on configural information).

This debate about the domain-specificity of face processing has been based primarily on results of fMRI studies. Numerous fMRI experiments have demonstrated clear face-specific patterns of activation in posterior fusiform gyrus (Kanwisher et al., 1997). However, the degree to which non-face objects activate the same areas appears to be modulated by expertise: car or bird experts show enhanced levels of activation in right posterior face-selective brain areas when confronted with objects from their respective expert category (Gauthier et al., 2000a). Likewise, extended training with a class of novel objects (greebles) results in a selective recruitment of the same face-sensitive brain areas (Gauthier et al., 1999). While such fMRI results suggest that cortical regions that are usually dedicated to the processing of faces can be activated by non-face objects once observers have gained expertise with such objects, they do not provide any information about the timing of such effects. If similar systematic expertise-related modulations could be demonstrated for the face-sensitive N170 component in response to non-face objects, this would suggest that perceptual expertise can already affect early perceptual processing stages that are usually regarded as face-selective.

A number of recent ERP studies have indeed reported effects of perceptual expertise on N170 latencies and amplitudes. As discussed in the previous section, the N170 delay for inverted as compared to upright faces has been linked to the disruption of configural processing produced by inversion. If perceptual expertise with a non-face category recruits brain areas that are involved in configural subordinate-level processing, presenting objects of expertise in an upside-down fash-ion should produce delays of N170 latencies that are comparable to the delays usually observed in response to inverted faces. This logic was adopted in an ERP study (Rossion et al., 2002b) where participants received intensive perceptual training with greeble stimuli, and ERPs to upright and inverted faces as well as upright and inverted greebles were recorded both before and after this training. As expected, the N170 was delayed for inverted as compared to upright faces. The critical observation was that following (but not prior to) perceptual expertise training, an inversion-induced N170 latency delay was also present for greeble stimuli. However, this training-induced N170 latency shift was observed only over the left hemisphere, which is neither in line with the N170 latency delay in response to inverted faces, nor with previous expertise-related effects observed in fMRI studies (Gauthier et al., 1999, 2000a). Both are either bilateral or tend to be more pronounced in the right hemisphere. Effects of long-term perceptual expertise on N170 latencies were reported by Busey and Vanderkolk (2005), who measured ERPs to upright and inverted faces and to upright and inverted fingerprints, separately for fingerprint experts and novices. While the usual N170 delay for inverted relative to upright faces was observed for both groups over the right hemisphere, only fingerprint experts showed a right-lateralized N170 delay for inverted as compared to upright fingerprints. Overall, the effects of perceptual expertise with non-face stimuli on N170 latencies that were found in these studies provide initial evidence that such stimuli may be processed configurally, similar to the kind of processing that is triggered in response to faces.

Other ERP investigations of links between perceptual expertise and the N170 component have measured expertise effects on N170 amplitudes. Tanaka and Curran (2001) presented pictures of birds and dogs to groups of bird or dog experts, and found that N170 amplitudes were larger in response to objects within observers' area of expertise than for objects outside this area (see also Gauthier et al., 2003, for similar findings). While these authors interpreted this result as evidence that perceptual expertise can modulate the activity of face-sensitive brain areas, in line with the subordinate level expertise model (Tarr and Gauthier, 2000), other interpretations remain possible. For example, experts may have attended more intensively to objects within their specific domain of expertise, resulting in a general attentional enhancement of early visual components, including the N170. As described in the first section, the N170 represents the face-sensitive part of the visual N1 component. This fact makes it often difficult to dissociate genuinely category-specific effects on N170 amplitudes from category-unspecific effects of task strategies or selective attention on visual processing (see also Carmel and Bentin, 2002 for a more detailed discussion of this issue).

To eliminate a possible confounding influence of attentional factors on expertise-related N170 amplitude modulations, Rossion et al. (2004) studied the effects of perceptual training with greebles on the N170 to faces in the context of a perceptual competition paradigm. On each trial, a greeble appeared at fixation, and a face in the left or right visual hemifield was added to this display after 600 ms. EEG was recorded before and after perceptual training with the greeble stimuli, and participants had to report the side on which the face was presented. N170 components to greebles were larger after training than before training, similar to the effects of long-term expertise reported by Tanaka and Curran (2001). Most importantly, the N170 in response to the lateral faces was reduced in amplitude after extensive perceptual training with greebles. Rossion et al. (2004) interpreted this result as demonstrating that once perceptual expertise with respect to a non-face object category has been acquired, stimuli in this category will begin to activate regions in occipitotemporal cortex that are preferentially activated by faces. Because faces and greebles compete for the same category-specific processing resources after perceptual training, N170 amplitudes to faces are reduced. It should also be noted that the greeble stimuli used in this experiment were asymmetrical, to rule out the concern that these effects are due to the fact that greebles are face-like in terms of their overall configuration and symmetry (see Xu et al., 2005). In a more recent study that used a similar perceptual competition paradigm (Rossion et al., 2007), analogous N170 amplitude reductions in response to lateral faces were found when participants viewed centrally presented cars. Critically, these effects were more pronounced for car experts than for novices.

In summary, the observation that long-term perceptual expertise or perceptual training with specific object categories can modulate the N170 component provides evidence that the face-selective brain processes that are reflected by this component should not be regarded as domain-specific perceptual modules that are exclusively dedicated to face processing, but instead as face-sensitive mechanisms that can also be recruited, at least to some degree, during the configural processing of non-face objects (see also Bentin and Carmel 2002; Carmel and Bentin 2002; Rossion et al., 2002a, for further discussion of this issue). It should however also be noted that this debate is far from resolved. For example, in a study using MEG, Xu et al. (2005) found no evidence for any differential effect of car expertise on M170 amplitudes, and no correlation between the M170 to cars and successful car identification in car experts, which was interpreted as evidence that the M170 is linked to strictly domain-specific face brain processes (see also McKone and Robbins, Chapter 9, this volume, for further discussion).

Summary and conclusions

In the research reviewed in this chapter, the face-sensitive N170 component was employed to investigate the brain mechanisms that are responsible for our ability to perceive faces. This review has focused primarily on experiments that have studied links between the N170 and the structural encoding and configural processing of faces, and on studies that have investigated the domain-specificity versus domain-generality of the face processing mechanisms that are reflected by the N170. In addition to these questions, many other issues that are relevant to our understanding of face processing have been addressed by measuring the N170 component. These include effects of contextual priming (Bentin et al., 2002), contrast reversal (Itier and Taylor 2002), spatial attention (Eimer 2000a; Eimer et al., 2003), eccentricity and size (Jeffreys et al., 1992), or spatial frequency content (Goffaux et al., 2003; Holmes et al., 2005), as well as investigations of face-selective processing deficits in prosopagnosia (Bentin et al., 1999; Eimer and McCarthy 1999). These and many other recent studies have demonstrated that the N170 component is an immensely useful electrophysiological tool that can be used to study the time course and functional organization of human face processing.

One major task for future research will be to provide a more comprehensive account of how specific properties of faces are processed and represented at the level of the N170. A related goal is to clarify how different aspects of face processing that are reflected by the N170 are linked to specific activations of face-sensitive brain areas. To answer such questions, new methodological approaches may need to be developed. For example, the neural adaptation paradigms that have recently begun to be used in ERP studies of face processing have the potential to provide important new insights into the response profile of the N170 and its links to different aspects of face perception, and are likely to become one major focus of N170 research in the coming years. To identify the neural sources that underlie the N170 more precisely, traditional source localization methods may need to be complemented by face processing studies where EEG and fMRI activity is measured simultaneously (see Sadeh et al., 2008, for a demonstration of the validity of this approach). In addition to such methodological and conceptual developments, the application of N170 research to applied and clinical questions is likely to become more prominent. Issues such as the early development of face processing (see Johnson, Chapter 1, this volume), the social role of gaze perception (see Tipper and Bayliss, Chapter 28, this volume), the nature of face processing in autism (see Webb et al., Chapter 43, this volume), or the impairment of face perception in developmental prosopagnosia (see Duchaine, Chapter 42, this volume) have already begun to be studied with ERP methods, and the face-sensitive N170 component is likely to become a useful tool for addressing important questions in these fields.

Acknowledgments

This research was supported by the Economic and Social Research Council (ESRC), UK. Thanks to Bruno Rossion, Corentin Jacques, Gill Rhodes, and Monika Kiss for their comments. The author holds a Royal Society-Wolfson Research Merit Award.

References

Allison, T., Puce, A., Spencer, D.D., and McCarthy, G. (1999). Electrophysiological studies of human face perception. I: Potentials generated in occipitotemporal cortex by face and non-face stimuli. *Cerebral Cortex*, **9**, 415–430.

Batty, M. and Taylor, M.J. (2003). Early processing of the six basic facial emotional expressions. *Cognitive Brain Research*, **17**, 613–620.

Bentin, S. and Carmel, D. (2002). Accounts for the N170 face-effect: A reply to Rossion, Curran, & Gauthier. *Cognition*, **85**, 197–202.

Bentin, S. and Deouell. L.Y. (2000). Structural encoding and identification in face processing: ERP evidence for separate mechanisms. *Cognitive Neuropsychology*, **17**, 35–54.

Bentin, S., Allison, T., Puce, A., Perez, E. and McCarthy, G. (1996). Electrophysiological studies of face perception in humans. *Journal of Cognitive Neuroscience*, **8**, 551–565.

Bentin, S., Deouell, L.Y., and Soroker, N. (1999). Selective visual streaming in face recognition: evidence from developmental prosopagnosia. *Neuroreport*, **10**, 823–827.

Bentin, S., Sagiv, N., Mecklinger, A., Friederici, A., and von Cramon, Y.D. (2002). Priming visual face-processing mechanisms: Electrophysiological evidence. *Psychological Science*, **13**, 190–193.

Bentin, S., Taylor M.J., Rousselet, G.A. *et al.* (2007). Controlling interstimulus perceptual variance does not abolish N170 face sensitivity. *Nature Neuroscience*, **10**, 801–802.

Bötzel, K. and Grüsser, O.J. (1989). Electric brain potentials evoked by pictures of faces and non-faces: a search for face-specific EEG-Potentials. *Experimental Brain Research*, **77**, 349–360.

Bötzel, K., Schulze, S., and Stodieck, S.R.G. (1995). Scalp topography and analysis of intracranial sources of face-evoked potentials. *Experimental Brain Research*, **104**, 135–143.

Bruce, V. and Young, A. (1986). Understanding face recognition. *British Journal of Psychology*, **77**, 305–327.

Busey, T.A. and Vanderkolk, J.R. (2005). Behavioral and electrophysiological evidence for configural processing in fingerprint experts. *Vision Research*, **45**, 431–448.

Caharel, S., d'Arripe, O., Ramon, M., Jacques, C., and Rossion, B. (2009). Early adaptation to unfamiliar faces across viewpoint changes in the right hemisphere: evidence from the N170 ERP component. *Neuropsychologia*, **47**, 639–643.

Caharel, S., Poiroux, S., Bernard, C., Thibaut, F., Lalonde, R., and Rebai, M. (2002). ERPs associated with familiarity and degree of familiarity during face recognition. *International Journal of Neuroscience*, **112**, 1499–1512.

Carmel, D. and Bentin, S. (2002). Domain specificity versus expertise: factors influencing distinct processing of faces. *Cognition*, **83**, 1–29.

Deffke, I., Sander, T., Heidenreich, J., Sommer, W., Curio, G., Trahms, L., and Lueschow, A. (2007). MEG/EEG sources of the 170-ms response to faces are co-localized in the fusiform gyrus. *Neuroimage*, **35**, 1495–1501.

Eimer, M. (2000a). Attentional modulations of event-related brain potentials sensitive to faces. *Cognitive Neuropsychology*, **17**, 103–116.

Eimer, M. (2000b). Effects of face inversion on the structural encoding and recognition of faces - Evidence from event-related brain potentials. *Cognitive Brain Research*, **10**, 145–158.

Eimer, M. (2000c). Event-related brain potentials distinguish processing stages involved in face perception and recognition. *Clinical Neurophysiology*, **111**, 694–705.

Eimer, M. (2000d). The face-specific N170 component reflects late stages in the structural encoding of faces. *Neuroreport*, **11**, 2319–2324.

Eimer, M. and Holmes, A. (2002). An ERP study on the time course of emotional face processing. *Neuroreport*, **13**, 427–431.

Eimer, M. and Holmes, A. (2007). Event-related brain potential correlates of emotional face processing. *Neuropsychologia*, **45**, 15–31.

Eimer, M. and McCarthy, R.A. (1999). Prosopagnosia and structural encoding of faces: Evidence from event-related potentials. *Neuroreport*, **10**, 255–259.

Eimer, M., Holmes, A., and McGlone, F.P. (2003). The role of spatial attention in the processing of facial expression: an ERP study of rapid brain responses to six basic emotions. *Cognitive, Affective, and Behavioral Neuroscience*, **3**, 97–110.

Gauthier, I., Tarr, M.J., Anderson, A.W., Skudlarski, P., and Gore, J.C. (1999). Activation of the middle fusiform 'face area' increases with expertise in recognizing novel objects. *Nature Neuroscience*, **2**, 568–73.

Gauthier, I., Skudlarski, P., Gore, J.C., and Anderson, A.W. (2000a). Expertise for cars and birds recruits brain areas involved in face recognition. *Nature Neuroscience*, **3**, 191–197.

Gauthier, I., Tarr, M.J., Moylan, J., Skudlarski, P., Gore, J.C., and Anderson, A.W. (2000b). The fusiform 'face area' is part of a network that processes faces at the individual level. *Journal of Cognitive Neuroscience*, **12**, 495–504.

Gauthier, I., Curran, T., Curby, K.M., and Collins, D. (2003). Perceptual interference supports a non-modular account of face processing. *Nature Neuroscience*, **6**, 428–432.

George, N., Evans, J., Fiori, N., Davidoff, J., and Renault, B. (1996). Brain events related to normal and moderately scrambled faces. *Cognitive Brain Research*, **4**, 65–76.

George, N., Jemel, B., Fiori, N., Chaby, L., and Renault, B. (2005). Electrophysiological correlates of facial decision: Insights from upright and upside-down Mooney-face perception. *Cognitive Brain Research*, **24**, 663–673.

Goffaux, V., Gauthier, I., and Rossion, B. (2003). Spatial scale contribution to early visual differences between face and object processing. *Cognitive Brain Research*, **16**, 416–424.

Halgren, E., Raij, T., Marinkovic, K., Jousmäki, V., and Hari, R. (2000). Cognitive response profile of the human fusiform face area as determined by MEG. *Cerebral Cortex*, **10**, 69–81.

Harris, A. and Nakayama, K. (2008). Rapid adaptation of the M170 response: Importance of face parts. *Cerebral Cortex*, **18**, 467–476.

Haxby, J.V., Ungerleider, L.G., Clark, V.P., Schouten, J.L., Hoffmanm E.A., and Martin, A. (1999). The effect of face inversion on activity in human neural systems for face and object perception. *Neuron*, **22**, 189–199.

Haxby, J.V., Hoffman, E.A., and Gobbini, M.I. (2000). The distributed human neural system for face perception. *Trends in Cognitive Sciences*, **4**, 223–233.

Henson, R.N., Mattout, J., Singh, K.D., Bames, G.R., Hillebrand, A., and Friston, K. (2007). Population-level inferences for distributed MEG source localization under multiple constraints: Application to face-evoked fields. *Neuroimage*, **38**, 422–438.

Holmes, A., Winston, J.S., and Eimer, M. (2005). The role of spatial frequency information for ERP components sensitive to faces and emotional facial expression. *Cognitive Brain Research*, **25**, 508–520.

Hoffman, E. and Haxby, J. (2000). Distinct representations of eye gaze and identity in the distributed human neural system for face perception. *Nature Neuroscience*, **3**, 80–84

Itier, R.J. and Taylor, M.J. (2002). Inversion and contrast polarity reversal affect both encoding and recognition processes of unfamiliar faces: A repetition study using ERPs. *Neuroimage*, **15**, 353–372.

Itier, R.J. and Taylor, M.J. (2004). Source analysis of the N170 to faces and objects. *Neuroreport*, **15**, 1261–65.

Itier, R.J., Latinus, M., and Taylor, M.J. (2006). Face, eye and object early processing: What is the face specificity? *NeuroImage*, **29**, 667–676.

Itier, R.J., Alain, C., Sedore, K., and McIntosh, A.R. (2007). Early face processing specificity: It's in the eyes! *Journal of Cognitive Neuroscience*, **19**, 1815–1826.

Jeffreys, D.A. (1989). A face-responsive potential recorded from the human scalp. *Experimental Brain Research*, **78**, 193–202.

Jeffreys, D.A., Tukmachi, E.S.A., and Rockley, G. (1992). Evoked-potential evidence for human brain mechanisms that respond to single fixated faces. *Experimental Brain Research*, **91**, 351–362.

Jemel, B., Schuller, A.M., Cheref-Khan, Y., Goffaux, V., Crommelinck, M., and Bruyer, R. (2003). Stepwise emergence of the face-sensitive N170 event-related potential component. *Neuroreport*, **14**, 2035–2039.

Jemel, B., Pisani, M., Rousselle, L., Crommelinck, M., and Bruyer, R. (2005). Exploring the functional architecture of person recognition system with event-related potentials in a within- and cross-domain self-priming of faces. *Neuropsychologia*, **43**, 2024–2040.

Joyce, C. and Rossion, B. (2005). The face-sensitive N170 and VPP components manifest the same brain processes: The effect of reference electrode site. *Clinical Neurophysiology*, **116**, 2613–2631.

Kanwisher, N. (2000). Domain specificity in face perception. *Nature Neuroscience*, **3**, 759–763.

Kanwisher, N., McDermott, J., and Chun, M.M. (1997). The fusiform face area: A module in human extrastriate cortex specialized for face perception. *Journal of Neuroscience*, **17**, 4302–4311.

Kanwisher, N., Tong, F., and Nakayama, K. (1998). The effect of face inversion on the human fusiform face area. *Cognition*, **68**, B1–B11.

Leder, H. and Bruce, V. (2000). When inverted faces are recognized: The role of configural information in face recognition. *Quarterly Journal of Experimental Psychology Section A - Human Experimental Psychology*, **53**, 513–536.

Letourneau, S.M. and Mitchell, T.V. (2008). Behavioral and ERP measures of holistic face processing in a composite task. *Brain and Cognition*, **67**, 234–245.

McCarthy, G., Puce, A., Belger, A., and Allison, T. (1999). Electrophysiological studies of human face perception. II: Response properties of face-specific potentials generated in occipitotemporal cortex. *Cerebral Cortex*, **9**, 431–444.

Perrett, D.I., Mistlin, A.J., Chitty, A.J., *et al.* (1988). Specialized face processing and hemispheric-asymmetry in man and monkey - Evidence from single unit and reaction-time studies. *Behavioural Brain Research*, **29**, 245–258.

Rosburg, T., Ludowig, E., Dümpelmann, M., Alba-Ferrara, L., Urbach, H., and Elger, C.E. (2010). The effect of face inversion on intracranial and scalp recordings of event-related potentials. *Psychophysiology*, **47**, 147–157.

Rossion, B. (2008). Picture-plane inversion leads to qualitative changes of face perception. *Acta Psychologica*, **128**, 274–289.

Rossion, B. and Gauthier, I. (2002). How does the brain process upright and inverted faces? *Behavioral and Cognitive Neuroscience Reviews*, **1**, 63–75.

Rossion, B. and Jacques, C. (2008). Does physical interstimulus variance account for early electrophysiological face sensitive responses in the human brain? Ten lessons on the N170. *Neuroimage*, **39**, 1959–79.

Rossion, B., Gauthier, I., Tarr, M.J., Despland, P., Bruyer, R., Linotte, S., and Crommelinck, M. (2000). The N170 occipito-temporal component is delayed and enhanced to inverted faces but not to inverted objects: an electrophysiological account of face-specific processes in the human brain. *Neuroreport*, **11**, 69–74.

Rossion, B., Curran, T., and Gauthier, I. (2002a). A defense of the subordinate-level expertise account for the N170 component. *Cognition*, **85**, 189–196.

Rossion, B., Gauthier, I., Goffaux, V., Tarr, M.J., and Crommelinck, M. (2002b). Expertise training with novel objects leads to left-lateralized facelike electrophysiological responses. *Psychological Science*, **13**, 250–257.

Rossion, B., Joyce, C.A., Cottrell, G.W., and Tarr M.J. (2003). Early lateralization and orientation tuning for face, word, and object processing in the visual cortex. *Neuroimage*, **20**, 1609–1624.

Rossion, B., Kung, C.C., and Tarr, M.J. (2004). Visual expertise with nonface objects leads to competition with the early perceptual processing of faces in the human occipitotemporal cortex. *Proceedings of the National Academy of Science USA*, **101**, 14521–14526.

Rossion, B., Collins, D., Goffaux, V., and Curran, T. (2007). Long-term expertise with artificial objects increases visual competition with early face categorization processes. *Journal of Cognitive Neuroscience*, **19**, 543–555.

Rousselet, G., Husk, J.S., Bennett, P.G., and Sekuler, A.B. (2008). Time course and robustness of ERP object and face differences. *Journal of Vision*, **8**, 1–18.

Sadeh, V., Zhdanov, A., Podlipsky, I., Hendler, T., and Yovel G. (2008). The validity of the face-selective ERP N170 component during simultaneous recording with functional MRI. *Neuroimage*, **42**, 778–786.

Sagiv, N. and Bentin, S. (2001). Structural encoding of human and schematic faces: Holistic and part-based processes. *Journal of Cognitive Neuroscience*, **13**, 937–951.

Sams M., Hietanen, J.K., Hari, R., Ilmoniemi, R.J., and Lounasmaa, O.V. (1997). Face-specific responses from the human inferior occipito-temporal cortex. *Neuroscience*, **77**, 49–55.

Tanaka, J.W. and Curran, T. (2001). A neural basis for expert object recognition. *Psychological Science*, **12**, 43–47.

Tanaka, J.W. and Farah, M.J. (1993). Parts and wholes in face recognition. *Quarterly Journal of Experimental Psychology*, **46A**, 225–245.

Tarr, M.J. and Gauthier, I. (2000). FFA: a flexible fusiform area for subordinate-level visual processing automatized by expertise. *Nature Neuroscience*, **3**, 764–769.

Thierry, G., Martin, C.D., Downing, P.E., and Pegna, A.J. (2007a). Controlling for interstimulus perceptual variance abolishes N170 face selectivity. *Nature Neuroscience*, **10**, 505–511.

Thierry, G., Martin, C.D., Downing, P.E., and Pegna, A.J. (2007b). Is the N170 sensitive to the human face or to several intertwined perceptual and conceptual factors? *Nature Neuroscience*, **10**, 802–803.

Valentine, T. (1988). Upside-down faces - a review of the effect of inversion upon face recognition. *British Journal of Psychology*, **79**, 471–491.

Watanabe, S., Kakigi, R., and Puce, A. (2003). The spatiotemporal dynamics of the face inversion effect: A magneto- and electro-encephalographic study. *Neuroscience*, **116**, 879–895.

Xu, Y., Liu, J., and Kanwisher, N. (2005). The M170 is selective for faces, not for expertise. *Neuropsychologia*, **43**, 588–597.

Yin, R.K. (1969). Looking at upside-down faces. *Journal of Experimental Psychology*, **81**, 141–145.

Yovel, G. and Kanwisher, N. (2005). The neural basis of the face-inversion effect. *Current Biology*, **15**, 2256–2262.

Chapter 18

Neurophysiological Correlates of Face Recognition

Stefan R. Schweinberger

Introduction

Humans are social beings, and faces convey an enormous range of social information about identity, age, gender, mood, ethnicity, or current state and focus of attention of people, and this list is non-exhaustive. Despite the enormous importance of faces for social cognition, many researchers have been fascinated in particular by the fact that the human visual system can easily individuate literally hundreds of familiar people by their faces. This is true even though, on the one hand, individual encounters of faces (e.g. on photos) vary greatly in viewpoint, illumination, expression etc., and despite the fact that, on the other hand, human faces are all characterized by a very similar basic configuration of features. On that view, although today's perspective on disorders (see the respective contributions in this volume) tends to consider a range of social signals in the face beyond identity, it is unsurprising that prosopagnosia, the inability to recognize familiar people by their faces (Bodamer, 1947), continues to be considered by many as "the" most important disorder in face processing.

The present chapter is about neurophysiological correlates of those processes that mediate face recognition. By the term "recognition" I refer to the word in its specific sense, and hence to processes by which humans perceive the identity of familiar faces. Quite a few neurophysiological studies on face recognition do not acknowledge the important distinction between familiar and unfamiliar face processing. Although face recognition, in that specific sense, has been investigated in only a fraction of neurophysiological studies of face perception, we still face a wide topic: early models of familiar face recognition (best represented by Bruce and Young, 1986; cf. Figure 18.1 for an adapted version of this model) specified identification as involving a number of functional stages (or, for present purposes, neural computations). First, a detailed analysis of the visual stimulus and its image elements is performed during pictorial encoding. During structural encoding, this basic information about contour, shape, color, texture etc. is integrated into a uniform, holistic representation of the face. Subsequently, this representation needs to be compared with more permanently stored representations of familiar faces (termed "face recognition units," FRUs), and if a match is detected, the face may be recognized as familiar. If so, a person identity node (PIN) is activated (Burton et al., 1990). The idea is that PINs are convergence nodes which may be activated by faces, voices, or other individuating stimuli, and which then provide access to further semantic or episodic information (for instance, the context in which we learned to know the person, her or his occupation, place of living, and so forth), and to the name of that person. This is clearly not an all-or-none sequence of processes (e.g. sometimes we can easily recognize a face but yet are unable to retrieve the name). Also, the precise description and organization of these functional stages continues to be a matter of debate. But overall, Bruce and Young's model and its successors have done remarkably well in decades of subsequent research, and most current models continue to use this basic architecture when describing processes involved in face recognition (see the contributions in Schweinberger and Barton, in press).

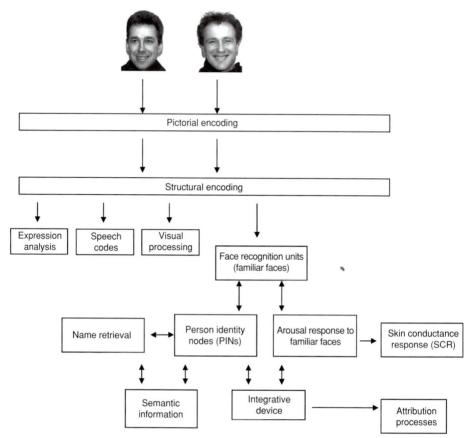

Fig. 18.1 An adaptation of the model of face recognition proposed by Burton et al. (1999) and Schweinberger and Burton (2003). Familiar faces are recognized when a stimulus-based representation that is formed during structural encoding sufficiently activates a stored representation of a familiar face in long-term memory (sometimes referred to as face recognition unit, FRU). Apart from eliciting an arousal response, individual recognition then enables access to semantic information about a person, and eventually supports retrieval of that person's name. Adapted from Schweinberger, S.R. and Burton, A.M. (2003). Covert recognition and the neural system for face processing. *Cortex*, **39**, 9–30. Reprinted with permission from Elsevier.

For the purpose of the present text, how can we approach neurophysiological correlates of face recognition? In its simplest form perhaps, neural correlates of recognition may be inferred from a difference between a repeated and an unrepeated presentation of a particular face. This is because such *repetition effects* show that the brain must have registered at some stage that the same face has occurred before.[1] Neural correlates of recognition can also be inferred when a difference in

---

[1] Note that this is similar to the kind of recognition tested in many studies probing episodic memory for pre-experimentally unfamiliar faces. While recognition in this sense may be said to have occurred even for an unfamiliar face when presented a second time, it needs to be acknowledged that there are substantial and qualitative differences in the mental representations of well-known familiar versus once-seen unfamiliar faces (cf. Burton and Jenkins, Chapter 15, this volume).

response is demonstrated between presentations of familiar and unfamiliar faces, and those *familiarity effects* demonstrate contact with a representation in some type of more permanent memory store for familiar (but not unfamiliar) faces. Moreover, recognition of familiar faces often (but not always) triggers *identification*, by means of retrieving unique semantic information about a known person, by retrieving her or his personal name, or both.

Here I will focus on effects related to face repetition and familiarity, and say much less about correlates of face identification that involve retrieval of semantic information or names, for two reasons: this emphasis is simply a reflection of research activity in the past 15 years, with comparatively less activity devoted to these post-perceptual identification processes. There are also good reasons to believe that equivalent mechanisms of retrieving semantic information or names of people can be triggered both by seeing a familiar person's face and by, for instance, hearing a person's voice (Hanley et al., 1989; Neuner and Schweinberger, 2000). In the model's terms, I will thus put some emphasis on those neurophysiological responses (most importantly, N170 and N250/N250r components of the event-related potential, ERP) which have been broadly related by many researchers to processes of structural encoding and individual face recognition.

Perhaps due to their sociobiological importance, the specificity debate—the question of whether or not humans perceive faces by a "special" set of mental routines or brain processes has absorbed many scientists for the past 40 years or so (cf. McKone and Robbins, Chapter 9, this volume). The question of whether or not particular ERP components are indeed selective for faces may be seen as a specific instance of this debate, though one that has been led in a rather heated manner recently (e.g. Bentin et al., 2007; Dering et al., 2009; Rossion and Jacques, 2008; Thierry et al., 2007). In fact, as will be seen in the next section, a debate around the face-selectivity of ERPs already dominated much early research in that field. I argue that to understand the underlying neural processes mediating face recognition, the specificity debate is of only secondary importance, and the main challenge is to investigate the functional significance of various neural responses in the context of cognitive models (such as the model sketched in Figure 18.1).

Historical perspective

"Early" studies (pre-1985)

Historically, localization of higher perceptual and cognitive function in the brain had started when Broca and Wernicke linked aspects of language processing with left hemisphere (LH) function. While language may be the most efficient means of exchanging many types of information, faces convey extremely rich and salient *non-verbal* communicative information. Nearly a century passed, however, before face processing was more systematically linked to right hemisphere (RH) function, based on behavioral data (Rizzolatti et al., 1971) and evidence from brain-lesioned patients (Milner, 1968; but see also Meadows, 1974; Damasio et al., 1982). Not surprisingly, the earliest neurophysiological studies on face recognition were dominated by then-popular ideas on functional hemispheric specialization. Accordingly, many of the first ERP studies on face perception confirmed the role of the RH. For instance, in anticipation of or in response to faces, larger contingent negative variations (CNV; Butler et al., 1981), P300 amplitudes (Small, 1983), or negative slow waves (Sobotka et al., 1984) were seen over the RH.

The vertex-positive potential (VPP)

ERP studies until around 1990 typically used only a few recording channels, and thus did not permit detailed topographical analyses, nor source localizations, of the measured signals. This limitation also held for a subsequent and systematic research series by Jeffreys and coworkers. Jeffreys' research aimed at the question of whether faces are perceived by "special" neuronal mechanisms (also see McKone and Robbins, Chapter 9, this volume), and thus he recorded ERPs while subjects—passively—watched either faces or different kinds of non-face objects (Jeffreys, 1989, 1996; Jeffreys and Tukmachi, 1992; also cf. Bötzel and Grüsser, 1989). Jeffreys observed a vertex-positive potential (VPP) at mid-central electrodes, with a latency of around 170 to 200 ms, that was consistently larger to faces than to non-face objects. This difference persisted for artificial facial configurations when face and non-face control objects were equated for visual complexity (e.g. by construing non-faces as scrambled configurations of potential facial features, cf. Figure 18.2).

The mid-1990s

Intracranial N200; scalp-recorded N170, and N250r. A few years later, Allison and colleagues (1994) recorded ERPs in epileptic patients from surface electrodes that were chronically implanted over striate and extrastriate cortex. They found a number of apparently face-selective potentials between around 200 and 300 ms (most prominently, a N200) at the surface of the fusiform gyrus and more lateral temporal regions, as well as longer-latency potentials over the inferior anterior temporal lobe. These loci corresponded well with regions of activation found in functional imaging studies, published in approximately the same time period (e.g. Sergent and Signoret, 1992).

Finally, the mid-1990s also saw the first reports on two new face-elicited ERP responses recorded from the scalp surface in healthy participants: First, a right-lateralized occipitotemporal N170 response selective to faces (compared to other visual stimuli) was demonstrated in two papers (Bentin et al., 1996; Bötzel et al., 1995). This response typically has a peak latency of around 150 to 190 ms. The careful and extensive report by Bentin became what today may well be the best-known ERP study on face perception (see also Eimer, Chapter 17, this volume).

Second, while it was soon recognized that the VPP and N170 were ERP correlates of face percep-tion (rather than recognition), the study of ERP correlates of face recognition also started almost at the same time. In 1995, an ERP correlate of the repetition of familiar (compared to unfamiliar) faces was first reported, again by two independent groups (Begleiter et al., 1995; Schweinberger et al., 1995). This response, with a peak latency of approximately 230 to 280 ms, has a right-later-alized inferior occipitotemporal scalp topography, with a maximum slightly anterior to what is seen for N170. This ERP correlate of familiar face repetitions was later termed the N250r ("r"for "repetition"; Schweinberger et al., 2002a), whereas it had been labeled "visual memory potential, VMP" (Begleiter) or "early repetition effect, ERE" (Schweinberger) in the initial reports.

1995 to 2000

Event-related magnetoencephalography and induced oscillatory brain responses. Magnetoencephalography (MEG) is a technique to measure the magnetic fields produced by electrical brain activity. The use of this technique to measure magnetic fields evoked by faces revealed prominent responses at latencies comparable to those in ERPs. These include an M170, an occipitotemporal MEG response around 140 to 180 ms (Halgren et al., 2000; Linkenkaer-Hansen et al., 1998). This response is typically considered as a magnetic counterpart of the electri-cal N170 (Liu et al., 2000), although it needs to be kept in mind that EEG and MEG differ in their relative sensitivity to radially and tangentially orientated brain sources. Perception of a face in an ambiguous stimulus (a "Mooney" face) was also shown to induce a burst of gamma oscillations (synchronizations of neuronal activity in the EEG in the 34–40 Hz frequency range) around 250 ms poststimulus (Rodriguez et al., 1999). Such induced EEG or MEG gamma responses are thought to be crucially involved in conscious perception (Engel and Singer, 2001). In this chapter,

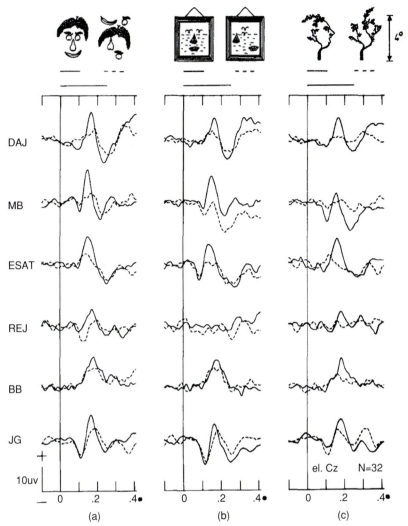

Fig. 18.2 Vertex-recorded visual evoked potentials in six subjects to three artificial facial configurations (full traces) and their respective non-face control stimuli (dashed traces) consistently show a prominent vertex-positive potential (VPP) for faces. With kind permission of Springer Science + Business Media, *Experimental Brain Research*, The vertex-positive scalp potential evoked by faces and by objects, **91**, 1992, 340–350, Jeffreys and Tukmachi.

although I will occasionally discuss findings from MEG or induced gamma band responses, I will largely restrain myself to the substantial literature on ERP correlates of face recognition.

Event-related potentials and cognitive models of face recognition

I will now consider face-sensitive ERPs and their supposed relationship to cognitive models defining different processes involved in familiar face recognition (Bruce et al., 1986; Burton et al.,

1990, 1999; Haxby et al., 2000; Schweinberger and Burton, 2003, see Figure 18.1 for an example).

Pictorial encoding/P100

Following a period during which many researchers strongly focused on N170 (sometimes disregarding other ERP effects visible in their data), several researchers noted that the earlier P100 also responds to faces as compared to other visual stimuli (Herrmann et al., 2005). Although substantial research remains to be done on this component, the face-elicited P100 may in part reflect top-down attentional processes related to face perception, and likely is related to an early pictorial encoding stage (Desjardins and Segalowitz, 2009).

Structural encoding/N170

The N170 is typically regarded as a marker for the structural encoding of faces. Rather than reiterating the full set of arguments for this conclusion (see Eimer, Chapter 17, this volume), I will focus on effects of repetition and familiarity on N170. In a large number of studies, the N170 component was not affected by familiarity of faces at all (for a few examples, see Bentin and Deouell, 2000; Eimer, 2000b), nor did it show sensitivity to face repetition (e.g. Cooper et al., 2007; Eimer, 2000b; Engst et al., 2006; Schweinberger et al., 1995). The majority of more recent reports corroborate these results. However, some other studies now suggest that the insensitivity of the N170 to repetition may be relative rather than absolute. For instance, a few studies have reported a small repetition-related modulation on the N170. While some studies report an increase (Jemel et al., 2005), others report a decrease (Itier and Taylor, 2002, 2004; Jacques and Rossion, 2006) in N170 amplitude. It is also important to note that, in a systematic series of experiments, Itier and Taylor (2002, 2004) found equivalent N170 repetition effects for upright, inverted and contrast-reversed (photographic negative) unfamiliar faces. Because both inversion and photographic negation massively disrupt face identification, this suggests that the N170 repetition effect was based on repetition of pictorial, rather than identity-related information.

A recent study by Caharel et al. (2009) reported a slight reduction, or adaptation, of a right occipitotemporal N170 for repeated as compared to unrepeated unfamiliar faces, even when viewpoint was changed between repetitions. While this is an interesting finding, it may be important to note that those results were obtained under quite specific conditions of very small inter-stimulus interval (150–350 ms) and long (3000 ms) and short (200 ms) presentation times for adaptor and test, respectively—conditions known to maximize face adaptation effects (Leopold et al., 2005). Yet, this N170 repetition effect was small, compared to a prominent N250r effect in the same study (cf. Figure 18.3). Evidence for small identity-specific repetition effects on N170 is accompanied by equally recent evidence for more prominent category-specific repetition effects on N170. Those results reveal a strong attenuation of the N170 whenever a current face was preceded by another face (compared to when the same face was preceded by a stimulus from a different category), irrespective of identity (Kloth et al., 2010; Maurer et al., 2008).

On balance, it seems fair to conclude that the N170 is mainly (though perhaps not exclusively) related to processes that precede individual face identification. The N170 therefore predominantly reflects the categorization of a stimulus as a face (or a face-like pattern) and the structural encoding of faces (cf. Eimer, Chapter 17, this volume, for a similar conclusion).

Individual face recognition/N250r

In contrast to the N170, the N250r ("r" for "repetition") component has consistently emerged as a neurophysiological correlate of face recognition. Before turning to the functional characteristics

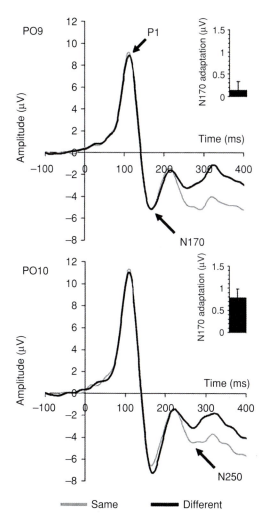

Fig. 18.3 ERP waveforms elicited by the second, frontally depicted face at two occipitotemporal electrodes (PO9 and PO10) for full-front faces immediately (SOA of 150–350 ms) preceded by same or different faces. Primes were always orientated 30 degrees to the right. Note the small right-lateralized N170 adaptation effect, together with the prominent N250r repetition effect. Data from Caharel et al. 2009. Reprinted from *Neuropsychologia*, **47** (3), Early adaptation to repeated unfamiliar faces across viewpoint changes in the right hemisphere: Evidence from the N170 ERP component, copyright 2009, with permission from Elsevier.

of this ERP response, I will briefly describe its spatiotemporal characteristics. The N250r is a negativity for repeated as compared to non-repeated familiar faces over inferior occipitotemporal regions, and typically is larger over the right hemisphere. N250r onsets between about 180 and 220 ms, and reaches a maximum between about 230 and 330 ms. With common average reference, the occipitotemporal negativity is invariably accompanied by frontocentral positivity in the same latency range. Source modeling suggested that this ERP is generated in fusiform gyrus, coinciding with a region that is activated by faces in fMRI studies, and that responds to face repetitions (e.g. Eger et al., 2005, cf. Figures 18.4 and 18.5).

Response to repetition

The N250r is, by definition, highly sensitive to repetitions of faces. The scalp-recorded N250r may also be reconciled with intracranial data, which show the earliest consistent face repetition effects peaking around 290 ms (Puce et al., 1999), and with MEG research which has identified the

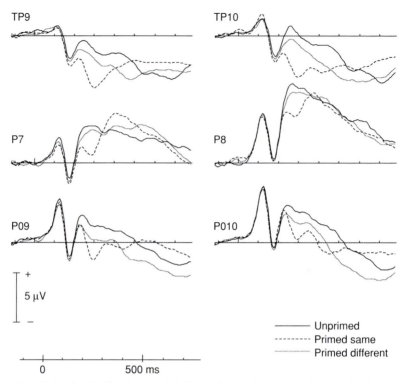

Fig. 18.4 ERPs elicited by familiar faces at inferior and posterior temporal electrodes (TP9, TP10, P7, P8, PO9, PO10). Familiar face repetition does not affect the N170, but starts to influence ERPs from about 200 ms onwards, an effect most prominent at more anterior and inferior locations. N250r repetition effects are similar in topography, but smaller in amplitude, for repetitions across different images as compared to same-image face repetitions. Reprinted from *Cognitive Brain Research*, **14** (3), Stefan R. Schweinberger, Esther C. Pickering, Ines Jentzsch, A. Mike Burton, and Jürgen M. Kaufmann, Event-related brain potential evidence for a response of inferior temporal cortex to familiar face repetitions, Copyright (2002), with permission from Elsevier.

M250r as a neuromagnetic analog of the N250r (Schweinberger et al., 2007). Although a clear N250r is seen for repetitions of familiar faces across different images, N250r is larger for repetitions using the same image (Schweinberger et al., 2002a; also cf. Figure 18.4), mirroring behavioral facilitation effects of face priming (Ellis et al., 1987). This suggests that the facial representations that mediate N250r exhibit a degree of image specific coding. Intriguingly, however, a recent study shows that compared with same-image priming, prime faces with massive linear geometrical distortions elicit equivalent N250r repetition effects (Bindemann et al., 2008; cf. Figure 18.6).

Response to familiarity

Several studies observed larger repetition-related N250r responses for familiar than unfamiliar faces (e.g. Begleiter et al., 1995; Pfütze et al., 2002; Schweinberger et al., 1995; see Herzmann et al., 2004, for a comparison of effects by personally familiar vs. famous faces). At least when repetitions are immediate (i.e. without other faces intervening between repetitions), unfamiliar faces also elicit some N250r effect (see also Itier and Taylor, 2004), although consistently a smaller one

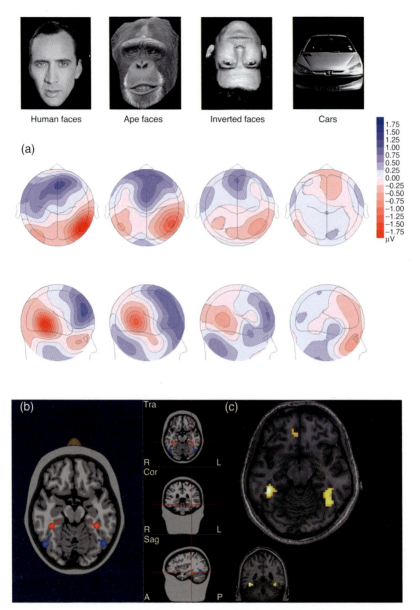

Fig. 18.5 (a) Top. Scalp topography of the N250r for different types of stimuli. Depicted is the ERP difference (voltage map, spherical spline interpolation, 110 degrees equidistant projection) between repeated and unrepeated stimuli for four categories including famous human faces. Data from Schweinberger et al. (2004) reproduced from *Neuroreport*, **15**, Schweinberger, S.R., Huddy, V., and Burton, A.M., N250r–A face-selective brain response to stimulus repetitions, pp. 1501–1505, Copyright 2004, with permission from Wolters Kluwer, Lippincott, Williams, and Wilkins. (b) Bottom, left. Best-fitting source model of the N250r (in red). Source model for the N170 (in blue) from the same data set is also shown for comparison. Data from Schweinberger et al. (2002a) reprinted with permission from Elsevier; replicated in Schweinberger et al. (2004). (c) Bottom, right. A similar fMRI study exhibits effects of face repetition priming in fusiform cortex. Data from Eger et al. (2005) with permission from Elsevier. Reprinted from *Cognitive Brain Research*, **14** (3), Stefan R. Schweinberger, Esther C. Pickering, Ines Jentzsch, A. Mike Burton, and Jürgen M. Kaufmann, Event-related brain potential evidence for a response of inferior temporal cortex to familiar face repetitions, Copyright (2002), with permission from Elsevier.

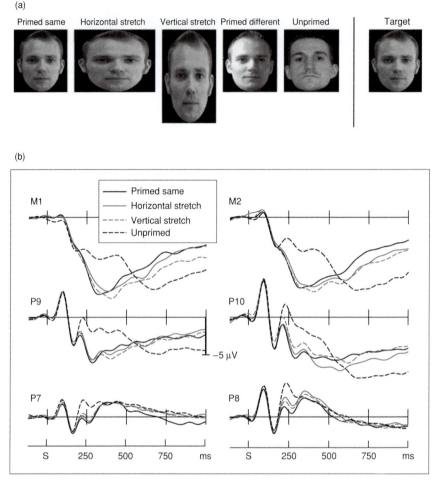

Fig. 18.6 Top. Priming conditions used in the study by Bindemann et al. (2008). Images are for illustration only, as famous faces were actually used in the study. Bottom. ERPs for the primed same condition, the horizontal and vertical stretch conditions, and the unprimed condition. N250r is virtually equivalent for priming by the same face image and priming from stretched onto unstretched faces, demonstrating that N250r does not simply reflect the superficial visual overlap between two face images, but may be related to person recognition. Data from Bindemann et al. (2008).

compared to familiar faces (Begleiter et al., 1995; Herzmann et al., 2004; Schweinberger et al., 1995). However, while N250r to repetitions of unfamiliar faces can be eliminated by backward masking of the prime (Dörr, 2008) or by other faces intervening between prime and target face (Pfütze et al., 2002), N250r to familiar faces is well preserved under those conditions.

Despite this, the N250r to familiar faces also is a somewhat transient phenomenon: while surviving a small number of two to four intervening stimuli (Pfütze et al., 2002), a direct comparison suggests that N250r is enhanced by emotional compared to neutral faces, but is reduced with increasing numbers of faces held in working memory (Langeslag et al., 2009). When hundreds of stimuli and ~30 min intervene between familiar face repetitions, N250r is very nearly eliminated, despite the fact that behavioral priming may persist under those circumstances (Schweinberger et al., 2002b; but see also Graham and Dawson, 2005). Collectively, these observations could suggest that the N250r reflects the re-activation of a facial representation in working memory (Schweinberger and Burton, 2003). On that view, the N250r to unfamiliar faces may be fragile because, once the active representation of an unfamiliar face is erased from visual working memory due to masking or interference, it cannot be reactivated via long-term memory, whereas this reactivation remains possible for familiar faces.

Response to inversion

The behavioral face inversion effect (Yin, 1969) refers to a disproportionate disruption of face recognition caused by inversion. Like N170, N250r is highly sensitive to inversion, but the pattern of effects dramatically differs from that seen for the N170: While N170 is increased (and delayed) by face inversion (Rossion et al., 1999, 2000; Wiese et al., 2009), N250r is reduced or abolished by inversion (Schweinberger et al., 2004; cf. Figure 18.5). The inversion effect on N170 still awaits a generally accepted explanation (see Eimer, Chapter 17, this volume), but the latency delay and amplitude increase have been taken as indicators of increased perceptual demands on structural encoding of inverted faces (Rossion et al., 2000; but see also Itier et al., 2007, for a more detailed account). A plausible explanation for the inversion effect on N250r suggests that this response reflects transient access to representations of familiar faces (Bindemann et al., 2008), and that the formation of these is hampered by inversion.

Attention and N250r

It has been presumed that, compared with other stimuli, faces are hard to ignore and capture attention (Vuilleumier, 2000; but see also VanRullen, 2006). Consistent with this idea, behavioral repetition priming was observed from familiar faces when shown as distractors during a prime phase, while participants performed a letter identification task. Moreover, although explicit memory for these faces was massively reduced by high versus low perceptual load during letter identification, the magnitude of priming was unaffected by perceptual load. Thus, explicit (recognition) and implicit (priming) memory for faces can be dissociated (Jenkins et al., 2002). It is therefore interesting whether N250r is moderated by attention. In a series of recent studies, participants attended to letter strings superimposed on briefly (200 ms) presented faces, and identified target letters ("X" vs. "N") embedded in strings of either six different (high load) or six identical (low load) letters. Letter identification was followed by probes, which were either repetitions of faces, new faces, or infrequent butterflies, to which participants responded. N250r amplitude was equivalent regardless of perceptual load at prime presentation, indicating that task-irrelevant face encoding was remarkably preserved even in a demanding letter identification task (Neumann and Schweinberger, 2008). Intriguingly, high perceptual load at prime presentation can eliminate (or strongly reduce) N250r to probe face repetitions, but only when the target at prime presentation is another face, and not when the target item is another visual object (Neumann and Schweinberger, 2009). These findings provide an interesting extension to behavioral evidence for capacity-limited and face-specific attention resources, and could suggest that no more than one face can be encoded at a time (Bindemann et al., 2005).

Semantic access and naming/N400, N400f and late slow waves

The ERP most frequently associated with semantic processing is N400 (Kutas and Hillyard, 1980), a negative component with central-parietal maximum. In the context of face recognition, an N400-like component with a latency of approximately 300 to 600 ms was consistently attenuated as a result of semantic (associative) priming (Dietl et al., 2005; Wiese and Schweinberger, 2008).

The topography of the N400 seems uninfluenced by whether people are recognized via faces or names (Schweinberger, 1996), suggesting that the N400 is a marker for postperceptual processing stages in person (rather than face) recognition. Other researchers (Eimer, 2000a) reported an enhanced negativity for familiar faces (termed N400f) and thought that this ERP may reflect the activation of stored representations of familiar faces. From today's viewpoint, N400f may more likely relate to those aspects of semantic processing that are triggered by familiar but not unfamiliar persons (i.e. identity-specific as opposed to visually derived semantic information; cf. Bruce et al., 1986).

Finally, there is also preliminary evidence that neural correlates of naming familiar faces start around 500 ms, a latency similar or slightly later than semantic access (Diaz et al., 2007). With regard to identification and naming, a long-standing controversy is whether access to a name invariably is subsequent to, and contingent on, access to semantic information about a person, or whether semantic access and name retrieval occur in parallel. Combined with a particular experimental design, a chronometric index of covert response preparation (the so-called lateralized readiness potential, LRP) permits powerful inferences with respect to the relative timing in processing different kinds of information from the same stimulus (e.g. semantic information and names, van Turennout et al., 1997). Although the controversy is likely to continue, results from the LRP tend to support parallel access to semantic information and names in face identification (Abdel Rahman et al., 2002, also cf. Figure 18.1).

Overall, the evidence reviewed in this section is in broad agreement with the idea that the occipitotemporal N170 indicates processes of detection and categorization of a stimulus as a face and its structural encoding. Processes of individual face recognition are consistently related to a subsequent ventral occipitotemporal N250r effect.[2] In addition, while relatively few studies have been performed to date on later processes of person identification, a central-parietal N400 has emerged as one correlate of access to semantic information about people.

Neurophysiological correlates of face learning and expertise

As faces become familiar, the nature of their mental representation also changes. While representations for unfamiliar faces are based on relatively low-level image descriptions, representations for familiar faces are much more robust against transformations in viewpoint or lighting (Hancock et al., 2000; see also Burton and Jenkins, Chapter 15, this volume). One important challenge is therefore to investigate how faces become familiar (Burton, 1994), and to determine neural processes accompanying successful learning.

A line of research initiated by Ken Paller (Paller et al., 1987) investigated ERPs to individual memorized words, and compared ERPs depending on whether or not items were successfully recalled later. This research revealed an ERP difference predictive of subsequent memory performance, termed Dm. In short, frontocentral ERPs during encoding were more positive for

---

[2] Neural correlates of individual recognition of faces are not necessarily completely absent for N170, or more generally before 180 ms—possibly particularly so for personally familiar faces. However, even where present, effects of individual recognition on the N170 are small, and need to be compared against strong and consistent effects seen in N250/N250r. Moreover, recent studies investigating effects of perceptual expertise using either basic-level (i.e. categorization) or subordinate-level (i.e. individuation) training, also consistently show that whereas basic-level training with faces or objects increases the N170, superordinate-level training increases an occipitotemporal N250 response, termed the "expert" N250 by those authors (Scott, Tanaka, Sheinberg, and Curran, 2006; Tanaka, Curran, Porterfield, and Collins, 2006; Tanaka and Pierce, 2009; see also next section)

items later recalled or recognized, compared to subsequently forgotten items. This difference held for considerable time periods (400–800 ms). Later, Werner Sommer demonstrated similar Dm effects for successfully learned faces (Sommer et al., 1991, 1995) and, based on topographical differences, suggested that the brain systems mediating Dm for faces dissociate from those mediating Dm for names (Sommer et al., 1997).

Subsequently, researchers focused on the recognition (rather than encoding) phase of learning experiments. Paller's team reported more positive ERPs from 300 to 600 ms to learned faces than to new faces. For faces learned by visual presentation only, this old-new ERP difference was confined to posterior electrodes. By contrast, old-new difference for faces learned with semantic information and names was seen over posterior and anterior electrodes. This suggests that the posterior portion of the ERP effect is a neural correlate of retrieval of visual face information, whereas its anterior portion reflects the retrieval of person-specific semantic information (Paller et al., 2000).

Learning is related to expertise, in that the latter may be regarded as the product of the former. The concept of expertise plays a special role in more recent rounds of the specificity debate, as it was held that faces only seem special because most people are more experienced in individuating faces than in individuating other object classes. While all people may be "experts" for faces, some acquire very considerable expertise for other domains, making them valuable individuals for investigating expertise effects. An early study by Jim Tanaka investigated ERPs in bird and dog experts. This study focused on N170, and found slightly enhanced amplitudes when experts categorized animals in their respective domain of expertise, compared to when categorizing animals outside their domain of expertise (Tanaka and Curran, 2001). Unfortunately, statistical analyses were reported for the N170 only. Thus, although later ERPs of approximately 200 to 350 ms may have more clearly discriminated between the expertise groups (cf. Tanaka and Curran, 2001, figure 2), this possibility remains unclear.

"Experts" differ from novices at least in two aspects of perceptual expertise: First, they acquire categorical expertise, through more frequent exposure to the category of objects from their domain of expertise. Second, experts acquire subordinate level expertise, when learning to differentiate between individual exemplars. In a recent series of extensive learning studies, novice participants learned to classify birds at either basic (e.g. wading bird, owl) or subordinate level. Subordinate but not basic-level training improved individual discrimination of trained exemplars from novel ones. While both basic- and subordinate-level training enhanced an N170, only subordinate-level training increased an N250 component (Scott et al., 2006). Later, Tanaka and Pierce (2009) ingeniously used a variant of this design to train Caucasian participants either to differentiate African American or Hispanic faces at the individual level, or to classify these faces at the basic level. While little effects of either basic- or subordinate-level training were seen for N170, subordinate-level training not only improved individual recognition, but also increased the so-called "expert" N250 component.

Of particular relevance, Tanaka's group also demonstrated that an occipitotemporal N250 was initially much larger to a highly familiar face (the participant's own face), compared to both a to-be-learned target face and non-target faces. After learning, however, the learned face elicited an N250 that was similar in magnitude to the N250 elicited by the own face (cf. Figure 18.7). Irrespective of the specificity debate, those findings suggested that N250 is a reliable index of face familiarity (Tanaka et al., 2006).

One limitation of the above studies is that learning and test was always performed using identical images. It could be argued that N250 learning effects for pre-experimentally unfamiliar faces may be specific to identical images, whereas natural face learning should create representations that are more robust for image transformations. However, there is now independent evidence

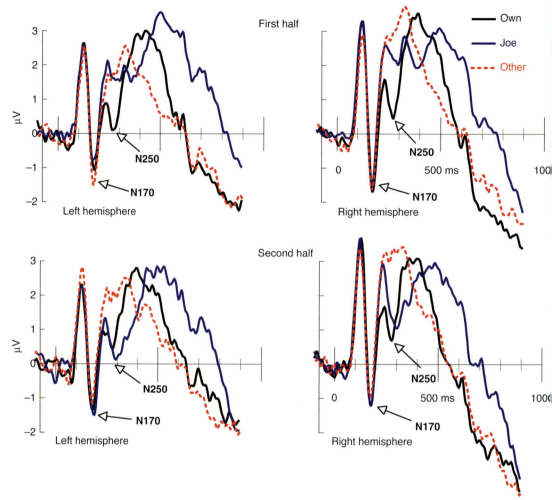

Fig. 18.7 The occipitotemporal N250 as an index of face familiarity. In the early stage of learning, a large N250 is elicited only be the own face, but not by a to-be-learned ("Joe") face. In a later stage of learning, the learned face elicits a larger N250, comparable to that elicited by the familiar own face. Data from the left and right hemisphere are pooled across a number of symmetrical inferior occipitotemporal sites. From James W. Tanaka, Tim Curran, Albert L. Poterfield, and Daniel Collins, Activation of Preexisting and Acquired Face Representations: The N250 Event-related Potential as an Index of Face Familiarity. *Journal of Cognitive Neuroscience*, **18:9** (September, 2006), pp. 1488–1497. © 2006 by the Massachusetts Institute of Technology. Figure courtesy of Jim Tanaka.

that the N250 is an index of the acquisition of face representation during learning, even when learning and test is based on different images of the same face (Kaufmann et al., 2009).

An open question is whether or not the N250 effect by subordinate-level training or learning of non-face objects should be regarded as identical to the N250 effect for learned faces. A comparison of source localization across studies tentatively suggests a more posterior source for the object-elicited N250 (e.g. compare Kaufmann et al., 2009; Schweinberger et al., 2002a, 2004;

Scott et al., 2006). However, a comparison of effects within the same study remains to be done. Despite this, evidence from brain lesions or functional imaging may well provide more conclusive evidence for the specificity debate, when compared to ERPs (McKone et al., 2007).

How many systems for the recognition of complex visual stimuli?

Based initially on patterns of co-occurrence among the associative visual agnosias (e.g. Farah, 1991), there has been a long and controversial debate about which (and how many) different systems for high-level visual recognition should be assumed. Using a divided visual field variant of perceptual priming, Marsolek presented behavioral evidence to suggest that the LH represents stimuli in an "abstractive," image-independent manner, and may be particularly important in representing words or written names, whereas the RH tends to represent stimuli in a concrete, image-dependent manner, particularly relevant for representing faces (e.g. Marsolek, 1995, 1999; Marsolek et al., 1992). On that view, many visual objects perhaps depend to some extent on both systems or types of visual representation.

While the right fusiform cortex area has been implicated in face recognition (Kanwisher and Yovel, 2006; Kanwisher et al., 1997), a region in the left fusiform gyrus was postulated as the "visual word-form area" (VWFA, Dehaene et al., 2001; McCandliss et al., 2003; also cf. Dien, 2009). It is thus relevant to consider studies investigating N250r in response to same-image versus across-image (or, for that matter, across-font) priming, from primes presented initially to the left or right visual fields and thus to the right or left hemispheres, respectively. In line with Marsolek's behavioral work, those studies suggest more image- or font-specific priming in the RH, and more abstractive priming in the LH, at the level of representation reflected in the ventral temporal N250r. Of particular interest, this specific gradient in asymmetry depending on the nature of priming was seen for both faces (Cooper et al., 2007) and words (Schweinberger et al., 2006).

Although evidence for and against face selectivity has been presented for both N170 and N250r, it is worth noting that experiments on the recognition of words or common objects have also revealed occipitotemporal N170 responses that distinguished between orthographic and non-orthographic stimuli (e.g. Bentin et al., 1999), though with a more left-lateralized topography. Similarly, repetition of objects (Henson et al., 2004) or words (Pickering and Schweinberger, 2003) can elicit N250r responses, though the magnitude and scalp topography of those responses differs systematically as a consequence of stimulus category (Martin-Loeches et al., 2005), with the word-elicited N250r exhibiting a consistent left lateralization (Pickering et al., 2003). At a broader level, and irrespective of issues of specificity, it therefore remains possible that (1) different variants of N170 and N250r responses relate to functionally similar processes of encoding and recognition, respectively, of various kinds of complex visual stimuli, (2) two systems related to the left and right fusiform regions support "abstractive" and "image-dependent" coding, respectively, and (3) the relative importance of those codes differs for different kinds of visual objects.

Methodological issues

While scalp-recorded ERPs offer superior temporal resolution, ERP source modeling faces limitations (Junghöfer et al., 1997; Michel et al., 2004), and even in ideal cases will not surpass a resolution of about 10 mm when localizing sources. By contrast, recent developments in fMRI methods significantly refined our ideas of how objects and faces are represented in ventral temporal cortex (Grill-Spector et al., 2006a). In particular, novel approaches of multivariate analyses for neuroimaging data allow for more precise decomposition of object(category)-dependent population responses (Kriegeskorte et al., 2008). Novel evidence from neuroimaging will likely continue to sharpen our ideas about the neural representation of faces, and the major future contribution of

EEG and MEG likely is to provide precise chronometric information of neural activation during face perception.

When interpreting ERPs from the scalp surface, electrical reference is a factor that explains many apparent discrepancies across labs in the responses recorded. With the benefit of hindsight, there is now good evidence that the VPP (Jeffreys, 1989) and the N170 (Bentin et al., 1996) likely are simply positive and negative maxima of the same underlying process (Itier et al., 2002; Joyce and Rossion, 2005; see also Eimer, Chapter 17, this volume). Given the importance for face perception of areas in ventral temporal cortex, we now know that it has been unfortunate for researchers to place the electrical reference at the mastoids or the earlobes, in close vicinity to precisely those areas—as has been common for decades of cognitive ERP research! As a result, the occipitotemporal maximum of many face-elicited ERPs was not noticed in those studies, including many reports on VPP as well as studies on face repetition effects. With today's multichannel EEG systems and sufficient whole-head sensor coverage, a common average reference not only enjoys the best biophysical justification (Lehmann, 1987; Michel et al., 2004), but also can be regarded as the most "neutral" reference for topographical analyses of face-elicited ERPs (Joyce et al., 2005; Schweinberger and Sommer, 1991).

Summary and conclusion

This chapter began with the assertion that, while much research has been performed on neurophysiological correlates of face perception, fewer studies specifically investigated processes that mediate face recognition—the perception of individual identity of familiar faces. This is because neuroscientists often did not incorporate into their experimental designs the important distinction, emphasized by cognitive models in the field (e.g. Bruce et al., 1986), between familiar and unfamiliar face processing. I have also argued that the specificity debate around faces, although interesting in its own right, is crucial neither for understanding the various processes that mediate individual face recognition, nor for elucidating the functional significance of neurophysiological responses as markers for the neural implementation of those processes.

Neurophysiological research in the past few years has been strongly focused on the N170, a putative correlate of the detection of a face-like visual configuration or structural encoding of faces. By contrast, the occipitotemporal N250/N250r can be considered as a correlate of the recognition of individual faces: While the N250r systematically responds to repetitions of individual facial identities, a similar N250 responds to the learning of previously unfamiliar faces. There is also evidence that a central-parietal N400 is a correlate of the access to semantic information for familiar people (rather than faces).

As an outlook, while effects of face priming or repetition have influenced this field for decades, the neural correlates of contrastive effects of perceptual adaptation (Leopold et al., 2001) are only beginning to be investigated. Both priming and adaptation can be considered "tools" to investigate the nature of neurocognitive representations, and a challenge for the future will be to develop models that specify mechanisms mediating both repetition priming and adaptation (Grill-Spector et al., 2006b; Huber, 2008). Such models will clearly need to consider data from various research domains. As one example, repetition of visual objects can induce changes in the power of EEG oscillations which, if they are not phase-locked to stimulus onset, are invisible in conventional ERPs. Intriguingly, such induced changes by object repetition seem to be maximal in the gamma band (30–80 Hz) around 220–350 ms, similar to the latency of N250r. It has been suggested that ERP and induced gamma may reflect complementary functional processes (Gruber and Müller, 2005). Also, induced changes in EEG power may correlate with activation changes seen in fMRI (Brookes et al., 2005), though the precise relationship between those signals is far from fully understood yet.

On a more practical side, while understanding face recognition will require neuroscientists to use familiar faces, the type of stimuli chosen will depend on the specific research question. Famous faces may be chosen when an experimental design requires large numbers of stimuli, though their disadvantage may be limited control over the stimulus images. While personally familiar faces likely represent the most "ecologically valid" category, researchers using those stimuli face many practical problems, since stimuli need to be individually mapped onto each participant, and only a limited number of faces is typically available. Learning studies often are extremely time-consuming, and it may be unclear how good a model experimental learning is for real-life familiarization with faces, but this approach permits full control over both the stimuli and the learning experience. In any case, it should be clear that, in order to understand the processes mediating face recognition, researchers need to use familiar faces for which robust representations have been acquired across various images.

It is clear that our seemingly effortless identification of an individual familiar face involves a complex cascade of processes, from encoding a holistic representation of the visual stimulus, comparison with stored representations of familiar faces in memory, access to semantic information about a person, to retrieval of that person's name. Considerable progress has been made in understanding the neurophysiological correlates of some specific processes in face recognition. In the future, both tailor-made experiments and the analysis of a multitude of neurophysiological responses will be required in order to promote further and more thorough understanding of the relationship between the cognitive system for face recognition and its neural implementation.

Acknowledgments

The author's research has been supported by the Deutsche Forschungsgemeinschaft (DFG), the Biotechnology and Biological Sciences Research Council (BBSRC, UK), the Wellcome Trust (UK), and the Royal Society (UK). Many thanks go to Roxane J. Itier and Holger Wiese for helpful comments.

References

Abdel Rahman, R., Sommer, W., and Schweinberger, S.R. (2002). Brain-potential evidence for the time course of access to biographical facts and names of familiar persons. *Journal of Experimental Psychology: Learning, Memory, and Cognition*, **28**, 366–373.

Allison, T., McCarthy, G., Nobre, A., Puce, A., and Belger, A. (1994). Human extrastriate visual cortex and the perception of faces, words, numbers, and colors. *Cerebral Cortex*, **5**, 544–554.

Begleiter, H., Porjesz, B., and Wang, W.Y. (1995). Event-related brain potentials differentiate priming and recognition to familiar and unfamiliar faces. *Electroencephalography and Clinical Neurophysiology*, **94**, 41–49.

Bentin, S. and Deouell, L.Y. (2000). Structural encoding and identification in face processing: ERP evidence for separate mechanisms. *Cognitive Neuropsychology*, **17**, 35–54.

Bentin, S., Allison, T., Puce, A., Perez, E., and McCarthy, G. (1996). Electrophysiological studies of face perception in humans. *Journal of Cognitive Neuroscience*, **8**, 551–565.

Bentin, S., Mouchetant-Rostaing, Y., Giard, M.H., Echallier, J.F., and Pernier, J. (1999). ERP manifestations of processing printed words at different psycholinguistic levels: Time course and scalp distribution. *Journal of Cognitive Neuroscience*, **11**, 235–260.

Bentin, S., Taylor, M.J., Rousselet, G.A., *et al.* (2007). Controlling interstimulus perceptual variance does not abolish N170 face sensitivity. *Nature Neuroscience*, **10**, 801–802.

Bindemann, M., Burton, A.M., and Jenkins, R. (2005). Capacity limits for face processing. *Cognition*, **98**, 177–197.

Bindemann, M., Burton, A.M., Leuthold, H., and Schweinberger, S.R. (2008). Brain potential correlates of face recognition: Geometric distortions and the N250r brain response to stimulus repetitions. *Psychophysiology*, **45**, 535–544.

Bodamer, J. (1947). Die Prosop-Agnosie. (Die Agnosie des Physiognomieerkennens). *Archiv für Psychiatrie und Nervenkrankheiten*, **179**, 6–53.

Bötzel, K. and Grüsser, O.J. (1989). Electric brain potentials-evoked by pictures of faces and non-faces - a search for face-specific EEG-potentials. *Experimental Brain Research*, **77**, 349–360.

Bötzel, K., Schulze, S., and Stodieck, S.R.G. (1995). Scalp topography and analysis of intracranial sources of face-evoked potentials. *Experimental Brain Research*, **104**, 135–143.

Brookes, M.J., Gibson, A.M., Hall, S.D., *et al.* (2005). GLM-beamformer method demonstrates stationary field, alpha ERD and gamma ERS co-localisation with fMRI BOLD response in visual cortex. *NeuroImage*, **26**, 302–308.

Bruce, V. and Young, A. (1986). Understanding face recognition. *British Journal of Psychology*, **77**, 305–327.

Burton, A.M. (1994). Learning new faces in an interactive activation and competition model. *Visual Cognition*, **1**, 313–348.

Burton, A.M., Bruce, V., and Hancock, P.J.B. (1999). From pixels to people: A model of familiar face recognition. *Cognitive Science*, **23**, 1–31.

Burton, A.M., Bruce, V., and Johnston, R.A. (1990). Understanding face recognition with an interactive activation model. *British Journal of Psychology*, **81**, 361–380.

Butler, S.R., Glass, A., and Heffner, R. (1981). Asymmetries of the contingent negative variation (CNV) and its after positive wave (APW) related to differential hemispheric involvement in verbal and nonverbal tasks. *Biological Psychology*, **13**, 157–171.

Caharel, S., d'Arripe, O., Ramon, M., Jacques, C., and Rossion, B. (2009). Early adaptation to repeated unfamiliar faces across viewpoint changes in the right hemisphere: Evidence from the N170 ERP component. *Neuropsychologia*, **47**, 639–643.

Cooper, T.J., Harvey, M., Lavidor, M., and Schweinberger, S.R. (2007). Hemispheric asymmetries in image-specific and abstractive priming of famous faces: Evidence from reaction times and event-related brain potentials. *Neuropsychologia*, **45**, 2910–2921.

Damasio, A.R., Damasio, H., and VanHoesen, G.W. (1982). Prosopagnosia: Anatomic basis and behavioral mechanisms. *Neurology*, **32**, 331–341.

Dehaene, S., Naccache, L., Cohen, L., Le Bihan, D., Mangin, J.F., Poline, J.B. et al. (2001). Cerebral mechanisms of word masking and unconscious repetition priming. *Nature Neuroscience*, **4**, 752–758.

Dering, B., Martin, C.D., and Thierry, G. (2009). Is the N170 peak of visual event-related brain potentials car-selective? *NeuroReport*, **20**, 902–906.

Desjardins, J. and Segalowitz, S.J. (2009). Deconstructing the P1 and N170 face-effect using independent component analysis. *Psychophysiology*, **46**, S24.

Diaz, F., Lindin, M., Galdo-Alvarez, S., Facal, D., and Juncos-Rabadan, O. (2007). An event-related potentials study of face identification and naming: The tip-of-the-tongue state. *Psychophysiology*, **44**, 50–68.

Dien, J. (2009). A tale of two recognition systems: Implications of the fusiform face area and the visual word form area for lateralized object recognition models. *Neuropsychologia*, **47**, 1–16.

Dietl, T., Trautner, P., Staedtgen, M., *et al.* (2005). Processing of famous faces and medial temporal lobe event-related potentials: a depth electrode study. *NeuroImage*, **25**, 401–407.

Dörr, P. (2008). The early repetition effect as a marker of facial representation stored in memory and its sensitivity to changes in viewpoint. Unpublished PhD thesis, Humboldt-University at Berlin.

Eger, E., Schweinberger, S.R., Dolan, R.J., and Henson, R.N. (2005). Familiarity enhances invariance of face representations in human ventral visual cortex: fMRI evidence. *NeuroImage*, **26**, 1128–1139.

Eimer, M. (2000a). Event-related brain potentials distinguish processing stages involved in face perception and recognition. *Clinical Neurophysiology*, **111**, 694–705.

Eimer, M. (2000b). Event-related brain potentials distinguish processing stages involved in face perception and recognition. *Clinical Neurophysiology*, **111**, 694–705.

Ellis, A.W., Young, A.W., Flude, B.M., and Hay, D.C. (1987). Repetition priming of face recognition. *Quarterly Journal of Experimental Psychology*, **39A**, 193–210.

Engel, A.K. and Singer, W. (2001). Temporal binding and the neural correlates of sensory awareness. *Trends in Cognitive Sciences*, **5**, 16–25.

Engst, F.M., Martin-Loeches, M., and Sommer, W. (2006). Memory systems for structural and semantic knowledge of faces and buildings. *Brain Research*, **1124**, 70–80.

Farah, M. (1991). Patterns of co-occurrence among the associative agnosias: Implications for visual object representation. *Cognitive Neuropsychology*, **8**, 1–19.

Graham, R. and Dawson, M.R.W. (2005). Using artificial neural networks to examine event-related potentials of face memory. *Neural Network World*, **15**, 215–227.

Grill-Spector, K., Sayres, R., and Ress, D. (2006a). High-resolution imaging reveals highly selective nonface clusters in the fusiform face area. *Nature Neuroscience*, **9**, 1177–1185.

Grill-Spector, K., Henson, R., and Martin, A. (2006b). Repetition and the brain: neural models of stimulus-specific effects. *Trends in Cognitive Sciences*, **10**, 14–23.

Gruber, T. and Müller, M.M. (2005). Oscillatory brain activity dissociates between associative stimulus content in a repetition priming task in the human EEG. *Cerebral Cortex*, **15**, 109–116.

Halgren, E., Raij, T., Marinkovic, K., Jousmäki, V., and Hari, R. (2000). Cognitive response profile of the human fusiform face area as determined by MEG. *Cerebral Cortex*, **10**, 69–81.

Hancock, P.J.B., Bruce, V., and Burton, A.M. (2000). Recognition of unfamiliar faces. *Trends in Cognitive Sciences*, **4**, 330–337.

Hanley, J.R., Young, A.W., and Pearson, N.A. (1989). Defective recognition of familiar people. *Cognitive Neuropsychology*, **6**, 179–210.

Haxby, J.V., Hoffman, E.A., and Gobbini, M.I. (2000). The distributed human neural system for face perception. *Trends in Cognitive Sciences*, **4**, 223–233.

Henson, R.N., Rylands, A., Ross, E., Vuilleumier, P., and Rugg, M.D. (2004). The effect of repetition lag on electrophysiological and haemodynamic correlates of visual object priming. *NeuroImage*, **21**, 1674–1689.

Herrmann, M.J., Ehlis, A.C., Ellgring, H., and Fallgatter, A.J. (2005). Early stages (P100) of face perception in humans as measured with event-related potentials (ERPs). *Journal of Neural Transmission*, **112**, 1073–1081.

Herzmann, G., Schweinberger, S.R., Sommer, W., and Jentzsch, I. (2004). What's special about personally familiar faces? A multimodal approach. *Psychophysiology*, **41**, 688–701.

Huber, D.E. (2008). Immediate priming and cognitive aftereffects. *Journal of Experimental Psychology-General*, **137**, 324–347.

Itier, R.J. and Taylor, M.J. (2002). Inversion and contrast polarity reversal affect both encoding and recognition processes of unfamiliar faces: A repetition study using ERPs. *NeuroImage*, **15**, 353–372.

Itier, R.J. and Taylor, M.J. (2004). Effects of repetition learning on upright, inverted and contrast-reversed face processing using ERPs. *NeuroImage*, **21**, 1518–1532.

Itier, R.J., Alain, C., Sedore, K., and McIntosh, A.R. (2007). Early face processing specificity: It's in the eyes! *Journal of Cognitive Neuroscience*, **19**, 1815–1826.

Jacques, C. and Rossion, B. (2006). The speed of individual face categorization. *Psychological Science*, **17**, 485–492.

Jeffreys, D.A. (1989). A face-responsive potential recorded from the human scalp. *Experimental Brain Research*, **78**, 193–202.

Jeffreys, D.A. (1996). Evoked potentials studies of face and object processing. *Visual Cognition*, **3**, 1–38.

Jeffreys, D.A. and Tukmachi, E.S.A. (1992). The vertex-positive scalp potential evoked by faces and by objects. *Experimental Brain Research*, **91**, 340–350.

Jemel, B., Pisani, M., Rousselle, L., Crommelinck, M., and Bruyer, R. (2005). Exploring the functional architecture of person recognition system with event-related potentials in a within- and cross-domain self-priming of faces. *Neuropsychologia*, **43**, 2024–2040.

Jenkins, R., Burton, A.M., and Ellis, A.W. (2002). Long-term effects of covert face recognition. *Cognition*, **86**, B43–B52.

Joyce, C. and Rossion, B. (2005). The face-sensitive N170 and VPP components manifest the same brain processes: The effect of reference electrode site. *Clinical Neurophysiology*, **116**, 2613–2631.

Junghöfer, M., Elbert, T., Leiderer, P., Berg, P., and Rockstroh, B. (1997). Mapping EEG-potentials on the surface of the brain: A strategy for uncovering cortical sources. *Brain Topography*, **9**, 203–217.

Kanwisher, N. and Yovel, G. (2006). The fusiform face area: a cortical region specialized for the perception of faces. *Philosophical Transactions of the Royal Society B-Biological Sciences*, **361**, 2109–2128.

Kanwisher, N., McDermott, J., and Chun, M.M. (1997). The fusiform face area: A module in human extrastriate cortex specialized for face perception. *Journal of Neuroscience*, **17**, 4302–4311.

Kaufmann, J.M., Schweinberger, S.R., and Burton, A.M. (2009). N250 ERP Correlates of the Acquisition of Face Representations across Different Images. *Journal of Cognitive Neuroscience*, **21**, 625–641.

Kloth, N., Schweinberger, S.R., and Kovács, G. (2010). Neural correlates of generic versus gender-specific face adaptation. *Journal of Cognitive Neuroscience*, **22**, 2345–2356.

Kriegeskorte, N., Mur, M., Ruff, D.A., *et al.* (2008). Matching categorical object representations in inferior temporal cortex of man and monkey. *Neuron*, **60**, 1126–1141.

Kutas, M. and Hillyard, S.A. (1980). Reading senseless sentences: brain potentials reflect semantic incongruity. *Science*, **207**, 203–205.

Langeslag, S.J.E., Morgan, H.M., Jackson, M.C., Linden, D.E.J., and Van Strien, J.W. (2009). Electrophysio-logical correlates of improved short-term memory for emotional faces. *Neuropsychologia*, **47**, 887–896.

Lehmann, D. (1987). Principles of spatial analysis. In A.S. Gevins and A. Remond (Eds.), *Handbook of electroencephalography and clinical neurophysiology. Vol. 1. Methods of analysis of brain electrical and magnetic signals*, pp. 309–354. Amsterdam: Elsevier.

Leopold, D.A., O'Toole, A.J., Vetter, T., and Blanz, V. (2001). Prototype-referenced shape encoding revealed by high-level aftereffects. *Nature Neuroscience*, **4**, 89–94.

Leopold, D.A., Rhodes, G., Muller, K.M., and Jeffery, L. (2005). The dynamics of visual adaptation to faces. *Proceedings of the Royal Society B-Biological Sciences*, **272**, 897–904.

Linkenkaer-Hansen, K., Palva, J.M., Sams, M., Hietanen, J.K., Aronen, H.J., and Ilmoniemi, R.J. (1998). Face-selective processing in human extrastriate cortex around 120 ms after stimulus onset revealed by magneto- and electroencephalography. *Neuroscience Letters*, **253**, 147–150.

Liu, J., Higuchi, M., Marantz, A., and Kanwisher, N. (2000). The selectivity of the occipitotemporal M170 for faces. *NeuroReport*, **11**, 337–341.

Marsolek, C.J. (1999). Dissociable neural subsystems underlie abstract and specific object recognition. *Psychological Science*, **10**, 111–118.

Marsolek, C.J. (1995). Abstract visual-form representations in the left cerebral hemisphere. *Journal of Experimental Psychology: Human Perception and Performance*, **21**, 375–386.

Marsolek, C.J., Kosslyn, S.M., and Squire, L.R. (1992). Form-specific visual priming in the right cerebral hemisphere. *Journal of Experimental Psychology: Learning, Memory, and Cognition*, **18**, 492–508.

Martin-Loeches, M., Sommer, W., and Hinojosa, J.A. (2005). ERP components reflecting stimulus identification: contrasting the recognition potential and the early repetition effect (N250r). *International Journal of Psychophysiology*, **55**, 113–125.

Maurer, U., Rossion, B., and McCandliss, B.D. (2008). Category specificity in early perception: face and word N170 responses differ in both lateralization and habituation properties. *Frontiers in Human Neuroscience*, **2**, 18.

McCandliss, B.D., Cohen, L., and Dehaene, S. (2003). The visual word form area: expertise for reading in the fusiform gyrus. *Trends in Cognitive Sciences*, **7**, 293–299.

McKone, E., Kanwisher, N., and Duchaine, B.C. (2007). Can generic expertise explain special processing for faces? *Trends in Cognitive Sciences*, **11**, 8–15.

Meadows, J.C. (1974). The anatomical basis of prosopagnosia. *Journal of Neurology, Neurosurgery, and Psychiatry*, **37**, 489–501.

Michel, C.M., Murray, M.M., Lantz, G., Gonzalez, S., Spinelli, L., and de Peralta, R.G. (2004). EEG source imaging. *Clinical Neurophysiology*, **115**, 2195–2222.

Milner, B. (1968). Visual recognition and recall after right temporal lobe excision in man. *Neuropsychologia*, **6**, 191–209.

Neumann, M.F. and Schweinberger, S.R. (2008). N250r and N400 ERP correlates of immediate famous face repetition are independent of perceptual load. *Brain Research*, **1239**, 181–190.

Neumann, M.F. and Schweinberger, S.R. (2009). N250r ERP repetition effects from distractor faces when attending to another face under load: Evidence for a face attention resource. *Brain Research*, **1270**, 64–77.

Neuner, F. and Schweinberger, S.R. (2000). Neuropsychological impairments in the recognition of faces, voices, and personal names. *Brain and Cognition*, **44**, 342–366.

Paller, K.A., Kutas, M., and Mayes, A.R. (1987). Neural correlates of encoding in an incidental learning paradigm. *Electroencephalography and Clinical Neurophysiology*, **67**, 360–371.

Paller, K.A., Gonsalves, B., Grabowecky, M., Bozic, V.S., and Yamada, S. (2000). Electrophysiological correlates of recollecting faces of known and unknown individuals. *NeuroImage*, **11**, 98–110.

Pfütze, E.-M., Sommer, W., and Schweinberger, S.R. (2002). Age-related slowing in face and name recognition: Evidence from event-related brain potentials. *Psychology and Aging*, **17**, 140–160.

Pickering, E.C. and Schweinberger, S.R. (2003). N200, N250r and N400 event-related brain potentials reveal three loci of repetition priming for familiar names. *Journal of Experimental Psychology: Learning, Memory, and Cognition*, **29**, 1298–1311.

Puce, A., Allison, T., and McCarthy, G. (1999). Electrophysiological studies of human face perception. III: Effects of top-down processing of face-specific potentials. *Cerebral Cortex*, **9**, 445–458.

Rizzolatti, G., Umiltà, C., and Berlucchi, G. (1971). Opposite superiorities of the right and left cerebral hemispheres in discriminative reaction time to physiognomical and alphabetical material. *Brain*, **94**, 431–442.

Rodriguez, E., George, N., Lachaux, J.P., Martinerie, J., Renault, B., and Varela, F.J. (1999). Perception's shadow: long-distance synchronization of human brain activity. *Nature*, **397**, 430–433.

Rossion, B., Campanella, S., Gomez, C.M., *et al.* (1999). Task modulation of brain activity related to familiar and unfamiliar face processing: An ERP study. *Clinical Neurophysiology*, **110**, 449–462.

Rossion, B., Gauthier, I., Tarr, M.J., *et al.* (2000). The N170 occipito-temporal component is delayed and enhanced to inverted faces but not to inverted objects: an electrophysiological account of face-specific processes in the human brain. *NeuroReport*, **11**, 69–74.

Rossion, B. and Jacques, C. (2008). Does physical interstimulus variance account for early electrophysiological face sensitive responses in the human brain? Ten lessons on the N170. *NeuroImage*, **39**, 1959–1979.

Schweinberger, S.R. (1996). How Gorbachev primed Yeltsin: Analyses of associative priming in person recognition by means of reaction times and event-related brain potentials. *Journal of Experimental Psychology: Learning, Memory, and Cognition*, **22**, 1383–1407.

Schweinberger, S.R. and Burton, A.M. (2003). Covert recognition and the neural system for face processing. *Cortex*, **39**, 9–30.

Schweinberger, S.R. and Burton, A.M. (in press). Person perception 25 years after Bruce and Young (1986). *British Journal of Psychology*, [Special Issue].

Schweinberger, S.R. and Sommer, W. (1991). Contributions of stimulus encoding and memory search to right hemisphere superiority in face recognition: Behavioural and electrophysiological evidence. *Neuropsychologia*, **29**, 389–413.

Schweinberger, S.R., Pfütze, E.-M., and Sommer, W. (1995). Repetition priming and associative priming of face recognition: Evidence from event-related potentials. *Journal of Experimental Psychology: Learning, Memory, and Cognition*, **21**, 722–736.

Schweinberger, S.R., Pickering, E.C., Jentzsch, I., Burton, A.M., and Kaufmann, J.M. (2002a). Event-related brain potential evidence for a response of inferior temporal cortex to familiar face repetitions. *Cognitive Brain Research*, **14**, 398–409.

Schweinberger, S.R., Pickering, E.C., Burton, A.M., and Kaufmann, J.M. (2002b). Human brain potential correlates of repetition priming in face and name recognition. *Neuropsychologia*, **40**, 2057–2073.

Schweinberger, S.R., Huddy, V., and Burton, A.M. (2004). N250r–A face-selective brain response to stimulus repetitions. *NeuroReport*, **15**, 1501–1505.

Schweinberger, S.R., Ramsay, A.L., and Kaufmann, J.M. (2006). Hemispheric asymmetries in font-specific and abstractive priming of written personal names: Evidence from event-related brain potentials. *Brain Research*, **1117**, 195–205.

Schweinberger, S.R., Kaufmann, J.M., Moratti, S., Keil, A., and Burton, A.M. (2007). Brain responses to repetitions of human and animal faces, inverted faces, and objects - An MEG study. *Brain Research*, **1184**, 226–233.

Scott, L.S., Tanaka, J.W., Sheinberg, D.L., and Curran, T. (2006). A reevaluation of the electrophysiological correlates of expert object processing. *Journal of Cognitive Neuroscience*, **18**, 1453–1465.

Sergent, J. and Signoret, J.L. (1992). Functional and anatomical decomposition of face processing: evidence from prosopagnosia and PET study of normal subjects. *Philosophical Transactions of the Royal Society B-Biological Sciences*, **335**, 55–62.

Small, M. (1983). Asymmetrical evoked potentials in response to face stimuli. *Cortex*, **19**, 441–450.

Sobotka, A., Pizlo, Z., and Budohoska, W. (1984). Hemispheric differences in evoked potentials to pictures of faces in the left and right visual fields. *Electroencephalography and Clinical Neurophysiology*, **58**, 441–453.

Sommer, W., Schweinberger, S.R., and Matt, J. (1991). Human brain potential correlates of face encoding into memory. *Electroencephalography and Clinical Neurophysiology*, **79**, 357–363.

Sommer, W., Heinz, A., Leuthold, H., Matt, J., and Schweinberger, S.R. (1995). Metamemory, distinctiveness, and event-related potentials in recognition memory for faces. *Memory and Cognition*, **23**, 1–11.

Sommer, W., Komoss, E., and Schweinberger, S.R. (1997). Differential localization of brain systems subserving memory for names and faces with event-related potentials. *Electroencephalography and Clinical Neurophysiology*, **102**, 192–199.

Tanaka, J.W. and Curran, T. (2001). A neural basis for expert object recognition. *Psychological Science*, **12**, 43–47.

Tanaka, J.W. and Pierce, L.J. (2009). The neural plasticity of other-race face recognition. *Cognitive Affective and Behavioral Neuroscience*, **9**, 122–131.

Tanaka, J.W., Curran, T., Porterfield, A.L., and Collins, D. (2006). Activation of preexisting and acquired face representations: The N250 event-related potential as an index of face familiarity. *Journal of Cognitive Neuroscience*, **18**, 1488–1497.

Thierry, G., Martin, C.D., Downing, P., and Pegna, A.J. (2007). Controlling for interstimulus perceptual variance abolishes N170 face selectivity. *Nature Neuroscience*, **10**, 505–511.

van Turennout, M., Hagoort, P., and Brown, C. (1997). Electrophysiological evidence on the time course of semantic and phonological processes in speech production. *Journal of Experimental Psychology: Learning, Memory, and Cognition*, **23**, 787–806.

Vuilleumier, P. (2000). Faces call for attention: evidence from patients with visual extinction. *Neuropsychologia*, **38**, 693–700.

VanRullen, R. (2006). On second glance: Still no high-level pop-out effect for faces. *Vision Research*, **46**, 3017–3027.

Wiese, H. and Schweinberger, S.R. (2008). Event-related potentials indicate different processes to mediate categorical and associative priming in person recognition. *Journal of Experimental Psychology: Learning, Memory, and Cognition*, **34**, 1246–1263.

Wiese, H., Stahl, J., and Schweinberger, S.R. (2009). Configural processing of other-race faces is delayed but not decreased. *Biological Psychology*, **81**, 103–109.

Yin, R.K. (1969). Looking at upside-down faces. *Journal of Experimental Psychology*, **81**, 141–145.

Chapter 19

Transcranial Magnetic Stimulation Studies of Face Processing

David Pitcher, Vincent Walsh, and Bradley Duchaine

Introduction

Neuropsychological patients exhibiting category-selective visual agnosias have provided unique insights into the cognitive functions of the human brain (Shallice, 1988; Moscovitch et al., 1997; Moro et al., 2008), and this has been especially true in the study of face processing (Bodamer, 1947; Farah, 2004). While cases of pure prosopagnosia resulting from cortical damage are extremely rare they still provide the strongest evidence that faces are processed in anatomically segregated neural networks in the human brain (Sergent and Signoret, 1992; McNeill and Warrington 1993; Rossion et al., 2003; Riddoch et al., 2008). Moreover, acquired prosopagnosics exhibiting selective deficits with specific aspects of face recognition (e.g. recognizing facial identity or recognizing facial expressions) provided evidence for the seminal cognitive model of face processing (Bruce and Young, 1986) as well as for subsequent cortical models of face processing (Haxby et al., 2000; Adolphs, 2002; Calder and Young, 2005). These models in turn provided cognitive frameworks with which to test how faces are recognized in the undamaged brain.

Over the past 15 years experimental techniques such as event-related potentials (ERPs), magnetoencephalograhy (MEG), and functional magnetic resonance imaging (fMRI) have been used to add to the evidence from neuropsychological and single unit studies to demonstrate where, when, and how faces are processed. However, unlike patient studies, neuroimaging techniques cannot demonstrate that a region is necessary for a particular cognitive function (Price and Friston, 2002). Transcranial magnetic stimulation (TMS), in contrast, can be used to draw causal inferences, as one of the effects of the cortical disruption induced by magnetic stimulation is to act as a "virtual lesion" lasting from tens of milliseconds up to approximately 1 hour, depending on the type of stimulation (Pascual-Leone et al., 2000; Walsh and Pascual Leone, 2003; Huang et al., 2005). TMS also avoids some of the potential difficulties of patient studies that can limit their interpretation such as individual differences in premorbid ability (Farah, 2004) and compensatory plasticity following the lesion (Robertson and Murre, 1999).

The greatest strength of TMS is that it can be delivered with a high degree of both spatial and temporal specificity (millisecond resolution). This specificity offers a unique advantage in psychological testing as TMS can be used to test where and when cognitive computations are performed (Walsh and Cowey, 2000; Walsh and Pascual-Leone, 2003). In this chapter we will briefly describe TMS, consider the small but growing number of studies that have used TMS to disrupt face processing, and discuss how TMS can be used in the future to better understand how faces are cortically represented in the human brain.

What is transcranial magnetic stimulation?

TMS is an experimental technique widely used in physiological studies of motor function and plasticity (Wassermann et al., 2008; Pascual-Leone et al., 2005). TMS can also be used to study cognitive processes by delivering an electromagnetic pulse over a targeted cortical area that can disrupt normal cognitive function (see Figure 19.1). A TMS pulse is produced by generating a large, rapidly changing electrical current that is passed through a metal coil. The current generates a magnetic field perpendicular to the coil orientation. When the coil is placed on the scalp of an experimental participant the magnetic field passes through the skull and induces an electrical field within the underlying cortex.

The size of the induced current depends on the amplitude and the rate of change of the current passing through the TMS coil. Typically the current in the coil is large, up to 8 kiloamperes (kA), with a swift rise time of roughly 200 microseconds (μs) and an overall duration of approximately 1 ms (Walsh and Cowey, 2000). The induced current alters the electrical state both inside and outside any affected nerve axons within range of the pulse (Nagarajan et al., 1993). The resulting voltage difference across the cell membrane causes it to depolarize, initiating an action potential. This difference raises the resting membrane potential of some neurons in the targeted cortical area while inducing others to fire.

The effects of the neural disruption induced by the TMS pulse on concurrent behavioral performance in experimental tasks can be measured using the standard behavioral tools of experimental psychology, e.g. performance accuracy, reaction times (RT), threshold procedures, etc. Furthermore by measuring performance during the delivery of TMS and when no TMS is delivered it is possible for subjects to act as their own experimental control group.

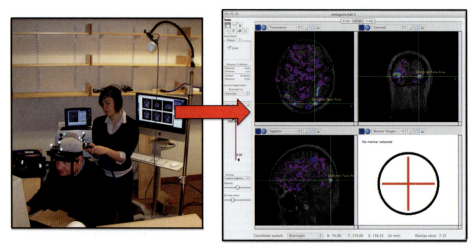

Fig. 19.1 Where and how a specific cortical area can be targeted using a TMS coil (in this case TMS is being delivered over the right occipital face area). On the right are images from the Brainsight neuronavigation software used to identify the TMS target site. The subject's individual MRI scan is shown overlaid with the results of a face-selective functional localizer (faces minus objects). The Polaris camera (seen in the top right of the photo) identifies the precise location of the experimental subject and the TMS coil by sensing the location of the silver balls. This location information can be tracked online using the Brainsight software to ensure precise TMS coil placement over the targeted area throughout the experiment.

The spatial resolution of TMS

The exact spatial resolution of TMS cannot be stated in mm or cm because the effects depend on the initial state of the brain, the stimulation intensity and frequency and the measure being taken of the effects of TMS. What one can do, however, is make sound inferences based on what is known about cortical organization. For example, phosphenes (perceived flashes of light induced by delivering TMS over V1) can be elicited with a resolution of 1 to 2 degrees of visual angle which equals a functional specificity mapped across 9 to 18 mm of early visual cortex (Kammer, 1999). Similarly, in the motor cortex muscles that are segregated by as little as 1 to 2 cm on the cortex can be selectively stimulated (Brasil-Nero et al., 1992; Wassermann et al., 1992; Singh et al., 1997). TMS has also been used to induce behavioral dissociations in spatially adjacent regions in the parietal cortex (Ashbridge et al., 1997), the left inferior frontal cortex (Gough et al., 2005) and the left occipitotemporal cortex (Duncan et al., 2010). The evidence from these studies demonstrates that the behavioral impairments of TMS in human studies can correspond with an effective spatial resolution of approximately 1 to 2cm.

Identifying TMS target sites

In any TMS experiment it is important to accurately position the TMS coil to ensure that the induced neural disruption is focused on the intended targeted cortical area. Single pulses of TMS can be used to functionally identify early visual cortex (by inducing phosphenes) and motor cortex (by inducing muscle twitches) but no such induced signature techniques exist for face-selective areas such as the occipital face area (OFA) or the superior temporal sulcus (STS). The optimal method for individually identifying these target sites in subjects is by using a stereotaxic neuron-avigation system (such as the Brainsight system seen in Figure 19.1). Such systems allow individual structural and functional MRI data to be coregistered with a subject's head in real space. This allows the TMS coil to be accurately positioned over the desired TMS target site.

Although localizing target sites with functional MRI data is the most accurate method (Pitcher et al., 2009), other studies have used individual structural scans and identified target sites based on mean Talairach co-ordinates for functionally defined areas reported in prior fMRI studies (Pitcher et al., 2007, 2008). A recent study that systematically compared different methods of TMS site localization reported that the differences between such methods lay in statistical power and therefore in the number of subjects required to find significant effects rather than in qualitative differences in the experimental effects (Sack et al., 2009).

The temporal resolution of TMS

The disruptive effects of TMS in healthy human subjects are most commonly assessed by correlating the induced neural disruption with a behavioral task that is dependent on the stimulated region. As such the best demonstration of the temporal duration of any TMS disruption will be evident in the behavioral results (Amassian et al., 1993; O'Shea et al., 2004; Pitcher et al., 2007). The duration of a TMS pulse is very brief, approximately 1 ms. By contrast the physiologically measurable effects at the neuronal level have been shown to range from hundreds of milliseconds up to a matter of seconds (Moliazde et al., 2005). However, the effects recorded from single neurons over these longer time periods do not appear to be relevant behaviorally. The recordings in this study were made in anesthetized animals and it is a common finding in human brain stimulation experiments that physiologically measurable effects that may last for several seconds in a passive subject do not survive if the subject uses the affected brain region/body part (Antal et al., 2007). For example, different TMS paired and quadpulse paradigms delivered over the motor cortex can change resting state motor evoked potentials (MEP) recorded from the hand and finger regions for several minutes after TMS if and only if the subject does not employ their motor cortex to move their hands and fingers (Silvanto et al., 2008). Thus the most important consideration when designing TMS experiments is the duration of the impairment to the behavioral performance being measured. Any task in a standard experiment will typically require the involvement of multiple brain regions and these regions will exhibit peaks of neural activity at different times. As a result it is important that the TMS is delivered in the correct time window because otherwise the induced neural disruption could occur either too early or too late to cause a behavioral impairment.

One way to effectively address this problem is to deliver single pulses of TMS to the target region at different time points after stimulus onset or after the commencement of behavioral monitoring (Amassian et al., 1993). Plotting the temporal pattern of the induced impairments will demonstrate when the TMS is most effective which demonstrates when the targeted area is likely to be most active during task performance. While single pulse TMS can give a very precise temporal activation pattern for a targeted region it necessarily requires a large number of temporal conditions (single pulses of TMS delivered at different times from stimulus onset). One way to reduce these conditions and to expand the duration of any TMS induced disruption is to use more than a single pulse such that the disruptive effects of two pulses of TMS will summate and thereby increase the effect of the induced behavioral disruption. This is well established in the physiological domain and has been adapted for behavioral experiments. Double pulse TMS separated by 40 ms has proven to be a reliable protocol for demonstrating when a variety of functionally distinct cortical areas exhibit peak processing (Juan and Walsh, 2003; O'Shea et al., 2004; Pitcher at al., 2007, 2008; Juan et al., 2008; Kalla et al., 2008; Duncan et al., 2010).

The summation of multiple TMS pulses is further demonstrated in longer repetitive TMS protocols. Rushworth and colleagues (2001) and Göbel and colleagues (2001) were the first to deliver TMS at a frequency of 10 Hz for 500 ms. The summation of five pulses of TMS has subsequently proven to be a robust TMS protocol across a wide variety of functionally distinct cortical areas (Bjoertomt et al., 2002; Lavidor et al., 2003; Wig et al., 2005; Beck et al., 2006; Muggleton et al., 2006; Pitcher et al., 2007, 2008, 2009; Campana et al., 2008; Duncan et al., 2010). Moreover the comparatively long duration of the impairment window makes it more likely that using this TMS paradigm will induce behavioral impairments.

The safety of TMS as an experimental tool

A concern in any TMS experiment is the health and safety of the subjects. The magnetic field generated by a TMS coil produces a loud clicking sound so earplugs are recommended for all experiments. Some subjects may experience headaches or nausea or may find the associated twitching and additional peripheral effects of TMS too uncomfortable. These subjects should be released from any obligation to continue in the experiment both for their own health and safety and additionally because such subjects are more likely to generate noisy data. More serious are the concerns that TMS may induce an epileptic seizure. As a guide, any subject with any personal or family history of epilepsy or other neurological condition should be precluded from participating in an experiment that does not involve investigation of that condition (Stewart et al., 2001).

Which face areas are accessible to TMS?

FMRI studies have identified several areas in the human brain that exhibit a larger neural response to images of faces than to images of objects (Haxby et al., 2000). These areas are thought to perform functionally different cognitive operations (Kanwisher and Yovel, 2006) and cortical models have been proposed that link these areas into distributed networks for face processing (Haxby et al., 2000; Adolphs, 2002; Calder and Young, 2005; Fairhill and Ishai, 2007) (Figure 19.2).

Not all of the face-selective areas identified with fMRI are accessible to TMS (see Figure 19.3). The range of the disruptive effects of TMS can only be inferred from previous experiments but it seems that a cortical area that is greater than 2 to 3 cm from the cortical surface is unlikely to be affected by a TMS pulse. This makes it likely that functionally defined face-selective areas such as the fusiform face area (FFA) (Kanwisher et al., 1997) and the anterior temporal lobe (Kriegeskorte et al., 2007; Tsao et al., 2008) are outside the range in which TMS can induce cognitive disruption. However it remains possible that future studies may find a way to address this technical issue. In this chapter we will discuss studies that have disrupted the occipital face area (OFA), the superior temporal sulcus (STS), and the face regions in the right somatosensory cortex.

TMS studies of the occipital face area

The OFA is a functionally defined face-selective region most typically located in the inferior occipital gyrus (Gauthier et al., 2000). Cortical models of face processing (Haxby et al., 2000) propose that the OFA represents facial features prior to further analysis in downstream face-selective areas such as the FFA (Grill-Spector et al., 2004) and the anterior temporal lobe (Kriegeskorte et al., 2007). This hypothesis is supported by evidence that the OFA shows a much

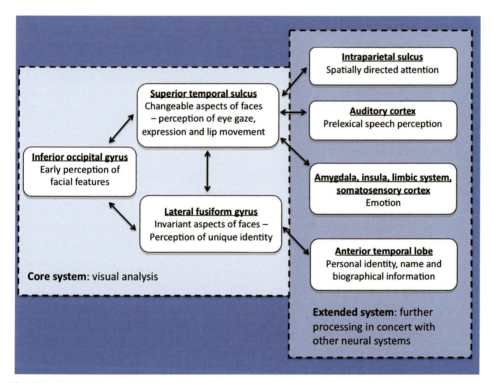

Fig. 19.2 The extended face processing cortical network. Figure adapted from the original model in *Trends in Cognitive Sciences*, **4**:6, Haxby, Hoffman and Gobbini, The distributed human neural system for face perception, © 2000, with permission from Elsevier.

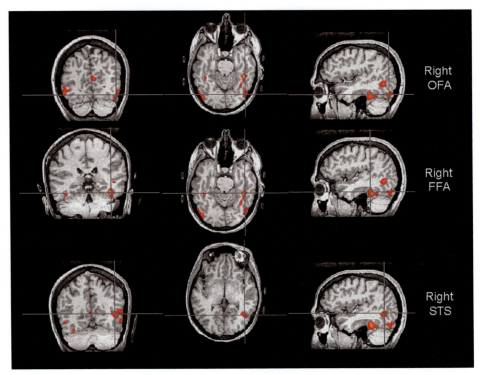

Fig. 19.3 The three core face selective regions in the occipitotemporal cortex shown in one participant. From the top to bottom; the right OFA, right FFA and the face selective region in the right STS. The intersection of the gray lines identifies the area illustrated in each row. From left to right: coronal slice, horizontal slice and sagittal slice. The areas have been identified using a standard functional localizer (the subtraction was faces minus objects). As can be clearly seen in this subject the OFA and the face-selective in the STS are on the cortical surface and accessible to TMS. By contrast the cortical depth of the FFA probably makes it outside the range of TMS.

larger preference for faces presented in the contralateral visual hemifield than the FFA (Hemond et al., 2007; Hsiao et al., 2008), a characteristic consistent with the OFA being earlier in the visual processing stream than the FFA. The hypothesis is also consistent with a recent study that used dynamic causal modeling (DCM) to demonstrate that the inferior occipital gyrus (the area of the brain that contains the OFA) sends information to the fusiform gyrus (the area of the brain containing the FFA) (Fairhill and Ishai, 2007).

Also consistent with this hierarchical view are the functionally different fMRI adaptation responses exhibited by the OFA and the FFA (Rothstein et al., 2005). In this study the stimuli were a series of faces morphed at different gradations between images of two famous faces (for example, Margaret Thatcher and Marilyn Monroe). Subjects were presented with two successive faces that were either identical or varied by 30% along the physical morphing dimension. In half of the 30% steps, the faces were perceived as the same identity (both Marilyn or both Margaret) while on the other half the faces were perceived to be two different identities (Marilyn then Margaret or vice versa). The neural response in the OFA changed (it was released from adaptation) in response to a within-category change or to a between-category change. By contrast the neural response in the FFA changed in response to a between-category change but not to a within-category change. This result indicates that the OFA is sensitive to physical changes in a face but not to identity changes and that identity computations are carried out in the FFA.

Neuropsychological evidence has demonstrated that the OFA is essential for accurate face processing. Bouvier and Engel (2006) performed a meta-analysis of neuropsychological patients exhibiting either cortical achromatopsia or prosopagnosia from reports that included details of behavioral testing and (in over half of the reported cases) detailed fMRI scans of the damaged brain areas. The majority of patients with face processing impairments had lesions encompassing the right inferior occipital gyrus (the cortical area usually containing the OFA in the undamaged brain) where fewer had lesions encompassing the right fusiform gyrus (the cortical area usually containing the FFA in the undamaged brain). Detailed single case studies of acquired prosopagnosics have complemented this lesion analysis by demonstrating that damage to the region typically encompassing the OFA (but importantly not to the right FFA) can cause severe prosopagnosia (Rossion et al., 2003; Steeves et al., 2006). While these neuropsychological studies suggest that the OFA is crucial for face processing the diffuse nature of the lesions in these patients makes specific claims about the functional role of the OFA problematic.

The spatial specificity of cortical disruption and its implications for any observed face-selective behavioral impairments are also issues directly relevant to TMS studies of the OFA. Demonstrating that any TMS impairment is specific to faces is important because the lateral occipital cortex, the region of the brain where the OFA is located, also contains functionally defined areas selective for other classes of visual object categories (see Figure 19.4). These include an area selective for objects, the lateral occipital area (LO) (Malach et al., 1995), and another for bodies, the extrastriate body area (EBA) (Downing et al., 2001). Moreover, distributed theories of object representation suggest that a face is represented across these functionally defined areas rather than only within areas showing a preferential response to faces (Haxby et al., 2001). It is therefore necessary to demonstrate that any behavioral impairment induced by delivering TMS over the OFA is face-selective and not the result of more general object recognition disruption.

A recent study has demonstrated that TMS delivered over the OFA is capable of selectively disrupting face discrimination while leaving object and body discrimination unaffected (Pitcher et al., 2009). In this study TMS was delivered over the right OFA, right EBA and right LO while participants made delayed match-to-sample same/different discrimination judgments to computer generated face, body and object stimuli. Each stimulus category (faces, objects, bodies) consisted of paired images morphed between two distinct exemplars. On different trials the level of morph was varied to produce trials of differing difficulty. Prior to the TMS experiments each subject was scanned using a standard fMRI region of interest (ROI) functional localizer that included images of faces, objects, scrambled objects, and bodies (Yovel and Kanwisher, 2004, 2005). The results of this localizer were used to identify the right OFA (faces minus objects), the right EBA (bodies minus objects) and the right LO (objects minus scrambled objects) individually in each subject. TMS was delivered concurrently with the presentation of a probe stimulus, at a frequency of 10Hz for 500 ms (see Figure 19.5).

Behavioral impairments in each task were manifested only when TMS was delivered over the area selective for that class of visual stimuli (see Figure 19.6). That is, TMS delivered over the right OFA disrupted face but not object or body discrimination, TMS over the right LO disrupted object but not face or body discrimination, and TMS over the right EBA disrupted body but not face or object discrimination. These results demonstrate that TMS possesses the necessary spatial resolution to selectively disrupt face processing at the right OFA.

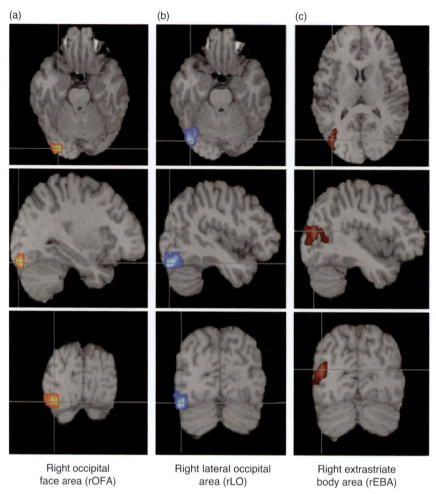

Fig. 19.4 The three TMS target sites in Pitcher et al. (2009). The locations in one participant of (a) the rOFA in yellow (faces minus objects), (b) the rLO in blue (objects minus scrambled objects), and (c) the rEBA in red (bodies minus objects).

What information does the OFA represent and when is it active?

Cortical models of face processing propose that the OFA is the first stage of a face processing network and that it computes the early perception of facial features (Haxby et al., 2000; Calder and Young, 2005). Higher visual areas such as the FFA and the anterior temporal lobe are believed to compute the invariant aspects of a face such as facial identity at higher stages of the network. This theory is consistent with feedforward models of visual perception that propose complex visual stimuli are recognized via a series of stages in which features of increasing complexity are extracted and analyzed along the visual processing stream (Ullman et al., 2002; Grill-Spector and Malach, 2004). Thus establishing the precise temporal dynamics of different face-selective cortical areas will provide a better understanding of how these face recognitions mechanisms may function.

Electrophysiological studies indicate when different phases of face processing are performed but the inverse problem (Slotnick, 2004) makes directly linking these temporal components to

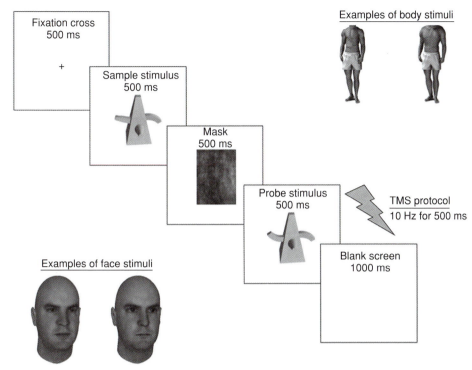

Fig. 19.5 The trial procedure and examples of the stimuli used in Pitcher et al. (2009). The first TMS pulse was delivered concurrently with the presentation of the probe stimulus.

functionally defined cortical areas identified in fMRI problematic. The N170 (Eimer, Chapter 17, this volume), a key face-selective ERP component that peaks 170 ms after stimulus onset (Bentin et al., 1996), is believed to result from neural activity in the FFA (Horovitz et al., 2004) or possibly the STS (Henson et al., 2003) but not from the OFA. Magnetoencephalography (MEG) studies report a face-selective response that peaks 100ms after stimulus onset, the M100 component (Liu et al., 2002; Itier et al., 2006). The functional properties of the M100 are similar to those attributed to the OFA in fMRI studies (Liu et al., 2010), in that it is sensitive to face parts and is associated with successful face detection but not with identification (Liu et al., 2002). This converging evidence suggests the possibility that the OFA and the M100 may be generated by the same underlying neural activity.

The hypothesis that the OFA represents face part information approximately 100 ms after stimulus onset can be directly tested by delivering TMS pulses at different time points while subjects perform a face task (Amassian et al., 1993; Juan and Walsh, 2003; O'Shea et al., 2004; Duncan et al., 2010). Pitcher et al. (2007) conducted a TMS study in which subjects discriminated face stimuli that varied either the face parts (the eyes and the mouth) or the spacing between these face parts (see Figure 19.7). Houses with varied parts and spacing (the manipulated house parts were the windows and the door) were used as control stimuli (Yovel and Kanwisher, 2004).

In the first experiment subjects performed a delayed match to sample same/different discrimination task. TMS was delivered at a frequency of 10Hz for 500 ms concurrently with the presentation of the second stimulus. This robust TMS protocol was used to establish whether the two sets of face stimuli were susceptible to disruption when TMS was delivered over the left and right

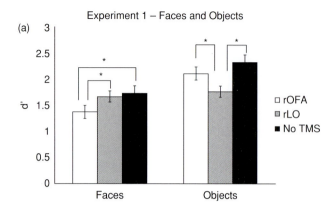

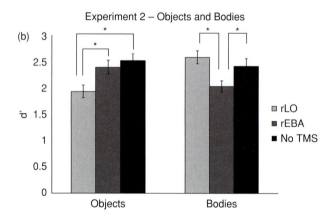

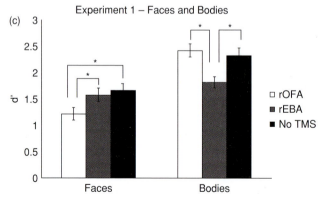

Fig. 19.6 Results from Pitcher et al. (2009) (error bars denote standard errors). In each panel, performance on two tasks is compared in three conditions: TMS to a site selective for that category, TMS to a site selective for another category, and no TMS. An asterisk (*) denotes a significant difference in Bonferroni corrected tests. (a) Faces and Objects. Face task performance was disrupted only by TMS to rOFA, and object task performance was impaired only by TMS to rLO. (b) Objects and Bodies. Object task performance was impaired only by TMS to rLO whereas performance on the body task was disrupted only by TMS to rEBA. (c) Faces and Bodies. Performance on the face task was impaired only by TMS to rOFA, and body task performance was disrupted only by TMS to rEBA.

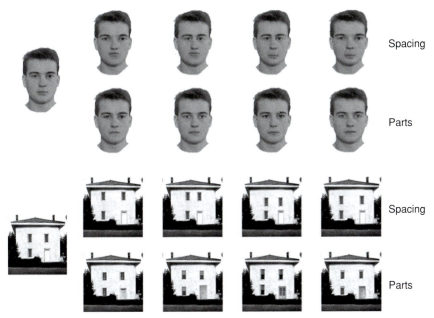

Fig. 19.7 Examples of the face and house stimuli used in Pitcher et al. (2007). Faces or houses were manipulated in one of two different ways. For the part set, the shapes of the parts (eyes and mouth in faces, windows and doors in houses) were manipulated to generate four different stimuli that differed in parts, but shared the same configuration. For the configuration set, the spacing between these parts was manipulated to generate four stimuli that shared the same parts, but differed in configuration (these stimuli were originally used in Yovel and Kanwisher, 2004).

OFA. The results demonstrated that only the face part stimuli were impaired and only when TMS was delivered over the right OFA. There were no impairments on the face spacing stimuli or the parts and the spacing house stimuli. There were also no significant impairments at the left OFA although there was a trend towards a face part impairment. This lack of a significant face effect at the left OFA is consistent with evidence from other methodologies which demonstrates that faces are preferentially processed in the right hemisphere (Young et al., 1985; Landis et al., 1986; Bentin et al., 1996; Yovel et al., 2003). It is also worth noting that the left OFA is typically further from the surface than the right OFA. The induced face part impairment at the right OFA fits nicely with fMRI evidence that the OFA processes face parts (Liu et al., 2010) and the sensitivity of the M100 to face parts (Liu et al., 2002). The lack of impairment for the face spacing is seemingly inconsistent with a recent study which has demonstrated that the OFA codes information about the spatial relations of face parts (Rhodes et al., 2009). It is possible that the spacing information coded in the OFA is not behaviorally relevant to face discrimination, or alternatively the spacing task in our TMS study may have been insensitive to TMS disruption at the rOFA. Future studies will be needed to resolve this issue.

Pitcher et al. (2007) next tested when the OFA is active in the face processing stream by delivering TMS at different points after stimulus onset while subjects again performed the face part task. Double pulse TMS separated by 40ms was delivered over the right OFA and vertex (as a control TMS site) in six distinct time windows after stimulus onset: 20 to 60ms, 60 to 100ms, 100 to 140ms, 130 to 170ms, 170 to 210ms and 210 to 250ms. These time windows were selected so that

TMS pulses coincided with the M100 (Liu et al., 2002) and the N170/M170 (Bentin et al., 1996; Liu et al., 2002) components reported in electrophysiological face processing studies.

The results showed a temporally discrete impairment window from 60 to 100ms; there were no impairments in any of the other time windows (see Figure 19.8). Thus the TMS data provide convincing evidence that the OFA processes face parts and does so in an early and temporally discrete time period.

TMS studies of facial expression processing

Cognitive and cortical models of face processing propose that categorization of facial expressions relies on different computations than categorization of facial identity (Bruce and Young, 1986; Haxby et al., 2000; Adolphs, 2002; Calder and Young, 2005; and Calder, Chapter 22; Kanwisher and Barton, Chapter 7, this volume), and two studies have used TMS to examine how expressions are computed and cortically processed in the human brain. Pourtois et al. (2004) delivered single pulse TMS over the right somatosensory cortex while subjects performed a matching task involving happy or fearful facial expressions. They targeted right somatosensory cortex because neuropsychological and neuroimaging evidence suggests that it performs a role in facial expression discrimination (Adolphs et al., 2000; Winston et al, 2003). These findings fit with theories of embodied cognition, which suggest that the right somatosensory cortex is a component in a sensorimotor cortical network that internally simulates an observed expression and that this simulation contributes to identifying the expressions of others (Goldman and Sripada, 2005; Niedenthal, 2007).

TMS increased the time it took for subjects to match fearful but not happy expressions. It is not clear why the perception of fearful faces was impaired while the happy faces were unaffected but some evidence suggests that recognition of negative expressions is more dependent on the right hemisphere than positive expressions (Adolphs et al., 1996; Vuilleumier and Pourtois, 2007). It is also worth noting that Pourtois et al. (2004) also reported that TMS to right STS disrupts the

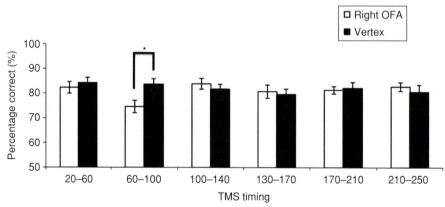

Fig. 19.8 Results of the TMS timing experiment taken from Pitcher et al. (2007). Double pulse TMS was delivered over right OFA and vertex at six different time windows after stimulus onset while subjects made sequential delayed match-to-sample judgments about the face part stimuli shown in Figure 19.7. The results show that TMS induced a disruption only when delivered 60 to 100ms after stimulus onset. This result suggests that the right OFA represents face parts early in the face processing stream.

perception of gaze but not expression. This finding is consistent with other evidence that STS is important for gaze perception (Haxby et al., 2000; Calder et al., 2007; also Adolphs and Birmingham, Chapter 29; Pelphrey and Vander Wyk, Chapter 30, this volume), and more importantly it indicates that TMS to STS can disrupt face processing.

Pitcher et al. (2008) examined how facial expressions are represented across visual and non-visual cortical areas by delivering TMS over the right occipital face area and the right somatosensory cortex. In the first experiment subjects performed a delayed match-to-sample discrimination task in which two stimulus faces displayed the same identity across different expressions (identity task) or two stimulus faces displayed the same expression across different identities (expression task). The expression task and the identity task were behaviorally matched for performance accuracy. TMS was delivered concurrently with the presentation of the probe stimulus (as in Pitcher et al., 2009) at a frequency of 10 Hz for 500 ms. The results demonstrated that TMS impaired the expression task but not the identity task when delivered over the right OFA and the right somatosensory cortex.

The expression task impairments at right somatosensory cortex partially replicated the results of Pourtois et al. (2004), although TMS in the Pitcher study did not selectively impair any specific expression discriminations. This is possibly due to the inclusion of a broader range of expressions in this study (happy, sad, fear, surprise, disgust, anger) that reduced the statistical power in the subsequent analysis and future testing will be required to further clarify this point (Hussey and Safford, 2009). While there is no reason to suppose that the right somatosensory cortex should contribute to identity computations, the lack of identity impairment at right OFA in this study is perhaps surprising. Cortical models of face processing (Haxby et al., 2000; Calder and Young, 2005), fMRI studies (Hoffman and Haxby, 2000; Yovel and Kanwisher, 2005) and patient data (Rossion et al., 2003; Bouvier and Engel, 2006) suggest that the OFA is involved in identity computations. However, as discussed above, studies, including one involving TMS (Pitcher et al., 2007), indicate that the OFA represents face part information (Liu et al., 2010). In the identity task, same pairs always differed in expression and hence discrimination based on face parts may not have been an effective strategy. This may have forced reliance on aspects of the face such as spacing between parts or surface reflectance that may be represented in other brain regions than right OFA.

In a follow-up TMS timing experiment Pitcher et al. (2008) used double pulse TMS separated by 40ms delivered at different time points to examine when the right OFA and the right somatosensory cortex contribute to facial expression discrimination. TMS was delivered in seven time windows while subjects performed the facial expression discrimination task. At right OFA TMS delivered 60 and 100 ms after stimulus onset impaired expression discrimination (see Figure 19.9). This replicates the TMS timing impairment on the face part task reported in the earlier study (Pitcher et al., 2007) and again demonstrates that the OFA makes an early and temporally discrete face processing contribution.

TMS delivered over right somatosensory cortex induced impairments in two partially overlapping time windows at 100 and 140 ms and again at 130 and 170 ms. This result suggests that in comparison with the visual analysis at right OFA the expression processing at right somatosensory cortex may be a relatively sustained process. The timing of this effect demonstrates that the contribution from non-visual cortical areas to expression discrimination co-occur with visually mediated face computations such as those producing the face-selective N170 component (Bentin et al., 1996). This timing effect is also consistent with studies that have reported that cortical areas outside the visual system exhibit a response earlier than the N170 in visual tasks involving facial expressions (Eimer and Holmes, 2002) and emotionally evocative images (Kawasaki et al., 2001).

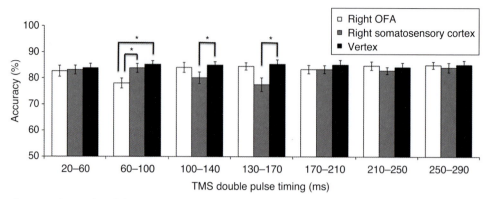

Fig. 19.9 The results of the double pulse TMS timing experiments from Pitcher et al. (2008). TMS impaired expression discrimination at 60 and 100 ms when delivered over right OFA. By comparison the impairment at right somatosensory cortex was later and longer at 100 and 140ms and again at 130 and 170ms.

Future possibilities

Given the importance of face processing research, there are surprisingly few TMS face studies. We believe that the small number of studies described in this chapter demonstrate that TMS can be employed to examine both how and when faces are cortically represented in the undamaged human brain. Briefly disrupting these areas with TMS will allow experimenters to ask new types of questions about the cortical face processing network. For example cortical models propose that both feedforward and feedback mechanisms connect the face processing areas (Haxby et al., 2000; Fairhill and Ishai, 2007). Evidence for feedback processes and the timing of these processes could be demonstrated by showing early and later impairments in a study that delivered TMS over a stimulated region at different points from stimulus onset (Pitcher et al., 2007, 2008).

Perhaps one of the most exciting applications of the TMS research reported here is the potential to combine transient disruption of the OFA with neuroimaging techniques such as fMRI or EEG. As was noted above, the OFA is believed to be the first stage of a face processing network and is thought to operate in combination with other face-selective areas, principally the FFA and STS. To date the FFA remains outside the range of TMS disruption and is largely studied using fMRI in humans. Disrupting the OFA via TMS and then measuring any subsequent downstream effects would offer a method of testing both the functional operation and the cortical connectivity in the face network. This could be achieved is by targeting TMS at the right OFA inside the fMRI scanner. This has been successfully achieved in both the dorsal premotor cortex (Bestmann et al., 2004) and the frontal eye fields (Ruff et al., 2006). However such studies are technologically challenging and require extensive resources. It may also be possible to disrupt the OFA using offline TMS techniques such as 1Hz TMS or using a theta stimulation protocol, the physiological effects of which can last up to an hour after stimulation (Huang et al., 2005) and the behavioral effects of which have been shown to outlast stimulation (Vallesi et al., 2007). Participants could be stimulated and quickly placed in the MRI scanner to search for any downstream effects. This technique has been successfully performed on the motor cortex (O'Shea et al., 2007).

TMS has also been successfully combined with EEG (Taylor et al., 2007; Fuggetta et al., 2009). The N170 (Eimer, Chapter Chapter 17, this volume) is a key face-selective EEG component

(Bentin et al., 1996) that is believed to result from neural activity in the FFA (Horovitz et al., 2004) or possibly the STS (Henson et al., 2003) but not from the OFA. TMS targeted at the OFA could potentially delay or reduce the N170 and thus demonstrate functional connectivity within the face network.

Summary and conclusions

At present only a small number of studies have used TMS to examine face processing. We therefore began the chapter with a brief description of how TMS works and how it can be applied experimentally. We then described the existing studies that have used TMS to disrupt different cortical areas implicated in the recognition and discrimination of faces. These included the OFA, the face area in the right somatosensory cortex, and STS. Some of these studies have exploited the temporal precision of TMS to determine the temporal profiles of cortical areas in the face-processing network. We concluded by describing the exciting future possibilities that the continued application of TMS can provide for face processing research.

References

Adolphs, R. (2002). Neural systems for recognizing emotion. *Current Opinion in Neurobiology*, **12**, 169–177.

Adolphs, R., Damasio, H., Tranel, D., and Damasio, A.R. (1996). Cortical systems for the recognition of emotion in facial expressions. *Journal of Neuroscience*, **16**, 7678–7687.

Adolphs, R., Damasio, H., Tranel, D., Cooper, G., and Damasio, A.R. (2000). A role for somatosensory cortices in the visual recognition of emotion as revealed by three-dimensional lesion mapping. *Journal of Neuroscience*, **20**, 2683–2690.

Amassian, V.E., Cracco, R.Q., Maccabee, P.J., Cracco, J.B., Rudell, A.P., and Eberle, L. (1993). Unmasking human visual perception with the magnetic coil and its relationship to hemispheric asymmetry. *Brain Research*, **605**, 312–316.

Antal, A., Terney, D., Poreisz, C., and Paulus, W. (2007). Towards unravelling task-related modulations of neuroplastic changes induced in the human motor cortex. *European Journal of Neuroscience*, **26**, 2687–2691.

Ashbridge, E., Walsh, V., and Cowey, A. (1997). Temporal aspects of visual search studied by transcranial magnetic stimulation. *Neuropsychologia*, **35**, 1121–1131.

Beck, D.M., Muggleton, N., Walsh, V., and Lavie, N. (2006). Right parietal cortex plays a critical role in change blindness. *Cerebral Cortex*, 16, 712–717.

Bentin, S., Allison, T., Puce, A., Perez, E., and McCarthy G. (1996) Electrophysiological studies of face perception in humans. *Journal of Cognitive Neuroscience*, **8**, 551–565.

Bestmann, S., Baudewig, J., Siebner, H.R., Rothwell, J.C., and Frahm, J. (2004). Functional MRI of the immediate impact of transcranial magnetic stimulation on cortical and subcortical motor circuits. *European Journal of Neuroscience*, **19**, 1950–1962.

Bjoertomt, O., Cowey, A., and Walsh, V. (2002). Spatial neglect in near and far space investigated by repetitive transcranial magnetic stimulation. *Brain*, **125**, 2012–2022.

Bodamer, J. (1947). Die Prosop-Agnosie. *Archiv Für Psychiatrie Und Nervenkrankheiten, Vereinigt Mit Zeitschrift Für Die Gesamte Neurologie Und Psychiatrie*, **118**, 6–53.

Bouvier, S.E., and Engel, S.A. (2006). Behavioral deficits and cortical damage loci in cerebral achromatopsia. *Cerebral Cortex*, 16, 183–191.

Brasil-Neto, J.P., Cohen, L.G., Panizza, M., Nilsson, J., Roth, B.J., and Hallett, M. (1992). Optimal focal transcranial magnetic activation of the human motor cortex: Effects of coil orientation, shape of the induced current pulse, and stimulus intensity. *Journal of Clinical Neurophysiology*, **9**, 132–136.

Bruce, V. and Young, A. (1986). Understanding face recognition. *British Journal of Psychology*, 77, 305.

Calder, A.J., Beaver, J.D., Winston, J.S., *et al.* (2007). Separate coding of different gaze directions in the superior temporal sulcus and inferior parietal lobule. *Current Biology*, **17**, 20–25.

Calder, A.J. and Young, A.W. (2005). Understanding the recognition of facial identity and facial expression. *Nature Reviews Neuroscience*, **6**, 641–651.

Campana, G., Pavan, A., and Casco, C. (2008). Priming of first- and second-order motion: Mechanisms and neural substrates. *Neuropsychologia*, **46**, 393–398.

Downing, P.E., Jiang, Y., Shuman, M., and Kanwisher, N. (2001). A cortical area selective for visual processing of the human body. *Science*, **293**, 2470–2473.

Duncan, K.J., Pattamadilok, C., and Devlin, J.T. (2010). Investigating occipito-temporal contributions to reading with TMS. *Journal of Cognitive Neuroscience*, **22**, 739–750.

Eimer, M. and Holmes, A. (2002). An ERP study on the time course of emotional face processing. *Neuroreport*, **13**, 427.

Fairhall, S.L. and Ishai, A. (2007). Effective connectivity within the distributed cortical network for face perception. *Cerebral Cortex*, 17, 2400–6.

Farah, M.J. (2004). *Visual agnosia: Disorders of object recognition and what they tell us about normal vision.* MIT Press Cambridge, MA.

Fuggetta, G., Rizzo, S., Pobric, G., Lavidor, M., and Walsh, V. (2009). Functional representation of living and nonliving domains across the cerebral hemispheres: A combined event-related potential/transcranial magnetic stimulation study. *Journal of Cognitive Neuroscience*, **21**, 403–414.

Gauthier, I., Tarr, M.J., Moylan, J., Skudlarski, P., Gore, J.C., and Anderson, A. W. (2000). The fusiform 'face area' is part of a network that processes faces at the individual level. *Journal of Cognitive Neuroscience*, **12**, 495–504.

Goldman, A.I. and Sripada, C.S. (2005). Simulationist models of face-based emotion recognition. *Cognition*, **94**, 193–213.

Gough, P.M., Nobre, A.C., and Devlin, J.T. (2005). Dissociating linguistic processes in the left inferior frontal cortex with transcranial magnetic stimulation. *Journal of Neuroscience*, **25**, 8010–8016.

Göbel, S., Walsh, V., and Rushworth, M.F. (2001). The mental number line and the human angular gyrus. *Neuroimage*, **14**, 1278–1289.

Grill-Spector, K. and Malach, R. (2004). The human visual cortex. *Annual Review of Neuroscience*, **27**, 649–677.

Grill-Spector, K., Knouf, N., and Kanwisher, N. (2004). The fusiform face area subserves face perception, not generic within-category identification. *Nature Neuroscience*, **7**, 555–62.

Haxby, J.V., Hoffman, E.A., and Gobbini, M.I. (2000). The distributed human neural system for face perception. *Trends in Cognitive Sciences*, **4**, 223–233.

Haxby, J.V., Gobbini, M.I., Furey, M.L., Ishai, A., Schouten, J.L., and Pietrini, P. (2001). Distributed and overlapping representations of faces and objects in ventral temporal cortex. *Science*, **293**, 2325–2430.

Hemond, C.C., Kanwisher, N.G., and Op de Beeck, H.P. (2007). A preference for contralateral stimuli in human object- and face-selective cortex. *Plos ONE*, **2**, e574.

Henson, R.N., Goshen-Gottstein, Y., Ganel, T., Otten, L.J., Quayle, A., and Rugg, M.D. (2003). Electrophysiological and haemodynamic correlates of face perception, recognition and priming. *Cerebral Cortex*, 13, 793–805.

Hoffman, E.A. and Haxby, J.V. (2000). Distinct representations of eye gaze and identity in the distributed human neural system for face perception. *Nature Neuroscience*, **3**, 80–84.

Horovitz, S.G., Rossion, B., Skudlarski, P., and Gore, J.C. (2004). Parametric design and correlational analyses help integrating fmri and electrophysiological data during face processing. *Neuroimage*, **22**, 1587–1595.

Hsiao, J.H., Shieh, D.X., and Cottrell, G.W. (2008). Convergence of the visual field split: Hemispheric modeling of face and object recognition. *Journal of Cognitive Neuroscience*, **20**, 2298–2307.

Huang, Y.Z., Edwards, M.J., Rounis, E., Bhatia, K.P., and Rothwell, J.C. (2005). Theta burst stimulation of the human motor cortex. *Neuron*, **45**, 201–206.

Hussey, E. and Safford, A. (2009). Perception of facial expression in somatosensory cortex supports simulationist models. *Journal of Neuroscience*, **29**, 301–302.

Itier, R.J., Herdman, A.T., George, N., Cheyne, D., and Taylor, M.J. (2006). Inversion and contrast-reversal effects on face processing assessed by MEG. *Brain Research*, **1115**, 108–120.

Juan, C.H. and Walsh, V. (2003). Feedback to V1: A reverse hierarchy in vision. *Experimental Brain Research*, **150**, 259–263.

Juan, C.H., Muggleton, N.G., Tzeng, O.J., Hung, D.L., Cowey, A., and Walsh, V. (2008). Segregation of visual selection and saccades in human frontal eye fields. *Cerebral Cortex*, 18, 2410–5.

Kalla, R., Muggleton, N.G., Juan, C.H., Cowey, A., and Walsh, V. (2008). The timing of the involvement of the frontal eye fields and posterior parietal cortex in visual search. *Neuroreport*, **19**, 1067–1071.

Kammer, T. (1999). Phosphenes and transient scotomas induced by magnetic stimulation of the occipital lobe: Their topographic relationship. *Neuropsychologia*, **37**, 191–198.

Kanwisher, N. and Yovel, G. (2006). The fusiform face area: A cortical region specialized for the perception of faces. *Philosophical Transactions of the Royal Society of London B*, **361**, 2109–2128.

Kanwisher, N., McDermott, J., and Chun, M.M. (1997). The fusiform face area: A module in human extrastriate cortex specialized for face perception. *Journal of Neuroscience*, **17**, 4302–4311.

Kawasaki, H., Kaufman, O., Damasio, H., *et al.* (2001). Single-Neuron responses to emotional visual stimuli recorded in human ventral prefrontal cortex. *Nature Neuroscience*, **4**, 15–16.

Kriegeskorte, N., Formisano, E., Sorger, B., and Goebel, R. (2007). Individual faces elicit distinct response patterns in human anterior temporal cortex. *Proceedings of the National Academy of Sciences of the USA*, **104**, 20600–20605.

Landis, T., Cummings, J.L., Christen, L., Bogen, J.E., and Imhof, H.G. (1986). Are unilateral right posterior cerebral lesions sufficient to cause prosopagnosia? Clinical and radiological findings in six additional patients. *Cortex*, **22**, 243–252.

Lavidor, M. and Walsh, V. (2003). A magnetic stimulation examination of orthographic neighborhood effects in visual word recognition. *Journal of Cognitive Neuroscience*, **15**, 354–63.

Liu, J., Harris, A., and Kanwisher, N. (2002). Stages of processing in face perception: An MEG study. *Nature Neuroscience*, **5**, 910–916.

Liu, J., Harris, A., and Kanwisher, N. (2010). Perception of face parts and face configurations: An fMRI study. *Journal of Cognitive Neuroscience*, 22, 203–211.

Malach, R., Reppas, J.B., Benson, R.R., *et al.* (1995). Object-related activity revealed by functional magnetic resonance imaging in human occipital cortex. *Proceedings of the National Academy of Sciences of the USA*, **92**, 8135–8139.

McNeil, J.E. and Warrington, E.K. (1993). Prosopagnosia: A face-specific disorder. *The Quarterly Journal of Experimental Psychology Section A*, **46**, 1–10.

Moliadze, V., Giannikopoulos, D., Eysel, U.T., and Funke, K. (2005). Paired-Pulse transcranial magnetic stimulation protocol applied to visual cortex of anaesthetized cat: Effects on visually evoked single-unit activity. *Journal of Physiology*, **566**, 955–65.

Moro, V., Urgesi, C., Pernigo, S., Lanteri, P., Pazzaglia, M., and Aglioti, S.M. (2008). The neural basis of body form and body action agnosia. *Neuron*, **60**, 235–246.

Moscovitch, M., Winocur, G., and Behrmann, M. (1997). What is special about face recognition? Nineteen experiments on a person with visual object agnosia and dyslexia but normal face recognition. *Journal of Cognitive Neuroscience*, **9**, 555–604.

Muggleton, N.G., Postma, P., Moutsopoulou, K., Nimmo-Smith, I., Marcel, A., and Walsh, V. (2006). TMS over right posterior parietal cortex induces neglect in a scene-based frame of reference. *Neuropsychologia*, **44**, 1222–1229.

Nagarajan, S.S., Durand, D.M., and Warman, E.N. (1993). Effects of induced electric fields on finite neuronal structures: A simulation study. *IEEE Transactions on Bio-Medical Engineering*, **40**, 1175–1188.

Niedenthal, P. M. (2007). Embodying emotion. *Science*, **316**, 1002–1005.

O'Shea, J., Johansen-Berg, H., Trief, D., Göbel, S., and Rushworth, M.F. (2007). Functionally specific reorganization in human premotor cortex. *Neuron*, **54**, 479–90.

O'Shea, J., Muggleton, N.G., Cowey, A., and Walsh, V. (2004). Timing of target discrimination in human frontal eye fields. *Journal of Cognitive Neuroscience*, **16**, 1060–1067.

Pascual-Leone, A., Amedi, A., Fregni, F., and Merabet, L.B. (2005). The plastic human brain cortex. *Annual Review of Neuroscience*, **28**, 377–401.

Pascual-Leone, A., Walsh, V., and Rothwell, J. (2000). Transcranial magnetic stimulation in cognitive neuroscience—virtual lesion, chronometry, and functional connectivity. *Current Opinion in Neurobiology*, **10**, 232–237.

Pitcher, D., Walsh, V., Yovel, G., and Duchaine, B. (2007). TMS evidence for the involvement of the right occipital face area in early face processing. *Current Biology*, **17**, 1568–1573.

Pitcher, D., Garrido, L., Walsh, V., and Duchaine, B.C. (2008). Transcranial magnetic stimulation disrupts the perception and embodiment of facial expressions. *Journal of Neuroscience*, **28**, 8929–8933.

Pitcher, D., Cha rles, L., Devlin, J.T., Walsh, V., and Duchaine, B. (2009). Triple dissociation of faces, bodies, and objects in extrastriate cortex. *Current Biology*, **19**, 319–324.

Pourtois, G., Sander, D., Andres, M., *et al.* (2004). Dissociable roles of the human somatosensory and superior temporal cortices for processing social face signals. *European Journal of Neuroscience*, **20**, 3507–3515.

Price, C.J. and Friston, K.J. (2002). Functional imaging studies of category specificity. In Forde, E.M. and Humphreys, G.W. (eds.), *Category Specificity in Brain and Mind*, pp. 427–447. Hove: Psychology Press.

Rhodes, G., Michie, P.T., Hughes, M.E., and Byatt, G. (2009). FFA and OFA show sensitivity to spatial relations in faces. *European Journal of Neuroscience*, **30**, 721–733.

Riddoch, M.J., Johnston, R.A., Bracewell, R.M., Boutsen, L., and Humphreys, G.W. (2008). Are faces special? A case of pure prosopagnosia. *Cognitive Neuropsychology*, **25**, 3–26.

Robertson, I.H. and Murre, J.M. (1999). Rehabilitation of brain damage: Brain plasticity and principles of guided recovery. *Psychological Bulletin*, **125**, 544–575.

Rossion, B., Caldara, R., Seghier, M., Schuller, A.M., Lazeyras, F., and Mayer, E. (2003). A network of occipito-temporal face-sensitive areas besides the right middle fusiform gyrus is necessary for normal face processing. *Brain*, **126**, 2381–2395.

Rotshtein, P., Henson, R.N., Treves, A., Driver, J., and Dolan, R.J. (2005). Morphing marilyn into maggie dissociates physical and identity face representations in the brain. *Nature Neuroscience*, **8**, 107–113.

Ruff, C.C., Blankenburg, F., Bjoertomt, O., *et al.* (2006). Concurrent tms-fmri and psychophysics reveal frontal influences on human retinotopic visual cortex. *Current Biology*, **16**, 1479–1488.

Rushworth, M.F., Ellison, A., and Walsh, V. (2001). Complementary localization and lateralization of orienting and motor attention. *Nature Neuroscience*, **4**, 656–661.

Sack, A.T., Cohen Kadosh, R., Schuhmann, T., Moerel, M., Walsh, V., and Goebel, R. (2009). Optimizing functional accuracy of TMS in cognitive studies: A comparison of methods. *Journal of Cognitive Neuroscience*, **21**, 207–221.

Sergent, J. and Signoret, J.L. (1992). Varieties of functional deficits in prosopagnosia. *Cerebral Cortex*, **2**, 375–88.

Shallice, T. (1988). *From neuropsychology to mental structure.* Cambridge: Cambridge University Press.

Silvanto, J., Muggleton, N., and Walsh, V. (2008). State-dependency in brain stimulation studies of perception and cognition. *Trends in Cognitive Sciences*, **12**, 447–454.

Singh, K.D., Hamdy, S., Aziz, Q., and Thompson, D.G. (1997). Topographic mapping of trans-cranial magnetic stimulation data on surface rendered MR images of the brain. *Electroencephalography and Clinical Neurophysiology*, **105**, 345–351.

Slotnick, S.D. (2004). Source localization of ERP generators. In Handy, T.C. (ed.), *Event-Related Potentials: A Methods Handbook*, (pp. 149–166). Cambridge, MA: The MIT Press.

Steeves, J.K., Culham, J.C., Duchaine, B.C., et al. (2006). The fusiform face area is not sufficient for face recognition: Evidence from a patient with dense prosopagnosia and no occipital face area. *Neuropsychologia*, **44**, 594–609.

Stewart, L., Ellison, A., Walsh, V., and Cowey, A. (2001). The role of transcranial magnetic stimulation (TMS) in studies of vision, attention and cognition. *Acta Psychologica*, **107**, 275–291.

Taylor, P.C., Nobre, A.C., and Rushworth, M.F. (2007). Subsecond changes in top down control exerted by human medial frontal cortex during conflict and action selection: a combined transcranial magnetic stimulation electroencephalography study. *The Journal of Neuroscience*, **27**, 11343–11353.

Tsao, D.Y., Moeller, S., and Freiwald, W.A. (2008). Comparing face patch systems in macaques and humans. *Proceedings of the National Academy of Sciences of the USA*, **105**, 19514–19519.

Ullman, S., Vidal-Naquet, M., and Sali, E. (2002). Visual features of intermediate complexity and their use in classification. *Nature Neuroscience*, **5**, 682–687.

Vallesi, A., Shallice, T., and Walsh, V. (2007). Role of the prefrontal cortex in the foreperiod effect: TMS evidence for dual mechanisms in temporal preparation. *Cerebral Cortex*, 17, 466–474.

Vuilleumier, P., and Pourtois, G. (2007). Distributed and interactive brain mechanisms during emotion face perception: Evidence from functional neuroimaging. *Neuropsychologia*, **45**, 174–194.

Walsh, V., and Cowey, A. (2000). Transcranial magnetic stimulation and cognitive neuroscience. *Nature Reviews Neuroscience*, **1**, 73–79.

Walsh, V. and Pascual-Leone, A. (2003). *Transcranial magnetic stimulation: A neurochronometics of mind*. Cambridge, MA: MIT Press.

Wassermann, E.M., Epstein, C., Ziemann, U., Walsh, V., Paus, T., and Lisanby, S (eds.). (2008). *Oxford Handbook of Transcranial Stimulation*. Oxford: Oxford University Press.

Wassermann, E.M., McShane, L.M., Hallett, M., and Cohen, L.G. (1992). Noninvasive mapping of muscle representations in human motor cortex. *Electroencephalography and Clinical Neurophysiology*, **85**, 1–8.

Wig, G.S., Grafton, S.T., Demos, K.E., and Kelley, W.M. (2005). Reductions in neural activity underlie behavioral components of repetition priming. *Nature Neuroscience*, **8**, 1228–1233.

Winston, J.S., O'Doherty, J., and Dolan, R.J. (2003). Common and distinct neural responses during direct and incidental processing of multiple facial emotions. *Neuroimage*, **20**, 84–97.

Young, A.W., Hay, D.C., McWeeny, K.H., Ellis, A.W., and Barry, C. (1985). Familiarity decisions for faces presented to the left and right cerebral hemispheres. *Brain and Cognition*, **4**, 439–450.

Yovel, G., and Kanwisher, N. (2004). Face perception: Domain specific, not process specific. *Neuron*, **44**, 889–898.

Yovel, G., and Kanwisher, N. (2005). The neural basis of the behavioral face-inversion effect. *Current Biology*, **15**, 2256–2262.

Yovel, G., Levy, J., Grabowecky, M., and Paller, K.A. (2003). Neural correlates of the left-visual-field superiority in face perception appear at multiple stages of face processing. *Journal of Cognitive Neuroscience*, **15**, 462–474.

Chapter 20

Computer-Generated Images in Face Perception

Thomas Vetter and Mirella Walker

Introduction

Researchers interested in human face perception encounter a research object consisting of thousands of individual human faces. To systematically investigate how faces are perceived, categorized, or recognized, they need control over the stimuli they use for their experiments. The problem is not only to get face images taken under comparable lighting conditions, distance from camera, angle, gaze direction, or facial expression but to get face stimuli with clearly defined similarities and differences. Another difficulty is to get natural-looking face stimuli varying on certain dimensions (e.g. distinctiveness or masculinity/femininity), but not on others (e.g. identity).

This problem motivated psychologists as well as computer scientists to generate computational models of human faces. In *face space* models (e.g. O'Toole et al., 1998; Valentine, 1991), every face is represented by a point in a highly dimensional continuous space. These models attempt to reflect the psychological representations by using similarity relations between faces as determinants for the distances between them. With such a continuous vector space concept, arbitrary faces can be generated by linearly combining exemplar faces, e.g. by superposing two exemplar faces or varying the distance of a face from the mean face.

Research in the field of computer graphics and vision strives to precisely synthesize any possible human face in a way that it is perceived as a real face and to parametrically describe or analyze any existing human face. To parametrically describe an unknown face means to relate it to a big set of exemplar faces reflecting the variety of faces in a society. So, the appearance of a face should be described along different dimensions with respect to the variability of these dimensions in the set of given faces. Synthesizing any possible face means to generate natural-looking faces that do not exist in reality but lie in the space of possible faces, which is spanned by the set of exemplar faces. This requires that the exemplar faces are organized in a meaningful way. Generating preferably realistic stimuli requires sophisticated computer graphics.

In this chapter we consider how researchers have tackled the problem of getting fully parametrized synthetic faces or control over the stimuli on the one hand and natural-looking faces or highly ecologically valid stimuli on the other at the same time. Towards the end of the chapter we present a new technology that fulfills both conditions.

An early method to synthesize faces: the caricature generator

There is a considerable amount of psychological literature concerning the different tasks and processes in face perception. Two major types of tasks can be distinguished (O'Toole et al., 1998): perception-based and memory-based tasks. One important thing about this distinction is that for memory-based tasks, such as face recognition, one needs to concentrate on the characteristics that make a face unique. To perform in perceptual tasks, such as social categorization or facial expression analysis, one needs to focus on the characteristics that a face shares with other faces. Thus the distinctiveness of a face (or its atypicality) is a crucial factor for face perception and recognition tasks.

Since the distinctiveness of a person's face is fixed with respect to a given population, researchers working with photographs as face stimuli encountered the difficulty that varying the distinctiveness of faces meant varying identity. This interconnection of distinctiveness and individual facial appearance set considerable limitations for experimental research, since other relevant factors for face perception such as attractiveness, likeability, or gender-typicality could not be controlled.

It is, perhaps, not surprising that one of the earliest psychological studies using computer-generated face images used face images with systematically enhanced or reduced distinctiveness (Rhodes et al., 1987). They found that caricatures (faces with enhanced distinctiveness) were more easily recognized than the veridical faces or anti-caricatures (faces with reduced distinctiveness). The face images were generated with the "caricature generator," a method to systematically manipulate a face's distinctiveness without changing its identity (Brennan, 1985). The first step was to digitize a photograph of a specific face and locate the major face features in a two-dimensional coordinate system by placing 169 key points in the face. Some of these points were connected by 37 lines resulting in a line drawing of the original photograph. This procedure was repeated on a series of other face photographs from the same gender. After scaling and translating them, so that the pupils were aligned, a norm face[1] was created by calculating the mean coordinates of every key point in this set of faces. To compare a specific line drawing with the norm face, the metric differences between all pairs of corresponding points in the two faces were represented as a vector. Finally, these differences were enhanced or reduced by lengthening or shortening the vector between the mean face and the veridical one, resulting in caricatures or anti-caricatures, respectively, of the face. This method also allowed researchers to morph between any two faces and to exaggerate the characteristics of a face compared to any other face.

This was a substantial step in the direction of having fully parametrized faces. The distinctiveness of the faces could not yet be described in absolute terms compared to a set of given faces, but could be described in terms of deviations from the veridical and a norm face. A disadvantage of this method was that since photographs capture much more detailed information of a face than line drawings do, the stimuli generated with this method have relatively low ecological validity. The line drawings look quite different from the faces we encounter in our everyday lives. The systematic reduction of the information in a face photograph to contour information is problematic, since images containing only contour information are much more difficult to recognize than photographs (Davies et al., 1978). The comparison of results gained with different types of stimuli supports the thesis that human face perception does not only rely on the spatial layout of changes in image intensity, which is coded in line drawings, but on these intensities themselves: "The relative pattern of light and dark within a face conveys important discriminating information about such things as hair and skin color, and three-dimensional shape from patterns of shading and shadows" (Hancock et al., 1996, p. 27).

---

[1] Please notice that the term *norm* has a different meaning in the psychological literature than in the context of mathematical vector space.

Manipulations of photographs

Since both control over stimuli and their ecological validity are important requirements in experimental psychological research, computer-generated and thus to some degree controlled stimuli were still quite far away from the final goal of looking natural. Taking one step closer to that goal was a technique that adapted and extended the general idea of caricaturing faces through exaggerating the distance from a stimulus face to a norm (Brennan, 1985) to photographs of faces (Benson and Perrett, 1991b). Similarly to the above described method, first key points had to be located in photographs of faces. These points were then compared to the corresponding points in a line drawing of an average or norm face of the same gender and age. The difficulty in changing the distinctiveness was to smoothly exaggerate the characteristics of a face by moving the key points in the photograph without losing too much of the photograph's quality (rendering). This problem was solved by building triangles of key points and changing the pixel values within these triangles relative to their boundaries (centroid-edge scan). These face images were evaluated in a face recognition experiment (Benson and Perrett, 1991a). Subjects were given sets of face images produced from the photographs of famous persons, differing only in their distinctiveness and were asked to choose the veridical face. Results indicated an effect of caricaturing: subjects showed a tendency to choose faces that were slightly more distinctive than the veridical ones. Another application of photographic caricatures aimed at investigating whether the position of a face on an identity trajectory could account for identification accuracy and distinctiveness ratings (Lee et al., 2000). It was shown that identification accuracy was best for caricatures and worst for anti-caricatures. Distinctiveness ratings were also higher for caricatures than for the veridical faces, but the ratings for the veridical faces and anti-caricatures did not significantly differ.

Around this time, an early method to computer-generate composite faces[2] was presented (Langlois and Roggman, 1990). Color photographs of faces with the same pose, expression, and taken under the same lighting conditions, were scanned into a computer and aligned so that the distance between the eyes and the lips was constant. Then faces of the same gender were averaged by computing the mean color intensities for all corresponding pixels from this set of images. These images were used to gather information about the perception of attractiveness. Attractiveness ratings increased with the number of images that were used to generate a composite face.

Like the caricature generator, these methods of generating composite faces (Langlois and Roggman, 1990) and producing caricatures of photographs (Benson and Perrett, 1991b) provided some control over the stimuli, since every face could be described in relation to other faces (e.g. being more/less distinct than the veridical face). However, they produced stimuli with much greater ecological validity.

The face-space framework

An important advance in the development of computer-generated face stimuli was initiated by the proposal of a theoretical face-space framework for the encoding of faces (Valentine, 1991). This face-space framework was able to give account of different findings from face perception and

---

[2] This method has its roots in Galton's photographic method of composite portraiture (Galton, 1883).

face recognition research, such as the distinctiveness-effect,[3] the so-called other-race-effect,[4] and the effect of inversion[5] by proposing that an individual face is mentally represented as a point in a highly dimensional space, whose dimensions correspond to the physical properties that are used to encode and discriminate between faces. The distance between any two points in this space represents the similarity between the corresponding faces. Summarizing his face space frame-work, Valentine (1991) states that it is not clear, yet, whether faces are coded in terms of their deviations from the norm or center of the space (norm-based coding), or whether they are coded in terms of absolute values on the dimensions of the space (exemplar-based). He observes the dilemma that "these theoretical issues may prove difficult to distinguish in experiments using photographs of faces as stimuli, but the use of "realistic" stimuli is essential to discover the processes by which people recognize faces" (Valentine, 1991, p. 201). As we will see in the next section, Valentine's theoretical framework gave future research in the development of computer-generated faces a new direction that finally led to face stimuli that were clearly defined and look-ing natural.

The abstract face space framework was used to build psychological as well as physical face space models by applying it to empirical image data. In this chapter we are focusing on the development of the physical models. For a discussion of the psychological models, see O'Toole (Chapter 2, this volume). The basis for physical models is the physical similarity between pairs of faces, which is further analyzed using linear systems analysis procedures (O'Toole et al., 1998). In a first step, individual faces have to be described or quantified. One early method to quantify faces is based on face photographs that are preprocessed in order to share the same facial width, frontal pose, and horizontal position of pupils (Sirovich and Kirby, 1987). Pixel intensities were used to code the faces (image-based coding). Then a principal component analysis (PCA) was run on a set of faces to get the dimensions on which these faces vary (eigenvectors). The first dimension captures the direction of maximum variability in the set of face images used. Every face can be recon-structed by a weighted sum of the eigenvectors and thus can be described in terms of its position in this multidimensional face space.

The problem with this method is that since the faces are only roughly aligned, the synthesis of new faces is limited. As long as only the pupils and the face width are in correspondence in dif-ferent faces, it is not yet possible to produce a realistic-looking mean face from two or more individual faces (morph), since the other feature points such as the tip of the nose or the corners of the mouth are not likely to lie on the same pixel. Thus a morphed face looks quite blurry (Figure 20.1).

Almost 10 years later this difficulty was solved (Hancock et al., 1996) using a recently developed technique to preprocess face images before subjecting them to PCA (Craw and Cameron, 1991). This technique demands that dozens of key points are located by hand in a set of face photographs coding for face shape. This allows for computing the average face shape by taking the mean value of every key point in this set of faces. The mean face shape as well as the face shapes of every individual face can be represented as a grid that connects some of these key points. Then the

---

[3] Distinctive faces are more accurately remembered than typical faces, whereas typical faces are faster classified as faces than distinctive faces. See, e.g. Going and Read (1974), Bartlett et al. (1984), and Light et al. (1979).

[4] Faces from the same cultural environment are more easily recognized than faces from a different envi-ronment. See, e.g. Goldstein and Chance (1980), Devine and Malpass (1985), MacLin and Malpass (2001), and O'Toole et al. (1994).

[5] Inversion strongly disrupts the face recognition process so that it is assumed that different features are used to recognize upright and inverted faces. See, e.g. Carey and Diamond (1977) and Diamond and Carey (1986).

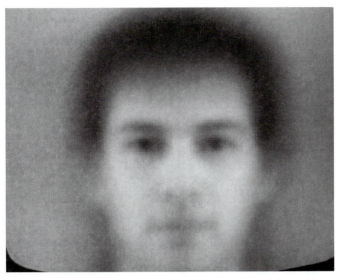

Fig. 20.1 This image shows the average face based on 115 faces (Sirovich and Kirby, 1987). Reproduced with permission of the Optical Society of America © 1987.

individual face shape can be warped to the average face shape. The resulting shape-free face codes for pixel intensities. This separation of shape and shape-free coding of faces before running the PCA allows not only for investigating the different accounts of these information in human face recognition, but also for smooth transitions in face space (morphing). The disadvantage of this method is that all faces have to be photographed under the same lighting conditions and with the same pose.

The three-dimensional morphable face model

Face modeling

Whereas in the previously described approaches the faces were aligned or set in correspondence by marking a limited set of key points by hand, the goal of the morphable face model approach was to construct a flexible three-dimensional face model, where all faces are in full correspondence (Blanz and Vetter, 1999). This face model was constructed on the basis of 200 laser scans from the heads of 100 male and 100 female adults who were between 18 and 45 years old (Cyberware™ 3030PS) (O'Toole et al., 1997; Troje and Bülthoff, 1996). Faces did not show any extra-facial cues, such as makeup, glasses, jewelry, beards, or moustaches. Every laser scan could be represented by two different kinds of information about the face: the three-dimensional head surface data and a two-dimensional reflectance or texture map. The correspondence problem was solved with an optic flow-based correspondence algorithm that could be applied to both kinds of information. This semi-automated procedure resulted in full correspondence between any two faces, meaning that not only some selected key points, such as the pupils or the tips of the noses, were in correspondence between two face images, but also any data points in the texture maps and on the head surfaces (Blanz and Vetter, 1999; Vetter and Poggio, 1997). An average face shape and an average texture map were computed and every face was coded as its deviation from this average face in terms of its three-dimensional head structure and its two-dimensional texture map. Then a PCA was performed to get the eigenvectors for the shape and the texture of the given set of faces. A wide range of new faces could be synthesized by forming linear combinations of the faces on which the database was built: transitions between any two individual faces (morphs or composite faces) or between an individual face and the average (caricatures and anti-caricatures), faces with the shape of an individual face A and the texture of an individual face B or the average face and vice versa, and faces that only vary along one single attribute such as gender, age or fullness of the face. To find the direction in our face space that best represents a specific attribute, every face in a set (S_i, T_i) is labeled according to this attribute (μ_i). Then weighted sums can be computed separately for shape and texture:

$$\Delta S = \sum_{i=1}^{m} \mu_i \left(S_i - \bar{S}\right), \ \Delta T = \sum_{i=1}^{m} \mu_i \left(T_i - \bar{T}\right).$$

Any database face can now be manipulated with respect to this attribute by adding or subtracting multiples of $(\Delta S, \Delta T)$ (Blanz and Vetter, 1999).

These different kinds of faces could be used as stimuli to investigate different research questions concerning human face perception and recognition. Since all faces generated with these methods can be precisely located on all dimensions in the face space, there is full control over the faces. This is an advantage for their use as stimuli in psychological experiments. A face can be described not only as, for example, more or less masculine or feminine or more or less distinctive than another face, but it can also be described in absolute terms. Another advantage of this face model stems from the modality of the input data. Since the laser scans provide three-dimensional information about faces, every face can be rendered under different clearly defined lighting conditions or views. Later in this chapter we will present applications of these image manipulation methods in psychological experiments.

Image processing

This method to manipulate faces in various ways can be applied to novel photographs of faces. Thus we are able to synthesize face images with extra-facial cues, such as hair and clothing, resulting in stimuli with much higher ecological validity. Any two-dimensional photograph of any human face can be selected as an input image. Using the analysis-by-synthesis-approach (Blanz and Vetter, 1999) we reconstruct the three-dimensional shape and surface reflectance of the head by fitting the three-dimensional model to the two-dimensional input image. The model coefficients are optimized along with a set of rendering parameters in order to produce an image as close as possible to the input photograph. This procedure results in a three-dimensional representation of the shape structure and its two-dimensional reflectance or texture map. This information can be used as the origin for the synthesis of new faces by applying any of the above described procedures to it. Finally the resulting head is rendered back into the original photograph using the rendering parameters estimated in the fitting process (Blanz et al., 2004). For an overview of the whole process, see Figure 20.2. In the second part of the next section we present two recent applications of these techniques in psychological experiments.

The three-dimensional morphable face model is highly flexible in generating different kinds of fully controlled face stimuli with high ecological validity since: 1) the dimensions obtained from PCA span a continuous space, 2) the database is built on three-dimensional input data, and 3) all faces are in full correspondence. The following sections present a selection of early applications of the three-dimensional morphable face model in psychological experiments.

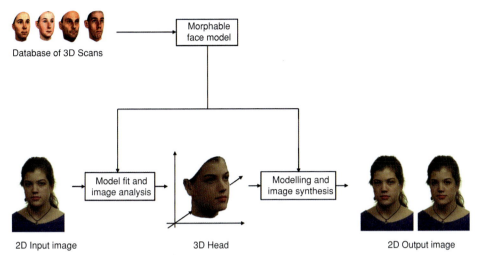

Fig. 20.2 The morphable face model is based on 200 exemplar three-dimensional representations of faces. Thus we can (a) analyze any face from a two-dimensional photograph by synthesizing it resulting in a three-dimensional head model of the input face and (b) manipulate this face in a natural-looking way. In this case, the face's masculinity/femininity was manipulated and the resulting heads were rendered back into the original photograph.

Applications of the three-dimensional morphable face model...
... on faces from the three-dimensional face database

This method to generate face stimuli was first used to conduct a psychological study that was aimed at investigating the different roles of three-dimensional shape and two-dimensional texture in the perception of attractiveness and age in faces (O'Toole et al., 1999). From a given set of 48 laser scans, three sets of faces were produced: the first set consisted of faces with the original three-dimensional shape and texture of the 48 individual faces; the second set of faces was produced by projecting the average texture on the individual shape of each face (texture normalized faces); the third set of faces was produced by projecting the original texture of each face on the average shape (shape normalized faces). In one experiment subjects were asked to make attractiveness ratings, in another experiment they were asked to estimate the age of faces. Results indicated that normalizing the faces led to higher attractiveness judgments and lower age judgments. And in both cases, the effect of shape normalization was bigger than the effect of texture normalization. The authors argued that since normalized faces are less distinctive or closer to the average face than the veridical faces, "some aspects of the averageness of faces can be linked reliably to the attractiveness and age of faces" (O'Toole et al., 1999a, p. 16).

In a third experiment, O'Toole and colleagues again isolated and separately manipulated the two- and three-dimensional information in faces in order to investigate the extent to which it is used to encode and recognize faces (O'Toole et al., 1999b). The three types of faces (normal faces with original shape and texture, shape normalized faces, texture normalized faces) were rendered from three different viewpoints (0% or frontal view, 30%, and 60%). Subjects learned frontal faces and had to recognize them at the same as well as different views. Recognition performance was best for normal faces, indicating that both the two- and three-dimensional information is used for face recognition.

Using the same three-dimensional morphable face model, face/anti-face pairs were generated (Blanz and Vetter, 1999) to investigate how the identity is extracted from faces and mentally represented (Leopold et al., 2001). For every face an identity trajectory was created that passed through the original face and the average face. The anti-face was defined as lying on the same axis but on the other side of the average face. The distinctiveness of a face could be systematically manipulated by changing its position on the identity trajectory (Figure 20.3).

Results showed that as long as there was no adaptation, the average identification threshold was 11% of the distance between the average face and a previously learned individual face and identification performance for the average face was at chance level. If subjects were adapted to the target's anti-face, the identification threshold was shifted to the other side of the mean, so that the average face was identified as being the corresponding person in over 60% of all cases. These results indicate that the average face—as proposed by the face space metaphor for the mental

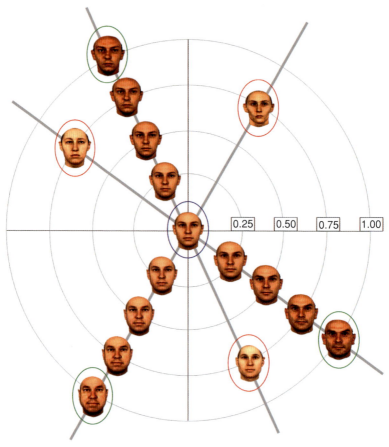

Fig. 20.3 For every face in this face space an identity trajectory can be generated that connects the original face (green) with the average face (blue). Anti-faces (red) lie on the same identity trajectory as the original face, but on the other side of the average face. Reprinted by permission from Macmillan Publishers Ltd: *Nature Neuroscience*, Prototype-referenced shape encoding revealed by high-level aftereffects, Leopold, O'Toole, Vetter, and Blanz © 2010.

representation of faces (Valentine, 1991)—"is particularly important in the interpretation of face structure. This is consistent with the well-studied "prototype effect," in which the central tendency of a collection of stimuli, though never actually seen, is classified or recognized more easily than particular exemplars" (Leopold et al., 2001, p. 92).

The three-dimensional morphable face model also allows the gender of faces to be isolated and manipulated to create gender continua between pairs of faces (Bülthoff and Newell, 2005). In this study, the endpoints of one gender continuum were faces only differing with respect to gender characteristics while the identity-related characteristics were held constant. This was done by first creating the average female face and the average male face from all 100 female and male faces in the database. Computing the trajectory between these two average faces resulted in a gender vector. This vector was then applied to different female faces from the database resulting in male versions of them. Subjects had to complete categorization and discrimination tasks. The results suggested that gender information in unfamiliar faces was not perceived categorically.

This wide range of face stimuli in psychological experiments created with the three-dimensional morphable face model demonstrates the power and flexibility of the face-space based approach in the synthesis of new clearly parametrized faces. However, the stimuli described so far did not have any non-facial features, such as hair or clothes, reducing their ecological validity. Even though the faces themselves may look very realistic, their isolation from such natural contexts makes them look quite different from what we normally encounter. Although this isolation of the facial appearance from other information can be an advantage for investigating some aspects of face perception and recognition, it is an obstacle for studying others.

… on novel photographs of faces

The first application of this method to generate synthetic stimuli with extra-facial features was aimed at investigating whether the femininity or masculinity of a face—independent of the gender of the stimulus person—leads to gender stereotyping (Walker and Vetter, 2006). First all photographs from the Feret database (Phillips et al., 1998) showing frontal Caucasian faces without glasses, beards, or moustaches were selected and pre-tested. Then three male–female pairs were selected that were well matched on various dimensions (e.g. attractiveness, likeability, age). These images were analyzed by synthesizing them with the three-dimensional morphable face model. The resulting heads were slightly manipulated by adding and subtracting a gender vector resulting in a feminized and a masculinized version of each head. The vector to enhance the femininity and masculinity of a face was equivalent to the one described above (Bülthoff and Newell, 2005). Finally the heads were rendered back into the original photographs (Figure 20.4). Results of the psychological study showed an effect of stereotyping on the basis of facial features. Feminine-looking stimulus persons were judged to be more socially skilled than masculine-looking ones, independent of their gender.

In a recent study (Walker and Vetter, 2009) we used this face model to quantify which information in faces is used for social judgments and to almost imperceptibly manipulate photographs of human faces in a way that changes the personality traits ascribed to the depicted person. In a first step we collected various social judgments about all 200 faces from the database underlying the morphable face model. We then projected the mean scores for every face and social dimension into the model. In a next step, we located in our face space vectors with maximum variability with respect to the different social dimensions. These vectors were applied to a set of three-dimensional database faces as well as to completely independent photographs of faces that were synthesized on the basis of our model. This procedure resulted in face images that are looking as realistic as the input images and affect the social judgments in the intended directions (Figure 20.5).

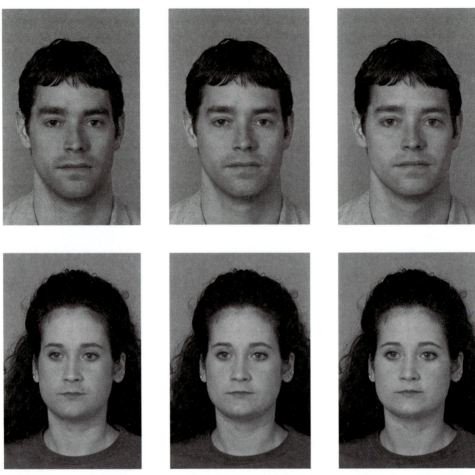

Fig. 20.4 In the left column are masculine versions and in the right column feminine versions of two original Feret database faces (middle column) (Walker and Vetter, 2006).

Summary and conclusions

Brennan's method to produce computer generated caricatured line-drawings developed in the mid-80s of the 20th century provided some control over the information in faces since one aspect of a face, its distinctiveness, could be precisely manipulated without changing other aspects of the face (Brennan, 1985). This method was then extended to generate more natural-looking carica-tures of faces (Benson and Perrett, 1991b). Around the same time a method to generate compos-ite faces was presented (Langlois and Roggman, 1990). All these approaches have in common that the generated faces can be described relative to other faces that were used to build them.

It was not until Valentine presented his abstract face-space framework (1991) that physical face spaces were developed. They could be used to analyze faces by reconstructing them on the basis of exemplar faces and to synthesize a wide range of novel faces by forming linear combinations of the exemplar faces (Hancock et al., 1996; O'Toole et al., 1993). Once the goal of parametrically describing or analyzing faces was reached, computer graphics researchers worked on achieving

Original face

Aggressiveness

Extroversion

Likeability

Risk seeking

Social skills

Trustworthiness

Fig. 20.5 A photograph from the FERET-database was manipulated by adding the six personality trait vectors in positive direction (Walker and Vetter, 2009).

the other goal, of synthesizing face images that look as natural as face photographs (Blanz and Vetter, 1999; Hancock et al., 1996).

This article provided an overview of the theoretical and technical steps taken to get a model of human faces that satisfied two demands for face stimuli for experimental research: full control over the information in faces enabling precise manipulations on the one hand, and high ecological validity of the stimuli, i.e. the ability to generate face stimuli that look very natural, on the other. The three-dimensional morphable face model combines these qualities with a third—high flexibility, which means that faces can be varied with respect to many dimensions (from rendering parameters such as view or lighting to social dimensions such as the perception of social skills or aggressiveness in faces).

Whereas computer graphics technology allows for synthesizing natural-looking faces with clearly defined impact on the perceiver, computer vision is still far away from the goal of analyzing faces with comparable accuracy to humans. It is already possible for a machine to recognize faces under different view or lighting conditions (O'Toole, Chapter 2, this volume) and to categorize faces into different social categories (such as age or gender), but facial expression and trait detecting machines are quite insensitive. The limitations are set by difficulties in estimating lightning parameters and analyzing facial characteristics such as ageing. Our goal is to overcome these difficulties in order to be able to analyze photographs of faces with the same exactness that is already reached for face synthesis. For now, the perception and interpretation of such subtle nuances is still restricted to humans.

References

Bartlett, J.C., Hurry, S., and Thorley, W. (1984). Typicality and familiarity of faces. *Memory and Cognition*, **12**, 219–228.

Benson, P.J. and Perrett, D.I. (1991a). Perception and recognition of photographic quality facial caricatures: Implications for the recognition of natural images. *European Journal of Cognitive Psychology*, **3**, 105–135.

Benson, P.J. and Perrett, D.I. (1991b). Synthesising continuous-tone caricatures. *Image and Vision Computing*, **9**, 123–129.

Blanz, V. and Vetter, T. (1999). A morphable model for the synthesis of 3d faces. *Proceedings of Siggraph'99*, 178–194.

Blanz, V., Scherbaum, K., Vetter, T., and Seidel, H.-P. (2004). Exchanging faces in images. *Computer Graphics Forum*, **23**, 669–676.

Brennan, S.E. (1985). Caricature generator: The dynamic exaggeration of faces by computer. *Leonardo*, **18**, 170–178.

Bülthoff, I. and Newell, F.N. (2005). Categorical perception of gender: No evidence for unfamiliar faces. *Technical Report, Max Planck Institute for Biological Cybernetics*, 1–26.

Carey, S. and Diamond, R. (1977). From piecemeal to configurational representation of faces. *Science*, **195**, 312–314.

Craw, I. and Cameron, P. (1991). Parameterising images for recognition and reconstruction. *Proceedings of the British Machine Vision Conference*, 367–370.

Davies, G., Ellis, H. and Shepherd, J. (1978). Face recognition accuracy as a function of mode of representation. *Journal of Applied Psychology*, **63**, 180–187.

Devine, P.G. and Malpass, R.S. (1985). Orienting strategies in differential face recognition. *Personality and Social Psychology Bulletin*, **11**, 33–40.

Diamond, R. and Carey, S. (1986). Why faces are and are not special: An effect of expertise. *Journal of Experimental Psychology*, **115**, 107–117.

Galton, F. (1883). *Inquiries into human faculty and its development*. London: Macmillan.

Going, M. and Read, J.D. (1974). Effects of uniqueness, sex of subject, and sex of photograph on facial recognition. *Perceptual and Motor Skills*, **39**, 109–110.

Goldstein, A.G. and Chance, J.E. (1980). Memory for faces and schema theory. *Journal of Psychology*, **105**, 47–59.

Hancock, P.J.B., Burton, M.A., and Bruce, V. (1996). Face processing: Human perception and principal components analysis. *Memory and Cognition*, **24**, 26–40.

Langlois, J.H. and Roggman, L.A. (1990). Attractive faces are only average. *Psychological Science*, **1**, 115–121.

Lee, K., Byatt, G., and Rhodes, G. (2000). Caricature effects, distinctiveness, and identification: testing the face-space framework. *Psychological Science*, **11**, 379–385.

Leopold, D.A., O'Toole, A.J., Vetter, T., and Blanz, V. (2001). Prototype-referenced shape encoding revealed by high-level aftereffects. *Nature Neuroscience*, **4**, 89–94.

Light, L.L., Kayra-Stuart, F., and Hollander, S. (1979). Recognition memory for typical and unusual faces. *Journal of experimental psychology. Human learning and memory*, **5**, 212–228.

MacLin, O.H. and Malpass, R.S. (2001). Racial categorization of faces. The ambiguous race face effect. *Psychology, Public Policy, and Law*, **7**, 98–118.

O'Toole, A.J., Abdi, H., Deffenbacher, K.A., and Valentin, D. (1993). Low-dimensional representation of faces in higher dimensions of the face space. *Journal of the Optical Society of America A*, **10**, 405–411.

O'Toole, A.J., Deffenbacher, K.A., Valentin, D., and Abdi, H. (1994). Structural aspects of face recognition and the other-race effect. *Memory and Cognition*, **22**, 208–224.

O'Toole, A.J., Vetter, T., Troje, N.F., and Bülthoff, H.H. (1997). Sex classification is better with three-dimensional head structure than with image intensity information. *Perception*, **26**, 75–84.

O'Toole, A.J., Wenger, M.J., and Townsend, J.T. (1998). Quantitative models of perceiving and remembering faces: Precedents and possibilities. In M.J. Wenger, and J.T. Townsend (eds.) *Computational, Geometric, and Process Perspectives on Facial Cognition*, pp. 1–38. Mahwah, NJ: Lawrence Erlbaum Associates.

O'Toole, A.J., Price, T., Vetter, T., Bartlett, J.C., and Blanz, V. (1999a). 3D shape and 2D surface textures of human faces: The role of 'averages' in attractiveness and age. *Image and Vision Computing*, **18**, 9–19.

O'Toole, A.J., Vetter, T., and Blanz, V. (1999b). Three-dimensional shape and two-dimensional surface reflectance contributions to face recognition: An application of three-dimensional morphing. *Vision Research*, **39**, 3145–3155.

Phillips, P.J., Wechsler, H., Huang, J., and Rauss, P.J. (1998). The feret database and evaluation procedure for face-recognition algorithms. *Image and Vision Computing*, **16**, 295–306.

Rhodes, G., Brennan, S.E., and Carey, S. (1987). Identification and ratings of caricatures: Implications for mental representations of faces. *Cognitive Psychology*, **19**, 473–497.

Sirovich, L. and Kirby, M. (1987). Low-dimensional procedure for the characterization of human faces. *Journal of the Optical Society of America, A*, **4**, 519–524.

Troje, N.F. and Bülthoff, H.H. (1996). How is bilateral symmetry of human faces used for recognition of novel views? *Vision Research*, **38**, 79–89.

Valentine, T. (1991). A unified account of the effects of distinctiveness, inversion, and race in face recognition. *The Quarterly Journal of Experimental Psychology*, **43A**, 161–204.

Vetter, T. and Poggio, T. (1997). Linear object classes and image synthesis from a single example image. *Pattern Analysis and Machine Intelligence*, **19**, 733–742.

Walker, M. and Vetter, T. (2006). Feminine-looking faces belong to friendly and helpful people - stereotyping with a parametric image model [Abstract]. *Journal of Vision*, **6**, 1067.

Walker, M. and Vetter, T. (2009). Portraits made to measure. Manipulating social judgments about individuals with a statistical face model. *Journal of Vision*, **9**, 1–13.

Chapter 21

Neurocomputational Models of Face Processing

Garrison W. Cottrell and Janet H. Hsiao

Until the day we can record from multiple neurons in undergraduates, understanding how humans process faces requires an interdisciplinary approach, including building computational models that mimic how the brain processes faces. Using machine learning techniques, we can often build models that perform the same tasks people do, in neurophysiologically plausible ways. These models can then be manipulated and analyzed in ways that people cannot, providing insights that are unavailable from behavioral experiments. For example, as we will see below, our model of perceptual expertise can be "raised" in an environment where its "parents" are cups or cans instead of faces, and the same kind of processing ensues. This demonstrates, at least from our point of view, that there is nothing special about faces as an object class per se; rather, it is what we have to do with them—fine level discrimination of a homogeneous class—that is special.

In this chapter, we will delineate two dimensions along which computational models of face (and object) processing may vary, and briefly review three such models (Dailey and Cottrell, 1999; O'Reilly and Munakata, 2000; Riesenhuber and Poggio, 1999). Subsequently, we will focus primarily on the model we are most familiar with (our own!) and how this model has been used to reveal potential mechanisms underlying the neural processing of faces and objects—the development of a specialized face processor, how it could be recruited for other domains, hemispheric lateralization of face processing, facial expression processing, and the development of face discrimination. At the end, we return to the Riesenhuber and Poggio model to describe the elegant way it has been used to predict functional magnetic resonance imaging (fMRI) data on face processing. The overall strategy of these modeling efforts is to sample problems that are constrained by neurophysiological and behavioral data, and to stress the ways in which models can generate novel hypotheses about the way humans process faces.

The model space

There are at least two dimensions along which neurocomputational models of face processing vary.[1] The first is the amount of fidelity to the known neural architecture and processing. The models created by O'Reilly and Munakata (2000) include realistic constraints on the neural units themselves, increasing large receptive fields in layers corresponding to V1, V2, V4, and the dorsal pathway, as well as inputs based upon known representations in lateral geniculate nucleus (LGN) (Figure 21.1). Images are transformed by a center-surround transform to the input layer. The final

---

[1] In this chapter we focus on neurocomputational models of face processing. Hence we will not be discussing, for example, models of face recognition from the field of computer vision. For a recent analysis of such models from a cognitive science point of view, see (O'Toole, Chapter 2, this volume).

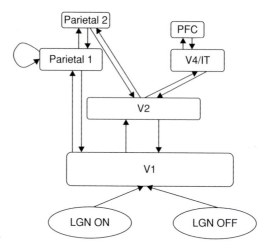

Fig. 21.1 Architecture of O'Reilly and Munakata's model.

layer corresponds to prefrontal categorization units. While this model is perhaps the most neuro-physiologically plausible, the (published) accounts of its use are on very simple stimuli.

The model of Riesenhuber and Poggio (1999) is based on the standard model of early visual processing in neuroscience, so their model is sometimes called "the Standard Model" (TSM) (Figure 21.2). They include alternating processing stages of pattern recognition, followed by spatial pooling of responses. These alternating stages are hypothesized to exist in V1, V2, and V4 (with increasingly large receptive fields). Further stages correspond to inferior temporal cortex (IT) and prefrontal cortex (PFC). Images are presented to the network and processed by Gabor filters representing the simple cells of the V1 layer. These units compute a weighted sum of their inputs, which results in them "firing" in proportion to how well the input matches with the Gabor filter. The stages alternate between units that compute weighted sums of their inputs (S-units, like the Gabor filters) to detect particular patterns, and units that compute the maximum of their inputs (C-units) in order to pool the responses of neurons on the previous layers. For example, a unit in the C1 layer fires if any S1 unit connected to it fires. All of the S1 units connected to the same C1 unit have the same orientation within a small area. So, the C1 unit "spatially pools" the S1 units' responses over a small region of space, similar to complex cells in V1. After four such layers (two S layers and two C layers), the next layer up contains units tuned to particular views of whole objects, which feed into view-invariant units. These, finally, provide input to a classification layer.

The models of Dailey and Cottrell (1999; and following models from our lab, which we dub here "The Model" (TM)), are the least biologically plausible, starting with a layer corresponding to V1 which directly feeds into a layer representing early IT, sometimes followed by a layer that represents category specific areas of IT, followed by the PFC (Figure 21.3a). The first layer units represent the magnitude response of Gabor filters, modeling complex cells in V1 over a very small region of space. The second layer projects the first layer inputs linearly onto cells whose receptive fields are the principal components of the first layer. That is, the second layer responds to *correlations* between the first layer units over a particular training set of images, resulting in global, holistic features, because they derive from inputs across the entire face. The next layer is either the category units or a layer of hidden units before the category units that are task-specific.

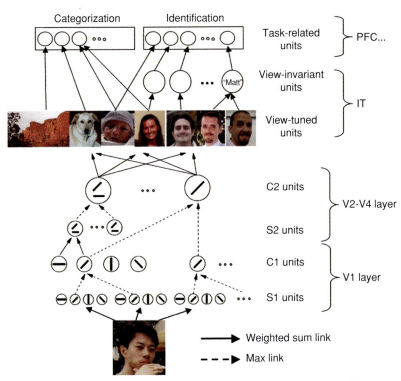

Fig. 21.2 Architecture of Riesenhuber and Poggio's model (aka "the Standard Model."). Reprinted by permission from Macmillan Publishers Ltd: *Nature Neuroscience*, Hierarchical models of object recognition in cortex, Riesenhuber and Poggio, © 1999.

The second dimension along which these models vary is the way in which the connection strengths are set. The O'Reilly and Munakata model starts with priors on the architecture in the form of receptive fields being retinotopically mapped, receiving inputs from localized regions of the layer before them, thus giving larger receptive fields at higher layers. These are then trained by the Leabra algorithm, a biologically plausible learning system that combines contrastive Hebbian learning (error driven), standard Hebbian learning (for structure learning), and k-winner take all competition, ensuring sparse representations at each layer.

TSM has connections set by hand for the first several layers, reflecting the same priors as the O'Reilly and Munakata model, with weights based roughly on physiological data. In some versions, later layers (e.g. the complex V1 to simple V2 connections (C1 to S2) in Cadieu et al. (2007)) are "trained" by greedy search of parameters that lead to C2 responses that are within some error tolerance of physiologically-measured V4 responses. In other versions (e.g. Jiang, et al., 2006), parameters of later layers are set by brute force search through parameter space to find parameters that lead to behavior that is not statistically significantly different from the desired behavior (e.g. responses of humans in a behavioral experiment). View-tuned units can be set by presenting the network with a face and setting the weights to the observed outputs of the C2 layer, and then view-invariant units can be tuned to these for each person.

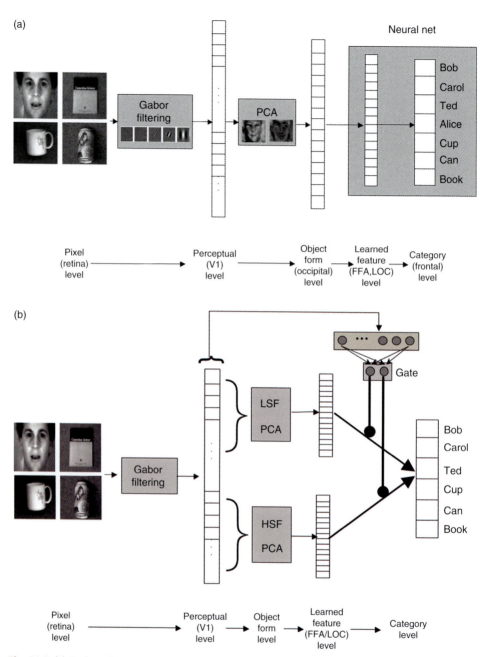

Fig. 21.3 (a) Basic architecture of Cottrell and colleagues' model (aka "The Model"). (b) Dailey and Cottrell's (1999) modular network.

Finally, in TM, as noted above, the first layer past the Gabor filters is trained in an unsupervised way by principal components analysis (PCA), capturing the statistical regularities over the training set. The next layer is trained by either a simple delta rule if there are no hidden units, or by backpropagation when there are. The network is usually trained to do the same general task required by human subjects (e.g. recognize a facial expression, a particular person, or an object) on a separate set of stimuli, and then tested on the same stimuli as used with the subjects. While backpropagation is not biologically plausible, similar representations can be learned using the contrastive Hebbian algorithm as used in Leabra, which is biologically plausible, as it is completely based on propagation of activations rather than errors.

The three modes of setting the connection strengths have different motivations and consequences. For the O'Reilly and Munakata model and TM, the motivation is to not to impose any preconceptions on the weights, except for the basic architectural constraints. The training tasks are the same sort of tasks people have to perform, and therefore the analysis of the final network involves analyzing the representations formed as a prediction about the actual neural representations. In the O'Reilly and Munakata model, a further motivation is to use a biologically plausible learning rule, so that the model as a whole, which uses biologically plausible units and connectivity patterns (including feedback between layers, a feature neither of the other two models shares), becomes a theory of how the object recognition system comes to be in the first place.

In TM, when there is a wealth of data concerning the task (as in the model of facial expression recognition; Dailey et al., 2002), the idea is to create a working model of the task that is at least neurally plausible, and then apply it to novel stimuli used in experimental settings to see how well it fits human data, and make predictions concerning neural representations for the tasks. There is no fitting to human data before testing it in the experimental setting; the model is simply trained to do the same task people do. When there is not a wealth of neurophysiological data (e.g. single-cell recordings in the fusiform face area (FFA) in humans are absent), the model can be used as an intuition pump to make predictions of what we would find were we able to (Tong et al., 2005, 2008).

In TSM, the motivation is quite different. Since the "training" is really a fit to human behavioral or monkey neural data, the idea is that, if the model architecture is neurally plausible, we can then analyze the resulting network's representations and behavior after the fitting process in ways that are unavailable in monkeys or humans. This analysis can provide a better understanding of the actual representations, and make novel predictions that can be tested.

In the following, while we mainly concentrate on TM and its variants, because it is the model we are most familiar with, we will also review an interesting result using TSM.

The development of the FFA and its right-hemisphere lateralization

What would turn a relatively generic object recognition system into a face recognition system? There are two main differences between face recognition and generic object recognition. First, faces are a type of visual stimuli that we are exposed to extensively from birth onwards. Hence they have both a primacy and a frequency advantage over objects in other categories. Second, faces must be categorized beyond the basic level—we must recognize individuals, even though in terms of basic features, we all look alike: we (almost) all have two eyes, two ears, a nose and a mouth, so fine-level discrimination is necessary to distinguish each other. It is clear that faces play a privileged role in our everyday lives, and our brains reflect this. FMRI studies have shown that an area within the fusiform gyrus (the FFA) responds more to faces than to other stimuli, especially in the right hemisphere (Kanwisher et al., 1997). The domain-specificity of this area has been challenged by some on the grounds that the FFA becomes more active after subordinate-level training on a new visual category (Gauthier et al., 1999), and hence that it is a visual expertise area, rather than a face-specific area. Whatever side one comes down on in this debate, it is still the case that, no matter what the FFA's role is, it is more active for faces *first*, and an account of how this comes to be is in order. In this section, we are going to introduce models accounting for the development of FFA and its right-hemisphere lateralization, in order to address how a specialized face processor may emerge under developmental constraints.

The development of the FFA

The model we describe here has been under development since 1990 (e.g. Fleming and Cottrell, 1990; Cottrell and Metcalfe, 1991; Dailey and Cottrell, 1999). As described above, the basic architecture of the model (TM) incorporates several known observations about visual anatomy (Figure 21.3a). In the first layer, Gabor filters (Daugman, 1985) are used to simulate neural responses in early visual areas such as V1 (Lades et al., 1993). The second layer uses PCA as a biologically plausible way (because it can be implemented using the generalized Hebbian algorithm; Sanger, 1989) to reduce the dimensionality of the information to simulate possible information extraction processes beyond V1, up to the level of lateral occipital regions; this layer can be thought of as the structural description layer from the classic Bruce and Young (1986) model. The next layer is an adaptive hidden layer that is trained by back propagation to learn features appropriate for a given task; when the task is face identification, it can be thought of as corresponding to the FFA. The fourth layer represents the output of the model, providing labels to the input; it may be analogous to frontal areas (Palmeri and Gauthier, 2004). Because the categories to be discriminated have a strong influence on the hidden layer, these are not just passive outputs; rather, they drive the kinds of representations developed through error feedback.

Dailey and Cottrell (1999) used TM to account for the development of the FFA. The model assumes two main developmental constraints: (1) infants' visual acuity is quite low in the high spatial frequencies (Teller et al., 1986); and (2) their goal is to differentiate their caregivers from each other and from the rest of the people they come in contact with. The model shows that these constraints are sufficient to drive the formation of a specialized face processing area. In order to implement the acuity constraint, they assumed separate spatial frequency input channels that were processed by a channel-specific PCA: there was a (relatively) low spatial frequency input channel and a (relatively) high spatial frequency input channel, and a separate PCA captured the covariances within each channel. By assuming separate spatial frequency input channels, they could model the developmentally appropriate input to the cortex as the low spatial frequency channel, and observe what effects that had on the model's performance. This representation can also be conceptualized as roughly modeling the left and right hemispheres: according to some theories, the right hemisphere has a relatively low spatial frequency bias and the left hemisphere has a relatively high spatial frequency bias (Sergent, 1982; Ivry and Robertson, 1998; cf. Hsiao et al., 2008; see also the next subsection). The two spatial frequency channels also had separate hidden layers before they reached the output layer (Figure 21.3b). The model assumed that the two spatial frequency networks competed for tasks through a gating network, which fed more error back to the module with the lower error (i.e. a "mixture of experts" model; Jordan and Jacobs, 1995). As shown in Figure 21.3b, the gating network mixed the hidden layers of the two spatial frequency modules and gave feedback to each module during learning in proportion to the value of the gating units. The entire network was trained through back-propagation of error with the generalized delta rule; it implemented a simple form of competition in which the gating units settled on a division of labor that minimized the network's output error. If the task being solved was best performed by the low spatial frequency network, then the gating network would learn to weight the low spatial frequency inputs to the output more highly, and the hidden units on that channel would be trained more on that task.

To examine how different learning experiences influence the development of representations, in particular the difference between basic- and subordinate-level categorization, the model was trained to either categorize four classes of 12 objects each at a basic level (i.e. books, faces, cups, and cans), or to individuate one of the classes into 12 different identities while continuing to simply categorize the other three classes of stimuli at the basic level. Consistent with behavioral data, the results showed that a strong specialization of the low spatial frequency module emerged when the model was trained to individuate faces while categorizing the other three classes of stimuli at the basic level; no other combinations of tasks and input stimuli showed a similar level of specialization. Further experiments showed why: a monolithic network trained on the low spatial frequency inputs generalized much better to new faces than a similar network trained only on the high spatial frequencies—which means that learning would proceed much faster in the low spatial frequency network. Thus, the model supported the hypothesis that something resembling a face processing "module", i.e. the FFA, could arise as a natural consequence of infants' developmental environment—poor visual acuity coupled with the goal of individuating people's faces—without being innately specified (see Johnson, Chapter 1, this volume for an alternate view).

Hemispheric lateralization in face processing

In face perception, it has been shown that a chimeric face made from two left-half faces from the viewer's perspective is usually judged more similar to the original face compared with that made from two right-half faces (Gilbert and Bakan, 1973; Brady et al., 2005; Figure 21.4). This *left-side bias* has been argued to be an indicator of right hemisphere (RH) involvement in face perception (Burt and Perrett, 1997), and may be related to visual expertise. For example, Hsiao and Cottrell (2009) found a RH bias in Chinese character experts. As noted above, fMRI studies of face processing usually find stronger FFA activation in the RH (e.g. Kanwisher et al., 1997). Similarly, electrophysiological studies of face processing usually show a stronger face-specific wave 170 ms after the stimulus onset over the RH (the so-called "N170," e.g. Rossion et al., 2003). In an expertise training study with artificial objects, Gauthier and colleagues found that an increase in holistic processing for the trained objects was correlated with increased right fusiform area activity (Gauthier et al., 1999; Gauthier and Tarr, 2002). Neuropsychological data also suggest a link between RH damage and deficits in face recognition and perception (e.g. Meadows, 1974). In short, RH lateralization in face and face-like processing has been consistently reported.

In order to account for this perceptual asymmetry phenomenon, Hsiao et al. (2008) developed a computational model that aimed to examine the fundamental processing differences between the two hemispheres, and the stage at which the information in the two hemispheres converges (cf. Dailey and Cottrell, 1999). It has been consistently reported that there is a hemispheric asymmetry in the perception of local and global features: an advantage for detecting global features when the stimuli are presented in the left visual field/RH, and an advantage for detecting local features when the stimuli are presented in the right visual field/left hemisphere (LH) (e.g. Sergent, 1982). In order to account for this hemispheric asymmetry, Ivry and Robertson (1998; cf. Sergent 1982)

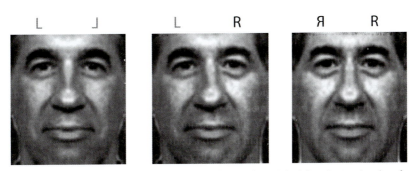

Fig. 21.4 Left chimeric, original, and right chimeric faces. The original face image is taken from the FERET database (Phillips et al., 2000).

proposed the double filtering by frequency (DFF) theory; the theory posits that information coming into the brain goes through two frequency filtering stages; stage one is an attentional selection
of the task-relevant frequency range; at stage two, the LH amplifies high frequency information,
whereas the RH amplifies low frequency information. Hsiao et al.'s (2008) hemispheric model
implemented this DFF theory.

In order to examine at what stage the information in the two hemispheres starts to converge,
Hsiao et al. (2008) compared three models with different timings of convergence (Figure 21.5).
Following the basic architecture of TM (Figure 21.3a), the model incorporated several known
observations about visual anatomy: Gabor filters simulated V1 neural responses; PCA simulated
possible information extraction processes up to the level of lateral occipital regions; the hidden
layers were by analogy with the fusiform area. With this level of abstraction, the timing of convergence may happen at three different stages: in the early convergence model, the convergence happened right after Gabor filters/V1; in the intermediate convergence model, it converged after the
PCA/information extraction stage; in the late convergence model, it had two separate hidden layers, and the convergence happened at the output layer. If the DFF manipulation was applied, it
was to the Gabor filters before the PCA stage in each model. This was done by attenuating the low
frequency Gabor filters for the LH and attenuating the high frequency Gabors for the RH.

In the simulations, two conditions were created: in the baseline condition, no frequency bias
(i.e. no DFF theory) was applied, and in the DFF condition, the information in the LH was biased
to high spatial frequency ranges whereas that in the RH was biased to low spatial frequency
ranges. The models' task was to map each face image to its identity; a localist representation was
used in the output layer, with each output node corresponding to each face identity. To examine
the models' fit to human data, the left side bias was defined as the size of the difference between
the activation of the output node representing the original face when the left chimeric face was
presented versus when the right chimeric face was presented; this activation reflected how much
the model "thinks" the all-left or all-right stimulus "looks like" the original stimulus. In the unbiased condition (no DFF theory applied), no left side bias was found, suggesting there is no a priori
bias in facial structure. In the DFF-biased condition, the early convergence model failed to produce the left side bias effect, whereas the intermediate and late convergence models did show the
effect (Figure 21.6a and b). In other words, the model showed that the combination of spatial
frequency bias *and* splitting of the information between left and right were sufficient to show the
left side bias, but neither alone can show the effect. This result suggests that the visual pathways

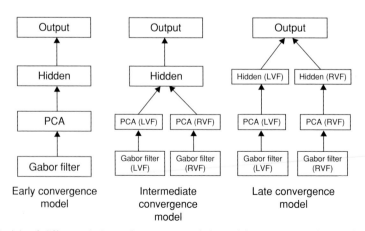

Fig. 21.5 Models of different timings of convergence (adapted from Hsiao et al., 2008).

may converge at an intermediate or late stage, at least after some information extraction has been applied to each separately; Hsiao et al. (2008) speculated that this convergence may be in the lateral occipital region in the visual stream (cf. Tootell et al., 1998). In addition, they trained the model to perform a recognition task on greebles, a novel type of object (Gauthier et al., 1998), and the results again showed that, when the DFF theory was applied, the early convergence model failed to produce the left side bias, whereas the intermediate and late convergence models did exhibit the bias (Figure 21.6c). This predicts that the left side bias will also be observed in expert object processing (cf. Hsiao and Cottrell, 2009).

Behavioral data accounted for by the model

In this section, we review some of the behavioral data accounted for by TM. We begin with facial expression recognition, as historically this is one of the first applications of our model. Next we discuss how the development of face discrimination can be accounted for solely by the PCA level of the model. Finally, we summarize a number of other experiments in modeling behavioral studies.

Facial expression processing

There has been a controversy concerning whether facial expression processing is "discrete" or "continuous." The proponents of the discrete view consider facial expressions as being perceived categorically, that is, facial expression recognition shows the operational definition of categorical perception: sharp boundaries between the categories (when subjects judge morphs between expressions) and greater discrimination of two faces along the morph continuum when they are near or cross a category boundary (Calder et al., 1996). On this view, facial expressions are placed in a category, and there are no underlying dimensions of similarity once they are categorized (but see Calder et al., 2000a, for a more nuanced view). Proponents of the continuous view point to data showing that when subjects make similarity judgments of facial expressions, and the data is subjected to a multidimensional scaling (MDS) procedure, a facial expression "circumplex" is revealed, where surprise is between happy and fear, and the other negative emotions are arranged

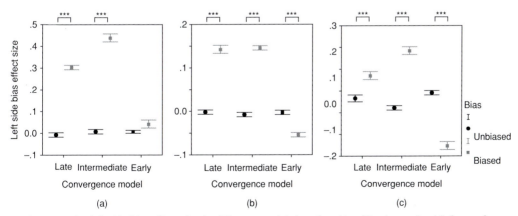

Fig. 21.6 The left side bias effect size in different models in a face identification task with faces of different expressions (left), a face identification task with faces in different lighting conditions (middle), and a greeble identification task with greebles in different lighting conditions (right). Images from Janet H. Hsiao, Danke X. Shieh, and Garrison W. Cottrell, Convergence of the Visual Field. Split: Hemispheric Modeling of face and Object Recognition. *Journal of Cognitive Neuroscience*, **20**(12), pp. 2298–2307. © 2008 by the Massachusetts Institute of Technology.

opposite happy (Russell, 1980). Under this view, facial expression perception is graded, and relies on an underlying two- or three-dimensional space, with two of the dimensions being valence and intensity.

The puzzle was intensified by Young et al. (1997), who used multiple measures from the same subjects when viewing images from a 15-way morph between the six basic emotions (six-way alternative forced choice (6-AFC), ranked choice (a second and third button push for any other emotions perceived), reaction time, discrimination and similarity measures) to reveal both data consistent with categorical perception, and data consistent with the dimensional view. For example, the ranked choice results showed that subjects were above chance at selecting the mixed-in category even at a morph level (70/30) when they were consistently picking the 70% category in the 6-AFC.

In Dailey et al. (2002), we modeled these results using a simple version of TM (Figure 21.3a with no hidden layer), and were able to fit *both* the data supporting categorical perception and the data supporting the dimensional view. We concluded that categorical perception is really the result of a simple decision process over a continuous representation (see also Ellison and Massaro, 1997, for a similar view), and that the data could be accounted for by a simple neurocomputational model trained to recognize facial expressions.

We modeled this experiment using TM trained on the six basic emotions using the Pictures of Facial Affect (POFA, Ekman and Friesen, 1976) dataset, excluding the subject "JJ," as he was the one used in the Young et al. experiment (i.e. the network in Figure 21.3a is trained with six outputs, one for each emotion, and no hidden units were used between the PCA and the outputs). We constructed image-quality morphs of JJ and tested the trained TM on them (it should be pointed out that the model had never been exposed to facial morphs or JJ), deriving the same measures from TM as were used with the human subjects (Dailey et al., 2002). For 6-AFC, we chose the most activated output unit as the model's choice. For ranked choice, we simply chose the second and third most activated outputs, and for reaction time, we used the uncertainty of the most activated output, where uncertainty is defined as the difference from 1 (the maximum possible output). The idea is that reaction time reflects certainty—an output of 0.9 will cause a faster button press than an output of 0.8. For similarity judgments (in order to apply MDS) with a model that only processes one face at a time, we presented the model with each face, and then correlated the responses of the model. Finally, to model discrimination between two faces, we use one minus the correlation (similarity). An interesting aspect of these last two measures is that they can be performed at any layer of the network, from the image pixels up to the output layer. We can then compare the results to the human data to see which layer of the model best accounts for the data. This led to some surprising results, as will be seen shortly.

First, the model finds fear the hardest expression to recognize, and often confused it with surprise, just as human subjects do. This is an emergent property of the model, since it was trained upon the majority agreed-upon category for each face. i.e. if 90% of the human subjects rated a face as surprised, and 10% rated it as fear, the model was trained to label the face as surprised. The (human) confusion between fear and surprise could therefore simply be a consequence of the similarity of the facial patterns and the categories we place them in. On this view, the reason why fear is the hardest expression to recognize is that it is not sufficiently differentiated from surprise in its appearance, rather than due to some more complex psychological account.

The model was able to account for the data consistent with categorical perception, showing high correlations ($r = 0.942$) with the human categorization responses to the morph stimuli (Figure 21.7a), and good correlations with the discrimination scores ($r = 0.65$).

The model was also able to account for the data consistent with the dimensional account. The human reaction times showed a characteristic "scalloped" shape—slower near the category boundaries and faster in the middle of a category, which Young et al. took to be inconsistent with the categorical account. Our model mirrored this (with correlation of $r = 0.677$), because of the way reaction time was modeled. The probability of a face being in a category drops smoothly as the morph moves farther away from the category, so the output goes down, and reaction time goes up. Furthermore, the ranked choice plots for the human subjects and the networks were very similar (Figure 21.7b).

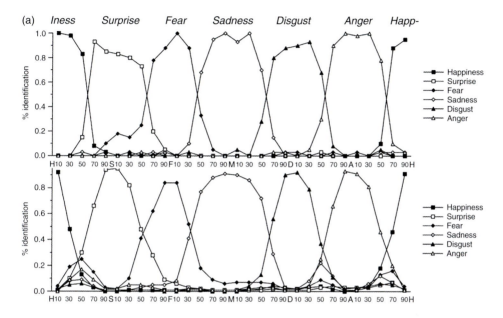

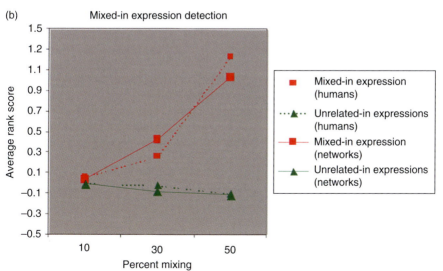

Fig. 21.7 Results of the expression recognition network. (a) Model results (bottom) versus human percentage of button push (top) for six morph sequences. (b) Model and human results for mixed-in expression detection. The data show that humans and the model both can detect the mixed-in expression at above chance levels at the 30% morph level, when both the networks and the humans are consistently rating the image as the majority (70%) expression.

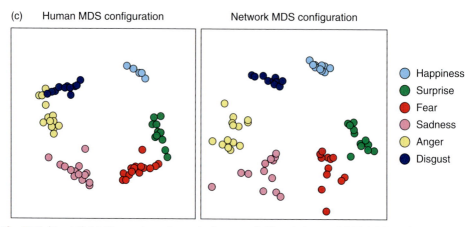

Fig. 21.7 (*Contd.*) (c) Circumplexes from the humans (left) and the model (right) based on similarity scores. The rotational orientation is meaningless. The order around the circumplex is matched by the model. Reproduced from Matthew N. Dailey, Garrison W. Cottrell, Curtis Padgett and Ralph Adolphs, 'EMPATH: A Neural Network that Categorizes Facial Expressions', *Journal of Cognitive Neuroscience*, **14**(8), pp. 1158–1173. © 2002 by the Massachusetts Institute of Technology.

A surprising result concerning the dimensional account is that the MDS of the model's *output* representation gave the same circumplex as the human data (Figure 21.7c). Hence, human similarity judgments of facial expressions can be accounted for by a simple pattern recognizer's judgment of the probability of the category, given the face, *not* by the underlying perceptual space (the PCA layer representation did not match the human circumplex as well as the output layer). This is, of course, quite counter to the categorical perception view, because that view is based on the idea of the actual *selection* of the highest likelihood category, and ignores the actual probability distribution over categories.

This model has also been used to account for cultural differences in facial expression recognition (Dailey et al., 2010). We conducted a cross-cultural facial expression recognition experiment using Japanese and American subjects viewing Japanese and American facial expressions, the first to demonstrate directly an ingroup advantage in facial expression (previous evidence was found via a meta-analysis of a number of experiments (Elfenbein and Ambady, 2002; see also Ambady and Weisbuch, Chapter 24, this volume). We then used the model to account for the ingroup advantage by training it on Japanese versus American expressions of emotion, and showed that the differences could be accounted for by experience.

The development of face processing

Face processing is typically described as holistic or configural. Holistic processing is typically taken to mean that the context of the whole face has an important contribution to processing the parts: subjects have difficulty recognizing parts of the face in isolation, and subjects have difficulty ignoring parts of the face when making judgments about another part (Tanaka and Farah, 1993). Configural processing means that subjects are sensitive to the relationships between the parts, e.g. the spacing between the eyes. These two, related, forms of processing, are characteristic of face processing, but they are somewhat oversold in the literature. People are also, of course, highly sensitive to *featural* differences between faces. Recently there has been a great deal of interest in the development of these sensitivities. In this section, we describe one such study and how we can account for the development of sensitivity to features and configuration in our model. Holistic processing can easily be captured by a model that uses whole-face template-like representations as ours does (the principal components of the Gabor filters are global representations of the face). It is interesting that this representation also captures featural differences.

The ability to discriminate faces develops throughout childhood. It has been shown that even children of 10 years of age do not achieve adult-level sensitivity to configural differences in faces (Mondloch, et al., 2002). What is the mechanism underlying this protracted developmental period? While there are likely to be a number of influences on development of face expertise, we used TM to investigate two that seemed potentially relevant. First, neuroplasticity studies have shown that changes in inputs to cortical areas lead to altered neural representations in several modalities, a result we assume carries over to changes in visual experience and hence higher level representations (Jenkins et al., 1987; Buonamono and Merzenich, 1998; Gauthier et al., 1999). Also, fMRI studies suggest that the FFA develops over many years in children (Scherf, et al., 2007). Hence, the first variable we investigate is increasing representational resources over time. Second, children meet an increasing number of people over time—first their immediate family, then classmates in elementary school, then more people in high school. It is possible that the social requirement of having to distinguish a greater number of individuals over the years drives the need to use configural information.

We investigated this question using only the first two layers of our model (Zhang and Cottrell, 2006), i.e. principal components analysis of Gabor filter representations. We simulated development qualitatively using a very simple manipulation of this preprocessing, i.e. how many people the model "knows," and how many principal components it uses to represent the data. These two variables were sufficient to account for the slower development of configural processing compared to featural processing, and how the child's performance improves with age. We trained the model on from 100 (19 individuals) to 500 faces (107 individuals) from the FERET face database (Phillips, et al., 2000), and evaluated them on the "Janes" images from Mondloch et al. (2002), which we describe shortly. Because human subjects had to discriminate the faces in that experiment, the evaluation of the model consisted of measuring the average discriminability of the face sets. We measured this at the PCA layer, using 1 minus the correlation between the representations of the faces as the discrimination measure, as in the expression recognition model. The rank order of the discriminability was then compared to the human subject data.

The Mondloch et al. (2002) images vary in several carefully controlled ways. Starting with "Jane," there are a number of variations of her face made by varying the distance between the eyes and the distance between the mouth and the nose. This is the configural set. Then, there are variations constructed by replacing her mouth or eyes with someone else's. This is the featural set. There is also a contour set, constructed by replacing the outside of her face with someone else's. Finally, there is the "cousin" set, which are simply pictures of different women of about the same age. Children ages 6, 8, and 10, as well as adults, were asked to discriminate pairs of faces, both upright and inverted. The results of children's performance on average, in order of best to worst, is: cousin > featural > contour > configural. The adult ranking is cousin > featural > configural > contour. For the inverted faces, the adult and child performance was ranked identically: featural > contour > configural (cousins were not tested in the inverted condition).

We found that in our model, when the number of the training images (and individuals) is small, the discriminability of the configural set is the lowest, which is also observed in children' performance. As the number of images increases, the discriminability of the configural set slowly catches up and exceeds that of the contour set, as observed in adults' performance. In parallel, we found that an increase of the number of components is able to account for the continuous improvement in the performance of all the Jane's sets, but does not cause a change in rank discriminability. Taken together, a "child" model exposed to a small number of people, and with a representation using a small number of resources will not discriminate faces as well as an adult, and the ranking of difficulty on the Jane's sets will mimic that of the children. An "adult" model exposed to a large number of people and with greater representational resources will have a better ability to discriminate the stimuli, and the rank order on the four sets matches that of the adults, both for upright and inverted faces. The careful reader will notice that these layers of model are *unsupervised*, so the increased representation of configural information is simply a consequence of the statistical structure of the face space as more individual faces are added, rather than the need to distinguish them, as hypothesized above.

Additional behavioral data accounted for

We do not have space to cover other behavioral effects that TM has been used to account for, hence we briefly summarize them. The model has been used to account for holistic processing effects in identity and expression, and the lack of interaction between them, as found by Calder and colleagues (Calder et al., 2000b; Cottrell et al., 2002). Of main interest here is that the model did not need separate processing pathways in order to show a lack of interaction (see Calder, this volume, for more discussion). In addition to the developmental work described above, the model has been used to account for age of acquisition effects in face processing (Lake and Cottrell, 2005). Although models of the other-race effect (ORE) have been built before (O'Toole et al., 1991), we have used our model to account for the other-race advantage in visual search (Haque and Cottrell, 2005; Levin, 2000). The basic idea of the model was that other race faces contain more information in the Shannon sense, and hence are more salient (see also (Zhang et al., 2007) for a similar account). Finally, the model has been used to account for priming effects in the discrimination of nonsense characters (McCleery et al., 2008). It had been shown that Chinese subjects primed to think of nonsense characters as a face discriminated them better than when they were primed to think of them as a Chinese character, when they differed configurally. We constructed a model virtually identical to our face processing model that recognized Chinese characters. We assumed that the priming caused the subjects to use either their face network or their Chinese character network. Since recognizing Chinese characters involves mapping similar characters (in different fonts) to the same category, it is a compressive mapping, lumping stimuli together and ignoring configural differences, while face processing is the opposite—it must differentiate between similar things (faces), and hence it involves an expansive mapping, spreading faces out in representational space, including on the basis of configural differences (see the next section for more discussion of this point). Hence when the Chinese character network is used, the nonsense characters were closer together in representational space, and more difficult to discriminate. When the face network is used, the nonsense characters are farther apart in representational space, and hence better discriminated, as in the behavioral data (McCleery et al., 2008).

The recruitment of the FFA: solving the "visual expertise mystery"

Although it remains highly controversial whether what makes faces "special" is that they are a domain of expertise or that they are faces per se (e.g. Bukach et al., 2006; McKone et al., 2007; McKone and Robbins, Chapter 9; Scott, Chapter 11, this volume), it is still of interest to account for the fMRI data on expertise learning. For example, Gauthier et al. (2000) showed that over-training in a new domain of expertise ("greebles", a novel type of object), activity in the FFA increased. They argued that the FFA's computational role may be fine level discrimination of homogeneous categories, such as faces, and as such, it becomes recruited for other expertise tasks (i.e. the expertise hypothesis). However, it is still incumbent upon modelers invested in this hypothesis to show *why* this happens mechanistically. We have called the question of why the FFA is recruited for other objects of expertise "the visual expertise mystery," and it has been a focus of research in our lab for many years.

The main result of the model, rather surprisingly to us, is that the features useful for discriminating members of a homogeneous class, whether it be faces, cups, cans, or books, are useful in discriminating members of other homogeneous classes. That is, there is nothing special about faces per se, rather, it is the fine-level discrimination process that encourages the development of universally useful features (Sugimoto and Cottrell, 2001; Joyce and Cottrell, 2004; Tong et al., 2005, 2008).

The basic assumption of the model is that (like the developmental model in Figure 21.3b) areas of cortex *compete* to solve tasks. The model assumes that there are two networks that share preprocessing up to the point of features specialized for a task (Figure 21.8). These correspond to two cortical areas that compete so that one becomes specialized for basic-level categorization (i.e. lateral occipital complex or other visual processing areas), and the other is specialized for subordinate-level (expert) categorization (i.e. the FFA). In our first simulation, similar to the model of the development of the FFA (Dailey and Cottrell, 1999; section one of this chapter), one network was trained to categorize four classes of 12 objects each (i.e. books, faces, cups, and cans) at a basic level (i.e. the basic network); the other network was trained to individuate one of the classes into its twelve identities, while continuing to simply categorize the other three classes of stimuli at the basic level (i.e. the expert network). Except for the difference in their tasks, the two networks were given identical processing resources in their hidden layers and received the same input during training. The results showed that, consistent with human data (Gauthier and Tarr, 1997), the model demonstrated the entry-level shift in reaction times, measured as the uncertainty of the output: it was just as fast for subordinate-level/expert responses as for basic-level ones (Joyce and Cottrell, 2004).

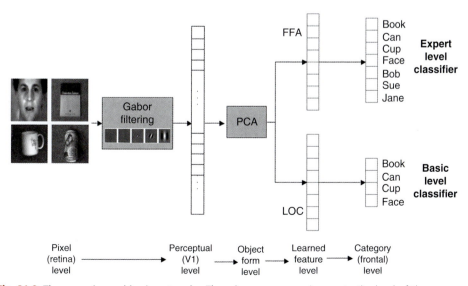

Fig. 21.8 The expertise and basic networks. They share preprocessing up to the level of the hidden units.

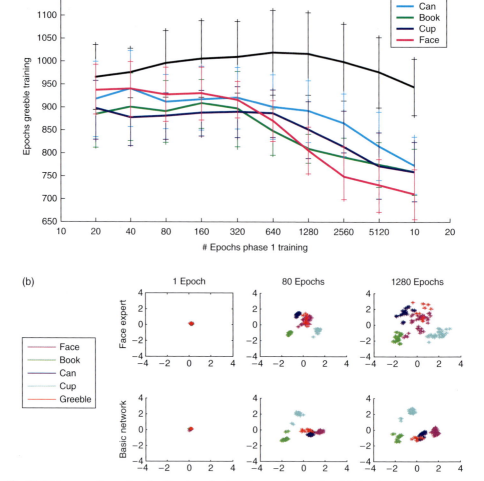

Fig. 21.9 The expertise network advantage for learning new expertise. (a) Number of epochs required to learn the greeble task versus training time on the first task; each line corresponds to a different type of expert network, except "Basic." All expert networks learn the greeble task faster. Error bars show standard errors. (b) Results of performing a PCA on the hidden unit activations of a face expert (top) and a basic level (bottom) network over training; the figure shows the second and third principal components. Note how basic-level networks grouped individual inputs while expert level networks spread individuals apart. This effect generalized to a novel category (here, greebles, in red): the greebles were differentiated by the expert network but not the basic network.

After learning the first task, the two networks were then placed in a competition to learn a new category of objects (e.g. greebles) at the subordinate/expert level. As shown in Figure 21.9a, the expert networks performed better in learning the new task than the basic network regardless of the kind of expertise that was acquired on the first task; in addition, the more training they received on the first task, the faster they learned the new task. This result suggests that in the expert networks, the features learned on the first task facilitated learning the second task.

This hypothesis is confirmed by an analysis of the hidden layer representations before training on the new task. We performed PCA of the hidden layer activations over learning of the first task, and plotted the projections of the stimuli on the second and third component in Figure 21.9b (the first component just represents the growth of the connections over time). What this shows is the position in representational space of each stimulus; the coordinates can be thought of as the firing rates of two "über-units" in response to each stimulus. As can be seen from the figure, the representations developed in the expert networks spread out the individuals in the representational space more than the basic networks did. Thus the expert networks were more sensitive to within-class variability, while the basic networks were only sensitive to between-class variability. This is because the expert networks had to differentiate among stimuli in the same class, and this lead to a representation that magnified small differences between the individuals. In contrast, the basic network needed to *ignore* differences between individuals. The red crosses shown in the figure correspond to the greeble stimuli projected into the space without training. It is clear that the reason that the greebles are learned faster is that the "spreading" transform by the expert network generalizes to the greeble stimuli. That is, the individual greebles are already differentiated by the representation even before training on them.

A common confusion concerning this result is that it seems to suggest that becoming an expert in one domain should facilitate the development of expertise in another domain. The prediction is somewhat more subtle than this. The model concerns competitions between multiple cortical areas, and what it says is that if a cortical area is used for visual expertise, that same area will be recruited for other domains of visual expertise. At some point, the amount of representational resources within the expertise area will be exhausted, and increased expertise in one domain may actually lead to *reduced* expertise in another. Indeed, it has been reported that the FFA is difficult to locate in bird experts (Kung et al., 2007). Of course, our results *do* suggest that being an expert in one domain facilitates acquiring expertise in a second domain. The problem is, it is difficult to test this prediction, since nearly every subject is a face expert to begin with. For the acquisition of expertise in a *third* domain, the predictions are less clear, and would depend on factors such as the amount of representational resources in the expertise area, the frequency of exposure in each domain, etc.

One criticism of this simulation was that the expert networks made more discriminations than the basic network, and this may have lead to more primitive representations in the basic network that were unable to do the expertise task. To respond to this criticism, Tong et al. (2005) conducted another simulation in which the number of output classes in the two networks was controlled instead of the input training set. They trained one network to categorize ten categories at the basic level (i.e. the basic network) and another network to categorize ten individual's faces at the individual level. Each network was trained on five images of each category or individual, but the networks' training sets were mutually exclusive. Then a novel category was used as a new expertise category that both networks had to learn to individuate. The results showed that the basic and expert networks took about the same length of time to train, showing that the tasks were now equally difficult. Nevertheless, the expert network still learned a new expert task more quickly, whether it was ships, swords, or lamps. Analysis of the network representations showed that this was for the same reason as in the previous simulation—representations were more spread out in the expertise network.

It is difficult to come up with a situation in which both the input images and the number of output categories for both basic and expert level categorization are controlled. However, Tran et al. (2004) conducted a simulation that used images of six letters in six different fonts, with letter categorization as the basic level task, while font categorization is the expert-level task. This is clearly an expertise discrimination, as similar-looking inputs (e.g. the letter "A" in six different fonts) must be separated into six different categories. After training two networks on these tasks, the networks were trained on greebles, and the font network was faster at learning the new expertise task. This is because the expert (font) network spread out the representation of the exemplars in the new category prior to training on them, while the letter network did not, just as in the face/object network. The conclusion is that it is the *type* of distinction that matters, not the number.[2]

In summary, these simulations consistently showed that the expert network always learned the new expertise category first, even when the first category of expertise was not faces. Further analyses showed that, compared with the basic network, the expert network spread the stimuli into broader regions of representational space; this is because subordinate-level categorization requires amplification of within-category variability. Consequently, this spreading transformation generalized to new objects and thus facilitated learning within-category identification of the new objects. In other words, the expert network had a head start in differentiating new objects from one another. Tong et al.'s study (2008) thus provides a computational explanation of why the FFA may be the location of processes for fine level discrimination of homogeneous categories that can be recruited for other expertise tasks (e.g. Gauthier et al., 2000).

The expertise hypothesis itself is, of course, controversial, and several research efforts have claimed to disprove it. For example, Rhodes et al. (2004) showed that butterfly experts showed more activation outside of FFA than within FFA. However, they also showed that the overlap with FFA increased when subjects were performing an individuation task, whether it was for objects of expertise or not. It is not surprising that there is activation outside of FFA for non-faces—after all, these objects have different shapes than faces, and activation outside of FFA could simply reflect differences in categorical, rather than individuating, representations. The increase in overlap with FFA when performing individuation tasks, however, does suggest that the FFA is playing a role in this task. The expertise hypothesis does not claim that it is only FFA that is activated by objects of expertise, nor does it claim that the FFA will be equally activated by faces and other objects of expertise. Hence we do not see a conflict between our model and these results.

The Standard Model, fMRI, and face discrimination

Although we have focused (perhaps overly so) on our own models, as noted in the introduction, there are models that are more neurophysiologically plausible, such as the Riesenhuber and Poggio (1999) HMAX model (Figure 21.2), often called the Standard Model (TSM). Again, the reason this is called the Standard Model is that it is based on the standard interpretation in neuroscience of what neurons in V1 (simple and complex) and V2 are thought to be doing. While TSM has for the most part been applied to modeling object recognition, it has also been applied to face processing, where similar points to ours have been made. For example, in Jiang et al. (2006), they show that the model does not require any special mechanism for face processing—it is just another form of object recognition. The difference between faces and objects in TSM is a quantitative one: units tuned to faces have more narrow tuning profiles than object-tuned units, due to the requirement to differentiate them from one another, leading to a sparse representation of faces (in this context, *sparse* means that few units are activated by any face).

Jiang et al. use TSM to model a face discrimination experiment in which faces vary either by configural or featural changes in the "different" condition. Complementary to our model, where holistic representations were shown to be sufficient to discriminate featural changes

---

[2] Or to put it another way, it is the distinction of type that matters, not the letters!

(Cottrell, et al., 2002), Jiang et al. were concerned with whether a model based on features could show sensitivity to configural differences in faces. The model is then used to make predictions concerning an fMRI experiment with facial morphs, which were confirmed by human experiments.

Jiang et al. model the fusiform face area with 180 view tuned units (VTUs, see Figure 21.2). These units are created by presenting the model with 180 training faces, and a radial basis function[3] unit is created that is tuned to each face by setting its weight vector to the pattern of activation on the C2 units. The set of faces used in the behavioral experiment is separate from the ones used to create the VTUs. These faces produce a pattern of activation across the 180 VTUs, depending on how similar the faces are to the training faces. As in TM, in order to model a discrimination experiment in a model that processes one face at a time, they assume that subjects store the activity pattern of the faces engendered on the VTUs, and compute the Euclidean distance between them. Unlike our model, one of the parameters of TSM is the number of elements of the activity pattern that are stored. Using only the most active units is seen as an efficient way to use memory. Also, since the model would never make errors when shown the same face image twice, noise is added to the units' activities, so that the model is capable of making mistakes on "same" trials. The standard deviation of this noise is one of the parameters of the model.

In order to fit the model to the human discrimination data, Jiang et al. use a brute force search through parameter space. The parameters are: (1) the number of afferents to the face units from the C2 units; (2) the standard deviation of the face units; (3) the number of unit activations stored in memory for face discrimination tasks; (4) the size of the noise variance used in storing the first face responses; and (5) the threshold for determining "same." The first two parameters constrain the tuning specificity of the face units—a small standard deviation results in tighter tuning, whereas a smaller number of afferents results in broader tuning. They find 35 sets of parameters that produce data that are not significantly different from the subject data, and the 35 networks' data are within the error bars of the human data for featural changes, configural changes, and inverted faces. This procedure achieves their goal of showing that their feature-based model is capable of producing data consistent with subject behavior with configurally-manipulated faces. The results are telling: the model predicts that face units will be relatively tightly tuned, with standard deviations of about 0.1, with connections to less than half the C2 units. Of note, the number of stored activations for comparing two faces comes out to be less than 10, suggesting only a very sparse representation of a face needs to be stored in memory in a discrimination task. To show this is a face-specific result, a model fit to an additional experiment using cars as stimuli for the human subjects required more broadly tuned units. Note that this can be seen as a similar story to the one we told with our model above: a small number of highly specific units fire for each face, which means that they will be spread out in representational space, whereas for a category like cars, broadly-tuned units will lead to a similar set of units being activated for most cars.

Since the model was directly fit to the data, it is important to show that the model "as is" can predict new data. Hence, to validate the model, Jiang et al. show that the same 35 networks with no further tuning can predict fMRI rapid adaptation (fMRI-RA) data on a completely different set of faces. The model and the human subjects are presented with morphed faces of varying distances from a set of prototypes. In a rapid adaptation paradigm, the BOLD response to one image is compared to the BOLD response to a different image presented immediately after the first.

---

[3] A radial basis function unit is a unit with a circular Gaussian response function; hence any deviation from its mean in any direction reduces the response only based on the distance from the mean. The mean for each unit is set to the responses of units at the previous layer (C2 units) for that unit's face. Tuning is set by the standard deviation of the Gaussian and by setting some components of the mean to 0.

If the BOLD response adapts, that is, it decreases from the presentation of the first image, this suggests that the two images are represented by a similar population of neurons. If the BOLD response recovers, then this suggests that they use a different population of neurons. The model predicted at what point the difference in BOLD adaptation response would asymptote. In the model, at some point, a completely separate population of units is activated by the two faces, so no further adaptation can occur. This prediction was confirmed. Importantly, this prediction did *not* follow from parameter sets that did not fit the behavioral data. Finally, they also performed a face discrimination task on the faces used in the scanner, and showed that the model's correlation with the human discrimination performance was significantly better when only the maximally activated units (less than 10) were used in the comparisons, as opposed to using all of the 180 unit activations. This finding supports the sparse representation prediction of the model.

Summary and conclusions

As noted at the outset, computational modeling is an important tool in trying to understand the nature of face representation and processing. As we have shown in this chapter, models can be manipulated in ways people cannot, in order to shed light on such questions as whether faces are special. We have shown here that, according to our model, at least, faces are only special to the extent that they are a class of stimuli for which we must discriminate individual members. This fine-level discrimination task requires transformations that separate representations of similar objects, and at least in our model, this transformation generalizes to novel objects. Hence when someone learns a new domain of expertise, this region of cortex is used to bootstrap the process of discriminating the new class.

Models can also be analyzed in ways that (currently) human brains cannot—down to the single-unit level. This kind of analysis can lead to predictions that are difficult to conceive of in the absence of a concrete model. An example from this chapter is the way in which Jiang et al. (2006) used their model to compare the behavioral predictions of sparse versus dense representations to suggest that representations in FFA are sparse. Another example is the prediction from the Dailey et al. (2002) EMPATH model that the similarity structure of facial expressions can be captured by the similarity of categorical representations.

We also discussed two ways in which models differ, in their degree of realism and their methods of parameter setting. The models we focused on the most here, TM and TSM, differ considerably along these dimensions, with TSM being more neurally realistic, while requiring a search for parameters to fit the data, and TM being less realistic, but using learning on a realistic task to set the parameters. While the use of backpropagation generally leads to the criticism of biological implausibility, more biologically plausible techniques for learning, such as those used in Leabra (O'Reilly and Munakata, 2000) should eventually lead to models that are biologically plausible in both their learning methods and their neural processing mechanisms.

One future direction, then, might be to first use the Leabra model to replicate many of the results in this chapter, extending the modeling effort to include interactions between the dorsal pathway and the ventral pathway. Since the dorsal pathway is believed by many to include a salience map, this approach could therefore add new dimensions to the modeling effort by explicating the role of attention in object and face recognition. This leads to a second observation and direction for future research: the models described here are all wrong in a fundamental way, in that they do not sample the environment with the eye movements that are required by a foveated retina. Indeed, eye movements have been shown to be functional in face recognition (Hsiao and Cottrell, 2009). Since we make about three eye movements per second, or about 173,000 per day, it seems important to take this factor into consideration when modeling human perception.

We look forward to new research that attempts to understand object and face perception in the light of such constraints.

Acknowledgments

This work was supported in part by NSF grant #SBE 0542013 to GWC for the Temporal Dynamics of Learning Center, an NSF Science of Learning Center; NIMH grant MH57075 to GWC; a grant by the James S. McDonnell Foundation to the Perceptual Expertise Network (Isabel Gauthier, PI); and the Research Grant Council of Hong Kong projects #HKU 744509H and #HKU 745210 to J.H. Hsiao.

References

Brady, N., Campbell, M., and Flaherty, M. (2005). Perceptual asymmetries are preserved in memory for highly familiar faces of self and friend. *Brain and Cognition*, **58**, 334–342.

Bruce, V. and Young, A. (1986). Understanding face recognition. *British Journal of Psychology*, **77**, 305–327.

Bukach, C.M., Gauthier, I., and Tarr, M. J. (2006). Beyond faces and modularity: the power of an expertise framework. *Trends in Cognitive Sciences*, **10**, 159–166.

Buonomano, D.V. and Merzenich, M.M. (1998). Cortical plasticity: From synapses to maps. *Annual Review of Neuroscience* **21**, 149–186.

Burt, D.M. and Perrett, D.I. (1997). Perceptual asymmetries in judgments of facial attractiveness, age, gender, speech and expression. *Neuropsychologia*, **35**, 685–693.

Cadieu, C., Kouh, M., Pasupathy, A., Conner, C., Riesenhuber, M., and Poggio, T.A. (2007). A Model of V4 Shape Selectivity and Invariance. *Journal of Neurophysiology*, **98**, 1733–1750.

Calder, A., Young, A., Perrett, D., Etcoff, N., and Rowland, D. (1996). Categorical perception of morphed facial expressions. *Visual Cognition*, **3**, 81–117.

Calder, A.J., Rowland, D., Young, A.W., Nimmo-Smith, I., Keane, J. and Perrett, D.I. (2000a) Caricaturing facial expressions. *Cognition*, **76**, 105–46.

Calder, A.J., Young, A., Keane, J., and Dean, M. (2000b). Configural information in facial perception. *Journal of Experimental Psychology: Human Perception and Performance*, **26**, 527–551.

Cottrell, G.W. and Metcalfe, J. (1991). EMPATH: Face, gender and emotion recognition using holons. In R.P. Lippman, J. Moody, and D.S. Touretzky (eds.), *Advances in Neural Information Processing Systems Vol. 3*, pp. 564–571. San Mateo, CA: Morgan Kaufmann.

Cottrell, G.W., Branson, K. and Calder, A.J. (2002). Do expression and identity need separate representations? In *Proceedings of the 24th Annual Cognitive Science Conference*, pp. 238–243, Fairfax, Virginia. Mahwah, NJ: Lawrence Erlbaum.

Dailey, M.N. and Cottrell, G.W. (1999). Organization of face and object recognition in modular neural network models. *Neural Networks*, **12**, 1053–1073.

Dailey, M.N., Cottrell, G.W., Padgett, C., and Adolphs, R. (2002). EMPATH: A neural network that categorizes facial expressions. *Journal of Cognitive Neuroscience*, **14**, 1158–1173.

Dailey, M.N., Joyce, C.A., Lyons, M.J., Kamachi, M., Ishi, H., Gyoba, J. and Cottrell, G.W. (2010). Evidence and a computational explanation of cultural differences in facial expression recognition. *Emotion*, **10**, 874–893.

Daugman, J.G. (1985). Uncertainty relation for resolution in space, spatial frequency, and orientation optimized by two-dimensional visual cortical filters. *Journal of the Optical Society of America A*, **2**, 1160–1169.

Ekman, P. and Friesen, W. (1976). *Pictures of Facial Affect*. Palo Alto, CA: Consulting Psychologists.

Elfenbein, H. and Ambady, N. (2002). On the universality and cultural specificity of emotion recognition: A meta-analysis. *Psychological Bulletin*, **128**, 203–235.

Ellison, J.W. and Massaro, D.W. (1997). Featural evaluation, integration, and judgement of facial affect. *Journal of Experimental Psychology: Human Perception and Performance*, **23**, 213–226.

Fleming, M. and Cottrell, G.W. (1990). Categorization of faces using unsupervised feature extraction. *Proceedings of the International Joint Conference on Neural Networks*, **2**, 65–70.

Gauthier, I., Skudlarski, P., Gore, J.C., and Anderson, A.W. (2000). Expertise for cars and birds recruits brain areas involved in face recognition. *Nature Neuroscience*, **3**, 191–197.

Gauthier, I. and Tarr, M.J. (1997). Becoming a 'greeble' expert: Exploring mechanisms for face recognition. *Vision Research*, **37**, 1673–1682.

Gauthier, I. and Tarr, M.J. (2002). Unraveling mechanisms for expert object recognition: bridging brain activity and behavior. *Journal of Experimental Psychology: Human Perception and Performance*, **28**, 431–446.

Gauthier, I., Tarr, M.J., Anderson, A.W., Skudlarski, P., and Gore, JC. (1999). Activation of the middle fusiform 'face area' increases with expertise in recognizing novel objects. *Nature Neuroscience*, **2**, 568–573.

Gauthier, I., Williams, P., Tarr, M.J., and Tanaka, J. (1998). Training 'Greeble' experts: A framework for studying expert object recognition processes. *Vision Research*, **38**, 2401–2428.

Gilbert, C. and Bakan, P. (1973). Visual asymmetry in perception of faces. *Neuropsychologia*, **11**, 355–362.

Haque, A. and Cottrell, G.W. (2005). Modeling the other race advantage with PCA. In *Proceedings of the 27th Annual Cognitive Science Conference*, pp. 899–904, La Stresa, Italy. Mahwah, NJ: Lawrence Erlbaum.

Hsiao, J.H. and Cottrell, G.W. (2009). Not all visual expertise is holistic, but it may be leftist: The case of Chinese character recognition. *Psychological Science*, **20**, 455–463.

Hsiao, J.H., Shieh, D.X., and Cottrell, G.W. (2008). Convergence of the visual field split: Hemispheric modeling of face and object recognition. *Journal of Cognitive Neuroscience*, **20**, 2298–2307.

Ivry, R.B. and Robertson, L.C. (1998). *The two sides of perception*. Cambridge, MA: MIT.

Jiang, X., Rosen, E., Zeffiro, T., VanMeter, J., Blanz, V., and Riesenhuber, M. (2006). Evaluation of a shape-based model of human face discrimination using fMRI and behavioral techniques. *Neuron*, **50**, 159–172.

Jenkins, W.M., Merzenich, M.M., and Ochs, M.T. (1987). Behaviorally controlled differential use of restricted hand surfaces induce changes in the cortical representation of the hand in area 3b of adult owl monkeys., *Society for Neuroscience*, **10**, 665.

Jordan, M. and Jacobs, R. (1995). Modular and hierarchical learning systems. In M. Arbib (ed.) *The Handbook of brain theory and neural networks*, Cambridge, MA: MIT Press.

Joyce, C. and Cottrell, G.W. (2004). Solving the visual expertise mystery. In H. Bowman and C. Labiouse (eds.) *Connectionist models of cognition and perception II: Proceedings of the eighth neural computation and psychology workshop*. World Scientific.

Kanwisher, N., McDermott, J. and Chun, M.M. (1997). The fusiform face area: a module in human extrastriate cortex specialized for face perception. *Journal of Neuroscience*, **17**, 4302–4311.

Kung, C-C., Ellis, C., and Tarr, M.J. (2007). Dynamic reorganization of fusiform gyrus: long-term bird expertise reduces face selectivity. Poster presented at the Cognitive Neuroscience Society (CNS) Annual Meeting, New York.

Lades, M., Vorbruggen, J.C., Buhmann, J., *et al* (1993). Distortion invariant object recognition in the dynamic link architecture. *IEEE Transactions on Computers*, **42**, 300–311.

Lake, B.M. and Cottrell, G.W. (2005). Age of Acquisition in Facial Identification: A connectionist approach. In *Proceedings of the 27th Annual Cognitive Science Conference*, pp. 1236–1241, La Stresa, Italy. Mahwah, NJ: Lawrence Erlbaum,

Levin, D.T. (2000). Race as a visual feature: using visual search and perceptual discrimination tasks to understand face categories and the cross-race recognition deficit. *Journal of Experimental Psychology: General*, **129**, 559–574.

McCleery, J.P., Zhang, L., Ge, L., *et al.* (2008). The roles of visual expertise and visual input in the face inversion effect: Behavioral and neurocomputational evidence. *Vision Research*, **48**, 703–715.

McKone, E., Kanwisher, N., and Duchaine, B.C. (2007). Can generic expertise explain special processing for faces? *Trends in Cognitive Sciences*, **11**, 8–15.

Meadows, J.C. (1974). The anatomical basis of prosopagnosia. *Journal of Neurology, Neurosurgery & Psychiatry*, **37**, 489–501.

Mondloch, C.J., Grand, R.L. and Maurer, D. (2002). Configural face processing develops more slowly than featural face processing. *Perception*, **31**, 553–566.

O'Reilly, R. and Munakata, Y. (2000). *Computational Explorations in Cognitive Neuroscience.* Cambridge, MA: MIT Press.

O'Toole, A.J., Deffenbacher, K.A., Abdi, H., and Bartlett, J.C. (1991). Simulation of 'other-race effect' as a problem in perceptual learning. *Connection Science,* **3**, 163–178.

Palmeri, T.J. and Gauthier, I. (2004). Visual object understanding. *Nature Reviews Neuroscience,* **5**, 291–303.

Phillips, P.J., Moon, H., Rauss, P.J., and Rizvi, S. (2000). The FERET evaluation methodology for face recognition algorithms. *IEEE Transactions on Pattern Analysis and Machine Intelligence,* **22**, 1090–1104.

Rhodes, G., Byatt, G., Michie, P.T., and Puce, A. (2004). Is the Fusiform Face Area Specialized for Faces, Individuation, or Expert Individuation? *Journal of Cognitive Neuroscience* **16**, 189–203.

Riesenhuber, M. and Poggio, T. (1999). Hierarchical Models of Object Recognition in Cortex. *Nature Neuroscience,* **2**, 1019–1025.

Rossion, B., Joyce, C.A., Cottrell, G.W., and Tarr, M.J. (2003). Early lateralization and orientation tuning for face, word, and object processing in the visual cortex. *Neuroimage,* **20**, 1609–1624.

Russell, J.A. (1980). A circumplex model of affect. *Journal of Personality and Social Psychology,* **39**, 1161–1178.

Sanger, T.D. (1989). Optimal unsupervised learning in a single-layer linear feed forward neural network. *Neural Networks,* **2**, 459–473.

Scherf, K.S., Behrmann, M., Humphreys, K. and Luna, B. (2007). Visual category-selectivity for faces, places, and objects emerges along different developmental trajectories. *Developmental Science,* **10**, F15–F30.

Sergent, J. (1982). The cerebral balance of power: Confrontation or cooperation? *Journal of Experimental Psychology: Human Perception and Performance,* **8**, 253–272.

Sugimoto, M., and Cottrell, G.W. (2001). Visual expertise is a general skill. In *Proceedings of the 23rd Annual Cognitive Science Conference,* pp. 994–999. Mahwah, NJ: Lawrence Erlbaum.

Tanaka, J.W. and Farah, M.J. (1993). Parts and wholes in face recognition. *Quarterly Journal of Experimental Psychology,* **46A**, 225–245.

Teller, D., McDonald, M., Preston, K., Sebris, S., and Dobson, V. (1986). Assessment of visual acuity in infants and children: the acuity card procedure. *Developmental Medicine and Child Neurology,* **28**, 779–789.

Tong, M.H., Joyce, C.A. and W. Cottrell, G.W. (2005). Are Greebles special? Or, why the Fusiform Fish Area (if we had one) would be recruited for sword expertise. *Proceedings of the 27th Annual Cognitive Science Conference.* Mahwah, NJ: Lawrence Erlbaum.

Tong, M.H., Joyce, C.A., and Cottrell, G.W. (2008). Why is the fusiform face area recruited for novel categories of expertise? A neurocomputational investigation. *Brain Research,* **1202**, 14–24.

Tootell, R.B.H., Mendola, J.D., Hadjikhani, N.K., Liu, A.K., and Dale, A.M. (1998). The representation of the ipsilateral visual field in human cerebral cortex. *The Proceedings of the National Academy of Sciences USA,* **95**, 818–824.

Tran, B., Joyce, C.A., and Cottrell, G.W. (2004). Visual expertise depends on how you slice the space. *Proceedings of the 26th Annual Conference of the Cognitive Science Conference.* Mahwah, NJ: Lawrence Erlbaum.

Young, A.W., Rowland, D., Calder, A.J., Etcoff, N.L., Seth, A., and Perrett, D.I. (1997). Facial expression megamix: Tests of dimensional and category accounts of emotion recognition. *Cognition,* **63**, 271–313.

Zhang, L. and Cottrell, G. (2006). Look Ma! No network: PCA of Gabor filters models the development of face discrimination. In *Proceedings of the 28th Annual Cognitive Science Conference,* Vancouver, BC, Canada. Mahwah, NJ: Lawrence Erlbaum.

Zhang, L., Tong, M.H., and Cottrell, G.W. (2007). Information attracts attention: A probabilistic account of the cross-race advantage in visual search. In *Proceedings of the 29th Annual Cognitive Science Society Meeting,* Nashville, TN. Mahwah, NJ: Lawrence Erlbaum.

Part III

Reading Faces

Chapter 22

Does Facial Identity and Facial Expression Recognition Involve Separate Visual Routes?

Andrew J. Calder

The idea that facial identity and facial expression are processed by separate visual routes has dominated face research for over 20 years and is at the heart of two prominent models of face perception. The Bruce and Young (1986) model constitutes an entirely functional or cognitive account, whereas Haxby et al. (2000) outlined a neuroanatomical framework (Figure 22.1). Both models contain a separate route for facial identity but differ in terms of the specificity of the expression route. In the Bruce and Young (1986) model, facial expressions are processed by a route dedicated to this facial property. By contrast, Haxby et al. (2000) proposed that the visual analysis of all "changeable" or dynamic facial properties, such as facial expressions, lipspeech, and eye gaze, are processed by a common anatomical route involving the superior temporal sulcus (STS), whereas a ventral temporal route, including the lateral fusiform gyrus, underlies the visual analysis of invariant (comparatively non-changeable) facial properties, such as identity. They further suggested that the two routes feed into an "extended" system that includes neural mechanisms involved in other cognitive processes that act in concert with the "core" face perception regions (inferior occipital gryrus, STS, and fusiform gyrus) to support the recognition of different facial cues (Figure 22.1); see Haxby and Gobbini (Chapter 6, this volume).

Evidence of some form of dissociation between facial identity and expression recognition comes from multiple sources, including cognitive studies of healthy volunteers (Bruce, 1986; Calder et al., 2000c; Campbell et al., 1996; Young et al., 1986), neuroimaging (George et al., 1993; Sergent et al., 1994; Winston et al., 2004), studies of brain-injured participants (Etcoff, 1984; Tranel et al., 1988; Young et al., 1993), and single-cell recording in non-human primates (Hasselmo et al., 1989). Hence, the idea that certain aspects of the mechanisms involved in recognizing expression and identity from the face are dissociable is not at issue. Rather, Andy Young and myself suggested that the more appropriate question is at what level does this dissociation occur (Calder and Young, 2005)? In particular, do the mechanisms underlying facial identity and facial expression recognition bifurcate at an early stage of processing, leading to separate *visual* routes underlying the perception and representation of each facial property as proposed by current models of face perception (Bruce and Young, 1986; Haxby et al., 2000), or does the bifurcation occur after the stage coding their visual representation, at a level corresponding to the extended system in Haxby et al.'s (2000) model? In this chapter I explore this issue further, drawing on research from multiple areas of face research.

I start by considering how research on the image-based analysis of facial images has informed this debate by demonstrating that a single representational system for facial identity and facial expression is not only computationally viable, but can simulate existing cognitive data demonstrating apparent dissociable processing of these two facial properties. In line with the

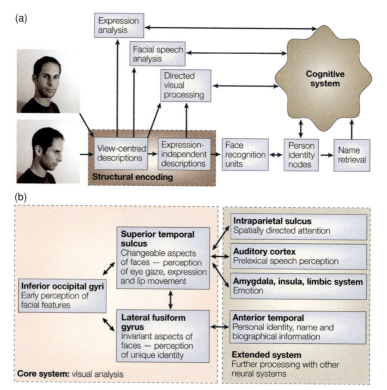

Fig. 22.1 (a) Bruce and Young's (1986) functional model of face processing. (b) Haxby, Hoffman, and Gobbini's (2000) distributed neural system for face perception. Part (a) modified with permission from the *British Journal of Psychology*, ©The British Psychological Society, and Nature Publishing Group. Part (b) Reprinted from *Trends in Cognitive Sciences*, **4**(6), Haxby, Hoffman, and Gobbini, The distributed human neural system for face perception, © 2000, with permission from Elsevier.

idea of a common representational framework, I discuss the increasing number of cognitive studies that provide support for this view. Next, I consider neuropsychological case studies of brain-injured patients and conclude that they provide, at best, limited evidence for separate visual routes processing facial identity and facial expression. Finally, I consider neuroimaging studies addressing both facial identity and facial expression processing which, contrary to the prevailing view, show that the fusiform gyrus contributes to the recognition of both facial properties. I conclude that research continues to reinforce our proposal that a common visual framework supports the representation of at least some aspects of facial identity and facial expression (Calder and Young, 2005).

Image-based analysis of faces

Researchers have commented that separate visual routes for facial identity and expression perception are required to avoid interference between the two facial properties. Work using image-based analysis techniques, such as principal component analysis (PCA) of pixel information (Calder et al., 2001) or the output of Gabor wavelets filters (Cottrell et al., 2002), speaks directly to the validity, or rather invalidity, of this conjecture by demonstrating that accurate recognition of facial expression and facial identity can be achieved by a single visuoperceptual system coding both facial characteristics. Of particular relevance, these studies also show that a single representational framework can produce an effective simulation of the apparent dissociable processing of these facial properties (Calder et al., 2001; Calder and Young, 2005; Cottrell et al., 2002). This builds on earlier research showing that image-based analysis techniques, such as PCA, independent component analysis (ICA), and Gabor wavelets, can reliably categorize a face's identity, expression, sex, race, and so on (Burton et al., 1999; Calder et al., 2001; O'Toole et al., 1993, 1994; Padgett and Cottrell, 1995; Turk and Pentland, 1991). Moreover, models based on image-based analysis techniques can simulate a number of face perception phenomena discussed in this volume, such as the composite illusion, a demonstration of holistic processing of faces (Cottrell et al., 2002); distinctiveness effects, showing that more distinctive faces are more readily recognized than typical faces (Burton et al., 1999; Hancock et al., 1996; O'Toole et al., 1994); the caricature effect, which demonstrates that exaggerating the distinctive features of faces can facilitate their recognition (Costen et al., 1995; Deffenbacher et al., 1998); and the other-race effect, the phenomenon that own-race faces are more readily discriminated or recognized than faces from other races (O'Toole et al., 1994); further discussion of image-based techniques can be found in the chapters by O'Toole (Chapter 2), Cottrell and Hsiao (Chapter 21), and Stewart Bartlett and Whitehill (Chapter 25) in this volume.

Before considering this approach any further, it is worth outlining briefly how techniques such as PCA are applied to the image-based analysis of faces. PCA and similar procedures attempt to describe or recode complex high-dimensional facial images in terms of a smaller set of principal components (PCs) that capture the relationships or correlations among sets of dimensions in the original faces. The original dimensions often comprise the pixel intensities of a standardized set of faces. For example, facial images made up of 100×200 pixels are originally represented by 20,000 dimensions. PCA identifies correlations between the pixel intensities so that each face can be recoded in terms of the weighted sum of a smaller number of PCs or eigenvectors (aka "eigenfaces"). In this sense, PCA recodes faces from a high-dimensional space (e.g. 20,000 pixel intensities) to a low-dimensional space (e.g. 20 to 50 eigenfaces). Because the eigenfaces have the same dimensionality as the original starting images, they can be displayed as the sorts of ghost-like facial images shown in Figure 22.2. This illustrates the first eight eigenfaces extracted from a PCA

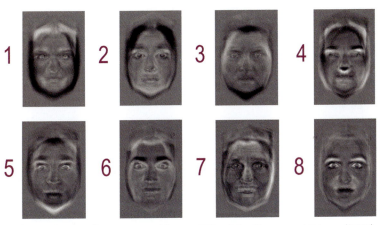

Fig. 22.2 The first eight eigenfaces extracted from a PCA of the Ekman and Friesen (1976) pictures of facial affect series. Reprinted from *Vision Research*, **41**(9), Calder, Burton, Miller, Young, Akamatsu, A principal component analysis of facial expressions © 2001, with permission from Elsevier.

of the Ekman and Friesen (1976) pictures of facial affect series, a standardized, widely used set that contains examples of facial expressions associated with six basic emotions (happiness, sadness, anger, fear, disgust, and surprise) plus neutral, "expressionless" faces.

Following the PCA, each face is associated with a component value for each PC. Submitting these data to additional statistical analysis, such as linear discriminant analysis (LDA), can provide a measure of how well the PCs discriminate between the faces' expression, identity, or sex. Using this procedure, Calder and colleagues showed that the PCA system does surprisingly well at discriminating exemplars of all three facial properties (Calder et al., 2001). Confusion matrices summarizing categorization of facial expressions by human participants and by a LDA of PCA data shows that their overall levels of performance are highly similar (Table 22.1). Moreover, for both matrices the most frequently selected label for each expression category is the intended emotion (i.e. the diagonal), and the patterns of confusions are also similar. For example, both matrices show that anger and disgust are confused with one another, as are sadness and neutral, and

Table 22.1 Confusion matrices for the Ekman and Friesen (1976) pictures of facial affect series. The top panel shows human participants' categorization of exemplars of seven facial expressions (vertical) using seven emotion labels (horizontal). The bottom panel shows the results of linear discriminant analyses (LDA) in which the same facial expressions are categorized on the basis of the faces' component values derived from a PCA of their pixel intensities and shape. Reprinted from *Vision Research*, **41**(9), Calder, Burton, Miller, Young, Akamatsu, A principal component analysis of facial expressions © 2001, with permission from Elsevier

	Human data						
	Anger	**Disgust**	**Fear**	**Happy**	**Neutral**	**Sad**	**Surprise**
Anger	**73%**	10%	2%	–	6%	4%	5%
Disgust	15%	**79%**	–	–	3%	1%	1%
Fear	1%	2%	**76%**	–	1%	2%	18%
Happy	–	–	–	**98%**	2%	–	–
Neutral	4%	1%	–	3%	**88%**	3%	1%
Sad	1%	8%	5%	–	9%	**74%**	3%
Surprise	–	–	10%	1%	–	–	**89%**
				Total correct		**82%**	

	PCA						
	Anger	**Disgust**	**Fear**	**Happy**	**Neutral**	**Sad**	**Surprise**
Anger	**86%**	14%	–	–	–	–	–
Disgust	17%	**72%**	–	11%	–	–	–
Fear	–	–	**97%**	3%	–	–	–
Happy	–	–	–	**98%**	2%	–	–
Neutral	–	–	–	1%	**69%**	23%	7%
Sad	–	–	–	2%	26%	**72%**	–
Surprise	–	–	6%	–	2%	–	**92%**
				Total correct		**84%**	

surprise is mistaken for fear. Unlike human participants, the LDA did not mistake fear for surprise, perhaps partly due to the system's superior categorization of fear expressions.

The particular advantage of techniques such as PCA is that they identify statistical regularities that are inherent in the input starting images with minimal assumptions. The PCA has no knowledge regarding which faces are displaying angry, sad, or happy expressions, etc., or their sex or identity. To this extent it is a "dumb" system, identifying commonalities between the statistical structures of different facial images without explicit reference to specific facial categories. PCA therefore provides an objective method of investigating the extent to which specific facial properties, such as identity, expression and sex, are represented by separate or shared visual features. To address this formally, we identified the 10 most important PCs for categorizing each of these three facial characteristics (Calder et al., 2001). Restricting the LDAs to information from these 10 PCs produced good categorization of all three. As shown in Figure 22.3 there was some overlap in the PCs identified for categorizing expression and identity (10%), or expression and sex (10%), and more substantial overlap for identity and sex (60%). Allowing the analyses to select more (14) PCs produced improved recognition rates and an increased overlap in the PCs coding both facial expression and facial identity (36%) (Figure 22.3). Further LDAs showed that good facial expression categorization could be achieved when the analysis was restricted to the 10 most important PCs for facial identity and *vice versa*, providing additional evidence that the two facial properties have overlapping visual features (Calder et al., 2001). By analogy then, we might infer that any process the brain uses to map regularities in the input image could deliver equivalent results, with a single multidimensional framework coding the visual representation of both facial identity and facial expression. This is not to say that the brain "does PCA," but rather that a form of linearized compact coding (analogous to PCA) provides a plausible psychological mechanism for the visual analysis and representation of different facial characteristics (identity, expression, sex, and race, etc.).

Another way to think about this framework is in terms of the "face space" metaphor, in which faces are coded as vectors in a multidimensional space, with the dimensions coding different facial features (Valentine, 1991; Valentine and Endo, 1992). Face space is generally restricted to the representation of facial identity, perhaps partly due to the prevailing idea that facial identity and facial expression are coded by distinct visual routes. However, PCA offers a suitable statistical

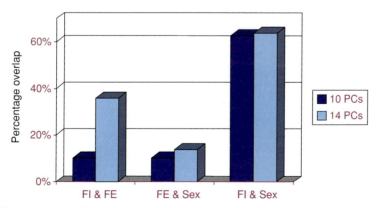

Fig. 22.3 The percentage of overlap between the 10 or 14 most important principal components (PCs) for categorizing the identity, expression and sex from faces. The overlap for the three pairs of facial properties is plotted separately; facial identity and facial expression (FI & FE), facial expression and sex (FE & Sex), and facial identity and sex (FI & Sex).

metaphor to extend the concept of face space to the representation of facial expression and indeed all facial properties, with the PCs forming the dimensions of face space (Calder et al., 2001). In this type of system, Bruce and Young's (1986) concept of a face recognition unit (FRU; i.e. representations of individual facial identities) could be conceived as a separate cluster of exemplars of the same identity: in other words, multiple representations of a single facial identity resulting from multiple encounters, for example. More specifically, these same-identity exemplars would form a densely packed cluster on dimensions important for coding facial identity, as opposed to all dimensions that might include those that are more important for facial expression, sex, race, and so on. Similarly, exemplars of the same expression would form a cluster on dimensions that are important for coding facial expressions; although as discussed, some dimensions are relevant to both facial identity and expression. In other words, the space would consist of high-density regions of the same identity or same expression interspersed with areas of low density.

We suggested that this sort of framework should be able to account for categorical perception of facial expression and facial identity (Calder et al., 2000b) whereby morphed or blended continua between two different expressions (posed by the same identity) or two identities (showing the same expression) are perceived in a stepwise, as opposed to continuous fashion. For example, in the case of facial expression continua, the morphs at one end of a continuum are perceived consistently as one expression, while the morphs at the other end are perceived as a second expression, with a distinct category boundary separating the two (Calder et al., 1996b; Young et al., 1997). Indeed, Cottrell and colleagues (Dailey et al., 2002) have shown that their EMPATH (EMotion PATtern recognition using Holons) model can produce an effective simulation of human data showing categorical perception of facial expressions (Young et al., 1997). In EMPATH, the visual representations of facial expressions are coded in a multidimensional space derived from a PCA of the output of Gabor filters placed over each facial image, as opposed to a PCA of pixel intensities used by Calder et al. (2001). The output of the PCA is then categorized as one of six facial expressions by a simple perceptron with six outputs (see Cottrell and Hsiao, Chapter 21, this volume).

A continuous multidimensional model in which exemplars are coded as vectors should also be able to account for caricature effects in facial expression perception, whereby computer-generated caricatures of facial expressions are recognized faster (Calder et al., 1997), rated as more intense exemplars (Calder et al., 2000b), and lead to greater brain activation of relevant areas than the original undistorted images (Morris et al., 1996; Phillips et al., 1997). In terms of face space, caricatures could be thought of as vectors with the same directionality as the original undistorted images but increased length. Interestingly, similar, although less marked, caricature effects have been found for facial identity (Benson and Perrett, 1991; Calder et al., 1996a; Rhodes et al., 1987). The smaller effects for identity than expression can be explained by the fact that expressions naturally vary in their intensity, whereas facial identities do not.

Cognitive research

Support for a single visual system coding facial identity and expression requires evidence that it can simulate the putative independent processing of these facial cues reported in cognitive research (Bruce, 1986; Calder et al., 2000c; Campbell et al., 1996; Young et al., 1986). This evidence was provided by Cottrell and colleagues (2002) who presented a simulation of cognitive data by Calder et al. (2000c) showing independent coding of configural information relating to each facial property.

Calder et al.'s (2000c) study used a variant of the composite effect. The original effect showed that aligning the top half of one person's face with the bottom half of a different person's face gave the illusion of a new facial identity (Young et al., 1987). This made it more difficult to recognize the identity shown in either of the two face halves when aligned, relative to a control condition in which the halves were misaligned so that they no longer formed a complete face. Calder and colleagues demonstrated an analogous effect for facial expressions, and in addition showed that the composite effects for facial identity and facial expression did not significantly interact or interfere with one another (Calder and Jansen, 2005; Calder et al., 2000c); suggesting separate configural or holistic analysis of facial identity and facial expression. This is illustrated in Figure 22.4 which shows data from an experiment in which participants were required to categorize the expression or identity shown in one half of three types of composite faces. These were prepared by combining the top and bottom face halves of two faces showing (1) different expressions posed by the same identity, (2) the same expression posed by different identities, or (3) different expressions posed by different identities. Reaction times (RTs) to report the expression in one face half (Figure 22.4b, top graph) were slowed when the two halves contained different expressions (i.e. different expression/same identity and different expression/different identity conditions) relative to when

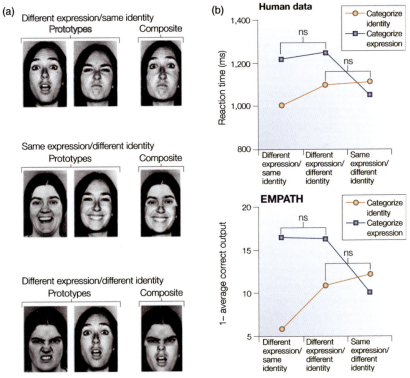

Fig. 22.4 (a) Composite facial expressions that combine the top and bottom halves of two different facial expressions posed by the same identity (top), the same expression posed by different identities (middle), and different expressions posed by different identities (bottom). (b) The top graph shows participants' mean correct reaction times to categorize the identity or expression shown in the top half of the composite faces. The bottom graph shows Cottrell, Branson, and Calder's (Cottrell et al., 2002) simulation of these data using a variant of Cottrell's EMPATH model. Reprinted from Calder and Young (2005), with permission from Nature publishing group; panels a and b modified with permission from American Psychological Association. Panel b also modified from Cottrell et al. (2002).

they contained the same expressions posed by different identities (i.e. same expression/different identity condition). Crucially, no further cost was found when the two halves contained different expressions *and* different identities relative to different expressions posed by the same identity. A corresponding effect was found when participants were asked to report the identity of one face half (Figure 22.4b, top graph); i.e. [different expression/same identity RTs] < [same expression/different identity conditions = different expression/different identity conditions RTs].

Cottrell, Branson, and Calder (2002) showed that this apparent independent processing of holistic cues to facial expression and identity could be modeled by a single representational framework coding both facial properties. This constituted an extended version of the EMPATH model in which the output of the PCA of Gabor filters fed into a single-layer neural network used to categorize the identity or expression of the face. As illustrated in Figure 22.4b (bottom graph), the model produced an impressive simulation of the human data (Cottrell et al., 2002).

These data suggest that other examples of apparent independent processing of facial identity and facial expression (Bruce, 1986; Campbell et al., 1996; Young et al., 1986) might also be accounted for by a single system, as opposed to a dual route account. Moreover, if the visual representation of these facial properties is coded, at least in part, by overlapping dimensions, then it follows that at least some studies should find that these two facial properties interact. This is indeed the case. Work has shown that "to-be-ignored" changes in facial identity interfere with participants' ability to categorize facial expressions (Ganel and Goshen-Gottstein, 2004; Schweinberger and Soukup, 1998; Schweinberger et al., 1999) in tasks using the Garner paradigm (Garner, 1976). In addition, the adaptation or aftereffect observed when prolonged exposure to a particular facial expression causes the perception of a subsequent test expression to be biased away from the adapter is significantly greater when the identity of the adaptation and test faces is the same relative to different (Campbell and Burke, 2009; Ellamil et al., 2008; Fox and Barton, 2007). Interestingly, these interference effects are often asymmetrical, such that to-be-ignored changes in facial identity affect perception of facial expression (Fox and Barton, 2007; Fox et al., 2008; Schweinberger and Soukup, 1998; Schweinberger et al., 1999), but not vice versa; but see Ganel and Goshen-Gottstein (2004) for symmetric interference. Important issues for future research are to provide an explanation of the asymmetry, and to explore whether computational models can simulate these effects. For example, since we encounter significantly more facial identities than facial expressions, this might result in facial identity being distributed over a larger number of dimensions (or PCs) than facial expressions, causing unattended facial identities to interfere more with facial expression recognition than vice versa.

By this point I hope you are persuaded that a single representational framework coding at least certain aspects of the visual representations of both facial identity and expression deserves serious consideration. Figure 22.5 presents a simplified, schematic version of the standard dual route account (Figure 22.5a) and a modified version (Figure 22.5b). Note, that I am not suggesting that all aspects of coding identity and expression from faces rely on common mechanisms. Rather, as illustrated in Figure 22.5b the idea is that the separate routes for these two facial characteristics bifurcate after the stage coding their visual representation, with facial expression representations projecting to areas involved in emotion, such as the amygdala, insula, and orbitofrontal cortex, and facial identity representations projecting to areas implicated in knowledge of people and semantic knowledge more generally, such as anterior temporal cortex. The framework also allows for some cross-over projections due to the fact that certain facial identities can elicit emotional reactions, while characteristic facial expressions are associated with particular identities, etc.

I also don't want to exclude the possibility that other visual routes are possible. As discussed, facial expressions and other changeable cues are conveyed by dynamic information, and a separate route involved in the visual analysis of facial motion may provide an additional input to brain regions in the extended system. Lander, Bruce, and colleagues (Lander and Bruce, 2000; Lander

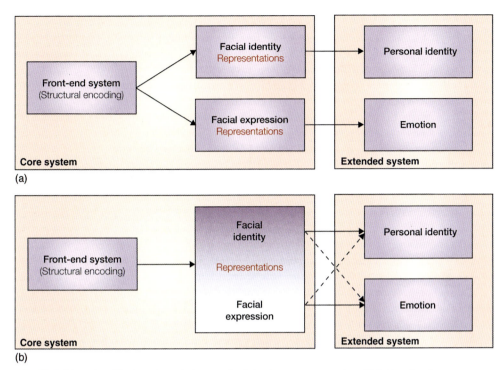

Fig. 22.5 (a) A simplified version of the standard dual route account in which the visual representation of facial identity and facial expression are coded by independent functional routes. (b) A modified system in which the visual form of facial identity and facial expression are coded in a single multidimensional framework with some dimensions coding facial expression, some facial identity, and others coding both. In this second model, the bifurcation between the facial expression and facial identity routes occurs after the stage coding their visual representation.

et al., 1999) have shown that dynamic information is also important for recognizing familiar facial identities, although to a lesser extent than it is for changeable facial cues. Hence, a parallel route processing dynamic information, particularly, although not exclusively from changeable facial cues such as facial expressions, seems highly likely. As I go on to discuss, however, the vast majority of research in face perception has used static facial images, and any conclusions are inevitably drawn primarily from research using these sorts of stimuli. With these factors in mind, Figure 22.5b may provide a schematic model of the recognition of facial identity and facial expression from *visual form*, but a similar system processing facial motion seems highly probable.

An obvious question is whether this type of model conflicts with studies of brain-injured patients suggesting that facial identity and expression recognition are dissociable processes. We have argued that it does not, because closer examination of these studies provides at best limited evidence for a double dissociation that is restricted to the facial domain (Calder and Young, 2005). Next, I reiterate some of the main arguments outlined in our previous review (Calder and Young, 2005) and consider new neuropsychological data relevant to this debate.

Neuropsychological research

Support for separate visual routes coding facial identity and facial expression requires a double dissociation between the recognition of these characteristics from the face but not other domains—that is, dissociation 1: impaired recognition of facial identity but not other identifying cues (e.g. the name, voice, etc.) in the context of preserved recognition of facial expression; *and* dissociation 2: impaired recognition of facial expression (but not other emotional impairments) with preserved recognition of facial identity. In the case of the latter dissociation, it is important to note that where the appropriate tests have been used, facial expression impairments are frequently accompanied by impaired recognition of emotion from other modalities and, or impaired experience of emotion (Hornak et al., 1996; Keane et al., 2002; Sprengelmeyer et al., 1996). Consequently, we suggested that these impairments should be conceived as emotion deficits rather than impaired access or damage to the visual representations of facial expressions (Calder and Young, 2005). To illustrate, Figure 22.6 shows that two separate groups of patients, one with frontal variant frontotemporal dementia the other with Huntington's disease, show very similar impairments on tests of facial *and vocal* emotional expression recognition matched for difficulty (Calder et al., Submitted; Keane et al., 2002). By contrast, their recognition of facial identity is preserved. Both of these conditions are also associated with altered emotional experience and personality (Bozeat et al., 2000; Craufurd and Snowden, 2002).

Patients showing selective or disproportionate impairments affecting one emotion, such as disgust (Calder et al., 2000a; Sprengelmeyer et al., 1996), or fear (Adolphs et al., 1994; Anderson and Phelps, 2000; Calder et al., 1996c; Sprengelmeyer et al., 1999), also show evidence of impaired recognition of the same emotion from other modalities and, or related emotional functions (e.g. emotional memory, emotion experience, fear conditioning, etc.) (Bechara et al., 1995; Calder et al., 2000a; Phelps et al., 1998; Scott et al., 1997; Sprengelmeyer et al., 1996, 1999). Thus, investigations of facial expression impairments to date provide little support for a separate *visual* route processing facial expressions; see Calder and Young (2005) for a more detailed discussion.

Evidence of the opposite dissociation—impaired recognition of identity from the face but not other identifying cues (i.e. prosopagnosia) without impaired facial expression recognition—also lacks convincing support. The literature contains a number of examples of neuropsychological cases showing impaired recognition of facial identity but not facial expression that support the idea that certain aspects of recognizing these two facial properties are dissociable (Bruyer et al., 1983; Parry et al., 1990; Tranel et al., 1988; Young et al., 1993). However, only those cases for which the facial identity impairment has been established as prosopagnosia (i.e. impaired recognition of identity from faces but not other identifying cues) address the debate concerning whether facial identity and facial expression are processed by separate *visual* routes. Other causes of

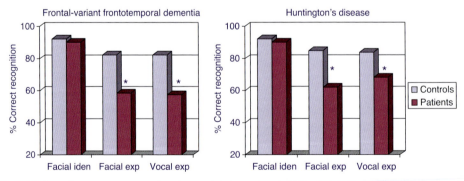

Fig. 22.6 Data from two groups of patients with frontal-variant frontotemporal dementia (left, Keane, et al., (2002)) and Huntington's disease (right, Calder et al. (2010)) on three tasks assessing recognition of facial identity, facial expressions, and vocal expressions. Asterisks indicate significant impairments.

impaired recognition of facial identity include impaired learning, and hence recognition, of faces encountered after, but not before, neurological damage (i.e. "prosopamnesia") (Hanley et al., 1990; Tippet et al., 2000; Tranel et al., 1988) and impaired access to knowledge of familiar people, affecting the recognition of identity from the face and other identifying cues (i.e. name, voice, etc.) (Ellis et al., 1989; Evans et al., 1995; Hanley et al., 1989). In addition, some earlier examples of impaired facial identity recognition with relatively preserved facial expression recognition did not exclude that the identity impairment arose from other cognitive deficits, such as amnesia or general semantic impairments (Etcoff, 1984; Parry et al., 1990). It is also important to exclude cases where impaired facial identity processing is demonstrated only by problems in face matching, because impaired matching of unfamiliar faces can occur in the absence of impaired recognition of familiar faces and vice versa (Young et al., 1993); see Young (Chapter 5, this volume).

Focusing only on studies that have excluded these alternative explanations of facial identity deficits leaves remarkably few studies demonstrating evidence of prosopagnosia with preserved facial expression recognition, and from what we have learnt in more recent years, there is uncertainty even with these.

The most frequently cited example is the case report of Mr W (Bruyer et al., 1983). Most tests of facial expression recognition in this study used a two-alternative choice procedure leading to ceiling performance in the patient and controls. In one experiment that did not suffer from this limitation the task was to find four examples of faces displaying the same expression as a target face from among an array of 16 different faces. Mr W's performance fell between the scores of left and right hemisphere lesion controls (Figure 22.7); data from neurologically intact controls were not reported and statistical comparisons were not conducted. Given that damage to either hemisphere can affect facial expression recognition (Bowers et al., 1985; Rapcsak et al., 2000; Young et al., 1993), it is difficult to conclude that Mr W's facial expression recognition is unimpaired in the absence of data from neurologically intact controls.

A further example of impaired recognition of facial identity with preserved facial expression recognition comes from Tranel et al. (1988). Three patients showing this pattern were described, but the facial identity recognition impairments were attributed to different causes (prosopagnosia, prosopamnesia, amnesia) and only "subject 1" showed prosopagnosia. Facial expression recognition was assessed using a standard task in which the patient was asked to categorize a series

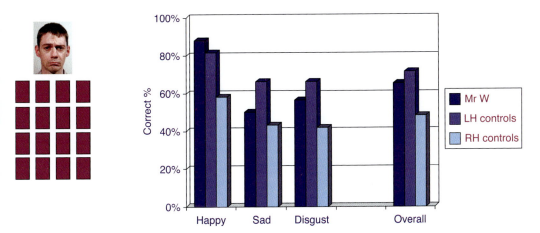

Fig. 22.7 Data from a facial expression matching task showing the performance of a prosopagnosic (Mr W) and left and right hemisphere lesion controls. Redrawn from Bruyer et al. (1983).

of facial expressions with one of six labels (happiness, sadness, anger, fear, disgust, and surprise). However, the authors used what would now be considered an unusual method of scoring in which two labels were assigned as correct for 20% of the stimuli. It is therefore unclear whether this may have overestimated subject 1's performance, who showed the worst facial expression recognition of the three patients.

More convincing evidence of prosopagnosia with preserved facial expression recognition comes from Riddoch et al. (2008) who reported this pattern in a patient (FB) with right occipitotemporal damage. However, on the basis of a previous case report by Baudouin and Humphreys (2006), Riddoch et al. suggested that FB's apparently normal performance in recognizing expressions may reflect the use of compensatory strategies. Baudouin and Humphreys (2006) showed that although a patient with a severe impairment in facial identity recognition showed comparatively good recognition of facial expressions, further investigation revealed that he was not processing expressions in the normal holistic manner (Calder and Jansen, 2005; Calder et al., 2000c), but instead was relying on salient individual features (e.g. smiling mouth, furrowed brow, etc.). This identifies an important issue relating to the relative difficulty of tests assessing facial identity and facial expression recognition that is frequently overlooked. For the former, participants are generally asked to provide identifying information for a series of faces belonging to any given famous individuals, whereas facial expression tasks tend to use a fixed alternative-choice procedure in which each expression is categorized as one of a limited number of alternatives; often six, but as few as two. Hence, facial expression tasks are more open to the application of compensatory strategies, and comparisons of performance with facial identity tasks are generally confounded by differences in difficulty. The two tasks also differ in other ways. For example, most facial expressions are frequently and personally encountered, whereas famous identities' faces are not.

As illustrated in Figure 22.8 from Shallice (1988), relative difficulty has important implications for interpreting neuropsychological dissociations because reduced cognitive resource (resulting from brain injury) can cause performance on a more difficult task to drop off more rapidly than an easier task involving the same cognitive system. Thus, a dissociation characterized by impaired recognition of facial identity but not facial expression recognition could potentially reflect the relative difficulty of the two tasks, rather than a genuine classical dissociation. For this reason, separate visual routes for recognizing facial identity and facial expression requires evidence of a double dissociation, comprising two classical dissociations that are restricted to the facial domain. In other words, a deficit that does not extend to the recognition of other identifying cues in the case of impaired facial identity recognition with preserved facial expression recognition, and does

Fig. 22.8 An illustration of how an apparent dissociation between the performance on a difficult and easy task can arise despite both being conducted by the same neural system. The more difficult task is affected more when the system's resource is depleted following brain damage. Redrawn from Shallice (1988) with permission from Cambridge University Press.

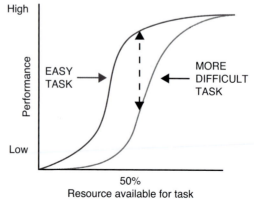

not affect other emotional tasks in the case of impaired facial expression recognition with preserved facial identity recognition. At present, there is no persuasive evidence of this double dissociation in the neuropsychological literature.

The same issues of strategy and relative difficulty apply to investigations of "developmental prosopagnosia" (aka congenital prosopagnosia) a condition defined by problems in face recognition that cannot be explained by a neurological or psychiatric condition (see Behrmann et al., Chapter 41; Duchaine, Chapter 42, this volume). Recent investigations of developmental prosopagnosics have provided evidence of impaired perception of facial identity in the context of preserved recognition of facial expressions (Duchaine et al., 2003; Humphreys et al., 2007). However, it is unclear whether facial expression recognition in these prosopagnosics is achieved with the same cognitive processes as controls. As discussed, this could be addressed with tasks such as the composite effect for facial expressions (Baudouin and Humphreys, 2006; Calder et al., 2000c).

There are more fundamental reasons to be cautious of using dissociations in developmental disorders to infer the organization of the healthy, normal face perception system. Foremost among these is that developmental conditions violate a fundamental assumption of dissociation logic; namely, that there is a disruption (following brain injury) to a previously normal functioning cognitive system. For this and other reasons, Bishop (1997) has warned that cognitive neuropsychology and developmental disorders are "uncomfortable bedfellows" that require different approaches. Karmiloff-Smith has similarly suggested that the dissociation logic is inappropriate for developmental disorders (Karmiloff-Smith et al., 2003). These researchers also propose that characterizing developmental impairments in terms of damage to discrete components or routes of cognitive models (e.g. damage to FRUs) or the facial identity route in the case of developmental prosopagnosia) places the emphasis on representational impairments at the expense of other possible explanations. For example, Maurer and colleagues showed that visual deprivation during a child's first 3 to 6 months of life, as a result of congenital cataracts that are later surgically corrected, causes a disproportionate, lasting impairment in configural versus featural processing of faces (Grand et al., 2001), see Maurer and Mondloch (Chapter 40, this volume). Of particular relevance, in one study they showed that a group of these individuals (aged 10–39 years) showed impaired performance on tasks assessing perception of facial identity, but preserved perception of facial expression and lipspeech (Geldart et al., 2002). Hence, delayed development of certain aspects of visual perception might provide a potential account of developmental prosopagnosia and why facial expression recognition is sometimes relatively preserved in this condition.

Developmental prosopagnosia remains a fascinating condition, however, and its study could provide important insights into the perceptual mechanisms involved in face perception.

In summary, support for separate visual routes coding facial identity and facial expression from neuropsychological studies requires evidence of a face-specific double dissociation, with one dissociation showing impaired recognition of identity but not expression from the face, and the other dissociation the opposite pattern. Where the appropriate tests have been used, patients showing impaired facial expression recognition in the context of intact facial identity recognition demonstrate concomitant problems on other emotional tasks. Consequently, they are perhaps best interpreted as showing emotional (i.e. non-face specific) impairments, rather than facial expression impairments per se. Although there are a number of reports of the opposite dissociation (i.e. impaired recognition of facial identity but not facial expression), the majority are silent with regard to the issue of whether the dissociation has a visuoperceptual origin and there are questions with the limited number of relevant examples that exist. Unfortunately, numerous published studies continue to brush over these details and use any demonstration of a dissociation between the two facial properties as support for separate neural coding of their *visual* representation. Research should also pay more careful attention to the relative difficulty of the facial identity and expression tasks, and the related issue of using compensatory strategies to recognize facial expressions.

Neuroimaging research

Earlier I discussed that Haxby et al.'s (2000) model includes neurologically separate routes for the visual analysis of facial identity and facial expression involving the fusiform gyrus and STS, respectively. Studies of brain-injured participants rarely provide the neurological precision or relevant information to address this proposed neurological dissociation (see Kanwisher and Barton, Chapter 7, this volume). In this respect, functional neuroimaging research provides a valuable addition to the current discussion.

Relatively few neuroimaging studies have investigated facial expression and facial identity perception in the same study, and those that exist provide little evidence of entirely separate visual routes. A notable exception used a functional magnetic resonance (fMR)-adaptation procedure (aka repetition suppression) to examine the effects of repeating the same facial identity or facial expression (Winston et al., 2004). The results showed that the fusiform gyrus and posterior STS were sensitive to the repetition of facial identity, whereas a more anterior section of STS was sensitive to repetition of facial expression. However, more recent work using a similar procedure has found that the fusiform gyrus is sensitive to both facial properties (Fox et al., 2009), posing a problem for the dual route account.

Fox et al. (2009) presented participants with adjacent pairs of morphed faces from continua ranging between two different facial identities or two different facial expressions. As discussed earlier, previous work has shown that perception of these continua operates in a stepwise rather than linear fashion (Beale and Keil, 1995; Calder et al., 1996b; Young et al., 1997). In the case of a facial identity continuum, the morphed faces in one half are perceived relatively consistently as one identity and the morphs in the other half as the second identity, with a perceptual category boundary separating the two (Beale and Keil, 1995). A previous fMRI study focusing on facial identity perception had shown that the presentation of consecutive pairs of morphed faces that crossed the category boundary, and were therefore seen as different identities, produced more fusiform gyrus activation than consecutive pairs from the same side of the category boundary, that were seen as the same identity (Rotshtein et al., 2005). Fox et al. (2009) replicated these findings and showed a highly similar pattern of fusiform gyrus activation for facial expression morphs; suggesting that the fusiform gyrus codes both facial properties. In addition, they showed similar sensitivity to facial identity and expression in posterior STS, but in accord with Winston et al. (2004), found that a more anterior section of STS was sensitive to repetition of facial expression alone.

Similarly, other neuroimaging research has found that the fusiform gyrus is involved in the perception of both facial identity and facial expression (Cohen-Kadosh et al., 2010; Fairhall and Ishai, 2007; Ganel et al., 2005; Narumoto et al., 2001). In one of these studies, Fairhall and Ishai (2007) employed dynamic causal modeling (DCM) to examine how effective connectivity between components of Haxby et al.'s (2000) model of face perception are modulated by viewing facial expressions or famous facial identities. Contrary to the Haxby et al. (2000) model, facial expression perception did not affect connectivity between the inferior occipital gyrus (IOG) and STS. Rather, both expression and identity conditions altered connectivity between the IOG and fusiform gyrus. The two conditions differed, however, in terms of their connectivity between the fusiform gyrus and other brain structures, with expressions and famous identities affecting connectivity to the amygdala and orbitofrontal cortex, respectively.

Intracranial recording in epilepsy patients has provided further evidence that ventral temporal cortex contributes to facial expression perception (Tsuchiya et al., 2008). Tsuchiya and colleagues recorded the electrophysiological response from electrodes in two sites—ventral temporal cortex, which included the fusiform gyrus, and lateral temporal cortex, which included the superior temporal sulcus and gyrus. Participants were presented with static or dynamic displays of facial expressions (happy and fear) posed by male and female models, together with static or dynamic radial checkerboard stimuli. Statistical analyses showed that recordings from the ventral site produced more accurate discrimination of happy versus fear expressions, male versus female faces, and faces versus checkerboards for both static and dynamic facial stimuli.

Tsuchiya et al.'s (2008) findings contrast with single-cell recordings in monkeys demonstrating that neurons responsive to facial expressions and facial identity were more likely to be located in STS and the more ventral inferotemporal region, respectively (Hasselmo et al., 1989). However, since other research has shown that monkey STS contains cells responsive to both facial proper-ties (Perrett et al., 1984), it is unclear whether a strict division between facial expression and identity perception in these two regions is warranted. Moreover, the implications of non-human primate research for the neural topography of human face perception may not be straightforward given recent work showing that face-sensitive "patches" in the monkey STS might constitute homologues of the face-sensitive regions in human ventral temporal cortex, including the lateral fusiform gyrus (Rajimehr et al., 2009; Tsao et al., 2003, 2008); see Freiwald and Tsao (Chapter 36, this volume).

In the earlier section discussing the PCA of facial expression images, I discussed that some PCs were found to code either facial identity or facial expression whereas others coded both. It is therefore interesting that Hasselmo et al. (1989) found that, in addition to selective coding of these facial properties by cells in macaque STS and inferotemporal cortex, a proportion of cells responded to both. Similarly, recordings from cells in monkey amygdala found a comparable pattern of selective and common coding of facial identity and facial expression, although here the majority of cells (64%) were sensitive to both (Gothard et al., 2007).

In summary, the majority of human neuroimaging studies addressing both facial identity and facial expression perception in the same study have found that the fusiform gyrus is sensitive to both facial properties (Cohen-Kadosh et al., 2010; Fairhall and Ishai, 2007; Fox et al., 2009; Ganel et al., 2005; Narumoto et al., 2001). Intracranial recordings in humans also implicate the ventral temporal cortex in facial expression perception (Tsuchiya et al., 2008). Common coding of facial identity and expression in ventral temporal cortex is difficult to reconcile with the idea that these facial properties are processed by entirely separate visual routes (Bruce and Young, 1986; Haxby et al., 2000), involving ventral temporal cortex (fusiform gyrus) for the visual analysis of facial identity and STS for the visual analysis of facial expressions (Haxby et al., 2000). Rather, the model shown in Figure 22.5b may provide a simplified representation of face perception in *ventral* temporal cortex, with the fusiform gyrus and IOG involved in the analysis of visual form coding both facial identity *and* facial expression. As discussed, a similar system may also underlie the analysis of these facial cues from dynamic information. Although this would play a greater role in coding facial expressions and other changeable cues relative to facial identity, there is evi-dence that dynamic information is used in some aspects of facial identity recognition. This dynamic route may involve the superior temporal sulcus (Haxby et al., 2000); however, the STS may contribute in other ways.

Recent neuroimaging research provides initial evidence that a mid-anterior section of STS is sensitive to facial expression but not facial identity (Fox et al., 2009; Winston et al., 2004). Since these studies used static facial images, the exact contribution of this region is currently unclear, as is its relationship to posterior STS, which is engaged by a number of face processing tasks. One potential explanation of the disproportionate role of the STS in facial expression perception may relate to this region's role in multisensory integration (Calder and Young, 2005). Emotional signals are inherently multimodal, comprising visual (facial, body), vocal, and dynamic components that are known to interact (Aviezer et al., 2008; de Gelder and Vroomen, 2000; Hietanen et al., 2004; Massaro and Egan, 1996). Neurophysiological recordings in monkeys indicate that this interaction or integration involves the STS (Barraclough et al., 2005; Oram and Perrett, 1996), while neuroimaging in humans shows that unimodal presentations of facial and vocal expressions engage the same area of STS (Phillips et al., 1998). More recent evidence from magnetoencephalographic recordings further shows that human STS shows a super-additive response to congruent pairs of facial and vocal expressions of fear, consistent with the idea of multi-modal integration (Hagan et al., 2009). The contribution of the STS to facial expression processing may therefore relate to its wider role in the integration of visual, vocal, and dynamic information, whereby even unimodal signals prime these integrative mechanisms.

Integration mechanisms are also involved in the perception of other changeable facial properties, such as lipspeech and cues to social attention (i.e. eye gaze, head and body orientation). In the case of lipspeech, this is demonstrated by the McGurk illusion (McGurk and MacDonald, 1976), and neuroimaging research has demonstrated that cross-modal integration of facial and vocal speech takes place in STS (Calvert, 2001; Calvert et al., 2000; see Campbell, Chapter 31, this volume). Similarly, gaze, head and body orientation interact (Langton et al., 2004), and single cell recording in monkeys shows that this occurs in the STS (Perrett et al., 1992).

In contrast to emotion, speech, and social attention cues, identity is conveyed primarily by the visual form of a face. Of course, vocal information can also convey identity, but with the exception of highly distinctive or personally familiar people, recognition rates from the voice alone are significantly worse than those found for faces (Hanley et al., 1998). Hence, the reduced role of STS in perception of facial identity may relate to the decreased reliance of identity recognition on dynamic information, non-facial channels, and integration mechanisms in particular.

Overall, then, I suggest that the fusiform gyrus contributes to the analysis and representation of the visual form of both facial identity and facial expression. By contrast, the STS may play a disproportionate role in coding facial expressions and other changeable facial properties in relation to facial identity, by virtue of the relatively increased reliance of the former on dynamic information (Haxby et al., 2000) and mutimodal integration of visual form, dynamic and vocal cues. As already discussed, a major limitation of the work I have reviewed is that the vast majority has used still photographs of facial images. Hence, the conclusions, and indeed our understanding of the functional and neural basis of face perception in general, are derived largely from experiments that have used unnatural, static facial images. It is vital that future research makes greater use of dynamic facial stimuli; not least because dynamic information is more important for facial expression recognition than facial identity recognition, but also because the role of dynamic information in the perceptual and neural representation of facial identity requires further exploration.

Summary and conclusions

The idea that facial identity and facial expression are processed by entirely separate visual routes has represented the prevailing view in face perception research for over 20 years. In a previous article, Andy Young and myself questioned whether there is adequate empirical support for this proposal (Calder and Young, 2005). Here, I have explored this issue in more detail taking account of new studies of brain-injured patients, neuroimaging, and cognitive research. I conclude that research continues to reinforce our original conclusion that at least certain aspects of facial identity and facial expression recognition involve the same visual route. Strong support for separate visual routes would require evidence of a double dissociation in recognizing facial identity and facial expression following brain-injury that does not extend to the recognition of identity and expression from non-facial cues. One dissociation should show prosopagnosia with preserved facial expression recognition, and the second dissociation impaired facial expression recognition with preserved facial identity recognition. Currently, persuasive evidence of this independent processing is lacking. That is not to deny that neuropsychological research shows that recognition of facial identity and facial expression are dissociable processes, but the majority are largely silent with regard to whether this dissociation has a visuoperceptual origin or not, or suggest that the dissociation occurs after the stage coding their visual representations.

Additional support for a common representational framework coding facial identity and expression comes from cognitive studies of neurologically intact volunteers (Ellamil et al., 2008; Fox and Barton, 2007; Ganel and Goshen-Gottstein, 2004; Schweinberger and Soukup, 1998). In addition, where apparently independent processing has been found, research using image-based analysis of facial images shows that this can be accounted for by a single representational framework coding both facial properties (Calder et al., 2000c; Cottrell et al., 2002). Recent neuroimaging research showing that the fusiform gyrus is involved in processing both facial identity and facial expression further questions the idea of entirely separate neurological routes (Cohen-Kadosh et al., 2010; Fairhall and Ishai, 2007; Fox et al., 2009; Ganel et al., 2005; Narumoto et al., 2001). However, neuroimaging research has also shown that the mid/anterior STS might play a disproportionate role in facial expression perception (Fox et al., 2009; Winston et al., 2004). This may relate to the wider role of the STS in encoding biological motion and multisensory integration. However, this is far from clear and other explanations should be explored.

In summary, I suggest that the emerging framework for face perception incorporates a ventral temporal route (including fusiform gyrus) involved in the analysis of visual form associated with both facial identity and facial expression, and possibly other facial properties. Dynamic facial information is likely to be coded by a separate route, including the STS, as suggested by Haxby et al. (2000). However, once again, this may not be restricted to facial expression and other changeable cues, and might also be involved in processing dynamic cues to facial identity; although to a much lesser extent than changeable facial properties. The STS may also play an important role in the integration of form and motion of facial cues. This proposal stands in contrast to the standard account that includes separate visual routes for facial identity and facial expression, with the ventral route underlying the visual analysis of facial identity (Bruce and Young, 1986; Haxby et al., 2000) and a dorsal facial route (STS) involved in the analysis of facial expression and other changeable facial cues. To this extent, the dissociation I propose reflects the relative reliance of different facial properties on visual form (which conveys facial identity, expression and other facial cues) and motion and the integration of multiple cues, which relates primarily to changeable facial cues.

References

Adolphs, R., Tranel, D., Damasio, H., and Damasio, A. (1994). Impaired recognition of emotion in facial expressions following bilateral damage to the human amygdala. *Nature*, **372**, 669–672.

Anderson, A.K. and Phelps, E.A. (2000). Expression without recognition: Contributions of the human amygdala to emotional communication. *Psychological Science*, **11**, 106–111.

Aviezer, H., Ran, H., Ryan, J., *et al.* (2008). Angry, disgusted or afraid? Studies on the malleability of facial expression perception. *Psychological Science*, **19**, 724–732.

Barraclough, N.E., Xiao, D., Baker, C.I., Oram, M.W., and Perrett, D.I. (2005). Integration of visual and auditory information by STS neurons responsive to the sight of actions. *Journal of Cognitive Neuroscience*, **7**, 377–391.

Baudouin, J.-Y. and Humphreys, G.W. (2006). Compensatory strategy in processing facial emotions: Evidence from prosopagnosia. *Neuropsychologia*, **44**, 1364–1369.

Beale, J.M. and Keil, F.C. (1995). Categorical effects in the perception of faces. *Cognition*, **57**, 217–239.

Bechara, A., Tranel, D., Damasio, H., Adolphs, R., Rockland, C., and Damasio, A.R. (1995). Double dissociation of conditioning and declarative knowledge relative to the amygdala and hippocampus in humans. *Science*, **269**, 1115–1118.

Benson, P.J. and Perrett, D.I. (1991). Perception and recognition of photographic quality facial caricatures: implications for the recognition of natural images. *European Journal of Cognitive Psychology*, **3**, 105–135.

Bishop, D.V.M. (1997). Cognitive neuropsychology and developmental disorders: Uncomfortable bedfellows. *Quarterly Journal of Experimental Psychology. A, Human Experimental Psychology*, **50A**, 899–923.

Bowers, D., Bauer, R.M., Coslett, H.B., and Heilman, K.M. (1985). Processing of faces by patients with unilateral hemisphere lesions. 1. Dissociation between judgements of facial affect and facial identity. *Brain and Cognition*, **4**, 258–272.

Bozeat, S., Gregory, C., Lambon Ralph, M.A., and Hodges, J.R. (2000). Which neuropsychiatric and behavioural features distinguish frontal and temporal variants of frontotemporal dementia from Alzheimer's disease? *Journal of Neurology Neurosurgery and Psychiatry*, **69**, 178–186.

Bruce, V. (1986). Influences of familiarity on the processing of faces. *Perception*, **15**, 387–397.

Bruce, V. and Young, A.W. (1986). Understanding face recognition. *British Journal of Psychology*, **77**, 305–327.

Bruyer, R., Laterre, C., Seron, X., *et al.* (1983). A case of prosopagnosia with some preserved covert remembrance of familiar faces. *Brain and Cognition*, **2**, 257–284.

Burton, A.M., Bruce, V., and Hancock, P.J.B. (1999). From pixels to people: a model of familiar face recognition. *Cognitive Science*, **23**, 1–31.

Calder, A.J. and Jansen, J. (2005). Configural coding of facial expressions: The impact of inversion and photographic negative. *Visual Cognition*, **12**, 495–518.

Calder, A.J. and Young, A.W. (2005). Understanding facial identity and facial expression recognition. *Nature Reviews Neuroscience*, **6**, 641–651.

Calder, A.J., Young, A.W., Benson, P.J., and Perrett, D.I. (1996a). Self priming from distinctive and caricatured faces. *British Journal of Psychology*, **87**, 141–162.

Calder, A.J., Young, A.W., Perrett, D.I., Etcoff, N.L., and Rowland, D. (1996b). Categorical perception of morphed facial expressions. *Visual Cognition*, **3**, 81–117.

Calder, A.J., Young, A.W., Rowland, D., Perrett, D.I., Hodges, J.R., and Etcoff, N.L. (1996c). Facial Emotion Recognition after Bilateral Amygdala Damage: Differentially Severe Impairment of Fear. *Cognitive Neuropsychology*, **13**, 699–745.

Calder, A.J., Young, A.W., Rowland, D., and Perrett, D.I. (1997). Computer-enhanced emotion in facial expressions. *Proceedings of the Royal Society of London. Series B: Biological Sciences*, **B264**, 919–925.

Calder, A.J., Keane, J., Manes, F., Antoun, N., and Young, A.W. (2000a). Impaired recognition and experience of disgust following brain injury. *Nature Neuroscience*, **3**, 1077–1078.

Calder, A.J., Rowland, D., Young, A.W., Nimmo-Smith, I., Keane, J., and Perrett, D.I. (2000b). Caricaturing facial expressions. *Cognition*, **76**, 105–146.

Calder, A.J., Young, A.W., Keane, J., and Dean, M. (2000c). Configural information in facial expression perception. *Journal of Experimental Psychology: Human Perception and Performance*, **26**, 527–551.

Calder, A.J., Burton, A.M., Miller, P., Young, A.W., and Akamatsu, S. (2001). A principal component analysis of facial expressions. *Vision Research*, **41**, 1179–1208.

Calder, A.J., Keane, J., Young, A.W., Lawrence, A.D., and Barker, R.A. (2010). Emotion recognition impairments across different modalities in manifest Huntington's disease. *Neuropsychologia*, **48**, 2719–2729.

Calvert, G.A. (2001). Crossmodal processing in the human brain: insights from functional neuroimaging studies. *Cerebral Cortex*, **11**, 1110–1123.

Calvert, G.A., Campbell, R., and Brammer, M.J. (2000). Evidence from functional magnetic resonance imaging of crossmodal binding in the human heteromodal cortex. *Current Biology*, **10**, 649–657.

Campbell, J. and Burke, D. (2009). Evidence that identity-dependent and identity-independent neural populations are recruited in the perception of five basic emotional facial expressions. *Vision Research*, **49**, 1532–1540.

Campbell, R., Brooks, B., de Haan, E., and Roberts, T. (1996). Dissociating face processing skills: Decisions about lip-read speech, expression and identity. *Quarterly Journal of Experimental Psychology. A, Human Experimental Psychology*, **49A**, 295–314.

Cohen-Kadosh, K., Henson, R.N.A., Cohen Kadosh, R., Johnson, M.H., and Dick, F. (2010). Task-dependent activation of face-sensitive cortex: an fMRI adaptation study. *Journal of Cognitive Neuroscience*, **22**, 903–917.

Costen, N., Craw, I., and Akamatsu, S. (1995). Automatic face recognition: what representation? British Machine Vision Association (Scottish chapter). Meeting. Glasgow.

Cottrell, G.W., Branson, K.M., and Calder, A.J. (2002). Do expression and identity need separate representations? 24th Annual Meeting of the Cognitive Science Society, Fairfax, Virginia.

Craufurd, D. and Snowden, J.S. (2002). Neuropsychological and neuropsychiatric aspects of Huntington's disease. In G. Bates, P.S. Harper, and L. Jones (eds.) *Huntington's Disease*, pp. 62–94. Oxford: Oxford University Press.

Dailey, M.N., Cottrell, G.W., Padgett, C., and Adolphs, R. (2002). EMPATH: A neural network that categorises facial expressions. *Journal of Cognitive Neuroscience*, **14**, 1158–1173.

de Gelder, B. and Vroomen, J. (2000). The perception of emotions by ear and by eye. *Cognition & Emotion*, **14**, 289–311.

Deffenbacher, K.A., Vetter, T., Johanson, J., and O'Toole, A.J. (1998). Facial aging, attractiveness, and distinctiveness. *Perception*, **27**, 1233–1243.

Duchaine, B.C., Paerker, H., and Nakayama, K. (2003). Normal recognition of emotion in a prosopagnosic patient. *Perception*, **32**, 827–839.

Ekman, P. and Friesen, W.V. (1976). *Pictures of facial affect*, Palo Alto, CA: Consulting Psychologists Press.

Ellamil, M., Susskind, J.M., and Anderson, A.K. (2008). Examinations of identity invariance in facial expression adaptation. *Cognitive, Affective, & Behavioral Neuroscience*, **8**, 273–281.

Ellis, A.W., Young, A.W., and Critchley, E.M.R. (1989). Loss of memory for people following temporal lobe damage. *Brain*, **112**, 1469–1483.

Etcoff, N.L. (1984). Selective attention to facial identity and facial emotion. *Neuropsychologia*, **22**, 281–295.

Evans, J.J., Heggs, A.J., Antoun, N., and Hodges, J.R. (1995). Progressive prosopagnosia associated with selective right temporal lobe atrophy: A new syndrome? *Brain*, **118**, 1–13.

Fairhall, S.L. and Ishai, A. (2007). Effective connectivity within the distributed cortical network for face perception. *Cerebral Cortex*, **17**, 2400–2406.

Fox, C.J. and Barton, J.J.S. (2007). What is adapted in face adaptation? The neural representations of expression in the human visual system. *Brain Research*, **1127**, 80–89.

Fox, C.J., Oruc, I., and Barton, J.J.S. (2008). It doesn't matter how you feel. The facial identity aftereffect is invariant to changes in facial expression. *Journal of Vision*, **8**, 1–13.

Fox, C.J., Moon, S.Y., Iaria, G., and Barton, J.J. (2009). The correlates of subjective perception of identity and expression in the face network: an fMRI adaptation study. *Neuroimage*, **44**, 569–580.

Ganel, T. and Goshen-Gottstein, Y. (2004). Effects of familiarity on the perceptual integrality of the identity and expression of faces: the parallel-route hypothesis revisited. *Journal of Experimental Psychology: Human Perception and Performance*, **30**, 583–597.

Ganel, T., Valyear, K.F., Goshen-Gottstein, Y., and Goodale, M.A. (2005). The involvement of the "fusiform face area" in processing facial expression. *Neuropsychologia*, **43**, 1645–1654.

Garner, W.R. (1976). Interaction of stimulus dimensions in concept and choice processes. *Cognitive Psychology*, **8**, 98–123.

Geldart, S., Mondloch, C., Maurer, D., de Schonen, S., and Brent, H. (2002). The effects of early visual deprivation on the development of face processing. *Developmental Science*, **5**, 490–501.

George, M.S., Ketter, T.A., Gill, D.S., *et al.* (1993). Brain-regions involved in recognizing facial emotion or identity: An oxygen-15 PET study. *Journal of Neuropsychiatry and Clinical Neurosciences*, **5**, 384–394.

Gothard, K.M., Battaglia, F.P., Erickson, C.A., Spitler, K.M., and Amaral, D.G. (2007). Neural responses to facial expression and face identity in the monkey amygdala. *Journal of Neurophysiology*, **7**, 1671–1683.

Grand, R., Mondloch, C.J., Maurer, D., and Brent, H.P. (2001). Neuroperception. Early visual experience and face processing. *Nature*, **410**, 890.

Hagan, C.C., Woods, W., Johnson, S., Calder, A.J., Green, G.G.R., and Young, A.W. (2009). MEG demonstrates a supra-additive response to facial and vocal emotion in right superior temporal sulcus. *Proceedings of the National Academy of Sciences*, **106**, 20010–20015.

Hancock, P.J.B., Burton, A.M., and Bruce, V. (1996). Face processing: human perception and principal components analysis. *Memory and Cognition*, **24**, 26–40.

Hanley, J.R., Young, A.W., and Pearson, N. (1989). Defective recognition of familiar people. *Cognitive Neuropsychology*, **6**, 179–210.

Hanley, J.R., Pearson, N., and Young, A.W. (1990). Impaired memory for new visual forms. *Brain*, **113**, 1131–1148.

Hanley, J.R., Smith, S.T., and Hadfield, J. (1998). I recognise you but I can't place you: An investigation of familiar-only experiences during tests of voice and face recognition. *Quarterly Journal of Experimental Psychology. A, Human Experimental Psychology*, **51A**, 179–195.

Hasselmo, M.E., Rolls, E.T., and Baylis, G.C. (1989). The role of expression and identity in face-selective responses of neurons in the temporal visual cortex of the monkey. *Behavioural Brain Research*, **32**, 203–218.

Haxby, J.V., Hoffman, E.A., and Gobbini, M.I. (2000). The distributed human neural system for face perception. *Trends in Cognitive Sciences*, **4**, 223–233.

Hietanen, J.K., Leppänen, J.M., Illi, M., and Surakka, V. (2004). Evidence for the integration of audiovisual emotional information at the perceptual level of processing. *European Journal of Cognitive Psychology*, **16**, 769–790.

Hornak, J., Rolls, E.T., and Wade, D. (1996). Face and voice expression identification in patients with emotional and behavioural changes following ventral frontal lobe damage. *Neuropsychologia*, **34**, 247–261.

Humphreys, K., Avidan, G., and Behrmann, M. (2007). A detailed investigation of facial expression processing in congenital prosopagnosia as compared to acquired prosopagnosia. *Experimental Brain Research*, **176**, 356–373.

Karmiloff-Smith, A., Scerif, G., and Ansari, D. (2003). Double dissociations in developmental disorders? Theoretically misconceived, empirically dubious. *Cortex*, **39**, 161–163.

Keane, J., Calder, A.J., Hodges, J.R., and Young, A.W. (2002). Face and emotion processing in frontal variant frontotemporal dementia. *Neuropsychologia*, **40**, 655–665.

Lander, K. and Bruce, V. (2000). Recognizing famous faces: exploring the benefits of facial motion. *Ecological Psychology*, **12**, 259–272.

Lander, K., Christie, F., and Bruce, V. (1999). The role of movement in the recognition of famous faces. *Memory and Cognition*, **27**, 974–985.

Langton, S.R.H., Honeyman, H., and Tessler, E. (2004). The influence of head contour and nose angle on the perception of eye-gaze direction. *Perception & Psychophysics*, **66**, 752–771.

Massaro, D.W. and Egan, P.B. (1996). Perceiving affect from the voice and the face. *Psychonnomic Bulletin and Review*, **3**, 215–221.

McGurk, H. and MacDonald, J. (1976). Hearing lips and seeing voices. *Nature*, **264**, 746–748.

Morris, J.S., Frith, C.D., Perrett, D.I., *et al.* (1996). A differential neural response in the human amygdala to fearful and happy facial expressions. *Nature*, **383**, 812–815.

Narumoto, J., Okada, T., Sadato, N., Fukui, K., and Yonekura, Y. (2001). Attention to emotion modulates fMRI activity in human right superior temporal sulcus. *Cognitive Brain Research*, **12**, 225–231.

O'Toole, A.J., Abdi, H., Deffenbacher, K.A., and Valentin, D. (1993). Low-dimensional representation of faces in higher dimensions of the face space. *Journal of the Optical Society of America*, **10**, 405–411.

O'Toole, A.J., Deffenbacher, K.A., Valentin, D., and Abdi, H. (1994). Structural aspects of face recognition and the other race effect. *Memory and Cognition*, **22**, 208–224.

Oram, M.W. and Perrett, D.I. (1996). Integration of form and motion in the anterior superior temporal polysensory area (STPa) of the macaque monkey. *Journal of Neurophysiology*, **76**, 109–129.

Padgett, C. and Cottrell, G. (1995). Identifying emotion in static face images. *Proceedings of the 2nd Joint Symposium on Neural Computation* (University of California, San Diego, La Jolla, CA), **5**, 91–101.

Parry, F.M., Young, A.W., Saul, J.S.M., and Moss, A. (1990). Dissociable face processing impairments after brain injury. *Journal of Clinical and Experimental Neuropsychology*, **13**, 545–558.

Perrett, D.I., Hietanen, J.K., Oram, M.W., and Benson, P.J. (1992). Organization and functions of cells responsive to faces in the temporal cortex. *Philosophical Transactions of the Royal Society of London. Series B: Biological Sciences*, B**335**, 23–30.

Perrett, D.I., Smith, P.A.J., Potter, D.D., *et al.* (1984). Neurones responsive to faces in the temporal cortex: studies of functional organization, sensitivity to identity and relation to perception. *Human Neurobiology*, **3**, 197–208.

Phelps, E.A., LaBar, K.S., Anderson, A.K., O'Connor, K.J., Fulbright, R.K., and Spencer, D.D. (1998). Specifying the contributions of the human amygdala to emotional memory: A case study. *Neurocase*, **4**, 527–540.

Phillips, M.L., Young, A.W., Scott, S.K., *et al.* (1998). Neural responses to facial and vocal expressions of fear and disgust. *Proceedings of the Royal Society of London. Series B: Biological Sciences*, **265**, 1809–1817.

Phillips, M.L., Young, A.W., Senior, C., *et al.* (1997). A specific neural substrate for perceiving facial expressions of disgust. *Nature*, **389**, 495–498.

Rajimehr, R., Young, J.C., and Tootell, R.B.H. (2009). An anterior temporal face patch in human cortex, predicted by macaque maps. *Proceedings of the National Academy of Sciences of the United States of America*, **106**, 1995–2000.

Rapcsak, S.Z., Galper, S.R., Comer, J.F., *et al.* (2000). Fear recognition deficits after focal brain damage - A cautionary note. *Neurology*, **54**, 575–581.

Rhodes, G., Brennan, S.E., and Carey, S. (1987). Identification and ratings of caricatures: implications for mental representations of faces. *Cognitive Psychology*, **19**, 473–497.

Riddoch, J.M., Johnston, R.A., Bracewell, R.M., Boutsen, L., and Humphreys, G.W. (2008). Are faces special? A case of pure prosopagnosia. *Cognitive Neuropsychology*, **25**, 3–26.

Rotshtein, P., Henson, R.N.A., Treves, A., Driver, J., and Dolan, R.J. (2005). Morphing Marilyn into Maggie dissociates physical and identity face representations in the brain. *Nature Neuroscience*, **8**, 107–113.

Schweinberger, S.R., Burton, A.M., and Kelly, S.W. (1999). Asymmetric dependencies in perceiving identity and emotion: Experiments with morphed faces. *Perception and Psychophysics*, **6**, 1102–1115.

Schweinberger, S.R. and Soukup, G.R. (1998). Asymmetric relationships among perceptions of facial identity, emotion, and facial speech. *Journal of Experimental Psychology: Human Perception and Performance*, **24**, 1748–1765.

Scott, S.K., Young, A.W., Calder, A.J., Hellawell, D.J., Aggleton, J.P., and Johnson, M. (1997). Impaired auditory recognition of fear and anger following bilateral amygdala lesions. *Nature*, **385**, 254–257.

Sergent, J., Ohta, S., MacDonald, B., and Zuck, E. (1994). Segregated processing of identity and emotion in the human brain: a PET study. *Visual Cognition*, **1**, 349–369.

Shallice, T. (1988). *From neuropsychology to mental structure*. Cambridge: Cambridge University Press.

Sprengelmeyer, R., Young, A.W., Calder, A.J., *et al.* (1996). Loss of disgust - Perception of faces and emotions in Huntington's disease. *Brain*, **119**, 1647–1665.

Sprengelmeyer, R., Young, A.W., Schroeder, U., *et al.* (1999). Knowing no fear. *Proceedings of the Royal Society of London. Series B: Biological Sciences*, **266**, 2451–2456.

Tippet, L.J., Milller, L.A., and Farah, M.J. (2000). Prosopamnesia: A selective impairment in face learning. *Cognitive Neuropsychology*, **17**, 241–255.

Tranel, D., Damasio, A.R., and Damasio, H. (1988). Intact recognition of facial expression, gender, and age in patients with impaired recognition of face identity. *Neurology*, **38**, 690–696.

Tsao, D.Y., Freiwald, W.A., Knutsen, T.A., Mandeville, J.B., and Tootell, R.B.H. (2003). Faces and objects in macaque cerebral cortex. *Nature Neuroscience*, **6**, 989–995.

Tsao, D.Y., Moeller, S., and Freiwald, W.A. (2008). Comparing face patch systems in macaques and humans. *Proceedings of the National Academy of Sciences of the United States of America*, **105**, 19513–19518.

Tsuchiya, N., Kawasaki, H., Oya, H., Howard, M.A., and Adolphs, R. (2008). Decoding face information in time, frequency and space from direct intracranial recordings of the human brain. *PLoS ONE*, **3**, e3892.

Turk, M. and Pentland, A. (1991). Eigenfaces for recognition. *Journal of Cognitive Neuroscience*, **3**, 71–86.

Valentine, T. (1991). A unified account of the effects of distinctiveness, inversion, and race in face recognition. *Quarterly Journal of Experimental Psychology. A, Human Experimental Psychology*, **43A**, 161–204.

Valentine, T. and Endo, M. (1992). Towards an exemplar model of face processing: the effects of race and distinctiveness. *Quarterly Journal of Experimental Psychology*, **44A**, 671–703.

Winston, J.S., Henson, R.N.A., Fine-Goulden, M.R., and Dolan, R.J. (2004). fMRI-adaptation reveals dissociable neural representations of identity and expression in face perception. *Journal of Neurophysiology*, **92**, 1830–1839.

Young, A.W., McWeeny, K.H., Hay, D.C., and Ellis, A.W. (1986). Matching familiar and unfamiliar faces on identity and expression. *Psychological Research*, **48**, 63–68.

Young, A.W., Hellawel, D., and Hay, D.C. (1987). Configurational information in face perception. *Perception*, **16**, 747–759.

Young, A.W., Newcombe, F., de Haan, E.H.F., Small, M., and Hay, D.C. (1993). Face perception after brain injury: Selective impairments affecting identity and expression. *Brain*, **116**, 941–959.

Young, A.W., Rowland, D., Calder, A.J., Etcoff, N.L., Seth, A., and Perrett, D.I. (1997). Facial expression megamix: Tests of dimensional and category accounts of emotion recognition *Cognition*, **63**, 271–313.

Chapter 23

Attention and Automaticity in Processing Facial Expressions

Patrik Vuilleumier and Ruthger Righart

A great deal of information of the world around us is processed automatically. It would simply take too much mental energy and require too much capacity to be attentive and conscious of every event (Bargh and Chartrand, 1999). In social situations, this general principle of the nervous system is certainly very important as it allows the selection of relevant information from the many simultaneous cues available during interpersonal interactions.

The property of automaticity is not only important to swiftly express and perceive emotional behaviors during communication and social exchanges, but it may also be crucial for survival in order to rapidly detect and respond to certain threat situations (Darwin, 1998). Facial displays of emotions are often produced involuntarily and perceived effortlessly (Ekman, 1992). Furthermore, experimental studies have shown that specific facial expressions are involuntarily and covertly elicited after the perception of similar expressions in others (Dimberg et al., 2000). This automatic mimicry is important in communication, and may contribute to guide the recognition of expressed emotions in other people (Oberman et al., 2007).

An important ongoing debate is whether (and to what degree) expression perception proceeds automatically or under the control of selective attention. To address this issue adequately, however, a precise definition of the concept of "automaticity" would be needed, but this concept is still associated with many different psychological features—see extensive reviews in Schneider and Shiffrin (1977), Shiffrin and Schneider (1977), Posner and Petersen (1990), Bargh et al. (1996), Bargh and Chartrand (1999), Moors and De Houwer (2006). These include processing aspects of which we are not aware, and/or that do not require effort, and/or over which we have no or little control, or for which we have no conscious intention. Furthermore, the degree of automaticity is generally divided in a dichotomous manner, between information processing that is obligatory and effortless, and hence difficult to alter or suppress on the one hand, and information processing that is intentional and effortful, hence controlled and conscious on the other hand (Moors and De Houwer, 2006). However, different degrees might exist between fully conscious, voluntary processing and fully unconscious, automatic processing.

Attention serves to selectively represent relevant information at the expense of competing and irrelevant information, but the mechanisms and effects of attention are not unitary. Studies of visual perception have shown that selective attention may involve several components, such as orienting to sensory events, detecting signals for conscious processing, and maintaining a vigilant alert state (Posner and Petersen, 1990). Visual selection can operate on the basis of spatial location, feature information, or even object properties. To detect important events, some perceptual processes must automatically analyze sensory inputs prior to full attention (Öhman et al., 2001a), and it is thought that automatic processing of emotionally significant information may contribute to initiate and speed-up (the shift of) attention to a corresponding target (Vuilleumier, 2005).

Nevertheless, as we will review here, only some of these different aspects of automaticity and attention have been investigated for the perception of facial expression (and more generally speaking, for a number of situations in the domain of emotion processing). The great variety of methods and techniques used to study automaticity and attention for facial expressions in the past few years suggests that the time should now be ready for better breaking down the concepts of automaticity and attention into elementary constituents that are more tractable to investigations in cognitive neuroscience.

Below we review both the behavioral and neuroimaging literature on the automatic perception of facial expressions of emotion in healthy volunteers and patients with brain damage. In particular, we will focus on aspects of automaticity in face perception that relate to task goals (intentionality), attentional control (selectivity), and conscious awareness (reportability). For additional perspectives on the interaction between attention and automaticity, we also refer the reader to previous reviews by Bargh and Chartrand (1999), Öhman (2002), Winkielman and Berridge (2004), Pessoa (2005), Vuilleumier (2005), and Bishop (2008). As we will describe, behavioral and neuroimaging findings converge to support some degree of automaticity in processing facial expressions, in that distinctive features of emotional faces can be extracted unintentionally, rapidly, and sometimes even unconsciously, presumably through specialized (cortical and/or subcortical) pathways involving the amygdala and closely related brain structures. However, even though such automatic processing can persist regardless of some factors related to explicit task demands or voluntary attention, it is still amenable to modulations (amplified or attenuated) by other factors related to endogenous states in the observer. Based on extant findings, we will therefore suggest that automaticity in emotional face processing is likely to reflect distinct components that should be better disentangled at both the behavioral and neural level.

Behavioral studies on recognition of facial expressions

In the classic psychological model by Bruce and Young (1986), facial expressions were proposed to be analyzed independently from face identity (see also Calder, Chapter 22, this volume). This idea was extended in subsequent neural models of face processing (see Gobbini and Haxby, 2007; Haxby et al., 2000). The independency of expressions and identity processing in these models was primarily based on double dissociations that have been observed in several neuropsychological case studies (i.e. prosopagnosic patients are not able to recognize facial identity but still are able to recognize facial expressions, though such observations have been mixed (Humphreys et al., 2007; Rossion et al., 2003), whereas amygdala patients are unable to recognize facial expressions although they are able to recognize face identity (Young et al., 1996; but see a discussion of these data by Calder, Chapter 22, this volume). Likewise, functional neuroimaging studies (positron emission tomography and functional magnetic resonance imaging (fMRI)) showed that distinct brain regions are recruited for processing face identity and expression, including the lateral fusiform gyrus and superior temporal sulcus, respectively (see also the later section "Neuroimaging studies").

However, recent behavioral research suggests that face identity and expression are not processed entirely independently. By using an adapted version of the classical Garner interference paradigm (Garner, 1974), it was found that judgment of facial expressions is influenced by changes in identity, even if subjects are asked to ignore the identity dimension. For instance, researchers have examined different variations between identity and expression by morphing between two opposite expressions, and morphing between two identities (Schweinberger et al., 1999). Participants were then asked to make identity judgments (i.e. person A or person B) or facial expression judgments (i.e. happy or angry). It was found that identity could be classified independently from the facial expression, suggesting that expressions did not affect face identification. By contrast, irrelevant variations in identity or sex of faces produced a significant interference on the classification of facial expressions (Atkinson et al., 2005; Schweinberger and Soukup, 1998; Schweinberger et al., 1999). These results point to a relative segregation of facial expression and identity recognition processes, rather than completely independent coding (see also Calder and Young 2005). In other words, if face identity can modulate the efficiency of facial expression recognition, this might imply that the processing of expression is not entirely automatic and independent from other factors.

However, the neural substrates of these effects remain unclear. Several imaging studies have shown that emotional expressions in faces can modulate neural responses in extrastriate visual cortex, including fusiform areas typically associated with face categorization and identification (e.g. Morris et al., 1998; Vuilleumier et al., 2001) (Figure 23.1), suggesting that face identity and facial expression may interact at this stage. Fusiform activity is also affected by familiarity in some studies (e.g. Dubois et al., 1999; Leveroni et al., 2000; Pourtois et al., 2005a), although it may persist in patients with prosopagnosia (Rossion et al., 2003), indicating that it is not sufficient for conscious face recognition. However, both emotion and familiarity effects on fusiform responses might reflect feedback modulations from limbic areas associated with emotion and memory processes (Sugase et al., 1999; Vuilleumier et al., 2004), rather than intrinsic visual computations. Hence, it is unresolved whether face identity may influence the processing of expression independent from interactions between familiarity and affective processes.

Other results from different experimental paradigms have also shown that facial emotions are processed with apparent automaticity, even when expressions are task-irrelevant. For example, adaptations of the classical Stroop paradigm (Stroop, 1935) have used emotional stimuli to demonstrate that an irrelevant emotional facial expressions can slow-down performance on another task-relevant dimension, such as color naming (Van Honk et al., 2002) or gender decision (Etkin et al., 2006) for face targets, as well as categorization of emotional words (Stenberg et al., 1998). This effect has also been found more generally for color naming when the irrelevant affective dimension involved emotionally desirable or undesirable personality-trait adjectives (Pratto and John, 1991) or threat words (Mathews and McLeod, 1985), although these behavioral effects have not been replicated with schematic images of spiders presented during color naming (Kolassa et al., 2006). However, a similar Stroop-like effect has been shown with other emotional stimuli (words or pictures) on the categorization of facial expressions (Etkin et al., 2006; Righart and de Gelder, 2008b), as well as on a variety of other tasks (e.g. Hartikainen et al., 2000; Okon-Singer et al., 2007), suggesting that this emotional interference is not specific to facial expressions. Even though the exact mechanism underlying these effects is still debated (Williams et al., 1996; see recent discussion by Algom et al., 2004), the overall interpretation is that emotional facial expressions (and emotional stimuli in general) may affect response latencies involuntarily due to a diversion of attentional resources towards the task-irrelevant emotional cues.

More generally, even when subjects categorize a stimulus presented alone, their response times tend to be longer for faces with negative than neutral or positive emotions (see Calder et al., 2000; Eastwood et al., 2003; Tracy and Robins, 2008), contrasting with the facilitation seen for these stimuli in visual search or attentional tasks (see below). These slower judgments made on emotional stimuli might result from interference or inhibition induced by emotion signals on task-relevant cognitive processes, as noted above for Stroop paradigms (see also Armony et al., 1997). These effects could perhaps also reflect the fact that threatening cues do not only draw attention more strongly, but also hold attention longer than neutral information (Fox et al., 2001). Both of these effects might be further amplified in anxious people, even below clinical levels (see Fox and Zougkou, Chapter 26, this volume).

Finally, it should be noted that recent research suggests that involuntary distracting effects are not only produced by threat-related or basic emotions, but also arise with positive or complex

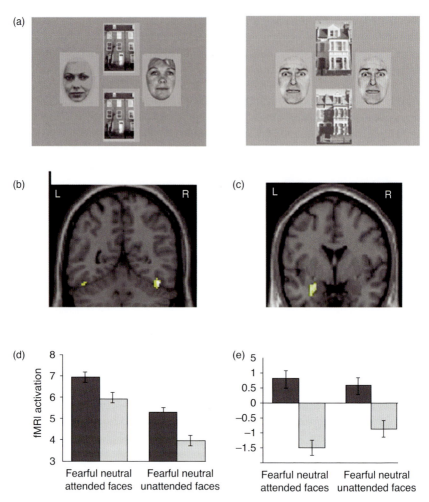

Fig. 23.1. Modulation of face processing by attention and emotion. (a) Illustration of the task. Each display included two faces and two houses, arranged in vertical and horizontal pairs. Faces could be arranged vertically and houses horizontally or vice versa in an unpredictable sequence. Both faces had a neutral expression, or both were fearful. At the beginning of each block of trials, a display with four boxes instructed subjects to attend and match only the vertical pair of stimuli or only the horizontal pair, in order to judge whether this pair showed the same or different pictures. (b) Fusiform activity was increased when subjects attended to faces versus houses at the relevant locations, regardless of emotion expression, whereas (c) amygdala activity was increased to fearful expression as compared to neutral faces, regardless of spatial attention. (d) Parameter estimates of activity across all conditions for the right fusiform gyrus, showing additive effects of attention and emotion; and (e) for the left amygdala, showing a similar magnitude of responses to fearful expression when faces appeared at the attended versus unattended locations. Error bars represent 1 SEM. Reprinted from Vuilleumier et al. (2001).

emotions like pride, embarrassment, and shame. These expressions of emotions could be reliably recognized, even under conditions with minimal attentional resources (Tracy and Robins, 2008). Nevertheless, response-times were generally found to be slower for fear relative to positive emotions happy and pride, converging with other evidence for a "negative threat bias" on response latencies in various tasks (Algom et al., 2004) as well as a "happy face advantage" observed in many previous studies (e.g. Kirita and Endo, 1995).

Taken together, these various behavioral paradigms have shown that the recognition of emotional facial expressions can proceed involuntarily and thus affect ongoing perceptual or attentional processes even if emotion is task-irrelevant. However, this may not be specific to faces, since similar effects may arise with other categories of emotional stimuli. Moreover, this may not take place entirely independently from the processing of other facial attributes or task characteristics that are presented at the same time, indicating that these involuntary processing may be controlled at least partly by other factors and, in that sense, not fully "automatic."

Behavioral studies on attention and awareness for facial expressions

Various behavioral studies have shown that facial expressions may be detected better or faster than neutral expressions. Such results come from experiments that manipulated attention (e.g. based on visual search or covert orienting) and/or suppressed awareness of the critical face stimuli (e.g. masking or rivalry), as we discuss below.

In a pioneer emotional visual search task, adapted from the classical search paradigm used in attention research (reviewed by Wolfe, 1998), Hansen and Hansen (1988) reported that subjects detected angry faces faster than happy faces, suggesting that an automatic pathway could process negative emotional expressions and speed-up face detection. Although it was later suggested that this effect was largely driven by low-level contrast differences between angry and happy face pictures (Purcell et al., 1996), the same results were later replicated using stimuli without such confounds (Öhman et al., 2001b; Eastwood et al., 2001). While threatening faces were found to be detected faster than friendly faces, no effect was found for sad faces, which suggests that this may not reflect a general effect of negative emotion (Öhman et al., 2001b). Importantly, in these tasks the slopes of the search functions (that is, the increased time that is needed to detect a facial expression as a function of the increasing number of distracters) is typically shallower for negative faces than for positive faces, although it is similar for inverted positive and negative faces. This suggests that the visual system is more efficient in guiding attention to the location of negative faces, but also that this detection is not completely independent from competition between simultaneous stimuli and relies on common resources to process distracters (i.e. it takes more time to find the face target when the crowd is larger). Thus, emotion cues do not appear to "bypass" attention, but rather facilitate attention by enhancing the perceptual saliency of face targets.

An effect of low-level facial features on attention is unlikely given that inverted faces do not produce the same results (e.g. Eastwood et al., 2001; Frischen et al., 2008). Moreover, schematic faces were found to produce a similar facilitation on search with very subtle differences in stimulus properties (Öhman et al., 2001b). Some features (e.g. eye vs. mouth-region, V vs. Λ-eyebrows) seem particularly critical to influence visual search for emotional faces, but only when embedded in a whole face configuration (rather than isolated) and when upright (rather than upside-down), suggesting that these features do not act as emotional cues if they are not perceived as face parts (Fox and Damjanovic, 2006; Eastwood et al., 2001; Öhman et al., 2001b). Thus, the critical visual information extracted from emotional faces during visual search appears to recruit face-selective processing rather than pop-out or elementary visual cues, because the same features presented alone without a face gestalt do not produce any effect. For instance, in one study (Schubö et al., 2006), participants were asked to either look for the presence of an emotional face with a discrepant expression, or for a stimulus with discrepant features. The feature stimuli were identical to faces, but lacked the eyes and surrounding oval, making them less face-like. Threatening faces were detected faster than friendly faces, but the threat features alone were not detected faster. Nevertheless, it remains unknown whether this sensitivity to emotional cues reflects a higher saliency of these facial features, or a selective tuning of expression recognition processes for specific features associated with emotional meaning (see Horstmann and Becker, 2008). The latter possibility would be consistent with other findings that eye-cues are crucial to mediate recognition of fear expression (Adolphs et al., 2005) and that the eyes drive the amygdala response to fearful faces (Whalen et al., 2004; but see Asghar et al., 2008).

Similar finding have been obtained with other stimulus materials evoking fear, like snakes, spiders, guns, and syringes (Öhman et al., 2001a; Blanchette, 2006), which suggests again that these effects are based on emotion rather than facial expressions per se. Furthermore, the influence of such emotional stimuli on search (or other attentional tasks) is typically modulated by affective characteristics of the observer, such as phobia or anxiety (Öhman et al., 2001a; see also Fox and Zougkou, Chapter 26, this volume). For instance, attention is directed faster to pictures of snakes than spiders in snake phobics (Öhman et al., 2001a), but vice versa in spider phobics (Lipp and Derakshan, 2005; Öhman et al., 2001a). This shows that these effects cannot be explained by intrinsic stimulus properties only. Instead, they reflect emotional appraisal processes that can be recruited without conscious intention and nevertheless modulated at least to some extent by internal states of the observer.

Similar biases in attention induced by emotion have been shown using various versions of the dot-probe paradigm. This paradigm was derived from Posner's covert orienting task (Posner et al., 1980), in which an exogenous cue induces a rapid covert shift of attention to the cued location (usually on the left or right side of the fixation). In the emotional version of this task, the target dot is replacing an emotional cue, such as a face, word, or scene. Several studies found that the detection of the target is faster when it replaces a threatening rather than a neutral facial expression (Mogg and Bradley, 1999; Pourtois et al., 2004a). Again, no such orienting effect is found when the face cue is inverted, suggesting that they are not due to simple low-level visual differences as in the traditional Posner paradigm. Similar cueing effects in dot-probe tasks have been reported for fear-relevant animals (Lipp and Derakshan, 2005) and for emotional words (MacLeod et al., 1986). In addition, reflexive attentional biases in search or dot-probe paradigms have also been found with positive facial expressions (such as happy among neutral faces, see Brosch et al., 2007; Lucas and Vuilleumier, 2008; Williams et al., 2005b).

As for search, spatial orienting effects in dot-probe tasks have usually been attributed to an automatic drawing or capture of attentional resources, but this is perhaps not the only explanation. An important distinction has been proposed between the initial orienting of attention to a new stimulus and the concomitant disengagement from another stimulus (Posner and Petersen, 1990). This distinction has been extended to emotional stimuli (Fox et al., 2001), by using a paradigm in which the target probe could be presented in an invalid location (other hemifield) or valid location (same hemifield) following a single emotional stimulus, allowing a pure measure of disengagement from the invalid location to the target. It was shown that participants took longer to disengage attention away from threat-related facial expressions as compared with positive or neutral faces, which was particularly the case for individuals with a high-level of anxiety; whereas there was no significant difference between faces in attracting attention to their own location. This disengagement effect was replicated in experiments using photographs but also schematic expressions of angry faces (Fox et al., 2001), but was not observed for sad facial expressions (Georgiou et al., 2005), suggesting that it may not result from negative emotions in general.

Taken together, these behavioral findings converge to indicate that the processing of facial expression (and other types of stimuli) may be unintentional and arise prior to receiving full attention, so as to increase the competitive saliency of an emotional stimulus among distractors and guide attention preferentially towards its location (see Frischen et al., 2008). However, although these characteristics constitute two major features of automaticity (see introduction above), they are still compatible with some sensitivity to top-down control and resource limitations. This is demonstrated not only by the fact that detection speed is dependent on the number of distracters in the search display (see above), but also by observations indicating that the detection advantage for emotional faces may depend on the type of target that is searched for. For instance, Hahn and Gronlund (2007) found shallower RT slopes for angry than happy face targets when participants had to search for any discrepant face among neutral items; but when they had a specific top-down goal for happy targets, the presence of angry distracters among neutral faces did not slow performance, suggesting that the involuntary attentional biases in search may depend on the combined influence of endogenous goals and stimulus characteristics (see also Bindemann et al., 2007).

One hypothesis has been put forward to propose that such automaticity in processing emotional facial expressions could occur only when the attentional system is not fully engaged by the main task, so that some attentional resources may be "spared" and "spill over" to emotion processing (e.g. Pessoa et al., 2002). Accordingly, emotional influences (from facial expressions or other stimulus materials) may be reduced under conditions of higher attentional load (Erthal et al., 2005; Okon-Singer et al., 2007), which has been taken to suggest that emotion processing is not automatic and depends on attention. However, in other studies it has been shown that the emotion effects occur irrespective of the imposed processing load (Mitchell et al., 2007; Righart and de Gelder, 2008b). This suggests that automaticity effects may still occur in conditions when attentional resources are limited. It should be noted however that a strict dichotomy between automatic processes and attentional control is probably oversimplified, as automaticity refers to several distinct dimensions (see review, Moors and De Houwer, 2006). This has been illustrated by an elegant behavioral study (Okon-Singer et al., 2007), in which emotional negative scenes were presented together with a competing task, under different levels of load. An interference was produced by negative emotional scenes on the judgment of a concurrent letter target presented at a different location, despite the fact that the presence of these scenes was task-irrelevant and detrimental for optimal performance; but this interference was found only when sufficient attention was available for target processing, not when processing load was increased by additional letter distractors. These results show that emotion processing is "automatic" (in that emotional distractors cannot be fully ignored even when they are counterproductive), but at the same time that it depends on task demands and attentional resources (in that interference is suppressed by additional competition). Moreover, a similar dissociation between the effect of attentional load and voluntary control has also been observed in experiments with masking procedures (Bahrami et al., 2008a,b) in which the visual representation of a stimulus that is not consciously seen can nevertheless be modulated by the task difficulty for another concurrent visible stimulus. It will be important to determine whether similar distinctions may apply to the processing of facial expressions, whose emotional meaning is not only very salient and effortlessly extracted, presumably due to human expertise in social processing (see Tracy and Robins 2008), but also conveyed by a single stimulus gestalt unlike the more complex semantics and layouts of objects in emotional scenes as those used by Okon-Singer et al. (2007).

Finally, another classic procedure to study the automatic effects of facial expressions on behavior is to use paradigms where affective reactions may be evoked even when the stimulus is processed minimally (Zajonc, 1980), for example during subliminal presentation after masking (e.g. Niedenthal, 1990; Murphy and Zajonc, 1993), binocular rivalry (Alpers and Gerdes, 2007;

Bannerman et al., 2008), or continuous flash suppression (Yang et al., 2007; Yoon et al., 2009). Several studies using such masking or suppression paradigms have revealed significant influences of unseen emotional faces on responses to a concurrent or subsequent stimulus, although it can sometimes be questioned whether the masked or suppressed face is truly invisible in all trails and all participants because of the high saliency of these stimuli and the high efficiency of face perception in humans (Pessoa, 2005). Subliminal presentation of faces may also influence other affective judgments made on faces (e.g. pleasantness) relative to conscious perception (Zajonc, 1980), and can affect behavioral decisions unrelated to face processing per se (Chen and Bargh, 1999). For example, it has been reported that subliminal (masked) presentation of happy and angry faces can influence subsequent behavioral actions of pouring and consuming a beverage: happy smiles that were seen subliminally caused participants to want more of a beverage, and like it better, whereas frowns had the opposite effect (Winkielman et al., 2005). Moreover, thirst was found to amplify these affective priming effects, suggesting that the effects on behavior could be changed by motivational states. Such findings further demonstrate the complex interactions between automatic and controlled processes, by showing that both conscious and unconscious mechanisms may act concurrently to influence perception and affective responses to facial expressions.

Taken together, behavioral studies indicate that facial expressions can be processed in a range of situations that imply automatic abilities, in the sense that these involve a lack of intention, focused attention, or even awareness. Yet, such automaticity does not preclude an effect of task load or top-down control, suggesting a need to better disentangle the role of distinct features of automaticity and to clarify their underlying cognitive mechanisms. Recent research in neuroscience and neuroimaging has delineated distributed brain networks selectively recruited during face processing tasks, showing differential responses to different conditions of automaticity, but still few have tried to tease apart these distinct facets of automaticity, as we will describe in the next section.

Neuroimaging studies of expression processing

The methods used in functional neuroimaging provide a major advantage to investigate automaticity in the perception of facial expression, as no direct verbal report or manual response is required to probe for an effect of emotion on brain responses, and different processing pathways can be assessed simultaneously.

Neuroimaging work has established that processing facial expressions of emotions recruits a number of brain areas including the amygdala (e.g. Morris et al., 1996), superior temporal sulcus (STS) (e.g. Narumoto et al., 2001), as well as the medial prefrontal and orbitofrontal cortex (e.g. Blair et al., 1999), insula (Critchley et al., 2002), and somatosensory areas (Pourtois et al., 2004b). In addition, extrastriate visual regions such as the fusiform face area (FFA), traditionally associated with face detection and identification (Grill-Spector et al., 2004), are also modulated by the emotional expression of faces, particularly when threat-related or fear-conditioned (e.g. Morris et al., 1998; Vuilleumier et al., 2001; Surguladze et al., 2003; Ganel et al., 2005). Such modulations of FFA by emotional expression may reflect feedback signals from the amygdala (Vuilleumier et al., 2004; Pourtois et al., 2010b) and seem to arise in a relatively automatic manner, without conscious control (Winston et al., 2002; Vuilleumier et al., 2002).

Differential responses to the nature and intensity of facial expressions are elicited in several of these brain regions, including FFA, amygdala, and OFC during tasks requiring passive viewing or judgments on facial dimensions other than their expression (i.e. gender-decision; Critchley et al., 2000; Morris et al., 1998; Surguladze et al., 2003). This suggests that some degree of "implicit" processing of emotional expression may take place in these regions even when task-irrelevant (but see Wright et al., 2007 for distinct task effects in OFC), consistent with behavioral findings reviewed above. By contrast, tasks requiring explicit categorization of facial expressions or subjective reports of elicited feelings have typically shown selective increases in higher-level areas in STS and medial prefrontal areas (for review, see Vuilleumier et al., 2003a), while amygdala activity may either be reduced as compared with implicit processing (Critchley et al., 2000) or passive viewing (Hariri et al., 2000; Lange et al., 2003), or sometimes increased instead (Gur et al., 2002). Differences between implicit and explicit processing might also partly be influenced by individual factors that are known to modulate emotional reactivity such as anxiety (Bishop et al., 2004), extraversion (Canli et al., 2002), attachment style (Vrtička et al., 2008), psychological well-being (Van Reekum et al., 2007), aggression tendency (Beaver et al., 2008; Passamonti et al., 2009), but also age (Gunning-Dixon et al., 2003) and even genotype (Hariri et al., 2002). Such modulations related to task contexts or individual factors might stem from changes in intrinsic responsiveness of the amygdala or its outputs by regulatory signals from ventromedial (Kim et al., 2003; Kim et al., 2004), and lateral prefrontal areas (Hariri et al., 2000), as well as anterior cingulate cortex (ACC) (Etkin et al., 2006; Van Reekum et al., 2007), acting together to balance reflexive responses to emotionally significant signals and endogenous control of attention to task-relevant information (Bishop et al., 2004).

Another important question is whether automaticity in facial expression processing is mediated at an early perceptual stage and/or later cognitive stage. Many studies have addressed this question by investigating the temporal dynamics of face perception with event-related potentials (ERPs). Results generally converge to suggest that the effects of emotion upon face perception may occur very rapidly and persist even when expression is task-irrelevant. Thus, the amplitude of early visual components such as the P100 is consistently modulated by facial expressions (Batty and Taylor, 2003; Pourtois et al., 2005b). P1 also predicts involuntary mimicry during presentations of angry or happy faces (Achaibou et al., 2008). As mimicry proceeds (to a great degree) automatically (Dimberg et al., 2000), this relation to the P1 amplitude accords with an involvement of pathways operating at an early stage of processing, prior to conscious and explicit recognition of emotion expressions. The P1 is not only enhanced for negative but also positive stimuli (Brosch et al., 2008). In addition, MEG work has shown that happy and sad faces presented in a one-back repetition task evoked larger response amplitude than neutral faces at approximately 110 ms, with possible sources in mid-occipital areas (Halgren et al., 2000). This finding therefore further suggests that early stages of visual processing may be affected by emotional face expression in an automatic way.

Another ERP component related to face-processing, the N170, is also influenced by emotion, particularly when the task requires categorizing the facial expression (Righart and de Gelder, 2008a) or when a categorical change of expression is induced in face pairs during same/different judgments (Campanella et al., 2002). However, similar effects can arise when the facial expression is task-irrelevant (Blau et al., 2007; Batty and Taylor, 2003; Morel et al., 2009; Righart and de Gelder, 2006; Stekelenburg and de Gelder, 2004; Williams et al., 2006a); And they do not seem to depend on low-level visual features, since similar effects are produced by schematic facial expressions (Krombholz et al., 2007). MEG recordings have also shown increases of the M170 to emotional versus neutral faces (e.g. Lewis et al., 2003).

However, it should be noted that emotion effects on the N170 have not been reported unequivocally (Eimer and Holmes, 2002; Holmes et al., 2003; Krolak-Salmon et al., 2001), and the effects may under some conditions reflect configural rather than purely emotional effects (see Ashley et al., 2004; Pourtois et al., 2010b). Future studies may reveal which factors underlie these inconsistencies. One factor that might be important is stimulus repetition, which may result in different effects for neutral and emotional faces: the M170/N170 amplitudes are initially larger for fearful and happy facial expressions, but tend to increase after repetition for neutral faces, while they remain similar for emotional facial expressions (Morel et al., 2009; but see Ishai et al., 2006; and Blau et al., 2007).

Other effects of facial expressions have been reported, including an early frontocentral positivity 120 ms after stimulus presentation (Eimer and Holmes, 2002), preceding the N170 associated with face recognition. Later components such as the P300, or sustained late positive potentials (between 550–750 ms), tend to be enhanced only during tasks requiring explicit attention to the facial expressions (Krolak-Salmon et al., 2001). Intracranial recordings in the amygdala also demonstrated long latency modulations (between 200–800 ms) when attention was explicitly directed at facial expression, not during gender-decision (Krolak-Salmon et al., 2004). These long-latency effects might be commonly observed when subjects are engaged in an explicit emotion recognition task, because similar responses were also observed for emotional words (Naccache et al., 2005). However, intracranial recordings in the amygdala may show earlier responses to emotional (fear) faces, starting approximately 130 ms post onset and continuing until further attentional enhancement around 700 ms (Pourtois et al., 2010a). Although caution is warranted in comparing intracranial EEG recordings with surface ERPs, this early latency is consistent with results of Eimer and Holmes (2002), and suggest that emotional face processing in the amygdala may take place at similar latencies as cortical effects associated with P1 but precede those associated with N170 (see also next section).

In summary, neuroimaging data on face processing support the notion that perceptual encoding of emotional face expressions can be fast, efficient, and unintentional, at least in conditions where faces are seen and attended but their emotional expression is task-irrelevant. This may allow emotional expression to be processed prior to attention and awareness, although unconscious responses might differ from conscious processing in several ways, as discussed next.

Neuroimaging studies of attention and awareness

Significant activations to emotional versus neutral faces have also been found in the amygdala when emotional faces are briefly presented and backward masked, particularly with fearful or angry expressions (e.g. Morris et al., 1998, 1999; Whalen et al., 1998), supporting the view that some threat signals could be processed automatically and unconsciously by this brain region (Öhman, 2002). Furthermore, differential responses to positive or negative expressions of masked faces were still observed in the ventral amygdala, while an undifferentiated arousal response was seen in the dorsal amygdala (Whalen et al., 1998). These data converge with differential skin conductance responses being evoked when angry faces are backward masked after aversive conditioning by a shock, relative to faces that were never paired with the shock (Esteves et al., 1994). Unconscious ERP effects have also been reported for the N170, showing a stronger negativity for fearful faces as compared with neutral faces, even when the images were backward-masked (Pegna et al., 2008), or rendered invisible by using a continuous flash suppression paradigm (Jiang et al., 2009). By contrast, awareness relative to masked presentation leads to differential fMRI responses in STS, insula, and visual cortex (Critchley et al., 2002).

However, it has been argued that the presentation-times used in these masking studies may not have prevented conscious access in all participants and that individuals may vary in their ability to detect faces in rapidly masked displays (Pessoa et al., 2005a). Nonetheless, other studies have used shorter target presentation-times (Liddell et al., 2005; L.M. Williams et al., 2006b), and still found differential responses in the amygdala, confirming previous results. These effects may not occur specifically for faces, as the amygdala has also been reported to be modulated by backwardly-masked emotional words that could not reach awareness (Naccache et al., 2005).

Nevertheless, automatic emotion responses after masking might be more effective with faces than with other types of stimuli, since amygdala responses to emotional faces have been shown to be driven by elementary facial features such as wide-open eyes and pupil size (Demos et al., 2008; Whalen et al., 2004; Yang et al., 2007; but see Asghar et al., 2008) or coarse low-frequency cues (Vuilleumier et al., 2003b; but see Said et al., 2009). Further, although these results show that backward masking is a useful method to test the automaticity of emotion processing, this procedure has many potentials flaws (e.g. due to failures of computer screens or beamers to ensure a reliable timing of stimulus presentation; see Wiens, 2006); and the remarkable efficiency and rapidity of human visual system might make it difficult to use the method successfully, unless extremely short duration are used (which may in turn preclude any meaningful visual information to be delivered to the retina in standard experimental conditions and require a strict control of fixation). There may also be individual differences in presentation-times that are necessary to achieve masking (Pessoa et al., 2005a). Furthermore, while amygdala responses to masked emotional faces might be reduced or suppressed with brief stimuli in observers who report no explicit awareness, similar amygdala activation may be observed when these individuals make false alarms and report emotional faces on trials without any masked stimulus (Pessoa and Padmala, 2007), indicating that fMRI responses in amygdala per se may not allow a distinction between stimulus-driven effects due to unconscious processing and top-down effects produced by conscious experience.

The amygdala responses to emotional expressions of unconsciously perceived faces have also been confirmed by imaging studies of binocular rivalry (Jiang and He, 2006; Pasley et al., 2004; M.A. Williams et al., 2004). In the latter paradigm, two images are presented, for example a face and a house, but each to one eye separately, such that one of the images dominates perception while the other is suppressed from awareness (Figure 23.2). By comparing brain activity during epochs in which the face was perceived but the house was suppressed, and vice versa, it was found that amygdala responses may increase for both fearful and happy faces, as compared with neutral faces, even when these are unseen and perception is dominated by house pictures. Interestingly, behavioral paradigms using continuous flash suppression (i.e. in which stimuli are invisible due to strongly suppressive nature of dynamic noise) have shown that fearful faces are detected faster (Yang et al., 2007). Future studies may reveal which features in the face and which task demands determine these differential results in neural and behavioral data.

Besides manipulating task demands and stimulus visibility, a third type of approach to test automaticity of expression processing is to investigate how changes in selective attention to faces may modify brain responses. Several fMRI studies have shown residual amygdala responses (as well as activations in other brain regions including fusiform and orbitofrontal cortex) when emotional faces are presented in unattended conditions or together with concurrent task-relevant stimuli, as compared with when they are presented in the focus of attention (Anderson et al., 2003; M.A. Williams et al., 2005a; Vuilleumier et al., 2001). These experiments have manipulated either spatial attention (e.g. Bishop et al., 2004; Ewbank et al., 2009; Vuilleumier et al., 2001) or object-based attention (e.g. Anderson et al., 2003), but found generally similar results, although it is possible that different visual selection mechanisms may have produced at least partly different results. In the latter attention studies, amygdala responses to fearful faces were often found to be unchanged during inattention, even though cortical responses in fusiform cortex were reduced (e.g. Vuilleumier et al., 2001), suggesting that expression processing in the amygdala does not depend on fully attentive processing in the visual cortex. However, other studies have suggested that amygdala activation may depend on the attentional resources that are available for facial expressions and is therefore seen only when attention is not fully engaged by the distracting task (Mitchell et al., 2007; Pessoa et al., 2002, 2005b; Silvert et al., 2007) (Figure 23.3). Thus, consistent with the perceptual load hypothesis (Lavie, 2005), the latter studies found increased activations in

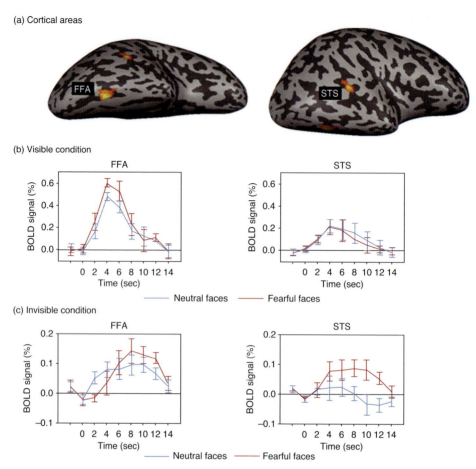

Fig. 23.2 FMRI responses to visible and invisible face images during interocular suppression. (a) Face-selective areas (FFA and STS) identified with an independent scan and depicted on the inflated right hemisphere of a representative observer. (b) Results for the visible condition. Each panel shows the time course averaged from six observers with scrambled faces as the baseline. Results from the left hemisphere are similar to the data shown here for the right hemisphere. Both the FFA and the STS had strong activations to visible neutral (blue curves and bars) and fearful (red curves and bars) faces. (c) Results for the invisible condition. Each panel shows the time course averaged across six observers.

the amygdala and fusiform cortex only under conditions of low attentional load for the main task, but not under conditions of high load (Pessoa et al., 2002, 2005b).

However, it should be noted that such effects of load do not preclude that some aspects of emotional face processing are stimulus-driven and unintentional when perceptual resources or task demands are appropriate, and converge with behavioral findings in visual search or Stroop studies showing that top-down factors related to current goals or prior expertise may affect the efficiency of automatic processes. Thus, differences in selective attention or perceptual load between conditions might influence amygdala activation on top of other more automatic processes, with both types of effects proceeding in parallel. Independent additive effects of spatial attention and emotion have been found in the fusiform cortex, but not in the amygdala (e.g. Vuilleumier

(d) Amygdala responses

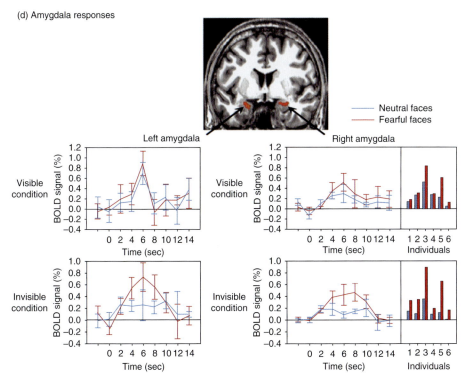

Fig. 23.2 (*Contd.*) (d) The bilateral amygdalae were identified with an independent scan. The average time course and individual BOLD amplitude are shown in each panel. Even when observers were not aware of the nature of the pictures presented in this condition, the FFA still showed substantial activation for both invisible neutral and fearful faces, whereas the STS only responded to invisible fearful faces. For both visible and invisible conditions, the amygdala showed stronger responses to fearful faces (red curves and bars) than neutral faces (blue curves and bars). Error bars stand for SE. Reprinted from *Current Biology*, **16**(20), Yi Jiang and Sheng He, Cortical Responses to Invisible Faces: Dissociating Subsystems for Facial-Information Processing, Copyright (2006), with permission from Elsevier.

et al., 2001). However, other top-down effects related to specific task demands or emotional contexts might potentially also act additively on stimulus-driven responses in the amygdala.

Further, high attentional load does not induce a complete suppression of amygdala activation to emotional faces in all paradigms (Pessoa et al., 2005b; Silvert et al., 2007), and does not only affect emotional processing but also impacts on other factors influencing amygdala activity. Thus, several fMRI studies found that inattention did not only reduce amygdala responses to negative facial expressions, but also increased responses to neutral faces (Silvert et al., 2007). The amygdala might even respond preferentially to potentially threatening stimuli under certain conditions of inattention (M.A. Williams et al., 2005a). These findings therefore suggest that high load or inattention can decrease the specificity of amygdala responses (Silvert et al., 2007), rather than just decrease its sensitivity. Interestingly, some researchers proposed that, rather than being specific to threat, amygdala responses may be particularly driven by ambiguous or unpredictable events (Whalen, 1998, 2007). This hypothesis has been supported by studies that showed different

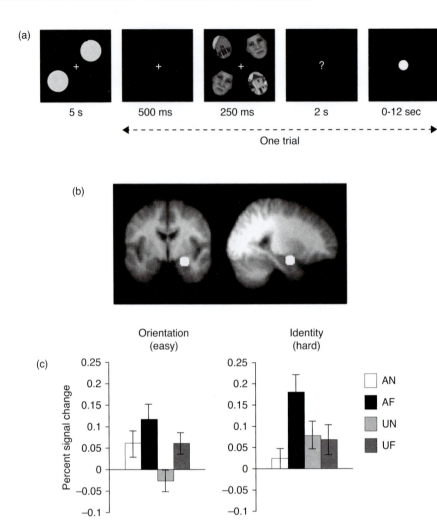

Fig. 23.3 Influence of attentional load on the processing of emotional facial expressions in the amygdala. (a) Illustration of the task used. Each trial began with an instruction screen indicating which task to perform (orientation or identity) and which pictures to match (diagonally aligned). Orientation judgments constituted a relatively easy task (low attentional load), whereas identity judgments constituted a more difficult task (high attentional load). (b) Region of interest in right amygdala. (c) Mean percent signal changes (±S.E.) in the amygdala ROI for attended neutral faces (AN), attended fearful faces (AF), unattended neutral faces (UN), and unattended fearful faces (UF) during the "easy" orientation task and in the "hard" identity task. In the latter condition ("hard identity task"), amygdala responses to unattended faces were unchanged for the fear expressions (UF) but increased for the neutral expressions (UN), relative to the former condition (easy task). Reprinted from *NeuroImage*, **38**(2), Laetitia Silvert, Jöran Lepsien, Nickolaos Fragopanagos, et al., Influence of attentional demands on the processing of emotional facial expressions in the amygdala, Copyright (2007), with permission from Elsevier.

amygdala response in situations where the meaning of facial expressions was determined by contextual information rather than facial traits (e.g. by using verbal stories (Kim et al., 2004) or gaze orientation to an object (Adams et al., 2003; N'Diaye et al., 2009)). This might explain why inattention could increase amygdala responses to otherwise neutral stimuli.

Likewise, other recent work has shown that the amygdala activity depends on the nature of threat conveyed by different categories of facial expressions, and that this modulation may differ for individuals with high as compared with low anxiety traits. For instance, the amygdala activates to fearful faces both when attended and unattended but is increased in individuals with higher anxiety specifically in unattended conditions (Ewbank et al., 2009), which is consistent with previous work (Bishop et al., 2004); whereas the same region shows increased responses to angry faces and increased effects of high anxiety only when faces are attended. This dissociation might reflect a differential biological significance of these two types of stimuli, in relation to undetermined signals of danger within the environment (fear) as opposed to a more direct form of threat (anger), consistent with the amygdala being part of a warning system that detects danger and triggers adaptive alert responses (Ewbank et al., 2009; see also LeDoux, 1996).

Changes in attention or load probably do not gate emotional processing in an all-or-none manner, and different brain regions involved in emotion processing may show different profiles of response and not always activate in a linear stepwise manner (see, e.g. Said et al., 2009). For instance, modulation by attention may occur at different stages of processing, which can only be distinguished by using techniques that achieve a high temporal resolution, such as electroen-cephalography (EEG) or magnetoencephalography (MEG). Results from ERP studies (Holmes et al., 2006) indicate that neural responses to emotional faces (over frontocentral sites) are pro-longed when attentional resources are sufficient (i.e. ERP differences starting at 160 ms and present for 700 ms) but much briefer when attentional resources are limited (effects eliminated beyond 220 ms). Such differences might or might not result in measurable differences in BOLD (blood-oxygen-level dependent) responses during fMRI studies. This highlights the major limita-tions of fMRI for dissociating changes in BOLD signals that are due to reduced duration versus reduced amplitude of neuronal responses. Under conditions of inattention (or unawareness), transient emotional responses might still persist in the amygdala or other pathways, but could produce reliable fMRI responses in some cases (e.g. Vuilleumier et al., 2001) or result in reduced or even abolished BOLD activation in other conditions (e.g. Pessoa et al., 2002). In keeping with this, intracranial recordings in patients implanted with depth-electrodes in the amygdala revealed the existence of an early activation to facial expressions (around 130 ms) which was similar for faces presented within or outside the focus of attention, whereas later activity in the same amygdala sites (after 700 ms) were strongly modulated by both emotion expression and selective attention (Pourtois et al., 2010b; see also Halgren et al., 1994). These findings are consistent with differential latencies of emotion effects and attention effects recorded by scalp ERPs (Holmes et al., 2003; Vuilleumier and Pourtois, 2007), possibly reflecting quicker affective categorization thresholds in the amygdala than explicit recognition and attention to faces (Vuilleumier, 2005).

Finally, another approach to investigate automatic processing of emotions is to examine how it can affect other cognitive processes, including attentional performance. Converging with behavioral studies on spatial orienting and visual search (see above), several neuroimaging studies determined specific neural correlates underlying involuntary biases or shifts of attention towards the spatial location of emotional faces. For example, the dot-probe paradigm has been used in an ERP experiment examining how the visual event-related potential P1 may change when a neutral visual target (probe) appears at the same location as an emotional face or as a neutral face (Pourtois et al., 2004b). An involuntary capture of attention was demonstrated in this paradigm by enhanced P1 amplitudes to the probe (indicating enhanced attention to its location) when the probe replaced a fearful face as compared with a neutral face; no such attentional effects were observed when the probe replaced a happy face (but for significant effects with another category of positive stimuli; see Brosch et al., 2008). Yet, faces and their expression were never relevant for task performance. These results thus show that facial expressions automatically drew attention to their spatial location and subsequently enhanced visual processing of the dot-probe. Further, source analyses demonstrated that the enhanced P1 response was preceded by differential activity in posterior parietal cortex on valid trials (target on the side of the emotional face), suggesting that the cueing effect was mediated by an influence of emotional faces on parietal regions involved in spatial attention, consistent with a role for these regions in spatial orienting (Posner and Petersen, 1990). In contrast, activation in medial frontal sources (presumably ACC) preceded the P1 responses to probes on invalid side (Pourtois et al., 2005c), consistent with a role of this region in controlling conflict. Similarly, fMRI results in the same paradigm demonstrated that emotional expression of peripheral faces modulated responses evoked by subsequent targets in both parietal and occipital areas (Pourtois et al., 2006).

Importantly, such cueing effects are not simply produced by the distinctive visual features of emotional expression in faces, but indisputably depend on their emotional value, as shown by an elegant fMRI study that used fear conditioning with angry faces in a dot-probe paradigm (Armony and Dolan, 2002). In the latter case, all faces had a similar angry expression but only one was aversively conditioned with a sound burst. Results showed greater activation in amygdala as well as in frontal and parietal areas when the dot-probe was preceded by the face that had acquired a negative valence by conditioning, suggesting that emotional responses could modulate attentional systems and influence spatial orienting. Again, these effects occurred even though the faces were actually not relevant to the task at hand. Moreover, because only two faces (one male, one female) were used and counterbalanced across participants, attentional orienting could not be due to low level differences in faces; but the conditioning effects may have relied on discriminating the sex and/or identity of these faces in addition to their valence. Hence, the involuntary effect of emotion on attention could apparently be elicited by extracting distinct identity cues paired with distinct affective values, presumably implicating associative learning in the amygdala rather than a mere categorization of specific facial features. In any case, the results of this study (Armony and Dolan, 2002) are consistent with behavioral and ERP results showing that negative facial expressions may capture attention to a spatial location in a reflexive manner. Likewise, the degree of automatic activation of the amygdala to emotional faces has also been related to behavioral facilitation of attention observed during visual search: faster detection latencies during search for emotional faces were found to be correlated with the magnitude of amygdala responses recorded during the presentation of masked facial expressions (Ohrmann et al., 2007).

In sum, neuroimaging findings confirm reciprocal influences between expression processing and selective attention or conscious awareness (Vuilleumier et al., 2003a). These results also suggest that the amygdala plays a central role in responding to emotional face information under a range of conditions where attention is not selectively directed to the location or the nature of faces, or where awareness is markedly reduced or even abolished. This is broadly consistent with a fair amount of automaticity of amygdala responses, in the sense of involuntariness and effective-ness of expression processing, allowing subsequent reflexive influences on various other processing domains. Such automaticity does not prevent additional modulations by context, goals, or task demands. Note that in neurophysiology, many other automatic or reflexive processes may also be modulated by volition or top-down factors, including for example pain, hunger, thirst, or even micturition—even when these are partly mediated by low-level (e.g. spinal) synaptic circuits. Besides the amygdala, other regions in STS and prefrontal areas are more often found to show an interaction between stimulus-driven and task-dependent responses to facial expressions.

However, much remains to be determined concerning the brain circuits underlying the exact sources and the sites of such modulations, and whether some aspects of automaticity (e.g. unawareness and inattention) depend on the recruitment of distinct neural pathways, such as subcortical rather than cortical routes (LeDoux, 1996), or instead reflect two (or more) distinct stages (or modes) of processing along the same cortico-subcortical pathways (see Rudrauf et al., 2008; Vuilleumier, 2005). Although controversial, some evidence for unconscious processing of facial expression through subcortical pathways has been provided by studies of neurological patients with cortical lesions, as we will review below.

Neurological patients and cortical–subcortical neural pathways

Neurological case studies provide invaluable information about the direct causal role of neural structures implicated in perceptual and cognitive processes. In accordance with animal studies (reviewed by LeDoux, 1996; Phelps and LeDoux, 2005), and imaging work in humans (reviewed above), studies in brain-damaged patients (Adolphs et al., 1994; Anderson and Phelps, 2001; Vuilleumier et al., 2004) have generally confirmed that the amygdala is necessary for rapid processing of emotional signals, including facial expression and other social cues in faces (such as gaze) (Cristinzio et al., 2010). Anatomic data in both primates and rodents have shown that the amygdala has bidirectional connections with widespread cortical and other subcortical regions (Aggleton et al., 1980; LeDoux et al., 1996; Sah et al., 2003). These connections do not only enable the efficient detection of emotional stimuli, but also the orchestration of a range of behavioral and physiological reactions, including feedback on sensory processing (LeDoux et al., 1996) and influences upon attentional systems (Vuilleumier, 2005). Hence, patients with amygdala lesions are not only impaired in recognizing emotional facial expressions (Adolphs et al., 1994, 2005; Cristinzio et al., 2007), but also fail to exhibit the typical modulation of emotion on perceptual processing and attention (Anderson and Phelps, 2001; Vuilleumier et al., 2004).

Strong support for automaticity in the perception of faces and emotion expressions has come from studies reporting that such processing may not depend on an intact primary visual cortex. Some neurological patients have a loss of vision due to occipital damage but can still report above chance level some stimuli in their blind visual field (blindsight), including facial expressions (de Gelder et al., 1999), and still show fear responses (i.e. startle reflex) when conditioned to a visual cue (Hamm et al., 2003). Furthermore, fMRI studies in such patients showed increased amygdala activation to fearful and fear-conditioned stimuli that were presented in the blind field (Morris et al., 2001; Pegna et al., 2005). These findings parallel the phenomenon of binocular rivalry in non-neurological subjects (Jiang and He, 2006; Pasley et al., 2004; M.A. Williams et al., 2004) (see above). Because this suppression for the representation of unseen stimuli in binocular rivalry is thought to arise in early visual areas including V1 (Polonsky et al., 2000), both phenomena of binocular rivalry in normal observers and blindsight in patients with occipital damage suggest that some emotional face information can be processed without V1, perhaps via a subcortical route involving pulvinar and/or superior colliculus and projecting directly to the amygdala (Morris et al., 2001; Pasley et al., 2004; M.A. Williams et al., 2004). However, alternative visual pathways may also exist via direct projections from the lateral geniculate nucleus (LGN) and pulvinar which project to other areas of visual cortex outside V1 (Cowey, 2010), as well as via reciprocal connections between visual pulvinar and inferior temporal cortex (including fusiform cortex in humans; see Clarke et al., 1999). All these routes could potentially support some form of recognition in the absence of V1, suggesting that results from blindsight should be treated with caution when considering the possible neural substrates of unconscious effects in these patients.

Some evidence from patients with lesions in the pulvinar confirms that a subcortical route via pulvinar to the amygdala might be important in emotion perception. A study reported that fear recognition was impaired for faces briefly presented in the hemifield contralesional to lateral (but not medial) pulvinar damage (Ward et al., 2007). Another patient with left pulvinar damage (Ward et al., 2005) also showed abnormal behavior in a color decision task in which targets were preceded by a brief task-irrelevant emotional picture. Unlike normal subjects (see also Okon-Singer et al., 2007), the patient's performance was not disrupted by the threatening stimuli, specifically when these were presented in his right visual field (contralateral to the pulvinar lesion). The authors concluded that such disruption of performance caused by brief emotional stimuli normally requires an intact subcortical route (Ward et al., 2005), while cortical processing could be responsible for disruption caused by longer stimulus presentations (which was actually preserved in this patient).

Taken together, these findings are usually taken to suggest a crucial role for subcortical routes for rapid and possibly unconscious processing of emotional faces, in agreement with functional imaging data showing a selective activation of pulvinar and superior colliculus together with amygdala in responses to fearful faces presented in masked conditions (e.g. Liddell et al., 2005; Morris et al., 1999; Pasley et al., 2004). Moreover, it is remarkable that visual processing functions in blindsight may be selectively tuned to low spatial frequency content (Sahraie et al., 2003), consistent with a predominant role of low spatial frequency information in subcortical visual pathways and a selective sensitivity of amygdala responses to coarse visual cues in fearful faces (Vuilleumier et al., 2003b).

Another alternative to this subcortical hypothesis is that coarse visual inputs might reach the amygdala and other distant (e.g. frontal) brain regions through a rapid feedforward sweep of cortical activations (Bullier, 2001; Kveraga et al., 2007), with distinction between conscious versus unconscious perception reflecting two different processing stages rather than two different pathways (Vuilleumier, 2005). Thus, amygdala responses to emotional expressions could be triggered by a limited amount of information, consisting of low spatial frequency cues conveyed by magnocellular visual inputs to the cortex, or simple "diagnostic" features of emotional stimuli (e.g. wide-open eyes in fearful faces). This initial emotional appraisal could then provide feedback signals to visual cortex where further processing may take place based on more detailed sensory information (e.g. high-spatial frequency information conveyed by parvocellular inputs). This could perhaps also explain why amygdala responses might be less discriminative of emotional versus neutral expression under conditions of reduced attention or reduced awareness (e.g. Silvert et al., 2007; Williams et al., 2005a; see above). Moreover, both the two-pathway or two-stage mechanisms would account for ERP data demonstrating that the emotional significance of faces can be encoded after short latencies (e.g. approximately 130 ms), prior to higher-level processes associated with categorical encoding of face stimuli (e.g. 170–200 ms). Accordingly, recent research using dynamic causal modeling of MEG data (Rudrauf et al., 2008) has provided support to the two-pathway hypothesis, by showing that the patterns of activation to emotional information was better explained by a network of regions including a fast subcortical or corticocortical pathway, rather than by a purely serial sequence of processing steps. However, more direct neurophysiological evidence is still needed to disentangle between these two hypotheses.

On the other hand, studies in patients with spatial neglect suggest that the automatic effects of facial expressions on attention and behavior do not depend on intact functioning of parietal and/or frontal areas involved in top-down attentional control. Neglect entails a loss of awareness for stimuli presented contralateral to the brain lesion, particularly when competing stimuli are simultaneously presented on the ipsilateral side (e.g. perceptual extinction). Unlike blindsight, V1 may still be intact and functionally activated despite spatial neglect (Driver and Vuilleumier, 2001). Neuropsychological findings in these patients indicate that faces with happy and angry facial expressions show less extinction relative to neutral faces when presented simultaneously across both visual fields (Fox, 2002; Vuilleumier and Schwartz, 2001), and are detected more rapidly than neutral face targets in visual search tasks (Lucas and Vuilleumier, 2008). This advantage for emotional faces is found on both sides of visual space, despite a pervasive attentional bias towards the neglected side. This suggests an additive influence of attention and emotion on face detection, which appears consistent with the idea that face processing in fusiform cortex is modulated by separate top-down influences from the parietal areas and amygdala (Vuilleumier, 2005). Other studies in neglect patients have shown that the explicit judgment of emotion in target faces can be influenced by a facial expression prime presented in the contralesional hemi-field even when the prime is extinguished (M.A. Williams and Mattingley, 2004), consistent with residual processing of unseen emotional faces.

Interestingly, systematic analyses of brain lesions in neglect patients suggest that those with the largest "benefits" in detection rates for emotional relative to neutral stimuli in visual search tasks had lesions centered on dorsolateral frontal and parietal regions, whereas those with weaker emotional biases had lesions in the basal ganglia and orbitofrontal regions more frequently, a pattern replicated for both emotional faces (Lucas and Vuilleumier, 2008) and emotional voices (Grandjean et al., 2008). The latter results are consistent with an important role of OFC in mediating some effects of emotion signals on behavior and attention through its connections with other frontal and parietal regions. A single-case study using fMRI in a neglect patient with visual extinction also found that fearful faces activated both the amygdala and orbitofrontal cortex, in addition to extrastriate cortex, under conditions where two stimuli (faces and houses) were presented simultaneously but with fearful faces being extinguished. These findings indicate that these regions could activate to emotional face expression even without awareness (Vuilleumier et al., 2002).

Altogether, studies of blindsight and neglect patients converge to suggest that emotional face expressions may be processed in the absence of awareness. While blindsight reveals that facial expressions are perceived without primary visual cortex, results from neglect patients add to the evidence that emotional influences on perception are not mediated by frontoparietal networks controlling spatial attention, and further suggest that orbitofrontal regions might be critically implicated in the interactions between attention and facial (or vocal) expression of emotions (Grandjean et al., 2008; Lucas and Vuilleumier, 2008). However, more research is needed to identify the exact neural pathways underlying the extraction of emotional face information in blindsight and neglect.

Automaticity beyond facial expressions of emotions

Recent studies have investigated whether other social affective features of the face, including first impressions (Todorov et al., 2007) and social judgments such as trustworthiness (Engell et al., 2007; Winston et al., 2002), may also be evaluated in an automatic manner. It was found that responses of the amygdala are sensitive to features that relate to trustworthiness, particularly when such evaluations are implicit and not directly task-relevant (Winston et al., 2002), although these responses are not only enhanced to highly untrustworthy but also highly trustworthy faces (Said et al., 2009). Moreover, amygdala responses were best predicted by the features related to consensus ratings (i.e. faces that everyone judged as determining lack of trust), whereas individual judgments of trustworthiness did not reliably account for amygdala activation. These responses have been considered to be automatic since the task demands were not directed to trustworthiness (i.e. subjects made trust ratings during a separate task) (Engell et al., 2007). Furthermore, (un)trustworthiness was found to be the best predictor of implicit amygdala responses to faces among a series of 14 personality trait dimensions, including attractiveness, aggressiveness, intelligence, caring, and so forth (Todorov and Engel, 2008), although such effects seem to reflect a more general response to negative valence and facial features typically associated with anger, such a frowns (Oosterhof and Todorov, 2008). An intact amygdala (perhaps together with the hippocampus and temporal pole) may be necessary to learn specific face-behavior descriptors related to trustworthiness (Todorov and Olson, 2008). Moreover, because prototypical facial features associated with judgments of trust may strongly depend on context and goals of current social interactions (e.g. whether an economic partner has the intention to cooperate, Singer et al., 2004), as well as past interactions, it is likely that implicit activation of amygdala by trustworthiness cues may reflect a more general "default mode" of the amygdala for the appraisal of potential threat and self-relevance (Vuilleumier and Sander, 2008), which can be modulated by several top-down factors. Future research should clarify whether amygdala responses to untrustworthy faces are also obtained in unconscious or implicit conditions (e.g. in blindsight patients, or during binocular rivalry and subliminal presentation in normal participants), and whether these "automatic" responses reflect their (un)trustworthiness during more conscious judgments in an explicit task.

Notably, affective preferences can be formed without cognitive elaboration and may dissociate from conscious judgments when faces are presented without conscious awareness judgments or judged explicitly (Zajonc, 1980). Kunst-Wilson and Zajonc (1980) have shown that learning to prefer some visual stimuli does not require explicit recognition of these stimuli. First impressions are indeed formed quickly, based on minimal information that is available (Bar et al., 2006). These formed impressions about a person's traits may influence the brain response to this person's face, even when the expression is neutral. For example, increased response of the insular cortex to neutral faces is observed when the person's behavior had previously been associated with disgust (Todorov et al., 2007). Past social interactions during exchanges in economic games (Singer et al., 2004) as well as perceived cooperation or conflicts during pseudo-interactive games (Vrtička et al., 2009) can also trigger differential responses to subsequent presentation of neutral faces in brain areas associated with affective appraisal and mentalizing, including STS, ventral ACC, and amygdala, suggesting automatic retrieval of past emotional associations even when the current task does not require explicit emotional judgments.

Future studies should further investigate whether these responses are truly automatic and persist during conditions of inattention or unawareness, and whether they can be controlled consciously by task demands and re-appraisal strategies. Moreover, although research on first impressions and trust suggests that other affective dimensions of faces beyond emotional expressions can be extracted rapidly, effortlessly and unintentionally, and thus considered as automatic, it remains to be determined whether these abilities are truly distinct or not from the exquisite sensitivity to more subtle and partial components of emotional expressions (see Oosterhof and Todorov, 2008).

Summary and conclusions

Whether the perception of facial expressions is dependent on attention and perceptual goals, or may arise in a relatively automatic way instead, has been debated for a long time in psychology and neuroscience. Different methods (psychophysics, ERPs, MEG, EMG, fMRI), different paradigms (e.g. backward-masking, Stroop-like interference, dot-probe paradigm, binocular rivalry, etc.), and different neurological populations (e.g. blindsight, neglect, amygdala-damaged patients) have been studied to answer questions about the neural substrates of automaticity in face and emotion processing, and the boundary conditions that may allow or constrain automaticity. However, automaticity is a relatively ill-defined notion that encompasses a number of distinct features, which may or may not apply for different processes involved in face expression recognition—including not only unawareness but also non-intentionality and goal-independence, lack of cognitive control, resistance of resource depletion, as well as efficiency and rapidity. Abundant empirical evidence supports the view that emotional face processing may exhibit several of these properties, as it can arise fast, efficiently, and involuntarily, in a stimulus-driven manner, independent of the current task requirements, without selective attention or without awareness; and that the amygdala and closely interconnected (cortical or subcortical) structures are critically involved in these aspects of automaticity.

Nevertheless, automatic processing can be modulated by various factors, which may or may not be under voluntary control, such as task demands, expectations, past experiences, personality traits, perceptual load or sensory competition. Hence, like other reflexive processes in the nervous system, the degree of emotion expression processing as well as its impact on other cognitive systems is likely to reflect both purely sensory driven effects and top-down influences due to internal states of the observer, probably acting and interacting at several different neural sites (e.g. in the amygdala proper and/or through its reciprocal connections with visual, parietal, and prefrontal cortical areas). Moreover, some aspects of automaticity in expression processing might not be specific to faces but extend to other categories of emotional or biologically relevant stimuli, even though it is likely that human expertise with face processing make the effects of facial expressions particularly efficient. Thus, taken together, both behavioral and neurophysiological findings suggest that processes associated with automaticity in face processing may primarily reflect some "default settings" in the brain rather than hard-wired, inflexible, and encapsulated processes. Top-down influences associated with voluntary control such as endogenous attention and explicit task goals may operate in parallel to these automatic processes, or may regulate their actual effectiveness and impact on other processes.

We are now just beginning to unveil the variety and complexity of such interactions between face recognition, emotion perception, executive control, and conscious awareness. Future research should more precisely tease apart the neural components underlying the different psychological properties associated with notions of automaticity and control.

References

Achaibou, A., Pourtois, G., Schwartz, S., and Vuilleumier, P. (2008). Simultaneous recording of EEG and facial muscle reactions during spontaneous emotional mimicry. *Neuropsychologia*, **46**, 1104–1113.

Adams, R.B., Gordon, H.L., Baird, A., Ambady, N., and Kleck, R.E. (2003). Effects of gaze on amygdala sensitivity to anger and fear faces. *Science*, **300**, 1536.

Adolphs, R., Tranel, D., Damasio, H., and Damasio, A. (1994). Impaired recognition of emotion in facial expressions following bilateral damage to the human amygdala. *Nature*, **372**, 669–672.

Adolphs, R., Gosselin, F., Buchanan, T.W., Tranel, D., Schyns, P., and Damasio, A.R. (2005). A mechanism for impaired fear recognition after amygdala damage. *Nature*, **433**, 68–72.

Aggleton, J.P., Burton, M.J., and Passingham, R.E. (1980). Cortical and subcortical afferents to the amygdala of the rhesus monkey (Macaca mulatta). *Brain Research*, **190**, 347–368.

Algom, D., Chajut, E., and Lev, S. (2004). A rational look at the emotional Stroop phenomenon: a generic slow-down, not a stroop effect. *Journal of Experimental Psychology: General*, **133**, 323–338.

Alpers, G.W. and Gerdes, A.B. (2007). Here is looking at you: emotional faces predominate in binocular rivalry. *Emotion*, **7**, 495–506.

Anderson, A.K. and Phelps, E.A. (2001). Lesions of the human amygdala impair enhanced perception of emotionally salient events. *Nature*, **411**, 305–309.

Anderson, A.K., Christoff, K., Panitz, D., De Rosa, E., and Gabrieli, J.D.E. (2003). Neural correlates of the automatic processing of threat facial signals. *Journal of Neuroscience*, **23**, 5627–5633.

Armony, J.L. and Dolan, R.J. (2002). Modulation of spatial attention by fear-conditioned stimuli: an event-related fMRI study. *Neuropsychologia*, **40**, 817–826.

Armony, J.L., Servan-Schreiber, D., Cohen, J.D., and LeDoux, J.E. (1997). Computational modeling of emotion: explorations through the anatomy and physiology of fear conditioning. *Trends in Cognitive Sciences*, **1**, 28–34.

Asghar, A.U.R., Chiu, Y-C., Hallam, G., *et al.* (2008). An amygdala response to fearful faces with covered eyes. *Neuropsychologia*, **46**, 2364–2370.

Ashley, V., Vuilleumier, P., and Swick, D. (2004). Time course and specificity of event-related potentials to emotional expressions. *Neuroreport*, **15**, 211–216.

Atkinson, A.P., Tipples, J., Burt, M., and Young, A.W. (2005). Asymmetric interference between sex and emotion in face perception. *Perception and Psychophysics*, **67**, 1199–1213.

Bahrami, B., Carmel, D., Walsh, V., Rees, G., and Lavie, N. (2008a). Spatial attention can modulate unconscious orientation processing. *Perception*, **37**, 1520–1528.

Bahrami, B., Carmel, D., Walsh, V., Rees, G., and Lavie, N. (2008b). Unconscious orientation processing depends on perceptual load. *Journal of Vision*, **8**, 1–10.

Bannerman, R.L., Milders, M., de Gelder, B., and Sahraie, A. (2008). Influence of emotional facial expressions on binocular rivalry. *Ophthalmic and Physiological Optics.*, **28**, 317–326.

Bar, M., Neta, M., and Linz, H. (2006). Very first impressions. *Emotion*, **6**, 269–278.

Bargh, J.A. and Chartrand, T.L. (1999). The unbearable automaticity of being. *American Psychologist*, **54**, 462–479.

Bargh, J.A. and Chen, M., and Burrows, L. (1996). Automaticity of social behavior: direct effects of trait construct and stereotype activation of action. *Journal of Personality and Social Psychology*, **71**, 230–244.

Batty, M. and Taylor, M.J. (2003). Early processing of the six basic facial emotional expressions. *Cognitive Brain Research*, **17**, 613–620.

Beaver, J.D., Lawrence, A.D., Passamonti, L., and Calder, A.W. (2008). Appetitive motivation predicts the neural response to facial signals of aggression. *Journal of Neuroscience*, **28**, 2719–2725.

Bindemann, M., Burton, A.M., Langton, S.R.H., Schweinberger, S.R., and Doherty, M.J. (2007). The control of attention to faces. *Journal of Vision*, **7**, 1–8.

Bishop, S.J. (2008). Neural mechanisms underlying selective attention to threat. *Annals N.Y. Academy of Sciences*, **1129**, 141–152.

Bishop, S.J., Duncan, J., Brett, M., and Lawrence, A.D. (2004). Prefrontal cortical function and anxiety: controlling attention to threat-related stimuli. *Nature Neuroscience*, **7**, 184–188.

Blair, R.J., Morris, J.S., Frith, C.D., Perrett, D.I., and Dolan, R.J. (1999). Dissociable neural responses to facial expressions of sadness and anger. *Brain*, **122**, 883–893.

Blanchette, I. (2006). Snakes, spiders, guns, and syringes: how specific are evolutionary constraints on the detection of threatening stimuli? *Quarterly Journal of Experimental Psychology*, **59**, 1484–1504.

Blau, V.C., Maurer, U., Tottenham, N., and McCandliss, B.D. (2007). The face-specific N170 component is modulated by emotional facial expression. *Behavioral and Brain Functions*, **3**, 7.

Brosch, T., Sander, D., and Scherer, K.R. (2007). That baby caught my eye… Attention capture by infant faces. *Emotion*, **7**, 685–689.

Brosch, T., Sander, D., Pourtois, G., and Scherer, K.R. (2008). Beyond fear. Rapid spatial orienting toward positive emotional stimuli. *Psychological Science*, **19**, 362–370.

Bruce, V. and Young, A. (1986). Understanding face recognition. *British Journal of Psychology*, **77**, 305–327.

Bullier, J. (2001). Integrated model of visual processing. *Brain Research Reviews*, **36**, 96–107.

Calder, A.J. and Young, A.W. (2005). Understanding the recognition of facial identity and facial expression. *Nature Reviews Neuroscience*, **6**, 641–651.

Calder, A.J., Young, A.W., Keane, J., and Dean, M. (2000). Configural information in facial expression perception. *Journal of Experimental Psychology: Human Perception and Performance*, **26**, 527–551.

Campanella, S., Quinet, P., Bruyer, R., Crommelinck, M., and Guérit, J-M. (2002). Categorical perception of happiness and fear facial expressions: an ERP study. *Journal of Cognitive Neuroscience*, **14**, 210–227.

Canli, T., Sivers, H., Whitfield, S.L., Gotlib, I.H., and Gabrieli, J.D.E. (2002). Amygdala response to happy faces as a function of extraversion. *Science*, **296**, 2191.

Chen, M. and Bargh, J.A. (1999). Consequences of automatic evaluation: Immediate behavioral predispositions to approach or avoid the stimulus. *Personality and Social Psychology Bulletin*, **25**, 215–224.

Clarke S., Riahi-Arya S., Tardif E., Eskenasy A.C., and Probst A. (1999) Thalamic projections of the fusiform gyrus in man. *European Journal of Neuroscience*, **11**, 1835–1838.

Cowey, A. (2010). The blindsight saga. *Experimental Brain Research*, **200**, 3–24.

Cristinzio, C., Sander, D. and Vuilleumier, P. (2007). Recognition of emotional face expressions and amygdala pathology. *Epileptologie*, **24**, 130–138

Cristinzio, C., N'Diaye, Seeck, M., Vuilleumier, P., and Sander, D. (2010). Integration of gaze direction and facial expression in patients with unilateral amygdala damage. *Brain*, **133**, 248–261.

Critchley, H., Daly, E., Phillips, M., *et al.* (2000). Explicit and implicit neural mechanisms for processing of social information from facial expressions: a functional Magnetic Resonance Imaging study. *Human Brain Mapping*, **9**, 93–105.

Critchley, H.D., Mathias, C.J., and Dolan, R.J. (2002). Fear conditioning in humans: the influence of awareness and automatic arousal on functional neuroanatomy. *Neuron*, **33**, 653–663.

Darwin, C. (1998). *The expression of emotion in man and animal*. New York: Oxford University Press (Original work published 1872.)

De Gelder, B., Vroomen, J., Pourtois, G. and Weiskrantz, L. (1999). Non-conscious recognition of affect in the absence of striate cortex. *NeuroReport*, **10**, 3759–3763.

Demos, K.E., Kelley, W.M., Ryan, S.L., Davis, F.C., and Whalen, P.J. (2008). Human amygdala sensitivity to pupil size of others. *Cerebral Cortex*, **18**, 2729–2734.

Dimberg, U., Thunberg, M., and Elmehed, K. (2000). Unconscious facial reactions to emotional facial expressions. *Psychological Science*, **11**, 86–89.

Driver, J. and Vuilleumier, P. (2001). Perceptual awareness and its loss in unilateral neglect and extinction. In S. Dehaene (ed.) *The Cognitive Neuroscience of Consciousness*, pp. 39–89. Cambridge, MA: MIT Press.

Dubois, S., Rossion, B., Schiltz, C., Bodart, J.M., Michel, C., Bruyer, R., and Crommelinck, M. (1999). Effects of familiarity on the processing of human faces. *NeuroImage*, **9**, 278–289.

Eastwood, J.D., Smilek, D., and Merikle, P.M. (2001). Differential attentional guidance by unattended faces expressing positive and negative emotion. *Perception and Psychophysics*, **63**, 1004–1013.

Eastwood, J.D., Smilek, D., and Merikle, P.M. (2003). Negative facial expression captures attention and disrupts performance. *Perception and Psychophysics*, **65**, 352–358.

Eimer, M. and Holmes, A. (2002). An ERP study on the time course of emotional face processing. *NeuroReport*, **13**, 427–431.

Ekman, P. (1992). An argument for basic emotions. *Cognition and Emotion*, **6**, 169–200.

Engell, A.D., Haxby, J.V., and Todorov, A. (2007). Implicit trustworthiness decisions: automatic coding of face properties in human amygdala. *Journal of Cognitive Neuroscience*, **19**, 1508–1519.

Erthal, F.S., De Oliveira, L., Mocaiber, I., *et al.* (2005). Load-dependent modulation of affective picture processing. *Cognitive, Affective, and Behavioral Neuroscience*, **5**, 388–395.

Esteves, F., Dimberg, U., and Öhman, A. (1994). Automatically elicited fear: conditioned skin conductance responses to masked facial expressions. *Cognition and Emotion*, **8**, 393–413.

Etkin, A., Egner, T., Peraza, D.M., Kandel, E.R., and Hirsch, J. (2006). Resolving emotional conflict: a role for the rostral anterior cingulate cortex in modulating activity in the amygdala. *Neuron*, **51**, 871–882.

Ewbank, M.P., Lawrence, A.D., Passamonti, L., Keane, J., Peers, P.V., and Calder, A.J. (2009). Anxiety predicts a differential neural response to attended and unattended facial signals of anger and fear. *NeuroImage*, **44**, 1144–1151.

Fox, E. (2002). Processing emotional facial expressions: the role of anxiety and awareness. *Cognitive, Affective, and Behavioral Neuroscience*, **2**, 52–63.

Fox, E. and Damjanovic, L. (2006). The eyes are sufficient to produce a threat superiority effect. *Emotion*, **6**, 534–539.

Fox, E., Russo, R., Bowles, R., and Dutton, K. (2001). Do threatening stimuli draw or hold visual attention in subclinical anxiety? *Journal of Experimental Psychology: General*, **130**, 681–700.

Frischen, A., Eastwood, J.D., and Smilek, D. (2008). Visual search for faces with emotional expressions. *Psychological Bulletin*, **134**, 662–676.

Ganel, T., Valyear, K.F., Goshen-Gottstein, Y., and Goodale, M.A. (2005). The involvement of the 'fusiform face area' in processing facial expression. *Neuropsychologia*, **43**, 1645–1654.

Garner, W.R. (1974). The processing of information and structure. Potomac, MD: Erlbaum.

Georgiou, G.A., Bleakley, C., Hayward, J., *et al.* (2005). Focusing on fear: attentional disengagement from emotional faces. *Visual Cognition*, **12**, 145–158.

Gobbini, M.I. and Haxby, J.V. (2007). Neural systems for recognition of familiar faces. *Neuropsychologia*, **45**, 32–41.

Grandjean, D., Sander, D., Lucas, N., Scherer, K.R., and Vuilleumier, P. (2008). Effects of emotional prosody on auditory extinction for voices in patients with spatial neglect. *Neuropsychologia*, **46**, 487–496.

Grill-Spector, K., Knouf, N., and Kanwisher, N. (2004). The fusiform face area subserves face perception, not generic within-category identification. *Nature Neuroscience*, **7**, 555–562.

Gunning-Dixon, F.M., Gur, R.C., Perkins, A.C., *et al.* (2003). Age-related differences in brain activation during emotional face processing. *Neurobiology of Aging*, **24**, 285–295.

Gur, R.C., Schroeder, L., Turner, T., *et al.* (2002). Brain activation during facial emotion processing. *NeuroImage*, **16**, 651–662.

Hahn, S. and Gronlund, S.D. (2007). Top-down guidance in visual search for facial expressions. *Psychonomic Bulletin and Review*, **14**, 159–165.

Halgren, E., Baudena, P., Heit, G., Clarke, J.M., and Marinkovic, K. (1994). Spatio-temporal stages in face and word processing. 1. Depth-recorded potentials in the human occipital, temporal and parietal lobes. *Journal of Physiology*, 88, 1–50.

Halgren, E., Raij, T., Marinkovic, K., Jousmäki, V., and Hari, R. (2000). Cognitive response profile of the human fusiform face area as determined by MEG. *Cerebral Cortex*, **10**, 69–81.

Hamm, A.O., Weike, A.I., Schupp, H.T., Treig, T., Dressel, A., and Kessler, C. (2003). Affective blindsight: intact fear conditioning to a visual cue in a cortically blind patient. *Brain*, **126**, 267–275.

Hansen, C.H. and Hansen, R.D. (1988). Finding the face in the crowd: an anger superiority effect. *Journal of Personality and Social Psychology*, **54**, 917–924.

Hariri, A.R., Bookheimer, S.Y., and Mazziotta, J.C. (2000). Modulating emotional responses: effects of a neocortical network on the limbic system. *NeuroReport*, **11**, 43–48.

Hariri, A.R., Mattay, V.S., Tessitore, A., *et al.* (2002). Serotonin transporter genetic variation and the response of the human amygdala. *Science*, **297**, 400–403.

Hartikainen, K.M., Ogawa, K.H., and Knight, R.T. (2000). Transient interference of right hemispheric function due to automatic emotional processing. *Neuropsychologia*, **38**, 1576–1580.

Haxby, J.V., Hoffman, E.A., and Gobbini, M.I. (2000). The distributed human neural system for face perception. *Trends in Cognitive Sciences*, **4**, 223–233.

Holmes, A., Vuilleumier, P., and Eimer, M. (2003). The processing of emotional facial expression is gated by spatial attention: evidence from event-related brain potentials. *Cognitive Brain Research*, **16**, 174–184.

Holmes, A., Kiss, M., and Eimer, M. (2006). Attention modulates the processing of emotional expression triggered by foveal faces. *Neuroscience Letters*, **394**, 48–52.

Horstmann, G., and Becker, S. (2008). Attentional effects of negative faces: Top-down contingent or involuntary? *Perception and Psychophysics*, **70**, 1416–1434.

Humphreys, K., Avidan, G., and Behrmann, M. (2007). A detailed investigation of facial expression processing in congenital prosopagnosia as compared to acquired prosopagnosia. *Experimental Brain Research*, **176**, 356–373.

Ishai, A., Bikle, P.C., and Ungerleider, L.G. (2006). Temporal dynamics of face repetition suppression. *Brain Research Bulletin*, **70**, 289–295.

Jiang, Y. and He, S. (2006). Cortical responses to invisible faces: dissociating subsystems for facial-information processing. *Current Biology*, **16**, 2023–2029.

Jiang, Y., Shannon, R.W., Vizueta, N., Bernat, E.M., Patrick, C.J., and He, S. (2009). Dynamics of processing invisible faces in the brain: Automatic neural encoding of facial expression information. *NeuroImage*, **44**, 1171–1177.

Kim, H., Somerville, L.H., Johnstone, T., Alexander, A.L., and Whalen, P.J. (2003). Inverse amygdala and medial prefrontal cortex responses to surprised faces. *NeuroReport*, **14**, 2317–2322.

Kim, H., Somerville, L.H., Johnstone, T., *et al.* (2004). Contextual modulation of amygdala responsivity to surprised faces. *Journal of Cognitive Neuroscience*, **16**, 1730–1745.

Kirita, T. and Endo, M. (1995). Happy face advantage in recognizing facial expressions. *Acta Psychologica*, **89**, 149–163.

Kolassa, I-T., Musial, F., Kolassa, S., and Miltner, W.H.R. (2006). Event-related potentials when identifying or color-naming threatening schematic stimuli in spider phobic and non-phobic individuals. *BMC Psychiatry*, **6**, 38.

Krolak-Salmon, P., Fischer, C., Vighetto, A., and Mauguiere, F. (2001). Processing of facial emotion expression: spatio-temporal data as assessed by scalp event-related potentials. *European Journal of Neuroscience*, **13**, 987–994.

Krolak-Salmon, P., Hénaff, M-A., Vighetto, A., Bertrand, O., and Mauguière, F. (2004). Early amygdala reaction to fear spreading in occipital, temporal, and frontal cortex: A depth electrode ERP study in human. *Neuron*, **42**, 665–676.

Krombholz, A., Schaefer, F., and Boucsein, W. (2007). Modification of N170 by different emotional expression of schematic faces. *Biological Psychology*, **76**, 156–162.

Kunst-Wilson, W.R., and Zajonc, R.B. (1980). Affective discrimination of stimuli that cannot be recognized. *Science*, **207**, 557–558.

Kveraga K., Boshyan J., and Bar M. (2007) Magnocellular projections as the trigger of top-down facilitation in recognition. *Journal of Neuroscience*, **27**, 13232–13240.

Lange, K., Williams, L.M., Young, A.W., *et al.* (2003). Task instructions modulate neural responses to fearful facial expressions. *Biological Psychiatry*, **53**, 226–232.

Lavie, N. (2005). Distracted and confused? Selective attention under load. *Trends in Cognitive Sciences*, **9**, 75–82.

LeDoux, J.E. (1996). *The emotional brain: the mysterious underpinnings of emotional life.* New York: Simon and Schuster.

Leveroni, C.L., Seidenberg, M., Mayer, A.R., Binder, J.R., and Rao, S.M. (2000). Neural systems underlying the recognition of familiar and newly learned faces. *Journal of Neuroscience*, **20**, 878–886.

Lewis, S., Thoma, R.J., Lanoue, M.D. *et al.* (2003). Visual processing of facial affect. *NeuroReport*, **14**, 1841–1845.

Liddell, B.J., Brown, K.J., and Kemp, A.H. (2005). A direct brainstem-amygdala-cortical alarm system for subliminal signals of fear. *Neuroimage*, **24**, 235–243.

Lipp, O.V. and Derakshan, N. (2005). Attentional bias to pictures of fear-relevant animals in a dot probe task. *Emotion*, **5**, 365–369.

Lucas, N. and Vuilleumier, P. (2008). Effects of emotional and non-emotional cues on visual search in neglect patients: Evidence for distinct sources of attentional guidance. *Neuropsychologia*, **46**, 1401–1414.

MacLeod, C., Mathews, A., and Tata, P. (1986). Attentional bias in emotional disorders. *Journal of Abnormal Psychology*, **95**, 15–20.

Mathews, A. and MacLeod, C. (1985). Selective processing of threat cues in anxiety states. *Behaviour Research and Therapy*, **23**, 563–569.

Mitchell, D.G.V., Nakic, M., Fridberg, D., Kamel, N., Pine, D.S., and Blair, R.J.R. (2007). The impact of processing load on emotion. *Neuroimage*, **34**, 1299–1309.

Mogg, K. and Bradley, B. (1999). Orienting of attention to threatening facial expressions presented under conditions of restricted awareness. *Cognition and Emotion*, **13**, 713–740.

Moors, A. and De Houwer, J. (2006). Automaticity: a theoretical and conceptual analysis. *Psychological Bulletin*, **132**, 297–326.

Morel, S., Ponz, A., Mercier, M., Vuilleumier, P., and George, N. (2009). EEG-MEG evidence for early differential repetition effects for fearful, happy and neutral faces. *Brain Research*, **1254**, 84–86.

Morris, J.S., Frith, C.D., Perrett, D.I. *et al.* (1996). A differential neural response in the human amygdala to fearful and happy facial expressions. *Nature*, **383**, 812–815.

Morris, J.S., Öhman, A., and Dolan, R.J. (1998). Conscious and unconscious emotional learning in the human amygdala. *Nature*, **393**, 467–470.

Morris, J.S., Öhman, A., and Dolan, R.J. (1999), A subcortical pathway to the right amygdala mediating 'unseen' fear. *Proceedings of the National Academy of Sciences, USA*, **96**, 1680–1685.

Morris, J.S., de Gelder, B., Weiskrantz, L., and Dolan, R.J. (2001). Differential extrageniculostriate and amygdala responses to presentation of emotional faces in a cortically blind field. *Brain*, **124**, 1241–1252.

Murphy, S.T. and Zajonc, R.B. (1993). Affect, cognition, and awareness: affective priming with optimal and suboptimal stimulus exposures. *Journal of Personality and Social Psychology*, **64**, 723–739.

Naccache, L., Gaillard, R., Adam, C., *et al.* (2005). A direct intracranial record of emotions evoked by subliminal words. *Proceedings of the National Academy of Sciences*, **102**, 7713–7717.

Narumoto, J., Okada, T., Sadato, N., Fukui, K., and Yonekura, Y. (2001). Attention to emotion modulates fMRI activity in human right superior temporal sulcus. *Brain Research Cognitive Brain Research*, **12**, 225–231.

N'Diaye, K., Sander, D., and Vuilleumier, P. (2009). Interaction between facial emotion and gaze direction in the human amygdala: the role of self-relevance and expression intensity. *Emotion*, **9**, 798–806.

Niedenthal, P.M. (1990). Implicit perception of affective information. *Journal of Experimental Social Psychology*, **26**, 505–527.

Oberman, L.M., Winkielman, P., and Ramachandran, V.S. (2007). Face to face: blocking facial mimicry can selectively impair recognition of emotional expressions. *Social Neuroscience*, **2**, 167–178.

Öhman, A. (2002). Automaticity and the amygdala: nonconscious responses to emotional faces. *Current Directions in Psychological Science*, **11**, 62–66.

Öhman, A., Flykt, A., and Esteves, F. (2001a). Emotion drives attention: Detecting the snake in the grass. *Journal of Experimental Psychology: General*, **130**, 466–478.

Öhman, A., Lundqvist, D., and Esteves, F. (2001b). The face in the crowd revisited: a threat advantage with schematic stimuli. *Journal of Personality and Social Psychology*, **80**, 381–396.

Ohrmann, P., Rauch, A.V., Bauer, J., *et al.* (2007). Threat sensitivity as assessed by automatic amygdala response to fearful faces predicts speed of visual search for facial expression. *Experimental Brain Research*, **183**, 51–59.

Okon-Singer, H., Tzelgov, J., and Henik, A. (2007). Distinguishing between automaticity and attention in the processing of emotionally significant stimuli. *Emotion*, **7**, 147–157.

Oosterhof, N.N. and Todorov, A. (2008). The functional basis of face evaluation. *Proceedings of National Academy for Sciences USA*, **105**, 11087–11092.

Pasley, B.N., Mayes, L.C., and Schultz, R.T. (2004). Subcortical discrimination of unperceived objects during binocular rivalry. *Neuron*, **42**, 163–172.

Passamonti, L., Rowe, J.B., Ewbank, M., Hampshire, A., Keane, J., and Calder, A.J. (2008). Connectivity from the ventral anterior cingulated to the amygdala is modulated by appetitive motivation in response to facial signals of aggression. *NeuroImage*, **43**, 562–570.

Pegna, A.J., Khateb, A., Lazeyras, F., and Seghier, M.L. (2005). Discriminating emotional faces without primary visual cortices involves the right amygdala. *Nature Neuroscience*, **8**, 24–25.

Pegna. A.J., Landis, T., and Khateb, A. (2008). Electrophysiological evidence for early non-conscious processing of fearful facial expressions. *International Journal of Psychophysiology*, **70**, 127–136.

Pessoa, L. (2005). To what extent are emotional visual stimuli processed without attention and awareness? *Current Opinion in Neurobiology*, **15**, 188–196.

Pessoa, L. and Padmala, S. (2007). Decoding near-threshold perception of fear from distributed single-trial brain activation. *Cerebral Cortex*, **17**, 691–701.

Pessoa, L., McKenna, M., Gutierrez, E., and Ungerleider, L.G. (2002). Neural processing of emotional faces requires attention. *Proceedings of National Academy for Sciences USA*, **99**, 11458–11463.

Pessoa, L., Japee, S., and Ungerleider, L.G. (2005a). Visual awareness and the detection of fearful faces. *Emotion*, **5**, 243–247.

Pessoa, L., Padmala, S., and Morland, T. (200b5). Fate of unattended fearful faces in the amygdala is determined by both attentional resources and cognitive modulation. *Neuroimage*, **28**, 249–255.

Phelps, E.A. and LeDoux, J.E. (2005). Contributions of the amygdala to emotion processing: from animal models to human behavior. *Neuron*, **48**, 175–187.

Polonsky, A., Blake, R., Braun, J., and Heeger, D.J. (2000). Neuronal activity in human primary visual cortex correlates with perception during binocular rivalry. *Nature Neuroscience*, **3**, 1153–1159.

Posner, M.I. and Peterson, S.E. (1990). The attention system of the human brain. *Annual Review of Neuroscience*, **13**, 25–42.

Posner, M.I., Snyder, C.R.R., and Davidson, B.J. (1980). Attention and the detection of signals. *Journal of Experimental Psychology: General*, **109**, 160–174.

Pourtois, G., Grandjean, D., Sander, D., and Vuilleumier, P. (2004a). Electrophysiological correlates of rapid spatial orienting towards fearful faces. *Cerebral Cortex*, **14**, 619–633.

Pourtois, G., Sander, D., Andres, M., *et al.* (2004b). Dissociable roles of the human somatosensory and superior temporal cortices for processing social face signals. *European Journal of Neuroscience*, **20**, 3507–3515

Pourtois, G., Schwartz, S., Seghier, M.L., Lazeyras, F., and Vuilleumier, P. (2005a). Portraits or people? Distinct representations of face identity in the human visual cortex. *Journal of Cognitive Neuroscience*, **17**, 1043–1057.

Pourtois, G., Dan, E.S., Grandjean, D., Sander, D., and Vuilleumier, P. (200b5). Enhanced extrastriate visual response to bandpass spatial frequency filtered fearful faces: Time course and topographic evoked-potentials mapping. *Human Brain Mapping*, **26**, 65–79.

Pourtois, G., Thut, G., Grave de Peralta, R., Michel, C., and Vuilleumier, P. (2005c). Two electrophysiological stages of spatial orienting towards fearful faces: early temporo-parietal activation preceding gain control in extrastriate visual cortex. *Neuroimage*, **26**, 149–163.

Pourtois, G., Schwartz, S., Seghier, M.L., Lazeyras, F., and Vuilleumier, P. (2006). Neural systems for orienting attention to the location of threat signals: an event-related fMRI study. *Neuroimage*, **31**, 920–933.

Pourtois, G., Spinelli, L., Seeck, M., and Vuilleumier, P. (2010a). Temporal precedence of emotion over attention modulations in lateral amygdala: Evidence from human intracranial recordings. *Cognitive Affective and Behavioral Neuroscience*, **10**, 83–93.

Pourtois, G, Spinelli L, Seeck M and Vuilleumier P. (2010b). Modulation of face processing by emotional expression and gaze direction during intracranial recordings in right fusiform cortex. *Journal of Cognitive Neuroscience*, **22**, 2086–2107.

Pratto, F. and John, O.P. (1991). Automatic vigilance: the attention-grabbing power of negative social information. *Journal of Personality and Social Psychology*, **61**, 380–391.

Purcell, D.G., Stewart, A.L., and Skov, R.B. (1996). It takes a confounded face to pop out of a crowd. *Perception*, **25**, 1091–1108.

Righart, R. and de Gelder, B. (2006). Context influences early perceptual analysis of faces–An electrophysiological study. *Cerebral Cortex*, **16**, 1249–1257.

Righart, R. and de Gelder, B. (2008a). Recognition of facial expressions is influenced by emotional scene gist. *Cognitive, Affective, and Behavioral Neuroscience*, **8**, 264–272.

Righart, R. and de Gelder, B. (2008b). Rapid influence of emotional scenes on encoding of facial expressions: an ERP study. *Social Cognitive and Affective Neuroscience*, **3**, 270–278.

Rossion, B., Caldara, R., Seghier, M., Schuller, A-M., Lazeyras, F., and Mayer, E. (2003). A network of occipito-temporal face-sensitive areas besides the right middle fusiform gyrus is necessary for normal face processing. *Brain*, **126**, 2381–2395.

Rudrauf, D., David, O., Lachaux, J-P., *et al* (2008). Rapid interactions between the ventral and visual stream and emotion-related structures rely on a two-pathway architecture. *Journal of Neuroscience*, **28**, 2793–2803.

Sah, P., Faber, E.S.L., Lopez De Armentia, M., and Power, J. (2003). The amygdaloid complex: anatomy and physiology. *Physiology Review*, **83**, 803–834.

Sahraie A, Trevethan C.T, Weiskrantz, L., *et al.* (2003). Spatial channels of visual processing in cortical blindness. *European Journal of Neuroscience*, **18**, 1189–96.

Said, C.P., Baron, S.G. and Todorov, A. (2008). Nonlinear amygdala response to face trustworthiness: Contributions of high and low spatial frequency information. *Journal of Cognitive Neuroscience*, **21**, 519–528.

Schneider, W. and Shiffrin, R.M. (1977). Controlled and automatic human information processing: I. Detection, search, and attention. *Psychological Review*, **84**, 1–66

Schubö, A., Gendolla, G.H.E., Meinecke, C., and Abele, A.E. (2006). Detecting emotional faces and features in a visual search paradigm: Are faces special? *Emotion*, **6**, 246–256.

Schweinberger, S.R. and Soukup, G.R. (1998). Asymmetric relationships among perceptions of facial identity, emotion, and facial speech. *Journal of Experimental Psychology: Human Perception and Performance*, **24**, 1748–1765.

Schweinberger, S.R., Burton, A.M., and Kelly, S.W. (1999). Asymmetric dependencies in perceiving identity and emotion: experiments with morphed faces. *Perception and Psychophysics*, **61**, 1102–1115.

Shiffrin, R.M. and Schneider, W. (1977). Controlled and automatic human information processing: II. Perceptual learning, automatic attending, and a general theory. *Psychological Review*, **84**, 127–190.

Silvert, L., Lepsien, J., Fragopanagos, N., *et al.* (2007). Influence of attentional demands on the processing of emotional facial expressions in the amygdala. *Neuroimage*, **38**, 357–366.

Singer, T., Kiebel, S.J., Winston, J.S., Dolan, R.J., and Frith, C.D. (2004). Brain responses to the acquired moral status of faces. *Neuron*, **41**, 653–662.

Stekelenburg, J.J. and de Gelder, B. (2004). The neural correlates of perceiving human bodies: an ERP study on the body-inversion effect. *NeuroReport*, **15**, 777–780.

Stenberg, G., Wilking, S., and Dahl, M. (1998). Judging words at face value: interference in a word processing task reveals automatic processing of affective facial expressions. *Cognition and Emotion*, **12**, 755–782.

Stroop, J.R. (1935). Studies of interference in serial-verbal reaction. *Journal of Experimental Psychology*, **18**, 643–662.

Sugase, Y., Yamane, S., Ueno, S., and Kawano, K. (1999). Global and fine information coded by single neurons in the temporal visual cortex. *Nature*, **400**, 869–873.

Surguladze, S.A., Brammer, M.J., Young, A.W., *et al.* (2003). A preferential increase in the extrastriate response to signals of danger. *Neuroimage*, **19**, 1317–1328.

Todorov, A. and Engell, A.D. (2008). The role of the amygdala in implicit evaluations of emotionally neutral faces. *Social Cognitive and Affective Neuroscience*, **3**, 303–312.

Todorov, A. and Olson, I.R. (2008). Robust learning of affective trait associations with faces when the hippocampus is damaged, but not when the amygdala and temporal pole are damaged. *Social Cognitive and Affective Neuroscience*, **3**, 195–203.

Todorov, A., Gobbini, I., Evans, K.K., and Haxby, J.V. (2007). Spontaneous retrieval of affective person knowledge in face perception. *Neuropsychologia*, **45**, 163–173.

Tracy, J.L. and Robins, R.W. (2008). The automaticity of emotion recognition. *Emotion*, **8**, 81–95.

Van Honk, J., Schutter, D., d'Alfonso, A.A.L., Kessels, R.P.C., and de Haan, E.H.F. (2002). 1 Hz rTMS over the right prefrontal cortex reduces vigilant attention to unmasked but not to masked fearful faces. *Biological Psychiatry*, **52**, 312–317.

Van Reekum, C.M., Urry, H.L., Johnstone, T., *et al.* (2007). Individual differences in amygdala and ventromedial prefrontal cortex activity are associated with evaluation speed and psychological well-being. *Journal of Cognitive Neuroscience*, **19**, 237–248.

Vrtička, P., Andersson, F., Grandjean, D., Sander, D., and Vuilleumier, P. (2008). Individual attachment style modulates human amygdala and striatum activation during social appraisal. *PLOS One*, **3**, e2868.

Vrtička, P., Andersson, F., Sander, D.,and Vuilleumier, P. (2009). Memory for friends or foes: The social context of past encounters with faces modulates their subsequent neural traces in the brain. *Social Neuroscience*, **4**, 384–401.

Vuilleumier, P. (2005). How brains beware: neural mechanisms of emotional attention. *Trends in Cognitive Sciences*, **9**, 585–594.

Vuilleumier, P. and Pourtois, G. (2007). Distributed and interactive brain mechanisms during emotion face perception : evidence from functional neuroimaging. *Neuropsychologia*, **45**, 174–194.

Vuilleumier, P. and Sander, D. (2008). Trust and valence processing in the amygdala. *Social Cognitive and Affective Neuroscience*, **3**, 299–302.

Vuilleumier, P. and Schwartz, S. (2001). Emotional facial expressions capture attention. *Neurology*, **56**, 153–158.

Vuilleumier, P., Armony, J.L., Driver, J. and Dolan, R.J. (2001). Effects of attention and emotion on face processing in the human brain. An event-related fMRI study. *Neuron*, **30**, 829–841.

Vuilleumier, P., Armony, J.L., Clarke, K., Husain, M., Driver, J., and Dolan, R.J. (2002). Neural response to emotional faces with and without awareness: event-related fMRI in a parietal patient with visual extinction and spatial neglect. *Neuropsychologia*, **40**, 2156–2166.

Vuilleumier, P., Armony, J., and Dolan, R. (2003a). *Reciprocal links between emotion and attention.* In R.S.J. Frackowiak, K.J. Friston, C.D. Firth, *et al.* (eds.), *Human Brain Function*, pp. 419–444. San Diego, CA: Academic Press.

Vuilleumier, P., Armony, J.G., Driver, J., and Dolan, R.J. (2003b). Distinct spatial frequency sensitivities for processing faces and emotional expressions. *Nature Neuroscience*, **6**, 624–631.

Vuilleumier, P., Richardson, M.P., Armony, J.L., Driver, J., and Dolan, R.J. (2004). Distant influences of amygdala lesion on visual cortical activation during emotional face processing. *Nature Neuroscience*, **7**, 1271–1278.

Ward, R., Danziger, S., and Bamford, S. (2005). Response to visual threat following damage to the pulvinar. *Current Biology*, **15**, 571–573.

Ward, R., Calder, A.J., Parker, M., and Arend, I. (2007). Emotion recognition following human pulvinar damage. *Neuropsychologia*, **45**, 1973–1978.

Whalen, P.J. (1998). Fear, vigilance, and ambiguity: Initial neuroimaging studies of the human amygdala. *Current Directions in Psychological Science*, **7**, 177–188.

Whalen, P.J. (2007). The uncertainty of it all. *Trends in Cognitive Sciences*, **11**, 499–500.

Whalen, P.J., Rauch, S.L., Etcoff, N.L., McInerney, S.C., Lee, M.B., and Jenike, M.A. (1998). Masked presentations of emotional facial expression modulate amygdala activity without explicit knowledge. *Journal of Neuroscience*, **18**, 411–418.

Whalen, P.J., Kagan, J., Cook, R.G. *et al.* (2004). Human amygdala responsivity to masked fearful eye whites. *Science*, **306**, 2061.

Wiens, S. (2006). Current concerns in visual masking. *Emotion*, **6**, 675–680.

Williams, J.M., Mathews, A., MacLeod, C. (1996). The emotional Stroop task and psychopathology. *Psychological Bulletin*, **120**, 3–24.

Williams, L.M., Palmer, D., Liddell, B.J., Song, L. and Gordon, E. (2006a). The 'when' and 'where' of perceiving signals of threat versus non-threat. *NeuroImage*, **31**, 458–467.

Williams, L.M., Liddell, B.J. and Kemp, A.H. (2006b). Amygdala-prefrontal dissociation of subliminal and subliminal and supraliminal fear. *Human Brain Mapping*, **27**, 652–661.

Williams, M.A. and Mattingley, J.B. (2004). Unconscious perception of non-threatening facial emotion in parietal extinction. *Experimental Brain Research*, **154**, 403–406.

Williams, M.A., Morris, A.P., McGlone, F., Abbott, D.F., and Mattingley, J.B. (2004). Amygdala responses to fearful and happy facial expressions under conditions of binocular suppression. *The Journal of Neuroscience*, **24**, 2898–2904.

Williams, M.A., McGlone, F., Abbott, D.F., and Mattingley, J.B. (2005a). Differential amygdala responses to happy and fearful facial expressions depend on selective attention. *Neuroimage*, **24**, 417–425.

Williams, M.A., Moss, S.A., Bradshaw, J.L., and Mattingley, J.B. (2005b). Look at me, I'm smiling: visual search for threatening and nonthreatening facial expressions. *Visual Cognition*, **12**, 29–50.

Winkielman, P. and Berridge, K.C. (2004). Unconscious emotion. *Current Directions in Psychological Science*, **13**, 120–123.

Winkielman, P., Berridge, K.C., and Wilbarger, J.L. (2005). Unconscious affective reactions to maked happy versus angry faces influence consumption behavior and judgments of value. *Personality and Social Psychology Bulletin*, **31**, 121–135.

Winston, J.S., Strange, B., O'Doherty, J., and Dolan R.J. (2002). Automatic and intentional brain responses during evaluation of trustworthiness of face. *Nature Neuroscience*, **5**, 277–283.

Wolfe, J.M. (1998). *Visual search*. In H. Pashler (ed.) *Attention*, pp. 13–73. Hove: Psychology Press.

Wright, P., Albarracin, D., Brown, R.D., Li, H., He, G., and Liu, Y. (2007). Dissociated responses in the amygdala and orbitofrontal cortex to bottom-up and top-down components of emotional evaluation. *Neuroimage*, **39**, 894–902.

Yang, E., Zald, D.H., and Blake, R. (2007). Fearful expressions gain preferential access to awareness during continuous flash suppression. *Emotion*, **7**, 882–886.

Yoon, K.L., Hong, S.W., Joormann, J., and Kang, P. (2009). Perception of facial expressions of emotion during binocular rivalry. *Emotion*, **9**, 172–182.

Young, A.W., Hellawell, D.J., Van de Wal, C. and Johnson, M. (1996). Facial expression processing after amygdalotomy. *Neuropsychologia*, **34**, 31–39.

Zajonc, R.B. (1980). Feeling and thinking. Preferences need no inferences. *American Psychologist*, **35**, 151–175.

Chapter 24

On Perceiving Facial Expressions: the Role of Culture and Context

Nalini Ambady and Max Weisbuch

Introduction

Facial expressions are not random configurations of skin, bone, and muscle. Perceivers attribute meaning to expressive facial configurations and exhibit affective responses to suggest that the *meaning* of these configurations is processed preconsciously. Facial expressions thus clearly have communicative properties that bear some importance to perceivers. Such expressions are informative with respect to the future behavior of the expressing individual and with respect to the conditions of the broader social environment. For these reasons, we argue that appropriate responses to facial expressions are an important means by which people adapt to their social ecology. First, the meaning of others' facial expressions for perceivers' well-being should depend on context; for this reason, immediate responses to facial expressions should depend on contextual factors. Second, it is more important for individuals to adapt to the ingroup than to other groups; for this reason people should exhibit special sensitivity to ingroup facial expressions. This chapter reviews the evidence bearing on both of these postulates.

We first review the literature regarding the role of context in recognition of facial expressions. We then go on to review the literature regarding group membership and emotion recognition, with a special emphasis on the role of culture. Throughout, we focus our discussion on facial expressions of emotion if only because of available empirical literature.

Context and expression perception

Emotional expressions are not independent of the face on which they appear, the body and voice by which they are accompanied, nor of the situation in which they occur. The perceiver who narrowly attends to facial emotion but not to other aspects of the face, body, or voice is a perceiver prone to frequent misinterpretation and inappropriate response. For example, a smiling face might require a different interpretation and different response if the identity of that face is one's boss as opposed to one's child. Or consider the different meaning of a smile when combined with a nervous as opposed to confident voice. In this section, we consider several different meanings of "context" with respect to facial expressions from an ecological approach to social perception.

Ecological approaches to perception generally hold that perceptual processes adapt to the environment in which they have evolved, over the course of one's life as well as over generations (Gibson, 1979). According to such theories, perceiving is for doing in that perception is for extracting the actionable properties of things or the properties of things that are relevant to well-being—these self-relevant properties are described as *affordances*. For example, lowered eyebrows might afford danger if the eyebrow lowering individual is moving toward the self, is yelling loudly, and exhibits other facial bodily motions indicative of aggressive intent. The key point for the current purposes is that affordances are said to be readily communicated over multiple modalities and most effectively via the higher-order patterning (or "configuration") of cues, rather than single cues in isolation (Zebrowitz and Collins, 1997). McArthur and Baron (1983), in a position consistent with Gibson's, suggested that social perception proceeds in an ecologically-adaptive manner. They argued that perceivers extract invariants, or stable social properties, from higher-order patterns in the social stimulus array that are important for social adaptation. This social-ecological approach either implicitly or explicitly anticipated a number of findings with respect to the role of expressive context in the interpretation of facial expressions.

First, the social-ecological approach suggests that modalities combine to inform social perception and judgment. If so, then judgment of facial expression should be especially fast when other modalities impart the same information and are consistent. Moreover, judgment should be impaired or slowed down when other modalities impart information that is inconsistent with the facial expression. Multimodal facilitation is clearly demonstrated with infant identification of emotion expression. Walker-Andrews and colleagues (for a review, see Walker-Andrews, 2008) have demonstrated, for example, that 3-month-old infants can recognize facial expressions of emotion but only when accompanied by a corresponding vocal expression. Only later do infants develop the ability to recognize facial expressions in the absence of other communicative channels. Nonetheless, adults are especially fast and especially accurate in identifying facial emotion when the facial expression is accompanied by a congruent vocal expression (for a review, see de Gelder and Van den Stock, Chapter 27, this volume).

One particularly fascinating demonstration of multimodal interference utilized posed facial expression pictures. These facial expressions were seamlessly photoedited onto bodies that expressed a different emotion. For example, a prototypically angry face was placed on a body that was holding a dirtied-pair of underwear; a prototypically disgusted face was placed on a body that was a holding a fist in the air (as if about to strike a blow). Although participants were instructed to completely ignore the body and focus on the face in making their emotion decision, they were unable to do so. For example, disgust facial expressions were correctly identified 66% of the time when presented alone but when presented on a body holding a fist in the air, the face was incorrectly judged to be *angry* by 87% of participants (Aviezer et al., 2008). A second study demonstrated that results could be replicated with respect to changes in perceived valence of feelings. Disgust faces were placed on a clothed body that held dirtied underwear or on a topless muscular body with hands above the head (in a proud expression). When paired with the proud body, the disgust face was perceived to be exhibiting positive affect and remarkably was *never* identified as disgust but instead as pride 78% of the time. Conversely, when paired with the disgust body holding dirty underwear, the disgust face was perceived to be exhibiting negative affect was identified as disgust 81% of the time. Similar results were observed in comparing sad and fearful bodies attached to sad faces. Aviezer and colleagues demonstrated that differences in attention may account in part for the impact of bodies on the perception of facial emotion. Specifically, a final study utilized eye-tracking technology showed that participants fixated on the eye region of a disgust face paired with angry body. This pattern of attention was notable in that it is normally observed for *angry faces*; disgust faces normally elicit attention to the mouth/nose region (Calder et al., 2000). In summary, there is dramatic evidence that facial expressions of emotion are perceived with the help of bodily and vocal expressions.

The social-ecological approach also suggests that the basic elements of a facial expression—such as lowered brows and clenched mouth for anger—are contingent on the broader context of the face. This idea can be illustrated by the combination of eye gaze and emotion expression. Joy and anger appear to be considerably more intense and easier to identify when combined with direct than with averted gaze, whereas the opposite is true for sadness and fear (Adams and Kleck,

2003, 2005; see also, Bindermann et al., 2008; Graham and LaBar, 2007). Adams and his colleagues argue that congruence in motivational meaning (approach versus avoidance) speeds responses whereas incongruence slows responses. For example, both joy and direct gaze signal approach whereas both fear and averted gaze signal avoidance—hence both of these combinations should be and are processed especially quickly.

Third, the social-ecological approach implies that perceptually obvious but unexpressive elements of the human form (e.g. identity, race) can alter the apparent meaning of a facial expression. Indeed, the speed with which people are able to identify emotions also appears to be contingent on group membership in a manner consistent with stereotypes about target race or gender. For example, although emotion recognition typically occurs faster for happiness than for other (negative) emotions, this finding is reversed when white participants judge black targets (Hugenberg, 2005). And the interpretation of anger appears to depend on the race and gender of the target—specifically, perceivers are faster and more prone to make anger judgments when the target is a man or is black than when a woman or white, at least when perceivers are prejudiced (Hugenberg and Bodenhausen, 2003; Plant et al., 2004). And happy faces are most quickly and accurately categorized when those faces are female (Hugenberg and Szesny, 2006; see Hugenberg et al., Chapter 13, this volume).

Beyond emotion recognition, a number of theoretical accounts suggest that *automatic* responses to emotion expressions are adaptive (Dimberg, 1997; Ohman, 2002; Russell et al., 2003). According to such theories, emotions communicate something about the environment or the person expressing the emotion—those who effectively and efficiently respond to these emotions are likely to succeed within that environment. In other words, stimulus qualities can signal social meaning or "affordances" for the perceiver and it is those affordances which elicit automatic responses. For example, outgroup emotions may signal relative group status as when *outgroup fear* implicates the relative strength and safety of the ingroup, thereby producing positive affect for perceiver. Likewise, *outgroup happiness* may implicate the relative weakness and danger of the ingroup and hence negative affect for the perceiver. *Ingroup fear and happiness*, however, could directly implicate distress (Marsh et al., 2005) and safety (Knutson, 1996), respectively, for the self vis-à-vis the ingroup. Indeed, Weisbuch and Ambady (2008) demonstrated that negative facial expressions automatically elicit negative affect in ingroup perceivers but positive affect in outgroup perceivers. Likewise, facial joy automatically elicited positive affect in ingroup perceivers but negative affect in outgroup perceivers. In general, then, even automatic responses to others' facial expressions depended crucially on social identity communicated via the face.

In summary, context clearly plays a crucial role in interpretation and responses to facial expressions. In one study, whether a prototypically disgusted face appeared to exhibit anger or disgust depended entirely on what the body was doing (cf. Aviezer et al., 2008). In another study, affective responses to happy and fearful faces depended entirely on the social identities of expresser and perceiver (cf. Weisbuch and Ambady, 2008). From a social-ecological approach, this is only logical—people have adapted to their ecological niche which is captured in configurations rather than isolated elements.

Culture and emotion recognition

The ecological niche was considered locally in the previous section, with respect to body parts, facial features, and voices. Here, the focus is ecological niche writ broadly. Darwin (1872/1965) was perhaps the first to examine the likelihood of universal recognition of emotional facial expression when he sent questionnaires to his colleagues around the world, inquiring about local facial expressions. Unlike Darwin's leading questions (e.g. "Do people in your area raise their eyebrows in fear?"), Ekman and his colleagues (e.g. Ekman, 1971, 2003; Ekman and Friesen, 1969, 1971; Izard, 1969; Tomkins, 1962) traveled to different cultures, asked individuals in these cultures to pose emotion expressions, and asked individuals in still other cultures to identify the emotions. For example, they traveled to Papua New Guinea to visit a group of people who had never been exposed to other cultures. Ekman (1971) provided some of these individuals with scenarios (e.g. a dead pig on the ground) and videotaped them as they expressed the emotion they would feel in that circumstance. The facial expressions in these videotapes were remarkably similar to American facial expressions, and Americans were able to correctly identify the emotion in these expressions. Likewise, the tribesmen in New Guinea were able to identify the emotions of Americans. A recent meta-analysis examined cross-cultural facial expressions in 162 samples, with picture sets and raters from a great number of countries ranging from New Guinea to Malaysia to Germany to Ethiopia. Supportive of universality in facial emotion recognition, in only 3% of these cross-cultural samples was even a *single emotion* recognized at rates below chance (Elfenbein and Ambady, 2002).

Does universal emotion recognition exist? An ongoing debate

The findings from cross-cultural studies of emotion recognition have often been recruited as evidence that emotions are universally recognized in the face (Ekman, 1971, 1992). This topic is not without controversy, however, and critics have made several poignant arguments (Russell, 1994; Russell et al., 2003) that have elicited spirited replies (Ekman, 1992, 1999; Izard, 1992). We highlight the most prominent of these issues here. First, while posed facial emotions can be recognized across cultures at above-chance levels, accuracy is far from perfect and there is substantial cultural variability (Russell, 1994). In other words, people often do not recognize emotions from facial expressions and this tendency may be greater cross-culturally. Consequently, the argument that emotions are universally recognized may be more specious than the argument that emotions can be recognized across cultures at above-chance rates. Although this conclusion seems reasonable, scholars have made reasonable contentions that the conclusion is too conservative. For example, Ekman (1992) suggests that while emotions manifest certain facial patterns that can be universally recognized, individual differences in facial structure as well as cultural differences in emotion expression ("display rules") introduce considerable variability such that any evidence for pan-cultural emotion recognition is rather remarkable. In other words, a significant difference from chance is a more reasonable criterion for universality than is perfect emotion recognition. Both sides of this debate can probably agree that various sources of error render perfect recognition unlikely even if recognition *is* universal. And both sides probably recognize that statistical significance is arbitrary and that a more appropriate criterion might be effect size. Hence, it will be important for both sides of this debate to agree on a criterion for universality that is both more absolute than statistical significance and less lofty than perfection. In lieu of such a criterion, we review below what we believe to be evidence for middle-ground in this debate—namely, that emotion recognition is enhanced within cultures.

A second issue with universality described by critics is that the facial images used in recognition studies have typically been posed. There is some evidence that posed and spontaneous emotion expressions are controlled by different parts of the brain (e.g. Rinn, 1984), suggesting that these emotion expressions are likely to look different and hence recognition of posed emotions may not transfer to the recognition of spontaneous emotions (Russell, 1994). Conversely, Ekman (1999) has cogently argued that it would be illogical for people to readily interpret posed facial expressions if they had not often encountered them in actual social life. Although studies on spontaneous emotion recognition may or may not be crucial to the universalist position it seems reasonable to expect cross-cultural recognition of spontaneous emotion if cross-cultural recognition of posed expression exists. Several early studies (e.g. Ekman, 1971) appeared to demonstrate cross-cultural (American and Japanese) recognition of spontaneous emotion but these studies have been disputed on grounds of low rates of recognition (see above; Russell, 1994). And although a recent study on Olympic medal winners suggests cross-cultural recognition of spontaneous emotion (Matsumoto and Willingham 2006) another recent study suggests limited recognition of spontaneous facial emotion (Naab and Russell, 2007). This latter study utilized Ekman's (1980) photographs of pre-literature New Guineans' spontaneous expressive displays of emotion. Americans rated these photographs and although they identified the correct emotion at above-chance levels (chance in this study was about 8%), for more than half of the expressions, an alternative emotion was more often selected. And nearly all existing studies on spontaneous emotion expression have demonstrated that recognition of such displays is much lower (often at chance) than that of posed emotion displays (e.g. Motley and Camden, 1988; Wagner et al., 1986). In general, although there is evidence for cross-cultural recognition of spontaneous emotion in specific cultures, contradicting evidence also exists, suggesting that conclusions regarding universality in spontaneous emotion recognition may be premature pending further cross-cultural replications.

The final issue we will discuss here regards the nature of the facial expressions that are accurately recognized. Some scholars argue that rather than emotion, it is general dimensions of affect (pleasure/displeasure) and arousal (arousing/unarousing) that are universally recognized (e.g. Russell, 1994). The idea is that given a forced choice (as in many recognition studies), participants may choose the emotion that comes closest to the facial expression with respect to affect and arousal. This proposition has recently been supported by the argument that emotions are not a "natural kind" and instead exist only as learned conceptual apparatuses; by this same approach, affect is a natural kind that exists independent from language (Barrett, 2006). By this treatment, recognition of affect should be pan-cultural whereas pan-cultural recognition of emotion is a methodological artifact. This proposal remains controversial—for example, studies that do not require forced-choice do seem to provide some evidence for cross-cultural recognition of facial emotion (Boucher and Carlson, 1980; Izard, 1971).

These and other issues in universal emotion recognition belie a largely-agreed upon fact—cultures differ in facial emotion recognition.

The ingroup advantage in emotion recognition

Cross-cultural accuracy rates above chance do not translate into perfect cross-cultural accuracy—even after the seminal studies of Ekman and others, there was at least the possibility for cultural variation in emotion recognition (Elfenbein and Ambady, 2002). Indeed, an ingroup advantage has more recently been demonstrated, such that individuals better recognize same-culture emotional expressions than other-culture emotion expressions (Elfenbein and Ambady, 2002; Elfenbein et al., 2002). This ingroup advantage has been observed across a variety of studies and cultures and a meta-analysis revealed that there was an increase in accuracy when judging emotional expressions for members of a cultural ingroup (Elfenbein and Ambady, 2002). Moreover, this phenomenon extends from racial, ethnic, and cultural groups to less commonly studied groups, such as cat-lovers and basketball players (who are especially good at identifying emotions in cats and basketball players, respectively; Thibault et al., 2006).

Explanations based on cultural history

Several explanations for the ingroup advantage rely on historical differences among cultures, including language and display rules. First, the words used to describe particular emotions vary in both intensity and meaning across cultures, and some languages may be better at expressing emotional concepts than others (Harré, 1986; Matsumoto and Assar, 1992; Mesquita et al., 1997; Wierzbicka, 1986, 1992). In many cross-cultural studies of emotion, linguistic differences in emotion concepts are thus of primary concern. Yet two facts contradict a linguistic interpretation of the ingroup bias. First and foremost, the ingroup advantage extends to group-distinctions in which groups share a language. Clearly, if the same language is used a linguistic interpretation is unlikely. Second, many studies revealing an ingroup advantage have utilized a *balanced design*, where both of two groups rate emotions from both groups. Such designs typically result in a statistical interaction, whereby the emotion expressions of Group A are better recognized by Group A than Group B *and* the expressions of Group B are better recognized by Group B than Groups A. With these designs, linguistic shortcomings in recognition should reduce accuracy across the board rather than reducing accuracy on other-group emotions. For these reasons, language is unlikely to be a compelling explanation of the ingroup advantage.

A second possibility is that *display rules* and *decoding rules* account for the ingroup advantage in emotion recognition. In some cultures, for example, it may be considered inappropriate to reveal anger in public, or impolite to acknowledge another person's sadness. These rules regulate the social norms regarding the appropriateness of emotion displays, and as a result, affect the identification of emotional expressions (Ekman, 1971; Matsumoto, 1989, 1992). Yet as with the language argument, such display and decoding rules can explain main effects (e.g. certain groups being less expressive or less willing to identify emotions) but not the interaction normally observed with ingroup advantage in balanced designs (see above).

In short, historical difference accounts of cultural differences in emotion recognition are well-suited to explaining why different cultures exhibit different levels of recognition accuracy in general. Yet these same accounts are poorly suited to describing why, *across groups and cultures*, ingroup expressions are more accurately identified than outgroup expressions. We turn instead to social adaptation accounts of the ingroup advantage.

Explanations based on social adaptation

Social adaptation accounts of the ingroup advantage are based on the idea that emotion recognition is adaptive for the individual but that accurate recognition is especially adaptive for ingroup emotions. One example of such account relies on a motivational mechanism: because the ingroup is more important to individual survival and reproduction than are outgroups, people may be more motivated to identify ingroup emotion expressions. Consistent with this idea, Thibault and colleagues (2006) demonstrated that identification with the ingroup—over and above familiarity—was associated with a greater ingroup advantage. Although this single study is far from conclusive in that it did not manipulate motivation, the theoretical rationale is compelling and seems likely to, at least in some cases, contribute to an ingroup advantage.

There is more evidence for an account of the ingroup advantage that relies on *non-verbal accents*. This account starts with the idea that there are subtle differences in how emotions are expressed among groups and cultures, and that these non-verbal accents go beyond cultural norms or display rules (Elfenbein and Ambady, 2003a). For example, in one study, individuals from the Canadian province of Quebec and the west-central African country of Gabon posed emotional expressions revealing reliable cultural differences in the activation of facial muscles for the same posed emotions (Elfenbein et al., 2007). Given subtle stylistic differences in emotion expression, people who have greater familiarity with a group and its facial expressions should be better at decoding facial expressions of emotion. Indeed, in the first of two experiments, Elfenbein and Ambady (2003b) examined emotion recognition for Chinese and American participants differing in their exposure to China and the US (Chinese in China, recent Chinese immigrants to the

US, second-generation Chinese immigrants born in the US, and non-Chinese US citizens). As expected, increased cultural exposure led to greater speed and accuracy in the recognition of emotions.

The second experiment replicated the cultural exposure effects for Tibetans living in China and Africans living in the US. Tibetans living in China were more accurate at identifying facial expressions of emotions for Chinese targets than for American targets, and Africans living in America showed the reverse pattern, thus demonstrating the role of exposure in improving accuracy of emotion recognition. More broadly, emotion recognition across nations appears to be a linear function of distance, such that perceiver nations achieve greater accuracy within increased proximity to the expresser nation (Elfenbein and Ambady, 2003c). Since national proximity is closely tied to national familiarity, these results are again supportive of a non-verbal accents account of the ingroup advantage.

In general, there is currently more support for a non-verbal accents account than for a motivational account of the ingroup advantage in emotion recognition. Yet these accounts do not necessarily conflict with one another in that both suggest that the ingroup advantage in emotion expressions is adaptive for the perceiver; indeed, future research may reveal evidence for both processes. In summary, it is clear that there are culture- and group-specific elements to emotion recognition. Emotions are best recognized by the ingroup and this ingroup advantage is best explained as an adaptive response to familiar expressions.

Culture and context together: recent findings

The preceding sections distinguished culture from context but some might argue that culture is simply context writ large. And others would argue that role of context should depend on the perceivers culture. One recent study is particularly illustrative of this approach. Noting that some eastern cultures are more likely to utilize holistic principles in perception and draw non-focal context into focal visual perception, Masuda and colleagues (2008) argued that Japanese individuals should be more likely than Americans to be influenced by social context in ratings of facial emotion. To test this hypothesis, a focal face was drawn against a background of four non-focal faces that expressed either the same or a different emotion as the focal face. As compared to American ratings, Japanese ratings of focal faces were skewed in the direction of the non-focal faces. One possible cause of this pattern of results is that the Japanese participants were paying more attention to the surrounding faces than were American participants. Indeed, participants in this study also completed a recognition task with foils that varied either the emotion expression or clothing of either the foreground face or surrounding faces. Japanese and American participants were equivalent in their recognition of changes to the central emotion expression but Japanese participants were more accurate in identifying changes to the emotional expressions of the surrounding faces, supporting the view that Japanese attended more to the surrounding expressions and were thus more influenced by these in their judgments of the central expression. In a second study, eye-tracking analyses confirmed that Japanese participants looked at the non-focal faces more often and for longer than American participants, providing strong evidence that the perceptual influence of context may depend on culture.

Summary and conclusions

The perception of facial expressions is perhaps the most popular area of research on non-verbal behavior and one of the more popular areas in social neuroscience research. The dominant Western approach to investigating facial expressions has been to isolate the face from contextual elements. Yet it is becoming increasingly clear that facial expressions are perceived within the broader social and cultural context. We reviewed evidence that the identification of facial emotion depends on emotion expressed via body movement and via the voice. Moreover, non-emotional elements of context, such as gaze, gender, and race were all found to alter judgments of facial emotion. And we described evidence to suggest that context influences automatic responses to facial expressions: facial emotion produces the same affect in ingroup perceivers but opposing affect in outgroup perceivers. Beyond the perceptually local ecological niche manifested by bodies and facial features, the broader ecological niche (read: culture) also alters the perception of facial expressions. Facial expressions are most accurately identified by perceivers who share cultural background with expressers. This effect appears to be driven in part by familiarity suggesting that "non-verbal accents" exist and can make identification difficult for outgroup observers. Additionally, display and decoding rules as well as linguistic conventions can alter the interpretation of emotion. Finally, the many effects of context and culture on expression perception may be interactive, as illustrated by findings that context is especially influential in some cultures.

This state of affairs is only sensible in that the adaptive importance of facial expressions to the perceiver is likely to depend on the ecological setting in which those expressions occur. If nothing else, evidence for contextualized perception of facial expressions should highlight the importance of achieving ecological validity—after all, only rarely do perceivers encounter acontextual and disembodied facial expressions.

Acknowledgments

This work was supported by NIH grant R01 MH70833 to N.A and NIH grant F32MH078350–03 to M.W.

References

Adams, R.B. and Kleck, R.E. (2003). Perceived gaze direction and the processing of facial displays of emotion. *Psychological Science*, **14**, 644–647.

Adams, R.B. and Kleck, R.E. (2005). Effects of direct and averted gaze on the perception of facially communicated emotion. *Emotion*, **5**, 3–11.

Aviezer, H., Hassin, R., Ryan, J., *et al.* (2008). Angry, disgusted or afraid? Studies on the malleability of emotion perception. *Psychological Science*, **19**, 724–732.

Barrett, L.F. (2006). Are emotions natural kinds? *Perspectives on Psychological Science*, **1**, 28–58.

Bindemann, M., Burton, A.M., and Langton, S.R.H. (2008) How do eye-gaze and facial expression interact? *Visual Cognition*, **16**, 708–733.

Boucher, J.D. and Carlson, O.E. (1980). Recognition of facial expression in three cultures. *Journal of Cross-Cultural Psychology*, **11**, 263–280.

Darwin, C. (1965). *The expressions of the emotions in man and animals.* Chicago, IL: University of Chicago Press. (Original work published 1872.)

Dimberg, U. (1997). Psychophysiological reactions to facial expressions. In U. Segerstrale and P. Molnar (eds.) *Nonverbal communication: Where nature meets culture*, pp. 47–60. Mahwah, NJ: Erlbaum.

Ekman, P. (1971). Universals and cultural differences in facial expressions of emotion. In J.K. Cole (ed.) *Nebraska symposium on motivation*, pp. 207–283. Lincoln, NE: University of Nebraska Press.

Ekman, P. (1980). *The face of man.* New York: Garland Publishing Inc.

Ekman, P. (1992). Are there basic emotions? *Psychological Review*, **99**, 550–553.

Ekman, P. (1999). *Facial expressions.* In T. Dalgleish and M. Power (eds.) *Handbook of cognition and emotion*, pp. 301–320. New York: John Wiley & Sons.

Ekman, P. (2003). *Emotions Revealed.* New York: Henry Holt.

Ekman, P., and Friesen, W.V. (1969). The repertoire of nonverbal behavior: Categories, origins, usage and coding. *Semiotica*, **1**, 49–98.

Ekman, P., and Friesen, W.V. (1971). Constants across cultures in the face and emotion. *Journal of Personality and Social Psychology*, **17**, 124–129.

Elfenbein, H.A., and Ambady, N. (2002). On the universality and cultural specificity of emotion recognition: A meta-analysis. *Psychological Bulletin*, **128**, 203–235.

Elfenbein, H.A. and Ambady, N. (2003a). Universals and cultural differences in recognizing emotions. *Current Directions in Psychological Science*, **12**, 159–164.

Elfenbein, H.A. and Ambady, N. (2003b). When familiarity breeds accuracy: Cultural exposure and facial emotion recognition. *Journal of Personality and Social Psychology*, **85**, 276–290.

Elfenbein, H.A. and Ambady, N. (2003c). Cultural similarity's consequences: A distance perspective on cross-cultural differences in emotion recognition. *Journal of Cross Cultural Psychology*, **34**, 92–109.

Elfenbein, H.A., Mandal, M.K., Ambady, N., Harizuka, S., and Kumar, S. (2002). Cross-cultural patterns in emotion recognition: Highlighting design and analytical techniques. *Emotion*, **2**, 75–84.

Elfenbein, H.A., Beaupre, M., Levesque, M., and Hess, U. (2007). Toward a dialect theory: Cultural differences in the expression and recognition of posed facial expressions. *Emotion*, **7**, 131–146.

Gibson, J.J. (1979). *The ecological approach to visual perception*. Wilmington, MA: Houghton Mifflin.

Graham, R. and LaBar, K.S. (2007) Garner interference reveals dependencies between emotional expression and gaze in face perception. *Emotion*, **7**, 296–313.

Harré, R.M. (ed.). (1986). *The social construction of emotions*. Oxford: Basil Blackwell.

Hugenberg, K. (2005). Social categorization and the perception of facial affect: Target race moderates the response latency advantage for happy faces. *Emotion*, **5**, 267–276.

Hugenberg, K. and Bodenhausen, G. V. (2003). Facing prejudice: Implicit prejudice and the perception of facial threat. *Psychological Science*, **14**, 640–643.

Hugenberg, K. and Sczesny, S. (2006). On wonderful women and seeing smiles: Social categorization moderates the happy face response latency advantage. *Social Cognition*, **24**, 516–539.

Izard, C. E. (1969). The emotions and emotion contrstucts in personality and culture research. In R.B. Cattell (ed.) *Handbook of modern personality theory*. Chicago, IL: Aldine Press.

Izard, C.E. (1971). *The face of emotion*. New York: Appleton-Century-Crofts.

Izard, C.E. (1992). Basic emotions, relations among emotions, and emotion-cognition relations. *Psychological Review*, **99**, 561–565.

Knutson, B. (1996). Facial expressions of emotion influence interpersonal trait inferences. *Journal of Nonverbal Behavior*, **20**, 165–182.

Marsh, A.A., Ambady, N., and Kleck, R.E. (2005). The effects of fear and anger facial expressions on approach and avoidance related behaviors. *Emotion*, **5**, 119–124.

Masuda, T., Ellsworth, P.C., Mesquita, B., Leu, J., Tanida, S., and Van de Veerdonk, E. (2008). Placing the face in context: Cultural differences in the perception of facial emotion. *Journal of Personality and Social Psychology*, **94**, 365–381.

Matsumoto, D. (1989). Cultural influences on the perception of emotion. *Journal of Cross-Cultural Psychology*, **20**, 92–105.

Matsumoto, D. (1992). American-Japanese cultural differences in the recognition of universal facial expressions. *Journal of Cross-Cultural Psychology*, **23**, 72–84.

Matsumoto, D. and Assar, M. (1992). The effects of language on the judgments of universal facial expressions of emotion. *Journal of Nonverbal Behavior*, **16**, 85–99.

Matsumoto, D. and Willingham, B. (2006). The thrill of victory and the agony of defeat: Spontaneous expressions of medal winners of the 2004 Athens Olympic Games. *Journal of Personality and Social Psychology*, **91**, 568–581.

McArthur, L.Z. and Baron, R.M. (1983). Toward an ecological theory of social perception. *Psychological Review*, **90**, 215–238.

Mesquita, B., Frijda, N.H., and Scherer, K.R. (1997). Culture and emotion. In J.W. Berry, P.R. Dasen, and T.S. Sararwathi (eds.), *Handbook of cross-cultural psychology: Vol. 2. Basic processes and human development*, pp. 255–297. Boston, MA: Allyn and Bacon.

Motley, M. and Camden, C. (1988). Facial expression of emotion: A comparison of posed expressions versus spontaneous expressions in an interpersonal communication setting. *Western Journal of Speech Communication*, **52**, 1–22.

Naab, P.J. and Russell, J.A. (2007). Judgments of emotion from spontaneous facial expressions of New Guineans. *Emotion*, **7**, 736–744.

Ohman, A. (2002). Automaticity and the amygdala: Nonconscious responses to emotional faces. *Current Directions in Psychological Science*, **11**, 62–65.

Plant, E.A., Kling, K.C., and Smith, G.L. (2004). The influence of gender and social role on the interpretation of facial expressions. *Sex Roles*, **51**, 187–196.

Rinn, W.E. (1984). The neuropsychology of facial expression: A review of the neurological and psychological mechanisms for producing facial expressions. *Psychological Bulletin*, **95**, 52–77.

Russell, J.A. (1994). Is there universal recognition of emotion from facial expressions? A review of the cross-cultural studies. *Psychological Review*, **115**, 102–141.

Russell, J.A., Bachorowski, J., and Fernandez-Dols, J. (2003). Facial and vocal expressions of emotion. *Annual Review of Psychology*, **54**, 329–439.

Thibault, P., Bourgeois, P., and Hess, U. (2006). The effect of group identification on emotion recognition: The case of cats and basketball players. *Journal of Experimental and Social Psychology*, **42**, 676–683.

Tomkins, S.S. (1962). *Affect imagery, consciousness, Vol. 1. The positive affects*. New York: Springer.

Wagner, H., MacDonald, C., and Manstead, A. (1986). Communication of individual emotions by spontaneous facial expressions. *Journal of Personality and Social Psychology*, **50**, 737–743.

Walker-Andrews, A.S. (2008). Intermodal emotional processes in infancy. In M. Lewis, J. M., Haviland, and L. Feldman-Barrett (eds.) *Handbook of emotions*, pp. 364–375. New York: Guilford Press.

Weisbuch, M. and Ambady, A. (2008). Affective divergence: Automatic responses to others' emotions depend on group membership. *Journal of Personality and Social Psychology*, **95**, 1063–1079.

Wierzbicka, A. (1986). Human emotions: Universal or culture-specific? *American Anthropologist*, **88**, 584–594.

Wierzbicka, A. (1992). Talking about emotions: Semantics, culture, and cognition. *Cognition and Emotion*, **6**, 285–319.

Zebrowitz, L.A. and Collins, M.A. (1997). Accurate social perception at zero acquaintance: The affordances of a Gibsonian approach. *Personality and Social Psychology Review*, **1**, 204–233.

Chapter 25

Automated Facial Expression Measurement: Recent Applications to Basic Research in Human Behavior, Learning, and Education

Marian Stewart Bartlett and Jacob Whitehill

Introduction

Automatic facial expression measurement systems have been under development since the early 1990s. The early attempts worked well in highly controlled conditions but failed for spontaneous expressions, and real application environments. Automatic facial expression recognition has now advanced to the point that we are able to apply it to spontaneous expressions. These systems extract a sufficiently reliable signal that we can employ them in behavioral studies and begin to develop applications that respond to spontaneous expressions in real time.

Tools for automatic expression measurement will bring about paradigmatic shifts in a number of fields by making facial expression more accessible as a behavioral measure. Previous behavioral studies employed objective coding of facial expression by hand, which required extensive training and could take hours to code each minute of video. The automated tools will enable new research activity not only in psychology, but also in cognitive neuroscience, psychiatry, education, human–machine communication, and human social dynamics. Statistical pattern recognition on large quantities of video data can reveal emergent behavioral patterns that previously would have required hundreds of coding hours by human experts, and would be unattainable by the non-expert. The explosion of research in these fields will also provide critical information for computer science and engineering efforts to make computers and robots that interact effectively with humans and understand behavior. Moreover, automated facial expression analysis will enable investigations into facial expression dynamics that were previously intractable by human coding because of the time required to code intensity changes.

This chapter first overviews the state of the art in computer vision approaches to facial expression recognition, including methods for characterizing expression dynamics. The chapter then reviews behavioral studies that have employed automatic facial expression recognition to learn new information about the relationships of facial expression to internal state, and reviews the first generation of applications in learning and education that take advantage of the real-time expression signal.

State of the art in computer vision approaches to automatic facial expression measurement

Automated facial expression recognition systems have been under development since the early 1990s (e.g. Cottrell and Metcalfe, 1991; Mase 1991). While the early systems worked well for the face video on which they were developed, generalization to new individuals, and new camera conditions, even when approximately frontal and well lit, remained a major challenge. Performance on spontaneous expressions tumbled to near chance. Much of the current research has focused on achieving robustness through machine learning, or statistical models, where the system parameters are estimated from large data samples. Advances have also included more informative image features and robust motion tracking.

Automatic expression recognition systems share a similar overall architecture, shown in Figure 25.1. (1) The face is first localized in the image; (2) information about the image is extracted from the face region ("feature extraction"); and (3) this information used to make a decision about facial expression ("classification"). The most important ways in which expression recognizers differ is the type of features extracted, the method of classification, and the integration of information over time. Below we overview these steps, and review some of the strengths and weaknesses of current approaches. For a more thorough analysis and comparison, the reviewer is referred to the survey papers (Fasel and Luettin, 2003; Tian et al., 2003; Pantic and Rothkrantz, 2000; Zeng et al., 2009).

Feature types

Image features for expression recognition fall into three main categories: geometric features, motion features, and appearance-based features. Geometric features include the shape of the mouth or eye opening, relative distances between fiducial points such as the inner eyebrows, or relative positions of many points on a face mesh; (see Tian et al., 2001, for an example).

Motion features consist of displacements estimated by tracking individual feature points or tracking more complex shapes. Motion tracking continues to be a highly challenging area of computer vision research, in which even state-of-the-art tracking algorithms are subject to drift after a couple of seconds of tracking, and require re-initialization. Drift refers to an accumulation of position error over time. A particular challenge is that most tracking algorithms depend on a brightness constraint equation which assumes that brightness has neither been added nor subtracted from the image, but rather it has just moved. Facial expressions include numerous violations of this constraint, including lips parting to show the teeth, and wrinkling.

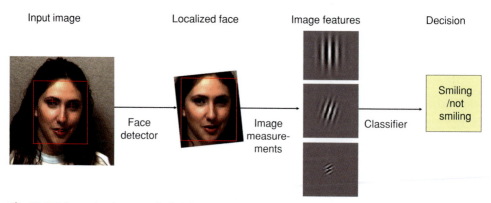

Fig. 25.1 Schematic of automatic facial expression recognition. Face image from RU-FACS database, Bartlett et al. (2006).

Appearance-based features attempt to extract information about the spatial patterns of light and dark in the face image. This information is typically extracted by applying banks of image filters on the pixel intensities. An image filter is like a template match. The more similar the image window is to the spatial pattern in the two-dimensional filter, the higher the output value. Commonly used features include Gabor filters (e.g. Bartlett et al., 2006), eigenfaces (e.g. Cottrell and Metcalfe, 1991), independent component filters (e.g. Donato et al., 1999), integral image filters (Wang et al., 2004; Whitehill et al., 2009), and histograms of edges at different spatial orientations (Levi and Weiss, 2004). Gabor filters, for example, are akin to a local Fourier analysis on the image obtained by applying templates of sine wave grating patches at multiple spatial scales, orientations, and positions on the image. Since the dimensionality of appearance-based feature vectors is high, on the order of tens of thousands of features, practical expression recognition systems typically require thousands of training images to achieve robust performance. Machine learning systems taking large sets of appearance-features as input, and trained on a large database of examples, are emerging as some of the most robust systems in computer vision for tasks such as face detection (Fasel et al., 2005; Viola and Jones, 2004), feature detection (Fasel, 2005; Vukadinovic and Pantic, 2005), identity recognition (Phillips et al., 2006), and expression recognition (Littlewort et al., 2006). Appearance-based features also don't suffer from drift, which is a major challenge for motion tracking.

Active appearance models (AAMs) integrate elements from geometric, tracking, and appearance-based approaches (Cootes et al., 2001; Huang et al., 2008; Lucey et al., 2006). AAMs are essentially a method for robust tracking of a set of facial landmarks by fitting the face image to a flexible face model. This flexible face model contains information not only about how landmark positions change with expression, but also how the image gray levels near the landmark points change in appearance. Robustness is achieved by constraining the motion tracking to fit statistical models of both the shape and appearance of the face. The approach requires a set of training images, usually of the individual face to be tracked, in which multiple landmark positions have been labeled as the face undergoes a range of facial expression changes that spans the tracking requirements in the run-time system. AAMs have performed well on individuals in which models have been trained, but have difficulty generalizing to novel individuals. Approaches to improve generalization of AAMs to novel faces is an area of active research. It is of note that AAM approaches to expression recognition typically use just the final landmark displacement information for expression recognition.

It is an open question which feature class, appearance-based, motion-based, or geometric, are best for expression recognition. Several studies that suggest that appearance-based features may contain more information about facial expression than displacements of a set of points (Donato et al., 1999; Zhang et al., 1998), although findings are mixed (e.g. Pantic and Patras, 2006). One compelling finding is that an upper-bound on expression recognition performance using hand-labeled feature positions (e.g. Michel and El Kaliouby, 2003) was found to be lower than the performance of a fully automated system using appearance-based features, tested on the same dataset (Littlewort et al., 2006). However there is no question that motion is an important signal, and may be crucial for detecting low intensity facial expressions. Ultimately, combining appearance-based and motion-based representations may be the most powerful, and there is some experimental evidence that this is indeed the case (e.g. Bartlett et al., 1999).

All three classes of features are highly affected by out-of-plane head rotations. Most systems require head pose to remain within about 10 to 20 degrees of a fully frontal view. Methods of handling out-of-plane rotation are an area of active research, and include learning view specific expression detectors for profile views (Pantic and Patras, 2006), or mapping onto a three-dimensional head model, rotating to frontal, and re-projecting (e.g. Bartlett et al., 2002).

As cameras and data storage become less expensive, multicamera approaches are emerging as one of the more effective ways to address this problem.

Classification methods

After image features are extracted from the face, a decision is made about facial expression based on the set of image measures. A few systems have used rule-based classifiers in which the mapping from feature values to facial expression is defined manually (e.g. Moriyama et al., 2002). For the most part, however, facial expression recognition systems use machine learning-based classifiers, such as neural networks (Tian et al., 2001), and more recent variants on neural networks such as support vector machines (Bartlett et al., 2006) and Adaboost (Tong et al., 2007; Whitehill et al., 2009), to make a decision about the facial expression in the image. Generally, the machine learning based classifiers, when trained on large amounts of data, give rise to more robust systems.

Methods of integrating over time

There is a large body of research showing that the dynamics of facial expressions (i.e. the timing and the duration of muscle movements) are crucial for interpretation of human facial behavior (Ekman and Rosenberg, 2005; Frank et al., 1993; Russell and Fernandez-Dols, 1997; Valstar et al., 2006). In recognition of this, several computational methods have been explored for integrating information over time, and this is an active area of current research. Approaches include employing spatiotemporal image features, such as spatiotemporal Gabor filters or motion energy filters (e.g. Yang et al., 2007). Another method is to compute expression estimates, using only spatial features for each video frame and then combining these with a dynamic time series model such as a HHM (e.g. Chang et al., 2006; De La Torre et al., 2007; el Kalioubi and Robson, 2005; Zhang et al., 2008;).

Levels of description

Another consideration in facial expression recognition is the level of categorization of the stimulus. One approach is to recognize facial expressions according to a categorical model, for example, at the level of basic emotions such as happy, sad, afraid, etc. However there may be many states of interest, such as stress, interest, and fatigue, or variants of an emotion, such as frustration, annoyance, and rage, and the facial configurations of these states may be unknown.

A second, more flexible approach is to recognize individual facial actions (facial action units (AUs); Ekman and Friesen, 1978), which can then be combined if categorical representations are required. An advantage of facial action systems is that they provide a more objective description of the facial expression, and enable discovery of new associations between facial movement and an emotional or cognitive state. The facial action coding system (FACS) (Ekman and Friesen, 1978) is a widely used method for coding facial expressions in the behavioral sciences. The system describes facial expressions in terms of 46 component movements, which roughly correspond to the individual facial muscle movements. Examples are shown in Figure 25.2. Because it is comprehensive, FACS has proven useful for discovering new associations between facial movements and affective or cognitive states (see Ekman and Rosenberg, 2005 for a review of facial expression studies using FACS). The primary limitation to the widespread use of FACS is the time required to manually code the individual facial actions by human experts. It takes over 100 hours of training to become proficient in FACS, and it takes approximately 2 hours for human experts to code a single minute of video. An automated system for facial action coding would enable a large range of new research in behavioral science.

Facial actions

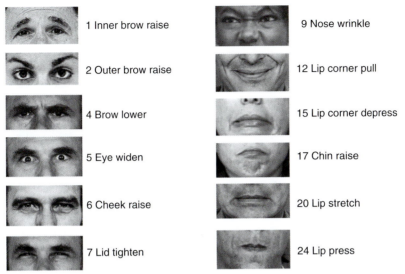

1 Inner brow raise	9 Nose wrinkle
2 Outer brow raise	12 Lip corner pull
4 Brow lower	15 Lip corner depress
5 Eye widen	17 Chin raise
6 Cheek raise	20 Lip stretch
7 Lid tighten	24 Lip press

Fig. 25.2 Sample facial actions from the Facial Action Coding System. The system defines 46 distinct facial movements. Reprinted from Insights on spontaneous facial expressions from automatic expression measurement, from *Dynamic Faces: Insights from Experiments and Computation*, edited by Cristabal Curio, Heinrich H. Bulthoff, Martin A. Giese, and the MIT Press.

Another parameterized expression coding system is the facial animation parameters (FAPS) in the MPEG4 video standard (Pandzic and Forchheimer, 2002). FAPS codes the movements of a set of 66 facial feature points. This coding standard is an important advance in terms of compatibility of multiple systems. A drawback is that it was developed by engineers with experience in speech animation, not facial expression. The set of feature points provide sparse information on many behaviorally relevant movements other than those immediately around the mouth, and it also encourages systems to ignore appearance changes, resulting in the plastic looking animations in computer generated films such as *Polar Express*. However, FACS is not well suited for coding speech movements. Some combination of the two systems may avoid the problems inherent in each.

Training images and spontaneous expressions

For the task of learning categorical models, often a set of undergraduates or professional actors will be used to pose the desired facial expression. However, these posed expressions often differ from their spontaneous counterparts. Spontaneous and posed expressions have different structural and temporal properties. Part of the reason for these differences is physiological. It is well known that there are two distinct neural pathways for posed and spontaneous facial expressions, each one originating in different areas of the brain (see Rinn, 1984, for a review). Subcortically initiated facial expressions (the spontaneous group) are characterized by synchronized, smooth, symmetrical, and ballistic muscle movements whereas cortically initiated facial expressions (posed expressions) tend to be less smooth, with more variable dynamics, and less synchrony among different muscles (Cohn and Schmidt, 2004; Frank et al., 1993; Schmidt et al., 2003). Because of these differences, it is important to employ databases of spontaneous expressions, such as the drowsiness example described later in this chapter. While this is recognized by many research groups, elicitation and verification of the desired states is a major research challenge (see Cowie, 2008.)

Approaches that focus on recognition of elemental facial movements such as facial actions have another set of challenges for development of training data. Such approaches require expert coding of face video, which is expensive and time consuming.

For both approaches, large numbers of training examples are required in order to recognize facial behavior with robustness. Moderate performance can be attained with tens of examples (Bartlett et al., 2003), and asymptotes with tens of thousands of examples (Whitehill et al., 2009). Experience in our lab has suggested that automated detection of facial actions, where the AU detectors were developed from a large number of training samples, provides a good foundation for subsequent recognition of subject states for which there may be a much smaller number of samples.

The precision of automated facial expression recognition systems depends on the richness of the training set. It is essential to not only have a good range of positive examples (e.g. images containing the target expression "happy") but also to have a good range of negative examples (images to which your system should respond "not happy"). The negative set is often overlooked, at great peril, as this can lead to false positives when the system is applied to real behavior (see Whitehill et al., 2009).

The computer expression recognition toolbox

A number of the system features described above have been combined into a end-to-end system for fully automated facial expression recognition, called the Computer Expression Recognition Toolbox (CERT). CERT was developed at developed at University of California, San Diego, originating from a collaboration between Ekman and Sejnowski (Bartlett et al., 1996, 1999, 2006; Donato et al., 1999; Littlewort et al., 2006). The current system automatically detects frontal faces in the video stream and codes each frame with respect to 40 continuous dimensions, including basic expressions of anger, disgust, fear, joy, sadness, surprise, contempt, a continuous measure of head pose (yaw, pitch, and roll), as well as 30 facial AUs from the FACS (see Figure 25.3).

The technical approach to CERT is an appearance-based, discriminative approach. As described above, these approaches have proven highly robust and fast for face detection and tracking (e.g. Viola and Jones, 2004), do not suffer from initialization and drift, which presents challenges for state of the art tracking algorithms, and take advantage of the rich appearance-based information in facial expression images. Face detection, as well as detection of internal facial features, is first performed on each frame using a generalization of the Viola and Jones face detector (Fasel et al., 2005). The automatically located faces are then aligned using a fast least squares fit on the detected features, and finally passed through a bank of Gabor filters at eight orientations and nine spatial frequencies (2:32 pixels per cycle at 1/2 octave steps). Output magnitudes are then normalized and passed to facial action classifiers.

Facial action detectors were developed by training separate support vector machines to detect the presence or absence of each facial action. The training set consisted of over 10,000 images that were coded for facial actions from the FACS, including over 5000 examples of spontaneous expressions. Tests on a benchmark dataset (Cohn-Kanade) show state of the art performance for recognition of basic emotions (98% correct detection for one vs. all, and 93% correct for seven

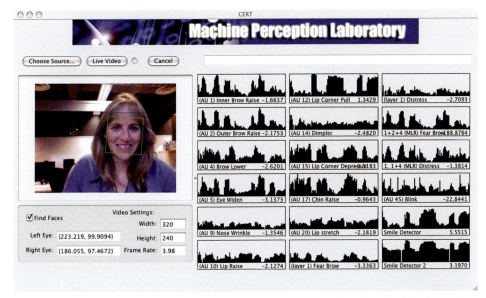

Fig. 25.3 Example of CERT running on live video. In each subplot, the horizontal axis is time and the vertical axis indicates the intensity of a particular facial movement. Reprinted from Bartlett et al. Computer Expression Recognition Toobox. Demo: 8th International IEEE Conference on Automatic Face and Gesture Recognition, 2008. © 2008 IEEE.

alternative forced choice of the six basic emotions plus neutral), and for recognizing facial actions from the FACS (mean 0.93 area under the ROC[1] curve for posed facial actions, 0.84 for spontaneous facial actions with speech). The system outputs a continuous value for each emotion and each facial action. These outputs are significantly correlated with the intensity of the facial action (Bartlett et al., 2006; Whitehill et al, 2009). More information about the facial expression detection system can be found in Bartlett et al., 2006.

This system was employed in some of the earliest experiments in which spontaneous behavior was analyzed with automated expression recognition (Bartlett et al., 2008). These experiments addressed automated discrimination of posed from genuine expressions of pain, automated detection of driver drowsiness, adaptive tutoring systems, and an intervention for children with autism. The analysis revealed information about facial behavior that was previously unknown, including the coupling of movements. These experiments are described in the next section, along with landmark studies from other research labs, which were among the first to employ computer vision for basic research into facial behavior.

---

[1] The Receiver Operator Characteristic curve (ROC) plots hits against false alarms as the decision threshold shifts from one extreme to the other. The area under the ROC is 0.5 for a system at chance and 1 for perfect detection. It is equivalent to per cent correct on a 2-alternative forced choice in which a target and non-target are randomly selected and the system must choose which is the target (Green and Swets, 1966).

Applications to basic research in human behavior, education, and medicine

Pain, fatigue, and stress

Automated discrimination of real from faked expressions of pain

Given the two different neural pathways for facial expressions, one may expect to find differences between genuine and posed expressions of states such as pain. The ultimate goal of this work is not the detection of malingering per se, but rather to demonstrate the ability of an automated system to detect facial behavior that the untrained eye might fail to interpret, and to differentiate types of neural control of the face. It holds out the prospect of illuminating basic questions pertaining to the behavioral fingerprint of neural control systems, and thus opens many future lines of inquiry.

In a study by Littlewort and colleagues (2009), CERT was applied to spontaneous and posed facial expressions of pain (Figure 25.4). In this study, 26 participants were videotaped under three experimental conditions: baseline, posed pain, and real pain. The real pain condition consisted of cold pressor pain induced by submerging the arm in ice water. The study assessed whether the automated measurements were consistent with expression measurements obtained by human experts, and developed a classifier to automatically differentiate real from faked pain in a subject-independent manner from the automated measurements. A machine learning approach was employed in a two-stage system. In the first stage, a set of 20 detectors for facial actions from the FACS operated on the continuous video stream. This data was then passed to a second machine learning stage, in which a non-linear support vector machine (SVM) was trained to detect the difference between expressions of real pain and fake pain. Measures of AU dynamics were extracted from the CERT outputs and passed to the real pain/faked pain classifier.

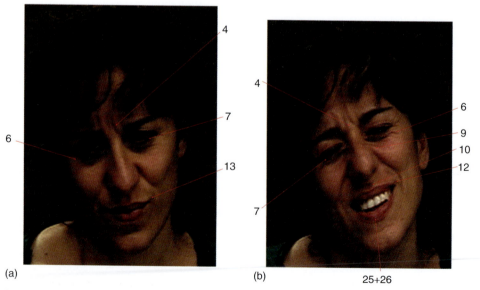

Fig. 25.4 Facial expression of faked pain (a) and real pain (b), with corresponding FACS codes.

Naïve human subjects tested on the same videos were at chance for differentiating faked from real pain expressions, obtaining only 49% accuracy, where chance is 50%. The automated system was successfully able to differentiate faked from real pain. In an analysis of 26 subjects displaying faked pain before real pain, the system obtained 88% correct for subject independent discrimination of real versus fake pain on a two-alternative forced choice. Moreover, the most discriminative facial actions in the automated system were consistent with findings using human expert FACS codes. In particular, in the faked pain condition the automated system output showed exaggerated activity of the brow lowering action (corrugator), as well as inner brow raise (central frontalis), and eyelid tightening, which were consistent with a previous study on faked versus real cold pressor pain that employed manual FACS coding (LaRochette et al., 2006).

The temporal event analysis performed significantly better than a SVM trained just on individual frames, suggesting that the real versus faked expression discrimination depends not only on which subset of AUs are present at which intensity, but also on the duration and number of AU events.

Pain or no pain?

In a related study, Ashraf et al. (2007) measured the ability of an automated facial expression recognition system to estimate pain intensity using a system developed at Carnegie Mellon University (CMU). Pain is typically assessed by patient self-report. Self-reported pain, however, is difficult to interpret and may be impaired or not even possible, as in young children or the severely ill. Behavioral scientists have identified reliable and valid facial indicators of pain. Until now they required manual measurement by highly skilled observers. Ashraf et al. developed an approach that automatically recognizes acute pain. Adult patients with rotator cuff injury were video-recorded while a physiotherapist manipulated their affected and unaffected shoulder. Skilled observers rated pain expression from the video on a 5-point Likert-type scale. From these ratings, sequences were categorized as no-pain (rating of 0), or pain (rating of 3, 4, or 5). Ratings of 1 or 2 were discarded as indeterminate. They explored machine learning approaches for pain-no pain classification using AAMs. Keyframes within each video sequence were manually labeled for the positions of internal facial landmarks, while in the remaining frames the positions of the landmarks were tracked automatically with the AAM. A set of appearance and shape features were then derived from the AAM and passed to a support vector machine for the pain/no-pain classification. The system achieved a hit rate of 81% for detecting pain versus no-pain. These results support the feasibility of automatic pain detection from video.

Automated detection of driver fatigue

It is estimated that driver drowsiness causes more fatal crashes in the US than drunk driving (Department of Transportation, 2001). Hence an automated system that could detect drowsiness and alert the driver or truck dispatcher could save many lives. Previous approaches to drowsiness detection by computer make presumptions about the relevant behavior, focusing on blink rate, eye closure, yawning, and head nods (Gu and Ji, 2004; Zhang and Zhang, 2006). While there is considerable empirical evidence that blink rate can predict falling asleep, it was unknown whether there were other facial behaviors that could predict sleep episodes. The work described here employed machine learning methods to real human behavior during drowsiness episodes. The objective of this study was to discover what facial configurations are predictors of fatigue. In this study, facial motion was analyzed automatically using CERT. In addition, we also collected head motion data using an accelerometer placed on the subject's head, as well as steering wheel data. (The automated yaw pitch and roll detectors had not been developed at the time of this study.)

In this study, 4 subjects participated in a driving simulation task over a 3-hour period between midnight and 3am. Video of the subjects' faces and time-locked crash events were recorded (Figure 25.5). The subjects' data were partitioned into drowsy and alert states as follows. The 1 min preceding a crash was labeled as a drowsy state. A set of "alert" video segments was identified from the first 20 min of the task in which there were no crashes by any subject. This resulted in a mean of 14 alert segments and 24 crash segments per subject.

In order to understand how each action unit is associated with drowsiness across different subjects, multinomial logistic ridge regression (MLR) was trained on each facial action individually. The five facial actions that were the most predictive of drowsiness by increasing in drowsy states were blink, outer brow raise, frown, chin raise, and nose wrinkle. The five actions that were the most predictive of drowsiness by decreasing in drowsy states were smile, lid tighten, nostril compress, brow lower, and jaw drop. The high predictive ability of the blink/eye closure measure was expected. However the predictability of the outer brow raise was previously unknown. We observed during this study that many subjects raised their eyebrows in an attempt to keep their eyes open. Also of note is that action 26, jaw drop, which occurs during yawning, actually occurred less often in the critical 60 s prior to a crash.

A fatigue detector that combines multiple AUs was then developed. An MLR classifier was trained using contingent feature selection, starting with the most discriminative feature (blink), and then iteratively adding the next most discriminative feature given the features already selected. MLR outputs were then temporally integrated over a 12-s window. Best performance of 0.98 area under the ROC was obtained with five features.

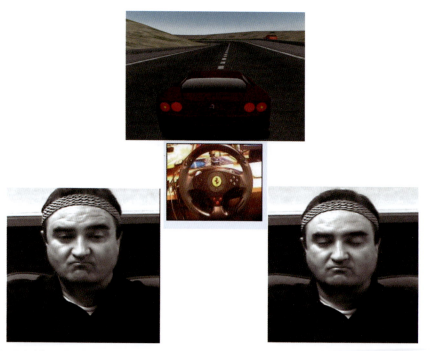

Fig. 25.5 Driving Simulation Task. Reprinted from Vural et al., Drowsy driver detection through facial movement and analysis. ICCV Workshop on Human Computer Interaction, 2007. © 2007 IEEE.

We also observed changes in the coupling of behaviors with drowsiness. For some of the subjects coupling between brow raise and eye openness increased in the drowsy state (Figure 25.6a,b). Subjects appear to have pulled up their eyebrows in an attempt to keep their eyes open. Head motion was next examined. Head motion increased as the driver became drowsy, with large roll motion coupled with the steering motion as the driver became drowsy. Just before falling asleep, the head would become still. See Figure 25.6c,d.

This is the first work to our knowledge to reveal significant associations between facial expression and fatigue beyond eyeblinks. The project also revealed a potential association between head roll and driver drowsiness, and the coupling of head roll with steering motion during drowsiness. Of note is that a behavior that is often assumed to be predictive of drowsiness, yawn, was in fact a negative predictor of the 60-s window prior to a crash. It appears that in the moments just before falling asleep, drivers may yawn less, not more, often. This highlights the importance of designing a system around real, not posed, examples of examples of fatigue and drowsiness.

Automatic detection of stress

Dinges et al. (2005) prototyped an automated system to discriminate between high and low levels of stress as expressed by a subject's face. The particular application that the research targeted was detection of stress in astronauts during space flight, but in fact the methods were quite general and were not tailored to this specific domain. In their experiment, 60 subjects completed a battery of computerized neurobehavioral tests, and the test sessions were video recorded. Tests were presented to each subject in both easy and difficult versions to induce stress of low and high levels, respectively. The high-stress version contained more difficult questions and allowed less time for answers.

The approach employed motion tracking followed by a dynamical model. The system tracks the face using a three-dimensional deformable face mesh that models both translation and rotation of the head (rigid motion) and deformations of the face itself (non-rigid motion). Feature vectors are then extracted from the face, including not only deformation parameters from the face mesh but also grayscale information from the eyes. These feature vectors are input to two dynamical models (HMMs), one trained on high-stress and the other trained on low-stress sequences. The two HMMs output a probability estimate that the sequence of input features were generated under high or low stress, respectively. Dinges et al. (2005) post-processed these probabilities with an additional discriminative classifier (support vector machine), for deciding high versus low stress. The system was tested for subject dependent recognition. From each subject video, four sequences were extracted of 5–10-s duration. Two sequences of each subject (one low and one high-stress) were employed to train the system, the other two sequences were used for testing performance. The overall accuracy was reported at 70% for a high- versus low-stress decision. This was above chance but below the 85% accuracy of human judges. This is moderate performance, but provides the first support to our knowledge for detection of stress states using automated expression measurement.

The science and technology of educating

Automated feedback for intelligent tutoring systems

There has been a growing thrust to develop tutoring systems and agents that respond to the students' emotional and cognitive state and interact with them in a social manner (e.g. D'Mello et al., 2007; Kapoor et al., 2007). Whitehill et al. (2008) investigated the utility of integrating automatic facial expression recognition into an automated teaching system. This work used expression to estimate the student's preferred viewing speed of the videos, and the level of difficulty, as perceived

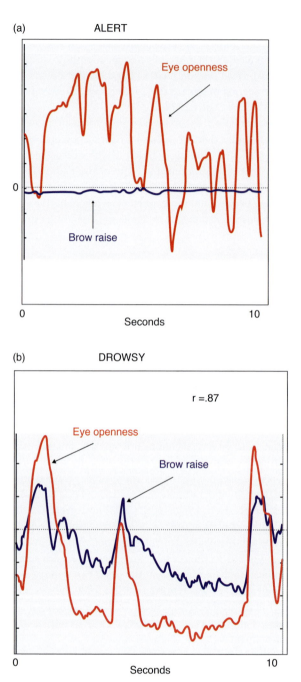

Fig. 25.6 Changes in movement coupling with drowsiniess. (a, b) Eye Openness (red) and Eye Brow Raise (AU2) (Blue) for 10 s in an alert state (a) and 10 s prior to a crash (b), for one subject.

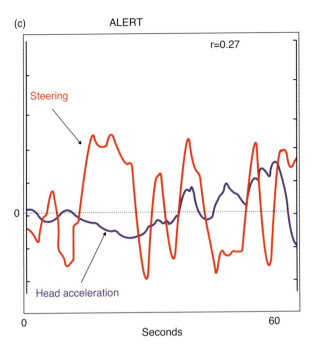

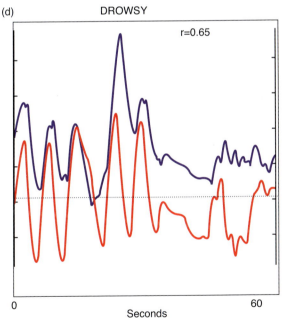

Fig. 25.6 (*Contd.*) (c, d) Head motion (blue) and steering position (red) for 60 s in an alert state (c) and 60 s prior to a crash (d) for one subject. Head motion is the output of the roll dimension of the accelerometer. (In grayscale, gray = blue, red = black.) With kind permission of Springer Science + Business Media, Data Mining Spontaneous Facial Behavior with Automatic Expression Coding, 2008, Bartlett.

by the individual student, of the lecture at each moment of time. This pilot study took first steps towards developing methods for closed loop teaching policies, i.e. systems that have access to real time estimates of cognitive and emotional states of the students and act accordingly.

In this study, eight subjects separately watched a video lecture composed of several short clips on mathematics, physics, psychology, and other topics. The playback speed of the video was controlled by the subject using a keypress. The subjects were instructed to watch the video as quickly as possible (so as to be efficient with their time) while still retaining accurate knowledge of the video's content, since they would be quizzed afterwards.

While watching the lecture, the student's facial expressions were measured in real-time by the CERT system (Bartlett et al., 2006). After watching the video and taking the quiz, each subject then watched the lecture video again at a fixed speed of 1.0. During this second viewing, subjects specified how easy or difficult they found the lecture to be at each moment in time using the keyboard.

For each subject, a regression analysis was performed to predict perceived difficulty and preferred viewing speed from the facial expression measures. The expression intensities themselves, as well as their first temporal derivatives, measuring the instantaneous change in intensity, were the independent variables in a standard linear regression. An example of such predictions is shown in Figure 25.7c for one subject.

The facial expression measures were significantly predictive of both perceived difficulty ($r = 0.75$) and preferred viewing speed ($r = 0.51$). The correlations on validation data were 0.42 and 0.29, respectively. The specific facial expressions that were correlated with difficulty and speed varied highly from subject to subject. The most consistently correlated expression was AU 45 ("blink"), where subjects blinked less during the more difficult sections of video. This is consistent with previous work associating decreases in blink rate with increases in cognitive load (Holland and Tarlow, 1972; Tada 1986).

Overall, this study provided proof of principle that fully automated facial expression recognition at the present state of the art can be used to provide real-time feedback in automated tutoring systems. The recognition system was able to extract a signal from the face video in real-time that provided information about internal states relevant to teaching and learning.

A related project that attempts to approximate the benefits of face-to-face tutoring interaction is a collaboration between the MIT media lab and the developers of AutoTutor (D'Mello et al., 2007). AutoTutor is an intelligent tutoring system that interacts with students using natural language to teach physics, computer literacy, and critical thinking skills. The current system adapts to the cognitive states of the learner as inferred from dialog and performance. A new affect sensitive version is presently under development (D'Mello, et al., 2008) which detects four emotions (boredom, flow/engagement, confusion, frustration) by monitoring conversational cues, gross body language, and facial expressions. Towards this end, they have developed a database of spontaneous expressions while interacting with the automated tutor, which will significantly advance the field.

Applications in neuropsychology and medicine

Facial expression perception and production in children with autism

Children with autism spectrum disorders (ASD) are impaired in their ability to produce and perceive dynamic facial expressions (Adolphs et al., 2001). Automated facial expression recognition systems can now be leveraged in the investigation of issues such as the facial expression recognition and production deficits common to children with ASD. Not only can these technologies assist in quantifying these deficits, but they can also be used as part of interventions aimed at reducing deficit severity.

(a)

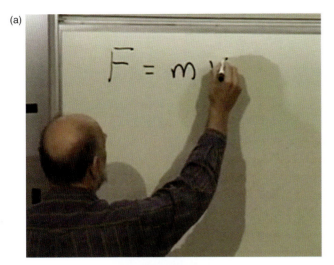

(b)

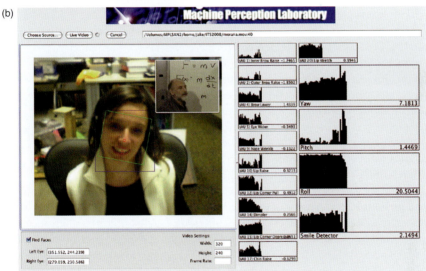

(c)

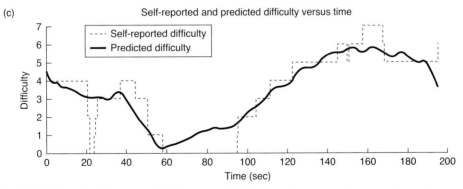

Fig. 25.7 (a) Sample video lecture. (b) Automated facial expression recognition is performed on subjects face as she watches the lecture. (c) Self-reported difficulty values (dashed), and the reconstructed difficulty values (solid) computed using linear regression over facial expression movements for one subject. Reprinted from Whitehill, Bartlett, and Movellan, Automatic Facial Expression Recognition for Intelligent Tutoring Systems, 2008 IEEE CVPR Workshop Sessions © 2008 IEEE.

The Let's Face It! training program (LFI!) (Cockburn et al., 2008) is an intervention for children with ASD that has been shown to significantly improve their face processing abilities. However, it is only capable of improving their receptive ability. In this project, we introduced CERT into LFI! in order to provide the children with immediate feedback on their facial expression production. In a prototype game, called SmileMaze, the system responds to the subject's smiles (Figure 25.8a). Such facial expression tasks engage children with autism and may aid in learning non-verbal behaviors essential for social functioning. Moreover, training in facial expression production may improve recognition, as perception and production have been shown to be linked in many areas of development.

This convergence of expertise from computer and behavioral science provides additional scientific opportunities beyond development of intervention games. For example, it enables us to more readily explore questions such as the effect of familiarity on recognition and generalization. Using CERT, we can capture and quantify training stimuli from the participant's environment, including parents, teachers, siblings, and friends. The use of familiar faces in the program may not only provide a more engaging environment for the participant, but may also facilitate generalization of learned skills from familiar faces to novel faces.

Facial expression recognition technology also enables us to develop an "Emotion Mirror" application (Figure 25.8b) in which players control the expressions of a computer-generated avatar and/or images and short video clips of real faces. Here, participants can explore the same expression on different faces. This aids in training a generalized understanding of facial expressions. It also knits expressive production and perception as it is the participant's own face that drives the expressions shown on the avatar and/or image.

A related project is underway at the MIT Media Lab (Madsen et al., 2008; Picard and Goodwin, 2008). They are developing new technology to help individuals with autism to capture, analyze, and reflect on a set of social-emotional signals communicated by facial and head movements in live social interaction. The system employs an ultramobile PC and miniature camera, which enables them to capture and analyze facial behavior of their own everyday social companions. The system then presents interpretations of the face and head movements, such as agreeing or confused. This approach with wearable technologies offers, for the first time, the ability to conduct *just-in-time in situ* assistance to help individuals with high functioning autism to learn facial expressions and underlying emotions in their own specific natural environments. A novel output display, called "emotion bubbles" was developed, in which each mental state was represented by a different color, and bubble size indicated the magnitude of that state.

The facial expression analysis employs a system developed by el Kaliouby and Robson (2005). This framework employs a commercial feature point tracker to obtain real-time measures of the locations of 24 features on the face. It uses the motion, shape, and color deformations of these features to classify 20 movement primitives including action units from the FACS, as well as 11 communicative gestures such as head nod or eyebrow flash. These measures are then passed to a dynamic Bayesian network to interpret the meaning of head and facial signals over time. The system was trained on a database of actors who displayed a range of cognitive and mental states. Rather than recognizing basic emotions, recognition is performed for the following six mental states: *agreeing, concentrating, disagreeing, interested, thinking,* and *confused*. This database, called the Mind-Reading database (Baron-Cohen et al., 2004) was collected with the objective of providing children with autism examples of facial expressions that are relevant in every day life.

Pilot studies were conducted with adolescents diagnosed as high functioning autism. Subjects watched the bubble display respond to their own facial expressions, and also attempted to elicit specific bubbles in their own conversations with their friends. Experimenters witnessed multiple instances of subjects adjusting their own conversation flow to try to elicit the desired bubble, thereby providing practice for both eliciting and understanding mental states of others.

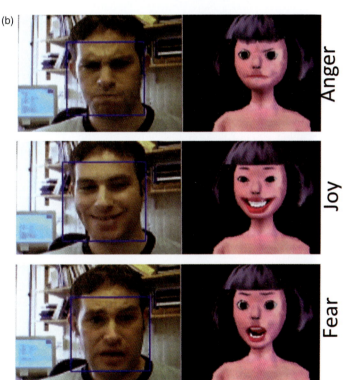

Fig. 25.8 Prototype intervention tasks for children with ASD. a: Smilemaze. The smilemaze responds in real time to smiles by the subject. (Reprinted from Cockburn et al., Smilemaze: A Tutoring System in Real-Time facial Expression Perception and Production for Children with Autism Spectrum Disorder. International Conference on Automatic Face and Gesture Recognition, Workshop on Facial and Bodily Expressions for Control and Adaptation of Games, 2008. © 2008 IEEE.) b. Emotion Mirror: An avatar responds to facial expressions of the subject in real-time. (Reprinted from Littlewort et al., Dynamics of facial expression extracted automatically from video. In IEEE Conference on Computer Vision and Pattern Recognition, Workshop on Face Processing in Video, 2004, © 2004 IEEE).

Automated facial expression analysis of psychiatric disorders

Wang et al. (2008) were the first to apply video-based automated facial expression analysis in neuropsychiatric research. They conducted case studies on two patients: one with schizophrenia and one with Asperger's syndrome. While it is well known that patients with schizophrenia exhibit impairments in facial expression including flattened affect, and "abnormal affect," there is little objective data on their facial behavior due to the time required for manual coding. Similarly, little objective data exists characterizing facial expression production in ASD. Studies such as this one will provide important information on facial expression production in these populations for relating to underlying neural pathology and social interaction deficits.

They employed a system for recognition of basic emotions that was trained on a dataset of 32 actors with evoked facial expressions. The evoked expressions were obtained by asking participants to describe a situation in their life pertaining to each emotion. These situations were recounted back to them by a psychiatrist and video recordings were taken during the recounting session. It was trained on four expressions plus neutral, and three intensities. This made a relatively small training set in machine learning terms (384 images, or 96 per class), but it is one of the very few systems to be trained on spontaneous expressions of basic emotions.

The evoked expression paradigm was then repeated for the patients. The automated system was used to measure dimensions such as the frequency of occurrence of the target facial expression, and the probability of the subjects expression given the model trained on the control subjects. This study obtained some general findings, such as reduced occurrences for sadness, anger, and fear for the patient with schizophrenia, and reduced occurrences of fear for the patient with Asperger's, as well as a poor match to the controls for fear.

This paper is a first step towards a larger study to compare the facial behavior of these patients to the distribution of facial behavior in the healthy population. Automated expression measurement facilitates such studies, and provides a consistent measurement tool for comparing populations, something typically not possible with manual coding studies due to intercoder variability. Approaches such as the one in this paper that are trained on full face expressions from healthy controls can indicate the degree to which expressions match the healthy population, but are less well suited to illustrating *how* they differ. Also, depending on the composition of the training set, they may be unable to differentiate some movements such as the zygomatic from the risorious, which move the lip corners obliquely versus laterally.[2] Systems that perform facial action coding may be better suited to making such discriminations.

Basic research in dynamic facial behavior

The dynamics of infant–mother smiles

Messinger et al. (2008) conducted the first application of automated measurement to study facial expression coupling in infant–parent interaction. They studied the facial behavior of mothers and infants during natural play sessions for two mother–infant dyads. The face analysis software was the system developed at CMU by Cohn, Kanade and colleagues based on AAM, described above. As is common with AAM-based methods, manual initialization of the face mesh, as well as intermittent re-initialization was necessary.

The facial behaviors that were analyzed with the automated system included smile (AU 12), eye constriction (AU 6), and mouth opening (25, 26). First, analysis of expression dynamics within

---

[2] The schizophrenic patient in a figure from the paper, for example, is smiling with the risorius, yet receives high scores for 'happy.'

subjects revealed that synchrony of smile-related movements differed for infants than for adults, For infants, correlations between mouth opening and smile strength, and mouth opening and eye constriction, were moderate to high, whereas for mothers, these correlations were lower and more variable.

Perhaps most demonstrative of the utility of automatic face measurement was the study of correlations between smile activity in one partner of the dyad and subsequent smile activity in the other partner. They investigated interaction between mother and infant by computing windowed cross-correlations of smile activity over time. The infant–mother smile activity exhibited changing (non-stationary) local patterns of association, providing a glimpse into turn-taking and the formation and dissolution of states of affective synchrony.

In this study, the automated system enabled analysis of expression dynamics that was previously not possible with manual FACS coding. While some important studies of dynamics exist (e.g. Frank et al., 1993), the coding of dynamics in these studies is coarse due to the time required for manual FACS coding of intensity, consisting of measures such as time to apex, duration of apex, and time to offset. Automated systems provided measurements of intensity on a frame-by-frame basis which facilitate new experiments on expression dynamics and coupling.

All smiles are not created equal

Ambadar et al. (2009) used automatic face analysis to study the morphological and dynamic characteristics of different types of spontaneous smiles, and more precisely, how these characteristics affect how smiles are perceived by other humans. All dynamics information except duration were measured automatically using an earlier version of the facial expression analysis software developed by Cohn and Kanade's group at CMU (Cohn and Kanade, 2007).

In Ambadar's experiment, 101 observers evaluated 122 different video sequences containing smiles. Each video sequence contained a single human subject spontaneously smiling while interacting with another human. The observers judged each video sequence to be either amused, embarrassed, nervous, polite, or other. Facial dynamics were then analyzed for three categories: amused, polite, and embarrassed/nervous.

Using the manual coding of the morphological characteristics (which AU was present) and automatic coding of the dynamics, the authors assessed which smile characteristics best distinguished each smile type from the others. Relative to perceived polite smiles, perceived amused smiles had larger amplitude, longer duration, more abrupt onset and offset, and more often included AU 6, open mouth, and smile controls. Relative to those perceived as embarrassed/nervous, perceived amused smiles were more likely to include AU 6 and have less downward head movement. Relative to those perceived as polite, perceived embarrassed/nervous smiles had greater amplitude, longer duration, more downward head movement, and were more likely to include open mouth.

Contrary to Ambadar et al.'s hypothesis, asymmetry between left and right side of the face was not significantly different across the three smile types. The researchers speculated that the facial expression analysis software, in its current version of development, may not have been sufficient to detect subtle facial asymmetries, especially when the faces analyzed are non-frontal, as often occurs in practice.

Human dynamic facial expression perception

Automated facial expression measurement also provides a way to test the *perception* of dynamic faces by providing a means for developing dynamic stimuli. Several recent studies have emerged which measure facial movements of a human subject, and then map them onto an avatar, which enables aspects of the face such as appearance features or dynamic features to be manipulated. Curio et al. (2008) employed this technology to enable new experiments on adaptation to dynamic facial expressions.

This study showed for the first time an aftereffect for dynamic facial expressions. Subjects adapted to anti-happy or anti-disgust expressions, where an anti-expression is a morph in the opposite direction to that of the original expression, relative to neutral. They were then tested for discrimination of reduced expressions, where a reduced expression is a morph in the same direction as the original expression, but attenuated. The task was a two-alternative forced choice of happy or disgust.

Adaptation to anti-happy facial motions increased the recognition rates for happy and decreased recognition rates for disgust, and vice versa. The aftereffect was much stronger for dynamic versus static adapting stimuli. (In both cases the test stimulus was dynamic. It would be interesting to look at cross-over to static test stimuli as well.) The study also showed that the aftereffect depended on identity. Both dynamic and static adaptation aftereffects were stronger when the identity of the adapting stimulus matched the identity of the test stimulus. This result contrasts other data from cognitive neuroscience suggesting separate encoding of expression and identity, although is consistent with some studies of static adaptation aftereffects (e.g. Ellamil et al., 2008; Fox and Barton, 2007). Please see Calder, Chapter 22, this volume for a more thorough discussion of whether identity and expression are processed by separate visual routes. Interestingly, there was no significant difference in forward versus reverse dynamic display on the adaptation aftereffect.

Another study by Boker and colleagues (in press) used automated facial expression measurement and synthesis to explore gender effects on head nods. It was previously shown that women tend to nod their heads more than men, and individuals of either gender nod more when speaking with a woman than a man. This study attempted to differentiate whether the increase in nodding when speaking with a woman was due to facial mimicry, or awareness of the gender of the conversant. In this study, subjects conversed with an avatar that was driven by another person, and the effects of changing the appearance or head motion of the avatar on the subject's non-verbal behavior was examined. An AAM was employed to drive the avatar, where identity was encoded by mean shape and appearance of the model, and changes in expression were encoded by the coefficients on the basis vectors that span shape and appearance for that person. Apparent gender was manipulated by changing mean shape and mean appearance to another confederate of the same or opposite gender. Voice pitch was altered to match the apparent gender. Head motion in both individuals was measured using motion capture.

They found that changing appearance of the avatar from one gender to another did not affect head nods in the subject, but that the motion dynamics of the avatar did. Thus the gender effect on head nods was related to dynamic aspects of the stimulus, and not to static appearance parameters related to gender. This finding supports the role of facial mimicry in the head nods. Of course, dynamics can influence perceived gender, as can the audio signal, pitch manipulations not withstanding. The facial dynamics of the avatar nevertheless accounted for more of the subjects head nod behavior than the gender of the avatar as indicated by appearance and voice pitch.

This team used a similar approach to investigate the effect of depression on face-to-face interaction (Boker at al., 2009). They specifically looked at the effects of dampened facial expressions and head movements. They found that attenuated head movements led to increased head nods and lateral head turns, and attenuated facial expressions also led to increased head nodding. These results are consistent with a hypothesis that the dynamics of head movements in dyadic conversation include a shared equilibrium, and contribute a new perspective on the effect of dampened affect on dyadic interaction.

A related line of research by Jonathan Gratch's group at USC has investigated the role of facial mimicry in eliciting social rapport. In these studies, two subjects interact through a computer monitor, where each subject views an avatar rendition of the other subject. Head pose is automatically tracked, and can either be rendered with fidelity, or with a manipulation such as displaying the head motion from the previous conversation. Such studies have shown a strong relationship between mimicry and ratings of rapport (Gratch et al., 2006, 2007).

Overall, this is a promising technique that will enable investigations of dynamic non-verbal behavior that were previously impossible.

Summary and conclusions

Automatic facial expression recognition has advanced to the point that we are now able to apply it to spontaneous expressions with some success. While the accuracy of automated facial expression recognition systems is still below that of human experts, automated systems already bring strengths to the table that enable new experiments into facial behavior that were previously infeasible. Automated systems can be applied to much larger quantities of video data than human coding. Statistical pattern recognition on this large quantity of data can reveal emergent behavioral patterns that previously would have required hundreds of coding hours by human experts, and would be unattainable by the non-expert. Moreover, automated facial expression analysis is enabling investigations into facial expression dynamics that were previously intractable by human coding because of the time required to code intensity changes. Automated facial expression technology such as CERT can be used in order to objectively characterize the distribution of facial expression productions in a large set of typically developing children and adults. Indeed, such a project is underway (Kang et al., 2008). This will provide a way to measure the degree to which facial expressions of patient populations diverge from norms, and describe the dimensions on which they diverge.

This chapter reviewed the state of the art in automated expression recognition technology, and outlined its capabilities and limitations. It then described a new generation of experiments that used this technology to study facial behavior and to develop applications in learning and education that take advantage of the real-time expression signal. The chapter also reviewed new experiments in dynamic face perception that have been enabled by this technology. Recent developments in expression tracking and animation have provided a way to parameterize and explore dynamic face space.

Tools for automatic expression measurement are beginning to bring about paradigmatic shifts in a number of fields by making facial expression more accessible as a behavioral measure. This chapter described how these tools are beginning to enable new research activity not only in psychology, but also in cognitive neuroscience, psychiatry, education, human–machine communication, and human social dynamics

References

Adolphs, R., Sears, L., and Piven, J. (2001). *Abnormal processing of social information from faces in autism.* Journal of Cognitive Neuroscience, **13**, 232–240.

Ambadar, Z., Cohn, J.F., and Reed, L.I. (2009). All Smiles are not created equal: morphology and timing of amused, polite, and embarrassed smiles as perceived by observers. *Journal of Nonverbal Behavior* **33**, 17–34.

Ashraf, A.B., Lucey, S. Chen, T., Prkachin, K., Solomon, P., Ambadar, Z., and Cohn, J.F. (2007). The painful face: Pain expression recognition using active appearance models. Proceedings of the ACM International Conference on Multimodal Interfaces (ICMI'07), Nagoya, Japan, 9–14.

Baron-Cohen, S., O. Golan, S. Wheelwright, and J. J. Hill. (2004). *Mind Reading: The Interactive Guide to Emotions*. London: Jessica Kingsley Publishers.

Bartlett, M. Stewart, Viola, P.A., *et al.* (1996). Classifying facial action. In *Advances in Neural Information Processing Systems 8*, pp. 823–829. Cambridge, MA: MIT Press.

Bartlett, M.S., Hager, J.C., Ekman, P., and Sejnowski, T.J. (1999). Measuring facial expressions by computer image analysis. *Psychophysiology*, **36**, 253–263.

Bartlett, M.S., Littlewort, G., Braathen, B., Sejnowski, T.J., and Movellan, J.R. (2003). A prototype for automatic recognition of spontaneous facial actions. In Becker, S., Thrun, S., and Obermayer, K. (eds.) *Advances in Neural Information Processing Systems*, Vol 15, pp. 1271–1278. Cambridge, MA: MIT Press.

Bartlett, M., Littlewort, G., Frank, M., Lainscsek, C., Fasel, I., and Movellan, J. (2006). Automatic recognition of facial actions in spontaneous expressions. *Journal of Multimedia*, **1**, 22–35.

Bartlett, M., Littlewort, G., Whitehill, J., *et al.* (2010). Insights on spontaneous facial expressions from automatic expression measurement. In Giese, M. Curio, C., Bulthoff, H. (eds.) *Dynamic Faces: Insights from Experiments and Computation*. Cambridge, MA: MIT Press.

Boker, S.M., Cohn, J. F., Theobald, B.-J., *et al.* (in press). Something in the way we move: Motion dynamics, not perceived sex, influence head movements in conversation. *Journal of Experimental Psychology: Human Perception and Performance*.

Boker, S.M., Cohn, J. F., Theobald, B.-J., Matthews, I., Brick, T., Spies, J.R. (2009). Effects of damping head movement and facial expression in dyadic conversation using real-time facial expression tracking and synthesized avatars. *Proc. Philosophical Transactions of the Royal Society B*, **364**, 3485–3495.

Chang, Y., Hu, C., Feris, R. and Turk, M. (2006). Manifold based analysis of facial expression. *Journal of Image and Vision Computing*, **24**, 605–614.

Cockburn, J., Bartlett, M., Tanaka, J., Movellan, J., Pierce, M., and Schultz, R. (2008). SmileMaze: A tutoring system in real-time facial expression perception and production for children with autism spectrum disorder. *Intl Conference on Automatic Face and Gesture Recognition, Workshop on Facial and Bodily expressions for Control and Adaptation of Games*.

Cohen, I., Sebe, N., Chen, L., Garg, A., and Huang, T.S. (2003). Facial expression recognition from video sequences: Temporal and static modelling. *CVIU Special Issue on Face Recognition*, **91**, 160–187.

Cohn, J. and Kanade, T. (2007). Automated facial image analysis for measurement of emotion expression. In J.A. Coan and J.B. Allen (eds.) *The handbook of emotion elicitation and assessment*. New York: Oxford University Press.

Cohn, J.F. and Schmidt, K.L. (2004). The timing of facial motion in posed and spontaneous smiles. *Journal of Wavelets, Multi-resolution and Information Processing*, **2**, 121–132.

Cootes, T., Edwards, G., and Taylor, C. (2001). Active appearance models. *Transactions on Pattern Analysis and Machine Intelligence*, **23**, 681–685.

Cottrell G. and Metcalfe, J. (1991). Face, gender, and expression recognition using holons. In D. Touretzky (ed.) *Advances in Neural Information Processing Systems*, **3**, 564–571.

Cowie, R. (2008). Building the databases needed to understand rich, spontaneous human behavior. Keynote talk, IEEE Conference on Automatic Face and Gesture Recognition.

Curio, C., Giese, M., Breidt, M., Kleiner, M., Bülthoff, H. (2008). Exploring human dynamic facial expression recognition with animation. International Conference on Cognitive Systems, University of Karlsruhe, Karlsruhe, Germany.

De la Torre, F., Campoy, J., Ambadar, Z. and Cohn, J.F. (2007). Temporal segmentation of facial behavior. Proceedings of the International Conference on Computer Vision, October, Rio De Janeiro, Brasil.

Dinges, D.F., Rider, R.L., Dorrian, J., *et al.* (2005). Optical computer recognition of facial expressions associated with stress induced by performance demands. *Aviation, Space, and Environmental Medicine*, **76**, b172–b182.

D'Mello, S., Picard, R., and Graesser, A. (2007). Towards an affect-sensitive autotutor. *IEEE Intelli- gent Systems*, Special issue on Intelligent Educational Systems, **22**, 53–61.

D'Mello, S., Jackson, T., Craig, S., *et al.* (2008). AutoTutor detects and responds to learners affective and cognitive states. Workshop on Emotional and Cognitive Issues at the International Conference of Intelligent Tutoring Systems, June 23–27, Montreal, Canada.

Department of Transportation (2001). Saving lives through advanced vehicle safety technology. USA Department of Transportation. Available at: http://www.its.dot.gov/ivi/docs/AR2001.pdf.

Donato, G., Bartlett, M.S., Hager, J.C., Ekman, P. and Sejnowski, T.J. (1999). Classifying facial actions. *IEEE Trans. Pattern Analysis and Machine Intelligence*, **21**, 974–989.

Ekman, P. and Friesen, W.V. (1978). *Facial Action Coding System*. Palo Alto, CA: Consulting Psychologists Press.

Ekman, P. and Rosenberg, E.L. (eds.) (2005). *What the face reveals: Basic and applied studies of spontaneous expression using the FACS*. Oxford: Oxford University Press.

el Kaliouby, R. and Robinson P. (2005). Real-time Inference of Complex Mental States from Facial Expressions and Head Gestures. In *Real-Time Vision for Human-Computer Interaction*, pp. 181–200. Berlin: Springer-Verlag.

Ellamil, M., Susskind, J.M. and Anderson, A.K. (2008) Examinations of identity invariance in facial expression adaptation. *Cognitive, Affective, & Behavioral Neuroscience*, **8**, 273–81.

Essa, I.A. and Pentland, A.P. (1995). Facial expression recognition using a dynamic model and motion energy. In *Proceedings of Fifth International Conference on Computer Vision*, 1995, June 20–23, pp. 360–367.

Fasel, B., and Luettin, J. (2003). Automatic facial expression analysis: Survey. *Pattern Recognition*, **36**, 259–275.

Fasel, I., Fortenberry B., Movellan J.R. (2005). A generative framework for real-time object detection and classification.,' *Computer Vision and Image Understanding* **98**, 182–210.

Fox, C.J. and Barton, J.J.S. (2007). What is adapted in face adaptation? The neural representations of expression in the human visual system. *Brain research*, **1127**, 80–89.

Frank, M.G., Ekman, P., and Friesen, W.V. (1993). Behavioral markers and recognizability of the smile of enjoyment. *Journal of Personality and Social Psychology*, **64**. 83–93.

Gratch, J., Okhmatovskaia, A., Lamothe, F., *et al.* (2006). Virtual Rapport. In *6th International Conference on Intelligent Virtual Agents*, Marina del Rey, CA.

Gratch, J., Wang, N., Okhmatovskaia, A., Lamothe, F., Morales, M and Morency, L-P (2007). Can virtual humans be more engaging than real ones? In *12th International Conference on Human-Computer Interaction*. Beijing, China.

Gratch, J., Wang, N., Gerten, J., Fast, E., and Duffy, R. (2007). Creating rapport with virtual agents. International Conference on Intelligent Virtual Agents, Paris, France.

Green, D.M. and Swets, J.A. (1966). *Signal Detection Theory and Psychophysics*. New York, Wiley.

Gu, H. and Ji, Q. (2004). An automated face reader for fatigue detection. In *Proceedings of the International Conference on Automated Face and Gesture Recognition*, pp. 111–116.

Holland, M.K. and Tarlow, G. (1972). Blinking and mental load. *Psychological Reports*, **31**, 119–127.

Huang, X., and Metaxas, D. (2008). Metamorphs: deformable shape and appearance models. *IEEE Trans. Pattern Analysis and Machine Intelligence*, **30**, 1444–1459.

Kang, G., Littlewort-Ford, G., Bartlett, M., Movellan, M., and Reilly, J. (2008). Facial expression production and temporal integration during development. Poster, UCSD Temporal Dynamics of Learning Center, NSF Site Visit.

Kaliouby, R. and Robinson, P. (2005). Real-time inference of complex mental states from facial expressions and head gestures. In: *Real-Time Vision for HCI*, pp. 181–200. Berlin: Spring-Verlag.

Kapoor, A. and Picard, R.E. (2005), Multimodal affect recognition in learning environments, ACM MM'05, November 6–11, 2005, Singapore.

Kapoor, A., Burleson, W., and Picard, R. (2007). Automatic prediction of frustration. *International Journal of Human-Computer Studies*, **65**, 724–736.

Koelstra, S. and Pantic, M. (2008). Non-rigid registration using free-form deformations for recognition of facial actions and their temporal dynamics, Proceedings of IEEE Int'l Conf. Automatic Face and Gesture Recognition (FG'08), Amsterdam.

Larochette, A.C., Chambers, C.T., Craig, K.D. (2006). Genuine, suppressed and faked facial expressions of pain in children. *Pain*, **126**, 64–71.

Levi, K. and Weiss, Y. (2004). Learning object detection from a small number of examples: The importance of good features. In: *Proceedings IEEE Computer Society Conference on Computer Vision and Pattern Recognition*, pp. 53–64, volume 2.

Littlewort, G., Bartlett, M., and Lee, K. (2009). Automatic coding of facial expressions displayed during posed and genuine pain. *Image and Vision Computing*, **27**, 1797–1803.

Littlewort, G., Bartlett, M., Fasel, I., Susskind, J., and Movellan, J. (2004). Dynamics of facial expression extracted automatically from video. In IEEE Conference on Computer Vision and Pattern Recognition, Workshop on Face Processing in Video.

Lucey, S., Matthews, I. Hu, C. Ambadar, Z. De la Torre, F., and Cohn, J.F. (2006). AMM derived face representations for robust facial action recognition. *Proceedings of the IEEE International Conference on Automatic Face and Gesture Recognition*, pp. 155–160, Southampton, April 2006.

Madsen, M., el Kaliouby, R., Goodwin, M., and Picard, R.W. (2008). Technology for just-in-time in-situ learning of facial affect for persons diagnosed with an autism spectrum disorder. Proceedings of the 10th ACM Conference on Computers and Accessibility (ASSETS), October 13–15, 2008, Halifax, Canada.

Mase, K. (1991). Recognition of facial expression from optical flow, *IEICE Transactions*, **74**, 3474–3483.

Messinger, D.S., Cassel, T.D., and Cohn, J.F. (2008). The dynamics of infant smiling and perceived positive emotion. *Journal of Nonverbal Behavior*, **32**, 133–155.

Michel, P. and el Kaliouby, R. (2003). Real time facial expression recognition in video using support vector machines. *Proceedings of the 5th international conference on Multimodal interfaces*, November, pp. 258–264.

Morecraft, RJ., Louie, J.L., Herrick, J.L., and Stilwell-Morecraft, K.S. (2001). Cortical innervation of the facial nucleus in the non-human primate: a new interpretation of the effects of stroke and related subtotal brain trauma on the muscles of facial expression. *Brain*, **124**, 176–208.

Morency, L.-P., Rahimi, A., and Darrell, T. (2003). Adaptive view-based appearance model. In *Proceedings of the 2003 IEEE conference on computer vision and pattern recognition*, **1**, 803–810.

Moriyama, T., Kanade, T., Cohn, J., *et al.* (2002). Automatic recognition of eye blinking in spontaneously occurring behavior. *Proceedings of the 16th international conference on pattern recognition*, pp. 78–81.

Pandzic, I. and Forchheimer, R. (eds.) *MPEG-4 Facial Animation: The Standard, Implementation and Applications*. New York: Wiley.

Pantic, M. and and I. Patras, I. (2006). Dynamics of facial expression: recognition of facial actions and their temporal segments from face profile image sequences. *IEEE Transactions on Systems, Man and Cybernetics - Part B*, **36**, 433–449.

Pantic, M., and Rothkrantz, L. (2000). Automatic analysis of facial expressions: the state of the art. *IEEE Transactions on Pattern Analysis and Machine Intelligence*, **22**, 1424–1445.

Phillips, J., Flynn, P., Scruggs T. (2006). Preliminary Face Recognition Grand Challenge Results. *Proceedings of the International Conference on Automatic Face & Gesture Recognition*, 15–24.

Picard, R.W. and Goodwin, M. (2008). Developing Innovative Technology for Future Personalized Autism Research and Treatment. *Autism Advocate, First Edition*, **50**, 32–39.

Rinn, W.E. (1984). The neuropsychology of facial expression: a review of the neurological and psychological mechanisms for producing facial expression. *Psychological Bulletin*, **95**, 52–77.

Rogers, C.R., Schmidt, K.L., Van Swearingen, J.M., *et al.* (2007). Automated facial image analysis: Detecting improvement in abnormal facial movement after treatment with Botulinum toxin A. *Annals of Plastic Surgery*, **58**, 39–47.

Russell, J.A. and Fernandez-Dols, J.M. (eds.) (1997). *The Psychology of Facial Expression*. New York: Cambridge University Press.

Schmidt, K.L., Cohn, J.F., and Tian, Y. (2003). Signal characteristics of spontaneous facial expressions: automatic movement in solitary and social smiles. *Biological Psychology*, **65**, 49–66.

Tada, H. (1986). Eyeblink rates as a function of the interest value of video stimuli. *Tohoku Psychologica Folica*, **45**.

Tian, Y.-L., Kanade, T., and Cohn, J. (2001). Recognizing action units for facial expression analysis. *IEEE Transactions on Pattern Analysis and Machine Intelligence*, **23**, 97–115.

Tian, Y.-L., Kanade, T., and Cohn, J. (2003). Facial expression analysis. In S.L.A. Jain (ed.), *Handbook of face recognition*, pp. 247–275. New York: Springer.

Tong, Y., Liao, W., and Ji, Q. (2007). Facial action unit recognition by exploiting their dynamic and semantic relationships. *IEEE Transactions on Pattern Analysis and Machine Intelligence*, **29**, 1683–1699.

Valstar, M., Gunes, H., and Pantic, M. (2007). How to distinguish posed from spontaneous smiles using geometric features. In *Proceedings of ACM Int'l Conf. Multimodal Interfaces (ICMI'07)*, pp. 38–45, November, Nagoya, Japan.

Valstar, M.F., Pantic, M., Ambadar, Z., and Cohn, J.F. (2006). Spontaneous vs. posed facial behavior: Automatic analysis of brow actions, *Proceedings of the ACM International Conference on Multimodal Interfaces*, pp. 162–170.

Viola, P. and Jones, M. (2004). Robust real-time face detection. *International Journal of Computer Vision*, **57**, 137–154.

Vukadinovic, D. and Pantic, M. (2005). Fully automatic facial feature point detection using Gabor feature based boosted classifers. In: *Proceedings of the IEEE International Conference on Systems, Man, and Cybernetics*, pp. 1692–1698, volume 2.

Vural, E., Cetin, M., Ercil, A., Littlewort, G., Bartlett, M., and Movellan, J. (2007). Drowsy driver detection through facial movement analysis. ICCV Workshop on Human Computer Interaction.

Wang, P., Barrett, F., Martin, E., *et al.* (2008). Automated video-based facial expression analysis of neuropsychiatric disorders. *Journal of Neuroscience Methods*, **168**, 224–238.

Wang, Y., Ai, H., Wu, B., and Huang, C. (2004). Real time facial expression recognition with adaboost. In *Proceedings of the 17th international conference on pattern recognition (ICPR 2004)*, **3**, 926–929.

Whitehill, J., Bartlett, M., and Movellan, J. (2008). Automated teacher feedback using facial expression recognition. Workshop on CVPR for Human Communicative Behavior Analysis, IEEE Conference on Computer Vision and Pattern Recognition.

Whitehill, J., Littlewort, G., Fasel, I., Bartlett, M., and Movellan, J. (2009). Toward practical smile detection. *Transactions on Pattern Analysis and Machine Intelligence*, **31**, 2106–2111.

Yacoob, Y. and Davis L. (1994). Computer spatio-temporal represatation of human faces. In: *Proceedings of the IEEE Computer Society Conference on Computer Vision and Pattern Recognition'94*, pp. 70–75.

Yacoob, Y and Davis, L.S. (1996). Recognizing human facial expressions from long image sequeces using optical flow. *IEEE Transactions PAMI*, **18**, 636–42.

Yang, P., Liu, Q., and Metaxas, D.N. (2007). Boosting coded dynamic features for facial action units and facial expression recognition. In *Proceedings of the 2004 IEEE conference on computer vision and pattern recognition*, pp. 1–6.

Zeng, Z., Pantic, M., Roisman, G.I., and Huang, T.S. (2009). A survey of affect recognition methods: Audio, visual, and spontaneous expressions. *IEEE Transactions on Pattern Analysis and Machine Intelligence*, **31**, 39–58.

Zhang, Y, Ji, Q., Zhu, Z., and Beifang Yi, B. (2008). Dynamic facial expression analysis and synthesis with MPEG-4 facial animation parameters. *IEEE Transactions on Circuits and Systems for Video Technology* **18**, 1383–1396.

Zhang, Z. and Zhang, J-S. (2006). Driver fatigue detection based intelligent vehicle control. In *Proceedings of the International Conference on Pattern Recognition*, pp. 1262–1265.

Zhang, Z., Lyons, M., Schuster, M., and Akamatsu, S. (1998). Comparison between Geometry-Based and Gabor-Wavelets-Based Facial Expression Recognition Using Multi-Layer Perception. In *Proceedings of the Third IEEE International Conference on Automatic Face and Gesture Recognitions*, pp. 454–459.

Chapter 26

Influence of Personality Traits on Processing of Facial Expressions

Elaine Fox and Konstantina Zougkou

Influence of personality traits on processing of facial expressions

Faces surprise, attract, and sometimes repel us. Indeed, the multitude of facial expressions that humans are capable of is particularly potent in capturing attention. This makes sense, of course, since facial expressions of emotion provide crucial information about the social environment, indicating—among many other things—the presence of danger or reward. For example, a happy facial expression indicates safety and security, while fearful or angry expressions are indicative of threat and aggression. Charles Darwin was one of the first scientists to propose that a small number of innate primary emotions exist. The evidence came from the observation that some facial expressions appear to be similar across widely different cultures and are present in several primate species, including humans, as well as in pre-linguistic children (Darwin, 1872/1998). In a well-known series of studies, Paul Ekman and his colleagues provided empirical support for the universality of the recognition of certain emotional expressions, such as anger, fear, happiness, disgust, and sadness (Ekman and Friesen, 1986; Ekman et al., 1969). While the validity of this research has been questioned on methodological grounds (Ortony and Turner, 1990; Russell, 1994; but see Ekman, 1994) there is nevertheless substantive evidence that at least some emotional expressions appear to be "special" and are prioritized for processing. In line with this, a number of key neural circuits have been identified that serve to rapidly detect and enhance the processing of salient facial expressions (Vuilleumier, 2005; see Vuilleumier and Righart, Chapter 23, this volume). It is likely that all humans will respond to particular facial expressions (e.g. anger, sad expressions) in a fairly uniform way but the evidence also suggests that the ability of these expressions to capture attention varies markedly across individuals (Mathews and Mackintosh 1998; Mogg and Bradley, 1998). The present chapter reviews evidence from a number of domains and we argue that common personality traits—that are distributed normally in the general population—can have a profound influence on the processing of facial expressions. We synthesize data from behavioral and neuroimaging research to illustrate that these personality traits are an important determinant of emotion processing.

General mechanisms of expression processing

Facial identity and expression processing: are there separate mechanisms?

To begin, it is worth considering whether the mechanisms underlying the recognition of facial identity are similar to those involved in the processing of facial expressions. Two current theoretical models suggest that the recognition of facial expressions is independent from recognition of facial identity (e.g. Bruce and Young, 1986; Haxby et al., 2000). At least some behavioral, neuropsychological and imaging findings support this distinction (e.g. Bruce, 1986; Calder et al., 2000; Campbell et al., 1996; Cottrell et al., 2002; Etcoff, 1984; George et al., 1993; Humphreys et al., 2007; Sergent et al., 1994; Tranel et al., 1988; Winston et al., 2004; Young et al., 1986; Young et al., 1993; see Calder, Chapter 22, this volume for more discussion). To give one example, selected patients with developmental prosopagnosia can show profound deficits in processing facial identity while their ability to recognize facial expressions remains intact (Duchaine et al., 2003; Humphreys et al., 2007).

Some evidence conflicts with this interpretation, however, and points to an interactive relationship between the processing of individual identity and the processing of facial expressions. For instance, in an adaptation paradigm where adaptation to a facial expression biases perception of expressions away from the adapting expression, there was a decreased aftereffect when the adapting and the test faces were of different identity. This suggests that expression adaptation relies on perceptual features that characterize an identity and there is therefore an interaction in the processing of facial identity and expressions (e.g. Ellamil et al., 2008; Fox and Barton, 2007). Imaging studies have also shown that the fusiform face area (FFA)—known to be involved in the processing of facial identity—also becomes activated when judging facial expressions (Cohen Kadosh et al., 2010; Fairhall and Ishai, 2007; Fox et al., 2009; Ganel et al., 2005; Narumoto et al., 2001). This activation of the FFA seemed to be sensitive to variations of facial expressions even when attention was captured by identity. In a review, Calder and Young (2005) concluded that the evidence supporting the independence of the visual representations of facial identity and expression is inconsistent. In a principal component analysis framework, they propose a single multidimensional system, incorporating largely, although not completely independent visual codes for facial identity and facial expression (Calder et al., 2001). This allows for a partial independence between these perceptual processes. Whatever the relationship between the various components of face processing, it is clear that the accurate and efficient processing of emotional and other *expressions* is crucial for social cognition. Our proposal is that there are identifiable individual differences in how efficiently such expressions are analyzed. In the present overview, we therefore focus on the processing of facial emotional expressions paying particular attention to the influence of common personality traits in influencing emotion processing.

Prioritization of expression processing

As we have seen, facial expressions provide crucial information regarding a person's internal state and intentions and therefore the rapid recognition of these expressions can facilitate efficient social interaction (Schupp et al., 2004). It comes as no surprise, therefore, that humans are especially efficient at recognizing emotionally relevant information displayed in the face. Given the affective significance of facial expressions, it is also no surprise that there are strong individual differences in how people respond to the expression conveyed by a face.

In the very early stages of life, reading emotional signals expressed by faces is the primary means by which infants can learn to navigate their social world. Recognizing a variety of expressions provides information about the mood state and intentions of caregivers and at a later stage of development provides extensive information about the affective salience of objects and people in the visual environment. Extensive research on human infants has indeed demonstrated that the ability to recognize and interpret emotional facial expressions emerges early in the postnatal period (see Leppänen and Nelson, 2009, for extensive review). It is of particular interest that at around the time that infants begin to show accurate discrimination among different facial expressions, they also begin to show a clear preference for fearful over happy or neutral expressions

(Kotsoni et al., 2001; Nelson and Dolgin, 1985). In addition to influencing looking time, it has been demonstrated that fearful expressions can also delay the disengagement of attention in 7-month-old infants (Peltola et al., 2008). In this study, infants were found to be less likely to move their eye-gaze from centrally presented fearful facial expressions to peripheral targets than from a non-fearful control face. It is of interest that a very similar pattern has been observed in adults (Georgiou et al., 2005). This study reported that university students took longer to respond to a peripheral target when a centrally presented face was fearful relative to when the central face expressed a sad, neutral or happy expression. The overall pattern of results indicates similar mechanisms in infants and in adults. However, it is of interest for the present overview that the delay in disengaging from fearful expressions in adults (Georgiou et al., 2005) was strongly modulated by individual differences in neuroticism or trait-anxiety.

Electrophysiological evidence also suggests that neural activity in 7-month-old infants and in adults is enhanced when viewing fearful expressions, relative to viewing happy or neutral facial expressions (Leppänen et al., 2007). Other ERP studies indicate that 7-month-old infants can distinguish between fearful, angry and happy facial expressions (Kobiella et al., 2008, Nelson and de Haan, 1996). Thus, both behavioral and neural measures indicate that young infants can distinguish among facial expressions and that fearful emotional expressions are particularly powerful in capturing as well as holding visual attention.

Another way to assess the prioritization of emotional facial expressions is to present arrays of faces with different expressions in a visual search task. Several studies have shown that participants are faster to identify an angry expression among an array of faces relative to identifying a happy expression (e.g. Eastwood et al., 2001; Fox et al., 2000; Hansen and Hansen, 1988; Öhman et al., 2001) a phenomenon known as the *threat superiority effect*. The role of different face parts in signaling threat has also been investigated. For example, schematic downwardly curved mouth regions (anger/sad) are detected more rapidly than upwardly curved mouth regions (smile) when presented in the context of a face (Fox et al., 2000), although no difference in detection time between the mouth regions of angry and happy expressions has been reported when photographs of real faces were used (Fox and Damjanovic, 2006). However, in photographs of real faces strong threat superiority effects are found when the *eye regions* of angry expressions are compared with the eye-regions of happy expressions (Fox and Damjanovic, 2006). Recent studies using ERP measures have also shown that facial expressions are determined to a large extent by crucial changes in the eye region of the face (Leppänen et al., 2008; Schyns et al., 2007). These findings are consistent with behavioral studies that highlighted the role of eyes in signaling threat (Bassili, 1979; Calder et al., 2000; Lundqvist et al., 1999).

In marked contrast to the foregoing, some studies have reported *happy superiority effects* (e.g. Calvo and Lundqvist, 2008; Juth et al., 2005; Williams et al., 2005). There are several methodological reasons that might explain why sometimes threat-related faces are noticed more efficiently, and why sometimes happy or positive expressions are detected more rapidly (Calvo and Lundqvist, 2008; Juth et al., 2005). One possibility that is rarely considered, however, is the notion that personality traits may have a strong influence on how visual attention is allocated to affectively salient stimuli. There is abundant empirical evidence from a variety of sources suggesting that people who report high levels of extraversion or sociability are more reactive to highly positive stimuli, whereas people who report higher levels of trait-anxiety or neuroticism tend to react more strongly to negative, especially threat-related stimuli (see Fox 2008, for review). These differences are obscured in general studies of emotion processing. The influence of individual differences in personality traits may therefore explain some of the apparent inconsistencies that are found in studies examining emotion processing.

Individual differences in processing of emotional expressions

The foregoing section suggests that humans can efficiently distinguish among different facial expressions and that highly relevant, especially threat-related, expressions are noticed earlier and attended to for longer periods. This pattern appears very early in life (around 7 months) and serves to draw attention towards the location occupied by affectively salient faces. In addition to drawing spatial attention to their location, there is also evidence that fearful facial expressions can lead to a direct enhancement of perceptual acuity (Phelps et al., 2006). In the present chapter we review evidence that these patterns of emotion processing can vary considerably depending on the expression of common personality traits. We argue that the understanding of how facial expressions are processed is incomplete without taking account of these fundamental personality-related individual differences. It is important to acknowledge, however, that facial expressions represent a category of highly significant social and biological stimuli but that many other classes of stimuli may have similar effects on attentional mechanisms. For example, snakes, spiders, guns and syringes are also detected rapidly in visual search tasks relative to neutral or positive stimuli (e.g. Brosch and Sharma 2005; Fox et al., 2007; Öhman et al., 2001).

Do a variety of personality traits influence processing of emotional expressions?

In recent years, it has been realized that personality-related differences can modulate the type of information (positive or negative valence) that captures attention. It has long been known that clinical conditions, such as anxiety and depression, are associated with differential processing of affective (especially negative) information (Williams et al., 1988). However, it is now clear that several personality traits vary normally in the population and that normal differences across these spectra can have profound effects on information processing biases (Fox, 2008, for extensive review). There is a general consensus that adult human personality is best described by variation on five broad factors–known as the "Big Five" (McCrae and Costa, 1987). These factors are: *extraversion, agreeableness, conscientiousness, neuroticism,* and *openness to experience.* Two of these factors (*neuroticism* and *extraversion*) have been linked with broad biobehavioral systems relating to avoidance and approach and are of most relevance here. Kagan (1994) has provided evidence for such broad variation in temperament in terms of how young children respond to unfamiliar situations. "Inhibited" children become distressed in novel situations and tend to avoid them whereas "uninhibited" children are highly sociable and tend to approach novel situations.

Neuroticism or negative affectivity (N-NA) is a higher order dimension of personality that has a genetic component and influences mood, cognition, behavior as well as a variety of neurobiological processes (Clark and Watson, 1991). There is good evidence that N-NA modulates the neurobiological circuitry that controls *aversion* or *avoidance of harm* (see Fox, 2008, for discussion). For example, evidence from a range of sources suggests that variation in self-reported N-NA affects the function of subcortical structures such as the amygdala and hippocampus, as well as regions of the prefrontal cortex including the dorsolateral prefrontal and anterior cingulate cortices (see Whittle et al., 2006, for comprehensive review). In contrast, *extraversion* or *positive affectivity* (E-PA) is considered to be a broad temperamental dimension that is associated with a variety of positive mood states, as well as changes in cognitive and neurobiological reactivity to positive events. Substantive evidence indicates that variation on self-reported E-PA influences the neurobiological circuitry involved with general *approach* or *appetitive* behaviors. In particular, there is strong evidence for a relationship between E-PA and the function of regions of the brain that receive rich dopaminergic projections, such as the amygdala and nucleus accumbens (NAcc), as well as cortical structures including the anterior cingulate and the dorsolateral prefrontal cortex (see Fox 2008; Whittle et al., 2006, for comprehensive reviews). Thus, it is highly likely that naturally occurring variation on the personality dimensions relating to neuroticism and extraversion will affect the processing of human facial expressions.

Personality research to date has tended to concentrate primarily on the dimension of neuroticism–or what might be called the *anxiety spectrum*—consisting of negative emotional states such as anxiety and depression. Fewer studies have examined extraversion—or a *happiness spectrum*—consisting of positive emotional states such as social activity, happiness and impulsiveness. Individuals who are high on the anxiety spectrum tend to be drawn towards negatively valenced information and are generally more reactive to stimuli associated with punishment. In contrast, individuals who are high on the happiness spectrum are more reactive to rewards and positive stimuli and their attention is also more likely to be drawn towards these events and objects (e.g. Davidson and Irwin, 1999). To a lesser extent, research has also examined differences in the *autistic spectrum*, the *psychopathic spectrum* and reward-drive and found that normal variation of these traits in the typical (healthy) population can also influence the nature of facial expression processing. For example, individuals with autistic or psychopathic spectrum traits are less able to recognize complex emotions in a face relative to individuals with few autistic or psychopathic spectrum traits (Ashwin et al., 2006; Golan et al., 2006; Marsh and Blair, 2008). In addition, high reward-drive individuals show increased attention to angry facial expressions in relation to low reward-drive individuals (Passamonti et al., 2008; Putman et al., 2004).

There are a rather limited number of studies that have measured both extraversion and neuroticism *in the same study* as possible determinants of facial expression processing. Rusting and Larsen (1998) assessed both of these personality traits in healthy participants and asked participants to assign negative, positive or neutral labels to words as well as to facial expressions. Those reporting higher levels of extraversion (i.e. high on the *happiness spectrum*) were faster in judging words and faces depicting a positive emotion relative to those depicting negative or neutral emotions. However, against expectation the reverse effect was not observed in individuals reporting high levels of neuroticism. In other words, those high on the *anxiety spectrum* were not faster to judge negative material relative to positive or neutral words or facial expressions. In a different task, Mauer and Borkenau (2007) also assessed individual differences in the happiness and anxiety spectra as determinants of emotional Stroop effects using words and faces. Here it was found that individuals with avoidance temperament (i.e. high on the *anxiety spectrum*) took longer than those with a low avoidance temperament to identify the color of words and facial expressions when they depicted unpleasant information relative to positive information. In contrast, the attention of those with an approach temperament (i.e. high on the *happiness spectrum*) tended to be captured by pleasant and positive information more than by negative information.

Individual differences in the recognition of emotional expressions

A small number of studies have focused on whether there are individual differences in the *recognition* of emotional facial expressions. Richards et al. (2002) used images of morphed facial expressions (each stimulus was prepared by blending two facial expressions) in an emotion identification task. Each facial expression stayed on the screen until the participants verbally identified which of six emotion labels (happiness, surprise, fear, sadness, disgust, anger, and happiness) described the facial expression. They found that socially anxious participants were more likely to describe blended expressions (e.g. combinations of fear and surprise or fear and sadness) as *fearful* than did participants reporting low levels of social anxiety. Given the nature of the task, these results might indicate a difference in how stimuli are *interpreted* rather than a difference in the ability to *detect* fearful facial expressions. To address this, the authors looked at descriptions of faces that included surprise, an expression often confused with fear. Socially anxious participants did not describe a facial expression in the continuum happiness–surprise as fearful any more than less socially anxious participants, indicating a heightened sensitivity for fearful expressions in socially anxious participants.

Surcinelli et al. (2006) reported a more direct assessment of the recognition of emotional facial expressions. They presented faces that depicted a particular facial expression and participants were required to judge among seven emotions (anger, sadness, happiness, fear, surprise, disgust and neutral). Individuals with high levels of self-reported trait anxiety were more accurate in recognizing fearful facial expressions compared with individuals reporting low-trait anxiety. There were no differences between the anxiety groups in terms of accuracy in recognizing a range of other facial expressions. However, a subsequent study using the same emotion recognition task was unable to replicate these results (R.M. Cooper et al., 2008). They found that low- and high-trait anxious individuals were equally accurate and fast in recognizing various emotions. R.M. Cooper et al. (2008) suggested that the contrasting results across the two studies could be the consequence of different cognitive processes assessed. For example, in Surcinelli et al.'s (2006) study, stimuli were presented for 10 s before participants were required to respond, while Cooper et al.'s participants were encouraged to respond as quickly and as accurately as possible. Thus, the high-trait anxious participants might have focused attention on the fearful faces to a greater extent in Surcinelli et al.'s (2006) study and this could have enhanced their accurate performance in recognizing the fearful expressions.

Individual differences in attentional processing of expressions

Processing of negative facial expressions

There is a large literature examining individual differences in the attentional processing of facial expressions. Much of this work has focused on neuroticism or anxiety-related traits and has found that people who report higher degrees of this trait are more likely to orient towards negative facial expressions such as anger (Bradley et al., 1998; Mogg and Bradley, 1999; Mogg et al., 2008) and fear (Fox, 2002; Mogg et al., 2008); show a reduced attentional blink to fearful expressions in a rapid steam of facial expressions (Fox et al., 2005); and take longer to disengage their attention from these expressions (Fox et al., 2001; Georgiou et al., 2005). Many different paradigms have been used to measure attentional bias, with some focusing more on the detection of affective stimuli (e.g. visual search; attentional blink task) and others focusing on the shifting of attention to a particular location. The majority of studies looking at the effect of anxiety on attentional processing have used variations on the "attentional probe" task. In a typical experiment, a pair of stimuli (words or pictures) is presented simultaneously for about half a second and when the stimuli disappear a *probe* to which people respond appears in either location. The usual finding is that when the probe appears in the same location as a negative stimulus anxious individuals are faster to detect it relative to when the probe appears following a neutral stimulus (e.g. MacLeod and Mathews, 1988; MacLeod et al., 1986). It has also been found using this paradigm that low anxious people often *avoid* threat-related stimuli so that they are *slower* to detect a probe that appears in the threatening location (e.g. Fox, 1993; MacLeod and Mathews, 1988). Several studies have used photographs of facial expressions using the attentional probe task (see Bar-Haim et al., 2007, for review). Individual differences in attentional processing of facial expressions have also been explored with a modification of the traditional Posner cueing paradigm, in which a target probe replaces a *single* cue that is presented to either the right or left-hand side of a computer screen. In Posner's original paradigm, the cue was a brief flickering of one of two boxes presented to the left or right-hand sight of the screen (Posner, 1980). In face perception, however, the cue is typically a happy, angry, or neutral facial expression. Fox and colleagues (Fox et al., 2001, 2002) have shown that when the target probe replaced the cue on the same side (valid trials) both high and low anxious individuals were equally fast in detecting the target regardless of the facial expression depicted in the cue, but when the target appeared in the *opposite* side from the cue (invalid trials), high anxious individuals were slower at detecting the target when the cue depicted angry facial expression. This pattern was interpreted as indicating that high levels of anxiety are associated with a delay in disengaging attention from a threat stimulus (Fox et al., 2001).

Other attentional paradigms have more specifically examined the enhanced *detection* of threat in anxious populations. For example, in the attentional blink paradigm participants are required to identify two successive targets, which are embedded in a stream of items presented rapidly one after the other in the same spatial location. An *attentional blink* (Raymond et al., 1992) is revealed by an inability to identify the second target (T2) when a response is required to the first target (T1). Responding to T2 when no response is required for T1 is the common control condition. An attentional blink generally occurs only when T2 is presented within about half a second of T1 (Raymond et al., 1992). Fox et al. (2005) modified this paradigm so that the magnitude of the attentional blink to different facial expressions could be assessed. As shown in Figure 26.1, T1 was

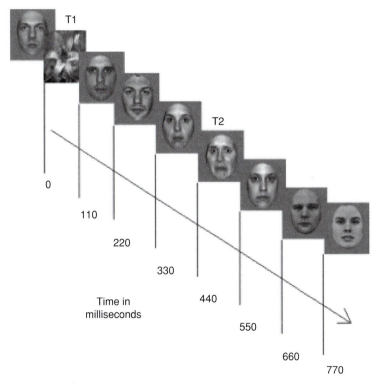

Fig. 26.1 An example of a typical trial to investigate the attentional blink effect. In this example, the first target T1 is a flower that has to be categorized on dual task trials or ignored on single task trials. The second target T2 (if present) was either a happy or a fearful expression and participants simply had to press a button if an emotional face appeared in the stream. In this example, T2 is a fearful facial expression. Figure was adopted from Fox et al. (2005) Anxiety modulates the degree of attentive resources required to process emotional faces. *Cognitive, Affective, & Behavioral Neuroscience,* **5**, 396–404. Permission was given by the Psychonomic Society and Palgrave Macmillan. Face stimuli were taken from the Karolinska Emotional Directed Faces (Lundqvist et al., 1998).

Fig. 26.2 The results reported in a study examining how self-reported anxiety can modulate the degree of attentional blink experienced for both happy and fearful facial expressions. As shown, performance was high when no T1 task was required (single task), but when T1 had to be attended (dual task) a substantial blink occurred for emotional expressions (happy and fearful) for both high and low anxious groups. However, for the high anxious group the degree of blink was significantly reduced for the fearful facial expressions. This suggests that this group were particularly tuned to the negatively valenced stimuli. Data are taken from Fox et al. (2005) Anxiety modulates the degree of attentive resources required to process emotional faces. *Cognitive, Affective, & Behavioral Neuroscience*, **5**, 396–404. Reproduced with permission from the Psychonomic Society and Palgrave Macmillan.

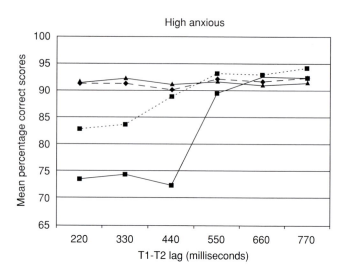

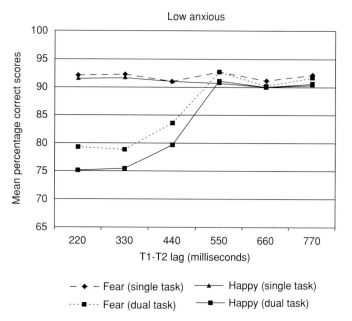

either a picture of flowers or mushrooms while T2 was either a happy or fearful face embedded in a series of neutral face distractors. It was found that the magnitude of the attentional blink was significantly reduced for fearful facial expressions in individuals reporting high levels of trait- and state-anxiety relative to those reporting low levels of anxiety (see Figure 26.2). These findings provide fairly direct evidence that higher levels of self-reported anxiety are associated with an enhanced perception of fearful facial expressions (Fox et al., 2005).

Other research has focused on the ability of different facial expressions to influence the rapid orienting of spatial attention. For example, when the eyes of a face shift towards the left or the

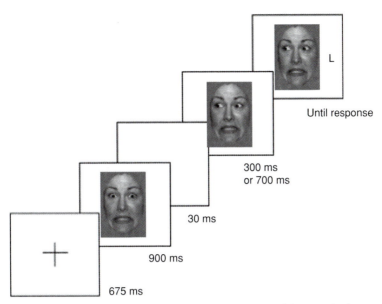

300 ms
or 700 ms

Until response

30 ms

900 ms

675 ms

Fig. 26.3 A typical sequence of events in a gaze cueing experiment. This example shows an incongruent averted gaze condition with a fearful expression. Illustrates procedure used by Fox et al. (2007). Anxiety and sensitivity to gaze direction in emotionally expressive faces. *Emotion*, **7**(3), 478–486. With permission from the American Psychological Association. Face stimuli were taken from the Karolinska Emotional Directed Faces (Lundqvist et al., 1998).

right as shown in Figure 26.3 this is a powerful and automatic cue to visual attention that is very difficult to override (Friesen and Kingstone, 1998). Several experiments by Hietanen and Leppänen (2003) suggest that the magnitude of this effect is not influenced by the emotional expression on the face. However, it is possible that the influence of emotional expression on the magnitude of the gaze cueing effect might be modulated by personality traits. This hypothesis was first tested in a study conducted by Andrew Mathews and colleagues (Mathews et al., 2003). In this and subsequent studies it was found that individuals reporting high levels of neuroticism (trait-anxiety) show an enhanced gaze cueing effect when the faces depicted fearful relative to happy facial expressions (Mathews et al., 2003; Putman et al., 2006; Tipples, 2006). Interestingly, a more recent study has replicated this pattern but also showed that it is not due to the negative connotation of the expression alone. As shown in Figure 26.4, trait-anxiety only affected the gaze cueing effect for fearful expressions and not for angry, happy or neutral expressions (Fox et al., 2007). Thus, for those who tend to worry and are generally more vigilant for danger (i.e. high on the anxiety spectrum) the eye-gaze of a person with a fearful facial expression represents a particularly potent cue that exerts a powerful influence on the direction of visual attention. Such a powerful influence on visual attention does not occur for those reporting lower levels of anxiety.

As the foregoing overview indicates, several behavioral experiments demonstrate that variation in a common personality trait (neuroticism) influences the attentional processing of facial expressions. This is unsurprising since personality traits play an important role in coordinating the affective response to a person's environment and facial expressions of emotion are powerful and salient social cues. The results are increasingly being complemented by a growing number of neuroimaging studies examining the neural correlates of facial expression processing. Using *functional*

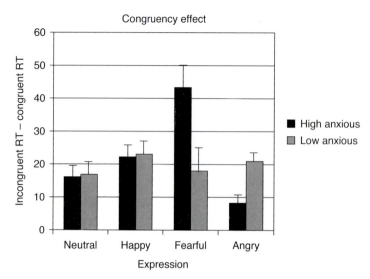

Fig. 26.4 Mean congruency effect (i.e., difference between congruent and incongruent trials) as a function of trait-anxiety and facial expressions. From Fox et al. (2007). Anxiety and sensitivity to gaze direction in emotionally expressive faces. *Emotion*, **7**(3), 478–486. With permission from the American Psychological Association.

magnetic resonance imaging (fMRI), it has been known for some time that the activity of the amygdala is significantly increased by the presence of fearful or angry facial expressions, even under conditions of reduced attention (Morris et al., 1996; Vuilleumier et al., 2001). These results suggest a potential neural mechanism that allows threat stimuli to be prioritized for processing (Vuilleumier et al., 2001). An interesting question concerns whether variation in self-reported anxiety might modulate this amygdala response to threat-related facial expressions. Studies using different paradigms have found converging results on this question (Bishop et al., 2004a; Etkin et al., 2004; Ewbank et al., 2009). Bishop et al. (2004a) used a well-established task in which two faces and two houses were presented in vertical and horizontal pairs around a central fixation cross (Vuilleumier et al., 2001). Participants had to determine whether either the vertically aligned pair or the horizontally aligned pair were the "same" or "different" on a series of trials. The results showed an enhanced response of the *left* amygdala to both unattended and attended fearful faces for those reporting higher levels of *state-anxiety*. Thus, variation on the state-anxiety spectrum was an important determinant of amygdala response to fearful facial expressions. Increased left amygdala activation that correlated with increased levels of anxiety in response to unattended (and borderline evidence for attended) fearful faces has been reported in a more recent study that used the same paradigm, with no difference between the two conditions (Ewbank et al., 2009). By contrast, angry faces produced a greater *right* amygdala response with increasing anxiety for the attended condition only. Ewbank et al. (2009) suggested that the different effects of attention on the neural response to anger and fear reflect the different natures of threat signaled by the two expressions. In contrast to fear, anger is normally used in face-to-face encounters and requires focused attention in order to allow full evaluation of aggressive threat that might involve consideration of several other factors (e.g. the aggressor's age, sex, identity, etc.).

In another study, participants were required to indicate the color (red, yellow, or blue) of both masked and unmasked facial expressions (Etkin et al., 2004). The *right* dorsal amygdala was activated by consciously perceived fearful expressions (200 ms presentation) and this activation was independent of the level of self-reported trait-anxiety. However, when the fearful expressions were *not* consciously perceived (i.e. backward masked), the right basolateral amygdala was activated only for those reporting relatively high levels of trait-anxiety. This result suggests an important neural mechanism that might underlie behavioral findings showing that the anxiety-related modulation of the capture of attention by threat-related facial expressions is most effective when the threat stimuli are not consciously perceived (Fox, 2002; Mogg and Bradley, 1999). It is interesting to note that with presentation of fearful expressions significant activations occurred only in the *right* amygdala in the Etkin et al. (2004) study, while Bishop et al. (2004a) and Ewbank et al. 2009 found *left* amygdala activation. Nevertheless, these studies demonstrate that amygdala activation to threat is modulated by individual variation within the normal range of an anxiety spectrum (state- or trait-anxiety).

ERP studies have also found that the neural response to threat-related facial expressions is modulated by variation on the anxiety spectrum. For example, using the N2pc component, which indicates a rapid attentional bias to a particular location it has been found that angry, but not happy, facial expressions elicit an enhanced N2pc, but only in participants that report relatively high levels of trait-anxiety (Fox et al., 2008). Other early ERP components elicited in response to negative facial expressions have also been shown to be modulated by non-clinical levels of self-reported anxiety (e.g. Bar-Haim et al., 2005; Rossignol et al., 2006).

Bishop et al. (2004b) addressed the question of whether variation within this normal range of trait-anxiety is associated with a reduced ability to implement top-down attentional control when processing threat-related facial expressions. Attentional control seems to be orchestrated by a network of cortical areas including the dorsolateral and ventrolateral prefrontal cortex (dlPFC, vlPFC) as well as the anterior cingulate cortex (ACC). A reduced recruitment of this circuitry was found in response to threat-related facial expressions as the degree of self-reported trait-anxiety increased (Bishop et al., 2004b), providing the first direct neural evidence for a weaker activation of cortical control mechanisms in anxious people when they are required to prevent distraction from threat-related distractors. It should be noted, however, that this result was not replicated in the study reported by Ewbank et al. (2009). In a more recent study, it has been suggested that the modulation of attentional control areas in the brain by normal variation in trait-anxiety may be a much more general phenomenon that is not just restricted to threat-related stimuli (Bishop 2009). This result is difficult to interpret, however, as attentional control is highly correlated with anxiety (e.g. Eysenck et al., 2007) and therefore the results may be more to do with individual variation in attentional control rather than anxiety per se (see Derryberry and Reed, 2002). This aside, however, there is growing evidence from fMRI and ERP studies that the neural response to threat-related facial expressions is strongly influenced by individual variation in a common personality trait.

Processing of positive facial expressions

Individual differences in the processing of positive expressions have not been investigated to the same degree as the modulation of attentional biases to negative faces. As we saw earlier, however, the speed of categorizing facial expressions as "positive" is highly correlated with the degree of extraversion reported (Rusting and Larsen 1998). In other words, higher scores on the *happiness spectrum* is associated with faster categorization of faces depicting a positive emotion relative to those depicting negative or neutral emotions. Neuroimaging evidence also indicates that the processing of positive facial expressions is modulated by extraversion (Canli et al., 2002). As shown in Figure 26.5, the degree of left amygdala activation to happy, but not fearful, facial expressions was positively correlated with self-reported levels of extraversion. Against expectation, however, no significant correlation was found between neuroticism and amygdala activation

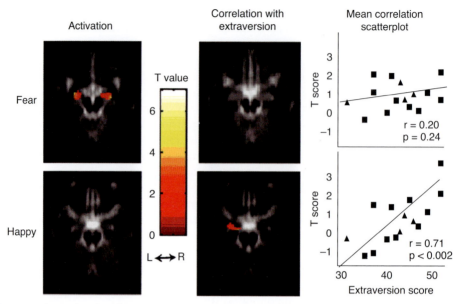

Fig. 26.5 Figure showing the response of the amygdala to emotional faces. The left part shows significant amygdala activation to fearful, but not happy, faces (red blobs). The middle shows that Extraversion is correlated with left amygdala activation to happy, but not fearful, faces (red blob). The right part shows participants mean activations (in T scores) as a function of extraversion. From Canli et al. (2002). Amygdala response to happy faces as a function of extraversion. *Science*, **296**, 2191. Reproduced with permission from AAAS.

in response to fearful or angry expressions in contrast to the reports discussed in the last section (Bishop et al., 2004a; Etkin et al., 2004; Ewbank et al., 2009). While self-report measures of neuroticism as used by Canli et al. (2002) and measures of trait and state-anxiety as used by Bishop et al. (2004a), Ewbank et al. (2009) and Etkin et al. (2004) are highly intercorrelated, these different measures may account for the different pattern of findings observed across these studies.

Further evidence for an enhanced neural response to positively valenced stimuli in extraverted individuals has been provided by studies that used pictures and words (e.g. Canli et al., 2001, 2004). Similarly, both amygdala and rostral ACC activation were enhanced when self-reported optimists were asked to imagine positive future emotional events relative to negatively toned events (Sharot et al., 2007). Thus, while there is a paucity of studies investigating the modulation of response to positive facial expressions there is growing evidence with non-facial positive affective stimuli that trait extraversion or trait optimism is likely to modulate such processing. As we mentioned earlier in this chapter, human facial expressions represent highly potent social stimuli and the modulation of expression processing by personality traits is likely to reflect much wider affective processing (see Fox 2008, for further discussion).

Separating current mood from personality traits

When discussing how common personality traits might influence expression processing, it is crucial to also examine the impact of current mood state on such processing. As discussed earlier, variation on self-reported N-NA relates to the intensity and frequency of negative mood states experienced just as variation on E-PA influences the degree to which positive mood states are experienced (Fox, 2008). This means that it is very difficult to separate out the effects of the personality trait on expression processing as opposed to the influence of current mood state. There is plenty of evidence that a happy mood state results in a positivity bias, for example. In a study reported by Canli et al. (2002) it was found that amygdala reactivity to happy expressions depended upon on the degree of E-PA reported. However, given that those reporting high levels of extraversion are also more likely to be in a positive mood state this result may have been due to the current mood state rather than the personality dimension. The same argument, of course, also holds for studies on N-NA and reactivity to negative situations. To the best of our knowledge there are no studies on facial expressions that directly examine the potential interaction of personality dimensions and current mood state. However, illustrative evidence comes from a study with words. Canli et al. (2004) measured the personality dimensions of neuroticism and extraversion as well as current mood state in a group of participants. An emotional Stroop task was presented in which negative, positive and neutral words were typed in different colors. The degree of activation in the ACC when responding to the color of positive words varied as a function of extraversion but not as a function of mood state. In contrast, the degree of activation in the ACC when responding to negative words was associated with current mood state not with self-reported neuroticism. Neither extraversion nor neuroticism was associated with decreased ACC activation. Extraversion was not associated with ACC activation to negative words and neuroticism was not associated with ACC activation to positive words. In addition, negative mood (but not neuroticism) was found to increase the functional connectivity between ACC and the left middle frontal gyrus and the left inferior parietal lobule during presentation of negative words. This functional connectivity was not observed for neuroticism (controlling negative mood) or extraversion and positive mood. These results demonstrate a strong double dissociation and suggest that personality traits and mood states may have different effects on neural reactivity to affective stimuli. It is important for future research on emotion expression processing to investigate the potential interaction between broad personality dimensions as well as current mood states in determining how an individual will respond to a potent social cue such as a facial expression.

Other personality dimensions

There are other elements of personality that vary across the normal population and that are known to influence expression processing. For example, variation on what has been termed the *autistic spectrum* can influence expression processing. Evidence suggests that individuals with autistic spectrum traits are less able to recognize complex emotions in a face in comparison to individuals without autistic spectrum traits (Golan et al., 2006; but see Corden et al., 2008). There is also evidence that people high on the autistic spectrum may use different processes (i.e. a more feature-based system) to recognize facial expressions (Ashwin et al., 2006).

Other research has examined variation in degrees of psychopathy in relation to processing of facial expressions. In a recent meta-analysis (Marsh and Blair, 2008), it has been found that individuals with antisocial personality behavior (psychopathic, aggressive, criminal, delinquent, or externalizing) were less accurate than individuals without antisocial behavior in identifying expressions of fear, sadness, and surprise (Blair et al., 2004; Dolan and Fullam, 2006; Hastings et al., 2008; Marsh and Blair 2008; Montagne et al., 2005). No differences were found between the two groups in the recognition of happy, angry and disgusted expressions. Interestingly, deficits in the recognition of fearful expressions were greater in relation to any of the other five emotions. Marsh and Blair (2008) suggested that a neurocognitive dysfunction underlies the difficulty in recognizing expressions of fear in people with antisocial behavior, since there is an association between fear recognition deficits and amygdala dysfunction (Adolphs et al., 1999; Calder et al., 1996).

A personality trait associated with Gray's (1990) behavioral approach system measuring the drive to pursue reward (or appetitive motivation) has been shown to be linked to anger (e.g. Carver 2004; A. Cooper et al., 2008; Harmon-Jones, 2003). High reward-drive individuals show increased attention to facial expressions depicting aggression (Passamonti et al., 2008; Putman et al., 2004) and ERP findings show that the magnitude of the ventromedial PFC response to angry facial expressions is linked with individual differences in reward-drive. Individuals with low reward-drive showed enhanced positive ERPs in response to angry faces, a pattern not observed in individuals with high reward-drive (Bediou et al., 2009). This finding is further supported by an fMRI study that found increased amygdala activation and reduced ventral ACC activation with presentation of angry faces in individuals with high reward-drive (Beaver et al., 2008). In addition, on another study the connectivity between the ventral ACC and the amygdala was more negative to individuals with lower reward-drive and less negative to individuals with higher reward-drive with presentation of angry facial expressions (Passamonti et al., 2008). Passamonti et al. (2008) suggested that the reduced negative connectivity in individuals with high reward-drive explains their interpretation of angry faces as more provocative than individuals with low-reward drive. In a study with individuals with intermittent explosive disorder, a psychiatric condition characterized by recurrent bursts of aggression, there was also no connectivity between amygdala and the ventromedial PFC with presentation of aggressive displays (Coccaro et al., 2007).

All together, these studies indicate that processing of facial expressions is modulated by personality traits and variation in neural activation.

Summary and conclusions

In this chapter, we have discussed evidence suggesting that emotion expression processing is a core cognitive ability that develops early in life. The ability to efficiently detect, identify and respond to facial expressions is a crucial component of social cognition. We have argued that this ability is influenced to an important degree by variation in a number of common personality dimensions. We focused on *neuroticism* and *extraversion* since these are two of the "Big Five" personality traits that are most relevant to expression processing. Evidence is now growing that normal variation on these common personality traits do play a role in how quickly and for how long emotional facial expressions are processed. Individuals reporting high levels of neuroticism or trait-anxiety tend to be drawn towards negatively valenced information whereas individuals reporting high levels of extraversion are more reactive to positive information (e.g. Davidson and Irwin 1999; Mauer and Borkenau 2007). The impact of these traits on the neural mechanisms underlying expression processing is also strong. The activity of the amygdala is significantly increased by the presence of fearful or angry facial expression in individuals high on the anxiety spectrum (Bishop et al., 2004a; Etkin et al., 2004; Ewbank et al., 2009) and by the presence of happy facial expressions in individuals reporting high levels of extraversion (Canli et al., 2002). We suggest that a complete understanding of the cognitive and neural mechanisms involved in the processing of facial expressions, should take individual differences in personality traits into account.

References

Adolphs, R., Tranel, D., Hamann, S., *et al.* (1999). Recognition of facial emotion in nine individuals with bilateral amygdala damage. *Neuropsychologia*, **37**, 1111–1117.

Ashwin, C., Wheelwright, S. and Baron-Cohen, S. (2006). Finding a face in the crowd: Testing the anger superiority effect in Asperger syndrome. *Brain & Cognition*, **61**, 78–95.

Bar-Haim, Y., Lamy, D. and Glickman, S. (2005). Attentional bias in anxiety: A behavioural and ERP study. *Brain & Cognition*, **59**, 11–22.

Bar-Haim, Y., Lamy, D., Pergamin, L., Bakermans-Kranenburg, M.J. and van Ijzendoorn, M.H. (2007). Threat-related attentional bias in anxious and nonanxious individuals: A metaanalytic study. *Psychological Bulletin*, **133**, 1–24.

Bassili, J.N. (1979). Emotion recognition: The role of facial movement and the relative importance of upper and lower areas of the face. *Journal of Personality and Social Psychology*, **37**, 2049–2058.

Beaver, J.D., Lawrence, A.D., Passamonti, L. and Calder, A.J. (2008). Appetitive motivation predicts the neural response to facial signals of aggression. *Journal of Neuroscience*, **28**, 2719–2725.

Bediou, B., Eimer, M., d'Amato, T., Hauk, O. and Calder, A.J. (2009). In the eye of the beholder: Individual differences in reward-drive modulate early frontocentral ERPs to angry faces. *Neuropsychologia*, **47**, 825–834.

Bishop, S. (2009). Trait anxiety and impoverished prefrontal control of attention. *Nature Neuroscience*, **12**, 92–98.

Bishop, S.J., Duncan, J. and Lawrence, A.D. (2004a). State anxiety modulation of the amygdala response to unattended threat-related stimuli. *Journal of Neuroscience*, **24**, 10364–10368.

Bishop, S., Duncan, J., Brett, M. and Lawrence, A.D. (2004b). Prefrontal cortical function and anxiety: Controlling attention to threat-related stimuli. *Nature Neuroscience*, **7**, 184–188.

Blair, R.J.R., Mitchell, D.G.V., Peschardt, K.S., *et al.* (2004). Reduced sensitivity to others' fearful expressions in psychopathic and nonpsychopathic offenders. *Personality and Individual Differences*, **37**, 1111–1122.

Bradley, B.P., Mogg, K., Falla, S.J. and Hamilton, L.R. (1998). Attentional bias for threatening facial expressions in anxiety: Manipulation of stimulus duration. *Cognition & Emotion*, **12**, 737–753.

Brosch, T. and Sharma, D. (2005). The role of fear-relevant stimuli in visual search: A comparison of phylogenetic and ontogenetic stimuli. *Emotion*, **5**, 360–364.

Bruce, V. (1986). Influences of familiarity on the processing of faces. *Perception*, **15**, 387–397.

Bruce, V. and Young, A. (1986). Understanding face recognition. *British Journal of Psychology*, **77**, 305–327.

Calder, A.J., Young, A.W., Rowland, D., Perrett, D.I., Hodges, J.R. and Etcoff, N.L. (1996). Facial emotion recognition after bilateral amygdala damage: Differentially severe impairment of fear. *Cognitive Neuropsychology*, **13**, 699–745.

Calder, A.J., Young, A.W., Keane, J. and Dean, M. (2000). Configural information in facial expression perception. *Journal of Experimental Psychology: Human Perception and Performance*, **26**, 527–551.

Calder, A.J., Burton, A.M., Miller, P., Young, A.W. and Akamatsu, S. (2001). A principal component analysis of facial expressions. *Vision Research*, **41**, 1179–1208.

Calder, A.J. and Young, A.W. (2005). Understanding the recognition of facial identity and facial expression. *Nature Reviews Neuroscience*, **6**, 641–651.

Calvo, M.G. and Lundqvist, D. (2008). Facial expressions of emotion (KDEF): Identification under different display-duration conditions. *Behavior Research Methods*, **40**, 109–115.

Campbell, R., Brooks, B., de Haan, E. and Roberts, T. (1996). Dissociating face processing skills: Decisions about lip-read speech, expression and identity. *Quarterly Journal of Experimental Psychology*, **49A**, 295–314.

Canli, T., Zhao, Z., Desmond, J.E., Kang, E.J., Gross, J. and Gabrieli, J.D.E. (2001). An fMRI study of personality influences on brain reactivity to emotional stimuli. *Behavioural Neuroscience*, **115**, 33–42.

Canli, T., Sivers, H., Whitfield, S.L., Gotlib, I.H. and Gabrieli, J.D.E. (2002). Amygdala response to happy faces as a function of extraversion. *Science*, **296**, 2191.

Canli, T., Amin, Z., Haas, B., Omura, K. and Constable, R.T. (2004). A double dissociation between mood states and personality traits in the anterior cingulated. *Behavioral Neuroscience*, **118**, 897–904.

Carver, C.S. (2004). Negative affects deriving from the behavioral approach system. *Emotion*, **4**, 3–22.

Clark, L.A. and Watson, D. (1991). Tripartite model of anxiety and depression: Psychometric evidence and taxonomic implications. *Journal of Abnormal Psychology*, **100**, 316–336.

Coccaro, E.F., McCloskey, M.S., Fitzgerald, D.A. and Phan, K.L. (2007). Amygdala and orbitofrontal reactivity to social threat in individuals with impulsive aggression. *Biological Psychiatry*, **62**, 168–178.

Cohen Kadosh, K., Henson, R.N.A., Cohen Kadosh, R., Johnson, M.H. and Dick, F. (2010). Task-dependent activation of face-sensitive cortex: An fMRI adaptation study. *Journal of Cognitive Neuroscience*, **22**, 903–917.

Cooper, A., Gomez, R. and Buck, E. (2008). The relationships between the BIS and BAS, anger and responses to anger. *Personality and Individual Differences*, **44**, 403–413.

Cooper, R.M., Rowe, A.C. and Penton-Voak, I.S. (2008). The role of trait anxiety in the recognition of emotional facial expressions. *Journal of Anxiety Disorders*, **22**, 1120–1127.

Corden, B., Chilvers, R. and Skuse, D. (2008). Avoidance of emotionally arousing stimuli predicts social-perceptual impairment in Asperger's syndrome. *Neuropsychologia*, **46**, 137–147.

Cottrell, G.W., Branson, K.M. and Calder, A.J. (2002). Do expression and identity need separate representations. 24th Annual Meeting of the Cognitive Science Society, Fairfax, Virginia.

Darwin, C. (1872/1998). *The expression of the emotions in man and animals*, 3rd edn. (P. Ekman, ed.). New York: Oxford University Press. (Original work published 1872.)

Davidson, R.J. and Irwin, W. (1999). The functional neuroanatomy of emotion and affective style. *Trends in Cognitive Science*, **3**, 11–21.

Derryberry, D. and Reed, M.A. (2002). Anxiety-related attentional biases and their regulation by attentional control. *Journal of Abnormal Psychology*, **111**, 225–236.

Dolan, M. and Fullam, R. (2006). Face affect recognition deficits in personality-disordered offenders: Association with psychopathy. *Psychological Medicine*, **36(11)**, 1563–1569.

Duchaine, B.C., Parker, H. and Nakayama, K. (2003). Normal recognition of emotion in a prosopagnosic. *Perception*, **32**, 827–838.

Eastwood, J.D., Smilek, D. and Merikle, P.M. (2001). Differential attentional guidance by unattended faces expressing positive and negative emotion. *Perception & Psycophysics*, **63**, 1004–1013.

Ekman, P. (1994). Strong evidence for universals in facial expressions: A reply to Russell's mistaken critique. *Psychological Bulletin*, **115**, 268–287.

Ekman, P. and Friesen, W.V. (1986). A new pan cultural facial expression of emotion. *Motivation & Emotion*, **10**, 159–168.

Ekman, P., Sorenson, E.R. and Friesen, W.V. (1969). Pan-cultural elements in facial displays of emotions. *Science*, **164**, 86–88.

Ellamil, M., Susskind, J.M. and Anderson, A.K. (2008). Examinations of identity invariance in facial expression adaptation. *Cognitive, Affective, & Behavioral Neuroscience*, **8**, 273–281.

Etkin, A., Klemenhagen, K.C., Dudman, J.T., *et al.* (2004). Individual differences in trait anxiety predict the response of the basolateral amygdala to unconsciously processed fearful faces. *Neuron*, **44**, 1043–1055.

Etcoff, N.L. (1984). Selective attention to facial identity and facial emotion. *Neuropsychologia*, **22**, 281–295.

Ewbank, M.P., Lawrence, A.D., Passamonti, L., Keane, J., Peers, P.V. and Calder, A.J. (2009). Anxiety predicts a differential neural response to attended and unattended facial signals of anger and fear. *NeuroImage*, **44**, 1144–1151.

Eyesnck, M.W., Derakshan, N., Santos, R. and Calvo, M. (2007). Anxiety and cognitive performance: Attentional control theory. *Emotion*, **7**, 336–353.

Fairhall, S.L. and Ishai, A. (2007). Effective connectivity within the distributed cortical network for face perception. *Cerebral Cortex*, **17**, 2400–2406.

Fox, C.J. and Barton, J.J.S. (2007). What is adapted in face adaptation? The neural representations of expression in the human visual system. *Brain Research*, **1127**, 80–89.

Fox, C.J., Moon, S.Y., Iaria, G. and Barton, J.J. (2009). The correlates of subjective perception of identity and expression in the face network: An fMRI adaptation study. *NeuroImage*, **44**, 569–580.

Fox, E. (1993). Allocation of visual attention and anxiety. *Cognition & Emotion*, **7**, 207–215.

Fox, E. (2002). Processing emotional facial expressions: The role of anxiety and awareness. *Cognitive, Affective & Behavioral Neuroscience*, **2**, 52–63.

Fox, E. (2008). *Emotion Science*. New York: Palgrave Macmillan.

Fox, E. and Damjanovic, L. (2006). The eyes are sufficient to produce a threat superiority effect. *Emotion*, **6**, 534–539.

Fox, E., Lester, V., Russo, R., Bowles, R.J., Pichler, A. and Dutton, K. (2000). Facial expressions of emotion: Are angry faces detected more efficiently? *Cognition & Emotion*, **14**, 61–92.

Fox, E., Russo, R., Bowles, R. and Dutton, K. (2001). Do threatening stimuli draw or hold visual attention in sub-clinical anxiety?. *Journal of Experimental Psychology: General*, **130**, 681–700.

Fox, E., Russo, R. and Dutton, K. (2002). Attentional bias for threat: Evidence for delayed disengagement from emotional faces. *Cognition & Emotion*, **16**, 355–379.

Fox, E., Russo, R. and Georgiou, G.A. (2005). Anxiety modulates the degree of attentive resources required to process emotional faces. *Cognitive, Affective, & Behavioral Neuroscience*, **5**, 396–404.

Fox, E., Mathews, A., Calder, A.J. and Yiend, J. (2007). Anxiety and sensitivity to gaze direction in emotionally expressive faces. *Emotion*, **7**, 478–486.

Fox, E., Derakshan, N. and Shoker, L. (2008). Trait anxiety modulates the electrophysiological indices of rapid spatial orienting towards angry faces. *NeuroReport*, **19**, 259–263.

Friesen, C.K. and Kingstone, A. (1998). The eyes have it! Reflexive orienting is triggered by non-predictive gaze. *Psychonomic Bulletin & Review*, **5**, 490–495.

Gallegos, D.R. and Tranel, D. (2005). Positive facial affect facilitates the identification of famous faces. *Brain & Language*, **93**, 338–348.

Ganel, T., Valyear, K.F., Goshen-Gottstein, Y. and Goodale, M.A. (2005). The involvement of the "fusiform face area" in processing facial expression. *Neuropsychologica*, **43**, 1645–1654.

George, M.S., Ketter, T.A., Gill, D.S., *et al.* (1993). Brain regions involved in recognizing facial emotion or identity: An oxygen-15 PET study. *Journal of Neuropsychiatry and Clinical Neurosciences*, **5**, 384–394.

Georgiou, G.A., Bleakley, C., Hayward, J., *et al.* (2005). Focusing on fear: Attentional disengagement from emotional faces. *Visual Cognition*, **12**, 145–158.

Golan, O., Baron-Cohen, S and Hill, J.J. (2006). The Cambridge mindreading (CAM) face-voice battery: Testing complex emotion recognition in adults with and without Asperger syndrome. *Journal of Autism and Developmental Disorders*, **36**, 169–183.

Gray, J.A. (1990). Brain systems that mediate both emotion and cognition. *Cognition & Emotion*, **4**, 269–288.

Hansen, C.H. and Hansen, R.D. (1988). Finding the face in the crowd: An anger superiority effect. *Journal of Personality and Social Psychology*, **54**, 917–924.

Harmon-Jones, E. (2003). Anger and the behavioral approach system. *Personality and Individual Differences*, **35**, 995–1005.

Hastings, M.E., Tangney, J.P. and Stuewig, J. (2008). Psychopathy and identification of facial expressions of emotion. *Personality and Individual Differences*, **44**, 1474–1483.

Haxby, J.V., Hoffman, E.A. and Gobbini, I.M. (2000). The distributed human neural system for face perception. *Trends in Cognitive Sciences*, **4**, 223–233.

Hietanen, J.K. and Leppänen, M. (2003). Does facial expression affect attention orienting by gaze direction cues? *Journal of Experimental Psychology: Human Perception & Performance*, **29**, 1228–1243.

Humphreys, K., Avidan, G. and Behrmann, M. (2007). A detailed investigation of facial expression processing in congenital prosopagnosia as compared to acquired prosopagnosia. *Experimental Brain Research*, **176**, 356–373.

Juth, P., Lundqvist, D., Karlsson, A. and Öhman, A. (2005). Looking for foes and friends: Perceptual and emotional factors when finding a face in the crowd. *Emotion*, **5**, 379–395.

Kagan, J. (1994). *Galen's Prophecy: Temperament in Human Nature.* New York: Basic Books.

Kobiella, A., Grossmann, T., Reid, V.M. and Striano, T. (2008). The discrimination of angry and fearful facial expressions in 7-month-old infants: An event-related potential study. *Cognition & Emotion*, **22**, 134–46.

Kotsoni, E., De Haan, M. and Johnson, M.H. (2001). Categorical perception of facial expressions by 7-month-old infants. *Perception*, **30**, 1115–1125.

Lander, K. and Metcalfe, S. (2007). The influence of positive and negative facial expressions on face familiarity. *Memory*, **15**, 63–69.

Leppänen, J.M., Hietanen, J.K. and Koskinen, K. (2008). Differential early ERPs to fearful versus neutral facial expressions: A response to the salience of the eyes?. *Biological Psychology*, **78**, 150–158.

Leppänen, J.M. and Nelson, C.A. (2009). Tuning the developing brain to social signals of emotions. *Nature Reviews Neuroscience*, **10**, 37–47.

Leppänen, J.M., Moulson, M.C., Vogel-Farley, V.K. and Nelson, C.A. (2007). An ERP study of emotional face processing in the adult and infant brain. *Child Development*, **78**, 232–245.

Lundqvist, D., Esteves, F. and Öhman, A. (1999). The face of wrath: Critical features for conveying facial threat. *Cognition & Emotion*, **13**, 691–711.

Lundqvist, D., Flykt, A. and Öhman, A. (1998). *The Karolinska Directed Emotional Faces (KDEF).* Stockholm: Department of Neurosciences Karolinska Hospital.

MacLeod, C. and Mathews, A. (1988). Anxiety and the allocation of attention to threat. *Quarterly Journal of Experimental Psychology. A, Human Experimental Psychology*, **40**, 653–670.

MacLeod, C., Mathews, A. and Tata, P. (1986). Attentional bias in emotional disorders. *Journal of Abnormal Psychology*, **95**, 15–20.

Marsh, A.A. and Blair, R.J.R. (2008). Deficits in facial affect recognition among antisocial populations: a meta-analysis. *Neuroscience and Biobehavioral Reviews*, **32**, 454–465.

Mathews, A. and Mackintosh, B. (1998). A cognitive model of selective processing in anxiety. *Cognitive Therapy and Research*, **22**, 539–560.

Mathews, A.M., Fox, E., Yiend, J. and Calder, A. (2003). The face of fear: Effects of eye-gaze and emotion on visual attention. *Visual Cognition*, **10**, 823–835.

Mauer, N. and Borkenau, P. (2007). Temperament and early information processing: Temperament-related attentional bias in emotional Stroop tasks. *Personality and Individual Differences*, **43**, 1063–1073.

McCrae, R.R. and Costa, P.T. (1987). Validation of the five-factor model across instruments and observers. *Journal of Personality and Social Psychology*, **52**, 81–90.

Mogg, K. and Bradley, B.P. (1998). A cognitive-motivational analysis of anxiety. *Behaviour Research and Therapy*, **36**, 809–848.

Mogg, K. and Bradley, B. (1999). Orienting of attention to threatening facial expressions presented under conditions of restricted awareness. *Cognition & Emotion*, **13**, 713–740.

Mogg, K., Garner, M. and Bradley, B.P. (2008). Anxiety and orienting of gaze to angry and fearful faces. *Biological Psychology*, **76**, 163–169.

Montagne, B., van Honk, J., Kessels, R.P.C., *et al.* (2005). Reduced efficiency in recognising fear in subjects scoring high on psychopathic personality characteristics. *Personality and Individual Differences*, **38**, 5–11.

Morris, J.S., Frith, C.D., Perrett, D.I., *et al.* (1996). A differential neural response in the human amygdala to fearful and happy facial expression. *Nature*, **383**, 813–815.

Narumoto, J., Okada, T., Sadato, N., Fukui, K. and Yonekura, Y. (2001). Attention to emotion modulates fMRI activity in human right superior temporal sulcus. *Cognitive Brain Research*, 12, 225–231.

Nelson, C.A. and de Haan, M. (1996). Neural correlates of infants' visual responsiveness to facial expressions of emotion. *Developmental Psychobiology*, 29, 577–595.

Nelson, C.A. and Dolgin, K. (1985). The generalized discrimination of facial expressions by 7-month-old infants. *Child Development*, 56, 58–61.

Öhman, A., Lundqvist, D. and Esteves, F. (2001). The face in the crowd revisited: A threat advantage with schematic stimuli. *Journal of Personality and Social Psychology*, 80, 381–396.

Ortony, A. and Turner, T.J. (1990).What's basic about basic emotions? *Psychological Review*, 97, 315–331.

Passamonti, L., Rowe, J.B., Ewbank, M., Hampshire, A., Keane, J. and Calder, A.J. (2008). Connectivity from the ventral anterior cingulated to the amygdala is modulated by appetitive motivation in response to facial signals of aggression. *NeuroImage*, 43, 562–570.

Peltola, M.J., Leppänen, J.M., Palokangas, T. and Hietanen, J.K. (2008). Fearful faces modulate looking duration and attention disengagement in 7-month-old infants. *Developmental Science*, 11, 60–68.

Phelps, E., Ling, S. and Carrasco, M. (2006). Emotion facilitates perception and potentiates the perceptual benefits of attention. *Psychological Science*, 17, 292–299.

Posner, M.I. (1980). Orienting of attention. *Quarterly Journal of Experimental Psychology*, 32, 2–25.

Putman, P., Hermans, E. and Van Honk, J. (2004). Emotional Stroop performance for masked angry faces: It's BAS, not BIS. *Emotion*, 4, 305–311.

Putman, P., Hermans, E. and Van Honk, J. (2006). Anxiety meets fear in perception of dynamic expressive gaze. *Emotion*, 6, 94–102.

Raymond, K.E., Shapiro, K.L. and Arnell, K.M. (1992). Temporary suppression of visual processing in an RSVP task: An attentional blink? *Journal of Experimental Psychology: Human Perception and Performance*, 18, 451–468.

Richards, A., French, C.C., Calder, A.J., Webb, B., Fox, R. and Young, A.W. (2002). Anxiety-related bias in the classification of emotionally ambiguous facial expressions. *Emotion*, 2, 273–287.

Rossignol, M., Anselme, C., Vermeulen, N., Phillippot, P. and Campanella, S. (2006). Categorical perception of anger and disgust facial expression is affected by non-clinical social anxiety: An ERP study. *Brain Research*, 1132, 166–176.

Russell, J.A. (1994). Is there universal recognition of emotion from facial expressions? *A review of cross-cultural studies. Psychological Bulletin*, 115 102–141.

Rusting, C.L. and Larsen, R.J. (1998). Personality and cognitive processing of affective information. *Personality and Social Psychology Bulletin*, 24, 200–213.

Schupp, H.T., Öhman, A., Junghöfer, M., Weike, A.I., Stockburger, J. and Hamm, A.O. (2004). The facilitated processing of threatening faces: An ERP analysis. *Emotion*, 4, 189–200.

Schyns, P.G., Petro, L.S. and Smith, M.L. (2007). Dynamics of visual information integration in the brain for categorizing facial expressions. *Current Biology*, 17, 1580–1585.

Sergent, J., Ohta, S., MacDonald, B. and Zuck, E. (1994). Segregated processing of identity and emotion in the human brain: a PET study. *Visual Cognition*, 1, 349–369.

Sharot, T., Riccardi, A.M., Raio, C.M. and Phelps, E. (2007). Neural mechanisms mediating optimism bias. *Nature*, 450, 102–106.

Surcinelli, P., Codispoti, M., Montebarocci, O., Rossi, N. and Baldaro, B. (2006). Facial emotion recognition in trait anxiety. *Anxiety Disorders*, 20, 110–117.

Tipples, J. (2006). Fear and fearfulness potentiate automatic orienting to eye gaze. *Cognition & Emotion*, 20, 309–320.

Tranel, D., Damasio, A.R. and Damasio, H. (1988). Intact recognition of facial expression, gender, and age in patients with impaired recognition of face identity. *Neurology*, 38, 690–696.

Whittle, S. Allen, N.B., Lubman, D. and Yucel, M. (2006). The neuroanatomical basis of affective temperament: Towards a better understanding of psychopathology. *Neuroscience and Biobehavioural Reviews*, **30**, 511–525.

Williams, J.M.G., Watts, F.N., MacLeod, C.M. and Mathews, A. (1988). *Cognitive Psychology and Emotional Disorders*. Chichester: Wiley.

Williams, M.A., Moss, S.A., Bradshaw, J.L. and Mattingley, J.B. (2005). Look at me, I'm smiling: Visual search for threatening and nonthreatening facial expressions. *Visual Cognition*, **12**, 29–50.

Winston, J.S., Henson, R.N.A., Fine-Goulden, M.R. and Dolan, R.J. (2004). fMRI-adaptation reveals dissociable neural representations of identity and expression in face perception. *Journal of Neurophysiology*, **92**, 1830–1839.

Vuilleumier, P. (2005). How brains beware: neural mechanisms of emotional attention. *Trends in Cognitive Sciences*, **9**, 585–594.

Vuilleumier, P., Armony, J.L., Driver, J. and Dolan, R.J. (2001). Distinct effects of attention and emotion on face processing in the human brain: An event related fMRI study. *Neuron*, **30**, 829–841.

Young, A.W., McWeeny, K.H., Hay, D.C. and Ellis, A.W. (1986). Matching familiar and unfamiliar faces on identity and expression. *Psychological Research*, **48**, 63–68.

Chapter 27

Real Faces, Real Emotions: Perceiving Facial Expressions in Naturalistic Contexts of Voices, Bodies, and Scenes

Beatrice de Gelder and Jan Van den Stock

Introduction

For a while, "Headless Body found in Topless Bar" counted as one of the funniest lines to have appeared in US newspapers. But headless bodies and bodiless heads figure only in crime catalogues and police reports and are not part of our daily experience, at the very least not part of the daily experience that constitutes the normal learning environment in which we acquire our face and body perception expertise. Yet, except for a few isolated studies, the literature on face recognition has not yet addressed the issue of context effects in face perception. By "context" we mean here the whole naturalistic environment that is almost always present when we encounter a face.

Why has context received so little attention and what, if any, changes would we need to make to mainstream models of face and facial expression processing if indeed different kinds of context have an impact on how the brain deals with faces and facial expressions? Discussions on context influences and their consequences for how we read and react to an emotion from the face have a long history (Fernberger, 1928). But the kind of context effects that were investigated in the early days would nowadays qualify as so called late effects or post-perceptual effects, related as they are to the overall (verbal) appraisal of a stimulus rather that to its online processing. In contrast, the context effects we have specifically targeted in recent studies are those that are to be found at the perceptual stage of face processing.

In this chapter we review recent investigations of three familiar naturalistic contexts in which facial expressions are frequently encountered: whole bodies, natural scenes and emotional voices (see also Ambady and Weisbuch, Chapter 24, this volume). In the first section we briefly review recent evidence that shifts the emphasis from a categorical model of face processing, based on the assumption that faces are processed as a distinct object category with their dedicated perceptual and neurofunctional basis, towards more distributed models where different aspects of faces (like direction of gaze and emotional expression) are processed by different brain areas and different perceptual routines and show how these models are better suited to represent face perception and face-context effects. In the second section we look in detail at one kind of context effect, as found in investigations of interactions between facial and bodily expressions. We sketch a perspective in which context plays a crucial role, even for highly automated processes like the ones underlying recognition of facial expressions. Some recent evidence of context effects also has implications for current theories of face perception and its deficits.

Making space for context effects in models of face perception

Older theories on face perception have tended to restrict scientific investigations of face perception to issues of face versus object categorization. The major sources of evidence for category specificity of face perception are findings about its temporal processing windows and neurofunctional basis. But this debate is not settled and recent evidence now indicates that the temporal and spatial neural markers of face categorization are also sensitive to some other non-face stimuli (for a review of such overlap between spatial and temporal markers of face and body specificity, see de Gelder et al., 2010). Furthermore, it is becoming increasingly clear that the presence of an emotional expression influences even those relatively early and relatively specific neural markers of category specificity like the N170 and the face area in the fusiform gyrus. Finally, distributed models as opposed to categorical models of face processing seem more appropriate to represent the relation between face perception, facial expression perception and perceptual context effects as they represent the various functional aspects of facial information and allow for multiple entry points of context into ongoing face processing. Finally, models must also include the role of subcortical structures shown to be important components of face and facial expression processes.

Face perception and categorization

Much of the face recognition literature has been dominated by the view that face processing proceeds at its own pace, immune to the surrounding context in which the face is encountered. In line with this, one of the major questions in the field continues to be that of the perceptual and neurofunctional bases of faces. An important assumption has been and continues to be that faces occupy a neurofunctional niche on their own, such that face representations coexists with but do not overlap with object representations, a view that in one sense or another is linked to the notion of modularity. Typical characteristics of modular processing as viewed in the eighties and brought to a broad audience by Fodor (1983) are mainly that processing is mandatory, automatic and insulated from context effects. What was originally a theoretical argument purporting to separate syntactic from the more intractable semantic aspects of mental processes became for a while the focus of studies using brain imaging (Kanwisher et al., 1997). A research program fully focused on category specificity is unlikely to pay attention to perceptual context effects on face processing. In contrast, more recent distributed models of face processing appear more suited to accommodate the novel context findings (de Gelder et al., 2003; Haxby et al., 2000).

Similarities between facial expressions and other affective signals in perceptual and neurofunctional processes

Seeing bodily expressions is an important part of everyday perception and the scientific study of how we perceive whole body expressions has taken off in the last decade. Issues and questions that have been addressed in face research are also on the foreground in research on whole body expressions (see de Gelder et al., 2010, for a review). This is not surprising, considering the fact that faces and bodies appear together in daily experience. It may be not so surprising that perception of faces and bodies show several similarities at the behavioral and neurofunctional level. For example, both faces and bodies are processed configurally, meaning as a single perceptual entity, rather than as an assemblage of features. This is reflected in the perceptual processes triggered when face and body stimuli are presented upside-down (the inversion effect): recognition of faces and bodies presented upside-down is relatively more impaired than recognition of inverted objects, like houses (Reed et al., 2003). Also, a comparison of perception of upright and inverted faces reveals that the time course of the underlying brain mechanisms is similar for upright and inverted bodies (Stekelenburg and de Gelder, 2004). The presence of a bodily expression of fear in the neglected field also significantly reduces attention deficits in neurological populations (Tamietto et al., 2007), just as has been reported for faces (Vuilleumier and Schwartz, 2001). As will be shown in detail in the later sections, perception of bodily expressions activates some brain areas that are associated with the perception of faces (for reviews, see de Gelder, 2006; Peelen and Downing, 2007; see also section 'Body context effects on facial expressions').

From a face module to a face processing network

Categorical models of face processing (e.g. Kanwisher et al., 1997) tend to assume that the core of face processing consists of a dedicated brain area or module that is functionally identified by contrasting faces with a small number of other object categories mostly by using passive viewing conditions. All other dimensions of face processing corresponding to other aspects of face information (emotion, age, attractiveness, gender…) are viewed as subsequent modulations of the basic face processing ability implemented in the brain's face area(s). In contrast, distributed models for face perception also consider other aspects of faces besides person identity (Adolphs, 2002; Adolphs et al., 2000; de Gelder and Rouw, 2000; de Gelder et al., 2003; Haxby et al., 1994, 1996, 2000; Hoffman and Haxby, 2000; Puce et al., 1996). In distributed models, different areas of the brain process different attributes of the face, such as identity (FFA and the occipital face area (OFA)), gaze direction (superior temporal sulcus (STS)) and expression and/or emotion analysis (OFC, amygdala, anterior cingulate cortex, premotor cortex, somatosensory cortex).

Clinical cases constitute critical tests for theoretical models, and patients suffering from a deficit in face recognition or prosopagnosia (Bodamer, 1947) have long served as touchstone for models of face processing (see also Behrmann et al., Chapter 41; Duchaine, Chapter 42; Calder, Chapter 22; Kanwisher and Barton, Chapter 7; and Young, Chapter 5, this volume). Available functional magnetic resonance imaging (fMRI) studies targeting face perception in prosopagnosics so far show inconsistent results (see Van den Stock et al., 2008b for an overview), but very few of those studies included facial expressions or compared emotional with neutral faces (see Calder, Chapter 22, this volume).

Configural processing as measured by the inversion effect is a hallmark of intact face processing skills and a few studies have reported that the normal pattern of the inversion effect does not obtain when a face perception disorder is present whether of acquired or of developmental origin (de Gelder and Rouw, 2000; but see McKone and Yovel, 2009). We investigated whether adding an emotional expression would normalize their face processing style with respect to the inversion effect. We presented neutral and emotional faces to patients with acquired prosopagnosia (face recognition deficits following brain damage) with lesions in FFA, inferior occipital gyrus (IOG) or both. Our study showed that emotional but not neutral faces elicited activity in other face related brain areas like STS and amygdala and, most importantly, that most of these patients showed a normal inversion effect for emotional faces as well as normal configural processing as measured in a part-to-whole face identity matching task when the faces were not neutral but expressed an emotion (de Gelder et al., 2003). In a follow up fMRI study with patients suffering from developmental prosopagnosia (prosopagnosia without neurological history), we presented neutral and emotional (fearful and happy) faces and bodies and the results showed normal activation in FFA for emotional faces (fearful and happy) but lower activation for neutral faces, compared to controls (Van den Stock et al., 2008b) (see Figure 27.1). Increased activation for emotional faces compared to neutral faces in FFA has since been reported in an acquired prosopagnosia case by others also (Peelen et al., 2009).

Electrophysiological studies are crucial for investigating distributed face models because the limited time resolution of fMRI does not allow one to conclude that all dimensions of facial information necessarily depend on activity in a single critical area like the fusiform face area. Studies using electroencephalogram (EEG) or magnetoencephalogram (MEG) data initially provided support for face modularity, in the sense that there appeared to be a unique time window for a

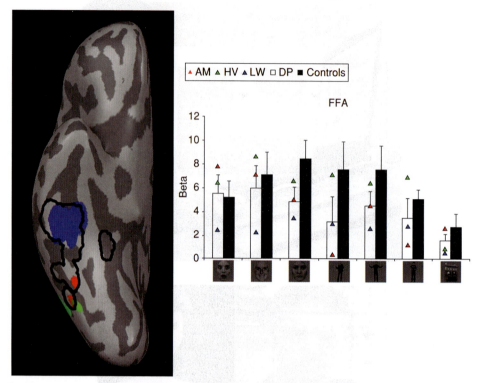

Fig. 27.1 Face-specific BOLD-activation in right fusiform face area (FFA) when comparing faces (fearful/happy/neutral) with houses. (Left) Areas are shown on an inflated right hemisphere. Activation maps of the control subjects are collapsed and displayed by the black contours. Activation of the individual developmental prosopagnosics (DPs) is plotted in color. (Right) Beta-values in the plotted areas. Conditions represent from left to right: fearful faces, happy faces, neutral faces, fearful bodies, happy bodies, neutral bodies and houses. White columns display the average value of three prosopagnosics, black columns show the average value of the controls. Triangles represent the individual values of the DPs. Error bars represent one standard error of the mean (SEM). © Beatrice de Gelder and Jan Van den Stock.

stimulus to enter the face processing system. EEG and MEG investigations into face perception have characterized two early markers in the temporal dynamics of face perception: a positive waveform around 100ms (P1) and a negative waveform around 170ms (N170) after stimulus onset indicating the time course of dedicated brain mechanisms sensitive to face perception. It is a matter of debate where in the brain these waveforms originate, whether in early extrastriate areas, STS or fusiform gyrus (FG) and what type of processing mechanism these waveforms reflect, whether global encoding, object categorization or configural processing (see de Gelder et al., 2006 for a review).

Face processing includes subcortical and cortical areas

Finally, we have shown, as have other groups, that patients with striate cortex damage can process and recognize faces presented in their blind visual field (Andino et al., 2009; de Gelder and Tamietto, 2007; de Gelder et al., 1999b; Morris et al., 2001; Pegna et al., 2005) and for which they have no conscious perception. For this and other reasons not relevant here, the involvement of subcortical structures in face perception also needs to be represented in a distributed model of face processing as we sketched in de Gelder et al. (2003). Masking studies performed with neurologically intact observers, studies on residual visual abilities for faces and facial expressions in cortically blind patients and on face processing skills of infants with immature visual cortex converge to provide tentative evidence for the importance of subcortical structures. Research indicates that the distributed brain network for face perception encompasses two main processing streams: a subcortical pathway from superior colliculus and pulvinar to the amygdala that is involved in rudimentary and mostly non-conscious processing of salient stimuli like facial expressions (de Gelder et al., 1999b, 2001, 2008; Morris et al., 1998b, 2001; Pegna et al., 2005) and a more familiar cortical route from the lateral geniculate nucleus (LGN) via primary visual cortex to OFA, FFA, and STS, subserving fine-grained analysis of conscious perception. Feedforward and feedback loops, especially between amygdala and striate cortex, OFA, FFA, and STS (Amaral and Price, 1984; Carmichael and Price, 1995; Catani et al., 2003; Iidaka et al., 2001; Morris et al., 1998a; Vuilleumier et al., 2004) support the interaction between these routes to contribute ultimately to a unified and conscious percept (Tamietto and de Gelder, 2010).

In summary, clinical phenomena like prosopagnosia and affective blindsight form an important contribution to the current understanding of face perception. Distributed face processing models that include subcortical structures and incorporate the many dimensions of faces like emotional expression appear to resonate best with the empirical data.

Body context effects on facial expressions

Of all the concurrent sources of affective signals that routinely accompany our sight of a facial expression, the body is by far the most obvious and immediate one. We review recent evidence for this perceptual effect and follow with a discussion of possible mechanisms underlying body context effects.

Perception of facial expression is influenced by the bodily expressions

Research on the simultaneous perception of faces and bodies is still sparse. Two behavioral studies directly investigated how our recognition of facial expressions is influenced by accompanying whole body expressions (Meeren et al., 2005; Van den Stock et al., 2007). Meeren et al. (2005) combined angry and fearful facial expressions with angry and fearful whole body expressions to create both congruent (fearful face on fearful body and angry face on angry body) and incongruent (fearful face on angry body and angry face on fearful body) realistically looking compound stimuli (see Figure 27.2). These were briefly (200 ms) presented one by one while the participants were instructed to categorize the emotion expressed by the face and ignore the body. The results showed that recognition of the facial expression was biased towards the emotion expressed by the body language, as reflected by both the accuracy and reaction time data. In a follow-up study, facial expressions that were morphed on a continuum between happy and fearful were once combined with a happy and once with a fearful whole body expression (Van den Stock et al., 2007). The resulting compound stimuli were presented one by one for 150ms, while the participants were instructed to categorize the emotion expressed by the face in a two-alternative forced choice paradigm (fear or happiness). Again, the ratings of the facial expressions were influenced towards the emotion expressed by the body and this influence was highest for facial expressions that were most ambiguous (expressions that occupied an intermediate position on the morph continuum). Evidence from EEG-recordings during the experiment shows that the brain responds to the emotional face-body incongruency as early as 115 ms poststimulus onset (Meeren et al., 2005).

The reverse issue, whether perception of bodily expressions is influenced by facial expression has not been studied so far. However, natural synergies between facial and bodily expressions predict emotional spill over between the face and the body as exists between the facial expression and the voice (de Gelder and Bertelson, 2003).

Possible mechanisms underlying body context effect

A few different explanations are suggested by body context effect. First, one may view these effects as providing support for a thesis that has a long history in research on facial expressions and states that facial expressions seen on their own are inherently ambiguous (Frijda, 1986). A different approach may be that emotions are intimately linked to action preparation and that action information is provided much more specifically by bodily than by facial expressions. A third consideration is that there may be considerable overlap between the neurofunctional basis of facial and bodily expressions such that showing either the face or the body also automatically triggers representation of the other.

Facial expressions may be inherently ambiguous

Does the strong impact of bodily expressions on judging facial expressions provide evidence for drawing the more radical conclusion that judgments of facial expressions are entirely context sensitive? Some recent studies have indeed suggested so. Adopting our methodology Aviezer et al. (2008) used disgust pictures with an average recognition of 65.6% in combination with contrasting upper body postures and contextual object cues like dirty underpants. Such low recognition rate does in fact provide a large margin for external influences on the face. Indeed, their results show that disgust faces are no longer viewed as expressing disgust when perceived with an incongruent body. This result is consistent with what has been known for a long time that the effect of the secondary information is the biggest where recognition rates of the primary stimulus are poorest (Massaro and Egan, 1996). It doesn't seem that this study provides good evidence that

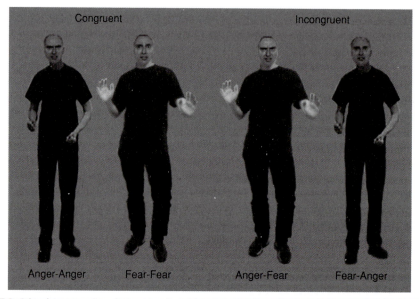

Fig. 27.2 Stimulus examples of congruent and incongruent face–body compounds (Meeren et al., 2005).

judgments of facial expressions are *entirely* malleable, since the effects it shows are for facial expressions that are rather ambiguous when they are viewed on their own.

Aviezer et al. (2008) rightly remark that a crucial issue is whether the context effects are postperceptual rather than truly perceptual (de Gelder and Bertelson, 2003). Their experiments unfortunately do not allow a conclusion one way or the other. They did not use rapid presentation or masking, the two classical means of exercising strategic control over the perceptual process. In all experiments they used untimed presentation with free exploration of the compound stimulus which allows the viewer to attend to the face and the body and ultimately to choose what information to base the response on, either on an ad hoc basis or also possibly depending on the particular emotion combination. The eye movement data they recorded do not settle the issue of rapid perceptual procedures in the observer. The eye movements effect they report cannot be deemed to reflect an underlying fast or rapid process, as the fixation latencies to enter either the upper or lower face area are on average around 1000 ms. In view of the fact that the latency to make a saccade is around 150 to 200 ms the reported latencies are very long indeed. Moreover, comparing their saccade latency values with RTs reported in Meeren et al. (2005) shows that on average RTs are about 200 ms faster and even more for the congruent conditions. This is remarkable since RTs are by definition a slower measure than saccades (Bannerman et al., 2009). The findings indicate that the long eye gaze latencies reflect gaze fixation under voluntary-attentional control. Participants look at the compound stimulus and as we have shown, rapidly (in EEG time at the P1, which is in the window around 100 ms) realizing the oddity of the compound stimulus and then explore and reassess the facial expression intentionally and apply a verbal label.

In fact, it is easy to imagine the opposite situation where the bodily expression completely loses its categorical identity in favor of the facial expression. In view of our limited understanding of what the critical components of bodily expressions are, it is currently still difficult to create stimuli where the specific information from body and face is well balanced such that what each contributes can reliably be compared. More importantly, the relative predominance of the face vs. the body when both are present and are equally attended to may very well depend on the specific emotion. This is already suggested by data from eye movement studies indicating that observers' fixation behavior during perception of bodily expressions is also a function of the emotion displayed. During perception of joy the observers tend to fixate on the head region, whereas during anger and fear most attention is devoted to the hands and arms. For sadness the subjects fixate on heads, arms, and hands, whereas the legs almost never attract the subjects' attention. This fixation behavior is emotion-specific and remains stable under different conditions: whether the subjects were asked to recognize the body postures or were just watching; for both incorrectly and correctly recognized emotions; for pictures with different response times; and during the time progression of the experiment (perceptual learning) (Ousov-Fridin et al., submitted).

One explanation may be provided by comparing the physical characteristic of different facial expressions. Components of different facial expressions may resemble each other, for example, upturned corners of the mouth characterize both smile and pain expressions. An example of this strategy is provided by the study just discussed. The role of the context would then be to glue the components together in the configuration reflecting the information from the context. But such a view prima facie goes against the notion that facial expressions are perceived configurally, and is difficult to combine with ERP data indicating that they are processed rapidly.

Emotional expressions involve the whole body in action

Bodiless heads are incomplete visual stimuli just as headless bodies are. To us the body to face context effect primarily suggests not that facial expressions are vague, imprecise or noisy, but that there is a very close link between both. An important aspect to consider when trying to explain that bodily postures influence the expression recognized on a face is provided by recent findings of overarching similarity in the perceptual (configural processing) (Reed et al., 2003) and neurofunctional (spatial and temporal overlap as shown in fMRI, EEG, and MEG) signature of facial and bodily expressions (Meeren et al., 2008; Stekelenburg and de Gelder, 2004; van de Riet et al., 2009). This suggests that faces as well as bodies can rapidly convey the same message and do so in very similar ways. The brain mentally completes the headless body or the bodiless head. This can obviously not be based on missing physical information as would for example be the case when only part of the face was shown or one component was missing. What triggers the brain's filling in may be, in the case of emotional body postures, the adaptive action the person is engaged in.

From a Darwinian evolutionary perspective, emotions are closely related to actions and therefore likely to involve the whole body rather than only the facial expressions. One view is that emotion provoking stimuli trigger affect programs (Darwin, 1872; Frijda, 1986; Panksepp, 1998; Russell and Feldman Barrett, 1999; Tomkins, 1963), which produce an ongoing stream of neurophysiologic change (or change in a person's homeostatic state) and are associated with evolutionary-tuned behaviors for dealing with stimuli of significant value. Along with the orbitofrontal cortex (OFC) and amygdala, the insula and somatosensory cortex are involved in the modulation of emotional reactions involving the body via connections to brain stem structures (Damasio, 1994, 1999; LeDoux, 1996). This function of the insula and somatosensory cortex may contribute to their important role in emotion perception.

Facial and bodily expressions share largely overlapping neurofunctional basis

Do the results just mentioned indicate that activation to facial expressions and to bodily expressions will almost always show complete overlap? As a matter of fact there is hardly any evidence in the literature to answer this question. For this reason we designed an fMRI study to investigate whether the brain shows distinctive activation patterns for perception of faces and bodies. We presented pictures of faces and faceless bodies that either showed a neutral, fearful or happy expression and asked participants to categorize the emotion expressed by the stimulus. To untangle brain activation related to faces and bodies, we compared how the brain responds to both categories (irrespective of emotional expression). Surprisingly, the results showed that the middle part of the fusiform gyrus (FG) that is typically associated with the perception of facial identity, is more activated for bodies than for faces (van de Riet et al., 2009). Previous studies have shown that there was at least partial overlap between the face-selective and body selective region within the FG (Hadjikhani and de Gelder, 2003; Peelen and Downing, 2005), and van de Riet et al. (2009) were the first to directly compare face and body related activation. In fact, perception of whole body expressions elicited a wider network of brain areas compared to faces, including other areas previously associated with perception of facial expressions, like STS. Other brain regions that were more active for bodies than for faces included the middle temporal/middle occipital gyrus (the so called extra-striate body area, EBA (Downing et al., 2001), the superior occipital gyrus and the parieto-occipital sulcus. When we consider more specifically the emotional information conveyed by the bodies and faces, again we observed a wider activation pattern specific for emotional bodies than for emotional faces. Interestingly, emotional body expressions activate cortical and subcortical motor areas like caudate nucleus, putamen and inferior frontal gyrus (IFG). This motor related activation may reflect the adaptive action component implied in the body expression, which is less pronounced in facial expressions (de Gelder et al., 2004a).

Since we used static images in this study, one may argue that the activity in areas associated with movement is related to the fact that there is more implied motion in the body expressions, compared to facial expressions. We therefore performed a follow up study in which we presented video clips of dynamic facial and bodily expressions that conveyed a neutral, fearful or angry expression instead of static picture stimuli. The results went in the same direction: bodies compared to faces activated more areas than vice versa, including the FG. Again, motor related areas were more activated by emotional body expressions (Kret et al., 2011).

Taken together these findings support the conclusion that bodily expressions activate a wider network of brain areas, including motor and action related regions.

Facial and bodily expressions in the context of scenes

When observing a stimulus that consists of a face and body with congruent expression (for example a fearful face on a fearful body) one expects that recognition will be close to 100% correct. But this is not necessarily the case. In fact, perception and recognition of an emotional action is also influenced by the particular setting or scene in which it occurs. For example, viewed in isolation the sprint to the finish of a man shaking off a competitor looks quite similar to the flight of a man running away from a robber holding a knife. Without the context information, the emotional valence may still be ambiguous. Faces and bodies routinely appear as part of natural scenes and our perceptual system seems to be wired to make the link between the expression and the environment in which it appears to us. But little is known about the mechanism underlying this. Appraisal theories of emotion (e.g. Scherer et al., 2001) acknowledge the importance of a visual event for our interpretation and evaluation of it and propose explanations for how we emotionally react to it. However, the primary focus in appraisal theories regards the emotional response of the observer to a stimulus, rather than the mere perception of the stimulus.

Hierarchical perception models tend to locate the possible effects of a scene context at a semantic level which occurs relatively late and takes place in relatively middle to high cognitive levels of processing (Bar, 2004). However, there is evidence that supports an early perceptual and neuroanatomical analysis of a scene. Tachitoscopic presentation of a scene contributes to subsequent processing of the spatial relations across the scene (Sanocki, 2003), and the rapid extraction of the gist of a scene may be based on low spatial frequency coding (Oliva and Schyns, 1997). The more semantic effects of scene processing occur at a later stage, around 400 ms after stimulus onset. For example, objects presented in their usual context are identified better (Davenport and Potter, 2004) and faster (Ganis and Kutas, 2003) and EEG data show the interaction occurs at about 390 ms after stimulus-onset. The functional neuroanatomy of contextual associations of objects comprises a network including parahippocampal cortex (PHC), retrosplenial cortex, and superior orbital sulcus (Bar, 2004).

However, the effects of the emotional gist of a scene may occur at an earlier level, in line with the evolutionary significance of the information. Few experimental studies currently exist on the influence of emotional scenes on the perception of faces and bodies. In the first explorations of this issue, we presented fearful, disgusted and happy faces embedded in a natural scene (see Figure 27.3 for an example). The affective valence of the scene was either fearful, disgusted or happy, and the face-scene combinations were emotionally congruent (e.g. fearful face in fearful scene) or incongruent (e.g. fearful face in happy scene). Participants were required to categorize the emotion expressed by the face. The results revealed faster response times and higher accuracies for the congruent stimulus pairs, showing that the emotional expression of a face is recognized better when it is embedded in a congruent scene (Righart and de Gelder, 2008b). The context effects hold up under different attentional conditions: it can be observed when participants are explicitly decoding the emotional expression of the face (Righart and de Gelder, 2008a) but also when they are primarily focused on the orientation of the face (Righart and de Gelder, 2006).

Fig. 27.3 Stimulus examples of congruent and incongruent face–scene compounds (Righart and de Gelder, 2008b).

This indicates that it reflects an early and mandatory process and suggests a perceptual basis. Our EEG studies support this view: when fearful faces are presented in a fearful scene, EEG recordings show a higher N170 amplitude compared to when the same faces are presented in a neutral scene (Righart and de Gelder, 2006).

To investigate how the emotion conveyed by scenes influences brain activity associated with perception of faces we used fMRI while subjects were shown neutral and fearful faces in both neutral and emotional scenes. We ran a parallel version of the experiment with neutral and fearful bodies instead of faces. The results showed that the activation level in FFA is modulated by the kind of scene in which it is presented. In particular, fearful faces elicit more activity than neutral faces, but more interestingly, fearful faces in threatening scenes trigger more activity than fearful faces in neutral scenes. Also, activity in body areas, like the extrastriate body area (EBA) (Downing et al., 2001) is influenced by the scene in which it is embedded: overall, fearful bodies trigger more activity than neutral bodies, but interestingly, neutral bodies in threatening scenes trigger more activity than neutral bodies in neutral scenes. On the other hand, the presence of a face or a body influences brain activity in areas that are associated with the processing of scenes, like the retrosplenial complex (RSC) and the parahippocampal cortex (PHC). In a behavioral experiment we presented participants with stimuli depicting an emotional body seen in the foreground against an emotionally congruent or incongruent background. Participants were instructed to categorize the emotion expressed by the foreground body and the results showed that especially negative emotions (fear and anger) were recognized faster in a congruent background, whereas this was not the case for happy expressions (Kret and de Gelder, 2010).

These findings suggest that the emotion conveyed by the scene "spills over" to the embedded face or body, and vice versa. Stated simply, a fearful face makes a neutral scene appear threatening, while a threatening scene makes a neutral face fearful.

Facial expressions in the context of the affective prosody of voices

Research focusing on human face and emotion perception has primarily targeted how visual stimuli are perceived, although in daily life facial expressions are typically accompanied by vocal expressions.

Human emotion recognition can be based on isolated facial or vocal cues (Banse and Scherer, 1996; Scherer et al., 1991) but combining both modalities results in a performance increase as shown by both increased accuracy rates and shorter response latencies (Gelder and Vroomen, 2000; de Gelder et al., 1999a, 1995; Dolan et al., 2001; Massaro and Egan, 1996). Detailed behavioral investigations into crossmodal influences between vocal and facial cues requires a paradigm in which both modalities are combined to create audiovisual pairs. The manipulation ideally consists of altering both the emotional congruency between the two modalities and a task that consists of emotion categorization based on only one of both information streams. For example, de Gelder and Vroomen (2000) presented facial expressions that were morphed on a continuum between happy and sad while at the same time a short spoken sentence was presented. This sentence had a neutral semantic meaning, but was spoken in either a happy or sad emotional tone of voice. Participants were instructed to attend to and categorize the face and ignore the voice in a two-alternative forced choice task. The results showed a clear influence of the task irrelevant auditory modality on the target visual modality. For example, sad faces were less frequently categorized as sad when they were accompanied by a happy voice. In a follow-up experiment, vocal expressions were morphed on a fear-happy continuum and presented with either a fearful or happy face, while participants were instructed to categorize the vocal expression. Again, the task irrelevant modality (facial expressions) influenced the emotional categorization of the target modality (vocal expressions). Furthermore, this experiment was repeated under different attentional demands, but the facial expression influenced the categorization of vocal expression in every attentional condition (Vroomen et al., 2001).

These findings suggest that affective multisensory integration is a mandatory and automatic process. However, based on these behavioral data, no direct claims can be made about the nature of this crossmodal bias effect. The findings could either reflect an early perceptual or later more cognitive or decisional effect. Neuroimaging methods with high temporal resolution are needed to provide information on the time course of when this bimodal crosstalk occurs. Studies addressing neural substrates of vocal expressions are few (de Gelder et al., 2004b; George et al., 1996; Ross, 2000) and primarily point to involvement of the right hemisphere. EEG investigations show that recognition of emotional prosody occurs already within the first 100 to 150 ms of stimulus presentation (Bostanov and Kotchoubey, 2004; de Gelder et al., 1999a; Goydke et al., 2004). The possibility that ecologically relevant audiovisual expressions may rely on specialized neural mechanisms has long been recognized in animal research and several studies have explored the relation between auditory and visual processing streams in non-human primate communication (Ghazanfar and Santos, 2004; Parr, 2004).

EEG studies addressing the timecourse of audiovisual integration point to an early integration of both modalities (around 110 ms after stimulus presentation) (de Gelder et al., 1999a; Pourtois et al., 2000), which is compatible with a perceptual effect. Supporting evidence for a mandatory nature of this integration is provided by studies with blindsight patients, who are unable, due to cortical damage, to consciously perceive visual stimuli presented in a segment of the visual field. When they are presented with auditory vocal expressions and at the same time visual facial expressions in their blind field, fMRI and EEG recordings are influenced by the facial expression of which they are unaware. This shows that the unconscious emotional information displayed by the face is processed by alternative brain pathways through which it influenced the brain responses to the consciously perceived vocal expressions.

Another question concerns where in the brain the integration of perceived vocal and facial expressions takes place. Heteromodal cortex is a logical candidate for multisensory integration (Mesulam, 1998). STS (Barraclough et al., 2005) and ventral premotor cortex (Kohler et al., 2002) have been shown to be involved in multisensory integration of biological stimuli. Functional imaging studies addressing the combined perception of emotional face-voice pairs (Dolan et al., 2001; Ethofer et al., 2006) show that fearful faces simultaneously presented with fearful voices activate the left amygdala. The role of the amygdala in emotional and face processing is well established (Zald, 2003) and connectivity data show that it receives inputs from both auditory and visual cortices (McDonald, 1998). These findings make this brain structure an important location for integration of affective bimodal inputs.

Recent studies have shown that next to facial expressions, bodily expressions are also prone to crossmodal affective influences. For example, recognition of dynamic whole body expressions of emotion are influenced not only by both human and animal vocalizations (Van den Stock et al., 2008a), but also by instrumental music (Van den Stock et al., 2009), suggesting the brain is well organized to combine affective information from different sensory channels.

Summary and conclusions

Real faces are part and parcel of their context and this consideration must play an important role in future models of face processing. Recent data show that bodily expressions, affective prosody, as well as the emotional gist of a natural scene all influence the recognition of facial expression. When a face is accompanied by a body or voice expressing the same emotion, or when it is presented in a congruent emotional scene, the recognition of facial expression typically improves, i.e. both the judgment accuracy and speed increase. Hence, both the immediate visual and auditory contexts function to disambiguate the signals of facial expression. Our behavioral and electrophysiological data suggest that this perceptual integration of information does not require high-level semantic analysis occurring relatively late at higher cognitive centers. Instead, the integration appears to be an automatic and mandatory process, which takes place very early in the processing stream, before full structural encoding of the stimulus and conscious awareness of the emotional expression are fully elaborated.

References

Adolphs, R. (2002). Neural systems for recognizing emotion. *Current Opinion in Neurobiology*, **12**, 169–177.

Adolphs, R., Damasio, H., Tranel, D., Cooper, G., and Damasio, A.R. (2000). A role for somatosensory cortices in the visual recognition of emotion as revealed by three-dimensional lesion mapping. *Journal of Neuroscience*, **20**, 2683–2690.

Amaral, D.G. and Price, J.L. (1984). Amygdalo-cortical projections in the monkey (Macaca fascicularis). *Journal of Comparative Neurology*, **230**, 465–496.

Andino, S.L., Menendez, R.G., Khateb, A., Landis, T., and Pegna, A.J. (2009). Electrophysiological correlates of affective blindsight. *Neuroimage*, **44**, 581–589.

Aviezer, H., Hassin, R.R., Ryan, J., *et al.* (2008). Angry, disgusted, or afraid? Studies on the malleability of emotion perception. *Psychological Science*, **19**, 724–732.

Bannerman, R.L., Milders, M., de Gelder, B., and Sahraie, A. (2009). Orienting to threat: faster localization of fearful facial expressions and body postures revealed by saccadic eye movements. *Proceedings of the Royal Society B*, **276**, 1635–1641.

Banse, R. and Scherer, K.R. (1996). Acoustic profiles in vocal emotion expression. *Journal of Personality and Social Psychology*, **70**, 614–636.

Bar, M. (2004). Visual objects in context. *Nature Review Neuroscience*, **5**, 617–629.

Barraclough, N.E., Xiao, D., Baker, C.I., Oram, M.W., and Perrett, D.I. (2005). Integration of visual and auditory information by superior temporal sulcus neurons responsive to the sight of actions. *Journal of Cognitive Neuroscience*, **17**, 377–391.

Bodamer, J. (1947). Die prosop-Agnosie. *Archiv fur Psychiatrie und Nervenkrankheiten*, **179**, 6–53.

Bostanov, V. and Kotchoubey, B. (2004). Recognition of affective prosody: continuous wavelet measures of event-related brain potentials to emotional exclamations. *Psychophysiology*, **41**, 259–268.

Carmichael, S.T. and Price, J.L. (1995). Limbic connections of the orbital and medial prefrontal cortex in macaque monkeys. *Journal of Comparative Neurology*, **363**, 615–641.

Catani, M., Jones, D.K., Donato, R., and Ffytche, D.H. (2003). Occipito-temporal connections in the human brain. *Brain*, **126**, 2093–2107.

Damasio, A.R. (1994). *Descartes' Error: Emotion, Reason, and the Human Brain*. New York, Grosset/Putnam.

Damasio, A.R. (1999). *The Feeling of What Happens*. New York: Harcourt Brace.

Darwin, C. (1872). *The expression of the emotions in man and animals*. London: John Murray.

Davenport, J.L. and Potter, M.C. (2004). Scene consistency in object and background perception. *Psychological Science*, **15**, 559–564.

de Gelder, B. (2006). Towards the neurobiology of emotional body language. *Nature Reviews Neuroscience*, 7, 242–249.

de Gelder, B. and Bertelson, P. (2003). Multisensory integration, perception and ecological validity. *Trends in Cognitive Science*, **7**, 460–467.

de Gelder, B. and Rouw, R. (2000). Configural face processes in acquired and developmental prosopagnosia: evidence for two separate face systems? *Neuroreport*, **11**, 3145–3150.

de Gelder, B. and Tamietto, M. (2007). Affective blindsight. *Scholarpedia*, **2**, 3555.

de Gelder, B. and Vroomen, J. (2000). The perception of emotions by ear and by eye. *Cognition and Emotion*, **14**, 289–311.

de Gelder, B., Vroomen, J., and Teunisse, J.P. (1995). Hearing smiles and seeing cries. The bimodal perception of emotion. *Bulletin of the Psychonomic Society*, **29**, 309.

de Gelder, B., Bocker, K.B., Tuomainen, J., Hensen, M., and Vroomen, J. (1999a). The combined perception of emotion from voice and face: early interaction revealed by human electric brain responses. *Neurosci Letters*, **260**, 133–136.

de Gelder, B., Vroomen, J., Pourtois, G., and Weiskrantz, L. (1999b). Non-conscious recognition of affect in the absence of striate cortex. *Neuroreport*, **10**, 3759–3763.

de Gelder, B., Pourtois, G., van Raamsdonk, M., Vroomen, J., and Weiskrantz, L. (2001). Unseen stimuli modulate conscious visual experience: evidence from inter-hemispheric summation. *Neuroreport*, **12**, 385–391.

de Gelder, B., Frissen, I., Barton, J., and Hadjikhani, N. (2003). A modulatory role for facial expressions in prosopagnosia. *Proceedings of the National Academy of Sciences U S A*, **100**, 13105–13110.

de Gelder, B., Snyder, J., Greve, D., Gerard, G., and Hadjikhani, N. (2004a). Fear fosters flight: A mechanism for fear contagion when perceiving emotion expressed by a whole body. *Proceedings of the National Academy of Sciences U S A*, **101**, 16701–16706.

de Gelder, B., Vroomen, J., and Pourtois, G. (2004b). Multisensory perception of emotion, its time course and its neural basis. In G. Calvert, C. Spence, and B.E. Stein (eds.) *Handbook of multisensory processes*. Cambridge, MA: MIT Press.

de Gelder, B., Meeren, H.K., Righart, R., Van den Stock, J., van de Riet, W.A.C., and Tamietto, M. (2006). Beyond the face: exploring rapid influences of context on face processing. *Progress in Brain Research*, **155**, 37–48.

de Gelder, B., Tamietto, M., van Boxtel, G., *et al.* (2008). Intact navigation skills after bilateral loss of striate cortex. *Current Biology*, **18**, R1128–R1129.

de Gelder, B., Van den Stock, J., Meeren, H.K., Sinke, C.B., Kret, M.E., and Tamietto, M. (2010). Standing up for the body. Recent progress in uncovering the networks involved in processing bodies and bodily expressions. *Neuroscience and Biobehavioral Reviews*, **34**, 513–527.

Dolan, R.J., Morris, J.S., and de Gelder, B. (2001). Crossmodal binding of fear in voice and face. *Proceedings of the National Academy of Sciences U S A*, **98**, 10006–10010.

Downing, P.E., Jiang, Y., Shuman, M., and Kanwisher, N. (2001). A cortical area selective for visual processing of the human body. *Science*, **293**, 2470–3.

Ethofer, T., Anders, S., Erb, M., *et al.* (2006). Impact of voice on emotional judgment of faces: an event-related fMRI study. *Human Brain Mapingp*, **27**, 707–714.

Fernberger, S.W. (1928). False suggestion and the Piderit model. *American Journal of Psychology*, **40**, 562–568.

Fodor, J. (1983). *The Modularity of Mind.* Cambridge, MA: MIT Press.

Frijda, N.H. (1986). *The emotions.* Cambridge: Cambridge University Press.

Ganis, G. and Kutas, M. (2003). An electrophysiological study of scene effects on object identification. *Brain Research. Cognitive Brain Research,* **16**, 123–144.

George, M.S., Parekh, P.I., Rosinsky, N., *et al.* (1996). Understanding emotional prosody activates right hemisphere regions. *Archives of Neurology,* **53**, 665–670.

Ghazanfar, A.A. and Santos, L.R. (2004). Primate brains in the wild: the sensory bases for social interactions. *Nature Reviews Neuroscience,* **5**, 603–616.

Goydke, K.N., Altenmuller, E., Moller, J., and Munte, T.F. (2004). Changes in emotional tone and instrumental timbre are reflected by the mismatch negativity. *Brain Research. Cognitive Brain Research,* **21**, 351–359.

Hadjikhani, N. and de Gelder, B. (2003). Seeing fearful body expressions activates the fusiform cortex and amygdala. *Current Biology,* **13**, 2201–2205.

Haxby, J.V., Hoffman, E.A., and Gobbini, M.I. (2000). The distributed human neural system for face perception. *Trends in Cognitive Sciences,* **4**, 223–233.

Haxby, J.V., Horwitz, B., Ungerleider, L.G., Maisog, J.M., Pietrini, P., and Grady, C.L. (1994). The functional organization of human extrastriate cortex: a PET-rCBF study of selective attention to faces and locations. *Journal of Neuroscience,* **14**, 6336–6353.

Haxby, J.V., Ungerleider, L.G., Horwitz, B., Maisog, J.M., Rapoport, S.I., and Grady, C.L. (1996). Face encoding and recognition in the human brain. *Proceedings of the National Academy of Sciences U S A,* **93**, 922–927.

Hoffman, E.A. and Haxby, J.V. (2000). Distinct representations of eye gaze and identity in the distributed human neural system for face perception. *Nature Neuroscience,* **3**, 80–84.

Iidaka, T., Omori, M., Murata, T., *et al.* (2001). Neural interaction of the amygdala with the prefrontal and temporal cortices in the processing of facial expressions as revealed by fMRI. *Journal of Cognitive Neuroscience,* **13**, 1035–1047.

Kanwisher, N., McDermott, J., and Chun, M.M. (1997). The fusiform face area: a module in human extrastriate cortex specialized for face perception. *Journal of Neuroscience,* **17**, 4302–4311.

Kohler, E., Keysers, C., Umilta, M.A., Fogassi, L., Gallese, V., and Rizzolatti, G. (2002). Hearing sounds, understanding actions: action representation in mirror neurons. *Science,* **297**, 846–848.

Kret, M.E. and de Gelder, B. (2010). Social context influences recognition of bodily expressions. *Experimental Brain Research,* **203**, 169–180.

Kret, M.E., Pichon, S., Grezes, J., and de Gelder, B. (2011). Similarities and differences in perceiving threat from dynamic faces and bodies. An fMRI study. *NeuroImage,* **54**, 1755–1762.

LeDoux, J.E. (1996). *The emotional brain: The mysterious underpinnings of emotional life.* New York: Simon and Schuster.

Massaro, D.W. and Egan, P.B. (1996). Perceiving affect from the voice and the face. *Psychonomic Bulletin and Review,* **3**, 215–221.

McDonald, A.J. (1998). Cortical pathways to the mammalian amygdala. *Progress in Neurobiology,* **55**, 257–332.

McKone, E. and Yovel, G. (2009). Why does picture-plane inversion sometimes dissociate perception of features and spacing in faces, and sometimes not? Towards a new theory of holistic processing. *Psychonic Bulletin & Review,* 16, 778–797.

Meeren, H.K., van Heijnsbergen, C.C., and de Gelder, B. (2005). Rapid perceptual integration of facial expression and emotional body language. *Proceedings of the National Academy of Sciences U S A,* **102**, 16518–16523.

Meeren, H.K., Hadjikhani, N., Ahlfors, S.P., Hamalainen, M.S., and de Gelder, B. (2008). Early category-specific cortical activation revealed by visual stimulus inversion. *PLoS ONE,* **3**, e3503.

Mesulam, M.M. (1998). From sensation to cognition. *Brain,* **121**, 1013–1052.

Morris, J.S., Friston, K.J., Buchel, C., *et al.* (1998a). A neuromodulatory role for the human amygdala in processing emotional facial expressions. *Brain*, **121**, 47–57.

Morris, J.S., Ohman, A., and Dolan, R.J. (1998b). Conscious and unconscious emotional learning in the human amygdala. *Nature*, **393**, 467–470.

Morris, J.S., de Gelder, B., Weiskrantz, L., and Dolan, R.J. (2001). Differential extrageniculostriate and amygdala responses to presentation of emotional faces in a cortically blind field. *Brain*, **124**, 1241–1252.

Oliva, A. and Schyns, P.G. (1997). Coarse blobs or fine edges? Evidence that information diagnosticity changes the perception of complex visual stimuli. *Cognitive Psychology*, **34**, 72–107.

Panksepp, J. (1998). *Affective neuroscience: The foundation of human and animal emotions*, New York: Oxford University Press.

Parr, L.A. (2004). Perceptual biases for multimodal cues in chimpanzee (Pan troglodytes) affect recognition. *Anim Cogn*, **7**, 171–178.

Peelen, M.V. and Downing, P.E. (2005). Selectivity for the human body in the fusiform gyrus. *Journal of Neurophysiology*, **93**, 603–608.

Peelen, M.V. and Downing, P.E. (2007). The neural basis of visual body perception. *Nature Reviews Neuroscience*, **8**, 636–648.

Peelen, M.V., Lucas, N., Mayer, E., and Vuilleumier, P. (2009). Emotional attention in acquired prosopagnosia. *Social Cognitive and Affective Neuroscience*, **4**, 268–277.

Pegna, A.J., Khateb, A., Lazeyras, F., and Seghier, M.L. (2005). Discriminating emotional faces without primary visual cortices involves the right amygdala. *Nature Neuroscience*, **8**, 24–25.

Pourtois, G., de Gelder, B., Vroomen, J., Rossion, B., and Crommelinck, M. (2000). The time-course of intermodal binding between seeing and hearing affective information. *Neuroreport*, **11**, 1329–1333.

Puce, A., Allison, T., Asgari, M., Gore, J.C., and McCarthy, G. (1996). Differential sensitivity of human visual cortex to faces, letterstrings, and textures: a functional magnetic resonance imaging study. *Journal of Neuroscience*, **16**, 5205–5215.

Reed, C.L., Stone, V.E., Bozova, S., and Tanaka, J. (2003). The body-inversion effect. *Psychological Science*, **14**, 302–308.

Righart, R. and de Gelder, B. (2006). Context influences early perceptual analysis of faces—an electrophysiological study. *Cerebral Cortex*, **16**, 1249–1257.

Righart, R. and de Gelder, B. (2008a). Rapid influence of emotional scenes on encoding of facial expressions: an ERP study. *Social Cognitive and Affective Neuroscience*, **3**, 270–278.

Righart, R. and de Gelder, B. (2008b). Recognition of facial expressions is influenced by emotional scene gist. *Cognitive, Affective & Behavioral Neuroscience*, **8**, 264–272.

Ross, E.D. (2000). Affective prosody and the aprosodias. In M.M. Marsel (ed). *Principles of behavioral and cognitive neurology*, 2nd edn, pp. 316 331. Oxford: Oxford University Press.

Russell, J.A. and Feldman Barrett, L. (1999). Core affect, prototypical emotional episodes, and other things called emotion: dissecting the elephant. *Journal of Personality and Social Psychology*, **76**, 805–819.

Sanocki, T. (2003). Representation and perception of scenic layout. *Cognitive Psychology*, **47**, 43–86.

Scherer, K.R., Banse, R., Wallbott, H.G., and Goldbeck, T. (1991). Vocal cues in emotion encoding and decoding. *Motivation and Emotion*, **15**, 123–148.

Scherer, K.R., Shorr, A., and Johnstone, T. (2001). *Appraisal processes in emotion: theory, methods, research*. New York: Oxford University Press.

Stekelenburg, J.J. and de Gelder, B. (2004). The neural correlates of perceiving human bodies: an ERP study on the body-inversion effect. *Neuroreport*, **15**, 777–780.

Tamietto, M. and de Gelder, B. (2010). Neural bases of the non-conscious perception of emotional signals. *Nat Rev Neurosci*, **11**, 697–709.

Tamietto, M., Geminiani, G., Genero, R., and de Gelder, B. (2007). Seeing fearful body language overcomes attentional deficits in patients with neglect. *Journal of Cognitive Neuroscience*, **19**, 445–454.

Tomkins, S.S. (1963). *Affect, imagery consciousness: Vol. 2. The negative affects*. New York: Springer Verlag.

van de Riet, W.A., Grezes, J., and de Gelder, B. (2009). Specific and common brain regions involved in the perception of faces and bodies and the representation of their emotional expressions. *Social Neuroscience*, **4**, 101–120.

Van den Stock, J., Righart, R., and de Gelder, B. (2007). Body expressions influence recognition of emotions in the face and voice. *Emotion*, **7**, 487–494.

Van den Stock, J., Grezes, J., and de Gelder, B. (2008a). Human and animal sounds influence recognition of body language. *Brain Research*, **1242**, 185–190.

Van den Stock, J., van de Riet, W.A., Righart, R., and de Gelder, B. (2008b). Neural correlates of perceiving emotional faces and bodies in developmental prosopagnosia: an event-related fMRI-study. *PLoS ONE*, **3**, e3195.

Van den Stock, J., Peretz, I., Grèzes, J., and de Gelder, B. (2009). Instrumental music influences recognition of emotional body language. *Brain Topography*, **21**, 216–220.

Vroomen, J., Driver, J., and de Gelder, B. (2001). Is cross-modal integration of emotional expressions independent of attentional resources? *Cognitive, Affective & Behavioral Neuroscience*, **1**, 382–387.

Vuilleumier, P., Richardson, M.P., Armony, J.L., Driver, J., and Dolan, R.J. (2004). Distant influences of amygdala lesion on visual cortical activation during emotional face processing. *Nature Neuroscience*, **7**, 1271–1278.

Vuilleumier, P. and Schwartz, S. (2001). Emotional facial expressions capture attention. *Neurology*, **56**, 153–158.

Zald, D.H. (2003). The human amygdala and the emotional evaluation of sensory stimuli. *Brain Research Brain Research Reviews*, **41**, 88–123.

Chapter 28

The Impact of Social Gaze Perception on Attention

Steven P. Tipper and Andrew P. Bayliss

A preference for attending to the eyes of other people is measurable on the day that a human infant is born (Batki et al., 2000). Whether this is a general preference for high-contrast regions of their visual world, or a more selective preference for the eye region of caregivers, the baby is certainly engaging in an incredibly important behavior. Making eye contact can aid the formation of the bond between caregiver and neonate (e.g. Robson, 1967), and detecting that someone is making you the focus of their attention is important for engaging efficiently in social interactions. Later, following the eyes of other people, thereby engaging in triadic "joint attention" between people and the objects they look at, will contribute to the development of "Theory of Mind" (see Baron-Cohen, 1995; Charman, 2003). Once fluent in the "language of the eyes", we continue to place great importance upon this facet of social behavior. Friendships are placed in jeopardy if one "blanks" another. Fights might break out if someone overreacts when they detect their partner is receiving undue visual attention from a mating competitor. Ultimately, we modulate our interactions with people by inferring their mental state: where people look gives us a window into their mind.

This chapter reviews research into the attention mechanisms underlying a critical behavior in social interactions. When we orient our attention to the location or object to which another person is attending based on the social attention signals derived from that person, we establish a state of joint attention. The study of joint attention, and social attention in general, has traditionally been confined to social (e.g. Argyle and Cook, 1976; Kleinke, 1986) and developmental laboratories (e.g. Scaife and Bruner, 1975; Farroni et al., 2000; Leekham et al., 1998). The research we focus on here, however, is from laboratories that study attention in adult subjects. That attention researchers have recently become interested in the various modes of social attention reflects the burgeoning field of social neuroscience. We discuss findings from studies that investigate social gaze as a cue to attention, and consider the perceptual mechanisms that may underlie these effects and their possible social functions.

We begin the chapter with an overview of gaze perception, and the use of eye stimuli as cues to attention. There is still debate as to whether gaze stimuli are "special" in terms of the attention processes engaged. However, there is evidence for the distinctive nature of gaze cues in their involvement in other aspects of social perception such as person identity and emotional expression perception. Further, the sensitivity to another person's gaze direction varies across individuals within normal populations and in clinical populations, and these individual differences provide further insights in to the key role of gaze cues in social cognition.

Gaze perception

Highly specialized mechanisms allow us to detect the direction of another person's eye gaze. Current frameworks for understanding these mechanisms are reviewed elsewhere (e.g. Emery,

Fig. 28.1 Illustrating the morphological differences between the eye regions of chimpanzees and humans, enabling more efficient gaze perception in the latter species.

2000; Frischen et al., 2007a; Nummenmaa and Calder, 2009; also Pelphrey and Vander Wyk, Chapter 30, this volume), but we give a brief overview here. The "unique morphology" of the human eye region lends itself to a relatively simple calculation of angular deviation of the eyeball within the orbit (Kobayashi and Kohshima, 1997; see Figure 28.1). The human eye is wider, the iris smaller, and has a larger, brighter sclera relative to that of other mammals. Contrast reversal—presenting the sclera as dark and the iris as white—causes human observers to make dramatic errors in gaze direction determination (Ricciardelli et al., 2000). This finding demonstrates the reliance of the system on contrast information, although the geometry of the eye is also a factor (cf. Ando, 2002). Direct gaze captures and/or holds our attention (Senju and Hasegawa, 2005) and prolonged direct gaze increases autonomic responses (Nichols and Champness, 1971).

When we see someone suddenly look somewhere, we will often follow their gaze to the same location. Work in the last 10 years or so has demonstrated that rapid covert attention shifts may underlie joint attention (e.g. Friesen and Kingstone, 1998; see Figure 28.2 for (a) examples of stimuli used, and (b) the resultant joint attentive state). We aim to describe how the "gaze cueing" paradigm has advanced our understanding of how cognitive systems responsible for perceiving and responding to social stimuli interact with spatial attention.

The gaze cueing paradigm

In the late 1990s, several laboratories began studying the attentional impact of seeing an averted gaze cue. Previous studies of gaze-following had been generally confined to developmental laboratories using naturalistic settings to understand joint attention in early childhood. However, the aim of subsequent research was to describe and study the attentional mechanisms that give rise to this joint attention, taking advantage of the high degree of control over stimuli presentation dimensions available in cognitive labs, yet retaining a degree of ecological validity (see Kingstone et al., 2003).

The basic paradigm is an adapted Posner cueing task (e.g. Posner, 1980; see Figure 28.3 for an example of a gaze cueing procedure). In general, a face is presented gazing to the left or right. The participant is asked to respond to a subsequent target appearing on the left or right of the screen with a speeded button press. Usually, the gaze direction of the model is unpredictive of target location, so the participant is instructed to maintain central fixation and ignore the gaze cue. Friesen and Kingstone (1998) presented a cartoon face, with black dots appearing as pupils looking left or right. Driver and colleagues showed a photograph to adults (Driver et al., 1999) and a computer generated face to infants (Hood et al., 1998), while Hietanen (1999) and Langton and Bruce (1999) showed photographs of averted heads as gaze cues. All demonstrated faster reaction times to targets appearing where the eyes were looking than to targets in different, uncued locations. This

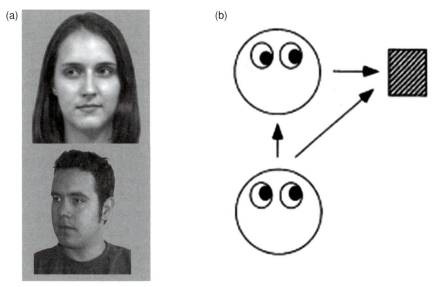

Fig. 28.2 Perceiving gaze cues, whether via averted gaze, or turned heads (a) results in a joint attentive state (b), whereby one individual attends an object based on the gaze signals of another individual who is looking at the same object. Adapted from Frischen, Bayliss and Tipper (2007a). *Psychological Bulletin*. Copyright © 2007 by the American Psychological Association. Adapted with permission.

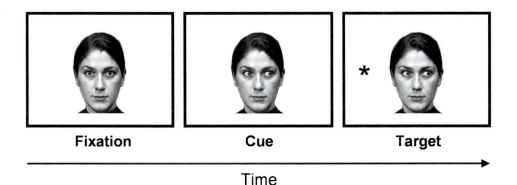

Fig. 28.3 An example of the displays shown to a participant on a computer screen in a gaze cueing experiment. Researchers have varied the manner of producing the gaze cue (horizontal vs. vertical looks; eyes move dynamically vs. sudden onset) the temporal dynamics of the displays (presence/absence of non-gazing face prior to cue onset; time between cue and target, "SOA"; offset of face prior to response) and participants' task (press a button to detect/localize/categorize target; look at target) in order to establish the attentional mechanisms underpinning joint attention. Stimuli from AR face database (Martinez and Benavente, 1998). Adapted from Frischen, Bayliss and Tipper (2007a). *Psychological Bulletin*. Copyright © 2007 by the American Psychological Association. Adapted with permission.

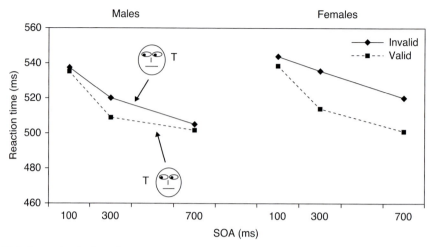

Fig. 28.4 Illustrative findings from a gaze cueing experiment. Dashed lines represent mean reaction times to categorize targets appearing at the gazed-at ("Valid") location, and are quicker than to targets appearing on the opposite side of the screen (solid lines, "Invalid" cues). Note that the "cueing effect" becomes stronger over time. Bayliss et al. (2005) found that the effect is markedly reduced in male subjects (left panel) by 700 ms after cue onset. However, female subjects are still consistently influenced by the cue at this longer SOA (right panel). This sex difference is discussed in the section on individual differences. From Sex Differences in Eye Gaze and Symbolic Cuing of Attention, *Quarterly Journal of Experimental Psychology, Section A* **58**.4 (2005) pp. 631–650. Taylor and Francis. Reprinted with permission of the publisher. http://www.informaworld.com.

difference in performance between congruent and incongruent trials is termed the "cueing effect", and is a classic marker of a shift of attention to the cued location (see Figure 28.4).

The development of this paradigm is clearly of interest to scholars investigating the nature of facial communication. However, there are many facets to the attention shift evoked by observed gaze shifts that also intrigue attention researchers. As it is important to integrate gaze cueing into previous attention research, the question as to whether the gaze cueing effect emerges as the result of an automatic shift of attention or through top-down voluntary control of orienting is a key issue (Posner, 1980; Corbetta and Shulman, 2002). This question is equally important to understanding joint attention, since a dominant view was that intentional attention sharing behavior emerged early reflecting a precursor to theory of mind (e.g. Baron-Cohen, 1995), while others suggested that low-level motion potentiated early reflex-like gaze following in infants (e.g. Moore and Corkum, 1994). Similarly, comparisons between the effects of gaze cues and other directional cues (e.g. arrows) challenge the uniqueness of gaze as a cue to attention and as a stimulus that interacts with other social cognitive mechanisms. Finally, placing gaze cueing in developmental and clinical contexts allows the field to test predictions borne out of research from social developmental theories and attention. We show that while clarity is yet to emerge on several key issues, the gaze cueing paradigm has yielded important information about the role of attention in social orienting.

Automatic or volitional orienting?

Do participants show facilitated processing of cued targets because they intentionally shift their attention to the looked-at location, that is endogenous, *controlled* orienting (Vecera and Rizzo,

2005); or because their attention system *reflexively* orients via exogenous processes to the looked-at location in an automatic manner (Stevens et al., 2008)? There are five features of gaze cues which appear to reflect properties of endogenous systems where processing is controlled and intentional. First, unlike exogenous/automatic shifts of attention, which can be fast (i.e. within 100 ms) gaze cued shifts of attention appeared to emerge relatively slowly (see Friesen and Kingstone, 1998; and Figure 28.4) consistent with volitional control (Jonides, 1981). Second, automatic exogenous shifts of attention are typically evoked by cues presented at the to-be-attended location, such as a flash of light in the periphery; whereas eye-gaze cues are central, and probably require a degree of higher-level processing to meaningfully derive the direction of gaze. Third, exogenous shifts of attention produce initial facilitation of processing at short intervals of around 100 ms, followed by a subsequent inhibition of processing at the cued location after 300 ms (i.e. Posner and Cohen, 1984: inhibition of return, IOR). Critically it initially appeared that gaze cues produce no evidence for subsequent IOR (e.g. Friesen and Kingstone, 2003b). Fourth, automatic exogenous shifts of attention appear to be mediated by the superior colliculus (Posner et al., 1985), whereas gaze cueing does not appear to be associated with this structure (e.g. Friesen and Kingstone, 2003a). Finally, endogenous voluntary control of attention is associated with a parieto-frontal system (e.g. Corbetta and Shulman, 2002). A patient, with damage to this system, described by Vecera and Rizzo (2005) failed to show gaze cueing attention shifts, suggesting top-down control over attention is necessary for gaze cueing.

Despite these initial observations, the overall balance of evidence would seem to support the opposite conclusion: That is, observing averted gaze triggers an automatic shift of attention, albeit with non-traditional characteristics. First, gaze cueing is observed even when the participants are motivated to orient away from gaze direction by being informed that the target will be presented at an uncued location on 80% of the trials (Driver et al., 1999; see also Friesen et al., 2004). The inability to prevent movement of attention when viewing a counter-predictive gaze shift argues against gaze cueing being a controlled voluntary process. Second, the assumption that gaze cued shifts of attention are slow has also been challenged. Hietenan and Leppanen (2003) produced significant gaze cueing effects within 14ms, suggesting that rapid automatic orienting is possible in some circumstances. Third, the subsequent inhibition (IOR) effect evoked by automatically evoked exogenous shifts of attention has now been demonstrated with gaze cues in optimized experimental designs (Frischen et al., 2007b; Frischen and Tipper, 2004). Finally, the neuropsychological data on gaze cueing is scarce, and there is a need for larger studies involving patients with difficulties with gaze perception.

Hence, the general features of the gaze cueing effect are that observing an averted gaze cue will produce an automatic, relatively long-lasting attention shift in the cued direction, independent of instruction. However, this automatic attention shift is derived from a cue that requires some processing more associated with "endogenous" orienting in order to convert the visual input into a spatial code (but see Vecera and Rizzo, 2005; Itier et al., 2007).

Gaze versus arrows

In everyday life, our attention is guided to peripheral events and objects by many types of cue. These can be biological, when someone uses declarative pointing to indicate the location of something interesting, or non-biological—an arrow on a roadsign, for example. In modern society, arrows are a common permanent proxy for a manual point or averted gaze, serving a social function by replacing a social cue. Nevertheless, they do not have the biological immediacy of a person pointing or looking. Perhaps one would therefore expect arrows to have weaker effects on attention. On the contrary, non-predictive arrows can have identical effects on attention as social gaze cues in terms of magnitude of impact on behavior (e.g. Tipples, 2002), individual differences (e.g. sex differences, Bayliss et al., 2005; Merritt et al., 2007) and even when placed in a rich social context (Bayliss and Tipper, 2005).

Although gaze and arrow cues appear to have similar effects, there are subtle differences that reflect the biological/social aspects of gaze cues. For example, participants find it easier to orient in the opposite direction of an arrow than a gaze cue (Friesen et al., 2004; see also Ristic et al., 2007; though see Tipples, 2008). The greater difficulty in disengaging attention from a gazed at location perhaps reflects the social nature of the cue. Furthermore, as we discuss later, arrow cues do not evoke the emotional responses that gaze cues do (e.g. Bayliss et al., 2006). Finally, evidence from split-brain patients suggests different neural mechanisms for gaze cueing (Kingstone et al., 2000) and arrow cueing (Ristic et al., 2002; Hietanen et al., 2006; Materna et al., 2008). The evidence therefore appears to support a role for a specialized system for analysing gaze direction (anterior superior temporal sulcus; Nummenmaa and Calder, 2009) sending inputs to a general attention system (inferior parietal sulcus; Materna et al., 2008). Other brain systems specifically involved in gaze may be engaged in parallel or subsequent to processing in these centers that give rise to the gaze effects on higher level social cognition that are absent with arrow cues are discussed elsewhere in this volume (Adolphs and Birmingham, Chapter 29; Pelphrey and Wyk, Chapter 30, this volume).

Gaze cueing and the oculomotor system

Joint attention can be established covertly where attention moves to a location without eye-movements, and in the above-cited examples, it is the covert attention shifts that have been studied. However, in natural scenarios, we move our attention about the world in concert with our fovea—that is, attention is shifted overtly with eye-movements. Certainly in the realm of social gaze, it is often necessary to overtly shift attention—to actually look, not just attend. This is how joint attention was classically measured in developmental set-ups (e.g. Scaife and Bruner, 1975). As well as the additional visual resolution attained by moving your eyes, this also gives your social partner the reciprocal indication that their original cue has been followed.[1] So what effects do gaze cues have on the oculomotor system?

Ricciardelli et al. (2002) showed that the preparation of a lateral eye movement, as instructed by a color cue, can be disrupted or facilitated by concurrently presented incongruent or congruent gaze, respectively. That is, if you plan an eye movement to the left, but see someone look right, then you will often accidentally look to the right, or at least be slower to execute your planned saccade (see also Kuhn and Kingstone, 2009). Mansfield et al. (2003) showed that even in the absence of a full overt eye movement, microsaccades are often elicited in the cued direction, suggesting that the oculomotor system represents the observed direction of gaze at an early stage and this leaks into the action system. Nummenmaa and Hietanen (2006) further investigated the influence of gaze cues on oculomotor planning by asking participants to make a vertically directed eye movement in the presence of an irrelevant horizontal gaze cue. They found that these vertical saccadic eye movements deviated from a straight path—curving away from the direction indicated by the gaze cue. This kind of effect had previously been shown following peripheral onset cueing (e.g. Sheliga et al., 1994; Tipper et al., 2001) and emerges due to the resolution of competition between saccade programs within neural population codes via lateral inhibition.

---

[1] This is a necessary condition for "shared attention"; note the subtle but important comparison with "joint attention"; the former occurs only where both protagonists are aware that each other is attending the same object, the latter however, does not require this level of understanding.

Recent neurophysiological work in macaques has uncovered neurons that appear to fulfill a functional definition of a saccadic "mirror neuron." Mirror neurons respond when an action is executed or observed being executed by another primate (di Pellegrino et al., 1992). Shepherd et al. (2009) showed cells in the inferior parietal lobe have similar response properties when observing averted gaze and when executing a gaze shift. However, further work is needed to determine the precise role of these neurons, as the activity of these cells may reflect spatial attention shifts in both cases. In another investigation looking into the overlap between gaze cueing and eye movements, Friesen and Kingstone (2003a) failed to find evidence for the "fixation offset effect", a classic property of the occulomotor system, in a gaze cueing paradigm. Normally, removal of the fixation cross in such tasks results in the release of the eye movement system, potentiating fast eye movements to peripheral locations. The lack of evidence for this fixation offset effect in a gaze perception paradigm may rule out a direct impact of gaze observation on at least the lower levels of the eye movement production system (i.e. the superior colliculus; see also Koval et al., 2005).

Hence it seems likely that the powerful nature of gaze cueing ensures fluent engagement of the eye movement system in response to observed averted gaze. However it is difficult to confirm that this is due to a direct effect of observed gaze on saccadic eye-movement control systems. Rather we suspect that this is likely an indirect effect via initial orienting of attention influencing subsequent saccade planning.

Face processing and gaze perception

The eyes are a crucial piece of the facial puzzle, so it is important to consider the impact that other processes relating to face perception may have on gaze processing—and vice versa. Do aspects of the face influence how effectively we can determine someone's direction of attention, and can they also affect the way we establish joint attention?

Head orientation

Very often, people must determine the direction of attention of a person whose head is not oriented directly towards them. For example, two cues to attention may directly oppose each other—the head may be pointing to the right, but the eyes are shifted to the left within the orbit. In this case, the direction of attention must be determined by combining the signals from the head and eye orientation to perceive the stimulus as "direct gaze"—someone is looking at you out of the corner of their eye. Furthermore there is evidence that the relationship between the body posture and head orientation must also be integrated. Perrett et al. (1992) provide a neural mechanism that explains how these three cues to attention are integrated and produce a percept that accurately depicts the direction of another's attention (see Langton et al., 2000; Pelphrey and Vander Wyk, Chapter 30, this volume, for reviews).

However, the system is vulnerable to interference between the multiple sources of information about social attention direction (Langton et al., 2000). The consequences for joint attention and gaze cueing are therefore of importance. One interesting finding of note here is that when a head is presented turned to the right or left, with the eyes gazing in a congruent direction (i.e. central within the orbit, hence looking in the same direction as the head is pointing), cueing in the direction of gaze is weaker than when the eyes are looking in an incongruent direction relative to head orientation (Hietanen, 1999). This could be because the latter is considered a more dynamic cue, implying an object has just captured the attention of the cueing face, and therefore could also be of immediate interest to the observer.

Bayliss and colleagues (Bayliss et al., 2004; Bayliss and Tipper, 2006a) were interested in how the global form of the face might influence the representation of gaze in the attention system. Previous work had suggested that inverting the face stimulus might disrupt accurate gaze perception (Jenkins and Langton, 2003; Schwaninger et al., 2005) and gaze cueing (Kingstone et al., 2000; Langton and Bruce, 1999; but see Tipples, 2005). That is, we don't efficiently establish joint attention with people if they are upside-down.

Bayliss and colleagues considered that this disruption of gaze cueing might reflect interactions between face- and spatial-centered frames of reference during face processing (e.g. Behrmann and Tipper, 1999). That is, because we rarely interact with upside-down faces, there is a natural tendency to process the face relative to its usual orientation and perhaps to assume that the face will shortly revert to the upright orientation. Consider the upside-down face in Figure 28.5a—if we represent inverted faces in a face-centered frame of reference, then the rightward gaze would simultaneously be represented as *leftward* gaze, disrupting gaze cueing due to the presence of two opposing directional signals. To test this, Bayliss et al. (2004) presented faces misoriented by 90 degrees (see Figure 28.5a). Here, the eyes in the face are looking up, but in a face-centered frame of reference, acting upon the canonical representation of an upright face, she is looking to the left. Bayliss et al. found that these stimuli caused shifts of attention both in the actual upward direction of gaze *and* in the leftward direction that the face would have been looking if it had appeared upright.

Hence, gaze perception is affected by global (Figure 28.5a) as well as local facial information (like contrast; Figure 28.5b). This tells us two things about gaze cueing. First, the representations of gaze direction are integrated with those of isomorphic face orientation prior to the execution of the attention shift, demonstrating that gaze direction is affording access to sophisticated mechanisms of face perception and spatial attention. Second, this sophistication comes with a puzzling cost since it demonstrates that orienting of attention via gaze can be executed to locations other than the currently looked-at location. This is at odds with one general aim of joint attention—to encourage orienting to the objects of another's gaze. Alternatively, it is possible that this effect emerges because the system predicts that a misoriented face will soon revert to the normal upright position.

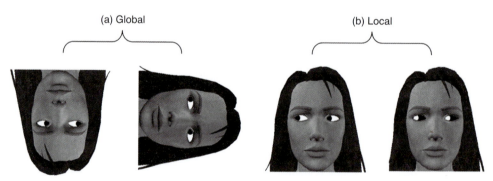

Fig. 28.5 Higher- and lower-order levels of facial processing influences gaze perception.
(a) Face perception may rely on configural processing of the global form, which is disrupted when isomorphically rotated. This may in turn affect gaze processing despite the fact that the local feature of interest—the eyes—are perfectly intact. (b) As discussed in the introduction, low-level features of the human eye make it easy to interpret gaze signals. This is demonstrated by contrast negation, which disrupts gaze processing despite the observer's knowledge that he/she is looking at a manipulated image.

In this way these data are in line with the idea that gaze cues contribute to predictions of the future actions and attentional states of another person (e.g. Pierno et al., 2006).

Facial identity

Many highly influential frameworks of face perception propose some degree of independence between the systems underlying the recognition of facial identity and the understanding of facial communication including emotion perception (Bruce and Young, 1986; Calder and Young, 2005) and eye gaze perception (Hoffman and Haxby, 2000). So, does the "gaze cueing" system know *who* does the cueing? While the gaze cueing effect appears to be operated by sophisticated attention mechanisms, initial work on this question suggested that it appears to be blind to the identity of the person acting as the cue. For example, Frischen and Tipper (2004) showed that orienting effects were of identical magnitude whether the same face was presented on 160 trials, or if a new face appeared on each and every trial of an experiment.

However, further work by Frischen and Tipper (2006) showed that gaze cues can be tied to the identity of the face, given appropriate circumstances. They presented a series of gaze cues (individuals looking either left or right) to participants, but unlike most studies, only presented targets alongside these faces on a few trials to ensure attention was maintained on the displays. Three minutes after viewing the faces in the gaze cueing trials they were presented again, this time looking straight ahead. Participants were required to detect or locate a peripheral target to the left or right (see Figure 28.6). Remarkably, despite the elapsed time, the attention-holding effect of direct gaze in the test display, the myriad intervening displays and multiple responses, reliable gaze cueing was measured in the direction that the face had *previously* looked. This was a quite specific effect being strongly lateralized (right hemisphere) and confined to famous faces. Both processing in the right hemisphere and famous faces can result in stronger memory representations, enabling retrieval of prior gaze states associated with each face (see also Deaner et al., 2007).

If gaze cueing subserves social cognitive functioning, then it would behove the system to track the reliability of different individuals' gaze cues over time. While people almost always look at the object that currently holds their interest, people are able to use their appreciation of the power of automatic joint attention to deceive others about their knowledge or intentions. For example, everyone knows that the last thing one should do when stuck in a long supermarket queue is to

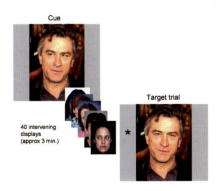

Cue

Target trial

40 intervening displays (approx 3 min.)

Fig. 28.6 Illustration of the adapted gaze cueing design implemented by Frischen and Tipper (2006). Participants did not respond to the initial presentation of (for example) Robert De Niro as (there was no target), but when he reappeared three minutes later, they were quicker to respond to a target if it appeared where he had initially looked. Hence, in some specific conditions we recall the attentional state of other people, and it can influence our social attention. From Long-term gaze cueing effects: Evidence for retrieval of prior states of attention from memory, Frischen and Tipper, *Visual Cognition*, 2006, Taylor and Francis. Reprinted by permission of the publisher (Taylor & Francis Group, http://www.informaworld.com).

look at the checkout assistant who appears to be opening a new desk, lest you alert other frustrated shoppers to the possibility of early escape from the purgatory of convenience retail. Instead, one looks elsewhere and monitors the situation peripherally until sure the checkout is indeed open before making your move. This is a familiar scenario, and certain individuals are even more expert at deception via gaze cues, successfully tricking people with their eyes time and again. For example, magicians use misdirection to great effect, and audience knowledge of certain deception usually does not diminish the illusion (see Kuhn and Land, 2006).

Bayliss and colleagues asked whether the record of an individual's joint attention history can be encoded by an observer (Bayliss and Tipper, 2006b; Bayliss et al., 2009). In a standard gaze cueing paradigm participants were required to categorize targets which were presented to the left and right. A range of faces with gaze oriented left and right were presented centrally and participants were informed that these were task-irrelevant. Each face appeared 12 times. However, critically, a subset of these faces always *looked at* the target (predictive, valid, and conforming to the social norm of looking at interesting things), while another subset of these faces always *looked away* from the target (counter-predictive, invalid, violating the social norm; see Figure 28.7).

The first finding of note was that the predictive nature of these gaze cues appeared to have no effect on attention, suggesting that while specific gaze cues may establish a memory trace (Frischen and Tipper, 2006), they do not influence the initial very rapid and automatic orienting of attention. Second, after 12 exposures to each face, when given a pair of faces containing one that had always looked at the target, and the other had always looked away, participants were more likely to choose the pro-predictive faces as being more trustworthy. Third, when asked which face they

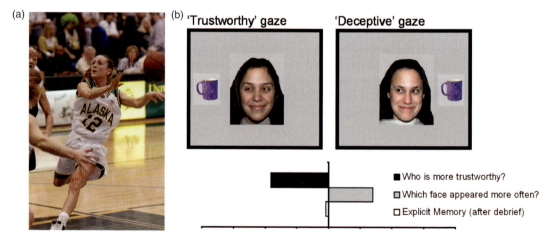

Fig. 28.7 (a) Gaze direction is such an effective cue that it can be easily used to deceive others of our knowledge or intentions, such as when employing the "no-look" pass in team ball games. (b) But using our eyes deceptively might have consequences. Bayliss et al. (2009) showed that people who consistently looked away from visual targets were perceived as less trustworthy than other faces who always looked at targets. The bar chart illustrates the relative bias in responses when asked the questions on the right. Deceptive faces were also committed to memory more fluently, since participants felt they had appeared more often, yet people were unable to notice the patterns of social gaze behavior. From Predictive gaze cues affect face evaluations: The effect of facial emotion, Bayliss, Griffiths, and Tipper, *European Journal of Cognitive Psychology*, 2009, Taylor and Francis. Reprinted by permission of the publisher (Taylor & Francis Group, http://www.informaworld.com).

felt appeared more often, they tended to choose the other individual—the one that always looked *away* from the target. This latter perceived frequency of occurrence bias may occur because it is important to commit the faces of deceptive individuals to memory in order to moderate future interactions with them. Finally however, even after a full debrief where the aims, procedure and contingencies were explained to participants, they were unable to identify which faces were responsible for helpful versus deceptive gaze cues, suggesting these effects are the result of implicit processes that are not available to conscious perception (Bayliss et al., 2009).

Emotion

Like gaze direction, facial expressions shed light on the mental states and likely future behavior of other people, making fluent recognition and interpretation of these signals of vital importance during social interactions. There is evidence that the perception of facial emotion and gaze direction influence one another. "Approach" emotions (e.g. anger) have been shown to be recognized quicker when the eyes of the face are directed straight ahead towards the viewer than when averted to the side. In contrast, "avoid" emotions (e.g. fear) are detected more rapidly when gaze is averted away from the viewer (Adams and Kleck, 2003). However, these findings have been questioned by Bindemann et al. (2008) who present multiple failures to replicate the effect, supporting more independence between emotion and gaze perception systems.

There have also been several investigations examining the opposite interaction, where facial emotion influences gaze cueing. It is somewhat surprising that the data thus far is perhaps more mixed than one would expect. In one study, Hietanen and Leppanen (2003) found no modulation of gaze cueing as a function of emotional expression, comparing neutral, happy, angry and fearful facial expressions. Similarly, Bayliss et al. (2007) demonstrated identical cueing effects for happy and disgusted faces. Further, Bonifacci et al. (2008) showed equivalent effects on overt orienting of gaze produced by angry and neutral faces, a result also described by Fox et al. (2002) with a covert orienting paradigm; similarly happy and neutral faces appear to produce equivalent cueing effects (Holmes, Richards and Green, 2006; Pecchinenda et al., 2008).

However, there does appear to be one emotional expression that reliably boosts gaze cueing: fear. Mathews et al. (2003) found that the eyes of fearful faces produced stronger gaze cueing effects than those of neutrally expressive faces. Critically, however, this pattern of data was attained in a group of participants with higher than average (yet subclinical) levels of anxiety (for further discussion of the interaction between facial expression processing and anxiety see Fox and Zougkou, Chapter 26, this volume). This interaction with anxiety might explain other failures to demonstrate modulation of cueing as a function of emotional expression (e.g. Hietanen and Leppanen, 2003). The findings of Mathews et al. have been replicated by several groups (Holmes et al., 2006; Pecchinenda et al., 2008; Tipples, 2006, Putman et al., 2006; Fox et al., 2007; Graham et al., 2009).

Interestingly, Tipples (2005) showed that simply widening the eyes of the gaze stimulus potentiates gaze cueing. It is important, therefore, even if modulation of gaze cueing is found in a non-anxious random sample, to rule out the quality of the gaze stimulus per se, rather than the interpretation of the specific emotion as the underlying cause. For example, in Figure 28.8, it is clear that the fear expression is also associated with much wider eyes than other emotional expressions, and hence the greater cueing effects with fearful faces due to the low-level salience of the gaze cues. Using an interesting approach, Pecchinenda et al. (2008) found emotional modulation of gaze cueing only when participants were required to evaluate the emotional content of the target stimuli. We feel that using context rich target stimuli, that evoke emotional states in the observer, along with an appreciation for potential individual differences along multiple dimensions will lead to a deeper understanding of interactions with emotional content and gaze cueing.

Fig. 28.8 A fearful expression classically involves a widening of the eyes, increasing the quality of the signal to be processed by the gaze perception system. When compared with happy and angry expressions, this increases gaze cueing magnitude, especially in anxious people. Is this because of the interpretation of the fear emotion leading to an imperative to follow the eyes to the inferred threat, or because gaze direction is represented more strongly due to the larger eye region as compared with the happy/angry face?

It is also interesting to investigate other, non-attentional, consequences of following the gaze of an emotional face. Bayliss and colleagues (2006, 2007) investigated whether evaluative judgments of objects are influenced by the combination of observed gaze direction and emotional expression. They found that, for example, an object that is looked at by a disgusted person is liked less than when looked at by a happy face (upper panels of Figure 28.9). In contrast the emotional expression has no effect on the evaluation of objects that were not the recipient of social attention (lower panels of Figure 28.9; see also Corneille et al., 2009).

Individual differences

The developmental disorder autism is characterized by a triad of symptoms relating to difficulties with social behavior, language delays, and rigid thinking (see Happé et al., 2006). Children with autism tend to make less eye contact, and their engagement in joint attention behavior is disrupted or delayed (e.g. Charman, 2003). These difficulties are in turn related to language impairments and delays (e.g. Leekam et al., 2000). Characterizing the differences between how eyes are processed by normally developing individuals and by people with autism may lead to a deeper understanding of how perceptual factors associated with the syndrome might contribute to the social difficulties faced by autistic individuals (see Happé and Frith, 2006 for a review of the "weak central coherence" account).

Gaze cueing in autism

Interestingly, despite the weaknesses in joint attention abilities in the autism spectrum, many gaze cueing studies have failed to find consistent deficits in autism spectrum disorder groups (e.g. Swettenham et al., 2003; Kyllianen and Hietanen, 2004; but see Ristic et al., 2005, for a notable exception and Nation and Penny, 2008, for review). Often where differences are found, they are not simple differences in overall cueing magnitude (e.g. hemispheric asymmetries; Vlamings et al., 2005 and spatial frequency biases, de Jong et al., 2008). This apparent paradox may reflect

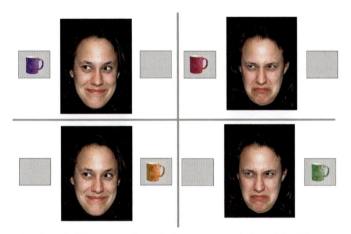

Fig. 28.9 The evaluation of objects are affected when presented alongside different emotion (disgust/happy) and gaze (towards/away) combinations. Objects that are looked-at are liked more if the face is happy as compared with if the face is disgusted, while objects that receive no attention (i.e. not looked at) are unaffected by the emotion of the gazing face. Reprinted from *Cognition*, **104** (3), Andrew P. Bayliss, Alexandra Frischen, Mark J. Fenske, Steven P. Tipper, Affective evaluations of objects are influenced by observed gaze direction and emotional expression, Copyright (2007), with permission from Elsevier.

findings that discriminating gaze direction is preserved in autism (e.g. Leekam et al., 1997), perhaps meaning that attention can act on these representations.

Whether gaze cueing in autism, where present, is based on the activation of precisely the same mechanisms as in normal samples is unclear. It is likely, however, that the use of gaze cues for higher-level social functions is impaired. For example, work by Pierno et al. (2006) suggests that gaze direction does not help autistic children infer the likely actions of other people (see also Becchio et al., 2007). Further issues worthy of pursuit concern whether preferences for looked-at objects are modulated by combined signals of gaze direction and emotional expression (Bayliss et al., 2007) and how face identity might interact with gaze perception in autism (Bayliss and Tipper, 2006a; Frischen and Tipper, 2006).

That is, while the attention systems of autistic groups appear to be sensitive to gaze direction to a certain degree, the next link in the chain of fluent social processing—linking this information to the current global social context—may be compromised. It is perhaps this level of processing that is impaired, leading to the difficulties that individuals with autism have with social attention. Hence, while intact gaze cueing in autism is at odds with their impaired overt orienting to gaze direction in naturalistic scenarios, it could instead reflect preserved low-level perceptual abilities needed for gaze cueing. What is impaired, though, is the full exploitation of these signals in a global social context.

Individual differences in non-clinical samples

Several groups of researchers have investigated individual differences within the normal population. For example, neonatal males tend to spend less time looking at faces and other social stimuli than neonatal females do (Batki et al., 2000; see also Connellan et al., 2000). Data such as these have led some authors to develop theories of autism based partly on sex differences in autism and the normal population (e.g. Baron-Cohen, 2002).

Previous work showing sex differences in infants led Bayliss et al. (2005) to predict that on average, normally developed adult male participants will be less sensitive to gaze cues than female adults. Bayliss et al. (2005) did indeed find such a consistent sex difference in gaze cueing, with stronger gaze cueing in normal adult females compared with normal adult males (see Figure 28.4). This effect was particularly strong at longer SOAs (700 ms). Interestingly this effect was not confined to "social" cue stimuli, since the same sex difference was observed with arrow cues. So although their prediction was derived from a sociodevelopmental theory of sex differences, Bayliss et al. (2005) posited the existence of a general sex difference in the attentional processing of directional stimuli (see also Merritt et al., 2007; Ristic et al., 2005; Tipples, 2008).

Further evidence of a role for sex differences in social orienting was presented by Deaner et al. (2007). They showed that familiarity with the faces used in a gaze cueing paradigm enhanced the strength of the resulting attention shift—but only for female subjects. Male participants showed a weak cueing effect for familiar and unfamiliar faces (see discussion of Frischen and Tipper, 2006 above).

Bayliss and Tipper (2005) conducted a second study investigating individual differences in gaze cueing in the normal population, using the "Autism Spectrum Quotient" (AQ; Baron-Cohen et al., 2001). This questionnaire is designed to assess autistic-like traits in clinical and non-clinical samples. On average, clinical autistic groups score higher than normally developed males, who in turn score higher than normally developed females. Bayliss and Tipper (2005) predicted that those scoring higher on the autism scale would be less influenced by observed gaze shifts. In their study, a rich social context was established on some trials with a gaze cueing face looking to the left or right while flanked by two faces of the opposite sex. The to-be-detected target was a red patch, appearing on one of the faces (see Figure 28.10). It is striking that even in this socially rich environment, the "social" nature of the gaze cues (left panels of Figure 28.10) failed to boost the cueing effects above that of arrows (right panels), even when the target was a face looked at by the cueing gaze (relative to targets that were tools).

However, Bayliss and Tipper (2005) also varied the coherence of the target objects, presenting intact objects on some trials (top panels of Figure 28.10) and scrambled objects (lower panels of Figure 28.10) on others. Here, the administration of the AQ revealed an interesting and consistent effect across two experiments. Participants with low AQ scores (i.e. those who revealed few autistic-like traits on the AQ) showed stronger attention shifts towards coherent target objects than scrambled target objects. In contrast, participants with higher than average scores on the AQ, revealed the opposite pattern, where gaze and arrow cues were more effective when targets appeared on scrambled objects. This pattern of results may relate to the finding that autism reflects more local/detailed perceptual processing styles in contrast to more global processing in controls (Happé and Frith, 2006).

It is interesting to discuss here a peculiar aspect of the literature, that the individual differences *within* the normal population seem to be more robust and revealing about the interactions between social attention and face processing (Deaner et al., 2007) and scene processing (Bayliss and Tipper, 2005), than differences between control and clinical samples. However, we repeat that comparing tasks with purely perceptual manipulations (e.g. de Jong et al., 2008) to those with richer stimulus contexts (Langton et al., 2006) may reveal important differences between the processing of social cues in clinical groups (see Becchio et al., 2007).

Summary and conclusions

The human brain has evolved systems able to compute the internal states of other people, to enable the complex social interactions that mediate the impressive achievements of culture and

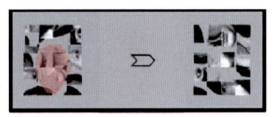

Fig. 28.10 Examples of the cue-target displays from Bayliss and Tipper (2005). Imbuing the display with a high degree of social content (top left) did not potentiate stronger gaze cueing overall compared with when an arrow cued attention (top right). However, consistent individual differences were found, with low AQ participants showing more cueing in conditions similar to the top two displays than when the potential target objects were scrambled (lower displays); whereas those with more autistic traits showed larger attention orienting effects towards the scrambled objects in the lower panels. The target to be located with a key-press was a red transparent patch presented over one of the peripheral objects. Stimuli from AR face database (Martinez and Benavente, 1998). Adapted from Bayliss and Tipper (2005). Reproduced with permission from *British Journal of Psychology* © The British Psychological Society.

society. One of these systems exploits another person's gaze direction to orient our attention to the same features of the environment that they are attending, allowing us to track their current interests and infer mental states enabling predictions of their future actions. Understanding the perceptual bases of social attention, determining the consequences for person and object perception in a social context, and appreciating individual differences in how the cognitive system utilizes gaze cues, are critical aims for social cognition.

Research over the last decade or so has demonstrated that averted gaze cues trigger an automatic shift of attention, even when the observer is trying to ignore the cue (e.g. Driver et al., 1999). While these attentional effects are fairly robust, they are heavily influenced by individual differences, though somewhat counter intuitively, these seem to be more clear cut in the normal (Bayliss et al., 2005) than clinical populations (i.e. autism; Swettenham et al., 2003). Further, other aspects of face processing appear to interact with gaze cueing in a highly specific manner (e.g. identity: Frischen and Tipper, 2006; emotional expression: Mathews et al., 2003). Moreover, the affective *consequences* for engaging in joint attention appear to be important and wide-ranging (e.g. Bayliss and Tipper, 2006a; Bayliss et al., 2007). For example, emotional reactions such as trust and liking can be evoked by patterns of gaze direction. Employing the approaches used in the studies from our laboratory to investigate the non-attentional consequences of social attention could be of use in studies of clinical populations (e.g. depression, autism, social anxiety) where interpersonal trust may be an issue, and as a technique of use to assess the effects of oxytocin or tryptophan on trust (Guastella et al., 2008; Williams et al., 2007). Finally, findings that viewing another person's gaze direction can influence how much a person likes a gazed at object has clear implications for advertising.

Future work should also utilize converging approaches to identify and understand the neural systems mediating perception of gaze direction and its links to attentional orienting systems. For example, neuropsychological data on gaze cueing are scarce, and there is a need for larger studies involving patients with difficulties with gaze perception. Such work could be supported by studies utilizing TMS to disrupt neural processing in regions such as STS, to better identify their role in gaze perception and attention. Finally, to further identify the neural networks that mediate gaze cueing, studies with fMRI to identify structures involved, and subsequent studies with MEG to analyze the sequential flow of information through the neural networks are important. In particular, the timing of neural events associated with the processing of gaze direction and execution of gaze-triggered attention shifts will provide significant insights into the origins of gaze cueing. Clearly, although progress has been made, further studies of the processes mediating gaze perception are necessary to improve our understanding of the social brain.

Acknowledgments

Steven Tipper is supported by a Wellcome Programme, and Andrew Bayliss is supported by a Leverhulme Early Career Fellowship and by a University of Queensland Postdoctoral Fellowship. Stimuli in Figures 28.6–28.9 are from the MacBrain Face Stimulus Set, developed by Nim Tottenham (tott0006@tc.umn.edu), supported by the John D. and Catherine T. MacArthur Foundation.

References

Adams, R.B. and Kleck, R.E. (2003). Perceived gaze direction and the processing of facial displays of emotion. *Psychological Science, 14*, 644–647.

Ando, S. (2002). Luminance-induced shift in the apparent direction of gaze. *Perception, 31*, 657–674.

Argyle, M. and Cook, M. (1976). *Gaze and mutual gaze.* Cambridge: Cambridge University Press.

Baron-Cohen, S. (1995). The eye direction detector (EDD) and the shared attention mechanism (SAM): Two cases for evolutionary psychology. In C. Moore and P. J. Dunham (eds.) *Joint attention: Its origins and role in development*, pp. 41–59. Hillsdale, NJ: Lawrence Erlbaum Associates, Inc.

Baron-Cohen, S. (2002). The extreme male brain theory of autism. *Trends in Cognitive Sciences, 6*, 248–254.

Baron-Cohen, S., Wheelwright, S., Skinner, R., Martin, J., and Clubley, E. (2001). The autism-spectrum quotient (AQ): Evidence from Asperger syndrome/high functioning autism, males and females, scientists and mathematicians. *Journal of Autism and Developmental Disorders, 31*, 5–17.

Batki, A., Baron-Cohen, S., Wheelwright, S., Connellan, J., and Ahluwalia, J. (2000). Is there an innate gaze module? Evidence from human neonates. *Infant Behavior and Development, 23*, 223–229.

Bayliss, A.P. and Tipper, S.P. (2005). Gaze and arrow cueing of attention reveals individual differences along the autism spectrum as a function of target context. *British Journal of Psychology, 96*, 95–114.

Bayliss, A.P. and Tipper, S.P. (2006a). Gaze cues evoke both spatial and object-centered shifts of attention. *Perception and Psychophysics, 68*(2), 310–318.

Bayliss, A.P. and Tipper, S.P. (2006b). Predictive gaze cues and personality judgments: Should eye trust you? *Psychological Science, 17*, 514–520.

Bayliss, A.P., di Pellegrino, G., and Tipper, S.P. (2004). Orienting of attention via observed eye gaze is head-centred. *Cognition, 94*, B1–B10.

Bayliss, A.P., di Pellegrino, G., and Tipper, S.P. (2005). Sex differences in eye gaze and symbolic cueing of attention. *Quarterly Journal of Experimental Psychology, 58A*, 631–650.

Bayliss, A.P., Paul, M.A., Cannon, P.R., and Tipper, S.P. (2006). Gaze cueing and affective judgments of objects: I like what you look at. *Psychonomic Bulletin and Review, 13*(6), 1061–1066.

Bayliss, A.P., Frischen, A., Fenske, M.J., and Tipper, S.P. (2007). Affective evaluations of objects are influenced by observed gaze direction and emotional expression. *Cognition, 104*, 644–653.

Bayliss, A.P., Griffiths, D., and Tipper, S.P. (2009). Predictive gaze cues affect face evaluations: The effect of facial emotion. *European Journal of Cognitive Psychology, 21*, 1072–1084.

Becchio, C., Pierno, A., Mari, M., Lusher, D., and Castiello, U. (2007). Motor contagion from gaze: the case of autism. *Brain, 130*, 2401–2411.

Behrmann, M. and Tipper, S.P. (1999). Attention accesses multiple reference frames: Evidence from visual neglect. *Journal of Experimental Psychology: Human Perception and Performance, 25*, 83–101.

Bindemann, M., Burton, A.M., and Langton, S.R.H. (2008). How do eye-gaze and facial expression interact? *Visual Cognition 16*, 708–733.

Bonifacci, P., Ricciardelli, P., Lugli, L., and Pellicano, A. (2008). Emotional attention: Effects of emotion and gaze direction on overt orienting of attention. *Cognitive Processing, 9*, 127–133.

Bruce, V. and Young, A. (1986). Understanding face recognition. *British Journal of Psychology, 77*, 305–327.

Calder, A.J., Beaver, J.D., Winston, J.S., *et al.* (2007). Separate Coding of Different Gaze Directions in the Superior Temporal Sulcus and Inferior Parietal Lobule. *Current Biology, 17*, 20–25.

Calder, A.J. and Young, A.W. (2005). Understanding the recognition of facial identity and facial expression. *Nature Reviews Neuroscience, 6*, 641–651.

Charman, T. (2003). Why is joint attention a pivotal skill in autism? *Philosophical Transactions of the Royal Society, London, B, 358*, 315–324.

Connellan, J., Baron-Cohen, S., Wheelwright, S., Batki, A., and Ahluwalia, J. (2000). Sex differences in human neonatal social perception. *Infant Behavior and Development, 23*, 113–118.

Corbetta, M., and Shulman, G.L. (2002). Control of goal-directed and stimulus-driven attention in the brain. *Nature Reviews Neuroscience, 3*, 201–215.

Corneille, O., Mauduit, S., Holland, R.W., and Strick, M. (2009). Liking products by the head of a dog: Perceived orientation of attention induces valence acquisition. *Journal of Experimental Social Psychology, 45*, 234–237.

de Jong, M.C., van Engeland, H., Kemner, C. (2008). Attentional effects of gaze shifts are influenced by emotion and spatial frequency, but not in autism. *Journal of the American Academy of Child and Adolescent Psychiatry, 47*, 443–454.

Deaner, R.O., Shepherd, S.V., and Platt, M.L. (2007). Familiarity accentuates gaze cueing in women but not men. *Biology Letters, 3*(1), 63–67.

di Pellegrino, G., Fadiga, L., Fogassi, L., Gallese, V., and Rizzolatti, G. (1992). Understanding motor events: A neurophysiological study. *Experimental Brain Research, 91*, 176–180.

Driver, J., Davis, G., Ricciardelli, P., Kidd, P., Maxwell, E., and Baron-Cohen, S. (1999). Gaze perception triggers reflexive visuospatial orienting. *Visual Cognition, 6*, 509–540.

Emery, N.J. (2000). The eyes have it: The neuroethology, function and evolution of social gaze. *Neuroscience and Biobehavioral Reviews, 24*, 581–604.

Farroni, T., Johnson, M.H., Brockbank, M., and Simion, F. (2000). Infants' use of gaze direction to cue attention: The importance of perceived motion. *Visual Cognition, 7*, 705–718.

Friesen, C.K., and Kingstone, A. (1998). The eyes have it! Reflexive orienting is triggered by nonpredictive gaze. *Psychonomic Bulletin and Review, 5*, 490–495.

Friesen, C.K., and Kingstone, A. (2003a). Covert and overt orienting to gaze direction cues and the effects of fixation offset. *Neuroreport, 14*, 489–493.

Friesen, C.K., and Kingstone, A. (2003b). Abrupt onsets and gaze direction cues trigger independent reflexive attentional effects. *Cognition, 87*, B1–B10.

Friesen, C.K., Ristic, J., and Kingstone, A. (2004). Attentional effects of counterpredictive gaze and arrow cues. *Journal of Experimental Psychology: Human Perception and Performance, 30*, 319–329.

Frischen, A. and Tipper, S.P. (2004). Orienting attention via observed gaze shift evokes longer term inhibitory effects: implications for social interactions, attention, and memory. *Journal of Experimental Psychology: General,* **133**, 516–533.

Frischen, A. and Tipper, S.P. (2006). Long-term gaze cueing effects: Evidence for retrieval of prior states of attention from memory. *Visual Cognition,* **14**, 351–364.

Frischen, A., Bayliss, A.P., and Tipper, S.P. (2007a). Gaze cueing of attention: Visual attention, social cognition and individual differences. *Psychological Bulletin,* **133(4)**, 694–724.

Frischen, A., Smilek, D., Eastwood, J.D., and Tipper, S.P. (2007b). Inhibition of return in response to gaze cues: Evaluating the roles of time course and fixation cue. *Visual Cognition,* **15(8)**, 881–895.

Fox, E., Mathews, A., Calder, A.J., and Yiend, J. (2007). Anxiety and sensitivity to gaze direction in emotionally expressive faces. *Emotion,* **7**, 478–486.

Fox, E., Russo, R., and Dulton, K. (2002). Attentional bias for threat: Evidence for delayed disengagement from emotional faces. *Cognition and Emotion,* **16**, 355–379.

Graham, R., Friesen, C.K., Fichtenholtz, H.M., and LaBar, K.S. (2009). Modulation of reflexive orienting to gaze direction by facial expression. *Visual Cognition,* **18**, 331–368.

Guastella, A.J., Mitchell, P.B., and Dadds, M.R. (2008). Oxytocin increases gaze to the eye region of human faces. *Biological Psychiatry,* **63**, 3–5.

Happé, F. and Frith, U. (2006). The weak central coherence account: Detail-focused cognitive style in autism spectrum disorders. *Journal of Autism and Developmental Disorders,* **36**, 5–25.

Happé, F., Ronald, A., and Plomin, R. (2006). Time to give up on a single explanation for autism. *Nature Neuroscience,* **9**, 1218–1220.

Hietanen, J.K. (1999). Does your gaze direction and head orientation shift my visual attention? *NeuroReport,* **10**, 3443–3447.

Hietanen, J.K. and Leppänen, J.M. (2003). Does facial expression affect attention orienting by gaze direction cues? *Journal of Experimental Psychology: Human Perception and Performance,* **29**, 1228–1243.

Hietanen, J.K., Nummenmaa, L., Nyman, M.J., Parkkola, R., Hämäläinen, H. (2006). Automatic orienting of attention by social and symbolic cues activates different neural networks: An fMRI study. *NeuroImage,* **33**, 406–413.

Hoffman, E.A. and Haxby, J.V. (2000). Distinct representations of eye gaze and identity in the distributed human neural system for face perception. *Nature Neuroscience,* **3**, 80–84.

Holmes, A., Richards, A., and Green, S. (2006). Anxiety and sensitivity to eye gaze in emotional faces. *Brain and Cognition,* **60**, 282–294.

Hood, B.M., Willen, J.D., and Driver, J. (1998). Adult's eyes trigger shifts of visual attention in human infants. *Psychological Science,* **9**, 131–134.

Itier, R.J., Villate, C., and Ryan, J.D. (2007). Eyes always attract attention but gaze orienting is task-dependent: Evidence from eye movement monitoring. *Neuropsychologia,* **5**, 1019–1028.

Jenkins, J. and Langton, S.R.H. (2003). Configural processing in the perception of eye-gaze direction. *Perception,* **32**, 1181–1188.

Jonides, J. (1981). Voluntary versus automatic control over the mind's eye's movement. In J. B. Long and A. D. Baddeley (eds.), *Attention and Performance IX,* pp. 187–203. Hillsdale, NJ: Erlbaum.

Kingstone, A., Friesen, C.K., and Gazzaniga, M.S. (2000). Reflexive joint attention depends on lateralized cortical connections. *Psychological Science,* **11**, 159–166.

Kingstone, A., Smilek, D., Ristic, J., Friesen, C.K., and Eastwood, J.D. (2003). Attention researchers! It is time to take a look at the real world. *Current Directions in Psychological Science,* **12**, 176–180.

Kleinke, C.L. (1986). Gaze and eye contact: A research review. *Psychological Bulletin,* **100(1)**, 78–100.

Kobayashi, H. and Kohshima, S. (1997). Unique morphology of the human eye. *Nature,* **387**, 767–768.

Koval, M.J., Thomas, B.S., and Everling, S. (2005). Task-dependent effects of social attention on saccadic reaction times. *Experimental Brain Research,* **167**, 475–480.

Kuhn, G. and Kingstone, A. (2009). Look away! Eyes and arrows engage oculomotor responses automatically. *Attention,* Perception and Psychophysics, **71**(2), 314–327.

Kuhn, G. and Land, M.F. (2006). There's more to magic than meets the eye! *Current Biology,* **16**(22), R950.

Kylliäinen, A. and Hietanen, J.K. (2004). Attention orienting by another's gaze direction in children with autism. *Journal of Child Psychology and Psychiatry,* **45**, 435–444.

Langton, S.R.H. and Bruce, V. (1999). Reflexive visual orienting in response to the social attention of others. *Visual Cognition,* **6**, 541–567.

Langton, S.R.H., Watt, R.J., and Bruce, V. (2000). Do the eyes have it? Cues to the direction of social attention. *Trends in Cognitive Sciences,* **4**, 50–59.

Langton, S.R., O'Donnell, C., Riby, D.M., and Ballantyne, C.J. (2006). Gaze cues influence the allocation of attention in natural scene viewing. *Quarterly Journal of Experimental Psychology,* **59**, 2056–2064.

Leekam, S.R., Baron-Cohen, S., Perrett, D.I., Milders, M., and Brown, S. (1997). Eye-direction detection: A dissociation between geometric and joint attention skills in autism. *British Journal of Developmental Psychology,* **15**, 77–95.

Leekam, S.R., López, B., and Moore, C. (2000). Attention and joint attention in preschool children with autism. *Developmental Psychology,* **36**, 261–273.

Mansfield, E.M., Farroni, T., and Johnson, M.H. (2003). Does gaze perception facilitate overt orienting? *Visual Cognition,* **10**, 7–14.

Martinez, A.M., and Benavente, R. (1998). The AR Face Database. *CVC Technical Report,* 24.

Materna, S., Dicke, P.W., and Their, P. (2008). Dissociable roles of the superior temporal sulcus and the intraparietal sulcus in joint attention: a functional magnetic resonance imaging study. *Journal of Cognitive Neuroscience,* **20**, 108–119.

Mathews, A., Fox, E., Yiend, J., and Calder, A. (2003). The face of fear: Effects of eye gaze and emotion on visual attention. *Visual Cognition,* **10**, 823–835.

Merritt, P., Hirshman, E., Wharton, W., Stangl, B., Devlin, J., and Lenz, A. (2007). Evidence for gender differences in visual selective attention. *Personality and individual differences,* **43**(3), 597–603.

Moore, C. and Corkum, V. (1994). Social Understanding at the End of the First Year of Life. *Developmental Review,* **14**, 349–372.

Nation, K. and Penny, S. (2008) Sensitivity to eye gaze cues in autism. Is it normal? Is it automatic? Is it social? *Development and Psychopathology,* **20**, 79–97.

Nichols, K.A. and Champness, B.G. (1971). Eye gaze and the GSR. *Journal of Experimental Social Psychology,* **7**, 623–626.

Nummenmaa, L. and Calder, A.J. (2009). Neural mechanisms of social attention. Trends in *Cognitive Sciences,* **13**, 135–43.

Nummenmaa, L. and Hietanen, J.K. (2006). Gaze distractors influence saccadic curvature: Evidence for the role of the oculomotor system in gaze-cued orienting. *Vision Research,* **46**, 3674–3680.

Pecchinenda, A., Pes, M., Ferlazzo, and Zoccolotti, P. (2008). The combined effect of gaze direction and facial expression on cueing spatial attention. *Emotion,* **8**, 628–634.

Perrett, D.I., Hietanen, J.K., Oram, M.W., and Benson, P.J. (1992). Organisation and functions of cells responsive to faces in the temporal cortex. *Philosophical Transactions of the Royal Society, London, B,* **335**, 23–30.

Pierno, A.C., Mari, M., Glover, S., Georgiou, I., and Castiello, U. (2006). Failure to read motor intentions from gaze in children with autism. *Neuropsychologia,* **44**, 1483–1488.

Pierno, A.C., Becchio, C., Wall, M.B., Smith, A.T., Turella, L., Castiello, U. (2006). When Gaze Turns into Grasp. *Journal of Cognitive Neuroscience,* **18**, 2130–2137.

Posner, M.I. (1980). Orienting of attention. *Quarterly Journal of Experimental Psychology,* **32**, 3–25.

Posner, M.I., and Cohen, Y.A. (1984). Components of visual orienting. In H. Bouma and D. G. Bouwhuis (eds.), *Attention and Performance XVII: Control of visual processing,* pp. 531–556. Hillsdale, NJ: Lawrence Erlbaum Associates.

Posner, M.I., Rafal, R.D., and Choate, L.S. (1985). Inhibition of return: Neural basis and function. *Cognitive Neuropsychology*, **2**, 211–228.

Putman, P., Hermans, E., and van Honk, J. (2006). Anxiety meets fear in perception of dynamic expressive gaze. *Emotion*, **6**, 94–102.

Ricciardelli, P., Baylis, G., and Driver, J. (2000). The positive and negative of human expertise in gaze perception. *Cognition*, **77**, B1–B14.

Ricciardelli, P., Bricolo, E., Aglioti, S.M., and Chelazzi, L. (2002). My eyes want to look where your eyes are looking: Exploring the tendency to imitate another individual's gaze. *NeuroReport*, **13**, 2259–2264.

Ristic, J., Friesen, C.K., and Kingstone, A. (2002). Are eyes special? It depends on how you look at it. *Psychonomic Bulletin and Review*, **9**, 507–513.

Ristic, J., Mottron, L., Friesen, C.K., Iarocci, G., Burack, J.A., and Kingstone, A. (2005). Eyes are special but not for everyone: The case of autism. *Cognitive Brain Research*, **24**, 715–718.

Ristic, J., Wright, A., and Kingstone, A. (2007). Attentional control and reflexive orienting to gaze and arrow cues. *Psychonomic Bulletin and Review*, **14**, 964–969.

Robson, K.S. (1967). The role of eye-to-eye contact in maternal-infant attachment. *Journal of Child Psychology and Psychiatry*, **8**, 13–25.

Scaife, M., and Bruner, J.S. (1975). The capacity for joint visual attention in the infant. *Nature*, **253**, 265–266.

Schwaninger, A., Lobmaier, J.S., and Fischer, M.H. (2005). The inversion effect on gaze perception reflects processing of component information. *Experimental Brain Research*, **167**, 49–55.

Sheliga, B.M., Riggio, L., and Rizzolatti, G. (1994). Orienting of attention and eye movements. *Experimental Brain Research*, **98**, 507–522.

Senju, A., and Hasegawa, T. (2005). Direct gaze captures visuospatial attention. *Visual Cognition*, **12**, 127–144.

Shepherd, S.V., Klein, J.T., Deaner, R.O., and Platt, M.L. (2009). Mirroring of attention by neurons in macaque parietal cortex. *Proceedings of the National Academy of Sciences*, **106**, 9489–9494.

Stevens, S.A., West, G.L., Al-Aidroos, N., Weger, U.W., and Pratt, J. (2008). Testing whether gaze cues and arrow cues produce reflexive or volitional shifts of attention. *Psychonomic Bulletin and Review*, **15**, 1148–1153.

Swettenham, J., Condie, S., Campbell, R., Milne, E., and Coleman, M. (2003). Does the perception of moving eyes trigger reflexive visual orienting in autism? *Philosophical Transactions of the Royal Society, London, B*, **358**, 325–334.

Tipper, S.P., Howard, L.A., and Paul, M.A. (2001). Reaching affects saccade trajectories. *Experimental Brain Research*, **136**, 241–249.

Tipples, J. (2002). Eye gaze is not unique: Automatic orienting in response to uninformative arrows. *Psychonomic Bulletin and Review*, **9**, 314–318.

Tipples, J. (2005). Orienting to Eye Gaze and Face Processing. *Journal of Experimental Psychology: Human Perception and Performance*, **31**, 843–856.

Tipples, J. (2006). Fear and fearfulness potentiate automatic orienting to eye gaze. *Cognition and Emotion*, **20**, 309–320.

Tipples, J. (2008). Orienting to counterpredictive gaze and arrow cues. *Perception and Psychophysics*, **70**, 77–87.

Vecera, S.P. and Rizzo, M. (2005). Eye gaze does not produce reflexive shifts of attention: Evidence from frontal-lobe damage. *Neuropsychologia*, **44**, 150–159.

Vlamings, P.H.J.M., Stauder, J.E.A., van Son, I.A.M., and Mottron, L. (2005). Atypical visual orienting to gaze- and arrow-cues in adults with high functioning autism. *Journal of Autism and Developmental Disorders*, **35**, 267–277.

Williams, J.H., Perrett, D.I., Waiter, G.D., and Pechey, S. (2007). Differential effects of tryptophan depletion on emotion processing according to face direction. *Social Cognitive and Affective Neuroscience*, **2**, 264–273.

Chapter 29

Neural Substrates of Social Perception

Ralph Adolphs and Elina Birmingham

Introduction

In their quest to understand what it is about our species that makes our behavior and ecology so distinct from any other mammal on the planet, writers frequently focus on the brain and on cognitive adaptations to function in a dynamic and complex environment. While there is lively debate about the details, a leading idea is that the social environment is the most important aspect of the human niche, and one adaptation relative to it is *social cognition*. This in turn fractionates into many different abilities, such as "mentalizing"(including our ability to conceive of other people's beliefs and to manipulate them in deception; Byrne and Whiten, 1988), cooperation (including the proximate mechanisms for it, such as altruistic punishment; Fehr and Gaechter, 2002), cheater detection (Cosmides and Tooby, 1992), and a collection of abilities for social learning that may be a prerequisite for the emergence of culture and civilization (Tomasello, 1999). It is easy to focus on these more central/"higher-level" cognitive abilities as distinctively human while forgetting that they are of course grounded in sensory information, and mechanisms for seeking out such information, in the first place. The sensory information is in the form of *social signals* from other humans, and social perception mediates between sensory processing and inferential cognition to generate social knowledge (Adolphs, 2009).

In this chapter we review what is known about the neural basis of the perception of such signals in humans. To begin, we briefly consider how to conceive of a social signal (Hauser, 1996). The main distinctions of interest are whether or not the characteristic *contains information*, and whether the characteristic is *static or changeable* (making it either a cue or a signal). If the characteristic does not contain information, then it is neither a cue nor a signal. If the characteristic contains information but the characteristic is static, i.e. it cannot be turned on or off, then the characteristic is a *cue*. If the characteristic contains information and is dynamic, i.e. it can be turned on and off (either intentionally or unintentionally), then the characteristic is a signal. One can imagine that there is a graded scale of social features, in terms of information content, changeability, and control, as follows:

1 The feature is purely incidental (e.g. physical height). In this case, the feature does not count either as a cue or a signal.

2 The feature is static (i.e. cannot be turned on or off) but contains information that the brain has developed perceptual mechanisms to detect and use (e.g. attractiveness is a relatively stable feature but carries information about fitness). In this case the feature is a cue.

3 The feature is dynamic, i.e. can be turned on or off, whether intentional or not, and the feature has signal value (e.g. peacock feathers or plumage that can be manipulated to become a display for the male's fitness and willingness to mate). This is a signal.

4 The feature is dynamic (can be turned on or off) and carries information, and is thus a signal, and the sender can strategically and dynamically utilize it (e.g. aspects of emotional facial expressions, deception).

It is helpful to provide some examples, which we do in Table 29.1. This table is not meant to be exhaustive or even comprehensive by any means; it is intended to provide a flavor of the diversity of social signals that we perceive, and to situate the particular ones on which this chapter will focus (in bold in the Table). We focus here on social signals from the face, including emotional expression and gaze direction. Social signals from face and gaze are the most widely studied of human social signals, perhaps reflecting the understanding that faces, and in particular eyes, are special social stimuli for humans. There are good reasons to believe that changes in facial expression and gaze should be thought of as signals that play an important and adaptive role in human social behavior (Schmidt and Cohn, 2001). It should be noted at the outset that all these signals interact: for instance, expressions of fear or anger can have different

Table 29.1 Overview of some social signals and cues

Signal/cue	Signaling function(s)	Dynamic (signal) or static (cue)?	Control by signaler	Example of situation where signal is sent
Pupil size	Empathic emotion	Dynamic	None	Emotional arousal
Blushing	Unwanted attention	Dynamic	Low (indirect regulation)	Excessive praise
Facial expression	Complex (Emotion, mental state)	Dynamic	Medium-High (both involuntary and deliberate)	Conversations; interacts with all below
Gaze direction	Attention, social interest and control	Dynamic	Low-High (visual capture to intentional eye contact)	Complex social interaction
Olfactory	Pheromones	Dynamic	None (except perfumes)	Infant-mother interaction
Vocal signals (e.g. pitch, tempo, energy)	Diverse	Dynamic	High	Conversation
Vocal signals-crying	Need/separation	Dynamic	Low	Hungry baby
Social touch	Bonding, mating	Dynamic	High	Infant-mother interaction
Head position	Attention, interest	Dynamic	High	Complex social interaction
Body posture	Emotion, attention, intention	Dynamic	High	Complex social interaction
Facial attractiveness	Fitness	Static	None (except cosmetics)	Mate selection
Skin color	Race	Static	None	Mate selection and group membership

Note: A signal is characteristic that contains information and is dynamic or changeable in nature, i.e. it can be turned on or off. Cues, on the other hand, contain information but are not changeable, i.e. cannot be turned on or off (e.g. attractiveness, ethnic skin color).

interpretations (and evoke different brain responses) depending on whether gaze is direct or averted (Adams et al., 2003, although see Bindemann et al., 2007; Graham and LaBar, 2007; Hess et al., 2007); single neurons in the primate temporal lobe code for highly specific conjunctions of faces, gaze, and head direction (Perrett et al., 1992; see also Rolls, Chapter 4, this volume); and facial expressions interact with vocal expression in both humans and monkeys (Ghazanfar and Logothetis, 2003).

Facial expressions

Together with the great apes, we have a complex musculature that permits a vast array of dynamic changes in the appearance of the face. Monkeys do not share the same musculature, and hence lack the same repertoire of possible feature changes (see Parr and Hecht, Chapter 35, this volume). What to call these changes has been a matter of some debate. A subset of them has been referred to as "expressions" ever since Charles Darwin analyzed their phylogeny and function in relation to emotion (Darwin, 1872). This theme was picked up in modern day and defended vigorously by Paul Ekman, who argued for six or seven so-called "basic" emotions that are thought to be expressed and perceived universally and as a result of specific neural programs. These basic emotions are happiness, surprise, fear, anger, disgust, sadness, and maybe contempt (Ekman, 1994). While some have taken up the problem of what precisely these so-called expressions actually express (Fridlund, 1994), taken issue with their universality (Russell, 1994), or with the concept of "emotion" in general (Griffiths, 1997), this has not detracted from the use of emotional facial expressions in a huge number of psychological and, more recently, neurological studies.

There are two prominent sources of debate regarding the processing of social information from faces: first, to what extent are the findings attributable to faces or information about faces, specifically (as opposed to intracategory classification, expertise, and stimulus variance), and what are the categories or dimensions along which social information is represented? The first issue relates to the debate about the modularity of face processing and the role of the fusiform face area, issues discussed in detail elsewhere in this volume (e.g. McKone and Robbins, Chapter 9, this volume); we will discuss the second.

The psychological study of emotional facial expressions has a long-standing tension between dimensional and categorical accounts. The six basic emotions described by Ekman can be represented in spaces of various dimensions; most common are the simplest, two-dimensional spaces of valence and arousal (Russell, 1980). Facial appearance as such, and the evaluations of others that we make automatically, have also been mapped onto two-dimensional spaces: for instance, Fiske has an evaluative space with dimensions of *warmth* and *competence* (Fiske et al., 2007), and Todorov et al. (Chapter 32, this volume) has a space with dimensions of *valence* and *dominance*. Another approach capitalizes on the fact that facial expressions vary along roughly continuous geometric parameters and can be morphed smoothly into one another. Mapping the variance in how we evaluate facial expressions into a similarity space often produces a "circumplex" structure using techniques such as multidimensional scaling (Russell, 1980) or principal components analysis (Calder et al., 2001b). This structure reflects the continuity between different facial expressions and their relatedness. Morphing the six basic emotions in all combinations also produces a circular manifold with parametric changes in the deformation from an average face towards each emotion prototype (Young et al., 1997).

Neural correlates of these dimensional accounts have been probed in a variety of studies. The clearest exploration of the valence-arousal two-dimensional space has been carried out using olfactory stimuli, since these permit an orthogonalization of the dimensions that is difficult to achieve with visual stimuli (where negative valence tends to have higher arousal than positive valence).

An initial study described BOLD responses in the amygdala that tracked arousal relatively independently of valence, and responses in the orbitofrontal cortex that tracked valence relatively independently of arousal (although lateral orbitofrontal cortex (OFC) responded more to unpleasant odors that were also fairly intense, indicating an interaction in line with more recent findings that lateral OFC codes for stimulus values that require a behavioral switch) (Anderson et al., 2003). This picture has been complicated by subsequent findings (Winston et al., 2005), and it is now thought that the amygdala encodes a more complex interaction between valence and arousal, likely reflecting a more abstract function (see below).

Categorical accounts begin with a classic model that first postulated separate processing of information about face identity (who somebody is) and facial expression (how they are feeling) (Bruce and Young, 1986), an idea that has received substantial neurological support from both functional imaging studies (Haxby et al., 2000; and Haxby and Gobbini, Chapter 6, this volume) as well as from putative double dissociations following focal lesions (Adolphs et al., 1994; Tranel et al., 1988; see Calder, Chapter 22; and Kanwisher and Barton, Chapter 7, this volume). As reviewed by Haxby and Gobbini (Chapter 6, this volume) the summary from these studies has been that regions in the ventral temporal cortex, notably in the lateral fusiform gyrus, show differential activation to identity but not expression of faces, whereas regions in the superior temporal sulcus (STS) show differential activation to changeable features of faces, such as emotional expressions and gaze shifts. There are also electrophysiological findings in monkeys that somewhat mirror this distinction (Hasselmo et al., 1989), and functional magnetic resonance imaging (fMRI) adaptation studies have suggested distinct neuronal populations coding identity and emotion (Winston et al., 2004).

This picture has recently been challenged to some extent. The challenge begins with the observation that, while there are cases of impaired recognition of certain emotions (but not all emotions) with sparing of identity recognition, there are no compelling cases of the converse (cf. Calder and Young, 2005). A substantial part of the problem lies in equating identity-and emotion-recognition tasks for difficulty—since the former typically depends on more subtle cues and requires distinguishing a unique face from a large or open set of others, it is generally more difficult to recognize identity than emotion. Given that the only entirely clear neurological dissociations are confounded by this pattern of differential difficulty, they do not constitute convincing evidence that emotion and identity recognition depend on anatomically separable substrates. In one alternative view, both identity and emotion are coded to varying degrees by partly overlapping neural structures, and the underlying principal components or factors generated by such distributed coding are then read out by high brain regions in order to perform identity or emotion recognition tasks (Calder and Young, 2005). In support of this idea, some fMRI studies have found responses in the ventral temporal cortex modulated both by expression and identity (Ganel et al., 2005), and our laboratory has found direct electrophysiological evidence that both changeable and dynamic aspects of facial expression are represented in the fusiform gyrus (Tsuchiya et al., 2008).

Going further into specific emotion categories: are there neural structures associated with processing specific individual emotions? So far, there is clear evidence only with respect to two emotions: fear and disgust. Fear has been linked to the amygdala; disgust to the insula (Calder et al., 2001a) (although anger processing has been variably linked to certain brain regions, such as sectors of prefrontal cortex (Blair et al., 1999; Harmer et al., 2001), and there are rare reports of happy (Fried et al., 1998) or sad (Dejjani et al., 1999) emotional experience linked to specific brain sites as well). With respect to recognition of emotions, one of the most investigated structures is the amygdala, which has been linked to fear recognition (Adolphs et al., 1994, 1999b; Calder et al., 2001a), and to the judgment of other traits from faces, including attractiveness

(Winston et al., 2007), valence, arousal (Adolphs et al., 1999a), and trustworthiness (Adolphs et al., 1998). Earlier lesion studies found that patients with bilateral damage to the amygdala were unable to make normal judgments of trustworthiness, in particular for those faces normally judged to look the most untrustworthy (Adolphs et al., 1998). Subsequent neuroimaging studies corroborated this initial finding (Winston et al., 2002), but more recent studies suggest that the amygdala's response to trustworthiness may be non-monotonic (Said et al., 2009), and may map onto an underlying valence dimension instead (Todorov and Engell, 2008)—consistent with non-monotonic interactions between valence and intensity seen in studies that used olfactory stimuli (Winston et al., 2005).

The amygdala's role in fear recognition has also been substantially revised in the last few years. A key insight here came from using an innovative method for revealing how viewers make use of information about specific facial features in order to discriminate emotions. This so-called "bubbles" method randomly and sparsely samples a face-space (one of several dimensions in which faces are represented and sampled) (Gosselin and Schyns 2001). The most common is the steerable pyramid space, which has a two-dimensional image plane (the pixel locations and intensities comprising an image of the face) and a third dimension of spatial frequency (usually discrete, in octaves). The "bubbles" method shows viewers random small pieces of this face space and asks them to perform a discrimination task; after many trials, the location of the sampling (the bubbles) in this space is then correlated with the performance accuracy (or other dependent measure driven by the stimulus, such as reaction time, or even regional brain activation) to derive a classification image that shows the effective information from the face (in terms of features located on the face, such as eyes or mouth, and in terms of spatial frequency bands) that viewers make use of to distinguish among emotions. The "bubbles" method is conceptually related to classical reverse correlation, with the difference that the randomly sampled space is a structured stimulus space as opposed to noise. This method has been used successfully to determine the features that distinguish among the six "basic" emotions (Smith et al., 2005). With respect to the amygdala, the bubbles method was used to demonstrate that damage to the amygdala precludes the ability spontaneously to make use of information from the eyes (Adolphs et al., 2005). This finding was consistent also with the observation that amygdala damage results in a failure to fixate the eye region of faces, both to images of eyes as well as when confronted with real people, with the consequence that high-spatial frequency information from the eye region of faces would not be available (Adolphs et al., 2005). These studies suggest that the amygdala is involved in actively seeking out socially relevant information. It may be that the amygdala's role in allocating attention and gaze to the eye region of faces reflects its role in alerting the organism to salient, ambiguous, or unpredictable stimuli of potential importance and value in the environment (Sander et al., 2003; Herry et al., 2007; Whalen, 1999).

It is as yet unclear how to relate this finding to a number of others regarding the amygdala's role in processing social signals. A theme that runs throughout the human and non-human primate literature on the consequences of amygdala lesions is that the amygdala is important for regulating approach-avoidance behaviors: monkeys as well as humans with amygdala lesions exhibit an unusual propensity to approach objects and conspecifics, suggesting that the amygdala serves to put a brake on an approach system as a function of the potentially threatening aspect of stimuli or context (Kennedy et al., 2009; Mason et al., 2006). This observation could fit with the amygdala's role in detecting unpredictable (Herry et al., 2007) or ambiguous (Whalen, 1999) stimuli, since these are precisely sources of potential threat, and the finding is consistent also with preferential neuronal responses within monkey amygdala to threatening faces (Gothard et al., 2007). These findings may also be related to the amygdala's response to faces that convey untrustworthiness (Winston et al., 2002)—reflected in lesion studies by patients endorsing unusually high ratings of trustworthiness and approachability to people from their faces (Adolphs et al., 1998)—and to personally directed deceit (Grezes et al., 2006).

Attempting to link together all these somewhat disparate findings on the amygdala is difficult and probably premature, although it is possible to form some initial hypotheses. Across the findings there is a theme of the amygdala processing highly salient stimuli. Salient stimuli would certainly include social stimuli, and in particular stimuli related to threat or danger. Saliency would also arise from mere ambiguity or unpredictability, although here it arises not from the signal value of the stimuli as such, but from the computational requirement to resolve that signal value. A key effort for future studies in primates will be to resolve the contributions of different amygdala nuclei, since these will certainly implement somewhat different functions. High-resolution fMRI may be able to provide some distinctions here, as will rare intracranial recordings in surgical patients.

Related to the issue of resolving individual amygdala nuclei is the question of investigating their detailed connectivity with neocortex and other brain structures. The amygdala does not operate in isolation, and many frameworks for understanding its function in animals have stressed a modulatory rather than an essential role.

Rather than being necessary for producing social behavior, the amygdala might then be thought of more as a component of a mechanism for seeking out and evaluating context-dependent social information (Amaral et al., 2003). This leaves open the question of what processes come into play once relevant social information has in fact been detected—given an emotional face with attention allocated to the relevant features, how do we link its perceptual representation to the retrieval of social knowledge that is necessary for its appraisal and evaluation? While we envision the amygdala as playing a role here as well, not only in the initial detection of relevant features, there are additional structures that allow us to construct a representation of the presumptive internal states (feelings, goals, intentions, thoughts) of a person from observation of their body state (such as the face). One of these mechanisms likely involves simulating, to some extent, the sensorimotor state of the observed person. In one study (Adolphs et al., 2000), we found that lesions of right somatosensory cortex impaired the visual recognition of facial emotion, across several negatively valenced emotions (it remains unclear if the differential impairment of certain emotions in that study reflects genuine emotion specificity or results from some other factor, such as the differential difficulty recognizing certain emotions on the task). That the somatosensory cortex on the right side was involved more than the left may be related to aspects of lateralized processing of emotion (which is complex and still incompletely understood; Borod et al., 1998).

This lesion study is supported by a study that used TMS to transiently inactivate the right somatosensory cortex (Pitcher et al., 2008; Pourtois et al., 2004), as well as by an fMRI study showing activation in right somatosensory cortex when viewing facial expressions of emotion (Winston et al., 2003). The idea that somatosensory cortices participate in the recognition of emotion by representing the body state of the other person inferred from observing their facial expression fits with a large and growing literature on simulation (Goldman and Sripada, 2005). It also fits with the more specific finding that lesions to insular cortex, an interoceptive somatosensory cortex concerned with representing sensations such as pain and nausea, is important for the recognition as well as the experience of disgust (Calder et al., 2001a,b; Kipps et al., 2007).

The simulation account does not require actual facial expressions in the viewer as the source of the simulation. However, normally there is subtle facial mimicry in viewers (Dimberg 1982), apparently even under conditions of subliminal viewing (Dimberg et al., 2000), suggesting an automatic response with respect to facial movements, similar to the well-known chameleon effect in social psychology (Chartrand and Bargh, 1999). People with complete facial paralysis are nonetheless able to recognize basic emotional expressions (Calder et al., 2000), suggesting that central representations of the somatosensory consequences of the expression are sufficient (although this does not completely rule out a role for facial mimicry in emotion recognition, since there is always the possibility that the emotion recognition tasks were simply insufficiently sensitive to detect an impairment).

The above outlined architecture, which we have reviewed previously in detail (Adolphs, 2002), has been fairly well supported for recognizing basic emotions from facial expressions. It is less clear what the neural substrates are for recognizing *social* emotions or other complex states (e.g. guilt, admiration, flirtatiousness). However, some of these have also been linked to the amygdala, especially in terms of information conveyed by the eye region of faces: once again, just as was the case for basic emotions, complex emotions and mental states signaled by the eyes depend on the amygdala (Adolphs et al., 2002).

One important issue concerns the automaticity and context-dependency of amygdala responses to emotional faces. One possibility is that amygdala responses are fairly bottom-up and driven by features in faces such as fearful eyes. In support of this idea is the finding that backward masked fearful eyes, even when they are not consciously perceived, result in greater amygdala activation than masked happy eyes (Whalen et al., 2004). However, this interpretation is challenged by a number of other findings. First, there is some evidence that amygdala responses depend on conscious perception and attention, at least to some extent. Pessoa et al. (2006), for instance, found stronger amygdala activation for masked fearful faces (relative to neutral faces) but only when observers could detect the face (presented for 67 ms), and not when the face was presented for 33 ms and without awareness. Second, amygdala activation is sensitive to the context in which facial expressions are shown: when framed positively (e.g. "She just found $500."), surprised facial expressions activate the amygdala less than when framed negatively (e.g. "She just lost $500.") (Kim et al., 2004). As we note below, facial expression also interacts with other cues, such as the direction of eye gaze. These effects of the context or frame on amygdala activation are likely related to the framing effects that have been observed in regard to value-based decision-making (De Martino et al., 2006).

Gaze direction

A person's gaze signals a variety of information. On a very basic level, gaze direction signals where someone is looking, and therefore where they are directing attention. When someone looks directly at us (direct gaze) it signals that they may be interested in social interaction–whether this is positive or negative in nature (Argyle and Cook, 1976; Kellerman et al., 1989; Kleinke, 1986; von Grunau and Anston, 1995). Likewise, when someone moves their gaze away from us and toward the periphery (averted gaze), it signals that they are attending to a potentially important event or stimulus in the environment. Humans are highly interested in where other humans are directing their attention, and have a strong tendency to look at other people's eyes (Birmingham et al., 2008; Henderson et al., 2005; Pelphrey et al., 2002; Walker-Smith et al., 1977; Yarbus, 1967) and to orient their attention to where other people are looking, an effect that has been variously termed *joint attention* and *social attention* (e.g. Butterworth and Cochran, 1980; Corkum and Moore, 1995; Friesen and Kingstone, 1998; Langton and Bruce, 1999; Morissette et al., 1995; Scaife and Bruner, 1975; Tipper and Bayliss, Chapter 28, this volume; see also Birmingham and Kingstone 2009 for a review of social attention research).

However, it is clear that gaze direction does not *always* signal where someone is attending. For instance when we see a colleague sitting at his desk and staring at the ceiling, we interpret this to mean that he is deep in thought; rarely would we consider the possibility that he is attending to something on the ceiling. At a more complex level than direction of attention, gaze direction carries information about a person's mental state. Basic mental states like intentions and desires can be inferred from gaze (e.g. "He wants the cookie because he is looking at it."). Baron-Cohen (1994, 1995) has even proposed a model with an "Eye Direction Detector" (EDD) as a key component of a "mind-reading system" that makes mental state attributions about other people. Computing gaze direction is assumed to be a prerequisite to establishing a state of *shared attention* (the *understanding* that you and another organism are attending to the same thing), which itself is critical for making complex attributions of mental state (e.g. pretend, know, think, believe, etc.). Thus, in Baron-Cohen's model the eyes are not only important indicators of another person's attention, they are the key input into a system that is responsible for the development of "theory of mind."

Supporting this idea, there is empirical evidence showing that many of the complex mental states can be correctly identified from eye information alone, suggesting that there is a "language of the eyes" that typically developing individuals are adept at reading (Baron-Cohen et al., 1997). One component of this language is likely to be gaze direction, which may interact with "eye-expression" (e.g. squinting or widening the eyes, furrowing or raising the brows), to create the final signal. It appears that the eyes are particularly critical for recognizing complex mental states, whereas information from the whole face is most important for identifying basic emotional states such as happiness, sadness, fear, and surprise (Adolphs et al., 2002; Baron-Cohen et al., 1997).

Gaze direction can also be manipulated in order to exert social control. For instance, people increase direct gaze when trying to be persuasive and deceptive (Mehrabian and Williams, 1969; Timney and London, 1973) and when trying to make friends (Pellegrini et al., 1970). Prolonged direct gaze, or staring, can signal dominance or threat (Ellsworth, 1975; Exline, 1971; Hillabrant, 1974), whereas averted gaze can signal social appeasement or be used to escape or avoid an uncomfortable social situation (Efran and Cheyne, 1974; Rubin et al., 1974). Gaze direction can be used to enhance attraction and liking; for instance, speakers who make eye contact with their audience are rated as more pleasant and less nervous than non-gazers (Cook and Smith, 1975). Even something as simple as a gaze shift toward the observer can increase attractiveness and like-ability ratings relative to a gaze shift away from the observer (Mason et al., 2005). Direct gaze has also been found to speed person categorization (Macrae et al., 2002).

Behavioral studies have shown that humans are very accurate at discriminating different gaze directions, in particular at detecting when another person is looking directly at them, i.e. making eye contact (Cline, 1967; Gibson and Pick, 1963; Lord and Haith, 1974). Humans are also very good at discriminating averted gaze (e.g. a 30-s arc shift in the looker's iris when seated 100 cm away from the observer, Symons et al., 2004), although acuity changes as the target moves further away from the looker and the observer. It appears that for discriminating relatively disparate gaze directions (e.g. left vs. right), performance is unaffected by viewing distance up to a certain critical distance (approximately 15 m), after which performance rapidly declines (Watt et al., 2007). This ability appears to rely on the relatively high contrast between the sclera and iris of the human eye (Kobayashi and Kohshima, 1997). One possibility is that we have an "expert system" dedicated to determining gaze direction based on the contrast polarity of the iris and pupil relative to the sclera (Ricciardelli et al., 2000; Sinha, 2000). Consistent with this proposal, when the contrast polarity of the eyes is reversed, the system erroneously computes gaze direction to be in the direction of the darkened sclera (Sinha, 2000).

What are the neural substrates of gaze perception? Recent work by Calder et al. (2007) suggests that there are distinct neurons in the anterior superior temporal sulcus (aSTS) that are involved in the separate coding of different gaze directions. Using an adaptation paradigm, Calder et al. showed that being repeatedly exposed to one gaze direction influences subsequent judgments of gaze direction—that is, adapting to leftward gaze led to a rightward bias in judgments (leftward gaze is judged as direct, and direct gaze is judged as right). This adaptation is also reflected in brain activation—adapting to leftward gaze led to a reduction in BOLD response in aSTS for left relative to right and direct gaze probes. This finding complements monkey single-cell recording studies finding specific aSTS cell populations responsive to direct and averted gaze (Perrett et al., 1985; Perrett et al., 1992). Indeed, lesions to monkey STS leads to a significant drop in gaze discrimination ability (e.g. Heywood et al., 1992). Human neuroimaging studies also find support for a role of the STS in gaze perception (e.g. Hoffman and Haxby, 2000; Pelphrey et al., 2004; although see Calder et al., 2002; George et al., 2001; Wicker et al., 1998).

Other structures involved in gaze perception are the amygdala (Hooker et al., 2003; Kawashima et al., 1999; Young et al., 1995), which seems to be particularly sensitive to direct gaze; intraparietal sulcus (George et al., 2001; Hoffman and Haxby, 2000), which is activated more strongly for averted gaze and may be involved in shifting attention to gazed-at locations; and medial prefrontal cortex (Calder et al., 2002), which is more responsive to averted gaze, possibly reflecting mental state attribution (i.e. theory of mind) via joint attention. Many of these same structures are involved in other aspects of perceiving social signals, as reviewed above for facial expressions. This observation, together with the above fMRI adaptation and electrophysiological findings, suggest that similar brain regions may process a variety of social signals, although neurons within them may show preferential tuning for one signal over others.

Despite our sensitivity to eye gaze direction, it is also clear that the perception of gaze direction is dependent on the context in which the eyes are found. As early as 1824, Wollaston made the observation that our perception of gaze direction depends not only on the position of the iris and pupil relative to the sclera, but also on the position of the head. He noticed that the perception of eye gaze is "pushed" in the direction that the head is pointed (Langton et al., 2004). That is, the direction of gaze is perceived to be somewhere between the angle of the head and the true line of regard of the eyes. Other studies have found an "overshooting" effect, in which gaze direction is pushed in the opposite direction that the head is pointed (Anstis et al., 1969, who comments that this effect was also observed by Cline 1967, and Gibson and Pick, 1963).

Posterior STS (pSTS) activity, in particular, seems to be influenced by the context in which gaze direction is being perceived (Nummenmaa and Calder, 2009; Pelphrey et al., 2003, 2004, see Pelphrey and Vander Wyk, Chapter 30, this volume, for a discussion of a distinction between aSTS and pSTS involvement in gaze perception). That is, pSTS activity seems to reflect the social relevance of the gaze signal to the specific situation at hand. For instance, consistent with the idea that direct gaze is a meaningful signal within social interactions, Pelphrey et al. (2004) found that pSTS activity was stronger when observers viewed a virtual reality depiction of a man approaching and shifting gaze toward the observer than when he approached and shifted his gaze away from the observer. In contrast, it seems that in less social tasks or when location information is critical to performance (e.g. localizing a target), averted gaze may be more meaningful, reflecting greater pSTS activity for averted gaze (Hoffman and Haxby 2000; Hooker et al., 2003; Pelphrey et al., 2003). Interestingly, while the STS of typically developing individuals is sensitive to intention conveyed by perceived gaze shifts, the STS of individuals with autism is not (Pelphrey et al., 2005).

Another source of interaction is between direction of gaze and facial expression. It has been argued that the meaning of a facial expression critically depends on the concurrent direction of gaze. For instance, direct gaze facilitates the processing of expressions signaling approach (such as anger), whereas averted gaze facilitates the processing of expressions signaling withdrawal (such as fear or disgust) (Adams and Kleck, 2003; although see Bindemann et al., 2007; Graham and LaBar, 2007; Hess et al., 2007 for contradictory results). This effect is correlated with amygdala activation: the amygdala is more strongly activated for ambiguous threat displays (anger faces coupled with averted gaze and fear faces coupled with direct gaze) than for clear threat displays (anger faces coupled with direct gaze and fear faces coupled with averted gaze), suggesting a role for the amygdala in processing threat-related ambiguity (Adams et al., 2003).

As for the STS, a general role may be proposed: extracting information that affords meaningful social communication from biological cues. One of these sources of social-communicative information is eye gaze, which may be used to infer the direction of attention (e.g. averted gaze) and indicates social interest from others (e.g. mutual gaze). However, STS selectivity is clearly not restricted to eye gaze, because meaningful mouth motion also activates STS (Calvert et al., 1998; Puce et al., 2000). Other studies have found STS activation in response to biological motion of heads (Hasselmo et al., 1989), hands (Bonda et al., 1996; Grèzes et al., 1999; Grafton et al., 1996; Rizolatti et al., 1996), and bodies (Bonda et al., 1996; Grossman et al., 2000; Kourtzi and Kanwisher, 2000). Thus, the STS may be more generally involved in resolving meaningful biological motion that conveys information about the attention, and intentions, of others, with a subset of cells specifically responsive to gaze cues.

Thus, it might be that there is an expert system for processing gaze, but that it is just part of a more general system dedicated to processing social-communicative cues. Indeed, the finding that gaze processing (particularly mutual gaze) recruits the amygdala and fusiform gyrus, areas known to be involved in emotional and face processing, provides further support for this notion.

Other signals from the face

Two other and less well understood social signals are pupil size and blushing. Both are mediated essentially entirely through the autonomic nervous system and are involuntary. Both pupil size and blushing are social signals because they convey information and can be turned on and off; even though these changes are not strategically available to the sender (one cannot voluntarily change one's pupil size or color of skin). Dilated pupils correlate with sympathetic autonomic activation, and depending on the context faces with more dilated pupils are perceived to look more attractive for this reason. Atropine, a blocker of muscarinic cholinergic neurotransmission that subserves parasympathetic activation, was used by 17th-century women to dilate their pupils (the name of the plant from which it was derived is "belladonna").

Two neuroimaging studies have examined brain responses evoked by manipulations in pupil size. One found robust activation of the amygdala in response to faces with more dilated pupils, regardless of other factors such as emotional expression or even perceived attractiveness (Demos et al., 2008). Indeed, the amygdala response was based on entirely covert perception of pupil size: viewers were unaware of any difference in pupil size. However, once one becomes aware that pupil size is being manipulated in the study, there is a clear subjective impression of a social perceptual difference (cf. fig. 1 in Demos et al., 2008). The authors conclude that the amygdala is automatically picking up facial cues related to arousal/interest, in line with ideas that the amygdala serves to alert the organism to biological salience whose details or outcomes are unpredictable or ambiguous in some way (Whalen, 1999). This role may be based in a very general mechanism of rapid habituation of neurons within the amygdala (Herry et al., 2007). The second study (Harrison et al., 2006) showed a clear interaction between pupil size and emotional facial expression: constricted pupils rendered sad faces sadder, an effect that was again covert (viewers were unaware that changes in pupil size were present in the study, let alone influencing their emotion judgments). In this case, constricted pupils modulated activation of the amygdala, and moreover resulted in an empathic constriction of pupils within the viewer.

These results relate to the findings we described earlier, that the amygdala appears to be sensitive to, and involved in using, information from the eye region of faces, possibly with a special sensitivity to the eye whites correlated with wide eyes (Adolphs et al., 2005; Whalen et al., 2004).

Some studies have linked this finding, together with the covert nature of the above pupil dilation, to non-conscious processing of eye information by the amygdala (Whalen et al., 2004). This idea has a long history, sparked by studies finding amygdala activation to non-conscious facial expressions of fear (Jiang and He, 2006) and amygdala activation in patients with blindsight due to lesions of striate cortex (Pegna et al., 2005). However, the basis for these effects is still debated. While a subcortical route of visual input to the amygdala through the superior colliculus and pulvinar thalamus has been postulated, this is difficult to reconcile with the known anatomy (Adolphs, 2008). Furthermore, the backward masked facial expressions or eyes used in several studies to investigate non-conscious processing introduce visual transients that may themselves be sufficient to result in amygdala activation.

These findings regarding the amygdala's role in detecting salient features, unpredictability, or ambiguity are consistent with more recent studies that tend to find non-monotonic responses along certain stimulus dimensions. For instance, the amygdala appears to respond to faces that signal either very low or very high trustworthiness (Said et al., 2009), or low or high attractiveness (Winston et al., 2007). In both cases, the extremes of the dimensional scale would correspond to stimuli that are especially salient in some way.

Social blushing is the "most peculiar and the most human of all expressions" (Darwin 1872/1965, p. 309). Blushing can be defined as the spontaneous reddening or darkening of the skin–and although this occurs on the face, ears, neck, and upper chest, we most commonly see the blush response on the face (given the conventional uses of clothing and hairstyles that cover most of the other areas). Blushing is caused by the dilation of small blood vessels under the skin, and is involuntary, making it impossible to fake. The signal value of blushing is not entirely clear. Blushing often accompanies facial expressions of shame or embarrassment, suggesting that it may signal to perceivers that one is aware of a social transgression (de Jong, 1999; Leary et al., 1992). However, we also blush in situations that should not elicit shame or embarrassment, such as when we receive praise, or when friends sing "happy birthday" to us, or even when we are the recipient of a prolonged stare. These latter examples suggest that social blushing may be the result of general self consciousness and undesired social attention (Leary et al., 1992), and the blush itself signals to others that one is not comfortable and would like people to attend elsewhere. However, blushing in non-Whites, which is difficult to detect, raises problems for the idea that blushes are social signals (especially if it is true that all races evolved from dark-skinned peoples of the African savanna; Johanson and White, 1979).

While we know that blushing affects how we evaluate blushers (e.g. seeing someone blush after they violate social norm reduces our negative evaluation of the blunder; de Jong, 1999), it is not known how the brain processes blushing faces. One conjecture is that color vision in primates specifically evolved to process variations in skin color, such as blushing, in conspecifics (Changizi et al., 2006). In support of this, trichromat primates tend to be bare faced, or at least have some bare body part (e.g. the rump of a chimpanzee); indeed, humans are the "naked ape", consistent with our status as socially advanced organisms. Furthermore, non-human primates also experience skin color changes that indicate aspects of their emotional state (e.g. sexual arousal; Wickler, 1967; Waitt et al., 2003). Thus, one possibility is that human blush perception is subserved by the interaction between mechanisms underlying facial expression perception and visuocortical areas supporting color perception.

Tying it all together

Various types of information from faces appear to be processed in a roughly hierarchical scheme extending from inferior occipital cortex through ventral temporal cortex to anterior temporal cortex. This progression of processing implements early perception (in occipital cortex) through recognition and memory for faces (in anterior temporal lobe) (Rotshtein et al., 2005; Haxby and Gobbini, Chapter 6; Freiwald and Tsao, Chapter 36, this volume). In humans as in monkeys there are regions of ventral temporal cortex that appear to be surprisingly specialized for face processing, although as we reviewed these regions already encode more than one dimension (e.g. both identity and emotion information is represented). The amygdala and superior temporal sulcus and gyrus (STS/STG) come into play as well, and it is possible that these regions obtain face information in part through parallel routes, perhaps subcortical (but see Adolphs, 2008), that may relate facial motion information and face information that cannot be consciously perceived (Jiang and He, 2006). At least at the single-unit level, there appears to be a great extent of intermingling of responses to different cues (Perrett et al., 1984) and the combinations of feature dimensions encoded by neurons is often very complex.

This constellation of cortical and subcortical regions in the temporal lobe representing and distinguishing between facial cues and signals then feeds into several mechanisms whereby social knowledge can be generated—mechanisms for social inference and attribution (see Figure 29.1). The neural regions involved in these attributions are diverse, and include regions in the temporoparietal junction involved in "theory of mind" (Saxe and Kanwisher, 2003) (although perhaps not uniquely so; see Mitchell, 2007), regions in the medial and orbital frontal cortex involved in similar processing and in linking face signals to their reward value, and regions in insular and somatosensory cortices that help us to figure out what other people think and feel through simulation routines.

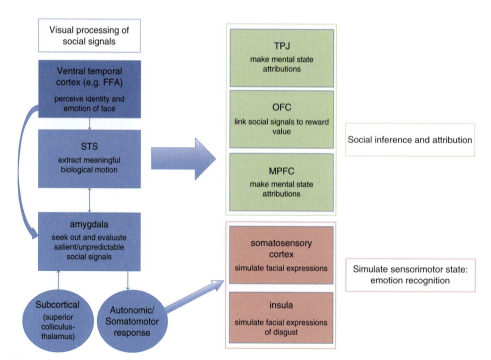

Fig. 29.1 Brain regions involved in visually processing social signals from the face feed into areas involved in social inference and attribution, and to areas involved in simulating sensorimotor states. FFA (fusiform face area), STS (superior temporal sulcus), TPJ (temporoparietal junction), OFC (orbital frontal cortex), MPFC (medial prefrontal cortex).

This picture also emphasizes the obvious importance of white matter connections between all these regions, a topic that has received scant attention and about which little is known. Some of the large white matter tracts, such as the inferior longitudinal fasciculus, inferior fronto-occipital fasciculus, and the uncinate fasciculus will all play a role in the feedforward cascade of face information conveyed from occipital regions anteriorly, as well as for mediating feedback. Indeed, we have found clear evidence for the importance of such white matter connections in mediating between occipital cortices and right somatosensory cortices in the facial emotion recognition (Philippi et al., 2008).

Two interesting directions for future research concern the full description of social signals from the face, and the automaticity of their recognition. We have Paul Ekman's basic emotions as the focus of much of the research on facial emotion; much less is known about the social emotions, or other facial signals at the neural level, even though this topic is investigated in psychology. We also have evidence for both automatic as well as strategic and context-dependent processing of facial signals, and it would be important to be able to map these onto their respective neural substrates. Finally, all these investigations will eventually need to take into account the issue of ecological validity: social signals are situated in a complex ecological setting, are dynamic, and are multimodal (Ghazanfar and Santos, 2004; see Penton-Voak and Morrison, Chapter 33, this volume). It will be important for researchers to continue to branch out from studying static pictures of faces to studying how we perceive dynamic social signals within rich, complex, real-world settings.

Summary and conclusions

We are skilled at reading a variety of social signals expressed by others. A central source of such socially meaningful signals is the face, which can be visually analyzed to understand a person's emotions, intentions, beliefs, and desires, along with information about that person's social status, approachability, age, and gender. In this chapter we reviewed what is known about the neural basis of the perception of such signals in humans, focusing on facial expression and gaze, and touching on lesser-studied signals such as pupil dilation and blushing. We reviewed the involvement of structures such as the insula, orbitofrontal cortex, amygdala, and superior temporal gyrus, which have been studied in some detail with respect to how they process social stimuli. We noted that social perception also involves information from other modalities and depends on the context in which signals occur.

References

Adams, R.B., Gordon, H.L., Baird, A.A., Ambady, N., and Kleck, R.E. (2003). Effects of gaze on amygdala sensitivity to anger and fear faces. *Science*, **300**, 1536.

Adams, R.B. and Kleck, R.E. (2003). Perceived gaze direction and the processing of facial displays of emotion. *Psychological Science*, **14**, 644–647.

Adolphs, R. (2002). Recognizing emotion from facial expressions: psychological and neurological mechanisms. *Behavioral and Cognitive Neuroscience Reviews*, **1**, 21–61.

Adolphs, R. (2008). Fear, faces, and the human amygdala. *Current Opinion in Neurobiology*, **18**, 1–7.

Adolphs, R. (2009). The social brain: neural basis of social knowledge. *Annual Review of Psychology*, **60**, 693–716.

Adolphs, R., Tranel, D., Damasio, H., and Damasio, A. (1994). Impaired recognition of emotion in facial expressions following bilateral damage to the human amygdala. *Nature*, **372**, 669–672.

Adolphs, R., Tranel, D., and Damasio, A.R. (1998). The human amygdala in social judgment. *Nature*, **393**, 470–474.

Adolphs, R., Russell, J.A., and Tranel, D. (1999a). A role for the human amygdala in recognizing emotional arousal from unpleasant stimuli. *Psychological Science*, **10**, 167–171.

Adolphs, R., Tranel, D., Hamann, S., *et al.* (1999b). Recognition of facial emotion in nine subjects with bilateral amygdala damage. *Neuropsychologia*, **37**, 1111–1117.

Adolphs, R., Damasio, H., Tranel, D., Cooper, G., and Damasio, A.R. (2000). A role for somatosensory cortices in the visual recognition of emotion as revealed by 3-D lesion mapping. *The Journal of Neuroscience*, **20**, 2683–2690.

Adolphs, R., Tranel, D., and Baron-Cohen, S. (2002). Amygdala damage impairs recognition of social emotions from facial expressions. *Journal of Cognitive Neuroscience*, **14**, 1264–1274.

Adolphs, R., Gosselin, F., Buchanan, T.W., Tranel, D., Schyns, P., and Damasio, A.R. (2005). A mechanism for impaired fear recognition after amygdala damage. *Nature*, **433**, 68–72.

Amaral, D.G., Capitanio, J.P., Jourdain, M., Mason, W.A., Mendoza, S.P., and Prather, M. (2003). The amygdala: is it an essential component of the neural network for social cognition? *Neuropsychologia*, **41**, 235–240.

Anderson, A.K., Christoff, K., Stappen, I., *et al.* (2003). Dissociated neural representations of intensity and valence in human olfaction. *Nature Neuroscience*, **6**, 196–202.

Anstis, S.M., Mayhew, J.W., Morley, T. (1969). The perception of where a face or television "portrait" is looking. *American Journal of Psychology*, **82**, 474–489.

Argyle, M. and Cook, M. (1976). *Gaze and mutual gaze.* Cambridge: Cambridge University Press.

Baron-Cohen, S. (1994). How to build a baby that can read minds: cognitive mechanisms in mindreading. *Cahiers de Psychologie Cognitive*, **13**, 513–552.

Baron-Cohen, S. (1995). *Mindblindness: An Essay on Autism and Theory of Mind.* Cambridge. MA: MIT Press.

Baron-Cohen, S., Wheelwright, S., and Jolliffe. T. (1997). Is there a "Language of the Eyes"? Evidence from normal adults, and adults with autism or Asperger syndrome. *Visual Cognition*, **4**, 311–331.

Bindemann, M., Burton, M.A., and Langton, S.R.H. (2007). How do eye gaze and facial expression interact? *Visual Cognition*, **6**, 708–733.

Birmingham, E. and Kingstone, A. (2009). Human social attention: A new look at past, present and future investigations. *The Year in Cognitive Neuroscience 2009, Annals of the New York Academy of Sciences*, **1156**, 118–140.

Birmingham, E., Bischof, W.F., and Kingstone, A. (2008). Gaze selection in complex social scenes. *Visual Cognition*, **16**, 341–355.

Blair, R.J.R., Morris, J.S., Frith, C.D., Perrett, D.I., and Dolan, R.J. (1999). Dissociable neural responses to facial expressions of sadness and anger. *Brain*, **122**, 883–893.

Bonda, E., Petrides, P. Ostry, D., and Evans, A. (1996). Specific involvement of human parietal systems and the amygdala in the perception of biological motion. *Journal of Neuroscience*, **16**, 3737–3744.

Borod, J.C., Koff, E., Yecker, S., Santschi, C., and Schmidt, J. (1998). Facial asymmetry during emotional expression: gender, valence and measurement technique. *Psychophysiology*, **36**, 1209–1215.

Bruce, V. and Young, A. (1986). Understanding face recognition. *British Journal of Psychology*, **77**, 305–327.

Butterworth, G. and Cochran, E. (1980). Towards a mechanism of joint visual attention in human infancy. *International Journal of Behavioral Development*, **3**, 253–272.

Byrne, R. and Whiten, A. (eds.) (1988). *Machiavellian Intelligence: Social Expertise and the Evolution of Intellect in Monkeys, Apes, and Humans.* Oxford: Clarendon.

Calder, A. and Young, A. (2005). Understanding the recognition of facial identity and facial expression. *Nature Reviews Neuroscience*, **6**, 641–651.

Calder, A.J., Keane, J., Cole, J., Campbell, R., and Young, A.W. (2000). Facial expression recognition by people with moebius syndrome. *Cognitive Neuropsychology*, **17**, 73–87

Calder, A.J., Lawrence, A.D., and Young, A.W. (2001a). Neuropsychology of fear and loathing. *Nature Reviews Neuroscience*, **2**, 352–363.

Calder, A.J., Burton, A.M., Miller, P., Young, A.W., and Akamatsu, S. (2001b). A principal component analysis of facial expressions. *Vision Research*, **41**, 1179–1208.

Calder, A.J., Lawrence, A.D., Keane, J., *et al.* (2002). Reading the mind from eye gaze. *Neuropsychologia*, **40**, 1129–1138.

Calder, A.J., Beaver, J.D., Winston, J.S., *et al.* (2007). Separate coding of different gaze directions in the superior temporal sulcus and inferior parietal lobule. *Current Biology*, **17**, 20–25.

Calvert, G.A., Brammer, M.J., and Iverson, S.D. (1998) Crossmodal identification. *Trends in Cognitive Science*, **2**, 247–253.

Changizi, M.A., Zhang, Q., and Shimojo, S. (2006). Bare skin, blood and the evolution of primate colour vision. *Biology Letters*, **2**, 217–221.

Chartrand, T. L. and Bargh, J. A. (1999). The Chameleon effect: the perception-behavior link and social interaction. *Journal of Personality and Social Psychology*, **76**, 893–910.

Cline, M.G. (1967). The perception of where a person is looking. *American Journal of Psychology*. **80**, 41–50.

Cook, M. and Smith, M.C. (1975). The role of gaze in impression formation. *British Journal of Social and Clinical Psychology*, **14**, 19–25.

Corkum, V. and Moore, C. (1995). Development of joint visual attention in infants. In C. Moore and P. J. Dunham (eds.), *Joint attention: Its origins and role in development*, pp. 61–83. Hillsdale, NJ: Erlbaum.

Cosmides, L. and Tooby, J. (1992). Cognitive adaptations for social exchange. In J. H. Barkow, L. Cosmides and J. Tooby (eds.), *The Adapted Mind: Evolutionary Psychology and the Generation of Culture*, pp. 163–228. New York: Oxford University Press.

Darwin, C. (1872/1965). *The Expression of the Emotions in Man and Animals*. Chicago. IL: University of Chicago Press. (Original work published 1872.)

Dejjani, B.-P., Damier, P., and Arnulf, I., *et al.* (1999). Transient acute depression induced by high-frequency deep-brain stimulation. *New England Journal of Medicine*, **340**, 1476–1480.

de Jong, P.J. (1999). Communicative and remedial effects of social blushing. *Journal of Nonverbal Behavior*, **23**(3), 197–217.

De Martino, B., Kumaran, D., Seymour, B., and Dolan, R. J. (2006). Frames, biases, and rational decision-making in the human brain. *Science*, **313**, 684–687.

Demos, K.E., Kelley, W.M., Ryan, S.L., Davis, F.C., and Whalen, P.J. (2008). Human amygdala sensitivity to the pupil size of others. *Cerebral Cortex*, **18**, 2729–2734.

Dimberg, U. (1982). Facial reactions to facial expressions. *Psychophysiology*, **19**, 643–647.

Dimberg, U., Thunberg, M., and Elmehed, K. (2000). Unconscious facial reactions to emotional facial expressions. *Psychological Science*, **11**, 86–89.

Efran, M.G. and Cheyne, J.A. (1974). Affective concomitants of the invasion of shared space: behavioral, physiological, and verbal indicators. *Journal of Personality and Social Psychology*, **29**, 219–226.

Ellsworth, P.C. (1975). Direct gaze as a social stimulus: the example of aggression. In P. Pilner, L. Krames, and T. Alloway (ed.) *Nonverbal communication of aggression*, pp. 53–76. New York: Plenum Press.

Ekman, P. (1994). Strong evidence for universals in facial expressions: a reply to Russell's mistaken critique. *Psychological Bulletin*, **115**, 268–287.

Exline, R.V. (1971). Visual interaction: The glances of power and preference. In J.K. Cole (ed.) *Nebraska Symposium on Motivation*, vol. **19**, pp.162–205. Lincoln, NE: University of Nebraska Press.

Fehr, E. and Gaechter, S. (2002). Altruistic punishment in humans. *Nature*, **415**, 137–140.

Fiske, S.T., Cuddy, A.J.C., and Glick, P. (2007). Universal dimensions of social cognition: warmth and competence. *TICS*, **11**, 78–83.

Fridlund, A.J. (1994). *Human Facial Expression*. New York: Academic Press.

Fried, I., Wilson, C. L., MacDonald, K. A., and Behnke, E. J. (1998). Electric current stimulates laughter. *Nature*, **391**, 650.

Friesen, C.K. and Kingstone, A. (1998). The eyes have it! Reflexive orienting is triggered by nonpredictive gaze. *Psychonomic Bulletin and Review*, **5**, 490–495.

Ganel, T., Valyear, K.F., Goshen-Gottstein, Y., and Goodale, M. A. (2005). The involvement of the "fusiform face area" in processing facial expression. *Neuropsychologia*, **43**, 1645–1654.

George, N., Driver, J., and Dolan, R.J. (2001). Seen gaze-direction modulates fusiform activity and its coupling with other brain areas during face processing. *NeuroImage*, **13**, 1102–1112.

Ghazanfar, A.A., and Logothetis, N.K. (2003). Facial expressions linked to monkey calls. *Nature*, **423**, 937–938.

Ghazanfar, A.A., and Santos, L.R. (2004). Primate brains in the wild: the sensory bases for social interactions. *Nature Reviews Neuroscience*, **5**, 603–616.

Gibson, J.J. and Pick, A. (1963). Perception of another person's looking. *American Journal of Psychology*, **76**, 86–94.

Goldman, A.I. and Sripada, C.S. (2005). Simulationist models of face-based emotion recognition. *Cognition*, **94**, 193–213.

Gosselin, F. and Schyns, P.G. (2001). Bubbles: a technique to reveal the use of information in recognition. *Vision Research*, **41**, 2261–2271.

Gothard, K.M., Battaglia, F.P., Erickson, C.A., Spitler, K.M., and Amaral, D.G. (2007). Neural responses to facial expression and face identity in the monkey amygdala. *Journal of Neurophysiology*, **97**, 1671–1683.

Grafton, S.T., Arbib, M.A., Fadiga, L., and Rizzolatti, G. (1996). Localization of grasp representation in humans by positron emission tomography: 2. Observation compared with imagination. *Experimental Brain Research*, **112**, 103–111.

Graham, R. and LaBar, K.S. (2007). Garner interference reveals dependencies between emotional expression and gaze in face perception. *Emotion*, **7**, 296–313.

Grèzes, J., Berthoz, S., and Passingham, R. (2006). Amygdala activation when one is the target of deceit: did he lie to you or to someone else. *Neuroimage*, 30, 601–608.

Grèzes, J., Costes, N., and Decety, J. (1999). The effects of learning and intention on the neural network involved in the perception of meaningless actions. *Brain*, **122**, 1875–1887

Griffiths, P.E. (1997). *What Emotions Really Are*. Chicago, IL: University of Chicago Press.

Grossman, E., Donnelly, M., Price, R., Pickens, D., Morgan, V., Neighbor, G., and Blake, R. (2000). Brain areas involved in perception of biological motion source. *Journal of Cognitive Neuroscience*, **12**, 711–720.

Harmer, C.J., Thilo, K.V., Rothwell, J.C., and Goodwin, G.M. (2001). Transcranial magnetic stimulation of medial-frontal cortex impairs the processing of angry facial expressions. *Nature Neuroscience*, **4**, 17–18.

Harrison, N.A., Singer, T., and Rothstein, P. (2006). Pupillary contagion: central mechanisms engaged in sadness processing. *Social Cognitive and Affective Neuroscience*, **1**, 5–17.

Hasselmo, M.E., Rolls, E.T., and Baylis, G.C. (1989). The role of expression and identity in the face-selective responses of neurons in the temporal visual cortex of the monkey. *Behavioral Brain Research*, **32**, 203–218.

Hauser, M.D. (1996). *The Evolution of Communication*. Cambridge, MA: MIT Press.

Haxby, J.V., Hoffman, E.A., and Gobbini, M.I. (2000). The distributed human neural system for face perception. *Trends in Cognitive Science*, **4**, 223–233.

Henderson, J.M., Williams, C.C., and Falk, R. (2005). Eye movements are functional during face learning. *Memory and Cognition*, **33**, 98–106.

Herry, C., Bach, D.R., Esposito, F., *et al.* (2007). Processing of temporal unpredictability in human and animal amygdala. *Journal of Neuroscience*, **27**, 5958–5966.

Hess, U., Adams, R.B. Jr., and Kleck, R.E. (2007). Looking at you or looking elsewhere: the influence of head orientation on the signal value of emotional facial expressions. *Motivation and Emotion*, **31**, 137–144.

Heywood, C.A., Cowey, A., and Rolls, E.T. (1992). The role of the face cell area in the discrimination and recognition of faces by monkeys. *Philosophical Transactions of the Royal Society of London B*, **335**, 31–38.

Hillabrant, W. (1974). The influence of locomotion and gaze direction on perceptions of interacting persons. *Personality and Social Psychology Bulletin*, **1**, 237–239.

Hoffman, E.A. and Haxby, J.V. (2000). Distinct representations of eye gaze and identity in the distributed human neural system for face perception. *Nature Neuroscience*, **3**, 80–84.

Hooker, C.I., Paller, K.A., Gitelman, D.R., Parrish, T.B., Mesulam, M.M., and Reber, P.J. (2003). Brain networks for analyzing eye gaze. *Cognitive Brain Research*, **17**, 406–418.

Jiang, Y. and He, S. (2006). Cortical responses to invisible faces: dissociating subsystems for facial-information processing. *Current Biology*, **16**, 2023–2029.

Johanson, D.C. and White, T.D. (1979). A systematic reassessment of early African hominids. *Science*, **203**, 321–330.

Kawashima, R. Sugiura, M, Kato, T., *et al.* (1999). The human amygdala plays an important role in gaze monitoring: a PET study. *Brain*, **122**, 779–783.

Kellerman, J., Lewis, J., and Laird, J.D. (1989). Looking and loving: the effects of mutual gaze on feelings of romantic love. *Journal of research in personality*, **23**, 145–161.

Kennedy, D.P., Gläscher, J., Tyszka, M., and Adolphs, R. (2009). Personal space regulation by the human amygdala. *Nature Neuroscience*, **12**, 1226–1227.

Kim, H., Somerville, L.H., Johnstone, T., *et al.* (2004). Contextual modulation of amygdala responsivity to surprised faces. *Journal of Cognitive Neuroscience*, **16**, 1730–1745.

Kipps, C.M., Duggins, A.J., McCusker, E.A., and Calder, A.J. (2007). Disgust and happiness recognition correlate with anteroventral insula and amygdala volume respectively in preclinical Huntington's Disease. *Journal of Cognitive Neuroscience*, **19**, 1206–1217.

Kleinke, C.L. (1986). Gaze and eye contact: a research review. *Psychological Bulletin*, **100**, 78–100.

Kobayashi, H. and Koshima, S. (1997). Unique morphology of the human eye. *Nature*, **387**, 767–768.

Kourtzi, Z. and Kanwisher, N. (2000). Activation in human MT/MST by static images with implied motion. *Journal of Cognitive Neuroscience*, **12**, 48–55

Langton, S.R.H. and Bruce, V. (1999). Reflexive visual orienting in response to the social attention of others. *Visual Cognition*, **6**, 541–568.

Langton, S.R.H., Honeyman, H., and Tessler, E. (2004). The influence of head contour and nose angle on the perception of eye-gaze direction. *Perception and Psychophysics*, **66**, 752–771.

Leary, M.R., Britt, T.W., Cutlip, W.D., and Templeton, J.L. (1992). Social blushing. *Psychological Bulletin*, **112(3)**, 446–460.

Lord, C. and Haith, M.M. (1974). The perception of eye contact. *Perception and Psychophysics*, **16**, 413–416.

Macrae, C.N., Hood, B.M., Milne, A.B., Rowe, A.C., and Mason, M.F. (2002). Are you looking at me? Eye gaze and person perception. *Psychological Science*, **13**, 460–464.

Mason, W.A., Capitanio, J.P., Machado, C.J., Mendoza, S.P., and Amaral, D. G. (2006). Amygdalectomy and responsiveness to novelty in rhesus monkeys: generality and individual consistency of effects. *Emotion*, **6**, 73–81.

Mason, M.F., Tatkow, E.P., and Macrae, C.N. (2005). The look of love: gaze shifts and person perception. *Psychological Science*, **16**, 236–239.

Mehrabian, A. and Williams, M. (1969). Nonverbal concomitants of perceived and intended persuasiveness. *Journal of Personality and Social Psychology*, **13**, 37–58.

Mitchell, J.P. (2007). Activity in right temporo-parietal junction is not selective for theory-of-mind. *Cerebral Cortex*, **18**, 262–271

Morissette, P., Ricard, M., and Decarie, T.G. (1995). Joint visual attention and pointing in infancy: A longitudinal study of comprehension. *British Journal of Developmental Psychology*, **13**, 163–175.

Nummenmaa, L. and Calder, A.J. (2009) Neural mechanisms of social attention. *Trends in Cognitive Sciences*, **13**, 135–143.

Pegna, A.J., Khateb, A., Lazeyras, F., and Seghier, M.L. (2005). Discriminating emotional faces without primary visual cortices involves the right amygdala. *Nature Neuroscience*, **8**, 24–25.

Pellegrini, R.J., Hicks, R.A., and Gordon, L. (1970). The effects of an approval-seeking induction on eye contact in dyads. *British Journal of Social and Clinical Psychology*, **9**, 373–374.

Pelphrey, K.A., Sasson, N.J., Reznick, S., Paul, G., Goldman, B.D., and Piven, J. (2002). Visual scanning of faces in autism. *Journal of Autism and Developmental Disorders*, **32**, 249–261.

Pelphrey, K.A., Singerman, J.D., Allison T., and McCarthy, G. (2003). Brain activation evoked by perception of gaze shifts: the influence of context. *Neuropsychologia*, **41**, 156–170.

Pelphrey, K.A., Viola, R.J., and McCarthy, G. (2004). When strangers pass: Processing of mutual and averted social gaze in the superior temporal sulcus. *Psychological Science*, **15**, 598–603.

Pelphrey, K.A., Morris, J.P., and McCarthy, G. (2005). Neural basis of eye gaze processing deficits in autism. *Brain*, **128**, 1038–1048.

Perrett, D.I., Hietanen, J.K., Oram, M.W., and Benson, P.J. (1992). Organization and functions of cells responsive to faces in the temporal cortex. *Philosophical Transactions of the Royal Society of London B*, **335**, 23–30.

Perrett D.I., Smith, P.A.J., Potter, D.D., *et al.* (1985). Visual cells in the temporal cortex sensitive to face view and gaze direction. *Proceedings of the Royal Society of London: Series B*, **223**, 293–317.

Perrett, D.I., Smith, P.A.J., Potter, D.D., *et al.* (1984) Neurones responsive to faces in the temporal cortex: studies of functional organization, sensitivity to identity and relation to perception. *Human Neurobiology*, **3**, 197–208.

Pessoa, L., Japee, S., Sturman, D., and Ungerleider, L.G. (2006). Target visibility and visual awareness modulate amygdala responses to fearful faces. *Cerebral Cortex*, **16**, 366–375.

Philippi, C., Mehta, S., Grabowski, T., Adolphs, R., and Rudrauf, D. (2008). The inferior fronto-occipital fasciculus mediates recognition of the facial expression of emotions. *Human Brain Mapping* 2008 conference.

Pourtois, G., Sander, D., Andres, M., *et al.* (2004). Dissociable roles of the human somatosensory and superior temporal cortices for processing social face signals. *European Journal of Neuroscience*, **20**, 3507–3515.

Puce, A., Smith, A., and Allison, T. (2000). ERPs evoked by viewing facial movements. *Cognitive Neuropsychology*, **17**, 221–239

Ricciardelli, P., Baylis, G., and Driver, J. (2000). The positive and negative of human expertise in gaze perception. *Cognition*, **77**, B1–B14.

Rizzolatti, G., Fadiga, L. Matelli, M., *et al.* (1996). Localization of grasp representations in humans by PET: 1. Observation versus execution. *Experimental Brain Research*, **111**, 246–252.

Rotshtein, P., Henson, R.N.A., Treves, A., Driver, J., and Dolan, R.J. (2005). Morphing Marilyn into Maggie dissociates physical and identity face representations in the brain. *Nature Neuroscience*, **8**, 107–113.

Rubin, J.Z., Stenberg, B.D., and Gerrein, J.R. (1974). How to obtain the right of way: an experimental analysis of behavior at intersections. *Perceptual and Motor Skills*, **39**, 1263–1274.

Russell, J.A. (1980). A circumplex model of affect. *Journal of Personality and Social Psychology*, **39**, 1161–1178.

Russell, J.A. (1994). Is there universal recognition of emotion from facial expression? A review of the cross-cultural studies, *Psychological Bulletin*, **115**, 102–141.

Said, C.P., Baron, S.G., and Todorov, A. (2009). Nonlinear amygdala response to face trustworthiness: contributions of high and low spatial frequency information. *Journal of Cognitive Neuroscience*, **21**, 519–528.

Sander, D., Grafman, J., and Zalla, T. (2003). The human amygdala: an evolved system for relevance detection. *Reviews in the Neurosciences*, **14**, 303–316.

Saxe, R. and Kanwisher, N. (2003). People thinking about thinking people. The role of the temporo-parietal junction in "theory of mind". *Neuroimage*, **19**, 1835–1842.

Scaife, M. and Bruner, J.S. (1975). The capacity for joint visual attention in the infant. *Nature*, **253**, 265–266.

Schmidt, K.L. and Cohn, J.F. (2001). Human facial expressions as adaptations: evolutionary questions in facial expression research. *Yearbook of Physical Anthropology*, **44**, 3–24.

Sinha, P. (2000). Last but not least: Here's looking at you, kid. *Perception*, **29**, 1005–1008.

Smith, M.L., Cottrell, G.W., Gosselin, F., and Schyns, P.G. (2005). Transmitting and decoding facial expressions. *Psychological Science*, **16**, 184–189.

Symons, L.A., Lee, K., Cedrone, C.C., and Nishimura, M. (2004). What are you looking at? Acuity for triadic eye gaze. Source: *Journal of General Psychology* **131**, 451–69.

Timney, B. and London, H. (1973). Body language concomitants of persuasiveness and persuasibility in dyadic interaction. *International Journal of Group Tensions*, **3**, 48–67.

Todorov, A. and Engell, A.D. (2008). The role of the amygdala in implicit evaluation of emotionally neutral faces. *Social Cognitive and Affective Neuroscience*, **3**, 303–312.

Tomasello, M. (1999). *The Cultural Origins of Human Cognition*. Cambridge, MA: Harvard University Press.

Tranel, D., Damasio, A.R., and Damasio, H. (1988). Intact recognition of facial expression, gender, and age in patients with impaired recognition of face identity. *Neurology*, **38**, 690–696.

Tsuchiya, N., Kawasaki, H., Oya, H., Howard, M.A., and Adolphs, R. (2008). Decoding face information in time, frequency and space from direct intracranial recordings of the human brain. *PLoS One*, **3**, e3892.

von Grunau, M. and Anston, C. (1995). The detection of gaze direction: A stare-in-the-crowd effect. *Perception*, **24**, 1297–1313.

Waitt, C., Little, A.C., Wolfensohn, S., Honess, P., Brown, A.P., Buchanan-Smith, H.M., *et al.* (2003). Evidence from rhesus macaques suggests that male coloration plays a role in female primate choice. *Proceedings of the Royal Society B*, **270**(Suppl), S144–S146.

Walker-Smith, G., Gale, A.G., and Findlay, J.M. (1977). Eye movement strategies involved in face perception. *Perception*, **6**, 313–326.

Watt, R., Craven, B., and Quinn, S. (2007). A role for eyebrows in regulating the visibility of eye gaze direction. *The Quarterly Journal of Experimental Psychology*, **60**, 1169–1177.

Whalen, P.J. (1999). Fear, vigilance, and ambiguity: initial neuroimaging studies of the human amygdala. *Current Directions in Psychological Science*, **7**, 177–187.

Whalen, P.J., Kagan, J., Cook, R.G., *et al.* (2004). Human amygdala responsivity to masked fearful eye whites. *Science*, **306**, 2061.

Wicker, B., Michel, F., Henaff, M.A., and Decety, J. (1998). Brain regions involved in the perception of gaze: a PET study. *NeuroImage*, **8**, 221–227.

Wickler, W. (1967). Socio-sexual signals and their intra-specific imitation among primates. In D. Morris (ed.), *Primate Ethology*, pp. 69–147. London: Weidenfeld and Nicolson.

Winston, J.S., Strange, B.A., O'Doherty, J., and Dolan, R.J. (2002). Automatic and intentional brain responses during evaluation of trustworthiness of faces. *Nature Neuroscience*, **5**, 277–283.

Winston, J.S., O'Doherty, J., and Dolan, R.J. (2003). Common and distinct neural responses during direct and incidental processing of multiple facial emotions. *NeuroImage*, **20**, 84–97.

Winston, J.S., Henson, R.N., Fine-Goulden, M.R., and Dolan, R.J. (2004). fMRI-adaptation reveals dissociable neural representations of identity and expression in face perception. *Journal of Neurophysiology*, **92**, 1830–1839.

Winston, J.S., Gottfried, J.A., Kilner, J.M., and Dolan, R.J. (2005). Integrated neural representations of odor intensity and affective valence in human amygdala. *The Journal of Neuroscience*, **25**, 8903–8907.

Winston, J.S., O'Doherty, J., Kilner, J.M., Perrett, D.I., and Dolan, R.J. (2007). Brain systems for assessing facial attractiveness. *Neuropsychologia*, **45**, 195–206.

Wollaston, W.H. (1824). On the apparent direction of eyes in a portrait. *Philosophical Transactions of the Royal Society of London B*, 247–256.

Yarbus, A.L (1967). *Eye movements and vision* (B. Haigh, Trans.) New York: Plenum Press. (Original work published 1965.)

Young, A.W., Aggleton, J.P., Hellawell, D.J., Johnson, M., Broks, P., and Hanley, J.R. (1995). Face processing impairments after amygdalotomy. *Brain*, **118**, 15–24.

Young, A.W., Rowland, D., Calder, A.J., Etcoff, N.L., Seth, A., and Perrett, D.I. (1997). Facial expression megamix: tests of dimensional and category accounts of emotion recognition. *Cognition*, **63**, 271–313.

Chapter 30

Functional and Neural Mechanisms for Eye Gaze Processing

Kevin A. Pelphrey and Brent C. Vander Wyk

Introduction

Faces provide a wealth of social information, including the bearer's identity (Bruce and Young, 1986), emotional state (Bassili, 1989; Ekman, 1982), focus of attention (Langton, 2000; Langton et al., 2000), and intentions (Baron-Cohen, 1995; Baron-Cohen et al., 2001). The capacity to extract socially relevant information from faces is fundamental to normal reciprocal social interactions and communication. Faces, generally, are highly salient to typically developing individuals (Goren et al., 1975; Johnson et al., 1991), even from the earliest stages of postnatal development (Johnson, Chapter 1, this volume). More specifically, it is the eyes that seem to preferentially draw a viewer's attention (Emery, 2000; Langton et al., 2000), garnering 70% or more of the fixations of adult viewers (Luria and Strauss, 1978; Noton and Stark, 1971; Walker-Smith et al., 1977).

The basic function of the eye, as a sense organ, is to take in sensory stimuli so as to permit an organism to navigate its environment. Unlike the other sense organs, the eye is highly direction-specific, which means that in order to sense a distal stimulus it needs to be oriented toward that stimulus. Consequently, eyes are often aimed at important things in the world, such as food, predators, mates, and targets of future action, be they objects or other animals. Since gaze orientation is itself often a perceptible stimulus, an onlooker able to detect and make use of this stimulus has at its disposal information about potentially important locations in the world, about what the gazer may know, and about what the gazer might do. Thus, from an evolutionary perspective gaze appears to warrant the attention it receives. Indeed, given the seeming importance of gaze direction, it is not surprising that many species, including some birds and snakes (Marr, 1982; Ristau, 1991), have mechanisms that are sensitive to gaze. Undoubtedly, it is primates, human and non-human, that make the most of gaze cues. Below we will review evidence that suggests that the primate gaze processing system consists of more than one information processing system. As illustrated in Figure 30.1, the anterior superior temporal sulcus (aSTS) performs the initial computation and representation of specific gaze direction. It passes this information along two dissociable processing streams. One stream, which involves regions in the inferior parietal cortex (IPC), drives attentional shifting mechanisms that subserve basic gaze following (Tipper and Bayliss, this volume). A second stream involves the posterior STS (pSTS), amygdala, and medial prefrontal cortex (mPFC), which collectively computes the social significance of gaze and permits higher-order social cognition such as joint or shared attention, at least in humans.

A system for computing gaze direction

Although eyes have captivated the imagination of writers, philosophers, and theologians for centuries, the scientific study of gaze perception only began in earnest in the 1960s. Research during this period focused on basic questions such as whether the perceptual system has sufficient power

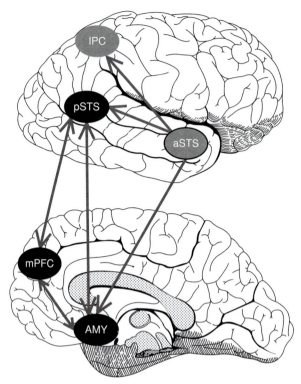

Fig. 30.1 Illustration of the brain mechanisms involved in eye gaze perception and their functional roles. Two neuroanatomical systems for different aspects of eye gaze processing are illustrated. The black markers indicate the components of a system for processing eye gaze as a cue to mental states. The grey markers highlight regions involved in processing eye gaze as an environmental cue. While dissociable, it is hypothesized that these two networks function together in the service of complex social cognitive functions that are reliant upon information from the eyes. AMY, amygdala (emotional contextualization of gaze); aSTS, anterior superior temporal sulcus (computation and representation of others' gaze direction); IPC, inferior parietal cortex (reorienting of spatial attention to observed gaze targets); mPFC, medial prefrontal cortex (integration of observed social and emotional cues); pSTS (representation of others' actions and intentions to act).

to discriminate the direction of eye gaze indicated by very minute changes within the eyes. In these studies, participants were presented with live confederates, pictures of a face, or even videos in which the gazer fixated on one of several targets in the environment. Participants were, typically, asked to determine the gazer's fixation target. This early work in the laboratory setting showed that people possess a remarkable ability to discriminate between different directions of gaze and to determine the point of regard with high accuracy. For example, at a distance of 2 m, participants could discriminate between different gaze directions that corresponded to differences as small as 1 mm in the iris, which amounts to acuity roughly equivalent to that needed to discriminate standard printed text (Cline, 1967; Gibson and Pick, 1963).

These experiments also permitted the investigation into how different parameters impact gaze discriminability. Researchers studied factors such as the distance of the participant from the gazer, the angle of the fixated target relative to the participant-gazer axis, and the angle of the gazer's head relative to the participant and to the direction of gaze. All of these factors were found to affect the ability to perceive gaze direction. For instance, eye gaze discriminability was found to diminish both as the distance from the perceiver to the gazer increased, and with reduced ambient brightness (Martin and Rovira, 1981). Participants tended to overestimate the gaze angle when gaze was averted relative to the perceiver (Anstis et al., 1969). And gaze perception is slightly more accurate for targets located directly horizontal and vertical to the eyes (Bock et al., 2008). The head direction of the gazer was also found to interact with perceived direction of gaze (Gibson and Pick, 1963; Loomis et al., 2008; Todorovic, 2006), a finding that echoes results from electrophysiological studies of neuron function in non-human primates, discussed below.

As researchers built a body of work delimiting the psychophysical factors that influence gaze perception, neuroscientists began to address basic issues in how the primate brain encodes and processes gaze. Seminal work involving electrophysiological recordings from the aSTS in the rhesus macaque revealed separate cell populations coding for direct and averted gaze (De Souza et al., 2005; Perrett et al., 1985, 1992). For instance, David Perrett and his colleagues studied the ways in which responses from face- and head-selective cells in the macaque brain are modulated by the direction of eye gaze and orientation of the face. Via direct neuronal recordings, they found that the majority of those cells selectively responsive to the sight of the face or head (versus other objects) were also sensitive to the orientation of the head such that different views (e.g. full face, profile, back or top of the head, face rotated by 45 degrees up or down) maximally activated different groups of cells. These same cells were not sensitive to rotation in the picture plane or changes in size/perceived distance. Within those cells sensitive to head orientation, many were also sensitive to gaze direction. In many cases, cells most responsive to the full face preferred eye contact, while cells tuned to the profile face preferred averted gaze. Therefore, sensitivity to gaze was often symmetric with, but could be asymmetric to, sensitivity to head orientation. This and other studies of the monkey brain provided critical, early evidence for the idea that diverse cell populations in and around the aSTS of the primate brain could be responsive to different directions of gaze. Behavioral and neural results in humans lead researchers to hypothesize that regions within the STS served as a specific module for the detection of eye-gaze direction. Simon Baron-Cohen hypothesized that regions within the STS might be the neural correlate of a hypothesized "eye direction detector" (Baron-Cohen, 1992, 1995) that was conserved through primate evolution. Evidence from human neuroimaging localized several areas active to face stimuli that included gaze shifts, including regions in the IPC and pSTS. Haxby and colleagues (2000) incorporated these regions as part of an extended system for processing faces (see also, Haxby and Gobbini, Chapter 6, this volume).

Recent evidence suggests that there are actually two cortical regions along the STS that are involved in different aspects of eye gaze processing: one in an anterior and one in the posterior portion of this neuroanatomical feature. The function of the anterior portion was described only recently, and relates to representation of gaze direction. We will return to the function of the pSTS later in this chapter. In an elegant functional magnetic resonance imaging (fMRI) study, Andy Calder and colleagues (2007) investigated whether the human aSTS contains representations of different gaze directions, as predicted by the work in non-human primates. In an fMRI-adaptation paradigm, they showed subjects faces gazing to the left, directly ahead, or to the right. Importantly, studies employing fMRI-adaptation have been shown to offer higher spatial resolution compared to more standard fMRI paradigms (e.g. Grill-Spector et al., 1999). Using this paradigm, they identified regions that decreased their response as a function of gaze direction repetition. It was reasoned that voxels exhibiting a declining response profile due to the repetition of a particular gaze direction were involved in coding that direction of gaze. They found that adapting to leftward gaze produced a reduction in BOLD response to left relative to right (and direct) gaze probes in the aSTS and IPC, while rightward gaze adaptation produced a corresponding reduction to right gaze probes.

Behaviorally, and replicating a prior experiment (Jenkins et al., 2006), averted gaze in the adapted direction was most often misidentified as direct gaze. This was the first evidence of distinct neuronal populations in the right aSTS of humans that are sensitive to different directions of gaze. If this region has the function of computing gaze direction, then it follows that its activity ought to be modulated by the many parameters that are known to influence the perception of gaze.

A brain system for processing gaze as an environmental cue

The direction of another person's eye gaze provides powerful information regarding the decisions they have made about whether something is important. While it is possible to dissociate eye movements and visual attention (Posner, 1980), under normal circumstances, eyes are often moved to fixate attended targets. Thus, another's gaze can be exploited as a cue to potential targets of interest in the environment, for example as an "early warning signal" to potential threats. The processes by which gaze directs attention have been studied in detail in humans (Adolphs and Birmingham, Chapter 29, this volume). At the same time, studies of gaze perception in non-human primates have generated mixed results. Some studies find that non-human primates do in fact utilize gaze cues (Brauer et al., 2005; Povinelli and Eddy, 1996; Povinelli et al., 1997; Tomasello et al., 1998; Ruiz et al., 2009) while others do not (Anderson et al., 1995; Itakura, 1996). The basic function of gaze following may be present in monkeys, but understanding the social significance may only be present in apes and humans (Emery, 1997). Thus, the mixed results may reflect differences in the degree to which the experiments required deeper understanding of gaze including its mentalistic significance.

As discussed above, the primate gaze processing system utilizes the aSTS to represent specific details of the direction of an observed gaze. An additional mechanism is needed to shift the organism's own attention along the observed gaze. Functional imaging research has identified a role for the IPC, including the intraparietal sulci (IPS), in gaze processing (Pelphrey et al., 2003, 2005; Wicker et al., 1998). Haxby and colleagues (2000) suggested that activations within the IPS reflect the coordination of gaze direction information with systems in the parietal cortex involved in orienting attention (Corbetta et al., 1993; Posner et al., 1984; Rushworth et al., 2001). These systems are initiated by viewing averted gaze (Driver et al., 1999; Friesen and Kingstone, 1998; Langton and Bruce, 1999). Specifically, the right IPC (as a component of the frontoparietal attentional network) plays a role in reorienting attention toward behaviorally relevant events (Corbetta and Shulman, 2002) and is connected to both the aSTS and pSTS (Harries and Perrett, 1991; Rozzi et al., 2006). Hence, the involvement of the inferior parietal lobule in processing gaze direction probably reflects the operation of attentional orienting mechanisms rather than perceptual representations of gaze. In sum, the evidence points to a neuroanatomical system comprised of the aSTS and IPC that serves to recognize different gaze directions and then uses this information to orient the observer's attention in line with the perceived gaze direction.

A brain system for processing gaze as a mental state cue

In addition to providing information about the spatial location of relevant targets, gaze provides information about the internal states of the gazer. For example, gaze direction also permits inferences about his emotional state. In particular, mutual gaze, (i.e. gaze perceived to be directed at the viewer's own eyes), seems to play a special role in social behaviors of human (Argyle and Dean, 1965; Argyle et al., 1974) and non-human primates (Redican, 1975). Mutual gaze often signals threat, approach and/or the intention to interact, while averted gaze can convey submission and/or the intention to avoid social interaction (e.g. Argyle and Cook, 1976; Baron-Cohen, 1995; Darwin, 1872/1965; Emery, 2000; Kleinke, 1986; Strongman and Champness, 1968). Because of its importance, a great deal of work has focused on the neural basis of distinctions between mutual and averted gaze. Studies of the rhesus macaque as well as a handful of functional neuroimaging studies in humans (George et al., 2001; Kawashima et al., 1999; Pelphrey et al., 2004; Wicker et al., 1998) have examined eye contact versus averted gaze. Human neuroimaging studies have generated mixed results, with some studies finding no difference in STS responses to mutual and averted gaze (George et al., 2001; Wicker et al., 1998), and others finding a greater response to mutual versus averted gaze localized in the amygdala (Kawashima et al., 1999) or the pSTS (Pelphrey et al., 2004). Comparisons between these studies are difficult because of methodological differences among them (e.g. static versus dynamic eye gazes, single mutual gaze fixation vs. multiple fixations, and analyses based on restricted regions of interest vs. whole-brain analysis at higher statistical thresholds). However, much of the confusion may arise because these studies did not always take into account the distinct inferences about others' minds that eye gaze permits: inferences about their intentions to act and inferences about their emotional state. Below we will review research that implicates the pSTS in processing the former and research that points to the amygdala and mPFC in the processing of the latter (Nishijo et al., 1988; Oschner et al., 2004; Rolls, 1992).

Because people tend to look at things they want or plan to act upon, successfully computing the direction of gaze and determining the target of attention provides a powerful source of information to infer intentions of others. This process, referred to as joint or shared attention (Baron-Cohen, 1995), builds on the gaze following described in the preceding section, but also requires an awareness that the other is attending. Joint attention processes have been studied in both human and non-human primates (Parr and Hecht, Chapter 35, this volume). Even very young humans seem to be sensitive to mentalistic implications of gaze, and by 12 months of age show increased looking when they observe someone failing to reach for a previously fixated upon target (Phillips et al., 2002; Sodian and Thoermer, 2004). However, as in simple gaze following, non-human primates' ability to engage in joint attention is unclear. Some have argued that higher level social cognition such as joint attention and Theory of Mind (ToM) are uniquely human capacities, while others have argued that lower primates have these abilities, but that they are more domain-specific than in humans. Thus, they will only be evinced contingent on the experimental set-up matching an ecologically valid situation (Lyons and Santos, 2006; Santos et al., 2006).

In functional neuroimaging studies, the pSTS has been consistently implicated in gaze processing, but it does not appear to consistently exhibit differential activity as a function of gaze direction, except when the different gaze directions signal different social intentions (Pelphrey et al., 2004). In the first fMRI study to examine the neural basis of eye movement processing, Puce and her colleagues (Puce et al., 1998) demonstrated that the pSTS responds more strongly to observed eye and mouth movements than it does to various non-biological-motion controls. This response to eye gaze, however, is subsumed under a broader pattern of selectivity for biological versus non-biological motion, as several early functional neuroimaging studies in humans implicated the pSTS in the visual perception of biological motion (for a review, see Allison et al., 2000). For example, Bonda and colleagues (Bonda et al., 1996) reported that the perception of point-light displays representing goal-directed hand actions and body movements selectively activates the pSTS relative to random motion.

Like the study by Bonda and colleagues (1996), most of the early studies of biological motion perception had used point-light displays conveying random or meaningless/unnamable motions as non-biological comparison stimuli. However, a subsequent imaging experiment (Pelphrey et al., 2003) contrasted four types of visual motion generated using virtual reality animation techniques: a walking robot, a grandfather clock, a disjointed mechanical figure, and a walking human. This experiment demonstrated that the pSTS responds more strongly to biological motion (as conveyed by a walking robot or walking human) than it does to non-meaningful but complex non-biological motion (a disjointed mechanical figure) or to complex and meaningful non-biological motion (the movements of a grandfather clock). It was noteworthy that the nearby and well-characterized motion-processing area, V5 (e.g. Zeki et al., 1991), responded strongly and equivalently to all four movements. Thus, it is not likely that the results from the pSTS can be accounted for by lower-level differences in the attentional value of the stimuli or differences in the amount of movement inherent in each stimulus. These results demonstrate that the pSTS appears to signal the presence of an animate agent in the environment, and is capable of distinguishing between the movements of another person and the complex motions of a recognizable machine.

While activity levels in the pSTS differentiate between biological and non-biological motion, the region is not homogeneous in its response to different kinds of biological motion. Instead, there is evidence for a somatotopic organization for different observed effectors in the pSTS. An fMRI study that compared the activity patterns in response to movements of the eyes, mouth, or hand (Pelphrey et al., 2005) discovered that the spatial distribution of hemodynamic response amplitudes differentiated between the movements in the pSTS. Specifically, there was an anterior-to-posterior distribution of mouth-to-eye movements within the pSTS such that mouth movements elicited activity along the mid-pSTS, while eye movements elicited activity in more superior and posterior portions of the right pSTS. Hand movements activated more inferior and posterior portions of the pSTS within the posterior continuing branch of the pSTS. Hand-evoked activity also extended into the inferior temporal, middle occipital, and lingual gyri.

This topography might reflect the role of particular body motions in different functional activities, or differential involvement of the pSTS in directing spatial attention and in social communication. From this perspective, the posterior/superior focus of eye movement-evoked activity is well-positioned in relation to the frontoparietal network thought to be important for spatially directed attention (Corbetta et al., 1993; Culham et al., 1998; Nobre et al., 1997; reviewed in Kastner and Ungerleider, 2000). Similarly, the more anterior focus of mouth activity is well-positioned near polysensory regions of the left and right middle STS and superior temporal gyrus, which are known to be involved in the integration of audio and visual components of speech (Calvert, 2001; Calvert and Campbell, 2003; Hikosaka, 1993; Hikosaka et al., 1998; Wright et al., 2003).

Further studies suggest that the pSTS is more broadly involved in deriving higher-level mentalistic descriptions from motion, and gaze in particular, for use in action interpretation and other inferences regarding the goals and intentions underlying observed actions. In one such study, participants viewed the face of a virtual female character that was present on the screen throughout the fMRI experiment (Pelphrey et al., 2003). At the beginning of a trial, a checkerboard would appear within the character's field of view. The female character would then make an eye gaze shift toward or away from the checkerboard. In this context, a gaze shift toward the checkerboard was consistent with the expectation that another person would look at a target appearing in their visual field. These trials are called "congruent." A shift away from the checkerboard would be inconsistent with this expectation, and would demand additional processing from regions involved in processing the intentions of actions. These trials are called "incongruent." It was observed that the pSTS, particularly in the right hemisphere, responded more strongly to an eye gaze when it was incongruent with the participant's expectations about what the female character ought to do in this particular context. It was concluded that the pSTS does not merely represent the surface features of biological motion, but also participates in integrating biological motion, or actions, with the social and/or physical context. In this way, the pSTS plays a role in analyzing and interpreting the intentions underlying observed biological motions. These conclusions were bolstered by other findings regarding a role for the pSTS in analyzing the intentions and dispositions of others as conveyed by biological motion (e.g. Brass et al., 2007; Castelli et al., 2000; Pelphrey et al., 2004; Saxe et al., 2004, Vander Wyk et al., 2009).

Moving away from the pSTS, two other brain regions, the amygdala and mPFC, have been implicated in aspects of eye gaze processing relevant to eye gaze as a mentalistic cue. With regard to the amygdala, Hooker and colleagues (Hooker et al., 2003) conducted an fMRI study in which subjects attempted to detect a particular directional cue provided either by gaze changes on an image of a face or by an arrow presented alone or by an arrow superimposed on the face. They found that increases in activity in the amygdala are associated with facilitated processing of gaze cues when a person is actively monitoring for emotional gaze events, whereas increases in the activity of the pSTS are related to the analysis of gaze cues that provide socially meaningful spatial information. Further, Kawashima and colleagues (Culham et al., 1998) identified amygdala activation to both direct and averted gaze, with the direct gaze condition showing significantly greater right amygdala activation than the averted gaze condition. The authors attributed the amygdala involvement to the emotional component of processing another person's gaze.

The mPFC has frequently been implicated in complex aspects of social cognition (e.g. Brunet et al., 2000; Castelli et al., 2000; Fletcher et al., 1995; Gallagher et al., 2000). Frith and Frith (1999) first proposed that, together with the anterior cingulate, the mPFC serves to process mental states of the self. These states can then be attributed to others in the process of inferring another person's thoughts and intentions. Consistent with this theory, there is a growing literature on the contributions of the mPFC to judgments of others who are more or less like oneself (e.g. Mitchell et al., 2006). Calder and colleagues (2002) conducted a positron emission tomography (PET) study in which they examined the role of the mPFC in eye gaze processing. The experiment involved three conditions in which the proportions of faces gazing at and away from the participant were as follows: 100% direct, 50% direct:50% averted, and 100% horizontally averted. Two control conditions were also included in which the eyes were averted down or the eyes were closed. Contrasts comparing the gaze conditions with each of the control conditions revealed mPFC involvement. Parametric analyses showed a significant linear relationship between increasing proportions of horizontally averted gaze and increased regional cortical blood flow (rCBF) in the mPFC. The opposite parametric analysis (increasing proportions of direct gaze) was associated with increased rCBF in a number of areas including the superior and medial temporal gyri. Their results demonstrated a considerable degree of overlap between the mPFC areas involved in eye gaze processing and theory of mind tasks. Similarly, using the previously mentioned incongruent versus congruent eye gaze paradigm in a sample of school-age children, mPFC activation was reported in response to the observation of eye movements (Mosconi et al., 2005). Williams and colleagues (2005) conducted a striking study in which they induced the experience of joint attention for the participant in the magnet, which allowed them to contrast joint and non-joint attention during the observation of another person's eye movements. They found that activity associated with joint attention was localized to ventromedial frontal cortex, the left superior frontal gyrus, cingulate cortex, and caudate nuclei. The region of ventromedial frontal cortex they identified overlaps greatly with the region of mPFC reported in numerous studies employing a wider variety of theory of mind tasks.

Summary and conclusions

Successfully navigating a social environment requires specialized mechanisms for perceiving important aspects of the people around oneself and using that information to modify one's behavior and cognition. In this regard, the direction of gaze is an especially important target for these mechanisms because of the rich information it provides about the environment and the mental states of the gazer. The psychophysical evidence reviewed here demonstrates that humans possess a perceptual apparatus sensitive enough to detect the visual features informative of gaze in many face-to-face situations. This computational feat is accomplished by taking into account visual details of the eyes, the position of the gazer's head, and the location of potential targets in the environment. Evidence from human and primate studies implicates the aSTS as the neural substrate of this computational process. Having computed the direction of gaze, this information is used as a cue to the internal mental states of the gazer, including their emotions and intentions, and is used to inform the attention system of potential targets in the environment. Research suggests that the former functions are performed by a network of regions that comprise the "social brain," including the pSTS, the amygdala, and the mPFC. The functions relating to attentional shifting, however, involve regions of the IPC. The continuous interaction of these systems is necessary for the successful generation of complex social behaviors, such as joint-attention and shared intentions.

In summary, we have reviewed evidence for the existence of three functionally and neuroanatomically dissociable eye gaze processing systems. These systems appear to map onto behavioral findings that distinguish between the ability to compute eye gaze direction per se, the ability to use eye gaze as an environmental cue, and the ability to use eye gaze as a cue to mental states. Eyes engage a system involved in determining the direction of another person's gaze via the aSTS. Outputs from this system are capable of guiding the reorientation of the subject's own direction of attention via the response of the IPC. Eye gaze also represents a class of biological motion cues which engages the pSTS for the analysis of intentions and psychological dispositions. Outputs from the aSTS constrain processing in the pSTS, linking the observed direction of gaze towards an object or person in the environment with the mentalistic information provided by the gaze shift.

We conclude by highlighting a few promising research directions for the field. One important direction involves charting the development of these brain mechanisms for eye gaze processing. Our understanding of early behavioral development in the domain of eye gaze processing would predict different developmental trajectories for each of the three mechanisms we have discussed (Johnson, Chapter 1, this volume). For example, we might predict that the ability to represent gaze direction comes on line first, with the emergence of the associated aSTS system. Shortly thereafter, the development of functional connections between the aSTS and the IPC might enable the system for the reorientation of the infant's own direction of attention in line with that of another person. Finally, and somewhat later, the development of pSTS, amygdala, and mPFC, and interconnections between these regions and the aSTS/IPC systems, support the emergence of the ability to link the observed direction of gaze towards an object or person in the environment with the mentalistic information provided by the gaze shift.

A second important direction involves the study of autism, a neurodevelopmental disorder that deeply affects multiple aspects of social cognition and social behavior. A large body of research demonstrates that individuals with autism exhibit early appearing deficits in using gaze information to understand the intentions and mental states of others, as well as to coordinate joint attention (Webb et al., Chapter 43, this volume). Currently, the brain mechanisms underlying these deficits are poorly understood. Given our growing understanding of the brain mechanisms supporting different aspects of gaze processing in typically developing people, the time is ripe for experiments to determine exactly which eye gaze processing mechanisms are affected in autism.

Acknowledgments

An award from the John Merck Scholars Fund and a Career Development Award from the National Institute of Mental Health to KAP supported the writing of this chapter.

References

Allison, T., Puce, A., and McCarthy, G. (2000). Social perception from visual cues: Role of the STS region. *Trends in Cognitive Science,* **4**, 267–278.

Anderson, J.R., Sallaberry, P., and Barbier, H. (1995). Use of experimenter-given cues during object-choice tasks by capuchin monkeys. *Animal Behavior,* **49**, 201–208.

Anstis, S.M., Mayhew, J.W., and Morley, T. (1969). Perception of where a face or television portrait is looking. *American Journal of Psychology,* **82**, 474–489.

Argyle, M., and Cook, M. (1976). *Gaze and mutual gaze.* Cambridge University Press: New York.

Argyle, M., and Dean, J. (1965). Eye-contact, distance and affiliation. *Sociometry,* **28**, 289–304.

Argyle, M., Lefebvre, L., and Cook, M. (1974). The meaning of five patterns of gaze. *European Journal of Social Psychology,* **4**, 125–136.

Baron-Cohen, S. (1992). How to build a baby that can read minds: cognitive mechanisms in mindreading. *Cahiers de Psychologie Cognitive,* **13**, 513–552.

Baron-Cohen, S. (1995). *Mindblindness: an essay on autism and theory-of-mind.* MIT Press: Cambridge, M.A.

Baron-Cohen, S., Wheelwright, S., Hill, J., Raste, Y., and Plumb, I. (2001). The reading the mind in the eyes test revised version: a study with normal adults, and adults with Asperger syndrome or high-functioning autism. *Journal of Child Psychology and Psychiatry,* **42**, 241–251.

Bassili, J.N. (1989). *On-line cognition in person perception.* Lawrence Erlbaum: Hillsdale, NJ.

Bock, S.W., Dicke, P., and Thier, P. (2008). How precise is gaze following in humans? *Vision Research,* **48**, 946–957.

Bonda, E., Petrides, M., Ostry, D., and Evans, A. (1996). Special involvement of human parietal systems and the amygdala in the perception of biological motion. *The Journal of Neuroscience,* **16**, 3737–3744.

Brass, M., Schmitt, R.M., Spengler, S., and Gergely, G. (2007). Investigating action understanding: inferential processes versus action simulation. *Current Biology,* **17**, 1–5.

Brauer, J., Call, J., and Tomasello, M. (2005). All great ape species follow gaze to distant locations and around barriers. *Journal of Comparative Psychology,* **119**, 145–154.

Bruce, V., and Young, A. (1986). Understanding face recognition. *British Journal of Psychology,* **77**, 305–327.

Brunet, E., Sarfati, Y., Hardy-Bayle, M.C., and Decety, J. (2000). A PET investigation of the attribution of intentions with a nonverbal task. *NeuroImage,* **11**, 157–166.

Calder, A.J., Lawrence, A.D., Keane, J., *et al.* (2002). Reading the mind from eye gaze. *Neuropsychologia,* **40**, 1129–1138.

Calder, A.J., Beaver, J.D., Winston, J.S., *et al.* (2007). Separate coding of different gaze directions in the superior temporal sulcus and inferior parietal lobule. *Current Biology,* **17**, 20–25.

Calvert, G.A., and Campell, R. (2003). Reading speech from still and moving faces: the neural substrates of visual speech. *Journal of Cognitive Neuroscience,* **15**, 57–70.

Calvert, G.A. (2001). Crossmodal processing in the human brain: insights from functional neuroimgaging studies. *Cerebral Cortex,* **11**, 1110–1123.

Castelli, F., Happe, F., Frith, U., and Frith, C. (2000). Movement and mind: a functional imaging study of perception and interpretation of complex intentional movement patterns. *NeuroImage,* **12**, 314–325.

Cline, M.G. (1967). The perception of where a person is looking. *American Journal of Psychology,* **80**, 41–50.

Corbetta, M., Miezin, F.M., Shulman, G.L., and Petersen, S.E. (1993). A PET study of visuospatial attention. *Journal of Neuroscience,* **13**, 1202–1226.

Corbetta, M., and Shulman, G.L. (2002). Control of Goal-directed and stimulus-driven attention in the brain. *Nature Reviews: Neuroscience,* **3**, 201–215.

Culham, J.C., Brandt, S.A., Cavanagh, P., Kanwisher, N.G., Dale, A.M., and Tootell, R.B.H. (1998). Cortical fMRI activation produced by attentive tracking of moving objects. *Journal of Neurophysiology,* **80**, 2657–2670.

Darwin, C.R. (1965). The expression of the emotions in man and animals. Chicago: University of Chicago Press (original work published 1872).

Driver, J., Davis, G., Ricciardelli, P., Kidd, P., Maxwell, E., and Baron-Cohen, S. (1999). Gaze Perception Triggers Reflexive Visuospatial Orienting. *Visual Cognition,* **6**, 509–540.

De Souza, W. C., Eifuku, S., Tamaru, R., Nishijo, H., and Ono, T. (2005). Differential characteristics of face neuron responses within the anterior superior temporal sulcus of macaques. *Journal of Neurophysiology,* **94**, 1252–1266.

Ekman, P. (1982). *Emotion in the human face.* Cambridge University Press: New York.

Emery, N.J. (1997). Gaze following and joint attention in rhesus monkeys (Macaca mulatta). *Journal of Comparative Psychology,* **111**, 286–293.

Emery, N.J. (2000). The eyes have it: the neuroethology, function and evolution of social gaze. *Neuroscience and Biobehavioral Reviews,* **24**, 581–604.

Fletcher, P.C., Happe, F., Frith, U., *et al.* (1995). Other minds in the brain—a functional imaging study of theory of mind in story comprehension. *Cognition,* **57**, 109–128.

Friesen, C.K., and Kingstone, A. (1998). The eyes have it! Reflexive orienting is triggered by nonpredictive gaze. *Psychonomic Bulletin and Review,* **5**, 490–495.

Frith, C.D., and Frith, U. (1999). Interacting Minds: a biological basis. *Science,* **286**, 1692–1695.

Gallagher, H.L., Happe, F., Brunswick, N., Fletcher, P.C., Frith, U., and Frith, C.D. (2000). Reading the mind in cartoons and stories: an fMRI study of theory of mind in verbal and nonverbal tasks. *Neuropsychologia,* **38**, 11–21.

George, N., Driver, J., and Dolan, R. (2001) Seen gaze-direction modulates fusiform activity and its coupling with other brain areas during face processing. *NeuroImage,* **13**, 1102–1112.

Gibson, J.J., and Pick, A.D. (1963). Perception of another person's looking behavior. *American Jounal of Psychology,* **76**, 386–394.

Goren, C.C., Sarty, M., and Wu, P.Y. (1975).Visual following and pattern discrimination of face-like stimuli by newborn infants. *Pediatrics,* **56**, 544–549.

Grill-Spector, K., Kushnir, T., Edelman, S., Avidan, G., Itzchak, Y., and Malach, R. (1999). Differential processing of objects under different viewing conditions in the human lateral occipital complex. *Neuron,* **24**, 187–203.

Harries, M.H., and Perrett, D.I. (1991). Visual processing of faces in temporal cortex: physiological evidence for a modular organization and possible anatomical correlates. *Journal of Cognitive Neuroscience,* **3**, 9–24.

Haxby, J.V., Hoffman, E.A., and Gobbini, M.I. (2000). The distributed human neural system for face perception. *Trends in Cognitive Sciences,* **4**, 223–232.

Hikosaka, K. (1993). The polysensory region in the anterior bank of the caudal superior temporal sulcus of the macaque monkey. *Biomedical Research,* **14**, 41–45.

Hikosaka, K., Iwai, E., Saito, H.-A., and Tanaka, K. (1988). Polysensory properties of neurones in the anterior bank of the caudal superior temporal sulcus. *Journal of Neurophysiology,* **60**, 1615–1637.

Hooker, C.I., Paller, K.A., Gitelman, D.R., Parrish, T.B., Mesulam, M.M., and Reber, P.J. (2003). Brain networks for analyzing eye gaze. *Cognitive Brain Research,* **17**, 406–418.

Itakura, S. (1996). An exploratory study of gaze-monitoring in non-human primates. *Japanese Psychological Research*, **38**, 174–180.

Jenkins, R., Beaver, J.D., and Calder, A.J. (2006). I thought you were looking at me: Direction-specific aftereffects in gaze perception. *Psychological Science*, **17**, 506–513.

Johnson, M.H., Dziurawiec, S., Ellis, H., and Morton, J. (1991). Newborns'preferential tracking of face-like stimuli and its subsequent decline. *Cognition*, **40**, 1–19.

Kastner, S., and Ungerleider, L.G. (2000). Mechanisms of visual attention in the human cortex. *Annual Review of Neuroscience*, **23**, 315–341.

Kawashima, R., Suguira, M., Kato, T., *et al.* (1999). The human amygdala plays an important role in gaze monitoring. *Brain*, **122**, 779–783.

Kleinke, C.L. (1986). Gaze and eye contact: a research review. *Psychological Bulletin*, **100**, 78–100.

Langton, S.R.H. (2000). The mutual influence of gaze and head orientation in the analysis of social attention direction. *Quarterly Journal of Experimental Psychology Section A: Human Experimental Psychology*, **53**, 825–845.

Langton, S.R.H., and Bruce, V. (1999). Reflexive visual orienting in response to the social attention of others. *Visual Cognition*, **6**, 541–567.

Langton, S.R.H., Watt, R.J., and Bruce, V. (2000). Do the eyes have it? Cues to the direction of social attention. *Trends in Cognitive Sciences*, **4**, 50–59.

Loomis, J.M., Kelly, J.W., Pusch, M., Bailenson, J.N., and Beall, A.C. (2008). Psychophysics of perceiving eye and head direction with peripheral vision: Implications for the dynamics of eye gaze behavior. *Perception*, **37**, 1443–1457.

Luria, S.M., and Strauss, M.S. (1978). Comparison of eye movements over faces in photographic positives and negatives. *Perception*, **7**, 349–358.

Lyons, D.E., Santos, L.R. (2006). Ecology, domain specificity, and the origins of theory of mind: is competition the catalyst? *Philosophy Compass*, **5**, 481–492.

Marr, D. (1982). *Vision: A computational investigation into the human representation and processing of visual information.* New York: Henry Holt and Co., Inc.

Martin, W.W., and Rovira, M.L. (1981). An experimental analysis of discriminability and bias in eye-gaze judgment. *Journal of Nonverbal Behavior*, **5**, 155–163.

Mitchell, J.P., Macrae, C.N., and Banaji, M.R. (2006). Dissociable medial prefrontal contributions to judgments of similar and dissimilar others. *Neuron*, **50**, 655–663.

Mosconi, M.W., Mack P.B., McCarthy, G., and Pelphrey, K.A. (2005). Taking an intentional stance on "eye-gaze" shifts: A functional neuroimaging study of social perception in children. *NeuroImage*, **27**, 247–252.

Nishijo, H., Ono, T., and Nishino, H. (1988). Single neuron responses in amygdala of alert monkey during complex sensory stimulation with affective significance. *Journal of Neuroscience*, **8**, 3570–3583.

Nobre, A.C, Sebestyen, G.N., Gitelman, D.R., *et al.* (1997). Functional localization of the system for visual spatial attention using positron emission tomography. *Brain*, **120**, 515–533.

Noton, D., and Stark, L. (1971). Eye movements and visual perception. *Scientific American*, **224**, 35–43.

Oschner, K.N., Ray, R.D., Cooper, J.C., *et al.* (2004). For better or for worse: neural systems supporting the cognitive down- and up-regulation of negative emotion. *NeuroImage*, **23**, 483–499.

Pelphrey, K.A., Morris, J.P., McCarthy G. (2005). Neural basis of eye gaze processing deficits in autism. *Brain*, **128**, 1038–1048.

Pelphrey, K.A., Morris, J.P., Michelich, C.R., Allison, T., and McCarthy, G. (2005). Functional anatomy of biological motion perception in posterior temporal cortex: an fMRI study of eye, moulth, and hand movements. *Cerebral Cortex*, **15**, 1866–1876.

Pelphrey, K.A., Mitchell, T.V., McKeown, M.J., Goldstein, J., Allison, T. and McCarthy, G. (2003). Brain activity evoked by the perception of human walking: controlling for meaningful coherent motion. *The Journal of Neuroscience*, **23**, 6819–6825.

Pelphrey, K.A., Singerman, J.D., Allison, T., and McCarthy G. (2003). Brain activation evoked by perception of gaze shifts: the influence of context. *Neuropsychologia*, **41**, 156–170.

Pelphrey, K.A., Viola, R.J., and McCarthy, G. (2004). When strangers pass. *Psychological Science*, **15**, 598–603.

Perrett, D.I., Hietanen, J.K., Oram, M.W., and Benson, P.J. (1992). Organization and functions of cells responsive to faces in the temporal cortex. *Philosophical Transactions of the Royal Society of London. Series B*, **335**, 23–30.

Perrett, D.I., Smith, P.A.J., Potter, D.D., Mistlin, A.J., Head, A.S., Milner, A.D., and Jeeves, M.A. (1985). Visual cells in the temporal cortex sensitive to face view and gaze direction. *Proceedings of the Royal Society of Londo*n, Series B, B223, **1232**, 293–317.

Phillips, A.T., Wellman, H.M., and Spelke, E.S. (2002). Infants' ability to connect gaze and emotional expression to intentional action. *Cognition*, **85**, 53–78.

Posner, M.I. (1980). Orienting of attention. *Quarterly Journal of Experimental Psychology*, **32**, 3–25.

Posner, M.I., Walker, J.A., Friedrich, F., and Rafal, R.D. (1984). Effects of parietal injury on covert orienting of visual attention. *Journal of Neuroscience*, **4**, 1863–1874.

Povinelli, D.J. and Eddy, T.J. (1996). Factors influencing young chimpanzees' (Pan troglodytes) recognition of attention. *Journal of Comparative Psychology*, **110**, 336–345.

Povinelli, D.J., Gallup, G.G. Jr, Eddy, T.J., *et al.* (1997). Chimpanzees recognize themselves in mirrors. *Animal Behavior*, **53**, 1083–1088.

Puce A., Allison, T., Benton, S., Gore, J.C., and McCarthy, G. (1998). Temporal cortex activation in humans viewing eye and mouth movements. *The Journal of Neuroscience*, **18**, 2188–2199.

Redican, W.K. (1975). Facial expressions in nonhuman primates. *Primate Behavior: Developments in Field and Laboratory Research*, **4**, 103–194.

Ristau, C.A. (1991). Before mindreading: Attention, purposes and deception in birds. In A. Whiten (ed.) *Natural Theories of Mind: Evolution, Development and Simulation of Everyday Mindreading*, pp. 209–222. Oxford: Basil Blackwell.

Rolls, E.T. (1992). Neurophysiology and functions of the primate amygdala. In: J. P. Aggleton (ed.) *The amygdala: neurobiological aspects of emotion, memory and mental dysfunction*, pp. 143–167. New York: Wiley-Liss.

Rozzi, S., Calzavara, R., Belmalih, A., Borra, E., Gregoriou, G., Matelli, M., and Luppino, G. (2006). Cortical connections of the inferior parietal cortical convexity of the Macaque monkey. *Cerebral Cortex*, **16**, 1389–1417.

Ruiz, A., Gomez, J.C., Roeder J.J., and Byrne, R.W. (2009). Gaze following and gaze priming in lemurs. *Animal Cognition*, **12**, 427–434.

Rushworth, M.F.S., Ellison, A., and Walsh, V. (2001). Complementary localization and lateralisation of orienting and motor attention. *Nature Neuroscience*, **4**, 656–661.

Santos, L.R., Flombaum, J.I., Phillips, W. (2006). The evolution of human mindreading: how non-human primates can inform social cognitive neuroscience. In S. Platek (ed.) *Evolutionary Cognitive Neuroscience*, pp. 433–456. Cambridge: MIT Press.

Saxe R., Xiao, D.K., Kovacs, G., Perrett, D.I., and Kanwisher, N. (2004). A region of right posterior superior temporal sulcus responds to observed intentional actions. *Neuropsychologia*, **42**, 1435–1446.

Sodian, B., and Thoermer, C. (2004). Infants' understanding of looking, pointing, and reaching as cues to goal-directed action. *Journal of Cognition and Development*, **5**, 289–316.

Strongman, K.T., and Champness, B.G. (1968). Dominance hierarchies and conflict in eye contact. *Acta Psychologia*, **28**, 376–386.

Todorovic, D. (2006). Geometrical basis of perception of gaze direction. *Vision Research*, **46**, 3549–3562.

Tomasello, M., Call, J., Hare, B. (1998). Five primate species follow the visual gaze of conspecifics. *Animal Behavior*. **55**, 1063–1069.

Vander Wyk, B.C., Hudac, C.M., Carter, E.J., Sobel, D.M., Pelphrey, K.A. (2009). Action understanding in the superior temporal sulcus region. *Psychological Science, 20*, 771–777.

Walker-Smith, G.J., Gale, A.G., and Findlay, J.M. (1977). Eye movement strategies involved in face perception. *Perception, 6*, 313–326.

Wicker B., Michel F., Henaff, M., Decety, J. (1998). Brain regions involved in the perception of gaze: a PET Study. *NeuroImage, 8*, 221–227.

Williams J.H.G., Waiter, G.D., Perra, O., Perrett, D.I., and Whiten A. (2005). An fMRI study of joint attention experience. *NeuroImage, 25*, 133–140.

Wright, T.M., Pelphrey, K.P., Allison, T., McKeown, M.J., and McCarthy, G. (2003). Polysensory interactions along lateral temporal regions evoked by audiovisual speech. *Cerebral Cortex, 13*, 1034–1043.

Zeki S., Watson, J.D., Lueck, C.J., Friston, K.J., Kennard, C., and Frackowiak R.S. (1991). A direct demonstration of functional specialization in human visual cortex. *The Journal of Neuroscience, 11*, 641–649.

Chapter 31

Speechreading: what's MISS-ing?

Ruth Campbell

Introduction

In this chapter I hope to demonstrate that watching speech as well as listening to it is very much part of what we do when we look at people, and that observing someone talking can relate to other aspects of face processing. The perception of speaking faces can offer insights into how human communication skills develop, and the role of the face and its actions in relation to those skills.

In developing these themes, I propose that cross-modal processing occurs at a relatively early cognitive processing stage in relation to speech processing and identifying aspects of the talker. To date, the cognitive processes involved in face processing and voice/speech processing have been considered as essentially separate unimodal systems; faces being processed wholly within a visual stream, speech within an acoustic stream. In considering speech processing, the role of vision—i.e. of seeing speech being spoken—has hardly been considered at all in most models, yet seeing speech impacts on auditory speech processing in a variety of ways in hearing people, as well as being the prime mode of access to speech for deaf people (Campbell, 2008). In relation to face processing, previous models suggest that cross-modal information comes into play only at a relatively late stage of processing, when we form representations of known individuals (e.g. recognizing someone we know from their voice: a processing stage that reflects semantic associations). Here, I propose that multimodal (audio-visual) processing is apparent early in cognitive processing for faces and for speech, A perceptual information processing stage (multimodal indexical speech structure: MISS) operates prior to obtaining information about who someone is or what they are saying. In turn, this suggests that some aspects of face processing can be considered as inherently multimodal: research on seeing speech highlights this assertion.

Preamble: seeing speech is special

Purely in terms of its signal qualities, speech is unlike other perceived face actions. Speech inheres in a continuously changing auditory or audio-visual signal that delivers recognizable language in structured and meaningful segments. Natural speech can be processed efficiently despite variations between or within talkers, and carries semantic import. In viewing a speaking face we attend to what it is saying, we "listen" to the talker. When we watch someone speak we notice small, fast movements of the face. While these include mouth movements they are not limited to those movements—hence "speechreading" rather than "lip-reading" (Campbell, 2006). What do we see? We might catch "ah" being spoken here, "p" or "mm" there. It's these segments, often called "visemes" since they can be readily mapped onto the phonemes of heard speech, that carry the message. The perception of non-speech facial actions, such as detecting and identifying emotional expression, does not require that we identify each small, fast-changing component of the face act over a time-frame of tenths of a second. What is more, the meaning of a spoken message—whether it is heard or speechread—depends crucially on the *words* that have been perceived to be spoken. By contrast, meaning gleaned from an expression on a face seems to be holistic and largely determined by the context in which the expression is seen. (de Gelder and Van den Stock, Chapter 27; Ambady and Weisbuch, Chapter 24, this volume).

Where researchers have been interested in speechreading, therefore, they have followed a speech processing perspective, and the critical questions are: which components of speech can be read from facial actions? What are the cognitive and cortical processes involved in audio-visual speech perception? Briefly addressing these questions will open up the main part of this chapter, which is to explore speechreading in the context of face processing and, in particular, how seeing speech might relate to other aspects of face processing.

Clearly, fewer speech segments can be distinguished by eye than by ear. Some estimates suggest that only a quarter to a third of the critical speech phonemes are visemically distinctive (Campbell, 2006). However, this is not always a bar to identifying the content of silent seen speech. Not only can context often provide a strong cue (the footballer swearing on the football pitch), but also many spoken words can be identified on the basis of a subset of their identifiable phonemes: That is, many words are over-determined when their constituent phonemes are considered. In this respect, speechreading silent speech is similar to listening to speech that is degraded, e.g. speech heard in noise. We may have had the experience of hearing words emerge from otherwise hard-to-hear speech in noise. Sometimes these are words which one has been primed to recognize (your own name, or a predictable end to a sentence), but another class of words also tends to emerge from the noise. These are words which have a unique segmental structure in relation to all other words: those whose phoneme combinations are unique, so that they could *only* lead to a single identification. The word "umbrella," for instance, is hard to mistake for any other word, even when some parts of it may be lost in noise when heard, or invisible when seen to be spoken. Words such as "airella" or "ubrenner" do not exist, so the target *must* be "umbrella." So, as well as sensitivity to the segmental structure of seen speech, successful speechreading requires sensitivity to the statistical structure of speech, insofar as that leads to word identification. Good speechreaders, especially deaf and deafened people who rely on speechreading, make use of this (Auer and Bernstein, 1997), while other verbal abilities, especially verbal working memory skills, can boost speechreading abilities further (Rönnberg, 2003).

Of course, for hearing people, silent speech is not the usual way in which we encounter seen speech. We generally experience speech audio-visually. Audio-visual integration of seen and heard speech occurs readily, and can be demonstrated at *all* levels of speech structure, from the subphonemic to the phrase (Campbell, 2008, for review). As far as the cortical substrates of seen speech are concerned, while many regions are implicated (and we will encounter these later in the chapter), two findings have been repeatedly demonstrated. Firstly, seen silent speech can activate parts of auditory cortex that had been thought to be dedicated to hearing: these are within Heschl's gyrus in the temporal plane (planum temporale) of the upper part of the lateral temporal lobe (Calvert et al., 1997; Pekkola et al., 2005). This suggests that at least some parts of this region may be specialized for the amodal processing of speech-like signals, rather than complex acoustic signals only. "Hearing by eye" is not just a figurative description of speechreading: "auditory" parts of the brain are distinctively and selectively responsive to seen speech. Secondly, posterior parts of the superior temporal gyrus in the lateral temporal lobes are especially sensitive to audio-visual speech congruence and synchronization, and are thought to play a key role in cross-modal integration of speech (see Figure 31.1).

These well-established findings set the scene for more recent research which focuses less on what the talker is saying and more on the characteristics of the talker herself. These are considered the *indexical* aspects of speech processing; those idiosyncratic characteristics of the talker which tell us about who they are, rather than what they are saying. One reason for this shift within speech processing research is to try to understand how speech content can be processed irrespective

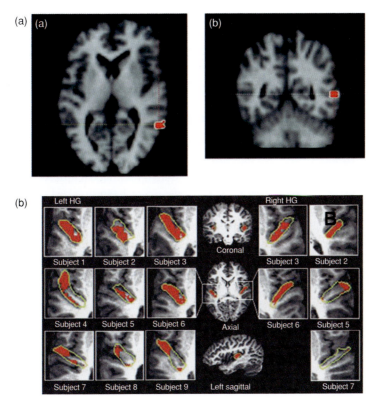

Fig. 31.1 Two cortical regions critically involved in processing seen speech: fMRI activation.
(a) Posterior superior temporal regions are especially sensitive to the audio-visual binding of seen and heard speech. This fMRI group analysis shows the region which was activated more strongly when observing synchronized audio-visual speech than non-synchronized audio-visual speech or auditory or visual speech alone The cluster of voxels from the group averaged data in (a) axial and (b) coronal sections localized to the ventral bank of the left superior temporal sulcus (x = −49, y = −50, z = 9),. The images are displayed in radiological convention so that the left of the image corresponds to the right hemisphere. Reprinted from *Current Biology*, Calvert, Campbell, and Brammer, Evidence from functional magnetic resonance imaging of crossmodal binding in the human heteromodal cortex © 2000 with permission from Elsevier. (b) Watching speech activates primary auditory cortex (a study at 3T). Individual activation patterns within the planum temporale (as determined by structural scanning) when watching silent monosyllables being spoken. Significant (Z>2.3, p<0.01, corrected), activations within Heschl's gyri (HG) are shown, overlaid on axial magnetic resonance images. The yellow line outlines Heschl's gyri, the medial parts of which accommodate primary auditory cortex. The statistical maps and the Heschl's gyrus outline are collapsed into a 2D image. The middle column displays coronal, axial, and left sagittal high-resolution MR images of subject 6 with overlaid activations. Reprinted from Pekkola, Ojanen, Autti et al. Primary auditory cortex activation by visual speech: an fMRI study at 3T, *NeuroReport*, **16**(2) with permission from Wolters Kluwer Health.

of who speaks it—and, conversely, to identify talker characteristics such as region of origin, age or gender from a sample of speech. For visual speech, this last point might sometimes seem trivial—after all if we can see the talker, we can see if it is a child or an old man. But other questions persist: can regional and non-native accents be discriminated from facial speech actions? Can we reliably match a seen, silent talker (as on a video-clip) to a separate, audio record of their speech? Does knowing what the talker's speech patterns look like affect our ability to process heard speech? These questions link readily with the concerns of the researcher in face processing. I will try to show some of those links in the sections that follow. In order to do this, I need to convince you that while few people can speechread efficiently, just about everyone shows some sensitivity to speech that they see, as well as speech that they hear.

Visual speech sensitivity: developmental and comparative evidence

The first place to look for evidence that we take account of what we see when we perceive a talker is in prelingual infants. Here, some very early acquired multimodal processing capacities are apparent. By the age of 8 weeks, hearing babies prefer to watch synchronized audio-visual speech and are disturbed when face and voice seem to slip out of synch (Dodd, 1979). Behavioral sensitivity to the visible shape and heard sound of a (native) vowel can be detected in 18-week-olds (Kuhl and Meltzoff, 1982; Patterson and Werker, 1999). Electrophysiological studies confirm that discriminating (mismatch) responses to a heard vowel followed by a seen facial action can be recorded from the scalps of 10-week-old infants (Bristow et al., 2009).

What function could be served by such multimodal sensitivity to speech in the prelingual infant? One possibility is that seeing what a speech sound looks like can help the infant learn to develop appropriate phoneme categories for their native spoken language. A recent study (Teinonen et al., 2008) presented 6-month-olds with stimuli from a synthesized auditory continuum spanning the heard speech sounds "ba" to "da." Stimulus items in the mid-range of the continuum were ambiguous between the two forms. Adults and older children typically show a categorical response to such ambiguous items and readily classify these ambiguous speech sounds as either "ba" or "da." They show categorical perception for these speech sounds. However, prelingual infants tend to respond randomly to the ambiguous mid-range stimuli, failing to show sharp categorical responses. In the Teinonen et al. study, when the 6-month-old infants were provided with an appropriate visual "anchor" of a seen "ba" and a seen "da" accompanying the relevant tokens within the ambiguous auditory mid-range, they quickly learned the appropriate *auditory* categorization.

In Teinonen et al.'s study, infants were required to make discriminative responses to auditorily ambiguous tokens, and were helped when they saw "ba" or "da" on the talker's face. What happens when auditory and visual syllables are quite different, and individually clearly perceived, but then combined in a synchronized audio-visual presentation? Depending on the material presented, people may report that they "hear" something that was different than the acoustic stimulus. The most dramatic of these are syllabic illusions involving consonants. For instance, hearing "ba" when "ga" is what appears on the talker's face, leads to the perception that "da" was uttered: the experience is of hearing "da." not the actual "ba" (McGurk effects; McGurk and MacDonald, 1976; see Campbell, 2008 for review). McGurk effects can be elicited in prelingual infants from around 20 weeks of age (Rosenblum et al., 1997; Burnham and Dodd, 2004). This suggests that some (multimodal) components of the appropriate phonological categories are already in place in very young infants.

There is much more evidence that the human infant with normal sensory capacities uses both vision and audition to develop an appropriate perceptual repertoire of speech-related information to guide their own developing language competencies in the first year of life (Lewkowicz, 2010). One feature of development in the second half of the first year of life is "perceptual narrowing." While a 6-month-old infant can distinguish between two similar heard speech sounds (e.g. an aspirated "pa," where the "p" requires a plosive, cheek-puffing action, and the aftercoming vowel is voiced late in the utterance, and "pa" spoken with an unvoiced "p"—no cheek puff and early voice onset), by the age of 8 to 10 months she will have "tuned in" to her native speech sound categories. In English, there is no distinction between the two variants of "pa," and by that age the child raised among English speakers loses the ability to distinguish those sounds. An infant reared in a language such as Hindi, where the aspirated and non-aspirated versions of "pa" can distinguish words, does not lose the ability to distinguish between them. So, from an early state in the child's development when she is sensitive to all or any possible distinctions in the speech that she hears, she soon becomes especially sensitive to the important contrasts within the language that surrounds her, losing some of her previous, more general, discriminatory powers (Werker and Tees, 2005. See Pascalis and Wirth, Chapter 37, this volume, for similar "perceptual narrowing" as a characteristic of the infant's ability to discriminate own- and other race/species faces).

Pons et al. (2009) reported perceptual narrowing for audio-visual speech processing in the second half of the first year of life. "ba" and "va" are easy to distinguish visually for English speakers—"ba" is produced with both lips touching (bi-labial), while "va" is made with the top teeth touching the bottom lip (labio-dental). In English, these are contrastive gestures: "ban" and "van" are different words. In Spanish, however, the distinction is not contrastive: "baño" may be pronounced with a bi-labial or a labio-dental gesture on the first consonant. The question then is, do Spanish infants show a different pattern of sensitivity to the visual forms of these utterances than English infants, and if so at what age? Pons et al. report that, when infants were trained to match a heard syllable to one which then appeared as a silent, seen speech gesture, the looking preference patterns of both English and Spanish 6-month-olds showed appropriate cross-modal matching for "ba" and for "va." However, while English infants aged eleven months retained this skill, Spanish infants of the same age showed reduced audio-visual discrimination between "ba" and "va."

While these studies clearly show a role for seen speech in early human speech perception, when considered in evolutionary terms these competencies may be based on broader multimodal abilities related to vocalization. The ability to detect correspondences between seen facial actions and heard vocalizations occurs in other primate species. "Coo" and "threat" calls of rhesus monkeys are produced with distinct facial actions and mouth shapes. Ghazanfar and Logothetis (2003) showed that monkeys were sensitive to the congruence between the acoustic signal qualities and those of the face image corresponding to these different calls. Monkeys are also able to match the visual size/age of a monkey "caller" to an appropriate heard vocalization. This is assumed to reflect the mapping of acoustic formant characteristics delivering characteristic resonance and pitch qualities of the vocal tract of the caller (Ghazanfar et al., 2007). To date, no studies have explored the perceptual bases for face-call matching in non-human primates. For example, the effects of structural changes in the facial image (Parr and Hecht, Chapter 35, this volume), and of "other-species effects" when monkeys view other primate species faces and calls (Pascalis and Wirth, Chapter 37, this volume) remain to be investigated.

The studies with rhesus monkeys suggest that identifying individuals in the group is one reason for this multimodal sensitivity—in addition to the utility of matching vision to audition in identifying the meaning of a call. It remains to be established whether domesticated animals, which show surprising abilities in processing human faces (sheep: Tate et al., 2006; Kendrick and Feng, Chapter 34, this volume; horses: Stone, 2010) and intentions (dogs: Hare and Tomasello, 2005) are able to match faces to voices, and whether they can distinguish different language users on the basis of their visible speech patterns.

Speechreading facial actions: movement of the face and point-light seen speech

What of normal adult capabilities? First of all, is a full facial image required to process who someone is and what they are saying? Point-light stimuli, generated by illuminated points distributed on the skin of the face, and which retain facial motion characteristics without facial forms or features, can be sufficient to identify familiar faces (Lander et al., 1999). Characteristic facial motion patterns are quickly learned for new faces (Lander and Davies, 2007). Familiar people can also be identified solely from their point-light seen speech patterns (Rosenblum et al., 2007b). Point-light faces can generate McGurk effects and enhance the comprehension of speech in noise (Rosenblum and Saldaña, 1996; Rosenblum et al., 1996). That is, the visible dynamic speech signature, alone, carries sufficient information to enable the identification of speech content and speech carrier. These demonstrations have been made with people who have been exposed to natural speaking faces, and (until it has been shown otherwise) we should assume that it is exposure to natural faces throughout the lifespan that has developed processing systems and representations that support these skills, and which allow strong correlations to emerge between the patterns of movement of face parts and phonetic classification of heard speech segments (Jiang et al., 2002; 2007).

Speechreading and facial identity processing

While point-light seen speech can be "read" for identity and content, a still image of a face, even if it is just a photographic snapshot, also provides speech cues. In Figure 31.2, we can easily see that Madonna might have been snapped saying "ah"—and not "mm" or "ff." Which cognitive systems are involved in identifying the image in that figure as Madonna, and which are involved in identifying the speech gesture that she seems to be making? Speech processing and face identification were characterized by Fodor (1983) as distinct cognitive modules (Fodor, 1983), with no (low-level) interaction between the two processes. In apparent support of this discrete modular view came clear neuropsychological evidence. Two patients were described with doubly dissociated abilities. One could recognize faces, but could not identify any images of seen speech. For instance, in one task the patients were each given a pile of photographs, each of which showed one of six different individuals. The models had been photographed from different viewpoints and posed different speech gestures, such as "oo," "mm," "ff," "th," "sh," "ee." One patient was able to sort the cards into separate piles on the basis of their identity, but not on the basis of the speech gesture. That patient had a left (posterior) temporal lesion. The other patient could sort and identify speech patterns from the cards, but not faces. She had a right (posterior) temporal lesion (Campbell et al., 1986). This finding was incorporated into the now-classical model of face processing (Bruce and Young, 1986), which proposed independence of processing streams for the two tasks. Figure 31.2 illustrates the cognitive stages in processing (familiar) faces, as described in the Bruce and Young model. It shows that while face recognition requires access to face recognition units (FRUs), seen speech does not. Similarly, facial expression processing is, on this model, independent of face identification.[1]

Not all people with face recognition problems show spared speechreading abilities. Some people have been identified with impaired face recognition abilities and lessened sensitivity to visual influence in speech perception—that is, with *associated* deficits in each domain (e.g. de Haan and Campbell, 1991; de Gelder et al., 1998). The impairments shown by these patients, who showed no other visual deficits, could be attributed to impaired structural encoding problems specific to faces—whatever the task. This is consistent with the Bruce and Young model and suggests, moreover, that speechreading requires some special face-related processing—that is, it appears to be a skill which falls within the face-processing domain, rather than something extrinsic to it.

---

[1] But see Calder, Chapter 22, this volume, for another perspective.

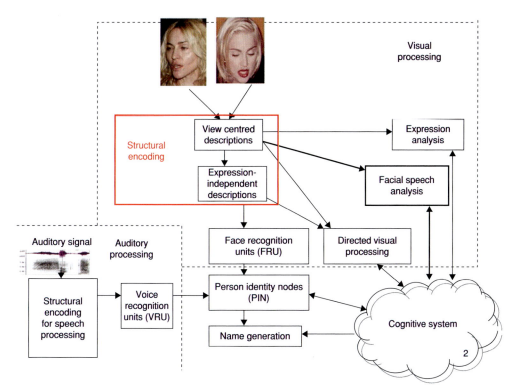

Fig. 31.2 Modeling the cognitive stages in face recognition and in face processing: independent modality-specific routes. This figure replicates Bruce and Young's (1986) model of face processing, showing independent visual processing streams for watching speech, expression processing and face recognition. A similar modality-specific model has been proposed for voice recognition (Belin et al., 2004); parts of it are sketched here. The two (unimodal) recognition systems are assumed to interact at the PIN level.

More problematic for the model are findings suggesting that speechreading may be sensitive to identity-related processing. Walker et al. (1995) showed that sensitivity to audio-visual fusions was affected by personal familiarity with the talker. They used McGurk material (see "ga" and hear "ba": think-you-hear "da"), and found that the influence of vision on audition was greatest when the face of the talker was unfamiliar. For familiar faces, dubbed to an unfamiliar voice, McGurk effects were much reduced. In the Bruce and Young model, the processing of a facial identity (FRU), and the identification of the person (multimodal person identification node: PIN) reflect discrete processing stages, and the model assumes that speechreading reflects processes at the structural encoding stage, independent of familiarity with the face or the person. If this were the case then every face, whether familiar or unfamiliar, should generate similar patterns of McGurk sensibility when dubbed to an (unfamiliar) voice. Since the familiarity of the face affected McGurk sensitivity, we must—assume at least some "backflow" of information about a familiar person (PIN-level) to structural processing stages to account for the Walker et al. finding. This is not an isolated example of effects of talker-familiarity in processing speech from faces. Using still photographs and a repetition priming paradigm, Campbell et al. (1996) found face-*identity* judgments were speeded when that individual had been seen earlier in a speech-matching phase of the study: that is, when respondents had become familiarized with the faces in the course of the experiment. Schweinberger and Soukup (1998) used a Garner (1974) interference paradigm, systematically changing possible sources of variation in the face image when sequences of images were presented for speeded speech gesture classification. Each image was of a face producing a different vowel— such as "ee," "oo," or "ah." Thus, in one phase of the study a single face was seen throughout, while in another phase different faces appeared. Varying the identity/familiarity of the face affected speed of identifying the seen vowel shape. Also, matching face images on the basis of the vowel shape was faster for personally familiar than unfamiliar faces.

From Schweinberger et al.'s study, two effects related to familiarity appear to be important: familiarity with a person helps identify their speech pattern, but also it is easier to identify the speech pattern when the face is the same from trial to trial, even when the face is unfamiliar. It is most efficient when one talker is seen throughout a series of presentations (priming), least efficient when many different facial instances of a talker are seen (interference). Similar effects have also been demonstrated in studies using more naturalistic material than photographs of speech. Several studies have shown a processing cost to speechreading words or connected speech when multiple talkers rather than a single talker are seen (Yakel et al., 2000; Kaiser et al., 2003; Kaufmann and Schweinberger, 2005). These findings confirm clinical reports that people with hearing loss may find it easier to speechread just one person, and have more difficulty in speechreading when different talkers speak. Observers tune in to the speech patterns of a model, so that switching between talkers carries a processing cost. These data echo findings for heard speech. It is harder to understand heard words (for example in a lexical decision task where the task is to respond to each spoken item) when spoken by different (unfamiliar) talkers compared with a single talker (Nygaard et al., 1994). Indexical properties (who is talking) affect seen speech processing just as they affect heard speech processing.

All these studies suggest that whether we consider faces, voices or speech content, processing is more sensitive to influences related to discriminating or identifying the talker than is acknowledged in many cognitive models. One way to accommodate these influences is to introduce or emphasize top-down effects. Thus, activation at the supramodal PIN level can in turn influence FRU or VRU activation which in turn influences processes "downstream" within structural encoding itself (Figure 31.2). However, as we will see, this may not be sufficient to account for all phenomena related to how we match talkers from their face or voice.

Indexical properties of the voice: identifying the talker across different modalities and matching face to voice

We can often identify a familiar person from their voice—though not usually as accurately or automatically as from the face (Belin et al., 2004). As Figure 31.2 shows, in the Bruce and Young (1986) model, the person identification system (PIN) describes the level at which all information relevant to identifying a familiar person may be represented and accessed. It is at this level that semantic knowledge about a person (their name, their profession and so forth) is associated with their facial appearance, and also their voice, gait and other identifying aspects of the individual person. It is also at the PIN level that multimodal information is accessible—for example, matching face and voice for a known person. However, empirical research has only recently explored the implications of this part of the model. For example, can we classify a voice as familiar or unfamiliar more efficiently when it is accompanied by the "right" face, and what if the "wrong" face accompanies the voice?

Schweinberger et al. (2007) presented familiar and unfamiliar voices to be discriminated. The voice, speaking a standard sentence, was synchronized to the face of the corresponding talker, or to another talking face, which could be familiar or unfamiliar. For familiar voices, the presence of the corresponding talking face improved, while a non-corresponding talking face impaired familiarity decisions, when compared with voice-alone decisions. Thus, making a decision about identity (indexical processing) from the voice is affected by seeing the face. This outcome occurred only when the faces were shown as dynamic, natural talking sequences: photographs of talkers had no effect on voice familiarity judgment (Schweinberger et al., 2007). Further evidence that the dynamic signature of the seen talker is crucial comes from a study by Rosenblum and colleagues. Rosenblum et al. (2007b) showed that familiar people can be identified from point-light displays of the face speaking. In a separate study, this team showed that one hour of (full) video familiarization with a previously unfamiliar talker enabled accurate matching of (natural) silent speech to voice (Rosenblum, 2007a; and see von Kriegstein et al., 2008). What all these studies suggest is that there appears to be a reasonably robust dynamic signature for speech that can discriminate talkers and which is available by eye as well as by ear. These studies add to those which demonstrate that the movement characteristics of a known person's face are stored as part of the representation of that individual, and that the dynamic signature of facial expressiveness and movement can be sufficient to identify familiar people (Lander et al., 1999, 2004; O'Toole et al., 2002).

But what of unfamiliar talkers? In Schweinberger et al.'s (2007) study, only weak improvements in unfamiliar voice identification occurred when watching the "correct" (unfamiliar) talker's face, and the interference effects of splicing such voices to non-corresponding faces were slight and non-significant. However, using different methodologies, cross-modal identity matches can be demonstrated for unfamiliar people. Typically, the perceiver first experiences the talker in just one modality and then tries to match that target talker when she is presented among distractors in the other modality. For example, if one hears a voice uttering a sentence, then one sees silent videotapes of two unfamiliar talkers, of similar gender, age and language background, identification of the talker is better than chance—even when the utterance is different for presentation and match conditions (Kamachi et al., 2003). The important clues that support this matching skill reside in the dynamic signature of the talker's speech, since matching a voice to a photograph, or a backward-running videotape of the talker, was no better than chance (Kamachi et al., 2003; Lachs and Pisoni, 2004a). Further studies established that such matching was most effective when the acoustic signal preserved all the spectral and temporal formant frequency information (although some was possible with reduced signal quality; see Lachs and Pisoni, 2004b), and confirmed the importance of the dynamic visual properties of the talker (i.e. by point-light displays—Lachs and Pisoni, 2004c; Rosenblum et al., 2006).

The role of dynamic information in learning to identify an unfamiliar face is nugatory (Christie and Bruce, 1998), so how can people match voice and face for individuals who they do not know? Neither simple talking speed nor extent of movement of the articulators is a reliable cue (Lander et al., 2007; Rosenblum et al., 2006). While structural aspects of natural voice quality (pitch and timbre) can provide cues to the size of the talker's vocal tract, these are usually insufficient for forensic identification purposes (Rose, 2002). Indeed, natural voice quality may not always be needed to identify a talker, as sine-wave speech experiments have shown (see Remez et al., 1997; Sheffert et al., 2002). Talker-specific cues are to be found in a combination of cues. Some of these are linguistic. For example, phonetic variation in the way that vowels are produced characterizes many regional accents and idiosyncratic speech patterns available to the hearer as variation in the acoustic formant frequency patterns (Mullenix et al., 1989). Variations in how a word is spoken can also be seen as changes in mouth shape or other visible aspects of speech (McGrath et al., 1984; Green, 1998). Because of this, it is possible to distinguish regional accents simply from watching the talker (Irwin et al., 2007).

Language-specific aspects of speechreading

Cross-modal matching for talker identity appears to be most effective when (auditory) words can be recognized (Lachs and Pisoni, 2004b). This is probably because representations of known spoken words are sufficiently phonetically detailed to allow idiosyncratic deviations from the norm to be readily detected and identified. In turn, this suggests that familiarity with the spoken language is important in processing talker variations. How are processes involving seen speech engaged when the language is unfamiliar and linguistic processing cannot proceed automatically? The language of the talker and the expectations of the viewer about the language being spoken affect susceptibility to visual influences and speechreading. McGurk effects which are robust for North American users of spoken English need not be so for users of another language, even when tested in their own language. For example, in Japanese or Chinese there is lowered susceptibility to the effects of vision on audition (Sekiyama and Tohkura, 1991; Sekiyama, 1994, 1997). It has been suggested that both phonological and cultural factors are important here (Sekiyama, 1994, 1997). Intriguing effects of language emerge when auditory speech is masked by noise and the participant is required to detect when speech has occurred. Under these conditions, seeing the talker improves detection when speech is in a familiar language, but can impair it when the language is unfamiliar (Kim and Davis, 2003).

However, we are not "blind" to seen speech in an unfamiliar language. Indeed, being able to see the talker can help the novice language learner learn distinctions that may be hard to make by ear alone (Hazan et al., 2006; Navarra and Soto, 2007). Distinguishing *between* languages can also be done by eye, though language familiarity affects its accuracy. Spanish-Catalan bilinguals were able to distinguish these two familiar languages by eye alone, but the task was impossible for English or Italian people who knew neither language, while Spanish monolinguals could perform the discrimination, but less accurately than the bilinguals (Soto-Faraco et al., 2007).

Moreover, the skill of distinguishing two languages by eye is evident prelingually in infants raised in bilingual homes. At 8 months old, bilingual (French–English) infants can distinguish talkers of the different languages when these are shown speaking silently (Weikum et al., 2007). We have already noted that monolingual infants "tune in" to their native language "by eye" in the second half of the first year of life, losing some of their earlier sensitivity in matching seen and heard utterances that may not be phonologically salient to the language to which they are exposed (Pons et al., 2009). It seems that bilingual children maintain sensitivity to auditory-visual speech utterances, which they then apply discriminatively to the talkers and languages that surround them. The representations (phonological, lexical) of the forms of familiar language and of languages that the child is learning find their way into processes that require or reflect visual speech processing.

All these recent studies are moving us towards more specific characterizations of the indexical signature for (seen) speech. Language-specific and talker-specific processes are implicated, and arise early in life. Recognizing individual voice characteristics (i.e. for matching to a face) are best when the language/s is/are familiar. However, the actual cues used by observers to match seen speech to the talker, and when processing audio-visual combinations, are still under-researched, although the dynamic signature of the talking face appears to be important. Unfamiliar, as well as familiar, faces can be matched to their voices—not perfectly but better than chance. What do these recent studies suggest about the cognitive structures involved in identifying a talker from their visible and acoustic speech patterns?

Multimodal indexical speech structure (MISS)

Taken together, these findings suggest a model such as that proposed in Figure 31.3. In distinction to other models (see Figure 31.2, and, e.g. Belin et al., 2004; Campanella and Belin, 2007;

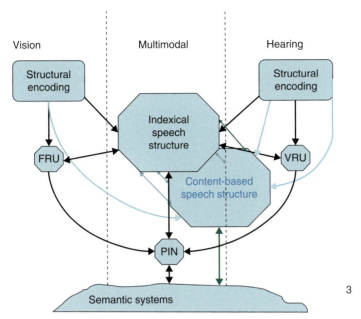

Fig. 31.3 MISS: A multimodal indexical speech structure system. This figure shows the relationship of MISS (see text) with content-based normative speech processing and with sensory-specific and multimodal familiarity detection systems: Face recognition units (FRU), Voice recognition Units (VRU), and person identification nodes (PIN) (Bruce and Young, 1986, and see Figure 31.1). Connector lines are black where they are salient to indexical processing, blue in relation to content processing and to interactions between content and indexical processing.

von Kriegstein et al., 2008), which posit separate visual and auditory structural analysis systems leading to modality-specific voice (VRU, voice recognition units) and face (FRU) activation, a multimodal indexical speech structure encoding component (MISS) takes inputs from both visual and auditory systems, in order to derive a multimodal speech-based representation. The contribution of each sensory modality to the structural analysis of seen-and-heard speech will differ depending on speechreading sensitivity and hearing status (see below). One function of MISS is to deliver a coherent signature of the potential identifying characteristics of any talker. MISS is conceived to work interactively with structural analysis for speech content, allowing content and carrier information to influence each other.[2]

Although not indicated in the figure, MISS is also likely to accommodate inputs from action and somatosensory systems. Some theorists suggest that it is the articulatory plan for making a speech gesture, not its auditory or visual outcome, that constitutes the primary speech representation (motor theory of speech perception: Liberman et al., 1967). Articulatory motor plans are "mirrored" in one's own speech as imitative speaking styles (Kerzel and Bekkering, 2000; Sams et al., 2005).

---

[2] The intention of Figure 31.3 is to highlight how the indexical part of a multimodal speech processing system may operate in relation to the components of a face processing system. As indicated in the previous sections, language (speech content) can affect indexical processing. That is, a single speech encoding system encompasses both indexical and normative content cue information. Both indexical and content analysis can proceed from a single cue or set of cues, with processing being distributed depending on task requirements.

From all these inputs, features characterizing idiosyncratic speech patterns can be derived. Activation within MISS allows unfamiliar voices (auditory input) and face actions (visual input) to be matched via their distinctive (unimodal) components. However, MISS also receives "top-down" activation from familiarity detection systems within the unimodal visual (FRU) and auditory (VRU) systems, both directly and via the amodal PIN. This allows knowledge of a known person's face or voice to constrain/inform processing of new input (i.e. detecting mismatched (known) face and voice), and accounts for the findings that familiarity with the individual makes face-voice matching more efficient. When, for example, a child hears the voice of someone who is out of view—and two people then come into view, MISS processing will have been involved in identifying the voice and matching the face to it. She will be alerted to the "face that owns the voice," whether that is a familiar or an unfamiliar one. Matching unknown faces to voices has forensic import, too: audiotapes of individuals may need to be matched to (silent) CCTV video footage.

One reason for proposing MISS rather than distinct modality-specific structural processing systems is that acoustic, visible and articulatory characteristics are tightly correlated (Munhall and Vatikiotis-Bateson, 1998; Yehia et al., 1998, 2002; Jiang et al., 2002; Davis and Kim, 2004). The affordances of the dynamic signature of speech across the different signal channels appears to be a primary aspect of speech processing, and operates efficiently at the segmental (consonant-vowel) level (Jiang et al., 2007). Given these correspondences, researchers are increasingly suggesting that conceptualizing speech processing as intrinsically multimodal may give more powerful insights than models that focus exclusively on the auditory pathway for speech (see Ghazanfar and Schroeder, 2006). Some other structural features are also apparent when speech is conceptualized as multimodal. For example, the relatively constant characteristics of voice such as timbre and pitch, which vary with the size and shape of the vocal tract, can be mapped onto visible indicators of size and shape of the talker such as their gender or age. Gender matching of face and voice is apparent in prelingual infants (Patterson and Werker, 2002). These are unlikely to depend on learned knowledge of faces and speech styles and may, rather, reflect some more general tendencies reflecting sensitivity to the acoustic properties of visible objects (small things tend to make high, low energy sounds; large things low, high energy sounds). All these features are more readily accommodated in a model that proposes a single multimodal structural system in relation to speech processing, rather than separate systems interacting only at a relatively late processing stage.

MISS cannot capture all aspects of the structural processing of speech/talker. Some remain stubbornly unimodal. Auditory adaptation effects demonstrate this. These occur when the repeated auditory presentation of a heard syllable shifts the categorization of an ambiguous syllable away from the direction of the "adapted" sound. Such effects are unaffected by the sight of the talker, whether for speech content (i.e. syllable category shift for McGurk stimuli; Roberts and Summerfield, 1981; Saldaña and Rosenblum, 1994) or voice identification (Schweinberger et al., 2008).

While audio-visual speech processing may rest on multimodal processing skills this does not mean that audio-visual speech processing is completely "automatic." Attentional processes are implicated in audio-visual speech processing, even for such apparently effortless perceptions as McGurk effects (Alsius et al., 2005). One aspect of how attention is allocated across modalities is that, normally, temporal synchronization of what is seen and what is heard leads to the perception of a unitary event. A recent neuropsychological case study suggests what happens when this "binding function" is missing (Hamilton et al., 2006). This patient, in distinction to most people, was worse at reporting audio-visual than auditory-alone speech and showed reduced susceptibility to McGurk illusions. The patient had bilateral parietal lesions, suggesting that parietal function needs to be intact to effect the seamless and apparently automatic perception that characterizes natural audio-visual speech processing (de Gelder and Bertelson, 2003). Input from different cortical systems needs to be effectively coordinated in order for MISS to function effectively.

Logically, the accurate identification of a spoken utterance needs to take account of indexical features such as accent or style of speech, embedded in language knowledge. Empirically, the auditory processing of speech (e.g. lexical decision) is more efficient when a single talker, rather than several talkers, is heard (Nygaard et al., 1994). For seen and heard speech, the advantages of a single talker over multiple talkers occur when training is in one modality, and testing in the other (e.g. Rosenblum et al., 2007a, Lander and Davies 2008). Here MISS is hypothesized to provide a means for "setting" speech content analysis to the perceived speech parameters of the talker. Memorial functions (VRU, FRU and PIN) then come into play when observers are exposed to specific talkers. Training participants to recognize voices paired with talkers' facial actions can enhance the later recognition of those voices when they are heard without facial actions (Sheffert and Olson, 2004; von Kriegstein et al., 2006, 2008).

To summarize: a multimodal structural processing stage is proposed which would allow visual and auditory speech (and possibly inputs from somesthetic and action systems too) to start to be analyzed prior to the identification of heard words or talkers faces (visual). Various research results point to the possibility of this structural multimodal stage. That is, structural aspects of face processing and structural aspects of speech processing may, independently, input into MISS. However, it is possible that MISS also enjoys more direct multimodal activation. The strongly correlated auditory (acoustic formants) and visual (face movement) consequences of speaking suggest more powerful multimodal mechanisms that detect correspondences between visual and auditory signal streams, whether or not face processing or voice analysis has been undertaken. This is an empirical question that awaits resolution.

Neuropsychological correlates: carrier and content in speech processing, a MISSing piece?

In addition to its cross-modal properties, MISS, as proposed here, makes a distinction between identifying a talker across modalities (matching a talker's voice to their face) and identifying the content of speech (e.g. from noisy audio-visual speech). That is, carrier and content may be distinguishable at this level. If a double dissociation were to be reported between content and carrier processing, whether for familiar or unfamiliar speech, that would constitute a telling line of evidence in support of MISS. Generally, of course, it is easier to identify a particular talker by face than by voice, and to identify a particular word by ear rather than by eye: modality itself offers asymmetric cues to carrier and content of speech. Nevertheless, we have seen that neuropsychological dissociations between carrier and content can be identified in the visual modality as dissociated skills for speechreading and for identifying faces or facial expressions (see Campbell et al., 1990). Is there neuropsychological evidence for a dissociation between content and carrier for speech? This has not yet been demonstrated in the multimodal domain, but several studies suggest a neuropsychological dissociation in *auditory* speech processing between content and voice identification, with right hemisphere mechanisms implicated in voice recognition, and left hemisphere ones for content (Assal et al., 1976; Landis et al., 1982; Kreiman and Van Lancker 1988; see Belin, 2006, for further discussion). Neuroimaging research with intact respondents supports the distinction: Voice identification usually activates right-hemisphere regions to a greater extent, while speech-content identification shows greater left-sided activation (Belin and Zatorre, 2003; von Kriegstein et al., 2003). Future research could usefully address these questions multimodally. "Temporary lesion" techniques such as repetitive transcranial magnetic stimulation

(Pitcher et al., Chapter 19, this volume) could be used to explore the contribution of localized cortical systems to natural speech processing, and would rule out explanations of anomalous perception in patients, where compensatory and long-term plasticity mechanisms may obscure interpretation.

Neuroimaging studies of speechreading

I have already mentioned two important regions involved in observing speaking faces. These are both in the superior parts of the temporal lobe and can include "auditory cortex" within Heschl's gyrus in the *planum temporale* as well as multimodal regions lateral and posterior to it (see Figure 31.1). But, of course, these are not the only regions involved. Regions sensitive to face processing including occipital, occipitotemporal and inferior temporal regions are also activated when watching a speaking face, but when watching speech, other regions are implicated too. These include inferior frontal, insular and inferior parietal regions, and even the auditory brainstem. These may show differently lateralized sensitivity depending on task. It should also be noted that processing of moving speaking faces and the processing of stilled facial speech forms can dissociate, following a "dorsal" and a "ventral" route, respectively (Calvert and Campbell, 2003; Campbell, 2008).

A superior temporal "hub" for multimodal processing of carrier and content?

The region comprising mid to posterior parts of the superior temporal gyrus and the posterior superior temporal sulcus inferior to it, bordering the middle temporal gyrus (pSTG/STS) is reliably activated in most studies of speechreading and audio-visual speech processing (e.g. Calvert et al., 1997; Möttönen et al., 2002; Wright et al., 2003; Capek et al., 2004, 2008; Hall et al., 2005; Murase et al., 2008; Stevenson and James, 2009). Posteriorly, this extends to the temporoparietal junction around the supramarginal gyrus (see Figure 31.1a). This highly multimodal region receives projections not only from auditory, visual and somatosensory cortical regions, but also from motor and action planning regions and more medial structures, too. What is its role in silent speechreading? To answer this question we need a model of information flow through the cortical areas involved.

In a simple feedforward model, seeing speech first activates visual regions of the occipital and inferior temporal lobes, then projects to multimodal p-STS—which can then generate activation within more "purely" auditory speech areas such as primary and secondary auditory cortex via back-projection. Depending on the task, activation may also flow into frontal regions (e.g. when a speech gesture has to be repeated). A MEG study (Nishitani and Hari, 2002) provided a close fit to this simple model. That is, on this model, the role of p-STS is to serve as a multimodal hub for processing speech, allowing projections both to higher order centers related to speech comprehension and production and also in the reverse direction to "sensory-specific" regions corresponding to the modality other than that in which the signal was experienced, as well as to the regions in which the signal was experienced.

It is important to note that p-STS specialization is not restricted to audio-visual and visual speech: it appears to be much more broadly based. Functionally, p-STS has been implicated in a broad range of processes relating to effective communication and intention processing (Brothers, 1990; Hein and Knight, 2008). So, as far as audio-visual and visual speech are concerned, the role of p-STS may reflect the convergence of at least three distinct functional specializations: Firstly, p-STS is especially sensitive to the perception of moving faces and their parts (e.g. Puce et al.,

1998; Allison et al., 2000; Haxby et al., 2002; Santi et al., 2003, and see Calder, Chapter 22, this volume). Secondly, p-STS/STG is implicated in auditory speech processing, where its preference for speech-like over non-speech-like, but similarly complex, acoustic patterns has been amply demonstrated (e.g. Rauschecker, 1997; Scott and Johnsrude, 2003, Binder et al., 2004). Finally, these regions are highly sensitive to the processing of perceived intentional actions and dispositions of others, however delivered (e.g. Saxe and Kanwisher, 2003; Pelphrey et al., 2005; Ghazanfar and Schroeder, 2006; Redcay, 2008).

Although p-STS is implicated in speech-content processing "by eye," its involvement in the identification of individuals from their facial movement patterns (i.e. indexical speech processing capabilities from visual displays such as point-light displays where face features are absent) has not yet been explored. STG/STS must be a "prime suspect" for a key role in indexical processing of seen speech given its involvement in identifying speech from point-light displays (Santi et al., 2003) and in auditory voice processing (Belin, 2006).

The extensive connectivity of p-STS with many other cortical regions underlines its role as a key cortical site for the cross-modal integration of auditory and visual speech, including projections to ostensibly sensory-specific regions (back-projection). Thus just listening to a familiar person's voice can generate activation in the fusiform gyrus, a region specialized for processing faces within the inferior temporal lobe. The fusiform gyrus is usually activated when looking at a face, but not when listening to sounds that are not like human speech. When listening to someone talk, activation in the fusiform gyrus is correlated with p-STS activation (von Kriegstein et al., 2003, 2008). Similarly, just watching someone speak (silent speech observation) leads to activation in (primary) auditory cortex, as we have seen (figure 1, Calvert et al., 1997; Pekkola et al., 2005). Activation in auditory cortex by silent speech is also dependent on p-STS activation (e.g. Calvert et al., 2000). Watching silent speech can even lead to neural potentials being recorded in the auditory brainstem, a subcortical, early "auditory" processing region (Musacchia et al., 2006, 2007). Again, it is likely that this reflects back-projection and is associated with p-STS activation.

Because p-STS has been implicated in most of these patterns, and because it is in p-STS that effects of seeing the talker on hearing speech can be robustly and reliably observed (Reale et al., 2007), it may follow that its role in *silent* speechreading is secondary to audio-visual speech processing and the perception of a unified audio-visual speech event (the "binding function": see Calvert et al., 2000; Miller and D'Esposito, 2005).However, it should be noted that people who are deaf from birth show *greater* activation in p-STS than hearing people, when they are speechreading. At the very least, this suggests that acoustic specification of voice does not have to be experienced in order for p-STS to show distinctive activation for silent speechreading.[3]

While p-STS may play a key role in speechreading and in audio-visual speech processing, some studies show no activation in p-STS, with key sites distributed in other regions, for both audio-visual (Bernstein et al., 2008) and visual (Campbell, 2008) speech observation. However, these demonstrations typically use special experimental material or require special responses which may not be relevant to natural speechreading. That is, they suggest that regions other than p-STS may be implicated in some distinctive aspects of seen speech analysis. More critical in relation to the simple feed-forward model for silent and audio-visual speech processing, the *timing* of the activations in sensory and supramodal regions does not always fit the proposal that p-STS is the

---

[3] Elsewhere in this handbook, it is proposed that p-STS supports another binding function: that of the (wholly visual) dynamic and non-dynamic aspects of facial expression perception (Calder, Chapter 22, this volume). A similar proposal has been made with respect to the integration of dynamic and non-dynamic visual information for processing silent speech (Calvert and Campbell, 2003; Campbell, 2006). This may underlie its special role in seen speech processing, especially in deaf people.

critical processing hub. For example, we would not expect silent speechreading to activate secondary auditory regions of the superior temporal lobe prior to activation in p-STS: yet this has been reported in independent studies (Möttönen et al., 2004; Besle et al., 2008), and is discussed further, below.

What of the distinction between carrier and content which motivated much of the discussion in this chapter? While posterior superior temporal regions can show distinctively lateralized sensitivity to carrier (right hemisphere) and content (bilateral/left hemisphere) for auditory speech (e.g. Belin and Zatorre, 2003), a similar pattern has not yet been shown for seen speech where, to date, studies have used a single talker and so are mute with respect to this issue. An anterior/posterior gradient along the superior temporal gyrus may reflect further functional specialization in relation to content/carrier. More anterior parts of STS/STG can be associated with perception of intentions (Hein and Knight, 2008), and with the extraction of meaning from heard speech (left anterior temporal regions: Scott et al., 2006). A further role for anterior parts of the (right) superior temporal gyrus is in identifying known conspecifics by voice (Belin, 2006; Petkov et al., 2008).

The role of the right anterior superior temporal gyrus in distinguishing different talkers was confirmed in a further neuroimaging study with humans. Formisano et al. (2008) used a multivariate statistical learning algorithm to "train" the discrimination of voice (three auditory identities) and content (three auditory vowels) from multi-voxel fMRI activation patterns within primary auditory cortex, and then examined which further temporal regions were associated with these "labeled-and-learned" discriminations. In the first place, the algorithm distinguished voice and content from the multi-voxel activation patterns within primary auditory cortex—and generalized accurately to new samples of talkers and content. The extended temporal regions associated with each of these patterns were distinctive. Right anterior temporal regions were implicated in voice recognition, while content discrimination was associated with bilateral activation along the length of the superior temporal gyrus.

The novelty of this approach, and its relevance to MISS, is that the algorithm worked efficiently in the absence of complex symbolic processes, such as phonetic feature recognition or specific spectrotemporal acoustic features of a particular voice: the only information given to the "pattern recognizer" was either voice or content identity. Because the auditory stimulus patterns came from unfamiliar talkers and were limited to monosyllables, one possible inference from this study is that (right) anterior superior temporal regions need not be conceptualized exclusively as "PIN" regions, intimately linked to conceptual and semantic knowledge about individuals and associations between known faces and their voices. Rather, it suggests that right anterior superior temporal regions may have a special role in processing stylistic, idiosyncratic voice features which may be particularly important for discriminating the speech carrier, whether they are familiar or not (and see Belin and Zatorre, 2003; von Kriegstein and Giraud, 2004).

The superior temporal gyrus and sulcus appear to be good candidate regions underpinning crucial aspects of processing seen speech, both in terms of mapping heard to seen speech, and identifying the talker from speech patterns. While specialized sub-regions may be implicated differentially (right anterior–carrier; left posterior–speech content), it is likely that processing is distributed along the gyrus and sulcus so that content and indexical information can be mutually informative. However, no study to date has explicitly explored this.

Other cortical regions implicated in speechreading: the role of frontal systems

Functional activation patterns indicate a network of interconnected regions supporting speechreading. Activation in insular cortex and in subcortical sub-Sylvian regions is reliably reported (e.g. Calvert et al., 1997; Hertrich et al., 2009). Seen speech can make special demands on regions associated with speech production. In particular, activation in inferior frontal regions, including partes opercularis/triangularis of the inferior frontal gyrus (BA 44/45) accompanies visual or audio-visual speech processing. Frontal activation often extends dorsally to the supplementary motor area (e.g. Campbell et al., 2006; Calvert and Campbell, 2003; Paulesu et al., 2003; Santi et al., 2003; Watkins et al., 2003; Miller and d'Esposito, 2005; Saito et al., 2005; Skipper et al., 2005; Hasson et al., 2007; Fridriksson et al., 2009). This suggests that access to articulatory representations of speech is important for speechreading and could mean that these regions are more accessible for speech that is seen (or seen-and-heard) than for speech that is simply heard. Seeing speech could then be considered to have a special role not only in relation to the binding of auditory and visual modalities in perception, but in the binding of speech perception and its production, whereby action-based representations refine the perceptual processing of speech (Studdert-Kennedy, 1983). The activation of representations based on articulatory properties of speech has further consequences—for example, it can lead to subvocal articulation of seen speech (Watkins et al., 2003) with concomitant activation in the observer's somatosensory cortex (Möttönen et al., 2005).

Timing and models of flow of activation

It is not yet clear to what extent regions implicated in the perception of seen speech exert their effects early or late in processing. Simple feed-forward models for speechreading (Nishitani and Hari, 2002; Campbell, 2008) will probably require modification In particular, there are indications from electrophysiological and MEG studies that there may be "super-fast" connections from occipital regions sensitive to dynamic visual events directly to auditory cortex, since responses within auditory cortex appear to be modulated by visual speech events at an earlier stage of processing than would be predicted if their source were polymodal p-STS (Möttönen et al., 2004; van Wassenhove et al., 2005; Besle et al., 2008; Hertrich et al., 2009).

Now, visible mouth movements often precede actual vocalization, and observers judge as synchronous a seen speech action that can be up to half a second in advance of the heard sound (Campbell and Dodd, 1980; Dixon and Spitz, 1980). Therefore it seems likely that seeing a particular speech gesture (temporarily) "sets" auditory processing strategy, and this is reflected in cortical "preparedness." One way to conceptualize this is as a temporary prioritization of forward connections from visual face processing regions (inferior temporal), to secondary auditory areas in more anterior parts of the temporal lobe. That is, local plastic changes in connection strengths come into play as seeing a face action prepares the observer for a (corresponding) auditory event (van Wassenhove et al., 2005; Hertrich et al., 2009). Such preparatory re-setting does not seem to involve p-STS—at least not in relation to early processing stages. The specificity and duration of such re-setting of the forward connections for audio-visual speech will be a fruitful area for further research.

The many regions implicated in speechreading, and the elaboration of the time course of events allowing a visual or audio-visual stimulus to be perceived as speech suggests not only that processing of carrier and of content is distributed across multiple brain sites, but that coherent, sustained activation of multiple sites is required for audio-visual percepts such as McGurk effects to be experienced as unitary events. Gamma-band oscillatory activity across multiple brain regions is a likely candidate for such temporal cohesion (Fingelkurts et al., 2003). This type of activity is associated with the detection of asynchrony in audio-visual speech (Doesburg et al., 2008) and with synchronized McGurk syllable perception (Kaiser et al., 2006). It is likely that future research will find more evidence that multiple perceptual and action systems contribute to the unitary experience of a speech event.

Taken together, neuroimaging findings are opening up interesting avenues for identifying the processes implicated in speechreading and audio-visual speech perception, and their time course. While many "classical" speech perception regions are involved, especially within superior temporal regions, and these include auditory processing regions, speechreading may implicate frontal and somesthetic circuits too—possibly to a greater extent than for hearing speech. p-STS clearly performs crucial integration functions with respect to seeing speech, however, some fast feedforward connections may sometimes bypass this route. Investigations of voice as well as speech processing further suggest that content and carrier can be distinguished by different cortical subsystems within superior temporal regions. The cognitive stages models (Figures 31.2 and 31.3) proposed to account for findings in visual and audio-visual processing do not always fit readily to cortical activation findings, but cortical data can inform these models.

Summary and conclusion

In this chapter I have shown that when we listen to speech we are highly sensitive to the sight of the talker, and this is evident early in infancy, before the child produces spoken language. In this sense we all speechread, even when we may not be able to understand much of a silent speechread utterance. Moreover we can match a speaker's face to their voice and cannot ignore who someone is when we hear them talk. Watching someone talk involves both speech processing and face processing—and processing speech involves both processing speech content and managing aspects of the identity of the talker (indexical properties—the carrier). While we do this readily for familiar people, we can also discriminate between unfamiliar individuals by matching their (silent) talking face with their voice. Since a spoken utterance has correlated dynamic properties across the face and the voice (the timing and extent of the actions are closely synchronized), I have suggested that an early multimodal processing system (MISS) operates to integrate the talking face and the heard voice at a structural (pre-identification) level.

Fodor (1983) proposed that cognitive input systems are domain specific and input driven (bottom-up). To take the last of these first: one aspect of the chapter is to illustrate the extent to which the input-driven aspect may need to be moderated. Examples abound of "top-down" influences on "automatic" audio-visual speech processing, and have been provided in this chapter. But what about domain-specificity? What domain is occupied by speechreading? In contrast to a simple interpretation of Fodorian modularity, which might locate face processing in a purely visual domain and speech processing in a purely acoustic one (and so speechreading would be brushed out of sight), our sensitivity to the sight of a talker who is speaking tells us that there are crucial multimodal processes involved—and some of these operate at a relatively low (input) level.

One message of this chapter is that two domains—each of which is inherently multimodal—underpin much of our ability to process communicative information. These are a content domain (primarily speech) and a carrier domain (who is doing the communicating, and how?) The cortical correlates for each of these domains can be identified and each of their distinctive cognitive characteristics can be described. The details of how these domains interact await discovery.

Acknowledgments

Much work for this chapter was done during a visit to the MARCS laboratory, University of Western Sydney, Australia. I am happy to acknowledge the hospitality of Denis Burnham, who invited me to present at Summerfest2008 and was gracious enough to let me stay on for a while. MARCS colleagues, especially Jeesun Kim and Chris Davis, and also Harold Hill, provided the necessary inspiration.

References

Allison, T., Puce, A., and McCarthy, G. (2000). Social perception from visual cues: role of the STS region. *Trends in Cognitive Sciences*, **4**, 267–278.

Alsius, A., Navarra, J., Campbell, R., and Soto-Faraco, S.S. (2005). Audiovisual integration of speech falters under high attention demands. *Current Biology*, **15**, 839–843.

Assal, G., Zander, E., Kremin, H., and Buttet, J. (1976). Discrimination des voix lors des lésions du cortex cérébral. *Arch Suisses de Neurologie, Neurochirurgerie et Psychiatrie*, **119**, 307–315

Auer, E.T., Jr. and Bernstein, L.E. (1997). Speechreading and the structure of the lexicon: computationally modeling the effects of reduced phonetic distinctiveness on lexical uniqueness. *Journal of the Acoustical Society of America*, **102**, 3704–3710.

Belin, P. (2006). Voice processing in human and non-human primates. *Philosophical Transactions of the Royal Society of London B*, **361**, 2091–2107.

Belin, P., Fecteau, S., and Bédard,C. (2004). Thinking the voice: neural correlates of voice perception. *Trends in Cognitive Science*, **8**, 129–136.

Belin, P. and Zatorre, R.J. (2003). Adaptation to speaker's voice in right anterior temporal lobe. *Neuroreport*, **14**, 2105–2109.

Besle, J., Fischer, C., Bidet-Caulet, A., Lecaignard, F., Bertrand, O., and Giard, M.H. (2008). Visual activation and audiovisual interactions in the auditory cortex during speech perception: intracranial recordings in humans. *Journal of Neuroscience*, **28**, 14301–14310.

Bernstein, L.E., Auer, E.T. Jr., Wagner, M., and Ponton, C.W. (2008). Spatiotemporal dynamics of audiovisual speech processing. *Neuroimage*, **39**, 423–435.

Binder, J.R., Rao, S.M., Hammeke, T.A., *et al.* (2004). Functional magnetic resonance imaging of human auditory cortex *Annals of Neurology*, **35**, 662–672.

Bristow, D., Dehaene-Lambertz, G., Mattout, J., *et al.* (2009). Hearing faces: how the infant brain matches the face it sees with the speech it hears. *Journal of Cognitive Neuroscience*, **21**, 905–921.

Brothers, L. (1990). The social brain: a project for integrating primate behaviour and neurophysiology in a new domain. *Concepts in Neuroscience*, **1**, 27–51.

Bruce, V. and Young, A.W. (1986). Understanding face recognition. *British Journal of Psychology*, **77**, 305–327.

Burnham, D. and Dodd, B. (2004). Auditory-visual speech integration by prelinguistic infants: perception of an emergent consonant in the McGurk effect. *Developmental Psychobiology*, **45**, 204–220.

Calvert, G., Bullmore, E., Brammer, M.J., *et al.* (1997). Activation of auditory cortex during silent speechreading. *Science*, **276**, 593–596.

Calvert, G. and Campbell, R. (2003). Reading speech from still and moving faces: the neural substrates of seen speech. *Journal of Cognitive Neuroscience*, **15**, 57–70.

Calvert, G.A., Campbell, R., and Brammer, M. (2000).Evidence from functional magnetic resonance imaging of crossmodal binding in the human heteromodal cortex. *Current Biology*, **10**, 649–665.

Campanella, S. and Belin, P. (2007). Integrating face and voice in person perception. *Trends in Cognitive Sciences*, **11**, 535–543.

Campbell, R. (2006). Audio-visual speech processing. In K. Brown, A. Anderson, L. Bauer, M. Berns, G. Hirst, and J. Miller (eds.), *The encyclopedia of language and linguistics*, pp. 562–569. Amsterdam: Elsevier.

Campbell, R. (2008). The processing of audio-visual speech: empirical and neural bases. *Philosophical Transactions of the Royal Society of London B*, **363**, 1001–1010.

Campbell, R. and Dodd, B. (1980). Hearing by eye. *Quarterly Journal of Experimental Psychology*, **32**, 85–99.

Campbell, R., Landis, T., and Regard, M.(1986). Face recognition and lipreading. A neurological dissociation. *Brain*, **109**, 509–521.

Campbell, R., Garwood, J., Franklin, S., Howard, D., Landis, T., and Regard, M. (1990). Neuropsychological studies of auditory-visual fusion illusions. Four case studies and their implications. *Neuropsychologia*, **128**, 787–802.

Campbell, R., Brooks, B., de Haan, E., and Roberts, T. (1996). Dissociating face processing skills: decision about lip-read speech, expression, and identity. *Quarterly Journal of Experimental Psychology A*, **49**, 295–314.

Capek, C.M., Bavelier, D., Corina, D., Newman, A.J., Jezzard, P., and Neville, H.J. (2004). The cortical organization of audio-visual sentence comprehension: an fMRI study at 4 Tesla. *Brain Research, Cognitive Brain Research*, **20**, 111–119.

Capek, C.M., MacSweeney, M., Woll, B., *et al.* (2008). Cortical circuits for silent speechreading in deaf and hearing people. *Neuropsychologia*, **46**, 1233–1241.

Christie, F. and Bruce, V. (1998). The role of dynamic information in the recognition of unfamiliar faces. *Memory and Cognition*, **26**, 780–790.

Davis, C. and Kim, J. (2004). Audio-visual interactions with intact clearly audible speech. *Quarterly Journal of Experimental Psychology A*, **57**, 1103–1121.

De Gelder, B. and Bertelson, P. (2003). Multisensory integration, perception and ecological validity. *Trends in Cognitive Science*, 10, 460–467.

de Gelder, B., Vroomen, J., and Bachoud Levi, A.C. (1998). Impaired speechreading and audio-visual speech integration in prosopagnosia. In R. Campbell and B. Dodd (eds.) *Hearing by eye II* pp. 195–207. Hove: Psychology Press/Erlbaum.

de Haan, E.H. and Campbell, R. (1991). A fifteen year follow-up of a case of developmental prosopagnosia. *Cortex*, **27**, 489–509.

Dixon, N.F. and Spitz, L. (1980). The detection of audio-visual desynchrony. *Perception*, **9**, 719–21.

Dodd, B. (1979). Lip reading in infants: attention to speech presented in- and out-of-synchrony. *Cognitive Psychology*, **11**, 478–484.

Doesburg, S.M., Emberson, L.L., Rahi, A., Cameron, D., and Ward, L.M. (2008). Asynchrony from synchrony: long-range gamma-band neural synchrony accompanies perception of audiovisual speech asynchrony. *Experimental Brain Research*, **185**, 11–20.

Fingelkurts, A.A., Fingelkurts, A.A., Krause, C.M., Möttönen, R., and Sams, M. (2003). Cortical operational synchrony during audio-visual speech integration. *Brain and Language*, **85**, 297–312.

Fodor, J.A. (1983). *Modularity of Mind: An Essay on Faculty Psychology*. Cambridge, MA: MIT Press.

Formisano, E., De Martino, F., Bonte, M., and Goebel, R. (2008). "Who" is saying "what"? Brain-based decoding of human voice and speech. *Science*, **322**, 970–973.

Fridriksson, J., Moser, D., Ryalls, J., Bonilha, L., Rorden, C., and Baylis, G. (2009). Modulation of frontal lobe speech areas associated with the production and perception of speech movements. *Journal of Speech and Language and Hearing Research*, **52**, 812–819.

Garner, W.R. (1974). *The Processing of Information and Structure*. New York: Erlbaum, Potomac, Wiley.

Ghazanfar, A.A. and Logothetis, N.K. (2003). Neuroperception: facial expressions linked to monkey calls. *Nature*, **423**, 937–938.

Ghazanfar, A.A. and Schroeder, C.E. (2006). Is neocortex essentially multisensory? *Trends in Cognitive Science*, **10**, 278–285.

Ghazanfar, A.A., Turesson, H.K., Maier, J.X., van Dinther,R., Patterson,R.D., and Logothetis, N.K. (2007). Vocal-tract resonances as indexical cues in rhesus monkeys. *Current Biology*, **17**, 425–430

Green, K.P. (1998). *The use of auditory and visual information during phonetic processing; implications for theories of speech perception*. In Campbell R, Dodd BM and Burnham D (eds.) *Hearing By Eye II*, pp. 3–26. Hove: Psychology Press.

Hall, D.A., Fussell, C., and Summerfield, A.Q. (2005). Reading fluent speech from talking faces: typical brain networks and individual differences. *Journal of Cognitive Neuroscience*, **17**, 939–953.

Hamilton, R.H., Shenton, J.T., and Branch Coslett, H. (2006). An acquired deficit of audio-visual speech processing. *Brain and Language*, **98**, 66–73.

Hare, B. and Tomasello, M. (2005). Human-like social skills in dogs? *Trends in Cognitive Science*, **9**, 439–444.

Hasson, U., Skipper, J.I., Nusbaum, H.C., and Small, S.L. (2007). Abstract coding of audiovisual speech: beyond sensory representation. *Neuron*, **56**, 1116–1126.

Haxby, J.V., Hoffman, E.A., and Gobbini, M.I. (2002). Human neural systems for face recognition and social communication. *Biological Psychiatry*, **51**, 59–67.

Hazan, V., Sennema, A., Faulkner, A., Ortega-Llebaria, M., Iba, M., and Chunge, H. (2006). The use of visual cues in the perception of non-native consonant contrasts. *Journal of the Acoustical Society of America*, **119**, 1740–1751.

Hein, G. and Knight, R.T. (2008). Superior temporal sulcus - It's my area: Or is it? *Journal of Cognitive Neuroscience*, **20**, 2125–2136.

Hertrich, I., Mathiak, K., Lutzenberger,W., and Ackerman, H. (2009). Timecourse of early audiovisual interactions during speech and nonspeech central auditory processing: a magnetoencephalography study *Journal of Cognitive Neuroscience*, **21**, 259–274.

Irwin, A., Thomas, S., and Pilling, M. (2007). Regional accent familiarity and speechreading performance. In J. Vroomen, M. Swarts and E. Kramer (eds.) *Proceedings of the international conference AVSP2007* ISCA available at: http://spitswww.uvt.nl/Fsw/Psychologie/AVSP2007/.

Jiang, J., Alwan, A., Keating, P.A., Auer, E.T., and Bernstein, L.E. (2002). On the relationship between face movements, tongue movements and speech acoustics. *Journal of Applied Signal Processing*, **11**, 1174–1188.

Jiang, J., Auer, E.T. Jr., Alwan, A., Keating, P.A., and Bernstein, L.E. (2007). Similarity structure in visual speech perception and optical phonetic signals. *Perception and Psychophysics*, **69**, 1070–1083.

Kaiser, A.R., Kirk, K.I., Lachs, L., and Pisoni, D.B. (2003)Talker and lexical effects on audiovisual word recognition by adults with cochlear implants. *Journal of Speech and Language and Hearing Research*, **46**, 390–404.

Kaiser, J., Hertrich, I., Ackermann, H., and Lutzenberger, W. (2006)Gamma-band activity over early sensory areas predicts detection of changes in audiovisual speech stimuli. *Neuroimage*, **30**, 1376–1382.

Kamachi, M., Hill, H., Lander, K., and Vatikiotis-Bateson, E. (2003). Putting the face to the voice: matching identity across modality. *Current Biology*, **13**, 1709–1714.

Kaufmann, J.M. and Schweinberger, S.R. (2005). Speaker variations influence speechreading speed for dynamic faces. *Perception*, **34**, 595–610.

Kerzel, D. and Bekkering, H. (2000). Motor activation from visible speech: evidence from stimulus response compatibility. *Journal of Experimental Psychology: Human Perception and Performance*, **26**, 634–647.

Kim, J. and Davis, C. (2003). Hearing foreign voices: does knowing what is said affect visual-masked-speech detection? *Perception*, **32**, 111–120.

Kreiman, J. and Van Lancker, D. (1988). Hemispheric specialization for voice recognition: evidence from dichotic listening. *Brain and Language*, **34**, 246–252.

Kuhl, P.K. and Meltzoff, A.N. (1982). The bimodal perception of speech in infancy. *Science*, **218**, 1138–1141.

Lachs, L. and Pisoni, D.B. (2004a). Cross-modal source identification in speech perception. *Ecological Psychology*, **16**, 159–187.

Lachs, L. and Pisoni, D.B. (2004b). Cross-modal source information and spoken word recognition. *Journal of Experimental Psychology: Human Perception and Performance*, **30**, 378–396.

Lachs, L. and Pisoni, D.B. (2004c). Specification of cross-modal source information in isolated kinematic displays of speech. *Journal of the Acoustical Society of America*, **116**, 507–518.

Lander, K. (2004). Repetition priming from moving faces. *Memory and Cognition*, **32**(4), 640–647.

Lander, K. and Davies, R. (2007). Exploring the role of characteristic motion when learnig new faces. *Quarterly Journal of Experimental Psychology*, **60**, 519–526.

Lander, K. and Davies, R. (2008). Does face familiarity influence speechreadability? *Quarterly Journal of Experimental Psychology*, **61**, 961–967.

Landis, T., Buttet, J., Assal, G., and Graves, R.(1982). Dissociation of ear preference in monaural word and voice recognition. *Neuropsychologia*, **20**, 501–504.

Lander, K., Christie, F., and Bruce, V. (1999). The role of movement in the recognition of famous faces. *Memory and Cognition*, **27**, 974–985.

Lander, K., Hill, H., Kamachi, M., and Vatikiotis-Bateson, E. (2007). It's not what you say but the way you say it: matching faces and voices. *Journal of Experimental Psychology: Human Perception and Performance*, **33**, 905–914.

Lewkowicz, D.J. (2010). Infant perception of audio-visual speech synchrony. *Developmental Psychology*, **46**, 66–77.

Liberman, A.M., Cooper, F.S., Shankweiler, D.P., and Studdert-Kennedy, M. (1967). Perception of the speech code. *Psychological Review*, **74**, 431–461.

McGrath, M., Summerfield, A.Q., and Brooke, N.M. (1984). Roles of lips and teeth in lipreading vowels, *Proceedings of the Institute of Acoustics (Autumn Meeting, Windermere)*, **6**, 401–408.

McGurk, H. and MacDonald, J. (1976). Hearing lips and seeing voices. *Nature*, **264**, 746–748.

Miller, L.M. and D'Esposito, M. (2005). Perceptual fusion and stimulus coincidence in the cross-modal integration of speech. *Journal of Neuroscience*, **25**, 5884–5893.

Möttönen, R., Krause, C.M, Tiippana, K., and Sams, M. (2002a). Processing of changes in visual speech in the human auditory cortex, *Brain Research, Cognitive. Brain Research*, **13**, 417–425.

Möttönen, R., Schürmann, M., and Sams, M. (2004). Time course of multisensory interactions during audiovisual speech perception in humans: a magnetoencephalographic study. *Neuroscience Letters*, **363**, 112–115.

Möttönen, R., Järveläinen, J., Sams, M., and Hari, R. (2005). Viewing speech modulates activity in the left SI mouth cortex. *Neuroimage*, **24**, 731–737.

Mullenix, J.W., Pisoni, D.B., and Martin, C.S. (1989). Some effects of talker variability on spoken word recognition, *Journal of the Acoustical Society of America*, 85, 365–378.

Munhall, K.G. and Vatikiotis-Bateson, E. (1998). The moving face during speech communication. In Campbell, R., Dodd, B. and Burnham, D. (eds.) *Hearing by eye II*, pp. 123–139. Hove: Psychology Press Ltd.

Murase, M., Saito, D.N., Kochiyama, T., *et al.* (2008). Cross-modal integration during vowel identification in audiovisual speech: a functional magnetic resonance imaging study. *Neuroscience Letters*, **434**, 71–76.

Musacchia, G., Sams, M., Nicol, T., and Kraus, N. (2006). Seeing speech affects acoustic information processing in the human brainstem. *Experimental Brain Research*, **168**, 1–10.

Musacchia, G., Sams, M., Skoe, E., and Kraus, N. (2007). Musicians have enhanced subcortical auditory and audiovisual processing of speech and music. *Proceedings of the National Academy of Sciences, U S A*, **104**, 15894–15898.

Navarra, J. and Soto-Faraco, S. (2007). Hearing lips in a second language: visual articulatory information enables the perception of second language sounds. *Psychological Research*, **71**, 4–12.

Nishitani, N. and Hari, R. (2002). Viewing lip forms: cortical dynamics. *Neuron*, **36**, 1211–1220.

Nygaard, L.C., Sommers, M.S., and Pisoni, D.B. (1994). Speech perception as a talker-contingent process. *Psychological Science*, **5**, 42–46.

O'Toole, A.J., Roark, D.A., and Abdi, H. (2002). Recognizing moving faces: a psychological and neural synthesis. *Trends in Cognitive Science*, **6**, 261–266.

Patterson, M.L. and Werker, J.F. (1999). Matching phonetic information in lips and voice is robust in 4.5-month-old infants. *Infant Behaviour and Development*, **22**, 237–247.

Patterson, M.L. and Werker, J.F. (2002). Infants ability to match phonetic and gender information in the face and voice *Journal of Experimental Child Psychology*, **81**, 93–115.

Paulesu, E., Perani, D., Blasi, V., Silani, G., Borghese, N.A. *et al.* (2003). A functional anatomical model for lipreading. *Journal of Neurophysiology*, **90**, 2005–2013.

Pekkola, J., Ojanen, V., Autti, T., *et al.* (2005). Primary auditory cortex activation by visual speech: an fMRI study at 3 T. *NeuroReport*, **16**, 125–128.

Pelphrey, K.A., Morris, J.P., Michelich, C.R., Allison, T., and McCarthy, G. (2005). Functional anatomy of biological motion perception in posterior temporal cortex: An FMRI study of eye, mouth and hand movements. *Cerebral Cortex*, **15**, 1866–1876.

Petkov, C.I., Kayser, C., Steudel, T., Whittingstall, K., Augath, M., and Logothetis, N.K. (2008). A voice region in the monkey brain. *Nature Neuroscience*, **11**, 367–374.

Pons, F., Lewkowicz, D.J., Soto-Faraco, S., and Sebastián-Gallés, N. (2009). Narrowing of intersensory speech perception in infancy. *Proceedings of the National Academy of Sciences, USA*, **106**, 10598–10602.

Puce, A., Allison, T., Bentin, S., Gore, J.C., and McCarthy, G. (1998). Temporal cortex activation in humans viewing eye and mouth movements. *Journal of Neuroscience*, **18**, 2188–2199.

Rauschecker, J.P. (1997). Processing of complex sounds in the auditory cortex of cat, monkey and man. *Acta Otolaryngologica (Stockholm) Suppl.* **532**, 34–38.

Reale, R.A., Calvert, G.A., Thesen, T., *et al.* (2007). Auditory-visual processing represented in the human superior temporal gyrus. *Neuroscience*, **145**, 162–184.

Redcay, E. (2008). The superior temporal sulcus performs a common function for social and speech perception: implications for the emergence of autism. *Neuroscience Biobehavioral Reviews*, **32**, 123–142.

Remez, R.E., Fellowes, J.M., and Rubin, P.E. (1997). Talker identification based on phonetic information. *Journal of Experimental Psychology: Human Perception and Performance*, **23**, 651–666.

Roberts, M. and Summerfield, Q. (1981). Audiovisual presentation demonstrates that selective adaptation in speech perception is purely auditory. *Perception and Psychophysics*, **30**, 309–314.

Rönnberg, J. (2003). Cognition in the hearing impaired and deaf as a bridge between signal and dialogue: A framework and a model. *International Journal of Audiology*, **42**, S68–S76.

Rose, P. (2002). *Forensic Speaker Identification*. London: Taylor and Francis/CRC Press.

Rosenblum, L.D. and Saldaña H.M. (1996). An audiovisual test of kinematic primitives for visual speech perception. *Journal of Experimental Psychology: Human Perception and Performance*, **22**, 318–331.

Rosenblum, L.D., Johnson, J.A., and Saldaña, H.M. (1996). Point-light facial displays enhance comprehension of speech in noise. *Journal of Speech and Hearing Research*, **39**, 1159–1170.

Rosenblum, L.D., Schmuckler, M.A., and Johnson, J.A. (1997). The McGurk effect in infants. *Perception and Psychophysics*, **59**, 347–357.

Rosenblum, L.D., Smith, N.M., Nichols, S.M., Hale, S., and Lee, J. (2006). Hearing a face: cross-modal speaker matching using isolated visible speech. *Perception and Psychophysics*, **68**, 84–93.

Rosenblum, L.D., Miller, R.M., and Sanchez, K. (2007a). Lip-read me now, hear me better later: cross-modal transfer of talker-familiarity effects. *Psychological Science*, **18**, 392–396.

Rosenblum, L.D., Niehus, R.P., and Smith, N.M. (2007b). Look who's talking: recognizing friends from visible articulation. *Perception*, **36**, 157–159.

Saldaña, H.M. and Rosenblum, L.D. (1994). Selective adaptation in speech perception using a compelling audiovisual adaptor. *Journal of the Acoustic Society of America*, **95**, 3658–3961.

Saito, D.N., Yoshimura, K., Kochiyama, T., Okada, T., Honda, M., and Sadato, N. (2005). Cross-modal binding and activated attentional networks during audio-visual speech integration: a functional MRI study. *Cerebral Cortex*, **15**, 1750–1760.

Sams, M., Möttönen, R., and Sihvonen, T. (2005). Seeing and hearing others and oneself talk. *Brain Research, Cognitive Brain Research*, **23**, 429–435.

Santi, A., Servos, P., Vatikiotis-Bateson, E., Kuratate, T., and Munhall, K. (2003). Perceiving biological motion: dissociating visible speech from walking. *Journal of Cognitive Neuroscience*, **15**, 800–809.

Saxe, R. and Kanwisher, N. (2003). People thinking about thinking people. The role of the temporo-parietal junction in "theory of mind". *Neuroimage*, **19**, 1835–1842.

Schweinberger, S.R., Casper, C., Hauthal, N., *et al.* (2008). Auditory adaptation in voice perception. *Current Biology*, **18**, 684–688.

Schweinberger, S.R., Robertson, D., and Kaufmann, J.M. (2007). Hearing facial identities. *Quarterly Journal of Experimental Psychology*, **60**, 1446–1456.

Schweinberger, S.R. and Soukup, G.R. (1998). Asymmetric relationships among perceptions of facial identity, emotion, and facial speech. *Journal of Experimental Psychology: Human Perception and Performance*, **24**, 1748–1765.

Scott, S.K. and Johnsrude, I.S. (2003). The neuroanatomical and functional organization of speech perception. *Trends in Neuroscience*, **26**, 100–107.

Scott, S.K., Rosen, S., Lang, H., and Wise, R.J. (2006). Neural correlates of intelligibility in speech investigated with noise vocoded speech—a positron emission tomography study. *Journal of the Acoustical Society of America*, **120**, 1075–1083.

Sekiyama, K. (1994). Differences in auditory-visual speech perception between Japanese and Americans: McGurk effect as a function of incompatibility. *Journal of the. Acoustical Society of Japan*, **15**, 143–158.

Sekiyama, K. (1997). Cultural and linguistic factors in audiovisual speech processing: the McGurk effect in Chinese subjects. *Perception and Psychophysics*, **59**, 73–80.

Sekiyama, K. and Tohkura, Y. (1991). McGurk effect in non-English listeners: few visual effects for Japanese subjects hearing Japanese syllables of high auditory intelligibility. *Journal of the Acoustical Society of America*, **90**, 1797–1805.

Sheffert, S.M. and Olson, E. (2004). Audiovisual speech facilitates voice learning. *Perception and Psychophysics*, **66**, 352–362.

Sheffert, S.M., Pisoni, D.B., Fellowes, J.M., and Remez, R.E. (2002). Learning to recognize talkers from natural, sinewave, and reversed speech samples. *Journal of Experimental Psychology: Human Perception and Performance*, **28**, 1447–1469.

Skipper, J.I., Nusbaum, H.C., and Small, S.L. (2005). Listening to talking faces: motor cortical activation during speech perception. *Neuroimage* **25**, 76–89.

Soto-Faraco, S., Navarra, J., Weikum, W.M., Vouloumanos, A., Sebastián-Gallés, N., and Werker, J.F. (2007). Discriminating languages by speech-reading. *Perception and Psychophysics*. **69**, 218–231.

Stevenson, R.A. and James, T.W. (2009). Audiovisual integration in human superior temporal sulcus: Inverse effectiveness and the neural processing of speech and object recognition. *Neuroimage*. **44**, 1210–1223.

Stone, S.M. (2010). Human facial discrimination in horses: can they tell us apart? *Animal Cognition*, **13**, 51–61.

Studdert-Kennedy, M. (1983). Perceptual processing links to the motor system. In M. Studdert-Kennedy (ed.) *The Psychobiology of Language*, pp. 29–39. Cambridge MA: MIT Press.

Tate, A.J., Fischer, H., Leigh, A.E., and Kendrick, K.M. (2006). Behavioural and neurophysiological evidence for face identity and face emotion processing in animals. *Philosophical Transactions of the Royal Society of London B*, **361**, 2155–2172.

Teinonen,T., Aslin, R.N., Alku, P., and Csibra,G. (2008). Visual speech contributes to phonetic learning in 6-month-old infants *Cognitio*, **108**, 850–855.

van Wassenhove, V., Grant, K.W., and Poeppel, D. (2005).Visual speech speeds up the neural processing of auditory speech. *Proceedings of the National Academy of Sciences USA*, **102**, 1181–1186.

von Kriegstein, K.V. and Giraud, A.L. (2004). Distinct functional substrates along the right superior temporal sulcus for the processing of voices. *Neuroimage*, **22**, 948–955.

von Kriegstein, K., Eger, E., Kleinschmidt, A., and Giraud, A.L. (2003). Modulation of neural responses to speech by directing attention to voices or verbal content. *Brain Research, Cognitive Brain Research*, **17**, 48–55.

von Kriegstein, K., Kleinschmidt, A., and Giraud, A.L. (2006) Voice recognition and cross-modal responses to familiar speakers' voices in prosopagnosia. *Cerebral Cortex* **16**, 1314–11313.

von Kriegstein, K., Dogan, O., Grüter, M., *et al.* (2008) Simulation of talking faces in the human brain improves auditory speech recognition. *Proceedings of the National Academy of Sciences USA*, **105**, 6747–6752.

Walker, S., Bruce, V., and O'Malley, C. (1995). Facial identity and facial speech processing: familiar faces and voices in the McGurk effect. *Perception and Psychophysics*, **57**, 1124–1133.

Watkins, K.E., Strafella, A.P., and Paus, T. (2003). Seeing and hearing speech excites the motor system involved in speech production *Neuropsychologia*, **41**, 989–994.

Weikum, W.M., Vouloumanos, A., Navarra, J., Soto-Faraco, S., Sebastián-Gallés, N., and Werker, J.F. (2007). Visual language discrimination in infancy. *Science*, **316**, 1159.

Werker, J.F. and Tees, R.C. (2005). Speech perception as a window for understanding plasticity and commitment in language systems of the brain. *Developmental Psychobiology* **46**, 233–234.

Wright, T.M., Pelphrey, K.A., Allison, T., McKeown, M.J., and McCarthy, G. (2003). Polysensory Interactions along lateral temporal regions evoked by audiovisual speech. *Cerebral Cortex*, **13**, 1034–1043.

Yakel, D.A., Rosenblum, L.D., and Fortier, M.A. (2000). Effects of talker variability on speechreading. *Perception and Psychophysics*. **62**, 1405–1412.

Yehia, H.C., Rubin, P.E., and Vatikiotis-Bateson, E. (1998). Quantitative association of vocal-tract and facial behavior. *Speech Communication* **26**, 23–43.

Yehia, H.C., Kuratate, T., and Vatikiotis-Bateson, E. (2002). Linking facial animation, head motion and speech acoustics. *Journal of Phonetics* **30**, 555–568.

Chapter 32

Personality Impressions from Facial Appearance

Alexander Todorov, Christopher C. Said,
and Sara C. Verosky

The study of personality inferences from facial appearance has a long history in psychology (Hollingworth, 1922; Secord, 1958; Shepherd, 1989). Work at the beginning of the 20th century was primarily focused on the accuracy of these inferences (Hollingworth, 1922; Laird, 1927; Pintner, 1918). In the fifties, the focus of research shifted to the cognitive mechanisms underlying such inferences (Secord, 1958). Subsequent social cognition research has followed this tradition with a focus on inferences of social categories (e.g. sex, age, race) and the implications of these inferences for social interaction (e.g. Eberhardt et al., 2006; Macrae et al., 2005; Quinn and Macrae, 2005). Parallel to this research, evolutionary and ecological psychologists have produced a large body of research on the determinants and consequences of facial attractiveness and facial maturity (Perrett et al., 1998; McArthur and Apatow, 1983; Montepare and Zebrowitz, 1998; Rhodes, 2006; Thornhill and Gangestad, 1993; also Penton-Voak and Morrison, Chapter 33; Zebrowitz, Chapter 3, this volume). Finally, with advances in cognitive neuroscience methods and the emergence of social neuroscience research (Adolphs, 2003), there have been multiple recent studies probing the neural correlates of personality inferences from faces (e.g. Adolphs et al., 1998; Aharon et al., 2001; Engell et al., 2007; O'Doherty et al., 2003; Said et al., 2009b; Winston et al., 2002).

In this chapter, we review several lines of research on personality impressions from faces. We discuss research on the accuracy of these impressions (first section: "The accuracy of personality impressions from faces"), the social consequences of these impressions (second section: "Consequences of personality impressions from faces"), the automaticity of forming these impressions (third section: "The automaticity of personality impressions from faces"), recent patient and functional magnetic resonance imaging (fMRI) studies exploring the neural basis of these impressions (fourth section: "Neuroimaging and patient studies of personality impressions from faces"), dimensional approaches to personality impressions from faces (fifth section: "Dimensional approaches to face evaluation"), and potential sources of individual differences in evaluation of faces (sixth section: "The role of individual differences in face evaluation").

The accuracy of personality impressions from faces

It has been known for a long time in psychology that people agree on their personality impressions from faces (Hollingworth, 1922, chapter 3). However, consensus or reliability of judgments is not equivalent to accuracy or validity of these judgments. A detailed review of the accuracy of judgments from facial appearance is beyond the scope of this chapter.[1] Instead, we briefly review selected studies and note the methodological challenges facing research on accuracy.

Early studies on the accuracy of judgments were conducted in the context of personnel selection and tested the relationship between judgments of intelligence from photographs and intelligence measures (Hollingworth, 1922; Laird, 1927). The evidence for the accuracy of judgment was mixed, with some studies failing to find a significant relationship (Laird, 1927, Chapter 6) and some studies finding modest positive correlations between judgments and IQ measures (Pintner, 1918). A meta-analysis of these early studies found an average correlation of .30 (Zebrowitz et al., 2002).

However, many of the earlier studies had methodological flaws (Shepherd, 1989). For example, in the study reporting the highest correlations between individual judgments of intelligence and IQ measures, the variance of IQ was unrepresentative of the general population, ranging from 18 to 171 for 11 individuals (Gaskill et al., 1927).[2] The correlation was almost perfect for individuals with IQ below 100 but negative for individuals with IQ above 100. Interestingly, recent studies have shown that judgments of intelligence correlate with measures of intelligence only for individuals below median attractiveness (Zebrowitz and Rhodes, 2004). This finding was predicted by the "bad genes" hypothesis, which posits that unattractive faces signal poor genetic fitness (e.g. individuals with Down syndrome).

In general, better controlled recent studies have confirmed the relationship between judgments of intelligence and IQ measures, although the correlations were weaker and were only valid for some age groups (e.g. childhood) but not others (e.g. later adulthood). Moreover, attractiveness accounted for these correlations, suggesting that people rely on attractiveness to infer intelligence (Zebrowitz et al., 2002). Because attractiveness happens to be weakly correlated with intelligence, judgments of intelligence predict actual intelligence.

Studies in social and personality psychology have also tested whether trait inferences from faces correlate with self-reports. Several studies have reported moderate correlations for self-reports of approachability, warmth, power and extraversion (Berry, 1991; Berry and Brownlow, 1989; Penton-Voak et al., 2006). However, other studies have failed to find significant correlations for agreeableness, conscientiousness (Pound et al., 2007), and suggestibility (Bachmann and Nurmoja, 2006). Studies have also used behavioral measures with one study finding positive but weak correlations between judgments of honesty and willingness to participate in experiments involving deception of other subjects (Bond et al., 1994) and another failing to find a significant relationship between judgments of honesty and observationally assessed honesty (Zebrowitz et al., 1996).

It is instructive to consider the question of accuracy in the context of studies in which subjects made personality judgments from dynamic video clips of social interaction (Carney et al., 2007), materials much richer than still images of faces. Although subjects were accurate—the accuracy increased for longer clips and clips drawn from the middle and the end of the 5-min interaction— the accuracies of judgments made after 5-s clips from the first minute of the interaction were low, with correlations of −0.12 for positive affect, 0.11 for negative affect, 0.07 for neuroticism, 0.02 for extraversion, 0.21 for openness to experience, −0.03 for agreeableness, 0.12 for conscientiousness, and 0.10 for intelligence.

---

[1] Unfortunately, to the best of our knowledge, there are no comprehensive reviews of research on the accuracy of personality impressions from *still images of faces*. There are, however, reviews on the accuracy of person impressions based on various materials, including dynamic videos, voice recordings, and still images. For a recent review, see Hall et al. (2008).

[2] For an unbiased estimate of the strength of the true relationship, the variability in the sample of faces should be representative of the variability of faces in the population (Hönekopp et al., 2006).

Recently, there has been a renewed interest in the accuracy of personality impressions with some studies suggesting that sexual orientation (Rule and Ambady, 2008) and aggressiveness (Carré and McCormick, 2008; Carré et al., 2009; Sell et al., 2009) can be inferred from faces at better than chance accuracy. The latter studies are particularly interesting because a plausible biological mechanism can be postulated in light of evidence that testosterone treatment of adolescents leads to increased craniofacial growth (Verdonck et al., 1999) and that fluctuations in testosterone correlate with aggressive behavior (Pound et al., 2008).

Although there is evidence for accuracy in some trait judgments, there is no evidence for accuracy in other judgments. Why, then, do people make these inaccurate judgments, and why are they made so reliably? One of the most intriguing explanations is the *overgeneralization hypothesis* (Zebrowitz, Chapter 3, this volume). Under this hypothesis, certain traits that are accurately revealed by face qualities such as emotion, age, or identity are erroneously perceived in people who merely resemble one of those categories. For instance, there is evidence that neutral faces that resemble the emotion anger are perceived as being low on the affiliation trait, whereas neutral faces that resemble the emotion happiness are perceived as high on affiliation (Montepare and Dobish, 2003; see also Said et al., 2009b). Similarly, babyfaced adults are perceived as having traits consistent with baby stereotypes, such as low social dominance and low intellectual capacity (McArthur and Apatow, 1983; Montepare and Zebrowitz, 1998). The overgeneralization hypothesis is not mutually exclusive with accuracy of impressions, and there is evidence that the two phenomena may interact in interesting ways. Initially inaccurate overgeneralizations can trigger a self-fulfilling prophecy, in which social interactions influenced by face impressions may lead to the actual development of the expected traits (Snyder et al., 1977). Conversely, there is evidence that in some cases, such as with adolescent baby-faced boys, a self-defeating prophecy can be triggered, leading to the behavioral development of the opposite of the perceived face trait (Zebrowitz et al., 1998a). A more complete discussion of these and other issues relating to overgeneralization can be found in Zebrowitz, Chapter 3, this volume.

To summarize, the degree to which trait inferences from faces are accurate will depend on the trait dimension, with some traits showing accuracy (e.g. extraversion) and others not (e.g. agreeableness). Currently, it is not clear what factors determine the degree of accuracy (see Hall et al., 2008). Even if trait judgments predict actual measures of personality, the correlations are fairly low for individual judges. The average correlations between judgments and personality measures are often obtained at the aggregated level of subjects. That is, the personality measures for the target faces are correlated with the mean personality judgments across subjects. As a general statistical rule, this aggregation produces higher correlations than correlations at the level of individual subjects (Dawes, 1970; Hönecopp, 2006). The latter are much weaker and for many subjects negative (e.g. Hollingworth, 1922; Pintner, 1918). For example, in one study, the range of correlations of individual judgments of intelligence and measures of intelligence was from −0.63 to 0.52 with a median correlation of 0.10 (Pintner, 1918). Moreover, facial cues that may have predictive utility are often overweighted in judgments. For example, the magnitude of the correlations between perceived intelligence and attractiveness is two to three times higher than the magnitude of the correlations between actual intelligence and attractiveness (Zebrowitz et al., 2002).

The most important methodological challenge facing research on accuracy concerns the sampling of the stimuli. It would be generally easy to select faces for which people show either good or dismal accuracy (see Laird, 1927, chapter 6, for examples). To establish that judgments are accurate though, one needs to ascertain the representativeness of the stimuli, a condition that would be difficult to satisfy in many situations.

Finally, researchers need to specify the mechanisms through which positive (or negative) correlations between trait inferences from faces and personality characteristics develop. These could range from self-fulfilling (Zebrowitz, 1999) and self-defeating prophecy effects, the latter producing negative correlations (Collins and Zebrowitz, 1995; Zebrowitz et al., 1998a,b), to effects of frequent expressions of specific emotions on facial structure (Malatesta et al., 1987).

Consequences of personality impressions from faces

Whether or not trait inferences from faces are accurate, they affect important social outcomes. The effects of attractiveness on various social outcomes have been extensively documented (Langlois et al., 2000). For example, attractive people have better mating success, job prospects, and earning potential than their less fortunate peers (Dipboye et al.1977; Frieze et al., 1991; Hamermesh and Biddle, 1994; Pashos and Niemitz, 2003; Rhodes et al., 2005). There is also an extensive literature on the effect of baby-faced appearance on social outcomes (Montepare and Zebrowitz, 1998; Zebrowitz, 1999). For example, in small claims court, baby-faced people were less likely to be found at fault than their mature-faced peers when they denied responsibility for intentional but not negligent actions (Zebrowitz and McDonald, 1991).

These findings clearly suggest that people act on their impressions from facial appearance (Hassin and Trope, 2000). The effects of appearance on social outcomes may be partly attributable to halo effects (Nisbett and Wilson, 1977), global evaluations that can influence the perception of specific traits. For example, attractiveness correlates with perceptions of intelligence, friendliness, and a host of other social evaluations (Eagly et al., 1991). Similarly, babyfaced appearance correlates with perceptions of honesty, intelligence, assertiveness, approachability, and many other evaluations (Montepare and Zebrowitz, 1998). Thus, variations on these basic dimensions can give rise to specific trait inferences relevant to the specific context. For example, attractive people may be perceived as more competent and, hence, paid a "premium" for their performance (Hamermesh and Biddle, 1994). Facially mature looking people may be perceived as more dominant (Keating and Bai, 1986; Keating et al., 1981), and these perceptions can influence their professional outcomes such as military rank attainment (Mazur and Mueller, 1996; Mazur et al., 1984; Mueller and Mazur, 1996). Similar halo effects may operate for social categories too. For example, several studies have found that race stereotypical face features predicted sentencing decisions (Blair et al., 2004; Eberhardt et al., 2006), presumably by activating general stereotypes that affected specific decisions.

However, variations on general dimensions such as attractiveness and facial maturity may not be sufficient to account for all effects of impressions from faces on social outcomes. For example, there have been a number of recent studies showing that inferences related to competence and leadership predict electoral success (Antonakis and Delgas, 2009; Ballew and Todorov, 2007; Little et al., 2007), even when variations on general dimensions are controlled (Hall et al., 2009; Poutvaara et al., 2009; Todorov et al., 2005; for a review see Olivola and Todorov, 2010). One of the surprising findings of this research was the specificity of the effects. People generally report that competence is the most important attribute for a politician and inferences of this attribute, but not inferences of attributes considered unimportant, predict electoral success (Hall et al., 2009). Moreover, inferences of competence remain a significant predictor of electoral success even when the analysis controls for age, babyfaced appearance, attractiveness, face familiarity, and a dozen personality impressions from the faces of political candidates (Olivola and Todorov, 2010).

How personality impressions from faces affect social outcomes appears to depend on the specific context of choices. The research findings suggest that the decision context determines the primary dimensions of importance and that inferences along these dimensions affect decisions (Brownlow, 1992; Brownlow and Zebrowitz, 1990; DeBruine, 2002; Little et al., 2007). For example, in the context of a war voters prefer masculine and dominant looking leaders.

Conversely, in the context of peace they prefer feminine and intelligent looking leaders (Little et al., 2007). Thus, researchers interested in predicting how impressions from faces affect decisions need to first determine the relevant personality dimensions for the context and then measure impressions on these dimensions.

The automaticity of personality impressions from faces

Facial attractiveness is one of the most thoroughly studied face properties (Rhodes 2006; Langlois et al., 2000; Penton-Voak and Morrison, Chapter 33, this volume) and the initial studies on the efficiency of impressions from faces focused on judgments of attractiveness (Locher et al., 1993; Olson and Marshuetz, 2005). Locher et al. (1993) showed that 100 ms exposure to faces was sufficient for subjects to discriminate between different levels of facial attractiveness. Olson and Marshuetz (2005) replicated these findings using extremely short subliminal exposures to faces (13 ms) suggesting that attractiveness is extracted automatically from facial appearance.

The findings that attractiveness can be perceived after brief exposures to faces have been extended to personality inferences (Ballew and Todorov, 2007; Bar et al., 2006; Todorov et al., 2009; Willis and Todorov, 2006). In addition to attractiveness, Willis and Todorov (2006) studied four other judgments: likeability, trustworthiness, competence, and aggressiveness. For all five judgments, judgments made after 100 ms exposure to faces were highly correlated with judgments made in the absence of time constraints. Additional time exposure did not improve these correlations. However, with increased exposure, judgments on different traits become less correlated with each other, suggesting that additional time allowed the subjects to form more differentiated impressions.

Bar et al. (2006) studied judgments of threat and intelligence. They showed that judgments of threat made after 39 ms exposure correlated highly with judgments made after 1700 ms. In contrast, judgments of intelligence made after brief exposures were much less consistent with judgments made after longer exposures. These findings suggest that survival-related traits with respect to immediate threat may have an advantage in visual processing over other traits.

Todorov et al. (2009, Exp. 2) studied judgments of trustworthiness after time exposures ranging from 17 ms to unlimited time. Similar to the findings of Bar et al. (2006), who did not observe consistency in judgments after extremely brief, subliminal exposures to faces (26 ms), Todorov et al. did not observe significant correlations between judgments made after 17 ms exposure and judgments made in the absence of time constraints. However, the correlation was significant for 33 ms exposure and increased as a sigmoid function of time exposure. The correlation increased dramatically with the increase in exposure from 33 to 100 ms and reached a plateau after 167 ms exposure.

At first blush, the findings of Bar et al. (2006) and Todorov et al. (2009) suggest that trait judgments from faces are not made after subliminal exposure, in contrast to judgments of attractiveness (Olson and Marshuetz, 2005). However, two possible reasons for the failure to obtain significant effects for trait judgments after subliminal exposure are that explicit judgment tasks may not be sensitive enough to detect such effects and that the face stimuli used in the studies were not extreme enough. In fact, in the study by Olson and Marshuetz (2005), the mean difference between attractive and unattractive faces was 5 points on a 10-point scale and the distributions were completely non-overlapping.

Todorov et al. (2009, Exp. 3) used faces generated by a computer model of face trustworthiness (Oosterhof and Todorov, 2008) in a subliminal priming paradigm. Extremely trustworthy or untrustworthy versions of faces were presented for 20 ms and immediately masked by the neutral version of the face, which was presented for 50 ms The subject's task was to judge the latter face.

Todorov et al. found that neutral faces were perceived as more trustworthy when they were preceded by trustworthy primes than when preceded by untrustworthy primes. This was the case even though an objective test of awareness failed to find any evidence for the awareness of the primes.

The findings reviewed in this section show that people can make a variety of trait inferences after extremely brief exposures to emotionally neutral faces, suggesting that such inferences are made automatically. There are several outstanding questions in this research. First, it is possible that the minimum time exposure of visual information necessary to make a trait judgment depends on the specific trait dimension. As argued by Bar et al. (2006), survival related trait inferences might have a visual advantage over other inferences. A second and related question is to what extent person inferences made after minimal exposure to faces are about specific traits (e.g. trustworthiness) or global dimensions (e.g. valence) (Todorov et al., 2009; Willis and Todorov 2006). As we outline in the section "Dimensional approaches to face evaluation" (see also Oosterhof and Todorov, 2008; Todorov et al., 2008a), trait inferences from faces are highly correlated with each other and it is possible that after extremely brief exposures, people make global valence related inferences rather than specific trait inferences. The specificity of inferences may also depend on the decision context and the relevance of the trait to this context (see section "Consequences of personality impressions from faces"). Finally, we know little about how social judgments are computed within a single glance of a face. Such rapid processing can rely on holistic information (Bar et al., 2006; Abbas and Duchaine, 2008; Santos and Young, 2008; Todorov et al., 2010) feature information (Cloutier et al., 2005; Cloutier and Macrae, 2007; Martin and Macrae, 2007; Schyns et al., 2008), or a combination of both (see also Rossion and Michel, Chapter 12; Tanaka and Gordon, Chapter 10, this volume).

Neuroimaging and patient studies of personality impressions from faces

Most of the cognitive neuroscience research on social judgments from faces has been on perceptions of attractiveness and trustworthiness (Adolphs et al., 1998; Aharon et al., 2001; O'Doherty et al., 2003; Todorov and Engell, 2008). Several fMRI studies have attempted to identify brain regions that show variable responses to different levels of facial attractiveness. A hypothesis in most of these studies is that perceptions of attractiveness should be related to activation in reward-related brain regions. Consistent with this hypothesis, the medial orbitofrontal cortex (mOFC) activated reliably across these studies, with greater activation as attractiveness increased (Cloutier et al., 2008; Kranz and Ishai, 2006; O'Doherty et al., 2003; Winston et al., 2007). Conversely, the lateral orbitofrontal cortex (lOFC) showed greater activation with decreasing levels of attractiveness (Cloutier et al., 2008; O'Doherty et al., 2003). This dissociation has been interpreted in light of evidence that mOFC activates in response to abstract monetary reward while the lOFC activates to abstract monetary punishment (O'Doherty et al., 2001). According to this interpretation, mOFC activates to attractive faces because they are rewarding, and lOFC activates to unattractive faces because they are not rewarding. However, the distinction between lOFC and mOFC is not a strict dissociation. There is evidence that rewarding gustatory stimuli can activate the lOFC (O'Doherty et al., 2002) and a fairly lateral OFC response to attractive faces has been found in one study (Aharon et al., 2001).

The nucleus accumbens (NAcc) has also been reported to respond more strongly to attractive faces in several studies (Aharon et al., 2001; Cloutier et al., 2008) and, like the mOFC, it has been interpreted with reference to its known role in reward processing (Breiter et al., 1997; Schultz 2000). However, many attractiveness studies have not reported NAcc activation (Kampe et al., 2001; Kranz and Ishai, 2006; O'Doherty et al., 2003; Winston et al., 2007). The reason for this discrepancy is not entirely clear, but one possibility is that the studies that found it only showed faces of the opposite gender of the subject, whereas the studies that did not find it showed both genders to each subject. As proposed by Cloutier et al. (2008), it may be possible that opposite gender-only paradigms put subjects in more of a mate-seeking context in which attractive faces of opposite gender are particularly rewarding.

The anterior cingulate cortex (ACC) shows greater activation to attractive faces than to unattractive faces, according to two studies (Winston et al., 2007; Cloutier et al., 2008). Because the ACC is known to generate and monitor autonomic states (Critchley, 2004; Teves et al., 2004), it is possible that its activity during the presentation of attractive faces reflects autonomic arousal. Support for this hypothesis comes from a study (Winston et al., 2007), in which only males showed increased pupil dilation—an indicator of autonomic arousal—and increased ACC activation to attractive faces.

Most studies on perceptions of face trustworthiness have focused on the amygdala, following a study by Adolphs et al. (1998). Adolphs and his colleagues tested three bilateral amygdala damage patients, other brain damage controls, and normal controls on perceptions of approachability and trustworthiness. Relative to the controls, bilateral amygdala damage patients showed a specific bias to give high ratings of trustworthiness and approachability to faces that were judged by normal controls as untrustworthy and unapproachable. In addition, participants who are given an intranasal dose of oxytocin, which is believed to work in part by dampening amygdala activity (Kirsch et al., 2005), make higher judgments of trustworthiness than controls (Theodoridou et al., 2009). Interestingly, in contrast to bilateral amygdala damage patients, some developmental prosopagnosics (Duchaine, Chapter 42, this volume) are able to make normal trustworthiness judgments (Todorov and Duchaine, 2008). These findings suggest that the neural systems that underlie face evaluation and processing of facial identity are at least partially dissociable.

Several fMRI studies with normal participants have confirmed the amygdala's involvement in perceptions of trustworthiness (Engell et al., 2007; Winston et al., 2002). Winston and his colleagues (2002) showed that the amygdala's response decreased with the trustworthiness of faces, as assessed by the subjects' judgments of the faces after the brain imaging session. Importantly, this was the case independent of the subjects' task in the scanner: judging trustworthiness or age of faces. Engell and his colleagues (2007) replicated the findings that the activation in the amygdala decreased with face trustworthiness, using only an implicit task to rule out the possibility that performance on implicit trials was influenced by prior performance on explicit trials. They also showed that the amygdala's response to face trustworthiness was driven by structural properties of the face that signal trustworthiness across perceivers rather than by idiosyncratic components of trustworthiness judgments (see section "The role of individual differences in face evaluation"). Todorov et al. (2008a) replicated these findings, using faces generated by a computer model of face trustworthiness.

Although all initial fMRI studies reported a linear amygdala response to face trustworthiness, two subsequent studies found a non-linear response (Said et al., 2009a; Todorov et al., 2008b). Using an explicit evaluation task, Said and colleagues showed that the response to extremely trustworthy and untrustworthy faces was larger than the response to faces in the middle of the continuum, although the response was more sensitive to differences at the negative end of the continuum. Using an implicit evaluation task, Todorov and colleagues (2008b) found a similar quadratic response in the left but not the right amygdala.

A similar non-linear response in the amygdala has also been observed for attractiveness (Winston et al., 2007). Most studies on attractiveness have either compared the effect of attractive faces to unattractive faces, or have looked at linear effects of attractiveness along a continuum. As noted in Winston et al. (2007), this may be the reason that so few studies have identified an amygdala response to attractiveness. Drawing from evidence that the amygdala responds both to positive and negative stimuli (Baxter and Murray, 2002), Winston et al. (2007) found quadratic effects of attractiveness in the amygdala, such that it responded strongly to very attractive and very unattractive faces, but weakly to faces in the middle of the continuum. Cunningham and his colleagues (Cunningham et al., 2008) have also observed a non-linear amygdala response to the valence of person names. Moreover, they found that the response was sensitive to the current goals of the subject. For instance, if the subject's task was to attend to the positivity rather than the negativity of the names, the response to positivity was enhanced.

What are we to make of all the consistencies and inconsistencies in the neuroimaging literature on attractiveness and trustworthiness? Although it is true that some regions such as the mOFC and NAcc activate in multiple studies on attractiveness, many other studies do not report them, and in any case the interpretation in studies that do find them is not always clear. Similar issues of interpretation confront research on face trustworthiness. Although the amygdala has been implicated in multiple studies, it is not clear under what conditions the amygdala's response is linear or non-linear, and there is surprisingly little overlap in activated regions other than the amygdala across studies.

Two main conclusions can be drawn from the literature. First, because of the diversity of results, looking for an "attractiveness network" or "trustworthiness network" may not be the best approach. As we argue below (section "Dimensional approaches to face evaluation"), some of the observed findings may be reinterpreted as responding to face valence or other general face qualities rather than to specific trait attributes. Further, there doesn't seem to be a set of brain regions that consistently varies with attractiveness or trustworthiness, at least at statistically significant levels; rather, the brain is engaged in diverse ways that heavily reflect task and motivational context. The challenge for future research would be to specify how context variables affect neural processes of face evaluation. Second, to the extent that some brain regions are more involved than others, neuroimaging does not tell us whether activation in these regions is necessary for social judgments, or merely a downstream consequence of judgments computed in other regions. As has been often noted, case studies of patients with localized brain damage can provide the causal information (Shallice, 1988) that neuroimaging cannot provide (Poldrack, 2006; Sarter et al., 1996).

Dimensional approaches to face evaluation

As mentioned above, trait judgments from faces are highly correlated with each other. For example, it is almost impossible to find social judgments that are uncorrelated with judgments of trustworthiness. Moreover, these correlations are sizeable (e.g. 0.83 with judgments of emotional stability, 0.75 with judgments of attractiveness, −0.76 with judgments of aggressiveness, 0.63 with judgments of intelligence, etc.; see Oosterhof and Todorov 2008). These high correlations suggest that there is a simple dimensional structure that accounts for most of the variance in social judgments. Using principal components analysis (PCA) on judgments of both natural and computer generated faces, Oosterhof and Todorov (2008) have shown that the first two components, best interpreted as valence/trustworthiness and power/dominance, account for most of the variance in judgments. This solution corresponds to other dimensional models of social perception (Fiske et al., 2007; Vigil, 2009; Wiggins, 1979; Wiggins et al., 1989). Trustworthiness judgments were closest to the first component and dominance judgments to the second component. For example, the correlations of trustworthiness judgments with the first and second components, derived from a PCA of 11 other trait judgments excluding trustworthiness and dominance, were 0.92 and −0.10, respectively. In contrast, dominance judgments were highly correlated with the second (0.87) but not with the first component (−0.20). The finding that trustworthiness judgments may serve as a proxy of general valence evaluation suggests that the amygdala may be involved not in assessments of face trustworthiness per se but in assessments of general valence in the service of approach/avoidance responses by the perceiver (Todorov, 2008).

This hypothesis was tested and confirmed by Todorov and Engell (2008). They reanalyzed the fMRI data from Engell et al. (2007) as a function of a large set of trait judgments. In the original study, the subject's ostensible task was to memorize faces and, hence, the instructions did not bias subjects to attend to a specific trait dimension. Todorov and Engell first selected face responsive voxels and then computed the average response in the face responsive regions to each face. Then they analyzed the correlations between the response to faces in face-selective regions and trait judgments of these faces. As shown in Figure 32.1, almost all trait judgments correlated with the

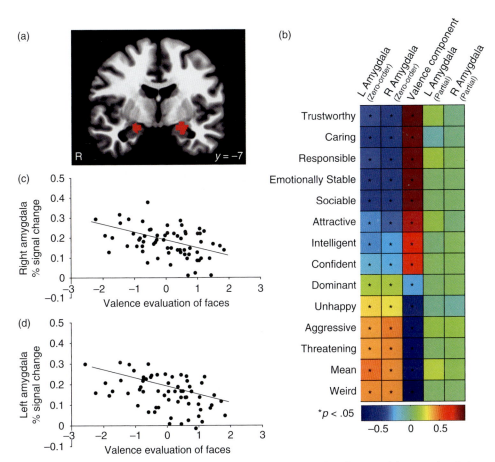

Fig. 32.1 The relation between the amygdala's response to emotionally neutral faces and variations of these faces on trait dimensions. (a) A coronal brain slice showing face responsive voxels in bilateral amygdala. (b) An intensity color plot showing correlations between the response in left and right amygdalae to faces and trait judgments of these faces. The first two columns show zero-order correlations and the fourth and fifth columns show partial correlations controlling for the valence content of the judgments. The third column shows the correlations between trait judgments and a valence component derived from a principal components analysis of the judgments. The traits are ordered according to their correlations with the valence component. Scatter plots of the amygdala's response to faces (c for right and d for left) and their values on the valence component. Each point represents a face. Reproduced from Todorov and Engell, The role of the amygdala in implicit evaluation of emotionally neutral faces, 2008, *Social Cognitive and Affective Neuroscience*, with permission from Oxford University Press.

amygdala response to faces. Positive traits correlated with decreases in the response and negative traits correlated with increases in the response. Moreover, the magnitude of the correlation varied systematically as a function of the valence content of the judgments, as assessed by the shared variance of the judgments with the first component of a PCA of the judgments. The more evaluative the judgment, the more strongly the amygdala was engaged. After controlling for the valence content of the judgments, the correlations between the amygdala response and trait judgments were no longer significant. The same pattern of responses was observed in a number of regions in occipital and inferior temporal cortices, although the magnitude of the correlations was smaller.

Given that judgments of trustworthiness and dominance are good approximations of the general dimensions of face evaluation, Oosterhof and Todorov (2008) built computer models representing how faces change along these dimensions (Figure 32.2). Specifically, they used a data-driven model in which faces are represented as points in a multidimensional space (Blanz and Vetter, 1999 and 2003; O'Toole, Chapter 2, this volume; Singular Inversions 2006; Vetter and Walker, Chapter 20, this volume). This model can generate an unlimited number of faces that are each linear combinations of the model dimensions. Judgments of randomly generated faces can be used to construct a novel dimension that is optimal in representing face variations along a particular social dimension.

Using this approach, Oosterhof and Todorov (2008; see also Todorov et al., 2008b) created dimensions that varied optimally in perceived trustworthiness and dominance. By investigating the range of faces along these dimensions, they showed that these judgments are based on similarity to facial cues that have adaptive significance. As shown in Figure 32.2d, exaggerating faces along the trustworthiness dimension resulted in angry faces on the negative end and in happy faces on the positive end of the dimension. (For convergent evidence from dynamic stimuli, see Oosterhof and Todorov, 2009). This finding suggests that valence evaluation of faces is based on cues initiating approach/avoidance behavior by the perceiver (Fridlund, 1994). Exaggerating faces along the dominance dimension resulted in extremely masculine, mature faces on the dominant end and in extremely feminine, baby-faced faces on the submissive end of the dimension. This finding is consistent with a rich body of evidence about the importance of neotenous and sexually dimorphic features in face perception (Perrett et al., 1998; McArthur and Apatow, 1983; Rhodes 2006; also Penton-Voak and Morrison, Chapter 33; Zebrowitz, Chapter 3, this volume). In general, the findings suggest that inferences along the valence/trustworthiness dimension are about the intentions of the person with respect to potential harm and inferences along the power/dominance dimension are about the capacity of the person to implement these intensions (cf. Fiske et al., 2007).

Dimensional approaches provide a parsimonious, powerful framework for the study of face evaluation. However, they may not be sufficient to account for judgments in specific contexts (Todorov, 2009). That is, while these models focus on identifying the commonalities among various judgments, interesting behavioral effects may be due to variance that is specific to a judgment, and not shared with general components. Further, the strong claim of dimensional models is that specific judgments can be represented within the dimensional framework. In fact, Oosterhof and Todorov (2008) showed that judgments of threat could be represented as a linear combination of untrustworthiness and dominance. However, their model was not particularly good at representing judgments of attractiveness, extraversion, and competence within the two-dimensional framework.

Finally, it is important to provide convergent evidence from other computer models (see Said et al., 2009a). For example, the computer model used by Oosterhof and Todorov (2008) is based on shape information and is not good at representing texture, an important determinant of face perception. Other techniques such as PCA methods (Brahnam, 2005) and reverse correlation

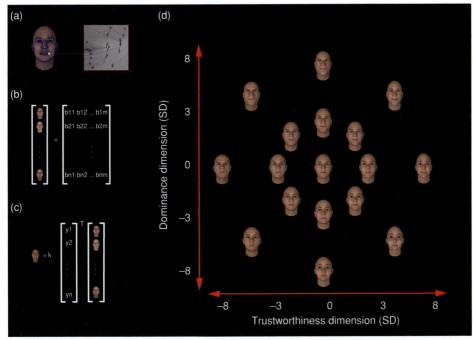

Fig. 32.2 Computer modeling of social judgments of faces. (a) Illustration of how the face model represents faces. Left: a surface mesh with fixed topology superimposed on the average face. Right: an expanded view of a section of the mesh, along with direction vectors specifying the linear changes in the vertex positions for the surface for one of the $m = 50$ shape dimensions. (b) A set of n random faces can be obtained by linear combinations of the m shape components, and represented in an n by m matrix. These dimensions are extracted from a principal component analysis of shape variations of the vertex positions and do not necessarily have inherent psychological meaning. Each row of the matrix contains the set of m weighting coefficients corresponding to a particular face. (c) Each of the n faces is rated by participants on a trait dimension and given an average score yj. Multiplication of the social judgments vector by the set of randomly generated faces yields a dimension that is optimal in changing faces on the trait dimension, which can be controlled with a tunable constant k. The figure shows the generation of one face along the trustworthiness dimension. (d) A two-dimensional model of evaluation of faces. Examples of a face with exaggerated features on the two orthogonal dimensions—trustworthiness plotted on the x-axis and dominance plotted on the y-axis—of face evaluation. The changes in features were implemented in a computer model based on trustworthiness and dominance judgments of n = 300 emotionally neutral faces (Oosterhof and Todorov, 2008). The extent of face exaggeration is presented in SD units. The faces on the diagonals were obtained by averaging the faces on the trustworthiness and dominance dimensions. The diagonal dimension passing from the 2nd to the 4th quadrant was nearly identical to a dimension based on threat judgments of faces. The other diagonal dimension passing from the 1st to the 3rd quadrant was similar to dimensions empirically obtained from judgments of likeability, extraversion, and competence. Reprinted from *Trends in Cognitive Sciences*, Todorov, Said, Engell, and Oosterhof, Understanding evaluation of faces on social dimensions, © 2008 with permission from Elsevier.

methods (Gosselin and Schyns, 2001; Mangini and Biederman, 2004), in which subjects make decisions on noisy images, may be particularly useful for discovering the cues used for face evaluation in a data-driven way. Reverse correlation methods have already been used to discover the cues used for judgments of expressions of emotions, gender, and identity (Schyns et al., 2002; Smith et al., 2005). They can also be used to study social judgments. For example, Dotsch et al. (2008) have used these methods to reveal the prototypical face representations of stigmatized out-groups.

The role of individual differences in face evaluation

As described in the first section, there is a surprising amount of consensus in judgments from faces, although this consensus varies as a function of the judged trait (Oosterhof and Todorov, 2008). The common statistic typically used to report consensus in judgments is Cronbach's alpha—a measure of the consistency of raters. However, as noted by Hönekopp (2006), this statistic describes reliability across samples of judges[3] and it is not clear how to interpret it at the level of individual raters. In fact, given a large sample of raters, Cronbach's alpha can be very high even when the inter-rater agreement is very low. Typically, the inter-rater agreement is not very high. For example, this agreement ranged from 0.09 to 0.47 (correlation coefficients) across 15 different trait judgments (Oosterhof and Todorov, 2008).[4] That is, the average shared variance between pairs of raters ranged from 0.8% to 22.1%. Thus, despite consensus in trait judgments, a large proportion of variance in these judgments is unaccounted for. Recent empirical work suggests that some of this variance may be attributable to individual differences (Engell et al., 2007; Hönekopp 2006). For example, Hönekopp (2006) estimated that half of the meaningful variance in attractiveness judgments is due to consensus contributions and half to idiosyncratic contributions.

We know very little about the sources of idiosyncratic variation in face evaluation. Whereas computer models of social judgments (Brahnam, 2005; Oosterhof and Todorov, 2008), which rely on averaging of judgments across judges, may be particularly appropriate for discovering consensual cues and their possible evolutionary and cultural origin, they may not be the best approach to capture cues to individual variations in judgments. Because the latter cues would differ across individuals, they would not be revealed in an average judgment. A key area for future research is the investigation of the determinants of individual variation in social judgments from faces. Likely candidates for these determinants are self-resemblance, similarity to faces of people with known personality dispositions, and individual differences in perceiver personality.[5]

Several studies have shown that faces that have been subtly manipulated to resemble the self (by morphing faces with the self face) are evaluated and treated more positively than control faces

---

[3] One way to understand this statistic is in terms of the agreement between the face ratings of two different groups of subjects. For example, an alpha of 0.90 indicates that this is the expected correlation between the mean observed face ratings (averaged across subjects) and the mean ratings of a new group of subjects with the same sample size.

[4] It should be noted that the subjects in Oosterhof and Todorov (2008) rated the faces three times and the agreement was computed from their mean ratings for each face. This procedure typically increases inter-rater agreement and, correspondingly, reliability. The inter-rater agreement from the first face ratings of the subjects was more modest, ranging from 0.04 to 0.35 across the 15 traits.

[5] For an interesting treatment of individual differences in face evaluation from the perspective of a Gibsonian approach in terms of social affordances and perceivers' attunements, see Zebrowitz (Chapter 3, this volume).

(Bailenson et al., 2006, 2008; DeBruine, 2002, 2005; Krupp et al., 2008). For example, subjects perceive self-resembling faces as more trustworthy (DeBruine, 2005), show more trusting behaviors in economic games with self-resembling partners (DeBruine, 2002; Krupp et al., 2008), and are more likely to vote for political candidates who resemble them (Bailenson et al., 2006, 2008).

The second source of idiosyncratic face evaluation may derive from learning about other people. While impressions of unfamiliar people are certainly influenced by their facial appearance (see sections "Consequences of personality impressions from faces" and "The automaticity of personality impressions from faces"), this does not mean these impressions are not changeable in light of new information (Todorov and Olson, 2008). In fact, such impressions can be rapidly changed based on minimal information (Bliss-Moreau et al., 2008; Johnson et al., 1985; Todorov et al., 2007; Todorov and Uleman, 2002, 2003, 2004). These processes are probably adaptive: people should be able to rapidly learn about other people and overwrite initial impressions. In addition, there is evidence that personality information can affect the evaluation of physical appearance (Gross and Croften, 1977; Hassin and Trope, 2000; Kniffin and Wilson, 2004; Paunonen, 2006). For instance, learning that someone is kindhearted or mean influences judgments of physical attractiveness (Hassin and Trope, 2000).

Given the importance of learning and consistent with the familiar face overgeneralization hypothesis (Zebrowitz, Chapter 3, this volume; Zebrowitz and Collins, 1997), an interesting possibility is that knowledge of familiar others can generalize to novel faces that resemble the faces of these others. Consistent with this possibility, Andersen and colleagues have demonstrated that participants' impressions of familiar others are affected by the similarity of those others to participants' own significant others (Andersen and Baum, 1994; Andersen and Cole, 1990). However, they have not yet investigated the role of physical similarity in this process. Indeed, there are very few experimental studies showing that experience with one set of faces leads to changes in judgments of another set of faces (Hill et al., 1990; Lewicki, 1985; Jones et al., 2007). In one such study, Hill et al. (1990) created an association between the length of faces and their fairness and then showed that this association influenced judgments of novel faces. In a more recent study, Jones et al. (2007) showed subjects composite faces whose constituent faces had been previously associated with either neutral or aversive sounds. They found that subjects preferred composites of faces previously paired with neutral sounds over composites of faces previously paired with aversive sounds. Together, these studies suggest that experience with familiar others may influence judgments about novel faces that resemble these familiar others.

Finally, perceiver goals, insofar as they persist through time, may also contribute to idiosyncratic variance in the evaluation of faces. For instance, the desire for certain personality characteristics (e.g. assertiveness) in a partner has been found to influence judgments of facial attractiveness. Specifically, Little et al. (2006) found that composites made from faces that were judged as attractive by individuals who value certain personality traits are seen as expressing those traits to a greater extent than composites from people who do not value those traits. Although trait judgments tend to be highly correlated with each other (see section "Dimensional approaches to face evaluation"), this study suggests that the relationship between specific judgments and overall evaluation may differ in a meaningful way across perceivers (see also Little and Perrett, 2002).

Traditionally, the focus of face evaluation research has been on the cues in the face that "signal" specific evaluations across perceivers. However, there is a large individual variation in these evaluations and, as we argued, this variation can originate in specific individual experiences with faces and self-resemblance. Future research needs to use statistical models (e.g. Hönekopp, 2006) to partition the variance in judgments of faces to variance due to consensus or properties of the face and variance due to the judge or idiosyncratic variance and then experimentally test what variables differentially affect these two sources of variance.

Summary and conclusions

People routinely make personality inferences from facial appearance, even though these inferences are not necessarily accurate. In the first section, we reviewed evidence for the accuracy of these inferences. Although there have been studies finding positive relationships between judgments from faces and measures of personality (Berry, 1991; Berry and Brownlow, 1989; Penton-Voak et al., 2006), there have been other studies failing to find such relationships (Bachmann and Nurmoja, 2006; Pound et al., 2007; Zebrowitz et al., 1996) and some finding negative relationships (Collins and Zebrowitz, 1995; Zebrowitz et al., 1998a,b). The most important methodological challenge for studies on accuracy is ascertaining the representativeness of face stimuli. This representativeness is a precondition for estimating the true relationship between personality inferences from faces and measures of personality. The most important conceptual challenge for studies on accuracy is positing plausible biological and social interaction mechanisms that can lead to positive or negative relationships between face inferences and measures of personality.

Although personality impressions from faces are not necessarily accurate, they affect important social outcomes ranging from sentencing decisions to electoral success (Blair et al., 2004; Eberhardt et al., 2006; Olivola and Todorov, 2010). In the second section ("Consequences of personality impressions from faces"), we reviewed evidence for the impact of these impressions. Interestingly, the degree to which personality inferences predict social outcomes depends on whether these inferences match the specific context of decision. For example, voters believe that competence is the most important attribute for a politician and inferences of competence from facial appearance, but not likeability, predict electoral success (Olivola and Todorov, 2010; Todorov et al., 2005). An important question for future research is how face inferences are integrated with other person information in decisions.

In the third section ("The automaticity of personality impressions from faces"), we reviewed studies showing that personality inferences are formed after extremely brief exposures to faces, suggesting that these inferences are automatic. For example, such inferences can be formed after as little as 40 ms exposure to faces (Bar et al., 2006; Todorov et al., 2009). Important questions for future research include whether some inferences have advantage in visual processing over other inferences and whether inferences made after rapid exposure are global, evaluative inferences linked to approach/avoidance responses rather than specific trait inferences.

In the fourth section ("Neuroimaging and patient studies of personality impressions from faces"), we reviewed cognitive neuroscience studies probing the neural basis of personality impressions from faces. Evidence from these studies suggests that such inferences engage brain regions implicated in reward-related and affective processing. However, although some regions— medial OFC in studies on attractiveness and amygdala in studies on trustworthiness—are consistently activated in fMRI studies, there is little overlap in other activated regions. The main challenge for future studies is to specify how context variables—task and motivational context—affect the processes of face evaluation and whether different processes engage different functional brain networks.

Although people make multiple trait inferences from faces, these inferences are highly intercorrelated. In the fifth section ("Dimensional approaches to face evaluation"), we reviewed recent dimensional approaches that posit that specific trait inferences can be represented within a two-dimensional space defined by valence/trustworthiness and power/dominance evaluation (Todorov et al., 2008b). Further, we reviewed evidence from data-driven methods that inferences along these dimensions are based on similarity to expressions signaling approach/avoidance behaviors and features signaling physical strength, respectively. Convergent evidence from other data-driven methods is needed to confirm these hypotheses. Finally, although dimensional models provide a parsimonious framework for the study of face evaluation, they may not be sufficient to account for face evaluation in specific contexts (see the second section).

The approaches reviewed in the fifth section are particularly useful for modeling consensus contributions to face evaluation or the facial properties that are uniformly perceived across perceivers to signal a specific quality. In the final section ("The role of individual differences in face evaluation"), we reviewed an ignored aspect of face evaluation: the idiosyncratic contributions of the perceivers to face evaluation. Findings that self-resemblance, learning, and personality differences affect the evaluation of faces suggest that these may be some of the determinants of idiosyncratic evaluation of faces. The challenge for future studies is to experimentally demonstrate these links.

The human face is a source of perennial fascination as a window to personality. Many people still believe that faces provide accurate information about personality and that important decisions can be based on this information (Hassin and Trope, 2000), although individual judgments are weakly correlated at best with personality measures. These impressions are formed rapidly, are consistent across observers, and are predictive of important social outcomes. The consistency in impressions is based on cues with adaptive significance such as similarity to emotional expressions (Montepare and Dobish 2003; Said et al., 2009b), neotenous features (Zebrowitz et al., 2003) and kin resemblance (DeBruine 2002, 2005).

Acknowledgments

We thank Jenny Porter for her help with the preparation of the chapter and Gill Rhodes for her insightful comments. Work on this chapter was supported by National Science Foundation grant NSF 0823749 and SAGE Young Scholar Award to AT.

References

Abbas, Z-A. and Duchaine, B. (2008). The role of holistic processing in judgments of facial attractiveness. *Perception*, **37**, 1187–1196.

Adolphs, R. (2003). Cognitive neuroscience of human social behavior. *Nature Reviews Neuroscience*, **4**, 165–178.

Adolphs, R., Tranel, D., and Damasio, A.R. (1998). The human amygdala in social judgment. *Nature*, **393**, 470–474.

Aharon, I., Etcoff, N., Ariely, D., Chabris, C.F., O'Connor, E., and Breiter, H.C. (2001). Beautiful faces have variable reward value: fMRI and behavioral evidence. *Neuron*, **32**, 537–551.

Andersen, S.M. and Baum, A. (1994). Transference in interpersonal relations: Inferences and affect based on significant-other representations. *Journal of Personality*, **62**, 459–497.

Andersen, S.M. and Cole, S.W. (1990). Do I know you?: The role of significant others in general social perception. *Journal of Personality and Social Psychology*, **59**, 384–399.

Antonakis, J. and Dalgas, O. (2009). Predicting elections: Child's play! *Science*, **323**, 1183.

Bachmann, T. and Nurmoja, M. (2006). Are there affordances of suggestibility in facial appearance? *Journal of Nonverbal Behavior*, **30**, 87–92.

Bailenson, J.N., Garland, P., Iyengar, S., and Yee N. (2006). Transformed facial similarity as a political cue: A preliminary investigation. *Political Psychology*, **27**, 373–385.

Bailenson, J.N., Iyengar, S., Yee, N., and Collins, N.A. (2008). Facial similarity between voters and candidates causes influence. *Public Opinion Quarterly*, **72**, 935–961.

Ballew, C.C. and Todorov, A. (2007). Predicting political elections from rapid and unreflective face judgments. *Proceedings of the National Academy of Sciences of the USA*, **104**, 17948–17953.

Bar, M., Neta, M., and Linz, H. (2006). Very first impressions. *Emotion*, **6**, 269–278.

Baxter, M.G. and Murray, E.A. (2002). The amygdala and reward. *Nature Reviews Neuroscience*, **3**, 563–573.

Berry, D.S. (1991). Accuracy in social-perception—contributions of facial and vocal Information. *Journal of Personality and Social Psychology*, **61**, 298–307.

Berry, D.S. and Brownlow, S. (1989). Were the physiognomists right— personality-correlates of facial babyishness. *Personlaity and Social Psycholology Bulletin*, **15**, 266–279.

Blair, I.V., Judd, C.M., and Chapleau, K.M. (2004). The influence of Afrocentric facial features in criminal sentencing. *Psychological Science*, **15**, 674–679.

Blanz, V. and Vetter, T. (1999). A morphable model for the synthesis of 3D faces. In *Proceedings of the 26th annual conference on Computer graphics and interactive techniques*, 187–194.

Blanz, V. and Vetter, T. (2003). Face recognition based on fitting a 3D morphable model. *IEEE Transactions on pattern analysis and machine intelligence*, **25**, 1063–1074.

Bliss-Moreau, E., Barrett, L.F., and Wright, C.I. (2008). Individual differences in learning the affective value of others under minimal conditions. *Emotion*, **8**, 479–493.

Bond, C.F., Berry, D.S., and Omar, A. (1994). The kernel of truth in judgments of deceptiveness. *Basic and Applied Social Psychology*, **15**, 523–534.

Boutet, I., Collin, C., and Faubert, J. (2003). Configural face encoding and spatial frequency information. *Perception and Psychophysics*, **65**, 1078–1093.

Brahnam, S. (2005). A computational model of the trait impressions of the face for agent perception and face synthesis. *Artificial Intelligence and Simulation of Behaviour Journal*, **1**, 481–508.

Breiter, H.C., Gollub, R.L., and Weisskoff, R.M. *et al.*(1997). Acute effects of cocaine on human brain activity and emotion. *Neuron*, **19**, 591–611.

Brownlow, S. (1992). Seeing is believing: Facial appearance, credibility, and attitude change. *Journal of Nonverbal Behavior*, **16**, 101–115.

Brownlow, S. and Zebrowitz, L.A. (1990). Facial appearance, gender, and credibility in television commercials. *Journal of Nonverbal Behavior*, **14**, 51–60.

Canli, T., Sivers, H., Whitfield, S.L., Gotlib, I.H., and Gabrieli, J.D.E. (2001). Amygdala response to happy faces as a function of extraversion. *Science*, **296**, 2191.

Carney, D.R., Colvin, C.R., and Hall, J.A. (2007). A thin slice perspective on the accuracy of first impressions. *Journal of Research in Personality*, **41**, 1054–1072.

Carré, J.M. and McCormick, C.M. (2008). In your face: Facial metrics predict aggressive behaviour in the laboratory and in varsity and professional hockey players. *Proceedings of the Royal Society of London: Biological Sciences*, **275**, 2651–2656.

Carré, J.M., McCormick, C.M., and Mondloch, C.J. (2009). Face structure is a reliable cue of aggressive behavior. *Psychological Science*, **20**, 1994–1998.

Chan, S.W., Norbury, R., Goodwin, G.R., and Harmer, C.J. (2009). Risk for depression and neural responses to fearful facial expressions of emotion. *The British Journal of Psychiatry*, **194**, 139–145.

Cloutier, J., Heatherton, T.F., Whalen, P.J., and Kelley, W.M. (2008). Are attractive people.rewarding? Sex differences in the neural substrates of facial attractiveness. *Journal of Cognitive Neuroscience*, **20**, 941–951.

Cloutier, J. and Macrae, C.N. (2007). Who or what are you?: Facial orientation and person construal. *European Journal of Social Psychology*, **37**, 1298–1309.

Cloutier, J., Mason, M.F., and Macrae, C.N. (2005). The perceptual determinants of person construal: reopening the social-cognitive toolbox. *Journal of Personality and Social Psychology*, **88**, 885–894.

Collins, M.A. and Zebrowitz, L.A. (1995). The contributions of appearance to occupational outcomes in civilian and military settings. *Journal of Applied Social Psychology*, **25**, 129–163.

Critchley, H.D. (2004). The human cortex responds to an interoceptive challenge. *Proceedings of the National Academy of Sciences of the United States of America*, **101**, 6333–6334.

Cunningham, W.A., Van Bavel, J.J., and Johnsen, I.R. (2008). Affective flexibility: Evaluative processing goals shape amygdala activity. *Psychological Science*, **19**, 152–160.

Dawes, R.M. (1970). An inequality concerning correlation of composites vs. composites of correlations. *Methodological Note*, **1**, 1–5. Oregon Research Institute.

DeBruine, L.M. (2002). Facial resemblance enhances trust. *Proceedings of the Royal Society B.*, **269**, 1307–1312.

Dipboye, R., Arvey, R., and Terpstra, D. (1977). Sex and physical attractiveness of raters and applicants as determinants of resume evaluations. *Journal of Applied Psychology*, **4**, 288–294.

Dotsch, R., Wigboldus, D.H.J., Langner, O., and van Knippenberg, A. (2008). Ethnic out-group faces are biased in the prejudiced mind. *Psychological Science*, **19**, 978–980.

Eagly, A.H., Ashmore, R.D., Makhijani, M.G., and Longo, L.C. (1991). What is beautiful is good, but…: A meta-analytic review of research on the physical attractiveness stereotype. *Psychological Bulletin*, **110**, 109–128.

Eberhardt, J.L., Davies, P.G., Purdie-Vaughns, V.J., and Johnson, S.L. (2006). Looking deathworthy: Perceived stereotypicality of Black defendants predicts capital-sentencing outcomes. *Psychological Science*, **17**, 383–386.

Engell, A.D., Haxby, J.V., and Todorov, A. (2007). Implicit trustworthiness decisions: Automatic coding of face properties in human amygdala. *Journal of Cognitive Neuroscience*, **19**, 1508–1519.

Fiske, S.T., Cuddy, A.J.C., and Glick, P. (2007). Universal dimensions of social cognition: warmth and competence. *Trends in Cognitive Sciences*, **11**, 77–83.

Fridlund, A.J. (1994). *Human facial expression: An evolutionary view*. San Diego, CA: Academic Press.

Frieze, I.H., Olson, J.E., and Russell, J. (1991). Attractiveness and income for men and women in management. *Journal of Applied Social Psychology*, **21**, 1039–1057.

Gaskill, P.C., Fenton, N., and Porter, J.P. (1927). Judging the intelligence of boys from their photographs. *Journal of Applied Psychology*, **11**, 394–403.

Gosselin, F. and Schyns, P.G. (2001). Bubbles: A technique to reveal the use of information in recognition. *Vision Research*, **41**, 2261–2271.

Gross, A.E. and Crofton, C. (1977). What is good is beautiful. *Sociometry*, **40**, 85–90.

Hall, C.C., Goren, A., Chaiken, S., and Todorov, A. (2009). Shallow cues with deep effects: Trait judgments from faces and voting decisions. In E Borgida, JL Sullivan and CM Federico (eds.) *The Political Psychology of Democratic Citizenship*, pp. 73–99. New York: Oxford University Press.

Hall, J.A., Andrzejewski, S.A., Murphy, N.A., Mast, M.S., and Feinstein, B.A. (2008). Accuracy of judging others' traits and states: Comparing mean levels across tests. *Journal of Research in Personality*, **42**, 1476–1489.

Hamermesh, D. and Biddle, J. (1994). Beauty and the labor market. *The American Economic Review*, **84**, 1174–1194.

Hassin, R. and Trope, Y. (2000). Facing faces: Studies on the cognitive aspects of physiognomy. *Journal of Personality and Social Psychology*, **78**, 837–852.

Hill, T., Lewicki, P., Czyzewska, M., and Schuller, G. (1990). The role of learned inferential encoding rules in the perception of faces: Effects of nonconscious self-perpetuation of a bias. *Journal of Experimental Social Psychology*, **26**, 350–371.

Hollingworth, H.L. (1922). *Judging human character*. New York: D. Appleton and Company.

Hönekopp, J. (2006). Once more: Is beauty in the eye of the beholder? Relative contributions of private and shared taste to judgments of facial attractiveness. *Journal of Experimental Psychology: Human Perception and Performance*, **32**, 199–209.

Hönekopp, J., Becker, B.J., and Oswald, F.L. (2006). The meaning and suitability of various effect sizes for structured rater x ratee designs. *Psychological Methods*, **11**, 72–86.

Johnson, M.K., Kim, J.K., and Risse, G. (1985). Do alcoholic Korsakoff's Syndrome patients acquire affective reactions? *Journal of Experimental Psychology: Learning, Memory, and Cognition*, **11**, 22–36.

Jones, B.C., DeBruine, L.M., Little, A.C., and Feinberg, D.R. (2007). The valence of experiences with faces influences generalized preferences. *Journal of Evolutionary Psychology*, **5**, 119–129.

Kampe, K.K.W., Frith, C.D., Dolan, R.J., and Frith, U. (2001). Reward value of attractiveness and gaze—Making eye contact enhances the appeal of a pleasing face, irrespective of gender. *Nature*, **413**, 589–589.

Keating, C.F. and Bai, D.L. (1986). Children's attributions of social dominance from facial cues. *Child Development*, **57**, 1269–1276.

Keating, C.F., Mazur, A., and Segall, M.H. (1981). A cross-cultural exploration of physiognomic traits of dominance and happiness. *Ethology and Sociobiology*, **2**, 41–48.

Kirsch, P., Esslinger, C., and Chen, Q. *et al.*(2005). Oxytocin modulates neural circuitry for social cognition and fear in humans. *Journal of Neuroscience*, **25**, 11489–11493.

Kniffin, K.M. and Wilson, D.S. (2004). The effect of nonphysical traits on the perception of physical attractiveness. Three naturalistic studies. *Evolution and Human Behavior*, **25**, 88–101.

Kranz, F. and Ishai, A. (2006). Face perception is modulated by sexual preference. *Current Biology*, **16**, 63–68.

Krupp, D.B., DeBruine, L.M., and Barclay, P. (2008). A cue of kinship promotes cooperation for the public good. *Evolution and Human Behavior*, **29**, 49–55.

Laird, D.A. (1927). *The psychology of selecting men* (2nd edition). New York: McGraw-Hill Book Company.

Langlois, J.H., Kalakanis, L., Rubenstein, A.J., Larson, A., Hallam, M., and Smoot, M. (2000). Maxims or myths of beauty? A meta-analytic and theoretical review. *Psychological Bulletin*, **126**, 390–423.

Lewicki, P. (1985). Nonconscious biasing effects of single instances on subsequent judgments. *Journal of Personality and Social Psychology*, **48**, 563–574.

Little, A.C. and Perrett, D.I. (2002). Putting beauty back in the eye of the beholder: evolution and individual differences in face preference. *The Psychologist*, **15**, 28–32.

Little, A.C., Burt, D., Penton-Voak, I.S., and Perrett, D.I. (2001). Self-perceived attractiveness influences human female preferences for sexual dimorphism and symmetry in male faces. *Proceedings of the Royal Society of London B*, **268**, 39–44.

Little, A.C., Burt, D.M., and Perrett, D.I. (2006). What is good is beautiful: face preference reflects desired personality. *Personality and Individual Differences*, **41**, 1107–1118.

Little, A.C., Burriss, R.P., Jones, B.C., and Roberts, S.C. (2007). Facial appearance affects voting decisions. *Evolution and Human Behavior*, **28**, 18–27.

Locher, P., Unger, R., Sociedade, P., and Wahl, J. (1993). At first glance: Accessibility of the physical attractiveness stereotype. *Sex Roles*, **28**, 729–743.

Macrae, C.N., Quinn, K.A., Mason, M.F., and Quadflieg, S. (2005). Understanding others: The face and person construal. *Journal of Personality and Social Psychology*, **89**, 686–695.

Malatesta, C.Z., Fiore, M.J., and Messina, J.J. (1987). Affect, personality, and facial expressive characteristics of older people. *Psychology and Aging*, **2**, 64–69.

Mangini, M.C. and Biederman, I. (2004). Making the ineffable explicit: Estimating the information employed for face classification. *Cognitive Science*, **28**, 209–226.

Martin, D. and Macrae, C.N. (2007). A face with a cue: Exploring the inevitability of person categorization. *European Journal of Social Psychology*, **37**, 806–816.

Mazur, A., Mazur, J., and Keating, C. (1984). Military rank attainment of a West Point class: Effects of cadets' physical features. *American Journal of Sociology*, **90**, 125–150.

Mazur, A. and Mueller, U. (1996). Channel modeling: From West Point cadet to general. *Public Administration Review*, **56**, 191–198.

McArthur, L.Z. and Apatow, K. (1983/4). Impressions of babyfaced adults. *Social Cognition*, **2**, 315–342.

Montepare, J.M. and Dobish, H. (2003). The contribution of emotion perceptions and their overgeneralizations to trait impressions. *Journal of Nonverbal Behavior*, **27**, 237–254.

Montepare, J.M. and Zebrowitz, L.A. (1998). Person perception comes of age: The salience and significance of age in social judgments. *Advances in Experimental Social Psychology*, **30**, 93–161.

Mueller, U. and Mazur, A. (1996). Facial dominance of West Point cadets as a predictor of later military rank. *Social Forces*, **74**, 823–850.

Nisbett, R.E. and Wilson, T.D. (1977). The halo effect: Evidence for unconscious alteration of judgments. *Journal of Personality and Social Psychology*, **35**, 250–256.

O'Doherty, J.P., Deichmann, R., Critchley, H.D., and Dolan, R.J. (2002). Neural responses during anticipation of a primary taste reward. *Neuron*, **33**, 815–826.

O'Doherty, J., Kringelbach, M.L., Rolls, E.T., Hornak, J., and Andrews, C. (2001). Abstract reward and punishment representations in the human orbitofrontal cortex. *Nature Neuroscience*, **4**, 95–102.

O'Doherty, J., Winston, J., Critchley, H., Perrett, D., Burt, D.M., and Dolan, R.J. (2003). Beauty in a smile: The role of medial orbitofrontal cortex in facial attractiveness. *Neuropsychologia*, **41**, 147–155.

Olivola, C.Y. and Todorov, A. (2010). Elected in 100 milliseconds: Appearance-based trait inferences and voting. *Journal of Nonverbal Behavior*, **34**, 83–110.

Olson, I.R. and Marshuetz, C. (2005). Facial attractiveness is appraised in a glance. *Emotion*, **5**, 498–502.

Oosterhof, N.N. and Todorov, A. (2008). The functional basis of face evaluation. *Proceedings of the National Academy of Sciences of the USA*, **105**, 11087–11092.

Oosterhof, N.N. and Todorov, A. (2009). Shared perceptual basis of emotional expressions and trustworthiness impressions from faces. *Emotion*, **9**, 128–133.

Pashos, A. and Niemitz, C. (2003). Results of an explorative empirical study on human mating in Germany: Handsome men, not high-status men, succeed in courtship. *Anthropologischer Anzeiger*, **61**, 331–341.

Paunonen, S.V. (2006). You are honest and therefore I like you and find you attractive. *Journal of Research in Personality*, **40**, 237–249.

Penton-Voak, I.S., Pound, N., Little, A.C., and Perrett, D.I. (2006). Personality judgments from natural and composite facial images: More evidence for a "kernel of truth" in social perception. *Social Cognition*, **24**, 607–640.

Perrett, D.I., Lee, K.J., and Penton-Voak, I. *et al.* (1998). Effects of sexual dimorphism on facial attractiveness. *Nature*, **394**, 884–887.

Pintner, R. (1918). Intelligence as estimated from photographs. *Psychological Review*, **25**, 286–296.

Poldrack, R.A. (2006). Can cognitive processes be inferred from neuroimaging data? *Trends in Cognitive Sciences*, **10**, 59–63.

Pound, N., Penton-Voak, I.S., and Brown, W.M. (2007). Facial symmetry is positively associated with self-reported extraversion. *Personality and Individual Differences*, **43**, 1572–1582.

Pound, N., Penton-Voak, I.S., and Surridge, A.K. (2008). Testosterone responses to competition in men are related to facial masculinity. *Proceedings of the Royal Society of London: Biological Sciences*, **276**, 153–159.

Poutvaara, P., Jordahl, H., and Berggren, N. (2009). Faces of politicians: Babyfacedness predicts inferred competence but not electoral success. *Journal of Experimental Social Psychology*, **45**, 1132–1135.

Quinn, K.A. and Macrae, C.N. (2005). Categorizing others: The dynamics of person construal. *Journal of Personality and Social Psychology*, **88**, 467–479.

Rhodes, G. (2006). The evolutionary psychology of facial beauty. *Annual Review of Psychology*, **57**, 199–226.

Rhodes, G., Simmons, L.W., and Peters, M. (2005). Attractiveness and sexual behavior: Does attractiveness enhance mating success? *Evolution and Human Behavior*, **26**, 186–201.

Rule, N.O. and Ambady, N. (2008). Brief exposures: Male sexual orientation is accurately perceived at 50 ms. *Journal of Experimental Social Psychology*, **44**, 1100–1105.

Said, C.P., Baron, S., and Todorov, A. (2009a). Nonlinear amygdala response to face trustworthiness: Contributions of high and low spatial frequency information. *Journal of Cognitive Neuroscience*, **21(3)**, 519–528.

Said, C.P., Sebe, N., and Todorov, A. (2009b). Structural resemblance to emotional expressions predicts evaluation of emotionally neutral faces. *Emotion*, **9**, 260–264.

Santos, I.M. and Young, A.W. (2008). Effects of inversion and negation on social inferences from faces. *Perception*, **37**, 1061–1078.

Sarter, M., Bernston, G.G., and Cacioppo, J.T. (1996). Brain imaging and cognitive neuroscience: Toward strong inference in attributing function to structure. *American Psychologist*, **51**, 13–21.

Schultz, W. (2000). Multiple reward signals in the brain. *Nature Reviews Neuroscience*, **1**, 199–207.

Schyns, P.G., Bonnar, L., and Gosselin, F. (2002). Show me the features! Understanding recognition from the use of visual information. *Psychological Science*, **13**, 402–409.

Schyns, P.G., Gosselin, F., and Smith, M.L. (2008). Information processing algorithms in the brain. *Trends in Cognitive Sciences*, **13**, 20–26.

Secord, P.F. (1958). Facial features and inference processes in interpersonal perception. In R. Tagiuri and L. Petrullo (eds.) Person perception and interpersonal behavior, pp. 300–315. Stanford, CA: Stanford University Press.

Sell, A., Cosmides, L., Tooby, J., Sznycer, D., von Rueden, C., and Gurven, M. (2009). Human adaptations for the visual assessment of strength and fighting ability from the body and face. *Proceedings of the Royal Society of London: Biological Sciences*, **276**, 575–584.

Shallice, T. (1988). *From neuropsychology to mental structure.* Cambridge: Cambridge University Press.

Shepherd, J. (1989). The face and social attribution. In A. W. Young and H. D. Ellis (eds.), *Handbook of Research on Face Processing*, pp. 289–320. Elsevier Science Publishers.

Singular Inversions. (2006). *FaceGen 3.1 Full SDK Documentation.* http://facegen.com

Smith, M., Cottrell, G., Gosselin, F., and Schyns, P.G. (2005). Transmitting and decoding facial expressions of emotions. *Psychological Science*, **16**, 184–189.

Snyder, M., Tanke, E.D., and Berscheid, E. (1977). Social perception and interpersonal behavior: On the self-fulfilling nature of social stereotypes. *Journal of Personality and Social Psychology*, **35**, 656–666.

Teves, D., Videen, T.O., Cryer, P.E., and Powers, W.J. (2004). Activation of human medial prefrontal cortex during autonomic responses to hypoglycemia. *Proceedings of the National Academy of Sciences of the United States of America*, **101**, 6217–6221.

Theodoridou, A., Rowe, A.C., Penton-Voak, I.S., and Rogers, P.J. (2009). Oxytocin and social perception: Oxytocin increases perceived facial trustworthiness and attractiveness. *Hormones and Behavior*, **56**, 128–132.

Thornhill, R. and Gangestad, S.W. (1993). Human facial beauty: Averageness, symmetry and parasitic resistance. *Human Nature*, **4**, 237–269.

Todorov, A. (2008). Evaluating faces on trustworthiness: An extension of systems for recognition of emotions signaling approach/avoidance behaviors. In A. Kingstone and M. Miller (eds.) The Year in Cognitive Neuroscience 2008, Annals of the New York Academy of Sciences, **1124**, 208–224.

Todorov, A. (2009). On the richness and limitations of dimensional models of social perception. *Behavioral and Brain Sciences*, **32**, 402–403.

Todorov, A. and Duchaine, B. (2008). Reading trustworthiness in faces without recognizing faces. *Cognitive Neuropsychology*, **25**, 395–410.

Todorov, A. and Engell, A. (2008). The role of the amygdala in implicit evaluation of emotionally neutral faces. *Social, Cognitive, and Affective Neuroscience*, **3**, 303–312.

Todorov, A., Loehr, V., and Oosterhof, N.N. (2010). The obligatory nature of holistic processing of faces in social judgments. *Perception*, **39**, 514–532.

Todorov, A. and Olson, I. (2008). Robust learning of affective trait associations with faces when the hippocampus is damaged, but not when the amygdala and temporal pole are damaged. *Social, Cognitive, and Affective Neuroscience*, **3**, 195–203.

Todorov, A. and Uleman, J.S. (2002). Spontaneous trait inferences are bound to actor's faces: Evidence from a false recognition paradigm. *Journal of Personality and Social Psychology*, **83**, 1051–1065.

Todorov, A. and Uleman, J.S. (2003). The efficiency of binding spontaneous trait inferences to actor's faces. *Journal of Experimental Social Psychology*, **39**, 549–562.

Todorov, A. and Uleman, J.S. (2004). The person reference process in spontaneous trait inferences. *Journal of Personality and Social Psychology*, **87**, 482–493.

Todorov, A., Mandisodza, A.N., Goren A., and Hall C.C. (2005). Inferences of competence from faces predict election outcomes. *Science*, **308**, 1623–1626.

Todorov, A., Gobbini, M.I., Evans, K.K., and Haxby, J.V. (2007). Spontaneous retrieval of affective person knowledge in face perception. *Neuropsychologia*, **45**, 163–173.

Todorov, A., Baron, S., and Oosterhof, N.N. (2008a). Evaluating face trustworthiness: A model based approach. *Social, Cognitive, and Affective Neuroscience*, **3**, 119–127.

Todorov, A., Said, C.P., Engell, A.D., and Oosterhof, N.N. (2008b). Understanding evaluation of faces on social dimensions. *Trends in Cognitive Sciences*, **12**, 455–460.

Todorov, A., Pakrashi, M., and Oosterhof, N.N. (2009). Evaluating faces on trustworthiness after minimal time exposure. *Social Cognition*, **27**, 813–833.

Verdonck, A., Gaethofs, M., Carels, C., and de Zegner, F. (1999). Effect of low-dose testosterone treatment on craniofacial growth in boys with delayed puberty. *European Journal of Orthodontics*, **21**, 137–143.

Vigil, J.M. (2009). A sociorelational framework of sex differences in the expression of emotion. *Behavioral and Brain Sciences*, **32**, 1–54.

Wiggins, J.S. (1979). A psychological taxonomy of trait descriptive terms: The interpersonal domain. *Journal of Personality and Social Psychology*, **37**, 395–412.

Wiggins, J.S., Philips, N., and Trapnell, P. (1989). Circular reasoning about interpersonal behavior: Evidence concerning some untested assumptions underlying diagnostic classification. *Journal of Personality and Social Psychology*, **56**, 296–305.

Willis, J. and Todorov, A. (2006). First impressions: Making up your mind after 100 ms exposure to a face. *Psychological Science*, **17**, 592–598.

Winston, J., O'Doherty, J., Kilner, J.M., Perrett, D.I., and Dolan, R.J. (2007). Brain systems for assessing facial attractiveness, *Neuropsychologia*, **45**, 195–206.

Winston, J., Strange, B., O'Doherty, J., and Dolan, R. (2002). Automatic and intentional brain responses during evaluation of trustworthiness of faces. *Nature Neuroscience*, **5**, 277–283.

Zebrowitz, L.A. (1999). *Reading faces: Window to the soul?* Boulder, CO: Westview Press.

Zebrowitz, L.A. (2004). The origins of first impressions. *Journal of Cultural and Evolutionary Psychology*, **2**, 93–108.

Zebrowitz, L.A. and Collins, M.A. (1997). Accurate social perception at zero acquaintance: The affordances of a Gibsonian approach. *Personality and Social Psychology Review*, **1**, 204–223.

Zebrowitz, L.A. and McDonald, S.M. (1991). The impact of litigants' babyfaceness and attractiveness on adjudications in small claims courts. *Law and Behavior*, **15**, 603–623.

Zebrowitz, L.A. and Rhodes, G. (2004). Sensitivity to "bad genes" and the anomalous face overgeneralization effect: Cue validity, cue utilization, and accuracy in judging intelligence and health. *Journal of Nonverbal Behavior*, **28**, 167–185.

Zebrowitz, L.A., Voinescu, L., and Collins, M.A. (1996). "Wide-eyed" and "crooked-faced": Determinants of perceived and real honesty across the life span. *Personality and Social Psychology Bulletin*, **22**, 1258–1269.

Zebrowitz, L.A., Andreoletti, C., Collins, M.A., Lee, S.Y., and Blumenthal, J. (1998a). Bright, bad, babyfaced boys: Appearance stereotypes do not always yield self-fulfilling prophecy effects. *Journal of Personality and Social Psychology*, **75**, 1300–1320.

Zebrowitz, L.A., Collins, M.A., and Dutta, R. (1998b). The relationship between appearance personality across the life span. *Personality and Social Psychology Bulletin*, **24**, 736–749.

Zebrowitz, L.A., Hall, J.A., Murphy, N.A., and Rhodes, G. (2002). Looking smart and looking good: Facial cues to intelligence and their origins. *Personality and Social Psychology Bulletin*, **28**, 238–249.

Zebrowitz, L.A., Fellous, J.M., Mignault, A., and Andreoletti, C. (2003). Trait impressions as overgeneralized responses to adaptively significant facial qualities: Evidence from connectionist modeling. *Personality and Social Psychology Review*, **7**, 194–215.

Chapter 33

Structure, Expression, and Motion in Facial Attractiveness

Ian S. Penton-Voak and Edward R. Morrison

From vain Narcissus who fell in love with his own reflection, to Helen of Troy's "face that launched a thousand ships" (Marlowe, 1604), poets and artists through the ages have contemplated beauty in the face. Everyday experience suggests that attractiveness is a highly salient aspect of both familiar and unfamiliar faces. This impression is backed up by findings showing that it only takes a fraction of a second to judge attractiveness: ratings of faces presented for only 100 ms correlate with ratings made when ample time is available to make the judgment (e.g. Locher et al., 1993; Willis and Todorov, 2006). In this chapter, we review recent developments in experimental facial attractiveness research. Following an outline of the important social consequences of facial attractiveness in social life, we briefly review the structural factors associated with attractiveness in both sexes taking a theoretical perspective largely influenced by evolutionary biology. We also discuss individual differences in preferences from this theoretical perspective. Attractiveness, however, is also affected by aspects of the face that are manifestly not static. Facial motion and expression involve changing configurations of the face and the execution of specific, discrete gestures that are likely to contribute to attractiveness and yet are largely neglected in the current literature. To finish the chapter, we review recent work looking at how an evolutionary viewpoint is also useful when considering attractiveness judgments when expressive or dynamic cues are present in stimuli.

Social consequences of attractiveness

The consequences of beauty have been well documented with many studies demonstrating the influence of attractiveness on social outcomes (reviewed in Berschied and Walster, 1974; Zebrowitz, Chapter 3, this volume). These studies swiftly came to the conclusion that attractiveness is a surprisingly important variable in human interaction.

The most striking early finding was the ubiquity of halo effects surrounding attractive people— the "beautiful is good" effect. Dion et al. (1972) presented photographs of people of different attractiveness and had them rated on various presumed characteristics. More attractive targets were assumed to have more positive personality attributes and better life outcomes such as career success and marital happiness. Even when targets are strangers and the only available source of information is physical appearance in a photograph, people still readily make such attributions, and, most importantly, they agree on the traits they perceive (e.g. Borkenau and Liebler, 1992; Penton-Voak et al., 2006). Irrespective of the platitude that "beauty is in the eye of the beholder", people also largely agree on the attractiveness of a face, typically showing high consensus on the attractiveness of a series of targets (Feingold, 1992; although see Hönekopp, 2006).

As a consequence of these halo effects, physical attractiveness is associated with preferential treatment in real life situations. Good-looking people fare better in employment (Hosoda et al., 2003) and may even be more likely to be acquitted in a trial (McCoun, 1990). An obvious area where attractiveness is an advantage is in being chosen as a sexual partner. In a classic study, Walster et al. (1966) organized a "computer dance" in which men and women were randomly matched as dates. From a large number of characteristics that were measured, only physical attractiveness predicted how much a date liked and desired future contact with his or her partner. Attractive people report more numerous mating opportunities (Rhodes et al., 2005a; Weeden and Sabini, 2007) and some studies have reported that they leave more off-spring in both non-industrial and industrial societies (Hill and Hurtado, 1996; Jokela, 2009). Attractiveness is also beneficial in the formation of same-sex alliances and friendships (Cash and Derlega 1978; Feingold 1988). Attractiveness clearly has an important influence on many aspects of our social lives.

Biological approaches to facial attractiveness

In parallel to social psychological work demonstrating the social consequences of attractiveness, researchers in other fields were laying foundations for the scientific study of both the function (why bother to make attractiveness judgments?) and the determinants (what facial traits do we prefer?) of attractiveness. Sociobiological theories derived from advances in the evolutionary biology were rapidly applied to human behaviours. Don Symons (1979) produced an early but influential treatment of this position in *The Evolution of Human Sexuality*. In this book, attractiveness judgments were proposed to be part of a suite of adaptive behaviours that served the ultimate biological "goal"—successful reproduction—of any sexual species.

This approach suggests that those morphological characteristics that are preferred should be reliable indicators of future fitness benefits. Thus, it proposes that attractiveness "works" by signaling a variety of qualities linked to fitness, such as health, reproductive value, and heritable genetic quality. So from an evolutionary point of view, the attractive face is a healthy one, or one with high reproductive value, or one that promises heritable benefits in offspring.

Preliminary evidence in favor of this biological approach to attractiveness comes from cross-cultural and developmental studies of attractiveness perception, which demonstrate that attractiveness is neither arbitrary nor culture bound. Firstly, not only do individuals within a culture tend to agree on the attractiveness of a face, but this consensus also applies to raters from other cultures (see Langlois, 2000 for a meta-analytic description of this effect). Secondly, and more critically, developmental studies have demonstrated that infants acquire adult like prefer-ences extraordinarily rapidly. When infants are shown a pair of faces that vary in (adult assessed) attractiveness, they show a visual preference for the attractive option (Langlois, 1987). Remarkably, infants between 14 to 151 hours from birth show the same preferences (Slater et al., 1998). Furthermore, children's behavior is influenced by attractiveness: infants interact more positively with adults wearing an attractive mask than with those wearing an unattractive mask, and prefer to play with an attractive doll than with an unattractive one (Langlois et al., 1990). Clearly, infants learn something about attractiveness rapidly, without any linguistic component and at a very young age. Such learning could be considered to be biologically predisposed and effectively "culture free."

Attractiveness and facial structure

The fact that people agree so readily on the attractiveness of strangers implies that there are systematic features that make a face beautiful. Three structural properties of faces have received the majority of research attention: symmetry, averageness, and sexual dimorphism. Each of these properties has a credible biological signalling role.

Symmetry

Many animals are bilaterally symmetrical, as symmetry is important for basic functions such as locomotion, vision, and audition. Symmetry, however, is never perfect, and individuals differ in the amount of asymmetry displayed in bilateral characteristics (such as limbs, ears, fingers, etc.). This fluctuating asymmetry (FA) is associated with homozygosity, parasite load, poor nutrition, and pollution (Møller and Swaddle 1997; Polak, 2003): developmental insults perturb the otherwise symmetrical body plan (Møller, 1999). Low FA is associated with high mating success across many species (Gangestad and Thornhill, 1997).

In humans, even though slight deviations from symmetry in non-facial bilateral traits (e.g. wrist and ankle width) are largely too subtle to be perceived, people with high measured FA are rated as less attractive than more symmetric individuals (Gangestad and Thornhill 1997; Thornhill et al., 1995). Interestingly, an asymmetrical body is negatively correlated with facial attractiveness (Gangestad et al., 1994), suggesting that a beautiful face is a signal of biological quality. Facial asymmetry itself is also unattractive in studies of real faces (Mealey et al., 1999; Penton-Voak et al., 2001; Scheib et al., 1999) and faces that have been manipulated to be more symmetrical become more attractive (Perrett et al., 1999; Rhodes et al., 1999).

In a meta-analysis, Rhodes (2006) found that symmetry was positively related to attractiveness in composite faces (see Figure 33.1), with quite a large effect size, and with a moderate effect size in unmanipulated photographs of faces. Rhodes, however, points out that few studies of the human face separate FA from directional asymmetry (a consistent departure from symmetry across a species), which is not a marker of mate quality. It may also be the case that it is not symmetry per se which is attractive, as facial symmetry predicts the attractiveness of hemifaces, which possess minimal cues to symmetry (Scheib et al., 1999). To counter the criticism that Schieb et al.'s hemifaces still contain cues to symmetry (e.g. in the lateral position of features on the midline such as the mouth and nose), Penton-Voak et al. (2001) created composites of groups of individual faces with high and low facial symmetry. These composite faces were made perfectly symmetric, and yet composites constructed from high symmetry faces were more attractive than those constructed from low symmetry faces, suggesting that some correlate of symmetry is also important in attractiveness judgments. It remains unclear whether facial symmetry, or indeed asymmetry in any other isolated bilateral trait, can function as a useful signal of biological quality: Gangestad and Scheyd (2005) suggest that facial symmetry has a very low correlation with body symmetry, and at best "weakly taps developmental instability."

As an alternative to symmetry signaling quality, some researchers have argued that preferences for symmetry may be a non-functional byproduct of the ease of processing of symmetrical stimuli in general (e.g. Enquist and Arak, 1994; Enquist and Johnstone, 1997). More recent work varying the orientation of faces, however, demonstrates the existence of higher level, face specific processes in symmetry detection (e.g. Little and Jones, 2003, 2006; Rhodes et al., 2005b, 2007). These findings are hard to reconcile with a perceptual bias explanation for symmetry preferences, and the existence of such specialized mechanisms has been taken as evidence for adaptations for symmetry detection in faces, despite the likely weak links between facial symmetry and underlying biological quality (Gangestad and Scheyd, 2005).

Averageness

Although the idea that average forms are in some way ideal can be traced back at least to Plato, Francis Galton (1878) was the first to provide empirical evidence that averageness is associated with attractiveness in human faces. By using photographic composites, Galton attempted to isolate the features common to a particular category (such as criminals, or army officers).

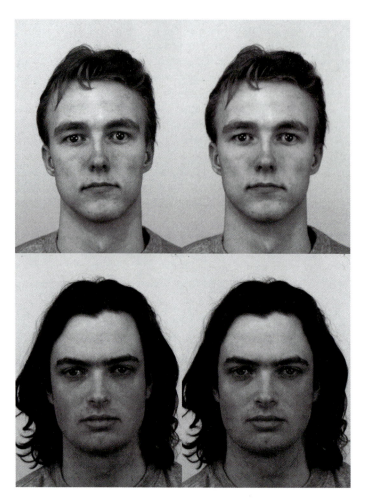

Fig. 33.1 Subtle changes in symmetry influence attractiveness. In forced choice, raters generally prefer symmetric (right) over asymmetric (left) versions of individual faces. Images from Lundqvist et al. (1998).

He famously noted that the resulting composite face was often considerably more attractive than the originals. More recently, digital computer techniques have allowed the morphing of individual faces to produce near photographic quality artificial facial composites (Rowland and Perrett, 1995). Using an early implementation of this technology Langlois and Roggman (1990) showed that computer-generated facial composites—average faces—were more attractive than the sum of their parts. This effect remained when symmetry was controlled (Rhodes et al., 1999) and when only profiles were used thus removing cues to symmetry (Valentine et al., 2004), and is not just a result of the smooth complexion of composites (Rhodes et al., 1999; see Figure 33.2). Averageness is also attractive in unmanipulated faces, and individual faces can be made more attractive by morphing their shape towards the population mean for that sex (Rhodes et al., 1999; Rhodes and Tremewan, 1996). Meta analysis indicates that averageness has a large effect on attractiveness with no differences due to face sex, or race (Rhodes, 2006).

The underlying biological argument for the appeal of average faces is similar to that for symmetry. Average traits may signal developmental stability and resistance to disease (Møller and Swaddle 1997) and heterozygosity (Thornhill and Gangestad, 1993), and hence be an honest

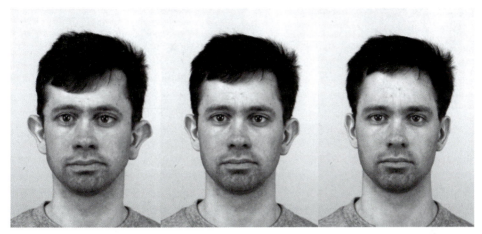

Fig. 33.2 The effects of averageness on attractiveness. An original face (center) morphed away from (left) and toward (right) the population average face shape. The majority of raters consider attractiveness to increase from left to right. Images from Lundqvist et al. (1998).

indicator of heritable quality. Yet, despite the appeal of average faces, the most attractive faces are not average. Optimally attractive faces differ systematically from the population mean. This principle was elegantly demonstrated for female faces by Perrett et al. (1994), who showed that an averaged composite of all faces in a group was less attractive than a composite made from a subset of the most attractive faces. Furthermore, this attractive composite became more attractive when its shape was caricatured to exaggerate the shape differences from averageness, neatly answering the potential criticism that the attractive exemplars from any given sample of faces are simply more representative of the true population average. These findings persisted with Japanese and Caucasian stimuli and raters, suggesting some cross-cultural stability in preferences.

Sexual dimorphism

Sex differences in facial structure provide a potential explanation for the attractiveness of non-average traits. Sexual dimorphism refers to differences in morphology between the sexes of the same species. Many animals are sexually dimorphic to varying degrees, in body size and structure (with stag's antlers, the peacock's tail, and the massive body size dimorphism in some pinnipeds remaining the classic examples). Exaggerated male traits are linked to mating success in a wide variety of species (Andersson, 1994).

The human face is sexually dimorphic too, so evolutionarily-minded researchers reasoned that it may also have been subject to sexual selection, and that dimorphism might affect attractiveness judgments. Largely, sexual dimorphism in faces is the result of sex steroid hormonal activity during puberty. Testosterone causes growth in the jaw and chin and makes the eyebrow ridge more prominent (Merow and Broadbent, 1990). Estrogen produces fuller lips and less growth in the lower region of the face, making the cheekbones more prominent (Enlow, 1990).

Masculine adult male faces also have higher levels of circulating testosterone (Penton-Voak and Chen, 2004), although the association is weak and is replicated inconsistently (e.g. Neave et al., 2003; Roney et al., 2006). A more robust finding is that men with more a masculine facial structure show higher levels of circulating testosterone after experimentally determined success in a competitive task than men with less masculine faces (Pound et al., 2009).

Preferences for androgen-related traits are thought to indicate sexual selection for putative indicators of "good genes." In "good genes" models of sexual selection, traits are proposed to be honest signals indicating desirable genetic qualities—such traits cannot be faked by individuals of lower "quality" because of their cost. Androgens are linked to the growth of secondary sexual characteristics in male mammals but have a suppressive action on active immune system function (Hillgarth and Wingfield, 1997). Traits that demonstrate successful development despite this immunosuppression may therefore represent an honest signal of health in males (Folstad and Karter, 1992), which may in turn lead to good condition in offspring.

Perrett et al. (1998) manipulated sexual dimorphism by exaggerating or diminishing the differences between the average male and female shapes (see Figure 33.3). Feminizing female faces in this way increased attractiveness. Femininity is also attractive in unmanipulated faces when measured (Cunningham, 1986; Cunningham et al., 1995; Johnson and Franklin, 1993; Jones and Hill, 1993; Koehler et al., 2004) or rated (Bruce et al., 1994; Dunkle and Francis, 1990; Koehler et al., 2004, O'Toole et al., 1998; Rhodes et al., 2003a). As women with feminine faces have higher levels

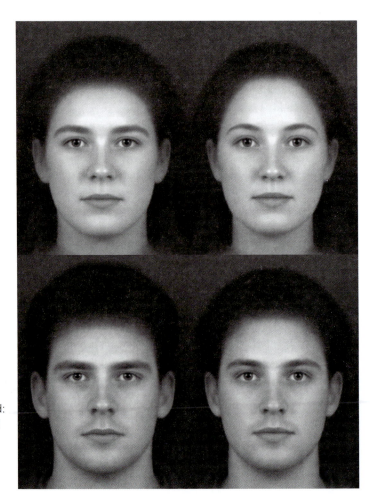

Fig. 33.3 Masculinized (left) and feminized (right) female and male faces. Reprinted by permission from Macmillan Publishers Ltd: *Nature*, Effects of sexual dimorphism on facial attractiveness, Perrett et al., **394**(6696) © 1998.

of estrogen metabolites in their urine (Law Smith et al., 2005), and estrogen is linked to various measures of reproductive health (Eissa et al., 1986; Dickey et al., 1993; Roumen et al., 1982), this finding provides a "smoking gun" suggesting that face preferences may have potentially important biological outcomes.

For male faces, however, sexual dimorphism (i.e. masculinity) is not universally attractive. Sometimes feminized faces are preferred (e.g. Perrett et al., 1998), but in other studies masculinized faces are favored (e.g. Johnston et al., 2001). In studies using composites, feminized male faces are largely preferred, but in studies with individual faces, masculinized faces are often more attractive. One limitation of studies of unmanipulated faces, however, is that masculinity is often rated rather than objectively defined, and hence its association with attractiveness may be the result of a halo effect. Nevertheless, masculinity is not clearly attractive in male faces, despite the fact that these studies use exactly the same techniques that generate reliable preferences for femininity in studies of female facial attractiveness. Perrett et al. (1998) suggest that this surprising conclusion may be because masculine faces are associated with negative personality traits such as coldness and dishonesty whereas feminine faces are associated with prosocial personality traits. Personality attributions may have a "kernel of truth," adding some credibility to this argument (Penton-Voak and Perrett, 2001; Penton-Voak et al., 2006; Todorov et al., Chapter 32, this volume).

Does facial attractiveness really signal mate quality?

These associations between the structure of faces and underlying biological properties such as endocrine status, suggest information relevant to mate choice is visible in human faces, and that people are sensitive to these traits. Preferences for these structural properties fit well with theoretical predictions from evolutionary biology for female faces, and are present (although less consistent) for male faces. But there are some empirical gaps in evolutionary explanations for preferences. Despite excellent theoretical reasons to expect attractiveness to signal health, relationships between medical health and facial attractiveness are weak when they are found at all (see Rhodes, 2006; Weeden and Sabini 2005 for reviews).

Links between health and attractiveness remain largely indirect: in addition to the evidence linking sex hormones to attractive facial traits outlined above, further evidence of associations between markers of biological quality and attractiveness judgments comes from studies of links between major histocompatability complex (MHC) genotype and facial attractiveness. The MHC is very polymorphic, with alleles that code for proteins that play an important role in immune responses (Havlicek and Roberts, 2009). Two studies have demonstrated that MHC heterozygosity (which may give an advantage to immune system function) is linked to facial attractiveness (Lie et al., 2008; Roberts et al., 2005; but see Coetzee et al., 2007; and Thornhill et al., 2003).

An appealing alternative to the possibility that small differences in attractiveness lead to differential reproductive outcomes has been proposed by Zebrowitz and Rhodes (2004). They propose that the function of attractiveness judgments may primarily be to avoid partners in very poor condition, rather than to make fine discriminations between the majority of individuals, who may vary little in fertililty or health. Certainly, very high levels of asymmetry, obvious cues to bad health (skin lesions, etc.) and large deviations from population average face shapes are likely to reflect ill health, and are traits best avoided in a mate from the perspective of reproduction. An aversion to such extreme traits (that provide valid cues to fitness) may then be overgeneralized to faces in the typical range, leading to preferences that are effectively byproducts of avoiding unhealthy individuals.

Individual differences in preferences

Despite general consensus in attractiveness judgments, preferences are not identical across all individuals. Perhaps some of the most interesting recent attractiveness research has attempted to reconcile variation in preferences with biological models that predict, at least at first glance, that there should be little variation between individuals in preferences. Hönekopp (2006) argues that the idea that raters agree on the attractiveness of faces is simplistic, and that the standard procedure for assessing agreement cannot even address the issue. He estimates that the relative contributions of what he labels "private" and "shared" taste vary according the stimulus set in question: if all faces in a given set are of similar attractiveness (a set of supermodels, for example), then private taste will be relatively more important than shared taste, whereas if the faces are of very different attractiveness, shared taste will dominate over private taste. Attraction also occurs in different contexts, such as short-term flings or long-term monogamous relationships, in which mate choice criteria may vary. Additionally, mutual mate choice in humans may introduce "market" considerations—choosers who are themselves "valuable" in a given mating market may have different preferences to those lower in value. Such considerations have led to a resurgence of interest in individual differences in attractiveness judgments.

One source of variability in judgments is likely to come from an individual's experience of faces. There are several studies showing that childhood experiences affect adult facial preferences: preferences for age, eye, and hair color are all influenced by parental characteristics (Bereczkei et al., 2002; Little et al., 2003; Perrett et al., 2002). Experimentally, exposure to faces that have been artificially manipulated in some way leads to higher attractiveness ratings of novel faces similarly manipulated (Buckingham et al., 2006; Little et al., 2005; Rhodes et al., 2003b). So, for example, following exposure to a set of faces with widely spaced eyes, novel faces with this trait would be rated as more attractive than those with narrowly spaced eyes. Exposure alone, however, is not always sufficient to generate preferences for faces. In a series of elegant experiments, Lisa DeBruine and colleagues have demonstrated that although opposite sex faces that resemble a given rater are considered trustworthy by that individual, they are rarely considered attractive. These findings make sense in the light of inclusive fitness theory: family members are more likely to resemble each other, and provide good social support, yet make poor reproductive partners due to the costs of inbreeding (see DeBruine et al., 2008, for review).

Other individual level variation in preferences has been hypothesized to reflect evolved facultative mating strategies that are dependent on environmental contingencies. In such facultative strategies, preferences may vary across circumstances in an adaptive fashion: e.g. a preference for cues to high body weight may be beneficial when food is scarce, but not in environments in which increased body weight is a possible predictor of ill health. Such behavioral variation is well documented in other species with individuals using diverse reproductive strategies, rather than using a single "best" strategy (e.g. fight–sneak copulation tactics; for reviews, see Brockmann 2001; Gross 1996). In humans, variation in face preferences within individuals, between individuals, and between cultures has been interpreted using this framework.

Strategic variation in preferences within individuals

Apparently strategic variation in preferences within the same individual has been reported in several studies. One body of work demonstrates that preferences for masculinity in male faces vary with the menstrual cycle phase of the rater. When women are in follicular phase of the menstrual cycle (when conception following intercourse is most likely), they prefer relatively masculinised (Johnston et al., 2001, Little et al., 2008; Penton-Voak and Perrett, 2000; Penton-Voak et al., 1999) and symmetrical male faces (Little et al., 2007a). The preference shift towards masculinity is greater in the context of a short-term rather than long-term relationship, and stronger in women in a committed relationship (Penton-Voak et al., 1999). Furthermore, irrespective of menstrual cycle phase, women prefer more masculine faces in the context of a short- rather than long-term relationship (Little et al., 2002). Women who currently have partners also prefer more masculine faces (Little et al., 2002).

These shifts in preference have been interpreted as providing evidence for a mixed mating strategy in women. Potentially, when choosing a mate women require men who provide two (possibly competing) types of benefit: first, mates offering heritable benefits to offspring (e.g. in terms of health) should be favored. Second, mates who offer paternal investment in offspring may also offer advantages over those that do not. Ideally, women may want a mate who offers good genes and paternal investment. However, men's own behavior may force women to adopt multiple strategies: evidence suggests that men offering heritable benefits (i.e. good genes as signaled by masculinity) are less likely to offer paternal investment than men without cues to heritable quality. For example, men with markers of heritable quality invest less time in relationships, are more dishonest to their partners, and sexualize other women more (e.g. Gangestad and Thornhill, 1997).

Women may trade off cues to good genes against cues to likely paternal investment when judging attractiveness of faces. Cues to paternal investment (i.e. the prosociality indicated by relative facial femininity) may be preferred in long-term relationships. Cues to good genes (i.e. facial masculinity and symmetry) may be preferred where parental investment is not expected (i.e. in short-term and extra-pair relationships), and during the fertile phases of the menstrual cycle to obtain genetic benefits in offspring by selecting short-term or extra-pair mates that have characteristics that suggest "good genes." Multiple mating strategies that appear to maximize investment from a primary partner and genetic quality from extra pair males have been observed in other species (Jennions and Petrie, 2000).

Strategic variation in preferences between individuals

Greater preferences for masculinity are also seen in women who consider themselves attractive (Little et al., 2001), or who are attractive by more objective measures (e.g. facial attractiveness and body shape; Penton-Voak et al., 2003), but only for long-term relationships. Women with a history of ill health also show weaker preferences for masculinity in men's faces (Scott et al., 2008). These findings indicate that women seem to adjust their preferences on the basis of their own mate value. High quality (i.e. masculine) men may be more willing to invest in relationships with high quality women compared with lower quality women. Conversely, women who perceive themselves as less competitive in the mating market may lack preferences for cues to good genes or actively prefer cues to direct benefits (such as paternal investment) in faces. Such "market forces" have been shown to influence men's and women's behavior when seeking a romantic partner (Pawlowski and Dunbar, 1999).

Cross-cultural variation in preferences

Tradeoffs of parental investment against heritable benefits may vary according to their value given local environmental conditions. Varying preferences across different populations may reflect conditional strategies, generating facultative adaptive responses to varying environmental stresses. Differences in environmental conditions could be ecological (e.g. pathogen prevalence) or cultural (societal tendencies towards low or high paternal investment). Gangestad and Buss (1993) showed that across a large sample of societies pathogen load is positively related to an individual's stated importance of physical attractiveness in mate choice. Given that attractiveness is supposed to indicate (broadly defined) health, this may represent an adaptive shift in preferences.

Specific examples of how different traits may be preferred in different cultures are given by a study showing that preferences for symmetry are more pronounced in the Hadza (a hunter-gatherer society in Tanzania) than in the UK (Little et al., 2007b). Additionally, preferences for masculinity tend to be more exaggerated in cultures with higher pathogen loads (e.g. Penton-Voak et al., 2004; Scott et al., 2008). These findings indicate that women, in particular, are sensitive to the relative benefits offered by different potential partners, and adjust their preferences according to local circumstances.

Non-structural aspects of attractiveness

Despite the success of the evolutionary approach in explaining both general preferences and individual differences in attractiveness judgments there are limitations in many studies to date, particularly in terms of the stimuli used. Many studies use photographs of faces, often with neutral expressions looking straight into the camera (direct gaze). This methodology is, of course, excellent in terms of experimental control, but largely ignores the social context in which attractiveness judgments are made. The literature largely treats the attractiveness of a face as a trait that is simply linked to its physical appearance. However, the feeling of attraction is also a motivational state where one individual is drawn to another. From a functional perspective, attraction is likely to facilitate the allocation of mating effort towards an opposite-sex target. Importantly, when an individual is expending resources in securing a mate, there should at least some chance of a successful outcome. Simply put, few men pursue supermodels, as they assume rejection is the likely outcome, and mating effort would be wasted. Recognising this, researchers have looked at the effects of factors such as emotional expression and gaze direction on attractiveness judgments: cues that indicate a likely return on mating "investment" should be valued.

Unsurprisingly, smiling increases attractiveness compared with neutral expression (Otta et al., 1996; Raines et al., 1990a,b; Schulman and Hoskins 1986), although this finding is sometimes absent for male faces (see Penton-Voak and Chang, 2008, for a review). Faces become more attractive when shifting gaze toward a viewer rather than away (Mason et al., 2005). Kampe et al. (2001) showed that direction of gaze affects the reward value of a face as measured by blood flow to the ventral striatum. Direct gaze increased the reward of attractive faces, but decreased the reward of unattractive faces. There are also behavioral interactions between these factors. Faces with direct gaze are preferred to versions of the same face with averted gaze, an effect that is particularly pronounced for attractive faces (Ewing et al., 2010). Attractive faces are particularly attractive when smiling towards rather than away from the viewer, but when gaze is averted attractive faces are preferred with a neutral expression (Jones et al., 2006). These findings are consistent with the idea that attractiveness judgments serve to allocate mating effort efficiently, i.e. towards a likely reward of reciprocated attraction. A face smiling towards you may be signaling sexual interest and/or friendly intentions, and it is therefore worthwhile valuing it. Likewise, if a face is attractive in another's eyes, it may have qualities you should also find attractive (Jones et al., 2007).

Although these experiments try to go beyond simple ratings of pictures by adding meaningful context of emotional content and the direction of social attention, they still suffer from the problem that they employ static stimuli. Real faces are seldom static, and evolved attractiveness preferences have presumably been selected in response to dynamic faces. Several recent studies have even shown that attractiveness ratings of the same face in photographs and videos may not correlate significantly. Rubenstein (2005) reported non-significant correlations with female pictures and videos, and both Lander (2008) and Penton-Voak and Chang (2008) found positive but non-significant correlations with male, but not female, stimuli. Roberts et al. (2009), however, demonstrated strong correlations between ratings of static and dynamic images for both male and female targets in a comprehensive study that varied rating conditions and video collection contexts. Although these results are somewhat contradictory, with three studies failing to replicate Rubenstein's findings, they do suggest that it is not necessarily easy to extrapolate attractiveness ratings from pictures to videos.

Social interaction inevitably involves facial dynamics as people talk and respond to each other. Research with static images may overestimate the importance of cues such as smiling (or even structural factors such as symmetry or sexual dimorphism), as such experiments typically manipulate only one or two variables at a time. Statistical significance in such experimental contexts may exaggerate the psychological significance of the variables under investigation in the real social situations in which attractiveness judgments are normally made. If the only difference between two faces is a smile, it is not surprising that the smiling one is more attractive. But a real person neither smiles continuously nor maintains unbroken eye contact with another (behavior which would be downright unnerving in real social interaction). Genuine interaction clearly involves a subtle interplay between smiling, gaze direction, and other non-structural aspects of the face.

Something in the way she moves

Our understanding of facial attractiveness must therefore eventually involve consideration of dynamic aspects of the face. Movement is known to be important in several facets of face perception with motion conveying cues to identity (Bassili, 1978; Bruce and Valentine, 1988; Knight and Johnston, 1997; Lander et al., 1999; Pike et al., 1997; Thornton and Kourtzi, 2002) and emotional expression (Bassili, 1978, 1979). Rubenstein (2005) showed that positive and negative emotional cues are an important cue to attractiveness in dynamic faces even when sitters are explicitly asked not to express emotion during filming. This suggests that dynamic images contain important social cues relevant to attractiveness. Indeed, Riggio et al. (1991) used ratings of behaviour from video sequences to argue that dynamic information was an important component of overall attractiveness independent of facial (static) beauty from photographs, although the study could not specify what aspects of movement were important in those judgments.

Just as digital morphing of images revolutionized the study of static facial attractiveness, motion-capture technology, which involves the digital recording of marker points on moving objects, is set to be an important technology in the study of facial movement. By recording the position of markers on faces, dynamic information can be isolated from underlying structure. This allows dynamic cues to be investigated with good control of static information by keeping structural cues in stimuli constant across conditions, by animating a given face with the motion from another. Using a form of such technology, we showed that there are differences between male and female facial motion (Gralewski et al., 2006; Figure 33.4), and that people can identify sex from these dynamic cues alone (Morrison et al., 2007, replicating earlier work by Hill and Johnston, 2001). Furthermore, these sex differences were linked to attractiveness, with female clips that were more easily identified as female being rated as more attractive. This findings parallels work with static faces reviewed above in which structural femininity is attractive in female faces (Perrett et al., 1998). Sex-typical male facial motion was not associated with attractiveness, which is again reminiscent of findings that structural masculinity is not always attractive. Male motion in this study did possess cues to attractiveness as inter-rater agreement between raters was high: as with structural cues to attractiveness, there is good consensus about clips that are attractive and those that are not.

One potential behavioral cue in motion is proceptivity—a suite of behaviors including sustained smiling, laughing and direct eye contact—which encourages dyadic interaction (Givens, 1978; Eibl-Eibsfeldt, 1989). Proceptivity potentially signals sexual interest, which may offer a direct

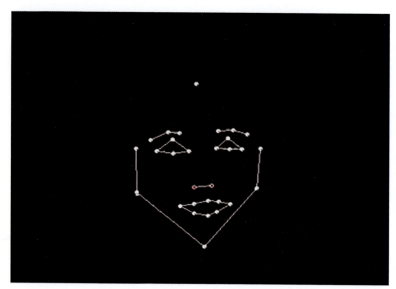

Fig. 33.4 A still frame from the shape normalized, line drawn stimuli used in Gralewski et al. (2006), Morrison et al. (2007, 2010) and Clark et al. (2009). Observers make reliable and consensual attributions of sex, attractiveness and proceptivity even to these impoverished dynamic displays.

benefit to the receiver, as mating effort toward the signaler is more likely to be rewarded (Mishra et al., 2007; Clark 2008). In addition, some researchers have speculated that skilled social behavior such as flirtation may be sufficiently difficult to serve as an honest signal of mate quality, potentially indicating benefits that may be inherited by offspring (i.e. "good genes"; Miller 2000). Moreover, proceptive behavior may also communicate social confidence, which may predict social status, or at the very least a prosocial orientation (i.e. a willingness to engage in social interaction).

Clark et al., (2009) had a series of wireframe clips rated for short- and long-term attractiveness, and independently, for flirtatiousness. Flirtatiousness is positively related to, but not synonymous with, attractiveness, as it predicted short-term attractiveness significantly better than long-term attractiveness. Furthermore, Morrison et al., (2010) demonstrated that women's preferences for male movement varied over the menstrual cycle. At more fertile times of the cycle, women found flirtatious motion particularly attractive. Preferences for sex-typical motion, however, did not vary across the menstrual cycle contrary to predictions made from static-face research. The lack of variation in preference for sex-typical movement is probably because the major sex-difference in facial movement is one of degree, with males moving their faces less than women overall. As proceptivity was associated with increased movement in this study, "masculine" movement (which is characterized by less movement overall than feminine movement) may signal social disengagement rather than biological quality. Social disinterest is unlikely to be considered attractive in any context. Increased preference for flirtatiousness when fertile makes adaptive sense by focusing women's attention on those males who are interested in mating and reducing mating effort towards unsuitable mates.

This idea of selective focusing of mating effort has also been explored by Clark et al. (2008), who filmed actors responding to questions proceptively and unreceptively (i.e. trying to discourage further interaction), and had the individuals rated for attractiveness. The facial videos were presented either as directed towards judges or towards the opposite-sex interviewer, a potential sexual rival. Unsurprisingly, actors in proceptive interviews were rated more attractive. But there were interesting interactions with direction of the signal, with some actors more attractive when responding towards the participant and others when responding towards the interviewer. Although only eight actors (four of each sex) were used, the data suggested that attractive actors were preferred when signaling towards the participant, and unattractive actors preferred when signaling towards the interviewer. If an attractive individual is signaling interest towards oneself, it may be adaptive to boost that individual's perceived attractiveness to focus mating effort. If, however, interest is coming from an unattractive individual, it may be adaptive to decrease his or her perceived attractiveness to avoid wasting mating effort.

It is possible that there are sex differences in the interpretation of signal direction and proceptive behavior, with the direction of socially relevant facial signals mattering more to males than females. Men (and indeed most male mammals) invest more resources in mating effort than women (as they are competing for access to a limited reproductive resource). Therefore, they may place greater weight on proceptive signals directed toward themselves as opposed to other males. In contrast, such signals may be relatively ubiquitous for females and may be discounted as a result. In support of this, Clark et al. (2008), found that men preferred smiling female faces presented directly and neutral female faces presented in profile. Women, on the other hand, did not alter preference as a function of direction.

Facing the future

These studies of dynamic and expressive faces illustrate that facial attractiveness is more than just the structural arrangement of a static face. Emotional expression, direction of gaze or behaviour, and the social content of facial movement all modulate what may be considered "baseline" attractiveness. But in pursuing more ecologically valid stimuli, we must ask to what extent evolutionary reasoning is still useful in explaining what makes them attractive. For example, it is intuitive that a smiling face should be more attractive than a neutral one, and that it should be particularly attractive with direct rather than averted gaze. Likewise, it is no surprise that proceptive behaviour should be attractive. So the question is, as ecological validity grows, does the value of the evolutionary approach wane?

We would argue that considering these data from a functional perspective still adds to our understanding of the area. Although standard social psychology can easily predict that smiling should be attractive because it signals positive intent, and that gaze direction should modulate the perceived target of such signals, the adaptive framework is still useful in its own right because it allows prediction in situations that are not immediately obvious. Our finding that women's preferences for proceptive movement are stronger when they are at the fertile point of their menstrual cycle is difficult to explain without a functional perspective. Likewise, evolutionary logic allows us to predict that there might be interactions between the direction in which positive behaviors are signaled and the sex and structural attractiveness of the signaler, based on the adaptive allocation of mating effort.

We believe that future studies of facial attractiveness should persevere with attempts to improve ecological validity and consider both structural and non-structural aspects of facial attractiveness. For example, our work using dynamic stimuli to date has yet to incorporate structural and dynamic cues to attractiveness simultaneously, and, as such, is as subject to criticisms of limited ecological validity as the static face literature. As attributions of personality made to static faces are important in attractiveness judgments, and motion clearly can carry personality information, the interaction between static and dynamic cues is likely to be an important and fruitful area for future research. For example, can the typically negative personality traits attributed to masculine male faces be overcome by prosocial dynamic information? Although the cues to mate quality available in static facial images may well tell us the sort of faces that we should find attractive, the cues available in dynamic stimuli may inform an individual of the sort of mate he or she may be able to obtain. In the context of an evolutionary history in which pair-bonded sexual relationships have been favored by selection, both static and dynamic social cues are likely to make an important contribution to attractiveness judgments.

Summary and conclusions

Possessing an attractive face is an enormous benefit in a wide range of social situations. Evolutionary theory has proved valuable in explaining facial attractiveness by proposing that a beautiful face is a signal of biological quality, and that human preferences for attractiveness have evolved via sexual selection. Three biologically-based aspects of facial structure have been linked to attractiveness: symmetry, averageness, and sexual dimorphism. Symmetry and averageness are thought to reflect ability to buffer developmental insults, and hence be a cue to good health and disease resistance. Sexual dimorphism is related to levels of sex hormones which are linked to fertility in women and putatively to "good genes" in men. These findings are internally consistent, but there is still some debate as to how successfully these putative cues of condition actually signal health.

There is growing realization, however, that facial attractiveness depends on more than just the structural arrangement of the face. Transient factors such as emotional expression and gaze direction influence perceptions of attractiveness. Other impressions gleaned from facial movement (such as attributions of flirtatious intent or social disengagement) also play a role in attractiveness judgments. Although considerations of these non-structural aspects of the face seems to move us away from the biological basis of attractiveness, an adaptationist framework is still useful for interpreting data and generating new hypotheses: movement may reveal aspects of mate quality as it does in other species (e.g. Maynard Smith, 1956), and give useful information regarding the likely success of mating attempts.

References

Andersson, M. (1994). *Sexual Selection*. Princeton, NJ: Princeton University Press.

Bassili, J.N. (1978). Facial motion in the perception of faces and of emotional expression. *Journal of Experimental Psychology: Human Perception and Performance*, **4**, 373–79.

Bassili, J.N. (1979). Emotion recognition: the role of facial movement and the relative importance of the upper and lower areas of the face. *Journal of Personality and Social Psychology*, **37**, 249–58.

Bereczkei, T., Gyuris, P., Koves, P., and Bernath, L. (2002). Homogamy, genetic similarity, and imprinting; parental influence on mate choice preferences. *Personality and Individual Differences*, **33**, 677–690.

Berscheid, E. and Walster, E. (1974). Physical attractiveness. *Advances in Experimental Social Psychology*, **7**, 157–215.

Borkenau, P. and Liebler, A. (1992). Trait inferences: sources of validity at zero acquaintance. *Journal of Personality and Social Psychology*, **62**, 645–57.

Brockmann, H.J. (2001). The evolution of alternative strategies and tactics. *Advances in the Study of Behavior*, **30**, 1–51.

Bruce, V. and Valentine, T. (1988). When a nod's as good as a wink: the role of dynamic information in facial recognition. In MM Gruneberg, PE Morrison, and RN Sykes (eds.) *Practical aspects of memory: Current research and issues*, pp. 169–174. Chichester: Wiley.

Bruce, V., Burton, A., and Dench, N. (1994). What's distinctive about a distinctive face? *Quarterly Journal of Experimental Psychology*, **47**, 119–41.

Buckingham, G., DeBruine, L.M., Little, A.C., *et al.* (2006). Visual adaptation to masculine and feminine faces influences generalized preferences and perceptions of trustworthiness. *Evolution and Human Behavior*, **27**, 381–389.

Cash, T.F. and Derlega, V.J. (1978). Matching hypothesis: Physical attractiveness among same-sexed friends. *Personality and Social Psychology Bulletin*, **4**, 240–43.

Clark, A.P. (2008). Attracting interest: Dynamic displays of proceptivity increase the attractiveness of men and women. *Evolutionary Psychology*, **6**, 563–74.

Clark, A.P., Reeve, F., and Penton-Voak, I.S. (2008). Smiling the wrong way: it only matters to men. Paper presented at HBES 2008, Kyoto, Japan.

Clark, A.P., Morrison, E.R., Jack, V., and Penton-Voak, I.S. (2009). Attractiveness in flux: female preferences for male facial motion depend on mating context and non-additive cues to prosociality and proceptivity. *Journal of Evolutionary Psychology*, **7**, 99–109.

Coetzee, V., Barrett, L., Greeff, J.M., Henzi, S.P., Perrett, D.I., and Wadee, A.A. (2007). Common HLA alleles associated with health, but not with facial attractiveness. *PLoS ONE*, **2**, e640.

Cunningham, M.R. (1986). Measuring the physical in physical attractiveness. Quais-experiments on the socio-biology of female facial beauty. *Journal of Personality and Social Psychology*, **50**, 925–35.

Cunningham, M.R., Roberts, A.R., Barbee, A.P., Druen, P.B., and Wu, C. (1995). "Their ideas of beauty are, on the whole, the same as ours": Consistency and variability in the cross-cultural perception of female physical attractiveness. *Journal of Personality and Social Psychology*, **68**, 261–79.

DeBruine, L.M., Jones, B.C., Little, A.C., and Perrett, D.I. (2008). *Social Perception of Facial Resemblance in Humans. Archives of Sexual Behavior*, **37**, 64–77.

Dickey, R.P., Olar, T.T., Taylor, S.N., Curole, D.N., and Matulich, E.M. (1993). Relationship of endometrial thickness and pattern to fecundity in ovulation induction cycles: effect of clomiphene citrate alone and with human menopausal gonadotrophin. *Fertility and Sterility*, **59**, 756–60.

Dion, K., Berscheid, E., and Walster, E. (1972). What is beautiful is good. *Journal of Personality and Social Psychology*, **24**, 207–13.

Dunkle, J.H. and Francis, P.L. (1990). The role of facial masculinity femininity in the attribution of homosexuality. *Sex Roles*, **23**, 157–67.

Eibl-Eibesfeldt, I. (1989): *Human Ethology*. New York: Aldine de Gruyter.

Eissa, M., Obhrai, M., Docker, M., Lynch, S., Sawers, R., and Newton, R. (1986). Follicular growth and endocrine profiles in spontaneous and induced conception cycles. *Fertility and Sterility*, **45**, 191–95.

Enlow, D.H. (1990). Faces. In DH Enlow (ed.) *Facial Growth*, 3rd. edn, pp. 1–24. Philadelphia, PA: Saunders.

Enquist, M. and Arak, A. (1994). Symmetry, beauty and evolution. *Nature*, **372**, 169–72.

Enquist, M. and Johnstone, R.A. (1997). Generalization and the evolution of symmetry preferences. *Proceedings of the Royal Society of London, B*, **264**, 1345–1348.

Ewing, L., Rhodes, G., and Pellicano, L. (2010). Have you got the look? Gaze direction affects facial attractiveness. *Visual Cogniton*, **18**, 321–330.

Feingold, A. (1988). Matching for attractiveness in romantic partners and same-sex friends: A meta-analysis and theoretical critique. *Psychological Bulletin*, **104**, 226–35.

Feingold, A. (1992). Gender differences in mate selection preferences: A test of the parental investment model. *Psychological Bulletin*, **112**, 125–39.

Folstad, I. and Karter, A.J. (1992). Parasites, bright males, and the immunocompetence handicap. *American Naturalist*, **139**, 603–22.

Galton, F. (1878). Composite portraits. *Journal of the Antrhopological Institute of Great Britain and Ireland*, **8**, 132–42.

Gangestad, S.W. and Buss, D.M. (1993). Pathogen prevalence and human mate preferences. *Ethology and Sociobiology*, **14**, 89–96.

Gangestad, S.W. and Scheyd, G.J. (2005). *The evolution of human physical attractiveness. Annual Review of Anthropology* **34**, 523–48.

Gangestad, S.W. and Thornhill, R. (1997). The evolutionary psychology of extrapair sex: the role of fluctuating asymmetry. *Evolution and Human Behavior*, **18**, 69–88.

Gangestad, S.W., Thornhill, R, and Yeo, R.A. (1994). Facial attractiveness, developmental stability, and fluctuating asymmetry. *Ethology and Sociobiology*, **15**, 73–85.

Givens, D.B. (1978). The nonverbal basis of attraction: Flirtation, courtship, and seduction. *Psychiatry*, **41**, 346–359.

Gralewski, L., Campbell, N., Morrison, E., and Penton-Voak, I. (2006). Analysis of facial dynamics using a tensor framework. *Journal of Multimedia*, **6**, 10–21.

Gross, M.R. (1996). Alternative reproductive strategies and tactics: Diversity within sexes. *Trends in Ecology and Evolution*, **11**, 92–98.

Havlicek, J. and Roberts, S.C. (2009). MHC-correlated mate choice in humans: A review. *Psychoneuroendocrinology*, **34**, 497–512.

Hill, K. and Hurtado, A.M. (1996). *Ache Life History: The Ecology and Demography of a Foraging People*. New York: Aldine de Gruyter, Hawthorne.

Hill, H. and Johnston, A. (2001). Categorizing sex and identity from the biological motion of faces. *Current Biology*, **11**, 880–85.

Hillgarth, N. and Wingfield, J.C. (1997). Testosterone and Immunosuppression in vertebrates: implications for parasite mediated sexual selection. In NE Beckage (ed.) *Parasites and Pathogens*, pp. 143–155. New York: Chapman and Hall.

Hönekopp, J. (2006). Once more: is beauty in the eye of the beholder? Relative contributions of private and shared taste to judgments of facial attractiveness. *Journal of Experimental Psychology: Human Perception and Performance*, **32**, 199–209.

Hosoda, M., Stone-Romero, E.F., and Coats, G. (2003). The effects of physical attractiveness on job-related outcomes: A meta-analysis of experimental studies. *Personnel Psychology*, **56**, 431–62.

Jennions, M.D. and Petrie, M. (2000). Why do females mate multiply? A review of the genetic benefits. *Biological Reviews*, **75**, 21–64.

Johnson, V.S. and Franklin, M. (1993). Is beauty in the eye of the beholder? *Ethology and Sociobiology*, **14**, 183–99.

Johnston, V.S., Hagel, R., Franklin, M., Fink, B., and Grammer, K. (2001). Male facial attractiveness: evidence for hormone-mediated adaptive design. *Evolution and Human Behavior*, **22**, 251–67.

Jokela, M. (2009). Physical attractiveness and reproductive success in humans: evidence from the late 20th century United States. *Evolution and Human Behavior*, **30**, 342–350.

Jones, D. and Hill, K. (1993). Criteria of facial attractiveness in five populations. *Human Nature*, **4**, 271–98.

Jones, B.C., DeBruine, L.M., Little, A.C., and Feinberg, D.R. (2006). Integrating gaze direction and expression in preferences for attractive faces. *Psychological Science*, **17**, 588–591.

Jones, B.C., DeBruine, L.M., Little, A.C., Burriss, R.P., and Feinberg, D.R. (2007). Social transmission of face preferences among humans. *Proceedings of the Royal Society of London B*, **274**, 899–903.

Kampe, K.K.W, Frith, C.D., Dolan, R.J., and Frith, U. (2001). Reward value of attractiveness and gaze: Making eye contact enhances the appeal of a pleasing face, irrespective of gender. *Nature*, **413**, 589–89.

Knight, B. and Johnston, A. (1997). The role of movement in face recognition. *Visual Cognition*, **4**, 264–73.

Koehler, N., Simmons, L.W., Rhodes, G., and Peters, M. (2004). The relationship between sexual dimorphism in human faces and fluctuating asymmetry. *Proceedings of the Royal Society of London B*, **271**, S233–S236.

Lander, K., Christie, F., and Bruce, V. (1999). The role of movement in the recognition of famous faces. *Memory Cognition*, **27**, 974–85.

Lander, K. (2008). Relating visual and vocal attractiveness for moving and static faces. *Animal Behaviour*, **75**, 817–822.

Langlois, J.H. and Roggman, L.A. (1990). Attractiveness faces are only average. *Psychological Science*, **1**, 115–21.

Langlois, J.H., Roggman, L.A., Casey, R J, Ritter, J.M., Riser-Danner, L.A., and Jenkins, V.Y. (1987). Infant preferences for attractive faces: Rudiments of a stereotype? *Developmental Psychology*, **23**, 363–369.

Langlois, J.H., Roggman, L.A., and Rieser-Danner, L.A. (1990). Infants' differential social responses to attractive and unattractive faces. *Developmental Psychology*, **26**, 153–159.

Langlois, J.H., Kalakanis, L, Rubenstein, A.J., Larson, A., Hallam, M., and Smoot, M. (2000). Maxims or myths of beauty? A meta-analytic and theoretical review. *Psychological Bulletin*, **126**, 390–423.

Law Smith, M.J., Perrett, D.I., Jones, B.C., *et al.* (2005). Facial appearance is a cue to oestrogen levels in women. *Proceedings of the Royal Society of London B*, **273**, 135–40.

Lie, H.C., Rhodes, G., and Simmons, L.W. (2008). Genetic diversity revealed in human faces. *Evolution*, **62**, 2473–2486.

Little, A.C. and Jones, B.C. (2003). Evidence against perceptual bias views for symmetry preferences in human faces. *Proceedings of the Royal Society of London B*, **270**, 1759–1763.

Little, A.C. and Jones, B.C. (2006). Attraction independent of detection suggests special mechanisms for symmetry preferences in human face perception. *Proceedings of the Royal Society B*, **273**, 3093–3099.

Little, A.C., Burt, D.M., Penton-Voak, I., and Perrett, D.I. (2001). Self perceived attractiveness influences human female preferences for sexual dimorphism and symmetry in male faces. *Proceedings of the Royal Society of London B*, **268**, 1–6.

Little, A.C., Jones, B.C., Penton-Voak, I.S., Burt, D.M., and Perrett, D.I. (2002). Partnership status and the temporal context of relationships influence human female preferences sexual dimorphism in male face shape. *Proceedings of the Royal Society of London B*, **269**, 1095–100.

Little, A.C., Penton-Voak, I.S., Burt, D.M., and Perrett, D.I. (2003). Investigating an imprinting-like phenomenon in humans Partners and opposite-sex parents have similar hair and eye colour. *Evolution and Human Behavior*, **24**, 43–51.

Little, A.C., DeBruine, L.M., and Jones, B.C. (2005). Sex-contingent face aftereffects suggest distinct neural populations code male and female faces. *Proceedings of the Royal Society of London B*, **272**, 2283–2287.

Little, A.C., Jones, B.C., Burt, D.M., and Perrett, D.I. (2007a). Preferences for symmetry in faces change across the menstrual cycle. *Biological Psychology*, **76**, 209–16.

Little, A.C., Apicella, C.L., and Marlowe, F.W. (2007b). Preferences for symmetry in human faces in two cultures: data from the UK and the Hadza, an isolated group of hunter-gatherers. *Proceedings of the Royal Society B*, **274**, 3113–3117.

Little, A.C., Jones, B.C., and DeBruine, L.M. (2008). Preferences for variation in masculinity in real male faces change across the menstrual cycle: Women prefer more masculine faces when they are more fertile. *Personality and Individual Differences*, **45**, 478–482.

Locher, P., Unger, R., Sociedade, P., and Wahl, J. (1993). At first glance: Accessibility of the physical attractiveness stereotype. *Sex Roles*, **28**, 729–743.

Lundqvist, D., Flykt, A., and Öhman, A. (1998). *The Karolinska Directed Emotional Faces – KDEF.* CD ROM from Department of Clinical Neuroscience, Psychology section, Karolinska Institutet, ISBN 91-630-7164-9.

Mason, M.F., Tatkow, E.P., and Macrae, C.N. (2005). The look of love: Gaze shifts and person perception. *Psychological Science*, **16**, 236–39.

Marlowe, C. (1604). *The tragical history of Dr Faustus.* London: Valentine Simmes.

Maynard Smith, J. (1956). Fertility, mating behaviour and sexual selection in Drosophila subobscura. *Journal of Genetics*, **54**, 261–279.

McCoun, R.J. (1990). The emergence of extralegal bias during jury deliberation. *Criminal Justice and Behavior*, **17**, 303–14.

Mealey, L., Bridgstock, R., and Townsend, G.C. (1999). Symmetry and perceived facial attractiveness: A monozygotic co-twin comparison. *Journal of Personality and Social Psychology*, **76**, 151–58.

Merow, W. and Broadbent, B. (1990). Cepahlometrics. In DH Enlow (ed.) *Facial Growth*, 3rd edn, pp. 346–395. Philadelphia, PA: Saunders.

Miller, G. (2000). *The mating mind: How sexual choice shaped the evolution of human nature,* London: Heineman.

Mishra, S., Clark, A.P., and Daly, M. (2007). One woman's behavior affects the attractiveness of others. *Evolution and Human Behavior*, **28**, 145–49.

Møller, A.P. (1999). Asymmetry as a predictor of growth, fecundity and survival. *Ecology Letters*, **2**, 149–56.

Møller, A.P. and Swaddle, J.P. (1997). *Asymmetry, developmental stability and evolution*. Oxford, Oxford University Press.

Morrison, E.R., Gralewski, L., Campbell, N., and Penton-Voak, I.S. (2007). Facial movement varies by sex and is related to attractiveness. *Evolution and Human Behaviour*, **28**, 186–92.

Morrison, E.R., Clark, A.P., Gralewski, L., Campbell, N., and Penton-Voak, I.S. (2010). Menstrual cycle increases preference for proceptive but not masculine facial movement. *Archives of Sexual Behaviour*, **39**, 1297–1304.

Neave, N., Laing, S., Fink, B., and Manning, J.T. (2003). Second to fourth digit ratio, testosterone and perceived male dominance. *Proceedings of the Royal Society of London B*, **270**, 2167–2172.

O'Toole, A.J., Deffenbacher, K.A.,Valentin, D., Mc-Kee, K., Huff, D., and Abdi, H. (1998). The perception of face gender: the role of stimulus structure in recognition and classification. *Memory and Cognition*, **26**, 146–60.

Otta, E., Abrosio, F.F.E, and Hoshino, R.L. (1996). Reading a smiling face: Messages conveyed by various forms of smiling. *Perceptual and Motor Skills*, **82**, 1111–21.

Pawlowski, B. and Dunbar, R.I.M. (1999). Impact of market value on human mate choice decisions. *Proceedings of the Royal Society of London B*, **266**, 281–85.

Penton-Voak, I.S. and Chang, H. (2008). Attractiveness judgments of individuals vary across emotional expression and movement conditions. *Journal of Cultural and Evolutionary Psychology*, **6**, 89–100.

Penton-Voak, I.S. and Chen, J.Y. (2004). High salivary testosterone is linked to masculine male facial appearance in humans. *Evolution and Human Behavior*, **25** 229–41.

Penton-Voak, I.S. and Perrett, D.I. (2000). Female preference for male faces changes cyclically: further evidence. *Evolution and Human Behavior*, **21**, 39–48.

Penton-Voak, I.S. and Perrett, D.I. (2001). Male facial attractiveness: perceived personality and shifting female preferences for male traits across the menstrual cycle. *Advances in the Study of Behavior*, **30**, 219–260.

Penton-Voak, I.S., Perrett, D.I., Castles, D.L., *et al.* (1999). Menstrual cycle alters face preference. *Nature*, **399**, 741–42.

Penton-Voak, I.S., Jones, B.C., Little, A.C., *et al.* (2001). Symmetry, sexual dimorphism in facial proportions and male facial attractiveness. *Proceedings of the Royal Society of London B*, **268**, 1617–23.

Penton-Voak, I.S., Little, A.C., Jones, B.C., Burt, D.M., Tiddeman, B.P., and Perrett, D.I. (2003). Female condition influences preferences for sexual dimorphism in faces of male humans (Homo sapiens). *Journal of Comparative Psychology*, **117**, 264–71.

Penton-Voak, I.S., Jacobson, A., and Trivers, R. (2004). Populational differences in attractiveness judgements of male and female faces: Comparing British and Jamaican samples. *Evolution and Human Behavior*, **6**, 355–70.

Penton-Voak, I.S., Pound, N., Little, A.C., and Perrett, D.I. (2006). Personality judgments from natural and composite facial images: More evidence for a "kernel of truth" in social perception. *Social Cognition*, **24**, 607–40.

Perrett, D.I., May, K.A., and Yoshikawa, S. (1994). Facial shape and judgements of female attractiveness. *Nature*, **368**, 239–42.

Perrett, D.I., Lee, K.J., Penton-Voak, I.S., *et al.* (1998). Effects of sexual dimorphism on facial attractiveness. *Nature*, **394**, 884–87.

Perrett, D.I., Burt, D.M., Penton-Voak, I.S., Lee, K.J., Rowland, D.A., and Edwards R. (1999). Symmetry and human facial attractiveness. *Evolution and Human Behaviour*, **20**, 295–307.

Perrett, D.I., Penton-Voak, I.S., Little, A.C., *et al.* (2002). Facial attractiveness judgements reflect learning of parental age characteristics. *Proceedings of the Royal Society Biological Sciences B*, **269**, 873–880.

Pike, G.E., Kemp, R.I., Towell, N.A., and Phillips, K.C. (1997). *Recognizing moving faces: the relative contribution of motion and perspective view information. Visual Cognition*, **4**, 409–37.

Polak, M. (2003). *Developmental instability: Causes and consequences.* New York: Oxford University Press.

Pound, N., Penton-Voak, I.S., and Surridge, A.K. (2009). Testosterone responses to competition in men are related to facial masculinity. *Proceedings of the Royal Society Biological Sciences B*, **276**, 153–59.

Raines, R.S., Hechtman, S.B., and Roesnthal, R. (1990a). Nonverbal behaviour and gender as determinants of physical attractiveness. *Journal of Nonverbal Behaviour*, **14**, 253–67.

Raines, R.S., Hechtman, S.B., and Roesnthal, R. (1990b). Physical attractiveness of face and voice: effects of positivity, dominance, and sex. *Journal of Applied Social Psychology*, **20**, 1558–78.

Rhodes, G. (2006). The evolutionary psychology of facial beauty. *Annual Review of Psychology*, **57**, 199–226.

Rhodes, G. and Tremewan, T. (1996). Averageness, exaggeration, and facial attractiveness. *Psychological Science*, **7**, 105–10.

Rhodes, G., Sumich, A., and Byatt, G. (1999). Are average facial configurations attractive only because of their symmetry? *Psychological Science*, **10**, 53–59.

Rhodes, G., Chang, J., Zebrowitz, L.A., and Simmons, L.W. (2003a). Does sexual dimorphism in human faces signal health? *Proceedings of the Royal Society of London B*, **270**, S93–S95.

Rhodes, G., Jeffery, L., Watson, T.L., Clifford, C.W.G., and Nakayama, K. (2003b). Fitting the mind to the world: Face adaptation and attractiveness aftereffects. *Psychological Science*, **14**, 558–566.

Rhodes, G., Simmons, L.W., and Peters, M. (2005a). Attractiveness and sexual behaviour: Does attractiveness enhance mating success? *Evolution and Human Behavior*, **26**, 186–201.

Rhodes, G., Peters, M., Lee, K., Morrone, M.C., and Burr, D. (2005b). Higher-level mechanisms detect facial symmetry. *Proceedings of the Royal Society B*, **272**, 1379–1384.

Rhodes, G., Peters, M., and Ewing, L.A. (2007). Specialised higher-level mechanisms for facial-symmetry perception: Evidence from orientation-tuning functions. *Perception*, **36**, 1804–1812.

Riggio, R.E., Widaman, K.F., Tucker, J.S., and Salinas, C. (1991). Beauty is more than skin deep: components of attractiveness. *Basic Applied Social Psychology*, **12**, 423–39.

Roberts, S.C., Little, A.C., Gosling, L.M., *et al.* (2005). MHC-heterozygosity and human facial attractiveness. *Evolution And Human Behavior*, **26**, 213–226.

Roberts, S.C., Saxton, T.K., Murray, A.K., Burriss, R.P., Rowland, H.M., and Little, A.C. (2009). Static and dynamic facial images cue similar attractiveness judgements. *Ethology*, **115**, 588–595.

Roney, J.R., Hanson, K.N., Durante, K.M., and Maestripieri, D. (2006). Reading men's faces: women's mate attractiveness judgments track men's testosterone and interest in infants. *Proceedings of the Royal Society B*, **273**, 2169–75.

Roumen, F.J.M.E., Doesburg, W.H., and Rolland, R. (1982). Hormonal patterns in infertile women with a deficient postcoital test. *Fertility and Sterility*, **38**, 24–47.

Rowland, D.A. and Perrett, D.I. (1995). Manipulating facial appearance through shape and color. *IEEE Computer Graphics and Applications*, **15**, 70–76.

Rubenstein, A.J. (2005). Variation in perceived attractiveness. *Psychological Science*, **16**, 759–62.

Scheib, J.E., Gangestad, S, and Thornhill, R. (1999). Facial attractiveness, symmetry and cues of good genes. *Proceedings of the Royal Society B*, **266**, 1913–17.

Schulman, G.I. and Hoskins, M. (1986). Perceiving the male versus the female face. *Psychology of Women Quarterly*, **10**, 141–53.

Scott, I., Swami, V., Josephson, S., and Penton-Voak, I.S. (2008). Context-dependent preferences for facial dimorphism in a rural Malaysian population. *Evolution and Human Behavior*, **4**, 289–96.

Slater, A., Schulenburg, C., Brown, E., *et al.* (1998). Newborn infants prefer attractive faces. *Infant Behavior and Development*, **21**, 345–54.

Symons, D. (1979). *The evolution of human sexuality.* Oxford: Oxford University Press.

Thornhill, R. and Gangestad, S.W. (1993). Human facial beauty: Averageness, symmetry, and parasite resistance. *Human Nature*, **4**, 237–69.

Thornhill, R., Gangestad, S.W., and Comer, R. (1995). Human female orgasm and mate fluctuating asymmetry. *Animal Behaviour*, **50**, 1601–15.

Thornhill, R., Gangestad, S.W., Miller, R., Scheyd, G., McCollough, J.K., and Franklin, M. (2003). Major histocompatibility complex genes, symmetry, and body scent attractiveness in men and women. *Behavioral Ecology*, **14**, 668–678.

Thornton, I.M. and Kourtzi, Z. (2002). A matching advantage for dynamic faces. *Perception*, **31**, 113–32.

Valentine, T., Darling, S., and Donnelly, M. (2004). Why are average face attractive? The effect of view of averageness on the attractiveness of female faces. *Psychonomic Bulletin Review*, **11**, 484–87.

Walster, E., Aronson, V., Abrahams, D., and Rottmann, L. (1966). Importance of physical attractiveness in dating behaviour. *Journal of Personality and Social Psychology*, **4**, 508–16.

Weeden, J. and Sabini, J. (2005). Physical attractiveness and health in western societies: A review. *Psychological Bulletin*, **131**, 635–653.

Weeden, J. and Sabini, J. (2007). Subjective and objective measures of attractiveness and their relation to sexual behavior and sexual attitudes in university students. *Archives of Sexual Behavior*, **36**, 79–88.

Willis, J. and Todorov, A. (2006). First impressions: Making up your mind after a 100-ms exposure to a face. *Psychological Science*, **17**, 592–598.

Zebrowitz, L.A. and Rhodes, G. (2004). Sensitivity to "bad genes" and the anomalous face overgeneralization effect: Cue validity, cue utilization, and accuracy in judging intelligence and health. *Journal of Nonverbal Behavior*, **28**, 167–185.

Part IV

Comparative and Developmental Perspectives

Chapter 34

Neural Encoding Principles in Face Perception Revealed Using Non-Primate Models

Keith M. Kendrick and Jianfeng Feng

Introduction

One of the long held assumptions in the field of face recognition research, namely that specialized processing of face cues was a facet of primate social evolution, was dispelled when we first published electrophysiological findings from sheep inferotemporal cortex reporting the presence of populations of face-sensitive neurons broadly similar to those found in monkeys (Kendrick and Baldwin, 1987). From our subsequent detailed behavioral, neuroanatomical mapping, and further electrophysiological studies in sheep (Tate et al., 2006) it has become clear that specialized face recognition systems in the brain are likely to have evolved more as a general facet of mammalian social evolution and are probably present in a number or ungulate and other mammalian species with complex social systems and well-developed visual acuity. As such, neurophysiological and behavioral studies on sheep face recognition can be considered broadly relevant as a model for helping to understand similar, although undoubtedly more complex, processes in humans.

The ability to recognize individual conspecifics from their facial features is not restricted to mammalian species with good visual acuity. It has also been shown in some bird species, such as budgerigars (Brown and Dooling, 1992), and even in some invertebrate ones, such as wasps (Tibbetts, 2002) and crayfish (Van der Velden et al., 2008). Both pigeons (Jitsumori and Yoshihara, 1997; Loidolt et al., 2003) and bees (Dyer et al., 2005) have also been shown to be able to discriminate between human faces or even human facial expressions. However, in these species their ability to discriminate between faces is probably primarily on the basis of simple feature encoding, as for other visual objects, and as yet there is no convincing evidence for the type of configural encoding of faces found in primates and sheep.

Face recognition in sheep

The first behavioral evidence for face recognition in sheep came from observations that maternal sheep found it difficult to recognize their lambs when the latter had their heads artificially colored (Alexander and Shillito-Walser, 1977). Subsequently, using various face discrimination paradigms it has been possible to show that sheep have a highly developed expertise. This was shown initially in a simple two-choice maze where sheep could immediately discriminate between face pictures of individuals with differential attraction (socially familiar vs. unfamiliar sheep or sheep vs. humans) in order to gain access to the individual whose face they had seen (Kendrick et al., 1995, 1996). Then, using food to reward accurate discrimination between individuals of similar attraction, it was shown both in a two choice maze, or with an operant response paradigm (with the sheep indicating choice by pressing one of two panels with its nose), that animals could recognize up to at least 25 pairs of sheep faces simultaneously (Kendrick et al., 2001a) and 4 to 5 pairs of human faces (Peirce et al., 2001). As with humans, they make use of configural cues for recognizing faces, exhibiting both classical inversion effects with both sheep and human faces (Kendrick et al., 1996; Peirce et al., 2001) and the ability to use internal face features for recognition of familiar sheep (Peirce et al., 2000), although not humans (Peirce et al., 2001). Recognition of familiar sheep faces with scrambled internal features is also impaired (Peirce et al., 2001).

Learning to recognize new faces in an experimental context tends to take a minimum of a least 30 to 40 trials for sheep faces, although learning new associations with faces socially familiar individuals and food rewards can take only 10 to 20 trials (Kendrick et al., 1996). With human faces novel individuals require on average about 75 trials and learning new reward associations with familiar faces 20 to 35 trials (Peirce et al., 2001).

Behavioral experiments have also revealed a right hemisphere advantage for face recognition in sheep with the half of the face appearing in the left visual field (from which information is processed by the right brain hemisphere) being utilized most for recognition of familiar sheep faces even under free-viewing circumstances (Peirce et al., 2000).

In terms of visual acuity for face recognition, computer morphing approaches have shown that sheep are able to discriminate between two sheep faces that are only 5% to 10% different from one another (Tate et al., 2006). They are also still able to discriminate above chance between faces that are one-third of normal size although accuracy is significantly reduced (full size $87.6\pm1.3\%$ correct vs. one-third size $65.0\pm2.5\%$ correct, paired t-test $t^9=6.46$, P<0.001). This may also explain why maternal ewes can take several weeks to recognize the faces of their lambs (Kendrick et al., 1996).

Less has been done to establish developmental aspects of face recognition expertise in sheep although lambs are unable to perform even the simplest discrimination of their mother's face from that of another sheep for at least 2 to 4 weeks after they are born (Kendrick, 1994). We have also had very little success in training sheep in face recognition tasks involving socially unfamiliar animals until they are at least 4 to 6 months of age. It seems likely therefore that it takes time and experience for a fully mature face recognition system to develop in this species, as it does in humans.

Face attraction and face emotion recognition in sheep

When sheep are socially isolated they show reduced behavioral and autonomic signs of psychological stress when they are able to view face pictures of individuals of their own breed (da Costa et al., 2004). They also show clear preferences for the faces of socially familiar animals (Kendrick et al., 1995, 1996). Females show marked changes in their relative attraction towards male and female faces as a function of their estrus cycle (Kendrick et al., 1995) and when they are sexually receptive will exhibit clear preferences for the faces of specific individual males (Fabre-Nys et al., 1997). Cross-fostering studies in both sheep and goats have also found that development of facial preference for one species over the other is determined by the species of the mother who rears them and with whom they have bonded (Kendrick et al., 1998, 2001b).

Sheep have been found to be able to discriminate accurately between both calm and stressed/anxious sheep faces and between human faces that are either smiling or angry. Here it was found that the animals preferred to chose calm or smiling versions of the same sheep and human faces respectively compared with stressed or angry ones (Elliker, 2006; Kendrick, 2008; Tate et al., 2006). This preference for calm as opposed to stressed/anxious faces even takes precedence over the preference for the faces of socially familiar compared to socially unfamiliar individuals (Tate et al., 2006).

In an operant discrimination experiment on five sheep we systematically varied the appearance of calm and stressed/anxious versions of the same sheep face to try and identify the main features the animals were relying on to discriminate between them. The single most important feature was the positioning of the ears (they tend to be lowered and pointing backwards when the animal is stressed); however, some other internal face features such as the eyes and nose may also play some role (Figure 34.1).

Neural substrates of face recognition in sheep

A number of studies have been carried out to map the neuroanatomical substrates involved in face recognition in sheep using quantification of expression changes in gene markers of neural activation (c-*fos* and *zif/268*). These have shown consistent activation in the medial and posterior inferior and superior temporal cortices, medial prefrontal and cingulate cortices and basolateral and basomedial amygdala and hippocampus during successful discrimination between or exposure to faces (Broad et al., 2000; da Costa et al., 2004; Ohkura et al., 1997). Face inversion also

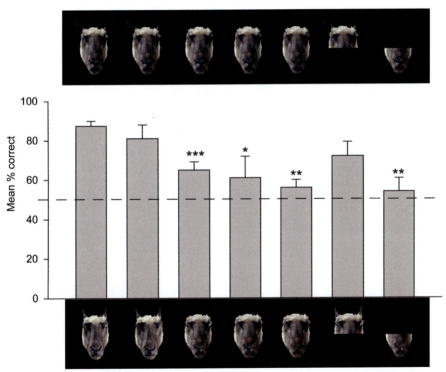

Fig. 34.1 Mean±sem correct choice of a calm (bottom) vs. stressed/anxious (top) version of the same sheep's face by five sheep following various manipulations of the face images (the first pair of images on the left are the control unaltered pictures). To avoid any possibility of the animals using subtle differences in face appearance to perform this discrimination, rather than emotion cues, the same version of the calm face was used in each case with alterations in ears, eyes, nose and mouth cause by stress/anxiety being substituted on calm face picture. ***P<0.001, **P<0.01, *P<0.05 compared with the unaltered pictures (left).

significantly reduces activation in the right medial inferior temporal cortex and bilaterally in the amygdala and hippocampus. In the temporal (see Figure 34.2) and frontal cortices and the amygdala activation is stronger in the right than in the left hemisphere (Broad et al., 2000; da Costa et al., 2004). When faces with a particularly strong attraction are shown (estrus females viewing males or socially isolated animals viewing a familiar breed of sheep) then dopamine reward centers such as the nucleus accumbens are also activated (da Costa et al., 2004; Ohkura et al., 1997).

The area of temporal cortex responding to face stimuli is quite large (at least 1cm^3). At this stage it is not clear whether sheep have a similar patch arrangement of face-sensitive regions that have been found in both monkeys and humans (see Freiwald and Tsao, 2009). However, it can been seen from dark field autoradiograms of c-*fos* and *zif/268* mRNA expression changes in Figure 34.2 that there are distinct clumps of activation hotspots in superior and inferior temporal cortex of sheep when they view faces which do not seem to occur when a non-face image, such as an inverted triangle is viewed.

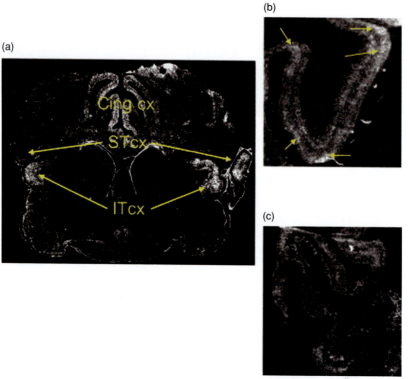

Fig. 34.2 Dark-field coronal section autoradiograms showing in (a) increased c-fos mRNA expression (white areas) in the left and right superior (STcx), inferior temporal (ITcx) and medial cingulated (Cing cx) cortices of sheep after discriminating between two faces. Expression levels in the temporal cortex are much stronger in the right hemisphere and there is some suggestion of patches.
(b) A higher magnification autoradiogram showing increased zif/268 mRNA expression in the right temporal cortex following exposure to a single sheep face stimulus in contrast to (c) which shows lower expression levels after exposure to a non-face stimulus (a white inverted triangle on a black background). Arrows in (b) indicate the presence of clusters of stronger expression which may be indicative of face-responsive patches.

It is clearly difficult to assess the extent to which the same brain regions that become activated during actual conscious perception of faces are also activated when a sheep forms a "mental" image of them, as has been shown in humans (O'Craven and Kanwisher, 2000). However, we have shown that similar c-*fos* expression changes occur in the region of temporal cortex that responds to faces when maternal ewes hear recordings of the bleats of their absent lambs but not scrambled sequences of these same bleats. The activation levels seen are very similar to those in response to an actual face picture of the lamb (Kendrick et al., 2001c). We have no evidence for vocalization-specific responses from neurons in this region so this is possibly the result of the animals forming a visual mental image of their lamb's face. This conclusion is further supported by some of the electrophysiological recording findings discussed in a later section.

While we have not investigated changes in molecular markers of neural plasticity during face learning paradigms per se we have found significant increases in mRNA expression of brain-derived nerve growth factor (BDNF) in the medial inferior temporal cortex, medial prefrontal cortex, hippocampus and basolateral amygdala of maternal sheep during the period when they learn to recognize their lambs There are also changes in mRNA expression of its receptor, *trk-B*, in the medial inferior temporal cortex at this time (Broad et al., 2002).

Face-specific evoked potentials?

As in humans (Truett et al., 1999) and monkeys (see Freiwald and Tsao, 2009) we have found some evidence for face-sensitive components of the visual evoked potential recorded by multiple (n = 64) electrodes in either right of left inferotemporal cortex. Figure 34.3 shows averaged evoked potentials following exposure to pairs of faces, inverted faces or non-face objects in a discrimination task. The primary components of the evoked potential are a P120 and a N300 and the P120 is largest for faces in both animals we have investigated with the profiles for inverted faces and non-face objects looking very similar. In both cases the animals were not able to do better than chance in discriminating between the inverted faces whereas performance was more than 80% correct for normal upright views of the same faces. With the non-face object pairs used the animals also discriminated between them with more than 80% correct. However, we have not investigated this extensively enough, or with single faces, as opposed to face-pair stimuli, to conclude categorically that this P120 component is truly face sensitive.

Characteristics of face-sensitive neurons in temporal and frontal cortices

The first study reporting face-sensitive neurons in the sheep temporal cortex found broadly similar general response properties as had been described in monkeys, namely large receptive fields, short latencies (80–180 ms) and with a similar population size (approximately 7%). Neuronal responses usually did not outlast the period of face presentation and many cells appeared best tuned to frontal views (Kendrick and Baldwin, 1987; Kendrick, 1991). However, an additional observation was that cells responded weakly or not at all to inverted faces. The most important difference with the studies on monkeys was that in the sheep different sub-populations of cells appeared to be categorizing for faces with specific behavioral or emotional significance rather than just faces or face features per se. Cells were either optimally tuned to respond to faces of sheep of the same breed, and maximally to social familiar individuals (sheep prefer to be with members of their own breed and form consortships with specific individuals); animals with horns and how large they were (the presence and size of horns provides information both on gender and social dominance) and a final subpopulation responded to faces of either

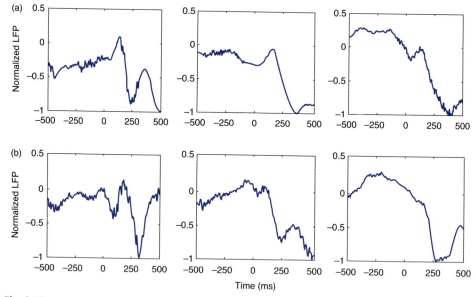

Fig. 34.3 Averaged local field potential recordings from 64 electrode arrays in the right temporal cortex of two sheep (a and b) showing visual evoked potentials during exposure to paired face, inverted face or non-face objects (gloves vs. phones or bucket vs. bin). For both sheep data are from the same face pairs presented normally or inverted and for 40–60 trials). Sheep a: faces 4 vs. 15 and sheep b faces 1721 vs. 1724). The LFPs are presented normalized to allow easier comparison. This was done by subtracting the baseline power during −100 to 0 ms and normalized by the absolute value of maximum negative peak. Upright faces clearly evoke a greater response, particularly in the P120 component.

dogs or humans (the two main classes of individuals sheep normally perceive as being a potential threat) (Kendrick and Baldwin, 1987). Of these categories the cells responding to horns and their size appeared to be relatively insensitive to identity (human faces with horns were just as effective as sheep or goats with horns) although the horns had to be viewed in the context of a face (Kendrick, 1994). There may well therefore be the same kind of norm-based encoding occurring in the temporal cortex of sheep (i.e. in this case a generic face with horns) as has been reported in monkeys (Leopold et al., 2006).

Faces were not the only body component encoded for by cells in the temporal cortex with a similar proportion of cells being found to be sensitive to the standard bipedal human body shape (even with the head region covered) and which did not respond to humans adopting a quadrupedal posture (Kendrick and Baldwin, 1989). In other studies we have also occasionally found cells highly specifically tuned to specific aggressive body movements in sheep such as foot stamping (Peirce and Kendrick, unpublished observations).

Subsequent single-electrode electrophysiological studies in both the medial frontal and temporal cortex regions have shown that cells can often be optimally tuned to the faces of one or two specific familiar sheep and/or humans (Kendrick et al., 2001a; Peirce and Kendrick, 2002). Furthermore, the response latencies of cells are longer the more selectively they are tuned to individual faces, suggesting a degree of hierarchical encoding (Kendrick, 1994; Peirce and Kendrick, 2002).

Face-sensitive cells in both temporal and frontal cortices can either be categorized as view dependent (responding selectively to front or profile views of faces) or view independent (responding equivalently to front and profile views). In the temporal cortex the relative distribution of these responses types is around 50:50 whereas in the frontal cortex it is around 70:30 in favor of the view independent type. Overall the response latencies are faster (approximately 50 ms) for the view-dependent cells compared with view independent ones once again implying a greater level of processing in the latter and potentially a degree of hierarchical encoding as well. Not only are the view dependent cells selective for face view but they are also very sensitive to a wide variety of manipulations of facial features and appearance and particularly by inversion. On the other hand the view independent cells show broadly equivalent responses to these manipulations and therefore appear relatively insensitive to both view and facial feature content (Tate et al., 2006). This further reinforces the possibility that the view independent cells are involved in higher level encoding of faces than are the view dependent ones. Similar view-independent cells responding to different views of specific individuals have also been reported in humans (Quian-Quiroga et al., 2005) and monkeys (Perrett et al., 1991). As in sheep, response latencies are longer for these view-independent cells in monkeys than for view dependent ones (Perrett et al., 1991).

In terms of the effects of learning and experience we have been able to show that the broad categories of differential encoding of faces we first reported (Kendrick and Baldwin, 1987) are not rigid. In subsequent single-cell recording studies where the sheep used had been exposed to the same familiar stockman for several years his face, but not those of other humans, his face was responded to by the majority of cells that encoded faces of socially familiar sheep. There were also a number of cells that responded highly selectively to just his face in the same way as other cells responded highly selectively to the faces of specific, socially familiar sheep (Kendrick et al., 2001a). Indeed, when we compared temporal and frontal cortex single-neuron response profiles across three different groups of sheep that had either had past and current extensive experience of another sheep and this stockman; or only past experience (they had not seen them for a year or more); or no experience of them at all, a number of principles emerged. As would be expected if learning is playing an important role, when the sheep had no experience of these two individuals no cells were found which encoded selectively for their faces and the stockman's face was not responded to by any sheep face selective cells. With the group that had not had experience of the sheep and stockman for a year or more then there were still many cells which responded to both of their faces along with other familiar sheep, whereas there were fewer responding to either of them selectively. This latter finding mirrored behavioral evidence that sheep faces can be remembered for up to 2 years or more, and suggests that forgetting the faces of previously familiar individuals involves a progressive loss of selective encoding for them (Kendrick et al., 2001a).

Generally speaking, neuronal responses to static faces in sheep inferotemporal and frontal cortex do not outlast the period of presentation. However, we have found that when using video sequences showing the eventual appearance of a familiar individual, that cells which normally only respond during the period of static presentation of its face will start to respond to parts of the video sequence which show that the individual is about to appear, and also when it is expected to appear but has been edited out of the film (Kendrick et al., 2001c). Further, and in support of our c-*fos* experiments already mentioned (Kendrick et al., 2001c), we have found evidence for face-sensitive cells in the frontal cortex responding to odors of the same individuals but when face and odor are combined there are no additive effects and very few other cells can be found which respond to odor stimuli alone. Only the view-independent face-sensitive cells showed this response to odor stimulation and the same was the case for the cells described above responding to the video sequences. It seems possible therefore that face-sensitive cells can respond to mental images of faces in sheep and that it is view-independent type cells which are of most importance in this context. Indeed, it is interesting that in humans view-independent face-sensitive cells in the medial temporal lobe can sometimes also respond to letters spelling an individual's name (Quian-Quiroga et al., 2005). Possibly in such cases the name of a familiar person might evoke a transient mental image of their face.

Face processing in left and right temporal cortex

Despite the fact that sheep, like humans, show a left visual field advantage (right brain hemisphere dominance) for recognizing faces (Peirce et al., 2000), and that molecular markers of neural activation are more strongly expressed in the right temporal cortex than in the left after the animal is exposed to face stimuli (Broad et al., 2000; da Costa et al., 2004; see Figure 34.2), we have so far been unable to establish any major significant difference in the tuning of cells to specific faces or face categories in the left and right temporal cortices (Kendrick, 2006; Kendrick and Baldwin, 1987; Peirce and Kendrick, 2002). A similar absence of inter-hemispheric differences in encoding by face sensitive cells has also been reported in monkeys (Perrett et al., 1988). There was a trend however for view-dependent cells in the right hemisphere to show more profound reductions in responses to face images where the left visual field half of the face (right half) was blocked out, and no effect whatsoever when the right visual side (left half) was blocked out (Tate et al., 2006).

There are however significant latency differences in the responses of higher order face-sensitive cells (those responding to a category of face or to faces of specific individuals) but not for those responding generically to both face and non-face stimuli (Peirce and Kendrick, 2002). With these higher-order, face-sensitive cells our single-electrode recordings have found responses in the left temporal cortex are, on average, about 50 to 100 ms slower than in the right. Indeed about 30% of cells in the left hemisphere had response latencies of greater than 300 ms compared with only about 5% on the right and this is likely beyond the time required to recognize the faces and may instead reflect memory or emotion processing aspects of face perception (Peirce and Kendrick, 2002).

There are always potential sampling error considerations that need to be taken into account with single recording electrode-based studies and so more recently we have confirmed these hemispheric latency differences in the temporal cortex using 64-electrode arrays capable of recording from up to around 250 single cells simultaneously. These have shown that overall response latencies in the left hemisphere are on average some 40 to 80 ms slower than those on the right for both cells showing excitatory or inhibitory responses when face discrimination on the basis of identity is required. However, when the basis for the discrimination is the respective emotional cues exhibited on the faces this latency difference disappears (Tate et al., 2006).

More recently we have applied partial Granger causality (Ladroue et al., 2009) to try to establish whether there are causal relationships between processing in the left and right temporal cortex and their directionality. Preliminary evidence using time-series data from local field potentials recorded from up to 60 different electrodes in each hemisphere has shown that following successful learning of a discrimination between two sheep faces to obtain a food reward there is an increased in the number of significant causal relations between electrodes in the right but not the left temporal cortex. Whereas before learning there are more frequent causal influences from the left to the right hemisphere after learning the right hemisphere becomes more dominant in this respect (Figure 34.4). This suggests that as faces become familiar, and are categorized more at an individual level, then the delayed response times seen in the left hemisphere may be as the result of the left temporal cortex receiving inputs via face processing networks on the right.

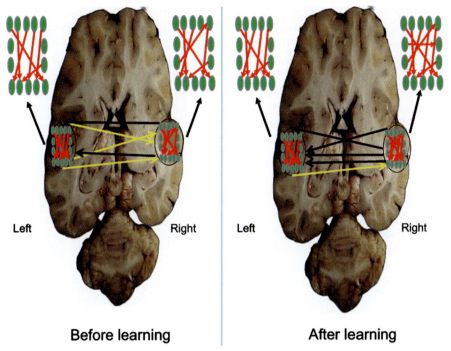

Before learning | After learning

Fig. 34.4 Significant causal connections within and between left and right temporal cortex of a sheep using partial Granger causality on local field potential data (Ladroue et al., 2009). The figure shows causal connectivity between 14 electrodes in each hemisphere and illustrates that the number increases within the right, but not the left hemisphere immediately successful (greater than 80% correct) discrimination learning of a face pair has been achieved (data are from 20 trials when the animal only achieved 70% correct—before learning, and the subsequent 20 trials when it achieved 95% correct—after learning). There is also a shift from more causal connection from left to right (yellow arrows) before learning to more from right to left (black arrows) after it. These changes were maintained in subsequent trials after learning had been established and were present when causality was calculated for all 60 electrodes used. Horizontal brain section adapted from Peters and Jaspers-Fayer (2002).

Sparse and population-based encoding principles

The face recognition system brings into sharp focus the ongoing debate as to whether sparse or population based codes or both are operating in the various cortical and subcortical networks involved. Only with the development of techniques where activities of multiple individual neurons can be recorded has it been possible to effectively address these different possibilities. In broad agreement with both monkey and human-based studies our single neuron recordings from repeated single-electrode penetrations in sheep temporal and frontal cortices have revealed strong support for sparse encoding (encoding of different faces being supported by a relatively small number of highly tuned and spatially distinct neurons) strategies being utilized by face-processing networks, with clear examples of hierarchical encoding and high level identity tuning of specific faces by very small numbers of cells rather than, for example, by many cells responding to more simple generic aspects of visual cues associated with faces. There also appears to be a degree of spatial clustering occurring, with cells with similar tuning to face categories or individuals often being encountered adjacent to one other on the same electrode track and distinct hotspots for specific face pairs being seen in multiarray recordings in the temporal cortex (Figure 34.5).

However, our multiarray recording experiments also provide compelling evidence that population-based, or "dense" encoding (where encoding is supported by a large network of less specifically tuned neurons such that different faces can be represented by large-scale overlapping populations) is occurring and it is clear that such population codes can hugely increase the representational capacity of neural networks (Rolls et al., 1997) as well as factors such as stimulus generalization. Activity profiles across recording arrays in the temporal cortex reveal distinct spatially discrete hot spots but also overlapping distributions with different face pairs evoking altered firing of a large proportion of neurons. Findings to date have shown that the array difference (an estimate of the reliability of the representation of a particular face stimulus across an array of neurons) variability in the population firing patterns when repeating stimuli is smallest with simple non-face objects and largest where different face identities are presented. The same animal face exhibiting different emotions (calm vs. stressed) is intermediate (Tate et al., 2006). Familiar/learned faces also tend to evoke changes in activity of fewer neurons than unfamiliar ones with the main difference being that fewer cells with excitatory responses are encountered (Tate et al., 2006). There seems therefore to be evidence for sparsening of population encoding as a face becomes familiar coupled with a greater degree of inhibitory activity in the network.

Overall therefore there appears to be both sparse and population-based representation of faces in sheep temporal cortex as in monkeys and humans. In monkey temporal cortex, for example, evidence for population based encoding in face patches has also been found (see Freiwald and Tsao, 2009). A combination of sparse and distributed representations offers a number of theoretical advantages. The most obvious of these is a reduction in the amount of overlap between representations, thereby limiting interference between stored memories and allowing greater ease in decoding carried out by downstream projection regions (Perez-Orive et al., 2002). Indeed, our single neuron studies have shown that as faces are forgotten their sparse representation weakens and more generic encoding increases. Unsurprisingly, we have seen that performance in discriminating faces becomes progressively weaker when they are not viewed for a long time (Kendrick et al., 2001a).

Theta-nested gamma oscillations and encoding

An immediate question following on from discussions of population encoding for faces in temporal cortex is how such population based responses are coordinated across widespread cortical networks which may extend for several millimeters or more. Oscillatory rhythms present one mechanism for this and we have found not only significant theta (4–8Hz) and gamma (30–70Hz) activity in local field potential recordings but also evidence that these two frequencies are coupled (Kendrick et al., 2009; theta phase and gamma amplitude) as has been reported in human neocortex (Canolty et al., 2006). Theta and gamma activities have been associated with various different aspects of cognitive functioning (Buzsaki et al., 2006) and with integration of visual feature processing (Csibra et al., 2000; Fries et al., 2001). Theta activity is remarkably synchronized across arrays of 64 electrodes (approximately 2mm × 2mm) in both left and right temporal cortex and after face pair discriminations are learned the amplitude of theta during stimulus presentation increases significantly as does the theta-gamma ratio, theta and strength of coupling between theta and gamma amplitude and theta phase (Kendrick et al., 2009) (see Figure 34.6). These changes

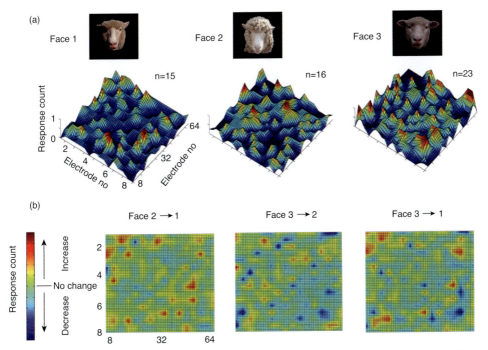

Fig. 34.5 A. Pseudocolor 3D representations of averaged activity changes in 244 single neurons in the right temporal cortex recorded by an 8 x 8 linear array of electrodes (2–4 neurons per electrode) during correct discrimination of three different face pairs (activity hot spots during face stimulus presentations are shown by yellow and red and low or no activity changes by light to dark blue). Data are averaged across 15–23 trials. It can be seen that in all cases there is a wide distribution of activity changes seen across the whole recorded network although with spatially distinct hotspots (red) where neurons which actually change their firing rate significantly in responses to the faces (p <0.05) occur. The pictures at the top show the face that was actually rewarded. B. Difference maps showing that overall differences in the respective patterns of activity changes evoked by the three different face stimuli are relatively small. The pseudocolor grids are arranged into 8 vertical columns with the first column being electrodes 1–8, the second 9–16, the third 17–24 etc.

can occur in a matter of a few minutes as a learning criterion of higher than 80% correct is achieved during a single training session. Interestingly, simultaneous multiunit activity recordings revealed no overall significant changes in neuronal firing rates in the temporal cortex as a result of learning face or non-face object pair discriminations, thereby further supporting the possibility of a population based code being important.

We have developed a neural network model which reproduces these oscillatory rhythm and neuronal firing rate observations in the temporal cortex and where changes to glutamatergic NMDA receptor coupling are sufficient to reproduce effects of learning (Kendrick et al., 2009). This model predicts that as a result of the changes in theta-nested gamma there is a slight desynchronization in the firing of the temporal cortex output neurons and that this produces a significant potentiation of the firing of downstream projection neurons through a more effective temporal spread of the inputs reaching them. As predicted by the model there was indeed a significant learning-evoked desynchronization of temporal cortex neurons recorded across the

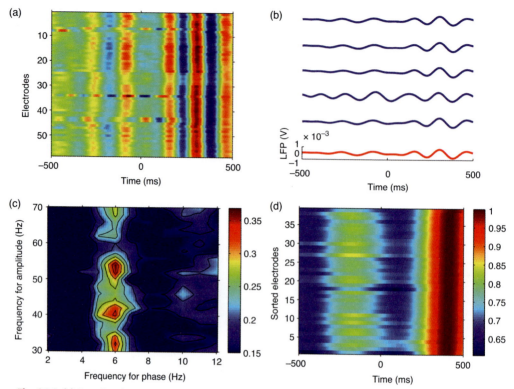

Fig. 34.6 (a) Pseudocolor representation of theta power across 58 recording electrodes in the right temporal cortex showing strong synchronization across the array. The face pair stimulus is presented at time 0. (b) Shows the filtered (4-8Hz) local field potential (LFP) for 5 of the electrodes (blue) and an overall mean across all electrodes (red). (c) Shows strong coherence in array recordings between theta phase (particularly 5–7 Hz: x-axis) and gamma amplitude (across the 30–70Hz frequency range: y-axis) after learning a face pair discrimination. The actual strength of coherence is shown by the pseudocolor scale on the right and contour lines above 0.2 indicate significance at p <0.001. (d) Shows an example of the large increase in theta amplitude shown in 40 of the electrodes during stimulus presentation following learning. The theta wave showing this increase starts at around 250–300 ms after the face-pair is presented at time 0. For the pseudocolor representation theta amplitude is normalized to the maximum level recorded in each case (i.e. a max of 1).

64 electrode arrays (Kendrick et al., 2009). Whether there is a corresponding facilitation of downstream responses in, for, example, the frontal cortex has yet to be confirmed.

Summary and conclusions

Specialized neural systems for encoding faces and face emotion cues have been found in sheep which are very similar to those described in human and non-human primates. Sheep exhibit highly sophisticated face identity and face emotion discrimination skills, use configural cues, and also show right hemisphere dominance in face processing. As such, sheep represent an important additional animal model for studying the processing capacities of this complex, and socially important, neural system. Findings have already provided evidence for both sparse and population-based encoding with small populations of cells encoding selectively for specific individuals or categories of individual but nevertheless with widespread and overlapping neuronal activity changes occurring across temporal cortex networks during the presentation of different faces. Of the more selective encoding cells both view dependent and view independent response profiles can be seen with the latter possibly being associated with metal imagery as well as perception. Both theta and gamma oscillations have been found to occur in the sheep temporal cortex and there is strong coupling between them. When animals have learned to discriminate between faces the amplitude or theta and coupling between the two frequencies increases and cause temporal changes in neuronal firing patterns which a network model predicts will potentiate responses by downstream neurons. Future experiments will hopefully be able to establish more precisely the differential encoding of face identity and face emotion components and the respective roles of the left and right brain hemispheres and inform further developments in modeling how temporal cortex networks combine these sparse and population based codes. It is clear that temporal as well as spatial aspects of encoding will prove to be of key importance.

References

Alexander, G. and Shillito-Walser, E. (1977). Importance of visual cues from various body regions in maternal recognition of the young in Merino sheep (Ovis aries). *Applied Animal Ethology*, **3**, 137–143.

Broad, K.D., Mimmack, M.L., and Kendrick, K.M. (2000). Is right hemisphere specialization for face discrimination specific to humans? *European Journal of Neuroscience*, **12**, 731–741.

Broad, K.D., Mimmack, M.L., Keverne E.B., and Kendrick, K.M. (2002). Increased BDNF and trk-B mRNA expression in cortical and limbic regions following formation of a social recognition memory. *European Journal of Neuroscience*, **16**, 2166–2174.

Brown, S.D. and Dooling, R.J. (1992). Perception of conspecific faces by budgerigars (*Melopsittacus-undulatus*). 1. Natural faces. *Journal of Comparative Psychology*, **106**, 203–216.

Buszaki, G. (2006). *Rhythms of the Brain*. Oxford: Oxford University Press.

Canolty, R.T., Edwards, E., Dalal, S.S., *et al.* (2006). High gamma power is phase-locked to theta oscillations in human neocortex. *Science*, **313**, 1626–1628.

Csibra, G., Davis, G., Spratling, M.W., and Johnson, M.H. (2000). Gamma oscillations and object processing in the infant brain. *Science*, **290**, 1582–1585.

Da Costa, A.P., Leigh, A.E., Man, M-S., and Kendrick, K.M (2004). Face pictures reduce behavioural, autonomic, endocrine and neural indices of stress and fear in sheep. *Proceedings of the Royal Society Biology B*, **271**, 2077–2084.

Dyer, A.G., Neumeyer, C., and Chittka, L. (2005). Honeybee (*Apis melifera*) vision can discriminate between and recognise images of human faces. *Journal of Experimental Biology*, **208**, 4709–4714.

Elliker, K. (2006). Recognition of emotion in sheep. PhD Thesis, University of Cambridge.

Fabre-Nys, C., Ohkura, S., and Kendrick, K. M. (1997). Male faces and odours evoke differential patterns of neurochemical release in the mediobasal hypothalamus of the ewe during oestrus: an insight into sexual motivation? *European Journal of Neuroscience*, **9**, 1666–1677.

Fries, P., Reynolds, J.H., Rorie, A.E., and Desimone, R. (2001). Modulation of oscillatory neuronal synchronization by selective visual attention. *Science*, **291**, 1560–1563.

Jitsumori, M. and Yoshihara, M. (1997). Categorical discrimination of human facial expressions by pigeons: a test of the linear feature model. *Quarterly Journal of Experimental Psychology*, **50**, 253–268.

Kendrick, K.M. (2008). Sheep senses, social cognition and capacity for consciousness. In C. Dwyer (ed.) *The Welfare of Sheep*, pp.135–158. Berlin: Springer.

Kendrick, K.M. (1991). How the sheep's brain controls the visual recognition of animals and humans. *Journal of Animal Science*, **69**, 5008–5016.

Kendrick, K.M. (1994). Neurobiological correlates of visual and olfactory recognition in sheep. *Behavioral Processes*, **33**, 89–112.

Kendrick, K.M. (2006). Brain asymmetries for face recognition and emotion control in sheep. *Cortex*, **42**, 96–98.

Kendrick, K.M., Atkins, K., Hinton, M.R., Broad, K.D., Fabre-Nys, C., and Keverne, B. (1995). Facial and vocal discrimination in sheep. *Animal Behaviour*, **49**, 1665–1676.

Kendrick, K.M., Atkins, K., Hinton, M.R., Heavens, P., and Keverne, B. (1996). Are faces special for sheep? Evidence from facial and object discrimination learning tests showing effects of inversion and social familiarity. *Behavioral Processes*, **38**, 19–35.

Kendrick, K.M. and Baldwin, B.A. (1987). Cells in temporal cortex of conscious sheep can respond to the sight of faces. *Science*, **236**, 448–450.

Kendrick, K.M. and Baldwin, B.A. (1989). Visual responses of sheep temporal cortex cells to moving and stationary human images. *Neuroscience Letters*, **100**, 193–197.

Kendrick, K.M., Hinton, M.R., Atkins, K., Haupt, M.A., and Skinner, J.D. (1998). Mothers determine sexual preferences. *Nature*, **395**, 229–230.

Kendrick, K.M., da Costa, A.P., Leigh, A.E., Hinton, M.R., and Peirce, J.W. (2001a). Sheep don't forget a face. *Nature*, **414**,165–166.

Kendrick, K.M., Haupt, M.A., Hinton, M.R., Broad, K.D., and Skinner, J.D. (2001b). Sex differences in the influence of mothers on the sociosexual preferences of their offspring. *Hormones and Behavior*, **40**, 322–338.

Kendrick, K.M., Leigh, A.E., and Peirce J. (2001c). Behavioural and neural correlates of mental imagery in sheep using face recognition paradigms. *Animal Welfare*, **10**, S89–101.

Kendrick, K.M., Zhan, Y., Fischer, H., Nicol, A.U., Zhang, X., and Feng, J. ((2009). Learning alters theta-nested gamma oscillations in inferotemporal cortex. *Nature Precedings*. Available online at http://precedings.nature.com/documents/3151/version/2

Ladroue, C., Guo, S., Kendrick, K.M., and Feng, J. (2009). Beyond element-wise interactions: defining group-to-group interactions for biological processes. *PLoS ONE*, **4**, e6899.

Leopold, D.A., Bondar, I.V., and Giese, M.A. (2006). Norm-based face encoding by single neurons in the monkey inferotemporal cortex. *Nature*, **442**, 572–575.

Loidolt, M., Aust, U., Meran, I., and Huber, L. (2003). Pigeons use item-specific and category-level information in the identification and categorization of human faces. *Journal of Experimental Psychology*, **29**, 261–276.

O'Craven, K.M. and Kanwisher, N. (2000). Mental imagery of faces and places activates corresponding stimulus-specific brain regions. *Journal of Cognitive Neuroscience*, **12**, 1013–1023.

Ohkura, S., Fabre-Nys, C., Broad, K.D., and Kendrick, K.M. (1997). Sex hormones enhance the impact of male sensory cues on both primary and association cortical components of visual and olfactory processing pathways as well as in limbic and hypothalamic regions in female sheep. *Neuroscience*, **80**, 285–297.

Peirce, J.W. and Kendrick, K.M. (2002). Functional asymmetry in sheep temporal cortex. *Neuroreport*, **13**, 2395–2399.

Peirce, J.W., Leigh, A.E., and Kendrick, K.M. (2000). Configurational coding, familiarity and the right hemisphere advantage for face recognition in sheep. *Neuropsychologia*, **38**, 475–483.

Peirce, J.W., Leigh A.E., da Costa A.P.C., and Kendrick, K.M. (2001). Human face recognition in sheep: lack of configurational coding and right hemisphere advantage. *Behavioral Processes*, **55**, 13–26.

Perez-Orive, J., Mazor, O., Turner, G.C., Cassenaer, S., Wilson, R.I., and Laurent, G. (2002). Oscillations and sparsening of odor representations in the mushroom body. *Science*, **297**, 359–65.

Perrett, D.I., Mistlin, A.J., Chitty, A.J., *et al.* (1988). Specialized face processing and hemispheric asymmetry in man and monkey: evidence from single unit and reaction time studies. *Behavioral Brain Research*, **29**, 245–58.

Perrett, D.I., Oram, M.W., Harries, M.H., *et al.* (1991). Viewer-centred and object-centred coding of heads in the macaque temporal cortex. *Experimental Brain Research,* **86,**159–73.

Peters, M. and Jaspers-Fayer (2002). *A laboratory manual for the dissection of the sheep brain.* Guelph, ON: The University of Guelph.

Rolls, E.T., Treves, A., and Tovee, M.J. (1997). The representational capacity of the distributed encoding of information provided by populations of neurons in the primate temporal visual temporal cortex. *Experimental Brain Research,* **114,** 149–162.

Quian Quiroga, R., Reddy, L., Kreiman, C., Koch, C., and Fried, I. (2005). Invariant visual representation by single neurons in the human brain. *Nature,* **435,** 1102–1107.

Tate, A.J., Fischer H., Leigh, A.E., and Kendrick, K.M. (2006). Behavioural and neurophysiological evidence for face emotion and face identity processing in animals. *Philosophical Transactions of the Royal Society B,* **361,** 2187–2198.

Tibbetts, E.A. (2002). Visual signals of individual identity in the wasp *Polistes fuscatus Proceedings of the Royal Society Biology B,* **269,** 1423–1428.

Truett, A., Puce, A, Spencer, D.D., and McCarthy, G. (1999). Electrophysiological studies of human face perception. I: Potentials generated in occipitotemporal cortex by face and non-face stimuli. *Cerebral Cortex,* **9,** 415–430.

Van der Velden, J., Zheng, Y., Patullo, B.W., and Macmillan D.L. (2008). Crayfish recognize the faces of fight opponents. *PLoS ONE,* **3,** e1695.

Chapter 35

Face Perception in Non-Human Primates

Lisa A. Parr and Erin E. Hecht

Introduction

Face recognition is one of the most important skills in primate social cognition, enabling the formation of long-lasting, interindividual relationships. Among humans, face recognition is associated with a variety of cognitive and neural specializations, suggesting that it has played an important role in shaping human societies. Humans, for example, are face experts. They are able to individuate faces, or recognize and remember many different individuals over a lifetime, often with only mere exposure. This is achieved developmentally through an orientation-dependent, configural processing strategy where it is not just the presence of specific features, such as the eyes, nose, and mouth, but the relative spatial arrangement of these facial features to one another that is compared (Maurer et al., 2002). Moreover, functional neuroimaging studies using both PET (positron emission tomography) and fMRI (functional magnetic resonance imaging) have identified a distributed network of brain regions important for face recognition (Haxby et al., 2000; see Haxby and Gobbini, Chapter 6; Kanwisher and Barton, Chapter 7, this volume), including a region in the medial temporal lobe that appears to be selectively tuned for faces compared to other ecologically important stimuli (Kanwisher et al., 1997; McCarthy et al., 1997; but see Tarr and Gauthier, 2000).

Despite the wealth of information available from human studies, much less is known about these face-processing skills in other species, or whether the cognitive and neural specializations for processing faces are unique to humans. This chapter will summarize existing research on face processing in non-human primates with the goal of understanding the evolution of this important socio-cognitive skill. It is organized into six main sections. In the first two it will describe different levels of configural processing and the importance of early visual expertise in face processing. In the third it will examine evidence for configural face processing in non-human primates by reviewing studies on the well-known face inversion effect. Then it will examine the social salience of faces by reviewing studies that employ a variety of gaze tracking and visual orienting techniques. In he fifth it will critically review studies on the individuation of faces, the ability to recognize individuals across various viewpoints, and manipulating configural cues directly. In the final section, neuroimaging studies will be reviewed to understand whether the neural correlates of face recognition in non-human primates involves a similar brain regions as humans (other important contributions are available in this volume). Table 35.1 provides a list of species studied and gives some information about their taxonomic classification and relatedness to humans.

Configural face processing: first- and second-order relational features

Numerous studies have demonstrated that human face recognition is critically dependent on the configural arrangement of facial features. In their seminal article, Diamond and Carey (1986)

Table 35.1 A list of species referenced in this chapter, arranged in ascending phylogenetic order with regard to when they last shared (millions of years ago, mya) a common ancestor with humans

New World Monkeys (parvorder Platyrrhini, 40 mya)	Cotton-top tamarin (*Saguinus oedipus*): Neiworth et al., 2007; Weiss et al., 2001
	Squirrel monkey (*Saimiri sciureus*): Phelps and Roberts, 1994; Pineda et al., 1994; Wright and Roberts, 1996
	Capuchin monkey (*Cebus apella*): Dufour et al., 2006; Pokorny and de Waal, 2009
Old World Monkeys (family Cercopithecidae, 23 mya)	Japanese macaque (*Macaca fuscata*): Eifuku et al., 2004; Kuwahata et al., 2004; Sugita, 2008; Tomonaga, 1994
	Pigtail macaques (*Macaca nemestrina*): Overman and Doty, 1982
	Long-tail macaque (*Macaca fascicularis*): Bruce, 1982; Dittrich, 1990; Hasselmo et al., 1989
	Rhesus macaque (*Macaca mulatta*): Dahl et al., 2007; Gothard et al., 2004; Gothard et al., 2007; Gothard et al., 2009; Hadj-Bouziane et al., 2007; Hasselmo et al., 1989; Hoffman et al., 2007; Keating and Keating, 1993; Mendelson, 1982; Moeller et al., 2008; Pascalis and Bachevalier, 1998; Parr et al., 2008; Parr et al., 1999, 2000; Pinsk et al., 2005; Rosenfeld and van Hoesen, 1979; Sato and Nakamura, 2001; Tao et al., 2003, 2006, 2008a,b; Vermeire and Hamilton, 1998; Wilson and Goldman-Rakic, 1994
	Tonkean macaque (*Macaca tonkeana*): Dufour et al., 2006
Apes (family Hylobatidae, 14 mya)	Gibbon (*Hylobates agilis*): Myowa-Yamakoshi and Tomonaga, 2001
Apes (family Hominidae, 5 mya)	Chimpanzee (*Pan troglodytes*): Martin-Malivel and Okada, 2007; Matsuzawa, 2007; Parr et al., 1998, 2000, 2006, 2009; Tomonaga, 1999, 2007; Tomonaga et al., 1993

differentiated two types of configural information present in faces, first- and second-order relational features. First-order relational properties refer to the general arrangement of facial features which is similar in every face. All faces, for example, have the same individual features, eyes, nose, mouth, etc., organized in the same general orientation. This type of configural information provides the means for recognizing faces at the basic categorical level, e.g. face versus non-face. Attraction to first-order relational cues in faces appears to have an innate component as newborn babies are more attracted to face-like patterns than non-face like patterns (Goren et al., 1975; Valenza et al., 1996). Similar innate preferences occur in non-human primates.

From birth, infant Japanese macaques show spontaneous gaze preferences to configural, face-like, patterns of dots compared to a linear arrangement (Kuwahata et al., 2004). An infant gibbon (13 days old) oriented more to face-like compared to non-face like drawings and, by 4 weeks of age, he oriented more towards familiar compared to unfamiliar conspecific's faces (Myowa-Yamakoshi and Tomonaga, 2001).

The second type of configural arrangement described by Diamond and Carey (1986) are second-order relational properties. These refer to the relative size, shape, and spatial arrangement of facial features with regard to one another, which are unique in every face (Maurer et al., 2002). This unique configuration of facial features establishes the formation of individual prototypes, enabling specific individuals to be distinguished from one another through the use of facial information alone. While first-order relational properties enable the identification of faces at a basic categorical level, second-order relational properties facilitate the subordinate-level classification of faces, e.g. the ability to distinguish Mary from Jane. Evidence for the individuation of faces in non-human primates and specific tests of second-order relational processing will be reviewed later in this chapter.

Expertise and configural processing

Configural processing, particularly second-order, is strongly influenced by an individual's expertise. Because humans have extensive experience with faces from birth, faces represent one of the few naturally occurring categories of stimuli for which people are experts (see Scott, Chapter 11, this volume). Experimental studies using Japanese macaques have shown that visual deprivation for up to 6 months followed by exposure to monkey faces led to a selective viewing preference, and better discrimination, for monkey faces compared to objects or human faces. However, early exposure to human faces led to the reverse pattern, which persisted even a year later after the monkeys had received visual exposure to both species (Sugita, 2008). Moreover, when tested using a visual paired comparison (VPC) task, which measures looking preferences for novel compared to familiar images, monkeys dishabituated to faces with altered features or altered spacing of features, but only for those species' faces for which they had received prior visual exposure (Sugita, 2008). In contrast, this skill in humans requires years (at least 5 years) to develop. Infant chimpanzees showed no preference for their mother's face compared to unrelated individuals in the first month of life but developed this preference at 2 months of age (Matsuzawa, 2007). This is similar to the experience-dependent perceptual narrowing effects for faces seen in human infants. Early in development, human infants show no differences viewing human or monkey faces, but by 9 months of age they selectively attend to human versus other-species faces (Pascalis et al., 2002). This early visual experience shapes the development of configural processing as evidenced by studies of human infants born with congenital cataracts, making them blind at birth. Their condition was surgically corrected in the first 6 months of life, but when tested later, they showed impaired configural processing of faces even though they had received years after normal visual input post-surgery (Le Grand et al., 2001).

These expertise effects are also present in human adults with normal rearing experience as "other race" effects (see Rossion and Michel, Chapter 12, this volume), and in adult monkeys as "other-species" effects (Pascalis and Bachevalier, 1998, see Pascalis and Wirth, Chapter 37, this volume). Using a VPC task, several studies have shown greater preferential looking at novel conspecific's faces, compared to other species' faces (rhesus: Pascalis and Bachevalier, 1998; Sugita, 2008; capuchin monkeys and Tonkean macaques: Dufour et al., 2006). Exposure to different species, and familiarity with different individuals of the same species, can also have effects on face processing in non-human primates throughout development. Early studies that measured evoked response potentials (ERPs), electrical activity across the brain, in squirrel monkeys, reflected greater amplitude components over lateral temporal-parietal cortex for monkey faces compared to human faces, with the strongest responses for familiar compared to unfamiliar monkeys (Pineda et al., 1994). Thus, differences in familiarity and expertise appear to be reflected by different patterns of brain activity.

An interesting recent study was the first to compare the influence of expertise on categorical perception in chimpanzees (Martin-Malivel and Okada, 2007). This study found that chimpanzees housed at a center where they saw few chimpanzees but many humans showed better discrimination of human faces compared to chimpanzee faces, and categorical perception of human faces. In contrast, chimpanzees housed at a different facility where they were familiar with many chimpanzees and humans did not show any species-biases for discrimination performance or categorical perception (Martin-Malivel and Okada, 2007). It should be noted that in this study, the chimpanzee subjects at both facilities discriminated both human and chimpanzee faces at near ceiling levels, with the worst performance occurring for the more human-familiar subjects when discriminating chimpanzee faces, for which they were still over 80% accurate. Thus, in both human and non-human primates, early attraction to faces is present from birth, undergoes similar perceptual narrowing during development, and early visual exposure to faces appears necessary for the normal development of configural processing.

The face inversion effect

By far the most widely used paradigm for studying the configural processing of face is the inversion effect, the phenomena by which rotating faces 180 degrees makes them difficult to recognize (Yin, 1969). This is because configural processing is orientation-dependent and turning faces upside down disrupts the configural arrangement of features. The most consistently replicated evidence for the inversion effect in non-human primates is for chimpanzees, although ironically, the first study in this species was the only one that failed to show inversion effects. This particular study asked a female chimpanzee to select a symbol representing the name of familiar human faces presented upright and inverted, for which she did equally well (Tomonaga et al., 1993). Thus, familiarity and specifically the symbolic naming of individuals may have contributed to this result.

Subsequently, Parr and colleagues tested the inversion effect in five chimpanzees using a computerized, matching-to-sample (MTS) task (Parr et al., 1998). In this study, chimpanzees used a joystick-controlled cursor to select one of two inverted stimuli that matched an upright sample on a computer monitor. Significant inversion effects were found for unfamiliar chimpanzee's faces, and human faces, the two species for which subjects had expertise, but not capuchin monkey faces or automobiles, categories for which subjects were naïve (Parr et al., 1998). Rhesus monkeys were also tested using the same computerized MTS task and they showed no evidence of familiarity-dependent inversion effects. These monkeys (N = 4) showed significant impairments discriminating inverted compared to upright faces of conspecifics, unfamiliar capuchin monkeys, and automobiles, but not the familiar category of human faces (Parr et al., 1999). A more recent replication using different rhesus subjects (N = 7) found significant inversion effects for all face categories, conspecifics, humans and chimpanzees, but not houses or clip art (Parr et al., 2008). In these two studies, the data for human faces was borderline in each case, against an inversion effect in Parr et al. (1998), but in favor of an inversion effect in Parr et al. (2008).

Studies of chimpanzees from other labs also support the inversion effect using a variety of stimuli and methods. Tomonaga (1999) found the inversion effect for unfamiliar human faces compared to houses in one chimpanzee (a different subject than in Tomonaga et al., 1993) using a MTS task. Similar results were found using a visual search task where the same chimpanzee was significantly faster to identify an upright human face and a human caricature face among four or 10 differently oriented distracters (Tomonaga, 2007). No differences were found in time required to find the target when stimuli were upright chairs or hands presented against inverted distracters of the same categories. A follow-up study presented different facial features and combinations of features and showed an upright superiority effect for the eyes and eyebrows, the eyes and nose, and the eyes and mouth, but not the nose and mouth, or nose, or mouth alone. A final study presented the inner features of the face, and the external contour, where faster identification times were found only for upright internal features when presented against inverted distracters (Tomonaga, 2007).

Evidence for the face inversion effect and its mechanisms in both New and Old World monkeys is less clear. Some studies have reported evidence of the face inversion effect in monkeys (cotton-top tamarins: Neiworth et al., 2007; pigtail macaques: Overman and Doty, 1982; Japanese macaques: Tomonaga, 1994; rhesus monkeys: Vermeire and Hamilton, 1998), while others have failed to find evidence of orientation-specific processing exclusive for faces (longtail macaques: Bruce, 1982; Dittrich, 1990; Gothard et al., 2004; Parr et al., 1999; rhesus monkeys: Rosenfeld and van Hoesen, 1979; cotton-top tamarins: Weiss et al., 2001).

In both Old and New World species, some authors have suggested a phylogenetic shift towards the use of configural cues when processing human and perhaps ape faces, compared to the faces of monkeys. Two squirrel monkeys showed significant inversion effects for human and ape faces, but not for monkey faces or scenery (Phelps and Roberts, 1994). Similarly, significant inversion effects were found in three rhesus monkeys using a same-different paradigm when discriminating inverted compared to upright human faces, but no differences were found for monkey faces or scenes (Wright and Roberts, 1996). However, there is little evidence beyond these data for any type of configural superiority for human faces (see Neiworth et al., 2007; Parr et al., 2008). In summary, studies of the inversion effect have consistently shown that chimpanzees are sensitive to the configural arrangement of facial features when processing familiar categories of faces like conspecifics and humans, while data from monkeys suggests different perceptual strategies that may be dependent on the task format and stimuli used. More comparative research in primates is needed before the similarities and differences in the importance of configural cues will be fully understood.

Selective viewing and paradigms and gaze patterns

Another popular method for studying face recognition in non-human primates is gaze tracking. This is used primarily to determine how subjects scan faces and what, if any, features are most salient. Reliably, these studies all confirm the importance of the eyes in subjects' scanning and recognition of faces. Kyes and Candland (1987), for example, used a viewing preference paradigm where baboons pressed a lever to control the duration that a slide would be visible. The stimuli consisted of the entire face, and specific facial features, of the dominant male in the subjects' social group. Subjects spent more time viewing the whole face compared to a covered face, and preferred to look at facial feature combinations where the eyes and particularly the eyes and nose were present. More sophisticated techniques involving eye-tracking provide more detailed information about how faces are scanned, including the location of the first fixation, fixation durations, and the sequence of fixations. The more non-invasive methods use infrared cameras to track corneal reflections, but more invasive methods surgically implant metallic coils into the sclera of the subject's eye and then track the movements of the eye using a two dimensional magnetic frame.

Mendelson (1982) used the corneal reflection technique to track the development of face preferences in infant rhesus monkeys. At 1, 3, and 7 weeks of age, monkeys were shown conspecific faces with gaze slightly averted and gaze directed at the subject. Their results showed that at 1 week of age, the monkeys spent equivalent amounts of time looking at the direct and averted gaze faces, but at 3 and 7 weeks of age, the monkeys looked less at the direct gaze faces. At 3 weeks of age, the monkeys also showed more emotional fussiness, perhaps indicating the beginning of when the direct gaze faces are viewed as socially significant. Direct gaze, for example, is considered aversive and threatening to rhesus monkeys, so these data represent a normal developmental trend for this species (Hinde and Rowell, 1962).

The analysis of scan patterns can also be divided into specific regions of interest, such as individual facial features. In the previously discussed study, the monkeys spent more time fixating on the eyes and ears compared to other facial regions, and this was consistent from week to week (Mendelson, 1982). Unlike humans, who scan faces in an inverted triangular pattern, across the eyes and down to stop at the nose and mouth, these monkeys appeared to ignore the mouth. The opposite scan patterns were found in adult rhesus monkeys viewing human faces (Sato and Nakamura, 2001). In this study, subjects made more fixations for longer total durations on a human face with direct compared to averted gaze. This suggests that the ecological salience of human and monkey faces may be different, although little detail is provided about the subjects' rearing history, only that they were experimentally naïve before the start of the study (Sato and Nakamura, 2001).

Keating and Keating (1993) used the scleral coil technique in rhesus monkeys to track viewing patterns for a familiar human face. The procedure first trained subjects to recognize a stimulus face ("go") from a variety of others ("no go") by pressing a lever when this, and only this, face appeared. Then, this face was edited by removal, replacement, or scrambling of facial features, and inversion. Subjects' recognition of the stimulus face was significantly impaired when the manipulation was to substitute the eyes or brow region, remove the chin, and for any of the inverted or scrambled feature manipulations. However, regardless of the type of manipulation, the majority of fixations were to the eyes. Interestingly, features were also graded by making them larger or smaller than the standard stimulus face and this had mixed results, with only deviations of eye shape reducing recognition. As stated earlier, this suggests that monkeys are highly attracted to eyes and less sensitive to the overall configuration of features.

Some similarities, but also notable differences, have been found in another study. Wilson and Goldman-Rakic (1994) showed rhesus monkeys photographs of conspecific faces, interesting pictures (common household items and scenery), and color fields. Monkeys looked longer at faces and pictures than color scenes but no differences were found between viewing time for faces and pictures. Moreover, this study examined changes in viewing preference for images after repeated exposure, memory effects. Monkeys spent less time looking at familiar faces and pictures compared to novel ones, but no differences were found for color scenes. The important difference was that when examining specific scan patterns for facial features, these authors showed monkeys were most attracted to regions of contour highlighted by specific facial features, such as eyes, ears, hairline, nose, mouth, and jawline. Therefore, while previous studies were unable to address the salience of faces compared to other interesting visual stimuli because no control stimuli were used, Wilson and Goldman-Rakic's study (1994) failed to support any particular salience for faces over other interesting pictures and, importantly, showed that monkeys may be more attracted to high contrast stimulus features, rather than to facial features, per se. The lack of appropriate control stimuli still persists in studies of face recognition in non-human primates and needs to be addressed before any major conclusions can be made about facial salience and feature salience, in particular.

Individual recognition: Individuating faces across viewpoints

One of the skills thought to emerge from configural face processing is the ability to individuate faces, or recognize individuals across different facial viewpoints. This skill is particularly aided by second-order configural processing. Although there is little doubt that monkeys living in large social groups are able to discriminate between individuals, the extent to which they are able to individuate conspecifics from faces alone, or whether this is based on configural processing, is unclear (Parr et al., 2008). Numerous studies in chimpanzees suggest that this species has a strong bias towards the use of configural cues when processing unfamiliar conspecific faces. In one of the first studies of its kind, chimpanzees were required to match the same unfamiliar individual across different facial viewpoints using an MTS task. They did this after only two exposures, suggesting rapid individuation of faces, even of unfamiliar individuals (Parr et al., 2000). Later, faces were manipulated by either fracturing/spacing the features apart, altering second-order configural cues, or fracturing and rearranging facial features, altering first- and second-order configural cues, or to show only inner facial features, preserving both first- and second-order configural features (Parr et al., 2006). Subjects were impaired matching the fractured, and fractured plus rearranged trials, but showed no impairments matching faces using only their inner features. When rhesus monkeys were tested on these same tasks using a comparable methodology, they failed to show evidence for individuation of faces of conspecifics (Parr et al., 2000, 2008), failed to show expertise effects for inverted stimuli (reviewed earlier, Parr et al., 1999, 2008), and failed to show any selective advantage for second-order configural processing (Parr et al., 2008).

Training monkeys to perform operant tasks like MTS or same-different discriminations takes time and many researchers prefer the automatic biases inherent in free viewing paradigms, like adaptation paradigms and VPC tasks. Gothard and colleagues (2004) combined a VPC task with eye-tracking in rhesus monkeys to demonstrate recognition of novel compared to familiarized individuals. This study also presented facial expressions but these data will not be covered here. After familiarizing subjects with a pair of identical photographs showing an unfamiliar conspecific face, they were presented with the same face paired with a new photograph of a novel individual, e.g. the test pair. Subjects spent more time viewing the novel individual than the familiarized one during the test pair presentation. These free viewing tasks are often used to demonstrate individual recognition, however, because the test pair showed the exact same photograph of the familiarized monkey paired with a novel individual, subjects could simply be showing increased attention to a novel photograph, not selective attention to a novel individual (see also Neiworth et al., 2007).

This problem was corrected in a second study (Gothard et al., 2009). They presented two different viewpoints of the same monkey in the familiarization pair, followed by a third view of the same monkey paired with a novel individual in the test pair. Eye-tracking was used to measure whether the monkeys viewed the familiar or novel individual for a longer period and on which facial features they fixated. Only two monkeys were tested with conspecific faces and they showed a preference for the novel individual's eye region. For human faces, two of three monkeys showed preferences for the eyes of the novel individual. These data showed that, indeed, subjects were able to detect similar individuals across different viewpoints, preferring to look at the novel individual when all of the actual photographs presented were novel. Next, the authors addressed whether the novelty preferences were dependent on configural processing by filtering the face stimuli (Gothard et al., 2009). When the faces were subjected to a high-pass filter, effectively removing the low-spatial frequency information that is important for configural processing, the monkeys attended to the novel face and viewed the eye region. This suggests a feature-based strategy. Interestingly, when the images were blurred using a low-pass filter, effectively removing high-spatial frequency information that is important for specific feature detection, subjects also attended to the eye region of the novel face. Although the authors conclude that monkeys show stronger configural processing for conspecific faces, there was actually no difference in the data between the two filter conditions. Moreover, the data showed that in all experimental conditions subjects primarily fixated on the eyes, a finding that overwhelmingly supports a feature-based processing strategy and, perhaps more specifically, an eye-detection strategy. This was even true when the faces were inverted, although further analyses showed that this was primarily due to the behavior of one monkey. Therefore, while this study is methodologically more sound that previous viewing preference studies, the inclusion of sophisticated eye-tracking techniques and ecologically valid experimental stimuli failed to provide any compelling evidence for selective advantages for configural processing in this species.

Using an oddity paradigm, Pokorny and de Waal (2009) tested the ability of capuchin monkeys to discriminate faces from familiar and unfamiliar conspecifics. An initial training phase presented four images, three of which were identical to the sample and the fourth showed a different individual (odd image). In the test phase, all four of the comparison images were different, three showed the same individual as in the sample but different facial viewpoints, while the fourth image showed a different monkey. These were combined so that individuals within a trial were either familiar (ingroup) or unfamiliar (outgroup) members. In the initial training phase, subjects were significantly faster to learn outgroup individuals compared to ingroup individuals. However, when different viewpoints of the same individual were presented (individual recognition task), there were no differences in performance on ingroup versus outgroup individuals. Subjects went on to generalize their performance to two separate transfer tasks involving all new images. Thus, this study shows that capuchin monkeys appear capable of individuating conspecific faces, although no strong advantages were found for familiar versus unfamiliar individuals (Pokorny and de Waal 2009). The study did not test specifically for whether the individual recognition involved reliance on configural cues.

A well-cited study of individual recognition and configural/holistic processing in rhesus monkeys is Dahl and colleagues (2007). These authors conducted three studies using an adaptation/dishabituation paradigm. According to this procedure, subjects are habituated to a photograph of a monkey and then the duration of viewing rebound, or dishabituation, to a novel photograph is measured. In the first experiment, three types of adaptation trials were presented, those in which the novel photograph was a different monkey (subordinate), a different species (basic), the same monkey with a configural face manipulation, e.g. the eyes spread apart (config-ural), or the same photograph of the original monkey rotated in a two-dimensional plane (same). Results showed greater rebound to subordinate pictures than same pictures for monkey faces, but not for animals, and to the configural faces than same/rotated faces. The authors concluded that subjects perform subordinate-level processing for monkey faces, but not for other animals, sug-gesting configural processing dependent on species expertise (Dahl et al., 2007). However, the "same" faces were identical to the original faces, only rotated. A true test of individual recognition and/or subordinate level processing would require comparing a different viewpoint (in-depth rotation) of the same monkey, rather than just rotating the picture in-plane, versus a different monkey's face (subordinate trial).

The authors next examined whether these rebound effects were due to holistic processing by showing composite images. In the original composite task, the top and bottom halves of two individual's faces are presented either aligned, with one part above the other to resemble a "typical" face, or misaligned so that the top and bottom parts are offset along their horizontal axis. People are slower to identify the top half individual when the face parts are aligned com-pared to misaligned (Young et al., 1987). This is because the configural face processing system automatically integrates features together and builds a holistic representation of face structure. While holistic processing makes it more difficult to identify the separate halves when aligned, performance is able to recover in the misaligned trials. Chimpanzees tested on the face composite task using a matching task, as opposed to a naming task, showed a spontaneous preference to match an aligned composite to a whole/unaltered face of the individual represented by the top face part, whereas they chose the individuals' face that was represented in the top and bottom parts equally when the faces were misaligned (Parr et al., 2006). Figure 35.1 shows an example of these manipulations.

Dahl and colleagues presented monkeys with both the aligned and misaligned composites, as described above, in the adaptation phase. After this, the novel image contained the same type of composite, aligned or misaligned, but now the individual in the bottom face part was new. The authors report greater rebound for aligned than misaligned composites, suggesting sensitivity to holistic processing. In explaining their results, however, the authors raise an interesting potential confound in their methods. Numerous studies, many of which have been reviewed above, have demonstrated that rhesus monkeys have a very robust preference to look at eyes, regardless of whether the pictures are human or monkey faces, or oriented in appropriate ways (Gothard et al., 2009; Keating and Keating, 1993; Wilson and Goldman-Rakic, 1994). Thus, the aligned composites may have received greater rebound compared to misaligned composites because of the proximity of the changed face part, the bottom half, to the eyes. The bottom face part is further away from the eyes in the misaligned condition, so may not have been as detectable. To address this, Experiment three recorded scanning patterns using eye-tracking and posed two hypotheses. First, if subjects were simply attracted to the bottom face part because it was closer to the eyes, there should be fewer eye fixations to the novel, aligned composite compared to the adaptation image,

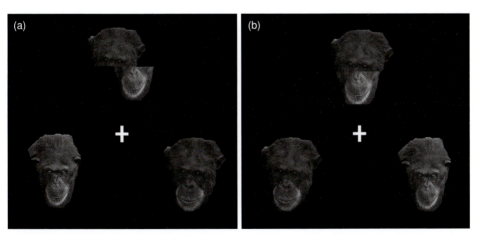

Fig. 35.1 Two types of composite trials shown to chimpanzees using an MTS format. The images on the top of each frame are the sample stimuli, the ones to match. Both of these show face composites where the top and bottom halves of two individuals are combined in a misaligned format (a), or aligned format (b). In each trial, subjects are free to match either the top or bottom half individual, whose unaltered faces are on the bottom of each frame, and are rewarded for either choice. For misaligned trials (a), subjects selected either individual about 50% of the time, however, in the aligned trials (b), subjects spontaneously preferred to select the individual represented by the top face part, lower left (Parr et al., 2006).

showing habituation, and this difference should be greater than for misaligned trials, where each part is processed separately. Alternatively, if subjects were processing faces holistically, then they should show renewed interest in the eye region of the novel images in aligned compared to misaligned trials, presumably because they see the novel aligned image as a new individual and explore the relevant face region, the eyes, even though these are identical between the adaptation and novel images. They claim their data support this latter, holistic processing, explanation, but several points must be considered. First, the justification for the first hypothesis is not clear, nor is it evident whether this hypothesis can be tested independently of holistic processing versus a feature-based mechanism, where attention is drawn to specific facial features such as eyes. If subjects are attracted to the bottom face part because of its proximity to the eyes, then fewer fixations would be expected for the eye region in both aligned and misaligned adaptation composites. It is not clear why the aligned condition would receive less rebound effects? Attraction to eyes alone would explain these effects. Second, eye fixations were not addressed in the other manipulations, such as the subordinate trials in Experiment 2, so it may be typical that fixations for eye regions are reduced in adaptation trials regardless of whether composites are used, and even when rebound effects occur. Third, there did appear to be fewer fixations on the eye region of misaligned compared to the aligned composites in both the adaptation and novel trials which, as suggested above, could be evidence of greater attention to specific facial features. However, the majority of these fixations to misaligned composites occurred in the region where the top and bottom face parts were joined, thus the middle of the offset region. This is a region of high contrast, and previous studies have shown monkeys to be extremely attracted to regions of high contrast for scenery, novel objects, and faces (Wilson and Goldman-Rakic, 1994). Therefore, any conclusion about how the eye-tracking data supports holistic processing should be interpreted with caution.

Finally, these authors claim that the use of free viewing paradigms, such as VPC, adaptation or habituation, has advantages over more operant paradigms, like same-different discrimination or matching-to-sample, because the latter formats "…produce systematically altered or idiosyncratic response strategies making it difficult to disentangle what monkeys are capable of learning from what they would do under natural circumstances" (Dahl et al., 2007). Although these authors fail to illuminate what these altered or idiosyncratic response strategies are, the data from free viewing paradigms has its own unnatural requirements, such as head fixation, training subjects to understand the reinforcement contingencies associated with fixating on the monitor, or food/water restrictions. Moreover, these paradigms have produced as many inconsistent findings in a variety of monkey species as those using the argued more unnaturalistic, trained paradigms (see the inversion effect, above).

Neuroimaging face processing in non-human primates

Extensive research in humans has identified a distributed network of brain regions involved in face processing. The "core" of this network consists of inferior occipital cortex ("occipital face area") and fusiform gyrus (the "fusiform face area" or FFA), which process the invariant, structural aspects of faces, and the posterior superior temporal sulcus (pSTS), which processes the changeable aspects of faces, like lip and body movements and facial expressions (Haxby et al., 2000; see Calder, Chapter 22, this volume). These regions are embedded in a large territory of occipitotemporal cortex that is involved in more general visual object processing (Haxby et al., 2001). In addition to the "core" is an "extended" network including the insula, amygdala, orbitofrontal cortex, and inferior prefrontal cortex (Haxby et al., 2000). An outstanding question, though, is to what degree these face processing networks are homologous in non-human primates and whether there are any species differences in anatomy or physiology which could account for the observed species differences in behavior, noted above.

Recent neuroimaging studies have demonstrated remarkable similarity in the activation of both core and extended networks during face processing tasks in humans, chimpanzees, and monkeys. For example, recently, Parr and colleagues (Parr et al., 2009) performed the first neuroimaging study of face processing in five chimpanzees using FDG-PET (^{18}F-flurodeoxy-glucose positron emission tomography). Overall, the face-responsive activity (compared to non-face objects) spanned broad regions of ventral occipitotemporal cortex, similar to the activity observed in human fMRI studies, including the inferior occipital gyri and fusiform gyrus, the superior temporal sulcus (STS), and frontolimbic regions that included the amygdala, orbitofrontal cortex, and inferior prefrontal cortex. A growing number of studies using fMRI in macaques have identified a similarly distributed network (see Freiwald and Tsao, Chapter 36; and Kendrick and Feng, Chapter 34, this volume). These face-selective regions in monkeys are concentrated in the fundus and lower bank of the anterior and posterior STS in rostral (aSTS-FA) and caudal regions (pSTS-FA) of inferotemporal cortex (area TE) respectively (Hadj-Bouziane et al., 2008; Hoffman et al., 2007; Moeller et al., 2008; Pinsk et al., 2005; Tsao et al., 2003, 2006, 2008a), in anterior temporal cortex on the medial ventral surface (area TEav) (Moeller et al., 2008; Tsao et al., 2008a), the amygdala (Hadj-Bouziane et al., 2008; Hoffman et al., 2007), and orbitofrontal and lateral prefrontal cortex (Hadj-Bouziane et al., 2008; Tsao et al., 2008a,b).

These data support a strong argument for functional homology between distributed networks for face processing in humans, chimpanzees, and macaques, comprised of distinct, but interconnected, regions spanning the rostral-caudal extent of occipitotemporal cortex, and some evidence for independent processing of face identity versus emotion (Eufiku et al., 2004; Gothard et al., 2007; Hasselmo et al., 1989; Hadj-Bouzaine et al., 2008). The human FFA and the macaque pSTS-FA, both situated in larger regions of object-selective cortex (Haxby et al., 2001), and the human STS-FA and the macaque aSTS-FA, both surrounded by cortex that processes the changeable aspects of faces and bodies, such as facial expressions and body movement, appear to perform similar functions and thus have been suggested to be functionally homologous (Pinsk et al., 2005). While very little evidence exists, these arguments could be extended to the chimpanzee face responsive regions in the fusiform gyrus and STS (Parr et al., 2009). However, despite these similarities, there are also notable differences in the functional responsiveness of these regions across species. The human FFA, for example, is responsive to faces but also to non-face objects relative to baseline and to objects for which people have developed expertise (Gauthier et al., 2000). By contrast, the macaque face patches show almost no response to non-face objects (Tsao et al., 2003). Both the human FFA and STS-FA distinguish between faces and body parts and between facial expressions versus neutral faces (Engell and Haxby, 2007; Morris et al., 2006; Schwarzlose et al., 2005), while studies disagree about whether similar distinctions can be made for macaque pSTS-FA and aSTS-FA (Hadj-Bouzaine et al., 2008; Pinsk et al., 2005). In addition, human face regions do not distinguish between macaque and human faces, while macaque face patches respond significantly more to conspecific than human faces (Tsao et al., 2003).

Despite these functional similarities, it remains highly problematic to assess the homology of these regions using more stringent anatomical criteria, particularly when it is known that visual regions are not always located in the same anatomical location across species, (Sereno 1998; Sereno and Allman, 1991), and there is known individual variability in the location of some regions, such as FFA, in humans (Kanwisher et al., 1997; Saxe et al., 2006). New techniques have aided this effort by making it possible to computationally deform and align flat maps of cortex of different species to identipotentially homologous regions with greater anatomical (sulcal) detail than looking at surface landmarks (van Essen et al., 2001). Using this approach,

Tsao and colleagues (2003) place the macaque pSTS-FA and human FFA in close proximity. Face-selective regions in the chimpanzee brain are also in regions comparable to the location of human FFA, although the selectivity of these regions has not been further validated (Parr et al., 2009). This makes it difficult to address the question posed earlier in this section, whether anatomical and/or physiological differences can be identified that may help to explain the behavioral differences seen in the face processing skills of monkeys, apes, and humans. It appears clear, though, that face recognition has played an important enough role in primate evolution that, through whatever mechanisms, there has been some dedication of neural circuitry to this important social skill and these selection pressures are likely to have been very similar in different species. While the idea of a "basic uniformity" in the primate neural architecture has appealing explanatory power, e.g. macaque or chimpanzee regions can be understood via their similarity to human regions, and vice versa, this stance also precludes investigations aimed at revealing neural adaptations that may have emerged during millions of years of divergent evolution, in different ecological and social environments (Preuss, 2006).

Summary and conclusions

Face recognition is a complex, yet highly efficient skill in humans involving both cognitive/ developmental and neural specializations. We are attracted to faces and face-like configurations from birth but develop face expertise slowly, achieving adult-like performance by early childhood. Around this time, a region in the medial temporal lobe, the fusiform gyurs, becomes specialized for processing faces compared to other visual stimuli. There is considerable debate as to whether these specializations are unique to humans and the extent to which some or all may be shared by related species of non-human primates. In this chapter, we review the evidence for face processing in non-human primates and conclude that chimpanzees share many of the same specializations for processing faces as humans, while the data from monkeys is less clear. The reason for this may be related to differences in the methods used to test monkeys compared to chimpanzees and humans, but a reasonable conclusion at this stage is that there are some fundamental differences in how monkeys process faces compared to hominoids.

Future studies on face processing in non-human primates should be extremely diligent in preparing tasks that can address outstanding questions in this research. First and foremost, to what extent are faces a special class of stimuli for monkeys, eliciting specific behavioral and cognitive response patterns similar to humans and chimpanzees, e.g. the inversion effect and composite face effects, to the exclusion of other stimulus categories? Unless faces are compared to other stimulus categories, no conclusions can be made regarding face-selectivity. Second, studies should incorporate a more ecological focus. While it is informative to understand how visual pictures are discriminated and what regions of the brain become selectively activated, face processing is a real world activity and studies should try and incorporate wherever possible the problems that primates face on a day-to-day basis, e.g. how do primates discriminate among the many individuals living in a social group and how are specific individuals recognized and remembered? Finally, comparative research on the neurobiology of face recognition is still in its infancy. Results to date raise the interesting possibility that increases in the complexity of the neural circuitry involved in face processing may underlie evolved increases in the complexity of face perception. In particular, it seems that the face-selective region in the fusiform gyrus may be linked to configural processing and, specifically, identity recognition. To address this question, it is essential that future research directly compare the homology of face processing regions across species, both in terms of function (association with behavioral markers of configural processing) and anatomy (cellular organization and connections with other regions). Moreover, the same questions raised in the second point should be incorporated into more sophisticated neuro-imaging procedures to bridge an understanding of cognitive and neural specializations in face processing from an ecologically-relevant perspective.

References

Bruce, C. (1982). Face recognition by monkeys: Absence of an inversion effect. *Neuropsychologia*, **20**, 515–521.

Collishaw, S.M. and Hole, G.J. (2002). Is there a linear or a nonlinear relationship between rotation and configural processing of faces? *Perception*, **31**, 287–296.

Dahl, C.D., Logothetis, N.K., and Hoffman, K.L. (2007). Individuation and holistic processing of faces in rhesus monkeys. *Proceedings of Biological Science*, **274**, 2069–2076.

Diamond, R. and Carey, S. (1986). Why faces are and are not special: An effect of expertise. *Journal of Experimental Psychology*, **115**, 107–117.

Dittrich, W. (1990). Representation of faces in longtailed macaques (Macaca fascicularis). *Ethology*, **85**, 265–278.

Dufour, V., Pascalis, O., and Petit, O. (2006). Face processing limitation to own species in primates: A comparative study in brown capuchins, Tonkean macaques and humans. *Behavioural Processes*, **73**, 107–113.

Eifuku, S., De Souza, W.C., Tamura, R., Nishijo, H., and Ono, T. (2004). Neuronal correlates of face identification in the monkey anterior temporal cortical areas. Journal of *Neurophysiology*, **91**, 358–371.

Engell, A.D. and Haxby, J.V. (2007). Facial expression and gaze-direction in human superior temporal sulcus. *Neuropsychologia*, **45**, 3234–3241.

Gauthier, I., Skudlarski, P., Gore, J.C. and Anderson, A.W. (2000). Expertise for cars and birds recruits brain areas involved in face recognition. *Nature Neuroscience*, **3**, 191–197.

Goren, C., Sarty, M. and Wu, P. (1975). Visual following and pattern discrimination of face-like stimuli by newborn infants. *Pediatrics*, **56**, 544–549.

Gothard, K.M., Erickson, C.A. and Amaral, D.G. (2004). How do rhesus monkeys (Macaca mulatta) scan faces in a visual paired comparison task? *Animal Cognition*, **7**, 25–36.

Gothard, K.M., Battaglia, F.P., Erickson, C.A., Spitler, K.M. and Amaral, D.G. (2007). Neural responses to facial expression and face identity in the monkey amygdala. *Journal of Neurophysiology*, **97**, 1671–1683.

Gothard, K.M., Brooks, K.N. and Peterson, M.A. (2009). Multiple perceptual strategies used by macaque monkeys for face recognition. *Animal Cognition*, **12**, 155–167.

Hadj-Bouziane, F., Bell, A.H., Knusten, T.A., Ungerleider, L.G. and Tootell, R.B. (2008). Perception of emotional expressions is independent of face selectivity in monkey inferior temporal cortex. *Proceedings of the National Academy of Sciences, USA*, **105**, 5591–5596.

Hasselmo, M.E., Rolls, E.T., and Baylis, G.C. (1989). The role of expression and identity in the face-selective responses of neurons in the temporal visual cortex of the monkey. *Behavioral Brain Research*, **32**, 203–218.

Haxby, J.V., Hoffman, E.A., and Gobbini, M.I. (2000). The distributed human neural system for face perception. *Trends in Cognitive Science*, **4**, 223–233.

Haxby, J.V., Gobbini, M.I., Furey, M.L., Ishai, L., Schouten, J.L. and Pietrini, P. (2001). Distributed and overlapping representations of faces and objects in ventral temporal cortex. *Science*, **293**, 2425–2430.

Hinde, R.A. and Rowell, T.E. (1962). Communication by postures and facial expressions in the rhesus monkey (Macaca mulatta). *Proceedings of the Royal Society of London B*, **138**, 1–21.

Hoffman, E.A. and Haxby, J.V. (2000). Distinct representations of eye gaze and identity in the distributed human neural system for face perception. *Nature Neuroscience*, **3**, 80–84.

Hoffman, K.L., Gothard, K.M., Schmid, M.C. and Logothetis, N.K. (2007). Facial-expression and gaze-selective responses in the monkey amygdala. *Current Biology*, **17**, 766–772.

Kanwisher, N., McDermott, J. and Chun, M.M. (1997). The fusiform face area: A module in human extrastriate cortex specialized for face perception. *Journal of Neuroscience*, **17**, 4302–4311.

Keating, C.F. and Keating, E.G. (1993). Monkeys and mug shots: cues used by rhesus monkeys (Macaca mulatta) to recognize a human face. *Journal of Comparative Psychology*, **107**, 131–139.

Kuwahata, H., Adachi, I., Fujita, K., Tomonaga, M., and Matsuzawa, T. (2004). Development of schematic face preferences in macaque monkeys. *Behavioural Processes*, **66**, 17–21.

Kyes, R.C. and Candland, D.K. (1987). Baboon (Papio hamadryas) visual preferences for regions of the face. *Journal of Comparative Psychology*, **101**, 345–348.

Le Grand, R., Mondloch, C.J., Maurer, D., and Brent, H.P. (2001). Early visual experience and face processing. *Nature*, **410**, 890.

Martin-Malivel, J. and Okada, K. (2007). Human and chimpanzee face recognition in chimpanzees (Pan troglodytes): Role of exposure and impact on categorical perception. *Behavioral Neuroscience*, **121**, 1145–1155.

Matsuzawa, T. (2007). Comparative cognitive development. *Developmental Science*, **10**, 97–103.

Maurer, D., Le Grand, R. and Mondloch, C.J. (2002). The many faces of configural processing. *Trends in Cognitive Science*, **6**, 255–260.

McCarthy, G., Puce, A., Gore, J.C. and Allison, T. (1997). Face-specific processing in the human fusiform gyrus. *Journal of Cognitive Neuroscience*, **9**, 605–610.

Mendelson, M.J. (1982). Visual and social responses in infant rhesus monkeys. *American Journal of Primatology*, **3**, 333–340.

Moeller, S., Freiwald, W.A., Tsao, D.Y. (2008). Patches with links: a unified system for processing faces in the macaque temporal lobe. *Science*, **320**, 1355–1359.

Morris, J.P., Pelphrey, K.A., and McCarthy, G. (2006). Occipitotemporal activation evoked by the perception of human bodies is modulated by the presence or absence of the face. *Neuropsychologia*, **44**, 1919–1927.

Myowa-Yamakoshi, M. and Tomonaga, M. (2001). Development of face recognition in an infant gibbon (Hylobates agilis). *Infant Behavior and Development*, **24**, 215–227.

Neiworth, J.J., Hassett, J.M. and Sylvester, C.J. (2007). Face processing in humans and new world monkeys: the influence of experiential and ecological factors. *Animal Cognition*, **10**, 125–134.

Overman, W.H. and Doty, R.W. (1982). Hemispheric specialization displayed by man but not macaques for analysis of faces. *Neuropsychologia*, **20**, 113–128.

Parr, L.A., Dove, T. and Hopkins, W.D. (1998). Why faces may be special: Evidence for the inversion effect in chimpanzees (Pan troglodytes). *Journal of Cognitive Neuroscience*, **10**, 615–622.

Parr, L.A., Winslow, J.T. and Hopkins, W.D. (1999). Is the inversion effect in rhesus monkeys face specific? *Animal Cognition*, **2**, 123–129.

Parr, L.A., Winslow, J.T., Hopkins, W.D. and de Waal, F.B.M. (2000). Recognizing facial cues: Individual recognition in chimpanzees (Pan troglodytes) and rhesus monkeys (Macaca mulatta). *Journal of Comparative Psychology*, **114**, 47–60.

Parr, L.A., Heintz, M. and Akamagwuna, U. (2006). Three studies of configural face processing by chimpanzees. *Brain and Cognition*, **62**, 30–42.

Parr, L.A., Heintz, M. and Pradhan, G. (2008). Rhesus monkeys (Macaca mulatta) lack face expertise. *Journal of Comparative Psychology*, **122**, 390–402.

Parr, L.A., Hecht, E., Barks, S.K., Preuss, T.M., and Votaw, J.R. (2009). Face selective brain activity in chimpanzees. *Current Biology*, **19**, 1–4.

Pascalis, O. and Bachevalier, J. (1998). Face recognition in primates: a cross-species study. *Behavioural Processes*, **43**, 87–96.

Pascalis, O., de Haan, M., and Nelson, C.A. (2002). Is face processing species-specific during the first year of life? *Science*, **296**, 1321–1323.

Phelps, M.T. and Roberts, W.A. (1994). Memory for pictures of upright and inverted primate faces in humans (Homo sapiens), squirrel monkeys (Saimiri sciureus), and pigeons (Columba livia). *Journal of Comparative Psychology*, **108**, 114–125.

Pineda, J.A., Sebestyen, G., and Nava, C. (1994). Face recognition as a function of social attention in nonhuman primates: An ERP study. *Cognitive Brain Research*, **2**, 1–12.

Pinsk, M.A., DeSimone, K., Moore, T., Gross, C.G., and Kastner, S. (2005). Representations of faces and body parts in macaque temporal cortex: a functional MRI study. *Proceedings of the National Academy of Sciences*, **102**, 6996–7001.

Pokorny, J.J. and de Waal, F.B.M. (2009). Face recognition in capuchin monkeys (Cebus paella). *Journal of Comparative Psychology*, **123**, 151–160.

Preuss, T.M. (2006). Who's afraid of Homo sapiens? *Journal of Biomedical Discovery Collaboration*, **1**, 17.

Rosenfeld, S.A. and Van Hoesen, G.W. (1979). Face recognition in the rhesus monkey. *Neuropsychologia*, **17**, 503–509.

Sato, N. and Nakamura, K. (2001). Detection of directed gaze in rhesus monkeys (Macaca mulatta). *Journal of Comparative Psychology*, **115**, 115–121.

Saxe, R., Brett, M. and Kanwisher, N. (2006). Divide and conquer: in defense of functional localizers. *NeuroImage*, **30**, 1088–1096.

Schwarzlose, R.F., Baker, C.I. and Kanwisher, N. (2005). Separate face and body selectivity on the fusiform gyrus. *Journal of Neuroscience*, **25**, 11055–11059.

Sereno, M.I. (1998). Brain mapping in animals and humans. *Current Opinion in Neurobiology*, **8**, 188–194.

Sereno, M.I. and Allman, J.M. (1991). Cortical visual areas in mammals. In A.G. Leventhal (ed.) *The Neural Basis of Visual Function*, pp. 160–172. London: Macmillan.

Sugita, Y. (2008). Face perception in monkeys reared with no exposure to faces. *Proceedings of the National Academy of Sciences, USA*, **105**, 394–398.

Tarr, M.J. and Gauthier, I. (2000). FFA: A flexible fusiform area for subordinate-level visual processing automatized by expertise. *Nature Neuroscience*, **3**, 764–769.

Tomonaga, M. (1994). How laboratory-raised Japanese monkeys (Macaca fuscata) perceive rotated photographs of monkeys: Evidence for an inversion effect in face perception. *Primates*, **35**, 155–165.

Tomonaga, M. (1999). Inversion effect in perception of human faces in a chimpanzee (Pan troglodytes). *Primates*, **40**, 417–438.

Tomonaga, M. (2007). Visual search for orientation of faces by a chimpanzee (Pan troglodytes): face-specific upright superiority and the role of facial configural properties. *Primates*, **48**, 1–12.

Tomonaga, M., Itakura, S. and Matsuzawa, T. (1993). Superiority of conspecific faces and reduced inversion effect in face perception by a chimpanzee. *Folia Primatologica*, **61**, 110–114.

Tsao, D.Y., Freiwald, W.A., Knuston, T.A., Mandeville, J.B. and Tottell, R.B. (2003). Faces and objects in macaque cerebral cortex. *Nature Neuroscience*, **6**, 989–995.

Tsao, D.Y., Freiwald, W.A. Tottell, R.B. and Livingstone, M.S. (2006). A cortical region consisting entirely of face-selective cells. *Science*, **311**, 670–674.

Tsao, D.Y., Schweers, N., Moeller, S. and Friewald, W.A. (2008a). Patches of face-selective cortex in the macaque frontal lobe. *Nature Neuroscience*, **11**, 877–879.

Tsao, D.Y., Moeller, S. and Friewald, W.A. (2008b). Comparing face patch systems in macaques and humans. *Proceedings of the National Academy of Sciences*, **105**, 19514–19519.

Valenza, E., Simion, F., Cassia, V.M., and Umilta, C. (1996). Face preference at birth. *Journal of Experimental Psychology: Human Perception and Performance*, **22**, 892–903.

Van Essen, D.C., Drury, H.A., Dickson, J., Harwell, J., Hanlon, D., and Anderson C.H. (2001). An integrated software suite for surface-based analyses of cerebral cortex. *Journal of the American Medical Information Association*, **8**, 443–459.

Vermeire, B.A. and Hamilton, C.R. (1998). Inversion effect for faces in split-brain monkeys. *Neuropsychologia*, **36**, 1003–1014.

Weiss, D.J., Kralik, J.D. and Hauser, M.D. (2001). Face processing in cotton-top tamarins (Saguinus oedipus). *Animal Cognition*, **4**, 191–205.

Wilson, F.A.W. and Goldman-Rakic, P.S. (1994). Viewing preferences of rhesus monkeys related to memory for complex pictures, colours and faces. *Behavioural Brain Research*, **60**, 79–89.

Wright, A.A. and Roberts, W.A. (1996). Monkey and human face perception: inversion effects for human faces but not for monkey faces or scenes. *Journal of Cognitive Neuroscience*, **8**, 278–290.

Yin, R.K. (1969). Looking at upside-down faces. *Journal of Experimental Psychology*, **81**, 141–145.

Young, A.W., Hellawell, D. and Hay, D.C. (1987). Configurational information in face perception. *Perception*, **16**, 747–759.

Chapter 36

Taking Apart the Neural Machinery of Face Processing

Winrich Freiwald and Doris Tsao

Introduction

Primate societies are based on face recognition. Telling apart the members of one's troop and inferring their mood or focus of attention are essential everyday operations that rely heavily on face recognition. In this chapter, we will present evidence that macaques have evolved a unique piece of neural machinery to support face recognition, consisting of six discrete patches of face-selective cortex in the temporal lobe. Though special, face recognition confronts the same fundamental challenge as all object recognition: identification of individuals belonging to a specific category despite a huge range in possible appearances. The specialized architecture of the face patch system—concentration of face cells into modules and spatial separation of modules—makes it possible to dissect the steps leading to invariant object recognition in unprecedented detail. We will discuss both anatomical experiments revealing the connectivity of the six face patches and electrophysiological experiments revealing the response selectivity of single units within the patches.

In the 1970s, Gross and colleagues reported the surprising discovery of cells in the macaque temporal lobe that responded selectively to particular biologically important forms such as faces and hands (Gross, 1973, 2002; Gross et al., 1972). This finding was subsequently confirmed by several labs who focused on face-selective cells, mapping their extent throughout different subdivisions of inferior temporal (IT) cortex (Baylis et al., 1987), and characterizing the invariance and selectivity properties of these cells in greater detail (Perrett et al., 1982, 1984, 1985, 1987, 1991, 1992; Young and Yamane, 1992; Logothetis and Sheinberg, 1996; Eifuku et al., 2004; Rolls, 2007). The difficulty of finding these cells, however, posed severe limits on the possibility of a deep understanding of how these cells are wired and what their precise function in face recognition is. The door to systematically understanding face cells opened ajar, when the discovery of face areas in humans suggested face cells may be locally concentrated.

One of the most surprising and reproducible discoveries in the entire functional magnetic resonance imaging (fMRI) literature is the finding that humans have several specialized regions in the temporal lobe that respond much more strongly to faces than to any other object class (Kanwisher et al., 1997; Puce et al., 1996). Similarly, in macaque monkeys, face-selective patches of cortex have been found in the temporal lobe (Pinsk et al., 2005; Rajimehr et al., 2009; Tsao et al., 2003). What is the contribution of such face-selective areas to face processing? In this chapter, we review insights into this question obtained from fMRI and electrophysiological experiments in macaque monkeys. We will present evidence that macaques have specialized face regions, and we will discuss their anatomical connectivity as well as functional properties measured with both fMRI and targeted electrophysiology.

The face system in macaque monkeys revealed by fMRI

The importance of face recognition for primates is likely the reason why both macaque and human temporal lobes host multiple face-selective regions. It is worthwhile noting that face cells have been found in other species, most notably in sheep (Kendrick and Baldwin, 1987) (see Kendrick and Feng, Chapter 34, this volume; yet it is unknown to date whether face cells in non-primate species are also organized into face-selective regions). How are these face selective regions organized in primates, what are the commonalities, and what are the differences between the species? Tsao et al. scanned 10 macaques and 13 human subjects using a stimulus set consisting of faces and objects in separate blocks (Tsao et al., 2008a). In most macaque monkeys they found six patches of face-selective cortex, so called "face patches," in each hemisphere of the temporal lobe. The location of the patches was consistent across hemispheres and individuals, with only slight variations across individuals.

Figure 36.1 illustrates the prototypical pattern of face patches in one animal. This animal had six discrete face patches in each hemisphere, distributed along the anteroposterior axis of the temporal lobe. These patches are organized into: one posterior patch on the lateral surface of TEO

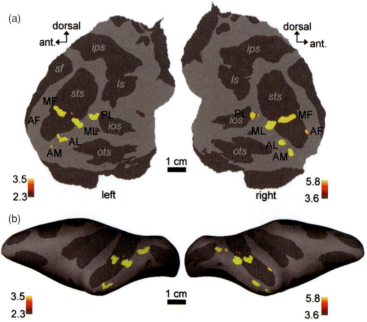

Fig. 36.1 Six patches of face-selective cortex in the macaque temporal lobe, shown on flattened cortical surfaces (a) and inflated hemispheres (b). Color scale bar indicates the negative common logarithm of the probability of error. Area initials: posterior face patch (PL), middle face patch in the STS fundus (MF), middle face patch on the lower lip of the STS (ML), anterior face patch in the STS fundus (AF), anterior face patch on the lower lip of the STS (AL), and anterior face patch on the ventral surface of IT just lateral and anterior to the AMTS (AM). Sulcal abbreviations: lunate sulcus (ls), inferior occipital sulcus (ios), occipito-temporal sulcus (ots), superior temporal sulcus (sts), intraparietal sulcus (ips), Sylvan fissure (sf).

("PL," for posterior lateral), two middle face patches in posterior TE, one located in the fundus of the STS ("MF," for middle fundus) and one on the lower lip of the STS ("ML," for middle lateral), and three patches in anterior TE, one located near the fundus of the STS ("AF," for anterior fundus), one on the lower lip of the STS and adjacent gyrus, in TEad ("AL," for anterior lateral), and one more medially on the ventral surface, just lateral and anterior to the AMTS, in TEav ("AM," for anterior medial). It is noteworthy that while face patches are organized, by and large, along the STS, areas PL and AM are located outside the STS. This may be the reason for the finding of Heywood and Cowey (1992) that bilateral lesions to the STS in monkeys have very little impact on their ability to recognize faces.

In humans, using the same stimuli, Tsao et al. found that across subjects the number of face areas varied between three and five, consisting of the occipital face area (OFA) (Kanwisher and Yovel, 2006), the superior temporal sulcus face area (STS-FA) (Hoffman and Haxby, 2000), the fusiform face area (FFA) (Kanwisher et al., 1997), plus one to two face regions located in the anterior collateral sulcus (Tsao et al., 2008a) (Figure 36.2). Thus the overall numbers of macaque and human face-selective regions are comparable.

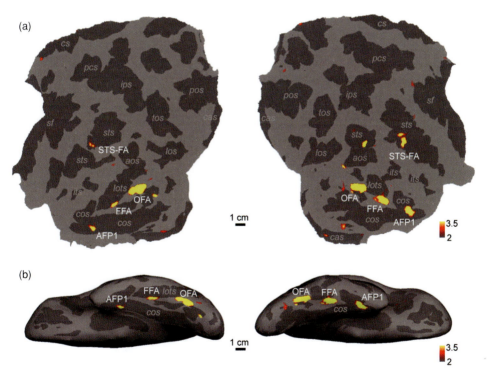

Fig. 36.2 Face-selective regions in the left and right temporal lobes of a human, superimposed on flattened cortical surface (a) and a ventral view of the inflated hemispheres (b). Face-region abbreviations: occipital face area (OFA), fusiform face area (FFA), superior temporal sulcus face area (STS-FA), anterior face patch 1 (AFP1). Sulcal abbreviations: anterior occipital (aos), lateral occipital (los), lateral occipito-temporal (lots), intraparietal (ips), inferior temporal (its), superior temporal (sts), parieto-occipital (pos), calcarine (cas), collateral (cos), transoccipital (tos), precentral (pcs), and Sylvan fissure (sf). Adapted from Tsao et al. (2008a).

The spatial patterning of macaque and human face-processing systems exhibits both a striking similarity and a striking difference. The striking similarity is the arrangement of areas along the occipitotemporal axis (compare Figures 36.1a and 36.2a); the striking difference is their location along the dorsoventral axis within the temporal lobe. While the macaque face patches are mostly located inside or close to the STS, all the human face-selective regions, with the exception of the STS-FA, are located further ventrally, primarily along or inside the collateral sulcus. Thus, if these areas are homologous, then a major shift of face area location must have occurred in the course of primate evolution following the split of catarrhine primates into hominoids and Old World monkeys. As of now, this evolutionary scenario is speculative as data on other primate species as well as a rigorous and more complete demonstration of homology are needed (see Parr and Hecht, Chapter 35, this volume; Parr et al., 2009).

Tsao et al. found that the macaque frontal lobe also contains three patches of face-selective cortex (Tsao et al., 2008b). Two patches were present in all animals scanned: one in the lateral orbital sulcus bilaterally ("PO," for prefrontal orbital), and one in ventrolateral prefrontal cortex, strongly biased to the right hemisphere ("PV," for prefrontal ventrolateral) (Figure 36.3). Since faces exert a powerful influence on primate behavior (e.g. when classifying a face as friend or foe, or trying to memorize a face), it is likely these face patches perform the function of translating perceptual information about faces into behavior. Most humans also show regions of

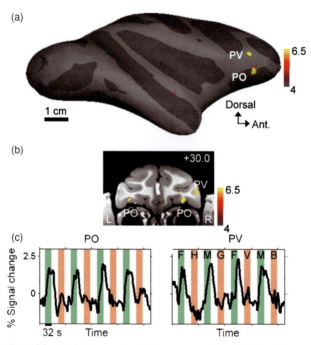

Fig. 36.3 Two patches of face-selective cortex in the macaque frontal lobe, shown on an inflated right hemisphere (a), and a coronal slice (b). (c) Mean time courses extracted from these two prefrontal face patches (averaged across four macaques, conventions as in Figure 36.1). Reprinted by permission from Macmillan Publishers Ltd: *Nature Neuroscience*, Patches of face-selective cortex in the macaque frontal lobe, Tsao et al., copyright (2008).

face-responsive cortex in the frontal lobe (Haxby et al., 1996), and in some subjects, frontal regions can be found that are not only face-responsive but also face-selective.

In particular, orbitofrontal cortex has been implicated in the control of mood, processing of emotions, and social reinforcement (Rolls, 1999), raising the possibility that it may be selective for facial expressions. When responses to neutral and expressive macaque faces were measured, it was found that all three prefrontal face patches responded more strongly to expressive than to neutral faces, with the difference reaching significance in PO, suggesting that PO may play a specific role in responding to the emotional content of faces (Tsao et al., 2008b). Temporal lobe face patches, by comparison, were only weakly modulated by facial expression.

In trying to understand the logic underlying the neural organization of face processing, it seems instructive to know what the cortex adjacent to the face patches is selective for. In both humans and macaques, body areas have been found adjacent to face areas (Pinsk et al., 2005; Schwarzlose et al., 2005; Tsao et al., 2003). Consistent with this finding, Tsao et al. observed a stronger response to bodies than to the other non-face object categories across the six macaque face patches, though importantly, the response to faces was significantly greater than that to bodies (Tsao et al., 2008a). Whether these body responses arise from the face-selective regions themselves, or from nearby regions, will require ultra-high-resolution fMRI and/or single-unit recordings to resolve. High-resolution fMRI shows that the human FFA does not respond to bodies (Schwarzlose et al., 2005), and targeted single-unit recordings show that the macaque middle face patch does not respond to bodies either (Tsao et al., 2006). Taken together, the available evidence suggests that bodies are processed by regions adjacent to but discrete from the face patches in both humans and macaques.

Connectivity of the face patch system

The architecture of the inferior temporal lobe has been studied by classic anatomical tracing. V4 sends strong projections to TEO from its central visual field representation (Ungerleider et al., 2008). TEO in turn sends strong feedforward projections to area TE (Saleem et al., 1993). The projection from TEO to TE shows a precise modularity, with single TEO sites projecting to two to five clusters in TE (Saleem et al., 1993) (Figure 36.4). These clusters are columnar, extending across all six cortical layers. Area TE, the highest purely visual stage of the ventral pathway, sends feedback projections to V4 and TEO, and feedforward projections to several polymodal brain sites including perirhinal cortex, frontal cortex, amygdala, and striatum (Cheng et al., 1997; Saleem and Tanaka, 1996; Suzuki et al., 2000; Webster et al., 1991, 1993, 1994).

While tracer studies demonstrate connections between specific nodes in TEO and TE (Saleem et al., 1993) (Figure 36.4), the need to sacrifice the animal to process the tissue prevents assessment of the functional properties of connected nodes. In general, to understand functional architecture, it is necessary to combine connectivity maps with functional topography. The organization of the face processing system of macaque monkeys into discrete, distributed nodes raises the question: Are the nodes connected to each other?

To determine the connectivity of individual face patches, Moeller et al. (2008) used electrical microstimulation combined with simultaneous fMRI. Stimulation of each of four targeted face patches produced strong activation specifically within a subset of the other face patches (Figure 36.5). Stimulation outside the face patches produced an activation pattern that spared the face patches. These results indicate that the face patches form a strongly and specifically interconnected network.

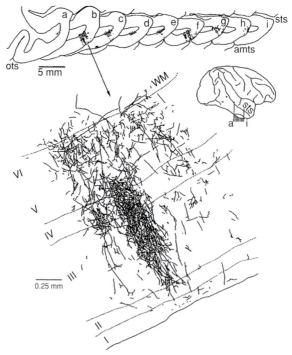

Fig. 36.4 Columnar projections in IT. Labeled terminals in TE following injections of the anterograde tracer Phaseolus vulgaris leucoagglutinin (PHA) in TEO (indicated by two red spots) form columnar clusters. Reproduced from *Cerebral Cortex*, Specific and Columnar Projection from Area TEO to TE in the Macaque Inferotemporal Cortex, Saleem, © 1993, with permission from Oxford University Press.

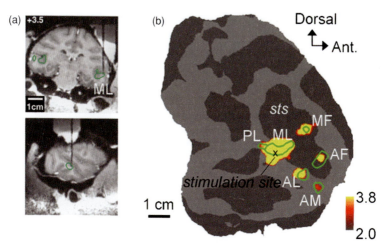

Fig. 36.5 Connectivity of temporal face patches revealed by microstimulation combined with fMRI. (a) Electrode position in relation to the face patches (green outlines) in sagittal and coronal MRI slices. The electrode targeted ML in the right hemisphere. (b) Areas significantly activated by microstimulation of ML overlaid on a flatmap. From *Science*, Patches with Links: A Unified System for Processing Faces in the Macaque Temporal Lobe, Moeller, Freiwald, and Tsao. Reprinted with permission from AAAS.

Single-unit and local field potential recordings in ML/MF

Tanaka and colleagues pioneered the study of tuning properties of IT neurons (Tanaka, 1996; Tanaka et al., 1991). Their work was centered on the concept of a "critical feature," defined as the simplest stimulus feature sufficient to elicit the maximum response in a cell. To identify critical features, they first probed a cell with many three-dimensional plant and animal models at different views, then took photographs of these objects and systematically simplified them to the point where further simplification would diminish the response (Kobatake and Tanaka, 1994). For example, the critical feature of a cell preferring a tiger might be two round black and white gratings arranged like a snowman (Tanaka, 2003). The main conclusion of these experiments was that most cells in TE are selective for moderately complex feature combinations, not for entire objects. Such cells are already present in V4 and TEO, but at a lower proportion, mixed with cells selective for simple features (such as color or orientation). Tanaka suggested that face cells may be distinct from most other IT cells in being resistant to stimulus simplification (Tanaka, 1996). However, results suggest that in the middle face patches ML and MF, face cells do respond to simplified stimuli (see below).

The face patches, forming discrete regions distributed along the entire length of the temporal lobe, offer ideal probes of the development of stimulus selectivity in IT cortex. Tsao and colleagues used functional imaging to localize face-selective regions in the macaque temporal lobe, and then recorded almost 500 single units within the middle face patches (ML and MF) to 96 images of faces and other objects (Tsao et al., 2006). They found 97% of all visually-responsive cells to be face selective, on average showing almost 20-fold larger responses to faces than to non-face objects (Figure 36.6).

In addition to the overwhelming response bias for face stimuli, many cells gave a significant response to a few particular non-face objects (the faint orange lines in Figure 36.6a to the right of the first 16 columns). In monkey M1, the two non-face objects that gave a mean response across the population exceeding the level of six average standard errors of the spontaneous activity distribution were a clock and an apple (Figure 36.6c). In monkey M2 the only non-face objects that elicited significant responses across the population were also round. The small but significant responses to round stimuli suggest that the coding of faces is based on analysis of visual shape in the middle face patch. Furthermore, the result shows that face cells, at least those located in ML/MF (in posterior TE, corresponding to an intermediate stage within IT cortex) do respond to simplified stimuli.

The local field potential (LFP) represents summated excitatory and inhibitory synaptic potentials in thousands of neurons around the electrode tip (Logothetis and Wandell, 2004). Figure 36.6d shows evoked LFPs recorded from monkey M1 and M2. In both monkeys tested, two large face-selective troughs with peak magnitudes at 130 ms and 200 ms were evident in the LFP (Tsao et al., 2006). These face-selective LFP troughs were observed at almost all recording sites in the middle face patch, providing further evidence that population activity within this face patch is strongly face selective. The existence of two face-selective troughs may suggest two discrete stages of face processing, possibly triggered by the arrival of feedforward and feedback/recurrent inputs, respectively (Lamme and Roelfsema, 2000).

Population analysis of the responses of middle face patch cells to the 96 image screening set, which included 16 different faces, showed that the population activity could be used not only to categorize faces from non-face objects, but also to distinguish different faces (Tsao et al., 2006), because many cells showed robust and differentiated responses to different faces (Figure 36.7).

The conglomeration of face cells into specialized cortical regions makes it technically feasible to test the perceptual function of face cells using microstimulation. Using this approach, Afraz et al.

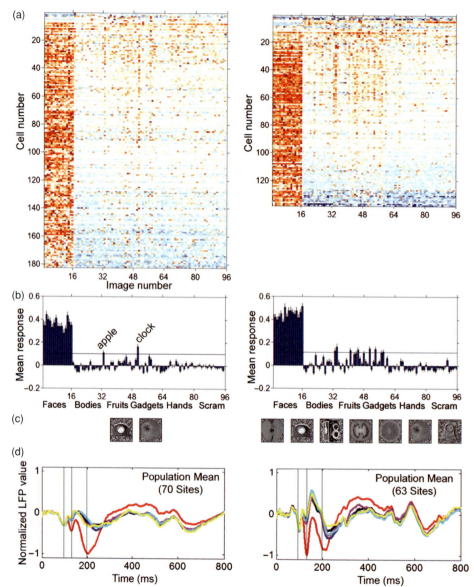

Fig. 36.6 Face selectivity of single units in the middle face patch. (a) Selectivity profiles of all visually responsive cells in monkeys M1 (182 cells) and M2 (138 cells) to 96 images of faces, bodies, fruits, gadgets, hands, and scrambled patterns (16 images/category). Each row represents one cell and each column one image. To compute selectivity profiles, for each cell responses to the 96 images were averaged over a 200 ms interval starting at the response latency, baseline subtracted, and normalized. (b) Average response to each of the 96 images across all visually responsive cells in monkeys M1 and M2. Error bars represent ±1 standard error. The black line indicates six average standard errors. (c) Non-face images that elicited a response above six average standard errors in monkeys M1 and M2. Images are sorted, from left to right, by increasing response magnitude. (d) Average evoked LFP responses, sorted by category, across 70 recording sites in monkey M1 and 63 recording sites in monkey M2. From *Science*, A Cortical Region Consisting Entirely of Face-Selective Cells, Tsao, Freiwald, Tootell, and Livingstone. Reprinted with permission from AAAS.

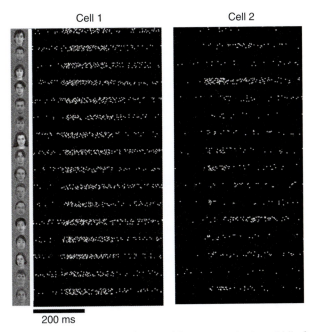

Fig. 36.7 Mechanisms for both detection and recognition operate in the middle face patch. (Left) Raster plot of a cell recorded from ML that responded strongly to all 16 screening faces. (Right) Another cell recorded from ML that reliably differentiated between the 16 screening faces.

(2006) obtained direct evidence that activity of face cells influences face detection. Monkeys were trained to discriminate between noisy pictures of faces and non-face objects. Through systematic sampling, cortical locations were identified where clusters of face-selective cells could be reliably recorded. When these regions were stimulated and the monkeys' perceptual choices were observed, a shift in the psychometric curve favoring detection of a face was found.

Summary and conclusions

The brain of the macaque monkey contains a specialized system of face-selective regions that is highly reproducible across individuals. This system consists of one posterior (PL), two middle (ML, MF), and three anterior (AL, AF, AM) face patches in the temporal lobe and three patches in the frontal lobe (PO, PV, PA). The distance between PL and AM in the anterior posterior direction is more than 20 mm. The face-patch system thus presents us with a new kind of functional organization in TE, more macroscopic than feature columns of inferotemporal cortex (approximately 0.5 mm in diameter, (Tanaka, 2003; Wang et al., 1996)), yet more delicate than the coarse partitioning of IT into anatomically defined subregions (Felleman and Van Essen, 1991; Seltzer and Pandya, 1994; Von Bonin and Bailey, 1947). The components of the face patch system are compact (a few millimeter in diameter), yet transgress area boundaries, with face patches located in posterior, middle, and anterior portions of IT (Felleman and Van Essen, 1991). Experiments combining microstimulation with fMRI show that the different face patches are strongly and specifically connected. Recordings from the two middle face patches have shown that these consist almost entirely of face-selective neurons (Tsao et al., 2006). The specialized architecture of the face patch system—concentration of face cells into modules and spatial separation of modules—makes it possible to dissect the steps leading to invariant object recognition in unprecedented detail. Future experiments can now target each face patch for study with large sets of face stimuli varied along multiple parameters, and during performance of a rich repertoire of face-related behaviors, to understand precisely what is being accomplished by the 6 + 3 natural steps of face processing carried out by face patches in the macaque brain.

References

Afraz, S.R., Kiani, R., and Esteky, H. (2006). Microstimulation of inferotemporal cortex influences face categorization. *Nature*, **442**, 692–695.

Baylis, G., Rolls, E., and Leonard, C. (1987). Functional subdivisions of the temporal lobe neocortex. *Journal of Neuroscience*, **7**, 330–342.

Cheng, K., Saleem, K.S., and Tanaka, K. (1997). Organization of corticostriatal and corticoamygdalar projections arising from the anterior inferotemporal area TE of the macaque monkey: a Phaseolus vulgaris leucoagglutinin study. *Journal of Neuroscience*, **17**, 7902–7925.

Eifuku, S., De Souza, W.C., Tamura, R., Nishijo, H., and Ono, T. (2004). Neuronal correlates of face identification in the monkey anterior temporal cortical areas. *Journal of Neurophysiology*, **91**, 358–371.

Felleman, D.J. and Van Essen, D.C. (1991). Distributed hierarchical processing in the primate cerebral cortex. *Cerebral Cortex*, **1**, 1–47.

Gross, C.G. (1973). Visual functions of inferotemporal cortex. In R. Jung (ed.) *Handbook of sensory physiology*, Vol. VII, Part 3B, pp. 451–482. Berlin: Springer.

Gross, C.G. (2002). Genealogy of the "grandmother cell". *Neuroscientist*, **8**, 512–518.

Gross, C.G., Rocha-Miranda, C.E., and Bender, D.B. (1972). Visual properties of neurons in inferotemporal cortex of the macaque. *Journal of Neurophysiology*, **35**, 96–111.

Haxby, J.V., Ungerleider, L.G., Horwitz, B., Maisog, J.M., Rapoport, S.I., and Grady, C.L. (1996). Face encoding and recognition in the human brain. *Proceedings of the National Academy of Sciences of the USA*, **93**, 922–927.

Heywood, C.A. and Cowey, A. (1992). The role of the "face-cell" area in the discrimination and recognition of faces by monkeys. *Philosophical transactions of the Royal Society of London. Series B, Biological sciences*, **335**, 31–37; discussion 37–38.

Hoffman, E.A. and Haxby, J.V. (2000). Distinct representations of eye gaze and identity in the distributed human neural system for face perception. *Nature Neuroscience*, **3**, 80–84.

Kanwisher, N., McDermott, J., and Chun, M. (1997). The fusiform face area: A module in human extrastriate cortex specialized for face perception. *Journal of Neurosciences*, **17**, 4302–4311.

Kanwisher, N. and Yovel, G. (2006). The fusiform face area: a cortical region specialized for the perception of faces. *Proceedings of the Royal Society of London Series B*, **214**, 501–524.

Kendrick, K.M. and Baldwin, B.A. (1987). Cells in temporal cortex of conscious sheep can respond preferentially to the sight of faces. *Science*, **236**, 448–450.

Kobatake, E. and Tanaka, K. (1994). Neuronal selectivities to complex object features in the ventral visual pathway of the macaque cerebral cortex. *Journal of Neurophysiology*, **71**, 856–867.

Lamme, V.A.F. and Roelfsema, P.R. (2000). The distinct modes of vision offered by feedforward and recurrent processing. *Trends in Neurosciences*, **23**, 571–579.

Logothetis, N.K. and Wandell, B.A. (2004). Interpreting the BOLD signal. *Annual Review of Physiology*, **66**, 735–769.

Moeller, S., Freiwald, W.A., and Tsao, D.Y. (2008). Patches with links: a unified system for processing faces in the macaque temporal lobe. *Science*, **320**, 1355–1359.

Parr, L.A., Hecht, E., Barks, S.K., Preuss, T.M., and Votaw, J.R. (2009). Face processing in the chimpanzee brain. *Current Biology*, **19**, 50–53.

Perrett, D.I., Rolls, E.T., and Caan, W. (1982). Visual neurones responsive to faces in the monkey temporal cortex. *Experimental Brain Research*, **47**, 329–342.

Perrett, D.I., Smith, P.A., Potter, D.D., *et al.* (1984). Neurones responsive to faces in the temporal cortex: studies of functional organization, sensitivity to identity and relation to perception. *Human Neurobiology*, **3**, 197–208.

Perrett, D.I., Smith, P.A., Potter, D.D., *et al.* (1985). Visual cells in the temporal cortex sensitive to face view and gaze direction. *Proceedings of the Royal Society of London. Series B*, **223**, 293–317.

Perrett, D.I., Mistlin, A.J., and Chitty, A.J. (1987). Visual neurones responsive to faces. *Trends in Neurosciences*, **10**, 358–364.

Perrett, D.I., Oram, M.W., Harries, M.H., *et al.* (1991). Viewer-centred and object-centred coding of heads in the macaque temporal cortex. *Experimental Brain Research*, **86**, 159–173.

Perrett, D.I., Hietanen, J.K., Oram, M.W., and Benson, P.J. (1992). Organization and Functions of cells responsive to faces in the temporal cortex. *Philosophical Transactions of the Royal Society of London, B*, **335**, 29–30.

Pinsk, M.A., DeSimone, K., Moore, T., Gross, C.G., and Kastner, S. (2005). Representations of faces and body parts in macaque temporal cortex: a functional MRI study. *Proceedings of the National Academy of Sciences of the USA*, **102**, 6996–7001.

Puce, A., Allison, T., Asgari, M., Gore, J.C., and McCarthy, G. (1996). Differential sensitivity of human visual cortex to faces, letterstrings, and textures: A functional magnetic resonance imaging study. *Journal of Neuroscience*, **16**, 5205–5215.

Rajimehr, R., Young, J.C., and Tootell, R.B. (2009). An anterior temporal face patch in human cortex, predicted by macaque maps. *Proceedings of the National Academy of Sciences of the USA*, **106**, 1995–2000.

Rolls, E.T. (1999). *The brain and emotion*. Oxford: Oxford University Press.

Rolls, E.T. (2007). The representation of information about faces in the temporal and frontal lobes. *Neuropsychologia*, **45**, 124–143.

Saleem, K.S. and Tanaka, K. (1996). Divergent projections from the anterior inferotemporal area TE to the perirhinal and entorhinal cortices in the macaque monkey. *Journal of Neuroscience*, **16**, 4757–4775.

Saleem, K.S., Tanaka, K., and Rockland, K.S. (1993). Specific and columnar projection from area TEO to TE in the macaque inferotemporal cortex. *Cerebral Cortex*, **3**, 454–464.

Schwarzlose, R.F., Baker, C.I., and Kanwisher, N. (2005). Separate face and body selectivity on the fusiform gyrus. *Journal of Neuroscience*, **25**, 11055–11059.

Seltzer, B. and Pandya, D.N. (1994). Parietal, temporal, and occipital projections to cortex of the superior temporal sulcus in the rhesus monkey: a retrograde tracer study. *Journal of Comparative Neurology*, **343**, 445–463.

Suzuki, W., Saleem, K.S., and Tanaka, K. (2000). Divergent backward projections from the anterior part of the inferotemporal cortex (area TE) in the macaque. *Journal of Comparative Neurology*, **422**, 206–228.

Tanaka, K. (1996). Inferotemporal cortex and object vision. *Annual Review of Neuroscience*, **19**, 109–139.

Tanaka, K. (2003). Columns for complex visual object features in the inferotemporal cortex: clustering of cells with similar but slightly different stimulus selectivities. *Cerebral Cortex*, **13**, 90–99.

Tanaka, K., Saito, H., Fukada, Y., and Moriya, M. (1991). Coding visual images of objects in the inferotemporal cortex of the macaque monkey. *Journal of Neurophysiology*, **66**, 170–189.

Tsao, D.Y., Freiwald, W.A., Knutsen, T.A., Mandeville, J.B., and Tootell, R.B. (2003). Faces and objects in macaque cerebral cortex. *Nature Neuroscience*, **6**, 989–995.

Tsao, D.Y., Freiwald, W.A., Tootell, R.B.H., and Livingstone, M.S. (2006). A cortical region consisting entirely of face-selective cells. *Science*, **311**, 670–674.

Tsao, D.Y., Moeller, S., and Freiwald, W.A. (2008a). Comparing face patch systems in macaques and humans. *Proceedings of the National Academy of Sciences of the USA*, **105**, 19514–19519.

Tsao, D.Y., Schweers, N., Moeller, S.M., and Freiwald, W.A. (2008b). Patches of face-selective cortex in the macaque frontal lobe. *Nature Neuroscience*, **11**, 877–879.

Ungerleider, L.G., Galkin, T.W., Desimone, R., and Gattass, R. (2008). Cortical connections of area V4 in the macaque. *Cerebral Cortex*, **18**, 477–499.

Von Bonin, G. and Bailey, P. (1947). *The neocortex of macaca mulatta.* Urbana, IL: Univeristy of Illinois Press.

Wang, G., Tanaka, K., and Tanifuji, M. (1996). Optical imaging of functional organization in the monkey inferotemporal cortex. *Science*, **272**, 1665–1668.

Webster, M.J., Bachevalier, J., and Ungerleider, L.G. (1993). Subcortical connections of inferior temporal areas TE and TEO in macaque monkeys. *Journal of Comparative Neurology*, **335**, 73–91.

Webster, M.J., Bachevalier, J., and Ungerleider, L.G. (1994). Connections of inferior temporal areas TEO and TE with parietal and frontal cortex in macaque monkeys. *Cerebral Cortex*, **4**, 470–483.

Webster, M.J., Ungerleider, L.G., and Bachevalier, J. (1991). Connections of inferior temporal areas TE and TEO with medial temporal-lobe structures in infant and adult monkeys. *Journal of Neuroscience*, **11**, 1095–1116.

Young, M.P. and Yamane, S. (1992). Sparse population coding of faces in the inferotemporal cortex. *Science* (Washington DC), **29**, 1327–1331.

Chapter 37

Recognizing the Faces of Other Species: What Can a Limited Skill Tell Us About Face Processing?

Olivier Pascalis and Sylvia Wirth

Imagine strolling in the countryside when suddenly a living creature appears nearby. Your brain will automatically and rapidly categorize it, so as to address the following important issues: Is it dangerous or not? Is it human or not? To survive, each species needs to detect dangerous species and conspecifics, and to discriminate ingroup and outgroup members, for safety and social purposes. This capacity is so crucial to survival, it is likely to have appeared early in the evolution of animal species, and to be conserved thereafter. This statement is supported by the fact that primate and non-primate species are able to perform basic categorical tasks at similar levels of performance and accuracy (see Kendrick and Feng, Chapter 34; Parr and Hecht, Chapter 35, this volume).

If the individual encountered is seen as human, then you may recognize him/her and make an adaptive behavioral response. Recognition of individuals at first sight is especially important for social species, and may have been pivotal for the development of primate societies with strong social relationships (Thierry, 1994). Some species rely on their olfactory system (e.g. hamster; Lai et al., 2005) or auditory system (e.g. birds; Moseley, 1979), exploiting appropriate or highly developed senses, whereas individuation in primates is primarily achieved via the visual system. Recognition can be based on several visual elements of an individual, but examination of the face leads to the fastest and most accurate identification.

Does this ability to process faces extend to faces of other species? Is the recognition system activated for all the stimuli encountered?

When looking at other species, we may stay at a categorical level, the basic level of abstraction: "It is a bird," whereas when looking at a human face, we will automatically process it on an individual level: "It is Gepetto" (Tanaka, 2001; Tanaka and Taylor, 1991). As individuation within another species may not be relevant to us, we are unlikely to process the face in detail, even if it has a very similar configuration to ours. If so, then this raises the question of the possibility that our face processing system is strictly limited to our own species.

In this chapter, we use phylogenetic, epigenetic, and neurophysiological data to characterize the specificity and limitations of the systems that support individual face recognition in human and non-human primates. The central question of the recognition of the faces of other species will allow us to explore the processes that lead to the remarkable face expertise that humans and non-humans develop for members of their own species.

We first review the literature on categorization/recognition abilities within and across species in human and non-human primates. We will evaluate whether it is possible to perceive other-species faces at the same level of expertise as for own species. We also describe the neural substrate and the current models of neuronal processing that supports face processing in human and non-human primates. Finally, we review the developmental data pertaining to face processing in human and non-human primates, challenging the view that face processing can be plastic in adults. In light of the evidence that children can process faces of the other species, we then argue that the species-specific expertise is the product of experience with one category of faces during development.

How do we categorize faces and how do we recognize individuals?

Viewing a face triggers two automatic and fast processes: *categorization* of the stimulus as a face belonging or not to our own group or species, and *recognition* of the face at an individual level. Those two visual processes are complementary and may even have common parts of their neural pathways (Ge et al., 2009) but they are not fully understood. It is unclear whether categorization has to be accomplished before recognition can occur, whether the two processes operate in parallel from different neural systems or they result from the same neural system. Moreover, it is unknown if individuation is restricted to faces of our own species, or if it can extend to faces of other species sharing the same configuration or arrangement of features.

The influential model proposed by Bruce and Young (1986) posits a stepwise model whereby categorization of faces according to their race, gender, etc. happens at an early stage of "structural encoding," before the "face recognition units" or the "person identity nodes" are involved. In this framework, categorization refers to the process by which information about a stimulus is used to relate the stimulus to classes exhibiting common traits, whereas individuation or recognition is the process by which unique traits are linked to an individual. According to Young's model, when presented with a face, we first determine automatically to which species it belongs, its gender, race, and then proceed to individuating information. However, opposing this sequential model, the recent work by Ge et al. (2009) shows that individuation and categorization can be achieved at different rates depending on the kind of face processed. In a cross-race study, the authors have replicated the finding that humans recognize individual faces from their own race more quickly and accurately than those of other races, whereas they categorize other races faster compared to their own race. To account for the discrepancy in recognition and categorization rates, one can hypothesize that looking at a face from a different race may automatically block the information from the face recognition units, preventing one from learning to identify individuals on face information alone. One caveat of this hypothesis is that, although it explains poorer performances for recognizing faces belonging to other own species, it does not explain better performances at categorizing them.

A second alternative hypothesis discussed by Ge et al. (2009) is that the amount of resources devoted to a face's categorical and individuating information depends on whether the face is ingroup and familiar versus outgroup and unfamiliar (Sporer, 2001). This hypothesis supposes that categorizing and recognizing are two separate processes that compete for resources. When looking at other race faces, more attention is devoted to categorical information than individuating information. The reverse is observed for faces of one's own race. In this framework, other-species faces may even receive less attention per se, as individuating the faces is usually not important.

An alternative hypothesis accounting for the poor recognition and better categorization of other races can be based on the model proposed by Valentine (1991). Valentine suggests that individual face exemplars are encoded as vectors within a space of facial features, whereby their coordinates represent deviation from a prototypical average. In this model, recognition arises from the separation of each individual vector from the average prototype. The average prototype held by each person represents the average of all faces ever encoded by this person and will therefore be unique. As argued by Nelson (2001), at birth the dimensions of the prototype are likely to be broad and largely unspecified as the development of the prototype depends largely on facial input. The resulting dimensions will differ according to the input received, with certain salient, individuating dimensions carrying more "weight" than others. Predominant exposure to faces of a specific gender, ethnicity, or species early in life will result in the dimensions of one's prototype becoming "tuned" towards such faces. Consequently, the face-space dimensions are optimal for the type of faces predominant in one's environment. When processing faces from other races, distances between different faces are small, because they are computed with inappropriate dimensions, leading to poorer recognition performance. However, it is likely that because faces from other races are further away from the prototypes and closer together as a group, they are easily categorized as different from the own race exemplars, and thus categorized faster. In this model, recognizing individual faces from other species is difficult as they are not represented within the appropriate face-space dimension.

Can humans process the faces of other species?

Our ability (or lack thereof) to recognize faces of other species brings to mind an amusing story from English folklore. During the Napoleonic wars, a French ship was wrecked off the Hartlepool coast. The Hartlepool fishermen were concerned about the possibility of French infiltrators and feared an invasion. Among the wreckage lay one wet and sorrowful looking survivor, the ship's pet monkey dressed in a military style uniform. Unfamiliar with what a Frenchman looked like, the fishermen came to the conclusion that this monkey was a French spy and should be sentenced to death. The unfortunate creature was to die by hanging. The Hartlepool monkey story represents one extreme example of poor discrimination abilities for other-species faces, as well as a nice illustration of the need of the "*entente cordiale*" at that time.

To our knowledge, the ability to recognize faces of other species has not been reported in the general population, or if it exists, it has not been quantified. It has been suggested, however, that any class of stimuli, even a non-face-like stimuli such as the silhouette of a dog, could be processed at an individual level like faces, provided that the expertise acquired is strong enough (Diamond and Carey, 1986; Gauthier and Tarr, 1997; Tarr and Gauthier, 2000). However, those studies investigated categorization and not recognition of individuals (for discussion see the "Can the face processing system show plasticity in adult life?" section).

The only report about humans being able to recognize animal faces comes from the neuropsychological literature. Prosopagnosia describes a specific form of visual agnosia that renders a person unable to recognize the faces of other humans (Bodamer, 1947; see Duchaine, Chapter 42, this volume). McNeil and Warrington (1993) described a man who had lost the ability to recognize human faces, who took up a job as a farmer and developed the ability to identify his sheep. However, as the normal face processing system was disrupted, it is possible that the patient learned to recognize the sheep's faces based on the neural system that normally supports visual object recognition.

Dogs' silhouettes and sheep's faces differ significantly from human faces and may not be appropriate to activate the face processing system. On the contrary, non-human primates that share with humans a similar face arrangement can be expected to be processed similarly. Campbell et al. (1997) explored this hypothesis by testing human subjects on their categorical perception of different computer-morphed faces of three categories: human–monkeys, monkey–cow, and human–cow faces. The authors showed that the perceptual discrimination boundaries for monkey–human morphs were less sharp than for monkey–cow or human–cow faces. A single category formed the basis for discrimination of both human and monkey faces, suggesting that similar mechanisms are involved in the processing of these two categories of stimuli. However, this was at a category level and recent studies do not support the view of common mechanisms, as face recognition appears to be specific to human faces. Dufour et al. (2004) showed that humans recognized human faces better than monkey faces in a two-alternative forced-choice task. Likewise, studies conducted with a visual paired comparison task where no instruction of recognition is given, showed that humans discriminate automatically between two human faces but not between two macaque faces (Pascalis and Bachevalier, 1998).

At the physiological level, there is also evidence suggesting that we process human faces and the faces of other species differently. Face-selective electrophysiological activity has been observed in event-related potential (ERP, recorded from the scalp) studies with adults, and consists of a negative deflection, with peak latency around 170 ms after stimulus onset (N170). This potential tends to be of larger amplitude and shorter latency for faces than other objects (Bentin et al., 1996; see Eimer, Chapter 17, this volume). It is influenced by stimulus inversion as the N170 is of larger amplitude and longer latency for inverted human faces compared to upright human faces. This inversion effect is particular to human face stimuli and has not been observed for animal faces (de Haan et al., 2002). In a similar way, faces of same and other species have been shown to have a different effect on measures of pupil constriction (Conway et al., 2008). The transient pupil constriction evoked by face viewing is greater for human faces than for macaque faces, and the magnitude of the constriction is sensitive to the upright effect for human but not for macaque faces.

Taken together, these elements provide solid evidence that the adult face processing system is somewhat species specific and lacks the flexibility to allow recognition of faces of other species at an individual level.

How do other species process faces?

A variety of social species possess remarkable face discrimination abilities. Tibbetts (2002) has found that wasps, who primarily rely on chemical signature for communication and identification of conspecifics, can also demonstrate hierarchical categorization (e.g. worker) based on facial visual pattern only. Dyer et al. (2005) have shown that honeybees are able to learn and recognize the picture of a human face when paired with a novel face, which is consistent with our existing knowledge of the visual ability of bees. Pascalis et al. (2006) pointed out, however, the limitation of this study is that recognition could be performed on the basis of very simple pattern processing, and is not necessarily related to face processing at all.

Kendrick and his collaborators found that the face processing system in sheep shares a lot of properties with the human face system (Kendrick et al., 2001; Kendrick and Feng, Chapter 34, this volume).

The adult face processing systems of non-human primates shares several similarities with the human one: eye scanning, region of interest, individual recognition on pictures, inversion (see Pascalis et al., 1999 for a review). We will only summarize the data from eye-tracking studies here. Dahl et al. (2007) with a classic habituation paradigm found that individual recognition in macaques was better for faces of conspecifics compared to faces of other species, and that, like humans, macaques show holistic processing. Gothard et al. (2009) found the same result and their detailed analysis of the eye scanning of the faces shows that whereas monkeys use both configural and feature-based processing to recognize the faces of conspecifics they use primarily feature-based strategies to recognize human faces. Those studies suggest the existence of a different strategy while processing the faces of other species.

A more recent study by Dahl et al. (2009) compared human and macaque scanning strategies when looking at faces of conspecifics or other species. Both species displayed the same pattern of scanning for their own- versus other-species faces: more attention was provided to the eye region for their own species, relative to other species.

Collectively, these behavioral results show the presence of a comparable and specialized face processing system in sheep and non-human and human primates (Kendrick et al., 2001; Parr, 2003).

Do human and non-human primates share comparable functional neuroanatomy of face processing?

The core of the human neural system for face processing as revealed by functional magnetic resonance imaging (fMRI) studies is of three cortical areas (see Freiwald and Tsao, Chapter 36, this volume, for figures illustrating the anatomy): the inferior occipital gyrus (occipital face area, OFA) that allows the creation of a global stimulus based on the parts of a face; the middle fusiform gyrus (fusiform face area, FFA) supporting recognition/discrimination of individuals, and the superior temporal sulcus (STS) that carries information relative to the direction of gaze, orientation, features of the faces (Haxby et al., 2000). These three areas are more activated in humans viewing human faces than other visual objects (Grill-Spector et al., 2004; Haxby et al., 2000; Puce et al., 1996) with the lateral FFA showing the strongest activation in the right hemisphere (Kanwisher et al., 1997). The activation in FFA is also found to be the most robust and to allow a wide range of face transformations. For example, fMRI levels of activation were found to be equally strong for cat, cartoon, and human faces despite different image properties (Tong et al., 2000).

Until recently, it was unknown whether the macaque brain had structural and functional equivalents to the face processing network found in human brains. The development of functional imaging carried out in the macaque has enabled identification of areas that showed strong preferential activation when animal or human were passively viewing faces when compared to other stimuli (Tsao et al., 2003; 2008; Freiwald and Tsao, Chapter 36, this volume). These areas are located in the posterior and anterior regions of the temporal lobe and appear to follow a similar organization in both species. In humans, in addition to the three main brain areas (OFA, FFA, and STS), Tsao and collaborators identified two additional areas in the anterior collateral sulcus. In the macaque, six regions located along STS (posterior face patch, anterior and middle face patches of the STS fundus; anterior and middle face patches on the STS lip) and the antero-medio-temporal sulcus has been identified. Extension of the brain surfaces obtained through computation suggests that the face selective areas in monkey and humans share spatial anatomical location. Comparison of functional activity obtained in humans and macaques shows that the most striking difference is that face perception in humans appears to be more lateralized to the right hemisphere than in the non-human primate (Tsao et al., 2008).

Are those regions responding only to own-species faces?

Surprisingly not. FFA discriminates faces from objects even when the material used is very far from photographic representation of own-species faces or even belongs to other species (Tong et al., 2000; Tsao et al., 2003). Tsao et al. (2003) compared functional activity in human and monkey exposed to the same sets of faces. They found the activity in the human FFA to be similar to both sets of stimuli whereas in the macaque, activation to macaque faces was greater than activation to human faces.

The tolerance for a wide array of face-like stimuli contrasts with the poor recognition abilities that primates express for stimuli drawn from other races or other species. This critical observation suggests that faces from other species are processed by the same areas as same-species faces.

In what follows, we explore the response properties of neurons that respond to faces to determine if a difference can be found in the neural network involved.

Can individual recognition be found at a neuronal level? Is it species specific?

Many single-unit studies in monkeys report neurons with higher activity to face stimuli than to other stimuli. Some cells exhibit higher firing rate when the animal was shown pictures of human faces (Desouza et al., 2005; Sugase et al., 1999; Young and Yamane, 1992), monkey faces (Tsao et al., 2006), or even cartoon-like faces (Kobatake and Tanaka, 1994) relative to other stimuli. Moreover, a subset of face cells exhibited selective firing across individuals and was found to encode the identity of the faces (Eifuku et al., 2004; Hasselmo et al., 1989; Matsumoto et al., 2005). These face cells have been found in humans as well: some neurons in the medial temporal lobe (hippocampus, parahippocampal cortex) are highly selective to particular individuals (Quiroga et al., 2005). Taken together, the data show that individual recognition can be found at the neuronal level. Moreover, a study by Eifuku et al. (2004) shows that the level of activity of cells in the anterior inferior temporal gyrus (ITG) is linked to recognition performance measured in a behavioral task. In their study, monkeys were trained to perform a match-to-sample task with human faces presented from different point of views. Responses in the anterior STS neurons depended on the orientation of the faces, whereas the anterior ITG neurons were sensitive to the facial identity. Interestingly, there was a significant correlation between the latency of neurons to respond to stimuli and the behavioral reaction time: frontal views of faces elicited the shortest neuronal latency and the fastest match response relative to other views. Similarly, in humans, a link between behavior and neuronal activity has been found in the temporal lobe. A selective increase in activity was not observed when human patients failed to recognize the stimulus (Quiroga et al., 2008).

Those studies have shown that successful recognition of individuals can be observed at a neuronal level or at least that neuronal activity correlates with recognition. Moreover, Eifuku et al. (2004) used both macaque and human faces and found that the recognition-dependent activity extends to other species. Although selective activity is found at the single cell level, several studies show that discrimination is better performed at the population level.

For example, Young and Yamane (1992) found that the identity of individuals could be decoded using the activity of groups of neurons that were selective along two dimensions of the physical properties of the stimuli. This implies that information is encoded at a population level with each cell participating in the representation of many faces. A study of the responses of cells in face patches (Tsao et al., 2006) suggests that categorization and identification processes are not separated in terms of neural pathways, but are embedded within the same population of neurons. All neurons that carry information relative to the identity also carry information relative to the category of stimuli. Tsao et al.'s results suggest that identification of faces arises from the combined activity of cells within a highly specialized area. In this model, the broad responses of single cells are not sufficient to determine identity. Only the activity of cells taken together in a population allows disambiguation of eventual overlap and supporting individuation.

So, if there is a representation of other-species faces in a "face" area, why are we so bad at recognizing the faces of other species? The key to understanding what is the neural basis for the better performance observed for same species may be to compare the tuning of neurons for same- and other-species faces. This could be done only by using sets of stimuli, from same and other species, in which the degree of variation between each individual's face is identical for both sets—these kinds of experiments remain to be done. One hypothesis is that networks of cells in the face areas may be poorly tuned to variables that afford disambiguation of faces of other species. Instead, networks may be finely tuned to variables allowing pattern separation of faces in own species. If this hypothesis is true, behavioral developmental data suggests that this tuning process occurs during early life. In the next two sections, we will review developmental data and describe possible plasticity of the system in adult to support this claim.

How does face processing change early in life?

A developmental approach is likely to help determine what the common processes in different species are before experience influences the system, if the developmental trend is similar across primates, and how flexible the system is to handle other-species faces.

Faces represent a highly attractive stimulus for infant primates, including humans (Goren et al., 1975), pigtailed macaques (*Macaca nemestrina*, Lutz et al., 1998), gibbons (*Hylobates agilis*, Myowa-Yamakoshi and Tomonaga, 2001) and chimpanzees (*Pan troglodytes*, Kuwahata et al., 2004). Some researchers have argued that primates may possess an innate face processing system that is predisposed to respond to conspecifics (e.g. Sackett, 1966). Two-month-old pigtailed macaques are already demonstrating a unique preference for their own species (Kim et al., 1999). The argument is also supported by several studies which have demonstrated that rhesus macaques raised without experience of other- or own-species monkeys will still prefer to look at faces of conspecifics (Fujita, 1987, 1993). This is not true for Japanese macaques, and it may be that rhesus monkeys have a hard-wired preference for their own species, while Japanese macaques have a more flexible preference that is influenced by experience. Challenging this hypothesis, a recent study by Sugita (2008) has illustrates the critical role of experience in the development of face processing in macaques. Infant Japanese macaques (*Macaca fuscata*) separated from their parents at birth and reared by humans in a faceless environment for a period of 6 to 24 months, showed a preference for both monkey and human faces over objects, but no preference for either category of faces when tested in a visual preference task. Furthermore, those monkeys were able to recognize both monkey and human faces. Following the face deprivation period, half of the monkeys were then introduced to fellow macaques and the other half to humans. When tested following a month of exposure to faces, monkeys exposed to human faces displayed a preference for human faces over objects, but also for human over monkey faces. They displayed no preference between monkey faces and objects. Consistent with this pattern of results, monkeys exposed to monkey faces preferred monkey faces over objects and over human faces, and showed no preference when human faces and objects were presented simultaneously. Furthermore, when tested for recognition, monkeys were only able to display recognition for faces from the category to which they were exposed. Those results highlight the crucial role of visual experience in the specialization of the face system toward own-species faces. The macaques are not displaying hard-wired preference for their own species but rather an experience-dependent preference.

This result fits with a study by Martin-Malivel and Okada (2007) which found that human-reared chimpanzee were better at processing human faces than chimpanzees faces compared to a group of chimpanzees who grew up in a own-species group.

Nelson (2001) hypothesized that in humans the representation of faces at birth is broad and develops according to the type of facial input received, tuning toward the predominant faces in the environment. In order to test whether experience tunes face processing, Pascalis et al. (2002) investigated the ability of 6- and 9-month-old infants to recognize faces from their own- (human) and other-species (rhesus macaque) using a standard infant recognition paradigm. Infants at both ages were able to demonstrate individual recognition with human faces, looking longer at a new human face compared to a previously seen human face. However, when tested with the monkey faces, only the 6-month-old group showed evidence of individual recognition. In contrast, 9-month-olds were unable to recognize which monkey face they had seen before. These findings suggest that the face system becomes "tuned" to human faces between 6 and 9 months of age (Pascalis et al., 2002).

In a follow-up study, Pascalis et al. (2005) investigated the impact of experience with other-species faces on the development of face processing from this unknown species. They provided the parents of 6-month-old babies with a book containing a selection of monkey faces, which they were instructed to show to their infant following a fixed schedule. They found that this exposure was sufficient to preserve recognition capabilities with monkey faces when the infants returned for testing at 9 months of age. Training experienced near the end of the tuning period appears to be effective for maintaining the ability to discriminate between individuals of other species. Thus, it is possible to alter the development of a cognitive system (for face processing) by providing training and learning via a book. However, it is still unclear how much training is necessary to produce other-species face processing skills at 9 months and for what period of time the long-term training will affect the face system.

Only a few studies have investigated the electrophysiological response elicited by own- versus other-species faces during infancy. De Haan et al. (2002) have found an "infant N170" in 6-month-olds that was elicited by faces at a latency of 290 ms followed by a positivity at 400 ms. They also examined the influence of stimulus inversion, for both human and monkey faces and found that in adults, inversion affected only the processing of human faces and not monkey faces, while in 6-month-olds, inversion affected the ERPs similarly for human and monkey faces. Around 12 months of age, the adult ERP patterns are observed (Halit et al., 2003). Those results show that 6-month-olds categorize both type of face pretty well and process them in the same way, but by 12 months of age, the processing of own- versus other-species faces has become different. Those results suggest that humans possess an evolved system for processing faces that becomes specialized as a consequence of exposure exclusively to faces from a single species. According to this interpretation, expert levels of face recognition are dependent upon both an evolved mechanism and experience (Pascalis and Kelly, 2009).

Can the face processing system show plasticity in adult life?

If infants can learn to recognize faces from another species, can adults do the same? Diamond and Carey (1986) found that dog experts showed comparable deficits with inverted dog profile stimuli as those found with human faces. In contrast, non-experts performed equally with upright and inverted dog stimuli. Therefore, they concluded that expertise with any complex stimulus category can produce effects like those observed in faces. Gauthier and colleagues (1997) have tested participants who have been trained to "expert" levels with a novel, artificially created category of stimuli. The stimuli in question are "greebles", a homogenous class of stimuli that were created to share the complex properties of the human face. Using these stimuli, Gauthier and Tarr (1997) found that greeble experts developed a configural processing strategy whereas controls used a featural strategy. This suggests that greeble experts develop a "greeble" processing very similar to face processing. However, the cognitive equivalence between processes involved in the tasks performed by greeble experts and face processing is open to debate: the experts were asked to categorize the items and not to recognize them at an individual level. It has been suggested that whereas novices categorize objects at the basic level of abstraction, perceptual experts identify objects in their domain of expertise at a more specific, subordinate level (Tanaka and Taylor, 1991). For example, a novice will identify a brown object with feathers and wings at the basic level of "bird," but an expert bird watcher will identify this same object at the subordinate level of "white crown sparrow." Thus, a hallmark of perceptual expertise is a downward shift in recognition to a more specific, subordinate level of abstraction. This brings expert categorization closer to face recognition. However, face expertise constitutes the most specific, downward shift in recognition where a familiar face is identified at the level of the unique individual (e.g. Gepetto) rather than categorized at the more generic level of race or gender (Tanaka, 2001). Thus, whereas categorization in experts is closer to individual recognition by one or two levels, it is still not equivalent to individual recognition.

Moreover, Robbins and McKone (2007), in a more tightly controlled replication and extension of Diamond and Carey's (1986) study, found no evidence for configural processing in dog experts.

There is not yet enough data to allow us to draw conclusions about the adult human's capacity to improve their individual face recognition abilities of other species.

Summary and conclusions

Thus, different levels of face processing can be powerfully studied via the use of other-species faces. Behavioral results, both in human and non-human primates, indicate that the species-specific face processing system is shaped progressively by experience. Differentiation in face processing by humans between own- or other-primate species is not present early in life, at which age other primate faces are processed in a similar fashion. How non-primate faces are processed by human adults awaits further studies.

Functional imaging data strongly suggests that human and non-human primates share a similar anatomical organization of the neural mechanisms supporting face processing. The activation of these areas is tolerant to variation in face stimuli such as cartoons or other primate faces, but is restricted to face-like stimuli. Likewise, response properties of individual neurons in macaques within face areas confirm the processing of a large variety of faces that encompasses human faces. Further studies are needed to clarify how neurons that respond to a large variety of face-like stimuli specifically afford better recognition of own-species faces. There is a related need to closely study the tuning of face cells to a variety of face stimuli. The physiological results confirm the flexible functional properties of the face processing system in primates, suggesting a common phylogenetic origin.

Given the epigenetic behavioral data, it is likely that cells become tuned with experience to the stimuli present in the environment, and thereby develop better disambiguation of faces belonging to the category that was the most often perceived. The importance of social interactions in developing specialization for only one type of face is also an important aspect that needs to be investigated in further detail (Martin-Malivel and Okada, 2007; Sugita, 2008.)

The ability to recognize faces in human and non-human primates stems from a conjunction of evolutionary inheritance and experience via exposure to faces present in the environment. Individuation is clearly a vital mechanism for any social species. By uncovering similarities across primate face systems, comparative studies allow us to understand the evolution of face processing capabilities in humans. Some researchers have argued that primates, including humans, may posses an innate face processing system that is predisposed to respond to conspecifics (Sackett, 1966). The argument is supported by a study showing that monkeys raised without experience of other own-species monkeys will still prefer to look at faces of conspecifics (Fujita, 1990). However, this proposal does not fit well with findings from the human infant literature (Pascalis et al., 2002) or with new data on monkeys raised without seeing faces (Sugita, 2008) which both suggest that face processing is highly shaped by experience at an early age. In our view, current evidence indicates that humans and non-human primates possess an evolved system for processing faces that becomes specialized as a consequence of exposure primarily to faces from a single species, thus limiting expertise.

References

Bentin, S., Allison, T., Puce, A., Perez, E., and McCarthy, G. (1996). Electrophysiological studies of face perception in humans. *Journal of Cognitive Neuroscience*, **8**, 551–565.

Bodamer, J. (1947). Die Prosop-agnosie. *Archive für Psychiatrie und Nervenkrankheiten*, **179**, 6–54. (English translation by Ellis, H.D. and Florence, M. (1990). *Cognitive Neuropsychology*, **7**, 81–105.)

Bruce, V. and Young, A. (1986). Understanding face recognition. *British Journal of Psychology*, **77**, 305–327.

Campbell, R., Pascalis, O., Coleman, M., Wallace, S.B., and Benson, P.J. (1997). Are faces of different species perceived categorically by human observers? *Royal Society Proceeding Biology*, **264**, 1429–1434.

Conway, C.A., Jones, B.C., DeBruine, L.M., Little, A.C., and Sahraie, A. (2008). Transient pupil constrictions to faces are sensitive to orientation and species. *Journal of Vision*, **8**, 17:1–11.

Dahl, C.D., Logothetis, N.K., and Hoffman, K.L. (2007). Individuation and holistic processing of faces in rhesus monkeys. *Proceedings in Biological Science*, **274**, 2069–2076.

Dahl, C.D., Wallraven, C., Bülthoff, H.H., and Logothetis, N.K. (2009). Humans and macaques employ similar face-processing strategies. *Current Biology*, **19**, 509–513.

De Souza, W.C., Eifuku, S., Tamura, R., Nishijo, H., and Ono, T. (2005). Differential characteristics of face neuron responses within the anterior superior temporal sulcus of macaques. *Journal of Neurophysiology*, **94**, 1252–1266.

Diamond, R. and Carey, S. (1986). Why faces are and are not special? *Journal of Experimental Psychology: General*, **115**, 107–117.

Dufour, V., Coleman, M., Campbell, R., Petit, O., and Pascalis, O. (2004). On the species-specificity of face recognition in human adults. *Current Psychology of Cognition*, **22**, 315–333.

Dyer, A.G., Neumeyer, C., and Chittka, L. (2005). Honeybee (*Apis mellifera*) vision can discriminate between and recognise images of human faces. *Journal of Experimental Biology*, **208**, 4709–4714.

Eifuku S., De Souza W.C., Tamura R., Nishijo H., and Ono T. (2004). Neuronal correlates of face identification in the monkey anterior temporal cortical areas. *Journal of Neurophysiology*, **91**, 358–371.

Fujita, K. (1987). Species recognition by five macaque monkeys. *Primates*, **28**, 353–366.

Fujita, K. (1990). Species preference by infant macaques with controlled social experience. *International Journal of Primatology*, **6**, 553–573.

Fujita, K. (1993). Role of some physical characteristics in species recognition by pigtail monkeys. *Primates*, **34**, 133–140.

Gauthier, I. and Tarr, M.J. (1997). Becoming a "Greeble" expert: Exploring the face recognition mechanism. *Vision Research*, **37**, 1673–1682.

Ge, L., Zhang, H., Wang, Z., Pascalis, O., Quinn, P.C., Kelly, D.J., Slater, A.M., and Lee, K. (2009). Two faces of the other-race effect. Recognition and categorization of Caucasian and Chinese faces. *Perception*, **38**, 1199–1210.

Goren, C., Sarty, M., and Wu, P.Y.K. (1975). Visual following and pattern discrimination of face-like stimuli by newborn infants. *Pediatrics*, **56**, 544–549.

Gothard, K.M., Brooks, K.N., and Peterson, M.A. (2009). Multiple perceptual strategies used by macaque monkeys for face recognition. *Animal Cognition*, **12**, 155–167.

Grill-Spector, K. Knouf, N., and Kanwisher, N. (2004). The FFA subserves face perception not generic within category identification. *Nature Neuroscience*, **7**, 555–562.

de Haan, M., Pascalis, O., and Johnson, M.H. (2002). Specialization of neural mechanisms underlying face recognition in human infants. *Journal of Cognitive Neuroscience*, **14**, 199–209.

Halit, H., de Haan, M., and Johnson, M.H. (2003). Cortical specialization for face processing: face-sensitive event-related potential components in 3-and 12-month-old infants. *NeuroImage*, **19**, 1180–1193.

Hasselmo, M.E., Rolls, E.T., and Baylis, G.C. (1989). The role of expression and identity in the face-selective responses of neurons in the temporal visual cortex of the monkey. *Behavioral Brain Research*, **32**, 203–218.

Haxby, J.V., Hoffmann, E.A., and Gobbini, M.I. (2000). The distributed human neural system for face perception. *Trends in Cognitive Science*, **4**, 223–233.

Kanwisher, N.G., McDermott, J., and Chun, M.M. (1997). The fusiform face area: a module in human extrastriate cortex specialized for face perception. *Journal of Neuroscience*, **17**, 4302–4311.

Kendrick, K.N., da Costa, A.P., Leigh, A.E., Hinton, M.R., and Peirce, J.W. (2001). Sheep don't forget a face. *Nature*, **441**, 165–166.

Kim, J.H., Gunderson, V.M., and Swartz, K.S. (1999). Humans all look alike: Cross-species face recognition in infant pigtailed macaque monkeys. Biennial meeting of the Society for Research in Child Development, April 15–18, Albuquerque, New Mexico.

Kobatake, E. and Tanaka, K. (1994). Neuronal selectivities to complex object features in the ventral visual pathway of the macaque cerebral cortex. *Journal of Neurophysiology*, **71**, 856–867.

Kuwahata, H., Adachi, I., Fujita, K., Tomonaga, M., and Matzuzawa, T. (2004). Development of schematic face preference in macaque monkeys. *Behavioral Processes*, **66**, 17–21.

Lai, W.-S, Ramiro, L.-L.R., Yu, A., and Johnston, R.E. (2005). Recognition of familiar individuals in golden hamsters: A new method and functional neuroanatomy. *Journal of Neuroscience*, **25**, 11239–11247.

Lutz, C.K., Lockard, J.S., Gunderson, V.M., and Grant, K.S. (1998). Infant monkeys' visual responses to drawings of normal and distorted faces. *American Journal of Primatology*, **44**, 169–174.

Martin-Malivel, J. and Okada, K. (2007). Human and chimpanzee face recognition in chimpanzees: Role of exposure and impact on categorical perception. *Behavioral Neuroscience*, **121**, 1145–1155.

Matsumoto, N., Okada, M., Sugase-Miyamoto, Y., Yamane, S., and Kawano, K. (2005). Population dynamics of face-responsive neurons in the inferior temporal cortex. *Cerebral Cortex*, **15**, 1103–12.

McNeil, J. E. and Warrington, E.K. (1993). Prosopagnosia: A face specific disorder. *Quarterly Journal of Experimental Psychology*, **46A**, 1–10.

Moseley, L.J. (1979). Individual auditory recognition in the least tern (*Sterna albifrons*). *Auk*, **96**, 31–39.

Myowa-Yamakoshi, M. and Tomonaga, M. (2001). Development of face recognition in an infant gibbon (*Hylobates agilis*). *Infant Behavior Development*, **24**, 215–227.

Nelson, C.A. (2001). The development and neural bases of face recognition. *Infant and Child Development*, **10**, 3–18.

Parr, L. (2003). The discrimination of faces and their emotional contents by chimpanzees (*Pan troglodytes*). *Annals New York Academy of Science*, **1000**, 56–78.

Pascalis, O. and Bachevalier, J. (1998). Face recognition in primates: a cross species study. *Behavioural Processes*, **43**, 87–96.

Pascalis O. and Kelly, D.J. (2009). On the development of face processing. *Perspective in Psychological Science*, **4**, 200–209.

Pascalis, O., Petit, O., Kim, J.H., and Campbell, R. (1999). Picture perception in primates: the case of face perception. *Picture Perception in Animals, Special issue of Current Psychology of Cognition*, **18**, 889–922.

Pascalis, O., de Haan, M., and Nelson, C.A. (2002). Is face processing species-specific during the first year of life? *Science*, **296**, 1321–1323.

Pascalis, O., Scott, L.S., Kelly, D. J., Shannon, R.W., Nicholson, E., Coleman M., and Nelson C.A. (2005). Plasticity of Face Processing in Infancy. *Proceedings of the National Academy of Science USA*, **102**, 5297–5300.

Pascalis, O., Kelly, D.J., and Caldara, R. (2006). What bees can *really* tell us about the face processing system in humans? A response to Dyer et al. (2005). *Journal of Experimental Biology*, **209**, 3266–3267

Puce, A., Allison, T., Asgari, M., Gore, J.C., and McCarthy, G. (1996). Differential sensitivity of human visual cortex to faces, letterstrings, and textures: A functional magnetic resonance imaging study. *Journal of Neuroscience*, **16**, 5205–5215.

Quiroga, R.Q., Reddy, L., Kreiman, G., Koch, C., and Fried, I. (2005). Invariant visual representation by single neurons in the human brain. *Nature, 435*, 1102–7.

Quiroga, R.Q., Mukamel, R., Isham, E.A., Malach, R., and Fried, I. (2008). Human single-neuron responses at the threshold of conscious recognition. *Proceedings of the National Academy of Science USA* **105**, 3599–604.

Robbins, R. and McKone, E. (2007). No face-like processing for objects-of-expertise in three behavioural tasks. *Cognition,* **103**, 34–79.

Sackett, G.P. (1966). Monkeys reared in isolation with pictures as visual input: Evidence for an innate releasing mechanism. *Science,* **154**, 1470–1473.

Sporer, S.L. (2001). Recognizing faces of other ethnic groups—An integration of theories. *Psychology Public Policy and Law,* **7**, 36–97.

Sugase, Y., Yamane, S., Ueno, S., and Kawano, K. (1999). Global and fine information coded by single neurons in the temporal visual cortex. *Nature,* **400**, 869–73.

Sugita, Y. (2008). Face perception in monkeys reared with no exposure to faces. *Proceedings of the National Academy of Sciences, USA,* **105**, 394–398.

Tanaka, J.W. (2001). The entry point of face recognition: Evidence for face expertise. *Journal of Experimental Psychology: General,* **130**, 534–543.

Tanaka, J.W., and Taylor, M. (1991). Object categories and expertise: Is the basic level in the eye of the beholder? *Cognitive Psychology,* **23**, 457–482.

Tarr, M.J. and Gauthier, I., (2000). FFA: A flexible fusiform area for subordinate-level visual processing automatized by expertise. *Nature Neuroscience,* **3**, 764–769.

Thierry, B. (1994). Emergence of social organizations in non-human primates. *Revue Internationale de Systémique,* **8**, 65–77.

Tibbetts, E.A. (2002). Visual signals of individual identity in the paper wasp (*Polistes fuscatus*). *Proceedings of the Royal Society of London, Series B: Biological Sciences,* **269**, 1423–1428.

Tong, F., Nakayama, K., Moscovitch, M., Weinrib, O., and Kanwisher N. (2000). Response properties of the human fusiform face area. *Cognitive Neuropsychoogy,* **17**, 257–279.

Tsao, D.Y., Freiwald, W.A., Knutsen, T.A., Mandeville, J.B., and Tootell, R.B.H. (2003). The representation of faces and objects in macaque cerebral cortex. *Nature Neuroscience,* **6**, 989–995.

Tsao, D.Y., Winrich A. Freiwald, W.A., Tootell, R.B.H., and Livingstone, M.S. (2006). A cortical region consisting entirely of face-selective cells. *Science,* **311**, 670–674.

Tsao, D.Y., Moeller, S., and Freiwald, W.A. (2008). Comparing face patch systems in macaques and humans. *Proceedings of the National Academy of Science USA,* **105**, 19514–19519.

Valentine, T. (1991). A unified account of the effects of distinctiveness, inversion, and race in face recognition. *Quarterly Journal of Experimental Psychology Section A: Human Experimental Psychology,* **43**, 161–204.

Young, M.P. and Yamane, S. (1992). Sparse population coding of faces in the inferotemporal cortex. *Science,* **256**, 1327–1331.

Chapter 38

The Neurodevelopment of Face Perception

Michelle de Haan

Faces are key components of everyday social interactions that can provide emotionally significant signals such as the warning of danger provided by a fearful face or the rewarding value of a familiar, smiling face. The neural systems underlying face processing must be able to rapidly and reliably register and react to complex and dynamic facial displays, while at the same time be able to learn from experience and be amenable to cognitive control. Evidence from a variety of sources suggests that this may be achieved in the brain through a multipathway neural system for face processing, with subcortical routes providing quick, but less detailed processing and cortical pathways providing slower, but more detailed and controlled processing. Developmental studies suggest that the emergence of face processing in infancy through adolescence may in part be characterized by shifts in the interplay between the subcortical and cortical systems. This chapter will review the evidence supporting this view by beginning with a brief description of the brain bases of face processing in adults, and then turning to studies of humans and non-human primates which have investigated the structural or functional development of these regions. The chapter will conclude that the brain structures involved in face processing and their interconnections mature along different timelines and become increasingly integrated during infancy and adolescence to support more complex and controlled use of facial social information. During the first postnatal years, normal amygdala development and typical visual experience appear to be two key factors for optimal development of face processing.

Faces: the basic brain network in adults

Processing of faces can be divided into perceptual processing, which involves distinguishing between different facial configurations, and conceptual processing, which involves understanding the meaning linked to a particular configuration. In adults, these processes are mediated by a distributed neural network involving subcortical and cortical areas. Visual information about faces is initially passed along two neural pathways: (1) a Subcortical System that is involved in detecting faces and directing visual attention to them and (2) a Core Cortical System that is involved in the detailed visual-perceptual analysis of faces. Both of these components interact with (3) an Extended Cortical-Subcortical System involved in further processing of faces such as the conscious processing of emotional intentions of others (Gobbini and Haxby, 2007; Haxby et al., 2000; Johnson, 2005).

In the *subcortical pathway* for face processing, information travels from the retina directly to the superior colliculus, then to the pulvinar and on to the amygdala (de Gelder et al., 2003; Johnson, 2005). This route is believed to process facial information quickly and automatically and to rely primarily on low spatial frequency information (reviewed in Johnson, 2005). Existence of such a pathway in humans is supported by studies showing that the emotional valence of facial expressions can be reliably discriminated even following lesions to the primary visual cortex that abolish conscious visual experience (Morris et al, 1999, 2001) and by studies showing that emotional expressions not consciously registered due to brief presentations and use of backward masking can still activate the amygdala (Whalen et al., 1998; but see Pessoa et al., 2006). The subcortical pathway could allow an initial rapid processing of basic features to be carried out before slower, conscious cortical processing is completed, and might also modulate this slower cortical processing (e.g. Tamietto and de Gelder, 2008). For example, projections from the amygdala to the occipital cortex may enhance visual processing of emotionally salient stimuli (Morris et al, 1998; Vuilleumier and Pourtois, 2007).

The *Core System* for visual analysis of faces receives input from the retina via the geniculo-striate pathway, and includes the inferior occipital gyrus (encompassing the lateral occipital area, of which the "occipital face area" is a subregion), fusiform gyrus (including the "fusiform face area"), and posterior STS (STS)/gyrus. The inferior occipital gyrus mediates the early perception of faces and passes this information to two areas: (1) the fusiform gyrus and (2) the STS/gyrus. There is evidence that the fusiform gyrus is primarily involved in the interpretation of the static components of facial expressions and identity (Kanwisher et al., 1997), while the superior temporal gyrus contributes to the recognition of the dynamic properties of facial expressions and eye gaze (Allison et al., 2000).

The *Extended System* receives input from, and in return communicates with, both the Subcortical System and Core Cortical System. It encompasses a variety of regions involved in the further processing of these inputs to allow activities important in social processing such as conscious emotional appraisal and interpretation of the intentions of others. The paralimbic and higher cortical areas such as the medial prefrontal cortex, somatosensory cortices, and the anterior cingulate are involved in longer-latency processing of the conscious representations of emotional states, in controlling behavior in social situations and in the planning of actions and goals. This chapter will focus mainly on the subcortical and core cortical systems and will cover only more limited examples from the extended system.

Development of the subcortical pathway

Newborns preferentially orient and attend to faces in the visual environment from just minutes to hours after birth (e.g. Johnson et al., 1991). According to one influential hypothesis, this early ability is mediated by the subcortical system which thereby provides a "face-biased" input to the developing cortex and enhances cortical activation to faces (Johnson and Morton, 1991; see also Leppänen and Nelson, 2009). This may ultimately play a role in establishing the specialization of cortical regions for face processing observed in the mature brain. While there is some debate as to the best way to describe the visual bias(es) that lead newborns to preferentially look to faces (for further discussion see de Haan et al., 2002a; Johnson, 2005; Lepannen and Nelson, 2009), the different views concur that such a bias exists and that it is likely to be mediated subcortically.

In older children, research on the role of subcortical structures in face processing has focused mainly on the role of the amygdala in processing emotions. One influential hypothesis is that amygdala activation is great in younger children and diminishes with age as prefrontal/cingulate cortex activation increases reflecting better cognitive control of social-emotional processing over adolescence (Killgore and Yurgelun-Tod, 2007; Rubia et al., 2006).

In this section, the structural and functional development of the subcortical face processing pathway will be reviewed. Emphasis will be on human studies but studies of non-human primates will be included when human evidence is limited or absent.

Structural development

Superior colliculus

The superior colliculus is a layered midbrain structure positioned below the thalamus whose most well-studied function is orienting the head and eyes to sensory stimuli. Structurally, the superior colliculus and its retinal inputs are believed to be mature by birth. For example, retinocollicular projections are present in human embryos by 12 to 13 weeks, and the mature layered pattern of the superior colliculus is observed in human embryos by 16 weeks (Jia et al., 2006). However, cortical inputs to the superior colliculus develop more slowly, with studies in non-human primates showing that these connections go through a stage of being stronger and more diffuse in the young than in the mature system (Webster et al., 1995). The development of these cortical inputs may underlie improvements in visual abilities during infancy such as the increased abilities in detection of targets in the nasal visual field over the first months of life (Lewis et al., 1985).

Little is known about the development of the connection from the superior colliculus on to the pulvinar, which terminates in the lateral pulvinar (Benvento and Fallon, 1975). A recent diffusion tensor imaging (DTI) study did confirm a pathway between the superior colliculus and the pulvinar in healthy adults in vivo (Leh et al., 2008).

Pulvinar

The pulvinar is a nucleus of the thalamus involved in visual processing and thought to play a role in visual spatial attention, attention-shifting, and perceiving the salience or relevance of visual stimuli (Robinson and Petersen, 1992). Like other thalamic nuclei connected to the frontal cortex, the pulvinar is larger in primates than other mammals, and larger in humans compared to chimpanzees or macques (Armstrong, 1980). This is likely due to the unique early development of the human pulvinar: in addition to the initial phase of cell proliferation in the diencephalon itself which is common to mammals, humans have a second phase of pulvinar growth between 18 to 34 weeks' gestation involving migration of cells from the proliferative zone in the telencephalon (Letinic and Rakic, 2001).

There is limited information about the postnatal structural development of the pulvinar in humans. Magnetic resonance imaging (MRI) studies show that T1 values in the pulvinar decrease with age during childhood following a different trajectory than cortical gray matter (Cho et al., 1997; Steen et al., 1997), though the exact details of the developmental pattern differ somewhat between studies.

With regards to connections, little is known about the development of the projection from the pulvinar to the amygdala, which links the medial pulvinar to the basolateral amygdala (Romanski et al., 1997). A recent DTI study in healthy human adults did not observe a connection between the pulvinar and the amygdala (such connections have been reported in monkeys), though connections between the pulvinar and the cortex were observed (Leh et al., 2008). These included connections with inferior temporal cortical areas and secondary visual areas in the occipital cortex (Leh et al., 2008). Studies with monkey studies have also reported connections between the pulvinar and inferior temporal cortex: the pulvinar projects directly to inferior temporal cortical regions (TE), and inferior temporal regions (TE, TEO) project back to the pulvinar. These connections appear similar in infant and adult monkeys (Sorenson and Rodman, 1996; Webster et al., 1995).

The DTI study with humans also reported a direct connection between the pulvinar and the primary visual cortex (Leh et al., 2008). This could indicate less separation between the subcortical and core cortical pathways than is typically described. However, the imaging method used could not distinguish feedforward and feedback connections thus it could well be a feedback connection.

Amygdala

The amygdala is a subcortical group of 13 interconnected nuclei located in the anterior portion of the medial temporal lobe (for a more detailed review of amygdala development, see Payne and Bachevalier, 2009). The lateral nucleus is believed to be particularly relevant to face processing, because anatomical studies in monkeys show it receives input from the pulvinar in the subcortical pathway, though a recent MRI study in humans did not find such a connection (Leh et al., 2008). The lateral nucleus also receives inputs of highly-processed visual information from the cortex regarding faces, facial expression, gaze direction, and body movements. The lateral nucleus projects back to cortical areas via the basal nucleus, both to higher-order cortical areas as well as primary sensory areas. It is thus able to modulate various parts of the cortical network for face processing, including early sensory regions such as the fusiform gyrus.

The human amygdala is first observed by 5 weeks of gestation, with its nuclei becoming discernible by the early stages of the second trimester. Data regarding the development of the connections of the amygdala come primarily from studies of monkeys. These studies suggest that most of amygdalocortical connections are already established by the time of birth or soon afterwards (Amaral and Bennett, 2000), including reciprocal connections with the inferior temporal cortex (Webster et al., 1991). However, these connections do undergo some changes over the first post-natal year. In infant monkeys the inferior temporal inputs to the lateral nucleus of the amygdala are more widespread than in adults, and become more refined from 1 week to 3 months (Rodman, 1994; Webster et al., 1991). For example, at a time when temporal cortex anterior to area TE remains immature, the infant amygdala receives additional inputs from areas posterior to TE. A functional interpretation of this anatomical refinement is that the amygdala receives increasingly refined and detailed visual information over this period (Payne and Bachevalier, 2009).

Myelination in the human amygdala begins in the first months of life, with some aspects appearing mature by 10 months of age (Brody et al., 1987; Kinney et al., 1988). Studies in monkeys indicate, however, that mature levels of myelination of amygdala output fibers are not reached until at least 3 years after birth (Machado and Bachevalier, 2003). Together, these findings suggest that there is an increase the amygdala's influence over other brain areas in the first postnatal years of life. Neuroimaging studies also indicate a protracted period of gray matter development from 4 to 18 years, with the volume of the right amygdala increasing in boys, but not in girls, over this time (reviewed in Payne and Bachevalier, 2009). The amygdala is also connected to the orbito-frontal cortex, a part of the Extended Cortical Pathway that plays an important role in social and emotional behavior, though little is known about the development of this connection.

Structural development of the subcortical pathway: summary

The components of the subcortical pathway for face processing are in place and largely mature by birth though little is known about the development of the connections between the components, with the exception of documentation of the early maturity of retinal inputs to the superior colliculus. There is evidence that the cortical connections of the subcortical pathway show contin-ued development. The limited anatomical evidence available suggests that the visual cortical inputs to the superior colliculus and the inferior temporal cortical inputs to the amygdala may develop more slowly postnatally compared to the inferior temporal cortical connections of the pulvinar.

Functional development

The functional development of subcortical pathway has been studied using several approaches including: (1) testing infants and children on marker tasks believed to rely on the subcortical pathway such as use of stimulus conditions to which the subcortical pathway is uniquely sensitive or insensitive, (2) testing children using electrophysiological or neuroimaging methods to measure activation of the subcortical pathway, and (3) testing children with damage to a component of the subcortical pathway.

Marker tasks

The subcortical and geniculostriate pathways differ in their retinal inputs, and researchers have exploited these differences in order to examine whether abilities differentially rely on the two pathways. One such difference is the representation of the visual field. The input to the subcortical pathway favors representation of the temporal visual field compared to the nasal visual field (Rafal et al., 1991) while the input to the geniculostriate pathway does not. This is illustrated in a recent neuroimaging study in human adults showing greater activation to temporal compared to nasal visual field stimulation in the superior colliculus but not in the lateral geniculate nucleus or visual cortical areas (V1–V3; Sylvester et al., 2007). Thus, the presence of temporal-nasal field asymmetries in favor of the temporal hemifield has been used as evidence of subcortical involvement (but see Bompas et al., 2008).

Investigators have used this approach to probe the neural bases of newborns' preferential orienting to faces. Human newborns show a preferential orienting to a face-like arrangement of three blobs (two "eye" blobs above a "mouth" blob) compared to the same arrangement inverted only in the temporal visual field and not the nasal visual field (Simion et al., 1998). This is not due to a general failure to orient discriminantly in the nasal visual field, as newborns preferentially orient to stripes equally well in both visual fields (Simion et al., 1998). This finding suggests that newborns' preferential orienting to faces is mediated by the subcortical pathway, and a recent study suggests that same pathway is also functioning in adults (Tomalski et al., 2009). Some caution, however, in interpreting this result is warranted, as the anatomic asymmetry in retinal projections is less striking in primates than in cats, and the functional MRI (fMRI) study described above cannot conclusively show whether the asymmetry in collicular activation was due to feedforward or feedback inputs.

Another difference between the subcortical and cortical pathways is that the cortical geniculostriate pathway receives chromatic information from short-, medium-, and long wave-length sensitive cones and achromatic information. The superior colliculus, however, does not receive input from short-wave length (S) cones thus rendering it insensitive to blue/yellow stimuli. Thus, one way in which investigators have tried to isolate the role of the subcortical pathway is by comparing responses to S-cone compared to achromatic stimuli. If a response is present for the latter but not for the former, it points to involvement of the retinotectal pathway in mediating that response. In particular, the superior colliculus is implicated, as the pulvinar does receive S-cone input. For example, patients with blindsight following hemispherectomy show their blindsight abilities for achromatic stimuli but not S-cone stimuli, suggesting that these residual visual abilities are mediated by the superior colliculus. This approach has not been commonly used to investigate questions of face perception or development.

It has also been suggested that the subcortical pathway relies mainly on low-spatial frequency information. A recent fMRI study in adults demonstrated that the superior colliculus, pulvinar, and amygdala were responsive to low spatial frequency information (especially in fearful faces) but not sensitive to high spatial frequency information, while the fusiform gyrus was sensitive primarily to high spatial frequencies (Vuilleumier et al., 2003). Given that newborns' vision is immature and relies more on low spatial frequency information, this might suggest that face processing initially involves primarily the subcortical system. A recent study showed that human newborns are able to process information from faces in the 0 to 1 cpd range but rely primarily on the 0 to 0.5 cpd range for individual face recognition (de Heering et al., 2008). Few developmental studies have examined the influence of spatial frequency content on the development of face processing, though some studies have examined whether atypical face processing in autistic spectrum disorder can be accounted for by abnormalities an atypical sensitivity to high spatial frequency information (e.g. Deruelle et al., 2008).

Marker tasks have also been used to investigate amygdala involvement in infant face processing. The eyeblink startle response is a reflex blink initiated involuntarily by sudden bursts of loud noise. In adults, these reflex blinks are augmented by viewing slides of unpleasant pictures and scenes, and they are inhibited by viewing slides of pleasant or arousing pictures and scenes (Lang et al., 1990, 1992). Based on work in animals, it has been argued that fear potentiation of the startle response is mediated by the central nucleus of the amygdala, which in turn directly projects to brain stem centers that mediate the startle and efferent blink reflex activity (Davis, 1989; Holstege et al., 1986). One study has shown that 5-month-old infants' blinks were augmented when they viewed angry expressions and were reduced when they viewed happy expressions, relative to when they viewed neutral expression (Balaban, 1995). These results suggest that by 5 months of age, portions of the amygdala circuitry underlying the response to facial expressions may be functional.

Electrophysiology and neuroimaging

Several fMRI studies have examined the development of brain activation to faces (reviewed in Gruyer et al., 2008). Few of these have reported activation in the superior colliculus or pulvinar. This might be because the small size, deep location, and/or proximity to pulsating vascular structures can make the superior colliculus difficult to image and/or because the aim of most developmental fMRI studies has been to probe other specific components of the brain face processing network such as the amygdala or fusiform face area. In adults, fMRI studies do show activation of the superior colliculus and pulvinar (and amygdala), even to masked fearful faces that are not consciously perceived (e.g. Liddell et al., 2004).

A large literature documents that the adult amygdala is activated by fearful faces, though it is also activated by other facial or emotional stimuli and does not respond to fearful faces under all conditions (reviewed in Costafreda et al., 2008). Overall, there is a evidence that amygdala activation by emotion is stronger in passive than active attention tasks (reviewed in Costafreda et al., 2008), and that activation may be more specific to fear in active attention tasks but more broadly to threatening or otherwise attention-getting stimuli that occur outside attention (reviewed in Adolphs, 2008).

With respect to developmental studies, several have reported activation of the amygdala in children for fearful faces compared to fixation (Baird et al., 1999; Gruyer et al., 2008; Thomas et al., 2001), nonsense images (Baird et al., 1999), neutral faces (Gruyer et al., 2008; Jones et al., 2009; but see Thomas et al., 2001), or other emotional faces (Lobaugh et al., 2006). Studies that have compared responses for children and adults have reported greater activation of the amygdala for fearful (Gruyer et al., 2008; Monk et al., 2003; but see Thomas et al., 2001) and sad (Killgore and Yurgelun-Todd, 2007) faces in children compared to adults. Some studies have found that, within the childhood age range (9–17 years), activation of the amygdala to fearful faces decreases with age (Killgore et al., 2001), while other studies testing a similar age range have not found such a relation (Gruyer et al., 2008; Yurgelun-Todd and Killgore, 2006).

Studies using brief stimulus presentations and masking to prevent conscious perception of the stimuli are particularly relevant as they provide more convincing evidence that any amygdala activation observed occurs via the subcortical pathway rather than via cortical routes. In one such study, adolescents showed amygdala activation for masked sad faces compared to baseline (Killgore and Yurgelun-Todd, 2007). Another study found no greater activation for masked angry than masked neutral faces in the amygdala in healthy adolescents but greater right amygdala activation to angry than neutral faces in those with generalized anxiety disorder (Monk et al., 2008)

There is mixed evidence as to whether children show activation of the amygdala to faces without emotional expressions (neutral faces), with some studies showing such activation (Thomas et al., 2001) and some not (Gruyer et al., 2008); there is also little evidence that positive emotions engage the amygdala (Gruyer et al., 2008: Killlgore and Yurgelun-Todd, 2007).

There are no neuroimaging studies of amygdala involvement in face processing in human infants; however event-related potential (ERP) studies provide some interesting hints. ERPs have limited temporal resolution and are believed to reflect primarily the activity of cortical neurons, and as such are not ideal for investigations of amygdala function. However, ERPs could detect amygdala function indirectly via its effect on cortical processing. One ERP component of interest in this context is the Nc component, believed to reflect attentional orienting to salient, attention getting or unpredictable stimuli (reviewed in de Haan, 2007). This description of the Nc coincides very well with a recent description of the role of the amygdala (Adolphs, 2008). The Nc is known to be influenced by the emotional content of stimuli in infants, with the pattern of responding showing developmental change over the first postnatal year when there is believed to be an increase in the amygdala's influence on cortical processing (Payne and Bachevalier, 2009). For example, the Nc is larger in response to the mother's face than a stranger's face at 6 months of age (de Haan and Nelson, 1997, 1999), but this differential responding disappears and then re-emerges as a larger response to strangers' faces in the second year (Carver et al., 2003). Similarly, the Nc does not differentiate happy from fearful expressions at 4 months, (Peltola et al., 2009) but shows a larger response to fearful faces by 7 months (de Haan et al., 2004; Nelson and de Haan, 1996; Peltola et al, 2009). Individual differences in the amplitude of the Nc have also been linked to fearful infant temperament (de Haan et al., 2004), which in turn has been linked to the amygdala (e.g. Schmidt et al., 1997). One study has analyzed the cortical sources of the infant Nc and reported sources in the prefrontal cortex including the cingulate cortex. As the amygdala has reciprocal connections with the orbitofrontal and cingulate cortex, potentially modulations of the Nc could reflect in part amygdala modulation of these cortical regions (Ghashghaei et al., 2007).

Another infant ERP component that may be modulated by the amygdala is the P400. The P400 is an occipital component in the infant ERP that is thought to be one of the precursors of the adult N170 face-sensitive component (for further discussion, see below). The adult N170 is typically larger amplitude to fearful faces than happy or neutral faces (e.g. Leppänen et al., 2007), a result which has been interpreted as reflecting amygdala enhancement of cortical processing. In 7-month-old infants, the P400 is also larger in amplitude to fearful than happy or neutral expressions, a finding that may reflect a similar mechanism of enhancement of cortical processing (Leppänen et al., 2007).

Brain injury

Loss of cerebral hemispheres A small number of reports have investigated visual abilities in infants who have lost both cerebral hemispheres. These investigations suggest that neural structures in the midbrain can mediate vision in foveal or macular regions but not beyond 5 degrees eccentricity. One of five children in one study responded only to a moving face or drum of black and white stripes (Werth, 2007). This result supports the idea that a subcortical pathway could underlie infants' early orienting to faces, as this is most robustly elicited by moving faces (Johnson et al., 1991).

Infant mesial temporal lobe lesions In patients with temporal lobe epilepsy due to mesial temporal sclerosis, the amygdala is one structure that is often damaged together with the hippocampus. Studies of such patients suggest onset of right mesial temporal sclerosis before the age of 5 to 6 years is associated with a particular difficulty in recognition of fearful faces compared to patients with patients with left mesial temporal lobe sclerosis, temporal lobe epilepsy due to other causes, or epilepsy outside the temporal lobes (Hlobil et al., 2008; McClelland et al., 2006; Meletti et al., 2003). In patients with early-onset right mesial temporal sclerosis requiring surgical treatment, emotion recognition difficulties remain following surgery (Hlobil et al., 2008; McClelland et al., 2006). These results have led investigators to argue that normal early development of the right amygdala plays a critical role in establishing the normal circuitry for emotion recognition and that other brain mechanisms are unable to compensate for injury occurring in the first years of life (McClelland et al., 2006; Meletti et al., 2003). It should be noted that the amygdala is not the only brain structure damaged in patients with mesial temporal sclerosis, and some have argued that the co-occurring damage to the hippocampus also plays a critical role in the observed deficits in emotion recognition (Meletti et al., 2003).

Summary: development of subcortical pathway

The limited available evidence suggests that the structures of the subcortical pathway are in place and operational to some extent very early in postnatal life. While there is little direct evidence, the studies available support the view that subcortical structures can mediate attentional orienting to faces in early infancy. There is continued development of the cortical connections of these subcortical structures and functional studies of the amygdala also indicate continued development into adolescence. Further studies are needed to understand how the functional development of the amygdala in face processing is influenced by development of inputs via the subcortical pathway, the intrinsic structure of the amygdala, and/or other cortical connections. Evidence from children with disease of the mesial temporal lobe involving the amygdala suggest that normal function of right amygdala in the first 5 to 6 years is necessary for establishing normal function in the mature system.

Development of core cortical pathway

With respect to developmental studies, interest in development of the core cortical pathway has focused mainly on understanding the development of specialization of cortical regions for face processing and how this process may go awry in developmental disorders of social communication such as autistic spectrum disorder.

Structural development

There is limited information about the structural development of the components of the Core Cortical System in humans.

Fusiform gyrus

The fusiform gyrus is located along the inferior occipitotemporal cortex. There is little evidence regarding its normative structural development, though several studies have noted structural abnormalities of the fusiform in developmental disorders associated with atypical face processing including autistic spectrum disorder (van Kooten et al., 2008) and 22q11.2 deletion syndrome (Glaser et al., 2007). Recent DTI studies in human adults and adolescents confirm a connection between the mid fusiform gyrus and the amygdala (Conturo et al., 2008; Smith et al., 2009), which is consistent with the results of functional studies suggesting such a pathway. For example, fMRI studies show that increased responses in the fusiform cortex to fearful faces are abolished by amygdala damage in the ipsilateral hemisphere (reviewed in Vuilleumier and Pourtois, 2007).

Superior temporal sulcus

The STS is a longitudinal fissure that separates the superior and middle gyri of the temporal lobes. The multisensory regions of the STS receive inputs from auditory, visual, and somatosensory areas and send diffuse connections to much of the frontal cortex including the orbital frontal and dorsolateral prefrontal cortex. The STS also has reciprocal connections to the amygdala, with feedback from the amygdala possibly providing a route by which responses to socially relevant stimuli can be amplified.

Evidence from monkeys suggests that connections of STS to inferotemporal cortex are basically in place and adult-like by 7 weeks (Rodman, 1994). One exception is that there are additional connections between the STS and primary visual cortex in infant monkeys that are not present in adults (Kennedy et al., 1989). In humans, neuroimaging studies indicate that the connections of the STS still undergo a protracted period of myelination, with the STS being the last part of the temporal lobe to show adult levels of myelination (Lenroot and Giedd, 2006).

Functional development

Processing of faces and face orientation

A small number of studies using positron emission tomography (PET), near infra-red spectroscopy (NIRS) or ERPs suggest that occipitotemporal cortical pathways are involved in infant face processing within the first postnatal months. In the single PET study in infants, 2-month-olds' activation in the inferior occipital gyrus and the fusiform gyrus, but not the STS, was greater in response to a human face than to a set of three diodes (Tzourio-Mazoyer et al., 2002). This study demonstrates that areas involved in face processing in adults can also be activated by faces by 2 months of age. The lack of finding of activation of the STS could indicate more protracted development of this component of the core cortical system.

This study provides the main direct evidence for cortical involvement in face processing by 2 months of age. It is likely, however, that cortical mechanisms are functional to some extent before this age. From a theoretical point of view, developing cortical systems are believed to be benefiting from the exposure to faces provided by the subcortical orienting systems from birth (Johnson and Morton, 1991). Behavioral studies demonstrating that infants less than 2 months of age can perform feats such as recognizing faces across changes in viewpoint (Turati et al., 2008) and recognize their mother's face (Pascalis et al., 1995) also suggest cortical involvement at this time. However, as the brain bases of performance on these behavioral tasks has not been clearly worked out and there are no imaging studies of face processing in children less than 2 months of age, the exact role of the core cortical system during this time remains an important question for further study.

ERP studies support the idea that cortical mechanisms are involved in face processing from at least 3 months of age. However they also suggest that, when cortical mechanisms do become involved, they are less "tuned in" to faces than in the mature system. These studies have focused on the development of the N170, a negative deflection over occipitotemporal electrodes that peaks approximately 170 ms after stimulus onset that is thought to reflect the initial stages of the perceptual analysis of faces (Bentin et al., 1996). Components of the Core System contribute to the N170, including regions of the fusiform gyrus (Shibata et al., 2002), the posterior inferior temporal gyrus (Bentin et al., 1996; Shibata et al., 2002), lateral occipitotemporal cortex (Bentin et al., 1996; Schweinberger et al., 2002), and the STS (Henson et al., 2003; Itier and Taylor, 2004). The N170 is typically of larger amplitude and/or longer latency for inverted than upright faces (e.g. Bentin et al., 1996; de Haan et al., 2002b; Rossion et al., 2000) but does not differ for inverted compared to upright exemplars of non-face object categories (Bentin et al., 1996; Rebai et al., 2001; Rossion et al., 2000), even animal (monkey) faces that share the basic eyes-nose-mouth arrangement with the human face (de Haan et al., 2002b). This N170 inversion effect parallels the behavioral inversion effect described above, and suggests the N170 is involved in relational encoding.

In infants as young as 3 months, two components believed to be precursors to the adult N170 are elicited during viewing of faces, the N290 and the P400 (Halit et al., 2003). Source analyses show that the generators of the infant N290 include similar regions to those identified for the adult N170, including the lateral occipital area bilaterally, and the fusiform gyrus and STS particularly on the right (Johnson et al., 2005). While these precursors are observable by 3 months, they differ from the N170 in adults in that: (1) an inversion effect specific to human faces is not seen until 12 months of age (even though there is evidence of discrimination between upright and inverted faces by at least 3 months of age), (2) response latencies are approximately 100 to 200 ms slower than adults, (3) even at 12 months of age, responses are spread over a longer time range compared to adults, and (4) the spatial distribution of both the N290 and P400 is more medial and shifts laterally (thereby becoming more adult-like) between 3 to 12 months of age. Together, these results suggest that components of the Core Cortical System are functioning by 3 months, but become more specific to human faces over the first year of life. They also suggest that processing of faces occurs more quickly and more discretely in time with age, and that the relative involvement or position of neural generators that contribute to these components changes with age (for discussion see de Haan et al., 2007).

The N170 continues to develop until well into adolescence. For example, its latency decreases consistently until approximately 14 years of age and its amplitude shows a U-shaped function with smaller amplitudes at 11 to 12 years than older or younger ages (Taylor et al., 2004). Larger amplitudes over the right hemisphere characteristic of adults are not consistently seen until 11 to 12 years (Taylor et al., 2004). Interestingly, an inversion effect on children's N170 is not seen until 8 to 11 years of age (Taylor et al., 2004). This result is consistent with neuroimaging studies finding a protracted development of the effect of face inversion on activity in the lateral and medial fusiform regions and STS (Passarotti et al.,) but it is at odds with infant studies indicating that such an effect is present by 12 months of age (Halit et al., 2001). This may reflect a different neural organization of the processing of face inversion with age (see below).

A small number of fMRI studies also suggest continued development of the Core Cortical System through childhood. Children from 10 years show greater activation of the fusiform gyrus while viewing faces than viewing houses (Aylward et al., 2005), natural or manufactured objects (Gathers et al., 2004; see Figure 38.1), scrambled faces (Passarotti et al., 2003) or a fixation (Lobaugh et al., 2006) and greater activation to direct than averted faces (Garrett et al., 2004). One of these studies that included an adult comparison group found that children showed a more distributed pattern of fusiform activation encompassing the medial and lateral regions while adults showed a more focused pattern of activity (Passarotti et al., 2003). Two studies of children younger than 10 years failed to find activation greater activation of the fusiform gyrus for faces compared to other stimuli in the classic FFA region, but both found evidence of such activation more posteriorly in the inferior occipital region (Aylward et al., 2005; Gathers et al., 2004; see Figure 38.1). These latter results appear to conflict with those mentioned above, where 2-month-olds showed activation of both the fusiform gyrus and inferior occipital region while viewing faces. One explanation for this apparent discrepancy is the differing comparison stimuli: the developing fusiform may be more active to faces than diodes as in the study with 2-month-olds (Tzourio-Mazoyer et al., 2002), but may not yet be sufficiently specialized to be more active for faces than houses or other objects, as found with the children younger than 10 years (Aylward et al., 2005; Gathers et al., 2004). This stands in contrast to the pattern for object- and place-related cortical activation, which shows an adult-like organization even in young children (Scherf et al., 2007).

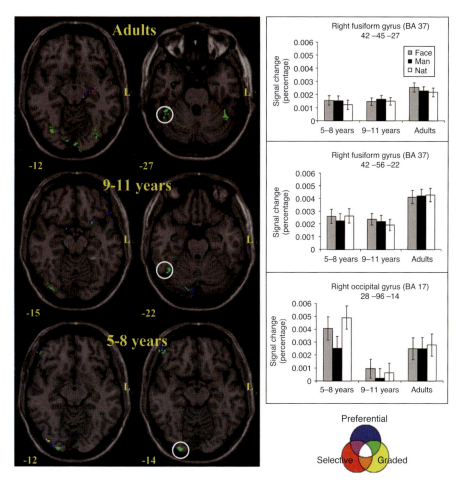

Fig. 38.1 Adults and older children show face-preferential activation the right fusiform region (1a, d and 1b, e respectively) while young children do so in a right occipital regions (1c, f). From Gathers et al., Developmental shifts in cortical loci for face and object recognition, *NeuroReport*, 15(10) © 2004 with permission of Wolters Kluwer Health.

These neuroimaging studies suggest that important developments in face processing occur at about 10 years of age, an idea that is consistent with prior conclusions from behavioral studies. According to the classic "encoding switch" hypothesis, younger children are poorer at encoding and remembering faces because they do so only in terms of featural information. At about 10 years of age, children switch encoding styles and begin to use relational information, resulting in improved face processing (Carey and Diamond, 1977; Diamond and Carey, 1977). More recent studies have demonstrated that young children (Freire and Lee, 2001) and even infants (Cohen and Cashon, 2001) are able to encode relational information and discount the strong version of the hypothesis wherein there is a complete switch. However, there is still evidence that reliance on relational information does increase with age (Mondloch et al., but see McKone and Boyer, 2006). In the neuroimaging studies activation in the fusiform region correlates with the size of the behavioral inversion effect for faces in both 12- to 14-year-old children (Aylward et al., 2005), and

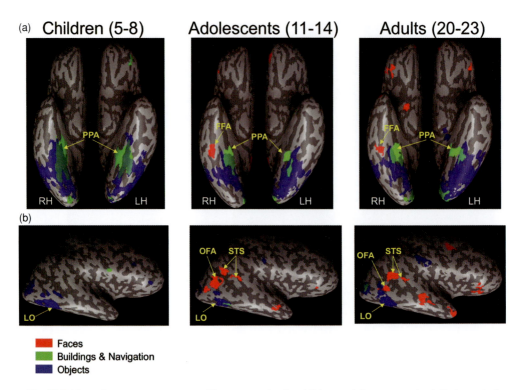

Fig. 38.2 Ventral stream category-specific topography for children, adolescents and adults in ventral cortex (a) and lateral right hemisphere (b). FFA, fusiform face area; LO, lateral occipital object area; OFA, occipital face area; PPA, parahippocampal place area; STS, superior temporal sulcus;. Figure from Scherf, Behrmann, Humphreys, and Luna, 2007, Visual category-selectivity for faces, places, and objects emerges along different developmental trajectories, *Developmental Science*, **10**, F15–F30.Wiley.

adults (Yovel and Kanwisher, 2005), possibly suggesting that improvements in relational encoding are linked to development of the fusiform region's role in face encoding.

There is a suggestion that the role of the STS may change with development. In contrast to the fMRI studies of children described above, where the inversion effect was linked to activation in the fusiform gyrus, infant ERP and NIRS studies suggest that the right STS discriminates between upright and inverted faces (Johnson et al., 2005; Otsuka et al., 2007). Another difference is that, while in adults the STS is sensitive to gaze direction, in infants fusiform generators, and not STS generators, mainly contribute to the ERP elicited by gaze direction (Grossmann and Johnson, 2007; see below). It is thus possible that the STS plays a different role in the face-processing network in infants than in adults, consistent with observations that the connections of the STS differ in infants compared to adults (Kennedy et al., 1989).

Facial identity The infant N170 does not appear to be sensitive to familiarity in facial identity (de Haan and Nelson, 1997, 1999). This finding is similar to that observed in adults, suggesting that, as in adults, the N170 reflects Core System processing of perceptual features that convey identity rather than recognition of familiarity personal identity. Less is known about development of the Extended System related to recognition of identity in infants, though studies have shown that more anterior and longer-latency components differentiate familiar from unfamiliar faces by 3 to 6 months of age (de Haan and Nelson, 1997, 1999; Pascalis et al., 1998). Interestingly, both NIRS and ERP studies show that familiar face recognition in infants is lateralized to the right fronto-temporal regions (Carlsson et al., 2008; de Haan and Nelson, 1997, 1999).

Face emotion

There is limited direct information about the involvement of the Core Cortical System in infants' or childrens' processing of facial expressions. Three ERP studies have examined 7-month-old infants' responses to fearful compared to happy or angry expressions (de Haan et al., 2004; de Haan and Nelson, 1998; Nelson and de Haan, 1996). These studies demonstrated that ERPs differed for happy compared to fearful faces by approximately 140 to 260 ms after stimulus onset, but ERPs did not differ from angry compared to fearful faces at any latency up to 1700 ms after stimulus onset. A more recent study demonstrated that the infant P400 component, like the adult N170, is larger to fearful faces (Leppänen et al., 2007). Studies of children between 4 and 14 years of age suggest that emotion does not greatly influence the N170 (de Haan et al., 1998; Batty and Taylor 2006), though one study found a faster latency for fearful than happy or angry expressions in 5-year-olds (de Haan et al.,1998) and a larger amplitude to fearful compared to other expressions is observed by 14 to 15 years (Batty and Taylor, 2006). Most neuroimaging studies of emotion processing in children have focused on the amygdala, but some also show that facial expressions of emotion do activate the fusiform gyrus (Wang et al., 2004) and superior temporal gyrus (Lobaugh et al., 2006). However, these findings were based on relatively small groups spanning a wide age range and without adult comparison.

Eye gaze

Four-month-old infants show a larger infant N170 to faces with direct than faces with averted gaze (Farroni et al., 2002). Four-month-olds show this response even if the head is turned, but not if the face is inverted (Farroni et al., 2004). It is not clear whether the abolition of the response when the face is inverted is, as for adults, due primarily to inversion of the eyes themselves or due to the inversion of the entire face. Interestingly, the N290 response to direction of eye gaze appears to be generated by the fusiform region rather than the superior temporal region, although both regions are involved at longer latencies (Johnson et al., 2005). Studies of older children have produced mixed results, with one study of 3.5- to 7-year-olds showing, as for adults, no influence of direction of gaze on the N170 (Grice et al., 2005) and another in 12-year-olds showing a larger N170 for direct than averted gaze (Senju et al., 2005). One study comparing children's N170 responses to eyes only with responses to full faces found that the response to eyes was much larger and quicker than to full faces (Taylor et al., 2001). The study also reported that the N170 to eyes matures more quickly, by 11 years, than the N170 to full faces which continues to develop until later in adolescence. In addition, the frontal positivity that in adults is the counterpoint to the posterior negative N170 is present only for eyes by 11 years but not yet for full faces. These results suggest developmental changes in the configuration of generators involved in processing of eyes compared to full face.

A study of event-related fMRI activity in 7- to 10-year-old healthy children confirms that the STS is activated by gaze shifts, and also indicate that the STS, middle temporal gyrus, and inferior parietal lobule are sensitive to the intentions underlying the stimulus character's eye movements. These findings suggest that the neural circuitry underlying the processing of eye gaze and the detection of intentions conveyed through shifts in eye gaze in children are similar to that found previously in adults, although the study did not make a direct comparison between children and adults (Mosconi, et al., 2005).

Brief summary: core cortical system

Neurophysiological and neuroimaging studies show that the components of the Core Cortical System are involved in face processing from infancy. Imaging studies provide direct evidence of involvement by 2 months of age, though behavioral studies indicate that the pathway maybe functioning to some extent even prior to this time. However, there are continued developmental changes in the system into adolescence. In particular, there is evidence that face-sensitivity of the system increases with age and that the system may become more focal and less distributed with age, although further more direct assessment of these possible developmental changes is warranted as not all studies have directly compared children of different ages or children with adults. There is also a suggestion that the relative roles and contributions of the STS and fusiform regions may vary from infancy to adolescence, possibly related to slower development of the STS. Few studies have attempted to directly examine interactions between the subcortical and cortical system in a developmental context.

Role of experience in the neurodevelopment of face processing

Current theories of the neurodevelopment of face processing emphasis the importance of experience, particularly for the shaping of cortical networks involved in face processing. One recent view suggests that there is an experience-expectant sensitive period in the development of face emotion processing, starting from 5-7 months of life and continuing for several years (Leppänen and Nelson, 2009). There is evidence consistent with the view that early experience has a lasting impact on face processing abilities. For instance, patients with congenital cataracts who were deprived of patterned visual input from birth until 2 to 6 months of age show deficits in particular aspects of face processing even after at least 9 years of "normal" visual input. These patients show normal processing of featural information in the face (e.g. subtle differences in the shape of the eyes and mouth), but show impairments in processing configural information (i.e. the spacing of features within the face; Le Grand et al., 2001). Studies with such patients also indicate that input to the right hemisphere is particularly important (Le Grand et al., 2003). These studies suggest that visual input during early infancy is necessary for the normal development of at least some aspects of face processing.

Experience with particular types of faces in the visual environment may also play a role in development of infants' abilities to recognize them. For example, studies have shown that in the first months of life infants are able to discriminate both own and other-race faces but, by 9 months, they show an adult-like pattern of better discrimination for own-race faces (Kelly et al., 2007); a similar pattern has been reported for discrimination of own-species versus other-species faces (Pascalis et al., 2002).

If experience plays an important role in normative development of expression recognition, infants who experience atypical early emotional environments should show an atypical pattern of abilities. For example, Pollak and colleagues have found that perception of the facial expression of anger, but not other expressions, is altered in children who are abused by their parents. Specifically, they report that, compared with non-abused children, abused children show a response bias for anger (Pollak et al., 2000), identify anger based on less perceptual input (Pollak and Sinha, 2002; Pollak et al., 2009), and show altered category boundaries for anger (Pollak and Kistler, 2002). ERP measures also support this pattern of findings: maltreated children show a larger target P3b to angry faces than happy or neutral faces (Pollak et al., 2001). These results suggest that atypical frequency and content of their emotional interactions with their caregivers results in a change in the basic perception of emotional expressions in abused children.

A recent study compared ERP responses to facial emotion in 3-year-old Romanian children who were institutionalized, those who had been institutionalized but now randomly assigned to foster care, and those always reared in families. While this study found general decrease in amplitude in increase in latency of the P1, N170, and Nc in institutionalized compared to family reared children, with those in foster care showing intermediate values, the groups did not differ in their response to emotional content: all three groups showed an enhancement of ERPs to fear compared to happy (Moulson et al., 2009).

Summary and conclusions

The neural system involved in face processing involves a widespread network of cortical and subcortical structures. There is evidence that subcortical structures are functioning from the start of postnatal life and may mediate the newborn's tendency to orient to faces in the visual environment. The subcortical system could thereby provide a face-biased input to cortical circuits and enhance the cortical processing of faces. With respect to the core cortical areas, the fusiform gyrus is activated by faces by 2 months of age and there is evidence for STS involvement within the first year as well. However, the pattern of functional activation of these areas varies with development.

Developments in neuroimaging will provide a useful tool for more detailed analysis of the development of subcortical and cortical systems for face processing and their interplay. Higher-strength magnets will allow better visualization of subcortical structures, which will provide important information given the prominent role these structures are given in models of infant face processing. Tools such as diffusion tensor imaging will provide better information about the development of connections between the components of these brain networks. This is important as available anatomical evidence suggests that connections undergo more dramatic developmental changes then the structures themselves. Studies with monkeys suggest that cortical inputs are initially more diffuse and become more refined with development. Understanding development of such inputs in humans is important as evidence also suggests that early experience has a lasting impact on functioning of the system.

References

Adolphs, R. (2008). Fear, faces and the human amygdala. *Current Opinion in Neurobiology*, **18**, 166–172.

Allison, T., Puce, A., and McCarthy, G. (2000). Social perception from visual cues: Role of the STS region. *Trends in Cognitive Science*, **4**, 267–278.

Amaral, D.G. and Bennett, J. (2000). Development of amygdalo-cortical connections in the macaque monkey. *Society for Neuroscience Abstracts*, **26**, 17–26.

Armstrong, E. (1980). A quantitative comparison of the hominoid thalamus. IV. Posterior association nuclei-the pulvinar and lateral posterior nucleus. *American Journal of Physical Anthropology*, **55**, 369–383.

Aylward, E.H., Park, J.E., Field, K.M., *et al.* (2005). Brain activation during face perception: Evidence of a developmental change. *Journal of Cognitive Neuroscience*, **17**, 308–319.

Baird, A.A., Gruber, S.A., Fein, D.A., *et al.* (1999). Functional magnetic resonance imaging of facial affect recognition in children and adolescents. *Journal of the American Academy of Child and Adolescent Psychiatry*, **38**, 195–199.

Balaban, M.T. (1995). Affective influences on startle in five-month-old infants: Reactions to facial expressions of emotion. *Child Development*, **66**, 28–36.

Batty, M. and Taylor, M.J. (2006). The development of emotional face processing during childhood. *Developmental Science*, **9**, 207–220.

Bentin, S., Allison, T., Puce, A., *et al.* (1996). Electrophysiological studies of face perception in humans. *Journal of Cognitive Neuroscience*, **8**, 551–565

Benvento, L.A. and Fallon, J.H. (1975). The ascending projections of the superior colliculus in the rhesus monkey. *Journal of Comparative Neurology*, **160**, 339–362.

Bompas, A., Sterling, T., Rafal, R.D., and Sumner, P. (2008). Naso-temporal asymmetry for signals invisible to the retinotectal pathway. *Journal of Neurophysiology*, **100**, 412–421.

Brody, B.A., Kinney, H., Kloman, A., and Gilles, F.H. (1987). Sequence of central nervous system myelination in human infancy: I. An autopsy study of myelination. *Journal of Neuropathology and Experimental Neurology*, **46**, 283–301.

Carlsson, J., Lagercrantz, H., Olson, L., Printz, G., and Bartocci, M. (2008). Activation of the right fronto-temporal cortex during maternal facial recognition in young infants. *Acta Paediatrica*, **97**, 1221–1225.

Carey, S. and Diamond, R. (1977). From piecemeal to configurational representation of faces. *Science*, **195**, 312–314.

Carver, L.J., Dawson, G., Panagiotides, H., *et al.* (2003). Age-related differences in neural correlates of face recognition during the toddlers and preschool years. *Developmental Psychobiology*, **42**, 148–159.

Cho, S., Jones, D., Reddick, W.E., Ogg, R.J., and Steen R.G. (1997). Establishing norms for age-related changes in proton T1 of human brain tissue in vivo. *Magnetic Resonance Imaging*, **15**, 1133–1143.

Cohen, L.B. and Cashon, C.H. (2001). Do 7-month-old infants process independent features or facial configurations? *Infant and Child Development*, **10**, 83–92.

Conturo, T.E., Williams, D.L., Smith, C.D., Gultepe, E., Akbudak, E., and Minshew, N.J. (2008). Neuronal fiber pathway abnormalities in autism: An initial MRI diffusion tensor tracking study of hippocamp-fusiform and amygdala-fusiform pathways. *Journal of the International Neuropsychology Society*, **14**, 933–946.

Costafreda, S.G., Brammer, M.J., David, A.S. and Fu, C.H.Y. (2008). Predictors of amygdala activation during processing of emotional stimuli: A meta-analysis of 385 PET and fMRI studies. *Brain Research Reviews*, **1**, 57–70.

Davis, M. (1989). The role of the amygdala and its efferent projections in fear and anxiety. In P. Tyrer (ed.), *Psychopharmacology of anxiety.* (pp. 52–79). Oxford: Oxford University Press.

de Gelder, B., and Stecklenburg, J.J. (2005). Naso-temporal asymmetry of the N170 for processing of faces in normal viewers but not in developmental prosopagnosia. *Neuroscience Letters*, **376**, 40–45.

de Gelder, B., Frissen, I., Barton, J., and Hadjukhani, M. (2003). A modulatory role for facial expressions in prosopagnosia. *Proceedings of the National Academy of Sciences USA*, **100**, 113105–13110.

de Haan, M. (2007). Visual attention and recognition memory in infancy. In M. de Haan (ed), *Infant EEG and event-related potentials*, pp. 101–143. Hove: Psychology Press.

de Haan, M. and Nelson, C.A. (1997). Recognition of the mother's face by six-month-old infants: A neurobehavioral study. *Child Development*, **68**, 187–210.

de Haan, M. and Nelson, C.A. (1998). Discrimination and categorisation of facial expressions of emotion during infancy. In A. Slater (ed.), *Perceptual Development.* (pp. 287–389). London: UCL Press.

de Haan, M. and Nelson, C.A. (1999). Brain activity differentiates face and object processing in 6-month-old infants. *Developmental Psychology*, **35**, 1113–1121.

de Haan, M., Nelson, C.A., Gunnar, M.R., and Tout, K. (1998). Hemispheric differences in brain activity related to the recognition of emotional expressions by 5-year-old children. *Developmental Neuropsychology*, **14**, 495–518.

de Haan, M., Humphreys, K., and Johnson, M.H. (2002a). Developing a brain specialized for face perception: A converging methods approach. *Developmental Psychobiology*, **40**, 200–212.

de Haan, M., Pascalis, O., and Johnson, M.H. (2002b). Specialization of neural mechanisms underlying face recognition in human infants. *Journal of Cognitive Neuroscience*, **14**, 199–209.

de Haan, M., Belsky, J., Reid, V., Volein, A., and Johnson, M.H. (2004). Maternal personality and infants' neural and visual responsivity to facial expressions of emotion. *Journal of Child Psychology and Psychiatry*, **45**, 1209–1218.

de Haan, M., Johnson, M.H., and Halit, H. (2007) Development of face-sensitive event-related potentials during infancy. In M. de Haan (ed). *Infant EEG and event-related potentials*, pp. 75–99. Hove: Psychology Press.

de Heering, A., Turati, C., Rossion, B., Bulf, H., Goffaux, V., and Simion, F. (2008). Newborns' face recognition is based on spatial frequencies below 0.5 cycles per degree. *Cognition*, **106**, 444–454.

Deruelle, C., Rondan, C., Salle-Collemiche, X., Bastard-Rosset, D., and Da Foseca, D. (2008). Attention to low- and high-spatial frequencies in categorizing facial identities, emotions and gender in children with autism. *Brain and Cognition*, **66**, 115–123.

Diamond, R. and Carey, S. (1977). Developmental changes in the representation of faces. *Journal of Experimental Child Psychology*, **23**, 1–22.

Farroni, T., Csibra, G., Simion, F., and Johnson, M.H. (2002). Eye contact detection in humans from birth. *Proceedings of the National Academy of Sciences USA*, **99**, 9602–9605.

Farroni, T., Johnson, M.H., and Csibra, G. (2004). Mechanisms of eye gaze perception during infancy. *Journal of Cognitive Neuroscience*, **16**, 1320–1326.

Friere, A. and Lee, K. (2001). Face recognition in 4- to 7-year-olds: Processing of configural, featural and paraphernalia information. *Journal of Experimental Child Psychology*, **80**, 347–371.

Garrett, A.S., Menon, V., MacKenzie, K., and Reiss, A.L. (2004). Here's looking at you kid. *Neural systems underlying face and gaze processing in fragile x syndrome. Archives of General Psychiatry*, **61**, 281–288.

Gathers, A.D., Bhatt, R., Corbly, C.R., Farley, A.B., and Joseph, J.E. (2004). Developmental shifts in cortical loci for face and object recognition. *NeuroReport*, **15**, 1549–1553.

Ghashghaei, H.T., Hilgetag, C.C., and Barbas, H. (2007). Sequence of information processing for emotions based on the anatomic dialogue between prefrontal cortex and amygdala. *Neuroimage*, **34**, 905–923.

Glaser, B., Schaer, M., Berney, S., Debbane, M., Vuilleumier, P., and Eliezb, S. (2007). Structural changes to the fusiform gyrus: A cerebral marker for social impairments in 22q11.1 deletion syndrome? *Schizophrenia Research*, **96**, 82–86.

Gobbini, M.I. and Haxby, J.V. (2007). Neural systems for recognition of familiar faces. *Neuropsychologia*, **45**, 32–41.

Golouboff, N., Fiori, N., Delalande, O., Fohlen, M., Dellatolas, G., and Jambaque, I. (2008). Impaired facial expression recognition in children with temporal lobe epilepsy: Impact of early seizure onset on fear recognition. *Neuropsychologia*, **46**, 1415–1428.

Grice, S., Halit, H., Farroni, T., Baron-Cohen, S., Bolton, P., and Johnson, M.H. (2005). Neural correlates of eye-gaze detection in young children with autism. *Cortex*, **41**, 342–353.

Grossmann, T. and Johnson, M.H. (2007). The development of the social brain in human infancy. *European Journal of Neuroscience*, **25**, 909–919.

Gruyer, A.E., Monk, C.S., McClure-Tone, E.B., *et al.* (2008) A developmental examination of amygdala response to facial expressions. *Journal of Cognitive Neuroscience*, **20**, 1565–1582.

Halit, H., de Haan, M., Johnson, M.H. (2003). Cortical specialisation for face processing: face-sensitive event-related potential components in 3- and 12-month-old infants. *Neuroimage*, **19**, 1180–1193.

Haxby, J.V., Hoffman, E.A., and Gobbini, M. (2000). The distributed human neural system for face perception. *Trends in Cognitive Sciences*, **4**, 223–233.

Henson, R.N., Goshen-Gottstein, Y., Ganel, T., Otten, L.J., Quayle, A., Rugg, M.D. (2003). Electrophysiological and haemodynamic correlates of face perception, recognition and priming. *Cerebral Cortex*, **13**, 793–805.

Hlobil, U., Rathore, C., Alexander, A., Sarma, S., and Radhakrishnan, K. (2008). Impaired facial emotion recognition in patients with mesial temporal lobe epilepsy associated with hippocampal sclerosis (MTLE-HS): Side and age of onset matters. *Epilepsy Research*, **80**, 150–157.

Holstege, G., Van Ham, J.J., and Tan, J. (1986). Afferent projections to the orbicularis oculi motoneural cell group: An autoradiographical tracing study in the cat. *Brain Research*, **374**, 306–320.

Itier, R.J. and Taylor, M.J. (2004). Source analysis of the N170 to faces and objects. *NeuroReport*, **15**, 1261–1265.

Jia, Q., Xiangtian, Z., Hua, Z., Gang, C., Ashwell, K., and Fan, L. (2006) Development of the human superior colliculus and the retinocollicular projection. *Experimental Eye Research*, **82**, 300–310.

Johnson, M.H. (2005). Subcortical face processing. *Nature Reviews Neuroscience*, **6**, 766–774.

Johnson, M.H. and Morton, J. (1991). Biology and cognitive development: The case of face recognition. Oxford: Blackwell.

Johnson, M.H., Dziurawiec, S., Ellis, H., and Morton, J. (1991). Newborns' preferential tracking of face-like stimuli and its subsequent decline. *Cognition*, **40**, 1–19.

Johnson, M.H., Griffin, R., Csibra, G., *et al.* (2005). The emergence of the social brain network: Evidence from typical and atypical development. *Development and Psychopathology*, **17**, 599–619.

Jones, A.P., Laurens, K.R., Herba, CM., Barker, G.J., and Viding, E. (2009). Amygdala hypoactivity to fearful faces in boys with conduct problems and callous-unemotional traits. *American Journal of Psychiatry*, **166**, 95–102.

Kanwisher, M., McDermott, J., and Chun, M.M. (1997). The fusiform face area: A module in human extrastriate cortex specialized for face perception. *Journal of Neuroscience*, **17**, 4302–4311.

Kelly, D.J., Quinn, P.C., Slater, A.M., Lee, K., Ge, L., and Pascalis, O. (2007). The other-race effect develops during infancy: evidence of perceptual narrowing. *Psychological Science*, **18**, 1084–1089.

Kennedy, H., Bullier, J., and Dehay, C. (1989). Transient projection fom the superior temporal sulcus to area 17 in the newborn macaque monkey. *Proceedings of the National Academy of Sciences USA*, 86, 8093–8097.

Killgore, W.D.S., Oki, M., and Yurgelun-Todd, D.A. (2001). Sex-specific developmental changes in amygdala responses to affective faces. *NeuroReport*, **12**, 427–433.

Killgore, W.D.S. and Yurgelun-Todd, D.A. (2007). Unconscious processing of facial affect in children and adolescents. *Social Neuroscience*, **2**, 28–47.

Kinney, H.C, Brody, B.A, Kloman, A., and Gilles, F. (1988). Sequence of CNS myelination in infancy. *Journal of Neuropathology and Experimental Neurology*, **47**, 217–234.

Lang, P.J., Bradley, M.M., and Cuthbert, B.N. (1990). Emotion, attention, and the startle reflex. *Psychological Review*, **97**, 377–395.

Lang, P.J., Bradley, M.M., and Cuthbert, B.N. (1992). A motivational analysis of emotion: Reflex-cortex connections. *Psychological Science*, **3**, 44–49.

Le Grand, R., Mondloch, C.J., Maurer, D., and Brent, H.P. (2001). Neuroperception: Early visual experience and face processing. *Nature*, **410**, 890.

Le Grand, R., Mondloch, C.J., Maurer, D., and Brent, H.P. (2003) Expert face processing requires visual input to the right hemisphere during infancy. *Nature Neuroscience*, **6**, 1108–1112.

Leh, S.E., Chakravarty, M.M., and Ptito, A. (2008). The connectivity of the human pulvinar: A diffusion tensor imaging tractography study. *International Journal of Biomedical Imaging*, **2008**, 789539.

Lenroot, R.K. and Giedd, J.N. (2006). Brain development in children and adolescents: Insights from anatomical magnetic resonance imaging. *Neuroscience and Biobehavioral Reviews*, **30**, 718–729.

Leppänen, J.M. and Nelson, C.A. (2009). Tuning the developing brain to social signals of emotions. *Nature Reviews Neuroscience*, **10**, 37–47.

Leppänen, J.M., Moulson, M.C., Vogel-Farley, V.K., and Nelson, C.A. (2007). An ERP study of emotional face processing in the adult and infant brain. *Child Development*, **78**, 232–245.

Letinic, K. and Rakic, P. (2001). Telencephalic origin of human thalamic GABAergic neurons. *Nature Neuroscience*, **4**, 931–936.

Lewis, T.L., Maurer, D., and Blackburn, K. (1985). The development of young infants' ability to detect stimuli in the nasal visual field. *Vision Research*, **25**, 943–950.

Liddell, B.J., Brown, K.H., Kemp, A.H., *et al.* (2004). A direct brainstem-amygdala-cortical "alarm" system for subliminal signals of fear. *Neuroimage*, **24**, 235–243.

Lobaugh, N.J., Gibson, E., and Taylor, M.H. (2006) Children recruit distinct neural systems for implicit emotional face processing. *NeuroReport*, **17**, 215–219.

Machado, C.J. and Bachevalier, J. (2003). Non-human primate models of childhood psychopathology: the promise and limitations. *Journal of Child Psychology and Psychiatry*, **44**, 64–87.

McClelland, S., Garica, R.E., Peraza, D.M., Shih, T.T., Hirsch, L.J., Hirsch, J., and Goodman, R.R. (2006). Facial emotion recognition after curative nondominant temporal lobectomy in patients with mesial temporal sclerosis. *Epilepsia*, **47**, 1337–1342.

McKone, E. and Boyer, B.L. (2006). Sensitivity of 4-year-olds to featural and second-order relational changes in face distinctiveness. *Journal of Experimental Child Psychology*, **94**, 134–162.

Meletti, S., Benuzzi, F., Nichelli, P., and Tassinari, C.A. (2003). Damage to the right hippocampal-amygdala formation during early infancy and recognition of fearful faces: neuropsychological and fMRI evidence in subjects with temporal lobe epilepsy. *Annals of the New York Academy of Sciences USA*, **1000**, 385–388.

Mondloch, C.J., LeGrand, R., and Maurer, D. (2002). Configural processing develops more slowly than featural processing. *Perception*, **31**, 553–566.

Monk, C., McClure, E.B., Nelson, E.E., *et al.* (2003). Adolescent immaturity in attention-related brain engagement to emotional facial expressions. *Neuroimage*, **20**, 420–428.

Monk, C.S., Telzer, E.H., Mogg, K., *et al.* (2008). Amygdala and ventro-lateral prefrontal cortex activation to masked angry faces in children and adolescents with generalized anxiety disorder. *Archives of General Psychiatry*, **65**, 568–576.

Morris, J.S., Ohman, A., and Dolan, R.J. (1999). A subcortical pathway to the right amygdala mediating "unseen" fear. *Proceedings of the National Academy of Sciences USA*, **96**, 1680–1685.

Morris, J.S., de Gelder, B., Weiskrantz L., and Dolan, R.J. (2001). Differential extrageniculostriate and amygdala responses to presentation of emotional faces in a cortically blind field. *Brain*, **124**, 1241–1252.

Mosconi, M.W., Mack, P.B., McCarthy, G., and Pelphrey, K.A. (2005). Taking an "intentional stance" on eye-gaze shifts: A functional neuroimaging study of social perception in children. *Neuroimage*, **27**, 247–252.

Moulson, M.C., Fox, N.A., Zeanah, C.H., and Nelson, C.A. (2009). Early adverse experiences and the neurobiology of facial emotion processing. *Developmental Psychology*, **45**, 17–30.

Nelson, C.A. and de Haan, M. (1996). Neural correlates of infants' visual responsiveness to facial expressions of emotion. *Developmental Psychobiology*, **29**, 577–595.

Otsuka, Y., Nakato, E., Kanazawa, S., Yamaguchi, M.K., Watanabe, S., and Kakigi, R. (2007). Neural activation to upright and inverted faces in infants measured by near infrared spectroscopy. *Neuroimage*, **34**, 399–406.

Pascalis, O., de Schonen, S., Morton, J., Deruelle, C., and Fabre-Grenet, M. (1995). Mother's face recognition by neonates: A replication and an extension. *Infant Behavior and Development*, **18**, 79–85.

Pascalis, O., de Haan, M., Nelson, C.A., and de Schonen, S. (1998). Long-term recognition memory for faces assessed by visual paired comparison in 3- and 6-month-old infants. *Journal of Experimental Psychology: Learning*, Memory and Cognition, **24**, 249–260.

Pascalis, O., de Haan, M., and Nelson, C.A. (2002). Is face processing species-specific during the first year of life? *Science*, **296**, 1321–1323.

Passarotti, A.M., Paul, B.M., Bussiere, J.R., Buxton, R.B., Wong, E.G., and Stiles, J.S. (2003). The development of face and location processing: an fMRI study. *Developmental Science*, **6**, 100–117.

Passarotti, A.M., Smith, J., DeLano, M., and Huang, J. (2007). Developmental differences in the neural bases of the face inversion effect show progressive tuning of face-selective regions to the upright orientation. *Neuroimage*, **34**, 1708–1722.

Payne, C. and Bachevalier, J. (2009). Neuroanatomy of the developing social brain. In M. de Haan and M.R. Gunnar (eds.) *Handbook of Developmental Social Neuroscience*, pp. 38–59. New York: Guilford Press.

Peltola, M.J., Leppänen, J.M., Maki, S., and Hietanen, J.J.K. (2009). Emergence of enhanced attention to fearful faces between 5 and 7 months of age. *Social, Cognitive and Affective Neuroscience*, **4**, 134–142.

Pessoa, L., Jappe, S., Sturman, D., and Ungerleider, L.G. (2006). Target visibility and visual awareness modulate the amygdala responses to fearful faces. *Cerebral Cortex*, **16**, 366–375.

Pollak, S.D. and Kistler, D.J. (2002). Early experience is associated with development of categorical representations for facial expressions of emotion. *Proceedings of the National Academy of Sciences USA*, **99**, 9072–9076.

Pollak, S.D. and Sinha, P. (2002). Effects of early experience on children's recognition of facial displays of emotion. *Developmental Psychology*, **38**, 784–791.

Pollak, S.D., Cicchetti, D., Hornung, K., and Reed, A. (2000). Recognizing emotion in faces: developmental effects of child abuse and neglect. *Developmental Psychology*, **36**, 679–688.

Pollak, S.D., Klorman, R., Thatcher, J.E., and Cicchetti, D. (2001). P3B reflects maltreated children's reactions to facial displays of emotion. *Psychophysiology*, **38**, 267–274.

Pollak, S.D., Messner, M., Kistler, D.J., and Cohn, J.F. (2009). Development of perceptual expertise in emotion recognition. *Cognition*, **110**, 242–247.

Posner, MI, and Cohen, Y. (1984). Components of visual orienting. In H. Bouma and D.G. Bouwhuis (eds) *Attention and performance X*, pp. 531–556. Hillside, NJ: Lawrence Erlbaum Associates.

Posner, M.I., Rafal, R.D., Choate, L.S., and Vaughan, J. (1985). Inhibition of return: Neural basis and function. *Cognitive Neuropsychology*, **2**, 211–228.

Rafal, R., Henik, A., and Smith, J. (1991). Extrageniculate contributions to reflex orienting in normal humans: A temporal hemifield advantage. *Journal of Cognitive Neuroscience*, **3**, 322–328.

Rebai, M., Poiroux, S., Bernard, C., and Lalonde, R. (2001). Event-related potentials for category-specific information during passive viewing of faces and objects. *International Journal of Neuroscience*, **106**, 209–226.

Reynolds, G.D. and Richards, J.E. (2005). Familiarization, attention and recognition memory in infancy: an event-related potential and cortical source localization study. *Developmental Psychology*, **41**, 598–615.

Robinson, D.L. and Petersen, S.E. (1992). The pulvinar and visual salience. *Trends in Neurosciences*, **15**, 127–132.

Rodman, H. (1994). Development of inferior temporal cortex in the monkey. *Cerebral Cortex*, **4**, 484–498.

Romanski, L.M., Giguere, M., Bates, J.F., and Goldman-Rakic, P.S. (1997). Topographic organization of medial pulvinar connections with the prefrontal cortex in the rhesus monkey. *Journal of Comparative Neurology*, **379**, 313–332.

Rossion, B., Gauthier, I., Tarr, M.J., *et al.* (2000). The N170 occipito-temporal component is delayed and enhanced to inverted faces but not to inverted objects: An electrophysiological account of face-specific processes in the human brain. *NeuroReport*, **11**, 69–74.

Rubia, K., Smith, A.B., Woolley, J., *et al.* (2006). Progressive increase of fronto-striatal brain activation from childhood to adulthood during event-related tasks of cognitive control. *Human Brain Mapping*, **27**, 973–993.

Sapir, A., Soroker, N., Berger, A., and Henik, A. (1999). Inhibition of return in spatial attention: Direct evidence for collicular generation. *Nature Neuroscience*, **2**, 1053–1054.

Scherf, K.S., Berhmann, M., Humprehys, K., and Luna, B. (2007). Visual category-selectivity for faces, places and objects emerges along different developmental trajectories. *Developmental Science*, **10**, F15–F30.

Schmidt, L.A., Fox, N.A., Rubin, K.H., *et al.* (1997). Behavioural and neuroendocrine responses in shy children. *Developmental Psychobiology*, **30**, 127–140.

Schweinberger, S.R., Pickering, E.C., Jentzsch, I., Burton, A.M., and Kaufmann, J.M. (2002). Event-related brain potential evidence for a response of inferior temporal cortex to familiar face repetitions. *Brain Research Cognitive Brain Research*, **14**, 398–409.

Senju, A., Tojo, Y., Yaghuchi, K., and Hasegawa, T. (2005). Deviant gaze processing in children with autism: an ERP study. *Neuropsychologia*, **43**, 1297–1306.

Shibata, T., Nishijo, H., Tamura, R., *et al.* (2002) Generators of visual evoked potentials for faces and eyes in the human brain as determined by dipole localization. *Brain Topography*, **15**, 51–63.

Simion, F., Valenza, E., Umilta, C., and Dalla Barba, B. (1995). Inhibition of return in newborns is temporo-nasal asymmetrical. *Infant Behavior and Development*, **18**, 189–194.

Simion, F., Valenza, E., Umilta, C., and Dalla Barba, B. (1998). Preferential orienting to faces in newborns: a temporal-nasal asymmetry. *Journal of Experimental Psychology: Human Perception and Performance*, **24**, 1399–1405.

Smith, C.D., Lori, N.F., Akbudak, E., *et al.* (2009). MRI diffusion tensor tracking of a new amygdalo-fusiform and hippcampo-fusiform pathway system in humans. *Journal of Magnetic Resonance Imaging*, **29**, 1248–1261.

Sorenson, K.M. and Rodman, H.R. (1996). The lateral geniculate nucleus does not project to area TE in infant or adult macques. *Neuroscience Letters*, **217**, 5–8.

Steen, R.G., Ogg, R.J., Reddick, W.E., and Kingsley, P.B. (1997). Age-related changes in the pediatric brain: Quantitative MR evidence of maturational changes during adolescence. *American Journal of Neuroradiology*, **18**, 819–828.

Stein, B.E. (1984). Development of the superior colliculus. *Annual Review of Neuroscience*, **7**, 95–125.

Sylvester, R., Josephs, O., Driver, J., and Rees, G. (2007). Visual fMRI responses in human superior colliculus show a temporal-nasal asymmetry that is absent in lateral geniculate nucleus and visual cortex. *Journal of Neurophysiology*, **97**, 1495–1502.

Tamietto, M. and de Gelder, B. (2008). Affective blindsight in the intact brain. *Neuropsychologia*, **46**, 820–828.

Taylor, M.J., Edmonds, G.E., McCarthy, G., and Allison, T. (2001). Eyes first! Eye processing develops before face processing in children. *NeuroReport*, **12**, 1671–1676.

Taylor, M.J., Batty, M., and Itier, R.J. (2004). The faces of development: A review of early face processing over childhood. *Journal of Cognitive Neuroscience*, **16**, 1426–1442.

Thomas, K.M., Drevets, W.C., Whalen, P.J., *et al.* (2001). Amygdala response to facial expressions in children and adults. *Biological Psychiatry*, **49**, 309–316.

Tomalski, P., Johnson, M.H., and Csibra, G. (2009). Temporal-nasal asymmetry of rapid orienting to face-like stimuli. *NeuroReport*, **20**, 1309–1312.

Turati, C., Bulf, H., and Simion, F. (2008). Newborns' face recognition over changes in viewpoint. *Cognition*, **106**, 1300–1321.

Tzourio-Mazoyer, N., de Schonen, S., Crivello, F., Reutter, B., Aujard, Y., and Mazoyer, B. (2002). Neural correlates of woman face processing by 2-month-old infants. *NeuroImage*, **15**, 454–461.

van Kooten, I.A., Palmen, S.J., von Cappeln, P., *et al.* (2008). Neurons in the fusiform gyrus are fewer and smaller in autism. *Brain*, **131**, 987–999.

Vuilleumier, P. and Pourtois, G. (2007). Distributed and interactive brain mechanisms during emotion face perception: Evidence from functional neuroimamging. *Neuropsychologia*, **45**, 174–194.

Vuilleumier, P., Armony, J.L., Driver, J., and Dolan, R.J. (2003). Distinct spatial frequency sensitivities for processing faces and emotion expressions. *Nature Neuroscience*, **6**, 624–631.

Wang, A.T., Dapretto, M., Hariri, A.R., Sigman, M., and Bookheimer, S.Y. (2004). Neural correlates of facial affect processing in children and adolescents with autism spectrum disorder. *Journal of the American Academy of Child and Adolescent Psychiatry*, **43**, 481–490.

Webster, M.J., Ungerleider, L.G., and Bachevalier, J. (1991). Connections of inferior temporal areas TE and TEO with medial temporal lobe structures in infant and adult monkeys. *Journal of Neuroscience*, **11**, 1095–1116.

Webster, M.J., Bachevalier, J., and Ungerleider, L.G. (1995). Transient subcortical connections of inferior temporal areas TE and TEO in infant macaque monkeys. *Journal of Comparative Neurology*, **352**, 213–226.

Werth, R. (2007). Residual visual function after loss of both cerebral hemispheres in infancy. *Investigative Ophthalmology and Visual Sciences*, **48**, 3098–3106.

Whalen, P.J., Raush, S.L., Etcoff, N.L., McInerney, S.C., Lee, M.B., and Jenike, M.A. (1998). Masked presentations of emotional facial expressions modulate amygdala activity without explicit knowledge. *Journal of Neuroscience*, **18**, 411–418.

Yovel, G. and Kanwisher, N. (2005). The neural basis of the behavioural face-inversion effect. *Current Biology*, **15**, 2256–2262.

Yurgelun-Todd, D.A. and Killgore, W.D. (2006). Fear-related activity in the prefrontal cortex increases with age during adolescence: A preliminary fMRI study. *Neuroscience Letters*, **406**, 194–199.

Chapter 39

Development of Face Processing Expertise

Kang Lee, Gizelle Anzures, Paul C. Quinn,
Olivier Pascalis, and Alan M. Slater

Faces are perhaps one of the most dominant category of visual stimuli in children's environments. From birth onwards, children encounter thousands of faces. These faces vary in terms of not only identity, but also gender, age, attractiveness, species, and race. Given the adaptive significance of face processing ability, the hypothesis about an innate disposition regarding this ability is appealing. However, the present chapter will also review evidence accumulated in the last few decades that suggests a prominent role of experience in shaping children's face processing expertise, which in turn forms a foundation for later face expertise in adulthood.

Multidimensional nature of faces

Faces are multidimensional visual stimuli. They provide rich sources of visual information with social significance. This information can be categorized in terms of its relative transient versus permanent nature. *Face states* refer to transient facial characteristics, such as emotional expression, whereas *face traits* are relatively more permanent and stable, such as species type, identity, race, gender, age, and attractiveness. The present chapter will focus on the latter type of facial information and review the corresponding research findings pertaining to developmental changes throughout infancy to adolescence in processing various bits of face trait information.

In this chapter we will first review the ongoing nature/nurture debate in the developmental literature that examines whether faces are indeed a special class of stimuli. The role of experience in developing species-specific face expertise and standards of attractiveness will be discussed. Second, we will review the research on infants' and children's categorization of different face types (e.g. male/female, own-/other-age, own-/other-race) and explore how the development of face categorization is influenced by experience. Third, we will discuss the evidence concerning the development of face identity discrimination and recognition and more specifically the controversy regarding whether such development undergoes a qualitative change during childhood. For the purposes of face discrimination and recognition, we will examine infants' and children's use of three types of facial information: featural information (i.e. individual features such as the eyes, nose, and mouth), configural information (i.e. the relations among individual features), and holistic information (i.e. the facial gestalt which fuses featural and configural information into an unbroken whole) (see Figure 39.1). Configural information itself can also be further differentiated based on the type of featural relation. First-order relations refer to the basic configuration of faces as two eyes above a nose and a mouth, whereas second-order relations refer to the spacing between individual facial features. However, to be consistent with the typical use of the term in the majority of the literature on face processing, the present chapter will use the term configural processing to refer to the processing of second-order relations.

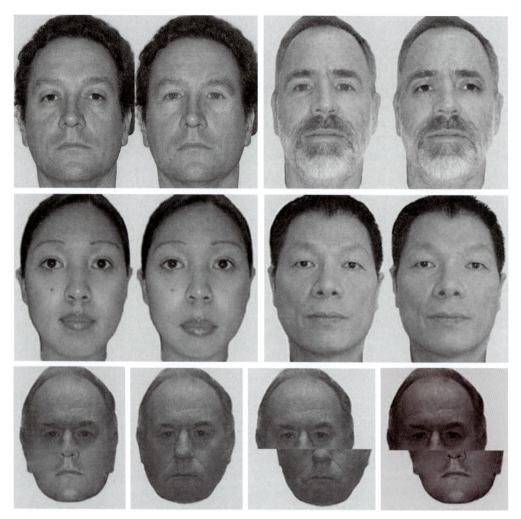

Fig. 39.1 Example of a featural change (i.e. eyes) made by switching the eyes of the two original faces on the left to make the two altered faces on the right (a). Example of configural changes (i.e. female face: spacing between the nose and mouth; male face: spacing between the eyes) with original faces on the left and altered faces on the right (b). Example of stimuli that can be used to examine holistic face processing (c). If asked to decide whether the top parts of two faces are identical or different, the composite faces in the left panel (which have different bottom parts) make it harder to simply process the top part of the face in isolation from the bottom part of the face—a task that is easier when the top and bottom parts of the face are segregated as shown in the right panel.

Nature versus nurture

A long-standing debate that continues to permeate the research on the development of face processing involves the origin of our face expertise. Are we born with an intrinsic predisposition to attend to faces, which in turn cultivates differential levels of expertise (e.g. discrimination/recognition) for face versus non-face stimuli? Or does our greater expertise for faces stem from our abundance of experience with faces relative to other visual stimuli? The adaptive appeal of the former alternative lies in newborns' ability to recognize conspecifics—an ability that offers significant contributions towards ensuring newborns' survival. The contention between these alternatives is clearly depicted in research examining young infants' relative preference for faces over non-face stimuli.

The notion that we may be born with an inherent predisposition to attend to faces is best supported by research findings which show that despite their lack of experience with faces, newborns exhibit longer fixations or greater orientation towards schematic faces relative to non-face stimuli (Fantz, 1963; Goren et al., 1975; Johnson and Morton, 1991; Johnson et al., 1991; Macchi Cassia et al., 2001; reviewed in Maurer, 1985; Maurer and Young, 1983; Mondloch et al., 1999), see Figure 39.2. Johnson and Morton (1991) and Morton and Johnson (1991) have proposed that this natural orientation and attentiveness towards faces may be driven by CONSPEC—a subcortical system containing very basic information regarding the visual structural characteristics of members of one's own species. These structural characteristics likely include a bounded area, an asymmetrical featural pattern with more elements on the upper portion of the bounded area, and a positive stimulus contrast (Johnson, 2005). On the other hand, CONLERN refers to a cortical system which accrues and retains fine details regarding the visual characteristics of conspecifics via experience with such conspecifics (Johnson and Morton, 1991; Morton and Johnson, 1991). Thus, one perspective holds that an initial biological predisposition to attend to faces is subsequently complemented by visual experience with conspecifics to develop face expertise. However, it should also be noted that the existing evidence regarding infants' preference for the first-order configuration of schematic faces does not directly implicate a preference for own-species configuration. Thus, if neural mechanisms such as CONSPEC and CONLERN do exist, they might not necessarily be species-specific. Nevertheless, both the existing behavioral evidence and the neural model of CONSPEC/CONLERN support the importance of experience in developing face expertise.

Although the role of experience in infants' developing face expertise has been readily accepted in the literature on face processing, the notion of an innate predisposition towards faces in particular has received some opposition. An alternative perspective holds that infants' seeming preference for faces over non-face stimuli can be attributed to certain properties of faces that are

 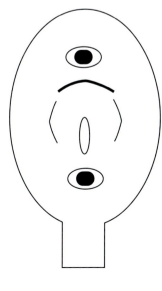

Fig. 39.2 Example of a face-like stimulus (left) that is preferred over a non-face stimulus (right) by infants.

nonetheless not face-specific. Kleiner (1987) and Mondloch et al. (1999), for example, showed that newborns' preference for the basic structure of faces (i.e. first-order relations) is secondary to stimulus energy. Previous studies have also shown that infants prefer stimuli with more elements on the top portion relative to the bottom portion, and that this preference exists regardless of whether or not the configuration of those elements is consistent with the first-order relations of facial features (Macchi Cassia et al., 2004; Simion et al., 2002a; Turati et al., 2002).

Despite these contentions, even Kleiner (1987) noted that a preference for a face-like structure in newborns may still prevail as long as stimulus energy is held constant across the contrasting stimuli. Newborns additionally show a preference for upright facial configurations relative to inverted configurations in schematic stimuli as well as in more realistic photographs of facial stimuli, as long as the upright configurations also possess a positive contrast that is characteristic of the natural faces that one would typically encounter (Farroni et al., 2005). Thus, despite the preference for top-heavy stimuli that appears to be independent of face specificity, newborns' attentional biases for top-heavy stimuli appears to be mediated by the nature of the stimulus contrast—with a face-like positive contrast driving the preference for the upright facial configuration (Farroni et al., 2005).

In addition to such early sensitivity to facial characteristics, further experience with faces does appear to build a preference for face stimuli so that by 6 to 8 weeks after birth, infants' preference for the basic structure of faces supersedes the initial influence of stimulus energy (Kleiner and Banks, 1987; Mondloch et al., 1999). Gliga et al. (2009) have also found that older infants at 6 months show a spontaneous preference for faces among an array of visual stimuli, so that their first look is more frequently directed towards face stimuli rather than to non-face stimuli (e.g. birds, cars, alarm clocks, shoes, and mobile phones). Six-month-olds' preference for faces is further reflected in their more frequent subsequent looking at faces relative to non-face objects (Gliga et al., 2009). However, it remains unknown whether the inherent preference for stimuli with disproportionately more elements on the top portion relative to the bottom portion originates from a general non-specific preference for such stimuli or whether a possible inherent preference for face-like structures generalizes to other stimuli. Regardless of its origins, infants' preference for top-heavy configurations ensures that they attend to faces.

In contrast to the questioned validity of an innate predisposition to attend to faces, Morton and Johnson's notion of CONLERN has been more readily accepted. In support of CONLERN, Mondloch et al. (1999) found that 12-week-old infants with more experience with faces showed more sophisticated face-like preferences (i.e. preference for a face with a positive contrast over a face with a negative contrast) relative to newborns and 6-week-old infants. Thus, despite the initial presence or absence of an innate predisposition to attend to faces, our abundance of experience with faces inevitably shapes an early preference for face-like stimuli.

Perceptual narrowing in face perception

Consistent with the nurture side of the nature–nurture debate, growing evidence suggests that greater experience with a particular face type leads to improved face processing abilities (e.g. better recognition abilities), whereas a lack of experience with a particular face type leads to relatively poorer face processing abilities (e.g. poor recognition). For example, adult humans demonstrate recognition memory for different human faces, but not for different monkey faces (Pascalis and Bachevalier, 1998; Pascalis et al., 2002), whereas adult monkeys demonstrate recognition memory for different monkey faces, but not for different human faces (Pascalis and Bachevalier, 1998). This pattern of results suggests that our greater experience with faces of members of our own species results in better recognition abilities for conspecifics, whereas our lack of experience with faces from other species results in poor recognition abilities for other species.

Nelson (1993, 2001) has suggested that discriminatory and recognition abilities may not be so species-specific early in development. Rather, infants may have the ability to process a broad range of face types. With increased experience with certain types of faces and the lack of contact with other types of faces, perceptual narrowing takes place that leads to increased discriminatory and recognition abilities with the highly experienced face types and decreased abilities to discriminate and recognize the infrequently experienced face types. This perceptual narrowing process is akin to a similar phenomenon in the language domain whereby younger infants are able to discriminate almost all phonemes in any language in the world but later become particularly sensitive to phonemes of the language to which they receive the most exposure in their environment (Kuhl, 1998; Werker and Tees, 1999).

In support of this idea, studies have found that 6-month-olds show recognition memory for different human faces as well as for different monkey faces (Pascalis et al., 2002, 2005). However, such recognition memory for individual monkey faces in the same species disappears by 9 months of age unless experience with such faces is provided (Pascalis et al., 2005). In addition, maintaining accurate recognition memory for monkey faces in the same species appears to require not just mere exposure to monkey faces, but rather, exposure to such faces accompanied by consistent individuation (i.e. repeatedly referring to each monkey face by a specific name) between such faces (Scott and Monesson, 2009). Such species-specific perceptual narrowing is also evident at the intersensory level by 8 months of age, with only younger 4- to 6-month-old infants demonstrating an ability to match a visual image of a monkey producing a given vocalization with its congruent auditory call (Lewkowicz and Ghazanfar, 2006).

This perceptual narrowing in face perception at the broader species level has also been found at the within-species level—that is, pertaining to different human races. Kelly et al. (2007a) showed that Caucasian infants at 3 months of age show recognition memory for individual faces within Caucasian, Chinese, Middle Eastern, and African races, but 6-month-olds only showed recognition memory for Caucasian and Chinese faces, and 9-month-olds only showed recognition memory for own-race Caucasian faces. In addition, Kelly et al. (2009) showed that Chinese infants undergo a similar course of perceptual narrowing in that increased exposure to Chinese faces leads to a recognition memory only for own-race Chinese faces at 9 months of age (see Figure 39.3).

It has been suggested that this perceptual narrowing in face recognition is due to a strengthening of the neural circuits that respond to frequently experienced faces, as well as a simultaneous weakening of the neural circuits that respond to infrequently experienced faces (Scott et al., 2007). As suggested by Scott et al. (2007), this Hebbian learning account of perceptual narrowing in face recognition may explain why 9-month-olds without prior exposure to monkey faces fail to show behavioral recognition for monkey faces (Pascalis et al., 2002), but nonetheless show some evidence of recognition abilities at the neural level via differential event-related potential responses to familiarized and novel monkey faces (Scott et al., 2006). Consistent with this notion of more efficient processing of conspecific faces relative to faces of other species, Pascalis et al. (2001) found that although 5- and 8-year-olds were above chance in their recognition of human, monkey, and sheep faces, they were most accurate in their recognition of human faces relative to the monkey and sheep faces. Improvement in the ability to recognize other-species monkey faces from 9 months of age to above chance levels by 5 years of age is likely due to general age-related changes in cognition (e.g. memory), as well as older children's possibly greater experience with animal faces (e.g. via storybook illustrations/photographs, videos, or direct encounters at zoos). This age-related improvement in recognition is also evident in 8-year-olds' greater accuracy in recognizing human, monkey, and sheep faces relative to 5-year-olds' performance (Pascalis et al., 2001). In addition, although both adults and 8-year-olds are better in their discrimination between

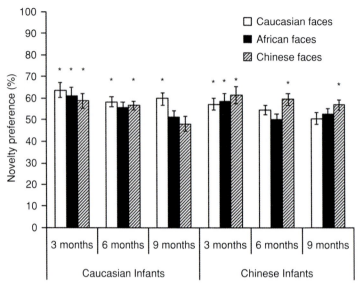

Fig. 39.3 Recognition performance of 3-, 6-, and 9-month-old Caucasian and Chinese infants for Caucasian, Asian, and African stimulus faces. With a significant preference for the novel face when paired with a familiarized face (i.e. novelty preference) as an indication of recognition memory, both Caucasian and Chinese infants show stable recognition memory for own-race faces, but an age-related decline in recognition memory for other-race faces (data from Kelly et al., 2007a, 2009).* indicates p <0.05.

human faces that differ only in configural information relative to their discrimination between monkey faces that differ only in configural information, adults still showed greater accuracy in their recognition of both face types relative to 8-year-olds (Mondloch et al., 2006a). Thus, although face recognition in general (i.e. regardless of type of species) improves with age, greater experience with one category of faces (e.g. conspecific faces) results in better recognition abilities for such faces.

Facial attractiveness

It is well established that humans are attracted to and beguiled by beautiful and attractive faces. Attractiveness is associated with mate choice (Shepherd and Ellis, 1972) and with positive psychological traits such as happier lives and pleasant personalities—"beauty is good" (Eagly et al., 1991). The tendency to prefer attractive faces appears to be largely inborn or at least developed very quickly after birth. Studies have shown that even newborns prefer, and thus look longer at attractive female adult faces relative to unattractive female adult faces (Slater et al., 1998, 2000). This early preference for attractiveness also generalizes to other types of faces, so that infants as young as 3 months prefer to look at attractive male adult faces over unattractive male faces (Samuels and Ewy, 1985) as well as at attractive cat and tiger faces relative to unattractive cat and tiger faces (Quinn et al., 2008a). Infants as young as 5 and 6 months old also prefer to look at attractive infant faces over unattractive infant faces (Langlois et al., 1991; Van Duuren et al., 2003), and 6-month-olds prefer to look at attractive other-race faces over unattractive other-race faces

(Langlois et al., 1991). By 6 months, infants also show the ability to form discrete categories of attractive and unattractive faces (Ramsey et al., 2004).

With regard to the specific aspects of faces that might contribute to their attractive appearance, previous studies have found that infants, like adults, show a preference for large eyes by 5 months of age (Geldart et al., 1999a). However, Geldart et al. (1999b) also showed that in contrast to adults' preference for faces with the internal facial features (i.e. eyes, nose, mouth) at a medium height and low height (i.e. large forehead and small chin), 5-month-olds prefer to look most at faces with the internal facial features at a high height (i.e. small forehead and large chin). Geldart et al. (1999b) have proposed that young infants' differential preference for faces with high-placed features may be a result of the viewpoint from which they typically view faces (i.e. when held by their caregivers, infants typically view faces from below the chin, which provides an image of faces with high-placed features).

Further support for the role of differential experience in cultivating standards of attractiveness is revealed in age-related changes in children's perception of the most attractive placement of the internal facial features (Cooper et al., 2006). Twelve-year-olds show the adult pattern of attractiveness preference, so that they judge faces with average-placed features as most attractive, followed by faces with low-placed features, and faces with high-placed features as least attractive—presumably because they have experience with both own-age peers and adults whose internal features are typically on an average location on the face (Cooper et al., 2006). Nine-year-olds, however, show no difference in their attractiveness judgments for faces with average-placed and low-placed features, presumably because of frequent experience with own-age peers' faces with low-placed features as well as frequent experience with adult faces with average-placed features (Cooper et al., 2006). In contrast, 3-year-olds with frequent exposure to own-age peers with low-placed features judge faces with low-placed features as more attractive relative to faces with high-placed features (Cooper et al., 2006). Thus, although some adult-like preferences for attractive facial characteristics may emerge during infancy, other preferences change over time and with differential experience.

In contrast to the changing preference for the height of the internal facial features, one aspect of facial attractiveness that remains relatively stable is the perception of average faces as attractive. It has been found that adults' attractiveness preference for averaged faces (Langlois and Roggman, 1990; Rhodes et al., 1999; Rubenstein et al., 1999; Valentine et al., 2004) is shared by infants as young as 6 months of age (Rubenstein et al., 1999). Langlois and Roggman (1990) proposed that adults' preference for averaged faces might arise from their ability to abstract a facial prototype or mathematical average of the faces they encounter. Thus, consistent with the notion that experience with faces shapes one's standards of attractiveness so that what is most familiar is most attractive, this cognitive averaging of faces has also been proposed to underlie infants' attractiveness preferences (Rubenstein et al., 1999). Indeed, it has been found that 6-month-olds (Rubenstein et al., 1999) and 3-month-olds (de Haan et al., 2001) are able to form a female prototype after familiarization with a number of individual female faces.

Direct support for the early use of facial prototypes in relation to the perception of attractiveness is provided by evidence showing that 8-year-olds, like adults, are sensitive to attractiveness aftereffects after a brief adaptation period to a series of faces that have been distorted in a particular way (Anzures et al., 2009). After adaptation to distorted faces, 8-year-olds' attractiveness preferences shifted towards the adapting distortion (see Figure 39.4), which suggests that, like adults, 8-year-olds are able to incorporate facial information from newly encountered faces into their existing face prototype (Anzures et al., 2009). Thus, not only do children as young as 8 years old make use of a face prototype as a reference for perceived attractiveness, but that face prototype is also constantly updated as new faces are encountered (Anzures et al., 2009).

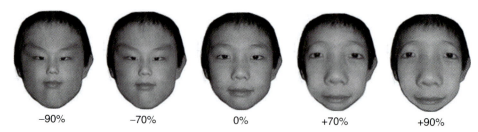

Fig. 39.4 Simulation of stimuli used in Anzures et al. (2009). Children adapted to -90% distorted faces increased their follow-up attractiveness ratings for -90% and -70% distorted faces. Children adapted to +90% distorted faces increased their follow-up attractiveness ratings for +90% and +70% distorted faces. (Note: The actual stimuli in Anzures et al. (2009) were faces of different Caucasian children for each level of distortion.)

Facial distinctiveness

In contrast to a face prototype's central location in one's face space, faces judged as high on distinctiveness are located further away from the central tendency, and thus appear less typical looking (Valentine, 1991). It has been found that children as young as 4 years old use both featural and configural information when judging facial distinctiveness (McKone and Boyer, 2006). Other studies, however, have alluded to developmental changes in children's sensitivity to featural and configural information when judging facial distinctiveness. Mondloch and Thomson (2008), for example, found that when undistorted faces were paired with their spatially distorted versions (i.e. eyes and mouth moved up or down), 4-year-olds were above chance in their distinctiveness judgments when the configural distortions among facial features were large, but they were at chance when such configural distortions were within the normal range of variability. Donnelly and Hadwin (2003) also showed that although even 6-year-olds were accurate in choosing the most unusual face from pairs of faces comprised of an undistorted and a Thatcherized face (i.e. inverted eyes and mouth in an upright face), young children's sensitivity to such featural and configural anomalies diminished but increased with age when the task was made more difficult by using Thatcherized monochrome "Mooney" face images. Relative to adults, 8-year-olds also give lower bizarreness ratings for upright faces with configural (i.e. spacing between the eyes, height of the eyes, or spacing between the nose and mouth) and Thatcherized distortions, which suggests that 8-year-olds are less sensitive to such featural and configural distortions (Mondloch et al., 2004). Alternatively, young children's apparent insensitivity to featural and configural distortions may be due to a greater tolerance for distinctive faces relative to adults, rather than to difficulty perceiving such physical distortions.

Facial categories

Faces can be processed at several category levels. Processing faces at a global or superordinate level (e.g. mammalian faces) is inclusive of many relatively more defined categories of faces. Basic-level processing involves a more differentiated processing of faces (e.g. human faces) relative to global-level processing. However, subordinate-level processing involves even more refined differentiation among face types (e.g. race, gender, and age of human faces)—with the most subordinate level involving the processing of individual identity. Information about how children process faces at the non-individual levels is in general lacking. There is some, albeit limited, research on how children categorize faces according to species, race, gender, and age to be reviewed below.

Investigations regarding the relative organization of different levels of face categories are even more limited, with only one study suggesting that race is a higher-level category that subsumes gender (Quinn et al., 2008b).

Species

The ability to form discrete facial categories for different species begins during early infancy. Infants as young as 3 months are able to form exclusive categories for cat and dog faces based on intact facial information, as well as internal facial features alone, or external facial features alone (Quinn and Eimas, 1996). It has also been found that 4-month-olds are able to form discrete categories of cats and dogs based on the head and face region (Spencer et al., 1997). Eye-tracking results suggest that the use of the head to categorize cats versus dogs reflects a pre-existing bias to attend to face information (Quinn et al., 2009). Although such early ability in categorizing animal faces according to their species can be found in infants without any experience with animals, Kovack-Lesh et al. (2008) did find that experience with pets facilitated older infants' categorization of such animals as cats and dogs.

Race

The only study to date that has examined racial categorization in infants found that the ability to form discrete categories based on the race of faces develops sometime between 6 and 9 months of age (Anzures et al., 2010). Caucasian 9-month-olds were able to form discrete categories of female Caucasian and Asian faces, whereas 6-month-olds were unable to do so (Anzures et al., 2010). Six-month-olds showed differential responsiveness (i.e. a significant increase in looking) to Caucasian faces after familiarization with Asian faces, but showed no such increase in looking at Asian faces after familiarization with Caucasian faces (Anzures et al., 2010).

Six-month-olds' asymmetrical pattern of responsiveness may be indicative of their developing, but as of yet, imperfect categorization abilities. Additionally, 6-month-olds' performance in the racial categorization task may have been influenced by a spontaneous preference for own-race faces. Infants' spontaneous preference for own-race faces (Bar-Haim et al., 2006; Kelly et al., 2005; 2007b) could have driven the observed increase in looking at own-race faces after familiarization with other-race faces, and would have hindered increased looking at the less preferred other-race faces after familiarization with own-race faces. Thus, it appears that young infants' racial categorization may be influenced by a spontaneous preference for the category/categories of faces with which they have the most experience, whereas older infants are able to form discrete categories of own-race and other-race faces. However, it is entirely unclear as to whether infants are able to form different categories for different other-race faces or simply treat all other-race faces as belonging to the same category. Further, the course by which racial categorization develops in childhood and how it reaches the adult level whereby adults in fact categorize other-race faces faster than own-race faces is also entirely unknown (Ge et al., 2009; Levin, 1996, 2000).

Gender

Research on children's categorization of the gender of faces has found that infants as young as 7 months can form an inclusive category of female adult faces (Cohen and Strauss, 1979). Older infants at 9 and 12 months are also able to form exclusive categories for color images of male and female faces by using hair and clothing cues (Leinbach and Fagot, 1993). However, by using black and white photographs of male and female adult faces, it has been found that infants as young as 5 months show differential responsiveness (i.e. increased looking) to a face from the novel gender category after habituation to four different faces from the contrasting gender category (Cornell, 1974). Another study by Younger and Fearing (1999) used color photographs of male and female faces and found that 10-month-olds, but not 7-month-olds, formed a category of male faces that excluded gender-ambiguous male faces, as well as a category of female faces that excluded gender-ambiguous female faces. Thus, the current literature suggests that infants can form exclusive categories of male and female faces sometime between 5 and 10 months of age, although the exact age at which they can do so needs to be verified with additional research.

Research on younger infants, however, shows an asymmetrical pattern of responsiveness in looking behavior in gender categorization tasks that parallels findings regarding younger infants' racial categorization of faces. Quinn et al. (2002) found an asymmetry in 3- to 4-month-olds' categorization of male and female faces. That is, infants looked longer at a novel female over a novel male after habituation to a number of different male faces, but they showed no preference for either of the novel faces at testing after habituation to a number of different female faces. This asymmetry was subsequently found to be driven by a spontaneous preference for female faces that in turn was attributed to infants' greater experience with female faces which is typically reinforced by the gender of the primary caregiver (i.e. mother). This speculation regarding infants' differential experience with male and female faces has been verified by Rennels and Davis (2008) who found that North American infants experience a significantly greater amount of interaction with female individuals relative to male individuals. In contrast, infants whose primary caregivers are male have a spontaneous preference for male instead of female faces (Quinn et al., 2002). Thus, differential experience with male and female faces results in a spontaneous preference for the more familiar face type, which likely drives the asymmetry in young infants' responsiveness in gender categorization tasks. Although experience seems to play an important role in infants' categorization of face gender, whether experience continues to play such a role in childhood remains largely unknown because of the lack of studies that examine face gender categorization beyond infancy. The only study to date that has examined gender categorization in children found that adults were significantly more accurate than 6- to 9-year-olds in their categorization of both adult and children's faces when sex-stereotyped cues such as hair were cropped from the stimuli (Wild et al., 2000). Thus, it appears as if greater experience with faces in general contributes to the improvement of gender categorization abilities using facial contour and internal facial features.

Age categories and age judgments

Sensitivity to facial age cues is evident at an early age. For example, Brooks and Lewis (1976) found that infants as young as 7 months show differential behavior towards young children and adults as measured by looking/gaze aversion and facial expressions. Studies with older age groups also show that young children can make accurate relative age judgments as well as categorical age judgments. Children as young as 2 years old can accurately group schematic faces under the broad categories of "baby," "boy," and "man" (Montepare and McArthur, 1986), and children as young as 3 years old can accurately rank colored photographs of young, middle-aged, and old female adult faces (Downs and Walz, 1981).

Children, like adults, also use a variety of similar facial cues when judging age. The paired relative age judgments (e.g. "which face is older?") of children as young as 2 years old are influenced by facial wrinkles and the height of the internal facial features, so that they judge schematic faces with low-placed features as younger looking and faces with wrinkles as older looking (Montepare and McArthur, 1986). In addition, a study by Jones and Smith (1984) showed that 4-year-olds use the eyes as a reference when judging facial age, so that ranking adult faces according to age was most *inaccurate* when the eye regions of photographs were masked relative to when other facial areas were masked. However, 4- to 6-year-olds can also use facial configuration (e.g. height of the internal facial features) and craniofacial shape (i.e. children's wide and short face/head shape versus adults' long and narrow face/head shape) to deduce which child/adult face from a pair is older (George et al., 2000). Similar to adults, children as young as 5 years old also rate schematic faces with large low-placed eyes and small noses as younger than faces with small high-placed eyes and long noses (Gross, 1997).

Despite children's early sensitivity to facial age cues, there is also evidence of age-related improvements in the accuracy of facial age judgments. Adults are better than children and adolescents, and adolescents are better than children at detecting an age difference between older adult faces that are proximal in age (Gross, 2004, 2007). However, this apparent developmental change in children's accuracy in facial age judgments is confounded by the potential influence of differential experience with faces from different age categories. Young children may have relatively less experience with adult faces or they may have experience with adult faces from a limited age range so that their facial age judgments and facial age categories for adult faces are broad or less refined relative to adults' age judgments and facial age categories. Thus, as with racial and gender categorization, facial age categorization and age judgments might also be influenced by differential experience with faces.

Processing of facial identity

Previous studies have established that the ability to process facial identity begins at birth. Several studies have shown that newborns are able to discriminate between their mother's face and a female stranger's face as evident by their longer looking at their mother's face (Bushnell, 2001; Bushnell et al., 1989; Pascalis et al., 1995). Such recognition abilities have also been replicated with female strangers' faces so that newborns demonstrate a preference for a novel female face after habituation to a different female face (de Heering et al., 2008; Gava et al., 2008; Pascalis and de Schonen, 1994; Turati et al., 2006, 2008).

However, newborns' recognition abilities are influenced by a number of factors. For example, newborns' facial recognition is limited to low spatial frequency presentation of faces (de Heering et al., 2008), and hindered by occluding the eyes (Gava et al., 2008). Newborns' recognition has also been limited to certain facial poses, so that they can recognize individuals across frontal and three-quarter poses, but are unable to generalize recognition when habituated or tested with pro-file poses (Turati et al., 2008). However, developmental changes in processing facial identity are evident in 12-month-olds' ability to recognize faces in profile (Rose et al., 2002). Developmental changes in speed of processing also influence infants' encoding of facial identity: relative to 12-month-olds, 7-month-olds require a longer habituation period when learning a new face (Rose et al., 2002). In addition, although newborns have shown recognition based on internal facial features alone (Turati et al., 2006), their recognition abilities appear to be primarily driven by their recognition of outer facial features such as hair and facial contour (Pascalis et al., 1995; Turati et al., 2006)—a finding supported by previous studies that have found that infants at 1 month and younger tend to fixate more on the outer regions of the face, whereas 2-month-olds devote more attention to the internal facial regions (Haith et al., 1977; Maurer and Salapatek, 1976).

Consistent with the notion that older infants fixate more on the internal regions relative to the external regions of the face, facial recognition in 4-month-olds appears to be facilitated by faces showing direct gaze (Farroni et al., 2007). Faces showing direct as opposed to indirect gaze elicited greater attention and most likely enhanced encoding of the faces, which subsequently led to a greater likelihood of facial recognition (Farroni et al., 2007). This recognition advantage for faces showing direct gaze extends into later childhood and adulthood, with children as young as 6 and adults showing enhanced recognition when faces are learned with a direct gaze (Hood et al., 2003), as well as enhanced recognition of faces with direct gaze at test (Hood et al., 2003; Smith et al., 2006).

Enhanced recognition of faces has also been associated with the types of information used to encode or process faces. One area of the developmental literature on face processing has focused on children's differential use of internal versus external facial regions. Another area of the literature has focused on children's use of isolated facial features, configural information, and holistic information.

Internal and external facial features

There have been mixed findings regarding children's differential reliance on internal and external facial regions (see Figure 39.5) for recognition purposes. Some studies cite an advantage in recognizing the external facial regions of adult faces among children younger than 14 years old (Campbell et al., 1999; Want et al., 2003), and an advantage in recognizing the internal facial regions of adult faces among children 14 years old and older (Campbell et al., 1999). However, there have been reports of the onset of an internal face advantage in the recognition of familiar peers at different ages: 9-year-olds (Campbell et al., 1995), 7-year-olds (Bonner and Burton, 2004), and 4-year-olds (Ge et al., 2008). An internal face advantage in the recognition of familiar adults has also been found in children as young as 5 years old (Wilson et al., 2007). Such seemingly contradictory findings regarding children's differential use of internal and external facial regions can be resolved if the familiarity of the face stimuli is taken into consideration. Studies that report an early internal face advantage have used highly familiar faces as stimuli. Thus, children's differential use of the internal and external regions of faces for recognition is likely mediated by their familiarity with such faces. This speculation is consistent with findings that adults' face recognition demonstrates a similar shift in reliance from external to internal facial regions as they become increasingly familiar with a face (Campbell et al., 1999; Clutterbuck and Johnston, 2004; Ellis et al., 1979; Young et al., 1985).

This internal face advantage in recognition of familiar faces is also likely driven by recognition of the eye region. Studies have generally found that children are better in their recognition of eyes relative to their recognition of mouths (Ge et al., 2008; Goldstein and Mackenberg, 1966; Hay and Cox, 2000; Pellicano and Rhodes, 2003; Pellicano et al., 2006) and noses (Ge et al., 2008; Goldstein and Mackenberg, 1966; Hay and Cox, 2000). Children as young as 4 years old are also better in their recognition of mouths relative to their recognition of noses (Ge et al., 2008).

Isolated features versus configural and holistic facial information

Research findings suggest that relative to the use of isolated facial features, using configural and holistic information is associated with better performance on recognition tasks (Carey and Diamond, 1977; Diamond and Carey, 1977; Yin, 1969). Sensitivity to configural and holistic information has been found to be related to early visual experience so that visual deprivation to the right hemisphere during the first 2 months after birth leads to impaired configural face processing (Le Grand et al., 2001, 2003) as well as impaired holistic face processing in adulthood (Le Grand et al., 2004; Mondloch et al., 2003a).

Despite this role of early visual experience on the development of configural and holistic processing, some researchers speculate that both are adult-like at a later age relative to featural face processing. This speculation was first proposed in the late 1970s with the introduction of the controversial encoding switch hypothesis (Carey and Diamond, 1977; Diamond and Carey, 1977)—a lingering

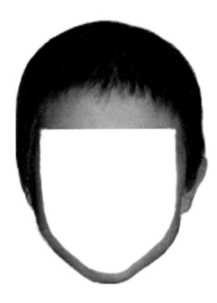
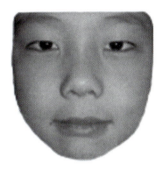

Fig. 39.5 Simulation of external and internal child face stimuli used in Ge et al. (2008).

contention in the literature. The encoding switch hypothesis proposes that young children encode faces in a piecemeal fashion (i.e. individual facial features) whereas older children—beginning at around the age of 10—encode the spatial relations between individual facial features. This hypothesis was based on findings regarding the effects of paraphernalia and inverting faces on children's recognition.

Using paraphernalia (e.g. hat, clothing, scarves, etc.) as a type of isolated feature, it was found that relative to 10-year-olds, 6- and 8-year-olds made more errors in their recognition of unfamiliar adults' faces (Carey and Diamond, 1977; Diamond and Carey, 1977) and unfamiliar children's faces (Diamond and Carey, 1977) in the presence of confounding paraphernalia (e.g. target face with a hat during learning phase followed by test showing the target face without the hat and the foil with the hat). However, more recent studies have suggested that young children's performance on recognition tasks involving paraphernalia is variable depending on the difficulty of the task (Baenninger, 1994; Flin, 1985). More importantly, Freire and Lee (2001, 2003) have shown that paraphernalia interferes with children's processing of both featural and configural information. Further, Freire et al. (2004) showed that children's face processing can be detrimentally affected by non-face factors such as the clothing that a target wears. Thus, Feire and Lee concluded that the paraphernalia effect is not a valid measure of children's reliance on face featural information.

Consistent with findings that adults' recognition of faces relative to non-face stimuli is disproportionately impaired when faces are presented in an inverted orientation due to the disruption of holistic processing (Yin, 1969, 1970), Carey and Diamond (1977) also used inversion as a measure of children's use of spatial relations among features (i.e. involved in both configural and holistic processing). Carey and Diamond (1977) found that 10-year-olds' recognition of faces was disproportionately impaired by inversion whereas 6- and 8-year-olds' recognition of faces and houses were equally impaired. This finding then became the cornerstone of the encoding switch hypothesis. However, since then, more recent findings show that inversion disproportionately impairs 3- to 4-year-olds' recognition of faces relative to their recognition of shoes (Picozzi et al., 2009). Inversion has also been found to disproportionately impair 3- to 5-year-olds' and

7-year-olds' recognition of faces relative to their recognition of cars (Picozzi et al., 2009) and dogs respectively (Crookes and McKone, 2009).

Thus, relatively recent research findings are inconsistent with a strict interpretation of the encoding switch hypothesis—one that proposes that children younger than 10 years old only use featural information in their recognition of faces and children 10 years and older only use configural and holistic information. Due to more recent evidence showing sensitivity to all three types of information at a young age, this strong version of the encoding switch hypothesis has been rejected. Current investigations have focused on age-related changes in the *relative* use of featural versus configural and holistic information in face recognition.

Infants' processing of featural, configural, and holistic facial information

Studies examining infants' use of facial information for recognition have found that sensitivity to changes in featural information precedes sensitivity to configural and holistic information. Newborns are able to detect changes in the shape of individual internal features to differentiate between different face-like configurations (Simion et al., 2002b). In contrast, in a task where the configural and featural changes were equated for discriminability in adults, sensitivity to configural changes among facial features (i.e. spacing between the eyes and spacing between the nose and mouth) was evident by 3 months of age (Quinn and Tanaka, 2009), and sensitivity to configural changes within the normal range of variability in adult faces emerges sometime between 3 and 5 months of age (Hayden et al., 2007a). However, 5-month-olds' sensitivity to configural information is limited to upright facial orientations (Bhatt et al., 2005).

With regards to infants' sensitivity to holistic information, infants as young as 4 months are able to process the internal and external regions of faces as a gestalt (Ferguson et al., 2009), but more refined holistic face processing develops later. Four-month-olds process the eyes and mouth separately from the rest of the face, whereas 6-month-olds process the mouth, but not the eyes, in relation to the entire face (Schwarzer et al., 2007). Holistic processing of both the mouth and eyes in relation to the entire face is evident in older 8-month-olds (Schwarzer and Zauner, 2003) and 10-month-olds (Schwarzer et al., 2007). In addition, similar to infants' sensitivity to configural information in upright faces, 7-month-olds' sensitivity to holistic information is also limited to upright facial orientations (Cohen and Cashon, 2001).

Children's processing of featural, configural, and holistic facial information

There exists a general consensus that children process facial identity as a gestalt. Like adults who are slower at making identity judgments for either the top or bottom portion of upright composite faces relative to their identity judgments for misaligned faces (Carey and Diamond, 1994; Le Grand et al., 2004; Michel et al., 2006; Young et al., 1987)—presumably because it is difficult to encode one aspect of the face in isolation from the entire face—7- and 10-year-olds are also slower and make more errors in their identity judgments for the top portion of upright composite faces of familiar classmates and familiarized adults (Carey and Diamond, 1994). Similar results have been found for composite face tasks requiring same/different judgments for the top portions of face pairs with 4-year-olds (de Heering et al., 2007) and 6-year-olds (de Heering et al., 2007; Mondloch et al., 2007) making more errors on upright composite faces with the same top halves than on upright misaligned faces. Developing holistic face processing abilities in 3-year-olds have also been shown via the composite face task (Macchi Cassia et al., 2009b). Like adults, 3- to 5-year-olds appear to utilize holistic processing (i.e. as measured by the composite face task) differentially, so that holistic processing is evident for faces, but not for cars (Macchi Cassia et al., 2009b).

Further evidence of children's holistic face processing has also been found using the part-whole paradigm—a procedure that has shown that when adults are familiarized with whole faces, then they are more accurate at identifying individual facial features in the context of the entire face than when presented in isolation (Davidoff and Donnelly, 1990; Donnelly and Davidoff, 1999; Leder and Carbon, 2004; Tanaka and Farah, 1993). A series of studies have found the whole-part advantage in 4-year-olds (Pellicano and Rhodes, 2003; Pellicano et al., 2006), 6-year-olds (Tanaka et al., 1998), and 8- and 10-year-olds (Seitz, 2002). However, despite young children's use of holistic face processing, there also exists evidence suggesting that younger children, relative to older children, rely more on isolated features. Hay and Cox (2000), for example, found that 9-year-olds were significantly better than 6-year-olds at recognizing whole faces, whereas 6-year-olds were significantly better than 9-year-olds at recognizing eye regions. Overall, the existing evidence regarding holistic processing fails to support the encoding switch hypothesis that young children encode faces in a piecemeal fashion, whereas older children—beginning at around the age of 10—encode the spatial relations between individual facial features.

In contrast to the consensus regarding children's holistic processing of facial identity, the literature on children's facial recognition has found mixed results regarding the relative use of featural and configural information. Baenninger (1994), for example, found no difference in 8-year-olds' use of featural and configural information in a recognition task relative to 11-year-old children. In contrast, other studies have shown that while 10-year-olds are adult-like in identity judgments of unfamiliar faces based on featural (i.e. eyes and mouth) changes, they are still immature in detecting identity changes based on configural information (see Figure 39.6) even after 14 years of age (Mondloch et al., 2002, 2003a,b). In addition, the distracting effects of paraphernalia have been found to be more detrimental to 4- to 7-year-olds' discrimination between target and distractor

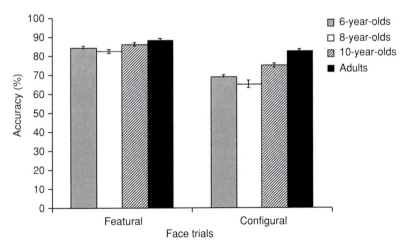

Fig. 39.6 Recognition performance of children and adults on configural and featural change face trials (adapted from Mondloch et al., 2002). On featural trials, 10-year-olds were adult-like in their face recognition. In contrast, on configural trials, children from all three age groups made significantly more recognition errors relative to adults.

faces differing in configural information relative to their discrimination between target and distractor faces differing in featural information—a finding which alludes to young children's more refined processing of individual features relative to their processing of configural information (Freire and Lee, 2001). Furthermore, studies have found chance performance among 4-year-olds on a recognition task involving configural changes for familiarized faces (Mondloch et al., 2006b) and familiar peers (Mondloch and Thomson, 2008).

These findings regarding children's difficulty in processing facial configural information appear to contradict the findings with infants: studies with children show that children as old as mid-adolescence perform poorly when asked to use configural information for recognition purposes, whereas infant studies show that young infants already use configural information in their recognition of faces (Bhatt et al., 2005; Hayden et al., 2007a; Quinn and Tanaka, 2009). This seeming contradiction may result from an important distinction in face recognition. The infant studies have specifically examined the ability to discriminate different facial configurations—a strictly perceptual indication of facial recognition. In contrast, studies on children's abilities have typically examined *identity* judgments—a mixture of perceptual and higher-order conceptual processes indicative of facial recognition. Thus, the existing evidence points to the conclusion that the ability to discriminate facial configural information is already present at infancy but to use such ability for recognizing facial identity may take a substantial amount of time to develop.

However, for several reasons, one should not take this finding as support for even the weaker version of the encoding switch hypothesis that, relatively speaking, children tend to rely on featural rather than on configural information for face recognition. First, most of the existing studies that compare children's featural and configural processing abilities have not matched the task difficulty with adults (see Quinn and Tanaka, 2009, for further discussion). The configural tasks may, in and of themselves, be more difficult than the featural tasks, even for adults. Thus, children's poorer performance in configural tasks relative to featural tasks may reflect discriminability differences among the faces used in the two tasks, rather than children's difficulty with face configural information per se. Second, all of the existing studies have not specifically manipulated and measured whether children's seeming difficulty with face configural information is indeed occurring at the encoding stage. One possibility is that children may be able to encode configural information as well as featural information, but they may have more difficulty in retaining the former in long-term memory relative to the latter. Both issues must be resolved before one can ascertain the validity of the encoding switch hypothesis.

Development of face space for facial identity

The majority of studies that examine face identity recognition have specifically focused on the different *types of facial information* that infants and children use. Relatively fewer studies have investigated developmental changes in the *degree of change* required to detect a difference in facial identity. One way of doing this is by examining infants' and children's face space for identity. Humphreys and Johnson (2007) found a developmental change in facial discrimination so that 4-month-olds' identity threshold required a larger deviation from a facial identity from one end of an identity continuum (i.e. different proportions of two facial identities) relative to 7-month-olds. In addition, 7-month-olds' identity threshold required a larger deviation from a facial identity from one end of an identity continuum relative to adults. Thus, identity processing becomes more refined with age so that a given identity encompasses a progressively smaller region in one's face space. However, it remains unknown how infants encode and retrieve face identity information. Considering previous findings that young infants can form a mental average of a number of individual faces (de Haan et al., 2001; Rubenstein et al., 1999), it is possible that infants might process faces in relation to a face prototype.

The norm-based coding model proposes that an average face prototype is abstracted from pre-viously encountered faces (Valentine, 1991). According to this model, discrete facial identities along a single trajectory are determined as a function of the distance and direction from the aver-age face prototype. Nishimura et al. (2008) found that 8-year-olds demonstrate adult-like identity aftereffects, so that after adaptation to a particular face identity, a previously neutral identity is perceived as an identity that is the computational opposite (e.g. in terms of shape/size of features and spacing between features) of the adapting face. Thus, by 8 years of age, children process facial identity relative to a face prototype that is abstracted from their previous and recent experience with faces.

Interaction between facial category and facial identity processing

Other evidence citing the influence of experience on children's face recognition shows that dif-ferential experience with facial categories mediates the ability to recognize different types of faces. Studies to date have specifically shown that differential experience with own- and other-race faces, male and female faces, and own- and other-age faces determines one's accuracy in facial recognition.

Race

Differential recognition of own- and other-race faces begins in infancy presumably because infants have an abundance of experience with own-race faces and little to no experience with other-race faces. The exact onset of the other-race effect depends on the nature of the face stimuli. When faces differ only in terms of internal features, 3-month-olds can differentiate between dif-ferent own-race faces but not between different other-race faces (Hayden et al., 2007b; Sangrigoli and de Schonen, 2004a). However, 3-month-olds' other-race effect is rather fragile—it may be eliminated when brief experience with other-race faces is introduced (Sangrigoli and de Schonen, 2004a). In addition, the introduction of external face contour can eliminate such an effect at 3 months of age. For example, when shown full faces with external contours from different races such as Caucasian, Chinese, Middle Eastern, and African faces, 3-month-old Caucasians without any exposure to other-race faces are nonetheless able to recognize such other-race faces (Kelly et al., 2007a). With increased exposure to own-race faces and continued lack of exposure to other-race faces, Caucasian infants by 6 months can only recognize Caucasian and Chinese faces, and Caucasian infants by 9 months can only recognize Caucasian faces. Thus, recognition ability for frequently encountered own-race faces is maintained, whereas recognition ability for infrequently encountered other-race faces disappears.

This other-race effect in older infants' recognition memory appears to be driven by differential processing of own- and other-race faces. That is, 8-month-olds demonstrate an other-race effect in their recognition memory, and they show holistic processing of the internal and external facial regions for upright own-race faces but not for upright other-race faces (Ferguson et al., 2009). In contrast, 4-month-olds show comparable recognition memory and holistic processing of the inter-nal and external facial regions for both own- and other-race faces (Ferguson et al., 2009). Thus, recognition memory for faces appears to rely at least partially on holistic face perception which is maintained with frequent experience with own-race faces.

This other-race effect in face recognition extends to the childhood (Chance et al., 1982; Feinman and Entwisle, 1976; Goodman et al., 2007; Pezdek et al., 2003; Sangrigoli and de Schonen, 2004b), adolescent (Walker and Hewstone, 2006), and adult (reviewed in Meissner and Brigham, 2001) years. However, later experience with other-race faces during the childhood and adolescent years is sufficient to eliminate this other-race effect in recognition (Goodman et al., 2007; Walker and

Hewstone, 2006). Experience with other races and lack of further experience with own-race faces in early childhood has also been shown to reverse this other-race effect in recognition. Korean adults who were adopted as children into Caucasian families in a predominantly Caucasian environment exhibited an advantage in their recognition of Caucasian faces relative to their recognition of Korean faces (Sangrigoli et al., 2005). Such differential recognition of familiar and unfamiliar races has been attributed to greater holistic processing as well as greater sensitivity to featural and configural information for familiar-race faces relative to unfamiliar-race faces (Hancock and Rhodes, 2008; Hayward et al., 2008; Michel et al., 2006; Rhodes et al., 2006; Sangrigoli and de Schonen, 2004b).

Gender

In addition to differential experience with own- and other-race faces, differential experience with male and female faces also influences developing recognition abilities. For example, 3- and 4-month-olds with female primary caregivers presented with either eight female or eight male faces are able to recognize a familiar female face, but are unable to recognize a familiar male face (Quinn et al., 2002); see Figure 39.7. Thus, differential experience with male and female faces cultivates different levels of representation (i.e. exemplar vs. summary) with greater recognition accuracy produced for the individual instances from the more familiar face category.

Research findings regarding recognition of male and female faces during the later childhood and adolescent years are variable, with some studies citing an own-gender advantage in recognition among female but not male children (Cross et al., 1971; Feinman and Entwisle, 1976) and adolescents (Cross et al., 1971; Ellis et al., 1973). Ge et al. (2008) also found an earlier own-gender advantage in 8-year-old females' recognition of isolated facial features (i.e. eyes, nose, mouth), whereas a cross-gender effect reflecting an own-gender advantage among both males and females emerged by 14 years of age, likely due to the gender-typing activities that increased with age.

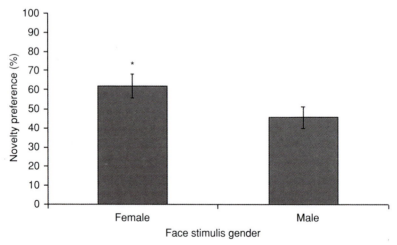

Fig. 39.7 Recognition performance of 3- to 4-month-olds for female and male faces (data from Quinn et al., 2002). A significant novelty preference in the female face condition but no such preference in the male face condition shows that young infants have a more sophisticated recognition memory for female faces. * indicates p < 0.05.

Age

A similar effect on children's recognition abilities exists for differential experience with faces from different age groups. For example, 3-year-olds who have younger siblings show comparable accuracy in their recognition of newborn and adult faces, whereas 3-year-olds without younger siblings show a significant impairment in their recognition of newborn faces relative to their recognition of adult faces (Macchi Cassia et al., 2009a). In addition, although a previous study by Goldstein and Chance (1964) failed to show an own-age bias in facial recognition, more recent evidence shows the contrary. Anastasi and Rhodes (2005) found an own-age bias in facial recognition among 5- to 8-year-olds and an older group of adults. Crookes and McKone (2009) have also shown an own-age bias in recognition among 5- to 6-year-olds and 10- to 11-year-olds who demonstrated better recognition of children's faces than adults' faces. Thus, the current literature suggests that experience with a particular face type may allow for more refined differentiation between the corresponding within-category exemplars, whereas a lack of experience with a particular face type leads to relatively impaired recognition of the corresponding within-category exemplars.

Summary and conclusions

A review of the developmental literature reveals early competence in face processing abilities with young infants showing a preference for face stimuli, a preference for attractive faces, categorization of various face trait attributes (i.e. species, race, gender, and attractiveness), and facial discrimination using featural, configural, and holistic cues. This early competence is then later refined as evidenced by age-related changes throughout childhood. Some of the refinements are likely due to the development of general cognitive abilities, whereas others (e.g. configural processing) may be face-specific.

Although biological factors may initially play some role in biasing the newborn's visual system towards faces in their environment, the existing evidence strongly suggests an important role for experience in the development of face processing expertise. The role of experience has been implicated in all aspects of the development of face processing expertise from infancy through childhood. For example, it is evident that experience plays a crucial role in infants' discrimination and children's identity judgments for different categories of faces (i.e. species, race, gender, age), with better recognition abilities for the more familiar face category (i.e. own-species, own-race, female, and own-age). However, considering the quasi-experimental nature of the existing studies, well-controlled investigations that directly manipulate experience (e.g. training studies) are needed to fully establish the causal linkage between differential experience and the development of face processing abilities.

The present review of the existing literature on the development of face processing has also revealed significant gaps in our research endeavor. While most of the recent exciting discoveries have been made with infants in all aspects of face processing, relatively limited knowledge has been gained about childhood except for the development of facial configural processing. Future studies need to examine how children's classification of faces at the basic and various subordinate category levels develops with age and to what extent such classification is related to their increasing abilities at processing faces at the individual level. This will, in turn, provide a comprehensive account of the formation of face processing expertise.

Acknowledgment

The preparation of this manuscript was supported in part by grants from NIH R01 HD046526, NSFC Grant No. 30528027 and 31028010, and NSERC.

References

Anastasi, J.S. and Rhodes, M.G. (2005). An own-age bias in face recognition for children and older adults. *Psychonomic Bulletin & Review*, **12**, 1043–1047.

Anzures, G., Mondloch, C.J., and Lackner, C. (2009). Face adaptation and attractiveness aftereffects in 8-year-olds and adults. *Child Development*, **80**, 178–191.

Anzures, G., Quinn, P.C., Pascalis, O., Slater, A., and Lee, K. (2010). Categorization, categorical perception, and asymmetry in infants' representation of face race. *Developmental Science*, **13**, 553–564.

Baenninger, M. (1994). The development of face recognition: Featural or configurational processing? *Journal of Experimental Child Psychology*, **57**, 377–396.

Bar-Haim, Y., Ziv, T., Lamy, D., and Hodes, R.M. (2006). Nature and nurture in own-race face processing. *Psychological Science*, **17**, 159–163.

Bhatt, R.S., Bertin, E., Hayden, A., and Reed, A. (2005). Face processing in infancy: Developmental changes in the use of different kinds of relational information. *Child Development*, **76**, 169–181.

Bonner, L. and Burton, M.A. (2004). 7–11-year-old children show an advantage for matching and recognizing the internal features of familiar faces: Evidence against a developmental shift. *The Quarterly Journal of Experimental Psychology*, **57**, 1019–1029.

Brooks, J. and Lewis, M. (1976). Infants' responses to strangers: Midget, adult, and child. *Child Development*, **47**, 323–332.

Bushnell, I.W.R. (2001). Mother's face recognition in newborn infants: Learning and memory. *Infant and Child Development*, **10**, 67–74.

Bushnell, I.W.R., Sai, F., and Mullin, J.T. (1989). Neonatal recognition of the mother's face. *British Journal of Developmental Psychology*, **7**, 3–15.

Campbell, R., Coleman, M., Walker, J., *et al.* (1999). When does the inner-face advantage in familiar face recognition arise and why? *Visual Cognition*, **6**, 197–216.

Campbell, R., Walker, J., and Baron-Cohen, S. (1995). The development of differential use of inner and outer face features in familiar face identification. *Journal of Experimental Child Psychology*, **59**, 196–210.

Carey, S. and Diamond, R. (1977). From piecemeal to configurational representation of faces. *Science*, **195**, 312–314.

Carey, S. and Diamond, R. (1994). Are faces perceived as configurations more by adults than by children? *Visual Cognition*, **1**, 253–274.

Chance, J.E., Turner, A.L., and Goldstein, A.G. (1982). Development of differential recognition for own- and other-race faces. *The Journal of Psychology*, **112**, 29–37.

Clutterbuck, R. and Johnston, R.A. (2004). Matching as an index of face familiarity. *Visual Cognition*, **11**, 857–869.

Cohen, L.B. and Cashon, C.H. (2001). Do 7-month-old infants process independent features or facial configurations? *Infant and Child Development*, **10**, 83–92.

Cohen, L.B. and Strauss, M.S. (1979). Concept acquisition in the human infant. *Child Development*, **50**, 419–424.

Cooper, P.A., Geldart, S.S., Mondloch, C.J., and Maurer, D. (2006). Developmental changes in perceptions of attractiveness: A role of experience? *Developmental Science*, **9**, 530–543.

Cornell, E.H. (1974). Infants' discrimination of photographs of faces following redundant presentations. *Journal of Experimental Child Psychology*, **18**, 98–106.

Crookes, K. and McKone, E. (2009). Early maturity of face recognition: No childhood development of holistic processing, novel face encoding, or face space. *Cognition*, **111**, 219–247.

Cross, J.F., Cross, J., and Daly, J. (1971). Sex, race, age, and beauty as factors in recognition of faces. *Perception & Psychophysics*, **10**, 393–396.

Davidoff, J. and Donnelly, N. (1990). Object superiority: A comparison of complete and part probes. *Acta Psychologica*, **73**, 225–243.

de Haan, M., Johnson, M.H., Maurer, D., and Perrett, D.I. (2001). Recognition of individual faces and average face prototypes by 1- and 3-month-old infants. *Cognitive Development*, **16**, 659–678.

de Heering, A., Houthuys, S., and Rossion, B. (2007). Holistic face processing is mature at 4 years of age: Evidence from the composite face effect. *Journal of Experimental Child Psychology*, **96**, 57–70.

de Heering, A., Turati, C., Rossion, B., Bulf, H., Goffaux, V., and Simion, F. (2008). Newborns' face recognition is based on spatial frequencies below 0.5 cycles per degree. *Cognition*, **106**, 444–454.

Diamond, R. and Carey, S. (1977). Developmental changes in the representation of faces. *Journal of Experimental Child Psychology*, **23**, 1–22.

Donnelly, N. and Davidoff, J. (1999). The mental representations of faces and houses: issues concerning parts and wholes. *Visual Cognition*, **6**, 319–343.

Donnelly, N. and Hadwin, J.A. (2003). Children's perception of the Thatcher illusion: Evidence for development in configural face processing. *Visual Cognition*, **10**, 1001–1017.

Downs, A.C. and Walz, P.J. (1981). Sex differences in preschoolers' perceptions of young, middle-aged, and elderly adults. *The Journal of Psychology*, **109**, 119–122.

Eagly, A.H., Ashmore, R.D., Makhijani, M.G., and Longo, L.C. (1991). What is beautiful is good, but… : A meta-analytic review of research on the physical attractiveness stereotype. *Psychological Bulletin*, **110**, 109–128.

Ellis, H., Shepherd, J., and Bruce, A. (1973). The effects of age and sex upon adolescents' recognition of faces. *Journal of Genetic Psychology*, **123**, 173–174.

Ellis, H.D., Shepherd, J.W., and Davies, G.M. (1979). Identification of familiar and unfamiliar faces from internal and external features: Some implications for theories of face recognition. *Perception*, **8**, 431–439.

Fantz, R.L. (1963). Pattern vision in newborn infants. *Science*, **140**, 296–297.

Farroni, T., Johnson, M.H., Menon, E., Zulian, L., Faraguna, D., and Csibra, G. (2005). Newborns' preference for face-relevant stimuli: Effects of contrast polarity. *PNAS*, **102**, 17245–17250.

Farroni, T., Massaccesi, S., Menon, E., and Johnson, M.H. (2007). Direct gaze modulates face recognition in young infants. *Cognition*, **102**, 396–404.

Feinman, S. and Entwisle, D.R. (1976). Children's ability to recognize other children's faces. *Child Development*, **47**, 506–510.

Ferguson, K.T., Kulkofsky, S., Cashon, C.H., and Casasola, M. (2009). The development of specialized processing of own-race faces in infancy. *Infancy*, **14**, 263–284.

Flin, R.H. (1985). Development of face recognition: An encoding switch? *British Journal of Psychology*, **76**, 123–134.

Freire, A. and Lee, K. (2001). Face recognition in 4- to 7-year-olds: Processing of configural, featural, and paraphernalia information. *Journal of Experimental Child Psychology*, **80**, 347–371.

Freire, A. and Lee, K. (2003). Person recognition by young children: Configural, featural, and paraphernalia processing. In O. Pascalis and A. Slater (eds.) *The Development of face processing in infancy and early childhood*, pp. 191–205. New York: Nova Science Publishers.

Freire, A., Lee, K., Williamson, K.S., Stuart, S.J.E., and Lindsay, R.C.L. (2004). Lineup identification by children: Effects of clothing bias. *Law and Human Behavior*, **28**, 339–354.

Gava, L., Valenza, E., Turati, C., and de Schonen, S. (2008). Effect of partial occlusion on newborns' face preference and recognition. *Developmental Science*, **11**, 563–574.

Ge, L., Anzures, G., Wang, Z., *et al.* (2008). An inner face advantage in children's recognition of familiar peers. *Journal of Experimental Child Psychology*, **101**, 124–136.

Ge, L., Zhang, H., Wang, Z., *et al.* (2009). Two faces of the other-race effect: Recognition and categorization of Caucasian and Chinese faces. *Perception*, **38**, 1199–1210.

Geldart, S., Maurer, D., and Carney, K. (1999a). Effects of eye size on adults' aesthetic ratings of faces and 5-month-olds' looking times. *Perception*, **28**, 361–374.

Geldart, S., Maurer, D., and Henderson, H. (1999b). Effects of the height of the internal features of faces on adults' aesthetic ratings and 5-month-olds' looking times. *Perception*, **28**, 839–850.

George, P.A., Hole, G.J., and Scaife, M. (2000). Factors influencing young children's ability to discriminate unfamiliar faces by age. *International Journal of Behavioral Development,* **24**, 480–491.

Gliga, T., Elsabbagh, M., Andravizou, A., and Johnson, M. (2009). Faces attract infants' attention in complex displays. *Infancy,* **14**, 550–562.

Goldstein, A.G. and Chance, J.E. (1964). Recognition of children's faces. *Child Development,* **35**, 129–136.

Goldstein, A.G. and Mackenberg, E.J. (1966). Recognition of human faces from isolated facial features: A developmental study. *Psychonomic Science,* **6**, 149–150.

Goodman, G.S., Sayfan, L., Lee, J.S., *et al.* (2007). The development of memory for own- and other-race faces. *Journal of Experimental Child Psychology,* **98**, 233–242.

Goren, C.C., Sarty, M., and Wu, P.Y.K. (1975). Visual following and pattern discrimination of face-like stimuli by newborn infants. *Pediatrics,* **56**, 545–549.

Gross, T.F. (1997). Children's perception of faces of varied immaturity. *Journal of Experimental Child Psychology,* **66**, 42–63.

Gross, T.F. (2004). Children's perceptions of and beliefs about facial maturity. *The Journal of Genetic Psychology,* **165**, 81–97.

Gross, T.F. (2007). Developmental changes in the perception of adult facial age. *The Journal of Genetic Psychology,* **168**, 443–464.

Haith, M.M., Bergman, T., and Moore, M. (1977). Eye contact and face scanning in early infancy. *Science,* **198**, 853–855.

Hancock, K.J. and Rhodes, G. (2008). Contact, configural coding and the other-race effect in face recognition. *British Journal of Psychology,* **99**, 45–56.

Hay, D.C. and Cox, R. (2000). Developmental changes in the recognition of faces and facial features. *Infant and Child Development,* **9**, 199–212.

Hayden, A., Bhatt, R.S., Reed, A., Corbly, C.R., and Joseph, J.E. (2007a). The development of expert face processing: Are infants sensitive to normal differences in second-order relational information? *Journal of Experimental Child Psychology,* **97**, 85–98.

Hayden, A., Bhatt, R.S., Joseph, J.E., and Tanaka, J.W. (2007b). The other-race effect in infancy: Evidence using a morphing technique. *Infancy,* **12**, 95–104.

Hayward, W.G., Rhodes, G., and Schwaninger, A. (2008). An own-race advantage for components as well as configurations in face recognition. *Cognition,* **106**, 1017–1027.

Hood, B.M., Macrae, C.N., Cole-Davies, V., and Dias, M. (2003). Eye remember you: The effects of gaze direction on face recognition in children and adults. *Developmental Science,* **6**, 67–71.

Humphreys, K. and Johnson, M.H. (2007). The development of "face-space" in infancy. *Visual Cognition,* **15**, 578–598.

Johnson, M.H. (2005). Subcortical face processing. *Nature Reviews Neuroscience,* **6**, 766–774.

Johnson, M.H., Dziurawiec, S., Ellis, H., and Morton, J. (1991). Newborns' preferential tracking of face-like stimuli and its subsequent decline. *Cognition,* **40**, 1–19.

Johnson, M.H. and Morton, J. (1991). *Biology and cognitive development: The case of face recognition.* Cambridge, MA: Basil Blackwell, Inc.

Jones, G. and Smith, P.K. (1984). The eyes have it: Young children's discrimination of age in masked and unmasked facial photographs. *Journal of Experimental Child Psychology,* **38**, 328–337.

Kelly, D.J., Quinn, P.C., Slater, A.M., *et al.* (2005). Three-month-olds, but not newborns, prefer own-race faces. *Developmental Science,* **8**, F31-F36.

Kelly, D.J., Quinn, P.C., Slater, A.M., *et al.* (2007a). The other-race effect develops during infancy: Evidence of perceptual narrowing. *Psychological Science,* **18**, 1084–1089.

Kelly, D.J., Liu, S., Ge, L., *et al.* (2007b). Cross-race preferences for same-race faces extend beyond the African versus Caucasian contrast in 3-month-old infants. *Infancy,* **11**, 87–95.

Kelly, D.J., Liu, S., Lee, K., *et al.* (2009). Development of the other-race effect in infancy: Evidence towards universality? *Journal of Experimental Child Psychology,* **104**, 105–114.

Kleiner, K.A. (1987). Amplitude and phase spectra as indices of infants' pattern preferences. *Infant Behavior and Development*, **10**, 49–59.

Kleiner, K.A. and Banks, M.S. (1987). Stimulus energy does not account for 2-month-olds' face preferences. *Journal of Experimental Psychology: Human Perception and Performance*, **13**, 594–600.

Kovack-Lesh, K.A., Horst, J.S., and Oakes, L.M. (2008). The cat is out of the bag: The joint influence of previous experience and looking behavior on infant categorization. *Infancy*, **13**, 285–307.

Kuhl, P.K. (1998). The development of speech and language. In T. J. Carew, R. Menzel, and C. J. Schatz (eds.), *Mechanistic relationships between development and learning*, pp. 53–73. New York: Wiley.

Langlois, J.H. and Roggman, L.A. (1990). Attractive faces are only average. *Psychological Science*, **1**, 115–121.

Langlois, J.H., Ritter, J.M., Roggman, L.A., and Vaughn, L.S. (1991). Facial diversity and infant preferences for attractive faces. *Developmental Psychology*, **27**, 79–84.

Leder, H. and Carbon, C.C. (2004). Part-to-whole effects and configural processing in faces. *Psychology Science*, **46**, 531–543.

Le Grand, R., Mondloch, C.J., Maurer, D., and Brent, H.P. (2001). Early visual experience and face processing. *Nature*, **410**, 890.

Le Grand, R., Mondloch, C.J., Maurer, D., and Brent, H.P. (2003). Expert face processing requires visual input to the right hemisphere during infancy. *Nature Neuroscience*, **6**, 1108–1112.

Le Grand, R., Mondloch, C.J., Maurer, D., and Brent, H.P. (2004). Impairment in holistic face processing following early visual deprivation. *Psychological Science*, **15**, 762–768.

Leinbach, M.D. and Fagot, B.I. (1993). Categorical habituation to male and female faces: Gender schematic processing in infancy. *Infant Behavior and Development*, **16**, 317–332.

Levin, D.T. (1996). Classifying faces by race: The structure of face categories. *Journal of Experimental Psychology*, **22**, 1364–1382.

Levin, D.T. (2000). Race as a visual feature: Using visual search and perceptual discrimination tasks to understand face categories and the cross-race recognition deficit. *Journal of Experimental Psychology: General*, **129**, 559–574.

Lewkowicz, D.J. and Ghazanfar, A.A. (2006). The decline of cross-species intersensory perception in human infants. *Proceedings of the National Academy of Sciences, USA*, **103**, 6771–6774.

Macchi Cassia, V., Simion, F., and Umilta, C. (2001). Face preference at birth: The role of an orienting mechanism. *Developmental Science*, **4**, 101–108.

Macchi Cassia, V., Turati, C., and Simion, F. (2004). Can a nonspecific bias toward top-heavy patterns explain newborns' face preference? *Psychological Science*, **15**, 379–383.

Macchi Cassia, V., Kuefner, D., Picozzi, M., and Vescovo, E. (2009a). Early experience predicts later plasticity for face processing: Evidence for the reactivation of dormant effects. *Psychological Science*, **20**, 853–859.

Macchi Cassia, V., Picozzi, M., Kuefner, D., Bricolo, E., and Turati, C. (2009b). Holistic processing for faces and cars in preschool-aged children and adults: Evidence from the composite effect. *Developmental Science*, **12**, 236–248.

Maurer, D. (1985). Infants' perception of facedness. In T. M. Field and N. A. Fox (eds.) *Social perception in infants*, pp. 73–100. Norwood, NJ: Ablex Publishing Corporation.

Maurer, D. and Salapatek P. (1976). Developmental changes in the scanning of faces by young infants. *Child Development*, **47**, 523–527.

Maurer, D. and Young, R.E. (1983). Newborn's following of natural and distorted arrangements of facial features. *Infant Behavior and Development*, **6**, 127–131.

Meissner, C.A. and Brigham, J.C. (2001). Thirty years of investigating the own-race bias in memory for faces: A meta-analytic review. *Psychology, Public Policy, and Law*, **7**, 3–35.

McKone, E. and Boyer, B.L. (2006). Sensitivity of 4-year-olds to featural and second-order relational changes in face distinctiveness. *Journal of Experimental Child Psychology*, **94**, 134–162.

Michel, C., Rossion, B., Han, J., Chung, C., and Caldara, R. (2006). Holistic processing is finely tuned for faces of one's own race. *Psychological Science*, **17**, 608–615.

Mondloch, C.J. and Thomson, K. (2008). Limitations in 4-year-old children's sensitivity to the spacing among facial features. *Child Development*, **79**, 1513–1523.

Mondloch, C.J., Lewis T.L., Budreau, D.R., *et al.* (1999). Face perception during early infancy. *Psychological Science*, **10**, 419–422.

Mondloch, C.J., Le Grand, R., and Maurer, D. (2002). Configural face processing develops more slowly than featural face processing. *Perception*, **31**, 553–566.

Mondloch, C.J., Le Grand, R., and Maurer, D. (2003a). Early visual experience is necessary for the development of some–but not all–aspects of face processing. In O. Pascalis and A. Slater (eds.) *The development of face processing in infancy and early childhood: Current perspectives*, pp. 99–117. New York: Nova Science Publishers, Inc.

Mondloch, C.J., Geldart, S., Maurer, D., and Le Grand, R. (2003b). Developmental changes in face processing skills. *Journal of Experimental Child Psychology*, **86**, 67–84.

Mondloch, C.J., Dobson, K.S., Parsons, J., and Maurer, D. (2004). Why 8-year-olds cannot tell the difference between Steve Martin and Paul Newman: Factors contributing to the slow development of sensitivity to the spacing of facial features. *Journal of Experimental Child Psychology*, **89**, 159–181.

Mondloch, C.J., Maurer, D., and Ahola, S. (2006a). Becoming a face expert. *Psychological Science*, **17**, 930–934.

Mondloch, C.J., Leis A., and Maurer, D. (2006b). Recognizing the face of Johnny, Suzy, and me: Insensitivity to the spacing among features at 4 years of age. *Child Development*, **77**, 234–243.

Mondloch, C.J., Pathman, T., Maurer, D., Le Grand, R., and de Schonen, S. (2007). The composite face effect in six-year-old children: Evidence of adult-like holistic face processing. *Visual Cognition*, **15**, 564–577.

Montepare, J.M. and McArthur, L.Z. (1986). The influence of facial characteristics on children's age perceptions. *Journal of Experimental Child Psychology*, **42**, 303–314.

Morton, J. and Johnson, M.H. (1991). CONSPEC and CONLERN: A two-process theory of infant face recognition. *Psychological Review*, **98**, 164–181.

Nelson, C.A. (1993). The recognition of facial expressions in infancy: Behavioral and electrophysiological evidence. In B. de Boysson-Bardies, S. de Schonen, P. Jusczyk, P. McNeilage, and J. Morton (eds.) *Developmental neurocognition: Speech and face processing in the first year of life*, pp. 187–198. Hingham, MA: Kluwer Academic Press.

Nelson, C.A. (2001). The development and neural bases of face recognition. *Infant and Child Development*, **10**, 3–18.

Nishimura, M., Maurer, D., Jeffery, L., Pellicano, E., and Rhodes, G. (2008). Fitting the child's mind to the world: Adaptive norm-based coding of facial identity in 8-year-olds. *Developmental Science*, **11**, 620–627.

Pascalis, O. and Bachevalier, J. (1998). Face recognition in primates: A cross-species study. *Behavioural Processes*, **43**, 87–96.

Pascalis, O. and de Schonen, S. (1994). Recognition memory in 3- to 4-day-old human neonates. *NeuroReport*, **5**, 1721–1724.

Pascalis, O., de Schonen, S., Morton, J., Deruelle, C., and Fabre-Grenet, M. (1995). Mother's face recognition by neonates: A replication and an extension. *Infant Behavior and Development*, **18**, 79–85.

Pascalis, O., Demont, E., de Haan M., and Campbell, R. (2001). Recognition of faces of different species: A developmental study between 5 and 8 years of age. *Infant and Child Development*, **10**, 39–45.

Pascalis, O., de Haan, M., and Nelson, C.A. (2002). Is face processing species-specific during the first year of life? *Science*, **296**, 1321–1323.

Pascalis, O., Scott, L.S., Kelly, D.J., *et al.* (2005). Plasticity of face processing in infancy. *PNAS*, **102**, 5297–5300.

Pellicano, E. and Rhodes, G. (2003). Holistic processing of faces in preschool children and adults.. *Psychological Science*, **14**, 618–622.

Pellicano, E., Rhodes, G., and Peters, M. (2006). Are preschoolers sensitive to configural information in faces? *Developmental Science*, **9**, 270–277.

Pezdek, K., Blandon-Gitlin, I., and Moore, C. (2003). Children's face recognition memory: More evidence for the cross-race effect. *Journal of Applied Psychology*, **88**, 760–763.

Picozzi, M., Macchi Cassia, V., Turati, C., and Vescovo, E. (2009). The effect of inversion on 3- to 5-year-olds' recognition of face and nonface visual objects. *Journal of Experimental Child Psychology*, **102**, 487–502.

Quinn, P.C. and Eimas, P.D. (1996). Perceptual cues that permit categorical differentiation of animal species by infants. *Journal of Experimental Child Psychology*, **63**, 189–211.

Quinn, P.C. and Tanaka, J.W. (2009). Infants' processing of featural and configural information in the upper and lower halves of the face. *Infancy*, **14**, 474–487.

Quinn, P.C., Yahr, J., Kuhn, A., Slater, A.M., and Pascalis, O. (2002). Representation of the gender of human faces by infants: A preference for female. *Perception*, **31**, 1109–1121.

Quinn, P.C., Kelly, D.J., Lee, K., Pascalis, O., and Slater, A.M. (2008a). Preference for attractive faces in human infants extends beyond conspecifics. *Developmental Science*, **11**, 76–83.

Quinn, P.C., Uttley, L., Lee, K., *et al.* (2008b). Infant preference for female faces occurs for same- but not other-race faces. *Journal of Neuropsychology*, **2**, 15–26.

Quinn, P.C., Doran, M.M., Reiss, J.E., and Hoffman, J.E. (2009). Time course of visual attention in infant categorization of cats versus dogs: Evidence for a head bias as revealed through eye tracking. *Child Development*, **80**, 151–161.

Ramsey, J.L., Langlois, J.H., Hoss, R.A., Rubenstein, A.J., and Griffin, A.M. (2004). Origins of a stereotype: Categorization of facial attractiveness by 6-month-old infants. *Developmental Science*, **7**, 201–211.

Rennels, J.L. and Davis, R.E. (2008). Facial experience during the first year. *Infant Behavior & Development*, **31**, 665–678.

Rhodes, G., Hayward, W.G., and Winkler, C. (2006). Expert face coding: Configural and component coding of own-race and other-race faces. *Psychonomic Bulletin & Review*, **13**, 499–505.

Rhodes, G., Sumich, A., and Byatt, G. (1999). Are average facial configurations attractive only because of their symmetry. *Psychological Science*, **10**, 52–58.

Rose, S.A., Jankowski, J.J., and Feldman, J.F. (2002). Speed of processing and face recognition at 7 and 12 months. *Infancy*, **3**, 435–455.

Rubenstein, A.J., Kalakanis, L., and Langlois, J.H. (1999). Infant preferences for attractive faces: A cognitive explanation. *Developmental Psychology*, **35**, 848–855.

Sangrigoli, S. and de Schonen, S. (2004a). Recognition of own-race and other-race faces by three-month-old infants. *Journal of Child Psychology and Psychiatry*, **45**, 1219–1227.

Sangrigoli, S. and de Schonen, S. (2004b). Effect of visual experience on face processing: A developmental study of inversion and non-native effects. *Developmental Science*, **7**, 74–87.

Sangrigoli, S., Pallier, C., Argenti, A.M., Ventureyra, V.A.G., and de Schonen, S. (2005). Reversibility of the other-race effect in face recognition during childhood. *Psychological Science*, **16**, 440–444.

Samuels, C.A. and Ewy, R. (1985). Aesthetic perception of faces during infancy. *British Journal of Developmental Psychology*, **3**, 221–228.

Schwarzer, G. and Zauner, N. (2003). Face processing in 8-month-old infants: Evidence for configural and analytical processing. *Vision Research*, **43**, 2783–2793.

Schwarzer, G., Zauner, N., and Jovanovic, B. (2007). Evidence of a shift from featural to configural face processing in infancy. *Developmental Science*, **10**, 452–463.

Scott, L.S. and Monesson, A. (2009). The origin of biases in face perception. *Psychological Science*, **20**, 676–680.

Scott, L.S., Shannon, R.W., and Nelson, C.A. (2006). Neural correlates of human and monkey face processing in 9-month-old infants. *Infancy*, **10**, 171–186.

Scott, L.S., Pascalis, O., and Nelson, C.A. (2007). A domain-general theory of the development of perceptual discrimination. *Current Directions in Psychological Science*, **16**, 197–201.

Seitz, K. (2002). Parts and wholes in person recognition: Developmental trends. *Journal of Experimental Child Psychology*, **82**, 367–381.

Shepherd, J.W. and Ellis, H.D. (1972). Physical attractiveness and selection of marriage partners. *Psychological Reports*, **30**, 1004.

Simion, F., Valenza, E., Macchi Cassia, V., Turati, C., and Umilta, C. (2002a). Newborns' preference for up-down asymmetrical configurations. *Developmental Science*, **5**, 427–434.

Simion, F., Farroni, T., Macchi Cassia, V., Turati, C., and Barba, B.D. (2002b). Newborns' local processing in schematic face like configurations. *British Journal of Developmental Psychology*, **20**, 465–478.

Slater, A., Von der Schulenburg, C., Brown, E., *et al.* (1998). Newborn infants prefer attractive faces. *Infant Behavior & Development*, **21**, 345–354.

Slater, A., Bremner, G., Johnson, S.P., Sherwood, P., Hayes, R., and Brown, E. (2000). Newborn infants' preference for attractive faces: The role of internal and external facial features. *Infancy*, **1**, 265–274.

Smith, A.D., Hood, B.M., and Hector, K. (2006). Eye remember you two: Gaze direction modulates face recognition in a developmental study. *Developmental Science*, **9**, 465–472.

Spencer, J., Quinn, P.C., Johnson, M.H., and Karmiloff-Smith, A. (1997). Heads you win, tails you lose: Evidence for young infants categorizing mammals by head and facial attributes. *Early Development and Parenting*, **6**, 113–126.

Tanaka, J.W. and Farah, M.J. (1993). Parts and wholes in face recognition. *Quarterly Journal of Experimental Psychology*, **46A**, 225–245.

Tanaka, J.W., Kay, J.B., Grinnell, E., Stansfield, B., and Szechter, L. (1998). Face recognition in young children: When the whole is greater than the sum of its parts. *Visual Cognition*, **5**, 479–496.

Turati, C., Simion, F., Milani, I., and Umiltà, C. (2002). Newborns' preference for faces: What is crucial? *Developmental Psychology*, **38**, 875–882.

Turati, C., Macchi Cassia, V., Simion, F., and Leo, I. (2006). Newborns' face recognition: Role of inner and outer facial features. *Child Development*, **77**, 297–311.

Turati, C., Bulf, H., and Simion, F. (2008). Newborns' face recognition over changes in viewpoint. *Cognition*, **106**, 1300–1321.

Valentine, T. (1991). A unified account of the effects of distinctiveness, inversion, and race in face recognition. *The Quarterly Journal of Experimental Psychology*, **43A**, 161–204.

Valentine, T., Darling, S., and Donnelly, M. (2004). Why are average faces attractive: The effect of view and averageness on the attractiveness of female faces. *Psychonomic Bulletin & Review*, **11**, 482–487.

Van Duuren, M., Kendell-Scott, L., and Stark, N. (2003). Early aesthetic choices: Infant preferences for attractive premature infant faces. *International Journal of Behavioral Development*, **27**, 212–219.

Walker, P.M. and Hewstone, M. (2006). A perceptual discrimination investigation of the own-race effect and intergroup experience. *Applied Cognitive Psychology*, **20**, 461–475.

Want, S.C., Pascalis, O., Coleman, M., and Blades, M. (2003). Recognizing people from the inner or outer parts of their faces: Developmental data concerning "unfamiliar" faces. *British Journal of Developmental Psychology*, **21**, 125–135.

Werker, J.F. and Tees, R.C. (1999). Influences on infant speech processing: Toward a new synthesis. *Annual Review of Psychology*, **50**, 509–535.

Wild, H.A., Barrett, S.E., Spence, M.J., O'Toole, A.J., Cheng, Y.D., and Brooke, J. (2000). Recognition and sex categorization of adults' and children's faces: Examining performance in the absence of sex-stereotyped cues. *Journal of Experimental Child Psychology*, **77**, 269–291.

Wilson, R.R., Blades, M., and Pascalis, O. (2007). What do children look at in an adult face with which they are personally familiar? *British Journal of Developmental Psychology*, **25**, 375–382.

Yin, R.K. (1969). Looking at upside-down faces. *Journal of Experimental Psychology*, **81**, 141–145.

Yin, R.K. (1970). Face recognition by brain-injured patients: A dissociable ability. *Neuropsychologia*, **8**, 395–402.

Young, A.W., Hay, D.C., McWeeny, K.H., Flude, B.M., and Ellis, A.W. (1985). Matching familiar and unfamiliar faces on internal and external features. *Perception*, **14**, 737–746.

Young, A.W., Hellawell, D., and Hay, D.C. (1987). Configurational information in face perception. *Perception*, **16**, 747–759.

Younger, B.A. and Fearing, D.D. (1999). Parsing items into separate categories: Developmental change in infant categorization. *Child Development*, **70**, 291–303.

Chapter 40

Sensitive Periods in Face Perception

Daphne Maurer and Catherine J. Mondloch

Human newborns are drawn towards face-like patterns, a bias that ensures they receive a wealth of experience with faces during the first few weeks of life. Yet their poor visual acuity and contrast sensitivity restrict the information they can process from faces, and they lack most, if not all, of the specialized mechanisms adults use to process faces differently from objects. Nonetheless this early input plays an important role in the development of adult-like expertise. The importance of early experience is shown by deficits in children who missed early visual experience because dense cataracts in both eyes blocked patterned visual input to the retina until the cataracts were removed surgically and the eye fitted with a compensatory contact lens. The deficits indicate that early visual experience is necessary to set up or preserve the neural architecture for the development of expert face processing. The examples we provide will demonstrate "sleeper effects": the impact of early visual deprivation on the development of a perceptual skill at a later age.

Background: functional visual input during infancy

Newborns' poor visual acuity and contrast sensitivity limit the information they can pick up from faces to the largest, most contrasty features: an outline of the head formed between the hair and the edge of the face, and dark blobs where the prominent internal features are located. Nevertheless, they are sensitive to the arrangement of those dark blobs: they orient preferentially toward visual stimuli comprised of a contour containing large dark elements arranged as facial features or dark elements arranged in any pattern in which the majority of elements are located toward the top of the figure. Newborns show this preference whether tested with schematic black-and-white drawings or facial photographs in which the features have been re-arranged (e.g. Macchi Cassia et al., 2004; Simion et al., 2002; Turati et al., 2006). Critical to this preference appears to be top-heaviness (more energy at the top), congruency (fit between the shape of the external contour and the distribution of internal elements) (Macchi Cassia et al., 2008), and a face-like pattern of phase contrast with features (or blobs) being darker than the background (Farroni et al., 2005; but see Dannemiller and Stephens, 1988). It is only later—at 2 to 4 months of age, that infants begin to prefer faces with the internal features in their correct location over faces with more visible energy or more high contrast elements in the top half (Turati et al., 2005; see also Mondloch et al., 1999). Nevertheless, the early attentional bias, and the fact that adults and children alike are attracted to infants, guarantee that human newborns will be drawn to human faces, and hence that they acquire a wealth of face experience during the first few weeks of life.

During the first 2 months of life, the information that babies extract from faces comes mainly from the external contour. When looking at real faces, young infants (less than 2 months old) are biased to process the external features rather than their internal details, perhaps because of the high contrast between the skin and hair. They typically scan only a limited part of the external contour (Hainline, 1978; Haith et al., 1977; Maurer and Salapatek, 1976) and, after repeated exposure to an individual face, they respond to changes in the external features but not to changes in the internal features, unless the external features were occluded during learning

(Turati et al., 2006). Such discriminations are based on information only from very low spatial frequencies (<0.5 cycles/degree), that is, very large features (de Heering et al., 2008). Newborns do pick up gross information from the internal features: they look longer at faces with direct gaze than with averted gaze if the faces are enface and upright (Farroni et al., 2006) and, by 2 to 3 days of age, they look longer at a face with an intense happy expression than a face with an intense fearful expression (but fail to discriminate fearful from neutral expressions, perhaps because the differences are more subtle) (Farroni, 2007). In addition, newborns look longer at attractive than at unattractive faces—even when the external contour is the same for all faces (Slater et al., 2000), and they discriminate Thatcherized versions of individual faces (upright faces containing inverted eyes and mouth) from their undistorted version when the faces are upright, but not inverted (Leo and Simion, 2009). Despite showing some sensitivity to internal features, newborns' first experience with faces is limited by their visual acuity and contrast sensitivity and hence conveys only limited information about the details of the internal structure of the face or how it varies between individuals or with changes in facial expression.

There are dramatic changes in sensitivity to internal details around the third month of life. Scanning shifts from an external bias to an internal bias favouring the eyes (Hainline, 1978; Haith et al., 1977; Hunnius and Geuze, 2004; Maurer and Salapatek, 1976) and face preferences depend on the correct arrangement of the internal facial features rather than top-heaviness and congruency (Turati et al., 2005; see also Mondloch et al., 1999). Moreover, beginning at 3 months infants show the first evidence of integrating the internal and external features of faces into a Gestalt: following habituation to the faces of two unfamiliar women, they treat a new face that recombines the internal features of one woman with the external features of the other as if it is completely novel (Cashon and Cohen, 2004). At the same time, babies show evidence of forming a prototype representing the average location and shape of the features in the faces they have seen recently (de Haan et al., 2001). New faces are compared to this prototype, allowing for the cumulative effect of experience. These changes launch a long developmental period during which children become increasingly sensitive to the details of internal features, and beginning at 5 months, the spacing among them (Hayden et al., 2007), with improvements in some face processing skills continuing past 10 years of age (Bruce et al., 2000; Mondloch et al., 2002, 2003a). These refinements lead to face expertise: the tuning of face processing to the characteristics of faces encountered in everyday life, namely, upright human faces, often only of one's own race or ethnic group and often only close to one's own age. As a result, discrimination and recognition for the expert category is better than for other types of faces or non-face objects.

Although infants possess only rudimentary face-processing skills, evidence from patients treated for congenital cataract and from monkeys deprived of face input for several months postnatally indicates that this early experience plays a key role in the ultimate development of expert face processing. We will provide evidence that early visual deprivation disrupts some (e.g. sensitivity to differences among faces in the spacing of features; holistic processing), but not all (e.g. sensitivity to differences among faces in the shape of individual features) aspects of face processing, that the deficits caused by early visual deprivation are face-specific, but that it is visual deprivation rather than the lack of input from faces per se that causes the deficits to occur. Finally, we will place this evidence from visually deprived monkeys and humans into a broader context showing the role of biased experience on the development of expert face processing.

Cataract-reversal patients

Our work with children treated for bilateral congenital cataract has allowed us to assess the influence on the development of face expertise of the input from faces during the first few months of life, a period before many hallmarks of face processing have emerged (e.g. configural processing; prototype formation; use of internal features for recognition) and during which effective face input is limited by poor acuity, poor sensitivity to contrast, and limited scanning. To do so, we developed a battery of tasks to measure different aspects of face processing and compared performance in children and adults with normal eyes to that of children and adults who missed visual input during infancy because it was blocked by dense, central cataracts. All individuals in the patient cohort were born with dense, central cataracts in one or both eyes that blocked all patterned input to the retina. The cataractous lenses were removed surgically during infancy and the eyes given compensatory contact lenses to focus visual input. The children's age at the end of visual deprivation varied from 2 months to more than a year. After treatment, the children had years of visual input from faces and objects with which to tune the system. However, because of the permanent deficit in visual acuity that emerges around 2 years of age (Lewis et al., 1995), the effective input never included the high spatial frequencies that define the sharp edges of features and limit acuity: they are unable to see a grating of 20 cycles per degree even at maximum contrast (Ellemberg et al., 1999). Cataract-reversal patients also require more contrast than normal to see mid-spatial frequencies (3–10 cycles per degree), unlike their normal sensitivity to low spatial frequencies (0.33–2 cycles per degree). Studies of adults with faces from which selective spatial frequencies have been filtered suggest that adults with normal eyes rely on mid spatial frequencies for the recognition of facial identity (reviewed in Ruiz-Soler and Beltran, 2006), although they can nevertheless perform many face tasks well based only on low spatial frequencies. Thus, the patient's deficits in acuity and contrast sensitivity limit the effective information they receive from faces even after treatment—and it is possible that residual deficits reflect the reduced input they receive throughout childhood from the mid spatial frequencies on which normal adults come to rely.

Final outcome

Face detection

Adults with normal eyes can rapidly detect that a stimulus is a face when it contains two eyes above a nose above a mouth—even when realistic facial features are not physically present, so long as this configuration can be inferred. For example, they can see a face in paintings by Archimbaldo in which the features are replaced by pieces of fruit or vegetables, in two-tone Mooney stimuli in which shadows have been altered to eliminate feature edges (see Figure 40.1), and in some random patterns of rocks, clouds, or white noise, at least when the images are upright (reviewed in Maurer et al., 2002). To measure the effect of early visual deprivation on the development of such skilled face detection, we tested patients treated for bilateral congenital cataract and normal controls with Mooney images forming 12 images of a face and 12 scrambled images formed by cutting the original images into eight pieces and reassembling the pieces (Mondloch et al., 2003b). The subject's task was to indicate whether the briefly presented image was a face or not. The 11 patients had missed patterned visual input for the first 2 to 6 months of life (M = 3.9 months), the period during which more complex face preferences emerge. Nevertheless, their accuracy (M = 92%) and reaction times (M = 824 ms) were as good as those of the control group (89% and 799 ms, respectively). Thus, early visual input from faces or other patterned visual stimuli is not necessary for the later development of normal face detection. In visually normal adults, upright Mooney faces activate the face-sensitive FFA (Kanwisher et al., 1998). Whether the neural correlates underlying face detection in our patient cohort are the same as those found in visually normal individuals remains unknown.

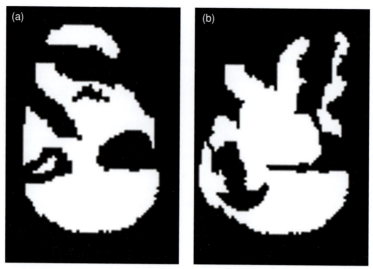

Fig. 40.1 An inverted Mooney face (a), and an inverted scrambled Mooney face (b) are shown. Reprinted from: Mondloch et al. (2003a). Early Visual Experience is Necessary for the Development of Some-but not all- Aspects of Face Processing. *The Development of Face Processing in Infancy and Early Childhood: Current Perspectives*. © 2003, Pascalis and Slater with permission from Nova Science Publishers, Inc.

Studies of infants immediately after treatment suggest that the patients' normal face detection likely reflects recovery from an earlier deficit. We have tested six patients within 10 minutes of their first receiving corrective contact lenses. All of the patients were at least 6 weeks old at the time of treatment, i.e. they were old enough that age-matched controls with normal visual experience no longer orient preferentially towards a head outline with three blobs arranged as facial features, *config*, when it is paired with a head outline with an inverted arrangement (Mondloch et al., 1999). Four patients were at least 12 weeks old at the time of treatment, i.e. were old enough that age-matched controls with normal visual experience orient preferentially towards a positive contrast schematic face when paired with a phase-reversed version (Mondloch et al., 1999). At the time of treatment two-thirds of the patients 6 weeks or older oriented preferentially towards *config*, and none of the patients 12 weeks or older preferred the positive contrast face (unpublished data). The patients' performance at the time of treatment resembles that of normal newborns, not age-matched controls, and suggests that the patients' ultimately normal performance represents recovery from an initial deficit. These results also indicate that the development of more complex face preferences over the first three months after birth in infants with normal eyes is driven by visual experience, presumably with faces.

Processing identity and changing aspects of faces

Human adults are experts at processing the identity of faces despite changes in their appearance that occur as the individual talks, changes facial expression, or looks off to the side. At the same time, they are good at deciphering the changeable cues: they can lip-read, decode facial expression, and detect precisely where the person is looking. To assess the effect of early visual deprivation on the development of these skills, we developed a match-to-sample task in which participants saw a face, and then saw three faces, one of which matched the first face on one dimension while varying on another. On two tasks, the matching face had the same identity as the target face, despite a change in point of view (e.g. from looking up to looking down) or in facial expression (e.g. from smiling to surprised). For these tasks, the participant was instructed to ignore the point of view and facial expression and to report which of the faces matched the identity of the target. On the three remaining tasks, the matching face had a different identity than the target, but matched the target in facial expression, vowel being mouthed, or the direction of eye gaze (despite a change in head orientation). For these tasks, the participant was instructed to ignore identity and to report which of the three faces matched the target on the relevant dimension. For all tasks, models wore surgical caps to eliminate superficial hair cues and encourage processing of the physiognomy of the face.

We tested 17 patients who had missed patterned visual input for the first 1.5 to 16 months of life (M = 105 days). Patients performed normally on the three tasks that required matching changeable aspects of the faces (vowel being mouthed, direction of gaze, facial expression), with accuracy as high and reaction times as low when deprivation lasted throughout the first year of life as when it ended during the first few months. These results indicate that sensitivity to the changeable aspects of faces that are important for social interactions can develop normally when the nervous system does not receive patterned visual input during the first year of life or functional input from high spatial frequencies at any point, at least for the gross types of discrimination tested in this experiment that likely depend on featural processing. In contrast, the patients made more errors than controls in matching facial identity despite changes in point of view, with a trend in the same direction for matching identity despite changes in facial expressions; their deficits were as large when deprivation ended by 2 to 3 months of age as when it lasted far longer. These results indicate that input during the first few months is necessary for the later development of normal sensitivity to the cues to identity that can be used across viewpoints and facial expressions. These cues arise from the bone structure of the face and the systematic way its visibility is altered as the head is rotated or the face adopts a non-neutral expression. We hypothesized that one such cue may be differences among faces in the spacing of features. To further assess for which cues to facial identity patients show a deficit, we developed a task that directly manipulated three cues to facial identity: facial features, the spacing among facial features (called *second-order relations*), and the shape of the external contour.

Cues to facial identity

Adults use a variety of cues to discriminate between faces and to recognize their identity: eye and hair colour, head shape, shape of individual features (chin, eyebrows, eyes, nose, mouth), skin texture, and the location of individual features, that is metric differences among faces in the location of features in relation to one another, a cue called *second-order relations*. To assess the influence of early visual experience on development of sensitivity to these various cues—and to understand the origin of the deficit in matching identity through changes in viewpoint and facial expression—we devised what has come to be known as the Jane task. Jane and her sisters are face images that were manipulated to create sets differing only in the shape of the external contour, only in the shape of the eyes and mouth, or only in the spacing among the internal features (see Figure 40.2). The task is a same/different sequential masking task in which the sets are blocked to emphasize the processing of contour, features, and spacing (second-order relations), respectively. For the spacing set, adults are much more sensitive to such small metric differences in upright human faces than in inverted faces, monkey faces, or houses (Mondloch et al., 2002, 2006; Rhodes et al., 2006; Robbins et al., 2008). (It is not possible to equate stimulus sets to make the same comparisons for features or contour.)

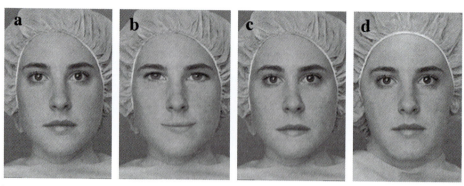

Fig. 40.2 An original face (a) and three altered versions: (b) Differs in the shape of the eyes and mouth: (c) Differs in the spacing among features; (d) Differs in the shape of the external contour. Reprinted from *Perception*, 2002, **31**(5), 553–566 with permission from Pion Limited, London.

We tested 14 patients who had been deprived of patterned visual input for the first 2 to 6 months of life (M = 4 months) and compared their accuracy to that of age-matched normative control groups (n = 36 per group). Patients performed normally on the contour and feature sets, but made significantly more errors than controls for the spacing set (Le Grand et al., 2001). This deficit is an example of a sleeper effect: visual input during the first 2 months of life, a period when the baby with normal eyes is not sensitive to even gross distortions of the spacing of facial features (Bertin and Bhatt, 2004; Bhatt et al., 2005), prevents the later normal development of sensitivity to feature spacing. To verify that featural processing is indeed normal after early deprivation, in a subsequent study we made 16 additional sisters with different eyes and mouths and administered a same/different discrimination task to a similar cohort of patients and visually normal adults. The task was comprised of 120 trials (60 "same" and 60 "different"). Even with this larger set of featural differences and the same sequential same/different task, patients treated for bilateral congenital cataract (n = 8) performed normally, with a mean accuracy of 0.90 (Mondloch et al., 2010). Thus, patterned visual input during early infancy and functional high spatial frequency input later in life are not necessary for the development of normal featural face processing.

A follow-up study suggests that it is specifically deprivation of visual input to the right hemisphere that leads to deficits in sensitivity to second-order relations (Le Grand et al., 2003). To determine the effects of early visual deprivation to the right versus the left hemisphere we took advantage of the fact that during early infancy, visual input to each eye is predominantly transmitted to the contralateral hemisphere. This is caused by the combined effects of two peculiarities of the newborn visual system: sensitivity to stimuli in the temporal visual field develops faster than sensitivity to stimuli in the nasal visual field (Lewis and Maurer, 1992) and cortically mediated transfer of visual information across hemispheres is not evident before 24 months of age (Liegeois et al., 2000). Therefore, left-eye congenital cataracts primarily deprive the right hemisphere of visual input, whereas right-eye congenital cataracts primarily deprive the left hemisphere. When tested on the Jane task, patients treated for left-eye congenital cataract performed like bilaterally deprived patients, whereas patients treated for right-eye congenital cataract performed like age-matched controls (Le Grand et al., 2003). That pattern suggests that it is visual input to the right hemisphere that is necessary for the later development of normal sensitivity to feature spacing.

Holistic processing

Adults with normal eyes process faces holistically—they glue the features together into a Gestalt, making it more difficult to parse the face so as to attend to the details of an individual feature. One demonstration of holistic processing is the composite face effect (e.g. Hole, 1994; Young et al., 1987): when the top half of one face is combined with the bottom half of another face, adults make errors in identifying the top half, presumably because holistic processing integrates it with the novel bottom half, creating the impression of a novel identity. The difficulty is manifested when adults are shown composite images formed from the top and bottom halves of different faces and asked to recognize a famous face based just on the top (or bottom) half or asked to make same/different judgments about the top halves of sequentially presented unfamiliar faces. If holistic processing is broken by misaligning the top and bottom halves, accuracy improves and reaction times decrease. Children show a composite face effect—better accuracy on misaligned than on aligned trials—that is as large as that seen in adults by 4 to 6 years of age (de Heering et al., 2007; Mondloch et al., 2007), and, like adults, they show no such effect for cars (Macchi Cassia et al., 2009b). Studies using a different measure (the part/whole effect) indicate that adults and children process upright faces, but not inverted faces or objects, holistically (Tanaka and Farah, 1993; Tanaka et al., 1998; Pellicano and Rhodes, 2003).

Patients with a history of early visual deprivation from cataract, however, fail to show any composite face effect whatsoever: their accuracy on aligned trials is just as high as their accuracy on misaligned trials and in fact, significantly higher than that of normal controls (Le Grand et al., 2004). This was the pattern we found when we tested 12 patients treated for congenital bilateral cataracts who missed early patterned visual input for the first 3 to 6 months of life (M = 4.6 months). The absence of a composite face effect suggests that cataract-reversal patients fail to process faces holistically, and hence can easily use their intact featural processing to make same/different judgments about the top (or bottom) half of the aligned composite face. Thus, early visual experience is necessary for the later development of holistic face processing. This is another example of a sleeper effect: young infants process faces in a piecemeal fashion and show the first manifestation of integrating information across the face (viz., the inner features and outer contour) at 3 months of age (Cashon and Cohen, 2004). Yet missing visual input during the period of piecemeal processing (the first 3 months) prevents the later development of holistic processing. Whether this deficit in holistic processing, like the deficit in sensitivity to second-order relations, results specifically from deprivation to the right hemisphere is not yet known.

Summary

In sum, patients treated for bilateral congenital cataract are able to develop normal face detection; normal sensitivity to changeable aspects of faces (direction of eye gaze, lipreading, facial expression), at least for the gross differences we tested, and normal sensitivity to differences between individual identities in the shape of the external contour and of internal features. These capabilities are normal later in life even when deprivation lasts throughout the first 6 months of life or even longer. Because we did not study these capabilities longitudinally, we do not know if the ultimately normal performance reflects a normal developmental trajectory or complete recovery from an earlier deficit, although our preliminary longitudinal studies of face detection point to the latter. It is tempting to conclude that the development of these capabilities is not subject to a critical period during which visual input from faces is necessary for normal development. However, that conclusion would be premature. Our results show only that visual input during early infancy is not necessary. It might well be the case that there is a period later in development during which such input is critical. To test that possibility, it is necessary to study children who began life with normal eyes and who then developed cataracts that blocked visual input for a period later in life. We are currently conducting such studies.

Our results also indicate that early patterned visual input is essential for the later normal development of holistic processing, normal sensitivity to metric differences between individual identities in the spacing of internal features (second-order relations), and normal ability to recognize the identity of individuals despite a change in point of view. Visual deprivation for as little as the first 2 to 3 months of life, a period during which poor acuity and limited scanning restrict the information babies with normal eyes can pick up from faces, is sufficient to prevent later normal development and, at least for sensitivity to the spacing of internal features, deprivation of the right hemisphere plays a key role. These sleeper effects may be inter-related: the spacing of features arises from the bone structure of the face, which does not change with rotation of the head, and which can often be inferred even when specific features are occluded (see McKone, 2008, for empirical evidence). Moreover, it is possible that holistic processing—which develops relatively early in the child with normal eyes (by age 4–6)—facilitates the development of acute sensitivity to spacing differences by allowing the proportionate relationships among features to be processed despite changes in viewing distance.

Specificity of deficits

Two questions arise about the specificity of the deficits we have reported in patients treated for congenital cataract. The first concerns whether the deficits we observed are specific to faces or reflect more general difficulties in object processing. The second concerns whether it is the lack of experiences with faces during early infancy that causes the observed deficits or the lack of patterned visual input more generally. The pattern of results across tasks implies that patients' deficits are face-specific: holistic processing and sensitivity to small differences in the spacing of features are both skills that adults with a normal visual history can apply well to faces, but not objects (Macchi Cassia et al., 2009b; Mondloch et al., 2006; Robbins et al., 2008; Tanaka and Farah, 1993). From this perspective, these deficits have to be face-specific, although the patients may have additional deficits in object processing, as suggested by elevated thresholds to integrate dot patterns into a global form (Lewis et al., 2002). Empirical evidence supports the face specificity of the deficits in sensitivity to metric differences in feature spacing: patients treated for bilateral congenital cataract performed normally on a similar task requiring differentiation of monkeys with the same spacing differences we had used previously with human faces and on a task requiring differentiation of houses based on the spacing between windows and between the windows and doors, but like the patients in our previous study, had deficits in sensitivity to the spacing among facial features in human faces (Robbins et al., 2010). This latter result suggests that early visual deprivation impairs specifically the exquisite sensitivity to spacing of facial features that adults are able to apply to upright human faces but normally not to other object categories. Whether the patients could develop expertise for another object category (e.g. dogs, cars, birds) is an open question.

The patients we studied were deprived not only of faces during the first few weeks and months of life, but were deprived of all patterned visual input. It is possible that patterned visual input during early infancy is necessary and sufficient to set up or preserve the neural architecture that is required for face expertise to develop later in life and that seeing faces during that period is not necessary. A recent study of monkeys suggests that seeing faces is not essential. Sugita (2008) raised monkeys in a complex visual environment but with no exposure to human or monkey faces for the first 0.5, 1, or 2 years of life. This visual input was sufficient for normal discrimination among human or monkey faces based on either just individual features or just the spacing among them at the end of deprivation. The ability of these monkeys to discriminate among faces based on featural or spacing differences even after 2 years of face deprivation (equivalent to roughly 8 years of age in humans) suggests that there is no critical period during which face input is necessary. Rather, Sugita's findings support the hypothesis that early visual input, but not experience with faces, is necessary for the setting up or preservation of the neural architecture that underlies adult-like expert face processing.

Other roles of experience: perceptual narrowing

Patterned visual input may be both necessary and sufficient to preserve the neural architecture that will ultimately underlie expert face processing. Experience with faces, though, is necessary to tune that expertise to the diet of faces experienced by each individual. As noted earlier, newborns orient preferentially towards top-heavy visual patterns, regardless of the extent to which the pattern resembles a human face (Macchi Cassia et al., 2004) as long as the contrast polarity is consistent with real faces (i.e. as long as the features are darker than the surrounding areas) (Farroni et al., 2005). Similarly, they look equally long at faces from their own racial/ethnic group as they do at faces from other groups (Kelly et al., 2005). Likewise, prior to experience with either human or monkey faces, Sugita's (2008) monkeys that were deprived of experience with faces while living in a visually rich environment, demonstrated a preference to look at monkey *or* human faces over objects and discriminated easily among monkey faces *and* among human faces.

Within the first few weeks of experiencing faces, both humans and monkeys show evidence of perceptual narrowing. Six-month-old infants discriminate among individual monkey faces as readily as among individual human faces, but 9-month-old infants fail the test for monkey faces while continuing to readily discriminate among human faces (Pascalis et al., 2002). This narrowing depends on biased exposure: infants typically see many human faces and few, if any, monkey faces. However, if the diet of faces is made more balanced between species, by exposing infants to named pictures of six monkeys between 6 and 9 months, infants continue to readily discriminate both human and monkey faces at 9 months of age (Pascalis et al., 2005). The attunement continues as children slowly acquire expertise in perceiving the small differences in feature spacing that distinguish individuals: by age 8, children, like adults, are more sensitive to such differences in upright human faces than upright monkey faces, with lower (and nearly equal) accuracy for inverted human faces and monkey faces (Mondloch et al., 2006). Anecdotal evidence suggests that once the system has narrowed, it is difficult to gain expertise in distinguishing among monkey faces, as evidenced by difficulties reported by animal handlers.

There is similar perceptual narrowing based on the race or ethnicity of the faces the infant sees over the first months of life but the timing and details differ from those for the species effect in enlightening ways. By 3 months, infants have a looking preference for faces from the racial/ethnic group(s) they encounter most often. Specifically, when tested with Middle Eastern, Chinese, African, and Caucasian faces, white babies growing up in a predominantly white area of a British city look preferentially toward white faces (Kelly et al., 2005) and Han Chinese babies growing up in China without exposure to foreigners look preferentially toward Chinese faces (Kelly et al., 2007a). When tested with white and black faces, white babies exposed predominantly to white faces in Israel look preferentially toward white faces, Ethiopian babies exposed predominantly to black faces in Ethiopia look preferentially toward black faces, and black Ethiopian babies growing up in an integrated refugee camp in Israel show no looking preference (Bar-Haim et al., 2006). Thus, by 3 months of age the ethnicity of the faces babies encounter has tuned their looking preferences.

There is conflicting evidence on when biased exposure to faces of one race (or ethnic group) begins to influence infants' ability to discriminate among, and recognize, faces. In one study,

3-month-old white French babies, showed evidence of discriminating among Caucasian but not Asian faces (Sangrigoli and de Schonen, 2004). In contrast, in another study, white British babies discriminated among faces in all four ethnic categories tested (Caucasian, Chinese, middle Eastern, and African) and it was only later that babies began to fail the discrimination/recognition test for other race faces (Kelly et al., 2007b), a precursor to adult's other-race effect, i.e. better accuracy in recognizing the identity of own-race than other-race faces. However, there is converging evidence that the system is plastic during infancy and able to learn to discriminate/recognize faces from a category to which there was originally little exposure. Thus, in the study of 3-month-old white French babies, familiarization with as few as three Asian faces was sufficient to induce discrimination among novel Asian faces (Sangrigloi and de Schonen, 2004) and babies overcome their initial inability to discriminate among male faces if growing up with a female caregiver or their initial inability to discriminate among female faces if growing up with a male caregiver (Quinn et al., 2002).

The results for attunement to species versus race/ethnic group are puzzling. On the one hand, in both domains there is perceptual narrowing or attunement to the types of faces the baby encounters. But the system shows signs of narrowing for race/ethnicity and sex (of caretaker) at 3 to 6 months of age, the period when babies can still readily discriminate among monkey faces. Moreover, the narrowing for species may be less modifiable by later input than that for race/ethnicity. The direction of the other-race effect can be completely reversed if the bias in the diet of face is reversed: Korean children adopted into French families between the ages of 3 and 9 later show an other-race effect as if they had grown up in a white community in France (Sangrigoli et al., 2005). Like white French adults and unlike Koreans who moved to France as adults, they are better at recognizing an unfamiliar face if it is Caucasian rather if it is Asian (but see de Heering et al., 2010, for a similar study showing the elimination but not the reversal of the other-race effect). In contrast, the direction of the other-species effect may be irreversible. Following the initial period of face deprivation, Sugita exposed the monkeys to either exclusively human or exclusively monkey faces for a period of 1 month. At the end of this one-month exposure, the monkeys showed a preference for only the exposed category of faces over objects and discriminated only among faces from that category. Subsequent exposure to the other category did not alter the narrowing: even after months of living in a monkey colony, the monkeys who saw human faces for the first month could discriminate among human but not monkey faces (Sugita, 2008) and it was only those faces that elicited neural responses in the superior temporal sulcus (Manaka and Sugita, 2008). This evidence from monkeys parallels that from human handlers, who despite many years on the job, continue to experience difficulty identifying the individual monkeys they care for.

One possibility is that the narrowing for species serves to define what is a face—and hence what is processed differently from objects. Although primate faces do elicit the neural markers of face processing—an N170 in the event-related potential and fMRI activation in the fusiform face area (FFA), both the amplitude of the N170 (de Haan et al., 2002) and the amount of FFA activation are smaller (Kanwisher et al., 1999). Thus, it is possible that when an adult looks at a monkey face, there is activation of networks involved in processing non-face objects but no or minimal activation of the networks beyond the FFA involved in processing facial identity (Maurer et al., 2007; Rotshtein et al., 2007). For that reason, exposure to monkey faces later in life may not be effective in inducing modifications in face processing networks. In contrast, faces from an unfamiliar race or ethnic group may continue to be processed as faces and hence maintain the potential to modify face processing networks.

Something similar may happen with inverted human faces. By 4 to 5 months of age, infants scan inverted faces differently from upright faces (Gallay et al., 2006), generalize habituation across point of view only for upright faces (Turati et al., 2004), and discriminate between faces with differences in feature spacing only if the faces are upright (Bhatt et al., 2005; Hayden et al., 2007). Thereafter, all of the specific face processing skills become tuned to upright faces: with upright faces, adults have faster face detection, show evidence of holistic processing, are better at perceiving differences in feature spacing, and, at least under some testing conditions, are better at picking up differences in feature shape (reviewed in Maurer et al., 2002). Inverted faces elicit a delayed N170 and, at least in some designs, less fMRI activation of the FFA (Kanwisher, et al., 1998; Rossion et al. 2000; Yovel and Kanwisher, 2005). As would be expected if inverted faces do not engage face processing networks beyond the FFA, it appears to be difficult, if not impossible, to train adults to distinguish accurately among inverted faces. Even after 1100 trials of training to distinguish a variety of inverted photos of twins, accuracy was poor, based on detection of tiny local featural differences, and did not lead to any signs of holistic processing (Robbins and McKone, 2003). The results of studies accessing whether it is possible to attain face-like expertise in adulthood for another object category are inconsistent (cf. Gauthier versus Robbins) and do not allow firm conclusions about whether there is a sensitive period for gaining such expertise.

Plasticity after infancy

Our work with patients treated for congenital cataract and the documentation of perceptual narrowing both provide evidence of plasticity during infancy. The finding of a reversal of the other-race effect in children adopted between 3 and 9 years of age suggests that plasticity persists beyond infancy for at least some types of face processing. The degree to which various aspects of the face-processing system remain plastic has not been investigated extensively, but there appears to be plasticity in adulthood for modifying sensitivity to differences between individual faces that belong to an initially unfamiliar race/ethnic group or age (see next section). One possibility is that faces from such unfamiliar categories are nevertheless processed as faces, not objects, and hence leave open the possibility that later exposure will modify their processing. Consistent with this hypothesis is evidence that the other-race effect can be largely overcome by training, even in adulthood, and that pre-school teachers and maternity ward nurses are better than other adults at discriminating among children's and infants' faces, respectively (see next section). Those findings suggest that the perceptual narrowing for sex, age and race/ethnicity may be modifiable at any age if the diet of faces changes.

Residual plasticity in adulthood

There is scattered evidence that the face processing skills of normal adults can be modified by training or a change in the types of faces that they have to differentiate—and hence that face processing remains plastic throughout life. Several studies have demonstrated that specialized face-processing mechanisms are tuned to own-age faces. When given a sequential matching to sample task, adults show an "other-age" effect: they are better at recognizing adults' faces than the faces of children or newborns and the advantage is seen only, or mainly, for upright faces (Kuefner et al., 2008; Macchi Cassia et al., 2009a,c). In contrast, pre-school teachers' accuracy at recognizing upright faces, the magnitude of their inversion decrement, and the strength of holistic processing they demonstrate do not differ for child versus adult faces (de Heering and Rossion, 2008; Kuefner et al., 2008). Interestingly, the size of their composite face effect for child faces as indexed by reaction time is correlated with the number of years of experience they have taught preschool (de Heering and Rossion, 2008). Similarly, nurses who have worked on a maternity ward for at least 2 years show a smaller other age advantage for upright adults' faces over infants' faces and, unlike other adults, an inversion decrement for both types of face (Macchi Cassia et al., 2009c).

However, experiencing a single infant for 9 months (one's own first child) is insufficient to induce this reduction in the other-age effect (Macchi Cassia et al., 2009a). Combined, these data suggest that face processing is modifiable at any age if it becomes important for the individual to individuate faces from an unfamiliar class and the individual is exposed to a large number of different faces over a protracted period.

The system may be more plastic during childhood: by age 3, children demonstrate the adult-like pattern of an other age advantage for upright adult over newborn faces, and an inversion decrement only for adult faces—unless they have a younger sibling who was born between age 1 and 3 and to whom they were exposed for an average of 15 months before the test (Macchi Cassia et al., 2009a). These results suggest that the system is still sufficiently plastic during early childhood that the introduction of one instance (or at most, a few instances) of a new category of faces (a single infant face) after the first year of life is sufficient to eliminate the initial advantage for adults' faces. The experience of an infant's face during childhood also appears to leave a trace that interacts with later adult experience: first time mothers who grew up with a younger sibling who was born when they were 1 to 7 years old show a reduced other-age advantage for adult over newborn faces and, unlike other adults, an inversion decrement for both categories. (Macchi Cassia et al., 2009a). This reduction of the other-age advantage for adults' over infants' faces is not apparent if the woman had the early experience but no child of her own or if she is a first time mother without a younger sibling. Note, however, that it is not possible to draw strong conclusions from these studies because the timing and duration of the experience with infants varied across the comparisons. Nevertheless, the comparisons suggest that the system remains plastic in adulthood, with the duration and variability of exposure needed to induce the plasticity related to whether or not it reinforces exposure received during childhood.

Similar evidence for plasticity of face processing in adulthood comes from studies of the other-race effect, the phenomenon that adults are better at recognizing a face in an old/new memory task if the face is from their own race/ethnic group than if it is from an unfamiliar group (see Meissner and Brigham, 2001 for a meta-analysis of 91 experiments). The effect does not influence face detection (Valentine and Endo, 1992), but does influence featural processing and the markers of face expertise, namely, holistic processing and processing of facial identity based on spacing of features (Hayward et al., 2008 Michel et al., 2006a,b; Tanaka et al., 2004). Each of these skills is better for faces from the viewer's own race/ethnic group. The other-race effect presumably reflects the relatively little experience the viewer has had with faces from the unfamiliar group, a hypothesis supported by a correlation between amount of self-reported contact and the size of the other-race effect (Meissner and Brigham, 2001). However, contact is not always sufficient to eliminate the other-race effect when it begins in adulthood, rather than childhood (e.g. Sangrigoli et al., 2005). Nevertheless, white university students who were at chance in recognizing Japanese faces improved after training not only on the trained faces but also novel examples: there was some improvement after short-term training with 30 faces (Elliott et al., 1973) and considerable improvement after 2 to 3 weeks of training with 67 to 94 faces, with no loss over 5 months (the longest period tested; Goldstein and Chance, 1985). Such successful training indicates that face processing can be tuned to an unfamiliar category of faces even in adulthood. It is consistent with evidence that the prototype(s) to which individual faces are compared is constantly updated by the diet of faces to which an individual is exposed (e.g. Webster et al., 2004; Rhodes et al., 2006) and is attributable, in part, to a shift to processing other-race faces at the individual rather than the basic level (Levin, 1996).

Additional evidence for the plasticity of face processing in adulthood comes from two studies that have been successful in training individuals with prosopagnosia, impaired face recognition of congenital origin or as a result of brain injury. In the first study, a congenital patient was trained over 14 months to classify faces on the basis of spacing cues: the spacing between the eyes and eyebrows and between the mouth and nose (DeGutis et al., 2007). During training, her accuracy on the task improved to normal levels and reaction times dropped from their original 10-fold elevation to normal levels. After training, she scored within the normal range on standardized tests of face recognition, a face-selective N170 emerged, and face-selective regions identified by fMRI showed greater coherence among one another. In the second study, a brain-injured patient profited, at least over the short-term (the only test point), from training that called attention to the characteristics of facial features ("This is Tracy. She has a large forehead and small eyes."). After this training, his accuracy was nearly perfect in recognizing the previously presented faces with a novel facial expression (Powell et al., 2008). Both of these studies suggest that face-processing networks may still be plastic during adulthood, although there aren't sufficient data to speculate about the most effective training protocol.

Summary and conclusions

Infants pay attention to faces from the moment of birth, but poor visual acuity and sensitivity to contrast limit the information they can extract to large details of high contrast. Newborns also lack most, if not all, of the specialized mechanisms adults use to process faces differently from objects. Despite these limitations, degraded input appears to set up or maintain the neural architecture that underlies the later development of adult-like expertise. We demonstrated this by considering the consequences of a natural experiment—children who missed early visual input because dense cataracts in both eyes blocked patterned visual input to the retina until the cataracts were removed surgically and the eye fitted with a compensatory contact lens. The role of later visual input is not yet clear. However, the specialization of expert face processing for the types of faces routinely distinguished (e.g. own species, own race, own age) indicates that later input plays a critical role in tuning the system. Visual experience tunes the system in several ways: it defines which stimuli the brain will process as faces (e.g. human, but not monkey faces; upright, but not inverted faces) and allows expertise to emerge later in life as there are changes in the diet of faces to which individuals are exposed (e.g. after moving to a new country; after becoming a teacher of young children). This remarkable and plastic system is what allows us to recognize hundreds of individual faces with ease on a daily basis.

Outstanding questions

1 Patients treated for congenital cataract perform normally on a difficult face detection task and on recognizing facial identity based on feature shape. Are the underlying neural mechanisms also normal or are patients recruiting different neural populations than normal controls (e.g. object areas)?

2 Patients perform normally on a delayed match-to-sample task in which they were asked to match prototypical expressions. Do they have normal sensitivity thresholds for emotional expressions (i.e. do they perform normally when tested with subtle or ambiguous expressions)?

3 Studies comparing bilateral versus unilaterally patients' sensitivity to second-order relations suggest that it is visual input to the right hemisphere that is necessary for the development of normal sensitivity to this cue to facial identity. Is visual input to the right hemisphere also necessary for the development or normal holistic processing?

4 Would extensive training improve cataract patients' holistic processing and/or sensitivity to second-order relations? And, if so, would the underlying neural mechanisms be identical to those seen in visually normal controls? Or would patients recruit different neural populations

to perform these tasks? Would the most effective training involve the presentation of faces filtered to contain only low spatial frequencies, of the type the patients missed during infancy? Or would any face input be adequate, as suggested by the face-deprived monkeys?

5 To date, most research has focused on the impact of early visual deprivation on the development of expert face processing. Does later deprivation (e.g. deprivation beginning after 6 months of age) produce a different pattern of deficits? What is the sensitive period for damage to each type of face processing?

6 Does the greater plasticity for other-race faces relative to other-species faces reflect differences in the extent to which these face categories are processed as faces versus objects?

7 Are the face-deprived monkeys of Sugita normal because they had some minimal exposure to faces on the first day of life or through reflections and shadows of their own face? Is there some minimum face exposure necessary to preserve the ability of the system to later specialize or is any patterned input sufficient?

Acknowledgments

This research was supported by grants from the Natural Sciences and Engineering Council (Canada) to DM and to CM. We thank Adélaïde de Heering for comments on an earlier version.

References

Bar-Haim, Y., Ziv, T., Lamy, D. and Hodes, R.M. (2006). Nature and nurture in own-race face processing. *Psychological Science*, **17**, 159–163.

Bertin, E. and Bhatt, R.S. (2004). The Thatcher illusion and face processing in infancy. *Developmental Science*, **7**, 431–436.

Bhatt, R.S., Bertin, E., Hayden, A. and Reed, A. (2005). Face processing in infancy: Developmental changes in the use of different kinds of relational information. *Child Development*, **76**, 169–181.

Bruce, V., Campbell, R.N., Doherty-Sneddon, G., *et al.* (2000). Testing face processing skills in children. *British Journal of Developmental Psychology*, **18**, 319–333.

Cashon, C.H. and Cohen, L.B. (2004). Beyond u-shaped development in infants' processing of faces: An information-processing account. *Journal of Cognition and Development*, **5**, 59–80.

Dannemiller, J.L. and Stephens, B.R. (1988). A critical test of infant pattern preference models. Child Development, **59**, 210–216.

De Gutis, J.M., Bentin, S., Robertson, L.C. and D' Esposito, M. (2007). Functional plasticity in ventral temporal cortex following cognitive rehabilitation of a congenital prosopagnosic. *Journal of Cognitive Neuroscience*, **19**, 1790–1802.

de Haan, M., Johnson, M.H., Maurer, D. and Perrett, D. (2001). Recognition of individual faces and average face prototypes by 1- and 3-month old infants. *Cognitive Development*, **16**, 659–678.

de Haan, M., Pascalis, O. and Johnson, M.H. (2002). Specialization of neural mechanisms underlying face recognition in human infants. *Journal of Cognitive Neuroscience*, **14**, 199–209.

de Heering, A. and Rossion, B. (2008). Prolonged visual experience in adulthood modulates holistic face perception. *Plos ONE*, **3**, e2317.

de Heering, A., Houthuys, S. and Rossion, B. (2007). Holistic face processing is mature at 4 years of age: Evidence from the composite face effect. *Journal of Experimental Child Psychology*, **96**, 57–70.

de Heering, A., Turati, C., Rossion, B., Bulf, H., Goffaux, V. and Simion, F. (2008). Newborns' face recognition is based on spatial frequencies below 0.5 cycles per degree. *Cognition*, **106**, 444–454.

de Heering, A., de Liedekerke, C., Deboni, M. and Rossion, B. (2010). The role of experience during childhood in shaping the other-race effect. *Developmental Science*, **13**, 181–187.

Ellemberg, D., Lewis, T.L., Maurer, D., Liu, C.H. and Brent, H. (1999). Spatial and temporal vision in patients treated for bilateral congenital cataracts. *Vision Research*, **39**, 3480–3489.

Elliott, E.S., Wills, E.J. and Goldstein, A.G. (1973). The effects of discrimination training on the recognition of white and oriental faces. *Bulletin of the Psychonomic Society*, **2**, 71–73.

Farroni, T., Johnson, M.H., Menon, E., Zulian, L., Faraguna, D. and Csibra, G. (2005). Newborns' preference for face-relevant stimuli: effects of contrast polarity. *Proceedings of the National Academy of Sciences, USA*, **102**, 17245–17250.

Farroni, T., Menon, E. and Johnson, M.H. (2006). Factors influencing newborns' preference for faces with eye contact. *Journal of Experimental Child Psychology*, **95**, 298–308.

Farroni, T., Menon, E., Rigato, S. and Johnson, M.H. (2007). The perception of facial expressions in newborns. *European Journal of Developmental Psychology*, **4**, 2–13.

Gallay, M., Baudouin, J.Y., Durand, K., Lemoine, C. and Lécuyer, R. (2006). Qualitative differences in the exploration of upright and upside-down faces in four-month-old infants: An eye-movement study. *Child Development*, **77**, 984–996.

Goldstein, A.G. and Chance, J.E. (1985). Effects of training on Japanese face recognition: Reduction of the other-race effect. *Bulletin of the Psychonomic Society*, **23**, 211–214.

Hainline, L. (1978). Developmental changes in visual scanning of face and nonface patterns by infants. *Journal of Experimental Child Psychology*, **25**, 90–115.

Haith, M.M., Bergman, T. and Moore, M. (1977). Eye contact and face scanning in early infancy. *Science*, **198**, 853–854.

Hayden, A., Bhatt, R.S., Reed, A., Corbly, C.R. and Joseph, J.E. (2007). The development of expert face processing: Are infants sensitive to normal differences in second-order relational information? *Journal of Experimental Child Psychology*, **97**, 85–98.

Hayward, W.G., Rhodes, G. and Schwaninger, A. (2008). An own-race advantage for components as well as configurations in face recognition. *Cognition*, **106**, 1017–1027.

Hunnius, S. and Geuze, R.H. (2004). Developmental changes in visual scanning of dynamic faces and abstract stimuli in infants: A longitudinal study. *Infancy*, **6**, 231–255.

Hole, G.J. (1994). Configurational factors in the perception of unfamiliar faces. *Perception*, **23**, 65–74.

Kanwisher, N., Stanley, D. and Harris, A. (1999). The fusiform face area is selective for faces not animals. *Neuroreport*, **10**, 183–187.

Kanwisher, N., Tong, F. and Nakayama, K. (1998). The effect of face inversion on the human fusiform face area. *Cognition*, **68**, B1–B11.

Kelly, D.J., Liu, S., Ge, L., Quinn, P.C., Slater, A.M., Lee, K., *et al.* (2007a). Cross-race preferences for same-race faces extend beyond the African versus Caucasian contrast in 3-month-old infants. *Infancy*, **11**, 87–95.

Kelly, D.J., Quinn, P.C., Slater, A.M., Lee, K., Ge, L. and Pascalis, O. (2007b). The other-race effect develops during infancy: Evidence of perceptual narrowing. *Psychological Science*, **18**, 1084–1089.

Kelly, D.J., Quinn, P.C., Slater, A.M., *et al.* (2005). Three-month-olds, but not newborns, prefer own-race faces. *Developmental Science*, **8**, F31–36.

Kuefner, D., Macchi Cassia, V., Picozzi, M. and Bricolo, E. (2008). Do all kids look alike? Evidence for an other-age effect in adults. *Journal of Experimental Psychology. Human Perception and Performance*, **34**, 811–817.

Le Grand, R., Mondloch, C.J., Maurer, D. and Brent, H.P. (2001). Neuroperception. Early visual experience and face processing. *Nature*, **410**, 890.

Le Grand, R., Mondloch, C.J., Maurer, D. and Brent, H.P. (2003). Expert face processing requires visual input to the right hemisphere during infancy. *Nature Neuroscience*, **6**, 1108–1112.

Le Grand, R., Mondloch, C.J., Maurer, D. and Brent, H.P. (2004). Impairment in holistic face processing following early visual deprivation. *Psychological Science*, **15**, 762–768.

Leo, I. and Simion, F. (2009). Face processing at birth: a Thatcher illusion study. *Developmental Science,* **12**, 492–498.

Levin, D.T. (1996). Classifying faces by race: The structure of face categories. *Journal of Experimental Psychology: Learning, Memory and Cognition,* **22**, 1364–1382.

Lewis, T.L., Ellemberg, D., Maurer, D., *et al.* (2002). Sensitivity to global form in glass patterns after early visual deprivation in humans. *Vision Research,* **42**, 939–948.

Lewis, T.L. and Maurer, D. (1992). The development of temporal and nasal visual fields during infancy. *Vision Research,* **32**, 903–911.

Lewis, T.L., Maurer, D. and Brent, H.P. (1995). Development of grating acuity in children treated for unilateral or bilateral congenital cataract. *Investigative Ophthalmology and Visual Science,* **36**, 2080–2095.

Liegeois, F., Bentejac, L. and de Schonen, S. (2000). When does inter-hemispheric integration of visual events emerge in infancy? A developmental study on 19- to 28-month old infants. *Neuropsychologia,* **38**, 1382–1389.

Macchi Cassia, V.M., Turati, C. and Simion, F. (2004). Can a nonspecific bias toward top-heavy patterns explain newborns' face preference? *Psychological Science,* **15**, 379–383.

Macchi Cassia, V.M., Valenza, E., Simion, F. and Leo, I. (2008). Congruency as a nonspecific perceptual property contributing to newborns' face preference. *Child Development,* **79**, 807–820.

Macchi Cassia, V.M., Kuefner, D., Picozzi, M. and Vescovo, E. (2009a). Early experience predicts later plasticity for face processing. *Psychological Science,* **20**, 853–859.

Macchi Cassia, V.M., Picozzi, M., Kuefner, D., Bricolo, E. and Turati, C. (2009b). Holistic processing for faces and cars in preschool-aged children and adults: Evidence from the composite effect. *Developmental Science,* **12**, 236–248.

Macchi Cassia, V.M., Picozzi, M., Kuefner, D. and Casati, M. (2009c). Why mixups don't happen in the nursery: Evidence for an experience-based interpretation of the other-age effect. *The Quarterly Journal of Experimental Psychology,* **62**, 1099–1107.

Manaka, Y. and Sugita, Y. (2008). Preference for face stimuli in monkeys before and after the first exposure to flesh faces. Poster presented to Society for Neuroscience, Washington.

Maurer, D., Le Grand, R.L. and Mondloch, C.J. (2002). The many faces of configural processing. *Trends in Cognitive Sciences,* **6**, 255–260.

Maurer, D., O' Craven, K.M., Le Grand, R., *et al.* (2007). Neural correlates of processing facial identity based on features versus their spacing. *Neuropsychologia,* **45**, 1438–1451.

Maurer, D. and Salapatek, P. (1976). Developmental changes in the scanning of faces by young infants. *Child Development,* **47**, 523–527.

McKone, E. (2008). Configural processing and face viewpoint. *Journal of Experimental Psychology. Human Perception and Performance,* **34**, 310–327.

Meissner, C.A. and Brigham, J.C. (2001). Thirty years of investigating the own-race bias in memory for faces: A meta-analytic review. *Psychology, Public Policy and Law,* **7**, 3–35.

Michel, C., Caldara, R. and Rossion, B. (2006a). Same-race faces are perceived more holistically than other-race faces. *Visual Cognition,* **14**, 55–73.

Michel, C., Rossion, B., Han, J., Chung, C-S. and Caldara, R. (2006b). Holistic processing is finely tuned for faces of our own race. *Psychological Science,* **17**, 608–615.

Mondloch, C.J., Lewis, T.L., Budreau, D.R., *et al.* (1999). Face perception during early infancy. *Psychological Science,* **10**, 419–422.

Mondloch, C.J., Le Grand, R. and Maurer, D. (2002). Configural face processing develops more slowly than featural face processing. *Perception,* **31**, 553–566.

Mondloch, C.J., Geldart, S., Maurer, D. and Le Grand, R. (2003a). Developmental changes in face processing skills. *Journal of Experimental Child Psychology,* **86**, 67–84.

Mondloch, C.J., Le Grand, R. and Maurer, D. (2003b). Early visual experience is necessary for the development of some-but not all- aspects of face processing. In O. Pascalis and A. Slater (eds.), *The development of face processing in infancy and early childhood*, pp. 99–117. New York: Nova.

Mondloch, C.J., Maurer, D. and Ahola, S. (2006). Becoming a face expert. *Psychological Science*, **17**, 930–934.

Mondloch, C.J., Pathman, T., Maurer D, Le Grand, R. and de Schonen, S. (2007). The composite face effect in six-year-old children: Evidence of adultlike holistic face processing. *Visual Cognition*, **15**, 564–577.

Mondloch, C.J., Robbins, R. and Maurer, D. (2010). Discrimination of facial features by adults, 10-year-olds and cataract-reversal patients. *Perception*, **39**, 184–194.

Pascalis, O., de Haan, M. and Nelson, C.A. (2002). Is face processing species-specific during the first year of life? *Science*, **296**, 1321–1323.

Pascalis, O., Scott, L.S., Kelly, D.J., *et al.* (2005). *Proceedings of the National Academy of Sciences*, **102**, 5297–5300.

Pellicano, E. and Rhodes, G. (2003). Holistic processing of faces in preschool children and adults. *Psychological Science*, **14**, 618–622.

Powell, J., Letson, S., Davidoff, J., Valentine, T. and Greenwood, R. (2008). Enhancement of face recognition learning in patients with brain injury using three cognitive training procedures. *Neuropsychological Rehabilitation*, **18**, 182–203.

Quinn, P., Yahr, J., Kuhn, A., Slater, A. and Pascalis, O. (2002). Representation of the gender of human faces by infants: A preference for female. *Perception*, **31**, 1109–1121.

Rhodes, G., Hayward, W.G. and Winkler, C. (2006). Expert face coding: Configural and component coding of own-race and other-race faces. *Psychonomic Bulletin and Review*, **13**, 499–505.

Robbins, R. and McKone, E. (2003). Can holistic processing be learned for inverted faces? *Cognition*, **88**, 79–107.

Robbins, R., Nishimura, M., Mondloch, C.J., Lewis, T.L. and Maurer, D. (2010). Deficits in sensitivity to spacing after early visual deprivation in humans: A comparison of human faces, monkey faces, and houses. *Developmental Psychobiology*, **52**, 775–781.

Rotshtein, P., Geng, J.J., Driver, J. and Dolan, R.J. (2007). Role of features and second-order spatial relations in face discrimination, face recognition, and individual face skills: Behavioral and functional magnetic resonance imaging data. *Journal of Cognitive Neuroscience*, **19**, 1435–1452.

Rossion, B., Gauthier, I., Tarr, M.J., *et al.* (2000). The N170 occipito-temporal component is delayed and enhanced to inverted faces but not to inverted objects: An electrophysiological account of face-specific processes in the human brain. *Neuroreport*, **11**, 69–70.

Ruiz-Soler, M. and Beltran, F.S. (2006). Face perception: An integrative review of the role of spatial frequencies. *Psychological Research*, **70**, 273–292.

Sangrigoli, S. and De Schonen, S. (2004). Recognition of own-race and other-race faces by three-month-old infants. *Journal of Child Psychology and Psychiatry, and Allied Disciplines*, **45**, 1219–27.

Sangrigoli, S., Pallier, C., Argenti, A.M., Ventureyra, V.A. and de Schonen, S. (2005). Reversibility of the other-race effect in face recognition during childhood. *Psychological Science*, **16**, 440–444.

Simion, F., Valenza, E., Macchi Cassia, V., Turati, C. and Umiltà, C. (2002). Newborns' preference for up-down asymmetrical configurations. *Developmental Science*, **5**, 427–434.

Slater, A., Bremner, G., Johnson, S., Sherwood, P., Hayes, R. and Brown, E. (2000). Newborn infants' preference for attractive faces: The role of internal and external facial features. *Infant and Child Development*, **1**, 265–274.

Sugita, Y. (2008). Face perception in monkeys reared with no exposure to faces. *Proceedings of the National Academy of Sciences of the United States of America*, **105**, 394–398.

Tanaka, J.W. and Farah, M.J. (1993). Parts and wholes in face recognition. *The Quarterly Journal of Experimental Psychology A*, Human Experimental Psychology, **46**, 225–245.

Tanaka, J.W., Kay, J.B., Grinnell, E., Stansfield, B. and Szechter, T. (1998). Face recognition in young children: When the whole is greater than the sum of its parts. *Visual Cognition*, **5**, 479–496.

Tanaka, J.W., Kiefer, M. and Bukach, C. (2004). A holistic account of the own-race effect in face recognition: evidence from a cross-cultural study. *Cognition*, **93**, B1–B9.

Turati, C., Macchi Cassia, V., Simion, F. and Leo, I. (2006). Newborns' face recognition: Role of inner and outer facial features. *Child Development*, **77**, 297–311.

Turati, C., Sangrigoli, S., Ruel, J. and de Schonen, S. (2004). Evidence of the face inversion effect in 4-month-old infants. *Infancy*, **6**, 275–297.

Turati, C., Valenza, E., Leo, I. and Simion, F. (2005). Three-Month-Olds' visual preference for faces and its underlying visual processing mechanisms. *Journal of Experimental Child Psychology*, **90**, 255–273.

Valentine, T. and Endo, M. (1992). Towards an exemplar model of face processing: The effects of race and distinctiveness. *Quarterly Journal of Experimental Psychology A*, **44A**, 671–703.

Webster, M.A., Kaping, D., Mizokami, Y. and Duhamel, P. (2004). Adaptation to natural facial categories. *Nature*, **428**, 557–561.

Young, A.W., Hellawell, D. and Hay, D.C. (1987). Configurational information in face perception. *Perception*, **16**, 747–759.

Yovel, G. and Kanwisher, N. (2005). The neural basis of the behavioral face-inversion effect. *Current Biology*, **15**, 2256–2262.

Part V

Disorders: Prosopagnosia, Neuropsychiatric, and Developmental Disorder

Chapter 41

Impairments in Face Perception

Marlene Behrmann, Galia Avidan, Cibu Thomas, and Mayu Nishimura

Introduction

The term "prosopagnosia" refers to the neuropsychological disorder in which individuals, who have normal sensory abilities, including low-level vision, as well as normal intellectual function and language abilities, are unable to recognize faces, sometimes even those of close family members. The anecdotal reports, included in the next section, obtained from three individuals with prosopagnosia, all of whom have participated in our investigations, capture the essence of their impairment. Prosopagnosia is intriguing for cognitive scientists not only because of the dramatic and compelling failures of facial recognition, but also because it affords a unique window into the underlying psychological and neural mechanisms that support normal face perception (see also Young, Chapter 5; Kanwisher and Barton, Chapter 7; and Duchaine, Chapter 42, this volume). In this chapter, we review some of the recent lessons gleaned from the study of prosopagnosia and the implications of these lessons for our understanding of normal face processing. A particular focus of this chapter is on the contrast between two prominent forms of prosopagnosia, one of which results from an acquired brain insult in an otherwise premorbidly normal individual and a second which appears to be lifelong and occurs in the absence of any obvious brain damage, at least as evident on conventional brain imaging. Whereas individuals in the former group are labeled as having "acquired prosopagnosia" (AP), those in the latter group are labeled as having "congenital prosopagnosia" (CP). The term "CP" has been used interchangeably in the literature with "developmental prosopagnosia" (DP) (see also chapter by Duchaine, Chapter 42, this volume) but we have chosen to reserve this latter term for individuals with explicit brain damage acquired early in life (e.g. see case of Farah et al., 2000) and to serve as a contrast with CP in which no frank brain damage is evident on conventional structural imaging.

AP and CP have many commonalities in their overt symptomatology, which we document below. Indeed, understanding the overlap in symptoms but also the differences in these two variants will be particularly revealing and we highlight those similarities and differences here. We acknowledge up front that there is considerable heterogeneity both among CP (Harris et al., 2005; Le Grand, et al., 2006; Minnebusch et al., 2007; Schmalzl et al., 2007) and among AP individuals (Barton, 2008; De Renzi, 1986; De Renzi et al., 1991; Epelbaum, et al., 2008), making it difficult to reach definitive, watertight general conclusions. Indeed, a clear future direction in the study of prosopagnosia will be to identify the varying subpatterns of both CP and AP (if they indeed exist) and the behavioral and neurological concomitants associated with such subpatterns. Despite the apparent heterogeneity, we outline characteristics that are common to the two groups, and point out differences where they exist, exercising caution throughout. Of course, any statements remain open to empirical challenge and we hope that our claims do indeed provoke further examination and testing.

In this chapter, we review two central issues: the first concerns the similarities and differences in the psychological representations of faces in AP and CP, and the second concerns the nature of the underlying neural representations of faces in these two populations. Before we embark on these two issues, however, we provide some additional description of both AP and CP and identify some well-established overlapping behavioral characteristics.

The deficit: acquired prosopagnosia and congenital prosopagnosia

Face perception

The obvious commonality across the AP and CP groups is that individuals in both groups experience marked difficulty in explicit face recognition. While AP is perhaps the better known disorder, because it has been recognized and reported many times since the initial documentation in the work of Bodamer (1947) and because it has been subject to careful scrutiny in many subsequent neuropsychological studies (for recent reviews, see Barton, 2008; Harris and Aguirre, 2007; Kanwisher and Barton, Chapter 7, this volume). Acquired prosopagnosia was also well publicized by Oliver Sacks' *Man who Mistook his Wife for a Hat* and many people are familiar with this book. CP, although recognized as an entity more recently, is becoming increasingly well recognized. From 2008 through early 2010, there were 34 published papers (as listed on PubMed) on AP and 22 on CP. Critically, the anecdotal reports of CP individuals, as illustrated below, capture the same essential features as the documented anecdotes from AP individuals. Here, we include anecdotes from three CP individuals, all of whom have participated in our studies.

> I'm not as badly off as some who don't recognize their families or even themselves, but I do have a hard time recognizing people I meet until I've seen them quite a few times (which can be very embarrassing). I also have a big problem in recognizing people out of context. The other day I saw a co-worker, whom I've known for a number of years and recognize easily at work, at a restaurant and I thought he might be someone I knew a long time ago. It took me several minutes to realize it was him and, of course, it was very embarrassing.

> I grew up in a small town of about 7000 people and most everyone knew everyone else. During high school I worked in the local movie theater and was quite good at selling the tickets, making change by hand and doing the reports that went with it. However, my Mom would say things like, "Mr. and Mrs. X, our neighbors" or "Mary from our church" told me that you are "stuck up." They went to the movies and you sold them a ticket but you didn't say hello to them. I never realized that they were people I knew or was supposed to know. I've always been amazed at how people recognized other people so easily.

> …Also, once after my husband and I had known each other for over 20 years and been married for 10 of them, we were out at a granddaughter's graduation and were separated for a few minutes while he parked the car. He put on a cap and I didn't recognize him when he came up and talked to Mom and me. He went on to help a friend get seated and I said to Mom "Who was that guy?" She was shocked and said "Jo, that was your husband!"

The recognition failures of these CP individuals are dramatic and mirror those of AP. It is also the case that severity per se does not distinguish the AP and CP groups: while there is a range of severity in both groups, there appear to be equally profoundly affected individuals in each group. For example, in one study, in response to a large set of over 100 photographs of famous individuals, all well known to the matched control participants, the CP group consisting of six individuals were able to identify, on average, approximately 40% of the faces, with performance ranging from 34–48%, while the three individuals with AP scored 17%, 34%, and 42% (Avidan et al., 2008; Behrmann et al., 2005). Note that the poor recognition performance for the prosopagnosic individuals is not attributable to a failure of semantic knowledge nor to a failure to label the face per se ("anomia"). Indeed, through questioning undertaken after the recognition experiment (e.g. "Do you know who Marilyn Monroe is?"), we confirm that the participants know the individuals whose faces are shown to them and that their failure to recognize the faces is not because they do not have the name or the semantic knowledge needed for the task.

This comparability of severity among the AP and CP individuals appears to be true not only for explicit recognition of known faces but also for the perception of novel faces, with similar performance across the two groups on a task of discriminating same/different pairs of novel faces (Avidan, et al., 2008; Behrmann, et al., 2005). In one version of this task, two novel faces were presented for an unlimited duration on a computer screen, and individuals simply indicated via button press whether the faces were same or different. When the faces were different, as shown in Figure 41.1, they could be two different gender faces (e.g. one male and one female) or two faces of the same gender albeit two different individuals (e.g. two different female faces). The CP subjects were significantly less accurate (85%) than the matched control subjects (96%) in face discrimination, although both groups performed significantly more accurately than the group of three AP subjects (70%), (F(2, 17) = 5.6, p <0.01). However, the improvement in accuracy in CP over AP apparently came at the cost of speed, as reflected in a speed-accuracy trade-off: the mean reaction time (RT) of the CP group (5285 ms) was significantly longer than that of the AP group (4235 ms), with both groups taking much longer to make decisions than the control group (1528 ms), (F(2, 17) = 7.8, p <0.01). The similarity across the two prosopagnosic groups was also evident on a measure of sensitivity, A', with the CP (0.88) and AP (0.85) groups showing reduced sensitivity, relative to the controls (0.98), (F(2, 17) = 4.1, p <0.05) (see Figure 41.1 for RT and accuracy scores). Taken together, the findings suggest that the problem exhibited by the individuals with prosopagnosia is one of deriving a sufficiently precise and accurate perceptual representation that can then be used to access semantic knowledge, and that this failure in the derivation of a rich visual representation is likely to be true for many, if not all, of the AP and CP individuals.

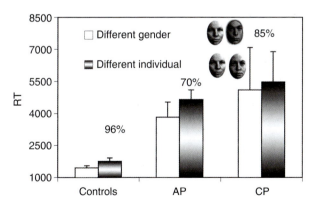

Fig. 41.1 Mean RT (and accuracy averaged across trial type) for trials that differ in gender (a male paired with a female face) or in identity (e.g. two different female faces) for the control participants, and CP and AP groups. The findings illustrate the increase in RT in the two prosopagnosic groups, relative to the controls, and the possible trade-off in speed and accuracy between the CP and AP groups, in the same/different discrimination task of novel faces. Faces obtained courtesy of Heinrich Bülthoff and Niko Troje (Max Planck Institute, Tübingen, Germany).

Eye movement patterns

Despite the overall similarities in behavioral profile, there are also some differences between the groups. One domain in which there may be some divergence between the two groups is in the eye movement patterns as the AP and CP individuals scan faces. There is some evidence that AP individuals fixate the mouth of the observed face more than the eyes, relative to controls (Bukach et al., 2008; Caldara, et al., 2005; Rossion et al., 2009), although this appears not to be the case in every AP individual (Stephan and Caine, 2009). In contrast, CP individuals tend to fixate the external features of faces, such as the hair, neck and chin, irrespective of whether the faces are recognized or not (Schwarzer, et al., 2007), and tend to show reduced dwell time on all inner features (Bate et al., 2008).

These latter findings are also consistent with some unpublished data that we have collected on three CP individuals whose eye movements were measured when they viewed familiar and unfamiliar faces. Our three CP individuals spent most of the scan time exploring the periphery of the face such as the outer contour and hair. Overall, the eye movement patterns in CP suggest that these individuals hunt the entire image for any clues that might be salient or informative, and this includes clues outside the inner features (perhaps the hairline, hairstyle, or earrings, etc). Importantly, none of the CP studies note the undue attention to the mouth region, as has been suggested for AP. Any differences in eye movements between the two groups do not appear to be an obvious result of a fundamental oculomotor deficit. Indeed, under controlled experimental conditions, the ability to discriminate gaze orientation is normal in both AP and CP individuals; that is, when the task requires attending to a particular facial feature, such as eye gaze, rather than the face as a whole, perception appears to be normal. This was demonstrated specifically in a study in six CPs and one AP individual who were able to discriminate between faces with averted and straight eye gaze as well as the normal controls, and in which the CPs and AP also showed expected adaptation aftereffects on gaze discrimination after adapting to leftward or rightward gaze (Duchaine et al., 2009). These findings suggest that prosopagnosic individuals can discern gaze direction normally. When they themselves direct gaze to a face, however, they do not do so normally and so it seems that the encoding or sampling of the faces is differentially affected in the two neuropsychological samples. Why the APs fixate the mouth for extended periods of time and why the CP individuals tend to fixate more on external features remains to be further evaluated and explained.

Of interest, a training program designed to alter the eye movement scanning of a 4-year-old with CP showed a positive outcome (Schmalzl et al., 2008), perhaps attesting further to the altered encoding of faces by individuals with face perception difficulties. At the outset, the prosopagnosic child, K, spent much time scanning the outer features of the face. The training involved teaching her to focus on the internal features of the face and this led to an improvement in her ability to recognize the trained faces but also resulted in some generalization to untrained faces. At this point, we still do not know what causes the abnormal scanning in the first place nor do we know whether the abnormal scan pattern is the cause or outcome of the face recognition deficit. Further studies of possible differences in eye movement patterns between the CP and AP groups are clearly warranted. Elucidating the patterns of encoding and of sampling the face input might shed light on possible group differences and might also be informative about the underlying deficit and possible compensatory reactions in the two prosopagnosic groups.

Facial expression recognition

A further domain in which there seems to be possible divergence between AP and CP is in the recognition of facial expressions. In one study that directly compares the CP and AP groups, along with controls, participants (three CP, two AP, and matched controls) completed a fine-grained expression recognition paradigm requiring a six-alternative forced-choice response to a continua of morphs across pairs of the six different basic facial expressions (e.g. fear and surprise, see Figure 41.2a) (Humphreys et al., 2007). Remarkably, the performance of all three CP individuals was indistinguishable from that of controls. This was true both when the expressions were largely unambiguous (i.e. 90% of one expression and 10% of a different expression), but, more critically, also when more subtle expressions were displayed (i.e. where the morph contained 70% of one expression and 30% of a different expression). In contrast, both individuals with AP displayed pronounced difficulties with the majority of expressions, even those that were relatively unambiguous and easily identified by the controls (see Figure 41.2b for accuracy and Figure 41.2c for LogRT).

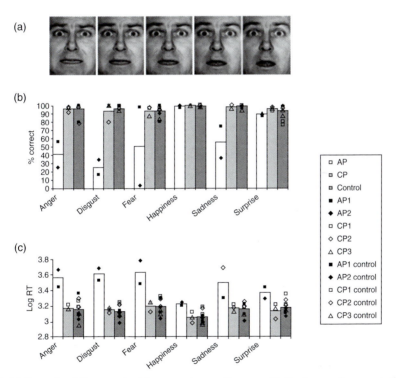

Fig. 41.2 (a) Example of the morphed fear-surprise continuum with the two ends representing unambiguous (90–10%) morphs, the second and fourth representing the 70–30% morphs and the centre representing 50–50% morph. (b) Unambiguous (90–10% morph) expression recognition accuracy and log reaction times for two acquired (AP1 and AP2) and three congenital prosopagnosics (CP1–3) and matched controls, labeled to reflect their yoking to the prosopagnosic individuals. Whereas the CPs and controls show similar patterns of performance both in accuracy and Log RT, this is not true for the APs. Figure reprinted from Humphreys et al. (2007). A detailed investigation of facial expression processing in congenital prosopagnosia as compared to acquired prosopagnosia. *Experimental Brain Research*, **176**, 356–373 with kind permission of Springer Science + Business Media.

The findings of preserved expression recognition in the CP individuals is consistent with the data from Dobel et al. (2007) who also report no difference between their CP and control subjects on emotional expression judgments, with the CP group scoring, on average, 92% correct, and with the data from several other CP individuals including YT (Bentin et al., 1999), EP (Nunn et al., 2001), TA (Jones and Tranel, 2001), NM (Duchaine et al., 2003) and KW (Bentin et al., 2007). We note, however, that not all CP individuals perform normally on expression recognition (Kress and Daum, 2003; Minnebusch, et al., 2007). The preservation of this expression recognition ability amongst some individuals is apparently not contingent on severity: in the Humphreys et al. (2007) study described above, some of the CP and AP individuals were matched on severity of identity impairment with the former showing good emotion comprehension while the latter did not. Of course it remains a possibility that the lesion site in AP is large enough to encompass cortical regions strongly associated with expression recognition, such as the superior temporal sulcus (Gobbini and Haxby, 2006), whereas the neural correlate of CP might be more limited and more circumscribed or might occur further downstream. Whether individuals with AP always evince impairments in expression recognition is also contentious. For example, Tranel and colleagues (1988) described a patient who scored 17/24 (controls 20.6) when asked to make a six-way categorization of facial expressions and Bruyer et al. (1983) also reported relative preservation of facial expression performance by their patient, Mr. W. Note, however, that Calder and Young (2005) in their comprehensive review of the dissociation between identity and recognition, critique some of these findings, leaving it open as to whether there are significant dissociations between identity and expression perception in AP.

Clearly, further research will be required to understand the conditions contributing to the preservation or impairment of emotional expression recognition in CP and AP. That some CP participants continue to be able to judge emotional expression notwithstanding the (sometimes profound) impairment in identity perception, however, attests to the possible dissociability of the processing of facial identity and of facial expression (a topic of ongoing, lively debate in itself; for example, see Calder and Young, 2005; Ganel et al., 2005).

Underlying psychological representations

Although we have made progress in understanding some aspects of both forms of prosopagnosia, we still do not have a definitive understanding of the nature (and perturbation) of the underlying psychological representations of faces in these populations. One useful framework for understanding the mental representation of facial identity is face-space, a multidimensional cognitive map in which individual faces are coded relative to the average of previously encountered faces, and in which the distance among faces represent their perceived similarity. The average of previously experienced faces is represented at the origin of the face-space, and individual identities are defined by unique vectors from the origin (Valentine, 1991). The distance from the origin represents the distinctiveness of a face because, by definition, typical faces should look more like the average face and therefore be located closer to the average. The direction from the origin represents how the face deviates from average, that is, along what particular facial dimension the face is distinct. Such a coding scheme results in a face-space layout such that the distance between two faces represents the perceived similarity of those faces (the smaller the distance, the more similar the faces), and many faces cluster around the average whereas few faces sparsely occupy the periphery. Face-space has been a useful framework to account for many empirical findings of face perception, including faster recognition of distinctive faces and enhanced recognition of caricatures (i.e. enhancing some distinctive facial feature, like Jay Leno's lower jaw) (e.g. Rhodes, 1987), because both increased distinctiveness and caricaturing moves the face away from the average into an area of lower spatial density, leading to fewer confusion errors.

A key question is whether individuals with AP and those with CP evince behavior that is consistent with the face-space representational schema. To examine this, six CPs and one AP individual, along with matched controls, completed a series of experiments involving judgments of facial identity (Nishimura et al., 2010). Digital images of male and female faces were morphed to varying degrees, relative to an average face, to create caricatures, anti-caricatures, and anti-faces (i.e. faces of the opposite identity; see Figure 41.3a). Across five behavioral tasks, CP individuals' performance was similar to that of the control group and was consistent with the face-space framework, whereas the AP individual's performance deviated significantly from both the control and the CP groups. For example, in one task, participants learned to classify morphs of two faces, Dan and Jim, as Team Dan or Team Jim and were then adapted to either anti-Jim (a face that differs from the average in a manner opposite to Jim) or anti-Dan. Comparison of participants' classification on the initial trials compared with the post-adaptation trials revealed shifts in classification (i.e. adapted to anti-Dan, participants classified a morphed average face more often as Dan than as Jim) and, moreover, this was equally true for the CPs and their matched controls (see Figure 41.3b and c). These results show that the CPs evince a normal identity aftereffect as reflected in the transient bias in perception of facial identity. In contrast, the single AP individual did not show the normal adaptation profile and, instead, showed a rather erratic and variable classification pattern suggesting that he did not share the same underlying face-space as the controls and CP (see Figure 41.3d). One might be surprised by the fact that the CP individuals perform so well—recall, though, that all that was required for this task is the initial acquisition of two identities, Jim and Dan, and that the CP individuals were clearly able to do this (see baseline of CP and controls on Figure 41.3b and c). Given this, they were then able to evince normal identity aftereffects on these two faces. Presumably, if they were required to differentiate between more than just two faces, or to make the distinction between faces after minimal training (e.g. just a single exposure), they might have had greater difficulty doing so than they did with the current paradigm that involved learning two faces over many trials.

A similar distinction between CP and AP was also seen in a subsequent set of experiments that employed caricatures and anti-caricatures as stimuli. Of note, physical deviation from a veridical image is equated between caricatures and anti-caricatures (each is morphed 50% relative to an average of a large set of faces but caricatures are morphed away from the average whereas anti-caricatures are morphed closer to the average), and notwithstanding the equivalent absolute manipulation of the image, observers perceive the anti-caricature to be less like the veridical image than the caricature (e.g. Benson and Perrett, 1981; Lee et al., 2000). This pattern of results is consistent with the face-space framework because anti-caricaturing results in moving the face into a high-density region, making recognition more difficult. If faces are coded relative to the average, then caricatures should be perceived as more distinctive than anti-caricatures, and they should also be perceived to be more like the original identity than anti-caricatures. The CP participants performed equivalently to the normal controls, perceiving caricatures as more distinctive than anti-caricatures (see Figure 41.4) and more like the original identity. The AP individual shows a similar pattern to the CP and the controls albeit not equivalent quantitatively.

Taken together, these findings differentiate between the behavioral profiles of CP and AP individuals, and suggest that, despite an inability to recognize individual identities, CPs perceive faces in a manner consistent with norm-based coding of facial identity. How the CPs acquired this face-space remains fascinating but puzzling given their lifelong difficulty with faces. One possibility is that their underlying face-space representation is supported by a feature-based strategy, rather than one that is holistic, and this would be consistent with the many observations that CP individuals tend to have more locally- rather than globally- or configurally-derived facial representations (Behrmann and Avidan, 2005). If so, this might suggest that even if they have what

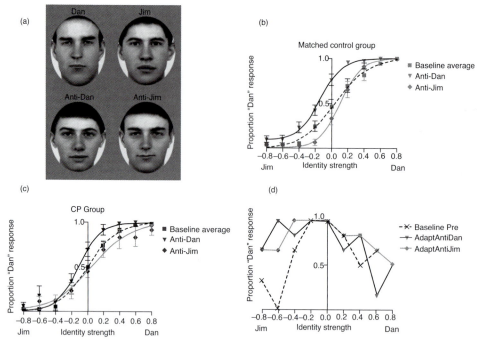

Fig. 41.3 (a) Examples of the Dan and Jim faces shown to participants for initial learning, as well as the anti-Dan and anti-Jim faces shown during adaptation. (b–d) Proportion "Dan" responses as a function of identity strength on pre-adaptation baseline trials and on post-adaptation Dan and Jim trials, for b) matched controls, c) CP group, and d) one AP individual. The point of subjective equality (PSE) is the identity strength at which the curve is equal to 0.5 on the y-axis, where observers are equally likely to respond "Team Dan" and "Team Jim." Reprinted from *Neuropsychologia*, Nishimura, Doyle, Humphreys, and Behrmann, Probing the face-space of individuals with prosopagnosia. Copyright (2010), with permission from Elsevier.

appears to be an intact face-space, this is not completely accurate as their mental representations are derived on the basis of features, rather than wholes, in contrast with the controls. Much work remains to be done to shed light on the nature of representations that support CP and AP face processing but these findings are potentially intriguing. We also note that because we only included one AP individual here, generalizing the result to other APs should be done with caution and replication of our findings will be helpful in understanding the generality of the AP pattern.

Consistent with the above results from the CP individuals showing that there is some integrity in the underlying face representations in these individuals, some, although apparently not all (Bentin, et al., 1999; De Haan and Campbell, 1991), individuals with CP show evidence of implicit processing of faces as evident in indirect RT or accuracy measures, or eye movement patterns. Controls' scanning patterns typically show a reduction in the number and duration of fixations, reduced attention to the inner features, and reduced sampling of regions in response to known than novel faces. A CP individual, AA, showed similar effects (such as fewer regions sampled and less attention to internal features), although these effects were not entirely normal as, unlike the controls, there was no difference in the fixation count and duration for famous versus novel faces (Bate, et al., 2008). That AA showed a reduction of sampling when re-viewing known faces that

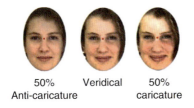

50% Anti-caricature   Veridical   50% caricature

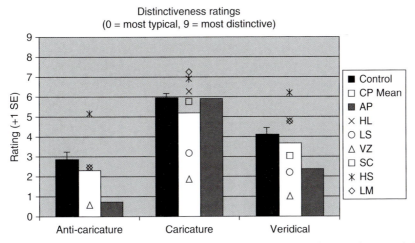

Fig. 41.4 Mean distinctiveness ratings for anti-caricatures, caricatures, and veridical images (original identities), for matched controls, CP group (and each individual separately too), and the AP individual. Reprinted from *Neuropsychologia*, Nishimura, Doyle, Humphreys, and Behrmann, Probing the face-space of individuals with prosopagnosia. Copyright (2010), with permission from Elsevier.

are unrecognizable in explicit tasks, is taken as evidence of an intact underlying structural description in this individual, and this is consistent with the findings reported above of a well-structured face-space in CP.

Finally, there is some evidence that, despite the marked impairment in explicit face recognition, CP individuals still have some familiarity representation, which manifests in the form of covert recognition. In one such study, participants completed a matching task with both famous (e.g. Bill Clinton, Harrison Ford) and unknown faces (celebrities in other countries) in which they decided whether two consecutive images share the same identity or not (Avidan and Behrmann, 2008). Critically, the level of face familiarity was orthogonal to the task at hand and this enabled us to examine whether the familiarity of a face enhanced identity matching, a finding that would implicate implicit face processing. As expected, the CP individuals were slower and less accurate overall than the control participants (see Figure 41.5 for data from RT; data using accuracy as the dependent measure yielded the same results). Not surprisingly, in trials with famous faces that were recognized, like the controls (Young et al., 1988), the CP individuals were faster and more accurate at matching different images of the same individual compared to trials with unknown faces (last bars in Figure 41.5 in each panel). Most critically, for both groups, matching performance for famous faces that were not explicitly recognized (as assessed in a separate testing session) fell at an intermediate level between performances on explicitly recognized famous faces and faces which are unknown. The facilitation for famous faces, even when not explicitly recognized, indicates that there is some level of processing that allows for differentiation between famous and unknown faces and, as such, these data provide evidence for the existence of implicit familiarity processing in CP.

A particularly dramatic demonstration of preservation of implicit knowledge of faces comes from the study of the severely congenitally prosopagnosic individual, TA, who was assessed at age 5 (Jones and Tranel, 2001). Of most relevance here is that the familiar faces that TA could not recognize overtly were discriminated covertly with skin conductance responses, paralleling an established finding in adults with acquired prosopagnosia (Bauer, 1984; Tranel and Damasio, 1985).

In a final recent study on implicit processing (Striemer et al., 2009), a single CP individual showed better performance in deciding whether a face was famous or not when the face was preceded by the correct name (referred to as the "true face effect") compared to the incorrect name (see also Young et al., 1988). This provides further support for the implicit processing of faces in CP. However, unlike the control participants, this CP individual did not show faster face classification when the face was preceded by a semantically related name than an unknown name (see also Barton et al., 2004). Based on these findings, the authors conclude that some individuals with CP may be able to acquire sufficient face-related information but that this is possible perhaps only to a limited degree. Consistent with this, patient KW reported by Bentin et al. (2007) did not show any evidence of implicit processing when matching faces with names but her performance was considerably more accurate and faster in a different matching task when the correct alternative had the same expression as the target face than when the expressions differed, showing some

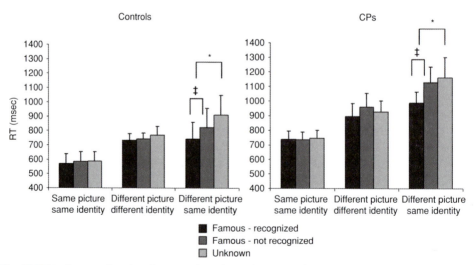

Fig. 41.5 Median reaction time for controls and CPs during the face identity matching task split by explicit recognition of the same faces tested beforehand on a face recognition task. As evident, both controls and CPs exhibited an intermediate level of processing in RT for famous faces who were not explicitly recognized (dark gray bars) during the "different picture, same identity" condition. *Significance level of p <0.05 on planned comparison test. ‡p values which were marginally significant (p =0 .06). From Avidan and Behrmann (2008a); Reproduced with permission from *Journal of Neuropsychology*, © The British Psychological Society.

implicit processing, even if only to a limited degree. As stated (almost repetitively now!), there remains much research to be done to understand how and why and under what conditions CP and AP individuals can or cannot process faces implicitly. This remains an exciting challenge not only for those interested in face perception but also for those interested in perception without awareness, more generally.

Underlying neural representations

To date, only a relatively small number of studies have conducted neural investigations of AP and CP, although an increasing number of studies are currently being undertaken and their data published. On some recent accounts (Gobbini and Haxby, 2006; Ishai, 2008), the face network is comprised of a posterior "core" network, including the fusiform gyrus (fusiform face area or FFA), the occipital face area (OFA) and the superior temporal sulcus (STS), and a more anterior "extended" network, including parts of the anterior temporal lobe and frontal cortex, some of which may be engaged in representing faces in working memory (Druzgal and D'Esposito, 2003; Morgan et al., 2008). Considerations of the structural and functional integrity of both core and extended regions is becoming increasingly important in considering the neural basis of both CP and AP as both regions appear to play a critical role in supporting intact face recognition (Fairhall and Ishai, 2007; Gobbini and Haxby, 2006; Ishai, 2008; for further discussion of the neural machinery underlying face perception, see Freiwald and Tsao, Chapter 36, this volume).

Neuroimaging: structural

In obvious and marked distinction with the CP individuals, the AP individuals suffer from prosopagnosia following an explicit insult to the brain (for example, following a traumatic brain injury, tumor, or vascular accident), and the site of damage in cases of AP has been well characterized in a series of papers reviewing large numbers of cases (Barton, 2003, 2008; Barton, et al., 2002; Bouvier and Engel, 2006). In summary, in almost all cases of acquired prosopagnosia, the lesion is to the occipitotemporal area, either bilaterally or just in the right hemisphere (Sergent and Signoret, 1992). For example, in a review of 10 cases with prosopagnosia, Barton (2008) observed that familiar face recognition is primarily a result of a lesion to the bilateral occipitotemporal cortices, although a unilateral (right lateralized) lesion will also suffice. Note, however, that in cases with a unilateral lesion, the deficit may not be as severe as the bilateral cases (De Renzi, et al., 1991).

  In recent years, there have been a number of detailed analyses of the lesion site in some cases with AP. For example, in a series of studies with one well known AP individual, PS, the authors revealed extensive lesions of the right inferior occipital cortex and left mid-fusiform gyrus, with minor damage to the left posterior cerebellum and the right middle temporal gyrus (for detailed anatomical data, see Sorger et al., 2007). Another example of detailed neuroanatomical analysis in AP is of patient MS who suffered from idiopathic herpes encephalitis and who has ventromedial damage bilaterally involving the lingual and the fusiform gyri, and the right temporal pole with the second, third, and fourth temporal gyri all implicated in the lesion (Arnott et al., 2008). As evident from these illustrative cases, the primary site of damage in most cases of AP is to the posterior "core" network and the necessary contribution of these posterior regions suggests a rather obvious conclusion that a lesion to one of these regions impairs the ability to recognize faces (for a related TMS study, see Pitcher et al., 2007; see also Pitcher et al., Chapter 19, this volume). There are, however, a few reported cases where the damage is to more anterior regions (Barton, 2008; Rapcsak, et al., 2001) and we also know that damage to more anterior regions can give rise to a form of anterograde amnesia called "prosopamnesia," in which the individual has difficulty learning new faces (Crane and Milner, 2002; Tippett et al., 2000; Williams et al., 2007). In contrast with prosopagnosia in which the individual is impaired at face recognition, and in which this deficit holds both for previously seen faces and for novel faces, individuals with prosopamnesia can discriminate between familiar and unfamiliar faces, and, with repeated exposure, can come to acquire facial representations. However, the ability to establish stable representations of previously unfamiliar faces is abnormal (Williams et al., 2007).

We also note that there is a growing literature describing cases of AP following degenerative conditions such as frontotemporal dementia and semantic dementia (Josephs, et al., 2009) and following temporal lobe atrophy which appears to be a separate syndromic variant of frontotemporal lobar degeneration (Chan, et al., 2009; Jourbert et al., 2004). Cases with these degenerative conditions show difficulties with face recognition but the details of their behavioral profile and the correspondence between the behavior and the brain alterations remains to be examined further and, although these cases are intriguing, we do not consider them in this chapter.

Although CP individuals do not have an obvious cortical lesion, there have been some attempts to identify possible structural abnormalities that might explain the face recognition impairment. For example, whereas almost all the studies endorse the absence of any obvious structural changes on conventional MRI (and, in fact, this is one of the criteria for inclusion in the CP group), two studies have indicated the presence of volumetric differences in the temporal cortex of CP individuals, relative to controls. In one study, in which both structural and functional measures were obtained (see below for more details), CP individual, YT, had a smaller right temporal lobe than the controls (Bentin et al., 1999). This was replicated in a group of six CP individuals in whom detailed volumetric measurement uncovered a smaller right anterior fusiform region and a larger right anterior and middle temporal gyrus (Behrmann et al., 2007). No volumetric differences were observed in the hippocampus or parahippocampal region in these individuals, suggesting that it is not the entire temporal cortex that is reduced but rather that it is the anterior portion of the fusiform gyrus, the pre-eminent structure for face processing that is only affected. Importantly, too, the reduction in the anterior fusiform volume is significantly correlated with the severity of the face recognition impairment (less volume, greater impairment). This finding is particularly intriguing in light of the recent reports of face-selective (and even selectivity for individual faces) activation in anterior inferior temporal cortex, as revealed in functional imaging of both humans and non-human primates (see below). While it is suggestive that the loss of anterior fusiform volume is associated with the face recognition decrement, what is not known from these volumetric studies is whether the alterations in the anterior fusiform region arises from a reduction in gray matter or white matter or both.

A recent investigation using voxel-based morphometry, however, has shed further light on this issue (Garrido, et al., 2009). An analysis based on segmentation of T1-weighted images from 17 CP and 18 controls revealed that the CPs had reduced gray matter volume in the right anterior inferior temporal lobe and in the superior temporal sulcus/middle temporal gyrus bilaterally. A voxel-based morphometry analysis based on the segmentation of magnetization transfer parameter maps showed that developmental prosopagnosics also had reduced gray matter volume in the right middle fusiform gyrus and the inferior temporal gyrus. Moreover, there was an association between a behavioral component (aggregation of several behavioral tasks) related to facial identity and gray matter volume in the left superior temporal sulcus/middle temporal gyrus plus the right middle fusiform gyrus/inferior temporal gyrus.

One recent investigation that has examined the structural status of the white matter tracts in CP quantified the macro- and microstructural integrity of the two major white matter tracts that project through the posterior regions of the distributed face network to the more anterior regions. In this study, Thomas and colleagues (2009) used diffusion tensor imaging (DTI) and tractography to map out the inferior longitudinal fasciculus (ILF) and inferior fronto-occipital fasciculus (IFOF), large white matter tracts which project through the fusiform gyrus and terminate, respectively, in the anterior temporal lobe or in the frontal lobe. The key result was that there was a significant difference in the density and volume of the fibers (number of fibers and number of voxels through which these project), as well as a reduction in structural coherence as reflected by the reduction in fractional anisostropy or coherence of these tracts in CP compared with controls (see Figure 41.6). Again, there was also a functional correlation with behavior in that the extent of the reduction in the inferior longitudinal fasciculus was associated with the decrement in face recognition. Note though that the correlation analysis was performed across all individuals who participated, not just the CP, given the small number of CP participants. These findings are

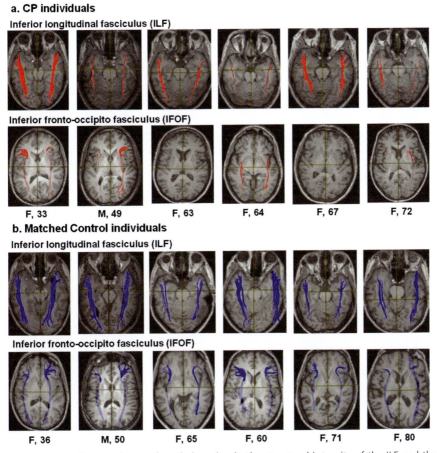

a. CP individuals

Inferior longitudinal fasciculus (ILF)

Inferior fronto-occipito fasciculus (IFOF)

F, 33   M, 49   F, 63   F, 64   F, 67   F, 72

b. Matched Control individuals

Inferior longitudinal fasciculus (ILF)

Inferior fronto-occipito fasciculus (IFOF)

F, 36   M, 50   F, 65   F, 60   F, 71   F, 80

Fig. 41.6 Tractography reveals a profound alteration in the structural integrity of the ILF and the IFOF in individuals with congenital prosopagnosia compared with their matched controls. Further analyses confirmed a reduction in the microstructural integrity of white matter along the trajectory of the ILF and IFOF in both hemispheres. Axial slices showing the bilateral ILF and the IFOF in (a) individuals with congenital prosopagnosia and (b) their matched controls. The gender and age of each individual with congenital prosopagnosia and their matched control is indicated below each slice. From Thomas et al. (2009), Reduced structural connectivity in ventral visual cortex in congenital prosopagnosia. *Nature Neuroscience*.

provocative as they seem to implicate a disconnection between more posterior "core" regions and more anterior "extended" regions of the face network. Whether the white matter decrement is the cause or outcome of the reduced gray matter volume (Garrido et al., 2009) remains to be determined. Note that there is growing evidence for similar perturbations of connectivity between posterior and more anterior cortical systems in other neurodevelopmental disorders like developmental dyslexia (Keller and Just, 2009), synesthesia (Rouw and Scholte, 2007), and congenital amusia (Peretz et al., 2009), suggesting that a more fundamental disruption in cortical circuitry supporting specific cognitive abilities may underlie a wide range of higher order cognitive processes (for further information regarding the neurodevelopment of face perception, see de Haan, Chapter 38, this volume).

Taken together, the analyses of the structural differences in CP, relative to control individuals, are beginning to uncover some subtle alterations in ventral temporal cortex, and while these changes are not visible on conventional MRI scanning, they are evident on other more detailed analyses. Further research is clearly needed to understand better the nature of these changes and whether they are the cause or effect of the behavioral difficulty in face recognition.

Neuroimaging: functional

Whereas the findings from the structural imaging studies are clearer for AP than for CP given the presence of an explicit lesion, the reverse holds true for the functional imaging studies. Thus, it is not surprising to see the absence of typical face-related activation in the AP individuals given the explicit brain damage, but the absence of major changes in vasculature in CP provides a unique opportunity to explore the functional integrity of the "core" and "extended" regions of the face network.

Although only a few functional MRI studies have examined the status of the ventral occipital network in AP individuals, their findings are interesting. For example, in two individuals with lesions that affected the fusiform gyrus per se, face selective activation was observed more posteriorly in either the right or left hemisphere and not in the normal fusiform face area per se (Marotta et al., 2001). In contrast, normal FFA activation was observed in a woman, PS, with AP following tissue loss in the right inferior lateral occipital lobe and the left medial temporal lobe. Despite the fact that the left OFA was affected, a normal pattern of face selectivity was observed in the right FFA (Rossion, et al., 2003; Schiltz, et al., 2006; Sorger, et al., 2007). A similar finding has been reported in which a normal pattern of face related activation was noted both in FFA and in STS in an AP patient, DF, with severe visual agnosia and prosopagnosia with damage to the OFA (Steeves, et al., 2006). In a more recent study of these same individuals, a comparison of faces to non-face objects elicited activation in all visual areas of the cortical face processing network that were spared subsequent to brain damage in both PS and DF (Steeves et al., 2009). Intriguingly, despite the lesion to the right OFA, there was a normal range of sensitivity to faces in the right FFA in both patients, but sensitivity to individual face representations, as explored via an adaptation protocol, revealed that the right FFA responses were abnormal. Not all AP individuals, however, continue to reveal face-selectivity: in two other individuals with brain damage sustained during childhood (GA, RP), there was reduction or elimination of face-selectivity (Hadjikhani and De Gelder, 2002) and similar activations for faces and houses were found in the typical FFA region. In fact, there was no face-selective activation in any area along the ventral visual pathway even when a permissive statistical threshold was used.

There are now a small series of functional imaging studies in CP but the results are rather controversial. Some individuals do not show any face-related activation (Bentin et al., 2007; Hadjikhani and de Gelder, 2002) whereas others apparently do. For example, in a group of 4 CP individuals, we (Avidan et al., 2005) reported a normal pattern of functional magnetic resonance imaging (fMRI) activation in the fusiform gyrus (FFA) and in other ventral occipitotemporal (VOT) areas, in response to faces, buildings and other objects, shown as line drawings (in a subsequent study we replicated these findings with three other CP individuals, too; Avidan et al., 2008). Of interest, these individuals performed a one-back task on these different stimulus classes and even though their behavioral performance was statistically significantly poorer than the matched controls, their cortical pattern of BOLD activation was equivalent to that of the control group. These same individuals also showed a normal pattern of adaptation (reduced BOLD signal to repeated over non-repeated stimuli) for faces and for other objects throughout ventral temporal cortex. A similar pattern has been reported by other groups. CP individual YT (who also showed reduced face selectivity in an event-related potential (ERP) study) exhibited face-related activation in ventral visual cortex that mirrored that of normal individuals in terms of site of activation, activation profile, and hemispheric laterality (Hasson, et al., 2003), and the CP individual studied by Degutis et al. (2007) showed significant face-related activation in the FFA and inferior occipital gyrus (IOG; akin to the OFA region). We have also obtained normal face-selective activation in the "core" regions using a protocol in which participants watch a series of vignettes (say of faces or of common objects) concatenated into a fluid movie (see Figure 41.7) (Avidan et al., 2008). As shown in Figure 41.7, all seven CP individuals show FFA activation remarkably like those of their matched typical controls. Other studies which typically examined face activation with three or four CP individuals (Minnebusch et al., 2009; Van den Stock et al., 2008) have obtained more mixed findings: whereas a subset of individuals evince normal face-related activation, others do not. And while some of the individuals reveal activation in, for example, FFA but not in IOG, others show the reverse. Clearly, these mixed findings are problematic and considerable effort is being made to understand this variability.

A number of possible explanations can be offered for this heterogeneity of findings. One immediate possibility is that the variability in the behavioral profile and the fMRI results (extent of activation of face-related cortex) is correlated with the severity of impairment. This issue clearly goes back to the question about the definition of CP and the means whereby this entity should be diagnosed. A further possible source of difference between these studies is the contrasts employed: whereas some studies compare face-related activation with that of object-related activation, others compare faces against scenes/places. There are also differences in the stimuli, with some studies using faces with neutral facial expressions while others used emotional faces. It is the case that as more imaging studies come to fruition, the range of possible outcomes and the extent to which face-related activation is normal or is indeed atypical in CP (or whether there is heterogeneity that is tied to severity or some other factor) will be clarified. One confounding problem that will need to be confronted in the fMRI data, however, is the reliability of the FFA or face-selective activation more generally as a marker of intact face processing. We know from studies that include the data from the individual participants (not just the group mean) that not every normal individual shows FFA activation. For example, in one study with typical adults, only 12 of the 15 participants showed fusiform activation for faces (Kanwisher et al., 1997), and whereas all 17 individuals did so in the right FFA in a more recent study (Yovel et al., 2008), only 15 out of 17 showed it in the left FFA, and 15/17 did so in the right OFA and 10/17 in the left OFA. In a study that we conducted, 14 out of 15 individuals showed face-selective right FFA activation but only seven showed it in the left FFA (Humphreys et al., 2008). Of course, the experimental conditions differ in these experiments–for example, some experiments use passive viewing and others require overt responses. And even if passive viewing is used, some studies like Kanwisher et al. (1997) have participants watch individual displays of faces or of a contrast category like houses, whereas in our study, participants watched a rich, colorful movie containing concatenated vignettes of faces, navigation scenes or houses in a fluid movie format. Given some variability even in the typical population, it will be critical to

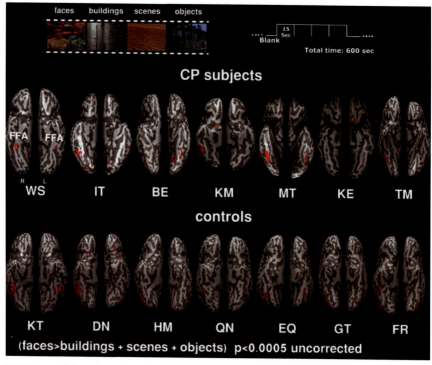

Fig. 41.7 Maps of face-related activation in the fusiform face area (FFA) of seven CP subjects and seven controls. For each subject, the data are presented on an inflated brain representation shown from a ventral view. As is evident, the CP individuals exhibit similar activation patterns to those of controls, thus indicating normal face-related activation in the fusiform gyrus. The maps were obtained from the motion picture experiment in which short video clips were presented to the subjects (top of figure) and face activation was obtained by contrasting the BOLD signal generated during the perception of faces with that of all other stimuli (buildings, scenes, objects) at $p<0.0005$ for each subject (uncorrected). Reprinted from Avidan et al. (2009), An Integrative Approach Towards Understanding the Psychological and Neural Basis of Congenital Prospopagnosia, © 2009, with permission from Cambridge University Press.

understand the distribution of face-related activation in the normal population, under differing experimental conditions, before we can reach definitive conclusions about CP.

There has only been one fMRI study conducted to date on an individual with prosopamnesia— this individual demonstrated normal attenuation of the PPA (parahippocampal place area; a region showing selective activation to houses) and FFA activation to repeated presentations of houses and familiar faces, respectively, but no adaptation in the BOLD signal to unfamiliar faces. These findings suggest that in developmental prosopamnesia, the FFA cannot maintain stable representations of previously unknown faces for subsequent recall or recognition (Williams, et al., 2007). Whether this individual really has a difficulty only for memory for new faces or also has some problem in discriminating novel faces is contested by some as she attained a score of 36/54 on the Benton Face Recognition test, which puts her below the normal score of 41.

The presence of FFA adaptation, as reported above, is observed both in prosopamnesia as well as in CP individuals with perceptual, rather than mnemonic, difficulties. Avidan and Behrmann

(2009) showed that six individuals with CP, all of whom have difficulties in perceptual discrimination as well as face recognition, all showed adaptation in FFA. Whether the FFA adaptation is mediated by the same computational mechanism in prosopamnesia and prosopagnosia remains to be determined. Interestingly, both the prosopamnesic and the prosopagnosic individuals do not exhibit entirely normal patterns of selectivity. In the former case, the FFA response is restricted to previously familiar but not unfamiliar faces and in the latter, there is a lack of selectivity in other regions in a contrast of famous versus unknown faces. These regions include left posterior cingulate and medial frontal anterior paracingulate cortex, sites previously documented in other studies of repetition priming with faces in association with familiarity and biographical knowledge. In addition to understanding the differences between these two disorders of face processing, a key question is how the initial representations (that show adaptation for faces in FFA) are acquired in the first place in these two types of individuals. This issue is closely related to the questions posed earlier in the discussion about the structure of face-space in CP and how identity aftereffects are mediated in these individuals. Issues about both the psychological and neural representations in CP are also relevant for the possibility of intervention and the potential for learning in individuals with prosopamnesia, and with prosopagnosia, more generally.

At present, there are only a few studies, which have used ERP or magnetoencephalography (MEG) to explore the physiology in CP compared to that of controls, and the findings are rather inconsistent. In normal individuals, there is a typical face selective waveform peaking at about 130 to 200 ms after stimulus onset that can be detected in both ERP (N170) and MEG (M170) and the neuronal origins of both the N170 and M170 might be located in the posterior fusiform gyri (Corrigan, et al., 2009; Deffke, et al., 2007). Some of the ERP studies have revealed reduced face selectivity in individuals with CP (Bentin et al., 1999, 2007; Kress and Daum, 2003) but, in one ERP study, the authors found that three CP participants exhibited normal N170 while only one subject exhibited reduced face selectivity in the N170 response (Minnebusch et al., 2007). Such heterogeneity is also apparent in a MEG study (Harris et al., 2005) in which two out of five CP individuals exhibited a normal response but the remaining three individuals did not exhibit a face selective response in their MEG pattern. A recent MEG study of seven CP individuals contrasted the MEG signal for familiar versus unfamiliar faces and upright versus inverted faces (Dobel et al., 2008). Compared to controls, the CP participants displayed a general decrease in brain activity, primarily over left occipitotemporal areas and this was unaffected by familiarity or orientation.

Summary and conclusions

A number of different populations suffer from some impairment in face processing. We have chosen two neuropsychological populations in whom to explore the brain–behavior relationship: individuals with AP and individuals with CP. We have explored the similarities and differences in these two populations, as revealed in a whole host of behavioral and neural investigations. While, on the surface, the behavioral manifestations for most, if not all, individuals are similar with respect to face recognition and discrimination (although bearing in mind that the expression recognition and eye movement patterns may differ), it is more difficult to understand whether there is any commonality in the neural basis of the behavioral difficulty. As reviewed above, in AP there is a clear lesion, most often to the posterior core regions of the face network, but in a smaller number of cases, to the more anterior regions. In CP, again in many but not all cases (see above for detailed discussion of the heterogeneity), face-selective activation of posterior regions is evident, but this is not so for more anterior regions observed in typical individuals. Furthermore, both volumetric and DTI measures suggest that there may be a lack of connectivity between the more posterior and anterior, extended regions. One possibility, albeit speculative, is to consider whether both forms emerge from a disruption of the distributed face network: lesions to nodes, either posterior or anterior, would certainly interfere with the effective communication of this network and reductions in structural connectivity, as revealed in CP, would have similar consequences. The idea of higher-level pattern recognition arising from a disconnection of key areas from each other is not novel. While this has always been a key concept in explaining neuropsychological disorders (Catani and Mesulam, 2008; Geschwind, 1965), increasing current evidence is accumulating both in the domain of faces (Fox et al., 2008) and in the domain of words (Epelbaum, et al., 2008), and has even been considered in the case of cortical–subcortical disconnections (Jacome, 1986). Clearly, more fine-tuned measures than simple ROI analyses that are in current use will be needed to better delineate the face network in typical individuals, and perhaps better methods for examining structural integrity in affected individuals, too. Improved methods for diagnosis of CP and more standardized behavioral measures both in and out of the scanner will help provide a broader and perhaps more consistent picture of incidence and variability in this population. It might be possible that computational models with sufficient precision might be able to predict the heterogeneity of symptoms in CP and AP depending on which component of the network is damaged, and these same models might provide some indications of the efficacy of intervention. Suffice it to say that the study of face recognition continues to intrigue scientists and the lay population alike, and the advent of more precise technology to examine neural structure and function and their relation to genetics offers an unprecedented examination of the cortical substrate of high-level pattern recognition.

References

Arnott, S.R., Heywood, C.A., Kentridge, R.W., and Goodale, M.A. (2008). Voice recognition and the posterior cingulate: an fMRI study of prosopagnosia. *Journal of Neuropsychology*, **2**, 269–286.

Avidan, G. and Behrmann, M. (2008). Implicit familiarity processing in congenital prosopagnosia. *Journal of Neuropsychology*, **2**, 141–164.

Avidan, G. and Behrmann, M. (2009). Functional MRI reveals compromised neural integrity of the face processing network in congenital prosopagnosia. *Current Biology*, **19**, 1146–1150.

Avidan, G., Hasson, U., Malach, R., and Behrmann, M. (2005). Detailed exploration of face-related processing in congenital prosopagnosia: 2. Functional neuroimaging findings. *Journal of Cognitive Neuroscience*, **17**, 1150–1167.

Avidan, G., Thomas, C., and Behrmann, M. (2009). An integrative approach to understanding the psychological and neural basis of congenital prosopagnosia. In M. Jenkins and L. Harris (eds.), *Cortical Mechanisms of Vision*, pp. 209–235. Cambridge: Cambridge University Press.

Barton, J.J.S. (2003). Disorders of face perception and recognition. *Neurologic Clinics*, **21**, 521–548.

Barton, J.J.S. (2008). Structure and function in acquired prosopagnosia: lessons from a series of 10 patients with brain damage. *Journal of Neuropsychology*, **2**, 197–225.

Barton, J.J.S., Press, D.Z., Keenan, J.P., and O'Connor, M. (2002). Lesions of the fusiform face area impair perception of facial configuration in prosopagnosia. *Neurology*, **58**, 71–78.

Barton, J.J.S., Cherkasova, M.V., and Hefter, R. (2004). The covert priming effect of faces in prosopagnosia. *Neurology*, **63**, 2062–2068.

Bate, S., Haslam, C., Tree, J.J., and Hodgson, T.L. (2008). Evidence of an eye movement-based memory effect in congenital prosopagnosia. *Cortex*, **44**, 806–819.

Bauer, R.M. (1984). Autonomic recognition of names and faces in prosopagnosia: a neuropsychological application of the Guilty Knowledge Test. *Neuropsychologia*, **22**, 457–469.

Behrmann, M. and Avidan, G. (2005). Congenital prosopagnosia: face-blind from birth. *Trends in Cognitive Science*, **9**, 180–187.

Behrmann, M., Avidan, G., Marotta, J.J., and Kimchi, R. (2005). Detailed exploration of face-related processing in congenital prosopagnosia: 1. Behavioral findings. *Journal of Cognitive Neuroscience,* **17**, 1130–1149.

Behrmann, M., Avidan, G., Gao, F., and Black, S. (2007). Structural imaging reveals anatomical alterations in inferotemporal cortex in congenital prosopagnosia. *Cerebral Cortex,* **17**, 2354–2363.

Benson, P.J. and Perrett, D.I. (1981). Perception and recognition of photographic quality facial caricatures: Implications for the recognition of natural images. *European Journal of Cognitive Psychology,* **3**, 105–135.

Bentin, S., Deouell, L.Y., and Soroker, N. (1999). Selective visual streaming in face recognition: evidence from developmental prosopagnosia. *NeuroReport,* **10**, 823–827.

Bentin, S., Degutis, J.M., D'Esposito, M., and Robertson, L.C. (2007). Too many trees to see the forest: performance, event-related potential, and functional magnetic resonance imaging manifestations of integrative congenital prosopagnosia. *Journal of Cognitive Neuroscience,* **19**, 132–146.

Bodamer, J. (1947). Die Prosop-agnosie. *Archiv für Psychiatrie und Nervkrankheiten,* **179**, 6–53.

Bouvier, S.E. and Engel, S.A. (2006). Behavioral deficits and cortical damage loci in cerebral achromatopsia. *Cerebral Cortex,* **16**, 183–191.

Bruyer, R., Laterre, C., Seron, X., Feyereisen, P., Strypstein, E., Pierrard, E., *et al.* (1983). A case of prosopagnosia with some preserved covert remembrance of familiar faces. *Brain and Cognition,* **2**, 257–284.

Bukach, C.M., Le Grand, R., Kaiser, M.D., Bub, D.N., and Tanaka, J.W. (2008). Preservation of mouth region processing in two cases of prosopagnosia. *Journal of Neuropsychology,* **2**, 227–244.

Caldara, R., Schyns, P., Mayer, E., Smith, M.L., Gosselin, F., and Rossion, B. (2005). Does prosopagnosia take the eyes out of face representations? Evidence for a defect in representing diagnostic facial information following brain damage. *Journal of Cognitive Neuroscience,* **17**, 1652–1666.

Calder, A.J. and Young, A.W. (2005). Understanding the recognition of facial identity and facial expression. *Nature Review Neuroscience,* **6**, 641–651.

Catani, M. and Mesulam, M. (2008). What is a disconnection syndrome? *Cortex,* **44**, 911–913.

Chan, D., Anderson, V., Pijnenburg, Y., Whitwell, J., Barnes, J., Scahill, R., *et al.* (2009). The clinical profile of right temporal lobe atrophy. *Brain,* **132**, 1287–1298.

Corrigan, N.M., Richards, T., Webb, S.J., Murias, M., Merkle, K., Kleinhans, N.M., *et al.* (2009). An investigation of the relationship between fMRI and ERP source localized measurements of brain activity during face processing. *Brain Topography,* **22**, 83–96.

Crane, J. and Milner, B. (2002). Do I know you? Face perception and memory in patients with selective amygdalo-hippocampectomy. *Neuropsychologia,* **40**, 530–538.

De Gutis, J.M., Bentin, S., Robertson, L.C., and D'Esposito, M. (2007). Functional plasticity in ventral temporal cortex following cognitive rehabilitation of a congenital prosopagnosic. *Journal of Cognitive Neuroscience,* **19**(11), 1790–1802.

de Haan, E.H.F. and Campbell, R. (1991). A fifteen year follow-up of a case of developmental prosopagnosia. *Cortex,* **27**, 489–509.

De Renzi, E. (1986). Current issues in prosopagnosia. In H. Ellis, M. A. Jeeves, F. Newcombe and A. W. Young (eds.), *Aspects of face processing,* pp. 243–252. Dordrecht: Martinus Nijhoff.

De Renzi, E., Faglioni, P., Grossi, D., and Nichelli, P. (1991). Apperceptive and associative forms of prosopagnosia. *Cortex,* **27**, 213–221.

Deffke, I., Sander, T., Heidenreich, J., Sommer, W., Curio, G., Trahms, L., *et al.* (2007). MEG/EEG sources of the 170-ms response to faces are co-localized in the fusiform gyrus. *Neuroimage,* **35**, 1495–1501.

Dobel, C., Bolte, J., Aicher, M., and Schweinberger, S.R. (2007). Prosopagnosia without apparent cause: Overview and diagnosis of six cases *Cortex,* **43**, 734–749.

Dobel, C., Putsche, C., Zwitserlood, P., and Junghofer, M. (2008). Early left-hemispheric dysfunction of face processing in congenital prosopagnosia: an MEG study. *PLoS one,* **3**, e2326.

Druzgal, T.J. and D'Esposito, M. (2003). Dissecting contributions of prefrontal cortex and fusiform face area to face working memory. *Journal of Cognitive Neuroscience*, **15**, 771–784.

Duchaine, B.C., Parker, H., and Nakayama, K. (2003). Normal recognition of emotion in a prosopagnosic. *Perception*, **32**, 827–838.

Duchaine, B., Yovel, G., Butterworth, E.J., and Nakayama, K. (2006). Prosopagnosia as an impairment to face-specific mechanisms: Elimination of the alternative hypotheses in a developmental case. *Cognitive Neuropsychology*, **23**, 714–747.

Duchaine, B.C., Jenkins, R., Germine, L., and Calder, A.J. (2009). Normal gaze discrimination and adaptation in seven prosopagnosics. *Neuropsychologia*, **47**, 2029–2036.

Epelbaum, S., Pinel, P., Gaillard, R., Delmaire, C., Perrin, M., Dupont, S., et al. (2008). Pure alexia as a disconnection syndrome: New diffusion imaging evidence for an old concept. *Cortex*, **8**, 962–974.

Fairhall, S.L. and Ishai, A. (2007). Effective Connectivity within the Distributed Cortical Network for Face Perception. *Cerebral Cortex*, **17**, 2400–2406.

Farah, M.J., Rabinowitz, C., Quinn, G.E., and Liu, G.T. (2000). Early commitment of neural substrates for face recognition. *Cognitive Neuropsychology*, **17**, 117–123.

Fox, C.J., Iaria, G., and Barton, J.J.S. (2008). Disconnection in prosopagnosia and face processing. *Cortex*, **44**, 996–1009.

Ganel, T., Valyear, K.F., Goshen-Gottstein, Y., and Goodale, M.A. (2005). The involvement of the "fusiform face area" in processing facial expression. *Neuropsychologia*, **43**, 1645–1654.

Garrido, L., Furl, N., Draganski, B., Weiskopf, N., Stevens, J., Tan, G.C., et al. (2009). Voxel-based morphometry reveals reduced grey matter volume in the temporal cortex of developmental prosopagnosics. *Brain*, **132**, 3443–3455.

Geschwind, N. (1965). Disconnection syndromes in animals and man. *Brain*, **88**, 237–294.

Gobbini, M.I. and Haxby, J.V. (2006). Neural systems for recognition of familiar faces. *Neuropsychologia*, **45**, 32–41.

Hadjikhani, N. and De Gelder, B. (2002). Neural basis of prosopagnosia. *Human Brain Mapping*, **16**, 176–182.

Harris, A.M. and Aguirre, G.K. (2007). Prosopagnosia. *Current Biology*, **17**, R7–8.

Harris, A.M., Duchaine, B.C., and Nakayama, K. (2005). Normal and abnormal face selectivity of the M170 response in developmental prosopagnosics. *Neuropsychologia*, **43**, 2125–2136.

Hasson, U., Avidan, G., Deouell, L.Y., Bentin, S., and Malach, R. (2003). Face-selective activation in a congenital prosopagnosic subject. *Journal of Cognitive Neuroscience*, **15**, 419–431.

Humphreys, K., Avidan, G., and Behrmann, M. (2007). A detailed investigation of facial expression processing in congenital prosopagnosia as compared to acquired prosopagnosia. *Experimental Brain Research*, **19**, 356–337.

Humphreys, K., Hasson, U., Avidan, G., Minshew, N., and Behrmann, M. (2008). Functional mapping of category-related object areas in high-functioning adults with autism. *Autism Research*, **1**, 52–63.

Ishai, A. (2008). Let's face it: it's a cortical network. *Neuroimage*, **40**, 415–419.

Jacome, D.E. (1986). Subcortical prosopagnosia and anosognosia. *American Journal of Medical Science*, **292**, 386–388.

Jones, R.D. and Tranel, D. (2001). Severe developmental prosopagnosia in a child with superior intellect. *Journal of Clinical and Experimental Neuropsychology*, **23**, 265–273.

Josephs, K.A., Whitwell, J.L., Knopman, D.S., Boeve, B.F., Vemuri, P., Senjem, M.L., et al. (2009). Two distinct subtypes of right temporal variant frontotemporal dementia. *Neurology*, **73**, 1443–1450.

Joubert, S., Felician, O., Barbeau, E., Sontheimer, A., Guedj, E., Ceccaldi, M., et al. (2004). Progressive prosopagnosia: clinical and neuroimaging results. *Neurology*, **63**, 1962–1965.

Kanwisher, N., McDermott, J., and Chun, M.M. (1997). The fusiform face area: a module in human extrastriate cortex specialized for face perception. *Journal of Neuroscience*, **17**, 4302–4311.

Keller, T.A. and Just, M.A. (2009). Altering cortical connectivity: remediation-induced changes in the white matter of poor readers. *Neuron*, **64**, 624–631.

Kress, T. and Daum, I. (2003). Developmental prosopagnosia: a review. *Behavioural Neurology,* **14,** 109–121.

Le Grand, R., Cooper, P.A., Mondloch, C.J., Lewis, T.L., Sagiv, N., de Gelder, B., *et al.* (2006). What aspects of face processing are impaired in developmental prosopagnosia? *Brain and Cognition,* **16,** 1584–1594.

Lee, K., Byatt, G., and Rhodes, G. (2000). Testing the face-space framework. *Psychological Science,* **11,** 379–385.

Marotta, J.J., Behrmann, M., and Genovese, C. (2001). A functional MRI study of face recognition in patients with prosopagnosia. *NeuroReport,* **12,** 959–965.

Minnebusch, D.A., Suchan, B., Ramon, M., and Daum, I. (2007). Event-related potentials reflect heterogeneity of developmental prosopagnosia. *European Journal of Neuroscience,* **25,** 2234–2247.

Minnebusch, D.A., Suchan, B., Koster, O., and Daum, I. (2009). A bilateral occipitotemporal network mediates face perception. *Behavioral Brain Research,* **198,** 179–185.

Morgan, H.M., Klein, C., Boehm, S.G., Shapiro, K.L., and Linden, D.E. (2008). Working memory load for faces modulates P300, N170, and N250r. *Journal of Cognitive Neuroscience,* **20,** 989–1002.

Nishimura, M., Doyle, J., Humphreys, K., and Behrmann, M. (2010). Probing the face-space of individuals with prosopagnosia, **48,** 1828–1841.

Nunn, J.A., Postma, P., and Pearson, R. (2001). Developmental prosopagnosia: should it be taken at face value? *Neurocase,* **7,** 15–27.

Peretz, I., Brattico, E., Jarvenpaa, M., and Tervaniemi, M. (2009). The amusic brain: in tune, out of key, and unaware. *Brain,* **132,** 1277–1286.

Pitcher, D., Walsh, V., Yovel, G., and Duchaine, B. (2007). TMS evidence for the involvement of the right occipital face area in early face processing. *Current Biology,* **17,** 1568–1573.

Rapcsak, S.Z., Nielsen, L., Littrell, L.D., Glisky, E.L., Kaszniak, A.W., and Laguna, J.F. (2001). Face memory impairments in patients with frontal lobe damage. *Neurology,* **57,** 1168–1175.

Rhodes, G., Brennan, S., and Carey, S. (1987). Identification and ratings of caricatures: Implications for mental representation of faces. *Cognitive Psychology,* **19,** 473–497.

Rossion, B., Caldara, R., Seghier, M., Schuller, A.M., Lazeyras, F., and Mayer, E. (2003). A network of occipito-temporal face-sensitive areas besides the right middle fusiform gyrus is necessary for normal face processing. *Brain,* **126,** 2381–2395.

Rossion, B., Kaiser, M.D., Bub, D., and Tanaka, J.W. (2009). Is the loss of diagnosticity of the eye region of the face a common aspect of acquired prosopagnosia? *Journal of Neuropsychology,* **3,** 69–78.

Rouw, R. and Scholte, H.S. (2007). Increased structural connectivity in grapheme-color synesthesia. *Nature Neuroscience,* **10,** 792–797.

Schiltz, C., Sorger, B., Caldara, R., Ahmed, F., Mayer, E., Goebel, R., *et al.* (2006). Impaired face discrimination in acquired prosopagnosia is associated with abnormal response to individual faces in the right middle fusiform gyrus. *Cerebral Cortex,* **16,** 574–586.

Schmalzl, L., Palermo, R., and Coltheart, M. (2007). Cognitive heterogeneity in genetically based prosopagnosia: A family study. *Journal of Neuropsychology,* **2,** 99–117.

Schmalzl, L., Palermo, R., Green, M., Brunsdon, R., and Coltheart, M. (2008). Training of familiar face recognition and visual scan paths for faces in a child with congenital prosopagnosia. *Cognitive Neuropsychology,* **25,** 704–729.

Schwarzer, G., Huber, S., Gruter, M., Gruter, T., Gross, C., Hipfel, M., *et al.* (2007). Gaze behaviour in hereditary prosopagnosia. *Psychology Research,* **71,** 583–590.

Sergent, J. and Signoret, J.-L. (1992). Functional and anatomical decomposition of face processing; Evidence from prosopagnosia and PET study of normal subjects. *Philosophical Transactions of the Royal Society of London B,* **335,** 55–62.

Sorger, B., Goebel, R., Schiltz, C., and Rossion, B. (2007). Understanding the functional neuroanatomy of acquired prosopagnosia. *Neuroimage,* **35,** 836–852.

Steeves, J.K., Culham, J.C., Duchaine, B.C., Pratesi, C.C., Valyear, K.F., Schindler, I., *et al.* (2006). The fusiform face area is not sufficient for face recognition: Evidence from a patient with dense prosopagnosia and no occipital face area. *Neuropsychologia,* **44,** 594–609.

Steeves, J., Dricot, L., Goltz, H.C., Sorger, B., Peters, J., Milner, A.D., *et al.* (2009). Abnormal face identity coding in the middle fusiform gyrus of two brain-damaged prosopagnosic patients. *Neuropsychologia,* **47**(12), 2584–2592.

Stephan, B.C. and Caine, D. (2009). Aberrant pattern of scanning in prosopagnosia reflects impaired face processing. *Brain and Cognition,* **69**, 262–268.

Striemer, C., Gingerich, T., Striemer, D., and Dixon, M. (2009). Covert face priming reveals a "true face effect" in a case of congenital prosopagnosia. *Neurocase,* **18**, 1–6.

Thomas, C., Avidan, G., Humphreys, K., Jung, K.J., Gao, F., and Behrmann, M. (2009). Reduced structural connectivity in ventral visual cortex in congenital prosopagnosia. *Nature Neuroscience,* **12**, 29–31.

Tippett, L.J., Miller, L.A., and Farah, M.J. (2000). Prosopamnesia: A selective impairment in face learning. *Cognitive Neuropsychology,* **17**, 241–255.

Tranel, D. and Damasio, A.R. (1985). Knowledge without awareness: An autonomic index of facial recognition by prosopagnosics. *Science,* **228**, 1453–1454.

Tranel, D., Damasio, A.R., and Damasio, H. (1988). Intact recognition of facial expression, gender, and age in patients with impaired recognition of face identity. *Neurology,* **38**, 690–696.

Valentine, T. (1991). A unified account of the effects of distinctiveness, inversion, and race in face recognition. *Quarterly Journal of Experimental Psychology,* **43A**, 161–204.

Van den Stock, J., van de Riet, W.A., Righart, R., and de Gelder, B. (2008). Neural correlates of perceiving emotional faces and bodies in developmental prosopagnosia: an event-related fMRI-study. *PLoS ONE,* **3**, e3195.

Williams, M.A., Berberovic, N., and Mattingley, J.B. (2007). Abnormal fMRI adaptation to unfamiliar faces in a case of developmental prosopagnosia. *Current Biology,* **17**, 1259–1264.

Young, A.W., Hellawell, D., and de Haan, E.H.F. (1988). Cross-domain semantic priming in normal subjects and a prosopagnosic patient. *Quarterly Journal of Experimental Psychology,* **40A**, 561–580.

Yovel, G., Tambini, A., and Brandman, T. (2008). The asymmetry of the fusiform face area is a stable individual characteristic that underlies the left-visual-field superiority for faces. *Neuropsychologia,* **46**, 3061–3068.

Chapter 42

Developmental Prosopagnosia: Cognitive, Neural, and Developmental Investigations

Bradley Duchaine

MJ, a 7-year-old boy, was an enigma to his mother. At home or when playing with unfamiliar children in public places, he was friendly and engaging. At school though he was a loner who tended to watch the other children play. His teachers regularly became exasperated with him when he failed to follow their instructions. MJ refused his teacher's request to take papers to a particular student, claiming that he didn't know who the student was. When told to stand next to a student named Casey, MJ stood next to the student he thought was Casey but his teacher became angry and she sent him to the end of the line. MJ's mother's claims that he was normal at home were met with disbelief by his teachers, and MJ's principal told his mother that his social problems were probably caused by her anxiety.

There were other oddities as well. MJ wasn't able to recognize the small number of neighbors they met regularly. He also confused his mother and his beloved aunt when they had similar hairstyles. When his aunt dramatically changed her hairstyle, MJ refused to believe that she was really his aunt, and he was mad at his mother for several days when she changed her hairstyle. In preschool, the only student MJ could identify was a Chinese girl—the only non-Caucasian student in the class. His mother thought MJ seemed overly obsessed with body weight and skin color, and he embarrassed her several times by referring to a child as "the fat boy" or "the brown girl."

MJ's one friend in kindergarten was a boy named Jacob. Upon running into Jacob and his parents at a soccer game, MJ failed to recognize him. The adults laughed off MJ's inability to recognize Jacob, but MJ's mother could see the same confused look on his face she'd seen many times before—a lack of recognition coupled with the look of someone who thinks they're being duped. Then, a couple of weeks later, MJ's older brother saw one of his former classmates at church. His name was also Jacob and he was roughly the same size and coloring as MJ's friend Jacob. Upon seeing his brother talking to this Jacob, MJ clearly thought this boy was his friend Jacob. His mother was astounded, and the realization hit her like a ton of bricks. MJ could not recognize people!

Background

MJ suffers from developmental prosopagnosia (DP), a condition defined by severe face recognition problems resulting from a failure to develop the necessary visual recognition mechanisms. Although it has been long recognized that severe face recognition deficits can follow brain damage (Bodamer, 1947/Ellis and Florence, 1990; Wigan, 1844), wider awareness of DP has only emerged in the last 10 years. In the literature DP is also often called *congenital prosopagnosia*, but here I will refer to it as *developmental prosopagnosia* because it is unclear whether face recognition abilities in DPs are atypical at birth. Face processing problems are also seen in other developmental disorders such as autism spectrum disorder (Dawson, et al., 2002) and Turner syndrome (Mazzola et al., 2006), but in DP intellectual function and social cognition is normal (Duchaine et al., 2010) and deficits to other abilities are limited.

Bornstein briefly described cases that appear to be DPs in a chapter on prosopagnosia (Bornstein, 1963), but McConachie (1976) was the first to publish a case study of a DP. AB was an intelligent 12-year-old girl who reported having severe difficulties recognizing faces that she was not extremely familiar with. She found recognition of her uniformed classmates especially challenging. Despite her reported difficulties, AB was able to hesitantly identify photographs of familiar faces and also scored normally on a test of unfamiliar face recognition. AB and her mother were unaware of any events that may have caused brain damage. Interestingly, AB's mother also reported face recognition problems which suggested a possible genetic cause. In a follow-up study 15 years later, AB showed clear difficulties in tests of face recognition as well as deficits with the recognition of facial expressions and within-class object recognition (de Haan and Campbell, 1991).

A few new cases of DP were reported in the 1990s (Bentin et al., 1999; Kracke, 1994; Temple, 1992), but it wasn't until the current decade that substantial numbers of prosopagnosics were investigated (Behrmann et al., 2005; de Gelder and Rouw, 2000; Duchaine, 2000; Kress and Daum, 2003). Awareness of the condition and research into it have benefited greatly from the emergence of the Internet. An email discussion group was created in late 1990s by a group of DPs, and Bill Choisser, an American DP, published an online book in 1997 about the condition and his experiences of it (Choisser, 1997). The internet has also provided a means for researchers and DPs to make contact. Several groups have websites aimed at recruiting research participants, and more than 5200 DPs have contacted the website Ken Nakayama and I created in 2002 (http://www.faceblind.org). Approximately 95% of these self-reported prosopagnosics are unaware of suffering any brain damage so severe face recognition problems appear to be much more often due to developmental problems than brain damage in adulthood (Duchaine and Nakayama, 2006). An estimate of the prevalence of DP based on self-report and interviews suggested that approximately 2% of the population experience significant face recognition difficulties in everyday life due to developmental problems (Kennerknecht et al., 2006). That the prevalence should be so high for such an ancestrally important ability is surprising, but it bears noting that modern environments place much greater demands on face recognition than ancestral environments did. Many people who experience difficulties recognizing the thousands of faces one encounters in modern life may not have experienced significant difficulties in ancestral environments.

Herein I will review recent research findings investigating DP. Like studies of acquired prosopagnosia, studies involving DP have addressed the cognitive and neural basis of face processing. However because DP is developmental in origin, it also holds promise as a means to better understand the developmental and the genetic basis of face processing. While our understanding of DP remains poor, the relatively rich cognitive, neural, and developmental theories of face recognition provide a framework that should allow rapid progress. In addition DP research may provide a model for investigating other selective developmental disorders. At present, only a handful of selective developmental disorders have been identified (Bishop, 2006; Garrido et al., 2009; Iaria et al., 2009; McCloskey et al., 1995; Ramus, 2003; Temple and Richardson, 2004; Van Zandvoort et al., 2007), but the late recognition of a developmental deficit affecting an ability as critical as face recognition suggests that other, possibly many other, selective developmental deficits may exist.

Experience of developmental prosopagnosia

Having lost their face recognition abilities due to brain damage, it is usually apparent to acquired prosopagnosics that they have face recognition deficits. DPs however are unable to appreciate first-hand that their face recognition abilities are deficient. Nearly all of the people who my laboratory work with were aware that they sometimes had trouble recognizing people but most did not attribute it to problems in their visual system. Many believed they were not trying hard enough or were not sufficiently interested in people. Jane Goodall, who has stated that both she and her sister are prosopagnosic, wrote:

> I used to think it was due to some mental laziness, and I tried desperately to memorize the faces of people I met so that, if I saw them the next day, I would recognize them. I had no trouble with those who had obvious physical characteristics—unusual bone structure, beaky nose, extreme beauty or the opposite. But with other faces I failed, miserably. Sometimes I knew that people were upset when I did not immediately recognize them—certainly I was. And because I was embarrassed, I kept it to myself. (Goodall and Berman, 1999.)

Like Dr Goodall, many DPs tested in my lab didn't recognize that they were prosopagnosic until they were adults.

Many DPs are slow to realize that they have difficulties with faces because they compensate for their prosopagnosia by relying on the many other cues available for person recognition. DPs report using hairstyles, voices, body shape, gait, and even characteristic facial expressions. Context is especially important for many DPs. DPs might recognize co-workers in the office where they are expecting to see them but have little hope of recognizing them when meeting them in the grocery store. Although they have severe problems with facial information, most DPs report that they do use the face for person recognition and their scores on famous face tests, although far worse than controls, show they can perceive and store some facial information (Behrmann et al., 2005; Duchaine and Nakayama, 2005; Duchaine et al., 2007b).

Not surprisingly, face recognition failures can create substantial difficulties for DPs. Their failure to acknowledge friends and acquaintances sometimes causes DPs to be seen as aloof or arrogant, and many of our DPs have discussed episodes in which their recognition failures have had major personal or professional consequences. For example, a DP who contacted our website stated:

> I was a public high school English teacher for ten years. I made all of my students sit in assigned seats the whole year. When the school required all students to wear navy blue polo shirts and khaki pants, I was adrift in a sea of blue shirts. The students felt like I disliked them because I didn't know who they were in the hall, even if class had just let out. The lunchroom was social hell. I couldn't even recognize the other faculty members, so I usually stayed in my classroom and locked the door.

A recent study in which 25 DPs were interviewed found that many reported chronic anxiety about offending others and most reported fear and avoidance of social situations in which face recognition would be challenging (Yardley et al., 2008). Many reported that DP had significant occupational ramifications, but most of the DPs did not view their prosopagnosia as debilitating but saw it instead as taxing.

A number of other deficits are commonly seen in DP, but it is important to note that dissociations between face recognition and most of these associated conditions have been reported. These associated deficits are similar to those often seen in acquired prosopagnosia which suggests that the two types of prosopagnosia involve deficits to similar mechanisms (Duchaine and Yovel, 2008). DP is defined by deficits with facial identity, but other aspects of face processing are also often impaired in DP including face detection (Garrido et al., 2008), expression recognition (Duchaine, 2000; Duchaine et al., 2006; Garrido et al., 2009), gender discrimination (Duchaine et al., 2006), and trustworthiness judgments (Todorov and Duchaine, 2008). Another type of social perception, biological motion perception, is also sometimes impaired in DP (Lange et al., 2009). DPs have not shown deficits with basic-level object recognition (Duchaine et al., 2006), but many have difficulties with individual item object recognition (often referred to as within-class recognition) (Behrmann et al., 2005; Duchaine and Nakayama, 2005; Duchaine et al., 2003a). Although it has yet to be formally documented, many DPs report difficulties with large-scale navigation (Duchaine et al., 2003b).

I'm often asked what DPs experience when they view a face. Although this is not a question that can be answered confidently, their performance on face perception tasks relative to people with normal face perception supports one possibility. Figure 42.1 shows an example item and upright and inverted scores on a test requiring participants to sort simultaneously presented faces in terms of their similarity to a target face (Duchaine et al., 2007b). In Figure 42.1b, the normal participants tend to cluster around the line which shows scores for which participants have made twice as many errors with inverted faces as with upright faces. The DPs however show a different pattern. Their scores are shifted primarily to the left because they made far more errors with upright faces than controls. Many DPs cluster around the line showing participants with equivalent errors with upright and inverted faces. The similarity of their scores with upright and inverted faces suggests that these DPs may process the upright and inverted faces with the same procedures (see also Behrmann et al., 2005; Nunn et al., 2001). In addition, the similarity of the DPs' upright scores and the normal subjects' inverted scores raises the possibility that DPs' experience of upright faces is similar to the percept that normal subjects experience when viewing inverted faces (See Figure 42.1c). For people with normal face perception, an inverted face is clearly a face, but the percept is not as rich as the percept of an upright face—the face's identity is not as apparent and its expression and attractiveness are more difficult to discern. If one imagines attempting to interact with a room full of inverted faces, it is easy to appreciate how challenging social situations can be for DPs.

Experimental studies of developmental prosopagnosia

The leading models of face processing (Bruce and Young, 1986; Gobbini and Haxby, 2007; Haxby et al., 2000) suggest that face processing is carried out by a hierarchically organized network of mechanisms, and recent neurophysiological work in macaques has definitely demonstrated that face processing involves a richly interconnected set of areas (Moeller et al., 2008; Tsao et al., 2006, 2008; see Freiwald and Tsao, Chapter 36, this volume). Given the many areas and connections that play a role in face processing, there are undoubtedly many different types of potential face processing deficits. Developing a taxonomy of face processing deficits in DP and an understanding of the developmental events that lead to them is a major challenge, and studies investigating DP so far have addressed relatively simple issues.

Cognitive studies of developmental prosopagnosia

A range of cognitive issues have been addressed in DP in recent years including the long debated question of whether the brain contains face-specific mechanisms (Diamond and Carey, 1986; Farah, 1996; Moscovitch et al., 1997; Rock, 1974; Yin, 1969). Like many acquired prosopagnosics, many DPs have difficulties with challenging object recognition tasks (Behrmann et al., 2005; Duchaine and Nakayama, 2005; Garrido et al., 2008). For example, eight out of 14 DPs in a recent study showed impairments on at least one of the seven old–new tests requiring discrimination of a set of similar objects from within a category and five of these DPs were impaired on four or more object tests (Garrido et al., 2008). Six of these DPs however showed no deficits on tests of object recognition, and other DPs have also shown dissociations between impaired face recognition and normal object recognition (Duchaine and Nakayama, 2005; Nunn et al., 2001; Yovel and Duchaine, 2006). The examples of apparently pure DP imply that the opposite dissociation may

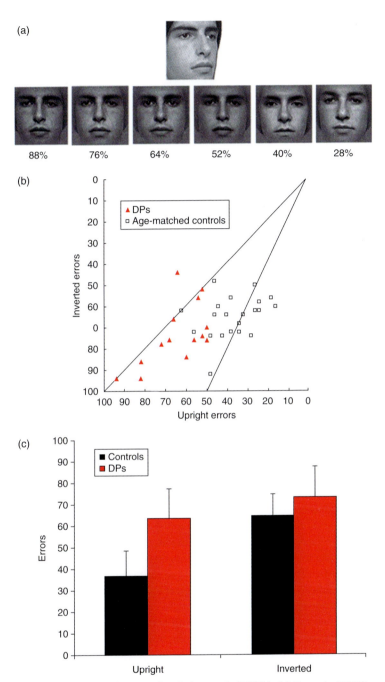

Fig. 42.1 Cambridge Face Perception Test (Duchaine et al., 2007b). (a) Example CFPT item. Participants have 1 min to sort the six faces in terms of their similarity to the target face above. Each participant sorted eight upright items and eight inverted items. (b) Individual scores on the CFPT for controls (black symbols) and DPs (red symbols). Each symbol represents the sum of errors for a participant on the upright items and the inverted items. Controls tend to cluster around the line on the right denoting scores for which inverted errors are twice the upright errors. Many DPs however cluster around the other line denoting equivalent upright and inverted errors. (c) Mean errors for controls and DPs on upright and inverted items. The DPs made as many errors with upright faces as the controls made with upright faces. Reproduced with permission from Social Cognitive Affective Neuroscience ©Oxford University Press.

also exist in developmental cases, and my colleagues and I have recently reported a woman with no evidence of brain damage who has normal face recognition and impaired object recognition (Germine et al., 2011).

While these dissociations between faces and objects are consistent with the possibility that DP can result from deficits to face-specific mechanisms, they do not provide definitive support for it. Many cognitive accounts of prosopagnosia have been proposed over the years, and most of these hypotheses are compatible with certain dissociations between face and object recognition. To more thoroughly address the nature of the mechanisms impaired in DP, my colleagues and I tested the predictions of all the alternatives to the face-specific hypothesis in a case that had shown good performance on a number of non-face visual recognition tests.

Edward was a man in his early 50s with no history of brain damage. He recalls difficulties with faces dating back to childhood. Several aspects of Edward's face processing are impaired including identity, expression, gender, and attractiveness (Duchaine et al., 2006) which suggest that his deficits begin early in the face processing stream. Magnetic resonance imaging (MRI) showed no lesions or obvious abnormalities. Two separate functional MRI (fMRI) sessions failed to find any face-selective voxels whereas all controls run with the same localizer scan showed areas of face-selective activation. Edward's normal performance on individual item object recognition showed that he did not suffer from a general problem involving within-class visual recognition (Damasio et al., 1982). Contrary to the predictions of an account proposing a general deficit with configural information (Behrmann et al., 2005; Levine and Calvanio, 1989), Edward discriminated changes to the spacing of parts of houses normally while scoring near chance on a matched face task. He scored normally on two tests of inverted face matching yet was impaired when the faces were upright. His normal performance with inverted faces demonstrates that Edward's problems with upright faces are not due to an inability to represent stimuli with particular properties such as non-decomposability (Farah 1990) or surface curvature (Kosslyn et al., 1995; Laeng and Caviness, 2001). Expertise accounts of prosopagnosia suggest that face recognition deficits are due to problems with mechanisms that apply special procedures to stimulus classes with which an observer has substantial experience (Diamond and Carey, 1986; Gauthier et al., 1998). One view of expertise proposes that expertise can be developed relatively quickly. To test whether Edward's prosopagnosia results from problems with the development of what we called rapid expertise we had him carry out a training procedure identical to those used to investigate rapid expertise. This training involved learning to identify 20 individual computer-generated stimuli greebles and also the family that each greeble belonged to (the five families were characterized by their body shapes). Edward's performance with greebles was comparable to the controls so his prosopagnosia does not appear to result from a rapid expertise deficit (Duchaine et al., 2004). Finally, to test whether he has general deficits with extended expertise (Diamond and Carey, 1986), we tested Edward with sequential matching tasks involving faces and human bodies. Bodies were chosen because several studies have shown that bodies, like faces, show substantial inversion effects (Reed et al., 2003, 2006; Yovel et al., 2010) which suggests that upright bodies receive special processing. Contrary to the predictions of the extended expertise view, Edward scored normally with the body task while showing a clear impairment with the face task. Taken together, Edward's results were inconsistent with all of the alternative account and so suggest that his prosopagnosia is caused by deficits to a face-specific mechanism (Duchaine et al., 2006). At present, Edward is the only prosopagnosic to have been tested in this manner so it will be important to see if future studies with acquired and developmental prosopagnosics find similar results (Duchaine and Garrido, 2008).

Edward did not have general problems with configural information, but two papers found evidence that general configural deficits may give rise to DP. In global-local tasks, participants are presented with a stimulus that has information at both the global level and the local level (Navon, 1977). One of the most common global-local stimuli consists of the same small letters (local) positioned to form a large letter (global). The local stimulus and global stimulus are usually one of two possibilities (e.g. S or H), and on a trial, the local and global letters can be either consistent or inconsistent. Participants can be asked to respond to the stimulus at one level or the other, and normal participants usually respond faster on global decisions than local decisions. In addition, trials with consistent global and local letters are usually responded to more quickly than trials with inconsistent letters due to interference from the to-be-ignored letter. However in one study with five DPs, the DP group were slower with global decisions than controls, experienced greater interference from inconsistent local information, and less interference from inconsistent global information than controls (Behrmann et al., 2005). In contrast, their performance with local letters was normal. Similarly, KW, another DP, was faster with local than global decisions and also showed larger interference from inconsistent local information and no interference from inconsistent global information (Bentin et al., 2007). However atypical non-face global processing is not seen in all DPs. A group of 14 DPs showed no signs of deficits on a global-local task (Duchaine et al., 2007a), and eight failed to show problems with a global form task (Le Grand et al., 2006). In addition, eight DPs performed normally on a task requiring discrimination of spacing changes in houses yet failed a comparable task with faces (Yovel and Duchaine, 2006). This group showed comparable deficits for spacing and part discrimination in faces which indicates that their problems with faces extend beyond what is usually considered global processing.

Studies of DP have also examined performance on different aspects of face processing and have used these results to make inferences about cognitive organization within face processing. Any recognition system that includes face-specific processes requires a means to detect the presence of faces in a visual scene. This process of face detection has received considerable attention in machine vision (Viola and Jones, 2004), but limited attention in human studies (Lewis and Edmonds, 2005; VanRullen, 2006). To investigate face detection in DP, 14 DPs were tested on two tasks requiring rapid detection of faces (Garrido et al., 2008). One task used stimuli consisting of a 5 × 5 array of grayscale images while the other used two-tone stimuli like the one shown in Figure 42.2a. Participants were asked to press a key as soon as they saw a face, and a substantial number of no-face trials were included in each task. Many of the DPs were less accurate and slower than controls, including several who showed deficits in both accuracy and response time. Figure 42.2b presents data for each DP and control on the task involving two-tone images. Note that, although many of the DPs were impaired, several scored normally and so appear to have normal face detection processes (Garrido et al., 2008). Eight DPs in another study also showed normal detection of Mooney faces (Le Grand et al., 2006).

The models of face processing mentioned above include mechanisms specialized for different aspects of face processing. In Bruce and Young's model (1986), the perception of identity, expression, and facial speech (for lip-reading) depend on separate modules, and Haxby and colleagues' neurocognitive model (2000) proposes that invariants aspects of faces such as identity and gender are processed in the fusiform face area (FFA) and changeable aspects of faces such as expression and gaze are processed in the face-selective region of the superior temporal sulcus (STS). However evidence in support of these divisions is limited. An influential review suggested that no unequivocal support for the distinction between identity and expression processing has been reported (Calder and Young, 2005), and support for the other divisions is even weaker. Although neuropsychological dissociations played an important role in the divisions of these models of face processing, many of the studies suffer from methodological limitations (Calder and Young, 2005; Duchaine and Weidenfeld, 2003).

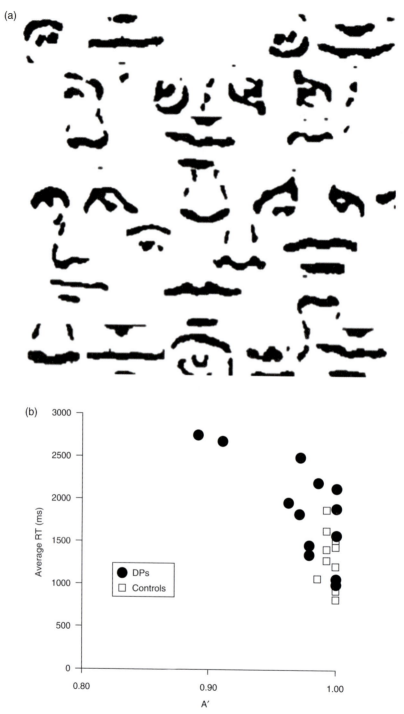

Fig. 42.2 Face detection (Garrido et al., 2008). (a) Example of a face present item in the two-tone face detection task. Face absent stimuli contained the same elements but the black regions creating the face were scrambled. The importance of orientation in face detection can be experienced by viewing the stimulus upside-down. (b) Each symbol shows performance for individual DPs (black circles) and controls (open squares). Reproduced with permission from *Journal of Neuropsychology* © The British Psychological Society.

For most face processing abilities that have been investigated, some DPs show normal perform-ance whereas others show impaired performance. Above I mentioned that Edward has expression recognition difficulties, and other DPs have also shown deficits with expression (Duchaine, 2000; Duchaine et al., 2003b). Several laboratories however have reported DPs with normal expression perception (Bentin et al., 2007; Duchaine et al., 2003b; Garrido et al., 2009; Humphreys et al., 2006; Nunn et al., 2001). Although a thorough investigation of gender discrimination in DP remains to be carried out, it appears that some DPs perceive gender normally (Behrmann et al., 2005; Nunn et al., 2001) whereas others do not (Behrmann et al., 2005; de Haan and Campbell, 1991; Duchaine et al., 2006). Some DPs who have contacted my laboratory have complained of difficulty reading eye gaze, but discrimination of eye gaze direction and perceptual adaptation to left and right gaze was normal in six DPs (Duchaine et al., 2009). Similarly, some DPs were normal and others were impaired in a task requiring that they sort faces based on attractiveness (Sadr et al., 2004), and two DPs made normal trustworthiness judgments whereas two DPs made judgments that were only weakly correlated with the judgments of controls (Todorov and Duchaine, 2008).

The dissociations between identity and these abilities fits well with modular models of face processing, but our understanding of the relationship between the mechanisms carrying out these computations will benefit from a thorough examination of the dissociations and associations seen in a large group of DPs. Such an investigation may show, for example, that some closely related abilities (e.g. gender and attractiveness) do not dissociate which would indicate that they rely on the same mechanisms. The dissociations between aspects of face processing may also provide some insight into the development of face processing mechanisms. The normal development of certain aspects of face processing in combination with deficits for the processing of facial identity indicates that the acquisition of these abilities depends on different developmental processes. However the unidirectional dissociations (impaired identity/normal ability with another aspect of face perception) identified so far leave open the possibility that the development of the mecha-nisms necessary for identity perception are more vulnerable to developmental disruption than the mechanisms that appear to be functioning normally. As a result, the identification of double dissociations in DPs would be valuable in that it would strongly suggest different developmental processes are involved in acquiring different face processing abilities.

A distinction between the perceptual representation of a face and its representation in memory is a common feature in most models and of facial identity recognition (Bruce and Young, 1986; Duchaine and Nakayama, 2006). Surprisingly little research has investigated this division in indi-viduals with developmental face recognition deficits, probably because most DP research is moti-vated by questions about high-level vision and so requires that DPs have deficits to perceptual processes contributing to identity recognition. Dissociations between normal perception and impaired memory have been reported in acquired prosopagnosia (Tippett et al., 2000), and my laboratory has tested a number of participants who score normally with identity perception but have severe deficits with identity memory.

Neural studies of developmental prosopagnosia

Research into the neural basis of face processing has flourished in recent years, and neuroimaging and neurophysiology have identified several face-selective responses (Bentin, 1996; Kanwisher et al., 1997; McCarthy et al., 1997). Nevertheless identifying atypical neural markers in DP has been challenging because the neural differences between DPs and controls are often not apparent. One reason for this difficulty is that participants with normal face processing show varied fMRI responses and event-related potentials (ERP) to faces so substantial differences are necessary to reveal abnormalities in small samples of DPs. The larger samples in several recent papers provide increased power for group comparisons, but it would be advantageous if methods were developed that allowed stronger inferences from single cases.

In the first fMRI paper published with a DP, YT showed a normal response in left FFA, right FFA, and right occipital face area (OFA) (Hasson et al., 2003). However in the left lateral occipital cortex, which houses the left OFA as well as an object-selective area, YT showed reduced selectivity for faces in the face area and for objects in the object area. Two of the paradigms used in the YT paper as well as two new paradigms were used to assess face-selective activity in four DPs (Avidan et al., 2005). In all paradigms, the DPs showed much stronger activation to faces than objects in the fusiform gyrus and also showed normal reduction of this response when faces were repeated (repetition suppression) in face-responsive regions in the fusiform gyrus and the lateral occipital cortex. Given the important role that these face-selective activations in ventral visual cortex are believed to play in face processing, these results were considered a surprise by many and suggested that this behaviorally striking developmental deficit results from either subtle neural abnormalities to these areas or impairments in other areas. Several single case studies however have found functional differences between DPs and controls. Edward, the DP discussed above, failed to show any face-selective voxels in two separate face localizer scans (Duchaine et al., 2006), and KW also showed no face-selective voxels in ventral temporal cortex (Bentin et al., 2007). Interestingly, these two DPs show very different behavioral abilities. Edward fails with a wide range of face processing tasks whereas K.W. performs normally with expression matching despite severe deficits with identity. SO showed a normal right FFA, but a weaker response to faces relative to objects at the left FFA and the temporal poles bilaterally than controls (von Kriegstein et al., 2006). Although Avidan et al., (2005) found normal adaptation to faces in four DPs, a recent paper did find atypical adaptation in one DP (Williams et al., 2007). This DP participant, referred to as C, shows an unusual pattern of abilities. She was impaired on tests of identity perception and unfamiliar face memory, but was able to successfully identify famous faces and reported that she was able to recognize faces after considerable exposure. When scanned she showed normal FFAs bilaterally and also bilateral parahippocampal place areas (PPA). Like controls, C showed adaptation to repeated familiar and unfamiliar places in PPA and also to repeated familiar faces in FFA. However consistent with her behavioral results, she failed to show a weaker response to repeated unfamiliar faces.

Neuroimaging has also been used to examine whether DPs have structural differences from controls. Volumetric MRI analysis with YT, one of the DPs who showed a normal fMRI response to faces in the ventral occipitotemporal cortex (Hasson et al., 2003), found that his temporal lobe was significantly smaller than controls (Bentin et al., 1999). A study with six DPs also found temporal lobe abnormalities (Behrmann et al., 2007). This analysis measured the volume of regions in the temporal lobes and found that the anterior fusiform gyrus was smaller in DPs than controls. The FFA is seen in regions of the posterior and mid-fusiform gyrus, so it is posterior to anterior fusiform (Behrmann et al., 2007). Interestingly, both the anterior and the posterior middle temporal gyrus were larger in DPs than controls. A recent study using voxel-based morphometry (VBM) found that DPs had less grey matter than controls in a number of regions that show face-selective responses (Garrido et al., 2009). Analyses of the T1-weighted images revealed that the 17 DPs had reduced grey matter volume in right anterior inferior temporal lobe and in the STS/middle temporal gyrus bilaterally. A separate analysis of the segmentation of magnetization transfer images also showed less grey matter volume in DPs in right middle fusiform gyrus and inferior temporal gyrus.

Diffusion tensor imaging (DTI) done in the six DPs in Behrmann et al. (2007) identified deficiencies in white matter fibers that connect ventral occipitotemporal regions with more anterior regions (Thomas et al., 2009). Using deterministic tractography, the authors identified the fronto-occipital fasciculus and the inferior longitudinal fasciculus for each DP and

17 controls. They found that the number of fibers and the number of voxels through which they passed was reduced in DPs when compared to controls. The mean fractional anisotropy in these tracts was also significantly lower in DPs than controls, possibly due to problems in the micro-structural integrity of the IFOF and ILF. Using the same dependent measures to compare callosal tracts, Thomas et al. (2009) did not observe any differences in the forceps minor, but did find a reduced number of voxels in the forceps major in DPs. This study indicates that deficits in the integrity of white matter tracts that pass through the temporal and occipital cortex are associated with DP.

Studies measuring ERPs in participants with normal face processing consistently find a negative component approximately 170ms (N170) after stimulus presentation that is much stronger for faces than for other stimuli (Bentin et al., 1996; see Eimer, Chapter 17; Schweinberger, Chapter 18, this volume), and measurement of the N170 provides a means to examine whether DPs have deficits in early face processing. YT, the DP discussed in the fMRI and the MRI paragraphs above, had a non-selective N170 in that his response to faces and non-face objects were comparable. Interestingly, the non-selectivity resulted from a stronger than normal response to non-face objects rather than a weaker response to faces. This led to suggestions that YT's face recognition systems processed both face and non-face representations due to early filtering deficits. Two DPs also showed a non-selective N170 due to a strong response to non-face objects (Kress and Daum, 2003), and MZ, who we will discuss further below, also showed a non-selective N170 due to a strong response to watches prior to face training (DeGutis et al., 2007) (see Figure 42.3). Some DPs however show normal face-selectivity in their response, which suggests that their prosopagnosia results from later processes. Five DPs were presented with faces and

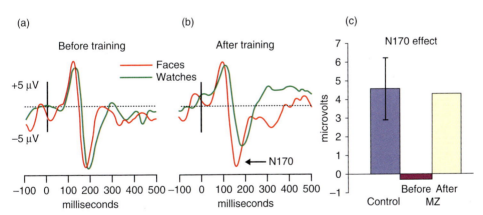

Fig. 42.3 The N170 in MZ before and after training (DeGutis et al., 2007). (a) Prior to face training, MZ's N170 was not selective for faces, because the amplitude to faces and watches is similar. (b) Following training, MZ's N170 is stronger to faces than to watches. Comparison with (a) shows that this selectivity emerged because the response to watches was weaker after training. (c) Difference in microvolts between the response to faces and watches. The difference in MZ's response after training is comparable to the average difference for controls. Errors bars represent the 95% confidence interval of the control mean. Reproduced with permission from Joseph M. DeGutis, Shlomo Bentin, Lynn C. Robertson, and Mark D'Esposito, Functional Plasticity in Ventral Temporal Cortex following Cognitive Rehabilitation of a Congenital Prospagnostic, *Journal of Cognitive Neuroscience*, **19**(11) (November, 2007), pp. 1790–1802. © 2007 by the Massachusetts Institute of Technology.

houses while their response was measured with magnetoencephalography (MEG) (Harris et al., 2005), a technique that also has high temporal resolution and measures many of the same neural sources as ERP (Hämäläinen et al., 1993). Three DPs had non-selective M170 responses similar to those discussed above, but two DPs had normal M170s. ERPs were recorded in these two DPs and they also manifested a face-selective N170 (Harris et al., 2005). Hence, as with fMRI, DPs show variability in their early response to faces and this heterogeneity indicates that DP results from impairments to different mechanisms in different individuals. In summary, neural measures have identified a number of neural abnormalities in DPs, but an integrated picture of the neural basis of DP remains to be worked out.

Developmental and genetic studies of developmental prosopagnosia

Given that DP is a failure of development, it is ironic that little research has investigated the developmental course of DP. At present, only a few reports of children with DP have been published and they only provide a snapshot of DP in childhood and no information about its developmental trajectory. Several parents with children with DP have told me that they noticed that their child was having difficulties with faces as early as 2 years of age. Often these individuals were aware of their own prosopagnosia and so were likely to be especially sensitive to their child's prosopagnosia. For most parents, identification of prosopagnosia in a child is challenging.

Marked differences between children with DP and adults with DP have not been identified (Jones and Tranel 2001; Schmalzl et al., 2008), but this comparison rests on limited findings. The youngest child tested so far was a 4-year-old girl, K, who showed perceptual deficits with faces (Schmalzl et al., 2008). Prior to face training, K made a large proportion of fixations to regions other than the inner face, with especially poor attendance of the eye region. Poor attention to the eyes has also been noted in acquired prosopagnosia (Rossion et al., 2009) and autism spectrum disorder (Dalton et al., 2005). K's results fit well with a hypothesis suggesting that DP may sometimes originate in a failure to attend to the face in early childhood (Johnson 2005). Infants and toddlers direct considerable attention to the face (Goren 1975; Johnson and Morton 1991; see de Haan, Chapter 38; Lee et al., Chapter 39, this volume), and diminished attention to the face may affect the tuning of face processing mechanisms. While this hypothesis provides a straightforward account of DP, it is also possible that DP children fail to attend to faces normally because of pre-existing high-level face processing deficits. Current evidence does not allow us to discriminate between these possibilities and it is likely that DP results from a variety of developmental disruptions. The presence of object recognition problems and navigational problems in some DP cases indicates that the prosopagnosia seen in these cases does not have its origins in lack of attention to faces (Duchaine and Yovel, 2008).

Although little is known about the developmental course of DP, recent studies have demonstrated that it sometimes runs in families. Many of the early papers hinted at this possibility (Bentin et al., 1999; Duchaine, 2000; McConachie, 1976), but de Haan (1999) was the first to test multiple members of the same family. Recent years have seen many families with multiple DPs reported (Duchaine et al., 2007a; Grueter et al., 2007; Kennerknecht et al., 2006; Schmalzl et al., 2008) so it now well established that DP can run in families. This finding fits well a twin study in the normal population that indicates that face processing ability is heritable (Wilmer et al., 2010). Given the complexity of the face processing system, it seems likely that DP will result from multiple genetic deficits but no genes associated with DP have been identified yet. Studies that have relied on self-reports of face recognition ability have found segregation patterns consistent with a dominant autosomal inheritance (Kennerknecht et al., 2006). There have been some suggestions that DP always runs in families (Kennerknecht et al., 2009), but in a group of 19 DPs in studies in my laboratory, only 58% were aware of genetic relatives who shared their prosopagnosia (Duchaine 2008).

Training studies with developmental prosopagnosics

Not surprisingly, the first question that most DPs ask when contacting me is whether treatment exists that will improve their face recognition. At present no proven treatment methods are available, but this is an area of active research and several studies have found encouraging results. The studies with DPs carried out involve training with behavioral tasks, but recent studies with normal participants showing that the neuropeptide oxytocin improves face memory (Rimmele et al., 2009; Savaskan et al., 2008) and increases fixations to the eye region (Guastello et al., 2008) also hold promise for DP.

Two DP children, one who was 8 years old and another who was 4, were taught to recognize familiar faces using the inner facial features rather than external information (Brunsdon et al., 2006; Schmalzl et al., 2008). In both cases, recognition of the familiar faces improved following training. Importantly, this training appeared to transfer to other faces. Recognition of unfamiliar faces improved in the 8-year-old (Brunsdon et al., 2006) and the 4-year-old increased her fixations of an unfamiliar set of faces (Schmalzl et al., 2008).

Training with MZ, an adult DP, involved discrimination of spacing differences between faces with similar features in an effort to improve her face configural processing (DeGutis et al., 2007). MZ engaged in several cycles of training followed by no training, and she reported that her everyday face recognition was markedly improved during training periods. MZ was tested with the same face recognition tasks before and after training, and her performance on them improved. Neural measures also indicated that her face recognition after training was carried out in a more typical fashion than prior to training. Before training she had a non-selective N170 due to a strong non-face response, but after training she showed a face-selective N170 because the amplitude of the non-face response had diminished (see Figure 42.3). In addition, her right OFA and right FFA showed increased functional connectivity following training (DeGutis et al., 2007).

Summary and conclusions

DP holds promise as a means to investigate a range of issues in face processing and may provide a useful model to better understand the development of neurocognitive mechanisms. Cognitive studies of DP provide support for the existence of face-specific processes, and dissociations between different types of face processing in DPs are consistent with leading models of face processing that propose separable mechanisms for various aspects of face processing. Research on the neural basis of DP has found abnormalities in a number of occipital and temporal regions that show face-selective responses in people with normal face processing, and so provide additional evidence that the integrity of these areas is necessary for face recognition. However, despite the progress made in recent years, much work remains to be done and connections between cognitive, neural, developmental, and genetic levels of explanation remain to be worked out.

Acknowledgments

This work was supported by a grant from the Economic and Social Research Council (RES-061–23-0400). Lucia Garrido and an anonymous reviewer provided valuable editing suggestions.

References

Avidan, G., Hasson, U., Malach, R., and Behrmann, M. (2005). Detailed exploration of face-related processing in congenital prosopagnosia: 2. Functional neuroimaging findings. *Journal of Cognitive Neuroscience*, **17**, 1150–1167.

Behrmann, M., Avidan, G., Marotta, J.J., and Kimchi, R. (2005). Detailed exploration of face-related processing in congenital prosopagnosia: 1. Behavioral findings. *Journal of Cognitive Neuroscience*, **17**, 1130–1149.

Behrmann, M., Avidan, G., Gao. F., and Black, S. (2007). Structural imaging reveals anatomical alterations in inferotemporal cortex in congenital prosopagnosia. *Cerebral Cortex*, **17**, 2354–2563.

Bentin, S., Allison, T., Puce, A., Perez, E, and McCarthy, G. (1996). Electrophysiological studies of face perception in humans. *Journal of Cognitive Neuroscience*, **8**, 551–565.

Bentin, S., DeGutis, J.M., D'Esposito, M., and Robertson, L.C. (2007). Too many trees to see the forest: Performance, ERP and fMRI manifestations of integrative congenital prosopagnosia. *Journal of Cognitive Neuroscience*, **19**, 132–146.

Bentin, S., Deouell, L.Y., and Soroker, N. (1999). Selective visual streaming in face recognition: evidence from developmental prosopagnosia. *Neuroreport*, **10**, 823–827.

Bishop, D.V. (2006). What causes specific language impairment in children? *Current Directions in Psychological Science*, **15**, 217–221.

Bornstein, B. (1963). *Prosopagnosia*. In L. Halpern, (ed.) *Problems in dynamic neurology*, pp. 283–318. Hadassah: Hadassah Medical School.

Bruce, V. and Young, A.W. (1986). Understanding face recognition. *British Journal of Psychology*, **81**, 305–327.

Brunsdon, R., Coltheart, M., Nickels, L., and Joy, P. (2006). Developmental prosopagnosia: A case analysis and treatment study. *Cognitive Neuropsychology*, **23**, 822–840.

Calder, A.J. and Young, A.W. (2005). Understanding the recognition of facial identity and facial expression. *Nature Reviews Neuroscience*, **6**, 641–651.

Choisser B (1997). *Faceblind!* Available at: http://www.choisser.com/faceblind (accessed 01 Dec 2009).

Dalton, K.M., Nacewicz, B.M., Johnstone, T., *et al.* (2005). Gaze fixation and the neural circuitry of face processing in autism. *Nature Neuroscience*, **8**, 519–526.

Damasio, A., Damasio, H., and Van Hoesen, G. (1982). Prosopagnosia: anatomic basis and behavioral mechanisms. *Neurology*, **32**, 331–341.

Dawson, G., Webb, S., Schellenberg, G.D. *et al.* (2002). Defining the broader phenotype of autism: genetic, brain, and behavioral perspectives. *Developmental Psychopathology*, **14**, 581–611.

de Gelder, B. and Rouw, R. (2000). Configural face processes in acquired and developmental prosopagnosia: Evidence for two separate face systems? *NeuroReport*, **11**, 3145–3150.

de Haan, E. (1999). A familial factor in the development of face recognition deficits. *Journal of Clinical and Experimental Neuropsychology*, **21**, 312–315.

De Haan, E.H. and Campbell, R. (1991). A fifteen year follow-up of a case of developmental prosopagnosia. *Cortex*, **27**, 489–509.

DeGutis, J., Bentin, S., Roberton, L.C., D'Esposito, M. (2007). Functional plasticity in ventral temporal cortex following cognitive rehabilitation of a congenital prosopagnosic. *Journal of Cognitive Neuroscience*, **19**, 1790–1802.

Diamond, R. and Carey, S. (1986). Why faces are and are not special: an effect of expertise. *Journal of Experimental Psychology: General*, **115**, 107–117.

Duchaine, B. (2000). Developmental prosopagnosia and configural processing. *NeuroReport*, **11**, 79–83.

Duchaine, B. and Garrido, L. (2008). We're getting warmer: Characterizing the mechanisms of face recognition with acquired prosopagnosia. *Cognitive Neuropsychology*, **25**, 765–768.

Duchaine, B. and Nakayama, K. (2005). Dissociations of face and object recognition in developmental prosopagnosia. *Journal of Cognitive Neuroscience*, **17**, 249–261.

Duchaine, B. and Nakayama, K. (2006). Developmental prosopagnosia: a window to content-specific processing. *Current Opinion in Neurobiology*, **16**, 166–173.

Duchaine, B. and Weidenfeld, A. (2003). An evaluation of two commonly used tests of unfamiliar face recognition. *Neuropsychologia*, **41**, 713–720.

Duchaine, B. and Yovel, G. (2007). Face recognition, in G. Westheimer (ed.) *The Senses: A Comprehensive Reference*, pp.330–59. London: Elsevier.

Duchaine, B., Murray, H., Turner, M., White, S., and Garrido, L. (2010). Normal social cognition in developmental prosopagnosia. *Cognitive Neuropsychology*, **25**, 1–15.

Duchaine, B.C., Nieminen-von Wendt, T., New, J., and Kulomaki, T. (2003a). Dissociations of visual recognition in a developmental agnosic: evidence for separate developmental processes. *Neurocase*, **9**, 380–389.

Duchaine, B., Parker, H., and Nakayama, K. (2003b). Normal recognition of emotion in a prosopagnosic. *Perception*, **32**, 827–838.

Duchaine, B.C., Dingle, K., Butterworth, E., and Nakayama, K. (2004). Normal greeble learning in a severe case of developmental prosopagnosia. *Neuron*, **43**, 469–473.

Duchaine, B., Yovel, G., Butterworth, E., and Nakayama, K. (2006). Prosopagnosia as an impairment to face-specific mechanisms: elimination of the alternative explanations in a developmental case. *Cognitive Neuropsychology*, **23**, 714–747.

Duchaine, B., Germine, L. and Nakayama, K. (2007a). Family resemblance: Ten family members with prosopagnosia and within-class object agnosia. *Cognitive Neuropsychology*, **24**, 419–430.

Duchaine, B., Yovel, G., and Nakayama, K. (2007b). No global processing deficit in the Navon task in 14 developmental prosopagnosics. *Social Cognitive Affective Neuroscience*, **2**, 104–113.

Duchaine, B., Jenkins, R., Germine, L., and Calder, A.J. (2009). Normal gaze discrimination and adaptation in seven prosopagnosics. *Neuropsychologia*, **47**, 2029–2036.

Ellis, H.D. and Florence, M. (1990). Bodamer's (1947) paper on prosopagnosia. *Cognitive Neuropsychology*, **7**, 81–105.

Farah, M.J. (1990). *Visual Agnosia*. Cambridge, MA, MIT Press.

Farah, M.J. (1996). Is face recognition "special"? Evidence from neuropsychology. *Behavioral Brain Research*, **76**, 181–189.

Garrido, L., Duchaine, B., and Nakayama, K. (2008). Face detection in normal and prosopagnosic individuals. *Journal of Neuropsychology*, **2**, 219–240.

Garrido, L., Eisner, F., McGettigan, C., *et al.* (2009). Developmental phonagnosia: a selective deficit to vocal identity recognition. *Neuropsychologia*, **47**, 123–131.

Garrido, L., Furl, N., Draganski, B., *et al.* (2009). VBM reveals reduced grey matter volume in the temporal cortex of developmental prosopagnosics. *Brain*, **132**, 3443–3455.

Gauthier, I., Williams, P., Tarr, M.J., and Tanaka, J. (1998). Training "greeble" experts: a framework for studying expert object recognition processes. *Vision Research*, **38**, 2401–2428.

Germine, L., Cashdollar, N., Düzel, E., and Duchaine, B. (2011). A new selective developmental deficit: Impaired object recognition with normal face recognition. *Cortex*, **47**, 598–607.

Gobbini, M. and Haxby, J.V. (2007). Neural systems for the recognition of familiar faces. *Neuropsychologia*, **45**, 32–41.

Goodall, J. and Berman, P. (1999). *Reason for Hope: A Spiritual Journey*. New York, Warner Books.

Goren, C., Sarty, M., and Wu, P.Y. (1975). Abstract visual following and pattern discrimination of face-like stimuli by newborn infants. *Pediatrics*, **56**, 544–549.

Guastello, A.J., Mitchell, P.B., and Dadds, M.R. (2008). Oxytocin increases gaze to the eye region of human faces. *Biological Psychiatry*, **63**, 3–5.

Hämäläinen, M., Hari, R., Ilmoniemi, R.J., Knuutila, J., and Lounasmaa, O.V. (1993). Magnetoencephalography—Theory, instrumentation, and applications to noninvasive studies of the working human brain. *Review of Modern Physics*, **65**, 413–497.

Harris, A., Duchaine, B., and Nakayama, K. (2005). Normal and abnormal face selectivity of the M170 response in developmental prosopagnosics. *Neuropsychologia*, **43**, 2125–2136.

Hasson, U., Avidan, G., Deouell, L.Y., Bentin, S., and Malach, R. (2003). Face-selective activation in a congenital prosopagnosic subject. *Journal of Cognitive Neuroscience*, **15**, 419–31.

Haxby, J.V., Hoffman, E.A., and Gobbini, M.I. (2000). The distributed human neural system for face perception. *Trends in Cognitive Science*, **4**, 223–233.

Humphreys, K., Avidan, G., and Behrmann, M. (2006). A detailed investigation of facial expression processing in congenital prosopagnosia as compared to acquired prosopagnosia. *Experimental Brain Research*, **176**, 356–373.

Iaria, G., Bogod, N., Fox, C.J., and Barton, J.J. (2009). Developmental topographical disorientation: Case one. *Neuropsychologia*, **47**, 30–40.

Johnson, M.H. (2005). Sub-cortical face processing. *Nature Reviews Neuroscience*, **6**, 766–774.

Johnson, M.H. and Morton, J. (1991). *Biology and cognitive development: The case of face recognition.* London: Blackwell.

Jones, R.D. and Tranel, D. (2001). Severe developmental prosopagnosia in a child with superior intellect. *Journal of Clinical and Experimental Neuropsychology*, **23**, 265–273.

Kanwisher, N., McDermott, J., and Chun, M. (1997). The fusiform face area: a module in human extrastriate cortex specialized for face perception. *Journal of Neuroscience*, **17**, 4302–4311.

Kennerknecht, I., Grueter, T., Welling, B., *et al.* (2006). First report of prevalence of non-syndromic hereditary prosopagnosia (HPA). *American Journal of Medical Genetics, A*, 140, 1617–1622.

Kennerknecht, I., Ho, T., and Wong, V. (2009). Prevalence of hereditary prosopagnosia (HPA) in Hong Kong Chinese population. *American Journal of Medical Genetics A*, **146**, 2863–2870.

Kosslyn, S., Hamilton, S.E., and Bernstein, J.H. (1995). The perception of curvature can be selectively disrupted in prosopagnosia. *Brain and Cognition*, **27**, 36–58.

Kracke, I. (1994). Developmental prosopagnosia in Asperger syndrome: presentation and discussion of an individual case. *Developmental Medicine and Child Neurology*, **36**, 873–886.

Kress, T. and Daum, I. (2003). Event-related potentials reflect impaired face recognition in patients with congenital prosopagnosia. *Neuroscience Letters*, **352**, 133–136.

Laeng, B. and Caviness, V.S. (2001). Prosopagnosia as a deficit in encoding curved surfaces. *Journal of Cognitive Neuroscience*, **13**, 556–576.

Lange, J., de Lussanet, M., Kuhlmann, S., *et al.* (2009). Impairments of biological motion perception in congenital prosopagnosia. *PLoS One*, **4**, e7414.

Le Grand, R., Cooper, P., Mondloch, C., *et al.* (2006). What aspects of face processing are impaired in developmental prosopagnosia? *Brain and Cognition*, **61**, 139–158.

Levine, D.N. and Calvanio, R. (1989). Prosopagnosia: a defect in visual configural processing. *Brain and Cognition*, **10**, 149–70.

Lewis, M.B. and Edmonds, A.J. (2005). Searching for faces in scrambled scenes. *Visual Cognition*, **32**, 903–920.

Mazzola, F., Seigal, A., MacAskill, A., Corden, B., Lawrence, K., and Skuse, D.H. (2006). Eye tracking and fear recognition deficits in Turner syndrome. *Social Neuroscience*, **1**, 259–269.

McCarthy, G., Puce, A., Gore, J.C., and Allison, T. (1997). Face-specific processing in the human fusiform gyrus. *Journal of Cognitive Neuroscience*, **9**, 605–610.

McCloskey, M., Rapp, B., Yantis, S., *et al.* (1995). A developmental deficit in localizing objects from vision. *Psychological Science*, **6**, 112–117.

McConachie, H. (1976). Developmental prosopagnosia. A single case report. *Cortex*, **12**, 76–82.

Moeller, S., Freiwald, W.A., and Tsao, D.Y. (2008). Patches with links: a unified system for processing faces in the macaque temporal lobe. *Science*, **320**, 1355–1459.

Moscovitch, M., Winocur, G., and Behrmann, M. (1997). What Is special about face recognition?: Nineteen experiments on a person with visual object agnosia and dyslexia but normal face recognition. *Journal of Cognitive Neuroscience*, **9**, 555–604.

Navon, D. (1977). Forest before trees: The precedence of global features in visual perception. *Cognitive Psychology*, **9**, 353–383.

Nunn, J.A., Postma, P., and Pearson, R. (2001). Developmental prosopagnosia: should it be taken at face value? *Neurocase*, **7**, 15–27.

Ramus, F. (2003). Developmental dyslexia: Specific phonological deficit or general sensorimotor dysfunction? *Current Opinion in Neurobiology*, **13**, 212–218.

Reed, C.L., Stone, V.E., Bozova, S., and Tanaka, J. (2003). The body-inversion effect. *Psychological Science*, **14**, 302–308.

Reed, C.L., Stone, V.E., Grubb, J.D., and McGoldrick, J.E. (2006). Turning configural processing upside down: part and whole body postures. *Journal of Experimental Psychology: Human Perception Performance*, **32**, 73–87.

Rimmele, U., Hediger, K., Heinrichs, M., and Klaver, P. (2009). Oxytocin makes a face in memory familiar. *Journal of Neuroscience*, **29**, 38–42.

Rock, I. (1974). The perception of disoriented figures. *Scientific American*, **230**, 78–85.

Rossion, B., Kaiser, M.D., Bub, D,, and Tanaka, J.W. (2009). Is the loss of diagnosticity of the eye region a common feature of acquired prosopagnosia? *Journal of Neuropsychology*, **3**, 69–78.

Sadr, J., Duchaine, B.C., and Nakayama, K. (2004). The perception of facial attractiveness in developmental prosopagnosia. *Journal of Vision*, **4**, 914.

Savaskan, E., Ehrhardt, R., Schulz, A., Walter, M., and Schächinger, H. (2008). Post-learning intranasal oxytocin modulates human memory for facial identity. *Psychoneuroendocrinology*, **33**, 368–374.

Schmalzl, L., Palermo, R., and Coltheart, M. (2008). Cognitive heterogeneity in genetically based prosopagnosia: A family study. *Journal of Neuropsychology*, **2**, 99–117.

Schmalzl, L, Palermo, R., Green, M., Brunsdon, R., and Coltheart, M. (2008). Training of familiar face recognition and visual scan paths for faces in a child with congenital prosopagnosia. *Cognitive Neuropsychology*, **25**, 704–729.

Temple, C. (1992). Developmental memory impairment: Faces and patterns. In R. Campbell (ed.) *Mental Lives: Case Studies in Cognition*, pp.199–215. London: Blackwell.

Temple, C.M. and Richardson, P. (2004). Developmental amnesia: A new pattern of dissociation with intact episodic memory. *Neuropsychologia*, **42**, 764–781.

Thomas, C., Avidan, G., Humphreys, K., Jung, K.J., Gao, F., and Behrmann, M. (2009). Reduced structural connectivity in ventral visual cortex in congenital prosopagnosia. *Nature Neuroscience*, **29**, 29–31.

Tippett, L.J., Miller, L.A., and Farah, M.J. (2000). Prosopamnesia: A selective impairment in face learning. *Cognitive Neuropsychology*, **17**, 241–55.

Todorov, A. and Duchaine, B. (2008). Reading trustworthiness in faces without recognizing faces. *Cognitive Neuropsychology*, **25**, 395–410.

Tsao, D.Y. and Freiwald, W.A. (2006). What's so special about the average face? *Trends in Cognitive Science*, **10**, 391–393.

Tsao, D.Y., Moeller, S., and Freiwald, W.A. (2008). Comparing face patch systems in macaques and humans. *Proceedings of the National Academy of Science USA*, **105**, 19514–19519.

Van Zandvoort, M.J.E., Nijboer, T.C.W., and De Haan, E.H.F. (2007). Developmental colour agnosia. *Cortex*, **43**, 750–757.

VanRullen, R. (2006). On second glance: Still no high-level pop-out effect for faces. *Vision Research*, **46**, 3017–3027.

Viola, P. and Jones, M. (2004). Robust real-time face detection. *International Journal of Computer Vision*, **57**, 137–154.

von Kriegstein, K., Kleinschmidt, A., and Giraud, A.L. (2006). Voice recognition and cross-modal responses to familiar speakers' voices in prosopagnosia. *Cerebral Cortex*, **16**, 1314–1322.

Wigan, A.L. (1844). *The Duality of the Mind*. London: Longman.

Williams, M.A., Berberovic, N., and Mattingley, J.B. (2007). Abnormal fMRI adaptation to unfamiliar faces in a case of developmental prosopamnesia. *Current Biology*, **17**, 1259–1264.

Wilmer, J.B., Germine, L., Chabris, C.F., *et al.* (2010). Human face recognition ability is specific and highly heritable. *Proceedings of the National Academy of Sciences USA*, **107**, 5238–5241.

Yardley, L., McDermott, L., Pisarski, S., Duchaine, B., and Nakayama, K. (2008). Psychosocial consequences of developmental prosopagnosia: A problem of recognition. *Journal of Psychosomatic Research*, **65**, 445–451.

Yin, R. (1969). Looking at upside down faces. *Journal of Experimental Psychology*, **81**, 141–145.

Yovel, G. and Duchaine, B. (2006). Specialized face perception mechanisms extract both part and spacing information: evidence from developmental prosopagnosia. *Journal of Cognitive Neuroscience*, **18**, 580–593.

Yovel, G., Pelc, T., and Lubetzky, I. (2010). It's all in your head: Why is the body inversion effect abolished for headless bodies? *Journal of Experimental Psychology: Human Perception and Performance*, **36**, 759–767.

Chapter 43

Face Processing in Autism

Sara Jane Webb, Susan Faja, and Geraldine Dawson

Introduction

Face processing and its role in the social phenotype of autism spectrum disorders (ASD) has received much attention in the past decade. Since 2000, over 120 empirical publications have addressed some aspect of face processing in ASD. Why is there an emphasis on faces? In ASD, many of the early signs (between 12 and 18 months) reflect the failure to attend to and use facial information, such as facial expressions, appropriately as reflected in poor eye contact, lack of attention to others, difficulties with joint attention, and failure to differentiate and respond appropriately to emotions. These abnormal early ASD symptoms are in stark contrast to the spontaneous attention and interest that young children without autism demonstrate toward people in their environment (see Johnson, Chapter 1, this volume for discussion of the typical development of face processing). Behavioral studies of individuals with ASD consistently note impaired performance on basic tests of face memory and face processing during the early and mid-childhood years. For adults with high functioning (HF) ASD who can converse about their abilities, many complain about the complexity of information within the face and difficulties processing facial information in *real time*. As compared with viewing static faces such as those often used in experimental measures of face processing, adults with HF ASD have commented that there are simultaneous pressures to respond, show that you are listening and paying attention, and recognize emotions. As a result, these individuals often report that they have less time to recognize faces and have to be "constantly tuned in." Specifically, in a recent project (Faja et al., 2008, 2009; Webb et al., 2009) one individual commented that "2D images don't mind if you stare. There are deadlines in recognizing people and (if you don't do it quickly) they are less than thrilled."

Background

The specific use of face information may be critical to the development of broader social and cognitive skills. For example, early attention preferences for social stimuli, such as orienting to a face when someone enters a room, provide opportunities for social engagement and facilitate the acquisition of later social and communication skills (e.g. Rochat and Striano, 1999). Joint attention, the ability to coordinate attention to an object or event with another person, in the first year is related to later language development (e.g. Tomasello, 1995). By 9 to 12 months of age, infants utilize facial expressions of others to guide their behavior toward novel objects and events (e.g. Feinman, 1982; Moore and Corkum, 1994). As well, face processing has been posited as important to the development of theory of mind (e.g. Baron-Cohen, 1995; Brothers et al., 1990).

Given the early development of face processing abilities and the supportive role face processing plays in the development of social and cognitive skills in the first years of life, impairment in the development of the face processing system may contribute to the social and cognitive impairments associated with ASD. However, face processing itself is not a simple process, but instead reflects a complex interconnected set of functions. This chapter will focus on how these processes contribute to face processing and how the impact of disruptions in any of these systems may contribute to the altered processing that is found in autism. These processes include: lower level visual processing, visual attention, early-stage processing of faces, memory for faces, and emotional significance of faces. Lastly, we will discuss preliminary evidence suggesting that face training may lead to subtle but important changes in the face processing system in individuals with ASD.

Lower-level visual processing

Faces pose the same problem for the brain as any other visual stimuli. Visible light reaches the eye, the retina converts light into patterned neural signals, and the retinal signals travel to the lateral geniculate nucleus (LGN), which in turn innervates the primary and secondary visual cortex. Two populations of retinal ganglion cells send separate projections to parvocellular and magnocellular layers of the LGN. For faces, the magnocellular system may be more sensitive to low spatial frequency (LSF) information, is thought to be a "fast" path to the amygdala, and would preferentially carry information about global information such as configural information (Costen et al., 1994). LSF information is also thought to support holistic processing and precedes processing of featural info (Goffaux and Rossion, 2006). It has been proposed that LSF information mediates fast, unconscious adjustments in social behavior (Johnson, 2005; Vuilleumier and Pourtois, 2007). The parvocellular system may be more sensitive to high spatial frequency (HSF) information about form and color, represents a "slow" path from the ventral extrastriate cortex to the anterior fusiform, and would preferentially carry information with detection of fine details (age and wrinkles), familiarity and featural information. Faces filtered for LSF appear blurred and features are difficult to detect. Filtering for HSF sharpens the features, making faces seem more like line drawings. Using such stimuli, a greater reliance on LSF than on HSF information in face processing has been supported by numerous studies on normal adults (e.g. Fiorentini et al., 1983; Schyns and Oliva, 1999), thus confirming the predominance of configural processing in face recognition (e.g. Tanaka and Farah, 1993).

In autism, recent evidence suggests that perception of faces may be biased toward HSF information. Deruelle et al. (2004) tested individuals with autism and Asperger's (AS) aged 5 to 13 years and found better performance when matching faces based on HSF faces than LSF. Similarly de Jong et al. (2008) showed a reliance on HSF information during attention orienting via gaze cuing in HF 7 to 13 year olds with PDD-NOS (pervasive developmental disorder–not otherwise specified). Adults with Asperger's may be impaired when identifying stimuli containing emotional expressions filtered for only LSF information (Katsyri et al., 2008).

Although little is known about the early development of this system in ASD, McCleery et al. (2008) found that high risk infants (i.e. infant siblings of children with autism who are at higher genetic risk for ASD) show enhanced differentiation of light/dark (luminance) information compared to low risk infants (infants with no family history of autism). The authors interpreted this as an abnormality of the magnocellular pathway.

Implications

What are the implications for a HSF bias in ASD? In general, a bias in HSF information would broadly impact visual processing. First, this bias could account for performance on local/global visual tasks. For example, some have argued that abnormal magnocellular processing may result in a deficit in perceiving global aspects of visual information (Milne et al., 2002; Greenaway and Plaisted, 2005, but see Carow et al., 2006). Second, increased HSF information may account for other behaviors such as the use of peripheral vision by affected individuals. Using peripheral vision or "lateral vision" may result from the need to filter out the overabundance of HSF detail information and the need to increase or facilitate movement perception. Thus, looking out of the corner of the eye may regulate or optimize perception and diminish local information.

Lower visual processing needs to be appreciated in a developmental context. McCleery et al. (2008) pose that a bias in lower level perceptual information may alter the visual world of infants, putting them at risk for visuoperceptual abnormalities, which in turn, could lead to the higher-level deficits in visual, social, communicative, and emotional behaviors associated with ASD. The ratio of magnocelluar/parvocelluar functioning may be an early risk marker (at least in siblings of children with ASD) or it might represent one endophenotype in which subtle variations in processing confer a risk for autism when combined with other deficits. As well, the visual system has known critical periods for structural organization; a narrow window of opportunity may be available for training the system correctly.

Visual attention

A second critical domain that likely contributes to impairments in face processing is the visual attention system. Attention is known to modulate stages of visual perception even early in development (e.g. Smith and Chatterjee, 2008). Within the first year, infants transition from reflexive orienting driven by the characteristics of external stimuli to volitional attention driven by the infant's own interests and needs. It is this internally driven, volitional attention system that facilitates the specialization of higher order visual processing circuits centered on response to the experiences that are present in the environment. Individuals with autism have been shown to have both difficulties in shifting and disengaging attention (Courchesne et al., 1994; Elsabbagh et al., 2009; Landry and Bryson, 2004; Townsend et al., 1996; Wainwright and Bryson, 1996), specifically during infancy (Zwaigenbaum et al., 2005). However, there is some evidence that these findings may be task dependent with spared reflexive orienting of visual attention (Iarocci and Burack, 2004).

Visual attention to faces

In adults with autism, Klin et al. (2002) found a lack of attention to faces during complex visual scene processing. In this study, adults with autism and with typical development watched the movie *Who's afraid of Virginia Woolf?* while their eye movements were recorded. Adults with autism as a group demonstrated less attention to the internal features of the face during the video than to other items. Within the autism group, individuals that attended to the mouth region had better social abilities than those that did not attend to the face at all. Thus, despite decreased attention to the eyes, attention to the mouth was seen as a compensatory mechanism. Similarly, Jones et al. (2008) found that 2-year-olds with ASD showed decreased attention to the eye region of the face and increased attention to the mouth; less attention to the eye region was associated with more social deficits. Merin et al. (2007) also found that a subgroup of high-risk infant siblings of children with ASD had diminished gaze to eyes relative to the mouth during a still face paradigm. About one-third of the 6-month-old group *at risk* for ASD demonstrated differences in their visual attention to their mother's faces.

Results using eye tracking to monitor visual attention to faces, however, have not been consistent, particularly among investigations using static faces as stimuli. Adolescents and adults with HF ASD have demonstrated fewer fixations to the internal region of the face containing the core features of eyes, nose, and mouth relative to controls (Pelphrey et al., 2002; Trepagnier et al., 2002). Greater attention to the mouth region than the eyes was also found in this population (Klin et al., 2002; Pelphrey et al., 2002). When attention was directed toward the face, fixations have also been found to be greater in the mouth than eye region (Neumann et al., 2006; Spezio et al., 2007). In contrast, two groups have found greater fixations to the eye region than the mouth in adults with ASD, although fixations were less than the control group (Hernandez et al., 2009; Sterling et al., 2008). Among children with HF ASD, differences were not detected compared with controls when viewing static faces with neutral or emotional expressions (van der Geest et al., 2002). However, children with ASD spent more time looking at faces in an inverted orientation compared to controls.

In younger toddlers with ASD, habituation measured by eye gaze suggests increased attention to the face. Using an infant controlled habituation paradigm, Webb et al. (2010) found that toddlers (aged 18 to 30 months) with more ASD symptoms spent more time examining new faces, compared to toddlers with ASD who had fewer symptoms, toddlers with developmental delay and toddlers with typical development. In the group with more ASD symptoms, attention to faces was also prolonged in comparison to attention to non-face stimuli (houses). Longer gazes to the face during habituation related to poorer social scores on the Vineland and lower verbal IQ.

Featural attention

Behavioral investigations are consistent with measures of eye gaze with respect to differences in attention to the face; children with autism may also attend to different aspects of the face. Although children with ASDs could recognize the faces of classmates, Langdell (1978) found that they were less able to judge identity using the eye region or upper part of the face, suggesting differential attention strategies among these more severely impaired children. Children with ASDs have also been reported to show better performance when recognizing isolated facial features and partially obscured faces than typical children (Hobson et al., 1988; Tantam et al., 1989). Using a paradigm designed to detect a holistic processing advantage over feature-based processing, Lopez et al. (2008) reported that children with ASD failed to show this advantage. Three groups have found evidence of holistic processing, but this may be due to focused attention toward certain regions of the face. Joseph and Tanaka (2003) found children with HF ASD demonstrated a holistic advantage, but only on trials that tested the mouth and not the eyes. Lopez et al. (2004) were able to elicit a holistic processing advantage via attention cuing. Among adults with HF ASD, holistic processing was detected only during trials testing the eye region, rather than the generalized advantage exhibited by controls (Faja et al., 2009). With familiar faces, which may elicit different attention patterns, Wilson et al. (2007) found that children with ASDs did not differ from children with developmental delay in a forced choice recognition paradigm regardless of whether the information included the full face, the inner face, or only the outer face area.

These results, taken together, suggest that children and adults with ASDs rely on different information from the face. The degree to which this is specific to ASD is unclear. Comparison children with developmental delay also have social deficits; thus deficits in social ability not the specific diagnosis may be related to alternative processing strategies. When comparisons were made between individuals with high cognitive ability and ASD versus typical controls, these differences in gaze and recognition of particular features persists suggesting that individuals with ASD may view faces differently in the absence of external cues to guide their attention.

Attention to the eyes

Eye contact and eye gaze serve important functions in social interaction and communication. Individuals with autism often display atypical eye contact (Baranek, 1999; Charman et al., 1997; Osterling et al., 2002), atypical gaze fixation patterns (Klin et al., 2002), and eye gaze processing impairments (Dawson et al., 1998; Mundy et al., 1986) that may contribute to their social cognitive deficits including differences in face processing ability. Directing attention explicitly to the eye region results in increased attention to the eyes by individuals with ASD. Cuing each trial with a cross hair that directed the participant to the region of the screen where the bridge of the nose would appear, adults with ASD demonstrated relatively more fixations within the eye region than the mouth region (Sterling et al., 2008). These results raise the possibility that minor manipulations in stimulus presentation or instructions may impact the pattern of responses by individuals with ASD, and may help to recruit face processing systems.

Neural correlates of visual attention

Several researchers have proposed that a failure to attend to the eye region underlies the difference between ASD and controls, particularly those detected via neuroimaging (see Pelphrey and Vander Wyk, Chapter 30, this volume for discussion of the neural basis of eye gaze processing). Attention to the face has been found to modulate the activation of the face fusiform gyrus among typically developing adults (Wojciulik et al., 1998). Using fMRI, numerous investigations have found hypoactivation of the face fusiform gyrus by individuals with ASD relative to controls (for review see Schultz, 2005). Hadjikhani et al. (2004) found no differences in fusiform activity between individuals with ASD and controls when stimulus presentation included a cross hair positioned on the bridge of the nose, explicit directions to look at the cross hair, and larger images. Finally, Dalton et al. (2005) found that fusiform activation was correlated with the amount of time spent looking at the eye region of the face by individuals with ASD.

Implications

The brain organizes around the information that is available and thus, attention is critical to creating functional neural circuits. Findings from adults with ASD suggest decreased attention to faces during complex situations with some compensatory ability to reduce the complexity of the input (e.g. Klin et al., 2002). During low demand tasks, such as when asked to attend to static two-dimensional faces, HF individuals may be able to complete the task, particularly in the presence of attention cues.

For infants and young children, the story may be more complex. Zwaigenbaum et al. (2005) suggests decreased attention shifting abilities from 6 to 12 months coincides with symptom onset. Young toddlers may need increased attention during basic processing such as when children orient to new stimuli on screen (e.g. Webb et al., 2009). This may result in difficulty flexibly shifting between important stimuli in their environment. Once children engage with a static face, longer processing (longer need for information processing, failure to disengage) is related to worse social skills. This is consistent with early impairments in joint referencing and joint attention (Sigman, 1998).

Early-stage processing of faces

Eyes are a critical source of information as well as an important feature on the face. Thus, to a large extent, the presence of this feature is critical to the identification of a face. However, the face is more than just the eyes. The overall positioning of features, such as the eyes residing above the nose (first order relations), and the spacing between features (second-order relations) is also of importance in encoding and recognizing faces (see Tanaka and Gordon, Chapter 10, this volume for discussion of holistic and configural face processing). Very soon after birth, neonates show a preference for stimuli that maintain the first order relations found in a face (Easterbrook et al., 1999). The development of sensitivity to second order relations has a much longer trajectory (Mondloch et al., 2002). Typically developing children are less likely to exhibit robust adult patterns on a variety of tasks (e.g. Carey and Diamond, 1977;

Carey et al., 1980; Thompson and Massaro, 1989), although adult-like behaviors can be elicited from preschoolers under certain task conditions (Freire and Lee, 2001; McKone and Boyer, 2006; Pellicano and Rhodes, 2003). Despite this long developmental trajectory, infancy may be a critical period for development of the networks supporting configural processing. Infants born with cataracts, which were removed within the first year, demonstrate deficits on facial configuration tasks in childhood (Le Grand et al., 2001).

Behavioral studies of face processing

Among individuals with ASD, there is indirect and direct evidence for reduced configural process-ing of faces. For instance, the face inversion effect–the decreased ability to recognize faces when presented in an inverted orientation—is less robust in individuals with ASD (Hobson et al., 1988; Langdell, 1978; Rose et al., 2007; Teunisse and de Gelder, 2003; but see Lahaie et al., 2006). Teunisse and de Gelder (2003) noted significant variability among individuals with ASD and a positive relation between recognition accuracy in the upright condition and social intelligence. Disruption of configural information with a split-face paradigm is also less disruptive to indi-viduals with ASD and task performance again was correlated with social IQ (Teunisse and de Gelder, 2003). In addition, the Thatcher illusion, which is thought to disrupt second-order relations, was detected as accurately by lower functioning children with ASD as controls (Rouse et al., 2004). A direct measure of configural processing among children with ASD revealed differ-ences on trials in which the eye region was probed, but not when the mouth region was tested (Wolf et al., 2009). Among HF adults with ASD, accuracy was reduced compared to controls in a direct measure of sensitivity to configural information (Faja et al., 2009). Reaction time suggested that adults with ASD did not detect large changes in the distances between features more quickly than smaller changes, which was the pattern for controls. Thus, although high-functioning adults with ASD are able to detect this information they may do so less automatically.

Neural correlates of early-state processing

The amplitude and latency of the ERP have been used to index and differentiate the allocation of neural resources and the temporal characteristics of information processing for faces. Many ERP studies have revealed a face-specific component, peaking at 130–170 ms after stimulus onset, which is related to early-stage processing of faces (Bentin et al., 1996; Botzel et al., 1995; Eimer 1998; 2000; George et al., 1996; see Eimer, Chapter 17, this volume). Using ERPs to assess the presence of face-specific processing among adolescents and adults with ASD has yielded mixed results. McPartland et al. (2004) found high-functioning individuals with ASD had slower N170 latencies in response to faces than objects (also see O'Connor et al., 2007). Similarly, O'Connor et al. (2005) found that a group of children with Asperger's had slower N170 latencies in response to facial expressions of emotions compared to controls. These findings were interpreted by O'Connor et al. (2005, 2007) to reflect impaired holistic and configural processing of faces. In contrast to these investigations, a recent investigation with a relatively large group of adults with HF ASD (N= 32) and age, gender and IQ-matched typical adults, revealed that early-stage face processing did not significantly differ between groups for the main comparison between faces and houses, but did differ for the comparison between inverted faces compared to upright faces (Webb et al., 2009a). Adults with ASD did not exhibit a differential N170 in the upright versus inverted conditions, while controls demonstrated greater amplitude but slower N170 responses to inverted compared to upright faces. Similar to other reports that have not differentiated indi-viduals with ASD from controls, we used a cross hair to direct attention to the eye region prior to the appearance of each face.

In a large sample of young children, the developmental precursor to the N170 has been found to be delayed to neutral faces and fear faces in 3- to 4-year-olds with ASD compared to typical peers (Dawson et al., 2004; Webb et al., 2006). Interestingly, when the same sample of children with ASD was followed up longitudinally at age 6, they exhibited more "typical" patterns of face/house discrimination (first order processing) at the prN170 and P400 (Webb et al., 2009b).

FMRI results have identified areas of critical significance to (novel) face processing, including the fusiform gyrus, amygdala, and prefrontal cortex. The fusiform gyrus has been found to be less active in HF ASD than in controls (e.g. Pierce et al., 2001; Pierce and Redcay, 2008; Schultz et al., 2000; for review Schultz, 2005; but see Bookheimer et al., 2008; Kleinhans et al., 2009). There is also preliminary evidence suggesting neuronal abnormalities in the fusiform gyrus (van Kooten et al., 2008). Habituation in the right amygdala during novel face viewing also may be abnormal compared to controls (Kleinhans et al., 2008). In children with ASD, differences in upright versus inverted face processing were not found in the fusiform gyrus, but in the prefrontal cortex and amygdala (Bookheimer et al., 2008). The connections between the amygdala and the fusiform (Kleinhans et al., 2008) as well as in the social brain network (Koshino et al., 2008; Pelphrey et al., 2007) have also been found to be under-activated in ASD.

Implications

To date, ERP data suggests that early-stage processing, which involves indexing first-order relations (e.g. face vs. object) are impaired early but not consistently later (after 6 years) in the development of ASD. Behavioral measurements with toddlers with ASD and *high-risk* infant siblings would be of interest in substantiating this. In contrast, configural processing including second order relations, holistic advantages and the inversion effect are poorly developed in ASD. Nonetheless, there is individual variability in the disruption to these specialized processing advantages for faces, which has been related by some investigations to the degree of social impairment. For both adults and children with ASD, more typical early-stage processing of faces has been found to be related to *less* severe social symptoms.

Memory for faces

Face memory involves recognition of familiar faces as well as learning and memory for new faces. Boucher et al. (1998) asked children with autism and verbal and chronological age matched comparison children to identify pictures of faces as either those of individuals working at their own school or "at another school" (i.e. individuals unfamiliar to the child). Children with autism correctly identified fewer faces; however only four out of the 19 children with an ASD performed below the lowest score of the comparison group suggesting considerable overlap. One potential source of variability may be symptom severity. In a large sample of children with ASDs, Klin et al. (1999) found that children with autism but not children with PDD-NOS performed worse than nonverbal mental age matched comparison children and verbal mental age matched comparison children on a test of face memory, although there were no differences between groups on a test of spatial memory.

For children with typical development (TD), memory is better for faces compared to non-face visual stimuli (Hauck et al., 1998). By contrast, children with autism do not always show superior memory for faces as compared to non-face stimuli (Hauck et al., 1998; Serra et al., 2003), and another study showed that they perform worse on a face memory as compared with a non-face memory task (Boucher and Lewis, 1992). Furthermore, in all three of these studies, the children with ASDs performed worse than comparison children. Of note, mental age differences between controls and children with ASD may contribute to this pattern. Chawarska and Volkmar (2007) found impaired (human and monkey) face memory in a sample of 1- to 3-year-olds with ASD and toddlers with more general developmental delay compared to toddlers with typical development.

In an older sample, adults with ASDs performed worse than chronological age and verbal IQ matched comparison groups on a test of unfamiliar face memory; their performance on the face memory test was also significantly worse than their performance on a test of memory for buildings. There were no differences between the autism group and verbal mental age matched comparison participants on these tests (Blair et al., 2002). This pattern was not replicated in a recent study conducted in our lab (Webb et al., 2009a). Adults with HF ASD were impaired on both face and house memory compared to controls with *both* groups demonstrating better performance on the face memory test than the house memory test. Although the tests were exactly similar in protocol, performance for the HF ASD group (N = 31) on the house and face versions of the test was highly correlated ($rs > 0.45$, $ps = 0.01$), while there were no relations for the Control group (N = 32) ($r = 0.12$, $r = 0.10$). This is in contrast to strong correlations (within both groups) between the immediate and delayed version for faces ($rs > 0.47$, $ps < 0.01$) and houses ($rs > 0.53$, $ps < 0.01$).

When assessed via fMRI, familiar faces have been shown to recruit the same regional activation in both adults and children with ASD as in matched controls (Pierce and Redcay, 2008; Pierce et al., 2004). One hypothesis is that increased fusiform activation to familiar faces may reflect enhanced attention and motivation. Consistent with this interpretation, Grelotti et al. (2005) found fusiform and amygdala activation during discrimination of Digimon characters in a child with autism who had a "special interest" in Digimon. The brain response to Digimon characters was greater than to other non-expertise categories and to unfamiliar faces. Taken together, these reports suggest that a failure to activate the fusiform to unfamiliar faces is not due to fundamental under-activation.

Implications

Several factors are particularly important when drawing conclusions about facial memory in autism. First, age is a significant confound. There is preliminary evidence to suggest that facial memory may be more impaired in childhood in individuals with ASD than during the adult period. It is unknown whether this reflects a longer period of developmental growth in this domain, is a downstream effect of developmental changes in early-stage processing of faces, or is an artifact of studies including more high functioning subjects in older age groups. Second, familiarity of the stimulus may influence performance. For example, familiarity may allow the use of verbal strategies to mediate visual memory, may link to more semantic information, and may reflect expertise effects. Lastly, many memory tasks can be completed using a variety of strategies. A reliance on parts based strategies may have contributed to the strong relation between performance on face and house memory in our ASD group (Webb et al., 2009a).

Facial emotional expressions

Relying on a variety of experimental designs, individuals with ASD fail to respond normally to affective facial displays (Bacon et al., 1998; Charman et al., 1997; Hall et al., 2003; Sigman et al., 1992), are impaired in the recognition of emotional expressions (e.g. Baron-Cohen et al., 1993; Braverman et al., 1989; Bormann-Kischkel et al., 1995; Hobson, 1986; Humphreys et al., 2007; Macdonald et al., 1989; Pelphreys et al., 2002), and have difficulty integrating multimodality affective information (Hobson et al., 1988; Loveland et al., 1997). However, a number of studies do not show atypical recognition of emotion expressions (Adolphs et al., 2001; Grossman et al., 2000; Ogai et al., 2003). The extent to which differences between individuals with ASD and controls are identified may be related to decreased verbal IQ in the ASD group.

Neural correlates of facial emotion processing

Conflicting evidence exists when "impairments" are defined via ERP processing of emotional expressions in children with ASD. In preschoolers aged 3 to 4 years, children with ASD did not differentiate a fear face from a neutral face either at early-stage processing components (precursor N170) or later stage components (slow wave) (Dawson et al., 2004). Slower responses to a face expressing fear were correlated with worse joint attention and social orienting. In older children, Wong et al. found normal patterns of ERP and behavioral responses to emotional expressions. However, using source localization, the children with autism showed slower and weaker responses to emotional expressions in regions responsible for face perception and emotion processing (Wong et al., 2008). Supporting these findings, we failed to find a difference in emotional face processing between high-functioning, 9-year-old children with autism compared with mental-aged-matched typically developing children (Burner et al., 2008). Of note, the sample studied by Dawson et al. (2004) differed not only in age but also was a lower-functioning group of children, in terms of IQ and language ability.

While the ERP literature remains limited in source localization of responses to emotional expressions, fMRI allows a more detailed analysis of structures such as the amygdalae and their role in face and emotion processing by individuals with ASD. The amygdala is involved in the processing of emotions from the face and it has reciprocal connections with the fusiform gyrus. Decreased amygdala activation has been found during processing of emotion expressions in individuals with ASD (Ashwin et al., 2007; Baron-Cohen et al., 2000; Critchley et al., 2000; Pelphrey et al., 2007; Wang et al., 2004). As well, the amgydala is not moderated by dynamic versus static emotion displays (Pelphrey et al., 2007) and may be atypically activated during neutral face processing (Bookheimer et al., 2008; Kleinhans et al., 2008).

Implications

Expression of emotion and facial emotion processing during real time interaction is a critical impairment in autism. Under experimental task constraints, some individuals with ASD, specifically those with higher verbal abilities, are able to perform emotion identification tasks comparably to controls. It is unclear if this reflects preserved basic emotion processing or compensatory abilities. And it is unclear whether these adults are able to perform similarly in real life situations. Like facial memory, younger children show greater impairment in this domain than older affected individuals. This may be because they have not developed alternative strategies nor received intervention/training to attend to the information that leads to successful performance.

Baron-Cohen et al. proposed that the abnormalities of the amygdala may be critical in the development of autism (e.g. Baron-Cohen et al., 2000). Amygdala anatomical abnormalities are well documented (e.g. Abell et al., 1999; Sparks et al., 2002) and anatomical variability in the amygdala has been found to be related to social growth (Munson et al., 2006). However, there is also evidence that basic amygdala functioning such as threat detection (Krysko and Rutherford, 2009) and fear potentiated startle (Bernier et al., 2005) is intact.

Intervention

Given the difficulties in recognizing and processing information contained in faces exhibited by individuals with ASD, several groups have developed interventions specifically targeting this domain. One approach to intervention with faces has targeted basic recognition ability. Faja and colleagues (2008) adapted training from the cognitive neuroscience literature that targeted perceptual expertise with faces but also emphasized configural processing, focus on the core features of the face, and emphasis on low spatial frequency information. The intervention was administered on a computer over 5 to 8 hours. Participants worked directly with a trainer who also briefly provided rule-based strategies for viewing faces at the beginning of each session. Adolescents and adults with HF ASD who received training met the behavioral criteria for expertise (i.e. were as efficient at recognizing individual faces as identifying their gender). After training, participants also were better able to detect differences in configural information (i.e. second order relations) than controls with ASD who did not receive training. Our group is currently examining changes in the N170 to faces before and after training in order to determine whether the training also affects neural plasticity.

Another group has developed a comprehensive package of computerized games, *Let's Face It*, aimed at children with ASD (Tanaka et al., 2003). The tasks progress in difficulty, build on internal motivation by permitting children to select the tasks they find most interesting, and had an average intensity of about 20 hours total. The activities include detecting faces from the background environment, matching on identity and emotional expression, and matching faces with different orientation in order to emphasize configural processing. Preliminary results suggested that, like adults, children with ASD also exhibit plasticity in their behavioral response to faces. Training improved recognition of faces and face parts relative to the wait-listed group (Wolf et al., 2009).

Finally, our group is in the process of analyzing the introduction of a face training module within a comprehensive early intensive intervention, the UW Early Start Denver Model. This intervention targeted recognition of familiar faces with toddlers and emphasized configural processing. Toddlers practiced identifying photos of their therapists, parents, and siblings in full face view as well as in images where parts of the face and head were naturally obscured (e.g. peaking around a corner or wearing a hat and glasses). Because the training was provided to all children in the treatment group, the effect of the face module cannot be tested in isolation. However, the intervention provides an avenue for investigating the interplay with other social skill development. We suggest that this integration of face training within more expansive social skills therapies may be the most effective means of influencing the system and generalizing basic processing skills.

Another approach to intervention with faces emphasizes the development of emotion recognition. Silver and Oakes (2001) presented a computer based emotion recognition intervention, *Emotion Trainer,* to children and adolescents with ASD for approximately 5 hours. Children who received training improved in their ability to recognize photographed emotions, cartoons with emotion-based situations and stories. Another group developed the *Frankfurt Test and Training of Facial Affect Recognition* (FEFA) to teach facial emotion recognition via the computer (Bolte et al., 2002, 2006) and adults who received training improved relative to controls in their recognition of emotional expressions in whole faces and within the eye region when isolated. Golan and Baron-Cohen (2006) also tested the effects of a computer intervention for emotion recognition, *Mind Reading,* with adults who have HFA. Participants who used the program had greater recognition of expressions, although they had difficulty generalizing these skills beyond the stimuli used in training. Baron-Cohen's group (2007) has also developed a DVD for young children targeting emotion recognition and featuring faces superimposed on toy vehicles such as trains (*The Transporters*), objects that are highly engaging to many children with ASD. Lastly, emotion recognition has also been incorporated in more comprehensive social skills interventions with measurable effects in emotion recognition (Bauminger, 2002; Solomon et al., 2004).

Implications

Relatively brief face training programs have produced modest change in the component processes that contribute to face processing, recognition, and emotion understanding. The larger impact of these trainings on social ability outside of the lab is still untested. One potential benefit may be that these trainings stimulate more typical system expression. Slowed processing or abnormal default circuitry may result in a failure to correctly and efficiently integrate facial information with speech, gesture and context and training may provide an opportunity to isolate, practice, and automate component skills. It is possible, that the increased social contact associated with participating in a training study may also be of benefit and comparisons of computer training done independently versus with in-person support will be of importance.

Discussion

Face processing in autism, we have begun to realize, mirrors the complexity and variability of the spectrum and does not lend itself to a simple conceptualizations of performance or causal pathway. Not all individuals with ASD have impairments in face processing or face impairments that manifest in the same way. There are some general themes that do appear in the data. First, behavioral tests tend to show more differences when controls are age matched instead of age and mental age matched. This issue is not unique to face processing. Differentiating how verbal/communicative and adaptive deficits contribute to performance is critical to understanding performance in individuals with ASD. Of note, children with developmental delay also have impairments in the social and communicative domain and thus, the specificity of the face processing atypicalities to the ASDs versus a general relation to social ability continues to be a critical question.

Second, tasks that specifically probe facial configuration processes have been consistent in showing impairments. Again, the source of these impairments is difficult to determine as differences in HSF/LSF processing and/or attention to mouths versus eyes may contribute to the results. ERP findings suggest that there are both attention (P1) and early-stage processing (N170) atypicalities in ASD even when attention is directed to the eye region.

Third, age and level of cognitive/language functioning are confounds in interpreting this body of work. The ability to automatically detect information contained in faces including identity, gaze, and emotion may be critical to the development of broader social and cognitive skills. During middle childhood and through adulthood, performance discrepancies between individuals with ASD and controls vary. At this time, it is unclear whether this reflects variability within the phenotype or the ability of some individuals to develop compensatory strategies.

Lastly, reconcilation of results must incorporate methodological differences. Specifically, a more important question is *how* and *why* individuals are succeeding or failing at these tasks and how this may lead to a better understanding of subgroups of individuals with the disorder. Follow-up investigations, as described in the study of prosopagnosia, with more complex batteries are necessary. As well, larger samples and longitudinal data will be critical to addressing these questions.

Overall, these findings suggest that the use of facial information, under real world circumstances, is critically impaired for many, if not most individuals with ASD. The DSM IV list of criteria for the social domain includes "marked impairments in the use of multiple nonverbal behaviors such as eye-to-eye gaze [and] facial expression… to regulate social interaction." The etiology of this impairment is not a simple determination. Face processing is not a unitary function in autism. The variability in performance across the autism phenotype, however, may make this a model system for understanding the brain systems impacted by autism and the differences in social capabilities of individuals with autism as they develop social skills over time. As described by adults with HF ASD, the challenges in real world face processing are numerous and differ across individuals. One describes his focus on the overall shape of faces and looking at noses noting, "I had to train myself to look at eyes, I notice moles and birthmarks a lot." When looking at a face, another commented, "I break it down into features. I match eyebrows, hair style, teeth. It's hard to see a gestalt and hard to recognize a lot of people also. I associate them with what they're wearing initially. It's not intuitive… Telling what mood they're in can be hard. I consciously look at the face and try to determine what they're thinking and feeling. I learned to do mental simulation of their feelings over time. It's not natural—like juggling and talking at same time." Another individual commented on his different strategies for viewing static stimuli, "I'm shy, so I don't look at faces in real life," while several other participants noted their awareness of being unable to stare at real people. This suggests the use of different gaze patterns in the lab and awareness of the inability to attend to real faces in ways that may aid recognition and memory. Finally, one man commented, "In real life, I'm trying to convey paying attention and listening. There is less social demand with a picture." These comments serve as a reminder to scientists of the importance of an integrated model of complex face processing systems in ASD and the necessity for connecting it to the day-to-day functioning of these individuals.

Summary and conclusions

Face processing and its role in the social phenotype of autism spectrum disorders (ASD) has gained a significant amount of attention in the past decade. Many of the early signs of autism reflect the failure to reference faces in an age appropriate manner. Despite the early development of the preference for and recognition of faces, the components involved in the processing and use of information from the face represent a network of systems that are complex unto themselves. We have proposed that face processing is neither a simple process nor one that is universally abnormal in individuals with autism. Several complementary processes that may contribute to impairment in face processing in individuals with autism have been described: lower-level visual processing, visual attention, early-stage processing of faces, memory for faces, and emotional significance of faces. The variability in performance on face processing tasks by individuals with ASD reflects an underlying variability in ability in face processing in the ASD spectrum, making face processing a model system for understanding the nature of social impairment in ASD.

Acknowledgments

The writing of this chapter was supported by the NIH UW Autism Center of Excellence (P50 HD055782) and NIH Shared Neurobiology of Fragile X and Autism (R03 HD057321) to the first author and the National Institutes of Neurological Disorders and Stroke T32NS007413 to the second author. Support was also provided by staff in the University of Washington Psychophysiology and Behavioral Systems Lab. Thank you to all of the participants and their families who have donated their time to research.

References

Abell, F., Krams, M., Ashburner, J., *et al.* (1999). The neuroanatomy of autism: a voxel-based whole brain analysis of structural scans. *Neuroreport,* **10**, 1647–1651.

Adolphs, R., Sears, L., and Piven, J. (2001). Abnormal processing of social information from faces in autism. *Journal of Cognitive Neuroscience,* **13**, 232–240.

Ashwin, C., Baron-Cohen, S., Wheelwright, S., O'Riordan, M., and Bullmore, E.T. (2007). Differential activation of the amygdala and the "social brain" during fearful face-processing in Asperger Syndrome. *Neuropsychologia,* **45**, 2–14.

Bacon, A.L., Fein, D., Morris, R., Waterhouse, L., and Allen, D. (1998). The responses of autistic children to the distress of others. *Journal of Autism and Developmental Disorders,* **28**, 129–142.

Baranek, G.T. (1999). Autism during infancy: a retrospective video analysis of sensory motor and social behaviors at 9–12 months of age. *Journal of Autism* and *Developmental Disorders*, **29**, 213–224.

Baron-Cohen, S. (1995). *Mindblindness: An essay on autism* and *theory of mind*. Learning, development, and conceptual change. Cambridge, MA: MIT Press.

Baron-Cohen, S., Spitz, A., and Cross, P. (1993). Do children with autism recognize surprise? A research note. *Cognition and Emotion*, **7**, 507.

Baron-Cohen, S., Ring, H.A., Bullmore, E.T., Wheelwright, S., Ashwin, C., and Williams S.C. (2000). The amygdala theory of autism. *Neuroscience and Biobehavioral Reviews*, **24**, 355–364.

Bauminger, N. (2002). The facilitation of social-emotional understanding and social interaction in high-functioning children with autism: intervention outcomes. *Journal of Autism and Developmental Disorders*, **32**, 283–298.

Bentin, S., Allison, T., Puce, A., Perez, E., and McCarthy, G. (1996). Electrophysiological studies of face perception in humans. *Journal of Cognitive Neuroscience*, **8**, 551–565.

Bernier, R., Dawson, G., Panagiotides, H., and Webb, S. (2005). Individuals with autism spectrum disorder show normal responses to a fear potential startle paradigm. *Journal of Autism and Developmental Disorders*, **35**, 575–583.

Blair, R.J., Frith, U., Smith, N., Abell, F., and Cipolotti, L. (2002). Fractionation of visual memory: agency detection and its impairment in autism. *Neuropsychologia*, **40**, 108–18.

Bölte, S., Feineis-Matthews, S., Leber S., Dierks, T., Hubl, D., and Poustka, F. (2002). The development and evaluation of a computer-based program to test and to teach the recognition of facial affect. *International Journal of Circumpolar Health*, **61**, 61–68.

Bölte, S., Hubl, D., Feineis-Matthews, S., Prvulovic, D., Dierks, T., Poustka, F. (2006). Facial affect recognition training in autism: Can we animate the fusiform gyrus? *Behavioral Neuroscience*, **120**, 211–216.

Bookheimer, S., Wang, A., Scott, A., Sigman, M., and Dapretto, M. (2008). Frontal contributions to face processing differences in autism: evidence from fMRI of inverted face processing. *Journal-International Neuropscyhological Society*, **14**, 922–932.

Bormann-Kischkel, C., Vilsmeier, M. and Baude, B. (1995). The development of emotional concepts in autism. *Journal of Child Psychology and Psychiatry*, and Allied Disciplines, **36**, 1243–1259.

Botzel, K., Schulze, S., and Stodieck, S.R.G. (1995). Scalp topography and analysis of intracranial sources of face-evoked potentials. *Experimental Brain Research*, **104**, 135.

Boucher, J. and Lewis, V. (1992). Unfamiliar face recognition in relatively able autistic children. *Journal of Child Psychology and Psychiatry*, and Allied Disciplines, **33**, 843–859.

Boucher, J., Lewis, V., and Collis, G. (1998). Familiar face and voice matching and recognition in children with autism. *Journal of Child Psychology* and *Psychiatry*, **39**, 171–181.

Braverman, M., Fein D., Lucci, D., and Waterhouse, L. (1989). Affect comprehension in children with pervasive developmental disorders. *Journal of Autism and Developmental Disorders*. **19**, 301–16.

Brothers, L., Ring, B., and Kling, A. (1990). Response of neurons in the macaque amygdala to complex social stimuli. *Behavioural Brain Research*, **41**, 199–213.

Burner, K., Webb, S.J., Dawson, G. (2008). Emotion processing in 9 year old children with autism. Unpublished data.

Carey, S. and Diamond, R. (1977). From piecemeal to configurational representation of faces. *Science*, **195**, 312–314.

Carey, S., Diamond, R., and Woods, B. (1980). The development of face recognition—A maturational component. *Developmental Psychology*, **16**, 257–269.

Carow, M., Mottron, L., Berthiaume, C., Dawson, M. (2006). Cognitive mechanisms, specificity and neural underpinnings of visuospatial peaks in autism. *Brain*, **129**, 1789–802.

Charman, T., Swettenham, J., Baron-Cohen, S., Cox, A., Baird, G., and Drew, A. (1997). Infants with autism: an investigation of empathy, pretend play, joint attention, and imitation. *Developmental Psychology*, **33**, 781–789.

Chawarska, K., and Volkmar, F., (2007). Impairments in monkey and human face recognition in 2-year-old toddlers with Autism Spectrum Disorder and Developmental Delay. *Developmental Science*, **10**, 266–279.

Costen, N.P., Parker, D.M., and Craw, I. (1994). Spatial content and spatial quantisation effects in face recognition. *Perception*, **23**, 129.

Courchesne, E., Townsend, J., Akshoomoff, N.A., *et al.* (1994). Impairment in shifting attention in autistic and cerebellar patients. *Behavioral Neuroscience*, **108**, 848–865.

Critchley, H.D., Daly, E.M., Bullmore, E.T., *et al.* (2000). The functional neuroanatomy of social behaviour. Changes in cerebral blood flow when people with autistic disorder process facial expressions. *Brain*, **123**, 2203–2212.

Dalton, K.M., Nacewicz, B.M., Johnstone, T., *et al.* (2005). Gaze fixation and the neural circuitry of face processing in autism. *Nature Neuroscience*, **8**, 519–526.

Dawson, G., Carver, L., Meltzoff, A.N., Panagiotides, H., McPartland, J., and Webb, S.J. (2002). Neural correlates of face and object recognition in young children with autism spectrum disorder, developmental delay, and typical development. *Child Development*, **73**, 700–717.

Dawson, G., Meltzoff, A., Osterling, J., and Rinaldi, J. (1998). Neuropsychological correlates of early symptoms of autism. *Child Development*, **69**, 1276–1285.

Dawson, G., Webb, S.J., Carver, L., Panagiotides, H., and McPartland, J. (2004). Young children with autism show atypical brain responses to fearful versus neutral facial expressions of emotion. *Developmental Science*, **7**, 340–359.

de Jong, M.C., van Engeland, H., and Kemner, C. (2008). Attentional effects of gaze shifts are influenced by emotion and spatial frequency, but not in autism. *Journal of the American Academy of Child & Adolescent Psychiatry*, **47**, 443–454.

Deruelle, C., Rondan, C., Gepner, B., and Tardif, C. (2004). Spatial frequency and face processing in children with autism and asperger syndrome. *Journal of Autism* and *Development Disorder*, **34**, 199–210.

Easterbrook, M.A., Kisilevsky, B.S., Muir, D.W., and Laplante, D.P. (1999). Newborns discriminate schematic faces from scrambled faces. *Canadian Journal of Experimental Psychology*, **53**, 231–241.

Eimer, M. (1998). Does the face-specific N170 component reflect the activity of a specialized eye processor? *Neuroreport*, **9**, 2945.

Elsabbagh, M., Volein, A., Holmboe, K., *et al.* (2009). Visual orienting in the early broader autism phenotype: disengagement and facilitation. *Journal of Child Psychology and Psychiatry*, **50**, 637–642.

Faja, S., Aylward, E., Bernier, R., and Dawson, G. (2008). Becoming a face expert: a computerized face-training program for high-functioning individuals with autism spectrum disorders. *Developmental Neuropsychology*, **33**, 1–24.

Faja, S., Webb, S.J., Merkle, K., Aylward, E., and Dawson, G. (2009). Brief report: face configuration accuracy and processing speed among adults with high-functioning autism spectrum disorders. *Journal of Autism and Developmental Disorders*, **39**, 532–538.

Feinman, S. (1982). Social Referencing in Infancy. *Merrill-Palmer Quarterly*, **28**, 445–470.

Fiorentini, A., Maffei, L., and Sandini, G. (1983). The role of high spatial frequencies in face perception. *Perception*, **12**, 195–201.

Freire, A. and Lee, K. (2001). Face recognition in 4- to 7-year olds: processing of configural, featural, and paraphernalia information. *Journal of Experimental Child Psychology*, **80**, 347–371.

George, N., Evans, J., Fiori, N., Davidoff, J., and Renault, B. (1996). Brain events related to normal and moderately scrambled faces. *Cognitive Brain Research*, **4**, 65–76.

Goffaux, V. and Rossion, B. (2006). Faces are "spatial"-holistic face perception is supported by low spatial frequencies. *Journal of Experimental Psychology Human Perception* and *Performance*, **32**, 1023–1039.

Golan, O. and Baron-Cohen, S. (2006). Systemizing empathy: teaching adults with asperger syndrome or high-functioning autism to recognize complex emotions using interactive multimedia. *Development and Psychopathology*, **18**, 591–617.

Greenaway, R. and Plaisted, K. (2005). Top-down attentional modulation in autistic spectrum disorders is stimulus-specific. *Psychological Science-Cambridge*, **16**, 987–994.

Grelotti, D.J., Klin, A.J., Gauthier, I., *et al.* (2005). FMRI activation of the fusiform gyrus and amygdala to cartoon characters but not to faces in a boy with autism. *Neuropsychologia*, **43**, 373–385.

Grossman, J.B., Klin, A., Carter, A.S., and Volkmar, F.R. (2000). Verbal bias in recognition of facial emotions in children with asperger syndrome. *Journal of Child Psychology and Psychiatry*, **41**,369–379.

Hadjikhani, N., Joseph, R.M., Snyder, J., *et al.* (2004). Activation of the fusiform gyrus when individuals with autism spectrum disorder view faces. *Neuroimage*, **22**, 1141–1150.

Hall, G.B., Szechtman, H., and Nahmias, C. (2003). Enhanced salience and emotion recognition in Autism: a PET study. *The American Journal of Psychiatry*, **160**, 1439–1441.

Hauck, M., Fein, D., Maltby, N., Waterhouse, L., and Feinstein, C. (1998). Memory for faces in children with autism. *Child Neuropsychology*, **4**, 187–198.

Hernandez, N., Metzger, A., Magne, R., Bonnet-Brilhault, F., Rouz, S., Barthelemy, C., and Martineau, J. (2009). Exploration of core features of a human face by healthy and autistic adults analyzed by visual scanning. *Neuropsychologia*, **47**, 1004–1012.

Hobson, R.P. (1986). The autistic child's appraisal of expressions of emotion. *Journal of Child Psychology and Psychiatry*, and Allied Disciplines, **27**, 321–342.

Hobson, R.P., Ouston, J., and Lee, A. (1988). What's in a face? The case of autism. *The British Journal of Psychology*, **79**, 441–453.

Humphreys, K., Minshew, N., Leonard, G.L., and Behrmann, M. (2007). A fine-grained analysis of facial expression processing in high-functioning adults with autism. *Neuropsychologia*, **45**, 685–695.

Iarocci, G. and Burack, J.A. (2004). Intact covert orienting to peripheral cues among children with autism. *Journal of Autism and Developmental Disorders*, **34**, 257–264.

Johnson, M.H. (2005). Subcortical face processing. *Nature Reviews Neuroscience*, **6**, 766–774.

Jones, W., Carr, K., and Klin, A. (2008). Absence of preferential looking to the eyes of approaching adults predicts level of social disability in 2-year-old toddlers with autism spectrum disorder. *Archives of General Psychiatry*, **65**, 946–954.

Joseph, R.M. and Tanaka, J. (2003). Holistic and part-based face recognition in children with autism. *Journal of Child Psychology* and *Psychiatry* and *Allied Disciplines*, **44**, 529–542.

Katsyri, J., Tiippana, K., Sams, M., Saalasti, S., and von Wendt, L. (2008). Impaired recognition of facial emotions from low-spatial frequencies in Asperger syndrome. *Neuropscyhologia*, **47**, 1888–1897.

Kleinhans, N.M., Richards, T., Sterling, L., *et al.* (2008). Abnormal functional connectivity in autism spectrum disorders during face processing. *Brain*, **131**, 1000–1012.

Kleinhans, N.M., Johnson, L.C., Richards, T., Mahurin, R., Greenson, J., Dawson, G., and Aylward, E. (2009). Reduced neural habituation in the amygdala and social impairments in autism spectrum disorders. *American Journal of Psychiatry*, **17**, 1–9.

Klin, A., Jones, W., Schultz, R., Volkmar, F., & Cohen, D. (2002). Visual fixation patterns during viewing of naturalistic social situations as predictors of social competence in individuals with autism. *Archives of General Psychiatry*, **59**, 809–816.

Klin, A., Sparrow, S.S., de Bildt, A., Cicchetti, D.V., Cohen, D.J., and Volkmar, F.R. (1999). A normed study of face recognition in autism and related disorders. *Journal of Autism and Developmental Disorders*, **29**, 499–508.

Koshino, H., Kana, R.K., Keller, T.A., Cherkassky, V.L., Minshew, N.J., and Just, M.A. (2008). fMRI investigation of working memory for faces in autism: visual coding and underconnectivity with frontal areas. *Cerebral Cortex*, **18**, 289–300.

Krysko, K.M. and Rutherford, M.D. (2009). A threat-detection advantage in those with autism spectrum disorders. *Brain and Cognition*, **69**, 472–480.

Lahaie, A., Mottron, L., Arguin, M., Berthiaume, C., Jemel, B., and Saumier, D. (2006). Face perception in high-functioning autistic adults: Evidence for superior processing of face parts, not for a configural face-processing deficit. *Neuropsychology*, **20**, 30–41.

Landry, R. and Bryson, S.E. (2004). Impaired disengagement of attention in young children with autism. *Journal of Child Psychology* and *Psychiatry*, **45**, 1115–1122.

Langdell, T. (1978). Recognition of faces: An approach to the study of autism. *Journal of Child Psychology* and *Psychiatry*, and Allied Disciplines, **19**, 255–268.

Le Grand, R.L., Mondloch, C.J., Maurer, D., and Brent, H.P. (2001). Neuroperception: early visual experience and face processing. *Nature*, **410**, 890.

Lopez, B., Donnelly, N., Hadwin, J.A., and Leekam, S.R. (2004). Face processing in high-functioning adolescents with autism: Evidence for weak central coherence. *Visual Cognition*, **11**, 673–688.

Lopez, B., Leekam, S.R., and Arts, G.R. (2008). How central is central coherence? Preliminary evidence on the link between conceptual and perceptual processing in children with autism. *Autism*, **12**, 159–171.

Loveland, K., Tunali-Kotoski, B., Chen, Y., Ortegon, J., Pearson, D., Brelsford, K., Gibbs, M. (1997). Emotion regulation in autism: verbal and nonverbal information. *Developmental Psychopathology*, **9**, 579–93.

Macdonald, H., Rutter, M., Howlin, P., *et al.* (1989). Recognition and expression of emotional cues by autistic and normal adults. *Journal of Child Psychology and Psychiatry*, and Allied Disciplines, **30**, 865–877.

McCleery, J.P., Zhang, L., Cottrell, G.W., Ge, L., and Wang, Z. (2008). The roles of visual expertise and visual input in the face inversion effect: Behavioral and neurocomputational evidence. *Vision Research*, **48**, 703–715.

McKone, E. and Boyer, B.L. (2006). Sensitivity of 4-year-olds to featural and second-order relational changes in face distinctiveness. *Journal of Experimental Child Psychology*, **94**, 134–162.

McPartland, J., Dawson, G., Webb, S., Panagiotides, H., and Carver, L. (2004). Event-related brain potentials reveal anomalies in temporal processing of faces in autism spectrum disorder. *Journal of Child Psychology* and *Psychiatry*, **45**, 1235–1245.

Merin, N., Young, G.S., Ozonoff, S., and Rogers, S.J. (2007). Visual fixation patterns during reciprocal social interaction distinguish a subgroup of 6-month-old infants at-risk for autism from comparison infants. *Journal of Autism* and *Developmental Disorders*, **37**, 108–121.

Milne, E., Swettenham, J., Hansen, P., Campbell, R., Jeffries, H., and Plaisted, K. (2002). High motion coherence thresholds in children with autism. *Journal of Child Psychology*, Psychiatry and Allied Disciplines, **43**, 255–264.

Mondloch, C.J., Le Grand, R., and Maurer, D. (2002). Configural face processing develops more slowly than featural face processing. *Perception*, **31**, 553–566.

Moore, C. and Corkum, V. (1994). Social understanding at the end of the first year of life. *Developmental Review*, **14**, 349.

Mundy, P., Sigman, M., Ungerer, J., and Sherman, T. (1986). Defining the social deficits of autism: the contribution of non-verbal communication measures. *Journal of Child Psychology* and *Psychiatry*, and Allied Discipline, **27**, 657–669.

Munson, J., Dawson, G., Abbott, R., *et al.* (2006). Amygdalar volume and behavioral development in autism. *Archives of General Psychiatry*, **63**, 686–693.

Neumann, D., Spezio, M.L., Piven, J., and Adolphs, R. (2006). Looking you in the mouth: abnormal gaze in autism resulting from impaired top-down modulation of visual attention. *Social Cognitive* and *Affective Neuroscience*, **1**, 194–202.

O'Connor, K., Hamm, J.P., and Kirk, I.J. (2005). The neurophysiological correlates of face processing in adults and children with Asperger's syndrome. *Brain* and *Cognition*, **59**, 82–95.

O'Connor, K., Hamm, J.P., and Kirk, I.J. (2007). Neurophysiological responses to face, facial regions and objects in adults with asperger's syndrome: an ERP investigation. *International Journal of Psychophysiology*, **63**, 283–293.

Ogai, M., Matsumoto, H., Suzuki, K., *et al.* (2003). FMRI study of recognition of facial expressions in high-functioning autistic patients. *Neuroreport*, **14**, 559–563.

Osterling, J.A., Dawson, G., and Munson, J.A. (2002). Early recognition of one year old infants with autism spectrum disorder versus mental retardation. *Development* and *Psychopathology*, **14**, 239–252.

Pellicano, E. and Rhodes, G. (2003). Holistic processing of faces in preschool children and adults. *Psychological Science*, **14**, 618–622.

Pelphrey, K.A., Sasson, N.J., Reznick, J.S., Paul, G., Goldman, B.D., and Piven, J. (2002). Visual scanning of faces in autism. *Journal of Autism* and *Developmental Disorders*, **32**, 249–261.

Pelphrey, K., Morris, J., McCarthy, G., and LaBar, K. (2007). Perception of dynamic changes in facila affect and identity in autism. *Social Cognitive and Affective Neuroscience*, **2**, 140–149.

Pierce, K. and Redcay, E. (2008). Fusiform function in children with an autism spectrum disorder is a matter of "who." *Biological Psychiatry*, **64**, 552–560.

Pierce, K., Haist, F., Sedaghat, F., and Courchesne, E. (2004). The brain response to personally familiar faces in autism: findings of fusiform activity and beyond. *Brain*, **127**, 2703–2716.

Pierce, K., Muller, R.A., Ambrose, J., Allen, G., and Courchesne, E. (2001). Face processing occurs outside the fusiform "face area" in autism: evidence from functional MRI. *Brain: a Journal of Neurology*, **124**, 2059–2073.

Rochat, P. and Striano, T. (1999). Emerging self-exploration by 2-month-old infants. *Developmental Science*, **2**, 206–218.

Rose, F.E., Lincoln, A.J., Lai, Z., Ene, M., Searcy, Y.M., and Bellugi, U. (2007). Orientation and affective expression effects on face recognition in Williams syndrome and autism. *Journal of Autism* and *Developmental Disorders*, **37**, 513–522.

Rouse, H., Donnelly, N., Hadwin, J.A., and Brown, T. (2004). Do children with autism perceive second-order relational features? The case of the Thatcher illusion. *Journal of Child Psychology* and *Psychiatry* and *Allied Disciplines*, **45**, 1246–1257.

Schultz, R.T., Gauthier, I., Klin, A., *et al.* (2000). Abnormal ventral temporal cortical activity during face discrimination among individuals with autism and asperger syndrome. *Archives of General Psychiatry*, **57**, 331–343.

Schultz, R.T. (2005). Developmental deficits in social perception in autism: the role of the amygdale and fusiform face area. *International Journal of Developmental Neuroscience*, **23**, 125–141.

Schyns, P.G. and Oliva, A. (1999). Dr. Angry and Mr. Smile: when categorization flexibly modifies the perception of faces in rapid visual presentations. *Cognition*, **69**, 243–265.

Serra, M., Althaus, M., de Sonneville, L.M., Stant, A.D., Jackson, A.E., and Minderaa, R.B. (2003). Face recognition in children with a pervasive developmental disorder not otherwise specified. *Journal of Autism and Developmental Disorders*, **33**, 303–317.

Sigman, M. (1998). The Emanuel Miller Memorial Lecture 1997, Change and continuity in the development of children with autism. *Journal of Child Psychology* and *Psychiatry*, **39**, 817–27.

Sigman, M.D., Kasari, C., Kwon, J.H., and Yirmiya, N. (1992). Responses to the negative emotions of others by autistic, mentally retarded, and normal children. *Child Development*, **63**, 796–807.

Silver, M. and Oakes, P. (2001). Evaluation of a new computer intervention to teach people with autism or Asperger syndrome to recognize and predict emotions in others. *Autism*, **5**, 299–316.

Smith, S.E. and Chatterjee, A. (2008). Visuospatial Attention in Children. *Archives of Neurology*, **65**, 1284.

Solomon, M., Goodlin-Jones, B.L., and Anders, T.F. (2004). A social adjustment enhancement intervention for high functioning autism, Asperger's syndrome, and pervasive developmental disorder NOS. *Journal of Autism and Developmental Disorders*, **34**, 649–668.

Sparks, B.F., Friedman, S.D., Shaw, D.W., *et al.* (2002). Brain structural abnormalities in young children with autism spectrum disorders. *Neurology*, **59**, 184–192.

Spezio, M.L., Adolphs, R., Hurley, R.S., and Piven, J. (2007). Abnormal use of facial information in high-functioning autism. *Journal of Autism and Developmental Disorders*, **37**, 929–939.

Sterling, L., Dawson, G., Webb, S.J., Murias, M., Munson, J., Panagiotides, H., and Aylward, E. (2008). The role of face familiarity in eye tracking of faces by individuals with autism spectrum disorders. *Journal of Autism and Developmental Disorders*, **38**, 1666–1675.

Tanaka, J.W. and Farah, M.J. (1993). Parts and wholes in face recognition. *Quarterly Journal of Experimental Psychology Series a Human Experimental Psychology*, **46**, 225.

Tanaka, J., Lincoln, S., and Hegg, L. (2003). A framework for the study and treatment of face processing deficits in autism. In H. Leder and G. Swartzer (eds.) *The development of face processing*, pp. 101–119. Berlin: Hogrefe Publishers.

Tantam, D., Monaghan, L., Nicholson, J., and Stirling, J. (1989). Autistic children's ability to interpret faces: A research note. *Journal of Child Psychology* and *Psychiatry*, **30**, 623–630.

Teunisse, J.P. and de Gelder, B. (2003). Face processing in adolescents with autistic disorder: The inversion and composite effects. *Brain* and *Cognition*, **52**, 285–294.

Thompson, L.A. and Massaro, D.W. (1989). Before you see it, you see its parts: evidence for feature encoding and integration in preschool children and adults. *Cognitive Psychology*, **21**, 334–362.

Tomasello, M. (1995). Language is not an instinct. *Cognitive Development*, **10**, 131.

Townsend, J., Harris, N.S., and Courchesne, E. (1996). Visual attention abnormalities in autism: delayed orienting to location. *Journal of the International Neuropsychological Society*, **2**, 541–550.

Trepagnier, C., Sebrechts, M.M., and Peterson, R. (2002). Atypical face gaze in autism. *Cyberpsychology and Behavior*, **5**, 213–218.

van der Geest, J.N., Kemner, C., Verbaten, M.N., and van Engeland, H. (2002). Gaze behavior of children with pervasive developmental disorder toward human faces: a fixation time study. *Journal of Child Psychology* and *Psychiatry* and *Allied Disciplines*, **43**, 669–678.

van Kooten, I.A., Palmen, S.J., von Cappeln, P., *et al.* (2008). Neurons in the fusiform gyrus are fewer and smaller in autism. *Brain*, **131**, 987–999.

Vuilleumier, P. and Pourtois, G. (2007). Distributed and interactive brain mechanisms during emotion face perception: evidence from functional neuroimaging. *Neuropsychologia*, **45**, 174–94.

Wainwright, J.A. and Bryson, S.E. (1996). Visual-spatial orienting in autism. *Journal of Autism* and *Developmental Disorders*, **26**, 423–438.

Wang, A.T., Dapretto, M., Hariri, A.R., Sigman, M., and Bookheimer, S.Y. (2004). Neural correlates of facial affect processing in children and adolescents with autism spectrum disorder. *Journal-American Academy of Child and Adolescent Psychiatry*, **43**, 481–490.

Webb, SJ, Dawson, G., Bernier, R., and Panagiotides, H. (2006). ERP evidence of atypical face processing in young children with autism. *Journal of Autism and Developmental Disorders*, **36**, 881–890.

Webb, SJ, Merkle, K., Murias, M., Richards, T., Aylward, E., and Dawson, G. (2009a). ERP responses differentiate inverted but not upright face processing in adults with ASD. *Social*, Cognitive & Affective Neuroscience. May **19**, Epub ahead of print.

Webb, S., Dawson, G., Bernier, R., Pangiotides, H. (2009b). Face and object memory in children with autism spectrum disorders: developmental change and continuity in ERP responses. Unpublished manuscript.

Webb, SJ, Jones, E., Merkle, K., Toth, K., Greenson, J., and Dawson, G. (2010). Increased attention to faces during habituation in toddlers with elevated autism symptoms. *Child Neurophysology*. March 18. Epub ahead of print.

Wilson, R., Pascalis, O., and Blades, M. (2007). Familiar face recognition in children with autism: the differential use of inner and outer face parts. *Journal of Autism and Developmental Disorders*, **37**, 314–320.

Wojciulik, E., Kanwisher, N., and Driver, J. (1998). Covert visual attention modulates face-specific activity in the human fusiform gyrus: fMRI study. *Journal of Neurophysiology*, **79**, 1574–78.

Wolf, J.M., Tanaka, J.W., Klaiman, C., *et al.* (2009). Specific impairment of face-processing abilities in children with autism spectrum disorder using the *Let's Face It!* skills battery. *Autism Research*, **1**, 329–340.

Wong, T.K., Fung, P.C., Chua, S.E., and McAlonan, G.M. (2008). Abnormal spatiotemporal processing of emotional facial expressions in childhood autism: dipole source analysis of event-related potentials. *European Journal of Neuroscience*, **28**, 407–416.

Zwaigenbaum L., Bryson S., Rogers T., Roberts W., Brian J., and Szatmari P. (2005). Behavioral manifestations of autism in the first year of life. *International Journal of Developmental Neuroscience*, **23**, 143–152.

Chapter 44

Facial Expression Perception in Schizophrenia and Mood Disorders

Mary L. Phillips

Introduction

Schizophrenia, major depressive disorder, and bipolar disorder are three major psychiatric illnesses, each associated with significant morbidity and mortality (Murray and Lopez, 1996) and social dysfunction. Schizophrenia can be considered as an illness characterized by a splitting of thoughts (cognition) from feelings (emotion; Bleuler, 1950). Indeed, a "flattening of affect" and a misinterpretation of social cues are common features of the illness, especially associated with symptoms such as persecutory delusions, that may result from misinterpretations of social interactions and events, that revolve around a person's relationship to others and role in society rather than neutral or impersonal themes (Young and Bentall, 1995). Major depressive disorder is associated with episodes of severe low mood—depression—during which there is frequently a tendency of individuals suffering from the illness to exhibit a negative emotional attentional bias (Beck, 1967), and an inability to perceive any environment, and particularly self-relevant events, as positive. Bipolar disorder is characterized by irritability, distractibility, emotional lability, and abnormalities in emotion processing, including the experience of emotions of inappropriately high intensity in relation to the social context in which they occur, and an inability to regulate mood. These three major psychiatric illnesses therefore have in common deficits in social perception, in particular, abnormal processing of socially salient information generated by others.

Faces, and facial expressions in particular, are among the most socially salient of all stimuli. It is therefore not surprising that impaired perception of facial expressions has been postulated to underlie the social-communicative problems in individuals with major psychiatric illness, including schizophrenia and mood disorders such as major depressive disorder and bipolar disorder (manic depression). This chapter will therefore first focus on examination of the extent to which abnormalities in facial expression perception characterize each of these three major psychiatric illnesses. The expansion of functional neuroimaging techniques to the study of psychiatric illnesses has also facilitated understanding of the neural basis of the facial emotion abnormalities in each of these illnesses that in turn may help provide a cognitive neuroscience framework for understanding the pathophysiological basis of these different illnesses. Furthermore, these techniques have more recently been applied to the study of neural system abnormalities in individuals in the early stages of these illnesses, namely, youth with, and those at high risk for, these illnesses. This chapter therefore includes a description of the main findings from such studies in these three psychiatric illnesses in adulthood, youth, and at risk populations. The chapter concludes with an integration of these findings toward development of neural models of abnormal facial expression perception for each of these illnesses.

Studies of facial expression labeling

Schizophrenia

Numerous studies have demonstrated facial expression labeling deficits in schizophrenia (Edwards et al., 2002; Mandal et al., 1998; Morrison et al., 1988), that in turn may relate to the observation of abnormal facial expression generation and flattened affect in individuals with schizophrenia (e.g. Kohler et al., 2008a,b). There are several questions, however, regarding the nature of the emotional expression labeling deficit in schizophrenia. First, it is unclear as to whether the facial expression labeling deficit is dependent upon the phase of illness (Mueser et al., 1997). Some studies reported greater deficits in chronic relative to acute stages of illness (e.g. Kucharska-Pietura et al., 2005). Other findings suggest that emotion labeling deficits are present from the onset of the disorder (Edwards et al., 2001), or that social dysfunction and emotional disturbance may pre-date disease onset (Baum and Walker, 1995; Cannon et al., 1990; Walker et al., 1993). A second question is the relative extent of the facial expression labeling deficit in schizophrenia versus other major psychiatric illnesses. Some studies, for example, compared performance of individuals with schizophrenia and those with mood disorders. These studies showed a greater overall impairment in schizophrenia (Feinberg et al., 1986; Loughland et al., 2002), although several recent studies have provided evidence for facial expression labeling deficits in individuals with mood disorders (see below). Third, it remains unclear as to whether the emotional expression labeling deficit in schizophrenia represents a generalized performance deficit (Archer et al., 1992; Feinberg et al., 1986; Johnston et al., 2001; Kerr and Neale, 1993; Kohler et al., 2000; Sachs et al., 2004; Salem et al., 1996; Whittaker et al., 2001), or a more specific emotional expression labeling deficit (e.g. (Borod et al., 1993; Hall et al., 2004; Penn et al., 2000; Heimberg et al., 1992; Silver et al., 2002; Walker et al., 1984). Another question is whether the facial expression labeling deficit is evident only to specific emotions. Some studies found that the emotion labeling deficit was more evident for negative emotional facial expressions (An et al., 2003; Bell et al., 1997; Borod et al., 1993; Davis and Gibson, 2000; Kline et al., 1992; Kucharska-Pietura et al., 2002; Mandal and Palchoudhury, 1985; Muzekari and Bates, 1977; Pilowsky and Bassett, 1980), such as fear (Evangeli and Broks, 2000), disgust (Mandal, 1987), and sadness (Silver et al., 2002). Other findings, however, indicate a misattribution of negative emotion labels to neutral faces in individuals with schizophrenia (Kohler et al., 2003). Finally, the extent to which facial expression labeling deficits are associated with specific symptoms of schizophrenia should be a focus of study. There is some evidence that facial emotion labeling deficits may be associated with cognitive impairment (Bozikas et al., 2004) or negative symptoms (Schneider et al., 1995) in individuals with schizophrenia. Paranoid symptoms, including persecutory delusions are common symptoms of schizophrenia, and may be associated with a tendency to misattribute emotional significance to emotionally neutral or ambiguous information. It has therefore been proposed that delusions may arise from an abnormal assignment of emotional meaning to otherwise non-salient stimuli in the environment (Kapur, 2003). In support of this hypothesis is evidence for an increased tendency in schizophrenic patients, relative to healthy subjects, to misclassify neutral facial expressions as disgusted or fearful (Kohler et al., 2003), and impaired facial emotional expression labeling particularly in schizophrenic individuals with paranoid symptoms (Combs et al., 2004).

Together, these findings indicate that individuals with schizophrenia have deficits in facial expression labeling, that: may predate illness onset and become worse with illness progression. These deficits are particularly evident for negative and neutral emotional facial expressions, and may be associated with specific symptoms associated with misperception of non-salient environmental stimuli as emotionally meaningful. These findings in turn suggest that schizophrenia may be associated with an inability to distinguish socially salient from non-socially-salient facial expressions, coupled with a tendency to misattribute undue meaning to less important—or unimportant—expressions. This facial expression perceptual abnormality may be associated with specific psychotic symptoms such as delusions, negative symptoms, or cognitive dysfunction.

Major depressive disorder

There have been several studies examining facial emotion recognition in individuals with major depressive disorder (MDD). Findings from these studies have demonstrated negative attentional biases to facial expressions in MDD, i.e. recognition of significantly more sadness in facial expressions of others than normal controls (Bouhuys et al., 1999; Gur et al., 1992; Matthews and Antes, 1992; Hale, 1998). Findings have also demonstrated impaired recognition of positive facial expressions (Suslow et al., 2001), and a bias away from the labeling of happy, but not sad, facial expressions as emotional that is unrelated to depression severity (Surguladze, et al., 2004). Other studies in MDD have reported specific deficits in the recognition of facial expressions of a variety of different emotions (Jaeger et al., 1987; Pursad and Polivy, 1993; Rubinow and Post, 1992). Yet others have reported a depression state impairment in the recognition of sad and happy, but not neutral faces (Mikhailova et al., 1996), more general impairments in visual perceptive tasks (Asthana et al., 1998), or impaired verbal labeling, but not matching, of all emotional (anger, happiness, sadness, fear, disgust, surprise) and neutral faces (Feinberg et al., 1986). Together, these findings indicate abnormal labeling of specific facial expressions, including a bias away from labeling expressions as happy, in MDD, which may coexist with a general visual perceptual deficit.

Bipolar disorder

There have been few studies that have examined facial expression labeling in bipolar disorder. Individuals in the manic phase of the disorder have specific impairments in the recognition of fear and disgust of unfamiliar others (Lembke and Ketter, 2002), and generalized deficits in the recognition of all emotional expressions (Getz et al., 2003). Other studies of bipolar individuals when remitted or euthymic have demonstrated impaired fear recognition (Yurgelun-Todd et al., 2000) and enhanced disgust recognition (Harmer et al., 2002), or no specific emotion recognition deficits (Venn et al., 2004). A further study reported that adolescents with bipolar disorder made more errors in labeling emotion displayed by faces of unfamiliar children (McClure et al., 2003): they mislabeled faces of peers, but not unfamiliar adults, as angry. Labeling of other emotions remained intact. An increasing number of studies in bipolar youth (typically focusing on ages 7–17 years) have also shown abnormal processing of emotional facial expressions, including abnormally elevated perception of threat from neutral faces (Rich et al., 2006), abnormally increased attention to threat faces (Brotman et al., 2007), and misperception of faces as being angry (McClure et al., 2003). Findings also indicate facial expression labeling deficits in youth at future genetic risk of developing bipolar disorder (Brotman et al., 2008).

Together, these findings suggest deficits in the labeling of facial expressions, particularly negative emotional expressions, in euthymic and symptomatic individuals with bipolar disorder. In contrast, other findings suggest enhanced recognition or no deficit in the recognition of negative emotional expressions in bipolar individuals when euthymic. Inconsistencies across studies may have resulted from methodological differences. No studies, however, have directly compared emotion labeling in bipolar individuals in the different phases of illness (remission, mania, and depression). It therefore remains unclear whether abnormalities in facial expression labeling in bipolar disorder are persistent or mood state-dependent. Additionally, most of these studies examined accuracy but not the nature of errors in labeling different categories of emotional facial expressions in bipolar disorder.

Interim summary

Findings from facial expression labeling studies point to differential patterns of abnormal facial emotion labeling in three major psychiatric illnesses: schizophrenia, MDD, and bipolar disorder. Findings to date suggest that schizophrenia may be characterized by an abnormal misattribution of emotional salience to otherwise unimportant, non-salient or "neutral" expressions, while MDD is characterized more by a an attentional bias away from labeling facial expressions as positive emotion. The few studies to date in bipolar disorder make it difficult to determine the precise nature of the facial expression labeling deficit in the illness, but suggest difficulties in labeling negative emotional expressions. Clearly, understanding of the pathophysiological bases of these major psychiatric illnesses is likely to come from studies that examine functional abnormalities in neural systems supporting facial expression perception in each illness, rather than from studies focusing only upon facial expression labeling per se. I therefore next turn to a brief description of neural systems for facial expression perception, and those studies that employed neuroimaging techniques to determine the nature of functional abnormalities in these neural systems in each illness.

Neural regions implicated in facial expression perception

A large number of animal, human lesion, and human neuroimaging studies have implicated different subcortical and medial temporal cortical regions, including the amygdala, striatum, hippocampus, and parahippocampal gyrus, during the encoding and retrieval of the emotional meaning of stimuli encountered in the environment. The amygdala and hippocampus are both activated during the successful encoding of emotionally-salient information (Dolcos et al., 2004; Kensinger and Corkin 2004; Maratos et al., 2001; Smith et al., 2004;), the viewing of emotional facial expressions (Gur et al., 2002a; Williams et al., 2001), and may interact via reciprocal projections (Krettek and Price 1977; Pitkanen et al., 2000). The hippocampus has been proposed to be involved in the resolution of conflicts between expectations and current percepts (Gray et al., 1995, 1998). The parahippocampal gyrus has multiple, direct connections with the hippocampus and amygdala and is involved in novelty detection (Schroeder et al., 2004), episodic and spatial memory (Malkova and Mishkin 2003; Tsukiura et al., 2002) and context appraisal (Sacchetti et al., 1999).

The ventral striatum, including rostroventral caudate nucleus and putamen, adjacent to, and contiguous with, the human homologue of the nucleus acumbens (Meredith et al., 1996; Prensa et al., 2003), has been implicated in anticipation of reward (Cooper and Knutson, 2008; Knutson and Wimmer, 2007; Knutson et al., 2001; 2005). More dorsal regions of the striatum, including the caudate nucleus, have been implicated in learning reward probability and reward cue-response reinforcement (Balleine et al., 2007; Delgado et al., 2003, 2004, 2005; Haruno and Kawato, 2006a,b; Haruno et al., 2004; Tricomi et al., 2004, 2006). Additionally, findings from a large number of animal, human lesion and human neuroimaging studies implicate different regions of the prefrontal cortex, including orbitofrontal cortex (OFC), dorsomedial prefrontal cortex, ventrolateral prefrontal cortex, and anterior cingulate gyrus (ACG), and suggest distinguishable roles of these regions, in the regulation of activity within subcortical limbic regions, including amygdala and striatum, in the response to emotionally-salient information, such as emotional facial expressions (Phillips et al., 2008). One study (Ghashghaei et al., 2007) examining output and input patterns of connections between prefrontal cortices and the amygdala in non-human primates, for example, provided novel evidence for connections from the amygdala to cortical layers I and II of OFC and ACG, which they interpreted as being implicated in the focus of attention to motivationally relevant stimuli.

These different neural regions implicated in emotion processing therefore have dissociable roles in processing of facial emotional expressions (Haxby et al., 2000). The evidence for specific functional abnormalities in these regions during emotional facial expression perception in schizophrenia, MDD and bipolar disorder is described in the next section.

Neural systems supporting facial expression perception in schizophrenia, major depressive disorder, and bipolar disorder

Schizophrenia

Many neuroimaging studies have focused upon examination of medial temporal cortical activity in schizophrenia, as functional abnormalities in this region may underlie the misattribution of salience to non-salient facial stimuli in the illness (Holt and Phillips, 2009). Differences in experimental design across studies (which may be sensitive to different stages of emotional appraisal) have led to reports of reduced, unchanged and elevated medial temporal cortical activity during emotional processing in schizophrenic relative to healthy individuals. Findings from these studies are summarized below.

Several functional neuroimaging studies have shown evidence for abnormal reductions in amygdala activity in schizophrenic relative to healthy individuals. In some of these studies, subjects performed a cognitive task (an explicit affect judgment or gender discrimination task; Gur et al., 2002b, 2007; Hempel et al., 2003; Johnston et al., 2005; Phillips et al., 1999; Williams et al., 2004, 2007) or underwent mood induction (Habel et al., 2004; Schneider et al., 1998) while viewing emotional facial expressions. In one recent study, the normal pattern of amygdala-prefrontal cortical functional connectivity during facial expression matching was found to be absent in schizophrenic relative to healthy individuals (Fakra et al., 2008). Some studies (Gur et al., 2002b, 2007; Hempel et al., 2003; Paradiso et al., 2003; Takahashi et al., 2004; Williams et al., 2007) reported reduced activity of the hippocampus as well as the amygdala in schizophrenic relative to healthy individuals. The majority of these studies used one of two designs: (1) a comparison of responses to emotional relative to neutral facial expressions (Das et al., 2007; Hempel et al., 2003; Paradiso et al., 2003; Phillips et al., 1999; Takahashi et al., 2004; Taylor et al., 2002; Williams et al., 2007), or (2) a comparison of responses to emotional 9 neutral faces during an explicit emotional judgment or mood induction task to responses to the same stimuli during a gender discrimination task (Gur et al., 2002b; Habel et al., 2004; Schneider et al., 1998).

Given that all of these studies were conducted in medicated patients, it is possible that treatment with antipsychotic medication played a role in these findings. Although there is evidence that antipsychotic treatment inhibits amygdala function (Greba et al., 2001; Pezze and Feldon, 2004), one study demonstrated diminished amygdala activity during sad mood induction in unaffected brothers of individuals with schizophrenia relative to healthy subjects without a schizophrenic relative (Habel et al., 2004). The latter finding suggested that functional impairment of the amygdala could represent a marker of genetic vulnerability to schizophrenia.

Three studies reported increased amygdala activity in schizophrenic relative to healthy individuals in response to happy (Kosaka et al., 2002), fearful (Holt et al., 2006a), and neutral (Holt et al., 2006a) facial expressions. Unlike the studies which found decreased amygdala activity to emotional facial expressions in schizophrenia, the baseline, comparator condition in two of these studies (Holt et al., 2006a; Kosaka et al., 2002) did not include faces. One study found elevated amygdala activity in schizophrenic relative to healthy individuals when fearful faces were incorrectly identified, but greater amygdala activity in healthy relative to schizophrenic individuals when fearful faces were correctly identified (Gur et al., 2007), suggesting that uncertainty about the emotion expressed by the faces may have led to elevated amygdala activity in schizophrenic individuals. In general, these studies which found abnormally increased medial temporal cortical activity in schizophrenia were minimally demanding from a cognitive standpoint, with an easy task which both groups performed at ceiling levels (Kosaka et al., 2002), or no task at all (Holt et al., 2006a). Furthermore, one of these studies and three additional studies found increased hippocampal and/or parahippocampal gyral responses to emotional (Holt et al., 2005, 2006a; Russell et al., 2007) and neutral or less fearful (Holt et al., 2006a; Surguladze et al., 2006) facial expressions in schizophrenic relative to healthy individuals.

One study failed to detect differences between healthy and schizophrenic individuals in amygdala activity, when comparing activity to emotional versus neutral facial expressions (Holt et al., 2006a).

Studies have indicated that schizophrenic individuals with active positive psychotic symptoms (paranoid subtype) show diminished amygdala activity to fearful facial expressions relative to nonparanoid patients (Williams et al., 2004) and healthy individuals (Phillips et al., 1999; Williams et al., 2004). These studies measured amygdala activity to fearful versus neutral faces, however; abnormally elevated amygdala responses to neutral facial expressions in the paranoid individuals may therefore have contributed to these findings. Consistent with this possibility is a parallel finding in one of these studies (Williams et al., 2004) of greater autonomic response (higher number of skin conductance responses) to neutral facial expressions, as well as to fearful expressions, in schizophrenic relative to healthy individuals. Similarly, a finding of a positive correlation between the magnitude of parahippocampal gyral activity to neutral facial expressions and severity of psychosis (Surguladze et al., 2006) supports this interpretation. Positive correlations between: (1) amygdala activity to sad facial expressions and thought disorder severity (Schneider et al., 1998); and (2) amygdala activity to dynamic representations of decreasing rather than increasing fearful facial expressions and levels of positive psychotic symptoms (Russell et al., 2007) provide additional evidence for a direct link between amygdala activity to neutral or ambiguous facial expressions and psychosis severity.

Together, these findings therefore suggest functional abnormalities in medial temporal cortical structures, including amygdala, hippocampus, and parahippocampal gyrus, in schizophrenia, that in turn may be associated with positive psychotic symptoms in the illness.

Studies of youth and individuals at high risk for schizophrenia

An increasing number of studies have reported social cognition (e.g. Pogue-Geile, 2008; Schiffman et al., 2004) and a general pattern of verbal and non-verbal cognitive deficits (e.g. Bearden et al., 2000; Cannon et al., 2000) in preschizophrenia children and adolescents, and in children and adolescents at familial risk of schizophrenia. While there is emerging parallel research examining functional abnormalities in neural regions associated with performance of specific cognitive tasks in these populations, these studies have not yet focused on examination of neural response during facial expression perception. This undoubtedly will be a focus of future research.

Major depressive disorder

An increasing number of functional neuroimaging studies employing emotional facial expressions have provided compelling evidence for a mood-congruent emotion processing bias in medial temporal cortex and striatum, but also in visual and prefrontal cortical regions implicated in emotion regulation, in depressed MDD individuals. One study for example (Lawrence et al., 2004) demonstrated increased activity within parahippocampus/hippocampus to mild sad facial expressions in depressed MDD relative to healthy individuals. Another study (Surguladze et al.,

2005) demonstrated a dissociation in neural activity to happy and sad facial expressions. In the latter study, healthy individuals demonstrated linear increases in activity in bilateral fusiform gyri and right putamen to expressions of increasing degree of happiness (neutral to mild happy to intense happy facial expressions), while depressed individuals demonstrated linear increases in activity in left putamen, left parahippocampal gyrus/amygdala, and right fusiform gyrus to expressions of increasing degree of sadness (neutral to mild sad to intense sad facial expressions). Similarly, in other studies, in response to sad faces, depressed MDD individuals demonstrated increased activity in left amygdala, ventral striatum, frontoparietal cortex and decreased activity in prefrontal cortex (Fu et al., 2004).

In further studies (Keedwell et al., 2005a,b), focusing on examination of neural activity to presentations of happy faces during happy mood induction, depressed MDD individuals showed increased activity within dorsomedial prefrontal cortex, that positively correlated with severity of anhedonia, while activity within striatum negatively correlated with anhedonia severity. These findings of abnormally elevated activity in prefrontal cortical regions implicated in emotion regulation in MDD in response to positive emotional facial expressions and positive mood induction suggest that abnormal recruitment of emotion regulatory neural regions in response to positive emotional stimuli may represent a potential biological mechanism for anhedonia in MDD.

Studies of MDD individuals before and after recovery from depressed episode have further indicated that the observed patterns of abnormally elevated medial temporal cortical and striatal activity to negative emotional facial expressions in MDD may ameliorate with successful treatments. For example, in one functional neuroimaging study (Sheline et al., 2001), abnormally elevated activity within the amygdala to masked fearful facial expressions reduced with antidepressant treatment. Other studies employing facial expressions have also shown an amelioration of baseline patterns of abnormal activity after antidepressant (selective serotonin reuptake inhibitor, SRI) treatment. Here, in response to happy faces (Fu et al., 2007), depressed MDD individuals demonstrated attenuated extrastriate cortical activity that subsequently increased following antidepressant treatment, while symptomatic improvement was associated with greater overall capacity in hippocampal and extrastriate regions. In contrast, abnormal patterns of increased activity in subcortical regions to sad facial expressions normalized after SRI treatment in these depressed MDD individuals (Fu et al., 2004). Similarly, in a recent study subgenual cingulate gyral and extrastriate cortical activity to sad facial expressions was reduced, while extrastriate activity to happy facial expression increased, after antidepressant treatment (Keedwell et al., 2009). Interestingly, in one study (Canli et al., 2005), amygdala activity to either positive or negative facial expressions predicted illness outcome: greater activity in amygdala at baseline predicted lower depression score 8 months later.

Recent research employing functional connectivity techniques has elucidated the extent to which changes in functional relationships between amygdala and striatal regions implicated in emotion processing and prefrontal cortical regions implicated in emotion regulation are associated with the treatment response. In one study, for example, (Chen et al., 2008), treatment-related increased functional connectivity to sad facial expressions was demonstrated between left amygdala, several prefrontal cortical regions implicated in emotion regulation, namely, right middle prefrontal cortex, inferior frontal gyrus, pregenual anterior cingulate, anterior mid-cingulate gyrus, thalamus, and striatum (caudate and putamen).

A more recent functional neuroimaging study examining the effect of cognitive behavioral therapy (CBT) showed that pre-treatment, MDD individuals showed elevated amygdala-hippocampal activity to sad faces, that normalized following 16 sessions of CBT (Fu et al., 2008b). Interestingly baseline dorsal anterior cingulate activity in depressed MDD individuals showed a significant relationship with subsequent clinical response.

Studies of youth and individuals at high risk for major depressive disorder

There have been few neuroimaging studies of child and adolescent MDD. One study (Thomas et al., 2001) reported blunted amygdala response to fearful facial expressions in children with depression, and exaggerated response in children with anxiety. In contrast, another, larger study (Roberson-Nay et al., 2006) found elevated amygdala activity in adolescents with MDD during incidental memory encoding of faces. In one later study (Monk et al., 2008), high-risk child and adolescent offspring of parents with MDD demonstrated greater amygdala and ventral striatal activity to fearful faces and lower ventral striatal activity to happy faces.

Together, these findings therefore suggest a relationship between abnormally elevated activity in neural regions, including amygdala and striatum, implicated in emotion processing to negative emotional facial expressions in particular in individuals with MDD during depressed episode, which would appear to ameliorate with successful treatment. Findings also suggest abnormally elevated activity in visual cortical regions to negative emotional facial expressions during the depressed episode, which also ameliorates with successful treatment. Connectivity between these regions and prefrontal cortical regions implicated in emotion regulation may increase with successful treatment, and may, in future studies, serve to predict future response to a given treatment intervention.

Bipolar disorder

Few functional neuroimaging studies have focused on examining neural activity to facial expressions in individuals with bipolar disorder. The few studies to date have demonstrated predominantly greater subcortical limbic activity (including amygdala, ventral striatum, and hippocampus) to a variety of different positive and negative emotional facial expressions in adult bipolar relative to healthy individuals during mania (e.g. Altshuler et al., 2005; Chen et al., 2006), depression (Chen et al., 2006) and even when euthymic (Hassel et al., 2008; Lawrence et al., 2004; Mahli et al., 2007) or in mixed mood states (experiencing symptoms of mania and depression (Blumberg et al., 2005; Yurgelun-Todd et al., 2000). Many of these studies employed face matching or implicit emotion processing tasks such as gender labeling of the emotional expressions. One recent study, however, reported reduced striatal activity to fearful facial expressions in bipolar individuals in mixed mood episode (having depressed and manic symptoms) relative to healthy individuals, but during passive viewing of fearful facial expressions presented later in the experiment (Killgore et al., 2008), suggesting that the nature of the face processing task impacts neural activity to these facial expressions, as has previously been demonstrated in healthy individuals (Lange et al., 2003). An important finding emerging from these studies that distinguishes bipolar from MDD individuals is abnormally elevated striatal and amygdala activity to *positive* emotional facial expressions in the former–even when they are experiencing subsyndromal depression symptoms (Lawrence et al., 2004). Furthermore, a later study showed differential patterns of abnormal functional connectivity between amygdala and OFC to happy facial expression in bipolar and MDD depressed individuals (Almeida et al., 2009).

Some studies have also demonstrated reduced lateral prefrontal cortical activity to fearful and happy facial expressions in bipolar relative to healthy individuals (Hassel et al., 2008; Yurgeuln-Todd et al., 2000), although one study showed increased activity in these regions in euthymic bipolar relative to healthy individuals during fearful and angry facial expression and identity matching (Robinson et al., 2008). Again, the task employed likely impacts patterns of abnormal lateral prefrontal cortical activity reported in bipolar relative to healthy individuals.

Medication may serve to attenuate this pattern of abnormal neural activity to some extent in bipolar individuals, although several studies indicate little impact of medication upon such activity in bipolar disorder (Phillips et al., 2008).

Bipolar youth

An increasing number of studies have now focused on the study of youth with bipolar disorder and those youth at future genetic risk of developing the illness. These studies have provided evidence of abnormally elevated amygdala activity to different facial expressions in these populations. One study, for example, has shown that bipolar youth show abnormally increased amygdala activity to neutral faces that were in turn perceived as more hostile by these than healthy, age-matched individuals (Rich et al., 2006). Neutral faces may therefore appear more ambiguous–or potentially threatening–to bipolar youth than their healthy counterparts. Other findings indicate increased amygdala and striatal activity (Dickstein et al., 2007; Pavuluri et al., 2007), and reduced lateral prefrontal cortical activity (Pavuluri et al., 2007) associated with the passive viewing of *happy* faces in euthymic bipolar relative to healthy, age-matched youth.

Functional connectivity analyses in bipolar youth have further revealed that, compared with age-matched controls, bipolar youth show less functional connectivity between the amygdala and a network of neural regions implicated in processing faces and emotional stimuli, including visual processing regions such as posterior cingulate/precuneus and fusiform gyrus/parahippocampal gyrus (Rich et al., 2008). These findings suggest that functional abnormalities in neural systems supporting facial expression perception may underlie the pathophysiology of bipolar disorder in youth. No studies to date have examined neural activity to facial expressions in bipolar disorder at risk youth.

Toward neural models of specific abnormalities in neural systems for facial expression perception in major psychiatric illnesses

The above findings point toward specific facial expression labeling and parallel functional abnormalities in neural systems supporting facial expression perception in each of three major psychiatric illnesses on which this chapter focuses. These findings can be integrated into neural models of abnormal emotion processing that characterize each of these illnesses as a first stage toward understanding of the potential pathophysiological processes that may distinguish these illnesses, and toward provision of potential biological targets for future treatment development for each illness.

Schizophrenia

Studies examining facial emotion labeling in individuals with schizophrenia show evidence for an attentional bias towards potential threat and attribution of threat to ambiguous or even neutral stimuli. The functional neuroimaging studies discussed above provide parallel, paradoxical findings regarding the processing of threat-related information in patients with schizophrenia, in that many suggest: *decreased* rather than increased amygdala activity to explicitly negative emotional stimuli. Of the studies showing increases in amygdala, hippocampal and parahippocampal gyral activity in schizophrenia, many of these increases in neural activity were to the *less negative or neutral* stimuli relative to the negative stimuli in the study. The tendency of individuals with schizophrenia to label neutral stimuli as negative, together with findings of an increase in amygdala activity to the less negative or neutral stimuli in a given experimental context rather than to the explicitly negative stimuli, suggests dysfunctional rather than decreased amygdala activity per se. Here, abnormal *increases* in amygdala activity occur to stimuli other than those depicting prototypical displays of fear. It is possible that the more neutral stimuli were emotionally ambiguous relative to the other, more explicitly fearful or negative stimuli in each of the experimental contexts. These findings suggest that a response bias in the amygdala to potentially *ambiguous,* rather than explicitly threatening, stimuli may be present in patients with schizophrenia, particularly in those individuals with positive symptoms or persecutory delusions (Phillips et al., 2003b).

These findings indicate the presence of an abnormal appraisal process such that sustained attention may occur to ambiguous, i.e. potentially threatening, rather than to overtly threatening stimuli in individuals with schizophrenia—particularly in those with persecutory delusions. If this is the case, then we would expect to observe increased activity in other regions linked functionally with the amygdala during the response to less negative relative to more negative emotional stimuli. Consistent with this are findings of increased hippocampal and parahippocampal gyral activity to neutral stimuli in patients with schizophrenia, particularly in those with positive symptoms. Thus, in schizophrenia, functional relationships between the amygdala, hippocampus and parahippocampal gyrus may therefore be disrupted, leading to abnormal assignment of salience to ambiguous, potentially threatening stimuli in the environment (Holt and Phillips, 2009).

Major depressive disorder

There are several neural models of MDD, most of which propose disproportionately elevated activity in subcortical (i.e. amygdala and striatal) regions relative to prefrontal cortex in response to emotionally-salient stimuli such as emotional facial expressions. One well-known model (Mayberg, 1997, 1999, 2005) has proposed reduced activity in dorsal lateral prefrontal cortex and increased activity in subgenual anterior cingulate gyrus, which reverses in remitted states. This is broadly supported by another model (Phillips et al., 2003b) that postulated increased activity within regions important for the identification of emotional stimuli and generation of emotional behavior, including amygdala, striatum, and prefrontal regions such as the subgenual cingulate gyrus and ventrolateral prefrontal cortex, and decreased activity within regions implicated in the effortful regulation of emotional behavior, including dorsomedial and dorsolateral prefrontal cortices. Similarly, Drevets and colleagues (Drevets et al., 1992, 1997, 2008) have proposed that the pattern of brain metabolic abnormalities in depression is characterized by increased glucose metabolism in myriad medial temporal cortical, ventromedial prefrontal cortical and striatal regions, including pre-and subgenual anterior cingulate gyrus, hippocampus, amygdala and parahippocampal gyrus, ventromedial striatum, medial thalamus, that may normalize with remission. The findings from facial expression labeling studies, and functional neuroimaging studies examining neural activity to negative and positive emotional facial expressions suggests that abnormally increased subcortical limbic activity in MDD may be more evident to negative rather than positive or neutral emotional facial expressions, and may represent a biological mechanism for the negative attentional bias observed clinically in MDD.

Bipolar disorder

Our recent neural model of emotion regulation that includes voluntary and automatic regulatory subprocesses, centered in different regions of PFC, hippocampus, and parahippocampus (Phillips et al., 2008) can be used as a theoretical framework to examine functional neural abnormalities in these neural systems that may predispose toward bipolar disorder. The most consistent findings in adult bipolar disorder and bipolar disorder in youth are those of studies employing facial expression perception paradigms that indicate abnormally elevated amygdala and striatal activity to positive and negative emotional facial expressions in bipolar disorder. More recent studies employing either automatic attentional control or automatic emotion regulation paradigms indicate abnormally reduced activity in ventromedial prefrontal cortical regions implicated in emotion regulation, including orbitofrontal cortical and dorsomedial prefrontal cortical regions, during automatic attentional control and automatic emotion regulation in adult bipolar disorder. Together, these findings therefore point to functional abnormalities between amygdala–striatal and prefrontal cortical regions during facial expression perception and during emotion regulation in bipolar disorder, but further study is required to elucidate the nature of these abnormalities in emotion regulatory neural systems, and the extent to which persistent versus mood state-dependent abnormalities in these neural systems can be dissociated, in bipolar disorder.

Summary and conclusions

This chapter has focused on examination of facial expression labeling deficits in each of three major psychiatric illnesses: schizophrenia, major depressive disorder, and bipolar disorder, and has shown that these illnesses can be distinguished by different patterns of facial expression labeling abnormalities. Schizophrenia is associated with deficits in facial expression labeling in general, which may predate illness onset and become worse with illness progression; are particularly evident for negative and neutral emotional facial expressions; and may be associated with specific symptoms associated with misperception of non-salient environmental stimuli as emotionally meaningful. Major depressive disorder is associated with abnormal labeling of specific facial expressions, including a bias away from labeling expressions as happy. Bipolar disorder is associated with difficulties in labeling negative emotional expressions.

In turn, the facial expression labeling abnormalities in each of these psychiatric illnesses is paralleled by functional abnormalities in neural regions supporting facial expression perception. In schizophrenia abnormal functional relationships between the amygdala, hippocampus, and parahippocampal gyrus may lead to abnormal assignment of salience to ambiguous, potentially threatening stimuli in the environment, which may underlie the difficulty in recognition of negative emotional stimuli, and the mislabeling of otherwise neutral stimuli as threatening. In major depressive disorder, abnormally increased subcortical limbic activity to negative, but decreased subcortical limbic activity to positive emotional facial expressions may underlie the negative attentional bias and bias away from labeling facial expressions as positive in the illness. In bipolar disorder, functional abnormalities between amygdala, striatal and prefrontal cortical regions during facial expression perception may underlie the difficulties in labeling facial expressions, as well as the mood dysregulation that typifies the illness.

Studies integrating facial expression labeling measures with measurement of activity in neural systems supporting emotion processing per se in schizophrenia, major depressive disorder and bipolar disorder are in their infancy. Findings from studies to date do suggest that these major psychiatric illnesses can be begun to be conceptualized as illnesses characterized by different patterns of functional abnormality in these neural systems. It is now important for future research in the area of clinical affective neuroscience to begin to elucidate the extent to which these functional abnormalities in facial expression labeling and underlying functional abnormalities in neural systems supporting facial expression perception can help increase understanding of the pathophysiological mechanisms for each illness, the extent to which they can provide biological targets to aid new treatment development, and the extent to which elucidation they can in turn provide insights into biological mechanisms underlying risk for future development of these illnesses.

References

Almeida, J.R., Versace, A., Mechelli, A., *et al.* (2009). Abnormal amygdala-prefrontal effective connectivity to happy faces differentiates bipolar from major depression. *Biological Psychiatry*, 66, 451–459.

Altshuler, L., Bookheimer, S., Proenza, M.A., *et al.* (2005). Increased amygdala activation during mania: a functional magnetic resonance imaging study. *American Journal of Psychiatry*, 162, 1211–1213.

An, S.K., Lee, S.J., Lee, C.H., *et al.* (2003). Reduced P3 amplitudes by negative facial emotional photographs in schizophrenia. *Schizophrenia Research,* **64**, 125–135.

Archer, J., Hay, D.C., and Young, A.W. (1992). Face processing in psychiatric conditions. *British Journal of Clinical Psychology,* **31**, 45–61.

Asthana, H.S., Mandal, M.K., Khurana, H., and Haque-Nizamie, S. (1998). Visuospatial and affect recognition deficit in depression. *Journal of Affective Disorders,* **48**, 57–62.

Auther, A.M., Lencz, T., Smith, C.W., Bowie, C.R., and Cornblatt, B.A. (2003). Overview of the First Annual Workshop on the Schizophrenia Prodrome. *Schizophrenia Bulletin,* **29**, 625–631.

Balleine, B.W., Delgado, M.R., and Hikosaka, O. (2007). The role of the dorsal striatum in reward and decision-making. *Journal of Neuroscience,* **27**, 8161–8165.

Baum, K.M., and Walker, E.F. (1995). Childhood behavioral precursors of adult symptom dimensions in schizophrenia. *Schizophrenia Research,* **16**, 111–120.

Bearden, C.E., Rosso, I.M., Hollister, J.M., Sanchez, L.E., Hadley, T., and Cannon, T.D. (2000). A prospective cohort study of childhood behavioral deviance and language abnormalities as predictors of adult schizophrenia. *Schizophrenia Bulletin,* **26**(2), 395–410.

Beck, A.T. (1967). *Depression: Causes and treatments.* Philadelphia, PA: University of Pennsylvania Press.

Bell, M., Bryson, G., and Lysaker, P. (1997). Positive and negative affect recognition in schizophrenia: a comparison with substance abuse and normal control subjects. *Psychiatry Research,* **73**, 73–82.

Bleuler, E. (1950). *Dementia Praecox or the Group of Schizophrenias.* New York: International University Press.

Blumberg, H.P., Donegan, N.H., Sanislow, C.A., *et al.* (2005). Preliminary evidence for medication effects on functional abnormalities in the amygdala and anterior cingulate in bipolar disorder. *Psychopharmacology,* **183**, 308–313.

Borod, J.C., Martin, C.C., Alpert, M., Brozgold, A., and Welkowitz, J. (1993). Perception of facial emotion in schizophrenic and right brain-damaged patients. *Journal of Nervous and Mental Disease,* **181**, 494–502.

Bouhuys, A.L., Geerts, E., and Gordijn, M.C. (1999). Depressed patients' perceptions of facial emotions in depressed and remitted states are associated with relapse: a longitudinal study. *Journal of Nervous and Mental Disease,* **187**, 595–602.

Bozikas, V.P., Kosmidis, M.H., Anezoulaki, D., Giannakou, M., and Karavatos, A. (2004). Relationship of affect recognition with psychopathology and cognitive performance in schizophrenia. *Journal of the International Neuropsychological Society,* **10**, 549–558.

Brotman, M.A., Rich, B.A., Schmajuk, M., *et al.* (2007). Attention bias to threat faces in children with bipolar disorder and comorbid lifetime anxiety disorders. *Biological Psychiatry,* **61**(6), 819–821.

Brotman, M.A., Skup, M., Rich, B.A., *et al.* (2008). Risk for bipolar disorder is associated with face-processing deficits across emotions. *Journal of the American Academy of Child and Adolescent Psychiatry,* **47**(12), 1455–1461.

Canli, T., Cooney, R.E., Goldin, P., *et al.* (2005). Amygdala reactivity to emotional faces predicts improvement in major depression. *Neuroreport,* **16**, 1267–1270.

Cannon, T.D., Mednick, S.A., and Parnas, J. (1990). Antecedents of predominantly negative- and predominantly positive-symptom schizophrenia in a high-risk population. *Archives of General Psychiatry,* **47**, 622–632.

Cannon, T.D., Bearden, C.E., Hollister, J.M., Rosso, I.M., Sanchez, L.E., and Hadley, T. (2000a). Childhood cognitive functioning in schizophrenia patients and their unaffected siblings: a prospective cohort study. *Schizophrenia Bulletin,* **26**, 379–393.

Cannon, T.D., Rosso, I.M., Hollister, J.M., Bearden, C.E., Sanchez, L.E., and Hadley, T. (2000b). A prospective cohort study of genetic and perinatal influences in the etiology of schizophrenia. *Schizophrenia Bulletin,* **26**, 351–366.

Chen, C.H., Suckling, J., Ooi, C., *et al.* (2008). Functional coupling of the amygdala in depressed patients treated with antidepressant medication. *Neuropsychopharmacology,* **33**, 1909–1918.

Combs, D.R. and Gouvier, W.D. (2004). The role of attention in affect perception: an examination of Mirsky's four factor model of attention in chronic schizophrenia. *Schizophrenia Bulletin,* **30**(4), 727–738.

Cooper, J.C., and Knutson, B. (2008). Valence and salience contribute to nucleus accumbens activation. *Neuroimage, 39*, 538–547.

Das, P., Kemp, A.H., Flynn, G., *et al.* (2007). Functional disconnections in the direct and indirect amygdala pathways for fear processing in schizophrenia. *Schizophrenia Research, 90*, 284–294.

Davis, P.J., and Gibson, M.G. (2000). Recognition of posed and genuine facial expressions of emotion in paranoid and nonparanoid schizophrenia. *Journal of Abnormal Psychology, 109*, 445–450.

Delgado, M.R., Stenger, V.A., and Fiez, J.A. (2004). Motivation-dependent responses in the human caudate nucleus. *Cerebral Cortex, 14*, 1022–1030.

Delgado, M.R., Miller, M.M., Inati, S., and Phelps, E.A. (2005). An fMRI study of reward-related probability learning. *Neuroimage, 24*, 862–873.

Dickstein, D.P., Rich, B.A., Roberson-Nay, R., Berghorst, L., Vinton, D., Pine, D.S., *et al* (2007). Neural activation during encoding of emotional faces in pediatric bipolar disorder. *Bipolar Disorders, 9*(7), 679–692.

Dolcos, F., Labar, K.S., and Cabeza, R. (2004). Interaction between the amygdala and the medial temporal lobe memory system predicts better memory for emotional events. *Neuron, 42*, 855–863.

Drevets, W.C., Videen, T.O., Price, J.L., Preskorn, S.H., Carmichael, S.T., and Raichle, M.E. (1992). A functional anatomical study of unipolar depression. *Journal of Neuroscience, 12*, 3628–3641.

Drevets, W.C., Price, J.L., Simpson, J.R., Jr., *et al.* (1997). Subgenual prefrontal cortex abnormalities in mood disorders. *Nature, 386*, 824–827.

Drevets, W.C., Price, J.L., and Furey, M.L. (2008). Brain structural and functional abnormalities in mood disorders: implications for neurocircuitry models of depression. *Brain Structure and Function, 213*, 93–118.

Edwards, J., Jackson, H.J., and Pattison, P.E. (2002). Emotion recognition via facial expression and affective prosody in schizophrenia: a methodological review. *Clinical Psychology Review, 22*, 789–832.

Edwards, J., Pattison, P.E., Jackson, H.J., and Wales, R.J. (2001). Facial affect and affective prosody recognition in first-episode schizophrenia. *Schizophrenia Research, 48*, 235–253.

Evangeli, M., and Broks, M.E. (2000). Face processing in schizophrenia: parallels with the effects of amygdala damage. *Cognitive Neuropsychiatry, 5*, 81–104.

Fakra, E., Salgado-Pineda, P., Delaveau, P., Hariri, A.R., and Blin, O. (2008). Neural bases of different cognitive strategies for facial affect processing in schizophrenia. *Schizophrenia Research, 100*(1-3), 191–205.

Feinberg, T.E., Rifkin, A., Schaffer, C., and Walker, E. (1986). Facial discrimination and emotional recognition in schizophrenia and affective disorders. *Archives of General Psychiatry, 43*, 276–279.

Freeman, D., Garety, P.A., and Phillips, M.L. (2000). An examination of hypervigilance for external threat in individuals with generalized anxiety disorder and individuals with persecutory delusions using visual scan paths. *Quarterly Journal of Experimental Psychology. A, Human Experimental Psychology, 53*, 549–567.

Fu, C.H., Williams, S.C., Cleare, A.J., *et al.* (2004). Attenuation of the neural response to sad faces in major depression by antidepressant treatment: a prospective, event-related functional magnetic resonance imaging study. *Archives of General Psychiatry, 61*, 877–889.

Fu, C.H.Y., Williams, S.C.R., Brammer, M.J., *et al.* (2007). Neural responses to happy facial expressions in major depression following antidepressant treatment. *American Journal of Psychiatry, 164*, 599–607.

Fu, C.H., Mourao-Miranda, J., Costafreda, S.G., *et al.* (2008a). Pattern classification of sad facial processing: toward the development of neurobiological markers in depression. *Biological Psychiatry, 63*, 656–662.

Fu, C.H., Williams, S.C., Cleare, A.J., *et al.* (2008b). Neural responses to sad facial expressions in major depression following cognitive behavioral therapy. *Biological Psychiatry, 64*, 505–512.

Getz, G.E., Shear, P.K., and Strakowski, S.M. (2003). Facial affect recognition deficits in bipolar disorder. *Journal of the International Neuropsychological Society, 9*, 623–632.

Ghashghaei, H.T., Hilgetag, C.C., and Barbas, H. (2007). Sequence of information processing for emotions based on the anatomic dialogue between prefrontal cortex and amygdala. *Neuroimage, 34*, 905–923.

Gray, J.A. (1998). Integrating schizophrenia. *Schizophrenia Bulletin,* **24**, 249–266.

Gray, J.A., Joseph, M.H., Hemsley, D.R., *et al.* (1995). The role of mesolimbic dopaminergic and retrohippocampal afferents to the nucleus accumbens in latent inhibition: implications for schizophrenia. *Behavioural Brain Research,* **71**, 19–31.

Greba, Q., Gifkins, A., and Kokkinidis, L. (2001). Inhibition of amygdaloid dopamine D2 receptors impairs emotional learning measured with fear-potentiated startle. *Brain Research,* **899**, 218–226.

Gur, R.C., Erwin, R.J., Gur, R.E., Zwil, A.S., Heimberg, C., and Kraemer, H.C. (1992). Facial emotion discrimination: II. Behavioral findings in depression. *Psychiatry Research,* **42**, 241–251.

Gur, R.C., Schroeder, L., Turner, T., *et al.* (2002a). Brain activation during facial emotion processing. *Neuroimage,* **16**, 651–662.

Gur, R.E., Loughead, J., Kohler, C.G., *et al.* (2007). Limbic activation associated with misidentification of fearful faces and flat affect in schizophrenia. *Archives of General Psychiatry,* **64**, 1356–1366.

Gur, R.E., Mcgrath, C., Chan, R.M., *et al.* (2002b). An fMRI study of facial emotion processing in patients with schizophrenia. *American Journal of Psychiatry,* **159**, 1992–1999.

Habel, U., Klein, M., Shah, N.J., *et al.* (2004). Genetic load on amygdala hypofunction during sadness in nonaffected brothers of schizophrenia patients. *American Journal of Psychiatry,* **161**, 1806–1813.

Hale, W.W., 3rd, Jansen, J.H., Bouhuys, A.L., and Van Den Hoofdakker, R.H. (1998). The judgement of facial expressions by depressed patients, their partners and controls. *Journal of Affective Disorders,* **47**, 63–70.

Hall, J., Harris, J.M., Sprengelmeyer, R., *et al.* (2004). Social cognition and face processing in schizophrenia. *British Journal of Psychiatry,* **185**, 169–170.

Harmer, C.J., Grayson, L., and Goodwin, G.M. (2002). Enhanced recognition of disgust in bipolar illness. *Biological Psychiatry,* **51**, 298–304.

Haruno, M., Kuroda, T., Doya, K., *et al.* (2004). A neural correlate of reward-based behavioral learning in caudate nucleus: a functional magnetic resonance imaging study of a stochastic decision task. *Journal of Neuroscience,* **24**, 1660–1665.

Haruno, M., and Kawato, M. (2006a). Different neural correlates of reward expectation and reward expectation error in the putamen and caudate nucleus during stimulus-action-reward association learning. *Journal of Neurophysiology,* **95**, 948–959.

Haruno, M., and Kawato, M. (2006b). Heterarchical reinforcement-learning model for integration of multiple cortico-striatal loops: fMRI examination in stimulus-action-reward association learning. *Neural Netw,* **19**, 1242–1254.

Hassel, S., Almeida, J.R., Kerr, N., *et al.* (2008). Elevated striatal and decreased dorsolateral prefrontal cortical activity in response to emotional stimuli in euthymic bipolar disorder: no associations with psychotropic medication load. *Bipolar Disorders,* **10**, 916–927.

Haxby, J.V., Hoffman, E.A., and Gobbini, M.I. (2000). The distributed human neural system for face perception. *Trends in Cognitive Science,* **4**, 223–233.

Heimberg, C., Gur, R.E., Erwin, R.J., Shtasel, D.L., and Gur, R.C. (1992). Facial emotion discrimination: III. Behavioral findings in schizophrenia. *Psychiatry Research,* **42**, 253–265.

Heining, M., Young, A.W., Ioannou, G., *et al.* (2003). Disgusting smells activate human anterior insula and ventral striatum. *Annals of the New York Academy of Sciences,* **1000**, 380–384.

Hempel, A., Hempel, E., Schonknecht, P., Stippich, C., and Schroder, J. (2003). Impairment in basal limbic function in schizophrenia during affect recognition. *Psychiatry Research,* **122**, 115–124.

Holt, D.J., Weiss, A.P., Rauch, S.L., *et al.* (2005). Sustained activation of the hippocampus in response to fearful faces in schizophrenia. *Biological Psychiatry,* **57**, 1011–1019.

Holt, D.J., Titone, D., Long, L.S., *et al.* (2006a). The misattribution of salience in delusional patients with schizophrenia. *Schizophrenia Research,* **83**, 247–256.

Holt, D.J., Kunkel, L., Weiss, A.P., *et al.* (2006b). Increased medial temporal lobe activation during the passive viewing of emotional and neutral facial expressions in schizophrenia. *Schizophrenia Research,* **82**, 153–162.

Holt, D.J., and Phillips, M.L. (2009).The human amygdala in schizophrenia . In Phelps, E.A. & Whalen, P.J. (Eds.) *The Human Amygdala* (pp. 344–361). New York: Guilford.

Hunter, E.C., Phillips, M.L., Chalder, T., Sierra, M., and David, A.S. (2003). Depersonalisation disorder: a cognitive-behavioural conceptualisation. *Behaviour Research and Therapy*, **41**, 1451–1467.

Hunter, E.C., Baker, D., Phillips, M.L., Sierra, M., and David, A.S. (2005). Cognitive-behaviour therapy for depersonalisation disorder: an open study. *Behaviour Research and Therapy*, **43**, 1121–1130.

Jaeger, J., Borod, J.C., and Peselow, E. (1987). Depressed patients have atypical hemispace biases in the perception of emotional chimeric faces. *Journal of Abnormal Psychology*, **96**, 321–324.

Johnston, P.J., Katsikitis, M., and Carr, V.J. (2001). A generalised deficit can account for problems in facial emotion recognition in schizophrenia. *Biological Psychology*, **58**, 203–227.

Johnston, P.J., Stojanov, W., Devir, H., and Schall, U. (2005). Functional MRI of facial emotion recognition deficits in schizophrenia and their electrophysiological correlates. *European Journal of Neuroscience*, **22**, 1221–1232.

Kapur, S. (2003). Psychosis as a state of aberrant salience: a framework linking biology, phenomenology, and pharmacology in schizophrenia. *American Journal of Psychiatry*, **160**, 13–23.

Keedwell, P.A., Andrew, C., Williams, S.C., Brammer, M.J., and Phillips, M.L. (2005a). A double dissociation of ventromedial prefrontal cortical responses to sad and happy stimuli in depressed and healthy individuals. *Biological Psychiatry*, **58**, 495–503.

Keedwell, P.A., Andrew, C., Williams, S.C., Brammer, M.J., and Phillips, M.L. (2005b). The neural correlates of anhedonia in major depressive disorder. *Biological Psychiatry*, **58**, 843–853.

Keedwell, P., Drapier, D., Surguladze, S., Giampietro, V., Brammer, M., and Phillips, M. (2009). Neural markers of symptomatic improvement during antidepressant therapy in severe depression: subgenual cingulate and visual cortical responses to sad, but not happy, facial stimuli are correlated with changes in symptom score. *Journal of Psychopharmacology*, **23**, 775–788.

Kensinger, E.A., and Corkin, S. (2004). Two routes to emotional memory: distinct neural processes for valence and arousal. *Proceedings of the National Academy of Sciences, USA*, **101**, 3310–5.

Kerr, N., Scott, J., and Phillips, M.L. (2005). Patterns of attentional deficits and emotional bias in bipolar and major depressive disorder. *British Journal of Clinical Psychology*, **44**, 343–356.

Kerr, S.L., and Neale, J.M. (1993). Emotion perception in schizophrenia: specific deficit or further evidence of generalized poor performance? *Journal of Abnormal Psychology*, **102**, 312–318.

Killgore, W.D., Gruber, S.A., and Yurgelun-Todd, D.A. (2008). Abnormal corticostriatal activity during fear perception in bipolar disorder. *Neuroreport*, **19**, 1523–1527.

Kline, J.S., Smith, J.E., and Ellis, H.C. (1992). Paranoid and nonparanoid schizophrenic processing of facially displayed affect. *Journal of Psychiatric Research*, **26**, 169–182.

Knutson, B., and Wimmer, G.E. (2007). Splitting the difference: how does the brain code reward episodes? *Annals of the New York Academy of Sciences*, **1104**, 54–69.

Knutson, B., Fong, G.W., Adams, C.M., Varner, J.L., and Hommer, D. (2001). Dissociation of reward anticipation and outcome with event-related fMRI. *Neuroreport*, **12**, 3683–2687.

Kohler, C.G., Bilker, W., Hagendoorn, M., Gur, R.E., and Gur, R.C. (2000). Emotion recognition deficit in schizophrenia: association with symptomatology and cognition. *Biological Psychiatry*, **48**, 127–136.

Kohler, C.G., Turner, T.H., Bilker, W.B., *et al.* (2003). Facial emotion recognition in schizophrenia: intensity effects and error pattern. *American Journal of Psychiatry*, **160**, 1768–1774.

Kohler, C.G., Martin, E.A., Milonova, M., *et al.* (2008a). Dynamic evoked facial expressions of emotions in schizophrenia. *Schizophrenia Research*, **105**, 30–39.

Kohler, C.G., Martin, E.A., Stolar, N., *et al.* (2008b). Static posed and evoked facial expressions of emotions in schizophrenia. *Schizophrenia Research*, **105**, 49–60.

Kosaka, H., Omori, M., Murata, T., *et al.* (2002). Differential amygdala response during facial recognition in patients with schizophrenia: an fMRI study. *Schizophrenia Research*, **57**, 87–95.

Krettek, J.E., and Price, J.L. (1977). Projections from the amygdaloid complex and adjacent olfactory structures to the entorhinal cortex and to the subiculum in the rat and cat. *Journal of Comparative Neurology,* **172**, 723–752.

Kucharska-Pietura, K., David, A.S., Dropko, P., and Klimkowski, M. (2002). The perception of emotional chimeric faces in schizophrenia: further evidence of right hemisphere dysfunction. *Neuropsychiatry, Neuropsychology, and Behavioral Neurology,* **15**, 72–78.

Kucharska-Pietura, K., David, A.S., Masiak, M., and Phillips, M.L. (2005). Perception of facial and vocal affect by people with schizophrenia in early and late stages of illness. *British Journal of Psychiatry,* **187**, 523–528.

Lange, K., Williams, L.M., Young, A.W., Bullmore, E.T., Brammer, M.J., Williams, S.C., *et al.* (2003). Task instructions modulate neural responses to fearful facial expressions. *Biological Psychiatry,* **53**(3), 226–232.

Lawrence, N.S., Williams, A.M., Surguladze, S., *et al.* (2004). Subcortical and ventral prefrontal cortical neural responses to facial expressions distinguish patients with bipolar disorder and major depression. *Biological Psychiatry,* **55**, 578–587.

Lembke, A., and Ketter, T.A. (2002). Impaired recognition of facial emotion in mania. *American Journal of Psychiatry,* **159**, 302–304.

Loughland, C.M., Williams, L.M., and Gordon, E. (2002). Visual scanpaths to positive and negative facial emotions in an outpatient schizophrenia sample. *Schizophrenia Research,* **55**, 159–170.

Malhi, G.S., Lagopoulos, J., Sachdev, P.S., Ivanovski, B., Shnier, R., and Ketter, T. (2007). Is a lack of disgust something to fear? A functional magnetic resonance imaging facial emotion recognition study in euthymic bipolar disorder patients. *Bipolar Disorders,* **9**, 345–357.

Malkova, L., and Mishkin, M. (2003). One-trial memory for object-place associations after separate lesions of hippocampus and posterior parahippocampal region in the monkey. *Journal of Neuroscience,* **23**, 1956–1965.

Mandal, M.K. (1987). Decoding of facial emotions, in terms of expressiveness, by schizophrenics and depressives. *Psychiatry,* **50**, 371–376.

Mandal, M.K., and Palchoudhury, S. (1985). Decoding of facial affect in schizophrenia. *Psychological Reports,* **56**, 651–652.

Mandal, M.K., Pandey, R., and Prasad, A.B. (1998). Facial expressions of emotions and schizophrenia: a review. *Schizophrenia Bulletin,* **24**, 399–412.

Maratos, E.J., Dolan, R.J., Morris, J.S., Henson, R.N., and Rugg, M.D. (2001). Neural activity associated with episodic memory for emotional context. *Neuropsychologia,* **39**, 910–920.

Matthews, G.R., and Antes, J.R. (1992). Visual attention and depression: Cognitive biases in the eye fixation of the dysphoric and non-depressed. *Cognitive Therapy and Research,* **16**, 359–371.

Mayberg, H.S. (1997). Limbic-cortical dysregulation: a proposed model of depression. *Journal of Neuropsychiatry and Clinical Neurosciences,* **9**, 471–481.

Mayberg, H.S., Liotti, M., Brannan, S.K., *et al.* (1999). Reciprocal limbic-cortical function and negative mood: converging PET findings in depression and normal sadness. *American Journal of Psychiatry,* **156**, 675–682.

Mayberg, H.S., Lozano, A.M., Voon, V., *et al.* (2005). Deep brain stimulation for treatment-resistant depression. *Neuron,* **45**, 651–660.

Mcclure, E.B., Pope, K., Hoberman, A.J., Pine, D.S., and Leibenluft, E. (2003). Facial expression recognition in adolescents with mood and anxiety disorders. *American Journal of Psychiatry,* **160**, 1172–1174.

Meredith, G.E., Pattiselanno, A., Groenewegen, H.J., and Haber, S.N. (1996). Shell and core in monkey and human nucleus accumbens identified with antibodies to calbindin-D28k. *Journal of Comparative Neurology,* **365**, 628–639.

Mikhailova, E.S., Vladimirova, T.V., Iznak, A.F., Tsusulkovskaya, E.J., and Sushko, N.V. (1996). Abnormal recognition of facial expression of emotions in depressed patients with major depression disorder and schizotypal personality disorder. *Biological Psychiatry,* **40**, 697–705.

Monk, C.S., Klein, R.G., Telzer, E.H., *et al.* (2008). Amygdala and nucleus accumbens activation to emotional facial expressions in children and adolescents at risk for major depression. *American Journal of Psychiatry,* **165**, 90–98.

Morrison, R.L., Bellack, A.S., and Mueser, K.T. (1988). Deficits in facial-affect recognition and schizophrenia. *Schizophrenia Bulletin,* **14**, 67–83.

Mueser, K.T., Penn, D.L., Blanchard, J.J., and Bellack, A.S. (1997). Affect recognition in schizophrenia: a synthesis of findings across three studies. *Psychiatry,* **60**, 301–308.

Murray, C.J., and Lopez, A.D. (1996). Evidence-based health policy—lessons from the Global Burden of Disease Study. *Science,* **274**, 740–743.

Muzekari, L.H., and Bates, M.E. (1977). Judgment of emotion among chronic schizophrenics. *Journal of Clinical Psychology,* **33**, 662–666.

Paradiso, S., Andreasen, N.C., Crespo-Facorro, B., *et al.* (2003). Emotions in unmedicated patients with schizophrenia during evaluation with positron emission tomography. *American Journal of Psychiatry,* **160**, 1775–1783.

Pavuluri, M.N., O'Connor, M.M., Harral, E., and Sweeney, J.A. (2007). Affective neural circuitry during facial emotion processing in pediatric bipolar disorder. *Biological Psychiatry,* **62**, 158–67.

Penn, D.L., Combs, D.R., Ritchie, M., *et al.* (2000). Emotion recognition in schizophrenia: further investigation of generalized versus specific deficit models. *Journal of Abnormal Psychology,* **109**, 512–516.

Persad, S.M., and Polivy, J. (1993). Differences between depressed and nondepressed individuals in the recognition of and response to facial emotional cues. *Journal of Abnormal Psychology,* **102**, 358–368.

Pezze, M.A., and Feldon, J. (2004). Mesolimbic dopaminergic pathways in fear conditioning. *Progress in Neurobiology,* **74**, 301–320.

Phillips, M.L., Williams, L., Senior, C., *et al.* (1999). A differential neural response to threatening and non-threatening negative facial expressions in paranoid and non-paranoid schizophrenics. *Psychiatry Research,* **92**, 11–31.

Phillips, M.L., Drevets, W.C., Rauch, S.L., and Lane, R. (2003a). Neurobiology of emotion perception I: The neural basis of normal emotion perception. *Biological Psychiatry,* **54**, 504–514.

Phillips, M.L., Drevets, W.C., Rauch, S.L., and Lane, R. (2003b). Neurobiology of emotion perception II: Implications for major psychiatric disorders. *Biological Psychiatry,* **54**, 515–528.

Phillips, M.L., Ladouceur, C.D., and Drevets, W.C. (2008). A neural model of voluntary and automatic emotion regulation: implications for understanding the pathophysiology and neurodevelopment of bipolar disorder. *Molecular Psychiatry,* **13**, 33–57.

Pilowsky, I., and Bassett, D. (1980). Schizophrenia and the response to facial emotions. *Comprehensive Psychiatry,* **21**, 236–244.

Pitkanen, A., Pikkarainen, M., Nurminen, N., and Ylinen, A. (2000). Reciprocal connections between the amygdala and the hippocampal formation, perirhinal cortex, and postrhinal cortex in rat. A review. *Annals of the New York Academy of Sciences,* **911**, 369–391.

Prensa, L., Richard, S., and Parent, A. (2003). Chemical anatomy of the human ventral striatum and adjacent basal forebrain structures. *Journal of Comparative Neurology,* **460**, 345–367.

Rich, B.A., Grimley, M.E., Schmajuk, M., Blair, K.S., Blair, R.J.R., and Leibenluft, E. (2008). Face emotion labeling deficits in children with bipolar disorder and severe mood dysregulation. *Development & Psychopathology,* **20**(2), 529–546.

Roberson-Nay, R., Mcclure, E.B., Monk, C.S., *et al.* (2006). Increased amygdala activity during successful memory encoding in adolescent major depressive disorder: An FMRI study. *Biological Psychiatry,* **60**, 966–973.

Robinson, J.L., Monkul, E.S., Tordesillas-Gutierrez, D., *et al.* (2008). Fronto-limbic circuitry in euthymic bipolar disorder: evidence for prefrontal hyperactivation. *Psychiatry Research,* **164**, 106–113.

Rubinow, D.R. and Post, R.M. (1992). Impaired recognition of affect in facial expression in depressed patients. *Biological Psychiatry,* **31**, 947–953.

Russell, T.A., Reynaud, E., Kucharska-Pietura, K., *et al.* (2007). Neural responses to dynamic expressions of fear in schizophrenia. *Neuropsychologia, 45*, 107–123.

Sacchetti, B., Lorenzini, C.A., Baldi, E., Tassoni, G., and Bucherelli, C. (1999). Auditory thalamus, dorsal hippocampus, basolateral amygdala, and perirhinal cortex role in the consolidation of conditioned freezing to context and to acoustic conditioned stimulus in the rat. *Journal of Neuroscience, 19*, 9570–9578.

Sachs, G., Steger-Wuchse, D., Kryspin-Exner, I., Gur, R.C., and Katschnig, H. (2004). Facial recognition deficits and cognition in schizophrenia. *Schizophrenia Research, 68*, 27–35.

Salem, J.E., Kring, A.M., and Kerr, S.L. (1996). More evidence for generalized poor performance in facial emotion perception in schizophrenia. *Journal of Abnormal Psychology, 105*, 480–483.

Schiffman, J., Walker, E., Ekstrom, M., Schulsinger, F., Sorensen, H., and Mednick, S. (2004). Childhood videotaped social and neuromotor precursors of schizophrenia: a prospective investigation. *American Journal of Psychiatry, 161*, 2021–2027.

Schneider, F., Gur, R.C., Gur, R.E., and Shtasel, D.L. (1995). Emotional processing in schizophrenia: neurobehavioral probes in relation to psychopathology. *Schizophrenia Research, 17*, 67–75.

Schneider, F., Weiss, U., Kessler, C., *et al.* (1998). Differential amygdala activation in schizophrenia during sadness. *Schizophrenia Research, 34*, 133–142.

Schroeder, U., Hennenlotter, A., Erhard, P., *et al.* (2004). Functional neuroanatomy of perceiving surprised faces. *Human Brain Mapping, 23*, 181–187.

Sheline, Y.I., Barch, D.M., Donnelly, J.M., Ollinger, J.M., Snyder, A.Z., and Mintun, M.A. (2001). Increased amygdala response to masked emotional faces in depressed subjects resolves with antidepressant treatment: an fMRI study. *Biological Psychiatry, 50*, 651–658.

Silver, H., Shlomo, N., Turner, T., and Gur, R.C. (2002). Perception of happy and sad facial expressions in chronic schizophrenia: evidence for two evaluative systems. *Schizophrenia Research, 55*, 171–177.

Smith, A.P., Henson, R.N., Dolan, R.J., and Rugg, M.D. (2004). fMRI correlates of the episodic retrieval of emotional contexts. *Neuroimage, 22*, 868–878.

Surguladze, S.A., Brammer, M.J., Young, A.W., *et al.* (2003). A preferential increase in the extrastriate response to signals of danger. *Neuroimage, 19*, 1317–1328.

Surguladze, S.A., Young, A.W., Senior, C., Brebion, G., Travis, M.J., and Phillips, M.L. (2004). Recognition accuracy and response bias to happy and sad facial expressions in patients with major depression. *Neuropsychology, 18*, 212–218.

Surguladze, S., Brammer, M.J., Keedwell, P., *et al.* (2005). A differential pattern of neural response toward sad versus happy facial expressions in major depressive disorder. *Biological Psychiatry, 57*, 201–209.

Surguladze, S., Russell, T., Kucharska-Pietura, K., *et al.* (2006). A reversal of the normal pattern of parahippocampal response to neutral and fearful faces is associated with reality distortion in schizophrenia. *Biological Psychiatry, 60*, 423–431.

Suslow, T., Junghanns, K., and Arolt, V. (2001). Detection of facial expressions of emotions in depression. *Perceptual and Motor Skills, 92*, 857–868.

Takahashi, H., Koeda, M., Oda, K., *et al.* (2004). An fMRI study of differential neural response to affective pictures in schizophrenia. *Neuroimage, 22*, 1247–1254.

Tarbox, S.I., and Pogue-Geile, M.F. (2008). Development of social functioning in preschizophrenia children and adolescents: a systematic review. *Psychological Bulletin, 134*, 561–583.

Taylor, S.F., Liberzon, I., Decker, L.R., and Koeppe, R.A. (2002). A functional anatomic study of emotion in schizophrenia. *Schizophrenia Research, 58*, 159–172.

Thomas, K.M., Drevets, W.C., Dahl, R.E., *et al.* (2001). Amygdala response to fearful faces in anxious and depressed children. *Archives of General Psychiatry, 58*, 1057–1063.

Tricomi, E.M., Delgado, M.R., and Fiez, J.A. (2004). Modulation of caudate activity by action contingency. *Neuron, 41*, 281–292.

Tricomi, E., Delgado, M.R., Mccandliss, B.D., Mcclelland, J.L., and Fiez, J.A. (2006). Performance feedback drives caudate activation in a phonological learning task. *Journal of Cognitive Neuroscience*, **18**, 1029–1043.

Tsukiura, T., Fujii, T., Takahashi, T., *et al.* (2002). Medial temporal lobe activation during context-dependent relational processes in episodic retrieval: an fMRI study. Functional magnetic resonance imaging. *Human Brain Mapping*, **17**, 203–213.

Venn, H.R., Gray, J.M., Montagne, B., *et al.* (2004). Perception of facial expressions of emotion in bipolar disorder. *Bipolar Disorders*, **6**, 286–293.

Walker, E., Mcguire, M., and Bettes, B. (1984). Recognition and identification of facial stimuli by schizophrenics and patients with affective disorders. *British Journal of Clinical Psychology*, **23**, 37–44.

Walker, E.F., Grimes, K.E., Davis, D.M., and Smith, A.J. (1993). Childhood precursors of schizophrenia: facial expressions of emotion. *American Journal of Psychiatry*, **150**, 1654–1660.

Whittaker, J.F., Deakin, J.F., and Tomenson, B. (2001). Face processing in schizophrenia: defining the deficit. *Psychological Medicine*, **31**, 499–507.

Williams, L.M., Das, P., Liddell, B.J., *et al.* (2007). Fronto-limbic and autonomic disjunctions to negative emotion distinguish schizophrenia subtypes. *Psychiatry Research*, **155**, 29–44.

Williams, L.M., Phillips, M.L., Brammer, M.J., *et al.* (2001). Arousal dissociates amygdala and hippocampal fear responses: evidence from simultaneous fMRI and skin conductance recording. *Neuroimage*, **14**, 1070–1079.

Williams, L.M., Das, P., Harris, A.W., *et al.* (2004). Dysregulation of arousal and amygdala-prefrontal systems in paranoid schizophrenia. *American Journal of Psychiatry*, **161**, 480–489.

Young H.F., and Bentall R. (1995). Hypothesis testing in patients with persecutory delusions: Comparison with depressed and normal subjects. *British Journal of Clinical Psychology*, **34**, 353–369.

Yurgelun-Todd, D.A., Gruber, S.A., Kanayama, G., Killgore, W.D., Baird, A.A., and Young, A.D. (2000). fMRI during affect discrimination in bipolar affective disorder. *Bipolar Disorders*, **2**, 237–248.

Chapter 45

Delusions and Faces

Robyn Langdon

Whatever could the study of delusional people tell us about the normal processes that healthy people use to extract information from the perception of faces, and vice versa? Delusions, or "false beliefs" according to the standard psychiatric nosology, are the archetypal signs of madness; they are first-rank markers of the pathological disconnect from normalcy and reality that is seen in schizophrenia, although they also occur in many neurological conditions (e.g. Alzheimer's disease). Traditional psychiatric approaches to delusions, of which there are two, are inconsistent with the idea that the study of face processing might inform understanding of the nature of delusional belief (and vice versa), which is the subject of this chapter.

One traditional approach has been to conceive of delusions, in particular, the so-called "primary" delusions, as psychologically irreducible or psychologically un-understandable (see Jaspers, 1913/1963; and also Spitzer, 1990, 1992, for discussion). Primary delusions purportedly spring into existence without a meaningful context to render the generation of the delusional content psychologically understandable. This "brute organic" view has tended to dominate when the delusional content is more fantastic, as occurs, for example, when a patient believes that she has a nuclear power station inside her stomach, or that she is controlled telepathically by an alien being from outer space. The alternate traditional approach, the psychodynamic view, has tended to dominate when the delusional content is more mundane, as occurs, for example, when a patient believes that his neighbors are plotting against him (a persecutory delusion), or that his partner is having an affair (delusional jealousy), or that he is a gifted composer (despite the fact that the patient plays no musical instrument and has never studied music: a grandiose delusion).[1] In these cases, the delusional content is often attributed to a motivation to protect or enhance a vulnerable self. Butler (2000a), for example, has described a patient with "reverse Othello syndrome" who was left a quadriplegic and unable to speak without an electronic communicator after a serious car accident. The patient had developed the self-protective delusion that his ex-partner continued to be loving and faithful, despite that the ex-partner had severed all contact with the patient soon after his accident (see McKay et al., 2005, for discussion).

Neither traditional approach suggests that the study of face processing might advance scientific understanding of delusions, although, to be fair, neither traditional approach rules out that the study of face processing in delusional people might be informative. A delusional person with schizophrenia might believe, for example, that aliens are inserting thoughts into her mind and she might also show a difficulty in recognizing facial expressions, and the study of her difficulties in facial expression recognition might advance understanding of how the normal cognitive system

---

[1] There is no simple mapping of the primary/secondary distinction onto the distinction between fantastic and mundane delusional content; for example, Cotard delusion, which is the delusional belief that one is dead (despite being able to walk and talk), often occurs in the context of depression, and so might be classed as a secondary delusion despite the bizarre delusional content.

for facial expression recognition is organized. It is less likely, however, that the study of her difficulties in facial expression recognition will explain what gave rise to the generation of her thought insertion delusion; and that's the sort of causal connection that interests me in this chapter—that is, the possibility of a direct causal connection between an impairment in the normal cognitive system for face processing and the generation of a particular type of delusional content. The particular type of delusional content that I want to focus on in this chapter involves a mistaken belief about the identity of oneself and/or other people. These "misidentification" delusions sometimes co-occur with persecutory delusions, and persecutory delusions, at least in schizophrenia, have been linked with deficits in facial expression recognition, in particular, a tendency to misidentify neutral facial expressions as disgusted or fearful (see Phillips, Chapter 44, this volume). However, while such deficits might exacerbate persecutory elaborations in a patient with a concurrent misidentification delusion, I think it less likely that such deficits will explain the generation of the patient's misidentification delusion. So, in this chapter, I want to focus on how the normal cognitive system for identifying familiar faces and people from the perception of faces might be disrupted so as to explain the generation of a misidentification delusion.

There are different types of misidentification delusion. Patients might believe, for example, that a loved one has been replaced by a visually similar stranger or impostor ("Capgras" delusion) or has been duplicated (a form of "reduplicative paramnesia"); they might believe that strangers around them are people who they know, but who are in disguise ("Frégoli" delusion); they might believe that another person's appearance has been changed into that of someone else ("inter-metamorphosis"); and they might even believe that the person they see reflected in the mirror is a stranger and not themselves ("mirrored-self misidentification" delusion). Misidentification delusions, like the other delusions with non-misidentification themes, have been thought of traditionally as either psychologically un-understandable or psychologically explicable only with regard to psychodynamic theorizing. Capgras delusion, for example, has been attributed to ambivalent feelings towards a loved one: love, on the one hand, and hate or anger, on the other hand. The Capgras patient then resolves this internal conflict by generating the impostor belief; anger is directed towards the impostor, while only love is felt for the true (but missing) loved one (see, e.g. Enoch and Trethowan, 1991, and Young, 2000, for discussion). More recently, however, "cognitive neuropsychiatry" has come to the fore as an influential alternative to the two traditional approaches to delusions.

Cognitive neuropsychiatry and delusions

Cognitive neuropsychiatry applies the logic and the methods of cognitive neuropsychology to explain symptoms, like delusions and hallucinations, which have historically been labeled "psychiatric" rather than "neurological." Cognitive neuropsychology, and its sibling, cognitive neuropsychiatry, have two main aims:

1 To use a model (or theory) of some relevant cognitive system (say for belief formation in the case of delusional patients) in order to account for a patient's symptoms in terms of what remains intact and what has been disrupted in that normal cognitive system; and

2 To study the patients with disorders of cognition (which might be acquired, developmental or psychiatric) in order to develop, test and modify a model (or theory) of the normal cognitive system.

When applied to delusions, the cognitive neuropsychiatric approach allows that delusions, which might seem psychologically un-understandable with regard to the common folk's psychology of why people come to believe what they do, might, nevertheless, still be psychologically

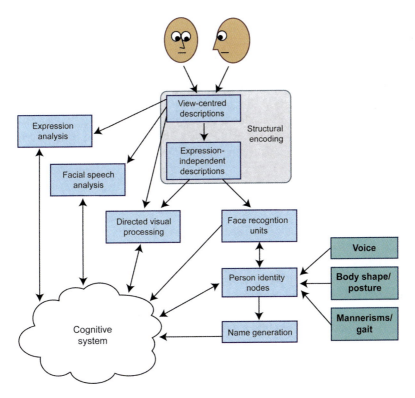

Fig. 45.1 Adaptation of Bruce and Young's (1986) model of face processing, as originally depicted in Ellis and Lewis (2001). (This original figure was published in *Trends in Cognitive Sciences*, 5(4), 149–156, © Elsevier 2001.) The original has been modified to include input to the Person identity nodes (PINs) from the processing of information about voice, body shape/posture and mannerisms/gait.

understandable with regard to disruptions in normal information processing (including normal face processing), many components of which are not directly accessible to consciousness. Cognitive neuropsychiatry also aims to develop testable (cognitive) psychological theories of delusions, unlike much of the post hoc psychodynamic theorizing that has occurred in the past.

Ellis (1998) described the application of cognitive neuropsychiatry to the study of the misidentification delusions as an exemplary vindication of the discipline. This was because cognitive neuropsychiatric research into the misidentification delusions has sparked some major advances with regard to each of the two main aims of the discipline. So, in the remainder of this chapter, I want to first illustrate how cognitive neurospychiatrists have used an influential cognitive model of face processing (that from Bruce and Young, 1986: see Figure 45.1) to explain the symptoms of their patients with a misidentification delusion, which is the first main aim of their discipline. Then, I want to review how cognitive neuropsychiatric theories and studies of the misidentification delusions, in particular, the Capgras delusion, have informed ongoing development of Bruce and Young's model, which accords with the second main aim of the discipline.

Patients DH and FE

Numerous authors have commented that the misidentification delusions often co-occur with right hemisphere brain dysfunction and impairments of face processing, although these impairments can be variable and sometimes relatively subtle (see, e.g. Young et al., 1993). In the cases of DH (Langdon et al., 2006) and FE (Breen et al., 2000a, 2001), however, the patients' face-processing impairments were marked, as was the evidence for right hemisphere brain damage.

DH was a 53-year-old male, who had sustained severe right frontotemporal brain damage after a suspected assault, about which he was amnesic. At the time of testing, he believed that a nursing sister in the hospital where he was being treated as an inpatient was his ex-partner. The two women differed in both facial appearance (although there were some similarities in build and coloring) and accent; the ex-partner had an Australian accent, while the nursing sister had a thick New Zealand accent. The ex-partner lived a distance from the hospital and never visited DH. Nevertheless, the two would speak together on the telephone from time to time, and sometimes DH might see the nursing sister on the ward, soon after one of these conversations. While he found such events confusing ("How could his ex-partner travel such a distance in such a short time?"), DH was not confused enough to shift his delusion. His delusion stayed fixed, despite this and other confusions—he was also perplexed as to why the hospital had employed his ex-partner, since she had never trained as a nurse, and why she was using a different name—this was very suspicious behavior.

Neuropsychological testing revealed that DH had a verbal IQ of 80 and a performance IQ of 63. He also showed poor visuospatial construction, slow processing speed, memory impairment, and executive dysfunction (e.g. poor planning and marked perseveration). While he was within the normal range on all subtests of the Visual Object Spatial Perception Test, with the exception of the Silhouettes subtest, his face processing was significantly impaired. He found it difficult to match unfamiliar faces, recall faces, recognize famous faces, and identify facial expressions. With regard to his processing of vocal information, he could identify gender from voice and could distinguish between Australian and Asian/European accents; however, he had significant difficulties in identifying familiar voices and vocal emotional expressions. He also failed to discriminate between Australian and New Zealand accents.

Langdon and colleagues drew upon Bruce and Young's model to account for the generation of DH's delusion. In particular, they focused on the conception of "person identity nodes" (PINs) as the entry points to biographical information about familiar persons, and the sites at which information about familiarity is integrated from the processing of familiar faces, as well as familiar voices and gait and other mannerisms. They proposed that the ex-partner's PIN was hyper-responsive in DH's face processing system because of much ill-feeling between himself and his ex-partner over money and property. The already hyper-responsive ex-partner PIN was then activated by his perception of mannerisms of the nursing sister that matched those of his ex-partner. With no, or only degraded, input to the PINs from the processing of structural and expression information from face and voice (see Figure 45.1), both of which were significantly impaired in DH, and both which might otherwise have interfered with the activation of the ex-partner PIN, there was sufficient activation of the PIN from the matching mannerisms to cause DH to mistakenly recognize the nursing sister as his ex-partner.

While the application of Bruce and Young's model to the explanation of DH's delusion was relatively straightforward, the explanation of FE's delusion was less so. FE was an 87-year-old male who had developed a mirrored-self misidentification delusion after a suspected transient ischemic attack. After his discharge from the hospital, FE began to treat his reflection in the mirror as that of another man. He tried to talk to this strange man, and was confused when the man did not reply. On one occasion, he looked into a full-length mirror, which was opposite his bed, and saw his wife in bed with another man! It seems that FE had recognized his wife's reflection in the mirror on this occasion, but not his own. He likewise recognized an experimenter's reflection in the mirror, but not his own, on another occasion. The following is adapted from an excerpt of a conversation between the neuropsychologist, Nora Breen, and FE, while they both stood side by side in front of a mirror (reported in full in Breen et al., 2000a):

> Examiner (pointing to the reflection of the examiner): Who does it look like? Have you seen this person in here before?
> FE: That's you.
> Examiner: So that's me in the mirror?
> FE: Yes.
> Examiner: That's my reflection?
> FE: Yes.
> Examiner (pointing to FE's reflection): And who is that?
> FE: I don't know what you would call him.

(Earlier in the interview, FE's initial response, on stepping in front of the mirror and looking into it, had been, "That's not me!")

FE knew about mirrors: he could define a mirror and tell you what it was used for; he could identify the mirrors among a group of objects; and he had no difficulty in recognizing objects reflected in a mirror. Neuropsychological testing revealed impaired copying, drawing, constructional skills, and visual memory, indicative of right hemisphere dysfunction. FE also had significant impairments of face processing. He had difficulty in matching unfamiliar faces and identifying famous faces and he misidentified the faces of strangers as familiar. He did, however, correctly identify 16/20 photographs of family members. He also correctly identified himself in a photograph, as well as his wife and son, although his recognition of his daughter from a photograph was less consistent.

Breen and colleagues acknowledged that, while it was tempting to speculate that FE's face processing deficits contributed to the generation of his mirrored-self misidentification delusion, it was perplexing that he could still recognize his own face in a photograph. Perhaps FE's face processing impairments simply co-occurred with his delusion, without being causally implicated. But then FE's test profile is very similar to that of another patient with a mirrored-self misidentification delusion, EF (Phillips et al., 1996). EF also identified her own face in a photograph, despite her other face processing deficits. That the same profile has been reported in at least two patients with a mirrored-self misidentification delusion makes it more plausible that some disruption to normal face processing, related to the identification of one's own face in a mirror versus a photograph, leads, at least in some cases, to the generation of a mirrored-self misidentification delusion.[2]

Phillips and colleagues speculated that the greater impairment in visual self-recognition compared to the recognition of other familiar persons in EF, along with her impairment in personal semantic memory, implicated disruption of a more specific, self-recognition process—a "self-identity node"—in the generation of her delusion. Such an account seems less plausible, however, in the case of FE; this is because FE was well oriented and provided a detailed personal history, including relevant names and dates throughout his life span, suggesting that he had no impairment of personal semantics. However, Phillips and colleagues had observed another interesting fact about EF, which hints at an alternate account of the possible role of face processing impairment in the generation of FE's (and perhaps EF's) mirrored-self misidentification delusion. They noted that EF's recognition of herself from photographs was less certain when the photographs

---

[2] Cognitive deficits which do not involve face processing (e.g. "mirror agnosia"—the inability to use knowledge of mirrors when interacting with mirrors) also appear to cause the generation of a mirrored-self misidentification delusion (see, e.g. Breen et al., 2001, for discussion of patient TE).

were recent compared to old. Perhaps FE was similar; perhaps the nature of face processing impairment which generated his mirrored-self misidentification delusion only became apparent when he had to match the most recent image of a face (in particular, the mirrored reflection of his own, here and now, face) with a poorly updated face recognition unit (FRU). In other words, rather than a specific difficulty in some self- (versus non-self-) face recognition process, perhaps FE was suffering from the beginnings of a general difficulty with updating the FRUs, which showed up first with regard to his updating of the FRU of his own face.

Future studies of patients with a mirrored-self misidentification delusion will hopefully untangle whether impairments of self-specific face recognition processes and/or deficits of more general face processing (e.g. updating of the FRUs) contribute to the generation of a mirrored-self misidentification delusion in at least some patients with this delusional belief. Whatever the outcome, future cognitive neuropsychiatric studies of patients with a mirrored-self misidentification will likely be important to advance scientific understanding of the functional architecture of (self versus non-self) face processing via different representational media (e.g. photographs—both recent and old, mirrored reflections and video recordings). Certainly, cognitive neuropsychiatric studies of the Capgras delusion have already had major ramifications with regard to modifying Bruce and Young's cognitive model of face processing.

The Capgras delusion and face processing

While cognitive neuropsychologists have, for many years, pursued the two main aims of their discipline with regard to prosopagnosia (i.e. the inability to recognize previously familiar faces) and the cognitive modeling of face processing, it has only been since the 1990s, and, in particular, since Ellis and Young's (1990) seminal paper, "Accounting for Delusional Misidentifications", that cognitive neuropsychiatrists have studied the misidentification delusions with similar aims in mind. Ellis and Young proposed that some of the major misidentification delusions might be explicable in terms of Bruce and Young's model, and incorporating Bauer's (1984) proposal of dual recognition routes for faces (one for covert recognition and the other for overt recognition). The Frégoli delusion, which is the delusional belief that strangers in the environment are people who one knows but who are in disguise, was proposed to stem from a defect involving inappropriate activation of the PINs and the associated cognitive system (i.e. in the absence of appropriate perceptual inputs). Intermetamorphosis, which is the delusional belief that the physical appearance of some other person has changed dramatically so as to match the appearance of someone else, was proposed to stem from inappropriate activation of the FRUs. Finally, and of most import with regard to the subsequent advance of cognitive neuropsychiatry, Capgras delusion, which is the delusional belief that a loved one has been replaced by a visually similar stranger or impostor, was proposed to stem from a sort of mirror image of prosopagnosia.

This was the idea that the stranger content which seeds a Capgras delusion is generated when the processes that support covert, autonomic recognition of familiar faces (indexed by skin conductance responses, SCRs) in prosopagnosic patients are impaired. In contrast, the visual processing of familiar faces, including activation of the appropriate FRUs and PINs, is still intact in the Capgras patients. So, a Capgras patient still recognizes his loved one's face, consistent with his developing a delusional belief that the loved one has been replaced by a visual look-a-like. However, he no longer experiences the heightened affective response which ought normally to accompany the visual percept of his loved one's face. So his experience is of seeing a stranger, who looks very like the loved one. Moreover, this "stranger" will typically claim to be the loved one and will act as if she is the loved one. Since impostors are unfamiliar people who resemble the real person and pretend to be the real person, the impostor delusion neatly explains the lack of affective response, despite the facts that the patient recognizes the loved one's face and that the stranger claims to be the loved one. Although, note here that the absence of an affective response to familiar faces is not sufficient to account for the presence of a Capgras delusion. This is because Tranel, Damasio, and Damasio (1995) have reported that patients with ventromedial brain damage, who are not delusional about the identity of their loved ones, also fail to autonomically discriminate between familiar and unfamiliar faces. But, in this chapter, I don't want to focus too much on the distinction between delusional and non-delusional cases of "candidate-Capgras"; I want to focus solely on why the stranger thought arises in the first place.

Ellis and Young's (1990) hypothesis predicted that patients with the Capgras delusion would show a reduced SCR to familiar faces and a lack of autonomic discrimination between familiar and unfamiliar faces. Their predictions were later confirmed by Ellis et al. (1997) in their SCR study of five psychiatric patients with the Capgras delusion, who failed to discriminate autonomically between photographs of well-known, although not personally familiar, faces (of, e.g. Elizabeth Taylor) and unfamiliar faces, and independently by Hirstein and Ramachandran (1997) in their single-case study of a neurological Capgras patient, DS. In addition to showing DS photographs of well-known, although not personally familiar, faces, Hirstein and Ramachandran had also shown DS photographs of faces of personally familiar people about whom he was delusional (his mother, father, and grandfather). They also included a photograph of DS himself since DS also tended to spontaneously self-report "self-duplication" beliefs (e.g. "For instance, on one occasion he volunteered, 'Yes they sent a check, but they sent it to the other DS.'"; p. 438). The sets of photographs of familiar faces were interspersed with the photographs of unfamiliar faces. Despite the fact that DS accurately recognized the identities of the familiar faces in the photographs (confirmed via personal communication with William Hirstein, 2009), he failed to discriminate autonomically across the sets of familiar faces and the unfamiliar faces.

More recently, Brighetti et al. (1997) have reported similar results in a Capgras patient, YY, a young female student who developed the Capgras delusion in the absence of known neurological insult and other psychiatric symptoms. Like DS, YY also failed to discriminate autonomically between the photographs of unfamiliar faces and the photographs of faces of personally familiar people. Brighetti and colleagues included 7 photographs of familiar people: (1) five family members for whom YY had had the Capgras delusion previously; (2) the father, about whom YY was still delusional; and (3) another family member, about whom the Capgras delusion had never developed. Brighetti and colleagues did not, however, include a photograph of YY herself, which might have been of additional interest since YY reported no self-duplication. Like DS, though, YY failed to show higher SCRs for any of the familiar faces compared to the unfamiliar faces. Also like DS, this was despite the fact that she correctly identified the familiar people whose faces she was shown in the photographs (confirmed via personal communication with Brighetti and colleagues, 2009, and reported in their paper, as follows, "YY has preserved abilities to recognise the structural features of faces as belonging to family members": p. 194). Of note, not one of the familiar faces generated an SCR which was larger than that triggered by the seven photographs of unfamiliar faces. In contrast, when YY scanned the faces of familiar people, about whom she had developed a Capgras delusion, her eye-movements differed from those recorded when she scanned the faces of familiar people about whom she was never delusional (see Brighetti et al., 1997, for further detail). The latter abnormality, it seems, was a consequence of her delusional beliefs about the people whose faces she saw.

While the reader might naturally ask why it was that YY was only delusional about the father at the time of testing, since the affective response was absent for all familiar persons, it is not uncommon for the Capgras delusion to centre on a single person—someone who is perhaps the most familiar to the patient, or perhaps the most salient, at a particular point in time. That YY was only delusional about the father at the time of testing is very important though; this is because Brighetti and colleagues have demonstrated that: (1) the lack of affective response is present for the face of a personally familiar individual, about whom a Capgras patient is delusional; and (2) the absence of an affective response to a loved one is not a consequence of the Capgras delusional belief. This is because the lack of affective response in YY was present for each of the personally familiar faces, including the face of someone about whom she was never delusional. To reiterate the point, Capgras patients show a general absence of affective response to all familiar faces, whether or not these are personally familiar (e.g. Ellis et al., 1997, had used famous, but not personally familiar, faces) and whether or not the familiar face is of the person who is the subject of a Capgras delusion (e.g. Hirstein and Ramachandran, 1997, had pooled their results for famous, but not personally familiar, faces and faces of personally familiar people, about whom DS was, or had been, delusional). In contrast, the abnormalities in visual scanpaths of faces, which YY showed, appeared to be a consequence of her delusional beliefs.

That overt and covert face recognition doubly dissociate in Capgras and prosopagnosic patients implied that a single-route model of face processing, as illustrated in Figure 45.1, is inadequate. But, just what sort of dual-route model is the best alternative?

Bauer (1984) had suggested two distinct neuroanatomical routes for face recognition: a ventral visual-limbic route via the inferior longitudinal fasciculus, which processes information about a face's familiarity and identity; and a dorsal visual-limbic route via the superior temporal sulcus and the inferior parietal lobule, which sustains covert face recognition. Breen et al. (2000b) influentially critiqued the neural plausibility of Bauer's proposal, in line with earlier comments made by Hirstein and Ramachandran (1997) and Tranel et al. (1995). Breen and colleagues proposed a single ventral pathway, with connections to the amygdala, so as to account for the SCR findings in prosopagnosic and Capgras patients. They also proposed a modification of Bruce and Young's model to incorporate two pathways after the FRUs: one pathway to connect the FRUs to the PINs and a second pathway to connect the FRUs to a system for generating an affective response, the strength of which is indexed by SCRs (see Figure 45.2). According to Breen and colleagues, the affective response system is not modality-specific—just like the PINs, it can receive input, not only from the FRUs but also from the processing of familiar voices, or a familiar person's mannerisms, or even the perception of that person's familiar belongings. They reasoned that the differential SCRs to familiar and unfamiliar faces in some prosopagnosic patients might reflect either a disconnection between otherwise intact FRUs and PINs or a degree of damage to the FRUs themselves. In the latter case, there would still be sufficient activation flowing from the FRUs to the affective response system to trigger larger SCRs for familiar compared to unfamiliar faces, but insufficient activation flowing from the FRUs to the PINs to support overt face recognition.

Breen and colleagues suggested two possible loci of damage in Capgras patients. Firstly, there might be a disconnection between an otherwise intact FRU module and an otherwise intact affective response system. In this case, the appropriate PIN would still be activated by the appropriately activated FRU, but there would be no concurrent input to the PIN from the affective response system. Since the affective response system is not modality-specific, this sort of damage would still allow a Capgras patient to identify the same loved one, who they deny face to face, when relying solely on voice (or gestures) for identification purposes. It seems that Hirstein and Ramachandran's (1997) patient, DS, was like this, at least according to the anecdotal reports of his parents who described DS as rejecting his father as an impostor when the two met face to face, while nevertheless treating his father just like his father when the two spoke together on the telephone. DS, it seemed, had a normal affective response when he heard his unseen father's voice (although this

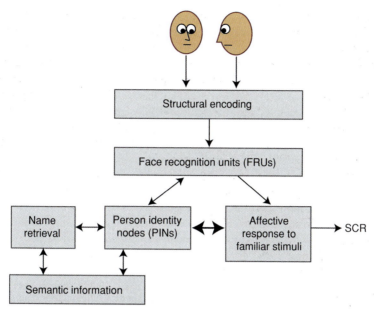

Fig. 45.2 A modification of Bruce and Young's (1986) model, adapted from Breen, Caine, and Coltheart (2000b). Models of Face Recognition and Delusional Misidentification: A critical review, Breen, Caine, and Coltheart, *Cognitive Neuropsychology*, 2000, Taylor and Francis, reprinted by permission of the publisher (Taylor and Francis Group, http://www.informaworld.com).

was not established empirically via the recording of SCRs), but not when he saw his father's face (which was established empirically). When he heard, but did not see his father, the concurrent activation of the father's PIN via a direct route (from the father's voice recognition unit: VRU) and via an indirect route (from the father's VRU by way of the affective response system) enabled DS to correctly identify his father. However, the lack of affective response to the visual percept of the father's face appears to have over-ridden whatever affective response was triggered by the father's VRU when DS both saw and heard his father at one and the same time (more on this later).

If Breen and colleagues are on the right track with regard to an affective response system which is not modality-specific, it is theoretically possible that delusional misidentification of familiar others might be driven primarily by some of the other senses, such as hearing or touch (see Lewis et al., 2001, for discussion). For example, an auditory version of a Capgras patient would be someone who experiences normal visual processing of a loved one's face (including activation of the FRU and the affective response system), but who fails to experience a normal affective response when the VRU of the loved one is activated. Such a patient might generate and maintain a stranger or an impostor delusion about the loved one's identity based primarily on his or her experiences when hearing the unseen loved one's voice. Cases of this type would be difficult to identify, since we usually see and hear our loved ones, at one and the same time, and since the visual modality appears to dominate (e.g. it appeared to dominate in the case of DS when he both saw and heard his father). There are reports, however, of at least three blind patients who reported Capgras-like delusions about other people (or a pet in one case) having been replaced (Reid et al., 1993; Rojo et al., 1991; Signer et al., 1990). These cases of blind Capgras would appear to support the suggestion that a Capgras-like delusion might be generated primarily via the absence of a heightened affective response to familiar voices. None of these blind Capgras cases involved the recording of SCRs to familiar and unfamiliar voices, however. That is why the case reported by Lewis et al. (2001) is of particular import. They recorded SCRs to voices in a female patient, HL, who was not blind, but who appeared to generate a stranger delusion about a loved one's identity when she heard her unseen loved one's voice. Three months prior to testing, HL, a 59-year-old female with schizoaffective disorder, had locked her son out of her flat, believing him to be an impostor. The following is adapted from an excerpt of an interview with HL (reported in full in Lewis et al., 2001):

> Examiner: I would like to ask you about the time when you locked your son out of your flat.
> HL: It's because of the voice I heard. My eyes were blurred at that moment and I was wondering when he went out, whether he was the same person as when he went in.
> Examiner: Why did you think he wasn't the same person?
> HL: He didn't come across as chirpy . . . or the person he was.

While suggestive, it is not clear-cut from the above exchange whether HL's delusion was triggered primarily by her failure to identify her son via his voice alone. Her meaning is difficult to decipher because of the communication deficits that are commonly associated with schizophrenia-related disorders. Nevertheless, regardless of the primary trigger for HL's delusion, her test performances were very interesting. She performed perfectly on the Warrington Recognition Test for Faces and showed differential SCRs to familiar and unfamiliar faces. In contrast, she differed from healthy controls in failing to show a significant SCR differential when hearing familiar and unfamiliar voices. The implications of Lewis et al.'s (2001) findings are twofold: (1) both familiar voices and familiar faces normally trigger a heightened affective response in healthy adults; and (2) the pathway from the VRUs to the affective response system was selectively disrupted in HL, leaving the pathway from the FRUs to her affective system intact. (Likely the pathways from the VRUs to the affective response system were similarly disrupted in the reported cases of blind Capgras.) Clearly future studies of SCRs to familiar faces and familiar voices in Capgras patients who are not blind will be important to establish more definitively whether the affective response system is accessible via separable pathways, which can be independently disrupted. To date, we have only anecdotal reports (e.g. of DS), which are suggestive of the reverse dissociation—that is, an intact pathway from the VRUs to the affective response system combined with a disrupted pathway from the otherwise intact FRUs.

The other sort of damage, which Breen and colleagues speculated might account for the Capgras delusion, is damage to the affective response system itself. Capgras patients with this sort of damage might be expected to experience a more pervasive absence of affective response to all manner of familiar stimuli. Perhaps this is what is happening in some of those Capgras patients who also report nihilistic delusions like Cotard delusion, which is the delusional belief that one is dead or does not exist. Butler (2000b), for example, has described RY, a 17-year-old male, who had sustained a severe traumatic brain injury after a car accident. RY described his environment as not real, and believed that he was dead, and in Hell. He also believed that his father had been replaced by a criminal double. Butler speculated that RY's delusions were secondary to his feelings of depersonalization, and that these delusions were elaborated via vivid dreams and nightmares, which RY could not distinguish from the reality. It seems that RY's depersonalization experiences, which may have stemmed from global damage to an affective response system, sometimes generated the Cotard delusional content and sometimes generated the Capgras delusional content. Wright, Young, and Hellawell (1993) have also reported another patient, KH, with sequential Cotard and Capgras delusions. KH was a 35-year-old male who met diagnostic criteria for a major depressive episode. His Cotard delusional content arose when he was feeling depressed, and so was focused on negative internalizing, while his Capgras delusional content arose when he felt paranoid, and so was focused on negative externalizing.

There is one other important set of data which accords well with Breen and colleagues' proposal of a bifurcation after the FRUs. This is a study of covert face recognition via autonomic indices (i.e. SCRs) and via behavioral indices (e.g. indirect priming and interference face processing measures: see Young, Chapter 5, this volume) in the same Capgras patient (Ellis et al., 2000). Whereas De Haan et al. (1992) had found intact covert recognition in their prosopagnosic patient, LF, whether they used autonomic or behavioral measures, suggesting that the autonomic and behavioral indices might reflect a common process, Ellis and colleagues found a dissociation; their Capgras patient BP showed an absence of differential SCRs to familiar and unfamiliar faces, alongside performances on indirect priming and interference face tasks that were similar to those of controls. It seems, therefore, that the covert recognition that is indexed by behavioral priming and interference measures is sustained by the direct pathway from the FRUs to the PINs, whereas the covert recognition that is indexed by autonomic measures requires a separate pathway, consistent with Breen and colleagues' proposal.

Since 2000, there has been some debate concerning whether or not further modification of the Bruce and Young model is required. Ellis and Lewis (2001) and Lewis and Ellis (2001), in particular, have expressed doubts about the existence of a bidirectional pathway between the affective response system and the PINs, as illustrated in Figure 45.2. In more detail, Lewis and Ellis (2001) have argued that such a pathway ought theoretically to make it possible for prosopagnosic patients, who show differential SCRs to familiar and unfamiliar faces, to use the activation flowing from the affective response system to the PINs to support overt face recognition, which they clearly cannot do. One response to Lewis and Ellis might be to argue that, while there is direct activation flowing from the affective response system to the PINs, the level of activation in a prosopagnosic patient, who shows differential SCRs to familiar and unfamiliar faces, is sufficient to support covert face recognition via behavioral indices, but is not sufficient to support overt face recognition, consistent with the performances of prosopagnosic patient, LF.(De Haan et al., 1992).

But then again, perhaps this debate is more important with regard to focusing our attention on the specific processes that are implied in the Breen, Caine, and Coltheart model, in particular, their inclusion of a direct connection from the PINs to the affective response system and vice versa. If the connection from the FRUs to the PINs is selectively disrupted in a prosopagnosic patient, then it follows that, when a known face is presented to that prosopagnosic patient, there will still be activation flowing from the activated FRU to the affective response system. But, contrary to Lewis and Ellis's (2001) suggestion, any purported flow on of activation from that affective response system to the PINs module cannot give rise to activation of that particular person's PIN, over and above any other PIN. This is because neither the affective response system nor the PINs module is able to identify whose face it is that is being presented. This is why I doubt that there is a direct connection from the affective response system to the PINs. Likewise I doubt any direct connection from the PINs to the affective response system. This is because Ellis et al. (2001) have shown that healthy people do not generate differential SCRs when they read the names of familiar and unfamiliar people as one might expect if activation flows from the PINs to the affective response system.

With regard to Capgras, Ellis and Lewis (2001) have also queried how precisely the Capgras patients, who have lost the connection between the FRUs and the affective response system, combine the information about activation flowing directly from the loved one's FRU to the loved one's PIN with the information about an absence of concurrent input to the PINs directly from the affective response system. I have similar concerns. For example, it seems difficult to mount a simple thresholds argument here—that is, to argue that the summed activation of the PIN is less than some critical threshold that is required for person identification. Take DS, for example; there appeared to have been sufficient activation of his father's PIN for him to identify his father when he relied solely on voice (and the father's PIN was activated directly from the VRU and indirectly by way of the VRU to the affective response system), but not enough activation for him to identify his father, when he both saw and heard his father (and the father's PIN was activated directly via the FRU and the VRU, and indirectly by way of the VRU to the affective response system).

One option might be to incorporate some sort of confirmation process before a FRU or a VRU, once activated, can, in turn, activate the PIN for person identification. In line with such an approach, Ellis (1998) has suggested that "a secondary, possibly confirmatory, signal is lacking and this may give rise to delusional belief which is most evident to the [Capgras] patient for those faces that normally engender a strong affective signal." (pp. 85–86). However, such a disconfirmation process cannot operate by blocking the flow of activation to the PINs, when the confirmatory affective signal is absent. This is because the Capgras patient, who will misidentify his loved one as an impostor when he sees his loved one in the flesh, will nevertheless correctly recognize a loved one's photograph as being the face of his loved one. He must therefore have been able to activate the appropriate PIN and to access the appropriate name and biographical information for overt recognition. And this correct overt identification of the face in the photograph (as being of the loved one) occurs, as it did for both DS and YY when they were shown the photographs of the faces of people about whom they were delusional, despite the fact that any confirmatory affective signal of familiarity must have been absent. The point here is that, for the Capgras patient, the face is identified as the right face—the face in the photograph and the face on the body of the person in front of the patient is the face of the loved one—but the identity of that real-life person (whose face matches that of the loved one) is wrong. This is precisely why the Capgras patients develop their delusional beliefs about replacement look-alikes or impostors. As Ellis and Lewis (2001) have tried to put it, the essential paradox of Capgras is that, "patients simultaneously recognize a [loved one's] face and, at the same time, deny its authenticity [as of the real person in daily life]" (p. 149).

How precisely does the model illustrated in Figure 45.2 explain the Capgras patient's intact recognition of his love one's face in a photograph combined with his misidentification of that same loved one, when seen in the flesh? The PIN of the loved one must have been sufficiently activated when the Capgras patient viewed the photograph of his loved one's face so as to allow the retrieval of the loved one's name and the associated biographical information that is required for overt face recognition, even though the confirmatory affective signal is missing. And yet, when the same patient sees his loved one's face in real life, the identity of that loved one is denied. Of note, this distinction might seem paradoxical, as Ellis and Lewis say, but it is not illogical. This is because we recognize a face as being the face *of* a certain person; we do not recognize a face as being the person. To try to put it another way, facial appearance is only a visual property of a person's physical appearance; facial appearance does not fundamentally constitute a person's identity. For example, a woman might pursue an extreme make-over involving extensive plastic surgery in the hope of "having the face of Jennifer Aniston", and, after her surgery, she might look in the mirror and say to her doctor, "You've done an amazing job. That's the face of Jennifer Aniston," but she does not become Jennifer Aniston; she is still the same person she was before the surgery and makeover, even though she now has the face of Jennifer Aniston. In the same way, the face of a loved one might conceivably be copied onto the head of a look-alike or an impostor, as the Capgras patients claim.

So, how are we to explain such a complex phenomenon with regard to the sort of cognitive model that is illustrated in Figure 45.2—one which posits bidirectional connections between the PINs and the affective response system and appears to locate all decisions about identity at the

PINs module? If the Capgras delusional content is triggered by a problem with person identity authentication and not a problem with the overt recognition of a known face, as appears to be the case, and conscious decisions of a person's identity in real life and of the identity of a known face in a photograph are both made at the level of the PINs, then perhaps we need to postulate different decision thresholds for PINs in different contexts. For example, person identification is an existential decision, which we make about real people in real life, and not a decision, which we make about photographs on paper. In the case of YY, there may have been sufficient activation of her father's PIN (even without the input from the affective response system) for her to recognize a photograph as being of her father's face, but not sufficient activation (without the additional input from the affective response) for her to authenticate his identity as that of her real father, in the flesh.

An alternative approach, however, is to remove the bidirectional pathways between the PINs and the affective response system, in accord with my previous arguments, and to incorporate a separate stage for person identity authentication: some form of integrative device which weighs up separable inputs from the PINs and the affective response system (see Figure 45.3). The functional role of this additional integrative device is to authenticate the identity of a real person. In contrast, activation of a PIN and subsequent access to name and biographical information might be sufficient for recognition of a known face, say in a photograph. Any significant discrepancy between the two separable inputs (from the PINs and from the affective response system) detected by the integrative device will generate doubt about the person's real identity—a stranger or an impostor suspicion, but not necessarily a Capgras delusion unless additional pathology related to an impairment of belief evaluation is also present (see Coltheart et al., 2011, for further discussion of the "two-factor" model of delusional belief—more on this later). How this hypothesized authentication process works remains a bit of a mystery, however. This is particularly so since the integrative device must weigh up more than a simple pooling of affective response signals

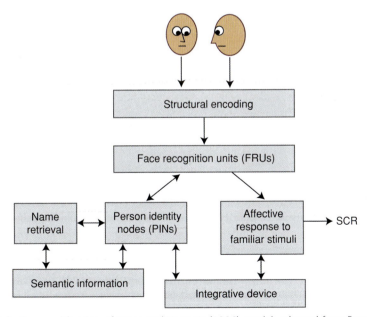

Fig. 45.3 A further modification of Bruce and Young's (1986) model, adapted from Breen, Caine, and Coltheart (2000b), Ellis and Lewis (2001) and Schweinberger and Burton. (2003). (The original article by Schweinberger and Burton was published in *Cortex*, **39**, 9–30, Schweinberger and Burton, Covert recognition and the neural system. © Elsevier 2003.)

(from different modalities of inputs) against the presence or not of an activated PIN. This is because the pooled affective response for DS appears to have been the same both when he saw and heard his father and rejected him as an impostor and when he heard his unseen father and accepted him as authentic.

So, the questions and the debates continue. One such debate centers on the distinction between explaining why a Capgras patient generates a stranger or an impostor thought in the first place (because, e.g. he lacks a normal heightened affective response to a loved one's face) and explaining why a Capgras patient adopts and maintains the stranger or impostor thought as a belief, despite its implausibility and despite the counter-arguments of others (Langdon and Coltheart, 2000). Ellis and Lewis (2001) have focused on individual differences in attributional biases (e.g. tendencies to externalize or internalize the cause of discordant events) so as to explain the latter, whereas Langdon and Coltheart have conceived of attributional biases as further nuancing the specific content of a patient's delusion, rather than accounting for the adoption and persistence of the delusion. Of perhaps more interest today, however, is the precise output of the integrative device— the information which likely constitutes the first thought that comes to mind when the Capgras patient perceives a loved one's face, after having suffered an impairment of autonomic face recognition (see, e.g. Langdon and Bayne, 2010, for discussion). Is the output, "this person is a stranger"? Or is it some paradoxical amalgam, "this person is an unfamiliar loved one"—some sort of duplicate of the original? Or is it even more specific; is it "this is not the authentic loved one"?

Summary and conclusions

My purpose in this chapter was not to "dot the i's and cross the t's" with regard to how a cognitive model of normal face processing might be fine-tuned so as to account for the findings of cognitive neuropsychiatric studies of misidentification delusions. My aims were far more modest. I sought firstly to contrast the cognitive neuropsychiatric approach with the traditional psychiatric approaches to delusions so as to highlight one of the main aims of cognitive neuropsychiatry— that is, to develop testable cognitive theories of delusions (including those which involve mistaken beliefs about the identity of oneself and/or other people) so as to render the generation of delusions psychologically understandable. I then illustrated how cognitive neuropsychiatrists have used the Bruce and Young model of face processing to explain the generation of misidentification delusions. DH's delusional misidentification of a nursing sister as his ex-partner became understandable given the evidence of his severe face and voice processing impairments and a conception of PINs as the sites for integrating cross-modal information about familiarity from faces, voices, mannerisms, gait, etc. The study of FE, who had a mirrored-self misidentification delusion, highlighted that future cognitive neuropsychiatric studies of self and non-self face processing using different representational media (e.g. photographs—recent and old, video recordings, mirror reflections) in patients with mirrored-self misidentification delusions (and other forms of misidentification delusions, for that matter[3]) will likely be informative with regard to advancing scientific understanding of the putative differences between self and non-self recognition.

---

[3] For example, if Capgras delusion stems from a loss of affective response when viewing the faces of familiar people, and this difficulty extends to viewing one's own face, why don't Capgras patients develop a mirrored-self misidentification delusion when they look at themselves in a mirror? Perhaps, the integrative device takes into account the context of standing in front of a mirror and the knowledge of how a mirror works.

I then went on to review cognitive neuropsychiatric research into the Capgras delusion. That overt and covert (autonomic) face recognition doubly dissociate in Capgras and prosopagnosic patients highlighted that Bruce and Young's original single-route model required modification so as to incorporate an affective response system and separate pathways after the face recognition units. That the overt recognition of familiar faces is intact in Capgras patients, while the authentication of the identity of a familiar loved one is disrupted, highlighted the distinction between overt face recognition and person identity authentication, and suggested the need for further modification of Bruce and Young's model to remove direct pathways between the PINs module and the affective response system and to incorporate a separate integrative device. How precisely the integrative device weighs up inputs from the PINs and an affective response system remains unclear, however, as does the precise output of the integrative device. Nevertheless, I think that future cognitive neuropsychiatric studies of the misidentification delusions will prove invaluable to answer these puzzles, and the likely new ones to come, so that we might further advance our scientific understanding of the normal (and the abnormal) processes for extracting information from the perception of faces.

References

Bauer, R.M. (1984). Autonomic recognition of names and faces in prosopagnosia: A neuropsychological application of the guilty knowledge test. *Neuropsychologia*, **22**, 457–469.

Breen, N., Caine, D., Coltheart, M., Hendy, J., and Roberts, C. (2000a). Towards an understanding of delusions of misidentification: Four case studies. *Mind & Language*, **15**, 74–110.

Breen, N., Caine, D., and Coltheart, M. (2000b). Models of face recognition and delusional misidentification: A critical review. *Cognitive Neuropsychology*, **17**, 55–71.

Breen, N., Caine, D., and Coltheart, M. (2001). Mirrored-self misidentification: Two cases of focal onset dementia. *Neurocase*, **7**, 239–254.

Brighetti, G., Bonifacci, P., Borlimi, P., and Ottaviani, C. (1997). "Far from the heart far from the eye": Evidence from the Capgras delusion. *Cognitive Neuropsychiatry*, **12**, 189–197.

Bruce, V. and Young, A.W. (1986). Understanding face recognition. *British Journal of Psychology*, **77**, 305–327.

Butler, P.V. (2000a). Reverse Othello syndrome subsequent to traumatic brain injury. *Psychiatry: Interpersonal & Biological Processes*, **63**, 85–92.

Butler, P.V. (2000b). Diurnal variation in Cotard's syndrome (copresent with Capgras delusion) following traumatic brain injury. *Australian and New Zealand Journal of Psychiatry*, **34**, 684–687.

Coltheart, M., Langdon, R., and McKay, R. (2011). Delusional belief. *Annual Review of Psychology*, **62**, 271–298.

De Haan, E.H.F., Bauer, R.M., and Greve, K.W. (1992). Behavioural and physiological evidence for covert face recognition in a prosopagnosic patient. *Cortex*, **28**, 77–95.

Ellis, H.D. (1998). Cognitive neuropsychiatry and delusional misidentification syndromes: An exemplary vindication of the new discipline. *Cognitive Neuropsychiatry*, **3**, 81–90.

Ellis, H.D. and Lewis, M.B. (2001). Capgras delusion: A window on face recognition. *Trends in Cognitive Sciences*, **5**, 149–156.

Ellis, H.D., Lewis, M.B., Moselhy, H.F., and Young, A.W. (2000). Automatic without autonomic responses to familiar faces: Differential components of covert face recognition in a case of Capgras delusion. *Cognitive Neuropsychiatry*, **5**, 255–269.

Ellis, H.D., Quayle, A.H., and Young, A.W. (2001). The emotional impact of faces (but not names): Face specific changes in skin conductance responses to familiar and unfamiliar people. In Ellis, H. and Macrae, N. (eds). *Validation in psychology: Research perspectives*, pp. 113–124. New Brunswick, NJ: Transaction Publishers. (This article also appeared in *Current Psychology: Developmental, Learning, Personality, Social*, 1999, **18**, 88–97.)

Ellis, H.D. and Young, A.W. (1990). Accounting for delusional misidentifications. *British Journal of Psychiatry*, **157**, 239–248.

Ellis, H.D., Young, A.W., Quayle, A.H., and de Pauw, K.W. (1997). Reduced autonomic responses to faces in Capgras delusion. *Proceedings of the Royal Society, London B*, **264**, 1085–1092.

Enoch, M.D. and Trethowan, W.H. (1991). *Uncommon psychiatric syndromes, 3rd Ed.* Oxford: Butterworth-Heinemann.

Hirstein, W. and Ramachandran, V.S. (1997). Capgras syndrome: A novel probe for understanding the neural representation of the identity and familiarity of persons. *Proceedings of the Royal Society, London B*, **264**, 437–444.

Jaspers, K. (1963). *General psychopathology.* (Translated by J. Hoening and M. Hamilton.) Manchester: Manchester University Press. (Original work published 1913.)

Langdon, R. and Bayne, T. (2010). Delusion and confabulation: Mistakes of perceiving, remembering and believing. *Cognitive Neuropsychiatry*, **15**, 319–345.

Langdon, R. and Coltheart, M. (2000). The cognitive neuropsychology of delusions. *Mind and Language*, **15**, 184–218.

Langdon, R., Cooper, S., Connaughton, E., and Martin, K. (2006). A variant of misidentification delusion in a patient with right frontal and temporal brain injury. *Neuropsychiatric Disease and Treatment*, **2**(Suppl. 3), 8.

Lewis, M.B. and Ellis, H.D. (2001). A two-way window on face recognition: Reply to Breen et al. *Trends in Cognitive Sciences*, **5**, 235.

Lewis, M.B., Sherwood, S., Moselhy, H., and Ellis, H.D. (2001). Autonomic responses to familiar faces without autonomic responses to familiar voices: Evidence for voice-specific Capgras delusion. *Cognitive Neuropsychiatry*, **6**, 217–228.

McKay, R., Langdon, R., and Coltheart, M. (2005). "Sleights of mind": Delusions, defences, and self-deception. *Cognitive Neuropsychiatry*, **10**, 305–326.

Phillips, M.L., Howard, R., and David, A.S. (1996). "Mirror, Mirror on the Wall, Who . . .?" Towards a Model of Visual Self-recognition. *Cognitive Neuropsychiatry*, **1**, 153–164.

Reid, I., Young, A.W., and Hellawell, D.J. (1993). Voice recognition impairment in a blind Capgras patient. *Behavioural Neurology*, **6**, 225–228.

Rojo, V.I., Caballero, L., Iruela, L.M., and Baca, E. (1991). Capgras' syndrome in a blind patient. *American Journal of Psychiatry*, **148**, 1272.

Signer, S.F., Van Ness, P.C., and Davis, R.J. (1990). Capgras's syndrome associated with sensory loss. *Western Journal of Medicine*, **152**, 719–720.

Spitzer, M. (1990). On defining delusions. *Comprehensive Psychiatry*, **31**, 377–397.

Spitzer, M. (1992). The phenomenology of delusions. *Psychiatric Annals*, **22**, 252–259.

Schweinberger S.R. and Burton, A.M. (2003). Covert recognition and the neural system for face processing. *Cortex*, **39**, 9–30.

Tranel, D., Damasio, A.R., and Damasio, H. (1995). Double dissociation between overt and covert recognition. *Journal of Cognitive Neurosciences*, **7**, 425–432.

Wright, S., Young, A.W., and Hellawell, D.J. (1993). Sequential Cotard and Capgras delusions. *British Journal of Clinical Psychology*, **32**, 345–349.

Young, A.W. (2000). Wondrous strange: The neuropsychology of abnormal beliefs. *Mind & Language*, **15**, 47–73.

Young, A.W. Reid, I., Wright, S. and Hellawell, D.J. (1993). Face processing impairments and the Capgras delusion. *British Journal of Psychiatry*, **162**, 695–698.

Index

Note: Entries in *italics* refer to figures and tables.

INDEX 903